CW01372046

BRITISH SHIPPING LAWS

KENNEDY & ROSE
LAW OF SALVAGE

SIXTH EDITION

AUSTRALIA
LBC Information Services Sydney
Sydney

CANADA AND USA
Carswell
Toronto—Ontario

NEW ZEALAND
Brookers
Auckland

SINGAPORE AND MALAYSIA
Sweet & Maxwell Asia
Singapore and Kuala Lumpur

BRITISH SHIPPING LAWS

KENNEDY AND ROSE
THE LAW OF SALVAGE

SIXTH EDITION

by

FRANCIS D. ROSE
M.A., B.C.L. (Oxon.), Ph. D. (Lond.), M.A. (Cantab.)
Barrister-at-Law (Gray's Inn)
Professor of Commercial Law
Director, Norton Rose Centre of Commercial Law
University of Bristol

Consulting Editors

The Hon. Sir David Steel, M.A. (Oxon.)
Admiralty Judge, High Court of Justice
Master of the Bench of the Inner Temple

Richard A.A. Shaw, M.A. (Oxon.)
Solicitor of the Supreme Court
Senior Research Fellow,
Institute of Maritime Law, University of Southampton
Consultant, Shaw and Croft, London

LONDON
SWEET & MAXWELL
2002

First Edition (1891)   By W.R. Kennedy, Q.C.
Second Edition (1907) By A.R. Kennedy
Third Edition (1936)   By His Honour Judge A.R. Kennedy, K.C.
Fourth Edition (1958) By Kenneth C. McGuffie
Fifth Edition (1985)   By David W. Steel Q.C. and Francis D. Rose
Sixth Edition (2002)   By Francis D. Rose

Published in 2002 by
Sweet & Maxwell Limited of
100 Avenue Road London NW3 3PF
http://www.sweetandmaxwell.co.uk
Typeset by Interactive Sciences Ltd, Gloucester
Printed by Athenaeum Press Ltd, Gateshead

A CIP catalogue record for this book
is available from the British Library

ISBN 0421 602309

All rights reserved. Crown copyright material is reproduced with the permission of the Controller of HMSO and the Queen's Printer for Scotland.
No part of this publication may
be reproduced or transmitted, in any form or by any means, or
stored in any retrieval system of any nature, without prior written
permission, except for permitted fair dealing under the
Copyright, Designs and Patents Act 1988, or in accordance with
the terms of a licence issued by the Copyright Licensing Agency in
respect of photocopying and/or reprographic reproduction.
Application for permission for other use of copyright material including
permission to reproduce extracts in other pubished works shall be
made to the publishers. Full acknowledgement of author, publisher and
source must be given.

No natural forests were destroyed to make
this product. Only farmed timber was used and re-planted.

ISBN 0-421-60230-9

©
Sweet & Maxwell
2002

**In memory of
GEOFFREY BRICE**, Q.C.
(12 April 1938—14 November 1999)

In memory of
GEOFFREY BRICE, Q.C.
(12 April 1938—14 November 1999)

ACKNOWLEDGMENTS

The forms and documents in Appendix A are reproduced with the kind permission of the Council of Lloyd's.

The Queen's Regulations. © Crown Copyright. Reproduced with the permission of the Controller of Her Majesty's Stationery Office.

The RNLI Regulations in Appendix D have been reproduced with the kind permission of the Royal National Lifeboat Institution.

PREFACE

Just as Lord Stowell made clear the principles of Admiralty law at the beginning of the nineteenth century, so did Lord Justice Kennedy draw together the principles of the law of maritime civil salvage at the end of that century. Since then, the shipping industry has changed dramatically, the business of salvage has largely passed from individual volunteers to professionals and the relationship between salvors and salvees has become dominated by contractual arrangements administered (in the main) privately by arbitrators. The turn of the millennia has heralded new developments. English law has been subjected to the International Salvage Convention of 1989, environmental services have been closely linked to salvage operations, the ubiquitous Lloyd's Form of salvage agreement has been substantially recast and, with its associated documents, has made the contractual regulation of salvage both more flexible and more complex.

Unlike his nineteenth century counterpart, the twenty-first century lawyer does not have the comfort of a uniform law and practice of salvage. Different rules may apply in different situations and the extent to which earlier decisions continue to inform the modern law is not always clear. Moreover, even in a world dominated by Lloyd's Form, parties are not bound to use either Lloyd's Form or, if they do, the latest edition; and the newly introduced Scopic Clause may or may not apply. Nevertheless, it is hoped that this book continues to provide a useful starting point to navigate towards the applicable law.

Scenes change and so do the players. David Steel, my co-author of the previous edition of this book, has become the Admiralty Judge and has had to relinquish his active involvement in the writing. Richard Shaw's participation has continued actively but subtly. My own preoccupations have not allowed me the time to draw on his reservoir of experience in salvage law as much as I would like to have done. However, his influence on the content of this work, through his involvement in the processes leading to the 1989 Salvage Convention and his published work, has been no less beneficial; in particular, his rapid and meritorious contributions at proof stage have been entirely in keeping with the spirit of the subject. I have also benefitted greatly from Nicholas Gaskell's commentary in *Current Law Statutes* on the salvage provisions of the Merchant Shipping Act 1995, which will endure as an invaluable source of learning on the effect of the Convention in English law. I am grateful also for assistance of various sorts from Michael Buckley, Michael Marks Cohen, Richard Olsen and John Willmer, Q.C., and to the staff of Sweet and Maxwell; they have been both indulgent and supportive and are owed the credit for preparation of the tables, appendices and index.

It is not common for authors to thank the authors of rival books. But Geoffrey Brice was no ordinary rival. The delay in producing the previous edition of this book produced one great advantage. It prompted Geoffrey to write his own book on maritime salvage (originally intended, I believe, to be

Preface

offered as an edition of this book). It consolidated Geoffrey's name as a leading authority on the subject, which he has influenced not only through his publications but in his work as a barrister and arbitrator, in the negotiations for the 1989 Convention and in his influence on the reformulation of the revised Lloyd's salvage forms. I would be surprised if many authors would have gone out of their way so often to keep a rival author up to date with developments in the subject. But no-one who knew Geoffrey would have expected anything different. Part of David Steel's tribute in the Admiralty Court to Geoffrey following his untimely death is reproduced in the supplement to the third edition of Geoffrey's book. I will content myself by dedicating this edition of this book to Geoffrey.

As with most authors, my final and greatest debt is to my family, in particular to my wife, Lynda, and our daughter Christabel. The final stages of writing took place over the best stretch of summer weather I can recall for a long time. Inevitably the weather changed the day the typescript was submitted. Christabel at least has the consolation that, unlike her brother and sister with the last edition of this book, she has missed the dubious pleasure of being press-ganged into helping prepare the index. As in most matters to do with salvage, one must expect the worst and hope for the best.

Francis Rose
4 Essex Court, Temple
11 November 2001

CONTENTS

	PAGE
Preface	ix
Table of Cases	xxix
Table of Statutes	lii
Table of Statutory Instruments	lix
Table of Conventions	lx
Abbreviations	lxiii

1. NATURE OF THE SUBJECT

	PARA.
Introduction	1
Elements of the law of salvage	1
Sources of the modern law	3
Terminology	13
Definition	16
Salvage operation	18
Civil salvage and military (prize) salvage	20
Underlying principles	21
Equitable basis	21
Twin bases of the law of salvage	26
Receipt of a benefit	28
Rights of salvors are essentially independent of contract	31
Restitution for unjust enrichment	33
Public policy	36
Professional salvors	42
Intention and voluntariness	48
Acceptance, prohibition and officiousness	50
Pre-Convention case law	52
Prohibition under the 1989 Salvage Convention, Art. 19	61
Remoteness of benefit	64
Implementation, content and period of application of the International Salvage Convention 1989	65
Implementation	65
Content, reservations and revision	66
Denunciation	66
Rights and duties of States and Public Authorities	67
Public authority control of salvage operations	69
Shipping casualties and oil pollution	70
Governing law	72
Contract and the general law of salvage	78
Extent of application of the International Salvage Convention 1989	81
Interpretation of the International Salvage Convention 1989	82
Interpretation of statutes	82
Interpretation of international conventions	83
Reference to previous domestic law	84
Reference to preparatory works	86

2. HISTORY

General	89
Admiralty jurisdiction	103
Introduction	103
Early jurisdiction over wreck	105
Extension of jurisdiction to preservation from shipwreck	109
The Act of 1713	110
The Act of 1753	112
The Act of 1809	113
Frauds by Boatmen Act 1813	114
Frauds by Boatmen Act 1821	115
Admiralty Court Act 1840	116
Wreck and Salvage Act 1846	117
Merchant Shipping Act 1854	118
Admiralty Court Act 1861	119
Naval Agency and Distribution Act 1864	120
County Courts Admiralty Jurisdiction Act 1868	121
Merchant Shipping Act 1894	122
Twentieth-century developments	123
International Conventions	127
Salvage at common law	129

3. SUBJECTS OF SALVAGE

1. GENERAL	150
Introduction	150
Summary	158
Involvement in navigation	160
The Merchant Shipping Act 1995	162
2. MARITIME PROPERTY	163
(a) General	163
(b) Navigable craft	168
Vessels, ships and boats	168
Boats and vessels propelled by oars	172
Navigation	174
(c) Property ancillary to navigable property	178
Contract	178
Apparel or equipment	179
Property on board the ship not owned by the shipowner	183
Ship's provisions	188
(d) Goods	190
Cargo	190
Personal effects and luggage	194
(e) Towed property	195
Pre-Convention law	196
Under the Salvage Convention 1989	200
(f) Wreck	201
Former definition	201
Flotsam, jetsam and lagan	204
Admiralty Court's current jurisdiction	205
Derelict	208
Wreck under the Salvage Convention 1989	213

3. FINANCIAL INTERESTS	216
Freight and hire	216
Freight generally	216
Charterparty remuneration	219
"Freight at risk"	229
Conclusions	231
Passage money	234
The "common law"	235
The International Salvage Convention 1989	242
4. AIRBORNE CRAFT	244
(a) Aircraft	244
History	244
Application of law of wreck and salvage to aircraft	250
Jurisdiction in respect of aircraft	252
Definition of "aircraft"	253
Salvage services by or to aircraft	255
Locality	256
(b) Hovercraft	257
5. LIFE SALVAGE	260
(a) Introduction	260
Definition	260
The modern law	260
(b) Pre-Convention English law	261
The common law rule and practice	261
The legal rule	261
The practice	262
Several salvors	263
Liability in Admiralty law	264
Effect of statutory changes	265
Explanation of the common law position	266
Life salvage by agreement	267
Life salvage under statute	273
Early statutes	273
Merchant Shipping Act 1894, ss.544–545	274
Principles of interpretation	275
Intention to save lives only	276
General rules	277
Extension to aircraft	278
Requirement that property be saved	279
Interest in property saved	280
Interest in property saved irrelevant to liability—the property need not have been "salved"	283
Saving of property immaterial if lives preserved but not salved	290
Extent of reward limited to value of property preserved	291
Discretionary payments of life salvage	292
The lives in question	293
"British waters"	294
Priority	297
(c) The Salvage Convention 1989 and English law	298
Current statutory provisions	298
Interpretation of the Convention	299
No personal liability	302
Entitlement to payment	303
Enforcing payment	304
Liability of one salvor to another	307
A trust of salvage proceeds?	308
Assessment	309
Discretionary Governmental life salvage payment	310

6. Liability	311
7. The Environment	312
8. Contract	313
9. Royal Fish	314
10. Excluded Subjects	317
Static structures, platforms and drilling units	318
General principle	318
Platforms and drilling units under Article 3	319
Personal effects and luggage	321
Contractual provision	327
Humanitarian cargoes	329

4. DANGER AND SALVAGE SERVICES

Overview	330
Danger	331
Danger as the foundation of salvage	332
Degree of danger	334
Vessels already damaged	335
Conditions of vessel	336
Type of danger	337
Danger to salvors	338
Knowledge of danger	339
Proof of danger	340
Evidence of danger	341
Signals	344
Non-physical danger ("liability salvage")	345
Property of no value	352
Classification of salvage services	354
Passive salvage	360
Location of danger—relevant waters	362
Categories of location	362
Pre-Convention law	363
Post-Convention law	369
Movement between inland and tidal waters	375
Duration	377
Importance	377
Salvage in stages	382
Duties on termination	390
Services in stages	391

5. ENVIRONMENTAL SERVICES

1. General	392
Background	392
SCOPIC	396
Damage to the environment	398
The relevant damage	399
Location	402
Cause of the damage	403
Responsibility for the damage	405
Encouraging environmental services	406
The policy behind Article 14	409

Duties to exercise due care to prevent or minimise damage to the environment 411
2. SPECIAL COMPENSATION 412
(a) Conditions for payment 412
Basic entitlement (Article 14.1) 413
   (i) A threat of damage to the environment 413
   (ii) Performance of salvage operations 413
   (iii) The incurring of expenses 414
   (iv) Article 13 reward less than basic entitlement to special compensation 414
Discretionary uplift (Article 14.2) 415
   (i) Basic entitlement to Article 14.1 compensation 415
   (ii) Prevention or minimisation of environmental damage 416
   (iii) Exercise of the tribunal's discretion 416
   (iv) Total special compensation not exceeding reward recoverable under Article 13 416
(b) The relationship between Articles 13 and 14 417
(c) Liability 422
(d) Amount of special compensation 423
The discretionary uplift: a two-tier discretion 424
Salvor's expenses 426
   The "fair rate" 428
   Period 431
The deductible salvage reward 433
   (i) Whose reward? 433
   (ii) The reward "under Article 13" 436
(e) Salvor's misconduct 438
(f) Shipowner's right of recourse 439

6. ENTITLEMENT TO CLAIM

1. GENERAL CONDITIONS FOR CLAIMS 441
Definition of salvor 443
2. PERSONAL SERVICE AND PROVISION OF PROPERTY ("CLASSIFICATION OF SALVORS") 445
(a) General 445
(b) The rule of personal service 448
(c) Possession or ownership of salving property 454
Owners of salving vessels 454
Chartered vessels 458
   Charterer not by demise and cargo-owner 459
   Demise charterparties 464
   Contractual provision for salvage 479
3. INTEREST IN SALVED PROPERTY 485
Salvor's relationship to salved property 485
The salved cargo 487
Salving crew 492
The salved ship 496
   (i) Generally 496
   (ii) Demise charterparties 499
   (iii) The Salvage Convention 1989 504
   (iv) Current position 509
Insurers 510

xv

7. VOLUNTARINESS

1. GENERAL CONSIDERATIONS	511
(a) Voluntariness in general	511
The two meanings of "voluntariness"	511
Voluntariness: the general rules	512
General rule as to voluntariness	515
Beneficiary of the pre-existing duty	516
(b) Moral obligation	522
(c) Pre-existing duty to owner of salved property	523
Beneficiary of pre-existing contractual or official duty	524
Pre-existing custom, usage or agreement	526
Pre-existing contract for work and labour	532
(d) Salvage under legal duty or authority	533
General principles	533
Statutory duties not precluding claims for salvage	534
The duties and the subjects of the duties	534
Duty to render assistance to persons in danger at sea	535
Duty to respond to information of distress	537
Duty to assist colliding ship	540
Duties under the Salvage Convention 1989	544
Public duties: salvage operations by or under the control of public authorities	545
The relevant public authorities	549
English law on salvage operations by public authorities	553
Salvage operations under the control of public authorities	556
(e) Self interest	557
(f) Gratuitous salvage	558
2. WHEN NON-VOLUNTEERS MAY CLAIM	563
(a) Contractual relationships	565
The master, officers and crew	565
General principle	565
Discharge by master	569
Abandonment of the vessel	570
Hostile capture	579
Salvage service	585
Parties governed by these rules	586
Pilots	588
Tugs	600
Towage	600
From towage to salvage	603
The effect of danger supervening	605
Effect on the contract	608
The tests for salvage by tugs	615
Towage as salvage *ab initio*	619
Towage contract providing "no salvage charges"	620
Burden of proving conversion of towage to salvage	621
Foyboatmen	625
Lloyd's agents and ship's agents	626
Passengers	632
Cargo owners	637
Sub-contractors	638
Employees	644
(b) Public Duties	645
Crown ships, officers and men	645
General principle	645
Extent of duty	648

Type of danger and degree of performance	651
Admiralty's consent to claim by commander or crew of Her Majesty's ships	652
Assessment of award	654
Beneficiaries of the duty	656
Place of performance of duty	658
Claims by the Crown itself: historical development	659
Claim by the Crown itself: present position	665
Officers and crew of other Crown ships	667
Her Majesty's ships: historical interpretation	699
Her Majesty's ships: present definition	673
The Royal Air Force, its officers and men	677
Royal Army	682
Coastguard officers and personnel	683
Statutory authorities and their servants	688
Receivers of wreck	694
Magistrates and other officials	696
(c) Lifeboat personnel	698

8. SUCCESS

1. GENERAL PRINCIPLES	716
Useful result	720
Salvage operation without useful result	721
Payment without useful result	722
Preservation of property	725
Requested services	727
Special contracts	728
The master's authority	729
Salvage agreements	731
Loss or damage after preservation	732
Meritorious contributions to success	733
Doubt as to value of service: court favours salvors	734
Services not contributing to success	735
Incompleted service leaving vessel in greater danger	736
Effect of other remedies	741
2. ENGAGED SERVICES	742
Engaged services today	754
Compensation for supersession of engaged services	756
The common law	757
Lloyd's Form	767

9. SALVAGE AGREEMENTS

1. TYPES OF SALVAGE AGREEMENT	779
Introduction	779
Agreements excluding salvage	784
Contractual salvage	790
Lloyd's Form of salvage agreement	791
2. PARTIES	793
General	795
The contracting salvors	794

xvii

Contents

The contracting salvees	795
3. AUTHORITY	796
General sources and specific provision	796
Pre-Convention and post-Convention law	796
LOF 2000	797
LSSAC 2000	799
General principles	800
Types of authority	801
Agent's actual authority, express and implied	801
Breach of warranty of authority	802
Apparent, or ostensible, authority	802
Usual authority	803
Authority of necessity	804
Authority by ratification	809
Agency and salvage	810
Salved vessel's master's power to bind shipowner	814
Reasonable necessity	817
Benefit	819
Settlement of claim	820
Arbitration	822
Authority of person other than master to bind salved vessel	823
Owners of salved cargo, freight, bunkers, etc.	824
Shipowner acting in personal capacity	825
Authority to bind persons other than shipowner	828
Salving vessel	833
Master's power to bind owners by salvage agreement	833
Master's power to bind officers and crew by salvage agreement	836
Power of owners to bind master and crew	841
Agreement with one of several salvors or salvees	845
Notification to principal	846
4. TERMS OF AGREEMENT	847
LOF 2000	849
5. EFFECT OF SALVAGE AGREEMENT	852
Prima facie effective	852
General principles	852
Independent assessment different	853
True salved values different	854
LOF 2000	856
Proof	857
Existence of agreement	857
Fairness of agreement	858
Invalidity	861
Admiralty jurisdiction still applies	862
Denial of salvage estopped	866
6. VITIATING FACTORS	876
Introduction	876
Common law vitiating factors	878
Admiralty law	880
The Salvage Convention 1989	883
The effects of vitiating factors	887
Fraud or collusion	891
Non-disclosure	895
Misrepresentation	905
Mistake	913
Compulsion and inequity of terms	925
Admiralty law generally	926
Admiralty law: inequitable terms alone	938
Admiralty law: inequitable settlements	941
Compulsion and unfair terms at common law	942

The Salvage Convention 1989	944
Inducements prohibited	952
Illegality	953
7. CONSTRUCTION	954
LOF 2000: overriding objectives	954
8. DISCHARGE	955
Grounds	955
Agreement or consent	956
Supervening circumstances	957
9. SCOPIC	960
Background	960
Application, invocation and exclusion	964
Parties	966
General terms	967
Security, liens and time limits	968
Appointment of SCR and Special Representatives	969
Duties of parties	970
Period of application, withdrawal and termination	971
Commencement of SCOPIC remuneration	971
Withdrawal	972
Termination	973
Relationship with Article 13 salvage reward	974
Relationship with Article 14 special compensation	975
SCOPIC remuneration	976
Assessment	976
Discount	977
Payment	978
Rights of recourse: general average	979
Dispute resolution	980

10. DUTIES OF PARTIES

1. INTRODUCTION	987
2. CONTRACTUAL LIABILITY	993
(a) General matters	993
Introduction	993
Origins of liability	994
Restrictions on liability	995
Application to salvage	996
Definition of salvage	997
(b) Implied terms	999
Contracts for the sale of goods	999
Contract of sale	999
Implied terms	1001
Qualification of liability	1002
Contracts for the supply of goods	1003
Contracts for the transfer of property in goods	1003
Contracts for the hire of goods	1004
Implied terms	1005
Qualification of liability	1006
Contracts for the supply of a service	1007
The contracts concerned	1007
Implied terms	1008
Variation of liability	1011
Care and skill	1013

Contents

Time for performance	1014
Consideration	1016
Personal performance	1019
Successful performance	1022
Common law implied terms	1024
(c) Failure of performance	1027
Breach of contract	1027
Time	1030
The effects of breach of a contract of salvage	1031
3. BEST ENDEAVOURS	1034
4. ENVIRONMENTAL SERVICES	1037
5. ASSISTANCE	1039
6. CO-OPERATION AND TERMINATION OF SERVICES	1044
1. Introduction	1044
2. General problems	1045
3. Entry to ports and harbours	1047
4. The duty of contracting States	1048
The content of the duty	1050
The relevant authority	1051
Time for performance	1052
Enforcement of the duty	1053
5. Co-operation between parties to salvage operations	1055
(a) The person(s) owing the duty	1059
(b) The duties owed	1060
6. Termination of services	1063
The place of safety	1063
Methods of termination	1066
7. Prolongation by public authority	1069
8. Non-acceptance of salved property	1070
Reimbursement under the salvage contract	1073
Duties and rights of the carrier	1075
Frustration or abandonment	1079
Duties and rights of salvors	1080
Redelivery to whom?	1083
Conclusion	1085
9. Summary	1085A

11. MISCONDUCT

1. INTRODUCTION	1086
Range of misconduct	1086
Effect of misconduct	1088
2. SALVEE'S DUTY TO SALVOR	1091
3. MISCONDUCT CAUSING DANGER	1096
Disentitlement?	1096
Former view	1096
Current view	1099
Proof	1100
Effects of claimant's fault	1101
Salvor's sister ship at fault	1103
4. SALVOR'S NEGLIGENCE DURING SALVAGE OPERATIONS	1104
The Tojo Maru	1104
The early authorities	1105
The duty of skill and care in Admiralty law	1105
The development os the law of negligence	1106
The jurisdiction of the Admiralty Court	1107

Contents

Counterclaims before 1873	1107
Dr Lushington's views on the effect of negligence	1108
Success and the theory of "more harm than good"	1110
The contractual duty of care	1112
Standard of care for contractual negligence	1114
Establishing negligence	1115
The modern law	1117
Duty of care	1117
Liability for breach of duty	1117
Effect of salvor's negligence	1117
Measure of damages for breach of salvage contract and assessment of salvage award	1118
Damages for negligence at common law	1120
Multiple claims	1123
5. Effect of Misconduct on Reward	1125
General principle	1125
Misconduct causing forfeiture	1126
Misconduct by some salvors: effect on claims of others	1128
Burden of proof lies on those who assert misconduct	1132
Misconduct causing diminution of award	1133
Misconduct causing diminution of award and partial or total deprivation of costs	1134
Misconduct causing only deprivation of costs	1135
To affect award, misconduct need not occasion actual damage	1136
Compound interest	1137

12. RESTRICTION ON CLAIMS

1. General	1138
2. Reduction of Liability	1140
Admiralty law	1140
The common law	1141
Statute	1143
Unfair Contract Terms Act 1977	1144
General provisions	1144
Sections 2–4 and 7	1145
Status of parties	1147
Contractual and tortious liability	1149
Relevant contractual clauses	1150
The requirement of reasonableness	1151
Effect of breach	1154
Death or personal injury	1155
Negligence liability generally	1156
Liability arising in contract	1157
Unfair Terms in Consumer Contract Regulations	1162
3. Sovereign Immunity	1163
Introduction	1163
The Crown	1166
Description	1166
Crown liability	1167
Limitation	1168
Crown property	1169
Crown proceedings	1170
State immunity	1171
Exceptions	1172
Admiralty proceedings	1175

Contents

4. HUMANITARIAN CARGOES	1178
5. LIMITATION OF LIABILITY	1182
Rationale and history	1182
Rationale	1182
History	1185
Scope of LLMC 1976	1188
Entitlement to limitation of liability	1190
(a) Under LLMC 1976	1190
Claims subject to limitation under LLMC 1976	1191
Counterclaims	1196
Unlimited liability	1197
(i) Claims not subject to limitation	1197
(ii) Claims excepted from limitation under LLMC 1976	1198
Conduct barring limitation	1201
6. LIMITATION OF ACTIONS	1205
The general position	1205
Commencement of limitation period(s)	1207
Extension of limitation period	1209
Claims subject to limitation	1210
Action relating to payment under the Convention	1211
Rights of recourse and actions for indemnities	1217

13. PROCEEDINGS

1. THE GENERAL POSITION	1220
High Court jurisdiction	1224
2. SECURITY	1225
(a) Introduction	1225
(b) Possession	1228
Introduction	1228
Possessory rights of first salvors	1229
Derelict	1230
Limitations on the right	1232
Property not derelict	1234
General rule	1234
Effect of owner's/master's right to possession	1236
Exceptions	1237
First salvors' rights of possession against second salvors	1240
Effect of salvor's conduct	1242
Possession and receiver of wreck	1246
(c) Maritime liens	1247
(d) Duty not to remove salved property	1253
(e) Provision of security	1255
Currency of security	1258
Amount and variation of security	1259
Form of security and liability of the Council of Lloyd's	1260
Liability for security	1261
Disputes as to security	1264
(f) Restriction on arrest or detention	1265
3. ARBITRATION	1266
Introduction	1266
Arbitration and the courts	1269
Stay of proceedings and security	1269
Continuing role of the court	1272
Reference to arbitration under Lloyd's Form	1273

Contents

The parties involved	1274
Participation, representation and service	1274
The relationships between the parties and the Council of Lloyd's	1277
Place of arbitration	1279
Appointment and tenure of arbitrator	1280
Appointment	1280
Termination of arbitrator's authority and appointment	1281
Arbitrator's duties and powers	1282
Arbitrator's duties	1282
Arbitrator's powers	1283
Procedure and evidence	1284
Preliminary meetings and consent orders	1285
Initial order for directions	1286
Disclosure of documents	1287
Experts, legal advisers and assessors	1288
The hearing	1289
The award	1290
Separate awards	1290
Open offers	1295
Fees, expenses and costs	1296
Effect of awards	1299
Publication of awards	1300
Correction of awards and additional awards	1301
Appeals and cross-appeals	1302
Parties to the appeal	1306
Appeal arbitrator's powers	1308
Appeal to the court	1309
Payment and enforcement of security under Lloyd's Form	1310
4. APPEALS AS TO AMOUNT OF SALVAGE AWARDED	1315
Appeals from court of first instance	1315
Appeal to the House of Lords	1318

14. SALVED VALUES

1. INTRODUCTION	1319
Issues	1319
Burden of proof	1320
2. AGREED VALUATION	1321
3. DISPUTED VALUATION	1322
Valuation of property by receiver	1322
Place and time of valuation	1323
Several salvage services	1326
Events after termination	1329
Qualifications on the general principle	1332
Evidence of salved values	1334
Sales	1336
Objective or subjective valuation	1338
Sound value	1339
Valuation for damages assessment	1343
Charterparty commitments	1344
No sale	1350
Deductions	1352
Scrap value	1355
Freight	1356
At risk of ship	1357

xxiii

Where salvage services terminate at port of destination	1358
Where salvage services terminate short of the port of destination	1359
If cargo salved is not carried on	1360
If cargo salved is carried on	1361
Cargo salved value	1368
Where salvage services terminate short of the port of destination	1370
Deductions from cargo salved value	1373
Other financial interests	1376
Derelicts	1378
Freight in salvage of derelict	1381
Abandonment	1381
No valid abandonment	1384
Life salvage	1385
4. APPRAISEMENT	1386

15. ASSESSMENT

1. CLAIMS GENERALLY	1387
Types of claims	1387
2. SALVAGE REWARDS IN GENERAL	1389
Salvage agreements and assessment	1389
The framework for assessment	1390
Material circumstances	1393
General approach	1396
The "salved fund"	1396
The value of the salved fund	1397
Guiding policies and principles	1398
Taking account of individual circumstances	1402
Eligible and "additional" circumstances	1404
3. MATERIAL CIRCUMSTANCES IN DETAIL	1407
Dangers	1411
Dangers to maritime property	1411
The safety of human lives	1412
Risk of legal liability	1415
Danger to navigation	1416
Damage to the environment	1417
Salvors' classification	1418
The services provided	1419
The skill and efforts of the salvors	1419
Risks run by salvors	1424
Risk of death and personal injury	1426
Risk of physical loss or damage	1427
Different risks to ship, cargo and freight	1429
Risk of financial loss	1433
Risk of responsibility or liability	1434
Time used and losses and expenses incurred by salvors	1435
Time: promptness and duration	1436
Losses and expenses incurred by the salvors	1439
The measure of success	1450
Public policy considerations	1453
Salvage services	1454
Environmental services	1456
Value of salved property	1457
Agreement for reward independently of success	1460

Contents

4. CURRENCY	1461
Currency correction	1461
Currency of award	1462
Inflation	1464
5. INTEREST	1466
Date from which interest may be awarded	1473
Interest upon judgments and arbitral awards	1475
6. TAXATION	1477

16. LIABILITY FOR PAYMENT

Introduction	1478
1. LIABILITY TO SALVOR	1479
General rule	1479
All interests in property benefited contribute	1479
Life salvage	1480
Exceptions to the general rule	1482
Life salvage	1482
Personal effects of passengers, master and crew	1482
Bottomry or respondentia	1482
Crown proceedings	1483
Sovereign immunity	1483
Defendants outside the jurisdiction	1484
Misconduct by salvor	1484
Salvor's remedies	1485
Payment of salvage by shipowner	1487
Liability to pay salvage	1488
Defences	1491
Agreements for fixed sum; agreements by shipowner to pay all salvage in first instance	1492
Estoppel	1492
Shipowner's remedies for reimbursement	1493
2. CONTRIBUTION RATEABLY ACCORDING TO SALVED VALUES	1495
General rule	1495
Different degrees of risk or difficulty	1497
Silver or bullion	1498
Justifications of the general rule	1499
Different risks	1500
Interests in salved property	1506
Contribution to life salvage	1514
3. DIVISION OF LIABILITY	1515
Introduction	1515
Interest not in fact benefited	1516

17. APPORTIONMENT OF SALVAGE PAYMENTS

1. GENERAL MATTERS	1519
How the question of apportionment may arise	1519
Jurisdiction and general principle on apportionment	1520
Salvage under £5,000	1521
Apportionment by the court	1522

xxv

Contents

Governing law	1523
2. Detailed Instances of Apportionment	1524
Apportionment amongst owners, master and crew of a salving vessel	1525
Share of owner of a salving vessel	1525
Master's share	1525
Crew's share; officers and seamen	1526
Passengers	1528
Extra shares	1528
Special rewards	1528
Crown ships	1529
Pilot	1530
Lifeboatmen	1530
Coastguard	1530
Apportionment amongst individual salvors not associated, *e.g.* as a crew	1531
Apportionment amongst various salving vessels or sets of salvors	1532
Where services contemporaneous	1532
Priority in time; general principle	1533
Wrongful dispossession; effect	1534
Share due to deceased salvor is awarded to his personal representatives	1535
3. Agreements for Apportionment	1536
Customary agreements for apportionment	1537
Seamen's salvage rights	1538
Salvors other than seamen	1540
Prior act of apportionment	1540

APPENDICES

A. Salvage Documents
  1. Lloyd's Standard Form of Salvage Agreement (LOF 1995)
  2. Lloyd's Standard Form of Salvage Agreement (LOF 2000)
  3. Lloyd's Standard Salvage and Arbitration Clauses
  4. Lloyd's Procedural Rules
  5. SCOPIC 2000 Clause
  5A. SCOPIC 2000 Appendix A
  5B. SCOPIC 2000 Appendix B
  5C. SCOPIC 2000 Appendix C
  6. ISU Lumpsum Sub-Contract Agreement
  7. Code of Practice between ISU and International Group of P&I Clubs
  8. Code of Practice between International Group of P&I Clubs and London Property Underwriters Regarding the Payment of the Fees and Expenses of the SCR under SCOPIC
  9. International Salvage Union Sub-Contract (Award Sharing) 1994
  10. Guarantee [for a Single Guarantor] to the Corporation of Lloyd's and to the Contractor in Connection with a Salvage Agreement on Lloyd's Form
  11. Guarantee [for two or More Guarantors] to the Corporation of Lloyd's and to the Contractor in Connection with a Salvage Agreement on Lloyd's Form
  12. Guarantee [for a Single Guarantor (Insured)] to the Corporation of Lloyd's and to the Contractor in Connection with a Salvage Agreement on Lloyd's Form [With Indemnity]
  13. Indemnity in Connection with a Salvage Agreement on Lloyd's Form [For Use with Guarantee by a Single Guarantor (Insured)]

Contents

14. Guarantee [for Two or More Guarantors (Insured)] to the Corporation of Lloyd's and to the Contractor in Connection with a Salvage Agreement on Lloyd's Form [With Indemnity]
15. Indemnity in Connection with a Salvage Agreement on Lloyd's Form [For Use with Guarantee by Two or More Guarantors (Insured)]
16. Salvage Guarantee Form I.S.U. 1
17. Salvage Guarantee Form I.S.U. 2
18. Salvage Guarantee Form I.S.U. 3
19. Salvage Guarantee Form I.S.U. 4
20. Salvage Guarantee Form I.S.U. 5

B. UNITED KINGDOM LEGISLATION
21. Aircraft (Wreck and Salvage) Order 1938
22. Hovercraft (Application of Enactments) Order 1972
23. Protection of Wrecks Act 1973
24. Civil Aviation Act 1982
25. Protection of Military Remains Act 1986
26. Merchant Shipping Act 1995
27. Merchant Shipping and Maritime Security Act 1997

C. INTERNATIONAL CONVENTIONS
28. (Brussels) Convention for the Unification of Certain Rules of Law respecting Assistance and Salvage at Sea 1910
29. (Brussels) International Convention for the Unification of Certain Rules relating to Assistance and Salvage of Aircraft or by Aircraft at Sea 1938
30. (Brussels) Protocol to Amend the Convention for Unification of Certain Rules of Law relating to Assistance and Salvage at Sea 1967
31. United Nations Convention on the Law of the Sea 1982
32. CMI Report to the International Maritime Organization
33. International Convention on Salvage 1989

D. RULES AND REGULATIONS
34. The Queen's Regulations for the Royal Navy
35. Royal National Lifeboat Institution Regulations

Page

Index   875

TABLE OF CASES

[References in these tables are to paragraph numbers.]

A.B. DONALDSON v. Dow & Carnie (1922) 10 Ll.L.Rep. 572 358
Aberdeen Arctic Co. v. Sutter (1862) 6 L.T. 229, H.L.; 10 W.R. 516 314
Aboukir, The (1905) 21 T.L.R. 200 .... 601, 607
Accomac, The [1891] P. 349; 66 L.T. 335; 7 T.L.R. 649; 7 Asp. M.L.C. 153 1316
Actaeon, The (1853) 1 Spinks 17; 1 Ecc. & Ad. 176; 164 E.R. 1026 98
Adam W. Spies, The (1901) 70 L.J.P. 25 .... 1096, 1101
Admiralty Commissioners v. Owners of M.V. Josefina Thorden and her cargo [1945] 1 All
    E.R. 344; 172 L.T. 186; 61 T.L.R. 22 .... 1331, 1479
—— v. Page [1921] 1 A.C. 137 .... 459, 464, 480, 670
—— v. Valverda (Owners) [1938] A.C. 173; *affirming* [1937] 1 K.B. 745; 107 L.J.K.B. 99;
    158 L.T. 281; 54 T.L.R. 305; 43 Com. Cas. 139; 59 Ll.L.Rep. 231, *reversing* [1936]
    1 K.B. 724 .... 3, 38, 455, 645, 652, 653, 659, 660, 662, 663, 781, 792, 863, 1460
Aeolus, The (1873) L.R. 4 A. & E. 29; 42 L.J. Adm. 814; 28 L.T. 41; 21 W.R. 704 .... 39, 590,
    591, 593
Africa, The (1854) 1 Spinks E. & A. 229; 1 Ecc. & Ad. 299; 8 L.T. 582; 164 E.R. 173 ... 528, 529,
    815, 833, 857, 956
Africa Occidental, The [1951] 2 Lloyd's Rep. 107 .... 357, 358, 698, 699, 701, 702, 705
Afrika, The (1880) 5 P.D. 192; 49 L.J.P. 63; 42 L.T. 403; 4 Asp. M.L.C. 266 ..... 1519, 1536, 1537,
    1538
Afro Produce (Supplies) Ltd v. Metalfa Shipping Co. Ltd (The Georgia) [1978] 2 Lloyd's
    Rep. 197 228
Agamemnon, The (1883) 5 Asp. M.L.C. 92 .... 493, 495
Aglaia, The (1888) 13 P.D. 160; 57 L.J. Adm. 106; 59 L.T. 528; 37 W.R. 255 .... 340, 341, 344,
    358, 590
Aitchison v. Lohre (1879) L.R. 4 App. Cas. 755; 2 Q.B. D. 501; 3 Q.B.D. 558; 49 L.J.Q.B.
    123; 41 L.T. 323; 28 W.R. 1; 4 Asp. M.L.C. 168 643
Akerblom v. Price, Potter, Walker & Co. (1881) 7 Q.B.D. 129; 50 L.J.Q.B. 629; 44 L.T.
    837; 29 W.R. 797; 4 Asp. M.L.C. 441 .... 8, 148, 593, 595, 596, 599, 603, 859, 861, 881, 930,
    931, 932
Albion, The (1861) Lush. 282 .... 27, 333, 358, 616
Albionic, The [1942] P. 81; 111 L.J.P. 1; 167 L.T. 148; 58 T.L.R. 154; 72 Ll.L.Rep. 91;
    affirming [1941] P. 99; 70 Ll.L.Rep. 257 ... 209, 515, 565, 569, 570, 573, 574, 575, 576, 577,
    579, 587, 1526
Aldora, The [1975] Q.B. 748; [1975] 2 W.L.R. 791; (1974) 119 S.J. 253; *sub nom.* Aldora,
    The; Tyne Tugs v. Owners of the Motor Vessels Aldora [1975] 2 All E.R. 69; *sub nom.*
Tyne Tugs v. Aldora (Owners); Aldora, The [1975] 1 Lloyd's Rep. 617 ..... 1467, 1468, 1473
Alenquer The, The Rene [1955] 1 W.L.R. 263; [1955] 1 Lloyd's Rep. 101 ... 717, 751, 752, 1111,
    1124, 1243, 1423
Alexander, The (1811) 1 Dods. 278; 165 E.R. 1310 181
Alfen, The (1857) Swab. 189; 166 E.R. 1088 .... 38, 459, 461, 462, 500, 501
Alfred, The (1884) 5 Asp. 214; 50 L.T. 511 .... 728, 730, 816, 820, 864
Alice, The (1868) L.R. 2 P.C. 245; 5 Moo. P.C.C. (N.S.) 333; 38 L.J. Adm. 5; 19 L.T. 678;
    17 W.R. 209; 3 Mar. L.C. 180; 16 E.R. 541 1317
Alice Richardson, The (1865) 3 M.L.C. Dig. 68 638
Alma, The (1861) Lush. 378; 7 L.T. 223; 1 M.L.C. 249; 167 E.R. 162 .... 357, 653
Alraigo, The [1984] 116 L.M.L.N. ;[1984] 123 L.M.L.N.;[1984] 4 L.M.C.L.Q. 690 361
Alsey Steam Fishing Co. Ltd v. Hillman (Owners) (The Kirkness) [1956] 2 Lloyd's Rep.
    651 1194
Altair, The [1897] P. 105; 66 L.J.P. 42; 76 L.T. 263; 8 Asp. M.C. 224 .... 930, 931, 1096, 1101
Ambatielos The, Cephalonia The [1923] P. 68 1247
Amelia Lauro, The (1940) 68 Ll.L.Rep. 12 .... 210, 333, 337, 357, 597, 598, 647
American Farmer, The (1947) 80 Ll.L.Rep. 672 .... 45, 215, 255, 357, 358, 636, 675, 681, 1126,
    1454, 1533

Table of Cases

American Sioux, The [1980] 1 W.L.R. 996; (1979) 124 S.J. 15; [1980] 3 All E.R. 154; [1980] 2 Lloyd's Rep. 224, C.A.; *reversing* [1980] 1 Lloyd's Rep. 620 1280
Amerique, The (1874) L.R. 6 P.C. 468; 31 L.T. 854; 23 W.R. 488 .... 1316, 1457
Amoco Cadiz, The [1984] 2 Lloyd's Rep. 304 1087
Andalusia, The (1865) 12 L.T. 584 .... 1437, 1438
Andalusian, The (1878) 3 P.D. 182 .... 178, 1411
Anders Knape, The (1879) 4 P.D. 213; 48 L.J. Adm. 53; 40 L.T. 684 .... 341, 357, 590, 593
Anderson Tritton & Co. v. Ocean Steamship Co. (1884) 10 App. Cas. 107; 13 Q.B.D. 651; 54 L.J.Q.B. 192; 53 L.J.Q.B. 161; 52 L.T. 441; 33 W.R. 433; 5 Asp. M.C. 202 .... 149, 816, 817, 827, 830, 831, 1489
Andrina, The (1870) L.R. 3 A. & E. 286; 22 L.T. 488; 3 Mar. L.C. 410 .... 357, 1445, 1528
Anna, The, Shipping Gazette, May 30, 1905 .... 1533, 1535
Anna Helena, The (1883) 49 L.T. 204; 5 Asp. M.L.C. 142 1432
Anna Mazarki, The (1931) 39 Ll.L.Rep. 194 341
Annapolis, The (1861) Lush. 355; 5 L.T. 37; 167 E.R. 150; *affirming* (1861) Lush. 295; 30 L.J.P.M. & A. 201; 4 L.T. 417; 167 E.R. 128 ...... 53, 64, 346, 358, 359, 601, 605, 606, 1096, 1097
Annie, The (1886) 12 P.D. 50; 56 L.J. Adm. 70; 56 L.T. 500; 35 W.R. 366; 6 Asp. M.L.C. 117 .... 279, 281
Antilope, The (1873) L.R. 4 A. & E. 33; 42 L.J.Adm. 42; 28 L.T. 74; 21 W.R. 464; 1 Asp. M.L.C. 513 1335
Appleby v. Myers (1867) L.R. 2 C.P. 651; 36 L.J.C.P. 331; 16 L.T. 669 610
Aquila, The (1798) 1 C. Rob. 37; 165 E.R. 87 .... 298, 696, 697, 1432
Archer H.M.S., The [1918] P. 1 24
Ardincaple, The (1834) 3 Hagg. 151; 8 L.T. 154; 166 E.R. 362 1414
Argentina, The (1888) 13 P.D. 191 1339
Argonaut, The, Shipping Gazette, December 3, 1884 .... 1380, 1382
Aries Tanker Corp. v. Total Transport Ltd [1977] 1 W.L.R. 185; 121 S.J. 117; [1977] 1 All E.R. 398; [1977] 1 Lloyd's Rep. 334; *affirming* [1976] 2 Lloyd's Rep. 256 474
Arno, The (1895) 72 L.T. 621; 11 T.L.R. 453; 8 Asp. M.L.C. 5 .... 1380, 1381, 1382, 1383
Arthur, The (1862) 6 L.T. 556; 1 M.L.C. 228 .... 815, 857, 881, 1397
Association and the Tomney, The [1970] 2 Lloyd's Rep. 59 212
Atkinson v. Woodhall (1862) 31 L.J.M.C. 174; 1 H. & C. 170; 36 L.T. 361; 26 J.P. 759; 10 W.R. 671; 8 Jur. (N.S.) 720; 1 Mar. L.C. 224 .... 141, 147, 1520
Atlantic, The (1925) 27 Ll.L.Rep. 196 1432
Atlas, The (1862) Lush. 518; 15 Moo. P.C. 329; 31 L.J.P.M. & A. 210; 6 L.T. 737; 10 W.R. 850; 8 Jur. (N.S.) 753; 10 W.R. 850; 1 Asp. M.C. 235; 15 E.R. 519 .... 717, 733, 894, 1109, 1125, 1132, 1423
Attorney General v. Blake [2001] 1 A.C. 268 952
—— v. Company of Proprietors of Margate Pier and Harbour [1900] 1 Ch. 749 549
—— v. Norstedt (The Triton) (1716) 3 Price 97 1250
—— v. Wilts United Dairies Ltd (1922) 91 L.J. (K.B.) 897 688
Attorney General of Hong Kong v. Reid [1994] 1 A.C. 324 952
Attorney General's Reference (No. 2 of 1999) [2000] 3 W.L.R. 195, C.A. 1202
August Korff, The [1903] P. 166; 72 L.J.P. 53; 89 L.T. 192 .... 38, 358, 490, 491, 493, 494, 495, 733, 734, 755
Auguste Legembre, The [1902] P. 123; 71 L.J.P. 53; 86 L.T. 358; 50 W.R. 622 .... 53, 55, 56, 57, 59, 60, 63, 703, 1528
Australian Steam Navigation Co. v. Morse (1872) L.R. 4 P.C. 222; 8 Moo. P.C. (N.S.) 482; 27 L.T. 357; 20 W.R. 728 .... 804, 807
Aztecs, The (1870) 3 Asp. M.L.C. 326; 21 L.T. 797 .... 333, 733

B.P. EXPLORATION CO, (LIBYA) LTD v. Hunt (No. 2) [1983] 2 A.C. 352; [1982] 2 W.L.R. 253; *affirming* [1981] 1 W.L.R. 232; 125 S.J. 165; *reversing* [1979] 1 W.L.R. 783; 123 S.J. 455 .... 610, 1462, 1466, 1468
B.V. Bureau Wijsmuller v. United States of America (The Pioneer Commander) (1983) 702 F. 2d 333 (U.S.C.A., 2nd Cir.) 341 1464
Baku Standard, The [1901] A.C. 549, P.C.; 70 L.J.P.C. 98; 84 L.T. 788 .... 1439, 1440, 1443, 1445
Baltimore, The (1817) 2 Dods. 132; 165 E.R. 1438 1528
Banda and Kirwee Booty, The (1866) L.R. 1 A. & E. 109; 35 L.J. Adm. 17; 12 Jur. (N.S.) 891 666
Banco, The [1971] P. 137 87

Table of Cases

Bankers Trust International Ltd v. Todd Shipyards Corp. (The Halcyon Isle) [1981] A.C. 221 1247
Barclays Bank Plc v. O' Brien [1994] 1 A.C. 180 942
Barefoot, The (1850) 6 L.T. 371; 14 Jur. 841 .... 210, 1126, 1234, 1242, 1243
Baring v. Day (1806) 8 East 57 .... 111, 144, 628
Barameda Enterprises Pty. Ltd v. O' Connor (The Tiruna) [1987] 2 Lloyd's Rep. 666 1195
Bartley, The (1857) Swab. 198 1412
Batavier, The (1853) 1 Spinks E. & A. 169; 164 E.R. 98 .... 333, 342, 377
Batty v. Metropolitan Realisations Ltd [1978] Q.B. 554; [1978] 2 W.L.R. 500; 122S.J. 63; [1978] 2 All E.R. 445; 245 E.G. 43; 7 Build. L.R. 1 1123
Baumwoll Manufacturer von Carl Scheibler v. Furness [1893] A.C. 8; 62 L.J.Q.B. 201; 68 L.T. 1; 9 T.L.R. 71; 7 Asp. M.L.C. 263 219
Beale v. Thompson (1803) 3 B. & P. 405; *reversed* (1804) 4 East 546 580
Beatsa, The (1937) 58 Ll.L.Rep. 85 .... 347, 359, 598, 1415, 1429, 1434, 1501
Beaver, The (1801) 3 C. Rob. 92; 165 E.R. 468 .... 48, 358, 522, 559, 567, 581, 582, 583, 586, 648
The Beaverford (Owners) v. The Kafiristan (Owners) [1938] A.C. 136; 106 L.J.P. 91; 157 L.T. 439; 53 T.L.R. 1010; 81 S.J. 844; 43 Com. Cas. 21; 19 Asp. M.L.C. 139; *reversing* [1937] P. 63 .... 78, 340, 488, 541, 542, 1096, 1099
Bedeburn, The [1914] P. 146; 83 L.J.P. 109; 111 L.T. 464; 80 T.L.R. 513; 12 Asp. M.C. 530 ... 39, 591, 597
Beldon v. Campbell (1851) 6 Exch. 886; 20 L.J. Ex. 342; 17 L.T. (O.S.) 257; 155 E.R. 805 ... 805, 820
Belgia, The (1941) 71 Ll.L. Rep. 21 .... 27, 208, 210, 358, 655, 657
Belgian Steamship (Salvage Claim, A (1941) 71 Ll.L.Rep. 82 597
Bell v. Lever Bros. Ltd [1932] A.C. 161; [1931] All E.R. 1; 101 L.J.K.B. 129; 146 L.T. 258; 48 T.L.R. 133; 76 S.J. 50; 37 Com. Cas. 98 913
Ben Gairn, The [1979] 1 Lloyd's Rep. 410 .... 1447, 1468, 1469, 1473
Bengali (ex Theophile Masart), The (1935) 52 Ll.L.Rep. 315 450
Bengloe, The (1940) 67 Ll.L.Rep. 307 .... 333, 341, 594, 598, 599
Benlarig, The (1888) 14 P.D. 3; 58 L.J. Adm. 24; 60 L.T. 238; 6 Asp. M.C. 360 .... 38, 358, 717, 734, 749, 736, 737, 738, 755, 1428
Bertie, The (1886) 55 .T. 520; 2 T.L.R. 690; 6 Asp. M.L.C. 26 .... 524, 666, 670
Bertil, The [1952] 2 Lloyd's Rep. 176 .... 347, 359, 1434
Betsey, The (1843) 2 W. Rob. 167; 2 Not. of Cas. 409; 1 L.T. (O.S.) 410; 7 Jur. 755; 166 E.R. 717 .... 861, 956, 957
Beulah, The (1842) 7 Jur. 207 .... 455, 603, 1536
Birckett v. Hayes [1982] 1 W.L.R. 816, C.A.; 126 S.J. 399; [1982] 2 All E.R. 70 1464
Birnam, The (1907) 76 L.J.P. 28; 96 L.T. 792; 10 Asp. M.L.C. 462 1525
Black Boy, The (1837) 3 Hagg. 386n; 166 E.R. 448n 1234
Blaireau, The (1804) 2 Cranch. 240 1128
Bland v. Ross (The Julia) (1860) 14 Moo. (P.C.) 210; Lush. 224; 15 E.R. 284 .... 1101, 1317
Blenden-Hall (1814) 1 Dods 414; 165 E.R. 1361 .... 1126, 1432, 1457, 1534
Blow Boat, The [1912] P. 217; 82 L.J.P. 24 174
Bluebird, The [1971] 1 Lloyd's Rep. 229 .... 1397, 1401
Boiler ex Elephant (1891) 64 L.T. 543 .... 208, 1397
Bold Buccleugh, The (1851) 7 Moo. P.C. 267; 19 L.T. (O.S.) 235; 13 E.R. 884 1247
Bomarsund, The (1860) Lush. 77; 167 E.R. 41 .... 343, 732
Boston, The (1833) 1 Sumn. 328 1128
Boston v. France, Fenwick & Co. Ltd (1923) 15 Ll.L.Rep. 85; 129 L.T. 766; 39 T.L.R. 441; 16 Asp. M.L.C. 239; 28 Com. Cas. 367; [1923] All E.R. 583 .... 691, 705
Boston Lincoln, The [1980] 1 Lloyd's Rep. 481 1427
Bosworth (No. 3), The [1962] 1 Lloyd's Rep. 483; 106 S.J. 689 1434
Bowbelle, The [1990] 1 W.L.R. 1330 .... 1203, 1204
Boyse v. Rossborough (1857) 6 H.L.C. 3; 7 I.C.L.R. 17 615
Bradley v. H. Newsom, Sons and Company [1919] A.C. 16; 88 L.J.K.B. 35; 119 L.T. 239 34 T.L.R. 613; 14 Asp. M.L.C. 340; 24 Com. Cas. 1; *reversing sub nom.* Newsum H. & Co. v. Bradley [1918] 1 K.B. 271; *reversing* [1917] 2 K.B. 112 ..... 208, 210, 211, 211, 1378, 1383, 1384
Bramley Moore, The [1964] P. 200 1182
Branken Moor, The (1837) 3 Hagg. 373; 166 E.R. 444 .... 590, 599
Branston, The (1826) 2 Hagg. 3n; 166 E.R. 146 .... 632, 633
Bremen, The (1906) 94 L.T. 380; 10 Asp. M.L.C. 229 1526

Table of Cases

Breydon Merchant, The [1992] 1 Lloyd's Rep. 373 .... 439, 1191, 1198
Briggs v. Merchant Traders' Ship Loan and Insurance Association (1849) 13 Q.B. 167; 18
    L.J.Q.B. 178; 13 Jur. 787 1494
Britain, The (1839) 1 W. Rob. 40; 70 L.T. 224; 166 E.R. 489 .... 835, 837, 843
British Empire, The (1842) 6 Jur. 608 .... 858, 881
British Inventor, The (1933) 45 Ll.L.Rep. 263 .... 26, 341, 357, 914
British Transport Commission v. Gourley [1956] A.C. 185 1477
Broadmayne, The [1916] P. 64; 85 L.J.P. 153; 114 L.T. 891; 60 S.J. 367; 32 T.L.R. 304 .... 671, 1170
Brown v. Stapyleton (1827) 4 Bing. 119; 5 L.J. (O.S.) C.P. 121; 12 Moore 334 .... 185, 188, 189, 192
—— v. Wilkinson (1846) 15 M. & W. 391 1185
Buffalo and Other Barges, The (1937) 58 Ll.L.Rep. 302 692
Bunge Corporation, New York v. Tradax Export S.A., Panama [1981] 1 W.L.R. 711; 125
    S.J. 373; [1981] 2 All E.R. 540; [1981] Lloyd's Rep. 1; *affirming* [1980] 1 Lloyd's
    Rep. 294; [1981] 2 All E.R. 524; *reversing* [1980] 2 Lloyd's Rep. 477 .... 1028, 1030
Burns Philip & Co. Ltd v. Gillespie Bros. Prt. Ltd (1947) 74 C.L.R. 148; 20 A.L.J. 490 806
Bushmills, The, Shipping Gazette, June 19, 1906 702

C.I.B.C. Mortgages Plc v. Pitt [1994] 1 A.C. 200 942
C.S. Butler, The (1874) L.R. 4 A. & E. 178; 43 L.J. Adm. 17; 30 L.T. 475; 22 W.R. 759;
    2 Asp. M.L.C. 237 .... 1111, 1423
Cadiz and The Boyne, The (1876) 35 l.t. 602; 3 Asp. M.L.C. 332 .... 15, 357, 358
Cairo, The (1874) L.R. 4 A. & E. 184; 43 l.j. Adm. 33; 30 L.T. 535; 22 W.R. 742; 2 Asp.
    M.L.C. 257 .... 277, 293, 358
The Caledonain Steamship Co. v. Hutton (The Medora) (1847) 5 Not. of Cas. 156 1317
Calypso, The (1828) 2 Hagg. 209; 116 E.R. 221 .... 20, 337, 358, 1334
Cambria, The, December 15, 1848 1233
Cambria, The (1923) 14 Ll.L.Rep. 170 .... 1432, 1528
Cambrian, The (1897) 8 Asp. M.L.C. 263; 76 L.T. 504 .... 357, 753, 755
Camellia, The (1883) 9 P.D. 27; 53 L.J.Adm. 12; 50 L.T. 126; 32 W.R. 495; 5 Asp. M.C.
    197 .... 717, 733, 734
Canova, The (1866) L.R. 1 A. & E. 54; 12 Jur. (N.S.) 528 .... 341, 342, 358, 620, 895, 904
Cape Packet, The (1848) 3 W. Rob. 122; 6 Not. of Cas. 565; 8 L.T. 582 ... 1105, 1108, 1422, 1423
Capella, The [1892] P. 70; 66 L.T. 388; 7 Asp M.C. 158 .... 1126, 1242, 1243
Capitan San Luis, The [1994] Q.B. 465 1204
Cargo ex Argos, The (1873) L.R. 5 P.C. 134 807
Cargo ex Capella, The (1867) L.R. 1 A. & E. 356; 16 L.T. 800 .... 541, 1096
Cargo ex Galem (1863) 2 Moo. P.C. (N.S.) 216; Br. & Lush. 167; 10 Jur. (N.S.) 477; 33
    L.J. Ad. 97; 9 L.T. 550; 12 W.R. 495 .... 1250, 1360
Cargo ex Honor, The (1866) L.R. 1 A. & E. 87; 35 L.J. Adm. 113; 15 W.R. 10; 12 Jur.
    (N.S.) 773 .... 626, 628, 629
Cargo ex Laertes, The (1887) 12 P.D. 187; 57 L.J. Adm. 108; 57 L.T. 502; 36 W.R. 111;
    6 Asp. M.C. 174 .... 490, 491
Cargo ex Loodianah, No. 1403, April 21, 1863, (1887) Vol. 2, p. 1854 1323
Cargo, The, ex Port Victor [1901] P. 243; 70 L.J.P. 52; 84 L.T. 677; 49 W.R. 578; 9 Asp.
    M.C. 182 .... 29, 31, 34, 41, 735, 1776, 1255, 1509, 1513
Cargo ex Sarpedon, The (1877) 3 P.D. 28; 37 L.T. 505; 26 W.R. 375; 3 Asp. M.C. 509 ... 267, 270, 280, 293, 725, 726, 727, 930
Cargo, The, ex Schiller (1877) 2 P.D. 145; 46 L.J. Adm. 9; 36 L.T. 714 ..... 99, 152, 204, 280, 284, 286, 288, 290, 291, 726, 1255, 1499
Cargo, The, ex Ulysses (1888) 13 P.D. 205; 60 L.T. 111; 58 L.J. Adm. 11; 6 Asp. M.C. 354 ... 358, 648, 650, 652, 655
Cargo, The, ex Woosung (1876) 1 P.D. 260; 35 L.T. 8; 25 W.R. 1; 3 Asp. M.L.C. 50 .... 357, 363, 669, 839, 895, 907, 932, 930, 939
Carmichael v. Brodie (The Sir Ralph Abercrombie) (1867) L.R. 1 P.C. 454; 4 Moo. P.C.
    (N.S.) 374; 16 E.R. 358 .... 2, 1446, 1528
Caroline, The (1861) Lush. 334; 5 L.T. 89; 1 Mar. L.C. 145; 167 E.R. 149 .... 496, 502
Carrie, The [1917] P. 224; 86 L.J.P. 178; 119 L.T. 128; 33 T.L.R. 573 ..... 515, 524, 525, 651, 655, 656
Carrier Dove, The (1863) 2 Moo. P.C. (N.S.) 243; 15 E.R. 893; Br. & L. 113 .... 1316, 1317
Case of Swans (1592) 7 Co. Rep. 15b 314

Table of Cases

Castellain v. Thompson (1862) 13 C.B. (N.S.) 105; 1 New Rep. 97; 32 L.P. (C.P.) 79; 7 L.T. 424; 11 W.R. 147; 1 Mar L.C. 259; 143 E.R. 41 .... 133, 145, 638
Castor, The [1932] P. 142; 101 L.J.P. 88; 147 L.T. 359; 48 T.L.R. 604; 18 Asp. M.C. 312 .... 233, 1341, 1342, 1348, 1528
Catherine, The (1848) 6 Not. of Cas. Suppl. xliii, (1848) 12 Jur. 682 .... 357, 854, 859
Cato, The (1930) 37 Ll.L.Rep. 33 .... 358, 853, 956, 1105, 1411, 1447
Cawarsand, The [1953] 1 Lloyd's Rep. 298 693
Cayo Bonito, The [1904] P. 310; 73 L.J.P. 93; 91 L.T. 102; 20 T.L.R. 576; 9 Asp. M.C. 603 ... 357, 358, 698, 703, 705
Cehave N.C. v. Bremer Handelsgesellschaft mbH, The Hansa Nord [1976] Q.B. 44; [1975] 3 W.L.R. 447; 119 S.J. 678; [1975] 3 All E.R. 739; [1975] 2 Lloyd's Rep. 445; *reversing* [1974] 2 Lloyd's Rep. 216 1028
Champion, The [1934] P. 1 .... 178, 1229, 1234, 1243
Chandler v. Blogg [1898] 1 Q.B. 32; 67 L.J.Q.B. 336; 77 L.T. 524; 8 Asp. M.L.C. 349; 14 T.L.R. 66; 3 Com. Cas. 18 178
—— v. Pearce [1904] 2 K.B. 422 178
Chaplin v. Hicks [1910] 2 K.B. 786; 80 L.J.K.B. 1292; 105 L.T. 285; 27 T.L.R. 458; 55 S.J. 580 763
Charcas, The (1908) Shipping Gazette, December 15 630
Charles, The (1872) L.R. 3 A. & E. 536; 26 L.T. 594; 21 W.R. 13 1525
Charles Adolphe, The (1856) Swab. 153; 166 E.R. 1069 .... 619, 1132
Charlotta, The (1831) 2 Hag. 361; 166 E.R. 275 685
Charlotte, The (1848) 3 Wm. Rob. 68 .... 333, 358, 448, 449, 454, 810, 857, 1393
Charlotte Wylie, The (1846) 2 W. Rob. 495; 5 Not. of Cas. 4; 166 E.R. 842 ... 341, 358, 645, 1486
Cheerful, The (1885) 11 P.D. 3; 55 L.J.P. 5; 54 L.T. 56; 34 W.R. 307; 5 Asp. M.L.C. 525 .... 717, 736, 739, 1411, 1422, 1423
Chetah, The (1868) L.R. 2. P.C. 205; 38 L.J. Adm. 1; 19 L.T. 621; 17 W.R. 233; 5 Moo. P.C. (N.S.) 278; 16 E.R. 520 .... 735, 1316, 1317
Chieftan, The (1846) 4 N. O.C. 459; 2 W. Rob. 450 .... 282, 822
China Navigation Co. Ltd v. Attorney General [1932] 2 K.B. 197; 101 L.J.K.B. 478; [1932] All E.R. 626; 147 L.T. 22; 48 T.L.R. 375; 18 Asp. M.L.C. 288 .... 658, 661, 688
China Pacific S.A. v. Food Corporation of India (The Winson) [1982] A.C. 439; [1981] 3 W.L.R. 860; 125 S.J. 808; [1981] 3 All E.R. 688; *reversing* [1981] Q.B. 403; [1980] 3 W.L.R. 891; 124 S.J. 614; [1980] 3 All E.R. 556; [1980] 2 Lloyd's Rep. 213; *reversing* [1979] 2 All E.R. 35; [1979] 1 Lloyd's Rep. 167 .... 15, 35, 363, 805, 806, 1488, 1999
Choka Star (No. 2), Thw [1989] 2 Lloyd's Rep. 42 829
Christy v. Row (1808) 1 Taunt. 300; 127 E.R. 849 1363
Cito, The (1881) 7 P.D. 5; 51 L.J. Adm. 1; 45 L.T. 663; 30 W.R. 836; 4 Asp. M.C. 468 .... 1380, 1381, 1383
Citos, The (1925) 22 Ll.L.Rep. 275 .... 690, 691, 693
City of Berlin, The (1877) 3 Asp. M.L.C. 491; 2 P.D. 187; 37 L.T. 307; 25 W.R. 793 1317
City of Calcutta, The (1898) 8 Asp. M.L.C. 442; 79 L.T. 517; 15 T.L.R. 108 .... 791, 820, 822
City of Chester, The (1884) 9 P.D. 182; 53 L.J.P. 90; 51 L.T. 485; 33 W.R. 104; 5 Asp. 311 .... 37, 38, 734, 735, 1392, 1393, 1428, 1439, 1442, 1457
City of Edinburgh, The (1831) 2 Hagg. 333; 166 E.R. 265 .... 591, 592
City of Lancaster, The (1929) 34 Ll.L.Rep. 381 .... 1315, 1316
City of Newcastle, The (1894) 71 L.T. 848; 7 Asp. M.L.C. 546 358
Clan Steam Trawling Co. Ltd v. Aberdeen Steam Trawling and Fishing Co. Ltd, 1908 S.C. 651; 45 Sc. L.R. 462; 15 S.L.T. 897 .... 515, 522, 530, 785, 857
Clan Sutherland, The [1918] P. 332; 88 L.J.P. 26 .... 1126, 1128
Clara, The, Shipping Gazette, November 22, 1905 1323
Clarisse, The (1856) Swab. 129; 12 Moo. P.C. 340; 8 L.T. 178; 14 E.R. 940 1316
Cleopatra, The (1877) 3 P.D. 145; 47 L.J.P. 72 1525
Clifton, The (1834) 3 Hagg. 117; 166 E.R. 349 .... 26, 37, 645, 651, 654, 683, 685
Collier, The (1866) L.R. 1 A. & E. 83; 12 Jur. (N.S.) 789 .... 484, 493, 499, 500, 531
Coltman v. Bibby Tankers Ltd (The Derbyshire) [1988] A.C. 276 169
Columbia, The (1838) 3 Hagg. 428; 166 E.R. 464 357
Columbus, The (1828) 2 Hagg. 178n; 166 E.R. 210 590
Colvin v. Newberry (1830) 7 Bing. 90; affirmed (1832) 1 Cl. & F. 283; 6 Bli. N.S. 167; 6 E.R. 923 464
Comitas, The (1934) 49 Ll.L.Rep. 43 1447

xxxiii

Table of Cases

Constable v. Gamble (Sir Henry Constable's Case) (1601) 5 Co. Rep. 106a; 77 E.R. 218; 2 Inst. 167 .... 91, 108, 202, 204
Constancia, The (1846) 2 W. Rob. 487; 4 Not. of Cas. 512; 11 L.T. 113; 10 Jur. 845; 166 E.R. 829 .... 33, 1247
Cook v. Dredging & Construction Co. Ltd [1958] 1 Lloyd's Rep. 334 174
Corcrest, The (1946) 80 Ll.L.Rep. 78 693
Coriolanus, The (1890) 15 P.D. 103; 59 L.J. Adm. 59; 63 L.T. 844 ...... 192, 587, 636, 1526, 1527, 1528
Cornelius Grinnell, The (1864) 2 M.L.C. 140 1445
Cornu v. Blackstone (1781) 2 Dougl. 641; 99 E.R. 406 131
Coromandel, The (1857) Swab. 205; 6 L.T. 371; 8 L.T 441; 166 E.R. 1097 .... 208, 209, 276
Corry v. Coulthard (1876) 3 Asp. M.L.C. 546 334
Cosmopolitan, The (1846) 6 N.O.C. Supp. xvii-xxviii 204, 208, 210
Cossman v. West (1887) 13 App. Cas. 160; 57 C.J.P.C. 17; 58 L.T. 122; 4 T.L.R. 65; 6 Asp. M.L.C. 233 .... 208, 209, 1229, 1233, 1234
Cox v. May (1815) 4 M. & S. 152; 105 E.R. 791 .... 1486, 1516
Craighall, The [1910] P. 207; 79 L.J.P. 73; 103 L.T. 236; 11 Asp. 419 174
Craigs, The (1880) 5 P.D. 186; 29 W.R. 446 1528
Cranstoun, The, unreported 1827 627
Crouan v. Stanier [1904] 1 K.B. 87 .... 479, 510
Crusader, The [1907] P. 196; 76 L.J.P. 102; 97 L.T. 20; 23 T.L.R. 382; 10 Asp. M.C. 442; affirming [1907] P. 15 .... 523, 629, 631, 815, 817
Crus V., The (1862) Lush. 583; 167 E.R. 266 .... 823, 891
Cumbrian, The (1887) 6 Asp. M.L.C. 151; 57 L.T. 205 .... 820, 857, 1492
Cunningham v. Harrison [1973] Q.B. 942; [1973] 3 W.L.R. 97; 117 S.J. 547; [1973] 3 All E.R. 463, C.A. 807
Currie v. M'Knight [1897] A.C. 97; 66 L.J.P.C. 19; 75 L.T. 457; 8 Asp. M.L.C. 193 89
Curtis v. Wild [1991] 4 All E.R. 172 176
Cutter v. Powell (1795) 6 T.R. 320; 101 E.R. 73 610
Cybele, The (1878) 3 P.D. 8; affirming (1877) 2 P.D. 224; 47 L.J. Adm. 86; 37 L.T. 773; 26 W.R. 345, C.A. 669, 672, 673, 693
Cythera, The [1965] 2 Lloyd's Rep. 454; Supreme Ct., New South Wales 16, 345, 358, 525

D.P.P. v. Manners [1978] A.C. 43 549
Dalewood, The (1943) 75 Ll.L.Rep. 88 .... 45, 357, 1454
Dalhousie, The (1875) 1 P.D. 271n; sub nom. The Azalea, 35 L.T. 9n; 3 Asp. M.L.C. 240a 670
Dantzic Packet, The (1837) 3 Hagg. 383; 8 L.T. 582; 166 E.R. 447 ... 1133, 1229, 1233, 1234, 1236, 1242, 1243
Dart, The (1899) 8 Asp. M.L.C. 481; 80 L.T. 23 .... 717, 734, 743, 735, 750, 752
Daulia Ltd v. Four Millbank Nominees Ltd [1978] Ch. 231; [1978] 2 W.L.R. 621; 121 S.J. 851; [1978] 2 All E.R. 557; 36 P. & C.R. 244 766
Re David Buckley v. Royal National Lifeboat Institution (1889) 43 Ch. D. 27; 59 L.J. Ch. 87; 62 L.T. 141; 41 Ch. D. 168 698
De Bay, The (1883) 8 App. Cas. 559; 52 L.J.P.C. 57; 49 L.T. 414; 5 Asp. 156 ... 1428, 1439, 1440, 1443, 1446, 1447, 1468
De Bussche v. Alt (1878) 8 Ch. D. 286; 47 L.J. Ch. 381; 38 L.T. 370; 3 Asp. M.L.C. 584 823
Debrett, The (1947) 81 Ll.L.Rep. 24 358
Delphinula, The (1947) 80 Ll.L.Rep. 459 .... 1111, 1120, 1122
Demosthenes, The (1926) 26 Ll.L.Rep. 99 358
Despina R., The [1979] A.C. 685; [1978] 3 W.L.R. 804; 122 S.J. 758; [1978] 1 All E.R. 421; [1979] 1 Lloyd's Rep. 1; affirming [1978] 2 W.L.R. 887; [1977] 3 W.L.R. 597; 122 S.J. 366; 121 S.J. 574; [1978] 2 All E.R. 764 1462
Dictator, Thee [1894] P. 64 1185
Dimitrios N. Bogiazides, The (1930) 37 Ll.L.Rep. 27 341
Domby, The (1941) 60 Ll.L.Rep. 161 .... 341, 601, 616
Domira, The (1914) 29 T.L.R. 557; 30 T.L.R. 521 1434
Donnelly v. Joyce [1974] Q.B. 454; [1973] 3 W.L.R. 514; 117 S.J. 488; [1973] 3 All E.R. 475; [1973] 2 Lloyd's Rep. 130 807
Donoghue v. Stevenson [1932] A.C. 562; 101 L.J.C.P. 119; 147 L.T. 281; 48 T.L.R. 494; 76 S.J. 396; 37 Com. Cas. 850 1120
Dorothy Foster, The (1805) 6 C. Rob. 89; 165 E.R. 860 .... 358, 1364

Table of Cases

Dorset Yacht Co. Ltd v. Home Office [1970] A.C. 1004; [1970] 2 W.L.R. 1140; 114S.J. 375; [1970] 1 Lloyd's Rep. 453; [1970] 2 All E.R. 294; *affirming* [1969] 2 Q.B. 412; [1969] 2 W.L.R. 1008; 113 S.J. 227; [1969] 2 All E.R. 564; *affirming* 113 S.J. 57; [1968] C.L.Y. 2638 1120
Dosseitei, The (1846) 10 Jur. 865 .... 344, 593, 1133
Dover Harbour Board v. The Ruby (1923) 14 Ll.L.Rep. 98 693
Driade, The [1959] 2 Lloyd's Rep. 311 .... 341, 357, 596, 597, 599, 616
Duc d' Aumale, The [1904] P. 60; 73 L.J.P. 8; 89 L.T. 486; 52 W.R. 319; 9 Asp. M.C. 502 ..... 541, 622, 1096, 1098, 1101
Due Checchi, The (1872) L.R. 4 A. & E. 35n; 26 L.T. 593; 20 W.R. 686; 1 Asp. 294 ... 1321, 1335
Dufferin, The (1849) 7 N.O.C. Supp. xxxiii 334
Duke of Clarence, The (1842) 1 W. Rob. 346; 8 L.T. 153; 166 E.R. 602 1420
Duke of Manchester, The (1847) 6 Moo. P.C. 90; *affirming* (1846) 2 W. Rob. 470; 4 Not. of Cas. 575; 10 Jur. 863; 166 E.R. 833 .. 261, 357, 512, 1125, 1389, 1402, 1411, 1412, 1423, 1424
Dunbar Cast, The [1902] W.N. 70 1527
Duncan v. Dundee, Perth and London Shipping Co. (1878) 5 R. 742; 15 Sc. L.R. 429; 5 Sess. Cas. (4th) 742 .... 29, 1255, 1491, 1508, 1513
Dundee, The (1823) 1 Hagg. 109 .... 1186, 1467
Dunlop Pneumatic Tyre Co. Ltd v. New Garage & Motor Co. Ltd [1915] A.C. 79 1448
Dunottar Castle, The [1902] W.N. 70 1528
Dygden, The (1841) 1 Not. of Cas. 115 1422

E.U., The (1853) 1 Spinks. 63; 8 L.T. 582; 164 E.R. 37 ... 289, 358, 717, 726, 727, 733, 734, 735, 1533
Earl of Eglinton, The (1855) Swab. 7; 8 L.T. 178; 166 E.R. 989 .... 38, 655, 1459
Eastern Monarch, The (1860) Lush. 81; 8 L.T. 441; 167 E.R. 43 .... 239, 358, 1385, 1514
Eastern Moon, The (1927) 28 Ll.L.Rep. 22 .... 1411, 1462
Eastwood, The (1943) 75 Ll.L.Rep. 91 .... 45, 1454
Ebor Jewel, The (1950) 83 Ll.L.Rep. 64 .... 1411, 1447
Edenmore, The [1893] P. 79; 69 L.T. 230 .... 782, 864, 1411, 1446, 1447, 1460
Edison, The [1932] P. 52; 101 L.J.P. 12; 147 L.T. 141; 48 T.L.R. 224; 37 Com. Cas. 182; 18 Asp. 276 1341
Edward Hawkins, The (1862) Lush. 5; 15 Moo. (P.C.) 486; 31 L.J. Adm. 46; 15 E.R. 578 ...... 717, 733, 735, 750
Effort, The (1834) 3 Hagg. 165; 166 E.R. 367 .... 1229, 1233, 1432
Egypt, The (1932) 44 Ll.L.R. 21 .... 389, 643
Eintracht, The (1874) 1 Asp. M.L.C. 198; 29 L.T. 857 289
Eisenach, The (1936) 54 Ll.L.Rep. 354; [1936] 1 All E.R. 855 .... 1347, 1350, 1411, 1462
Eleanor, The (1805) 6 C. Rob. 39 91
Eleanora Charlotta, The (1823) 1 Hagg. 156 .... 1247, 1249
Elin, The (1883) 8 P.D. 39 1250
Elise, The (1859) Swab. 436 .... 834, 837, 1126, 1238, 1528
Eliza, The (1862) Lush. 536; 7 L.T. 257; 1 Mar. L.C. 251; 167 E.R. 242 358
Elizabeth, The (1844) 8 Jur. 365; 3 L.T. (O.S.) 40 .... 341, 592, 593
Elkhound, The (1931) 39 Ll.L.Rep. 15 .... 358, 1528
Ella Constance, The (1864) 33 L.J. Adm. 189 .... 38, 333
Elliott Steam Tug Co. v. Admiralty Commissioners [1918] 2 K.B. 447; affirmed [1919] 1 K.B. 299, C.A.; affirmed [1921] 1 A.C. 137 H.L 464, 466, 467, 470, 472, 476, 670
Elliotta, The (1815) 2 Dods. 75 1397
Ellora, The (1862) Lush. 550; 167 E.R. 249 .... 338, 341, 357
Elpenor, The (1933) 47 Ll.L.Rep. 183 .... 1526, 1528
Elsie, The [1899] W.N. 54 358
Elton, The [1891] P. 265; 60 L.J.P. 69; 65 L.T. 232; 39 W.R. 703; 7 T.L.R. 434; 7 Asp. 66 ..... 142, 1255, 1484, 1490
Emilie Galline, The [1903] P. 106; 72 L.J.P. 38; 88 L.T. 743; 9 Asp. 401 .... 53, 54, 347, 358
Emma, The (1844) 2 W. Rob. 315; 3 Not. of Cas. 114; L.T. (O.S.) 17; 166 E.R. 774 ... 1335, 1431, 1495, 1497, 1498, 1499
Empire Gulf, The [1948] P. 168; [1948] L.J.R. 945; 92 S.J. 284; [1948] 1 All E.R. 564; 81 Ll.L.Rep. 255; 64 T.L.R. 214 1526
Empress of Australia and The Debrett, The (1947) 81 Ll.L.Rep. 24 .... 347, 358, 1434

Table of Cases

Enchantress, The (1860) Lush. 93; 30 L.J.P.M. & A. 15; 2 L.T. 574; 167 E.R. 49 .... 1519, 1525, 1536, 1537
Enchantress, The [1904] P. 310 .... 358, 455, 703
England, The (1868) L.R. 2 P.C. 253; 5 Moo. P.C.C. (N.S.) 344; 38 L.J. Adm. 9; 20 L.T. 46; 3 Mar. L.C. 216; 16 E.R. 545 1316
Envoy, The Shipp. Gaz., February 28, 1888 .... 43, 1454
Erato, The (1883) 13 P.D. 163; 57 L.J.P. 107 .... 37, 38, 357, 358, 1439, 1459, 1484
Escherheim, The Jade [1976] 1 W.L.R. 430; [1976] 1 All E.R. 920; \1976] 2 Lloyd's Rep. 1; *affirming* [1976] 1 W.L.R. 339; 120 S.J. 197; [1976] 1 All E.R. 441; [1976] 1 Lloyd's Rep. 81; *affirming* [1975] 1 W.L.R. 83; 119 S.J. 46; [1974] 3 All E.R. 307; [1974] 2 Lloyd's Rep. 188 .... 83, 1224, 1273
Esso Petroleum Co. Ltd v. Customs & Excise Commissioners [1976] 1 W.L.R. 1; 120 S.J. 49; [1976] 1 All E.R. 117; *affirming* [1975] 1 W.L.R. 406; 119 S.J. 205; *reversing* [1973] 1 W.L.R. 1240; 117 S.J. 680 240
Etrib, The (1930) 37 Ll.L.Rep. 262 .... 596, 598, 1530
Eugene, The (1834) 3 Hagg. 156; 166 E.R. 364 1534
Eugenia, The [1964] 2 Q.B. 226; [1964] 2 W.L.R. 114; 107 S.J. 931; [1964] 1 All E.R. 161; [1963] 2 Lloyd's Rep. 381; *reversing* [1963] 2 Lloyd's Rep. 155; [1963] C.L.Y. 3200 959
Eugenie, The (1844) 3 Not. Of Cas. 430 .... 339, 590
Europa, The (1863) Br. & Lush 89; 2 Moo. P.C.C. (N.S.) 1; 15 E.R. 803 24
Ewell Grove, The (1835) 3 Hagg. 209; 166 E.R. 384 .... 8, 654, 1392, 1434, 1457
ex p. Ferguson (1871) L.R. 6 Q. B. 280 .... 170, 207

F.D. LAMBERT, THE [1917] P. 232n; 119 L.T. 119; 1 Asp. 278 .... 210, 649
Fairbairn v. Vennootschap G. Ver Vries ZN (The Pergo) [1987] 1 Lloyd's Rep. 582 .... 1432, 1473
Fairless v. Thorsen, The Good Intent and The Prince Christian (1774) Mars. Ad. Cas.130 ... 91
Fairport, The (1882) 8 P.D.48; 52 L.J.P. 25; 48 L.T. 536; 31 W.R. 656; 5 Asp. 62 .... 1443, 1443, 1447
Falcke v. Scottish Imperial Insurance Co. (1886) 34 Ch. D. 234; 56 L.J. Ch. 707; 56 L.T. 220; 35 W.R. 143; 3 T.L.R. 141 .... 6, 33, 130
Farnley Hall, The (1881) 4 Asp. 499; 46 L.T. 216 .... 2, 1446
Favourite, The (1844) 2 W. Rob. 255; 5.L.T. 773 .... 144, 357, 359, 627, 628, 629
Federal Commerce & Navigation Co. Ltd v. Molena Alpha Inc. (The Nanfri) [1978] Q.B. 927; [1978] 3 W.L.R. 309; 122 S.J. 347; [1978] 3 All E.R. 1006; *affirmed* [1979] A.C. 757; [1978] 3 W.L.R. 991; 122 S.J. 843; [1979] 1 All E.R. 307; [1979] 1 Lloyd's Rep. 201 221
Felix, The (1853) 1 Spinks E. & A. 23n; 9 L.T. 302; 164 E.R. 14n 344, 599
Fenix, The (1855) Swab. 13 210
Fenton v. City of Dublin Steam Packet Co. (1838) 8 A. & E. 835; 8 L.J.Q.B. 28; 1 P. & D. 103 464
Ferriby, The (1948) 81 Ll.L.Rep. 246 358
Fibrosa Spolka Akcyjna v. Fairbairn, Lawson, Combe, Barbour Ltd [1943] A.C. 32; 111 L.J.K.B. 433; 86 S.J. 232; [1942] 2 All E.R. 122; 167 L.T. 101; 58 T.L.R. 308 610
Firefly, The (1857) Swab. 240; 29 L.T. (O.S.) 147; 166 E.R. 1116 .... 853, 857, 881
Firethorn, The (1948) 81 Ll.L.Rep. 178 .... 215, 1519, 1522, 1528
Fisher v. The Oceanic Grandeur (1972) 127 C.L.R. 312; [1972] 2 Lloyd's Rep. 396 ..... 41, 50, 54, 524, 641, 643, 785, 787, 841, 933, 1411
Five Steel Barges (1890) 15 P.D. 142; 59 L.J. Adm. 77; 63 L.T. 499; 39 W.R. 127; 6 Asp. M.L.C. 580 .... 21, 28, 29, 31, 233, 358, 601, 613, 616, 617, 1255, 1507, 1508, 1509, 1513
Fleece, The (1850) 3 W. Rob. 278; 7 Not. of Cas. 534; 166 E.R. 966 .... 1126, 1354, 1479, 1486
Flore, The (1929) 34 Li. L. Rep. 172 .... 53, 54, 57, 358
Florence, The (1852) 16 Jur. 572; 19 L.T. (O.S.) 304 .... 210, 565, 567, 568, 580, 572, 575, 576, 577, 581, 1126, 1432
Fortitude, The (1843) 2 W. Rob. 217; 2 Not. of Cas. 515; 2 L.T. (O.S.) 229; 8 Jur. 23 ... 115
Fothergill v. Monarch Airlines Ltd [1981] A.C. 251 88
Fountain, The (1866) L.R. 1 A. & E. 58 333
France, Fenwick Tyne and Wear Co. Ltd v. H.M. Procurator General (The Prins Knud) [1938] A.C. 667; [1942] A.C. 667; 111 L.J.P.C. 126; 167 L.T. 278; 58 T.L.R. 388, P.C. 20
Frances Mary, The (1827) 2 Hagg. 90 1397
Francis and Eliza, The (1816) 2 Dods. 115; 165 E.R. 1433 .... 358, 645, 650, 651

Table of Cases

Frederick, The (1838) 1 W. Rob. 16; 1 Hag. Adm. 211; 166 E.R. 480 .... 590, 593
Friesland, The [1904] P. 345; 73 L.J.P. 121; 91 L.T. 324 .... 620, 787, 837, 843
Frisia, The [1960] 1 Lloyd's Rep. 90; *affirming* [1959] 2 Lloyd's Rep. 193; [1959] C.L.Y. 3108 1477
Fulham, The [1899] P. 206; [1899] P. 251, C.A.; 68 L.J.P. 75; 81 L.T. 19; Asp. M.C. 559 ..... 1223, 1246
Funchal, The (1837) 3 Hagg. 386n; 166 E.R. 448 .... 591, 599
Fusilier, The (1865) 3 Moo. P.C. 51; Br. Of Lush. 341; 5 New Rep. 453; 12 L.T. 186; 11 Jur. (N.S.) 289; 13 W.R. 592; 2 Mar. L.C. 177; 16 E.R. 19 ... 26, 27, 261, 264, 266, 275, 277, 285, 293, 726, 727, 1428, 1479, 1481

G.N.R. v. Swaffield (1874) L.R. 9 Ex. 132 1073
Gaetano and Maria, The (1882) 7 P.D. 137; 51 L.J. Adm. 67; 46 L.T. 835; 3 W.R. 766; 4 Asp. M.C. 470 4
Galatea, The (1858) Swab. 349; 4 Jur. (N.S.) 1064 .... 592, 593, 601, 605, 607, 613
Ganges, The (1869) L.R. 2 A. & E. 370; 38 L.J. Adm. 61; 22 L.T. 73; 3 Mar. L.C. 342 .... 1140, 1537, 1540
Gapp v. Bond (1887) 19 Q.B.D. 200; 56 L.J.Q.B. 438; 57 L.T. 437; 35 W.R. 683; 3 T.L.R. 621 173
Garden City, The [1982] 2 Lloyd's Rep. 382 1202
Gark v. Straits Towing Ltd and Sayer, The Belize [1966] 2 Lloyd's Rep. 277 .... 516, 779
Gas Float Whitton No. 2, The (Wells v. The Owners of the Gas Float Whitton No. 2) [1897] A.C. 337; 76 L.T. 663; 66 L.J.P. 99; 13 T.L.R. 422; 8 Asp. M.L.C. 272; *affirming* [1896] P. 42; *affirming* [1895] P. 301; 65 L.J.P. 17; 66 L.J.P. 99; 76 L.T. 663; 4 Asp. M.C. 110 ...... 15, 152, 154, 157, 158, 165, 173, 179, 193, 195, 196, 206, 217, 230, 244, 245, 248, 318, 320
Gatoil International Inc. v. Arkwright-Boston Manufacturers Mutual Insurance Co. (The Sandrina) [1985] A.C. 255 .... 84, 88
Gaupen, The (1925) 22 Ll.L.Rep. 371; [1925] W.N. 138 .... 1323, 1329
Geertje K., The [1971] 1 Lloyd's Rep. 285 .... 332, 334, 705
Geestland, The [1980] 1 Lloyd's Rep. 628 .... 848, 1304, 1306, 1457, 1488
General Iron Screw Collier. Co. v. Schurmanns (1860) 1 J. & H. 180; 29 L.J. Ch. 877; 70 E.R. 712; 4 L.T. 138; 8 W.R. 732; 6 Jur. (N.S.) 883 294
General Palmer, The (1884) 5 Not. of Cas. 159n 598, 1401, 1411, 1437, 1520
General Tyre and Rubber Co. v. Firestone Tyre Co. Ltd [1975] 1 W.L.R. 819 1473
Genessee, The (1848) 12 Jur. 401 .... 38, 289, 733, 734, 1533
Georg, The [1894] P. 330; 71 l.t. 22; 7 App. M.L.C. 476 1397
George Booker & Co. v. Pocklington Steamship Co. Ltd [1899] 12 Q.B. 690 .... 479, 480, 481
George Dean, The (1857) Swab. 290; 30 L.T. (O.S.) 220; 6 W.R. 263; 166 E.R. 1143 .... 1323, 1361
George Gordon, The (1884) 9 P.D. 46; 53 L.J.P. 28; 50 L.T. 371; 32 W.R. 596; 5 Asp. M.L.C. 216 .... 1136, 1245
Germania, The [1904] P. 131; 73 L.J.P. 59; 9 Asp. M.C. 358; 90 L.T. 296 .... 357, 1095, 1323, 1325, 1330
Gertrude, The (1861) 30 L.J. Adm. 130 .... 208, 1229, 1232
Gipsy Queen, The [1895] P. 176; 72 L.T. 454; 43 W.R. 359; 11 T.L.R. 296; 39 S.J. 344; 7 Asp. M.L.C. 586; 11 R. 766 .... 1317, 1522, 1525
Glaisdale, The (1945) 78 Ll.L.Rep. 477; affirming 403 .... 341, 601, 608, 614
Glannibanta, The (1876) 1 P.D. 283; 24 W.R. 1033; *sub nom.* The Transit, 34 L.T. 934; 3 Asp. M.L.C. 233; 2 Char. Pr. Cas. 18 1317
Glasbrook Bros Ltd v. Glamorgan County Council [1925] A.C. 270 688
Glasgow Packet, The (1844) 2 W. Rob. 306 .... 1234, 1235, 1237, 1240, 1242, 1243
Glaucus, The (1948) 81 Ll.L.Rep. 262 .... 336, 341, 345, 383, 386, 600, 1411
Glenberg, The (1940) 67 Ll.L.Rep. 437 .... 531, 603
Glenduror, The (1871) L.R. 3 P.C. 589; 24 L.T. 499 1316
Glenfruin, The (1885) 10 P.D. 103; 54 L.J. Adm. 49; 52 L.T. 769; 33 W.R. 826 .... 488, 494, 502
Glengaber, The (1872) L.R. 3 A. & E. 534; 1Asp. 401; 41 L.J. Adm. 84; 27 L.T. 386; 21 W.R. 168 .... 541, 1096, 1103
Glengyle, The [1898] A.C. 519; 67 L.J.P. 87; *affirming* [1898] P. 97 ... 43, 45, 47, 1316, 1318, 1454, 1457, 1457
Glenmorven, The [1913] P. 141; 82 L.J.P. 113; 29 T.L.R. 412 .... 341, 601, 607, 620, 789

Table of Cases

Glider Standard Austria S.H., *In re* [1965] P. 463; [1965] 3 W.L.R. 568; 109 S.J. 649; [1965] 2 All E.R. 1022; [1965] 2 Lloyd's Rep. 189 248
Glory, The (1849) 14 Jur. 676; 8 L.T. 582 .... 1134, 1136, 1240, 1243, 1245
Gloxinia, The (1901) 18 T.L.R. 227 148
Glynoeron, The (1905) 21 T.L.R. 648 1245
Golden Sands, The [1975] 2 Lloyd's Rep. 166 .... 703, 705
Goldman v. Thai Airways International Ltd [1983] 1 W.L.R. 1186 1203
Golondrina, The (1867) L.R. 1 A. & E. 334 .... 358, 1528
Good Helmsman, The (1950) 84 Ll.L.Rep. 207 626
Goring, The [1988] A.C. 831 .... 89, 368
Gorliz, The [1917] P. 233n; 119 L.T. 123; 14 Asp. M.L.C. 282 656
Goulandris, The [1927] P. 182; 96 L.J.P. 85; 137 L.T. 90; 43 T.L.R. 308; 17 Asp. M.C. 209 ... 532, 1247, 1249, 1252
Governor Raffles, The (1815) 2 Dods. 14; 165 E.R. 1400 .... 16, 358, 580, 581
Graces, The (1844) 2 W. Rob. 294; 3 L.T. (O.S.) 320; 8 Jur. 501; 166 E.R. 765 .... 857, 1411, 1436
Grand Champion Tankers Ltd v. Nordpipe A/S (The Marion) [1984] A.C. 563 1202
Granhill, The [1951] 2 Lloyd's Rep. 13 .... 45, 47, 1454
Great Northern Railway Co. v. Swaffield (1874) L.R. 9 Ex. 132; 43 L.J. Ex. 89; 30 L.T. 562 807
Great Peace v. Tsavliris (The Great Peace) (2001) 151 N.L.J.R. 1696 913
Greenspan v. Slate (1953) 12 N.J. 426 .... 51, 807
Gregerso, The [1973] Q.B. 274; [1971] 2 W.L.R. 955; 115 S.J. 74; [1971] 1 All E.R. 961; [1971] 2 Lloyd's Rep. 220 .... 53, 348, 563, 690, 691, 693
Griffiths v. Kerkemeyer (1977) 139 C.L.R. 161 807
Grill v. General Iron Screw Collier Co. (1866) L.R. 1 C.P. 600; *affirmed* L.R. 3 C.P. 476; 37 L.J.CP. 205; 18 L.T. 485; 16 W.R. 796 1107
Guernsey Coast, The (1950) 83 Ll.L.Rep. 484 .... 357, 702, 705
Gurtner v. Beaton [1993] 2 Lloyd's Rep. 368 1204
Gustaf, The (1862) Lush. 506 1250
Guthrie v. North China Insurance Co. Ltd (1900) 6 Com. Cas. 25; 17 T.L.R. 79; *affirmed* 18 T.L.R. 412; 7 Com. Cas. 130 .... 1380, 1382, 1383

H.M Hayes, The (1861) Lush. 355; 5 L.T. 37; 1 Mar. L.C. 127; 167 E.R. 150 618
H.M.S. Thetis (1835) 3 Hagg. 14; 6 L.T. 914; 166 E.R. 312; *affirmed* 2 Knapp. 390; 8 L.T. 1543 .... 212, 389, 450, 451, 661, 663, 666, 1317, 1432
Hain SS. Co. v. Tate & Lyle (1936) 41 Com. Cas. 350; [1936] 2 All E.R. 597; 155 L.T. 177; 52 T.L.R. 617; 80 S.J. 687; 19 Asp. M.L.C. 62; 55 Lloyd's Rep. 159, H.L. 137
Hamtun, The [1999] 1 Lloyd's Rep. 883 .... 26, 333, 335, 1390
Happy Return, The (1828) 2 Hagg. 198; 166 E.R. 217 .... 111, 144, 627, 628, 629, 631
Harlow, The [1922] P. 175; 91 L.J.P. 119; 126 L.T. 763; 38 T.L.R. 375; 15 Asp. M.C. 498 ... 178
Harmonides, The [1903] P. 1; 72 L.J.P. 9; 87 L.T. 448; 51 W.R. 303; 19 T.L.R. 37; 9 Asp. M.L.C. 354 .... 1341, 1343
Harriot, The (1842) 1 W. Rob. 439; 1 Not. of Cas. 613; 8 L.T. 581; 166 E.R. 636 .... 528, 529
Harris v. Sheffield United Football Club Ltd [1988] Q.B. 77, C.A. 688
Hartford v. Jones (1698) 1 Ld. Raym. 393; 91 E.R. 1161; *sub nom.* Hartford v. Jones (1698) 2 Salk. 654 .... 131, 132, 140
Harvest Home, The [1904] P. 407; *varied* [1905] P. 177; 74 L.J.P. 65 .... 1096, 1101, 1102
Hassel, The [1959] 2 Lloyd's Rep. 82 .... 38, 743, 747, 766, 753, 756, 758, 761, 763, 764
Hastings v. Seman's Village [1946] 4 D.L.R. 695 808
Hebe, The (1844) 2 W. Rob. 246; 2 L.T. (O.S.) 404; 166 E.R. 747 ... 357, 590, 593, 597, 598, 1354
Hector, The (1853) 3 Hagg. 90; 166 E.R. 339 .... 27, 37, 1440, 1467
Hedley Byrne & Co. Ltd v. Heller & Partners Ltd [1964] A.C. 465; [1963] 3 W.L.R. 101; 107 S.J. 454; [1963] 2 All E.R. 575; [1963] 1 Lloyd's Rep. 485; *affirming* [1962] 1 Q.B. 396; [1961] 3 W.L.R. 1225; 105 S.J. 910; [1961] 3 All E.R. 891 905
Hedwig, The (1853) 1 Spinks E. & A. 19; 164 E.R. 11 .... 344, 598, 599
Heemskerk, The (1941) 70 Ll.L.Rep. 35 .... 208, 210
Hektor, The (1930) 36 Ll.L.Rep. 264 1447
Helen and George, The (1858) Swab. 368; 8 L.T. 335; 166 E.R. 1170 ..... 852, 861, 881, 891, 894, 907, 929, 930, 939
Helenus and Montagu, The [1982] 2 Lloyd's Rep. 39 .... 1473, 1530
Helmsing Schiffahrts GmbH & Co. A.G. v. Malta Drydocks Corp. [1977] 2 Lloyd's Rep. 444 1472

Table of Cases

Helmsman, The (1950) 84 Ll.L.Rep. 207 .... 333, 347, 359
Helvetia, The (1849) 8 Asp. 264n 752, 755
Henry, The (1810) Edwards 192; 2 Eng. Pr. Cas. 32; 165 E.R. 1079 .... 358, 815
Henry, The (1851) 15 Jur. 183; 16 L.T. (O.S.) 553 .... 38, 338, 891, 894, 902, 907, 908, 912, 926
Henry Ewbank, The (1833) 11 Fed. Cas. No. 6376 .... 27, 37
Herbert Fearn, The (1920) 4 Ll.L.Rep. 86 576
Hermione, The [1922] P. 162; 91 L.J.P. 136; 126 L.T. 701; 15 Asp. M.L.C. 493; [1922] All
    E.R. Rep. 570 801
Hertha, The (1940) 67 Ll.L.Rep. 370 598
Hestia, The [1895] P. 193, 64 l.j.p. 82; 72 l.t. 264 .... 31, 717, 732, 733, 748, 766, 779, 752, 963
Heye v. North German Lloyds (1887) 33 Fed. Rep. 60 (District Court, S.D., of New York);
    (1888) 36 Fed. Rep. 705 (Circuit Court of Appeals) 322
Himalaya, The (1857) Swab. 515 1525
Hingston v. Wendt (1876) 1 Q.B.D. 367; 45 L.J.Q.B. 440; 34 L.T. 664; 24 W.R. 864 ...... 133, 816,
    1493
Hjemmett, The (1880) 5 P.D. 227; 49 L.J.P. 66; 42 L.T. 514; 4 Asp. M.L.C. 274 .... 601, 613
Hoffman, The (1922) 10 Ll.L.Rep. 13 1432
Hohenzollern, The [1906] P. 339; 76 L.J.P. 17; 95 L.T. 585; 22 T.L.R. 778; 10 Asp. M.L.C.
    296 .... 1341, 1343
Hollandia, The [1983] 1 A.C. 565 76
Homewood, The (1928) 31 Ll.L.Rep. 336 .... 60, 336, 341, 358, 600, 603, 607, 617
Hong Kong Fir Co. Ltd v. Kawasaki Kisen Kaisha Ltd [1962] 2 Q.B. 26; [1962] 2 W.L.R.
    474; 106 S.J. 35; [1962] 1 All E.R. 474; [1961] 2 Lloyd's Rep. 478; *affirming* [1961]
    2 W.L.R. 716; 105 S.J. 347; [1961] 2 All E.R. 257; [1961] 1 Lloyd's Rep. 159 1027
Hope, The (1838) 3 Hagg. 423; 6 L.T. 479; 166 E.R. 462 .... 636, 1255, 1528
Hopper v. Burness (1876) 1 C.P.D. 137; 45 L.J.K.B. 377; 34 L.T. 528; 24 W.R. 612 1363
Horlock v. Beal [1916] 1 A.C. 486; 85 L.J.K.B. 602; 114 L.T. 193; 32 T.L.R. 251; 60 S.J.
    236; [1915] 3 K.B. 638 580
Howard, The (1975) 91 L.Q.R. 502 233
Huddart Parker Ltd v. The Mill Hill (1950) 81 C.L.R. 502 843
Hudson Light, The [1970] 1 Lloyd's Rep. 166 1530
Hunter v. Prinsep (1808) 10 East. 378; 103 E.R. 818 1363

I.C. POTTER, THE (1870) L.R. 3 A. & E. 292; 40 L.J. Adm. 9; 23 L.T. 603; 19 W.R. 335;
    3 Mar. L.C. 506 .... 377, 601, 605, 613, 618
I Congreso del Partido, The [1983] 1 A.C. 244; [1983] 2 Lloyd's Rep. 171; [1983] Com.
    L.R. 58; *affirming* [1982] Com. L.R. 171 1175
Ida, The (1860) Lush. 6; 1 L.T. 417 1107
Ilo, The [1982] 1 Lloyd's Rep. 39 .... 1473, 1530
Inca, The (1858) 12 Moo. P.C. 189 1397
Inchmaree, The [1899] P. 111; 68 L.J.P. 30; 80 L.T. 201; 8 Asp. M.C. 486 .... 41, 357, 834, 835,
    838, 841, 843, 921
India, The (1842) 1 W. Robb. 406; 8 L.T. 153; 166 E.R. 625 ... 289, 357, 717, 735, 737, 1241
Industrie Chimiche Italia Centrale v. Alexander G. Tsavliris & Sons Maritime Co. (The
    Choko Star)(No. 1) [1987] 1 Lloyd's Rep. 508, C.A. 831, 1270
Industry, The (1835) 3 Hagg. 203 37
Inna, The [1938] P. 148; 107 L.J.P. 110; 159 L.T. 439; 54 T.L.R. 744; 60 Ll.L.Rep. 414 854,
    946, 962, 1250, 1251, 1389
Iodine, The (1844) 3 Not. of Cas. 140 .... 648, 651, 654, 655, 660, 662, 894, 930
Ionic, The, Shipping Gazette, July 28 1893 .... 1434, 1448
Ios I., The [1989] 1 Lloyd's Rep. 321 1295
Island Tug and Barge Ltd v. S.S. Makedonai (Owners) (The Makedonia) [1958] 1 Q.B.
    365 1477
Italia, The (1906) 10 Asp. M.L.C. 284; 95 L.T. 398 1526

J.P. DONALDSON, THE (1897) 67 U.S. 599 (U.S.S.C.) 197
James Armstrong, The (1875) 33 L.T. 390; 3 Asp. M.L.C. 46; L.R. H. & E. 380 .... 1323, 1330,
    1365, 1443, 1447, 1536
James Brand, The, Shipping Gazette, July 17, 1903 1442
James Buchanan & Co. Ltd [1978] A.C. 141 83
Jane, The (1831) 2 Hagg. 338; 166 E.R. 267 .... 454, 1446, 1528
Janet Court, The [1897] P. 59; 66 L.J.P. 34; 76 L.T. 172; 8 Asp. 223 .... 357, 1432

Table of Cases

Jassy, The [1906] P. 270; 75 L.J.P. 93; 95 L.T. 363; 10 Asp. M.L.C. 278 673
Jebara v. Ottoman Bank [1972] 2 K.B. 254; [1928] A.C. 269 807
Jenkins v. Pharmaceutical Society of Great Britain [1921] 1 Ch. 392; 90 L.J. Ch. 47; 124
    L.T. 309; 37 T.L.R. 54; 65 Sol. 116 698
Johanne Dybwad, The (1926) 25 Ll.L.Rep. 119 .... 1405, 1415, 1432, 1434
Johannes, The (1835) 6 Not. Of Cas. 288 .... 39, 592, 597
Johannes, The (1848) 6 Not. of Cas. 288 591
Johannes, The (1860) Lush. 182 .... 261, 266, 294, 296
John and Jane, The (1802) 4 C. Rob. 216, 165 E.R. 590 210
John and Thomas, The (1822) 1 Hagg. 157n; 166 E.R. 56 .... 1136, 1245
Jonge Andries, The (1857) Swab. 226; affirmed (1857) 11 Moo. P.C. 313 .... 590, 592, 593, 855,
                                                                                                                  895, 904, 957
Jonge Bastiaan, The (1804) 5 C. Rob. 322; 165 E.R. 791 .... 56, 717, 733, 734, 1498, 1533
Jorgensen v. Neptune Steam Fishing Co. Ltd (1902) 4 F. (Ct. of Sn. Cas.) 992; 39 Sc. L.R.
    765; 10 S.L.T. 206 296
Joseph Harvey, The (1799) 1 C. Rob. 306 .... 339, 591, 592, 593, 597, 599
Joyce v. Williamson (1782) 3 Doug. 164; 99 E.R. 593 1482
Jubilee (1879) 4 Asp. M.L.C. 275; 42 L.T. 594 .... 338, 344, 357, 600
Julia Maria, The (1921) 7 Ll.L.Rep. 23 1432
Junior Books Ltd v. Veitchi Co. Ltd [1983] 1 A.C. 520; [1982] 3 W.L.R. 477; 126 S.J. 538;
    [1982] 3 All E.R. 201; [1982] Com. L.R. 221; 79 L.S. Gaz. 1413; 21 B.L.R. 66 1098
Jupiter, The, Shipping Gazette, August 9, 1901 1440

KALETAN, THE (1914) 30 T.L.R. 572 .... 240, 1356
Kangaroo, The [1918] P. 327; 88 L.J.P. 5 .... 53, 56, 60, 359, 556
Kate B. Jones, The [1892] P. 366; 69 L.T. 197; 7 Asp. M.L.C. 332 .. 357, 629, 630, 631, 782, 864,
                                                                                                                                1460
Kathleen, The (1874) L.R. 4 A. & E. 269; 43 L.J. Adm. 39; 31 L.T. 204; 23 W.R. 350 1380,
                                                                                                                                 1381
Kauss, The (1901) 20 T.L.R. 326 .... 1096, 1101
Kedah, The (1948) 81 Ll.L.Rep. 217 .... 1126, 1129, 1234, 1239, 1243, 1244
Keighley Maxsted & Co. v. Durant [1901] A.C. 240; 70 L.J.K.B. 662; 84 L.T. 777; 17
    T.L.R. 527; 45 So Jo. 536 809
Kenora, The [1921] P. 90; 90 L.J.P. 181; 37 T.L.R. 263; 5 Ll.L.Rep. 115 .... 597, 1126, 1128, 1530
Killeena, The (1881) 6 P.D. 193; 51 L.J. Adm. 11; 45 L.T. 621; 30 W.R. 339; 4 Asp. M.C.
    472 .... 733, 735, 1528
Kilmaho, The (1900) 16 T.L.R. 155 .... 728, 737, 750, 752, 820, 930
Kimes v. United States [1953] A.M.C. 1335 (U.S., C.A. 2nd Circuit), 1338 504
King, The (in his office of Admiralty) v. Forty-nine Casks of Brandy (1836) 3 Hagg. 257 202,
                                                                                                                   203, 204, 208
King, The v. Property Derelict (1825) 1 Hagg. 383 208
—— v. Two Casks of Tallow (1837) 3 Hagg. 294 .... 203, 208
King Oscar, The (1848) 6 Not. of Cas. 384 .... 597, 599
Kingalock, The (1854) 1 Spinks E. & A. 263; 8 L.T. 334; 18 Jur. 409; 164 E.R. 153 .... 38, 619,
                                                                                                       895, 897, 898, 989, 903
Kirby, The (1934) 49 Ll.L.Rep. 50 702
Kolpino, The (1904) 73 L.J.P. 29 1127
Koninklijke Rotterdamsche Lloyd (N.V.) v. Western Steamship Co. Ltd (The Empire
    Jamaica) [1957] A.C. 386 1202
Kostas Melas, The [1981] 1 Lloyd's Rep. 18 1293
Krypton and Other Barges, The [1954] 2 Lloyd's Rep. 451 692

L. SCHULER A.G. v. Wickman Machine Tool Sales Ltd [1974] A.C. 235 1028
Lady Durham, The (1835) 3 Hagg. 196; 166 E.R. 378 1485
Lady Egidia, The (1862) Lush. 513; 167 E.R. 234 617
Lady Gwendolen, The [1965] P. 294 1202
Lady Katherine Barham, The (1861) Lush. 404; 5 L.T. 693; 1 Mar. L.C. 184 1246
Lady Worsley, The (1855) 2 Spinks 253; 164 E.R. 417 .... 358, 1126, 1232
Laomedon, The (1925) 23 Ll.L.Rep. 230 .... 383, 490, 557
Larpool, The (1941) 70 Ll.L.Rep. 72 1526
Leda, The (1856) Swab. 40 294

xl

Table of Cases

Le Jonet, The (1872) L.R. 3 A. & E. 556; 41 L.J. Adm. 95; 27 L.T. 387; 21 W.R. 83 .... 357, 565, 571, 576, 579, 585, 1445
Lennard's Carrying Co. v. Asiatic Petroleum Co. [1915] A.C. 705 1202
Leo, The (1862) Lush 444; 31 L.J. Adm. 78; 6 L.T. 58 1485
Leon Blum, The [1915] P. 90; 85 L.J.P. 1; 114 L.T. 320; 31 T.L.R. 582 .... 27, 41, 522, 605, 606, 613, 617, 620, 784, 787, 814, 827, 844, 1140, 1538, 1540
L'Esperance, The (1811) 1 Dods. 48 1397
Lepanto, The [1892] P. 122; 66 L.T. 623 .... 209, 716, 717, 733, 740, 750, 752, 864, 1460
Leptir, The (1885) 5 Asp. M.L.C. 411; 52 I.T. 768 .... 1380, 1381, 1384
Liffey, The (1887) 58 L.T. 351; 6 Asp. M.L.C. 255 .... 22, 31, 48, 557, 559, 924, 1245
Lindfield, The (1894) 10 T.L.R. 606 .... 1317, 1457
Lipson v. Harrison (1853) 22 L.T. (O.S.) 83; 2 W.R. 10 .... 31, 134, 144, 146
Lista, The (1946) 79 Ll.L.Rep. 401 .... 1429, 1502, 1504
Lister v. Stubbs (1890) 45 Ch. D. 1 .... 952, 1094
Little Joe, The (1860) Lush. 88; 2 L.T. 473; 6 Jur. (N.S.) 783; 167 E.R. 46 .... 344, 358
Lively, The (1848) 3 W. Rob. 64; 6 Not. of Cas. 206; 166 E.R. 887 626
Liverpool, The [1893] P. 154; 68 L.T. 719; 7 Asp. M.L.C. 340; I.R. 601 ... 40, 339, 341, 601, 603, 605, 609, 617
Liverpool City Council v. Irwin [1977] A.C. 239; (1976) 238 E.G. 879, H.L. 812, 841
Livietta, The (1883) 8 P.D. 24; 52 L.J.P. 81; 48 L.T. 799; 31 W.R. 643; 5 Asp. M.L.C. 132 ... 1525, 1533
Lloyd v. Grace, Smith & Co. [1912] A.C. 716; 81 L.J.K.B. 1140; 56 S.J. 723; [1911–1913] All E.R. 51; 107 L.T. 531; 28 T.L.R. 547; *reversing* [1911] 2 K.B. 489 893
Lloyd's Bank Ltd v. Bundy [1975] Q.B. 326; [1974] W.L.R. 501; 118 S.J. 714; [1974] 3 All E.R. 757; [1974] 2 Lloyd's Rep. 366 900
Loch Tulla, The (1950) 84 Ll.L.Rep. 62 .... 749, 766, 756, 757, 760, 762, 763, 764
Lockwoods, The (1845) 9 Jur. 1017 .... 685, 734, 739, 1105, 1422, 1423
Lomonosoff, The [1912] P. 97; 90 L.J.P. 141; 37 T.L.R. 151 .... 49, 359, 557, 559, 651, 656, 682
London Corporation, The [1935] P. 70 1121
London Merchant, The (1837) 3 Hagg. 394; 166 E.R. 451 .... 38, 359, 685, 1414
Longford, The (1881) 6 P.D. 60; 50 L.J. Adm. 28; 44 L.T. 254; 29 W.R. 491 ..... 1431, 1495, 1498, 1499
Lord Dufferin, The (1848) 7 N.O.C. xxxiii 16, 35, 655, 661
Lord Warden and Admiral of the Cinque Ports v. H.M. in his Office of Admiralty, etc. (in the Matter of a Whale) (1931) 2 Hagg. 438 .... 314, 315
Louisa, The (1843(2 W. Rob. 22; 7 Jur. 182; 2 Not. of Cas. 149; 166 E.R. 664 ... 1397, 1433, 1445, 1447, 1448, 1506, 1520, 1535, 1538, 1540
Louisa, The (1848) 3 W. Rob. 99; 6 Not. of Cas. 531; 8 L.T. 440; 12 Jur. 946; 166 E.R. 900 1133
Louisa, The (1813) 1 Dods, 317; 165 E.R. 1324 .... 20, 648, 651
Luigi Accame, The (1938) 60 Ll.L.Rep. 106 .... 39, 341, 357, 592, 593, 597, 598, 599
Lustre, The (1834) 1 Hagg. 154; 166 E.R. 363 .... 647, 654, 660, 662, 688
Luxor (Eastbourne) Ltd v. Cooper [1941] A.C. 108; 110 L.J.K.B. 131; 85 S.J. 105; [1941] 1 All E.R. 33; 164 L.T. 313; 57 T.L.R. 213; 46 Com. Cas. 120 766
Lycaon, The (1949) 82 Ll.L.Rep. 691 1440
Lyles v. Southend on Sea Corp. [1905] 2 K.B. 1549
Lyrma (No. 2), The [1978] 2 Lloyd's Rep. 30 .... 25, 855, 1250, 1251, 1323, 1389

MSC ROSA M, THE [2000] 2 Lloyd's Rep. 399 1204
MacGregor Laird, The [1953] 2 Lloyd's Rep. 59 .... 359, 625, 837, 941
McRae v. Commonwealth Disposals Commission (1950) 84 C.L.R. 377 914
Maasdam, The (1893) 69 L.T. 659; 10 T.L.R. 31; 7 Asp. M.L.C. 400; 6 R. 716 .... 26, 357, 766, 756, 756, 761, 763, 764
Mac, The (1882) 7 P.D. 122; 46 L.T. 907; 51 L.J. Adm. 81; 4 Asp. M.L.C. 555; *reversing* (1882) 7 P.D. 38 .... 170, 178, 294
Madoera, The (1946) 79 Ll.L.Rep. 486 1533
Madras, The [1898] P. 90; 67 L.J.P. 53; 78 L.T. 325; 8 Asp. M.L.C. 397 .... 357, 607, 610, 614, 616, 1443
Magdalen, The (1861) 1 M.L.C. 189; 31 L.J. Adm. 22; 5 L.T. 807 .. 894, 1105, 1109, 1125, 1422, 1423, 1453
Mahesan v. Malaysian Housing Society [1979] A.C. 374; [1978] 2 W.L.R. 444; 122 S.J. 31; [1978] 2 All E.R. 405 .... 894, 952

Table of Cases

Makedonia, The [1958] 1 Q.B. 365; [1958] 2 W.L.R. 256; 102 S.J. 1241; [1958] 1 All E.R. 236; [1958] T.R. 63; 36 A.T.C. 376; [1957] 2 Lloyd's Rep. 575 .... 43, 45, 448, 453, 456, 496
Maliu Head, Shipping Gazette, November 20, 1903 1526
Manchester Trust v. Furness, Withy & Co. [1895] 2 Q.B. 539; 73 L.T. 110; 44 W.R. 178; 8 Asp. M.L.C. 57; 1 Comm. Cas. 39; 14 R. 739; *sub nom.* Manchester Trust Ltd v. Turner, Withy & Co. Ltd, 64 L.J.Q.B. 766; 11 T.L.R. 530 .... 469, 813
Mardorf Peach & Co. Ltd v. Attica Sea Carriers Corporation of Monrovia (The Laconig) [1977] A.C. 850; [1977] 2 W.L.R. 286; 121 S.J. 134; [1977] 1 All E.R. 545; [1977] 1 Lloyd's Rep. 315; *reversing* [1976] Q.B. 835; (1976) 2 W.L.R. 668; 120 S.J. 231; [1976] 2 All E.R. 249; [1976] 1 Lloyd's Rep. 395 219
Marechal Suchet, The [1911] P. 1; 80 L.J.P. 51; 26 T.R.L. 660; 11 Asp. M.C. 553 ... 623, 702, 1096
Margaret, The (1828) 2 Hagg. 48n 527, 529, 1140
Margery, The [1902] P. 157; 71 L.J.P. 83; 86 L.T. 863; 50 W.R. 654 .. 41, 620, 638, 815, 833, 841, 842
Marguerite Molinos, The [1903] P. 160; 72 L.J.P. 56; 89 L.T. 192 .... 358, 703, 1136, 1245
Marie, The (1882) 7 P.D. 203; 47 L.T. 737; 5 Asp. M.C. 27 .... 1136, 1239, 1243, 1245
Maria, The [1992] 2 Lloyd's Rep. 167 1295
Maria Jane, The (1850) 14 Jur. 857; 8 L.T. (N.S.) 582 .... 483, 494, 499, 529, 567
Mari Chandris, The (1941) 69 Ll.L.Rep. 166; [1942] P. 94; 111 L.J.P. 68; 167 L.T. 276; 71 Ll.L.Rep. 225 .... 1445, 1528
Mariposa, The [1896] P. 273; 65 L.J.P. 104; 76 L.T. 54 .... 235, 237, 357, 363, 815, 819
Maritime Liens, The (1980) 1247
Mark Lane, The (1890) 15 P.D. 135; 63 L.T. 468; 39 W.R. 47 .... 38, 936, 938
Marlborough, The (1943) 76 Ll.L.Rep. 102 .... 698, 699, 701, 705
Marquis of Huntly, The (1835) 3 Hagg. 246 1535
M. Arnus, The, November 11, 1918 1526
Mars, The (1921) Ll.L.Rep. 567 1432
Mars and Other Barges, The (1948) 81 Ll.L. Ep. 42 .... 40, 563, 688, 690, 693
Martha, The (1859) Swab. 48; 166 E.R. 1226 .... 1126, 1234, 1243
Martin Luther, The (1857) Swab. 287; 2 M.L. Cas. 216 .... 454, 1432, 434, 1525
Mary, The (1842) 1 W. Rob. 448; 2 Not. of Cas. 27; 7 Jur. 404 .... 262, 339, 344, 363
Mary Ann, The (1823) 1 Hagg. 158; 166 E.R. 57 .... 38, 647, 660
Mary Pleasants, The (1857) Swab. 224; 166 E.R. 1107 .... 659, 661, 1490
Mason v. Le Blaireau (1804) 6 U.S. 238; 2 Crouch. 240 .... 33, 34
Massalia, The [1959] 1 W.L.R. 787; *affirmed*, [1961] 2 Q.B. 276; [1960] 3 W.L.R. 701; 104 S.J. 850; [1960] 2 All E.R. 529; [1960] 1 Lloyd's Rep. 594 .... 959, 1067
Master of Trinity House v. Clark (1815) 4 M. & S. 288 670
Matatua, The (1924) 20 Ll.L.Rep. 5 .... 377, 597, 598, 599, 1530
Matheson v. Smiley [1932] 2 D.L.R. 787; [1932] 1 W.L.R. 758; 40 Man. R. 247 (Can.) 51, 807
Matti, The [1918] P. 314; 87 L.J.P. 179; 34 T.L.R. 582 670
Maude, The (1876) 36 L.T. 26; 3 Asp. M.L.C. 338 ... 357, 749, 766, 751, 752, 756, 761, 762, 764, 766
The Mayor etc., of Southport v. Morris [1893] 1 Q.B. 359 178
Meandros, The [1925] P. 61; 94 L.J.P. 37; 132 L.T. 750; 41 T.L.R. 236; 16 Asp. M.L.C. 476 ... 16, 30, 357, 457, 477, 1491, 1512, 1513
Mecca, The [1895] P. 95; 64 L.J.P. 40; 71 L.T. 711; 43 W.R. 209; 11 T.L.R. 139; 39 S.J. 132; 7 Asp. M.L.C. 91
Medina, The (1876) 2 P.D. 5; 35 L.T. 779; 25 W.R. 156; *affirming* (1876) 1 P.D. 272; 3 Asp. M.L.C. 220; 45 L.J. Adm. 81 ..... 235, 236, 238, 240, 269, 270, 293, 357, 363, 726, 861, 907, 927, 1125, 1255
Medora, The (1853) 1 Spinks. E. & E. 17; 10 L.T. 791; 164 E.R. 10 341
Meg Merrilies, The (1837) 3 Hagg. 346 1255
Melanie (Owners) The v. The San Onofre (Owners) [1925] A.C. 246; 94 L.J.P. 17; 132 L.T. 567; 41 T.L.R. 206; 16 Asp. M.L.C. 479 .... 542, 733, 735, 1317, 1440
—— v. The San Onofre (No. 2) (Owners) (1919) 35 T.L.R. 507; [1919] W.N. 154 542
—— v. The San Onofre (Owners)(No. 3) (1919) [1927] A.C. 162n 542
Melmore Head, The (1945) 78 Ll.L.Rep. 102 358
Melpomene, The (1873) L.R. 4 A.& E. 129; 42 L.J. Adm. 45; 29 L.T. 409 .... 38, 746, 751, 755, 1434
Merchants' Marine Insurance Co. v. North of England Protection and Indemnity Association (1926) 23 Com. Cas. 165 178

Table of Cases

Merannio, The (1927) 28 Ll.L.Rep. 352 .... 345, 347, 348, 358, 1411, 1415, 1434
Meridian Global Funds Management Asia Ltd v. Securities Commission [1995] 2 A.C.
  500, N.Z. 1202
Mersey Docks and Harbour Board Trustees v. Gibbs (1866) 11 H.L.C. 686 1054
Metcalfe v. Britannia Ironworks Co. (1877) 2 Q.B.D. 423; 46 L.J.Q.B. 443; 36 L.T. 451;
  25 W.R. 720; 3 Asp. M.L.C. 407 1363
Michael, The (1805) 2 Hag. Adm. 178n; 166 E.R. 210 590
Micosta S.A. v. Shetland Islands Council (The Mihalis) [1984] 2 Lloyd's Rep. 525 1054
Midland Bank Trus Co. Ltd v. Hett, Stubbs and Kemp [1979] Ch. 384; [1978] 3 W.L.R.
  167; (1977) 121 S.J. 830; [1978] 3 All E.R. 571 1123
Milburn & Co. v. Jamaica Fruit Importing Co. of London [1900] 2 Q.B. 540; 69 L.J.Q.B.
  860; 83 L.T. 321; 4 Com. Cas. 331; 5 Com. Cas. 346 1509
Miliangos v. George Frank (Textiles) Ltd [1976] A.C. 443; [1977] Q.B. 489; [1976] 3
  W.L.R. 477; 120 S.J. 450; [1976] 3 All E.R. 599; [1976] 2 Lloyd's Rep. 434 ...... 1462, 1464,
                                                                                                                1472
Millie, The [1940] P. 1 1194
Minneapolis, The [1902] P. 30; 71 L.J.P. 28; 86 L.T. 263; 9 Asp. M.L.C. 270 .... 1527, 1528
Minnehaha, The (1861) 15 Moo. P.C. 133; Lush. P.C. 335; 30 L.J.P.M. & A. 211; 4 L.T.
  810; 9 W.R. 925; 7 Jur. (N.S.) 1257; 15 E.R. 444 .... 40, 605, 609, 959, 1317
Miranda, The (1866) L.R. 3 A. & E. 561; 41 L.J. Adm. 82; 27 L.T. 389; 21 W.R. 84 .... 485, 490,
                                                                                                              491, 493, 496
Missouri's Cargo, The (1832) Sprague 260 1128
Mitchell v. Darthez (1836) 2 Bing. N.C. 555; 5 L.J.C.P. 154; 2 Scott. 771; 1 Hodges 418 1363
Modavia, The (1931) 39 Ll. Rep. 58 .... 45, 1411, 1437, 1454
Monarch, The (1886) 12 P.D. 5; 56 L.J. Adm. 114; 50 L.T. 204; 35 W.R. 292 591
Monarch Airlines Ltd v. London Luton Airport Ltd [1998] 1 Lloyd's Rep. 403 1204
Mons, The [1932] P. 109 1250
Morgana, The [1920] P. 442; 89 L.J.P. 232; 124 L.T. 254; 36 T.L.R. 747; 15 Asp. M.L.C.
  160 663
Morris v. C.W. Martin & Sons Ltd [1966] 1 Q.B. 716; [1965] 3 W.L.R. 276; 109 S.J. 451;
  [1965] 2 All E.R. 725; [1965] 2 Lloyd's Rep. 63; 109 S.J. 1021 1081
Mount Cynthos, The (1937) 58 Ll.L.Rep. 18 .... 333, 341, 616, 1528, 1531
Mud Hopper No. 4, The (1879) 40 L.T. 462; 4 Asp. M.L.C. 103 1443
Mudlark, The [1911] P. 116; 80 L.J.P. 117; 27 T.L.R. 385 178
Mulgrave, The (1827) 2 Hagg. 77; 166 E.R. 172 .... 454, 815, 852, 853
Munro v. Willmott [1949] 1 K.B. 295; [1949] L.J.R. 471; 64 T.L.R. 627; 92 Sol. Jo. 662 361
M. Vatan, The [1990] 1 Lloyd's Rep. 336 .... 1430, 1505

NAGASAKI SPIRIT, THE [1997] A.C. 455 .... 396, 410
National Defender, The [1970] 1 Lloyd's Rep. 40 (U.S.D.C.S.D.N.Y.) ... 4, 336, 431, 432, 435,
                                                                                                        523, 524, 641, 1411
National Westminster Bank plc v. Morgan [1986] A.C. 686 901
Naysmyth, The (1885) 10 P.D. 41; 54 L.J. Adm. 63; 52 L.T. 392; 33 W.R. 736; 5 Asp. M.C.
  364 .... 837, 843
Nellie, The (1873) 2 Asp. M.L.C. 142; 29 L.T. (N.S.) 516; 2 M.L.C. 142 .... 725, 733, 749
Neptune, The (1824) 1 Hagg. 227; 12 Moo. P.C. 346 .... 8, 565, 566, 1116, 1117, 1316
Neptune, The (1856) Swab. 129; (1858) 12 Moo. P.C. 346 1423
New Australia, The [1958] 2 Lloyd's Rep. 35 .... 347, 359, 1434
Newman v. Walters (1804) 3 Bos. & Pul. 612; 127 E.R. 330 .... 134, 137, 138, 139, 141, 143, 144,
                                                                          147, 357, 565, 567, 582, 590, 593, 597, 632, 633, 809, 823
New Zealand Shipping Co. Ltd v. A.M. Satterwhaite & Co. Ltd, The Eurymedon [1975]
  A.C. 154; [1974] 2 W.L.R. 865; 118 S.J. 387; [1974] 1 All E.R. 1015; sub nom.
  Eurymedon, The [1974] 1 Lloyd's Rep. 534 827
Nicholas Witzen, The (1837) 3 Hagg. 369 1531
Nicholson v. Chapman (1793) 2 Hy. Bl. 254; 126 E.R. 536 .... 130, 132, 140
—— v. Leith Salvage and Towage Co., 1923 S.C. 409 (Ct. of Session); 14 Ll.L.Rep. 244 356,
                                                                                                      492, 1140, 1537, 1538, 1540
Nicolai Heinrich, The (1853) 17 Jur. 329; 6 L.T. 615 1447
Nicolaou Georgis, The [1951] 2 Lloyd's Rep. 215 1522
Nicolina, The (1843) 2 W. Rob. 175; 166 E.R. 720 1528
Nile, The (1875) L.R. 4 A. & E. 449; 44 L.J. Adm. 38 .... 465, 525, 666, 670
Nimrod, The (1850) 14 Jur. 942; 7 Not. of Cas. 570 .... 1136, 1245

xliii

Table of Cases

Ningpo, The (1923) 16 Ll.L.Rep. 392 .... 358, 359, 788, 1325, 1326, 1330
Noordland, The [1893] P. 153n 1527
Norddeutscher Lloyd v. "Cairnhill", Cargo and Freight (1920) 5 Ll.L.Rep. 386 336
Norden, The (1853) 1 Soinks 185; 8 L.T. 335; 164 E.R. 107 .... 454, 1438
Noreuro Traders Ltd v. E. Hardy & Co. (1923) 16 Ll.L.Rep. 319 1462
Norma, The (1860) Lush. 124; 3 L.T. 340; 1 Mar. L.C. 7; 167 E.R. 58 .. 22, 732, 753, 1323, 1362, 1364, 1365
Norman, The [1960] 1 Lloyd's Rep. 1 84
Normandy, The [1904] P. 187; 73 L.J. P. 55; 90 L.T. 351; 52 W.R. 634; 20 T.L.R. 239; 9 Asp. M.L.C. 568 174
North Goodwin No. 16, The [1980] 1 Lloyd's Rep. 71 530
Northern Fishing Co. (Hull) Ltd v. Eddom (The Norman) [1960] 1 Lloyd's Rep. 1 1202
Norwhale, The [1975] 1 Q.B. 589 83
Notre Dame de Fourviere (1923) 14 Ll.L.Rep. 276 .... 636, 1528

OCEAN, THE (1843) 2 W. Rob. 91; 1 L.T. (O.S.) 58; 166 E.R. 689 358
Ocean Hound, The (1950) 84 Ll.L.Rep. 5 .... 702, 705
Oceanic Grandeur, The (1972) 127 C.L.R. 312; [1972] 2 Lloyd's Rep. 396 .. 356, 357, 358, 1538, 1539
OLL Ltd v. Secretary of State for Transport [1977] 3 All E.R. 897 683
Omoa and Cleland Coal and Iron Co. v. Huntley (1877) 2 C.P.D. 464; 37 L.T. 184; 25 W.R. 675 464
Optima, The (1905) 10 Asp. M.L.C. 147 .... 1248, 1252
Orbona, The (1853) 1 Spinks E. & A. 161; 8 L.T. 582; 164 E.R. 93 .... 1238, 1446
O'Reilly v. Mackman [1983] 2 A.C. 237 1053
Orelia, The [1958] 1 Lloyd's Rep. 441 .... 345, 357
Oscar, The (1829) 2 Hagg. 257 .... 1392, 1447
Ottercaps, The (1876) Pritchard Adm. Dig., 3rd ed. Vol. 2, 2094 358
Ousel, The [1957] 1 Lloyd's Rep. 151 690
Ovre and The Conde de Zubiria, The (1920) 2 Ll.L.Rep. 21 .... 53, 57, 333, 341, 347, 359
Owners of Dredger Liesbach v. Owners of Steamship Edison [1933] A.C. 449 ...... 1121, 1343
Owners of S.S. Hatfield v. Owners of S.S. Glasgow (The Glasgow) (1914) 13 Asp. M.L.C. 33 1091
Owners of the S.S. Melanie v. Owners of the S.S. San Onofre [1925] A.C. 246 ...... 716, 717, 736, 739

PACIFIC, THE (1931) 41 Ll.L.Rep. 83 .... 46, 295, 296, 1454
Pacific Colocotronics, The [1981] 2 Lloyd's Rep. 40; [1980] 1 Lloyd's Rep. 366 .... 359, 788
Palmer v. Rouse (1858) 3 H. & N. 505; 27 L.J. Ex. 437; 31 L.T. (O.S.) 220; 22 J.P. 773; 6 W.R. 674; 157 E.R. 569 .... 202, 206
Pa Mar, The [1999] 1 Lloyd's Rep. 338 .... 78, 357, 391, 805, 806, 817, 866, 1461
Pampa, The (1925) Ll.L.Rep. 496 1432
Pan Oak, The [1992] 2 Lloyd's Rep. 36 795
Pantanassa, The [1970] P. 187; [1970] 2 W.L.R. 981; (1969) 114 S.J. 372; [1970] 1 Lloyd's Rep. 153; [1970] 1 All E.R. 848 232
Papayanni v. Hocquard (The True Blue) (1866) L.R. 1 P.C. 250 1446
Parker v. London County Council [1904] 2 K.B. 501 549
Parsons v. B.N.M. Laboratories Ltd [1964] 1 Q.B. 95 1477
Pelton S.S. Co. v. North of England Protection and Indemnity Association (1925) 22 Ll.L.Rep. 510 178
Pembroke, The [1995] 2 Lloyd's Rep. 290 1204
Pepper (Inspector of Taxes) v. Hart [1993] A.C. 593 86
Perfective, The (1949) 82 Ll.L.Rep. 873 .... 332, 341, 1411, 1433, 1447
Pergo, The [1887] 1 Lloyd's Rep. 582 .... 210, 1410, 1413, 1419, 1428
Pericles, The (1863) Br. & L. 80; 167 E.R. 308 .... 338, 607
Perks v. Clark [2001] 2 Lloyd's Rep. 431 (CA) 169
Perla, The (1857) Swab. 230; 8 L.T. 612; 166 E.R. 1111 .... 1109, 1411, 1423, 1528
Pertotrade Inc. v. Smith [2000] 1 Lloyd's Rep. 486 952
Petter, The (1942) 72 Ll.L.Rep. 134 .... 1519, 1525
Phantom, The (1866) L.R. 1 A. & E. 58; 14 W.R. 774; 12 Jur. (N.S.) 529 .... 333, 338, 881, 937, 957
Philippine Admiral, The [1977] A.C. 373 1175

Table of Cases

Pickwick, The (1852) 1 Jur. 669 .... 210, 479, 510
Pierce v. Bemis (The Lusitania) [1986] Q.B. 384 .... 107, 208, 212
Pinnas, The (1888) 59 L.T. 526; 6 Asp. M.L.C. 313 ...... 378, 1135, 1234, 1238, 1243, 1440, 1443
Place v. Potts (1855) 5 H.L.C. 383; 24 L.J. Ex. 225; 25 L.T. (O.S.) 284; 3 W.R. 574; 10 E.R. 948 33
Planet, The, Shipping Gazette, January 31, 1902 1528
Polpen Shipping Co. Ltd v. Commercial Union Assurance Co. Ltd [1943] 1 K.B. 161; 112 L.J.K.B. 198; [1943] 1 All E.R. 162; 168 L.T. 143; T.L.R. 106; 74 Ll.L.Rep. 157 .... 178, 248
Port Caledonia and the Anne, The [1903] P. 184; 72 L.J.P. 60; 89 L.T. 216 .... 53, 57, 333, 347, 359, 934
Port Hunter, The [1910] P. 343; 80 L.J.P. 1; 103 L.T. 550; 11 Asp. M.C. 492; 26 T.L.R. 610 .... 1317, 1457
Port Jackson Stevedoring Pty. Ltd v. Salmond & Spraggon (Australia) Pty. Ltd, The New York Star [1981] 1 W.L.R. 138; (1980) 124 S.J. 756; [1980] 3 All E.R. 257; *reversing* [1979] 1 Lloyd's Rep. 298; *affirming* [1979] 1 Lloyd's Rep. 445 827
Portreath, The [1923] P. 155; 92 L.J.P. 116; 129 L.T. 475; 16 Asp. M.C. 227; 39 T.L.R. 356 .... 210, 565, 570, 574, 577, 579
Post Office v. Estuary Radio Ltd [1968] 2 Q.B. 740 .... 83, 87
Poustanic Wielkopolski [1989] Q.B. 279 266
Premuda, The (1940) 67 Ll.L.Rep. 9 .... 53, 377, 924
President of India v. La Pintada CNSA (La Pintada) [1985] A.C. 104 1467
President Van Buren, The (1924) 132 L.T. 253; 16 Asp. 444 1101
Pretoria, The (1920) 5 Ll.L.Rep. 112 .... 53, 57
Pride of Canada (1863) Br. & L. 208; 3 New Rep. 93; 9 L.T. 546; 1 M.L.C. 406; 167 E.R. 338 .... 1520, 1538, 1539, 1540
Prince Frederick William, The (1872) L.R. 3 A. & E. 512 484
Prince of Wales, The (1848) 6 Not. of Cas. 39; 12 Jur. 163 .... 341, 358
Princess Alice, The (1849) 3 W. Rob. 138; 6 Not. of Cas. 584 .... 37, 335, 338, 340, 600
Prins Knud (No. 1), The (1940) 67 Ll.L.Rep. 458; (1941) 68 Ll.L.Rep. 100 .... 341, 597
Prins Knud (No. 2), The (1941) 68 Ll.L.Rep. 100 .... 597, 631
Prinz Heinrich, The (1888) 13 P.D. 31; 57 L.J. Adm. 17; 58 L.T. 593; 36 W.R. 511 .... 267, 728, 828, 817, 867, 934, 1255, 1492, 1493, 1494
Prometheus, The (1949) 82 Ll.L.Rep. 859; *affirming* (1948) ibid. 172 .... 864, 1460
Pubnico Virgo, The [1975] 1 Lloyd's Rep. 448 .... 1433, 1477
Punta Lara, The (1910) 26 T.L.R. 268 1527
Purissima Concepcion, The (1849) 2 W. Rob. 181; 7 Not. of Cas. 150; 8 L.T. 178; 13 Jur. 967; 166 E.R. 930 .... 142, 144, 627, 629, 697, 1420
Pyrenee, The (1863) Br. & L. 189; 3 New Rep. 250; 167 E.R. 330 1488

QUEEN ELIZABETH, THE (1949) 82 Ll.Rep. 803 .... 44, 46, 334, 345, 357, 462, 620, 788, 827, 1411, 1454, 1458, 1533, 1538
Queen Mab, The (1835) 3 Hagg. 242; 166 E.R. 395 .... 263, 685, 686, 726, 735

R. v. Caldwell [1982] A.C. 341 1204
—— v. Judge of City of London Court (1883) 12 Q.B.D. 115 325
—— v. Kelly [1982] A.C. 665; [1981] 1 W.L.R. 387; 125 S.J. 607; [1981] 2 All E.R 1098; [1981] Crim. L.R. 707; [1981] 2 Lloyd's Rep. 384; 73 Cr. App. R. 310; *affirming* [1981] Q.B. 174; [1981] 2 W.L.R. 112; 125 S.J. 47; [1981] 1 All E.R. 370; [1981] Crim. L.R. 44; [1981] 1 Lloyd's Rep. 313; *sub nom.* R. v. Kelly Murphy and Avison (1980) 72 Cr. App. R. 47 293
—— v. Lawrence [1982] A.C. 510 1204
R.G. Mayor (t/a Granville Coaches) v. P. & O. Ferries Ltd (The Lion) [1990] 2 Lloyd's Rep. 144 1204
Racer, The (1874) 2 Asp. M.L.C. 317; 30 L.T. 904 344
Raft of Timber, The (1844) 2 W. Rob. 251; 3 L.T. 58; 166 E.R. 749 139
Raikes, The (1824) 1 Hagg. 246; 166 E.R. 88 .... 38, 455
Raisby, The (1885) 10 P.D. 114; 54 L.J. Adm. 65; 53 L.T. 56; 33 W.R. 938; 5 Asp. M.C. 473 .... 368, 864, 1484, 1485, 1488, 1489
Ranger, The (1845) 3 N.O.C. 589; 9 Jur. 119 .... 331, 333, 377, 735, 1095
Rapid, The (1838) 3 Hagg. 419 .... 654, 1255
Rasche, The (1873) L.R. 4 A. & E. 127; 42 L.J. Adm. 71; 22 W.R. 240 1528

Table of Cases

Ratata, The [1898] A.C. 513; 78 L.T. 797; 47 W.R. 156; 14 T.L.R. 500; 8 Asp. M.L.C. 427 622
Red Rover, The (1850) 3 W. Rob. 150 529
Red Sea Tankers Ltd v. Papachristidis (The Hellespont Ardent) [1997] 2 Lloyd's Rep. 547 1202
Refrigerant, The [1925] P. 130; 95 L.J.P. 11; 134 L.T. 26; 16 Asp. M.L.C. 559 .... 601, 605, 616, 1101
Renpor, The (1883) 8 P.D. 115; 52 L.J. Adm. 49; 48 L.T. 887; 31 W.R. 640; 5 Asp. M.C. 98 .... 26, 230, 240, 268, 271, 279, 363, 720, 725, 726, 727, 731, 779, 815, 819, 1511, 1513
Repulse, The (1845) 2 W. Rob. 396; 4 Not. of Cas. 166; 7 L.T. 225; 9 Jur. 738; 166 E.R. 805 .... 852, 891, 956
Resultatet, The (1853) 17 Jur. 178; 8 L.T. 178 .... 853, 857, 860, 891, 907, 911
Reward, The (1841) 1 W. Robb. 174; 8 L.T. 704 335
Rhodes, Re (1890) 44 Ch. D. 94; 59 L.J. Ch. 298; 62 L.T. 342; 38 W.R. 385 807
Rhodian River, The [1984] 1 Lloyd's Rep. 373; [1978] J.B.L. 410 803
Rialto, The [1891] P. 175; 60 L.J.P. 71; 64 L.T. 540 .... 930, 934, 936, 937
Re Richardson, Shuldham v. Royal National Lifeboat Institution (1887) 56 L.J. Ch. 784; 57 L.T. 17; 35 W.R. 710 698
Rilland, The [1979] 1 Lloyd's Rep. 455 .... 1411, 1473, 1474
Rising Sun, The (1837) Ware 378 1128
Rilland, The [1979] 1 Lloyd's Rep. 455 199
River Rima, The [1988] 1 W.L.R. 758 84
Robert Dixon (1879) 5 P.D. 54; 42 L.T. 344; 28 W.R. 716; 4 Asp. M.L.C. 246; *affirming* 4 P.D. 121 .... 622, 1096, 1097, 1100, 1101
Rosa Luxemburg, The (1934) 49 Ll.L.Rep. 292 .... 42, 45, 57, 63, 597, 598, 1454, 1530
Rosalie, The (1853) 1 Spinks E. & A. 188; 18 Jur. 337; 164 E.R. 109 .... 358, 363, 647, 651, 655, 660, 1423, 1426, 1443
Rosario, The (1876) 2 P.D. 41; 46 L.J.P. 52; 35 L.T. 816; 3 Asp. M.L.C. 334 .... 1519, 1520, 1538
Rosenhaugh, The (1854) 1 Spinks 267; 164 E.R. 155 589
Roumelian, The (1933) 45 Ll.L.Rep. 267 .... 341, 1530
Royal Arch, The (1857) Swab. 269; 30 L.T. (O.S.) 198; 6 W.R. 191; 166 E.R. 1131 1252
Royal Bank of Scotland v. Etridge (No. 2) [2001] 3 W.L.R. 1021 942

S.C. LOVELAND CO. v. U.S.A. [1963] A.M.C. 260 .... 197, 198
S.S. Mary Louisa, The 268
S.S. Pharmaceutical Co. Ltd v. Quantas Airways Ltd [1991] 1 Lloyd's Rep. 288 1203
Sabina, The (1842) 7 Jur. 1182 .... 1250, 1354
Sachs v. Miklos [1948] K.B. 23; [1948] L.J.R. 1012; 64 T.L.R. 181; [1948] 1 All E.R. 361
Saint Anna, The [1980] 1 Lloyd's Rep. 180 795
St Blane, The [1974] 1 Lloyd's Rep. 555 .... 262, 1422, 1423
St John Pilot Commissioners v. Cumberland Railway and Coal Co. [1910] A.C. 208 (P.C.); 79 L.J.P.C. 67; 101 L.T. 498; 26 T.L.R. 52; 11 Asp. M.L.C. 312 178
St Machar, The (1939) 65 Ll.L.Rep. 119 178
St Melante, The (1947) 80 Ll.L.Rep. 588 .... 1411, 1477
Saint Nicholas, The (1860) Lush. 29; 167 E.R. 15 1528
St Patrick, The (1930) 35 Ll.L.Rep. 231 .... 342, 603, 607, 622
Salacia, The (1829) 2 Hagg. 262; 166 E.R. 240 .... 633, 857, 1392, 1433, 1477, 1528
Salawati, The (1929) 34 Ll.L.Rep. 37 .... 348, 784
Salomon v. Customs & Excise Commissioners [1967] 2 Q.B. 116 .... 83, 87
Saltburn, The (1894) 7 Asp. 474; 71 L.T. 19; 6 R. 702 .... 1442, 1538, 1539
Salvital, The [1998] 1 Lloyd's Rep. 185 1087
Samick Lines Co. Ltd v. Owners of the Antonis P.
Samos (The Antonis P. Lemos) [1985] A.C. 711 83
Samuel, The (1851) 15 Jur. 407; 17 L.T. (O.S.) 204 .... 208, 357, 966, 1242
San Demetrico, The (1941) 69 Ll.L.Rep. 5 .... 210, 357, 565, 570, 574, 1528, 1531, 1535
Sandsend, The, Shipping Gazette, May 22, 1903 1537
San Onofre, The [1917] P. 96; 86 L.J.P. 103; 116 L.T. 800; 14 Asp. M.C. 74 ..... 1340, 1341, 1342, 1386, 1317
Sandefjord, The [1953] 2 Lloyd's Rep. 557 .... 39, 345, 597
Santiago, The (1900) 9 Asp. 147; 83 L.T. 439 .... 592, 93, 594, 717, 1528, 1530
Santipore, The (1854) 1 Spinks E. & A. 231; 164 E.R. 134 .... 38, 357, 734, 1533

Table of Cases

Sappho, The (1871) L.R. 3 P.C. 690; L.R. 3 A. & E. 142; 40 L.J. Adm. 47; 24 L.T. 795; 19 W.R. 24 .... 493, 494, 495, 522, 529, 565, 586, 641
Sarah, The (1878) 3 P.D. 39; 37 L.T. 831; 3 Asp. M.L.C. 542 .... 358, 1528, 1537, 1538
Sarah, The (1800) 1 C. Rob. 312n; 165 E.R. 188 27
Sarah Bell, The (1845) 4 Not. Of Cas. 144; 6 L.T. 371 .... 209, 577
Sarah Jane, The (1843) 2 W. Rob. 110; 8 L.T. 335; 166 E.R. 696 .... 837, 840, 843, 1528
Saratoga, The (1861) Lush. 318; 167 E.R. 140 .... 346, 359, 603, 605, 617, 1443
Sardonyx, The Shipping Gazette, April 4, 1901 1530
Sarpen, The [1916] P. 306; 85 L.J.P. 209; 114 L.T. 1011; 13 Asp. M.C. 370; 32 T.L.R. 575; 60 S.J. 538 .... 459, 465, 524, 641, 671
Saunders (Executrix of the Estate of Rose Maud Gallie) v. Anglia Building Society [1971] A.C. 1004; [1970] 3 W.L.R. 1078; *sub nom.* Saunders v. Anglia Building Society, 114 S.J. 885; *sub nom.* Saunders (Executrix of the Estate of Rose Maud Gallie) v. Anglia Building Society (formerly Northampton Town and County Building Society) [1970] 3 All E.R. 961 920
Sava Star, The [1995] 2 Lloyd's Rep. 134 ... 41, 446, 485, 490, 491, 492, 496, 505, 509, 516, 518, 523, 525, 544, 634, 637, 1418
Scaramanga v. Stamp (1880) 5 C.P.D. 295; 49 L.J.Q.B. 674; 42 L.T. 840; 28 W.R. 691; 4 Asp. M.L.C. 295 1446
Scheldestad, The (1933) 45 Ll.L.Rep. 269 .... 45, 1454
Schuster v. M'Kellar (1857) 7 E. & B. 704; 26 L.J.Q.B. 281; 3 Jur. (N.S.) 1320 464
Scindia, The (1865) L.R. 1 P.C. 241; 4 Moo. P.C.C. (N.S.) 84'6 E.R. 248; affirming (1865) 2 Asp. M.L.C. (O.S.) 232 .... 1128, 1317
Scout, The (1872) L.R. 3 A. & E. 512; 41 L.J. Adm. 42; 26 L.T. 371; 20 W.R. 617 493
Scrutton Ltd v. Midland Silicones Ltd [1962] A.C. 446; [1962] 2 W.L.R. 186; 106 S.J. 34; [1962] 1 All E.R. 1; *sub nom.* Midland Silicones v. Scrutton [1961] 2 Lloyd's Rep. 365; *affirming* [1961] 1 Q.B. 106; [1960] 3 W.L.R. 372; *affirming* [1959] 2 Q.B. 171; [1959] 2 W.L.R. 761; 103 S.J. 415; [1959] 2 All E.R. 289; [1959] 1 Lloyd's Rep. 289 827
Sea and Land Securities Ltd v. William Dickinson & Co. Ltd [1942] 2 K.B. 65; 111 L.J.K.B. 698; 167 L.T. 173; 58 T.L.R. 210; 72 Ll.L.Rep. 133; [1942] 1 All E.R. 503 ... 222
Selina, The (1842) 2 Not. of Cas. 18 .... 1250, 1354
Sembawang Salvage Pte Ltd v. Shell Todd Oil Services Ltd [1993] 1 N.Z.L.R. 97 .. 193, 1252
Semco Salvage and Marine Pte Ltd v. Lancer Navigation Co. Ltd (The Nagasaki Spirit) [1997] A.C. 455;[1997] L.M.C.L.O. 321; *affirming* [1996] 1 Lloyd's Rep. 449, C.A.; *affirming* [1995] 2 Lloyd's Rep. 44 .... 83, 312, 410, 428, 429, 430, 1391
Services Europe Atlantique Sud v. Stockholms Rederiaktiebolag SVEA (The Folias) [1979] A.C. 685 .... 1462, 1464
Seven Seas Transportation Ltd v. Atlantic Shipping Co. S.A. [1975] 2 Lloyd's Rep. 188 220
Shallcross v. Wright (1850) 12 Beav. 558; 19 L.J. Ch. 443; 16 L.T.O.S. 267; 14 Jur. 1037; 50 E.R. 1174 809
Silesia, The (1880) 5 P.D. 177; 43 L.T. 319; 29 W.R. 156 .... 930, 1434, 1446, 1447, 1448
Silia, The [1981] 2 Lloyd's Rep. 534; [1981] Com. L.R. 256 .... 180, 183, 188, 795
Silver Bullion, The (1854) 2 Slinks. 70; 164 E.R. 312; *sub nom.* Sir Robert Peel, The 4 L.T. 742 .... 273, 647, 683, 685, 941
Simon v. Taylor [1975] 2 Lloyd's Rep. 338 .... 49, 336, 357, 561, 638
Skibladner, The (1877) 3 P.D. 24; 47 L.J. Adm. 84; 38 L.T. 150 1528
Skinner v. Secretary of State for Transport [1995] T.L.R. 2 683
Slaney, The [1951] 2 Lloyd's Rep. 538 .... 601, 603
Smith v. Brown (1871) L.R. 6 Q.B. 729; 40 L.J.Q.B. 214; 24 L.T. 808; 36 J.P. 264; 19 W.R. 1165; 1 Asp. M.L.C. 56 93
Snark, The [1900] P. 105; 69 L.J.P. 41; 82 L.T. 42; 48 W.R. 279; 16 T.L.R. 160; 44 S.J. 209; 9 Asp. M.L.C. 50 1087
Soblomsten, The (1866) L.R. 1 A. & E. 293; 36 L.J. Adm. 5; 15 L.T. 393; 15 W.R. 591 1363
Societe Anonyme des Minerais v. Grant Trading Inc. (The Ert Stefanie) [1989] 1 Lloyd's Rep. 349 1202
Societe Franco-Tunisienne D'Armement Tunis v. Sidermar SpA (The Massalia) [1961] 2 Q.B. 278; [1960] 3 W.L.R. 701; 104 S.J. 850; [1960] 2 All E.R 529; [1960] 1 Lloyd's Rep. 594 .... 614, 1079
Societe Maritime Caledonienne v. The Cynthera and her Cargo, The Cynthera [1965] 2 Lloyd's Rep. 454, N.S.W.S.C. 337
Solle v. Butcher [1950] 1 K.B. 671; [1949] 2 All E.R. 1107; 66 (Pt. 1) T.L.R. 448 913

xlvii

Table of Cases

Solway Prince, The [1896] P. 120; 65 L.J.P. 45; 74 L.T. 32 .... 58, 524, 532, 639
Somes v. British Empire Shipping Co. (1860) 8 H.L. C. 338; 30 L.J.Q.B. 229; 28 L.J.Q.B. 220; 27 L.J.Q.B. 397; E.B. & E. 353; 5 Jur. (N.S.) 675; 6 Jur. (N.S.) 761; 8 W.R. 707; 2 L.T. 547 806
Southern Venturer, The [1953] 1 Lloyd's Rep. 428 1526
Southsea, The (1933) 44 Ll.L.Rep. 373 .... 1407, 1414, 1434
Spaight v. Tedcastle (1881) 6 App. Cas. 217; 44 L.T. 589; 29 W.R. 761; 4 Asp. M.L.C. 406 1101
Span Terza, The [1984] 1 Lloyd's Rep. 119 795
Spirit of Ages, The (1857) Swab. 286; 30 L.T. (O.S.) 189; 166 E.R. 1141 .... 1522, 1538
Spree, The [1893] P. 147; 69 L.T. 628; 7 Asp. M.L.C. 397; I.R. 584 1527
Stag Line Ltd v. Foscolo Mango & Co. Ltd [1932] A.C. 328 .... 83, 84
Stanmore, The (1897) 13 T.L.R. 165 617
Star of Persia, The (1887) 6 Asp. M.L.C. 220; 57 L.T. 839 .... 1315, 1316
Steedman v. Scofield [1992] 2 Lloyd's Rep. 163 .... 170, 172, 176
Stella, The (1867) L.R. 1 A. & E. 340; 36 L.J. Adm. 13; 16 L.T. 335; 15 W.R. 936 ..... 1320, 1323, 1330
Stiklestad, The [1926] P. 205; 95 L.J.P. 161; 136 L.T. 479; 17 Asp. M.L.C. 191; *affirmed* 43 T.L.R. 118 .... 357, 540, 747, 752, 753, 758
The Stonedale No. 1 (Owners) v. Manchester Ship Canal Co. [1956] A.C. 1 1194
Strang, Steel & Co. v. A. Scott & Co. (1889) 14 App. Cas. 601; 59 L.J.P.C. 1; 61 L.T. 597 326
Strathgarry, The [1895] P. 264; 64 L.J.P. 59; 72 L.T. 202 .... 377, 728, 833, 931, 930, 935, 1437
Strathnaver, The (1875) 1 App. Cas. 58; 34 L.T. 148; 3 Asp. M.LC. 113 ... 333, 358, 600, 618
Suevic, The [1908] P. 154; 77 L.J.P. 92; 98 L.T. 188; 11 Asp. M.L.C. 16 .... 333, 341, 357, 1385, 1514
Sunheath, The (1925) 22 Ll.L.Rep. 361 .... 1323, 1324, 1329
Sunniside, The (1883) 8 P.D. 137; 52 L.J. Adm. 76; 49 L.T. 401; 31 W.R. 859 .... 1440, 1442, 1443, 1447, 1535
Susan V. Luckenbach, The [1951] P. 197; [1951] 1 T.L.R. 165; [1951] 1 All E.R. 753; 84 Ll.L.Rep. 538; *affirming* (1950) 84 Ll.L.Rep. 318 .... 488, 542, 1103
Sutton v. Buck (1810) 2 Taunt. 302 (Exchequer Chamber); 127 E.R. 1094 130
Swan, The (1839) 1 W. Rob. 68; 166 E.R. 499 .... 266, 341, 358, 527, 528, 529
Sybron Corp. v. Rochem Ltd [1984] Ch. 112; [1983] I.C.R. 80; [1983] 3 W.L.R. 713; 127 S.J. 391; [1983] 2 All E.R. 707; I.R.L.R. 253 913
Sylvan Arrow, The [1923] P. 220; 92 L.J.P. 119; 130 L.T. 157; 16 Asp. M.C. 244; 39 T.L.R. 655 477
Symons v. Baker [1905] 2 K.B. 723; 74 L.J.K.B. 965; 93 L.T. 548; 54 W.R. 159; 21 T.L.R. 734; 49 S.J. 714; 10 Asp. M.L.C. 129 .... 672, 693
Syria, The (1874) Shipp. Caz., July 7, 1874 385

Tafelberg, The (1941) 71 Ll.L.Rep. 189 .... 38, 337, 357, 597, 598
Tantalus (Master and Crew) v. Telemachus, Her Cargo and Freight (The Telemachus) [1957] P. 47 1447
Tarbert, The [1891] P. 372; 90 L.J.P. 353; 125 L.T. 800; 37 T.L.R. 831; 15 Asp. M.L.C. 423; 8 Ll.L.Rep. 119 .... 290, 357, 601, 717, 735, 748, 751
Tees, The, Pentucket, The (1862) Lush. 505; 1 Mar. L.C. 251 .... 358, 1525
Teh Hu (Owners) and Owners of Her Cargo and Freight v. Nippon Salvage Co. Teh Hu, The [1970] P. 106; [1969] 3 W.L.R. 1135; 113 S.J. 792; [1969] 2 Lloyd's Rep. 365; *sub nom.* Teh Hu, The Owners of Turbo-Electric Bulk Carrier Teh Hu v. Nippon Salvage Co. of Tokyo [1969] 3 All E.R. 1200; *affirming sub nom.* Teh Hu, The 113 S.J. 467; [1969] 2 Lloyd's Rep. 7; *sub nom.* Teh Hu, The, Owners of Turbo-Electric Bulk Carrier Teh Hu v. Nippon Salvage Co. of Tokyo [1969] 3 All E.R. 8 .... 21, 24, 1323, 1329, 1464, 1465
Telemachus, The [1957] P. 47; [1957] 2 W.L.R. 200; 101 S.J. 112; [1957] 1 All E.R 72; [1956] 2 Lloyd's Rep. 490; [1957] T.R. 1; 50 R. & I.T. 319; 35 A.T.C. 497 .... 35, 496, 567
Tervaete, The [1922] P. 259; 91 L.J.P. 213; 128 L.T. 176; 16 Asp. M.C. 48; 38 T.L.R. 825 ..... 345, 477
Tesaba, The [1982] 1 Lloyd's Rep. 397 .... 1224, 1488
Texaco Southampton, The [1983] 1 Lloyd's Rep. 94 .... 562, 603, 643
Thalatta, The, Shipping Gazette, May 26, 1905 .... 605, 613

Table of Cases

The Beaverford v. The Kafiristan [1938] A.C. 136; 106 L.J.P. 91; 157 L.T. 439; 53 T.L.R. 1010; 81 S.J. 844; 43 Com. Cas. 21; 19 Asp. M.L.C. 139; *reversing* [1937] P. 63 .... 22, 36, 767, 866, 1103
Telata, The [1982] 1 Lloyd's Rep. 397 1254
Theodore, The (1858) Swab. 351; 8 L.T. 335; 166 E.R. 1163 ..... 860, 862, 928, 937, 946, 947
Theseus, The (1925) 23 Ll.L.Rep. 136 .... 488, 491, 493, 495, 557
Thetis, H.M.S. (1834) 2 Knapp. 390; 8 L.T. 154; *affirming* (1833) 3 Hagg. 14; 6 L.T. 914 .... 37, 522, 1434, 1446
Thomas Allen, The (1886) 12 App. Cas. 118; 56 L.T. 285; 3 T.L.R. 188; 6 Asp. M.L.C. 99 .... 341, 1316, 1317
Thomas Blyth, The (1860) Lush. 16; 167 E.R. 8 1444
Thomas Fielden, The (1862) 32 L.J. Adm. 61 .... 1392, 1412, 1437
Thomas v. Howell (1874) L.R. 18 Eq. 198 698
Thompson v. H. & W. Nelson [1913] 2 K.B. 523; 82 L.J.K.B. 657; 108 L.T. 847; 29 T.L.R. 422; 12 Asp. M.L.C. 351
Thornley v. Hebson (1819) 2 B. & Ald. 513 1234
Three Rivers District Council v. Governor and Company of the Bank of England (No. 3) [2000] 2 W.L.R. 1220 1054
Titan, The (1923) 14 Ll.L.Rep. 484 174
Tojo Maru, The [1972] A.C. 242; [1971] 2 W.L.R. 970; [1971] 1 All E.R. 1110; [1971] 1 Lloyd's Rep. 341; *affirming sub nom.* N.V. Bureau Wijjsmuller v. Owners of M.V. Tojo Maru [1970] P. 21; [1969] 3 W.L.R. 902; [1969] 3 All E.R. 1179; [1969] 2 Lloyd's Rep. 193; *reversing* [1969] 2 W.L.R. 594; [1969] 2 All E.R. 155; [1969] 1 Lloyd's Rep. 133 .... 5, 6, 9, 23, 26, 32, 78, 766, 767, 768, 769, 899, 1013, 1104, 1105, 1107, 1110, 1112, 1115, 1118, 1119, 1122, 1124, 1196, 1397, 1401, 1423
Topa Topa, The (1935) 50 Ll.L.Rep. 211 .... 45, 1454
Toscana, The [1905] P. 148; 93 L.T. 392; 53 W.R. 405; 21 T.L.R. 329; 49 S.J. 350; 10 Asp. M.L.C. 108 1527
Tower Bridge, The [1936] P. 30; 105 L.J.P. 33; 154 L.T. 565; 52 T.L.R. 153; 18 Asp. M.L.C. 594; 53 Ll.L.Rep. 171 .... 355, 358, 359, 377, 539, 1439
Towle v. The Great Eastern (1864) 2 M.L.C. 148 (U.S. District Court of Admiralty, Southern District of New York) 634
Tranter v. Watson (1703) 2 Ld. Raym. 931 1247
Trekieve, The (1942) 72 Ll.L.Rep. 1 1315
Trelawney, The (1801) 3 C. Rob. 216n; (1802) 4 C. Rob. 223 .... 337, 358, 531, 572, 651, 1255
Tres, The (1936) 55 Ll.L.Rep. 16 339
Tresco, The (1944) 77 Ll.L.Rep. 514 1447
Trevorian, The (1940) 66 Ll.L.Rep. 45 .... 341, 616
Tribels, The [1985] 1 Lloyd's Rep. 128 .... 1245, 1259
Troilus The, viz. Idomeneus, The (1925) 22 Ll.L.Rep. 299 383
Troilus, The; Troilis (Cargo Owners) v. Glenogle (Owners, Masters and Crew) [1951] A.C. 820; [1951] 2 T.L.R. 22; 95 S.J. 465; [1951[2 All E.R. 40; [1951] 1 Lloyd's Rep. 467; *affirming sub nom.* The Troilus [1950] P. 92; 66 T.L.R. (Pt. 1) 182; 94 S.J. 113; [1950] 1 All E.R. 103; 83 Ll.L.Rep. 195; [1950] P. 92; *affirming* (1949) 82 Ll.L.Rep. 681 ..... 31, 33, 334, 336, 340, 345, 357, 382, 387, 470, 1321, 1411
True Blue, The (1843) 2 W. Rob. 176; 2 Not. of Cas. 413; 3 L.T. 182; 7 Jur. 756; 166 E.R. 721 .... 602, 815, 852, 853, 857, 881, 957
True Blu, The (1886) L.R. 1 P.C. 250; 4 Moo. P.C. (N.S.) 96; 16 E.R. 252 .... 1317, 1432
Trumpeter, The (1947) 80 Ll.L.Rep. 263 .... 215, 1134, 1243, 1244
Tsakiroglou & Co. Ltd v. Noblee Thorl GmbH [1962] A.C. 93 1067
Tsiropinas, The (1935) 51 Ll.L.Rep. 87 .... 338, 341, 345, 591, 597, 598, 1530
Tubantia, The [1924] P. 78; 93 L.J.P. 148; 131 L.T. 570; 40 T.L.R. 335 .... 208, 212, 389, 1229, 1230
Two Friends, The (1799) 1 C. Rob. 271; 1 Eng. P.R. Cas. 130; 165 E.R. 174 131,
Two Friends, The (1844) 2 W. Rob. 349; 3 L.T. 246; 8 Jur. 1011; 166 E.R. 786 .... 454, 457, 581, 1255, 1247

UMBERLEIGH, THE (1931) 39 Ll.L.Rep. 155 .... 46, 1454
Undaunted, The (1860) Lush. 90; 29 L.J. Adm. 176; 2L.T. 520 .... 358, 726, 727, 747, 749, 751, 752, 753, 1101
Unique, The (1939) 65 Ll.L.Rep. 75 1096

Table of Cases

Unique Mariner (No. 1), The [1978] 1 Lloyd's Rep. 438 ...... 9, 767, 810, 878, 880, 882, 895, 896, 902, 906, 915, 918, 919
Unique Mariner (No. 2), The [1979] 1 Lloyd's Ep. 37 .... 9, 31, 78, 80, 731, 775, 753, 755, 756, 760, 761, 762, 764, 767, 768, 769, 919
Upcerne, The [1912] P. 160; 81 L.J.P. 110; 107 L.T. 860; 28 T.L.R. 370; 12 Asp. M.L.C. 281 173
Upnor, The (1826) 2 Hagg. 3 210
Uranus, The (1924) 18 Ll.L.Rep. 439 1432

VALSESIA, THE [1927] P. 115; 96 L.J.K.B. 38; 136 L.T. 544; 43 T.L.R. 144; 17 Asp. M.C. 207; 26 Ll.L.Rep. 222 .... 778, 1093, 1094
Vandyck, The (1882) 5 Asp. M.L.C. 17; *affirming* (1881) 7 P.D. 42 ... 53, 54, 60, 62, 347, 358
Velox, The [1906] P. 263; 75 L.J.P. 81; 95 L.T. 271; 10 Asp. M.C. 277 .... 350, 359, 1429, 1430, 1434, 1500, 1501, 1502, 1503, 1504, 1505
Veritas, The [1901] P. 304; 70 L.J.P. 75; 85 L.T. 136; 50 W.R. 30; 9 Asp. M.C. 237 1250
Vesta, The (1828) 2 Hagg. 189; 166 E.R. 214 .... 1497, 1499
Victoria Laundry (Windsor) Ltd v. Newman Industries Ltd [1949] 2 K.B. 528; 65 T.L.R. 274; [1949] 1 All E.R. 997 1119
Victoria Peak, The (1947) 80 Ll.L.Rep. 527 .... 336, 357
Vine, The (1825) 2 Hagg. 1; 166 E.R. 145 .... 448, 449, 451, 454
Viscount, The [1966] 1 Lloyd's Rep. 328; 116 New L.J. 754 .... 702, 857
Vlierboom v. Chapman (1844) 3 M. & W. 230; 13 L.J. Ex. 384; 8 Jur. 811 1363
Volant, The (1842) 1 W. Rob. 383 1186
Vrede, The (1861) Lush. 322; 30 L.J. (P.M. & A.) 209 .... 139, 446, 632, 633
Vrouw Margaretha, The (1801) 4 C. Rob. 103; 165 E.R. 551 .... 339, 358

WALKER v. Rowe [2000] 1 Lloyd's Rep. 116 1469
Walpole v. Ewer, Sitt. After Trin. Term. (1789); Park, System of the Law on Marine Insurances (8th Ed., 1842), p. 899 .... 1482, 1510
Ward v. McCorkill, The Minnehaha (1861) 15 Moo. (P.C.) 133; Lush P.C. 335; 30 L.J.P.M. & A. 211; 4 L.T. 810; 9 W.R. 925; 7 Jur. (N.S.) 1257; 15 E.R. 444 ... 602, 604, 606, 609, 612, 613, 615, 617, 621, 624, 1096
Warrior, The (1862) Lush. 476; 6 L.T. 133; 1 Mar. L.C. 204; 167 E.R. 214 ..... 565, 569, 570, 573, 575, 576, 577, 579
Waterloo, The (1820) 2 Dods. 433 ... 3, 41, 459, 462, 484, 500, 522, 526, 527, 528, 529, 529, 567, 784, 857
Waterman S.S. Corp. v. Dean (The Fairisle) (1948) 171 F. 2d 408 (U.S.C. A., 4th Cir.) 1464
Watson v. Fireman's Fund Insurance Co. [1922] 2 K.B. 355 333
—— v. R.C.A. Victor Company Inc. (1934) 50 Ll.L.Rep. 77 .... 89, 178, 191, 245, 248
Watt, The (1843) 2 W. Rob. 70; 6 L.T. 371; 166 E.R. 681 .... 626, 1420, 1432, 1528
Watteau v. Fenwick [1893] 1 Q.B. 346; 67 L.T. 831; 56 J.P. 839; 41 W.R. 222; 9 T.L.R. 133; 37 Sol. Jo. 117; 5 R. 143 .... 803, 813
Waverley, The (1871) L.R. 3 A. & E. 369; 40 L.J. Adm. 42; 24 L.T. 713 .... 619, 815, 853, 937, 957
Wear Packet, The (1855) 2 Spinks E. & A. 256; 164 E.R. 419 695
Weeks v. Ross [1913] 2 K.B. 229; 82 L.J.K.B. 925; 108 L.T. 423; 23 Cox. C.C. 337; 12 Asp. M.C. 307; 77 J.P. 182; 29 T.L.R. 369 179
Weir v. Union Steamship Co. [1900] A.C. 525; 69 L.J.Q.B. 809; 83 L.T. 91; 9 Asp. M.L.C. 111; 5 Com. Cas. 363 670
Wells v. The Owners of the Gas Float Whitton No. 2 [1897] A.C. 337⁷6 L.T. 663; 66 L.J.P. 99; 13 T.L.R. 422; 8 Asp. M.L.C. 272, H.L.; *affirming* [1896] P. 42, C.A.; 8 Asp. M.L.C. 110; *reversing* [1895] P. 301; 8 Asp. M.L.C. 85; 65 L.J.P. 17; 66 L.J.P. 99; 76 L.T. 663 153
Werra, The (1886) 12 P.D. 52; 56 L.J.P. 53; 56 L.T. 580; 35 W.R. 552; 6 Asp. M.L.C. 115 ...... 334, 341, 1414, 1415
Wertheim v. Chicoutimi Pulp Co. [1911] A.C. 301; 80 L.J.P.C. 91; 16 Com. Cas. 297; 104 L.T. 226 1119
Westbourne, The (1889) 14 P.D. 132; 58 L.J.P. 78; 61 L.T. 156; 38 W.R. 56; 5 T.L.R.599; 6 Asp. M.L.C. 405 .... 937, 957, 958
Westdeutsche Landesbank Girozentrale v. Islington LBC [1996] A.C. 669 1467
Westar Marine Services v. Heerema Marine Contractors (1985) 621 F. Supp. 1135 1405
Westminster, The (1841) 1 W. Rob. 229; 8 L.T. 153 .... 357, 1127, 1414, 1415, 1486

1

Table of Cases

Whippingham, The (1934) 48 Ll.L.Rep. 49 .... 349, 359, 1415, 1434
White Star, The (1866) L.R. 1 A. & E. 68 .... 333, 601, 605, 616
Wilhelm Tell, The [1892] P. 337; 61 L.J.P. 127; 69 L.T. 199; 41 W.R. 205; 7 Asp. M.L.C. 329; I.R. 551 .... 1442, 1536, 1538, 1539, 1540
Wilhelmine, The (1842) 1 N.O. C. 376 .... 331, 340, 341, 342, 344, 591
Willem III, The (1871) L.R. 3 A. & E. 487; 25 L.T. 386; 20 W.R. 216; 1 Asp. M.L.C. 129 ..... 276, 279, 294, 295, 321, 326
William Beckford, The (1801) 3 C. Rob. 355; 165 E.R. 492 .... 26, 27, 37
William Brandt Junior, The (1842) 2 Not. of Cas. Suppl. Lxviii 606, 957
William Lushington, The (1850) 7 N.O.C. 261 .... 728, 857, 862
Wilsons, The (1841) 1 W. Rob. 172; 166 E.R. 537 654
Winkfield, The [1902] P. 42; 71 L.J.P. 21; 85 L.T. 668; 50 W.R. 246; 9 Asp. M.L.C. 259; 18 T.L.R. 178 1121
Winsor, The; China Pacific S.A. v. Ford Corp. of India, The [1982] A.C. 939; [1981] 3 W.L.R. 860; 125 S.J. 808; [1981] 3 All E.R. 688; [1982] 1 Lloyd's Rep. 117; *reversing* [1981] Q.B. 403; [1980] 3 W.L.R. 891; 124 S.J. 614; [1980] 3 All E.R. 556; [1980] 2 Lloyd's Rep. 213; *reversing* [1970] 2 All E.R. 35; [1979] 1 Lloyd's Rep. 167 ...... 378, 380, 1021, 1077, 1079, 1082, 1085, 1445
Wladyslaw Lokietek, The [1978] 2 Lloyd's Rep. 520 1202
Wordsworth, The (1898) 88 Fed. Rep. 313 334
Wright v. British Railways Board [1983] 2 A.C. 773; [1983] 3 W.L.R. 211; [1983] 2 All E.R. 698 1464

XHINA OCEAN SHIPPING CO. (OWNERS OF XINGCHENG) v. Andros (Owners the Andros) (The Andros) [1987] 1 W.L.R. 1213, Hong Kong 1218

YAN YEAN, THE (1883) 8 P.D. 147; 52 L.J. Adm. 67; 49 L.T. 186; 31 W.R. 950; 5 Asp. M.C. 135 1126
Ydun, The [1899] P. 236 549
Yolaine, The [1995] 2 Lloyd's Rep. 7 .... 1352, 1473
Young v. S.S. Scotia [1903] A.C. 501; 72 L.J.P.C. 115; 89 L.T. 374; 9 Asp. M.L.C. 485 673

ZEPHYR, THE (1827) 2 Hagg. 43; 166 E.R. 160 .... 530, 727
Zephyrus, The (1842) 1 W. Rob. 329; 1 Not. of Cas. 338; 8 L.T. 153; 6 Jur. 304; 166 E.R. 596 .... 115, 261, 263, 685, 686, 726, 735, 1478
Zeta, The (1875) L.R. 4 A. & E. 460; 44 L.J. Adm. 22; 33 L.T. 477; 24 W.R. 180 .. 208, 210, 1107, 1245

TABLE OF STATUTES

[See also the Appendices for Statutes set out there.]

1275	Statute of Westminster I (3 Edw. 1, c. 4) 105, 111	1847	Harbours, Docks and Piers Clauses Act—*cont.*	
1276	Statute of Westminster (4 Edw. 4, st. 2)—		s. 56	1192
	s. 2 105	1853	Merchant Shipping Law Amendment Act (16 & 17 Vict., c. 131)—	
1353	Wreck of the Sea Act (27 Edw. 3, c. 13) 106		s. 40	663
1389	Jurisdiction of Admiral Deputy Act (13 Ric. 2, st. 1, c. 5) ... 91	1854	Merchant Shipping Acts Amendment Act—	
1391	Admiralty Jurisdiction Act (15 Ric. 2, c. 3) 91, 114		s. 39	663
			s. 59	273
1400	Admiralty Jurisdiction Act (2 Hen. 4, c. 11) 91		s. 61	273
			s. 62	273
1713	12 Anne, c. 18 .... 110, 111, 112, 113, 129, 655		Merchant Shipping Act (17 & 18 Vict., c. 104) 118, 206	
1717	Stranded Ships Act (4 Geo. 1, c. 12) 111		s. 445	695
			s. 458 .... 277, 284, 288, 293	
1733	Responsibility of Shipowners Act (7 Geo. II, c. 15) 1186		ss. 458–459	273
			s. 459	282
1753	Stealing Shipwrecked Goods Act (26 Geo. II, c. 19) 112		s. 460 .... 118, 147, 1506	
	s. 9 113		s. 467	118
1809	Frauds of Boatmen Act (49 Geo. III, c. 122) 113, 114		s. 468	286
			s. 484 .... 663, 669	
	s. 9 271		s. 485	652
1813	Frauds of Boatmen Act (53 Geo. III, c. 87) 114		Merchant Shipping Repeal Act (17 & 18 Vict, c. 120)	118
			s. 4	273
1821	Frauds of Boatmen Act (1 & 2 Geo. IV, c. 75)—		Sched.	273
	s. 8 .... 115, 271	1857	Court of Probate Act (20 & 21 Vict., c. 77)	95
	s. 31 115		Matrimonial Causes Act (20 & 21 Vict., c. 85)	95
	Cinque Ports Act (1 & 2 Geo. 4, c. 76) 113	1859	High Court of Admiralty Act (22 & 23 Vict., c. 6)	95
	s. 4 115			
	s. 20 115	1861	Admiralty Court Act (24 & 25 Vict., c. 10)	119
1832	Privy Council Appeals Act (2 & 3 Will. 4, c. 92)—		s. 9	273
	s. 3 98		s. 14	119
1833	Judicial Committee Act (3 & 4 Will. 4, c. 41)—	1862	Merchant Shipping Amendment Act (25 & 26 Vict., c. 63)—	
	ss. 1–2 98			
1838	Judgments Act 1467, 1475		s. 33	542
1840	Admiralty Court Act (3 & 4 Vict., c. 65) 116, 117		s. 49 .... 118, 122, 1506	
		1863	Statute Law Revision Act (26 & 27 Vict., c. 125)	105
1846	Wreck and Salvage Act (9 & 10 Vict., c. 99) 117, 118, 273	1864	Naval Agency and Distribution Act (27 & 28 Vict., c. 24) ...	120
	s. 15 695			
	s. 19 271		s. 122	120
1847	Harbours, Docks and Piers Clauses Act (10 & 11 Vict., c. 27)—	1868	County Courts Admiralty Jurisdiction Act (31 & 32 Vict., c. 71) 121, 123	
	s. 1 1047	1873	Supreme Court of Judicature Act (36 & 37 Vict., c. 66)	1475
	s. 52 1047			

Table of Statutes

1873 Merchant Shipping Act (36 & 37 Vict., c. 85)—
  s. 16 .... 541, 542
  Supreme Court of Judicature Acts (36 & 37 Vict., c. 66) ... 96, 98, 104, 143, 146, 247
1894 Merchant Shipping Act (57 & 58 Vict., c. 60) ... 110, 113, 123, 128, 276, 277, 588
  Pt. II 207
  Pt. IX 123, 207
  s. 255(1) 207
  s. 313(1) 168
  s. 422 540
  s. 503 .... 1186, 1202
  ss. 510–571 122
  ss. 538–543 113
  s. 544 ...... 113, 179, 230, 273, 274, 288
   (1) 240, 277, 294
   (2) 282, 297
   (3) 292, 310
  ss. 544–545 1514
  ss. 544–546 .... 279, 284, 305
  s. 545 .... 113, 277
  s. 546 .... 179, 230, 288
  s. 547 123
   (2) 123
   (3) 123
  s. 548 123
  s. 549 123
  s. 557 .... 663, 670
   (1) 663, 664, 669, 781, 1460
  s. 565 123
  s. 571 113
  s. 742 .... 168, 169, 172, 245
  s. 745 541
  s. 748 123
  Sched. 22 541
1898 Merchant Shipping (Mercantile Marine Fund) Act (61 & 62 Vict., c. 44)—
  s. 1(1)(b) 292
1906 Marine Insurance Act (6 Edw. 7, c. 41) 488
  s. 46 1446
  s. 33 1028
  s. 65(1) 486
   (2) 486
  s. 78 486
   (4) 637
  s. 80 670
   (3) 670
1911 Maritime Conventions Act (1 & 2 Geo. 5, c. 57)—
  s. 4(2) 540
  s. 6 535
  ss. 6–8 7
  s. 8 .... 4, 176, 1205, 1209

1916 Merchant Shipping (Salvage) Act (6 & 7 Geo. 5, c. 41) ... 664, 669, 781
  s. 1 .... 465, 466, 663, 671
1920 Air Navigation Act (10 & 11 Geo. 5, c. 80) 245, 679
  s. 11 .... 244, 245, 247, 249, 677
1924 Carriage of Goods by Sea Act (14 & 15 Geo. 5, c. 22) 83
1925 Supreme Court of Judicature (Consolidation) Act (15 & 16 Geo. 5, c. 49) 104
  s. 22 123
  s. 33 123
  s. 226 123
  Sched. 6 123
1932 Merchant Shipping (Safety and Load Line Convention) Act (22 & 23 Geo 5, c. 9)—
  s. 26(1) 539
1934 County Courts (Amendment) Act (24 & 25 Geo. 5, c. 17)—
  s. 13(8) 123
  s. 34 123
  Sched. V, Pt. I 123
1936 Air Navigation Act (26 Geo. 5 & 1 Edw. 7, c. 44) ... 249, 677, 679
1940 Merchant Shipping (Salvage) Act (3 & 4 Geo. 6, c. 43) ... 665, 781, 1460
  s. 4(3) 664
1943 Law Reform (Frustrated Contracts) Act (6 & 7 Geo. 6, c. 40) 1067
  s. 1(1) 610
   (2) 610
   (3) 610
  s. 2(3) 610
1944 Prize Salvage Act (7 & 8 Geo. 6, c. 7) 652
1947 Fire Services Act (10 & 11 Geo. 6, c. 41)—
  s. 3(4) 688
  Crown Proceedings Act (10 & 11 Geo. 6, c. 44) 781, 1163, 1167, 1169, 1170, 1429, 1460
  ss. 1–2 1167
  s. 2 1054
  s. 8 781
   (2) 1529
  s. 13 1170
  s. 15 1170
  s. 17 1166
  s. 21 1170
  s. 38(2) 1166, 1169
  s. 40(1) 1167
   (2)(g) 1167
  ss. 41–53 1166
  s. 89 664
   (2) 664

liii

Table of Statutes

1949 Merchant Shipping (Safety Conventions) Act (12, 13 & 14 Geo. 6, c. 43)—
    s. 22 536
  Civil Aviation Act (12, 13 & 14 Geo. 6, c. 67)—
    s. 51 .... 249, 252
    s. 70(1) 677
    s. 87(4) 249
    s. 109 249
    Sched. 12 677
    Sched. 14, Para. 3 249
    Sched. 16 249
1950 Arbitration Act (14 Geo. 6, c. 27) 125
    s. 27 1280
1956 Administration of Justice Act (4 & 5 Eliz. 2, c. 46) 101, 104, 124, 181
    s. 1(1)(q) 33
    s. 3 181
    s. 45(4) 371
    s. 57(2) 123
    Sched. 1
        para. 4(1) 260
        para. 8(1) 260
    Sched. 2 123
1959 County Courts Act (7 & 8 Eliz. 2, c. 22) 124
    ss. 55–61 123
1964 Diplomatic Privileges Act (c. 81) 1171
  Scrap Metal Dealers Act (c. 69) 113
1965 Nuclear Installations Act (c. 57)—
    ss. 7–11 1199
1967 Misrepresentation Act (c. 7)—
    s. 2(1) 905
      (2) 889, 905
1968 Consumer Relations Act (c. 18) 1171
  Hovercraft Act (c. 59) 259, 260
    s. 1(1) 259
      (h) 191, 259
      (j) 191
      (3) 191
    s. 2(1) 260
      (2) 260
      (3) 171, 260
      (3A) 260
    s. 4(1) 257
  Fisheries Act (c. 77)—
    s. 17 207
1969 Employer's Liability (Defective Employment) Act (c. 37) ... 169
1970 Administration of Justice Act (c. 31) 101, 125
1971 Carriage of Goods by Sea Act (c. 19) 192
    s. 1(2) 1446
      (2)–(3) 1188

1971 Carriage of Goods by Sea Act —cont.
    s. 1(7) 191, 192
    Sched., Art. 1 (c) 191, 192
      Art. III, r. 6bis 1218
      Art. IV, r. 4 1446
  Wild Creatures and Forest Laws Act (c. 47)
    s. 1(1) 314
  Prevention of Oil Pollution Act (c. 60) 82
    s. 12 70
1973 Supply of Goods (Implied Terms) Act (c. 13) 994
1975 Arbitration Act (c. 3) 125
1976 Sex Discrimination Act (c. 65) 169
1977 Unfair Contract Terms Act (c. 50) 1002, 1006, 1011, 1012, 1143, 1144, 1162
    Pt. I 1144
    Pt. II 1144
    Pt. III 1144
    s. 1(1) 1149
      (2) 1146, 1156
      (3) 1145
    s. 2(1) 1155
      (2) 1156
      (3) 1149
    ss. 2–4 .... 1145, 1146
    ss. 2–7 1147
    s. 3 .... 1157, 1158
      (1) 1157
      (2) 1157
        (b) 1160
    s. 4(1) 1150
      (2) 1150
    s. 5 1145
    s. 6 1145
      (1) 1002
      (2)(a) 1002
      (3) 1002, 1152
    s. 7 .... 1145, 1148
      (1) 1006
      (2) 1006
      (3) 1006, 1152
      (3A) 1006
      (4) 1006, 1152
    s. 8 1084
    s. 9 1154
    s. 11(1) 1152
      (2) 1152
      (3) 1152
      (4) 1153
      (5) 1150
    s. 12 .... 1002, 1148
      (1) 1001, 1148
      (2) 1001
        (a) 1001
        (b) 1001
      (3) 1148
    s. 13(1) 1001

Table of Statutes

1977 Unfair Contract Terms Act
—cont.
- s. 14 .... 1153, 1155
  - (2) 1001
  - (3) 1001
  - (6) 1001
- s. 15 1001
- s. 27 1144
- s. 29(1) 1144
- s. 32 1145
- Sched. 1, Para. 2(a) 1148, 1156
- Sched. 2 1152

1978 Interpretation Act (c. 30)—
- s. 17(2)
  - (a) 252
  - (b) 249
- s. 43 540
- Sched. 6, Pt. VII, para. 6 540
- State Immunity Act (c. 33) 1163, 1171
  - s. 1 1163
    - (1) 1171
  - s. 2(1) 1172
    - (2) 1172
  - s. 3(1) 1172
    - (2) 1172
    - (3) 1172
  - s. 5 1173
  - ss. 6–8 1173
  - s. 9 1173
  - s. 10 1171
    - (1)–(2) 1175
    - (3) 1176
    - (4) 1176
      - (a) 1176
      - (b) 1176
    - (5) 1177
    - (6) 1172, 1173, 1175
  - s. 11 1173
  - s. 14(1) 1171
    - (2) 1172
  - ss. 14–16 1171
  - s. 17(4) 1174

1979 Arbitration Act (c. 42) 794
- Sale of Goods Act (c. 54) ... 994, 1008, 1024, 1030
  - s. 2(1) 999
  - ss. 2–5 1025
  - ss. 7–10 1025
  - s. 8 1024
    - (1) 999
    - (2) 999
    - (3) 999
  - s. 10 .... 1024, 1030
  - s. 13 .... 1025, 1029
  - ss. 13–15–1025
  - s. 14 .... 1024, 1030
    - (1) 1024
  - s. 15 .... 1024, 1029
  - s. 16(3) 1024
  - s. 17 1024
  - s. 20(2) 1024

1979 Sale of Goods Act—cont.
- s. 29(3) 1024
- s. 35(1) 1024
- s. 37(1) 1024
- s. 49(1)–(2) 1024
- s. 50(1) 1024
- s. 51(1) 1024
- s. 55
  - (1) 1002, 1024
  - (2) 1002
- Merchant Shipping Act (c. 39) ... 127, 1187

1980 Limitation Act (c. 58) 1205
- s. 2 1205
- s. 5 1205
- s. 9 1205
- s. 24 1205
- s. 39 1205

1981 Supreme Court Act (c. 54) ... 102, 104, 171, 321, 1169
- s. 16(2) 20
- s. 20 153
  - (1)(a) 1224
  - (c) 153, 316
  - (s) 316
  - (2)(e) 1224
  - (h) 1224
  - (i) 296
  - (j) 145, 248, 252, 296, 1224
  - (iii) 243, 755
  - (k)–(l) 252
  - (q) 33
  - (6) 252, 279, 296
  - (7) 296
    - (a) 252
    - (b) 252
- ss. 20–24 321
- s. 21 1223
  - (3) 1249
- s. 24(1) 321
  - (2) (c) 1170
  - (3) 1169
- s. 21(3) 252
- ss. 20–24 124
- s. 22(2) 171
- s. 24(1) 171, 173, 176, 247, 252
- s. 27 20
- s. 29 1170
- s. 31 1053
- s. 33(1) 1223
- s. 35 1223
- s. 35A 1467, 1468
- s. 37 1226
- s. 61(1) 20
- Sched. 1, Para. 2 (c) 20
- Sched. 5 260

1982 Civil Aviation Act (c. 16) ... 249, 253
- s. 70(2) 249
- s. 87 .... 191, 252, 256, 279
  - (1) 251, 255
  - (2) 251, 255, 358, 677, 678

Table of Statutes

1982	Civil Aviation Act—*cont.*	
	s. 87(3)	255
	(4)	249
	s. 91	251, 279
	s. 97	253
	(7)	252
	s. 109	279
	Sched. 16	279
	Civil Jurisdiction and Judgments Act (c. 27)	124, 1224
	Supply of Goods and Services Act (c. 29)	994, 1024, 1026
	Pt. I	994, 1003, 1004, 1005, 1011
	Pt. II	994, 1007, 1010, 1011
	Pt. III	994
	s. 1(1)	1003
	(2)	1003, 1012
	(3)	1003
	s. 2(2)	1012
	ss. 2–4	1005
	s. 3	1012
	s. 4	1012
	s. 5	1005
	s. 6(1)–(2)	1004
	(3)	1004
	ss. 6–10	1005
	s. 7	1012
	s. 11(1)	1006
	(2)	1006
	(3)	1005
	s. 12(1)	1007
	(2)	1007
	(3)	1007
	(4)	1008, 1018
	(5)	1008
	s. 13	1008, 1010, 1013
	ss. 13–14–1020, 1021, 1022, 1023	
	ss. 13–15	1008, 1019
	s. 14	1008, 1010, 1014
	s. 15	1016, 1017, 1018, 1019
	s. 16(1)	1011
	(2)	1011
	(3)	1011
	(a)	1008
	(b)	1008
	(4)	1011
	s. 17(2)	1006
	(3)	1006
	s. 18(1)	1010
	Sched. 1, Para. 2,(g)	1012
	Criminal Justice Act (c. 48)—	
	s. 74	536
1984	County Courts Act (c. 28)	124
	ss. 26–29	125
	s. 31	125
	s. 69	1467
	s. 74	1467
1985	Companies Act (c. 6)—	
	s. 395	187
1985	Dangerous Vessels Act (c. 22)—	
	s. 1	1047
1986	Insolvency Act (c. 45)—	
	ss. 15–16	187
1987	Pilotage Act (c. 21)—	
	s. 16	1101
	s. 31(1)	588
1988	Merchant Shipping Act (c. 12)—	
	s. 48	366
	Sched. 5	366
1993	Merchant Shipping (Registration, etc.) Act (c. 22)—	
	s. 8(3)	535, 536, 540
	Sched. 4, Para. 6(2)	535, 536, 540
1994	Value Added Tax Act (c. 23)—	
	s. 30	1477
	Sched. 8, Group 8	1477
	Merchant Shipping (Salvage and Pollution) Act (c. 28)	66, 128, 1209
	s. 1	65, 66
	(5)	65
	(6)	310
	(10)	310
	s. 8(6)	70
	s. 10	297
	(4)	65
	Sched. 1	66
	Sched. 2, Para. 1(2)	310
	Sched. 4	297, 310
1995	Merchant Shipping Act (c. 21)	18, 66, 81, 82, 84, 87, 128, 169, 298, 307, 316, 368, 375, 534, 694, 722, 1046, 1187, 1205, 1496
	Pt. IX	207, 250, 694
	s. 1(3)	169, 310, 534
	s. 39	787, 841, 843, 846, 945, 1539, 1540
	(1)	644, 1537, 1538, 1539
	(2)	644, 1539
	s. 41	1247, 1540
	s. 92	539, 540, 541, 542, 543
	(1)(a)	540
	(b)	540
	(3)	540
	(4)	534, 541
	s. 93	537, 538
	(1)	537, 539
	(2)	534, 538
	(3)	534, 536
	(4)	538
	(5)	538
	(6)	534, 539
	(7)	539
	ss. 94–100	1046
	s. 128(1)	70, 1049
	s. 129	70
	s. 137	70, 71, 1047, 1049, 1054
	(1)	70

Table of Statutes

1995 Merchant Shipping Act—*cont.*
- s. 137(2) 70
- (3) 70
- (4) 70, 71
- (5) 70, 71
- (6) 70
- (7) 70
- (9) 70
- ss. 137–141 69
- s. 138 .... 71, 1054
- (1) 71
- (2) 71
- (3) 71
- (4) 71
- s. 139 71
- s. 141 70
- s. 153 1199
- s. 182 1169
- s. 185 .... 127, 1187
- (1) ... 1190, 1191, 1194, 1198
- (1)–(2) 1188
- (2) ... 1190, 1192, 1198, 1199
- (4) 1188, 1200
- s. 187 1102
- s. 190 .... 07, 176, 1209, 1214
- s. 192 654
- s. 201 1192
- s. 224 .... 514, 534, 535, 536, 678
- (1) ... 07, 66, 74, 76, 330, 368, 375, 395, 1049, 1496, 1521
- (2) 07, 66, 81, 169, 298, 310, 330, 368, 375, 414, 723
- (3) 66
- (4) 65
- (5) 66
- (6) 65, 81
- (7) 66
- s. 225 1322
- (1) 1322
- (2) 1322
- (3) 1322
- (4) 1322
- ss. 225–227 1169
- s. 226 .... 111, 1223, 1246
- (1)(a) 286
- s. 227 1223
- s. 228 1521
- (1) 1521
- (2) 1521
- (3) 1521
- (4) 1521
- (5) 1520
- (6) 1521
- (7) 1521
- s. 229 1522
- (1) 1522
- (2) 1520, 1522
- (3) 1522
- (4) 1522
- s. 230
- (1) 1167, 1170

1995 Merchant Shipping Act—*cont.*
- s. 230(2) ... 658, 664, 665, 667, 677, 838, 1167
- (3) 652, 668, 674, 679
- (4) 652, 679
- (5) 653, 679
- (6) 652, 679
- (7) 664
- (8) 652
- s. 231 .... 114, 687, 695
- (1) 694
- (2) 694, 695
- (3) 695
- (4) 688, 695
- ss. 231–247 695
- ss. 231–255 1223
- s. 232 111
- (1) 694
- (2) 694, 695
- (3) 694
- (4) 694
- s. 233 111
- s. 234 114
- s. 236 .... 22, 1246
- s. 237 1246
- s. 241 107
- s. 244 111
- s. 248 1521
- 684
- (1) 694
- (2) 694
- (3) 695
- (4) 694
- s. 250 688
- (4) 684
- s. 252 687
- (3) 170
- ss. 252–253 688
- s. 255(1) 17, 1169, 1521
- s. 293 .... 70, 1048
- s. 310 .... 258, 260
- s. 311(1) 169
- s. 312(2) 07
- (a) 294, 310
- (b) 294
- s. 313(1) ... 169, 169, 173, 176, 245, 310, 534, 1169, 1538, 1540
- (2)(a) 1521, 1522
- s. 314 .... 113, 535
- (2) 207
- s. 315 309
- (1) 70
- Sched. 7 .... 127, 1187
- Pt. I 1188
- Art. 1.1 1190
- Art. 1.3 1190
- Art. 1.4 1190
- Art. 1.5 1190
- Art. 1.6 1190
- Art. 2.1 1191
- Art. 2.2 ... 1191, 1194
- Pt. I Art. 3 1198

lvii

1995 Merchant Shipping Act—*cont.*
Sched. 7, Pt. II 1188, 1190
para. 3(1) 1192
para. 4
(1) 1198
(2) 1199
(3) 1199
para. 12 1190
Sched. 11 66
Pt. I ... 08, 66, 162, 330,
375, 395, 678, 1300
art. 1(a) ... 368, 375
art. 10 535
art. 12.1 678
art. 13.1(b) ... 395
art. 13.2 1496
Pt. II ... 07, 66, 162, 298,
375, 555
art. 3 1214
art. 5 723
para. 1 02
para. 2 368
(1) 81, 375
para. 3
(1) 514, 534,
536
(2) 536
para. 4 414
para. 5(1)(a) 169
para. 6 ...... 74, 76, 12–5
para. 7 81
Sched. 12 535
Sched. 13, para. 43(6) 207
Sched. 14, para. 11 113
1996 Arbitration Act (c. 23) 792, 822,
1281, 1284, 1309
s. 1(b) 1266
s. 3 1279
s. 9
(1) 1269
(4) 1269
s. 11 .... 1226, 1271, 1272
(2) 1271
s. 12 .... 1209, 1280, 1304

1996 Arbitration Act—*cont.*
s. 13 1205
ss. 13–14 1274
s. 16 1280
ss. 23–27 1275
s. 28 1297
s. 33 1275
s. 34 1284
s. 36 1275
s. 37 1288
s. 38 1283
s. 39 1291
(1)–(2) 1291
(3) 1291, 1294
(4) 1291
s. 41 1205
s. 47(1)–(2) 1290
(3) 1290
s. 49 .... 1137, 1467, 1468, 1469,
1471
(1) 1475
(1)–(2) 1469
(3) 1475
(4) 1475
s. 56 1297
s. 58 1299
ss. 59–65 1296
s. 63 1296
s. 64 1296
s. 65 1296
s. 66 1299
ss. 67–71 1309
s. 69 1469
s. 70(2)(a) 1309
s. 79 1209
s. 81 1314
1997 Merchant Shipping and Maritime Security Act (c. 28)—
s. 15 1187
1998 Late Payment of Commercial Debts (Interest) Act (c. 20) 1466, 1467
1999 Contracts (Rights of Third Parties) Act ... 879, 1038, 1098, 1277

TABLE OF STATUTORY INSTRUMENTS

[*See also the Appendices for Statutory Instruments set out there.*]

1938 Aircraft (Wreck and Salvage) Order 1938 (S. R. & O. 1938 No. 136) 249, 278, 679
    art. 2 .... 179, 250
        (b) 207
1964 Aircraft (Wreck and Salvage) Order in Council 1964 (S.I. 1964 No. 489) 679
1965 RSC—
    Ord. 75 102
1972 Hovercraft (Application of Enactments) Order 1972 (S.I. 1972 No. 971)—
    art. 4 1170
    art. 8 .... 191, 1167
        (1) 258
        (1) 207
1980 Air Navigation Order 1980 (S.I. 1980 No. 1965)—
    Art. 95 253
    Sched. 1, Pt. I 253
1982 Supply of Services (Exclusion of Implied Terms) Order 1982 (S.I. 1982 No. 1771) 1008
1983 Supply of Services (Exclusion of Implied Terms) Order 1983 (S.I. 1983 No. 902) 1009
1985 Supply of Services (Exclusion of Implied Terms) Order 1985 (S.I. 1985 No. 1) 1008
1986 Merchant Shipping Act 1979 (Commencement No. 10) Order 1986 (S.I. 1986 No. 1052) 1187
1994 Unfair Terms in Consumer Contracts Regulations—
    reg. 5(1) 943
        (5) 943

1994 Unfair Terms in Consumer Contracts Regulations—*cont.*
    Sched. 2 943
    Merchant Shipping (Salvage and Pollution) Act (Commencement No. 2) Order 1994 (S.I. 1994 No. 2871) 65
    Unfair Contract Terms in Consumer Contracts Regulations 1994 (S.I. 1994 No. 3159) 1162
1997 Merchant Shipping (Oil Pollution, Preparedness, Response and Co-operation Convention) Order 1997 (S.I. 1997 No. 2567) 1049
1998 Civil Procedure Rules 97
    Pt 49 102
    Practice Direction 49F PD 102, 1386
    Merchant Shipping (Convention on Limitation of Liability for Maritime Claims) (Amendment) Order 1998 (S.I. 1998 No. 1258) 1187, 1189, 1198
    Merchant Shipping (Oil Pollution Preparedness, Response and Co-operation) Regulations 1998 (S.I. 1998 No. 1056) 1049
1999 Unfair Contract Terms in Consumer Contracts Regulations 1999 1162
    reg. 3(1) 1162
    The Civil Courts (Amendment) (No. 2) Order 1999 (S.I. 1999 No. 1011) 124, 1224

lix

TABLE OF CONVENTIONS

[*See also the Appendices for Conventions set out there.*]

1910 Convention for the Unification of Certain Rules of Law Respecting Assistance and Salvage at Sea 12, 17, 73, 85, 88, 127, 234, 298, 305, 398, 953, 1226, 1397, 1453
- art. 1 17
- art. 2 .... 719, 755, 1319
- art. 3 45
- art. 4 512
- art. 5 .... 504, 413
- art. 5.1 .... 68, 69
- art. 7 .... 884, 885, 886
- art. 8 ... 332, 540, 1088, 1394, 1408, 1424, 1450
- art. 9 68
- art. 10 .... 1205, 1209
- art. 11 .... 535, 1164
- art. 13 68
- art. 14 1164

International Convention for the Unification of Certain Rules of Law with respect to Collision Between Vessels—
- Art. 7 1209

1919 Paris Convention 245
- Art. 23 245

1924 Brussels International Convention for the Unification of Certain Rules Relating to Bills of Lading 83

International Convention for the Unification of Certain Rules Relating to the Limitation of the Liability of Owners of Sea-Going Vessels 1186

1926 International Convention for the Unification of Certain Rules Concerning the Immunity of State-Owned Ships 1164, 1171
- Protocol 1171

International Convention for the Unification of Certain Rules Relating to Maritime Liens and Mortgages
- Art. 2.3 1247

1929 Convention for the Unification of Certain Rules Relating to International Carriage by Air 1203

1938 International Convention for the Unification of Certain Rules relating to Assistance and Salvage of Aircraft or by Aircraft at Sea 10, 12, 249
- Art. 2 250

1944 Chicago Convention 254

1955 Hague Protocol—
- Art. 25 1203

1957 International Convention for the Unification of Certain Rules Relating to the Limitation of the Liability of Owners of Sea-Going Ships 1186
- art. 1.1 1201
- art. 1.6 1202

1967 International Convention for the Unification of Certain Rules Relating to Maritime Liens and Mortgages—
- Art. 4.1(v) 1247

1968 Brussels Convention on Jurisdiction and Enforcement of Judgments 124, 1224

1969 International Convention for Oil Pollution Damage 1199
- Protocol 1199

1972 European Convention on State Immunity 1171

1973 International Convention for the Prevention of Pollution from Ships (MARPOL) 70

Protocol Relating to Intervention on the High Seas in Cases of Marine Pollution by Substances other than Oil 70

1976 Brussels Salvage Protocol 10

London Convention on Limitation of Liability for Maritime Claims (LLMC) 128, 1186, 1190, 1193, 1194, 1200, 1202
- art. 1 1190
- art. 1.2 1190
- art. 1.6 1204
- art. 2 1188
- art. 2.1 .... 1191, 1194, 1195

lx

Table of Conventions

1976 London Convention on Limitation of Liability for Maritime Claims (LLMC) —*cont.*
- art. 2.1(c) 1198
- (d) 1195
- (d)-(f) 1190
- art. 2.2 .... 1194, 1195
- arts. 2–3 1188
- art. 3 1198
- art. 3.2 1192
- art. 4 .... 1194, 1203
- art. 5 1196
- art. 15 1189
- art. 15.1 1190
- arts. 16–23 1187

1981 Montreal CMI Draft Salvage Convention 128
- art. 3–2(1)(d) 332
- art. 13 394

1982 United Nations Convention on the Law of the Sea 70, 534

1989 International Convention on Salvage ... 2, 8, 12, 65, 67, 72, 73, 81, 82, 83, 85, 87, 88, 128, 159, 162, 177, 194, 200, 213, 234, 243, 260, 261, 284, 292, 298, 311, 312, 330, 351, 369, 374, 376, 400, 411, 442, 443, 444, 514, 556, 564, 741, 742, 754, 870, 876, 878, 879, 882, 890, 925, 944, 945, 1059, 1060, 1062, 1220, 1248, 1388, 1453, 1456, 1457, 1468
- art. 1 .... 18, 65, 163, 169, 230, 396
- (a) 70, 161, 243, 306, 330, 443, 444, 513, 947
- (a)-(c) 162
- (b) 164, 404
- (c) 166, 230, 243, 327
- (d) 162, 398, 949
- (e) 353, 429, 1211, 1214
- art. 1.1 1410
- art. 2 .... 74, 81, 1397
- art. 3 .. 162, 174, 200, 318, 319, 320
- art. 4 68
- art. 4.1 1164
- art. 4.2 .... 1049, 1164
- art. 5 .... 545, 546, 550, 553, 556, 1069, 1165
- art. 5.1 .... 546, 548, 549, 551, 553, 554, 555, 556
- art. 5.2 ..... 443, 546, 551, 554, 556
- art. 5.3 ..... 76, 547, 549, 551, 552, 553, 554, 556, 1052
- art. 5.7 1224
- art. 6 .... 10, 396, 408
- art. 6.1 .. 77, 80, 164, 167, 243, 408, 444, 798, 818, 834, 951, 1211, 1291

1989 International Convention on Salvage—*cont.*
- art. 6.2 .... 62, 796, 816, 832
- art. 6.3 .... 404, 408, 886, 950
- art. 7 .... 796, 879, 886, 888, 889, 1215
- (a) ... 944, 946, 947, 948, 950, 951
- (b) 944, 951
- art. 8 ...... 396, 407, 443, 444, 1214
- art. 8.1 .... 443, 1059, 1117
- (a) 407, 1037, 1086
- (b) 404, 407, 989, 1013, 1037, 1089
- (c)-(d) 1019, 1036, 1040, 1041
- (d) 1037, 1043, 1059, 1404, 1406
- art. 8.2 .... 544, 1056, 1059
- (a) ... 407, 1037, 1059, 1059, 1060
- (b) 404, 407, 989, 1037, 1089
- (c) 381, 989, 1021, 1062, 1067, 1070, 1082, 1438
- art. 8.3 .... 544, 1394
- art. 9 .... 69, 70, 404, 546
- art. 10 .... 67, 1214
- art. 10.1 ... 535, 536, 538, 540, 987
- art. 10.2 .... 81, 535
- art. 10.3 .... 534, 535
- arts. 10–11 10
- art. 11 .... 67, 81, 404, 443, 1048, 1049, 1053
- art. 12 ... 19, 441, 719, 1068, 1450, 1451
- art. 12.1 .... 19, 721, 1450
- art. 12.2 .... 19, 722, 724, 1450
- art. 12.3 .. 486, 491, 505, 507, 508, 509
- arts. 12–13 1017
- arts. 12–19 504
- art. 13 ..... 312, 394, 396, 397, 407, 410, 413, 415, 416, 417, 418, 421, 423, 427, 430, 433, 435, 436, 436, 437, 971, 974, 977, 978, 979, 1402, 1406, 1408, 1417, 1418, 1419, 1451, 1520
- art. 13.1 .. 410, 418, 419, 425, 443, 1395, 1403, 1404, 1405, 1406, 1436, 1453, 1455, 1456, 1521, 1522
- (a) 1457
- (b) 404, 407, 410, 418, 1117, 1399, 1405, 1411, 1417, 1421, 1456
- (c) ... 719, 1450, 1451, 1456
- (d) 332, 1405, 1411
- (e) 359, 1117, 1399, 1405, 1411, 1412, 1413, 1421
- art. 13.1
- (f) 377, 1435, 1438

lxi

Table of Conventions

1989 International Convention on Salvage—*cont.*
- art. 13.1(g) 309, 338, 1409, 1410, 1411, 1413, 1424, 1427, 1460
- (h) 377, 410, 418, 1014
- (i) 1455
- (j) 410, 1409, 1410, 1455
- art. 13.2 .. 81, 435, 948, 949, 1218, 1395, 1488, 1491, 1496
- art. 13.3 .... 435, 1319, 1397
- arts. 13–14 196
- arts. 13–19 536
- art. 14 .... 19, 312, 352, 395, 397, 404, 407, 409, 410, 412, 413, 414, 415, 417, 419, 421, 422, 423, 424, 426, 427, 429, 430, 431, 432, 435, 436, 437, 438, 443, 960, 961, 964, 972, 975, 991, 1198, 1211, 1218, 1388, 1408, 1441, 1456, 1494
- art. 14.1 .... 18, 412, 413, 414, 415, 416, 417, 418, 422, 423, 425, 429, 431, 433, 434, 436, 975
- art. 14.2 .... 18, 414, 415, 416, 418, 419, 423, 424, 425, 429, 430, 433, 975
- art. 14.3 .. 414, 418, 426, 427, 428, 429, 430, 432, 949, 1408
- art. 14.4 .. 416, 417, 420, 423, 429, 434
- art. 14.5 .... 404, 438, 981, 1089
- art. 14.6 .... 440, 1218
- art. 15 .... 1520, 1523
- art. 15.1 443
- art. 15.2 76
- art. 16 .... 298, 301, 723
- art. 16.1 .... 299, 300, 302, 1211
- art. 16.2 .. 299, 301, 303, 304, 308, 309, 310, 404, 408, 443
- art. 17 .... 514, 516
- art. 18 ... 438, 443, 543, 1088, 1089, 1117, 1214
- art. 19 .... 45, 61, 62, 63, 193, 1214
- art. 20.1 .... 443, 1214, 1247
- art. 21 .... 443, 1214, 1226, 1249, 1291
- art. 21.1 .... 1256, 1257, 1262
- art. 21.2 .... 1260, 1488
- art. 21.3 .... 990, 1253
- art. 22 .... 1256, 1291, 1293
- art. 22.1 .... 443, 1291
- art. 22.2 .... 1256, 1291

1989 International Convention on Salvage—*cont.*
- art. 23 ...... 1205, 1210, 1211, 1212, 1217, 1219
- art. 23.1 .... 1205, 1207, 1218, 1219
- art. 23.2 .... 1209, 1218
- art. 23.3 .... 1218, 1219
- art. 24 .... 443, 1212, 1466
- art. 25 .. 68, 1049, 1165, 1170, 1176
- art. 26 ... 68, 329, 1178, 1179, 1180, 1181
- art. 27 .... 67, 81, 1049, 1300, 1390
- art. 28.1 65
- art. 28.2 65
- art. 28.3 65
- arts. 28–33 1049
- arts. 28–34 66
- art. 29 12
- art. 29.1 65
- art. 29.2 65
- art. 30 .... 66, 81
- art. 30.1 81
  - (a)-(b) 81
  - (d) 214
- art. 30.2 81
- art. 31.1 66
- art. 31.2 66
- art. 31.3 66
- art. 32.1 66
- art. 32.2 66
- art. 32.3 66
- art. 33 66
- art. 34 66
- Attachment 2 440

1990 International Convention on Oil Pollution Preparedness, Response and Co-operation (OPRC) 70, 1049

1993 International Convention on Maritime Liens and Mortgages—
- Art. 2 1248
- Art. 4.1 (c) 1247

1996 Protocol to the International Salvage Convention 1989 1198

2000 Council Regulation (EC) No. 44/2001 of 22 December 2000 on Jurisdiction and the Recognition and Enforcement of Judgments in Civil and Commercial Matters (2000) 44 OJ L12 .... 124, 1224

ABBREVIATIONS

[Abbreviated book and statute citations, omitting books to which full references are given. Standard abbreviations are omitted.]

A.J.A.	Administration of Justice Act
Abbott	*Abbott's Law of Merchant Ships & Seamen*, 14th ed. (1901), eds. J. P. Aspinall, B. Aspinall and H. S. Moore
Arnould	*Arnould's Law of Marine Insurance and Average*, 16th ed. (1982–97), eds. Sir M. J. Mustill and J. C. B. Gilman
Beawes	Beawes, *Lex Mercatoria Rediviva*, 6th ed. (1813), ed. Joseph Chitty
Benjamin	*Benjamin's Sale of Goods*, 5th ed. (1997) by A. G. Guest *et al.*
Birks	P. Birks, *An Introduction to the Law of Restitution* (revised ed., 1989)
Bowstead	*Bowstead & Reynolds on Agency*, 16th ed. (1996)
Brice	G. Brice, *Maritime Law of Salvage*, 3rd ed. (1999), with Supp. (2001)
C.C.A.	County Courts Act
C.J.A.	Criminal Justice Act
C.M.I.	Comité Maritime International
C.P.A.	Crown Proceedings Act
Carver	*Carver's Carriage by Sea*, 13th ed. (1982) ed. R. Colinvaux
Charlesworth & Percy	*Charlesworth & Percy on Negligence*, 8th ed. (2001)
Chitty	*Chitty on Contracts*, 28th ed. (1999)
Clerk & Lindsell	*Clerk & Lindsell on Torts*, 17th ed. (1995)
Dicey & Morris	*Dicey and Morris on the Conflict of Laws*, 13th ed. (2000)
Gaskell	"Merchant Shipping Act 1995", *Current Law Statutes 1995* (1996), Vol. 2
Goff and Jones	Goff & Jones, *The Law of Restitution*, 5th ed. (1998)
Halsbury	*Halsbury's Laws of England*, 4th ed. (1973–1983), eds. Lord Hailsham of St. Marylebone *et al.*
I.M.O.	International Maritime Organisation
Jackson	D. C. Jackson, *Enforcement of Maritime Claims*, 3rd ed. (2000)
Kennedy	*Kennedy's Civil Salvage*: 4th ed. (1958), ed. K. C. McGuffie, 5th ed. (1985)
L.O.F.	Lloyd's Standard Form of Salvage Agreement
L.P.R.	Lloyd's Procedural Rules
L.S.S.A.C.	Lloyd's Standard Salvage and Arbitration Clauses
Lloyd's Form	*See* L.O.F.
Lowndes & Rudolf	Lowndes & Rudolf, *The Law of General Average and the York-Antwerp Rules*, 12th ed. (1997), ed. D. J. Wilson and J. H. S. Cooke
M.C.A.	Maritime Conventions Act
M.S.	Merchant Shipping
Marsden	Marsden, *The Law of Collisions at Sea*, 12th ed. (1998) with Supp. (1999), ed. S. Gault *et al.*
Marvin	Marvin, *Wreck and Salvage* (1858)
Park	Park, *A System of the Law of Marine Insurance*, 8th ed. (1842), ed. F. Hildyard
Pritchard	*Pritchard's Digest of Admiralty and Maritime Law (Pritchard's Admiralty Digest)*, 3rd ed. (1887), eds. J. C. Hannen and W. T. Pritchard
Roscoe	*Roscoe's Admiralty Practice*, 5th ed. (1931), ed. G. Hutchinson
Rose	Rose, *The Modern Law of Pilotage* (1984)
S.C.A.	Supreme Court Act
S.G.A.	Sale of Goods Act

Abbreviations

S.G.S.A.	Supply of Goods and Services Act
S.I.A.	State Immunity Act
Scrutton	*Scrutton on Charterparties and Bills of Lading*, 20th ed. (1996), ed. S. C. Boyd *et al.*
Shaw	R. Shaw, "The 1989 Salvage Convention and English Law" [1996] L.M.C.L.Q. 202
Shawcross & Beamont	Shawcross & Beaumont, *Air Law*, 4th ed. (1991), ed. P. Martin *et al.*
Summerskill	Summerskill, *Oil Rigs: Law and Insurance* (1979)
Temperley	*Temperley's Merchant Shipping Act*, 7th ed. (1976), eds. M. Thomas and D. Steel
Treitel	Sir G. Treitel, *The Law of Contract*, 10th ed. (1999)
U.C.T.A.	Unfair Contract Terms Act (1977)
Wildeboer	I. H. Wildeboer, *The Brussels Salvage Convention* (1964)
Wiswall	*The Development of Admiralty Jurisdiction and Practice since 1800* (1970)

CHAPTER 1

NATURE OF THE SUBJECT

Introduction

Elements of the law of salvage

The law of maritime salvage is an ancient and important part of the wider law governing marine perils and safety at sea. Its basic principles in English law were laid down by decisions of the Admiralty Court[1] (hereafter referred to as "Admiralty law")[2] but the modern law is primarily governed by the International Convention on Salvage 1989 (hereafter "the Salvage Convention 1989" or "the Convention").[3]

The definition of salvage is considered below.[4] It suffices to indicate here the elements of the law of salvage considered in this book. The law of salvage applies where (i) there is a recognised *subject of salvage*[5] (ii) which has come into a position of *danger* necessitating a *salvage service* to preserve it from loss or damage[6] and (iii) a person falling within the classification of *salvors*[7] (traditionally called a *volunteer*[8]) (iv) is successful or meritoriously contributes to *success* in preserving the subject from danger.[9] In the days of sail, salvage was frequently effected by various individual acts, without the conclusion of a contractual relationship between the parties. But the availability of instantaneous means of communication and the increased use of steam- and, more recently, motor-driven vessels has resulted in services in the nature of salvage having come more frequently to be governed in part at least by an *agreement* or *contract*.[10] In either case, both the provider and the recipient of salvage services have been held to owe *duties* to each other.[11] These were much less defined before the role of contract increased but the

---

[1] See *post*, Chap. 2.
[2] See further *post*, Chap. 2.
[3] See also the Merchant Shipping Act (MSA) 1995, Sched. 11, Part II, para. 1; Lloyd's Standard Salvage and Arbitration Clauses (LSSAC) 2000, cl. 33.
[4] See *post*, §§16–20.
[5] See *post*, Chap. 3.
[6] See *post*, Chap. 4.
[7] See *post*, Chap. 6.
[8] See *post*, Chap. 7.
[9] See *post*, Chap. 8.
[10] See *post*, Chap. 9.
[11] See *post*, Chap. 10.

Nature of the Subject

court has always been alert to discourage *misconduct* during salvage operations.[12]

2   On termination of salvage services, the *salved values* of the preserved property can be calculated.[13] These provide the upper limit of the salvor's *reward*[14] and the most fundamental of all the relevant factors which must be considered in its *assessment*, if not already the subject of a binding agreement.[15] The award to the salvor is intended to represent a reasonable *remuneration* for his efforts, *reimbursement* for his loss or expenditure, plus an additional element of *reward* to reflect the judicially promoted *public policy*[16] of encouraging individuals to salve property imperilled at sea. All recognised beneficiaries of salvage services must in principle make a *contribution* to the reward,[17] although special rules apply to proceedings concerning the Crown and the immunity of foreign sovereign States.[18] The reward should be *apportioned* amongst the various salvors who have participated in the successful salvage.[19]

Salvors' *remedies* for enforcing their claim include a *maritime lien* in support of a right to proceed *in rem* or *in personam*.[20] Salvage claims are the subject of the court's *Admiralty jurisdiction*, although it has become overwhelmingly more common over the last century or so for salvage claims to be dealt with not judicially but by *arbitration*.[21]

Sources of the modern law[22]

3   From time immemorial, the merit of rewarding maritime salvors appears to have been recognised as self-evident. Thus, Lord Stowell, the Admiralty Judge who established the foundations of English Admiralty law, has said[23]:

> "It is what the law calls *jus liquidissimum*, the clearest general right that they who have saved lives and property at sea should be rewarded for such salutary exertions."

---

[12] See *post*, Chap. 11.
[13] See *post*, Chap. 14.
[14] In some of the older cases, the payment due to the salvor is referred to as compensation. See, e.g. Carmichael v. Brodie (The Sir Ralph Abercrombie) (1867) L.R. 1 P.C. 454, 458, per Dr Lushington; *The Farnley Hall* (1881) 4 Asp. 499, 501, *per* Brett L.J. However, the word compensation is better used to describe compensation for loss, which is remediable by an award of damages.
[15] See *post*, Chap. 15.
[16] See *post*, §§ 36–41.
[17] See *post*, Chap. 16.
[18] See *post*, Chap. 12.
[19] See *post*, Chap. 17.
[20] See *post*, Chap. 13.
[21] *ibid*.
[22] A fuller historical summary appears in Chap. 2.
[23] *The Waterloo* (1820) 2 Dods. 433, 435–436.

Introduction

Expressed in such general terms, whether or not accepted as a form of natural equity,[24] it demonstrates at least an affinity with the broad principle against unjust enrichment: that the recipient of a benefit at the plaintiff's expense should make restitution, a vital principle in Roman law, which legal system has provided one of the strongest influences on the law administered by the Admiralty Court.[25] However, salvage has also appeared in the various ancient maritime and commercial codes, such as the laws of Oleron, which, along with other writings and custom, have influenced the development of English, as well as other national, maritime laws.[26] As Lord Roche has observed[27]:

> "The law of salvage as administered by the Court of Admiralty is a maritime law derived from ancient and various sources and developed and built upon by decisions of the Court."

Despite the ubiquity of the concept of salvage, the applicable law has not developed identically in all jurisdictions, and it cannot be assumed that the resulting law in other jurisdictions, at least where not clearly based on English law, will necessarily be applicable to an English case. In a bottomry case, Brett L.J. said[28]:

> "Now the first question raised on the argument before us was what is the law which is administered in an English Court of Admiralty, whether it is English law, or whether it is that which is called the common maritime law, which is not the law of England alone but the law of all maritime countries. About that question I have not the smallest doubt. Every Court of Admiralty is a court of the country in which it sits and to which it belongs. The law which is administered in the Admiralty Court of England is the English maritime law. It is not the ordinary municipal law of the country, but it is the law which the English Court of Admiralty either by Act of Parliament or by reiterated decisions and traditions and principles has adopted as the English maritime law; and about that I cannot conceive that there is any doubt. It seems to me that this is what every judge in the Admiralty Court of England has promulgated (Lord Stowell and those before him, and Dr Lushington after him), and I do not understand that the present learned judge of the Admiralty Court [Sir Robert Phillimore] differs in the least from them. He says that this case must be determined by the general maritime law as administered in England—that is in other words by the English maritime law."

---

[24] See *post*, §§ 21–25.
[25] See further *post*, Chap. 2.
[26] For a modern introduction to the relevant sources and literature, see, *e.g.* Wiswall.
[27] *Admiralty Commissioners v. Valverda (Owners)* [1938] A.C. 173, 200.
[28] *The Gaetano and Maria* (1882) 7 P.D. 137, 143. *cf. The National Defender* [1970] 1 Lloyd's Rep. 40, 43 (U.S. D.C., S.D. N.Y.).

Nature of the Subject

5   More recently, Lord Diplock has stated[29]:

> "Outside the special field of 'prize' in times of hostilities, there is no 'maritime law of the world,' as distinct from the internal municipal laws of its constituent sovereign states, that is capable of giving rise to rights or liabilities enforceable in English Courts. Because of the nature of its subject-matter and its historic derivation from sources common to many maritime nations, the internal municipal laws of different states relating to what happens on the seas may show greater similarity to one another than is to be found in laws relating to what happens upon land. But the fact that the consequences of applying to the same facts the internal municipal laws of different sovereign states would be to give rise to similar legal rights and liabilities should not mislead us into supposing that those rights or liabilities are derived from a 'maritime law of the world' and not from the internal municipal law of a particular sovereign state."

6   From the middle of the nineteenth century, the judicially declared law applied in the Admiralty Court came to be increasingly influenced, though to an apparently limited extent, by the law applied in common law and Chancery cases,[30] most apparently where the common law courts dealt with the related subject of general average.[31] Awareness of the applicability of general English law (both case law and statute) to salvage has become more manifest since the last quarter of the nineteenth century—since the creation of a unified High Court of Justice[32] and the advent of technological developments.

7   The greater size of modern ships, and the increasing availability to salvors of reliable, powerful and accurately manoeuvrable power-driven vessels and equipment, have meant that most salvage operations can now only be undertaken by the professional salvage industry, which has grown accordingly. In common with other industries, the salvage industry has come to employ standard form contracts, most notably[33] Lloyd's Standard Form of Salvage Agreement (No Cure—No Pay) ("Lloyd's Form"), the most recent version being known by the code LOF 2000.[34] LOF 2000 contains provision for its terms to be supplemented by the SCOPIC clause.[35]

8   Lloyd's Form provides for the determination of salvage claims by arbitration. Since most modern salvage operations have been governed by Lloyd's Form and the resulting awards have been confidential to the parties and unpublished, the number of salvage cases coming before the courts has

---

[29] *The Tojo Maru* [1972] A.C. 242, 290–291.
[30] See further *post*, Chap. 2.
[31] See, *e.g.* Bowen L.J.'s famous dictum in *Falcke v. Scottish Imperial Insurance Co.* (1886) 34 Ch. D. 234, 248–249; *post*, §33.
[32] See *post*, Chap. 2.
[33] Though certainly not exclusively.
[34] See *post*, App. 2.
[35] See *post*, §§ 966–986.

Introduction

considerably decreased. This has not necessarily been detrimental to the development of the law, for the success of Lloyd's Form arbitrations has been facilitated by the comprehensive settlement of the guiding legal principles in the nineteenth century and the fact that, once it is clear that there is a salvage service (which is established by entry into a Lloyd's Form contract[36]), the arbitrator is basically left with the task of assessing, and possibly apportioning, the reward, which involves not so much questions of law as the balancing of a number of established factors and their application to the facts of the individual case in hand in the light of the arbitrator's experience. As has long been clear, most salvage cases depend upon their facts[37] and, to that extent and because judgments in Admiralty have traditionally not discriminated between the fact and the law, law reports have a limited utility in the resolution of salvage awards,[38] particularly as the factual matrix of salvage cases inevitably alters over the years. Most recently, it has been the nature of certain cargoes that has been the cause of interest, especially persistent hydrocarbon oils, liquefied natural gas, dangerous chemicals and nuclear materials. The settled principles of the law of salvage are normally sufficiently adaptable to resolve legal difficulties arising from novel situations, although practical problems may limit the efficacy of the law's role in dealing with such cases.

The scope of Lloyd's Form has been enlarged over the years, yet its principal object has always been to have matters referred to arbitration, it being for the arbitrator to resolve them in accordance with the law of salvage. Of course, the applicable law is qualified where the contract so provides and principles of the common law of contract may therefore apply.[39] The more radical interpretation of this approach has been to assume that the Admiralty law of salvage has been subordinated to the common law of contract. Thus, Lord Diplock has said[40]:

9

> "The proper approach to this question in the year 1971, as it seems to me, is to consider first what would be the salvage contractor's liability under the general English law of contract, and then to examine what, if any, differences flow, either in principle or on the authority of previous decisions, from the special characteristics of salvage services."

Whether or not Lord Diplock's approach is in principle correct, his remarks must now be read subject to the statutory implementation of the Salvage Convention 1989.

Parliament's early intervention in the law of salvage has been, *inter alia*, to extend the area of Admiralty jurisdiction to the saving of property within the

10

---

[36] See *post*, §§ 868–870.
[37] *The Ewell Grove* (1835) 3 Hagg. 209, 220–221.
[38] *Akerblom v. Price, Potter, Walker & Co.* (1881) 7 Q.B.D. 129, 132. *cf. The Neptune* (1824) 1 Hagg. 227, 235, n. 2.
[39] See especially *The Unique Mariner (No. 1)* [1978] 1 Lloyd's Rep. 438; *The Unique Mariner (No. 2)* [1979] 1 Lloyd's Rep. 37; *The Tojo Maru* [1972] A.C. 242.
[40] *The Tojo Maru* [1972] A.C. 242, 292.

Nature of the Subject

body of a county and the courts authorised to exercise Admiralty jurisdiction.[41] It has also amplified the subjects in respect of which salvage may be awarded, expressly incorporating salvage of lives, aircraft and hovercraft.[42]

11 As well as expressing originally domestic policy, statute has also been the vehicle for incorporating international conventions into English law. However, until recently, this process has been of minimal importance in purely salvage matters. A meeting sponsored by the Comité Maritime International (CMI) in 1905 led to an attempted international unification of salvage law in the Brussels Salvage Convention of 1910.[43] That Convention substantially reproduced the principles of English law, which made its enactment largely unnecessary in the United Kingdom, although some of its provisions found their way into the Maritime Conventions Act 1911.[44] There followed subsequent international agreements on particular subjects.[45]

12 The most significant international exercise for the English law of salvage arose as a result of the invitation of the Inter-Governmental Maritime Consultative Organisation (IMCO)—now the International Maritime Organisation (the IMO)—to the Comité Maritime International (the CMI) to prepare a draft international Convention on Salvage to replace the Brussels Salvage Convention 1910. This was introduced in Montreal in 1981 and its final form was settled at a Diplomatic Conference held at the IMO headquarters in London in 1989.

Specifically, the International Salvage Convention 1989 recited that "substantial developments, in particular the increased concern for the protection of the environment, have demonstrated the need to review the international rules presently contained in [the Brussels Salvage Convention 1910]".[46] More generally, the aim of the 1989 Convention was to provide a modernised and comprehensive restatement of the law of salvage. The 1989 Convention does not specifically purport to supersede the 1910 Convention, to which the United Kingdom was a party. However, implementation of the 1989 Convention would at least be potentially inconsistent with obligations owed by one party to another party to the 1910 Convention. Accordingly, the United Kingdom has denounced the 1910 Convention.[47]

---

[41] See *post*, Chap. 2.
[42] See *post*, Chap. 3.
[43] See *post*, App. 28.
[44] ss. 6–8 (enacting Arts. 6 and 10–11 of the Convention). See now the Merchant Shipping Act 1995, ss.190, 224(1)–(2), 312(2), Sched. II, Pt I, paras 10, 15, Pt II, para. 3.
[45] See the Brussels Salvage Convention on Aircraft 1938 and the Brussels Salvage Protocol 1967; *post*, Apps 29–30.
[46] The recitals are not reproduced in the text of the Convention contained in the Merchant Shipping Act 1995, Sched. 11, Pt 1.
[47] The 1989 Convention became effective in the U.K. on January 1, 1995 and internationally on July 14, 1996 (*i.e.* under Art. 29 of the Convention, one year after the date on which 15 States had expressed their consent to be bound by it).

Introduction

Terminology

A few brief words are appropriate concerning the terminology in this book. **13** The book deals essentially with *salvage* (and, to a limited extent, *wreck*), which expressions are defined below.[48] The great majority of cases deal with claims that a person has rendered a *salvage service*, possibly under a *salvage agreement*, and is therefore classifiable as a *salvor*. These descriptions may prove to be not entirely accurate. In particular, since the terms of a salvage contract generally override the underlying law of salvage, a contractual salvor may more precisely be described as a "Contractor". However, the traditional descriptions are usually convenient. The object of a salvage service is a subject of salvage—basically property in danger—the most obvious example of which is a ship or vessel. Frequently, it is convenient to use the words "vessel", "casualty" or "defendant" interchangeably, though not necessarily accurately, particularly since other subjects of salvage are often involved. The manifestly convenient autonym to salvor—*salvee*—has so far not gained common currency but is so easily intelligible and clear as to justify its use also.

Before 1875, the tribunal dealing with Admiralty cases was the independent **14** High Court of Admiralty. After that date, Admiralty jurisdiction was exercised within a single High Court of Justice, first within the Probate, Divorce and Admiralty Division then, after 1971, within the Queen's Bench Division by allocation to an Admiralty Court presided over by a specifically designated Admiralty Judge. For convenience, the court exercising Admiralty jurisdiction will be referred to throughout this book as the Admiralty Court and the presiding judge as the Admiralty Judge, whatever the date of the relevant events and whether or not the judge's usual work was in Admiralty.[49] In modern times the tribunal is more frequently an arbitrator appointed under Lloyd's Form, but his function is to apply the law administered in the Admiralty Court.

Strictly speaking, the law to be administered is English law rather than one **15** particular type of English law, albeit predominantly the Admiralty law developed by the judges of the original Admiralty Court, often termed maritime law,[50] though those expressions in their broader sense incorporate the relevant law derived from various sources. English law is notorious for its being classifiable in many, not always discrete, ways. It may be divided by its subject-matter, as between the criminal law and the non-criminal law, which latter category is in this sense traditionally referred to as the common law or the civil law. Salvage also has a division into civil and military (prize)

---

[48] At §§ 16–20 (salvage) and 201–215 (wreck).
[49] See further *post*, Chap. 2. "The Admiralty Court" and "the Admiralty Judge" are not strictly synonymous, for the judge may, and in previous years habitually did, sit with nautical assessors.
[50] See *ante*, §§ 4–5; *post*, §33.

Nature of the Subject

salvage.[51] On the other hand, the law may be distinguished according to its sources, as between statute law, laid down by Parliament, and the common law laid down by the judges. This judge-made common law may itself be divided into, first, common law *stricto sensu* (as developed by the common law courts) and equity (as developed in the Court of Chancery)—which together make up the home-grown common law of England—and, secondly, the civil law deriving through canon law ultimately from Roman law, which itself has a professedly "equitable" nature.[52] The meaning of these expressions, particularly of "common law," must be discerned from the sense in which they are used. Suffice it to say that "common law" will normally be used either to refer to judge-made law (possibly including equity) apart from the civil law or, more commonly, to include the civil law, so as to distinguish all judge-made law from statute law.[53]

Definition

16 Lord Stowell once declared[54]:

> "It has been said that no exact definition of salvage is given in any of the books. I do not know that it has, and I should be sorry to limit it by any definition now."

However, this dictum most obviously emphasises the necessarily flexible approach of the Admiralty Court to the practical problems arising under the law of salvage rather than precluding the essaying of a workable definition.

A salvage service, in the view of the Court of Admiralty, may be described sufficiently for practical purposes as a service which confers a benefit by saving or helping to save a recognised subject of salvage when in danger from which it cannot be extricated unaided, if and so far as the rendering of such service is voluntary in the sense of being attributable neither to a pre-existing obligation nor solely for the interests of the salvor.[55] More prosaically, a claim for salvage has been described as an unliquidated monetary claim, the cause of action for which accrues and is complete at the date of termination of the services.[56]

---

[51] See *post*, §17.
[52] See *post*, §§ 21–23.
[53] The sense used in *The Gas Float Whitton No. 2* [1896] P. 42, 63, *per* Lord Esher M.R.; and *China Pacific S.A. v. Food Corporation of India (The Winson)* [1983] A.C. 939, 957D. *cf. The Cadiz and The Boyne* (1876) 3 Asp. M.L.C. 332, 334, *per* Sir Robert Phillmore.
[54] *The Governor Raffles* (1815) 2 Dods. 14, 17.
[55] See also *The Cythera* [1965] 2 Lloyd's Rep. 454, 459; *The Meandros* [1925] P. 61, 68; and *The Lord Dufferin* (1848) 7 N.o.C. xxxiii (Bombay S.C.), where Sir T. Erskine Perry C.J. said, at xxxiii–xxxiv:
> "Without attempting to lay down a complete definition of what salvage is,—for all definitions in law are said to be dangerous,—it does not seem open to objection to hold that salvage occurs whenever assistance is rendered to a ship at sea which is in such a dangerous position that in all human probability she will not be able to extricate herself by her unassisted efforts."

[56] *The Teh Hu* [1969] 2 Lloyd's Rep. 7, 12, *per* Brandon J.

Definition

In regard to the preservation of life and property at sea, the word "salvage" is used indifferently in legal parlance to denote the salvor's service and the salvor's reward.

It was also employed in former times to signify the property saved, for the salvor's reward was once frequently made by delivery of some portion of the specific articles saved or recovered rather than by payment of money, as it invariably is now.[57] In the part of the Merchant Shipping Act 1995 dealing with salvage and wreck, unless the context otherwise requires, the expression "salvage" included all expenses properly incurred by the salvor in the performance of the salvage services.[58]

The full title of the Brussels Salvage Convention 1910 reflected a distinction drawn in some jurisdictions between services rendered to a vessel which is still manned ("assistance") and services to unmanned vessels ("salvage"), although the Convention was expressed to apply "without any distinction being drawn between these two kinds of service (*viz.*, assistance and salvage)."[59] The distinction has never been made in English law. **17**

Salvage operation

Article 1 of the International Salvage Convention 1989 provides: **18**

"For the purposes of this Convention—
(a) Salvage operation means any act or activity undertaken to assist a vessel or any other property in danger in navigable waters or in any other waters whatsoever."

It is clear from Article 1 that the Convention is concerned with action undertaken to assist vessels or property. Although the Convention and the Merchant Shipping Act 1995 also contain some provision for services which are (actually or potentially) beneficial to human lives or the environment, they are dependent on action taken to assist maritime property.

What Article 1 does not expressly state is whether, to qualify as salvage under the Convention, it is sufficient that the relevant act or activity has the *effect* of assisting maritime property or whether that must have been the actor's *intention*. In practice, it is unlikely that the distinction can be or will be made. Furthermore, at common law, the former was sufficient; and this will probably also be the position under the Convention.

---

[57] "This compensation ... at present is commonly made by payment in money; but in the infancy of commerce was more frequently made by the delivery of some portion of the specific articles saved or recovered": Abbott, 1st ed. (1802), 320. This passage was retained unchanged in all editions of Abbott, down to the fourteenth, in 1901. It remains accurate.

[58] s.255(1).

[59] Convention for the Unification of Certain Rules of Law Respecting Assistance and Salvage at Sea, Signed at Brussels, September 23, 1910, Art. 1.

Nature of the Subject

19   A further issue is whether there can be a salvage operation where the subject of salvage has little or no value. The point may be important because, in cases of low awards for property salvage, the Salvage Convention 1989, Art. 14 authorises special compensation for "environmental salvage" "*[i]f the salvor has carried out salvage operations*".[60] If the subject of salvage is valueless, it is arguable that there is not the requisite danger for there to be a salvage operation. However, this argument is discussed and rejected below.[61]

The value of the salved property is also relevant to satisfying the requirement of success or, under the Convention, a "useful result".[62] However, this requirement is a prerequisite of an award of salvage following on a salvage operation, not of whether there is a salvage operation in the first place. The distinction between a salvage operation and a useful result is made clear by the Convention's references to "[s]alvage operations which have had a useful result" and "if the salvage operations have had no useful result".[63] There may therefore be a salvage operation without a useful result in preserving property. If it were otherwise, there would have been an unintended limitation on the Convention's provisions for special compensation.

Civil salvage and military (prize) salvage

20   The Admiralty Court recognises two kinds of salvage, *viz.*, military salvage and civil salvage. Military salvage is such a service as may become the ground of a demand for reward in the court sitting as a Prize Court[64] and consists of the rescue of property from the enemy in time of war.[65] Civil salvage is such a service as may become the ground of a demand for reward in the court on the civil side of its jurisdiction; it includes the preservation of life or property from dangers which may be encountered in times of peace and war. Similar principles apply to both forms of salvage. Thus Lord Stowell has said that[66]:

> "It will be found, I think, that both these forms of salvage resolve themselves into the equity of rewarding spontaneous services, rendered in the protection of the lives and property of others. This is a general principle of natural equity."

---

[60] Art. 14.1 (emphasis added). See also the reference to "salvage operations" in Art. 14.2. See generally *post*, Chap. 5.
[61] *Post*, §§ 352–353.
[62] Art. 12.
[63] Art. 12.1 and 12.2 respectively.
[64] A court of the Queen's Bench Division. See Supreme Court Act (SCA) 1981, ss 27, 61(1), Sched. 1, para. 2(c). Appeals lie to the Privy Council: *ibid.*, s.16(2).
[65] See generally Colombos, *Law of Prize* (3rd ed., 1949); Halsbury (4th ed.), Vol. 37 (1982), §§ 1301–1387.
[66] *The Calypso* (1828) 2 Hagg. 209, 217–218.

Underlying principles

Indeed, the same act or circumstances may justify awards of both civil and military salvage,[67] and the Prize Court has an equitable jurisdiction to award remuneration in respect of civil salvage services rendered to a vessel before her seizure in prize.[68]

However, the particular rules applied in the law of prize salvage are not identical to those applicable to civil salvage.[69] Moreover, the law of prize salvage is of virtually no practical importance today. So it is with civil salvage only that this work is concerned. It is convenient as a general practice, therefore, to omit the adjective "civil".

Underlying principles

Equitable basis

The jurisdiction of the Admiralty Court has consistently been described **21** throughout its history as being of a peculiarly equitable character, seeking to do what is fair and just both to salvors and to the owners of the property which is saved.[70] Thus Sir Christopher Robinson, in the course of his judgment in *The Calypso*,[71] said of both military and civil salvage:

> "I doubt whether these services are essentially different, and whether they are not to be referred to one common origin, which takes away the effect of this distinction. It will be found, I think, that both these forms of salvage resolve themselves into the equity of rewarding spontaneous services, rendered in the protection of the lives and property of others. This is a general principle of natural equity: and it was considered as giving a cause of action in the Roman law; and from that source it was adopted, by jurisdictions of this nature, in the different countries of Europe....
>
> Considering all salvage, therefore, to be founded on the equity of remunerating private and individual services, a Court of Justice should be cautious not to treat it on any other principle."

Resort has been made to the equitable principles underlying salvage not **22** only as providing a general justification for, or approach to, the application of the law of salvage in general but also for moral support in the solution of particular problems, such as the value of freight salved,[72] whether or not a

---

[67] *The Louisa* (1813) 1 Dods. 317. However, where prize proceedings are pending, the judge may assess the reward for civil salvage then let his judgment await the determination of proceedings in the Prize Court.

[68] *France, Fenwick Tyne and Wear Co. Ltd v. H.M. Procurator General (The Prins Knud)* [1938] A.C. 667.

[69] See *supra*, n. 65.

[70] *The Teh Hu* [1970] P. 106, 124, *per* Lord Denning M.R. See also *Five Steel Barges* (1890) 15 P.D. 142, 146.

[71] (1828) 2 Hagg. 209, 217–218.

[72] *The Norma* (1860) Lush. 124, 127, *per* Dr Lushington: "But in Salvage we have to decide on purely equitable principles."

vessel in the same ownership as a wrongdoing vessel could claim salvage,[73] and the inapplicability of statutory forfeiture to a salvor who failed to notify the receiver of wrecks of his possession of a wreck which he believed to be his own.[74] At the beginning of the nineteenth century, the equitable nature of Admiralty jurisdiction was perceived to relate to the general approach of the court rather than to specific rules which it applied. Equity in Admiralty has, therefore, been a traditionally more fluid concept than in Chancery and it is this feature that Lord Stowell revealed when he said in the *The Juliana*[75]:

> "I know that that system [the common law], admirable in its construction, and still more in its actual administration, resting most properly on its ancient and approved technical rules is, on that account, sometimes unable to reach the real justice of a case, which it therefore leaves to other jurisdictions to discover and apply. No small part of the Chancery jurisdiction is built upon this very foundation. That exercise of jurisdiction is not seldom so applied to maritime contracts ... A Court of Law works its way to short issues, and confines its views to them. A Court of Equity takes a more comprehensive view, and looks to every connected circumstance that ought to influence its determination upon the real justice of the case. This Court certainly does not claim the character of a Court of General Equity; but it is bound, by its commission and constitution, to determine the cases submitted to its cognisance upon equitable principles, and according to the rules of natural justice."

23 There are principles of the maritime law of salvage which have developed alongside and demonstrate great affinity with principles evolved in Chancery, particularly in the area of illegitimate pressure.[76] But until 1875, when the ancient courts became merged in a unified High Court, the similarity in the equity applied in Admiralty and in Chancery derived principally from the method of applying the law and the appeal to general principle in reaching conclusions, rather than from the rules applied. The Court of Chancery was concerned with different factual situations and, originally at least, in appealing to general flexible notions of fairness and justice to ameliorate the over-rigid effects of the existing body of law laid down for non-Admiralty cases by the common law courts. In time, equity in Chancery became systematised in, and came to describe, a particular firm body of rules, while equity in Admiralty continued to retain its fluid character.

---

[73] *The Beaverford v. The Kafiristan* [1938] A.C. 136, 147, *per* Lord Wright: "But the maritime law of salvage is based upon principles of equity."

[74] *The Liffey* (1887) 6 Asp. M.L.C. 255, 256. See now MSA 1995, s.236.

[75] (1822) 2 Dods. 504, 520–521. See also *The Liffey* (1887) 6 Asp. M.L.C. 255, 256, *per* Sir James Hannen P.: "In this court happily we deal with matters on equitable principles, and we are not tied down to the strict rules of the common law. It appears to me that, on every principle of justice, this man must be entitled to something in the nature of salvage."

[76] See *post*, Chap. 9. *cf. The Tojo Maru* [1972] A.C. 242, 291.

Underlying principles

From the mid-nineteenth century, however, Admiralty Judges have had **24** overt resort to rules of equity as it is understood in Chancery, whilst continuing the traditional Admiralty approach. The process was boosted by the merger into the new High Court in 1875, prompting Sir Robert Phillimore on one occasion to refer to the Admiralty Court's "newly confirmed equitable jurisdiction." The equitable doctrine of laches was applied to the enforcement of maritime liens in 1869[77] and in 1918 to the extension of the limitation period in the Maritime Conventions Act 1911, s.8.[78] Five years later, Sir Henry Duke P. upheld salvors' possessory rights with the equitable remedy of injunction.[79]

More recent decisions indicate, without denying the tribunal's inherent **25** flexibility in assessing salvage rewards, that a party's appeal to equity should, to be successful, refer, as in Chancery, to a settled rule rather than to a general notion of fairness. Thus, in 1969, with respect to the question whether salvage could be assessed to take account of currency fluctuations, Salmon L.J. said[80]:

> "The salvors rely upon salvage having been described in some of the cases as a peculiarly equitable jurisdiction. But equity operates according to principles which today are considerably more rigid than those of the common law. I know of no principle of equity nor any decision which is of help to the salvors."

It would not be correct, however, to assimilate too closely the different elements of English law.[81] It is sufficient to note now that the Admiralty Court continues its ancient equitable jurisdiction in adopting a flexible approach to do justice to all the parties in individual cases but that the more rigid rules of equity developed in Chancery may also be invoked where relevant, though they must be applied according to their settled principles.

Twin bases of law of salvage

The ancient practice of rewarding salvage services is founded upon two **26** main considerations, which will be considered in turn.[82] The first, more often than not assumed, is that salvors should be paid for benefits conferred[83]—for historical and jurisdictional reasons, fundamentally for benefits to property,[84] although the judicial inclination and now the statutory rule have provided also

---

[77] *The Europa* (1863) Br. & Lush. 89.
[78] *HMS Archer* [1918] P. 1.
[79] *The Tubantia* [1924] P. 78.
[80] *The Teh Hu* [1970] P. 106, 130. *cf.* Brandon J.'s justification for the priority of salvage liens on specified equitable principles in *The Lyrma (No. 2)* [1978] 2 Lloyd's Rep. 30, 33, 34.
[81] *cf.* the attempted use of the concept of inequality of bargaining power: *post*, Chap. 9.
[82] *Post*, §§ 28–30.
[83] See *The Hamtun* [1999] 1 Lloyd's Rep. 883, 898.
[84] See, *e.g.* Brett M.R.'s reasoning in *The Renpor* (1883) 8 P.D. 115; *post*, §266.

Nature of the Subject

for the reward of life salvage.[85] This extension is justifiable on humanitarian grounds and derives from the general equitable notions motivating the Admiralty Court. The second consideration, which finds expression in a number of ways with particular regard to the assessment of rewards, is that of public policy of encouraging persons to become salvors, though not unduly so,[86] by liberal rewards.[87] Thus, Dr Lushington said[88]:

> "But direct benefit is not the sole principle upon which salvage reward is required to be paid. I am of opinion that the payment of salvage depends upon more general principles; and, in saying this, I think I am supported both by Lord Stowell[89] and Story J. Salvage is not governed by the ordinary rules which prevail in mercantile transactions on shore. Salvage is governed by a due regard to benefit received, combined with a just regard for the general interests of ships and marine commerce.[90] All owners of ships and cargoes and all underwriters are interested in the great principle of adequate remuneration being paid for salvage services; and none are more interested than the underwriters of the cargo."

27   Story J.'s dictum was as follows[91]:

> "Salvage, it is true, is not a question of compensation *pro opera et labore*. It raises to a higher dignity. It takes its source in a deeper policy. It combines with private merit and individual sacrifices larger considerations of the public good, of commercial liberality, and of international justice. It offers a premium by way of honorary reward, for prompt and ready assistance to human sufferings; for a bold and fearless intrepidity; and for that affecting chivalry, which forgets itself in an anxiety to save property, as well as life. Treated as a mere question of compensation for labor and services, measured by any common standard on land or at sea, the salvage of one moiety is far too high. But treated, as it should be, as *a mixed question of public policy and private right*, equally important to all commercial nations, and equally encouraged by all, a moiety is no more than may justly be rewarded."[92]

---

[85] See *post*, Chap. 3.

[86] See, *e.g. The Maasdam* (1893) 7 Asp. M.L.C. 400, 402, where Sir Francis Jeune P. expected that salvage awards which unduly encouraged owners to put pressure on their masters ought to be reconsidered as to their amount.

[87] Recently reiterated by the House of Lords in *The Tojo Maru* [1972] A.C. 242, 267, 273–274, 280–281, 289, 294.

[88] *The Fusilier* (1865) Br. of Lush. 341, 347. See also *The Clifton* (1834) 3 Hagg. 117, 120–121, *per* Sir John Nicholl.

[89] Presumably in *The William Beckford* (1801) 3 C. Rob. 355, 355–356.

[90] The potential detriment to commerce may similarly be a reason for discouraging salvage claims for a modest service. See, *e.g. The British Inventor* (1933) 45 Ll.L Rep. 263, 266.

[91] *The Henry Ewbank* (1883) 11 Fed. Cas. (Case No. 6376) 1166, 1170; originally reported at 1 Sumn. 400 (Massachusetts Circuit Court); emphasis added. Dr Lushington again cited Story J. in *The Albion* (1861) Lush. 282, 284, and *The Fusilier* (1865) Br. & Lush. 341, 347. See also *The Leon Blum* [1915] P. 90, 102, *per* Sir Samuel Evans P. and, to the same effect, *The Sarah* (1800) 1 C. Rob. 312n, 313n; *The William Beckford* (1801) 3 C. Rob. 355, 355–356, *per* Lord Stowell; *The Hector* (1853) 3 Hagg. 90, 95, *per* Sir John Nicholl.

[92] It is no longer the practice to award a moiety.

Underlying principles

Mercantile, proprietary and humanitarian considerations are not the only motivations for the salvage public policy. In wartime, the peculiar British national interest in preserving all forms of shipping which could possibly be utilised for the public good was considered a relevant factor in assessing salvage.[93]

Receipt of a benefit

28 The foundation of liability to pay or to contribute to the payment of a salvage reward is that each and every interest which has received a benefit from the salvage service provided must contribute.[94]

Thus, in *Five Steel Barges*,[95] Sir James Hannen P. uttered the following classic statement:

> "The jurisdiction which the Court exercises in salvage cases is of a peculiarly equitable character. The right to salvage may arise out of an actual contract; but it does not necessarily do so. It is a legal liability arising out of the fact that property has been saved, that the owner of the property who has had the benefit of it shall make remuneration to those who have conferred the benefit upon him, notwithstanding that he has not entered into any contract upon the subject. I think that proposition equally applies to the man who has had a benefit arising out of the saving of the property."

29 This statement was approved in *The Cargo ex Port Victor*,[96] where Sir Francis Jeune P., whose judgment was affirmed by the Court of Appeal, said[97]:

> "To rest the jurisdiction of the Admiralty Court upon an implied request from the owner of the property in danger to the salvors, or on an implied contract between the salvors and owner with the relinquishment of the *res* for consideration, is, I think, to confuse two different systems of law and to resort to a misleading analogy. The true view is, I think, that the law of Admiralty imposes on the owner of property saved an obligation to pay the person who saves it simply because in the view of that system of law it is just he should; and this conception of justice naturally imposes a proportionate obligation on any person whose interest in the property is real, though falling short of that ownership.
>
> I see no reason, therefore, why I should not follow the view of Lord Hannen,[98] and of the Scottish Court of Session,[99] that a man who has had

---

[93] *The Belgia* (1941) 71 Ll.L. Rep. 21.
[94] See *post*, Chap. 16.
[95] (1890) 15 P.D. 142, 146.
[96] [1901] P. 243.
[97] *ibid.*, 249.
[98] In *Five Steel Barges*, *supra*, n. 95.
[99] In *Duncan v. Dundee Shipping Co.* (1878) 5 R. 742.

a benefit arising out of the saving of the property is liable to a claim for salvage no less than the actual owner of it."

30 To the same effect, Sir Henry Duke P. held, in *The Meandros*,[1] that:

"upon the principles which are administered in Courts possessing Admiralty jurisdiction, salvage creates a legal liability arising out of the fact that a property has been saved whereby the owner, who has had the benefit of the service, has to make remuneration to those who have conferred the benefit. It has been said, more widely than it is necessary to express an opinion upon in this case, that any person whose interest in the property is real—though it fall short of ownership—may be liable in respect of salvage, and it has been said, further, in comprehensive terms, that 'owner' includes all persons who are collectively or singly owners."

Three observations can be made on these statements.

Rights of salvors are essentially independent of contract

31 As the preceding *dicta* indicate, whilst the nature of the service, or in rare cases the amount of its reward, may be fixed by agreement, the underlying principle is that "the obligation on ship and cargo to pay for salvage services is imposed by law irrespective of any contract, express or implied,[2] to that effect."[3] In *The Hestia*,[4] an agreement was made by the *S.S. Escalona* to tow the disabled *Hestia* from sea to a place of safety for £3,000. The *Escalona* succeeded in bringing the *Hestia* to shallower water, where she anchored, but was unsuccessful in completing the salvage, which was done by another vessel. It was contended that the *Escalona*, having failed to perform the agreement, was not entitled to any salvage reward, even though she might have contributed to the ultimate safety of the *Hestia*. Bruce J. said[5]:

"I cannot assent to this argument. No doubt it is well established that, where there is a contract to perform a specified service for a specified remuneration, nothing becomes due under the contract until the specified service has been completely performed. Although the service may have been partly performed yet, as the contract is not divisible, no obligation arises out of it to pay any part of the stipulated remuneration, and the

---

[1] [1925] P. 61, 68.
[2] *e.g.* from the implied obligations in a towage contract.
[3] *The Troilus* [1950] P. 92, 110, *per* Denning L.J. See also *Lipson v. Harrison* (1853) 22 L.T. (O.S.) 83, 84, *per* Wightman L.J.; *The Liffey* (1887) 6 Asp. M.L.C. 255, 256 ("It is perfectly plain that salvage does not depend upon any contract, because the whole thing could be done without the shipowner having any knowledge on the subject"); *Five Steel Barges* (1890) 15 P.D. 142, 146; *The Cargo ex Port Victor* [1901] P. 243, 249; *The Unique Mariner* (No. 2) [1979] 1 Lloyd's Rep. 37, *per* Brandon J.
[4] [1895] P. 193.
[5] *ibid.*, 199–200.

Underlying principles

existence of an express contract negatives the presumption which might otherwise arise of an implied contract to pay for the work done according to its value.

If salvage claims were dependent upon contract, I should have great difficulty in holding that the *Escalona* was entitled to anything, even on the assumption that she had rendered some service. But salvage claims do not rest upon contract. Where property has been salved from sea perils, and the claimants have effected the salvage, or have contributed to the salvage, the law confers upon them the right to be paid salvage reward out of the proceeds of the property which they have saved or helped to save.

No doubt the parties may by contract determine the amount to be paid; but the right to salvage is in no way dependent upon contract, and may exist, and frequently does exist, in the absence of any express contract, or of any circumstances to raise an implied contract. The way in which an agreement affects the question of salvage is laid down by Kennedy J. thus[6]:

> 'A salvage agreement is an agreement which fixes, indeed, the amount to be paid for salvage, but leaves untouched all the other conditions necessary to support a salvage award, one of which is the preservation of some part at least of the *res*, that is, ship, cargo, or freight.'

In the present case I think I must regard the claim of the *Escalona* as if there had been no agreement; and then the question arises, what did the *Escalona*, in fact, do, towards the preservation of the property?"

More recently, Lord Diplock pointed out in *The Tojo Maru*[7] that: **32**

> "except in the case of derelicts, the rendering of salvage was consensual. It involved the acceptance by the owner of a vessel which was in peril of an offer by the salvor to try to save it for a reward upon a *quantum meruit* in the event of success. To twentieth century English lawyers this has the essential characteristics of a contract. But to lawyers in the eighteenth and the first part of the nineteenth centuries the similarities between salvage services and contracts for work and labour were less apparent. There was no room for any consensual element in the case of derelicts; and even where there was a consensual element the implied promises lacked mutuality in that the salvor assumed no obligation to continue to provide his services. He could withdraw at any time, yet claim a reward if his services had contributed to the successful saving of the ship. One does not, therefore, find the judges of the Court of Admiralty before 1875 applying the concept of contract to salvage services."

---

[6] 1st ed., p. 42. See further *post*, Chap. 9.
[7] [1972] A.C. 242, 292.

Nature of the Subject

The basic principles upon which the law of salvage is founded remain prima facie applicable today. But, since the demise of the ancient Admiralty Court in 1875 and the emergence of professional salvors, the use of the Lloyd's Form of salvage agreement has become standard.

Restitution for unjust enrichment[8]

33   Whether a salvor should be entitled to recover a salvage reward is a specific variation of the general question whether the recipient of an unrequested benefit should be liable to make a payment for it to the person conferring it. The general common law rule is contained in a famous dictum of Bowen L.J. in the Court of Appeal, on appeal from the Chancery Division. He clearly saw the need to distinguish the approach of the Admiralty Court[9]:

> "The general principle is beyond all question, that work and labour done or money expended by one man to preserve or benefit the property of another do not according to English law create any lien upon the property saved or benefited, nor, even if standing alone, create any obligation to repay the expenditure. Liabilities are not to be forced upon people behind their backs any more than you can confer a benefit upon a man against his will.
>
> There is an exception to this proposition in the maritime law. I mention it because the word 'salvage' has been used from time to time throughout the argument, and some analogy is sought to be established between salvage and the right claimed by the Respondents. With regard to salvage, general average, and contribution, the maritime law differs from the common law. This has been so from the time of the Roman law downwards. The maritime law, for the purposes of public policy and for the advantages of trade, imposes in these cases a liability upon the thing saved, a liability which is a special consequence arising out of the character of mercantile enterprises, the nature of sea perils, and the fact that the thing saved was saved under great stress and exceptional circumstances. No similar doctrine applies to things lost upon land, nor to anything except ships or goods in peril at sea."

By "maritime law", his Lordship clearly meant "Admiralty law", though the narrower latter expression makes his statement strictly inaccurate because general average, which is founded on similar principles to those underlying

---

[8] See generally S. M. Waddams [1989] L.M.C.L.Q. 59, 76–80; F. D. Rose, "Restitution and Maritime Law", in E. Schrage (ed.), *Unjust Enrichment and the Law of Contract* (Kluwer, The Hague, 2001), 367.

[9] *Falcke v. Scottish Imperial Insurance Co.* (1886) 34 Ch.D. 234, 248–249. See also *The Tojo Maru* [1972] A.C. 242, 268, *per* Lord Reid. *cf. Mason v. Le Blaireau* (1804) 6 U.S. 238, 266 (2 Cranch 240, 266), where, in the U.S. Supreme Court, Marshall C.J. said: "If the property of an individual on land be exposed to the greatest peril, and be saved by the voluntary exertions of any persons whatever, if valuable goods be rescued from a house in flames, at the imminent hazard of life by the salvor, no remuneration in the shape of salvage is allowed." He did not say no remuneration at all would be allowed, a proposition which certainly would not accurately represent the modern law in the U.S.

Underlying principles

salvage, was in fact largely taken over and developed by the common law courts,[10] albeit it has recently reverted to the Admiralty jurisdiction again.[11]

Bowen L.J.'s general rule has come increasingly to be seen as an exception to the main principle underlying the modern English law of restitution: that, subject to the particular rules applicable to the type of situation in hand, a defendant receiving a benefit at the expense of the plaintiff in circumstances where he would be prima facie unjustly enriched, must make restitution to the plaintiff for it.[12] This principle undoubtedly finds expression in the law of salvage, although the latter's association with the general law of restitution has been doubted because, *e.g.*, of the method of assessing the defendant's liability otherwise than by direct reference to his gain at the plaintiff's expense[13] and of the predominant but otherwise distorting role of public policy.[14] Lord Wright, an eminent commercial lawyer and pioneer of the modern English law of restitution, once said that "general average, like salvage, is still essentially a matter of maritime equity and should be kept apart from common law or equitable ideas of quasi-contract."[15]

34

Nonetheless, the obligation to pay salvage has been seen as one creating a "civil contract"[16] or a "quasi-contract".[17] The similar previous description of the major common law component of what is now termed the law of restitution of obligations having in some respects effects similar to contracts provoked their theoretical justification, particularly in the nineteenth century, as types of implied contracts. The misleading association with contract has been rejected in both salvage cases, as seen above[18] and in non-maritime cases,[19] and recently leading maritime lawyers have confidently included salvage within the modern law of restitution for unjust enrichment.[20] Undoubtedly, there are particular rules which are peculiar to the law of salvage. However, its identification with the general law of restitution is not simply an academic exercise but enables resort to a greater body of authoritative guidance for

35

---

[10] See *The Constancia* (1846) 2 W. Rob. 487. *cf. Place v. Potts* (1855) 5 H.L.C. 383.

[11] See SCA 1981, s.20(2) (q), re-enacting the Administration of Justice Act (AJA) 1956, s.1(1)(q).

[12] Goff & Jones, Chap. 1; Birks, Chap. 1. *cf. The Cargo ex Honor* (1866) L.R. 1. A. & E. 87, 91, where it was said to be unjust that for extraordinary services only ordinary remuneration should be allowed.

[13] Birks, 304–308.

[14] *Mason v. Le Blaireau* (1804) 6 U.S. 238, 266 (2 Cranch 240, 266), U.S.S.C., *per* Marshall C.J., explaining on grounds of public policy the liberal remuneration of salvage at sea: "It is perhaps difficult, on any other principle, to account satisfactorily for the very great difference which is made between the retribution allowed for services at sea and on land."

[15] *Legal Essays and Addresses* (1939), 55.

[16] "which seems to be the true foundation of a salvage claim": *The Lord Dufferin* (1849) 7 Not. of Cas. Supp. xxxiii (Bombay S.C.J.), xxxv, *per* Sir T. Erskine Perry C.J.

[17] *The Telemachus* [1957] P. 47, 48, in argument by J. B. Hewson, later Admiralty Judge as Hewson J.

[18] *Ante*, §§ 31–32.

[19] Goff & Jones, pp. 5–11.

[20] See *e.g.* Goff & Jones, Chap. 18; Jackson, Chap. 26. *cf. China-Pacific S.A. v. Food Corp. of India (The Winson)* [1979] 2 All E.R. 35, 38.

Nature of the Subject

resolution of practical issues, such as the principle of denying restitution to an officious intervener.[21]

Public policy

36   Judgments in salvage cases contain innumerable references to a public policy, emanating from the Admiralty Court, in making salvage awards.[22] The policy is so well entrenched that it might appear to be the prime justification for making salvage awards such that, regardless of any other possible theoretical justification of the law of salvage, the obligation to pay a salvage reward might be maintained to exist *sui generis*. In fact, the right to claim salvage is dependent on similar requirements to those for other restitutionary rights. The public policy of encouraging salvage services by the prospect of generous rewards plays a general role in shaping the court's attitude to questions arising in salvage cases. But it is a role which derives from the central purpose of encouraging salvage by, wherever possible, inflating the salvor's reward for his services rather than to impose an obligation where none is otherwise assumed to exist.

37   The public policy to be applied by the court in assessing salvage rewards in fact requires the balancing of a number of disparate elements in the exercise of the tribunal's discretion in making an award. To begin with, the salvor must in principle have conferred a benefit on the salvee, for which at least a notional *quantum meruit* is assumed to be payable.[23] The importance of this is underlined by the fact that, where salved values are low, the salvor's minimum entitlement to a reasonable remuneration for his services may be reduced if the result of the award would be to deprive the salvee of a real benefit from the services,[24] although that does not mean that the reward may not fall upon an individual owner with some severity.[25] As Sir Christopher Robinson has said[26]:

> "the Court endeavours always to combine the consideration of what is due to the owners, in the protection of property, with the liberality due to the salvors in remunerating meritorious services."

This general approach indicates that rewards are not assessed simply on the basis of the value of the benefit conferred nor on a *quantum meruit* for work

---

[21] See *post*, §§ 50–60.
[22] See *e.g.*, *The Jane* (1831) 3 Hagg. 338, 343–344; *The Beaverford v. The Kafiristan* [1938] A.C. 136, 147, *per* Lord Wright ("the policy as to maritime law favours the grant of awards for meritorious salvage in order to encourage the rendering of salvage services").
[23] See *The Clifton* (1834) 3 Hagg. 117, 121.
[24] *The City of Chester* (1884) 9 P.D. 182, 202; *The Erato* (1888) 13 P.D. 163, 165.
[25] *The Industry* (1835) 3 Hagg. 203, 204.
[26] *HMS Thetis* (1833) 3 Hagg. 14, 62. See also *The Princess Alice* (1849) 3 W. Rob. 138, 140, *per* Dr Lushington, who, at 143, expressed a tendency to be lenient to unsuccessful salvors as to costs so as not to discourage their providing and claiming for salvage services. See now *post*, Chap. 8.

and labour[27] but that they are simply two of the elements to be considered.[28]

The prime factor is undoubtedly the judicially promoted policy of encouraging salvors by rewards which, wherever possible, greatly exceed a notional *quantum meruit* for their services. Thus, the courts have always borne in mind, particularly where salved values are high,[29] the risk which salvors run of getting little by reason of the comparatively small value of the property saved and also, despite the general requirement of success, getting nothing at all, however strenuous and heroic their efforts have been, by reason of the failure of those efforts to save the property in peril.[30] The court has been inclined to particular generosity where especially effective means of salvage are employed,[31] although not so as to devalue other meritorious claims.[32] In *The Ella Constance*,[33] Dr Lushington said:

38

"It is of great importance and of great value to property salved that the service should be performed with celerity, and I have ever held with regard to steamships that their power to perform services with a rapidity which belongs to no other description of vessel, and in a manner which can be effected by no other class of vessel, is that which entitles them to a higher rate of reward, for thereby, not only are the services performed in an infinitely more convenient way, but risk to property is saved."

In the overwhelming majority of salvage cases nowadays the vessel is a power-driven vessel, whether a tug or a merchant ship, and the chief instrument in effecting the service is the motor power. The increased size and value

---

[27] *The William Beckford* (1801) 3 C. Rob. 355, 355–356; *The Henry Ewbank* (1853) 11 Fed. Cas. (Case No. 6376) 1166, 1170 (see *ante*, §27); *The Clifton* (1834) 3 Hagg. 117, 120–121; *The Industry* (1835) 3 Hagg. 203, 204.

[28] See also *The Hector* (1823) 3 Hagg. 90, 95; *The Industry* (1835) 3 Hagg. 203, 204.

[29] *The Earl of Eglinton* (1855) Swab. 7, 8.

[30] *The Mary Ann* (1823) 1 Hagg. 158, 160–161; *The Melpomene* (1873) L.R. 4 A. & E. 129; *The City of Chester* (1884) 9 P.D. 182, 202; *The Henry* (1851) 15 Jur. 183, 184; *The Erato* (1888) 13 P.D. 163; *The Mark Lane* (1890) 15 P.D. 135, 137; *The Tafelberg* (1941) 71 Ll.L. Rep. 189, 196. In *The Hassel* [1959] 2 Lloyd's Rep. 82, Lord Merriman P. compensated an engaged vessel which was deprived of the opportunity of a substantial award, saying (at 89), "It does not matter whether it is done on the basis of one of the cases I quoted or whether it is done on the basis of the public policy of encouraging the readiness and willingness of salvors to come rapidly to the assistance of vessels in grave distress." cf. *The Sarah* (1800) 1 C.Rob. 312n., 313n., where Lord Stowell compared the policy of requiring ships to pay for the provision of lighthouses even where no immediate use was derived from them. An agreement to provide salvors with some remuneration independently of success will tend to diminish an award; see *post*, Chap. 8.

[31] See *The Raikes* (1824) 1 Hagg. 246 (the first claim for services rendered by a steamship); *The London Merchant* (1837) 3 Hagg. 394, 399, 401; *The Santipore* (1854) 1 Spinks E. & A. 231, 234; *The Alfen* (1857) Swab. 189, 190; *The Ella Constance* (1864) 33 L.J. Adm. 189, 193; *The Kingalock* (1854) 1 Spinks E. & A. 263, 267. The first use in Great Britain of steam power to propel a boat appears to have been in 1778 at Dalswinton in Scotland (*James Nasmyth, An Autobiography*, published 1883). But it was not until later that the steamship became a practical commercial proposition. Steamships were built in rapidly increasing numbers from about 1820. cf. *Admiralty Commissioners v. Valverda (Owners)* [1938] A.C. 173, 198–199.

[32] See *The Genessee* (1848) 12 Jur. 401, 402.

[33] (1864) 33 L.J. Adm. 189, 193.

Nature of the Subject

of modern vessels exposes them to the risk of considerable loss or damage which would discourage their employment for salvage purposes without the inducement of a substantial reward.[34] The availability of efficient, manoeuvrable, power-driven vessels has facilitated the establishment of professional salvors, whose existence has been particularly favoured by the court.[35]

39   The favour shown to especially capable salvors is occasionally reflected in a tendency to discriminate against other salvors. In *The Sandefjord*,[36] a pilot advised the casualty not to accept available assistance from tugs but that lifeboats should lay out a kedge anchor, which was successfully hauled on to refloat her. Willmer J. took account of the grave risk to the pilot of censure or withdrawal of his licence if the operation had been unsuccessful. He continued[37]:

> "But I do not think that it would be right, or in accordance with public policy, to make an extravagant award in favour of the plaintiff in this case on the basis that he took such a grave risk, because I do not want it to go out from this court that pilots are to be encouraged lightly to disregard offers of assistance made by tugs whose services are available. The awarding of salvage is governed largely by considerations of public policy and by the desirability of encouraging seafaring folk to take risks for the purpose of saving property. But it is, I think, no part of the business of this court to encourage pilots, or any other class of seafaring folk, to take undue risks such as may arise if it is thought that they are to be highly rewarded for refusing to accept the assistance of tugs which are offering help."

40   This approach is in part provoked by the general rule against sanctioning salvage claims by persons not falling within the description of "volunteers", denying salvage to persons who are expected to provide the service in question without recovering a salvage reward.[38] The reconciliation of this rule with the general public policy of encouraging salvage[39] may actively encourage the claimant's adherence to his original task. Similarly, lifeboatmen, who are deemed to act gratuitously, are unlikely to receive generous rewards for their services.[40] On the other hand, the court has become less disinclined to

---

[34] *The City of Chester* (1884) 15 P.D. 182, 203. See also *The Benlarig* (1888) 14 P.D. 3, 6; *The August Korff* [1903] P. 166, 174.

[35] See *post*, §§ 42–47.

[36] [1953] 2 Lloyd's Rep. 557.

[37] *ibid.*, 560–561. See also *The Johannes* (1835) 6 Not. of Cas. 288; *The Aeolus* (1873) L.R. 4 A. & E. 29; *The Bedeburn* [1914] P. 146, 151; *The Luigi Accame* (1938) 60 Ll.L. Rep. 106, 110.

[38] See Chap. 7.

[39] See, *e.g. The Mars and Other Barges* (1948) 81 LL.L. Rep. 452, 458, *per* Willmer J.: "what I have to do is hold the balance between two aspects of public policy—one which demands that the court do nothing lightly to encourage claims of this character on the part of public servants, and the other one which prompts the court, where it is satisfied that services going beyond the public duty have been rendered, to encourage the enterprise of the men who have performed those service."

[40] See *post*, §§ 698–705.

Underlying principles

recognise the conversion of towage into salvage services, particularly since tugs are required to continue so far as possible to assist the tow even when the original obligation has become incapable of performance.[41] And public policy has supported the decision that the court should, in an appropriate case, encourage, not discourage, salvage by a sister-ship or by a cargo-owner, *e.g.*, a large oil company with a fleet of tugs and tankers.[42]

The Admiralty Court's professedly equitable salvage jurisdiction is such as **41** to allow it to implement the policy of encouraging salvage in a reluctance to uphold agreements which are in some way inequitable,[43] particularly if they oust the right to salvage[44] or are in the form of settlements of sums which the court considers to be an inadequate reward.[45] But the equitable jurisdiction is exercised in the promotion of the general public policy. Thus, although the court has long disapproved of any kind of misconduct on the part of salvors,[46] it has not been inclined to disfavour over-zealous conduct in the course of meritorious services. As Stephen J. observed in delivering the judgment of the High Court of Australia in *Fisher v. The Oceanic Grandeur*[47]:

> "the main object of the law of salvage is, by the incentive of monetary gain, to encourage seafarers to render assistance to vessels in danger and the fact that their response is, to a greater or lesser extent, the product of that incentive cannot adversely reflect upon them."

Similarly, Brandon J. has said[48]:

> "The principle of the lenient approach to mistakes is an important one. It derives from the basic policy of the law relating to salvage services, which is to encourage, rather than discourage, the rendering of such services. The principle is especially important in cases involving life salvage, where its application demands that salvors should not in general be criticised if, faced with conflict between saving life on the one hand, and preserving property on the other, they err on the side of the former at the expense of the latter."

Professional salvors

The underlying principle of public policy in salvage cases is further **42** reflected by the special measure of generosity with which the court encourages the initiative and enterprise that go into the building and maintenance of

---

[41] See, *e.g. The Minnehaha* (1861) 15 Moo. P.C. 133, 154; *The Liverpool* [1893] P. 154, See *post*, Chap. 7.
[42] *The Sava Star* [1995] 2 Lloyd's Rep. 134, especially at 140, 144.
[43] See *post*, Chap. 9.
[44] See, *e.g. The Waterloo* (1820) 2 Dods. 433, 436; *The Margery* [1902] P. 157, 167, 170; *The Leon Blum* [1915] P. 90, 102; *post*, Chap. 9.
[45] See, *e.g. The Inchmaree* [1899] P. 111. 117. *cf. The Cargo ex Woosung* (1876) 1 P.D. 260, 270–271; *post*, Chap. 9.
[46] See Chap. 11.
[47] (1972) 127 C.L.R. 312, 336; [1972] 2 Lloyd's Rep. 396, 408.
[48] [1974] 1 Lloyd's Rep. 555, 560–561, *per* Brandon J.

salvage equipment and organisations of which at least one prime *raison d'être* is the performance of salvage services:

> "Persons whose principle business is that of rendering assistance to disabled vessels, whether they are vessels ashore or afloat, are, in the fullest sense of the word, professional salvors ... Everyone knows that a professional salvor is entitled to be remunerated, and ought to be remunerated, by a Court dealing with salvage upon a different footing from anyone or any other company ... who maintain their salvage vessels mainly for their own personal advantage."[49]

The scale upon which such professional salvors are rewarded varies, however, according to their degree of commitment to and involvement in salvage work.

43 A number of judges have demonstrated the reasons for and advantages of encouraging professional salvors. In *The Envoy*,[50] salvage services had been rendered by two steam-tugs off the coast of Devonshire in fine weather and with a moderate sea. After referring to these circumstances, favourable to the defendants, Butt J. said:

> "To my mind, one of the most important functions of this court is to encourage the maintenance of powerful and efficient steam-tugs around our coasts, to be in constant readiness to assist vessels in distress. Not only in the course of the year is a large amount of property saved by these means, but a considerable sacrifice of life is prevented. Therefore, the principle we go upon is not that of a *quantum meruit*, but of giving such an award as will encourage people to keep vessels of adequate size and dimensions ready to go out."

These motives were amplified by Gorell Barnes J., at first instance, in *The Glengyle*[51]:

> "The maintenance and establishment of salvage steamers such as the *Hermes* and the *Newa* are for the general benefit of owners and underwriters and others interested in seagoing vessels and their cargoes, and the crews and passengers of such vessels, and ... the Admiralty Court will be liberal in its awards in respect of services rendered by salvage

---

[49] *The Rosa Luxemburg* (1934) 49 Ll.L.Rep. 292, 300, *per* Langton J.
[50] Shipp. Gaz. W.S., February 28, 1888.
[51] [1898] P. 97; affirmed *ibid.* (CA); [1898] A.C. 519. £19,000 awarded on a salved value of £76,596. The case established the particular method of treatment of professional salvors, rejecting the following persuasive argument of counsel for the defendants [1898] P. 97, 105, that: "in practice tugs are not so liberally awarded as steamers not specially built for the purpose, the object being to induce such vessels with valuable cargoes and perhaps mails to assist other vessels in distress, which, without adequate remuneration, they will not do." The argument ignores the fact that both professional and non-professional salvors are encouraged anyway. The point of the case was whether professional salvors should receive additional encouragement.

steamers, even though the awards may fall somewhat heavily on individual owners. The owners of salvage steamers invest a large amount of capital in them and maintain them and their crews, divers, and appliances at great expense, and have no remuneration to look forward to except that which may be earned by occasional salvage services."

In the Court of Appeal, A.L. Smith L.J. stressed the importance of encouraging a network of suitably located salvage stations[52]:

"it is of the highest importance to foster the maintenance of salvage vessels around our coasts and in localities such as in the case here."

More recently, Pilcher J. in *The Makedonia*[53] demonstrated the twin advantages of professional salvors—their ready availability and the skilled services which they are especially capable of providing:

"It is, I think, common knowledge that for some 60 years or more companies incorporated in various countries, and whose names are household words in the shipping community, have carried on the business of professional salvors, maintaining salvage vessels and salvage equipment at strategic points. Such companies employ highly skilled personnel, and it has been recognised by the courts of this country, at least since the year 1898, when *The Glengyle*[54] was decided, that services rendered by salvage vessels of this character are deserving of and should receive a particularly generous award."

A number of the factors relevant to the enhancement of awards to professional salvors are revealed in the judgment of Willmer J. in *The Queen Elizabeth*[55]: **44**

"The *Bustler* is a good deal bigger than the other tugs which were engaged in this case. She is a tug of 4,200 i.h.p., and she is equipped with a very wide range of modern salvage equipment. She carries a full salvage crew, including three radio operators, to enable her to keep constant radio watch. I am told, as a matter of history, that she was built as a rescue tug for the Admiralty during the war, and has been maintained as a salvage vessel by her present demise charterers. The evidence is that she is normally kept on station in a state of immediate readiness to proceed to sea at a moment's notice, to any point where her services may be required. The *Metinda III* is a somewhat smaller salvage vessel of 1,275 i.h.p., but she, also, is equipped with a good deal of powerful salvage equipment."

---

[52] [1898] P. 97, 111. See also *ibid.*, 112; [1898] A.C. 519, 522.
[53] [1958] 1 Q.B. 365, 374.
[54] *Supra*.
[55] (1949) 82 Ll.L. Rep. 803, 814. Other relevant matters include the carrying of search-lights, divers repair facilities and a large quantity of fuel.

These plaintiffs claim that they are entitled to special consideration in asking for an award of salvage, having regard to the fact that they belong to the class of professional salvors whose normal method of livelihood is by the performance of salvage operations, and they rely on the well-known principle whereby a special measure of generosity is to be accorded to such salvors in order to encourage the initiative and enterprise that go to the maintenance of such salvage equipment and organisations."

45 Clearly, professional salvors cannot be especially encouraged to operate unless salvage awards to them enable them, first, to cover the general running expenses of maintaining vessels and equipment in a state of readiness—and not just the particular expenses of the salvage operation in issue—and, secondly, also to ensure that they are appropriately rewarded on top of that. In *The Scheldestad*,[56] it was not disputed that before the salvors could get anything out of the services they must receive £3,000. Bateson J. awarded them £6,000 on a value of £8,900. Similarly, Langton J. in *The Rosa Luxemburg*[57] rejected the argument that tugs of professional salvors rendered no more than any useful tug could have done, or that they did not in that case come directly from a special salvage station—albeit he bore in mind that it was not a case where the special equipment was of special value to the salved vessel.[58] In *The American Farmer*,[59] it was even intimated that professional salvors who went out to offer salvage services should be rewarded even if they made no contribution to the success of salvage operations, although the tugs in question did in fact render a service in standing by.

The generosity felt towards professional salvors has been demonstrated consistently in a long line of cases.[60] Now that salvage is much more likely than not to be undertaken by professional salvors, it has become a normal part of the assessment of rewards.

46 A distinction must be drawn, however, between those professional salvors whose normal method of livelihood is the performance of salvage operations

---

[56] (1933) 45 Ll.L. Rep. 269. See also *The Glengyle* [1898] A.C. 519, 522; *The Modavia* (1931) 39 Ll.L. Rep. 58, 61; *The Dalewood* (1943) 75 Ll.L. Rep. 88, 91; and *The Makedonia* [1958] 1 Q.B. 365, 375–376:
"... the claimants ... were professional salvors ... [T]hey employ experienced service personnel, and it is well known ... that professional salvors who keep salvage tugs on station have special arrangements which they make for the remuneration of the master and crew of those salvage vessels."

[57] (1934) 49 Ll.L. Rep. 292.

[58] cf. *The Modavia* (1931) 39 Ll.L. Rep. 58 (£5,000 awarded on salved values of nearly £170,000 to tug maintained by Dover Harbour Board for salvage purposes, for a short—alleged by the defendants to be only a few minutes—service, for which she was out of harbour for about two hours); *The Granhill* [1951] 2 Lloyd's Rep. 13 (£2,400 awarded for a short simple service, near base, in good weather, on salved values of nearly £186,000).

[59] (1947) 80 Ll.L. Rep. 672, 689.

[60] In addition to the other cases cited in this section, see *The Umberleigh* (1931) 39 Ll.L. Rep. 155; *The Pacific* (1931) 41 Ll.L. Rep. 83 (award of £6,000 on salved values of £22,000); *The Topa Topa* (1935) 50 Ll.L. Rep. 211 (£20,000 awarded on salved values of £72,000; salvage vessels maintained exclusively for salvage services); *The Eastwood* (1943) 75 Ll.L. Rep. 91.

and those professional salvors for whom salvage is only part of their work. As it was put in *The Queen Elizabeth*,[61] salvage awards to the first class of plaintiff are bread and butter, whereas to the second class they may be described as jam. In that case, Willmer J. tried to give effect to the fact that claimants were "primarily and in the first instance professional salvors."[62] But he took account of the fact that the immediate availability of their tugs was because they were at the time performing an ordinary commercial adventure—a towage operation—so that the reward need not be quite so high as in the case of vessels being used solely for salvage.[63]

In *The Granhill*,[64] the same judge made it quite clear that a company **47** normally engaged in ordinary towage business in the River Weser was not within the same class of professional salvor as described by Gorell Barnes J. in *The Glengyle*.[65] It was not a case of vessels or equipment which had no source of remuneration other than salvage awards. Nonetheless, he conceded that the court must always bear in mind the policy of encouraging the business enterprise of providing, fitting and maintaining salvage vessels and equipment and reward it accordingly—but not with the full measure of generosity accorded to those who live predominantly by salvage.[66] Almost no salvor lives by salvage work alone. That is only economically feasible where he can obtain governmental financial support, which is only likely to be forthcoming, if at all, where there is a particular public interest in the relevant operations, *e.g.* to avert environmental damage.

Intention and voluntariness

Provided the general requirements for a salvage reward are present, a **48** salvage claim will not fail for want of clear proof that the salvor intended to provide a service with the express aim of securing a salvage reward. If he intends to provide towage and the tow is in danger, he will receive a salvage reward.[67] Nor is it necessary for the salvor to intend to benefit someone other than himself, for he may be rewarded as a salvor where he has salved property which he mistakenly believed to belong to himself.[68] He may, therefore, recover salvage where he intends to act other than for the salvee's benefit, for example, for his own self-preservation.[69]

His intention is relevant, however, not so much in the sense of the positive **49** motivation for his acting, but in that a salvage claim which in all other respects

---

[61] (1949) 82 Ll.L. Rep. 803, 821. See also *The Glengyle* [1898] A.C. 519, 523.
[62] (1949) 82 Ll.L. Rep. 803, 820.
[63] See *ibid.*, 814.
[64] [1951] 2 Lloyd's Rep. 13.
[65] *Ante*, §36.
[66] He awarded the professional salvors—who were not the sole salvors—£15,000 on salved values of £6,208,000.
[67] See *post*, Chap. 4.
[68] *The Liffey* (1887) 6 Asp. M.L.C. 255.
[69] *The Lomonosoff* [1912] P. 97. See also *The Beaver* (1801) 3 C. Rob. 292.

satisfies the necessary conditions for a reward will fail if the plaintiff performs the service with the intention, however formed, of not claiming salvage,[70] thus with the presumed intention of conferring a voluntary benefit on the salvee.[71] This reasoning encompasses those categories of salvors, traditionally categorised as volunteers, whose performance by virtue of a pre-existing obligation excludes their entitlement to salvage.[72] It also justifies the exclusion from reward of rescuers such as lifeboatmen who are, at least before the danger arises, true volunteers, providing in principle a gratuitous service under no obligation to do so, and with the clear intention of preserving lives, which would normally justify a salvage award. However, they intend to confer this benefit voluntarily, without payment, and their inability to claim life salvage is thus consistent with the general public policy applied in salvage to reward those who are induced to preserve from danger by the attraction of a generous award. Where a claimant does not fall within one of the recognised categories of volunteers, any attempted exclusion of the right to salvage must be clearly proved.[73]

Acceptance, prohibition and officiousness

50 It is a principle of the general law of unjust enrichment that a person should not normally be obliged to pay for a benefit which he has neither requested nor freely accepted with the knowledge that it is to be paid for—particularly if that benefit is the provision of a service from which no tangible benefit results which can in some way be restored to the plaintiff.[74] It is not entirely clear from the cases how far this principle applies in Admiralty law to salvage cases. Where salvage services are contracted for in the absence of any form of illegitimate pressure or otherwise freely accepted, the obligation to pay a reward is clear.[75] At the other extreme, where a salvor is guilty of positive misconduct, he will be deprived of any potential right to reward.[76] The intermediate cases were complicated by the judicial promotion of salvorial zeal. As has been observed[77]:

> "the main object of the law of salvage is, by the incentive of monetary gain, to encourage seafarers to render assistance to vessels in danger and

---

[70] *cf. Simon v. Taylor* [1975] 2 Lloyd's Rep. 338 (Sing. HC), where, without having to decide the point, Chua J. said: "[The divers] thought they had every right to take the cargo from the submarine because the submarine was in international waters and that anyone fishing in it could take it. The evidence is clear that what the four divers did was motivated not by any intention to salve for the benefit of the owners of the cargo but solely for their own benefit. The four divers did not render any services in the nature of salvage services."
[71] See Goff & Jones, pp. 47–53, 58–63.
[72] See *post*, Chap. 7.
[73] See *post*, §§ 784–789.
[74] Goff & Jones, pp. 16–26, 63–65.
[75] See *post*, Chap. 9.
[76] *Post*, Chap. 11.
[77] *Fisher v. The Oceanic Grandeur* (1972) 127 C.L.R. 312, 336; [1972] 2 Lloyd's Rep. 396, 408; *ante*, para. 35.

the fact that their response is, to a greater or lesser extent, the product of that incentive cannot adversely reflect upon them."

51 The prevailing attitude of the Admiralty Court, however, was that a salvee is only liable to pay salvage if the service was provided with his consent or, if not with his actual consent, in circumstances where a prudent salvee would have consented and the salvor has not acted contrary to the positive opposition of the salvee. This was largely confirmed by the Brussels Salvage Convention 1910, Art. 3[78] and in turn by the International Salvage Convention 1989, Art. 19.[79] Article 19 provides:

"Services rendered notwithstanding the express and reasonable prohibition of the owner or master of the vessel or the owner of any other property in danger which is not and has not been on board the vessel shall not give rise to payment under this Convention."

It is convenient to consider the approach of the Admiralty Court to prohibition of salvage services before considering the effect of Article 19 of the 1989 Convention.

Pre-Convention case law

52 There are common law cases in other jurisdictions which suggest that an officious intervenor might nonetheless be able to recover salvage where, contrary to the unreasonable opposition of the salvee, he saves lives in danger.[80] This would seem to be in accordance with sound public policy, and derives some support from the rule that persons acting in consequence of a statutory obligation to assist in preservation of life at sea are not simply by virtue of that fact precluded from recovering salvage.[81]

53 The leading Admiralty law authority for the test to be applied is *The Vandyck*.[82] In that case, a tug assisted in disentangling a ship from a collision, thereby rescuing it from a position of great danger and providing a service of direct benefit to both vessels. The tug recovered salvage from the second as well as the first vessel, although it had acted without a request from or engagement by the second. The Court of Appeal applied the test proposed by the Privy Council in *The Annapolis*[83]: where salvage services are rendered to property in danger, without a request from or engagement by the recipient of

---

[78] "Persons who have taken part in salvage operations notwithstanding the express and reasonable prohibition on the part of the vessel to which the services were rendered have no right to any remuneration."

[79] The language of the Brussels Salvage Convention 1910, Art. 3 refuses reward to the *providers* of the prohibited services. The language of the Salvage Convention 1989, Art.19 does so with reference to the *service* prohibited.

[80] *Matheson v. Smiley* [1932] 2 D.L.R. 787; *Greenspan v. Slate* (1953) 12 N.J. 426.

[81] *Post*, Chap. 7.

[82] (1882) 5 Asp. M.L.C. 17, CA, affirming Sir Robert Phillimore, whose judgment is also reported at (1881) 7 P.D. 42.

[83] (1861) Lush. 355, 375.

those services, the recipient is nevertheless liable to pay a salvage reward if the services are rendered when a vessel is so circumstanced that a prudent man would accept them.[84] No express acceptance was required, nor should it have been.

> "In many cases the urgency of the case may be too great to admit of previous discussion, and if a salvor were required to prove such agreement before he could recover, it is to be feared that there would be much slackness in cases which most require energy and activity."[85]

Moreover, it would nearly always be unjust for the defendant to retain the benefit of the services provided without paying for them. Bucknill J. stated it to be a proposition which seemed to fit with the cases cited to him in *The Premuda*[86]:

> "that salvage cannot be rendered to property unless the owners either expressly assent to the services being rendered or unless there is a constructive acceptance, the meaning of 'constructive acceptance' being that the circumstances were such that any reasonable man who owned the property would have accepted the services on a salvage basis, whether he, in fact, accepted them or not."

54 Whether or not the test laid down in *The Vandyck* was satisfied was a question of fact in each case,[87] although there must have been sufficient evidence to justify the tribunal in coming to the conclusion that the proffered services should have been accepted in the circumstances of each case.[88]

A salvor will be entitled to a salvage reward if the salvee consents to the service provided in circumstances of danger. Unless there is an express agreement for remuneration otherwise than on salvage terms, the court will not permit the salvee to take the benefit of a salvage service without paying the proper remuneration. Without deciding whether the salvee's consent was necessary, it was said in the High Court of Australia in *Fisher v. The Oceanic Grandeur*[89]:

---

[84] See also *The Auguste Legembre* [1902] P. 123, 129; *The Emilie Galline* [1903] P. 106 (where the claim was rejected); *The Port Caledonia and The Anna* [1903] P. 184, 190–191 (where the claim against *The Anna* was rejected); *The Kangaroo* [1918] P. 327, 331; *The Ovre and The Conde de Zubiria* (1920) 2 Ll.L. Rep. 21 (where the claim was rejected); *The Pretoria* (1920) 5 Ll.L. Rep. 112 (where the claim was rejected); *The Flore* (1929) 34 Ll.L. Rep. 172; *The Gregerso* [1973] Q.B. 274, 284.
[85] *ibid.*, 375.
[86] (1940) 67 Ll.L. Rep. 9, 15. The cases in question are not specifically cited in the report. The proposition was put by Mr Gordon Willmer K.C., later Willmer L.J.
[87] See, *e.g. The Flore* (1929) 34 Ll.L. Rep. 172, 176, *per* Bateson J.: "the question I have to ask is whether any reasonable person would have taken the services of these tugs for the purpose of extinguishing the fire in the circumstances of this case."
[88] See *The Emilie Galline* [1903] P. 106, 112.
[89] (1972) 127 C.L.R. 312, 339; [1972] 2 Lloyd's Rep. 396, 410, *per* Stephen J.

"Consent will no doubt be lacking when acts are done in disobedience to a master's orders, but the relevant consent is consent to the acts performed, and not to their legal characterisation and consequences. It is for the Court to determine whether the acts constitute salvage services; I have decided that they were of that character and so long as the doing of the acts was assented to by the master of the salved vessel the requirement of consent is satisfied. Accordingly, even if, as I have assumed for present purposes, consent is a prerequisite to salvage award, I find that there existed the necessary element of consent in the present case."

55 The main support for the view that the salvor can override the wishes of the salvee appeared in *The Auguste Legembre*.[90] Two tugs from Falmouth, the *Victor* and the *Dragon*, offered to assist in the towage by another tug (the *Helen Peele*, accompanied by a lifeboat) of a disabled French steamer in the entrance of the Bristol Channel to Cardiff Roads. The French captain engaged the *Victor* but refused the *Dragon*. The master of the *Victor* said he would not tow without a third tug, though there was no evidence of any clear answer or that the master of the *Dragon* heard any answer that was given. It was not absolutely necessary to have a third tug but the *Victor* wanted a third, in case it was needed, and the *Dragon* joined in the service. All three tugs recovered salvage, Gorell Barnes J. said[91]:

"With regard to the *Dragon*, the question is one partly of law and partly of nautical skill. It is a legal question in this sense, that although the tug's services were not directly accepted, but in fact were refused, by the master of the steamship, the tug did at the request of the *Victor* make fast ahead for the reasons I have given, and rendered a towage service of a valuable character towards Cardiff; and, legally speaking, if those services were rendered in such circumstances that they ought to have been accepted, although, according to his evidence, the master of the steamship did not wish to have them, yet an award would be made of some amount, on the well-known principle.[92] Therefore I think it would be a nautical question whether, having regard to the circumstances of the case, and what might be anticipated at that time of year and in that locality, it was reasonably prudent and necessary to have a third tug. The Elder Brethren think it was, because, although the weather had moderated, it was in the middle of December, when the wind seems to have been flying about from quarter to quarter, and no one could be certain as to what would take place before they got to Cardiff. That is the reason why the *Victor* took this third tug ahead, and although I think in fact it did not turn out to be necessary, it was a reasonable thing to do. Therefore the *Dragon* must not be excluded, although the award should be of a moderate character."

[90] [1902] P. 123.
[91] *ibid.*, §§ 128–129.
[92] See *ante*, §53.

He awarded £325 to the *Helen Peele*, £75 to the lifeboatmen, £500 to the *Victor* and £100 to the *Dragon*.

56 The approach in *The Auguste Legembre* has its merits. The policy of encouraging salvage services should ensure that salvors are rewarded where they override protests made in their interests, for example where they contribute to salvage despite the protests of a master who seeks to discourage them because in his opinion salvage is impracticable and to deter them from risking their lives.[93] Similarly, a token protest should not deprive salvors of their rightful reward where they as well as the defendants run the risk of danger. In *The Kangaroo*,[94] a motor-vessel in convoy during the First World War dropped behind due to engine trouble. Another vessel in the convoy, the *S.S. Politician*, made an offer to the commander of the escorting ship to tow the *Kangaroo*. The commander accepted the offer and ordered her to take the *Kangaroo* in tow. The master of the *Kangaroo* said that he protested but accepted the services without further protest and was assisted in rejoining the convoy. Hill J. held[95]:

> "In these circumstances I have no doubt that the service is a salvage service. It matters not that the *Politician* was acting under orders; as regards the *Kangaroo* she was a volunteer and, in truth, she received her orders only because she volunteered. It seems to me to matter as little that the *Kangaroo* accepted under orders or under protest. That may be an important fact in considering whether the *Kangaroo* was in risk. But when a ship, which is in risk, accepts a service, it is none the less an acceptance, and none the less a salvage service, because some one else whose orders the ship must obey has ordered the ship to accept, or because the acceptance is under protest. Ships in convoy, no doubt, owe duties to one another, but to tow gratuitously for 900 miles a ship in peril is not one of them."

57 *The Auguste Legembre*[96] has been followed in a number of cases,[97] and with express approval.[98] However, reservations were expressed in *The Pretoria*,[99] where Hill J. said of it:

> "That case is the high water mark of authority in favour of granting a salvage award against a ship whose Master was unwilling to accept the service. [Counsel] says . . . that the decision does not cover a case where

---

[93] See *The Jonge Bastiaan* (1804) 5 C. Rob. 322, 323.
[94] [1918] P. 227.
[95] *ibid.*, 331–332.
[96] *Supra*, n. 90.
[97] See *The Kangaroo* [1918] P. 227; *The Pretoria* (1920) 5 Ll.L. Rep. 112; *The Rosa Luxemburg* (1934) 49 Ll.L. Rep. 292; *The Flore* (1929) 34 Ll.L. Rep. 172.
[98] See *ibid.*, 176, *per* Bateson J.: "I think that the *Auguste Legembre* case, which was decided in 1902 by the late Lord Gorell, is sound sense and good law. It has been the law for so long that even if I wanted to I should hesitate long before I took any other view."
[99] (1920) 5 Ll.L. Rep. 112, 113–114.

the owner has, to the knowledge of the alleged salvors, refused to have any salvage assistance on the ground that he is going to recover the property by his own exertions. I need not decide that. If *The Auguste Legembre* applies, the highest at which the decision can be put . . . is this: That salvage is earned if the services, though not accepted or requested by the owner, were rendered in such circumstances that they ought to have been accepted."

Other cases have shewn that salvage claims are likely to fail where the vessel is capable of extricating itself from danger by its own exertions.[1]

To similar effect is the speech of Sir Francis Jeune P. in *The Solway Prince*[2]:   **58**

"There need not, of course, in some cases of salvage, such as those of the rescue of a derelict, be any actual assent of the owner of the *res* or his servants to his property being saved—that is the characteristic difference between the legal consequences of the preservation of property by land and of some property at sea. But it appears to me impossible that the property of any owner can be salved without his sanction, express or implied, in any case in which anything that is done without his knowledge; and that where, as here, the owner has merely allowed some one else to employ persons to endeavour to rescue his property on the terms of being paid for their work and labour, such a sanction is certainly not expressed, and cannot be implied. If the owner made such a contract with such persons himself, provided there be no change in the nature of the service, and it may be necessary to add, provided that the transaction is not shewn to have been inequitable . . . , I think that there can be no doubt that the contracting parties could not claim a remuneration on salvage principles."

The difficulty posed by *The Auguste Legembre*[3] was its apparent tendency to encourage, or at least to permit, awards of salvage to persons who have compelled defendants to receive services which they neither requested nor wanted, and indeed refused. It therefore appears to be inconsistent with the general rule of English law denying restitution to officious intervenors and to the particular policy rules denying salvage to claimants who have been guilty of misconduct[4]; in particular, the engagement of the third tug in *The Auguste Legembre* might have been considered an unnecessary additional expense.   **59**

These inherent problems are, however, reconcilable on a proper appreciation of the case and similar decisions. In essence, *The Auguste Legembre*   **60**

---

[1] See *The Port Caledonia and The Anna* [1903] P. 184, 190–191; *The Ovre and the Conde de Zubiria* (1920) 2 Ll.L. Rep. 21; *The Pretoria* (1920) 5 Ll.L. Rep. 112. *cf. The Flore* (1929) 34 Ll.L. Rep. 172, 176.
[2] [1896] P. 120, 126.
[3] *Supra*, n. 90.
[4] See *post*, Chap. 11.

represents a particular application of the sound general test in *The Vandyck*[5] that salvage is payable where services are rendered when a vessel is so circumstanced that a prudent man would accept them. To begin with, it is clear that the services provided must genuinely be salvage services, so no claim will be allowed merely for the conferment of non-necessary services.[6] It must also be noticed that in none of the cases was there evidence of a clear refusal to accept the proffered services.[7] Where there is a blanket refusal, ignoring it is likely to deprive the claimant of any reward for his services. This will not necessarily be so, for a court might decide that satisfaction of the test in *The Vandyck* will automatically justify salvage because there is a general public interest in salving property in distress at sea. At least, the master's protest may be ineffective where rejection of the available services is prejudicial to other interests in the adventure. Even where additional services are not strictly necessary, a salvor is entitled to incur reasonable expense in performing the contract service, and the engagement of the extra tug in *The Auguste Legembre* was perhaps justifiable on that basis.[8] Admittedly, once a tug becomes entitled to claim salvage, it is entitled to remuneration on a salvage scale, but it is noteworthy that the *Dragon's* portion of the reward in *The Auguste Legembre* was lower than that of the other salving vessels.[9] The court, therefore, has been careful not to sanction an additional burden on the defendant.

Prohibition under the 1989 Salvage Convention, Art. 19

61   Article 19 of the International Salvage Convention 1989 adopts the general approach of the Admiralty Court to prohibited salvage services but in specific terms. Salvage services will not give rise to payment under the Convention if (i) they are *expressly* prohibited, (ii) they are *reasonably* prohibited, and (iii) the prohibition is by a *specified* person (*i.e.*, the owner or master of the vessel or the owner of any other property in danger which is not and has not been on board the vessel).[10] The pre-Convention case law provides guidance on the application of the first two of these conditions.

62   However, the third condition, which is new to the 1989 Convention, is less transparent. In particular, it may seem unclear on first impression why or when "the owner of any property in danger which is not and has not been on board the vessel" should seek to prohibit salvage operations. Article 19 can only apply where there is a prima facie entitlement to a salvage reward. It does not

---

[5] (1882) 5 Asp. M.L.C. 17; *ante*, § 53.
[6] See the cases *supra*, n. 1. *cf. The Homewood* (1928) 31 Ll.L. Rep. 336, where the claimants towed away an anchored, unmanned vessel without informing anyone.
[7] In *The Auguste Legembre*, *supra*, n. 90, the evidence was inconclusive. In *The Kangaroo*, *supra*, n. 94, the protest was perhaps mainly formal but in any case "acceptance" was present in the particular circumstances of the case.
[8] See also *The Rosa Luxemburg* (1934) 49 Ll.L. Rep. 292, 301 (engagement of the *Vulcan*).
[9] See also *ibid.*, 305 (reward to *Vulcan*).
[10] A salvor may also fail to recover part or all of his potential reward on the basis of the rules on misconduct discussed *post*, Chap. 11.

provide that, where a potential salvee has not prohibited salvage operations, he will become liable for salvage even if the normal pre-conditions for salvage have not been satisfied. Thus, it might be thought, property which has not been on board the vessel should not be liable to salvage anyway, so it is unnecessary to authorise its owner to prohibit an operation to salve it.

The answer is probably that, first, where property in danger has been on board a vessel in danger, it is convenient and right that, consistently with the Convention's other provisions on who is authorised to make decisions in relation to salvage,[11] the decision whether to prohibit salvage should rest with the owner or the master of the ship alone; and this is what the first part of Article 19 provides. But it is not the case that all property which is the subject of salvage services is or has been carried on a vessel, particularly under the extended range of subjects of salvage to which the 1989 Convention applies.[12] Therefore, in such a case, the second part of Article 19 authorises the owner of such property to prohibit salvage operations.[13]

Certainly, it seems right that the owner of a subject of salvage which is not being, and has not been, carried on a vessel should have the power (reasonably) to forbid salvage operations. But this is not exactly what Article 19 provides. By referring to "the vessel", Article 19 assumes its application solely to a situation where a vessel is involved. If so, either the owner of property which has not been carried on board a vessel cannot prohibit salvage operations (which seems unreasonable) or such owner's right to prohibit has to be found in the pre-Convention law (which reduces the scope of the code which the Convention was designed to provide).

However, Article 19 can be given a more comprehensive interpretation if its second part is construed to refer to "property which is not and has not been on board *a* [rather than *the*] vessel".

Remoteness of benefit

A salvage claim will fail if the resulting benefit is too remote in that it is not a direct consequence of the salvage service. In *The Annapolis*,[14] the *Annapolis*, drifting on the tide after a collision, became entangled with the *Golden Light* and together they drifted towards the anchored *H.M. Hayes*, an American ship. The *Annapolis* was pulled away from the *Golden Light* by the *Storm King*, the tug which had previously been towing her, and another tug. The *Storm King* returned to assist two other tugs to disentangle the *Golden Light* from the *H.M. Hayes*, which she had fouled and with which she was drifting towards *HMS Majestic*. The *Storm King* recovered salvage from the *Golden Light* but not from the *H.M. Hayes*.[15] The Privy Council decided that salvage was payable, even without express request for or acceptance of the service, if

---

[11] See the International Salvage Convention 1989, Art. 6.2; *post*, Chap. 9.
[12] See *post*, Chap. 3.
[13] See also Brice, §§ 1–135 to 1–136.
[14] (1861) Lush. 355.
[15] Nor from the *Annapolis*, which she was contractually bound to tow.

the circumstances were such that, if an offer had been made, any prudent man would have accepted it.

> "But in the present case the *H.M. Hayes* received only indirectly a benefit from the service rendered to the *Golden Light*. There was not only no acceptance of the service by her, but there was nothing done by the *Storm King* with a view to her benefit. She received benefit indirectly, as Her Majesty's ship *Majestic*, or any other ship lying higher up the river than the *H.M. Hayes*, may have received benefit."[16]

The Privy Council's opinion was applied to the similar circumstances of *The Vandyck*,[17] where Lord Coleridge C.J. said[18]:

> "In accordance with this judgment, I am of opinion that the danger, to entitle salvors to recover remuneration, must be direct and immediate. It must not be indirect, because it would be obvious that, were it not otherwise, every ship within a certain distance which might or might not have suffered, might be considered liable to pay salvors for averting the danger."

Implementation, content and period of application of the International Salvage Convention 1989

Implementation

65   The International Salvage Convention 1989 was open for signature at the Headquarters of the International Maritime Organisation ("IMO")[19] from July 1, 1989 to June 30, 1990 and has subsequently remained open for accession.[20] States have been able to express their consent to be bound by the Convention by: (a) signature without reservation as to ratification, acceptance or approval; (b) signature subject to ratification, acceptance or approval, followed by ratification, acceptance or approval; or (c) accession.[21] Certain provisions of the Convention were incorporated into LOF 1990[22] and therefore became effective as a matter of contract between parties contracting on those terms prior to the Convention's coming into force. As a matter of public international law, the Convention entered into force one year after the date on

---

[16] (1861) Lush. 355, 375.
[17] (1882) 5 Asp. M.L.C. 17.
[18] *ibid.*, 19.
[19] The International Salvage Convention 1989, Art. 1 states that, "For the purposes of this Convention . . . (f) Organisation means the International Maritime Organisation. (g) Secretary-General means the Secretary-General of the Organisation."
[20] International Salvage Convention 1989, Art. 28.1.
[21] International Salvage Convention 1989, Art. 28.2. Ratification, acceptance, approval or accession is effected by the deposit of an instrument to that effect with the Secretary-General of the IMO: *ibid.*, Art. 28.3.
[22] See LOF 1990, cl. 2, incorporating Arts. 1(a)–(e), 8, 13.1, 13.2 first sentence, 13.3 and 14. See also LOF 1995, cl. 2 and Appendix. See now LOF 2000, cl. 2.

which 15 States had expressed their consent to be bound by it,[23] in fact therefore entering into force on July 14, 1996. However, the Convention came into force as part of United Kingdom municipal law before that date, on January 1, 1995.[24] It does not affect any rights or liabilities arising out of any salvage operations started or other acts done before that date.[25]

Content, reservations and revision

The Convention, which is subject to revision,[26] is in several languages, including English.[27] It is deposited with the Secretary-General of the IMO, who is responsible for recording and notifying details of its current status.[28] The Convention may be implemented municipally either as it stands or subject to the terms of permitted reservations. The United Kingdom has implemented the Convention on the basis of those reservations of which it has availed itself and subject to other provisions ensuring congruity between the Convention and English law generally.[29] So far as English law is concerned, of course, it must be remembered that the Convention is effective only on the terms upon

---

[23] International Salvage Convention 1989, Art. 29.1. The U.K. deposited its instrument of ratification on September 29, 1994. See also *ibid.*, Art. 29.2: for a State which expresses its consent to be bound by the Convention after its entry into force, such consent takes effect one year after such expression.

[24] Merchant Shipping (Salvage and Pollution) Act 1994, ss. 1, 10(4); Merchant Shipping (Salvage and Pollution) Act 1994 (Commencement No. 2) Order 1994 (S.I. 1994 No. 2971). Since there is no "State party" to a Convention until it comes into force internationally, that description in U.K. legislation has been specifically extended to the U.K. in relation to the period between the Convention's municipal and its international effectiveness: Merchant Shipping (Salvage and Pollution) Act 1994, s.1(5); Merchant Shipping Act 1995, s.224(6).

[25] Merchant Shipping Act 1995, s.224(4).

[26] The Convention provides for its revision by a conference convened by the IMO, which the Secretary-General must do if requested by eight State parties, or one fourth of the States parties, whichever is the higher number: International Salvage Convention 1989, Art. 32.1–2. Any consent to be bound by the Convention after the date of entry into force of an amendment shall be deemed to apply to the Convention as amended: *ibid.*, Art. 32.3. If the U.K. agrees to a revision of the Convention, Sched. 11 to the Merchant Shipping Act 1995 may be modified by Order in Council, a draft of which must first be approved by a resolution of each House of Parliament: *ibid.*, s.224(3), (7). However, such modification shall not affect any rights or liabilities arising out of any salvage operations started or other acts done before the day on which the modification comes into force: *ibid.*, s.224(5).

[27] International Salvage Convention 1989, Art. 34: "The Convention is established in a single original in the Arabic, Chinese, English, French, Russian and Spanish languages, each text being equally authentic."

[28] See International Salvage Convention 1989, Art. 33.

[29] The Merchant Shipping Act 1995, s.224(1), Sched.11, Pt I gives effect to the International Salvage Convention 1989, Arts 1–27 verbatim. The remainder of the Convention comprises Chapter V—Final Clauses (Arts. 28–34) and Attachments 1 (the "Common Understanding": see *post*, § 395) and 2 (on General Average: see *post*, § 440). These remaining provisions include matters dealing with the U.K.'s position in public international law as a State party to the Convention, and so in general not directly relevant to the municipally implemented terms of the Convention. Art. 30 (permitting reservations to the Convention but only capable of being given effect in the light of the reservations actually made) and Attachment 1 (the "Common Understanding") together with other provisions necessary to give the Convention effect in relation to English law generally are implemented by the Merchant Shipping Act 1995, s.224(2), Sched. 11, Pt II ("Provisions Having Effect in Connection With the Convention").

which it has been given effect municipally.[30] The main provisions of the Convention were originally enacted verbatim, together with complementary provisions, as a Schedule to the Merchant Shipping (Salvage and Pollution) Act 1994.[31] The provisions of the 1994 Act have in turn been consolidated into the Merchant Shipping Act 1995.[32] Accordingly, most references in this book to the English legislation giving effect to the Salvage Convention 1989[33] are to the 1995 Act.

Denunciation

Any State party may, by the deposit of an instrument of denunciation with the Secretary-General of the IMO, denounce the Convention at any time after the expiry of one year from the date on which the Convention enters into force for that State.[34] A denunciation takes effect one year, or such longer period as may be specified in the instrument of denunciation, after the deposit.[35]

Rights and Duties of States and Public Authorities

67   The Salvage Convention 1989 essentially deals with the private rights and duties of parties to salvage operations. To that extent, it does not need to deal specifically with the interests of the State or public authorities, and there is not likely to be a conflict between the Salvage Convention 1989 and provisions dealing with the role of public authorities. However, in certain cases the Convention imposes duties on States parties to it and specifically preserves the interests of States in matters which do or may affect salvage.

Two of the duties on States parties to the Convention are vague: one is to take account of the need for co-operation between interested parties to ensure the efficient and successful performance of salvage operations[36]; the other is to encourage, as far as possible and with the consent of the parties, the publication of salvage arbitration awards.[37] More directly, States parties are required to adopt the measures necessary to enforce the duty imposed on masters to render assistance to persons in danger of being lost at sea.[38]

68   The Convention is more specific in safeguarding the interests of States parties. First, uncontroversially, it maintains the principle of State immunity for State-owned, non-commercial vessels and cargoes.[39] Secondly, expanding

---

[30] For the most part, the relevant terms of the Convention and the relevant parts of the Merchant Shipping Act 1995 are identical.
[31] Merchant Shipping (Salvage and Pollution) Act 1994, s.1, Sched.1.
[32] Merchant Shipping Act 1995, s.224(1)–(2), Sched.11.
[33] In the Merchant Shipping Act 1995, the International Salvage Convention 1989 is referred to as "the Salvage Convention": ss 224(1), 255(1).
[34] International Salvage Convention 1989, Art. 31.1–2.
[35] International Salvage Convention 1989, Art. 31.3.
[36] Salvage Convention 1989, Art. 11. See *post*, § 1048.
[37] Salvage Convention 1989, Art. 27. See *ante*, § 1300.
[38] Salvage Convention 1989, Art. 10. See *post*, § 534.
[39] Salvage Convention 1989, Arts 4 and 25. See *post*, §§ 1163–1177. See also Salvage Convention 1989, Art. 26 (humanitarian cargoes); *post*, §§ 1178–1181.

on similar provision in the Brussels Salvage Convention 1910,[40] the Salvage Convention 1989, Art. 5.1 provides that:

"This Convention shall not affect any provisions of national law or any international convention relating to salvage operations by or under the control of public authorities."

Thirdly, Article 9 provides that:

"Nothing in this Convention shall affect the right of the coastal State concerned to take measures in accordance with generally recognised principles of international law to protect its coastline or related interests from pollution or the threat of pollution following upon a maritime casualty or acts relating to such a casualty which may reasonably be expected to result in major harmful consequences, including the right of a coastal State to give directions in relation to salvage operations."

Public authority control of salvage operations

Article 5.1's preservation of other national law or international Convention provisions clearly means that such provisions override the terms of the Salvage Convention 1989 where they specifically relate to salvage operations by or under the control of public authorities. It is not clear that Article 5.1 preserves such other provisions where they relate to matters such as wrecks or pollution[41] which are not specifically concerned with salvage but nevertheless fall within the definition of "salvage operations" in the Salvage Convention 1989.[42] Most likely, a tribunal will wish to avoid apparent conflict between different Conventions and national laws so, if such provisions do fall within that definition, they will be given effect despite any possible contradiction of the Salvage Convention 1989. Article 9, preserving coastal States' rights to take measures to counter pollution, was included in the Convention as a political measure to secure agreement to it and is generally assumed to add little, if anything, of substance. If, however, Article 5.1 were given a restrictive interpretation, so as only to preserve other provisions specifically concerned with salvage, Article 9 might have some, other than clarificatory, function in preserving a State's right to give directions in relation to salvage operations while giving effect to measures to counter pollution. However, Article 9 merely preserves States' rights arising other than under the Salvage Convention 1989 and does not create new powers or obligations.[42a]

69

---

[40] The Brussels Salvage Convention 1910, Art. 13 provided: "This Convention does not affect the provisions of national laws or international treaties as regards the organisation of services of assistance and salvage by or under the control of public authorities, nor, in particular, does it affect such laws or treaties on the subject of the salvage of fishing gear."
[41] See, *e.g.* Merchant Shipping Act 1995, ss 137–141 ("Shipping casualties").
[42] Art. 1(a). See *ante*, §18.
[42a] In October 2001 the Legal Committee of the IMO resolved to conduct a study, in conjunction with the CMI, of the relevant legal rules of national and international law relating to "places of refuge". It recognised that Art. 9 would form a central part of this study.

Nature of the Subject

Shipping casualties and oil pollution

70 So far as concerns the United Kingdom,[43] the rights most obviously preserved by the Salvage Convention 1989, Arts. 5.1 and 9 are those contained in a number of international Conventions to which it is a party and which are given effect by the Merchant Shipping Act 1995, Pt VI, dealing with the prevention of pollution.[44]

The Secretary of State has the functions of taking or co-ordinating measures to prevent, reduce and minimise the effects of marine pollution.[45] In particular, the Merchant Shipping Act 1995, s.137 confers powers on him where an accident[46] has occurred to or in a ship and he believes that oil from the ship will or may cause pollution on a large scale in the United Kingdom or United Kingdom territorial waters and that the use of the powers conferred by the section is urgently needed.[47] For the purpose of preventing or reducing oil pollution or the risk of it, the Secretary of State may give directions as respects the ship or its cargo to: the owner[48] or any person in possession of the ship; the master; or any salvor or his servant or agent who is in possession of the ship and in charge of the salvage operation.[49] Such directions may require the person to whom they are given to take or refrain from taking any action of any kind whatsoever.[50] In particular, they may require: that the ship is or is not to be moved, or is to be moved to a specified place, or is to be removed from a

---

[43] See the Merchant Shipping Act 1995, s.315(1): "Except for sections 18 and 193(5), this Act extends to England and Wales, Scotland and Northern Ireland."

[44] *i.e.*, the International Convention for the Prevention of Pollution from Ships 1973 (MARPOL), the Protocol relating to Intervention on the High Seas in Cases of Marine Pollution by Substances other than Oil 1973, the 1978 Protocol to the 1973 Convention, the International Convention on Oil Pollution Preparedness, Response and Co-operation 1990 (the OPRC Convention) and any other international Convention relating to the prevention, reduction or control of pollution of the sea or other waters by matter from ships, including agreements providing for the modification of such agreements: Merchant Shipping Act 1995, s.128(1). Her Majesty may also provide by Order in Council that the powers under these Conventions shall, in such way as is provided by the Order(s), apply to a ship which is not a U.K. ship and which is for the time being outside U.K. waters; *ibid.*, s.141. The preceding provisions are without prejudice to any rights or powers exercisable by Her Majesty's Government exercisable apart from those provisions whether under international law or otherwise: *ibid.*, s.137(7). See also *ibid.*, s.129, authorising the implementation of provisions of the United Nations Convention on the Law of the Sea 1982.

[45] Although he has delegated their exercise, the Secretary of State continues to have these functions: Merchant Shipping Act 1995, s.293. The provisions in the Merchant Shipping Act 1995, s.137 (the subject-matter of the ensuing discussion) derive from the Prevention of Oil Pollution Act 1971, s.12, as amended by the Merchant Shipping (Salvage and Pollution) Act 1994, s.8(6). As he was entitled to do by the 1971 Act, the Secretary of State delegated his functions to the Marine Pollution Control Unit (MPCU), which was set up within the Department of Transport in 1978 to provide expert advice to the Secretary of State and to co-ordinate responses to disasters. The MPCU was previously a part of the Department of Transport Marine Directorate, becoming in April 1994 an executive agency of the Department, and eventually part of the Maritime and Coastguard Agency.

[46] "Accident" includes the loss, stranding, abandonment of or damage to a ship: Merchant Shipping Act 1995, s.137(9).

[47] Merchant Shipping Act 1995, s.137(1).

[48] This includes, in relation to the ship to or on which an accident has occurred, the owner at the time of the accident (Merchant Shipping Act 1995, s.137(9)), thereby preventing such an owner from avoiding liability by abandoning or attempting to transfer ownership or control before a direction is given under the section.

[49] Merchant Shipping Act 1995, s.137(2).

[50] Merchant Shipping Act 1995, s.137(3).

Governing Law

specified area or locality; that the ship is not to be moved to a specified place or area, or over a specified route; that any oil or other cargo is or is not to be unloaded or discharged; or that specified salvage measures are or are not to be taken.[51] If he believes that these powers are or have proved to be inadequate, the Secretary (or anyone authorised by him[52]) may, as respects the ship or its cargo, take any action of any kind whatsoever.[53] In particular, he may: take such action as he has power to direct to be taken; undertake operations for the sinking or destruction of the ship, or any part of it, of a kind which is not within the means of any person to whom he can give directions; and/or undertake operations which involve taking over control of the ship.[54]

Every person concerned with compliance with directions given or action taken under the Merchant Shipping Act 1995, s.137 must use his best endeavours to avoid any risk to human life.[55] Furthermore, it is an offence not to comply with any requirement of a direction given under section 137.[56] Compensation is not payable for loss suffered as a result of the lawful exercise of powers under section 137, though such loss is insurable.[57] However, if any action[58] taken by virtue of section 137[59] was not reasonably necessary to prevent or reduce oil pollution or was such that the good it did or was likely to do was disproportionately less than the expense incurred or damage suffered as a result of the action, a person thereby incurring expense or suffering damage is entitled to recover compensation from the Secretary of State.[60] 71

Governing Law

The law governing a dispute is determined by the principles and rules of the conflict of laws.[61] Unless it is pleaded that foreign law governs the question at issue, the English *lex fori* is automatically applied. Until the recent implementation of the International Salvage Convention 1989, the basic law governing salvage was the "common law" developed in the Admiralty Court and 72

---

[51] Merchant Shipping Act 1995, s.137(3).
[52] Merchant Shipping Act 1995, s.137(5). Following the recommendations in Lord Donaldson's Report on *Salvage and Intervention and their Command and Control* (Cm. 4193, 1999), these powers are delegated to an individual known as the "Secretary of State's Representative" ("SOSREP").
[53] Merchant Shipping Act 1995, s.137(4).
[54] Merchant Shipping Act 1995, s.137(4).
[55] Merchant Shipping Act 1995, s.137(6).
[56] Merchant Shipping Act 1995, s.139.
[57] See, *e.g.* the Institute Time Clauses (Hulls) 1/10/83, cl. 7; Institute Time Clauses (Hulls) 1/11/95, cl. 7; Institute Voyage Clauses (Hulls) 1/10/83, cl. 5 (the pollution hazard clause).
[58] Including compliance with a direction not to take some specified action: Merchant Shipping Act 1995, s.138(3).
[59] More specifically, "any action duly taken by a person in pursuance of a direction given to him under section 137, or any action taken under section 137(4) or (5)": Merchant Shipping Act 1995, s.138(1).
[60] Merchant Shipping Act 1995, s.138(1). In considering whether this subsection applies, account shall be taken of: the extent and risk of oil pollution if the action had not been taken; the likelihood of the action being ineffective; and the extent of the damage which has been caused by the action (Merchant Shipping Act 1995, s.138(2)). Jurisdiction to hear and determine any claim arising under s.138 falls within the Admiralty jurisdiction of the High Court and the Court of Session: Merchant Shipping Act 1995, s.138(4).
[61] See generally *Dicey & Morris*.

as amended by statute,[62] matters not falling within Admiralty law would in principle be governed by the common law proper.[63] Where it is pleaded and found that a foreign law applies, that law should be given effect. However whether the prima facie applicable law is English or foreign, it may be subject to contractual provision; or it may be subject to statutory provision, which may itself be displaced by contract unless the statute is mandatory.

73   Though, given their international character, maritime cases normally provide a plentiful source of material on the conflict of laws, they have not done so in cases of salvage. To a very large extent this must be because of London's leading position as a forum for the settlement of issues of maritime law and the substantial practice, in modern times at least, of using Lloyd's Form, under which it is agreed that issues will be determined by arbitration in London,[64] and that the agreement and the arbitration will be governed by English law.[65] Moreover, international unification of salvage law has been promoted this century by widespread acceptance of the Brussels Salvage Convention 1910. It is therefore reasonable to observe that

> "maritime law has, in this instance, found its own solution of questions of conflict and it would seem that no useful purpose is served by the introduction of rules of conflict into questions which are so essentially international in character that conflicts are best solved by the process of unification of the law."[66]

Unfortunately, the desirability of a unified approach to conflicts problems cannot prevent their surfacing if they in fact exist, the possibility of which may be exploited if it is recognised. Certainly, international uniformity is diminished if the Brussels Salvage Convention 1910 is not completely superseded by the 1989 Convention, which in any event has a fractured application where States parties implement it subject to reservations.

74   In practice, if a Conflicts problem were to arise, it would be in the unusual case where a party contests jurisdiction. Article 2 of the Convention states that "This Convention applies whenever judicial or arbitral proceedings[67] relating

---

[62] See *ante*, §15.
[63] *e.g.* in respect of services not governed by salvage law.
[64] LOF 1995, cl. 1(c); LOF 2000, cl. I.
[65] LOF 1995, cl. 1(g); LOF 2000, cl. J.
[66] H.C. Gutteridge and K. Lipstein, "Conflict of Laws in Matters of Unjustifiable Enrichment" (1941) 7 C.L.J. 80, 82–83. This observation is the full extent of the discussion on salvage in L.A. Collins (ed.), *Dicey & Morris on the Conflict of Laws* (12th ed., 1993), p. 1478. See further J. Bird, "Choice of Law", Chap. 3 of F.D. Rose (ed.), *Restitution and the Conflict of Laws* (Mansfield Press, Oxford, 1995), p. 82.
[67] For the purposes of the Merchant Shipping Act 1995, "judicial proceedings" are defined in Sched. 11, Pt II, para. 6, as follows:
"References in the Convention to judicial proceedings are references to proceedings—
(a) in England and Wales, in the High Court or the county court;
(b) in Scotland, in the Court of Session or in the sheriff court;
(c) in Northern Ireland, in the High Court;
and any reference to the tribunal having jurisdiction (so far as it refers to judicial proceedings) shall be construed accordingly."

to matters dealt with in the Convention are brought in a State Party." Applied literally, this would enable a claimant to enforce the Convention by the mere act of instituting such proceedings. This would not be a legitimate means of giving the Convention effect internationally. Article 2 must be subject to the *lex fori*'s recognition that the tribunal has jurisdiction under its normal jurisdictional rules. If it does not have jurisdiction, an English tribunal will not be required to speculate on the applicable law. If it does have jurisdiction, the Merchant Shipping Act 1995 settles the question, for Article 2 of the Convention expressly stipulates that the Convention applies to matters with which it deals, and the Act has the force of law.[68]

If it were successfully argued that the law applicable to a question of salvage was not governed by the Convention then, on the basis that salvage is part of the law of restitution for unjust enrichment and therefore subject to its conflicts rules, the proper law should be the law of the place of enrichment, *i.e.* the law of the place where the salvee benefitted from the salvage service.[69]

The potential necessity of having to work out which law governs a question of salvage is in practice reduced (though not eliminated) by two factors. First, the widely used Lloyd's Form is stated to be governed by English law. LOF 1995 states that: "This Agreement and Arbitration thereunder shall except as otherwise provided by governed by the law of England, including the English law of salvage."[70] LOF 2000 provides that: "This agreement and any arbitration hereunder shall be governed by English law."[71]

75

Secondly, the International Salvage Convention 1989 has the force of law[72] in the United Kingdom.[73] The Convention applies whenever judicial or arbitral proceedings[74] relating to matters dealt with in the Convention are brought in a State party.[75]

76

The Convention provides for the possibility of a proper law other than English law in Article 15.2, which states that the apportionment of a salvage reward between the owner, master and other persons in the service of each salving vessel shall be determined by the law of the flag of that vessel; but, if the salvage has not been carried out from a vessel, the apportionment shall be determined by the law governing the contract between the salvor and his servants.[76] Furthermore, the extent to which a public authority under a duty to

---

[68] s.224(1).
[69] See further J. Bird and R. Stevens, Chaps. 3 and 5 of F.D. Rose (ed.), *Restitution and the Conflict of Laws* (Mansfield Press, Oxford, 1995).
[70] LOF 1995, cl. 1(g).
[71] LOF 2000, cl. J (headed "Governing Law").
[72] On the effect of a statute's having "the force of law", see *The Hollandia* [1983] 1 A.C. 565.
[73] Merchant Shipping Act 1995, s.224(1).
[74] For the purposes of the Merchant Shipping Act 1995, "judicial proceedings" are defined *ibid.*, Sched. 11, Pt II, para. 6: see *ante*, § 74n.
[75] Art. 2.
[76] For the English law on apportionment, see *post*, Chap. 17.

perform salvage operations may avail itself of the rights and remedies provided for in the Convention shall be determined by the law of the State where such authority is situated.[77]

77 However, the standardising effect of Lloyd's Form and of the 1989 Convention is subject to the parties' general ability to agree otherwise (*i.e.* that a foreign law shall apply).[78] Thus, Article 6.1 of the Convention provides that: "This Convention shall apply to any salvage operations save to the extent that a contract provides expressly or by implication." Article 6.1, therefore, safeguards the use of standard form contracts such as Lloyd's Form where parties so agree. Indeed, since it is sufficient for "*a* contract" to provide otherwise, it is not necessary for such contrary provision to be in a salvage contract; it may be in a charterparty or contract for the carriage of goods by sea.[79] However, the ability to contract out of the general law or of the Convention is qualified. In particular, nothing in Article 6 shall effect the application of Article 7 (annulling or modifying "unfair" contracts)[80] or[81] duties to prevent or minimise damage to the environment.[82] Moreover, the wording of Article 6.1 suggests that provisions of the Convention may not be excluded merely because the contract is inconsistent with it; it may be necessary for the contract expressly or impliedly to exclude the Convention as such.

Contract and the general law of salvage

78 The rights and obligations of parties to a salvage operation arise in principle from the maritime law, without the necessity of a contract. Where the parties' relationship is governed by contract, the question arises: whether the general law of salvage applies to the contract so far as it is not excluded by the terms of the contract; or whether the general law of salvage is inapplicable except in so far as it is incorporated into the contract, whether expressly or by implication. Since the original purpose of Lloyd's Form was not to provide a self-contained regime governing the parties' relationship but to provide for arbitration as the means of determining their rights and liabilities (whatever they might be), it seems correct to state that "it provides for salvage remuneration to be fixed by an independent arbitrator *in accordance with the principles of the English law of salvage*".[83]

However, in *The Unique Mariner (No. 2)*[84] Brandon J. stated that the rights and obligations of parties to a Lloyd's Form contract are governed by the terms, express or implied, of that contract but that the general maritime law of salvage only applies in so far as it is expressly or impliedly incorporated into

---

[77] International Salvage Convention 1989, Art. 5.3.
[78] In the case of Lloyd's Form, see *supra*, §75.
[79] See *post*, Chap. 9.
[80] See *post*, Chap. 9.
[81] The Convention erroneously uses the word "nor".
[82] See *post*, Chap. 5.
[83] *The Pa Mar* [1999] 1 Lloyd's Rep. 338, 361, *per* Clarke J., adopting the words of John Willmer, Q.C., the Lloyd's appeal arbitrator (emphasis added).
[84] [1979] 1 Lloyd's Rep. 37.

such contract.[85] Brandon J. followed Lord Diplock's approach in *The Tojo Maru*[86] that the proper approach to determine the obligations of contractors under Lloyd's Form is to consider, first, what would be the salvage contractor's liability under the general English law of contract and then to examine what, if any, differences flow, either in principle or on the authority of previous decisions, from the special characteristics of salvage services.

It is manifestly right that, so far as the contract makes express provision, the terms of the contract must prevail; and successive revisions of Lloyd's Form have made increasing provision for the content of the contract beyond the basic scheme for arbitration, particularly with a view to altering the position which would apply at common law. But it is not a necessary consequence that the contract should prima facie supersede the common law entirely; this, it is suggested, is neither the intention behind Lloyd's Form nor the true position at common law. 79

The opposite approach is taken by the International Salvage Convention 1989, Art. 6.1[87] of which provides that the terms of the Convention "shall apply to any salvage operations save to the extent that a contract otherwise provides expressly or by implication." Article 6.1 therefore gives effect for most practical purposes to a general rule that the the general maritime law of salvage, so far as it is contained in the Convention, prevails except to the extent that it is excluded. So far as an issue is not dealt with by the Convention and the parties' relationship is not governed by contract,[88] the common law of salvage will continue to apply. This would normally also be the case where the relationship between parties is governed by a contract; but, if the approach of Brandon J. in *The Unique Mariner (No. 2)*[89] is applied, the terms of the Convention (as modified by the contract) and of the contract (prima facie excluding the common law) will form a complete code governing the relationship of parties to a salvage contract. 80

Extent of application of the International Salvage Convention 1989

The International Salvage Convention 1989 applies between the States parties[90] to it. Their treaty obligations require them to give effect to the 81

---

[85] *ibid.*, 50–51. *The Beaverford (Owners) v. The Kafiristan (Owners)* [1938] A.C. 136, 144–145, 153–154, *per* Lord Wright.

[86] [1972] A.C. 242, 292, *per* Lord Diplock; followed in *The Unique Mariner (No. 2)* [1979] 1 Lloyd's Rep. 37, 50–51.

[87] Quoted *ante*, § 77.

[88] Which is, of course, nowadays rare.

[89] *Supra*, § 78.

[90] An Order in Council made for the purpose of declaring that a specified State is a party to the Convention in respect of a specified country or territory shall, subject to any subsequent such Order, be conclusive evidence of the fact: Merchant Shipping Act 1995, s.224(2), Sched. 11, Pt II, para. 7. The term "State party" appears in Arts 2, 10.2, 11, 13.2 and 27 of the Convention. Since there is no "State party" to a Convention until it comes into force internationally, that description in U.K. legislation has been specifically extended to the U.K. in relation to the period between the Convention's municipal and international effectiveness: Merchant Shipping Act 1995, s.224(6).

Convention municipally, the extent to which they do so being a matter of public international law rather than for domestic tribunals. The Convention itself expressly permits departure from its basic provisions. An important method by which this may occur is an intrinsic part of the Convention: contrary contractual provision.[91] Other departures are effective to the extent that a State party has availed itself of reservations permitted to the Convention Article 30.1 of the Convention ("Reservation")[92] provides[93]:

> "Any State may, at the time of signature, ratification, acceptance, approval or accession, reserve the right not to apply the provisions of this Convention:
> (a) when the salvage operation takes place in inland waters and all vessels involved are of inland navigation;
> (b) when the salvage operation takes place in inland waters and no vessel is involved;
> (c) when all interested parties are nationals of that State;
> (d) when the property involved is maritime cultural property of prehistoric, archaeological or historic interest and is situated on the sea-bed."

On deposit of its instrument of ratification with the IMO, the United Kingdom exercised its option to make the reservations (a), (b) and (d) permitted by Article 30.1, but not (c). The United Kingdom's entitlement to give effect to these reservations has so far been exercised in relation to (a) and (b)[94] and remains to be exercised in relation to (d).

Interpretation of the International Salvage Convention 1989

Interpretation of statutes

82   The main point to be borne in mind when considering a statute is that (subject to overriding European Union law, which is currently irrelevant to the present discussion) Parliament is supreme and its legislation must be given effect. Unfortunately, however, this is not necessarily a straightforward process, given the different methods available for discovering the intention of Parliament and/or for achieving a just result within the framework of the legislation.[95]

[91] See Art. 6.1; *post*, Chap. 12.
[92] Art. 30 as such is not directly reproduced in the Merchant Shipping Act 1995. Given that it is concerned with decisions to be made prior to, and the terms of, the Convention's implementation, direct inclusion would have been inappropriate. Art. 30.1(a)–(b) is, however, expressly given effect in the Merchant Shipping Act 1995, s.224(2), Sched. 11., Pt II, para. 2(1): see *post*, §§ 369–374.
[93] Reservations made at the time of signature are subject to confirmation upon ratification, acceptance or approval: Art. 30.2. Any State which has made a reservation to the Convention may withdraw it in accordance with Art. 30.2.
[94] Merchant Shipping Act 1995, s.224(2), Sched. 11, Pt II, para. 2(1). See *post*, Chap. 12.
[95] See F.A.R. Bennion, *Statutory Interpretation: A Code* (3rd ed., Butterworths, London, 1992).

Interpretation of the International Salvage Convention 1989

Where a statute codifies the law, there are two approaches to the role of the pre-existing law. One is to ignore the previous law and simply to attempt to give effect to the words of the statute. Given the primacy of statute law, this makes sense where the terms of the statute appear to differ from the common law.[96] However, whether or not this approach is correct in principle, it is of course insufficient where the words of the statute do not yield a clear answer. The second approach helps to overcome that difficulty and to avoid wasting accumulated wisdom. It permits reference to the prior law.

There are several possible reasons for legislation. Thus, the Merchant Shipping Act 1995 consolidates the merchant shipping legislation, including the enacted International Salvage Convention 1989, which in part codifies and declares the common law of salvage. However, the primary reason for legislation is to change the law, in which case resort may legitimately be had to the previous law to demonstrate how the position has altered or how a particular problem could sensibly be resolved but *ex hypothesi* not to dictate how the new law should be applied.

Interpretation of international conventions[97]

International conventions are binding between the parties to them in public international law but become effective in municipal law through domestic legislation.[98] There may, therefore, be an inclination to interpret the terms of the enacting statute simply as a piece of domestic legislation. Indeed, it has been common for international conventions to be rewritten in local style for municipal implementation; and a convention may, as in the case of the International Salvage Convention 1989, expressly give States parties licence to make their own decisions on how some of its provisions may be implemented, in which case a localised attitude to the relevant provision may well be appropriate. However, although the primary duty of the court is to give effect to the act of the Parliament of the United Kingdom, rather than implement its international Treaty obligations, where Parliament's intention is to give effect to those obligations, it follows that the enacting statute should be construed so as to do so. This requires sensitivity to the fact that the convention may well not have been drafted in the way that English statutes are normally drafted, and that it is intended to be applied in different legal systems in accordance with the consensus arrived at by the parties to the Convention. The more insular approach to construction followed by English courts when the United Kingdom played a more dominant role in international shipping has therefore given way to a broader, more internationalist approach. Interpretation of the provisions of an international convention should not be unduly

83

---

[96] In principle, of course, a codifying statute should simply repeat the common law; though, of course, one of its aims may be to clarify the law where the common law is unclear.

[97] See N.J.J. Gaskell, "The Interpretation of Maritime Conventions at Common Law", in J.P. Gardner (ed.), *United Kingdom Law in the 1990s* (1990).

[98] Indeed, the Carriage of Goods by Sea Act 1924 enacted the Hague Rules into English Law prior to the final formulation of the Brussels International Convention for the Unification of Certain Rules of Law Relating to Bills of Lading 1924. See now the Carriage of Goods by Sea Act 1971.

Nature of the Subject

literalist or constrained by technical rules of English law or English legal precedent but should be on broad principles of general acceptance so as to achieve a uniform approach internationally in giving effect to the intentions and terms of the convention[99] and the United Kingdom's obligations thereunder,[1] so far as that is not inconsistent with the words of the statute.[2]

Reference to previous domestic law

84 There may be a temptation for English lawyers in particular to rely on previous English law in interpreting the 1989 Convention. It is their native law, they are familiar with it and, by virtue of the number of salvage cases traditionally determined in England and according to English law, it has served as a kind of international law of salvage. However, the importance of recognising the temptation is, of course, not to justify submission to it but to enable it to be resisted.

It is permissible to trace statutory provisions back through their legislative antecedents[3] and it has been the practice to assume that words used in the English language which have already in the particular context received judicial interpretation may be presumed to be used in the sense judicially imputed to them.[4] However, these guidelines are of limited utility in relation to the terms of the International Salvage Convention 1989 and can in any case only be of use so far as they assist in the object of giving effect to the legislation in question.

85 The 1989 Convention derives in part from the Brussels Salvage Convention 1910. A large part of the 1910 Convention reflected then current English law and so was not enacted in the United Kingdom; other parts were enacted in provisions which have become part of the Merchant Shipping Act 1995. So far as provisions of the Convention are traceable to pre-existing English law, it should be possible to refer to that law to assist in interpreting the Convention. However, it will be necessary to take account of the fact that English salvage law and practice may have evolved differently after 1910 from how it would have developed if the 1910 Convention had applied to it, and to the fact that the style and content of the 1989 Convention may produce substantive differences from previous formulations of the law.

---

[99] *Stag Line Ltd v. Foscolo Mango & Co. Ltd* [1932] A.C. 328, 350, *per* Lord Macmillan; *James Buchanan & Co. Ltd* [1978] A.C. 141, 152, *per* Lord Wilberforce; *Samick Lines Co. Ltd v. Owners of the Antonis P. Lemos (The Antonis P. Lemos)* [1985] A.C. 711, 717, 725–726. See also *Semco Salvage and Marine Pte Ltd v. Lancer Navigation Co. Ltd (The Nagasaki Spirit)* [1997] A.C. 455, 468–471, *per* Lord Mustill.

[1] *Salomon v. Customs & Excise Commissioners* [1967] 2 Q.B. 116; *Post Office v. Estuary Radio Ltd* [1968] 2 Q.B. 740; *The Norwhale* [1975] 1 Q.B. 589, 598; *The Escherheim; The Jade* [1976] 1 W.L.R. 430, 436.

[2] *The Escherheim; The Jade* [1976] 1 W.L.R. 430, 436.

[3] See *Gatoil International Inc. v. Arkwright-Boston Manufacturers Mutual Insurance Co. (The Sandrina)* [1985] A.C. 255; *The River Rima* [1988] 1 W.L.R. 758.

[4] *Stag Line Ltd v. Foscolo Mango & Co. Ltd* [1932] A.C. 328, 343, *per* Lord Atkin. *cf. The Norman* [1960] 1 Lloyd's Rep. 1.

Interpretation of the International Salvage Convention 1989

Reference to preparatory works

The English courts have traditionally resisted resort to extra-statutory **86**
materials in interpreting Acts of Parliament but it has now been held that,

> "subject to any question of Parliamentary privilege, the rule excluding reference to Parliamentary material as an aid to statutory construction should be relaxed so as to permit such reference where
> (a) legislation was ambiguous or obscure or led to absurdity,
> (b) the material relied upon consisted of one or more statements by a Minister or other promoter of the Bill together if necessary with such other Parliamentary material as was necessary to understand such statements and their effect and
> (c) the statements relied upon were clear."[5]

The ability to consult the *Hansard* report of Parliamentary debates is, however, of little practical importance so far as the International Salvage Convention 1989 is concerned, as they do little to elaborate on the scope of its provisions.

"It is now fully established that when an Act of Parliament is passed so as **87**
to give effect to an International Convention, we can look at the Convention so as to help us to construe the Act . . . and this is so even though the Act of Parliament does not mention the Convention."[6] So far as the International Salvage Convention 1989 is concerned, this observation is, of course, almost superfluous, as the Convention is largely reproduced in a Schedule to the Merchant Shipping Act 1995 itself.

More important in this situation, therefore, is the ability to consult works **88**
which are preparatory to the Convention. As Lord Wilberforce has put it[7]:

> "the use of *travaux préparatoires* in the interpretation of treaties should be cautious . . . [but] . . . there may be cases where such *travaux préparatoires* can profitably be used. These cases should be rare, and only where two conditions are fulfilled, first, that the material involved is public and accessible, and secondly, that the *travaux préparatoires* clearly and indisputably point to a definite legislative intention."

---

[5] *Pepper (Inspector of Taxes) v. Hart* [1993] A.C. 593 (the words quoted appear in the headnote).
[6] *The Banco* [1971] P. 137, 151E, per Lord Denning M.R. See also *ibid.*, 157D–F (Megaw L.J.), 161B (Cairns L.J.); *Salomon v. Customs & Excise Commissioners* [1967] 2 Q.B. 116; *Post Office v. Estuary Radio Ltd* [1968] 2 Q.B. 740.
[7] *Fothergill v. Monarch Airlines Ltd* [1981] A.C. 251, 278. See also *Gatoil International Inc. v. Arkwright-Boston Manufacturers Mutual Insurance Co. (The Sandrina)* [1985] A.C. 255, especially 263.

Nature of the Subject

Five categories of *travaux préparatoires* for the International Salvage Convention 1989 can be identified in the following, descending, order of importance[8]: (i) the proceedings of the 1989 Diplomatic Conference in London at which the text of the Convention was finalised; (ii) the proceedings of the Legal Committee of the International Maritime Organisation (an inter-governmental body) 1983–1988, discussing the Draft Convention formulated in Montreal in 1981 by the Comité Maritime International (a private, non-governmental body)[9]; (iii) the proceedings of the CMI from 1978–1981 leading up to the Montreal Draft[10]; (iv) the Brussels Salvage Convention of 1910, which the 1989 Convention superseded; and (v) the *travaux préparatoires* of the Brussels Convention 1910.[11]

---

[8] See Gaskell, 21–242.
[9] The IMO proceedings are being edited for publication in conjunction with the IMO by the Institute of Maritime Law of the University of Southampton.
[10] In particular, a Report was prepared on behalf of the CMI and submitted to the IMO Legal Committee at its 52nd session in 1984: see LEG 52/4, 3 July, 1984. See *post*, App. 32.
[11] See generally Shaw [1996] L.M.C.L.Q. 202.

CHAPTER 2

HISTORY

General

The history of the development of English law and the English judicial system is generally well-known but merits some brief restatement here for readers who may be unfamiliar with it.[1] The most ancient source of English law is the common law, developed in different ways in different localities but systematised into a unified body of law by the common law courts, principally the Courts of King's (or Queen's) Bench, Common Pleas and Exchequer. At times, the rules of common law administered in these courts were perceived to be insufficient, overly rigid or unjust. Amelioration of these difficulties was essayed by the development of a collateral system of more flexible rules of "equity" in the High Court of Chancery. These rules of common law *stricto sensu* and equity together constitute the home-grown common law of England as declared and developed by the judges.

The English common law was successfully exported to many of the countries once forming part of the British Empire. It is distinguishable from that other great system of law, the Roman civil law. Roman law has also provided the foundation of the present municipal law of many countries, including most of the continent of Europe and Scotland.[2] Yet, despite the Roman conquest, it has had little influence on English law, except by derivation through the mediaeval canon lawyers. After the Reformation, their descendants continued their established practice in ecclesiastical and Admiralty matters, which were

89

---

[1] A fuller study than can be attempted here in outline is most rewarding. Wiswall, *The Development of Admiralty Jurisdiction and Practice since 1800* (1970), has provided a helpful introduction and some useful references. See also the discussion in *The Goring* [1987] Q.B. 687 CA, and [1988] 1 A.C. 831.

[2] The maritime laws of England and Scotland are in fact treated as the same. See *Currie v. M'Knight* [1897] A.C. 97, 101–102, *per* Lord Halsbury L.C.:

"I cannot doubt that on such [maritime] questions it is the law of Great Britain that prevails, and that Scottish Admiralty Courts and English Admiralty Courts administer the same law. The Admiralty law, as we know it, differs from the common law of England, and the common law of Scotland differs from the common law of England. But the reason is obvious—the laws of England and Scotland were derived from different sources in respect of these two branches of the law. The Admiralty laws were derived both by Scotland and England from the same source; and as it is said by no mean authority that the Admiralty law was derived from the laws of Oleron, supplemented by the civil law, it would be strange as well as in the highest degree inconvenient if a different maritime law prevailed in two different parts of the same island."

See also *Watson v. RCA Victor Company Inc.* (1934) 50 Ll.L. Rep. 77, 81.

governed by the civil law in which its practitioners, who congregated in Doctors' Commons, were required to be proficient.

90   The Crown, which originally dealt with maritime affairs, delegated them to the Lord High Admiral. He in turn appointed a "Deputy" or "Lieutenant" to adjudicate on offences and disputes.[3] Thus was established an Admiral's Court, with general jurisdiction over Admiralty matters, although vice-admirals and certain other courts had a localised jurisdiction in Admiralty.[4]

The most prominent feature of the relationship between the Admiralty Court and the common law courts was the attempts of the latter to restrain the encroachment on their province of the former. They achieved this and more.

91   By statute, the Admiral's jurisdiction was restricted to things done upon the sea[5]; all matters which arose within the body of a county, whether on land or on water and including questions concerning wreck, were declared to be triable only at common law,[6] and penalties were imposed on litigants wrongly suing in Admiralty.[7] Parliament thus restricted by reference to locality the original jurisdiction of the Admiralty Court.[8] It also enabled the common law courts to help themselves, by means of statutory interpretation. Thus, "wreck" under the Act of 1391[9] was in *Sir Henry Constable's Case*[10] held to encompass that which was cast at ebb tide upon the shelf below the flood mark, the Admiral having previously exercised jurisdiction below the high-water mark. Services rendered not on the high seas[11] but within the body of a county[12]

---

[3] The Admiralty Judge was appointed as the Deputy of the Queen in her Office of Admiralty until 1875, when he became not formally the Admiralty Judge but simply one of Her Majesty's Judges, along with other High Court Judges, following the reforms of the Judicature Acts: see *post*, §§ 96–98. However, Sir Robert Phillimore (appointed 1867) continued to be known as such rather than as Phillimore J. (which he became in 1875 until his retirement in 1883).

[4] None of these, not even the High Court of Admiralty, as it formally became, were, by 1713 at least, a Court of Record.

[5] 13 Ric. II, st.1, c.5 (1389).

[6] 15 Ric. II, c.3 (1391).

[7] 2 Hen. IV, c.11 (1400).

[8] See, however, *Fairless v. Thorsen, The Good Intent and The Prince Christian* (1774) Mars. Ad. Cas. 130, from which it appears that the court would exercise jurisdiction, in certain cases, when the claim arose in areas where no prohibition had previously issued from the common law courts. Once a prohibition had issued (see *post*, §92), the court seems to have regarded the area as permanently out of its jurisdiction; see *The Eleanor* (1805) 6 C. Rob. 39, 40, *per* Lord Stowell. As to disregard of the statutes in very early days, see *Select Pleas in the Court of Admiralty* (Selden Society), Vol. I, Introduction.

[9] *Supra*, n. 6.

[10] *Constable v. Gamble (Sir Henry Constable's Case)* (1601) 5 Co. Rep. 106a.

[11] "The expression 'high seas,' when used with reference to the jurisdiction of the Court of Admiralty, includes all oceans, seas, bays, channels, rivers, creeks, and waters below low-water mark, and where great ships could go, with the exception only of such parts of such oceans, &c., as were within the body of same county:" *The Mecca* [1895] P. 95, 107, *per* Lindley L.J.

[12] "Body of a county" originally meant above low-water mark in an English county, but later "that arm or branch of the sea which is within the *fauces terrae* where a man may reasonably discerne between shore and shore is, or at least may be, within the body of a county": Hale, *De Jure Maris*, Harg. Law Tracts, p. 10. This view prevailed; thus, the Solent and Southampton Water, most of the Thames estuary, and the River Humber, were later held to be within the body of a county and therefore not within the jurisdiction of the Court of Admiralty.

General

gave no right to reward in the Admiralty Court until the nineteenth century, although there were rights to reward for services within the body of a county under various statutes which could be enforced within the framework of the common law.[13]

The common law courts also usurped jurisdiction over some Admiralty questions by means of legal fictions, so that certain maritime matters were deemed to have occurred within the jurisdiction of the common law courts. The common law courts maintained their position by the issue of writs of prohibition, preventing the trial at Admiralty of matters they deemed to be within their own jurisdiction.[14] 92

The implications of this tension between the courts so far as the law of salvage is concerned are considered in a little more detail below. It may be noted at this stage, however, that the jurisdiction of the Admiralty Court was not shaped simply by judge-made law, but also by statute law. Acts of Parliament have been instrumental, as will be seen, not only in altering the range of matters to be dealt with in Admiralty but also in re-designating which courts would deal with those matters. In particular, in the nineteenth century, Parliament gave authority in salvage matters to inferior courts.[15] 93

The nineteenth century was in many ways the most notable in the history of Admiralty law and practice. On the legal side, the century came in with a new Admiralty Judge, Sir William Scott, later Lord Stowell,[16] who received a great deal of prize work from the early nineteenth-century European and American wars. This, together with the growth in regular law reporting, enabled him to establish the basis of much modern Admiralty law, particularly of salvage and prize, by his elucidation of its governing principles—work which was ably continued by his successors in the High Court of Admiralty.[17] 94

In parallel with the systematisation of the law of Admiralty, its practice and procedure were subjected to substantial reform which coincidentally (as with the shift from written to oral evidence) wore down some of the distinctions between the common law and Admiralty Courts. 95

The Court of Probate Act of 1857 and the Matrimonial Causes Act 1857 contained the seeds of much to come and presaged the destruction of the

---

[13] See *post*, §§110–123.
[14] See *supra*, n. 8. Use was made of prohibition even at the eve of the formal abolition of the separate Admiralty and common law courts. See, *e.g. Smith v. Brown* (1871) L.R. 6 Q.B. 729.
[15] See further *post*, §117.
[16] Sir William Scott, Admiralty Judge 1798–1827; created Lord Stowell 1821. See E. S. Roscoe, *Lord Stowell: His Life and the Development of English Prize Law* (Constable, London, 1916); H. J. Bourguignon, *Sir William Scott, Lord Stowell* (CUP, Cambridge, 1987).
[17] Sir Christopher Robinson, 1828–1833; Sir John Nicholl, 1833–1838; Dr Stephen Lushington, 1838–1867; Sir Robert Phillimore, 1867–1875 (then Phillimore J. 1875–1883: see *supra*, n. 3). On Dr Lushington, see S. M. Waddams, "Dr Lushington's Contribution to the Law of Maritime Salvage (1838–67)" [1989] L.M.C.L.Q. 59; *Law, Politics and the Church of England: The Career of Stephen Lushington, 1782–1873* (CUP, Cambridge, 1992).

preservation of the practice of civil law and non-civil law matters between, on the one hand, the doctors[18] and proctors of the civil law courts and, on the other, the attorneys and solicitors of the common law courts, the financial implications of which for the practitioners had caused so much rivalry between the different courts. The ecclesiastical courts lost their jurisdiction over wills, intestacies and matrimonial matters to new courts, the Court of Probate and the Court for Divorce and Matrimonial Causes. Shortly afterwards, civilians and non-civilians were for the most part permitted to practice in each others' courts.[19] This would not have necessarily disabled the civilians from retaining their identity and surviving successfully. But the 1857 Act expressly permitted the dissolution of Doctors' Commons, in which the civilians had congregated and practised, and the distribution of its property amongst its members. By 1860, this had been done and the Admiralty Registry and sittings of the Admiralty Court had moved from the premises.

96 Within two decades, the High Court of Admiralty itself ceased its independent existence, and the Admiralty Court became completely disassociated from and independent of the Admiralty.[20] Under the Judicature Acts 1873–1975, a new Supreme Court of Judicature was established, composed of a High Court of Justice and a Court of Appeal. The separate Courts of Chancery, Queen's Bench, Common Pleas, Exchequer and Admiralty, along with other existing courts, were abolished and their functions transferred to five, then soon three, Divisions of the unified High Court. In practice, the work of the new Divisions was similar to that of the courts they replaced. The Chancery Division acquired the work of the Court of Chancery. The Queen's Bench, Common Pleas and Exchequer Divisions—combined into one Queen's Bench Division in 1880—replaced the common law courts. And the Probate, Divorce and Admiralty Division took over, and to a certain extent reunited, the work of the civil law based courts.[21]

97 Thus, shortly after the melting of the barrier between common law and civil law practitioners, the previously rival common law and Admiralty courts were merged into one High Court, with jurisdiction to try all matters. One of the most famous achievements of the legislation of the 1870s was the much vaunted fusion of the administration of law and equity whereby, having decided in principle what the rights of litigants were at common law, a judge became entitled, or even obliged, in all Divisions of the High Court to exercise his discretion to make his decision according to the rules of equity, which in cases of conflict were to prevail over those of the common law. The significance of the bringing together of the civil law courts with those of common

---

[18] Civil law advocates had to be Doctors of Civil Law of the Universities of Oxford or Cambridge.

[19] High Court of Admiralty Act 1859. The civilians retained their monopoly in ecclesiastical matters.

[20] But see Wiswall, p. 111.

[21] It is perhaps not inappropriate in a book dealing with the law of salvage and wreck to recall Sir A. P. Herbert's perception of the unified jurisdiction in the new Probate, Divorce and Admiralty Division as a general one over wrecks—of wills and marriages, as well as ships.

General

law and equity is less frequently remarked. It is not here a question of applying different systems of law to similar facts but of recognising that Admiralty law is basically concerned with different subject-matter from that dealt with elsewhere. Thus, having identified those matters, such as salvage, which properly fall within the Admiralty jurisdiction, the application of the civil law survives in providing the principles which govern the matter and the procedures, such as the action *in rem*, with which it can be dealt. Other matters which are not of their nature necessarily Admiralty matters, such as the effect on a contract (which happens to be a salvage contract) of some vitiating factor might be dealt with simply by applying the rules of common law and/or equity in any Division of the High Court, and even if a special rule developed at Admiralty were applicable.[22] In such a case, the fact that the contract was concerned with what was an otherwise Admiralty matter and might require consideration in the context of what was otherwise an Admiralty suit[23] would make it more convenient but not necessary that it be dealt with in Admiralty. In theory, matters of any description might be heard in any Division of the High Court, although in practice matters would be instituted in or transferred to the most appropriate Division.

Paradoxically, the Judicature Acts' policy of simplifying the judicial system complicated it in one important respect in Admiralty. Previously, appeals from the Admiralty Court went directly to the Privy Council,[24] whereas appeals from the courts of common law and equity went through two stages—to the Exchequer Chamber and to the Lords Justices in Chancery respectively, then to the House of Lords. The establishment of one Supreme Court of Judicature was designed to provide a single High Court, with first instance jurisdiction, and a single Court of Appeal, to assume the appellate jurisdiction of the Exchequer Chamber, Lords Justices in Chancery and Privy Council. Any further right of appeal to the House of Lords was originally abolished but, on an outcry by the House, then reinstituted, so that Admiralty cases acquired a second appeal stage which they had never previously had.[25] **98**

The grouping together of the subjects to be dealt with by the Probate, Divorce and Admiralty Division was explicable on historical grounds but neither manifestly appropriate nor necessary. In fact, Admiralty matters were ably dealt with in the Division because they were normally heard by an experienced Admiralty lawyer—albeit their monopoly over the development **99**

---

[22] See Chap. 9.
[23] According to the traditional terminology, procedure is by way of *action* at common law, but by *suit* in equity or in Admiralty. The Civil Procedure Rules now refer to *claims*.
[24] Since 1832. See the Judicial Committee Act 1833, ss 1–2 and the Privy Council Appeals Act 1832, s.3, which transferred to the Privy Council the jurisdiction of the High Court of Delegates over Admiralty and ecclesiastical appeals.
[25] At least this development prevented an Admiralty Judge from claiming not to be bound by a decision of the House of Lords. *cf. The Actaeon* (1853) 1 Spinks 176, 177.

of Admiralty law had disappeared, for another judge of the Division (or possibly of any other Division) who had little or no experience of Admiralty law might hear the case, and appellate judges most frequently had no Admiralty background.[26] Nautical assessors have for centuries been able to sit with and offer advice to judges on nautical matters, but the judge still had to decide on the law.

100 Other, non-Admiralty, maritime cases were conveniently dealt with in the Queen's Bench Division, along with other cases of a different nature factually but governed by similar principles of the general law of contract, tort, restitution and so on. Yet, even there, shipping cases were commonly dealt with in a distinct fashion. In 1895, a Commercial Court was created as part of the Queen's Bench Division by a resolution of the judges of that Division. Its actual purpose was to provide a more expeditious and less formal forum for hearing commercial causes. It thus became the regular court for determination of shipping cases of a non-Admiralty nature. Whereas the reasons for establishing the Commercial Court were not similarly applicable to Admiralty cases, its establishment made clear what was also clear in other areas, that specialist cases could be dealt with in a specialist court within the most appropriate Division. Indeed, proposals were mooted in the 1930s for a "Judge in Admiralty" of the King's Bench Division (after the abolition of the Probate, Divorce and Admiralty Division) to handle both Admiralty and commercial maritime cases, and, alternatively and more ambitiously, for the establishment of a fourth, Admiralty and Commercial, Division of the High Court, but nothing was done.[27]

101 Reallocation of Admiralty business came eventually after a general review of the judicial system and a tremendous expansion in family law work in the 1960s. Under the Administration of Justice Act 1970, the Probate, Divorce and Admiralty Division was replaced by a new Family Division. The probate work of the old Division was dispersed to the Chancery Division. For Admiralty matters, a new Admiralty Court was created as part of the Queen's Bench Division, acquiring the Admiralty work of the old Probate, Divorce and Admiralty Division (together with more commercial maritime matters which had been allocated to Admiralty jurisdiction by the Administration of Justice Act 1956).

102 This arrangement prevails today, the jurisdiction and procedure of the Admiralty Court currently being governed by the Supreme Court Act 1981[28] and the Civil Procedure Rules.[29]

---

[26] *cf.* the discussion of *The Cargo ex Schiller* (1877) 2 P.D. 145, *post*, §§ 284–288.
[27] See Wiswall, pp. 144–145.
[28] ss 20–24. See *post*, § 1224.
[29] CPR, Pt 49 and Practice Direction—Admiralty. These replace RSC, Ord. 75.

Admiralty jurisdiction

Introduction

Five aspects of the Admiralty Court's jurisdiction over Admiralty, and in particular salvage, matters, may be distinguished. First, the Admiralty Court's jurisdiction derives from two sources. Much of it derives from its original or *inherent* jurisdiction. But this has been altered by its *statutory* jurisdiction: on several occasions, Parliament has extended its jurisdiction—conferred new jurisdiction on it—or otherwise altered its jurisdiction. Secondly, the court's jurisdiction may be defined by reference to the locality over which it extends. The original jurisdiction of the High Court of Admiralty extended to the saving of property, and to the saving of life with property only when the services were rendered upon the high seas. Services within the body of a county gave no right to reward in the High Court of Admiralty until the nineteenth century. There were, however, rights to reward for services within the body of a county under various statutes which could be enforced within the framework of the common law. The distinction between the high seas and the body of a county is now of no more than historical interest. Legislation of the nineteenth century extended the original salvage jurisdiction of the High Court of Admiralty to include the body of a county.

Thirdly, jurisdiction may be defined according to function. If the judge is conducting the original hearing of the case, he exercises his instance jurisdiction. Alternatively, he may exercise an appellate or supervisory jurisdiction over the decisions of arbitrators. A court's jurisdiction may also be described by reference to the subject-matter of the case before it. Today, the Admiralty Court exercises a civil jurisdiction—one basically over claims between individuals. But it formerly exercised a limited criminal jurisdiction and moreover had a special jurisdiction of a military nature, in questions of prize—although it then sat as a distinct Prize Court (now part of the Queen's Bench Division), a function which is of minimal importance today. Finally, jurisdiction may be described according to the procedures and powers exercised. The Admiralty Court has, along with the common law courts, a jurisdiction *in personam*, over people. But it also has the uniquely civil law based jurisdiction *in rem*, over certain property.

However it originated, Admiralty jurisdiction today is placed firmly on a statutory basis. When the High Court of Admiralty was abolished and the unified High Court of Justice set up, the old Admiralty jurisdiction, inherent and statutory, was retained on a statutory basis by the Judicature Acts 1873–1875. These were superseded in turn by the Supreme Court of Judicature (Consolidation) Act 1925, the Administration of Justice Act 1956, and now the Supreme Court Act 1981.

Early jurisdiction over wreck

The earliest history of Admiralty jurisdiction so far as the subject-matter of this book is concerned relates to dealings with property which, through misfortune, had become wreck. The encouragement of efforts to prevent this fate and the determination of rewards for such efforts were matters that came into the picture at a later time.

In ancient times, wreck appears to have meant all shipwrecked goods, whether found at sea or cast up on land. As wreck, they belonged to the Crown.[30] However, by certain charters and by statute, the rights of the Crown were from an early date restricted to unclaimed wreck within those meanings. It was provided in 1275, by a statute worded to the effect that neither the ship nor anything in it could be adjudged wreck where a living being escaped therefrom, that, where the owner established his title, the goods were not to be called wreck and were to be handed to their owner on payment of salvage to those who had saved and kept them.[31]

106 In 1353, the first statute relating to salvage provided for jurisdiction of an essentially local character.[32] Jurisdiction of such nature was to continue for several centuries. The terms of the statute are, therefore, worth setting out here:

> "And in case that any Ships, going out of the said Realm and Lands, or coming to the same, by Tempest or other Misfortune, break upon the Sea Banks, and the Goods come to the Land, which may not be said Wreck,[33] they shall be presently without Fraud or evil Device delivered to the Merchants to whom the goods be, or to their servants, by such Proof as before is said,[34] paying to them that have saved and kept the same, a proper reward for their work[35]; that is to say, by the Discretion of the Sheriffs and Bailiffs, or other our Ministers, in Places Guildable, where other Lords have no Franchise, and by the Advice and Assent of four or six of the best or most sufficient discreet Men of the Country; and if that be within the Franchise of other Lords, then it shall be done by the Stewards and Bailiff, or Wardens of the same Franchises, and by the Advice of four or six discreet Men of the Country, as afore is said, without any delay."

---

[30] Statute de praerogativa regis, 17 Edw. II, c.11, temp. incert.

[31] Statute of Westminster I (1275). The wording of the Act was probably one of the factors leading to the enactment of later statutes aimed at those who wounded or killed or prevented persons leaving ships so that they drowned: see *post*, §§110 *et seq*. In 1276, the statute 4 Edw. I, st. 2, s.2, provided that coroners should inquire into cases of wreck and value the same. The Act of 1275 was repealed by the Statute Law Revision Act 1863.

[32] 27 Edw. III, c.13 (1353).

[33] See the Statute of Westminster I (1275).

[34] The Act had first dealt with cases of robbery of shipwrecked goods. The proof of ownership required in such cases and in salvage was "by his Marks, or by his Chart, or Cocket." In later times, at least, a cocket was an exporter's general entry outwards endorsed by the exporter and certified by an export officer. The word was an anglicised version of "*quo quietus est*," to signify that customs requirements had been met. The use of the form was not discontinued until 1853.

[35] The original wording is "payauntez a eux que les averont sauvez et gardez convenablement pur lour travaill" or "paiant a ceux qi les avont sauvez & gardez convenablement pr leur travaill." The word "travaill" means "work" or "labours." The translation in the book of statutes, "travel," does not take into account the alteration in the meaning of that word in the past 100 years or more, and to adhere to it would be to make the phrase almost meaningless at the present day.

The rights of the Crown to unclaimed wreck found on the high seas were 107
at an early date granted to the Admiral. These grants (more technically
described as civil droits of Admiralty) thus became proprietary rights or
perquisites of the Admiral. With the establishment of the Admiral's Court,
later the High Court of Admiralty, all wreck found at sea unclaimed or not,
came within the jurisdiction of that court, and it rewarded salvors.

In the course of time, however, the meaning of the word "wreck" altered.
Instead of meaning shipwrecked goods on sea or land belonging, because
unclaimed, to the Crown, it was restricted to goods cast up on land by the sea
and did not depend upon whether or not the Crown had a right to it. In many
areas of the coast, the original rights of the Crown to wreck of this kind, where
unclaimed by the owner, were the subject of piecemeal grants to lords of
manors and to towns.[36]

By the time of *Sir Henry Constable's Case*[37] in 1601, at least, the meaning 108
of wreck was firmly established and what had formerly been wreck at sea was
by then distinguished by the terms flotsam, jetsam and lagan or derelict. In
addition civil droits of Admiralty might also encompass *deodands*, that is,
personal chattels which were the immediate cause of a person's death or were
found upon a corpse floating on the sea or cast upon the shore. The right to
salvage for saving and keeping wreck was equally well established and
decisions as to ownership and the assessment of a proper reward in cases of
dispute appear to have been matters for justices of the peace, coroners, or local
courts according to the circumstances, depending upon who claimed to be
entitled to the goods, whether the original owner, the Crown, or grantee of
rights to unclaimed wreck being a lord of the manor in whose manor the goods
were cast up or a coast town with a local franchise court. Flotsam, jetsam,
lagan and derelict remained matters for the High Court of Admiralty, vice-
admirals and certain courts having a localised jurisdiction in Admiralty. The
courts of common law at Westminster do not appear to have been often
concerned with questions of salvage but the right to salvage was recognised
and the salvor's right was protected by a possessory lien which could be
pleaded in defence to an action of detinue or trover brought by the owner of
goods claiming their return.[38]

Extension of jurisdiction to preservation from shipwreck

Up to the first part of the eighteenth century, what may be called the land 109
jurisdiction, as opposed to the Admiralty jurisdiction, was concerned with

---

[36] Thus, today the Merchant Shipping Act 1995, s.241 provides that Her Majesty and Her Royal successors are entitled to all unclaimed wreck found in the U.K. or in U.K. waters except in places where Her Majesty or any of Her Royal predecessors has granted the right to any other person. In *Pierce v. Bemis (The Lusitania)* [1986] Q.B. 384, the Admiralty Judge held that the Crown had no rights to unclaimed wreck outside territorial waters.
[37] *Constable v. Gamble, Sir Henry Constable's Case* (1601) 5 Co.Rep. 106.
[38] See *post*, §§ 129 *et seq*. The doctrine of implied contract grew up later; and express contracts to pay for work and labour, made on the high seas, were probably not a matter for the common law courts until later, if they ever were.

wreck alone, and the Admiralty jurisdiction was concerned mainly if not entirely, with flotsam, jetsam, lagan and derelict. All these are the products or the consequences of shipwreck. Both jurisdictions were concerned with ownership and rights to salvage in cases of shipwrecked goods.

It is not known when the High Court of Admiralty began to reward salvors who rendered services, to ships and cargo, having as their object the *prevention* of disaster, or salvage in the modern sense.[39] It is certain, however, that in consequence of quarrels between that court and the courts of common law, its fortunes were at a low ebb by the end of the seventeenth century and that its jurisdiction had been excluded by prohibition from many waters, for example, estuaries, where ships might take refuge in storms. Once there, it was to the entire advantage of those on shore that the ship and cargo should become wreck, including those who had rights, as grantees from the Crown, to unclaimed wreck subject to payment of salvage, salvors who would be entitled to reward either from them or from the shipowner or his personal representatives if able to establish ownership, and all whose intentions were to plunder without regard to legal rights either of salvage or ownership. It is possible, too, that salvage in the modern sense was still in its infancy or unknown in the Admiralty Court, so that vessels whilst on the high seas but close in and in danger of shipwreck on land could not expect the assistance of salvors, who would receive no reward from that source for their efforts.

The Act of 1713

110 The legislature accordingly intervened to protect ships and their owners. It was intended by the Act 12 Anne, c.18 (1713), the first of a line of statutes which led up to the salvage provisions of the Merchant Shipping Act 1894, to prevent shipwreck, wherever possible, by providing for rewards to be paid for salvage services in the modern sense rendered on or near the coast, and for the assessment of such reward, in cases of dispute, by justices of the peace. The provisions of the Act, which, as will be seen,[40] actually had no connection with Admiralty jurisdiction, may be summarised as follows.

111 The 1713 Act referred first to the Statute of Westminster I (1275)[41] and to the complaints which had been made by British and foreign merchants that their ships and cargoes had been plundered on shore and when anything had been saved it had been swallowed up by exorbitant demands for salvage. In view of the losses to merchants and to the revenues of the Crown,[42] therefore, it was enacted that sheriffs, justices of the peace, customs officers and other public officers to whom application was made[43] should have power, when a

---

[39] Marsden, in *Select Pleas of the Admiralty*, suggests 1653, but this was an isolated case. Whether and if so to what extent the practice continued is at present a matter of doubt. There are cases of salvage of vessels, of a completely modern kind, at least as early as 1781, to be found in practitioners' notebooks amongst the Admiralty Court records in the Public Record Office.

[40] *Post*, §111.

[41] The wording of this Act referred to the escape of a living being from a shipwreck.

[42] Blackstone's *Commentaries* treated salvage under the heading revenue of the Crown. No mention was made of the jurisdiction of the High Court of Admiralty.

[43] See *Baring v. Day* (1806) 8 East 57; *The Happy Return* (1828) 2 Hagg. 198, 205.

ship or vessel was in danger of stranding or was stranded, to order the rendering of assistance to such ship or vessel in distress[44] by persons on shore[45] and also by any ship or vessel riding at anchor nearby,[46] whose master was to be bound to send boats to assist. For the encouragement of such persons, reasonable salvage was to be paid within 30 days to the master or commanding officer of the ship rendering assistance and to all others so employed by those interested in the vessel or cargo, and in default the vessel was to remain in the custody of the customs until the reward had been paid or security had been given to the satisfaction[47] of those entitled to the salvage. In the event of disagreement as to what was a reasonable sum, which could in effect be fixed by the customs officer, since he was one of those entitled to payment and had custody of the ship or goods saved, provision was made for the nomination of three justices of the peace to adjust the amount of reward. Such adjustment was to be binding on all parties and recoverable in an action at law to be brought in any of Her Majesty's Courts of Record. The Act also provided, significantly, that any person making holes in a ship in distress or stealing her pumps or doing anything tending to her loss or destruction was to be guilty of felony[48] and that the Act was to be read quarterly on Sundays in seaport towns (and upon the coasts) throughout the kingdom.[49] Finally, all claims to ownership of wreck and of flotsam, jetsam and lagan were declared unaffected by the provisions of the Act.[50]

In fact, the Act of 1713, which was made perpetual in 1717,[51] had no connection whatever with Admiralty jurisdiction, for neither the High Court of Admiralty nor any other court of Admiralty jurisdiction was a Court of Record.[52] The 1713 Act was not entirely successful in its effect, as can be deduced from a subsequent statute passed 40 years later.

The Act of 1753

The preamble to the Act 26 Geo. II, c.19 (1753) referred to the fact that, **112** "notwithstanding the good and salutary laws" already in force, "many wicked enormities had been committed to the disgrace of the nation" in plundering and destroying vessels in distress and stealing goods. Further penalties were accordingly provided in such cases, and against persons beating or wounding or wilfully obstructing the escape of those on board such vessels, and persons who put out false lights to lure vessels into danger, all of these acts being made felonies. A new principle was also introduced, providing for salvage reward to persons rendering voluntary services, that is to say, not under the

---

[44] This appears to be the original meaning of "in distress", *i.e.* in danger of stranding, or stranded.
[45] See now MSA 1995, ss 232–233.
[46] See now MSA 1995, s.233.
[47] See now MSA 1995, s.226.
[48] Expressly without benefit of clergy.
[49] The provision was in sufficient practical detail to direct that the reading should be before the sermon.
[50] See now MSA 1995, s.244.
[51] By the Act 4 Geo. 1, c.12 (1717). It has since been subsumed into MSA 1995.
[52] This was definite at least by 1713.

orders of justices, customs officers and others having powers under the Act of 1713. It was also enacted that, whenever a vessel was stranded in future, all those having powers and duties under the former Act should meet together and proceed to their duties. Further provisions were also made as to the adjustment of the amount of salvage; and the customs were given power to raise unpaid salvage by bill of sale, in addition to the earlier mere powers of detention. The Act is of some length and these are only some of the important provisions enacted in it.

The Act of 1809

113   In 1809, the Act 49 Geo. III, c.122 provided against depredations of boatmen and others in the harbours, bays and rivers of England by cutting cables[53] in order to take up and sell the anchors later and to endanger the ships to which the anchors had belonged. A large number of sections accordingly regulated future sales and markings of anchors and also extended the salvage provisions of the Act of 1713 to them, including assessment by justices of reward for saving anchors.[54] These, however, were not the most important part of the Act. Most significantly, section 9 provided, for the first time, that the High Court of Admiralty was to have some jurisdiction, albeit only on appeal from justices, in salvage under the series of statutes now under consideration. This is the beginning of the gradual process which later led to the virtual complete transference to the Admiralty Court of all such salvage jurisdiction in this country. The section also introduced, for the first time, a specific right to salvage reward for being instrumental in saving the life or lives of any person or persons on board a ship or vessel.[55] The existing jurisdiction of the Admiralty and other courts was expressly to be unaffected by any provisions of the Act.[56]

Frauds by Boatmen Act 1813

114   In 1813, the statute 53 Geo. III, c.87 continued the 1809 Act. Several new provisions included the conferment of rights for carriages to pass over land in order to reach vessels and goods for the purposes of salvage services.[57] More importantly, it gave the Admiralty Court, concurrently with the common law

---

[53] It was not until a later period that anchor chain superseded rope.

[54] These provisions are in considerable detail. The purpose was (a) to make it difficult to sell anchors, and cable stolen from ships after the cables had been cut, and (b) to provide for payment of salvage which, under controlled conditions, would only be paid for bona fide recovery of anchors and cable following a genuine parting of the latter. It is probable that (b) was subject to abuse and this provision was later dropped. But the provisions as to (a) were to be found, to some extent amended, under the heading of "Marine Store Dealers" in MSA 1894, ss 538–543. Sections 538–542 of the 1894 Act were in turn repealed and replaced by the Scrap Metal Dealers Act 1964.

[55] Subsequently MSA 1894, s.544. The provisions as to foreign ships in s.545 of the 1894 Act were not introduced until 1862. On life salvage now, see *post*, Chap. 3.

[56] There were several Acts making similar provision within the area of the Cinque Ports. This area is now set out in the Cinque Ports Acts 1821. The Cinque Ports jurisdiction in salvage was expressly preserved by MSA 1894, s.571 and MSA 1995, s.314 and Sched. 14, para. 11.

[57] See now MSA 1995, ss 231 and 234.

courts, jurisdiction over salvage matters arising between high and low water marks, a jurisdiction which had previously been expressly denied by the Acts of 1389[58] and 1391,[59] and *Sir Henry Constable's Case*.[60]

Frauds by Boatmen Act 1821

115 With reference to questions which had arisen as to the jurisdiction of the Courts of Record at Westminster and of the High Court of Admiralty, in cases of salvage of ships and goods between high and low water mark, it was again enacted in 1821, in section 31 of the Act 1 & 2 Geo. IV, c.75, that there should be concurrent jurisdiction in such cases. The scope of this section has not always been regarded as being very clear. Possibly the jurisdiction which the Admiralty Court had under the series of statutes relating to salvage, of which the Act of 1821 formed part, was on appeal from justices. It may be, therefore, that section 31 was intended to do no more than settle objections raised by the common law to an appellate jurisdiction related to services in waters which were within the body of a county. It is, however, usually taken to have meant an extension of the jurisdiction of first instance.[61] In the same year, the Admiralty Court expressly obtained, concurrently with the Admiralty Court of the Cinque Ports, appellate jurisdiction over salvage awards made by Commissioners of the Cinque Ports and jurisdiction to order the sale of property saved to defray salvage.[62]

Admiralty Court Act 1840

116 The Admiralty Court Act 1840[63] was not part of the previous series of statutes, under which it was not clear that the Admiralty Court was other than an appellate tribunal, but was of major importance. Speaking of the 1840 Act, Dr Lushington said[64]:

> "It was not, I apprehend, intended to confer any new, separate and distinct powers on this Court, but merely to enable the Court to exercise its ordinary jurisdiction to the full extent."

It did this by conferring jurisdiction, concurrently with that of the courts of law and equity, from the area of the high seas to which the Admiralty Court had previously been restricted, towards the land, so that it included the body of counties, not only in salvage cases, but in cases of collision, towage, necessaries and other matters. In the case of salvage, however, the jurisdiction

---

[58] *Ante*, §91, n. 5.
[59] *Ante*, §91, n. 6.
[60] *Ante*, §108.
[61] *cf.* Dr Lushington's interpretation of s.8 of the Act in *The Zephyrus* (1842) 1 W. Rob. 329.
[62] 1 & 2 Geo. IV, c.76, ss 4, 20.
[63] 3 & 4 Vict. c.65.
[64] *The Fortitude* (1843) 2 W. Rob. 217, 222.

was restricted to "all claims and demands whatsoever in the nature of salvage for services rendered to . . . any ship or sea-going vessel."

Wreck and Salvage Act 1846

117 In 1846, the Wreck and Salvage Act brought about further important changes. The rights to salvage separately conferred by various previous Acts were consolidated. For the first time, the High Court of Admiralty was given such jurisdiction as a court of first instance whenever the sum claimed under the statutes exceeded £200 and the parties preferred not to refer the dispute to the justices. Otherwise, the justices' jurisdiction was continued as regards assessment, and also distribution. But power was given to the Commissioners of Admiralty to appoint salvage commissioners with the same jurisdiction as the justices. The appellate jurisdiction of the High Court of Admiralty was also continued. The former restriction in the Act of 1840 relating to "ships and seagoing vessels" was removed and the court was given jurisdiction to decide, subject to the limits of amount, upon all claims and demands whatever in the nature of salvage for services performed (except to unclaimed property which was to be sold as droits of Admiralty and the reward fixed by receivers), whether in the case of ships or vessels, or of any goods or articles found either at sea or cast upon the shore, and whether such services should have been performed upon the high seas or within the body of a county. The Act of 1846 completed the process begun by that of 1840 in relation to the inherent jurisdiction of Admiralty origin. At the same time, it gave to the court statutory jurisdiction (subject to limits of value) which had formerly been the exclusive province (save on appeal) of justices, in relation to the statutory rights to salvage reward of non-Admiralty origin.

A further important provision of the 1846 Act was its apparent clear authorisation of awards for salvage of life, for which the court had claimed no inherent jurisdiction.[65]

Merchant Shipping Act 1854

118 The Wreck and Salvage Act 1846 was repealed by the Merchant Shipping Repeal Act 1854 and largely re-enacted in the Merchant Shipping Act of the same year, section 467 being the special jurisdiction section relating to the High Court of Admiralty. The 1854 Act established the court's jurisdiction over causes in which arbitration was involved and generally "whether the services in respect of which salvage is claimed were performed upon the high seas, or within the body of any county, or partly in one place and partly in the other, and whether the wreck is found at sea or cast upon the land, or partly in the sea and partly on land." Under the Act,[66] justices of the peace had jurisdiction over claims of up to £200, which was increased in 1862 in respect also of claims arising outside the United Kingdom to £1,000,[67] thus in practice

---

[65] See *post*, § 273.
[66] s.460.
[67] M.S. Amendment Act 1862, s.49.

limiting the Admiralty Court's instance jurisdiction to sums above that amount.

Admiralty Court Act 1861

Among a number of provisions introduced by the Admiralty Court Act 1861, the Admiralty Court was finally constituted a Court of Record[68] and jurisdiction in respect of life salvage was extended.[69]   **119**

Naval Agency and Distribution Act 1864

In this Act, it was provided that the Admiralty Court should have exclusive jurisdiction over questions concerning the distribution of Royal Navy salvage.[70]   **120**

County Courts Admiralty Jurisdiction Act 1868

The 1868 Act conferred on county courts both the original salvage jurisdiction of the High Court of Admiralty and the statutory jurisdiction under the Merchant Shipping Acts,[71] subject to limits of value based on the value of the property saved.   **121**

Merchant Shipping Act 1894

In 1894, the legislation governing salvage and merchant shipping generally was, with certain amendments, consolidated in the Merchant Shipping Act 1894. Part IX of the Act[72] dealt with wreck and salvage. The 1894 Act removed all salvage jurisdiction from justices of the peace in England and from the judge of "any county court,"[73] and transferred it to those county courts which had been given Admiralty jurisdiction by the County Courts Admiralty Jurisdiction Act 1868. The Merchant Shipping Act 1894 was the mother Act on merchant shipping for exactly 101 years[73a] but was frequently amended.   **122**

Twentieth-century developments

The provisions of the Merchant Shipping Act, 1894, ss 547 *et seq.*, relating to the determination of salvage disputes, were abolished, as regards England, by the repeal of subsections (2) and (3) of section 547 so far as relating to the   **123**

---

[68] s.14.
[69] See further Chap. 9.
[70] s.22.
[71] See Raikes and Kilburn's *Admiralty Jurisdiction and Practice in County Courts* (1896). There was only one edition of this work.
[72] ss 510–571.
[73] Who had been substituted for previous alternatives to the justices—namely, a county court judge or a stipendiary magistrate—by the Merchant Shipping Amendment Act 1862, s.49.
[73a] It came into force on January 1, 1895 (MSA 1894, s.748) and was repealed by the Merchant Shipping Act 1995, which came into force on January 1, 1996 (*ibid.*, s.316(2)).

High Court in England and of section 565 (Jurisdiction of the High Court in salvage) by the Supreme Court of Judicature (Consolidation) Act 1925, s.226 and Sched. 6, and by the repeal of sections 547, 548 and 549, as respects the summary determination in a county court of disputes as to salvage, by the County Courts (Amendment) Act 1934, ss 13(8), 34, and Sched. V, Pt I. The latter Act also repealed part of section 22(1) of the former, in which reference was made to the summary procedure. So far as concerns the statutory jurisdiction of the Admiralty Court in the determination of salvage disputes, the provisions of the Act of 1894 ceased to have effect. The Act of 1925 substituted others, forming party of section 22, with which section 33 was to be read. These provisions were in turn repealed by the Administration of Justice Act 1956, s.57(2) and Sched. 2. Three years later, the Admiralty jurisdiction of the county courts was restated by the County Courts Act 1959, ss 55–61.

124 The Admiralty jurisdiction of the High Court is now to be found in the Supreme Court Act 1981, ss 20–24,[74] replacing the relevant provisions of the Administration of Justice Act 1956. Three years after the Supreme Court Act 1981 was passed, the County Courts Act 1959 was repealed and the legislation governing the jurisdiction of county courts consolidated in the County Courts Act 1984.[75] However, the Admiralty jurisdiction of county courts was abolished in 1999.[76]

United Kingdom membership of the European Communities has also affected Admiralty jurisdiction, by virtue of the Admiralty provisions of the Civil Jurisdiction and Judgments Act 1982 (until February 28, 2002) and (from March 1, 2002) the E.C. Council Regulation on Jurisdiction and the Recognition and Enforcement of Judgments in Civil and Commercial Matters 2000.[77]

125 So far as concerns the *fora* in which matters concerning salvage are determined, it has been noted above that the Administration of Justice Act 1970 abolished the Probate, Divorce and Admiralty Division of the High Court and transferred Admiralty matters to an Admiralty Court of the Queen's Bench Division.[78] Of far greater practical importance, however, has been the triumph of arbitration over adjudication in salvage matters, principally under the auspices of Lloyd's Form, and subject to the Arbitration Acts 1950, 1975, 1979 and 1996.[79] The essentially confidential nature of the arbitration process has in one respect inhibited the development of the law of salvage, by restricting open consideration of its response to changes in shipping practices.

126 The predominant use of standard forms of salvage agreement, prompted by the growth of professional salvors which has been permitted by the availability

[74] See *post*, Chaps. 16, 17.
[75] See ss 26–29 and 31. The salvage jurisdiction of county courts was of minimal importance, however.
[76] The Civil Courts (Amendment) (No. 2) Order 1999 (S.I. 1999 No. 1011).
[77] See *post*, § 1224.
[78] *Ante*, § 96.
[79] See *post*, Chap. 13.

of reliable power-driven vessels, is a reflection of technological and practical changes which have had several implications for salvage jurisdiction over the twentieth century, particularly with regard to new subjects of salvage. Not all of these implications have as yet been clearly dealt with by the courts or the legislature. Thus, the availability of reliable power-driven vessels has also prompted development of the time charterparty, the remuneration for which, known as hire, is a subject of value, the preservation of which would appear to justify a salvage reward, although this has not, as yet, been clearly recognised. This is in part, at least, because certain subjects of salvage, such as time-charter hire, bunkers and containers, have an identity with other, firmly established, subjects of salvage, namely the ship and the cargo, which has inhibited separate consideration.[80] On other matters, Parliament has extended salvage jurisdiction either by domestic instigation, as with hovercraft,[81] or consequent upon international agreement, as with aircraft.[82]

International Conventions

Somewhat curiously, in this area of international concern, international negotiations originally produced little direct effect on the law of salvage. The Brussels Salvage Convention of 1910 substantially reflected English law and was not formally enacted as part of it.[83] However, as part of the wider maritime law, salvage was of course affected by other international conventions implemented in English law. In particular, the London Convention on Limitation of Liability for Maritime Claims 1976 ("LLMC 1976") extended the privilege of limited liability to salvors. LLMC 1976 was enacted in the Merchant Shipping Act 1979 and now has effect by virtue of the Merchant Shipping Act 1995.[84] Prior to LLMC 1976's coming into force by virtue of municipal legislation, it was implemented contractually in Lloyd's Form.   **127**

Lloyd's Form has proved to be a useful and flexible method of adjusting to changing circumstances in other respects. A growing problem with the development of large oil tankers was that it encouraged salvors (whose remuneration has traditionally been to salve property) to endeavour to prevent or minimise environmental damage and to receive at least some payment for doing so. Early provisions to this end were included in LOF 1980. These in turn contributed to the Montreal Draft Salvage Convention of 1981,[85] which eventually became the International Salvage Convention 1989, provisions of which were implemented as a matter of contract in Lloyd's Form before the 1989 Convention was eventually enacted into English law. The Convention was enacted in the Merchant Shipping (Salvage and Pollution) Act 1994. The 1994 Act was combined the following year in the consolidation of the merchant shipping legislation and the repeal of the Merchant Shipping Act   **128**

[80] See *post*, Chap. 3.
[81] See *post*, Chap. 3.
[82] See *post*, Chap. 3.
[83] See *ante*, Chap. 1. But see especially § 11.
[84] s.185 and Sched. 7. See *post*, Chap. 12.
[85] See *ante*, Chap. 1.

History

1894 by the Merchant Shipping Act 1995. The Convention came into force on July 14, 1996.[86]

Salvage at common law

129 As shewn earlier in this chapter, salvage jurisdiction not of Admiralty origin was always on a local basis and for a long period was, by a series of statutes beginning with 12 Anne, c.18, 1713, given to justices of the peace. Apart from the provisions in this series, whereby the courts at Westminster were given express powers to enforce the justices' awards, the jurisdiction of the courts of common law does not appear, save in exceptional cases, to have been required. These Acts, furthermore, provided for the detention and sale of salved property in order to meet claims for salvage, whereas the courts of common law had no similar powers; they never possessed any procedure *in rem*. Just as their procedure was unsuited to the enforcement of salvors' rights, so the substantive law of these courts was generally of a limited nature, although its scope became wider as the common law developed.

130 The attitude of the common law courts has traditionally been that, as a general rule, a person cannot be required to pay for receipt of something which might be classified as a benefit but which he has not requested. Thus, mere preservation of another's property by itself neither constitutes a debt nor does it create liability to make restitution to the preservor.[87]

The ubiquity of entitlement to salvage rewards internationally might have tended at one time to encourage the common law courts to recognise an entitlement at law for rewards for salvage services. Thus, the Court of King's Bench recognised in *Hartfort v. Jones, etc.*,[88] in 1698, the rights of an unpaid salvor by way of defence. If he were sued in trover or in detinue by the owner of salved property and he had neither received nor had tendered to him an adequate recompense for his services, he was recognised as having a possessory lien as security for his compensation. The report is as follows:

> "Trover for goods. The defendant pleads that they[89] were in a ship, and that the ship took fire, and that they hazarded their lives to save them; and therefore they are ready to deliver the goods, if the plaintiff will pay them 4l. for salvage, &c. The plaintiff demurred generally. And Holt C.J. held, that they might retain the goods until payment, as well as a taylor, or an hostler, or a common carrier. And salvage is allowed by all nations, it being reasonable, that a man shall be rewarded who hazards his life in the service of another."

---

[86] See *ante*, Chap. 1.
[87] See *Nicholson v. Chapman* (1793) 2 Hy. Bl. 254; *Falcke v. Scottish Imperial Insurance Co.* (1886) 34 Ch.D. 234 (see *ante*, § 33); Goff & Jones, Chap. 17.
[88] (1698) 1 Ld. Raym. 393 (91 E.R. 1161); *sub nom. Hartfort v. Jones* (1698) 2 Salk. 654 (91 E.R. 556). *cf. Sutton v. Buck* (1810) 2 Taunt. 302 (Exchequer Chamber).
[89] *Quaere*: the goods or the defendants?

Salvage at common law

That *Hartfort v. Jones* is of a limited effect, recognising a defence but not **131** a right to sue, is commonly assumed to be confirmed by a passage in Lord Mansfield's judgment in *Cornu v. Blackstone*.[90] While Great Britain and France were at war, a French privateer captured an English ship. The master and mate of the English ship signed a ransom bill, binding the owner to pay ransom. The privateer kept the mate hostage and released the English ship. British frigates then captured the privateer, with the mate and ransom bill on board, but the bill was secreted and not delivered up. It was held that the privateer could recover upon the ransom bill against the owner of the English ship.[91] In his judgment, Lord Mansfield C.J. said[92]:

> "It is said, that, by the law of nations, the recapture puts an end to the ransom bill; and the argument is, that the Court of Admiralty decrees salvage for retaking the ransom bill. But what are the cases brought to prove this position? None of them were litigated but the last, and, there no ransom bill was forth-coming. Upon what was salvage given in that case? They[93] seem to have mistaken the nature of salvage. They seem to consider it as a debt which may be exacted. *But no man can be compelled to pay salvage, unless he chooses to have the property back.* They have confounded distinct subjects."

Lord Mansfield is not obviously attempting to state the position at common law. Not only does he not appear to distinguish between the positions at law and in Admiralty, his reference to the Admiralty Court suggests that his statement was derived from his view of Admiralty law. If so, it cannot stand with the subsequently established rule[94] that a salvor does have an action *in personam*.

Lord Mansfield's view may have appeared not unfair at a time when a **132** defendant frequently lost possession of his property and did not wish to regain it along with personal liability to pay salvage. Such a situation, if it existed, would clearly have become unrealistic with passage of time. The less practical such a view, the more unrealistic *Hartfort v. Jones* appears. Unless it is explicable on the ground that a common law lien is available to support a claim for salvage which is upheld in Admiralty, it provides the salvor with security for an invalid claim at common law. Furthermore, *Hartfort v. Jones* paradoxically represents the very reverse of the general common law rule subsequently established in *Nicholson v. Chapman*[95] that the preservor of

---

[90] (1781) 2 Dougl. 641.
[91] According to Lord Mansfield, "It is sound policy, as well as good morality, to keep faith with an enemy in time of war. This is a contract, which arises out of a state of hostility, and is to be governed by the law of nations, and the eternal rules of justice:" *ibid.*, 648. But the ransoming of ships captured from the king's subjects and of goods aboard such ships was soon prohibited, by 22 Geo. 3, c.25.
[92] (1781) 2 Dougl. 641, 648–649. (emphasis added).
[93] *Quaere*: the parties or the cases?
[94] From 1799 at least. See *The Two Friends* (1799) 1 C. Rob. 271, 277.
[95] (1793) 2 Hy. Bl. 254. See also *Falcke's* case, *supra*, n. 87.

property may be entitled to reasonable recompense but is definitely not entitled to a lien.

133 It is clearly established that at common law a possessory lien is available in support of claims for salvage[96] and general average[97]; and also in analogous cases. In *Hingston v. Wendt*,[98] a vessel went ashore with cargo on board. The master put the plaintiff ship agent in possession of the ship and cargo, authorising him, as his agent, to do what was for the benefit of all concerned. The plaintiff did work and incurred expenditure in discharging the cargo and bringing it to a place of safety, where he took possession of it; the expenditure was not to enable the ship-owner to perform his contract and earn freight but was extraordinary expenditure for the purpose of saving the property at risk, the cargo. The hull broke up and became a wreck. Blackburn J. said[99]:

> "The case is very analogous to general average and to salvage, in both of which there is a lien."

He held the plaintiff entitled to a lien against the cargo owner, enforceable against the subsequent owner of the cargo who, on taking possession of the cargo, became liable to pay the plaintiff his reasonable expenses.

134 Three circumstances were recognised generally at common law in which the preservor could claim a remedy: where he could prove an employment for reward, either express or implied from the facts; where the defendant freely accepted the benefit, with the opportunity of not doing so; and where liability was imposed by law.

However, the cases in which the plaintiff has recovered at common law in the absence of an express contract are rare.[1] The paucity of cases in the area of maritime salvage is no doubt primarily a product of the Admiralty Court's being the more suitable and advantageous forum. But one, perhaps the only, case in which a salvor has recovered at common law is *Newman v. Walters*.[2]

135 In that case, the ship being in danger, the master and part of the crew left her. Thereupon, at the request of the remaining crew, a passenger who had been a ship's captain took command and brought the ship safely to port. His merits in saving the vessel were acknowledged by the owner to the underwriters in a letter wherein he expressed his desire to remunerate the passenger, declaring that £200 was the least he should receive and that whatever more might be allowed would afford him satisfaction. The passenger brought an *indebitatus assumpsit* and claimed for salvage of the vessel, for work and

---

[96] *Hartfort v. Jones, supra.*
[97] See F. D. Rose, *General Average: Law and Practice* (1997), 81–82.
[98] (1876) 1 Q.B.D. 367; *cf. Castellain v. Thompson* (1862) 13 C.B. (N.S.) 105.
[99] (1876) 1 Q.B.D. 367, 373.
[1] See *Lipson v. Harrison* (1853) 22 L.T. (O.S.) 53.
[2] (1804) 3 Bos. & Pul. 612.

labour in saving her, for work and labour generally, and upon a *quantum meruit*. At trial before Lord Alvanley C.J., the jury gave a verdict for £400. A rule *nisi* for a new trial was moved: first, on the ground that the plaintiff was under the circumstances of the case not entitled to recover anything; and, secondly, on the supposition that he was entitled to recover, that the jury had given too much. The rule was granted on the first ground but subsequently discharged.

The authority of the decision, as supporting claims for salvage at common law, can be judged by consideration, in reverse order, of the three possible justifications listed above.[3]

136 Lord Alvanley C.J. justified his original decision on the basis that liability was imposed by law. Relying on a recent decision of Lord Stowell in the Admiralty Court,[4] his view was that a passenger could claim salvage in such circumstances and he seems to have assumed that the approach of the Admiralty Court was applicable in the case in hand. As has been shewn, this approach, even if justifiable in principle, does not accord with the general experience of the common law. And the other two judges expressly confined their decisions to another ground.

A second reason why the defendant might be liable to salvage is that he has freely accepted the benefit conferred, having been able to reject it—a rationale which, founded on consent, might hint at liability which is explicable on a contractual basis were it not for the fact that it would rarely be possible to construct a contract in such a case, for the consideration would be past and therefore insufficient. The free acceptance explanation was neither considered nor alluded to in the case. Moreover, it is unlikely ever to succeed since a defendant retaking possession of his own goods really has no choice in whether to accept the benefit.[5]

137 The true *ratio decidendi* of *Newman v. Walters* is to be found in the narrow orthodox common law reasoning of Heath and Rooke JJ. Heath J. noted the defendant's acknowledgment of the plaintiff's merits and that the ship was saved by his skill, and said[6]:

> "It seems to me, therefore, to be the same as if he had given express orders to the plaintiff for his conduct. *Omnis ratihabitio retro-trahitur et mandato priori aequiparatur.*"

Rooke J.'s judgment is to similar effect and deliberately narrow[7]:

> "Under the special circumstances of the case, I think the Plaintiff is entitled to recover. The Plaintiff, who was a mere passenger, might have

---

[3] §46.
[4] (1799) 1 C. Rob. 306.
[5] *cf. Hain SS. Co. v. Tate & Lyle* (1936) 41 Com. Cas. 350.
[6] (1804) 3 Bos. & Pul. 612, 617.
[7] *ibid.*, 617.

gone on shore in the boat without danger, but being desired by the mate and all the crew to stay and take command of the ship, he did so. This may be considered as a retainer by the only persons who were the agents of the owners at the time. When he comes on shore, one of the owners recognises his conduct and approves of all that he has done. On this special ground I am clearly of opinion that this action may be supported."

In other words, the owner had ratified the plaintiff's employment as his agent for providing the service in question. And it is an implied term of an agency relationship that an agent should receive reasonable remuneration. Standing in for the master at the request of the owner's remaining representatives on board, the plaintiff on the facts acted as the owner's agent and with authority to do so: as Heath J. indicated, subsequent ratification is equivalent to prior authorisation. But in most circumstances salvors do not act as agents, and certainly do not do so simply *qua* salvors.

138 This narrow basis for the court's decision would explain why the case has had limited impact at common law. Lord Alvanley C.J.'s judgment supports a wider basis of liability which might arguably have been more widely relied upon. But it clearly became unnecessary for this to be so: at the time *Newman v. Walters* was decided, there was no existing body of authoritative case law on salvage but Lord Stowell was systematically laying down the foundations of the law of salvage in the Admiralty Court.

139 Shortly after *Newman v. Walters*, Lord Tenterden in his great work on merchant shipping law referred to the availability to the salvor of a possessory lien at common law then went on to state that[8]:

"This [*i.e.*, the salvor's] compensation, if the parties cannot agree upon it, may be the same law [*i.e.*, the common law] be ascertained by a jury in an action brought by the salvor against the proprietor of the goods."

The statement survived until the last edition of the book.[9] Forty years after *Newman v. Walters*, in dismissing a claim for salvage of a raft of timber found flotsam in Yarmouth harbour, because it was not a proper subject of salvage,[10] Dr Lushington in the Admiralty Court said that[11]:

"the party on whose behalf the application is made must seek elsewhere in a Court of Common Law the assistance to which he considers himself entitled."

---

[8] Abbott, 3rd ed. (1808), p. 383.
[9] *ibid.*, 14th ed. (1901), 461. But see n. (e) on that page.
[10] See *post*, Chap. 3.
[11] *Raft of Timber* (1844) 2 W. Rob. 251, 255.

Salvage at common law

Yet these statements build little on *Newman v. Walters*. In particular, Dr Lushington merely refers the claimant to the common law without indicating that he will obtain a remedy or, if so, what its nature or extent might be. Indeed, he subsequently cast doubt on the actual decision in *Newman v. Walters*.[12]

As Hill J. has pointed out, a right to salvage at common law, if not governed by principles identical to those pertaining in Admiralty, might benefit the salvor in not requiring him to prove danger. But a number of factors have militated against elucidation of the common law position in relation to maritime salvage. First, it must be admitted that the common law courts have conceded the justice in awarding payments to maritime salvors. Thus, in *Nicholson v. Chapman*,[13] Eyre C.J. said:

> "The only difficulty that remained with any of us, after we had heard this case argued, was upon the question whether this transaction could be assimilated to salvage? The taking care of goods left by the tide upon the banks of a navigable river, communicating with the sea, may in a vulgar sense be said to be salvage; but it has none of the qualities of salvage, in respect of which the laws of all civilized nations, the Laws of Oleron, and our own laws in particular, have provided that a recompence is due for the saving, and that our law has also provided that this recompence should be a lien upon goods which have been saved. Goods carried by sea are necessarily and unavoidably exposed to the perils which storms, tempests and accidents (far beyond the reach of human foresight to prevent) are hourly creating, and against which, it too often happens that the greatest diligence and the most strenuous exertions of the mariner cannot protect them. When goods are thus in imminent danger of being lost, it is most frequently at the hazard of the lives of those who save them, that they are saved. Principles of public policy dictate to civilized and commercial countries, not only the propriety, but even the absolute necessity of establishing a liberal recompence for the encouragement of those who engage in so dangerous a service.
>
> Such are the grounds upon which salvage stands; they are recognized by Lord Chief Justice Holt in the case which has been cited from Lord Raymond and Salkeld [*Hartfort v. Jones*[14]]. But see how very unlike this salvage is to the case now under consideration. In a navigable river within the flux and reflux of the tide, but at a great distance from the sea, pieces of timber lie moored together in convenient places . . . ."

The common law courts have never clearly acknowledged a right of action for salvage at common law or, if there were such a right, whether it was governed by the same principles as applied in Admiralty. Indeed, it was said

---

[12] See *The Vrede* (1861) Lush. 322.
[13] (1793) 2 Hy. Bl. 254, 257.
[14] *Supra*.

in the Court of Exchequer in 1862[15] that counsel could cite no case in which an action at common law had been held sustainable by a seaman to enforce his claim as a salvor. Moreover, despite acknowledgement that the common law might have a general power to order payment for services conferred in an emergency,[16] the rarity with which that power has been exercised has discouraged litigation to that end.[17] Very probably, a salvor suing at common law would lie under the disadvantage of having his remuneration meted out to him upon the basis merely of fair compensation for work and labour done, rather than as the policy-motivated enhanced reward given in Admiralty. Indeed, not only would this equally be true if he proved a contract of employment such as would entitle him to recover something upon a *quantum meruit*, but the proof of a contract on such a basis would only affirm that remuneration were on the basis of reasonable recompense rather than reward. If, by inference from its being double the sum contemplated by the owner as reasonable, the £400 given by the jury for the service in *Newman v. Walters* were generous by common law standards and equivalent to an Admiralty reward, there are now no means of knowing this.

142 Of course, Admiralty jurisdiction has always had the great advantages of proceedings *in rem* and maritime liens, and these must have contributed greatly to persuading claimants not to resort to the common law courts. Jeune J. has said[18]:

> "It is indeed possible that the reason why... actions for salvage at common law are so rare is that the facility of bringing all parties before the court gave advantages which the common law jurisdiction could not afford."

143 The formerly exclusive jurisdictions of the courts of Admiralty, common law and equity were by the Judicature Acts 1873–1875 vested in a single High Court of Justice, each Division of which is empowered to exercise the different jurisdictions. This integration, plus the modern practice of salvage's being rendered according to the terms of the Lloyd's Form of salvage contract, have further diminished any possibility of resort to any common law liability to salvage. This can be seen from an examination of the extent to which *Newman v. Walters* might be thought to support contractually based liability at common law.

144 In *Lipson v. Harrison*,[19] the Court of Queen's Bench held that a seaman could not sue at law for services rendered by the order of his own captain

---

[15] *Atkinson v. Woodall* (1862) 31 L.J.M.C. 174.
[16] See, *e.g. Nicholson v. Chapman, supra*, at p. 258, *per* Eyre C.J.
[17] See generally Rose (1989) 9 O.J.L.S. 167.
[18] *The Elton* [1891] P. 265, 270. See also *Lipson v. Harrison* (1853) 22 L.T. (O.S.) 83, 84, *per* Lord Campbell C.J.; *The Lord Cranstoun*, Unreported, *per* Lord Stowell, cited in *The Purissima Concepcion* (1849) 3 W. Rob. 181, 184.
[19] (1853) 22 L.T. (O.S.) 83.

because he could shew no contract with the owner of the salved ship. Wightman J. said[20]:

> "The proceedings in the Admiralty Court do not depend upon contract; and the only authority for the plaintiff is the case of *Newman v. Walters*; but in that case there was some evidence of a contract."

But that is to misinterpret the case. The confined, agency rationale of *Newman v. Walters* does not provide support for general liability at common law on a contractual basis. Purported ratification cannot generally surmount the obstacle that the completed (*i.e.* past) service provides no consideration for the contract. Of course, in modern circumstances, a salvor will almost invariably be able to claim on the basis of a contract to salve entered into before operations commence, on the Lloyd's Form. Even were such a contract concluded after completion of salvage services it will be valid, for both parties provide consideration by agreeing to be bound by the contract and to forebear from enforcing their rights under the general law of salvage. *Pace* Lord Alvanley C.J. there may have been no such rights at common law, but such a contract would have been upheld in the Admiralty Court, albeit not as a contract of work and labour as at common law but as a contract of salvage to which the general provisions of the Admiralty law of salvage were applicable.[21]

It is now immaterial whether a contract of salvage is to take effect in Admiralty or at common law for "any claims in the nature of salvage" fall (and, since 1875, have been stipulated as falling[22]) within the Admiralty jurisdiction of the Supreme Court, and will therefore be governed by Admiralty principles. Whether the common law provided its own basis for salvage claims is therefore now purely academic. Of course, where services to raise sunken property are rendered other than in a case where they justify a salvage reward or general average contribution, a contract will generally be necessary to secure compensation, in which case, of course, only parties to that contract will be liable to pay.[23]

If further explanation of the non-development of salvage claims at common law were necessary, it is to be found in the recognition of the Admiralty Court as the proper and most suitable forum for maritime claims.[24] This is obviously so nowadays, and there is provision for transferring to the Admiralty Court proceedings which properly belong there. It was even so after the rivalry over the demarcation between the jurisdictions of the formerly rival courts had all but ceased, before the Judicature Acts 1873–1875.

145

146

---

[20] *ibid.*, 84.
[21] See *Baring v. Day* (1806) 8 East 57, 75; *The Happy Return* (1828) 2 Hagg. 198, 205–206; *The Favorite* (1844) 2 W. Rob. 255; *The Purissima Concepcion* (1849) 3 W. Rob. 181.
[22] See now SCA 1981, s.20(2)(j).
[23] *Castellain v. Thompson* (1862) 13 C.B. (N.S.) 105.
[24] *Lipson v. Harrison* (1853) 22 L.T. (O.S.) 83, 84, *per* Lord Campbell C.J.

147 The view was expressed in *Abbott*[25] that:

> "This [common law] right seems not to have been exercised for a long time, and to have been taken away by s.460 of the Merchant Shipping Act 1854 (now ss 547, 548, 571 of the Merchant Shipping Act 1894)."

Presumably the Act explains *Atkinson v. Woodall*[26] rather than the attitudes of the common law judges. In *Atkinson v. Woodall*, a seaman of the salvage vessel brought an action at law, for money had and received, to recover his share of salvage money which had been awarded by justices under the Merchant Shipping Act 1854, s.460 "to the owner, captain and crew", but without apportionment, and paid over to the owner. The Court of Exchequer held that such an action was not maintainable: such matters were provided for by the Merchant Shipping Act and the rules of Admiralty jurisdiction. Wilde B. observed[27]:

> "The division of salvage is essentially a matter of Admiralty jurisdiction, and Mr Joyce [counsel for the plaintiff] has not been able to cite any case[28] in which an action at common law has been held sustainable by a seaman to enforce his claim as a salvor. I think a decision of this court, which would have the effect of withdrawing these questions from the rules of Admiralty jurisdiction, and substituting a jury, would be a most mischievous decision."

148 It was conceded by the court that, if the owner had offered to pay a portion of the salvage to the plaintiff and the plaintiff accepted the offer but the owner refused to pay, then the plaintiff might have recovered the sum at common law, as money had and received or on an account stated. In *The Gloxinia*,[29] the Admiralty Court awarded salvage and apportioned it amongst the owners, master and crew. The master authorised the owners to receive his share, from which the owners claimed to deduct a share of costs. The master brought an action on the Admiralty side of the county court, which the Divisional Court of the Probate, Divorce and Admiralty Division held the county court judge was right to dismiss:

> "This was not an Admiralty action at all, there being no question either as to salvage or apportionment which was in dispute. It was an ordinary common law claim for money had and received, and should have been brought on the common law side."[30]

---

[25] 14th ed. (1901), p. 961, n. 3.
[26] (1862) 31 L.J.M.C. 174.
[27] *ibid.* at p. 176.
[28] Presumably not even *Newman v. Walters, supra.*
[29] (1901) 18 T.L.R. 227.
[30] *ibid.*, 228, *per* Sir Francis Jeune P.

Salvage at common law

Important points of salvage law have, of necessity, been decided in courts exercising the common law jurisdiction.[31] But it is in the Admiralty Court that the rights of salvors normally have practical effect, and the rules which govern and define them are to be found, for the most part, in decisions of that court, and are based upon the principles of maritime law as there understood and adopted.

---

[31] See, e.g. *Akerblom v. Price, Potter, Walker & Co.* (1881) 7 Q.B.D. 129; *Anderson Tritton & Co. v. Ocean Steamship Co.* (1884) 10 App. Cas. 107 (both shipowners' claims against cargo-owners for general average contribution to payments for salvage services).

CHAPTER 3

SUBJECTS OF SALVAGE

1. GENERAL

Introduction

150 All interests which have benefited from salvage services are in principle liable to contribute to payment of the salvage reward. This is so even if the owner of a particular item of property is not expressly made a party to the salvage contract which is normally concluded. Where there is such a contract, the question then arises as to the nature of his liability, if any—whether it is governed by the general law or by terms similar to those contained in the salvage contract.[1]

Certain items, *e.g.* the personal effects of passengers, the master and crew, are excluded from consideration for salvage purposes. Other items may be given separate consideration or dealt with together with another. Thus, the ship's apparel has been identified as a subject of salvage but is usually treated together with the shipowner's other property, principally the ship. Yet property in common ownership may be dealt with separately, as is normal with the ship and cargo belonging to the shipowner.

151 It is necessary to identify separate subjects of salvage in order to value the interests preserved and to quantify the fund in respect of which the salvor is to be rewarded. The two processes of identification and assessment are not always seen as separate. Thus, the treatment of time charter hire is, if at all, normally considered as part of the question of valuing the ship.[2] But its classification as a subject of salvage in its own right has independent relevance.

Qualification as a subject of salvage is, therefore, essential to ascertain (i) for which items salvage may be claimed, (ii) who is liable to contribute, and (iii) what is the extent of the contribution due from each such person.

152 A number of items clearly fell within the inherent jurisdiction of the Admiralty Court, namely: the vessel, its apparel, cargo, freight and wreck.

---
[1] See *post*, Chap. 9.
[2] See *post*, Chap. 14.

Introduction

Further subjects were specifically made part of its jurisdiction by statute, namely: lives, aircraft and hovercraft. The intervention of Parliament—in amalgamating the ancient Admiralty Court into the new High Court in 1875, specifically legislating for previously unrecognised subjects of salvage, and placing Admiralty jurisdiction on a statutory basis—has promoted the view expounded in *The Gas Float Whitton No. 2*[3] that the Admiralty Court has no salvage jurisdiction over a subject which was not formally identified as a subject of salvage by judicial decision by 1875 or by legislation.

153 The Supreme Court Act 1981, s.20 outlines in detail the matters which are within the Admiralty jurisdiction but nevertheless acknowledges the possibilities of other matters in a sweeping-up clause which provides for any other Admiralty jurisdiction which the Admiralty Court had before the commencement of the Act.[4] This provides some support for the view that an acknowledged part of the Admiralty jurisdiction, namely salvage, might accommodate a previously unrecognised, though not expressly excluded, subject of salvage. This would be consistent with the exercise of the High Court's jurisdiction on the common law side, where the court has long shewn itself to be sufficiently flexible to adapt to formerly undecided points. It would also be desirable to prevent the unjust enrichment of the owner of property which has been preserved from loss or damage at sea.[5] Nonetheless, the traditionally conservative approach of the Admiralty Court in this area may make the court reluctant to act without good cause in advance of possible Parliamentary action, especially since the implementation of the Salvage Convention 1989. Thus, despite the obvious practical importance of clear legislative or judicial guidance on the liability, in the absence of a contract, of the owner of, for example, an oil rig which has been preserved from loss or destruction,[6] the status of novel subjects of salvage is a matter of some controversy.

154 The Admiralty Court's jurisdiction over salvage matters was summarised succinctly and accurately by Lord Watson in *The Gas Float Whitton No. 2*[7]:

> "I think it was rightly assumed in the Courts below that the law which must determine what are the proper subjects of maritime salvage is to be sought in the decisions and practice of the Admiralty Courts of England, and in the statutes which from time to time have been passed by the Legislature for the purpose, mainly, of protecting ships and cargoes and their wreck against depredation."

---

[3] [1896] P. 42; [1897] A.C. 337. See *post*, §§154–157. Cf. *The Cargo ex Schiller* (1877) 2 P.D. 145.

[4] s.20(1)(c). See *Jackson*, Chap. 2.

[5] Although the application of that principle would not *per se* indicate the basis on which the plaintiff should be remunerated. See *ante*, §§ 33–35.

[6] See *post*, §§ 318–320.

[7] *Wells v. The Owners of the Gas Float Whitton No. 2* (*The Gas Float Whitton No. 2*) [1897] A.C. 337, 346; affirming [1896] P. 42; reversing [1895] P. 301.

Subjects of Salvage

The importance of the case lies, however, in the specific definition of subjects of salvage given in the Court of Appeal by Lord Esher M.R.[8]

155   The facts were as follows. An unmanned gas float was moored in tidal waters to give light to vessels. It was shaped like a ship or boat but was neither intended nor fitted for navigation. Indeed, there was evidence that it could not be used for navigation and that it was next to impossible to tow it. It got adrift in a gale and the plaintiffs helped to secure it until a Trinity House yacht took charge. The plaintiffs successfully brought an action *in rem* for salvage services in the county court at Hull, the judge holding that the gas float was a ship or vessel and a wreck, so as to entitle him to exercise statutory jurisdiction. The Divisional Court[9] disagreed with his reasoning but affirmed his decision on the basis that he had jurisdiction at common law, the object being a structure used in connection with navigation and exposed in the ordinary course of its use to the perils of the sea. But neither reason was acceptable to the Court of Appeal or the House of Lords, both of which pronounced against the plaintiff's claim.

156   The House of Lords unanimously approved the exhaustive judgment of the Court of Appeal delivered by Lord Esher M.R., who concluded[10]:

> "I come, therefore, to the conclusion that by the common or original law of the High Court of Admiralty the only subjects in respect of the saving of which salvage reward could be entertained in the Admiralty Court were ship, her apparel and cargo, including flotsam, jetsam, and lagan, and the wreck of these and freight; that the only subject added by statute is life salvage; and that the county court has no right to exercise jurisdiction with regard to any other subject-matter than that which might be entertained by the High Court of Admiralty. Whether salvage could be granted for the saving of what is called a lightship may be doubtful. I incline to think not: if it could be, it is only because the lightship would be held to be a ship. As to some instances which were proposed—such as the *Victory* in Portsmouth Harbour—I have no doubt that she is a ship. So was the *Dreadnought*, used for years as a hospital. So is a ship used as a coal hulk. But the thing in question on this appeal is not a ship in any sense."

157   It was stressed in the House of Lords that the gas float *Whitton No. 2* was neither intended to be used, nor in fact used, for the purpose of being navigated or of carrying cargo or passengers, and the "suggestion that the gas

---

[8] See *post*, §147.
[9] Sir Francis Jeune P. presided but the law reports differ as to whether he sat with Barnes J. or Bruce J. Barnes J., more commonly known as Gorell Barnes J., was the only other judge of the Admiralty Division apart from the President. But Bruce J. (Kennedy J.'s immediate senior in the Queen's Bench Division) occasionally sat in Admiralty cases, so Barnes J. may well have been substituted by oversight by one of the reporters.
[10] [1896] P. 42, 63–64.

stored in the float can be regarded as cargo carried by it is more ingenious than sound."[11] Lord Herschell said[12]:

> "I do not think the extension of it [admiralty jurisdiction] to a floating beacon can be justified merely because it is property connected with navigation; and I think it would not be easy to define the limits of the jurisdiction if it were so extended. All buoys, every object intended to assist the navigation of vessels and guard them from danger, would, if exposed to perils of waters, be, I suppose, equally the subject of salvage claims. Would the lights which are found on piers and landing-stages be in the same category? And in that case must the claim be confined to the light or beacon, or would it extend to the whole structure on which it is erected, or of which it not infrequently forms part? Apart from this difficulty, however, I think it is enough to say that, in my judgment, it would not be right by judicial decision to add to the subjects to which the doctrine of salvage has hitherto been confined by the maritime law of this country."

Lord Macnaghten dealt as follows with the argument from policy of embracing subjects such as the gas float in question[13]:

> "It is, as the learned President says, 'certainly in the interests of navigation and commerce that beacons, valuable in themselves and for their utility, should be preserved from destruction.' There would be much force in the appellants' argument if it were clear that the proposed extension of the doctrine of salvage would conduce to the preservation of beacons. But these beacons are for the most part, if not always, left unguarded—they are easily set adrift. And the hope of earning reward by the restoration of lost property is not perhaps the best preservative against loss. Then, too, one must bear in mind the inconveniences which might arise from the legal rights of salvors in regard to detention of property when that property is the subject of salvage."

Summary

158 Two rules emerge from the judgments in *The Gas Float Whitton No. 2*. The first, which was not essential for the decision, was that the only possible subjects of salvage in Admiralty law were those which had been recognised as such by 1875. The second was that in Admiralty law subjects of salvage included only property involved in navigation. At the same time, it was acknowledged that other subjects could be brought within the law of salvage by legislation. On a broad, but not on a narrow, interpretation of *The Gas Float Whitton No. 2*, aircraft and hovercraft could be regarded as property

---
[11] [1897] A.C. 337, 343.
[12] *ibid.*, 345–346.
[13] *ibid.*, 349.

Subjects of Salvage

involved in navigation. But the point is now mainly academic since Parliament enacted legislation to apply the law of salvage to them,[14] as it had previously done to apply it to the preservation of human lives.[15]

Legislating for life salvage regularised a practice which had been followed in the Admiralty Court, when assessing a salvage award, of taking account of meritorious factors not directly related to property salvage. One further such factor is the avoidance of liability to third parties—"liability salvage"[16]—which has not been treated as a distinct subject of salvage.

159 Avoidance of liability to third parties is a potentially important, though not necessary, element of a growing concern of the late twentieth century—environmental damage—which has become an ancillary subject of salvage of a special kind by virtue of the International Salvage Convention 1989.[17]

The Convention's treatment of environmental damage builds on earlier steps to take account of it by contract, in Lloyd's Form.[18] Parties are generally free to contract as they wish in matters of a salvage nature, but the terms of their agreement will be given effect under the law of contract, rather than under the law of salvage. It is a further question whether the principles of the law of salvage, rather than just ordinary contractual rules, are to be applied in enforcing the contract.[19]

Involvement in navigation

160 It is a condition for the application of the law of general average that the property in question be involved in a maritime adventure in the nature of a voyage.[20] No such requirement has been recognised in the law of salvage. And a salvage reward may certainly be recovered in respect of property not involved in a maritime voyage at the time at which the service is rendered. But the policy of encouraging salvage was developed in support of maritime trade.[21] Furthermore, whereas fixed objects at sea have been excluded from the classification of subjects of salvage,[22] where that classification has been satisfied, the subjects in question have been involved in maritime voyages. It is suggested, therefore, that in cases of doubt the test whether something is or was at the time it became a casualty involved in navigation is a useful guideline to whether something is a subject of salvage.

161 Such a test might have allayed the fears of those who feared the application of the International Salvage Convention 1989 to diamond rings found in lakes or motor vehicles falling into rivers and being hauled out by other vehicles or

---

[14] See *post*, §§ 243–258.
[15] See *post*, §§ 259–310.
[16] See generally *post*, §§ 345–350.
[17] See *post*, Chap. 5.
[18] See *post*, § 395.
[19] See further *ante*, §§ 31–32.
[20] F. D. Rose, *General Average: Law and Practice* (1997), 16–17.
[21] See *ante*, §§ 36–47.
[22] *Ante*, § 155.

a crane operating from land. In the case of events occurring in inland waters, the difficulty has been overcome in English law by the exclusion of the Convention where no vessel is involved or all the vessels involved are of inland navigation.[23]

The proposed test could be of use in regulating the application of the International Salvage Convention 1989. However, the Convention applies in English law to any act or activity undertaken to assist "a vessel or any other property"[24] in danger in any waters except in prescribed circumstances in inland waters.[25] The Convention itself imposes no restriction on "any other property".

The Merchant Shipping Act 1995

The Merchant Shipping Act 1995 does not deal with subjects of salvage comprehensively and in detail. The provisions of the International Salvage Convention 1989, which it enacts, contain some broad general definitions dealing with the traditional scope of the law of salvage,[26] a definition of a more recent "subject of salvage" (environmental damage)[27] and an exclusion (platforms and offshore drilling units).[28] In addition the Act includes the Convention's general exclusion of claims for life salvage, though subject to Conventional and Conventionally sanctioned national modifications of the general position.[29]

162

The current range of subjects of salvage will now be discussed in turn. It may be noted that, although the law of salvage is underlain by a policy of supporting commercial activity[30] and although goods carried on board a vessel for private purposes are in practice not subjects of maritime claims, in general, classification as a subject of salvage is not dependent on the purpose for which the item in question is in or on relevant waters.

2. MARITIME PROPERTY

(a) General

The main rule laid down by the Admiralty Court is that the law of salvage is concerned with (primarily sea-going) vessels and cargo being transported by sea other than for personal purposes, together with freight being earned for

163

---

[23] See *post*, § 369.
[24] Art. 1(a).
[25] See Art. 1(a).
[26] Art. 1(a)–(c).
[27] Art. 1(d). See *post*, Chap. 5.
[28] Art. 3. See *post*, §§ 318–320.
[29] Merchant Shipping Act 1995, Sched. 11, Pt I, Art. 16; Pt II, para. 5. See post, §§ 298 and 310.
[30] See *ante*, Chap. 1.

Subjects of Salvage

such carriage. For convenience, these can be described as maritime property.

The position is basically the same under the International Salvage Convention 1989, Article 1 of which provides:

"For the purposes of this Convention—
(a) Salvage operation means any act or activity undertaken to assist a vessel or any other property in danger in navigable waters or in any other waters whatsoever.
(b) Vessel means any ship or craft, or any structure capable of navigation.
(c) Property means any property not permanently and intentionally attached to the shoreline and includes freight at risk."

164 In short, under the Convention, a salvage operation is any action undertaken to assist any property which is not permanently and intentionally attached to the shoreline and which is in danger in relevant waters[31]; and Article 1(b) simply explains one particular, though major, example of such property. The remainder of this chapter includes detailed discussion of particular subjects of salvage; but under the Convention it is sufficient that a potential subject of salvage falls within the broad principle just stated, and not necessary that it fits neatly into previously recognised classifications. By Article 6.1, the Convention applies unless the subject in question is excluded.

165 However, the general principle in Article 1 should not be construed too widely. One interpretation of its applicability to any property not permanently and intentionally attached to the shoreline is that it will embrace property which, though normally so attached, has become detached, whether as a result of the danger or otherwise. The point is important because, of course, property which is the product of human construction will rarely, if ever, be incapable of detachment from the shoreline; and, if property does become detached, there are good reasons why salvage services should be encouraged. Nevertheless, in the absence of clear evidence of intention to depart from the general exclusion from salvage in *The Gas Float Whitton No. 2*[32] of static objects, it may be assumed that the Convention does not alter the law in this respect.

166 Article 1(c)'s reference to freight at risk applies the Convention to a traditional subject of salvage, though it is not clear whether this specific extension to one particular subject of salvage (i) simply confirms the Admiralty law position on freight at risk, (ii) implies that the Conventional definition is otherwise exclusive, or (iii) implies that the Conventional definition is inclusive. The third interpretation is preferred.

---

[31] The relevant waters are discussed *post*, §§ 362–376.
[32] *Supra*, n. 8.

Of course, most of the provisions of the Convention may be overridden by agreement[33] and in modern practice salvage is commonly carried out under contract. The contract may therefore specify the subjects to which it applies. Accordingly, Box 2 of LOF 2000 describes the "Property to be salved" as:

167

"The vessel:
her cargo freight bunkers stores and any other property thereon but excluding the personal effects or baggage of passengers master or crew
(referred to in this agreement as 'the property')"

(b) Navigable craft

Vessels, ships and boats

The most obvious item of maritime property to form a subject of salvage is a ship or vessel. The ship was the first item identified by Lord Esher M.R. in his famous judgment in *The Gas Float Whitton No. 2*[34] as a subject in respect of the saving of which salvage could be rewarded by the Admiralty Court.

168

The provisions of the Merchant Shipping Acts have applied variously to ships and/or vessels. Thus, unless the context otherwise requires, section 313(1) of the Merchant Shipping Act 1995 states that " 'ship' includes every description of vessel used in navigation."[35]

Article 1 of the International Salvage Convention 1989 provides:

169

"For the purposes of this Convention—
(a) Salvage operation means any act or activity undertaken to assist a vessel or any other property in danger in [relevant waters].[36]
(b) Vessel means any ship or craft, or any structure capable of navigation."

The law prior to the Merchant Shipping Act 1995 does not provide clear and consistent guidance on the interpretation of the words "ship" and "vessel". Those terms and variants thereof[37] have been employed in different ways

---

[33] Art. 6.1.
[34] *Ante*, §156.
[35] The current definition includes vessels "propelled by oars", which were specifically excluded from the definition of "ship" in MSA 1894, s.742.
[36] See *post*, §§ 369–376.
[37] See also *Perks v. Clark* [2001] 2 Lloyd's Rep. 431, CA.

Subjects of Salvage

in different legislation,[38] as they are in the Merchant Shipping Act 1995,[39] and the courts seem to have been concerned with giving effect to the policy behind the legislation in question, or in particular to not applying the legislation to inappropriate situations (*e.g.* where maritime rules would prejudice personal injury claimants), than to providing consistent definitions of ships and vessels.

170 It was decided under previous merchant shipping legislation that the words of inclusion in the definition of "ship" and *mutatis mutandis* of "vessel" in that legislation were not to be read as meaning "shall be confined to," but are inclusive rather than exclusive.[40] Indeed, it has been said that the policy of the legislature was to enlarge, rather than to narrow, the definition of a ship.[41]

A vessel is usually a hollow receptacle used or capable of being used for transporting goods or people on water.[42] A wider definition of "vessel" is specifically provided for in provisions of the Merchant Shipping Act 1995 relating to the removal of wrecks. They apply to "every article or thing or collection of things being or forming part of the equipment, cargo, stores or ballast of the vessel".[43]

171 Obviously the most important type of vessel, and the one which has provoked the most frequent judicial interpretation of its meaning, is the "ship". The Admiralty jurisdiction provisions of the Supreme Court Act 1981 are expressed to apply, variously, to cargo, goods, materials, apparel, equipment, wreck, aircraft, hovercraft, other property and—in most instances—to ships. The word "vessel" is used once only, in the definition of "ship". Unless the context otherwise requires, "ship" includes any description of vessel used in navigation and, except in certain cases, includes a hovercraft.[44]

---

[38] Conversely, ships have fallen within other descriptions for the purposes of particular legislation: *e.g.* a ship has been held to be an "establishment" within the Sex Discrimination Act 1976 (*Haughton v. Olau Line Ltd* [1986] 1 W.L.R. 504) and "equipment" within the Employer's Liability (Defective Employment) Act 1969 (*Coltman v. Bibby Tankers Ltd (The Derbyshire)* [1988] A.C. 276).

[39] Thus, the MSA 1995, s.224(2), Sched. 11, Pt II, para. 5(1)(a) authorises the Secretary of State to make discretionary payments for saving life from "any United Kingdom ship": see *post*, § 310. A "United Kingdom ship" is *generally* defined as a ship registered in the U.K. under MSA 1995, Pt II: see *ibid.*, ss 1(3), 313(1).

Moreover, "[the] Secretary of State may by order provide that a thing designed or adapted for use at sea and described in the order is or is not to be treated as a ship for the purposes of any specified provision of this Act or of any instrument made thereunder": MSA 1995, s.311(1). The contemplated exercise of this power, particularly in relation to offshore craft, has not taken place.

[40] *ex p. Ferguson* (1871) L.R. 6 Q.B. 280.

[41] *ibid.*, 291, 292; *The Mac* (1882) 7 P.D. 122, 130, *per* Brett L.J.; *ibid.*, 131, *per* Cotton L.J. See also M. Summerskill, *Oil Rigs: Law and Insurance* (1979), Chap. 2.

[42] See *Steedman v. Scofield* [1992] 2 Lloyd's Rep. 163, 166, *per* Sheen J.

[43] MSA 1995, s.252(3).

[44] SCA 1981, s.24(1): " 'ship' includes any description of vessel used in navigation and (except in the definition of 'port' in section 22(2) and in subsection (2)(c) of this section) includes, subject to section 2(3) of the Hovercraft Act 1968, a hovercraft". On hovercraft, see *post*, §§ 257–259.

Boats and vessels propelled by oars

The Merchant Shipping Act 1894, s.742 defined "vessel" to include "any ship or boat, or any other description of vessel used in navigation" and "ship" to include "every description of vessel used in navigation not propelled by oars".

The word "boat" may be used with reference to larger vessels; though, if so, it is commonly used as part of a compound expression, such as steamboat, ferry boat or fishing boat. Normally, it is understood to apply to small, open vessels and to convey "the concept of a structure, whether it be made of wood, steel or fibreglass, which by reason of its concave shape provides buoyancy for the carriage of persons or goods. Thus, a lifeboat differs from a liferaft in that the boat derives its buoyancy from its shape, whereas a raft obtains its buoyancy from some method of utilizing air receptacles."[45] Lord Esher M.R., in his judgment in *Gapp v. Bond*,[46] held that the term "vessel" in the Bills of Sale Act 1878 would not include a raft or a Thames wherry but would include anything beyond a mere boat. "Boat" clearly would cover a wherry and it might perhaps cover a raft.

In *A Raft of Timber*,[47] Dr Lushington refused to treat a raft as a ship. "This," he said, "is neither a ship nor sea-going vessel; it is simply a raft of timber."[48] But, as Lord Herschell has pointed out in *The Gas Float Whitton No. 2*,[49] "rafts are frequently so constructed as to be in a sense navigated: they are capable of being and are steered. They often have crews resident on board; they are used for the transport, from place to place, by water, of the timber of which they consist, and sometimes of timber placed upon them."

In *Edwards v. Quickenden and Forester (No. 2)*,[50] where a racing skiff and a racing eight were in collision in the Thames, it was held that neither was a "vessel" on the grounds that "vessel" includes any ship or boat or any other description of vessel used in navigation, and "ship" includes every description of vessel not propelled by oars, so that no craft solely propelled by oars was a vessel and the provisions of the Maritime Conventions Act 1911 as to apportionment of blame were inapplicable.

Mention of "boats" and the exclusion of vessels "not propelled by oars" does not appear in the definitions of "ship" in the Supreme Court Act 1981, s.24(1) and the Merchant Shipping Act 1995, s.313(1) or the definition of "vessel" in the Salvage Convention 1989, Art. 1(b), so that both boats and vessels propelled by oars are now both prima facie included.

---

[45] *Steedman v. Scofield* [1992] 2 Lloyd's Rep. 163, 165, *per* Sheen J., holding that a jet ski was not a boat.
[46] (1887) 19 Q.B.D. 200.
[47] (1844) 2 W.Rob. 251.
[48] *ibid.*, 255.
[49] *The Gas Float Whitton No. 2* [1897] A.C. 337, 345.
[50] [1939] P. 261.

Navigation

174 As Lord Herschell's comment in *The Gas Float Whitton No. 2*[51] indicates, the definition of a ship or vessel may involve consideration of various relevant factors rather than simply an application of a precise general test. A particularly important part of the definition in the Merchant Shipping Act 1995 is that the object in question is both a "vessel" and "used in navigation."[52] This will normally exclude an object the position of which is fixed, such as a pier[53] or a floating buoy.[54] The exclusion would, therefore, also appear to embrace an oil rig.[55] However, the mere fact that an object is habitually moored may not be decisive. Thus, in one case, the view was expressed that a reclamation dredger, which was shaped like a ship and moving from one place of working to another as required, was not only a ship but also used in navigation.[56]

175 Objects which are constructed for use in navigation are, naturally, most commonly regarded as ships or vessels. It is particularly relevant that they are used for the carriage of goods and/or passengers[57] and also relevant that they have their own means of propulsion and direction, though this is not essential.[58] An object, such as a flying boat, which is capable of propulsion on water but primarily built for other purposes may not be regarded as a ship or vessel[59]; nor may an object in the process of construction for navigation but in an unfinished state, such as an unregistered ship just launched.[60] But an object which has been capable of independent, ordered navigation is likely to be considered to remain a ship or vessel, though it has become incapable of navigation, at least so long as there is a reasonable belief in its ability to regain its former capacity.[61] If a vessel is capable of navigation, she may be regarded as a vessel though not navigating on the sea.[62]

176 However, the definition of "ship" in the national legislation[63] is restricted to vessels which are "used in navigation", and therefore does not apply to

---

[51] *Supra*, n. 49.
[52] *cf. Steedman v. Scofield* [1992] 2 Lloyd's Rep. 163.
[53] *The Normandy* [1904] P. 187; *The Craighall* [1910] P. 207.
[54] [1897] A.C. 337; *The Upcerne* [1912] P. 160.
[55] See further Summerskill, Chap. 2. See also the Salvage Convention 1989, Art. 3; *post*, §§ 318–320.
[56] *Cook v. Dredging & Construction Co. Ltd* [1958] 1 Lloyd's Rep. 334, *per curiam*. See also *The Titan* (1923) 14 Ll.L.Rep. 484. *cf. The Blow Boat* [1912] P. 217.
[57] See *The Mac* (1882) 7 P.D. 126.
[58] *The Mac* (1882) 7 P.D. 126; *St John Pilot Commissioners v. Cumberland Railway and Coal Co.* [1910] A.C. 208 (P.C.); *The Mudlark* [1911] P. 116; *The Harlow* [1922] P. 175; *The Champion* [1934] P. 1; *The St Machar* (1939) 65 Ll.L.Rep. 119 (Ct of Sn).
[59] *Polpen Shipping Co. Ltd v. Commercial Union Assurance Co. Ltd* [1943] 1 K.B. 161. See also *Watson v. RCA Victor Co.* (1934) 50 Ll.L.Rep. 77.
[60] *The Andalusian* (1878) 3 P.D. 182.
[61] *Pelton S.S. Co. v. North of England Protection and Indemnity Association* (1925) 22 Ll.L.Rep. 510; *Merchants' Marine Insurance Co. v. North of England Protection and Indemnity Association* (1926) 23 Com. Cas. 165. See also *Chandler v. Blogg* [1898] 1 Q.B. 32.
[62] *Corbett v. Pearce* [1904] 2 K.B. 422; *Weeks v. Ross* [1913] 2 K.B. 229. *cf. The Mayor, etc., of Southport v. Morris* [1893] 1 Q.B. 359.
[63] SCA 1981, s.24(1); MSA 1995, s.313(1).

something which is otherwise a vessel but which is not used in navigation. In *Steedman v. Scofield*[64] Sheen J. said:

> "Navigation is the nautical art or science of conducting a ship from one place to another. The navigator must be able (1) to determine the ship's position and (2) to determine the future course or courses to be steered to reach the intended destination. The word 'navigation' is also used to describe the action of navigating or ordered movement of ships on water. Hence, 'navigable waters' means waters means waters on which ships can be navigated. To my mind the phrase 'used in navigation' conveys the concept of transporting persons or property by water to an intended destination. A fishing vessel may go to sea and return to the harbour from which she sailed, but that vessel will nevertheless be navigated to her fishing grounds and back again.
>
> 'Navigation' is not synonymous with movement on water. Navigation is planned or ordered movement from one place to another."

Accordingly—and even though, like a fishing boat, a jet ski must presumably leave and return to its resting place in planned fashion either side of use for its intended purpose—Sheen J. held that a jet ski was not a vessel so as to attract the shorter limitation period applying to vessels under the merchant shipping legislation.[65] Likewise, a sailing dinghy on a reservoir was held not to be a vessel in *Curtis v. Wild*.[66] It was held that "used in navigation" meant proceeding from an originating place A to a terminus B for the purpose of discharging people or cargo at the destination point, and not simply use for pleasure purposes by people who were messing about in boats.

177 However, the definition of "vessel" in the Salvage Convention 1989, Art. 1[67] is not restricted to vessels used in navigation and extends to "any structure *capable of navigation*", which presumably means currently capable of navigation rather than capable of being made so. Thus, it includes a vessel such as a sailing dinghy (which is a vessel). It is less clear whether a jet ski constitutes a vessel for the purposes of the Convention since, on the reasoning in *Steedman v. Scofield*,[68] it is not a vessel and, if it is not used in navigation, arguably not something capable of being so used. It does, however, fall within the Convention's application to other property not permanently and intentionally attached to the shoreline,[69] an extension which considerably reduces the need to bring mobile waterborne objects within the definition of "ship" or "vessel" for salvage purposes.

---

[64] [1992] 2 Lloyd's Rep. 163, 166.
[65] Under the Maritime Conventions Act 1911, s.8. See now MSA 1995, s.190.
[66] [1991] 4 All E.R. 172 (QB, Manchester).
[67] See *ante*, § 169.
[68] [1992] 2 Lloyd's Rep. 163.
[69] See *ante*, § 163.

(c) Property ancillary to navigable property

Contract

178 The following discussion must be read in the light of any contractual inclusion or exclusion of property to be considered as a subject of salvage. Thus, Box 2 of LOF 2000 includes within the "Property to be salved" " . . . bunkers stores and any other property thereon . . . ".

Apparel or equipment

179 The ship, her apparel and the wreck of these were expressly included within the subjects of salvage identified in *The Gas Float Whitton No. 2*[70] as being recognised at common law. And the statutory provisions relating to salvage specifically incorporated the apparel of ships or vessels[71] and of aircraft[72] within their purview. That it has been applied in connection with sailing ships, steamships and aircraft may suggest that "apparel" is an elastic term. It is a word which does not appear expressly to have been the subject of definition, either judicial or statutory, and it is in fact not now used in writs, pleadings or judgments. This is because those objects which might appear to fall within the definition are normally dealt with under some other description, principally as part of the ship or vessel. This reveals the perfectly sensible and well-established practice of treating as one all the property owned by the shipowner and distinguishing it from cargo not owned by him.

180 It is a practice which is reflected in the similar, but not identical, context of the court's exercise of its admiralty jurisdiction *in rem*. In *The Silia*,[73] the plaintiff time charterers wished to enforce an arbitration award against the shipowners. A Dutch company which had supplied stores to the vessel issued a writ *in rem* against her, in consequence of which she was appraised and sold together with everything on board belonging to the owners, including unused fuel oil (bunkers) and lubricating oil. The plaintiffs argued that the oil was not part of the ship, so that the proceeds of its sale were not part of the fund available to third parties who had obtained judgment *in rem*, and execution could be levied on the proceeds by any judgment creditor of the owners. The plaintiffs obtained a charging order *nisi* on the proceeds of sale of the oil but their application for the order to be made absolute was refused by Sheen J.

181 The question was whether the oil fell within the definition of "ship" so as to be within the court's Admiralty jurisdiction under the Administration of Justice Act 1956, s.3, then in force[74]:

[70] [1896] P. 42, 63; affmd [1897] A.C. 337.
[71] See MSA 1894, ss 544, 546. These provisions have now been repealed.
[72] See Aircraft (Wreck and Salvage) Order 1938, Art. 2.
[73] [1981] 2 Lloyd's Rep. 534.
[74] See now SCA 1981, s.21.

Property on board the ship not owned by the shipowner

"What I have to decide is whether the word 'ship' in s.3 has a limited meaning, and means no more than the hull, machinery and spare parts, or whether 'ship' has a wider meaning and means the hull, machinery and everything on board which is the property of her owners."

He held it to be the latter. In his judgment, the proceeds of sale of the oil were part of the *res* and, as such, available to judgment creditors *in rem*. He said[75]:

"I have no doubt that in the context of an action *in rem* the word 'ship' includes all property aboard the ship other than that which is owned by someone other than the owner of the ship . . .

If one goes back to the days before ships were driven by power derived from coal or oil a warrant served on a ship covered everything that belonged to it as part of its equipment, even to sails and rigging which are detached from it.[76] The personal property of the captain and crew are exempt. For many years before the 1956 Act was enacted it was the practice of the Admiralty Court to treat bunkers as part of the 'ship', unless they were shewn to be the property of charterers. If Parliament intended that an action *in rem* should be brought against the hull and machinery, and not against oil in the tanks, Parliament would have used language that made that clear. The language of the 1956 Act suggests that for this purpose no definition of 'ship' was needed and that the practice prevailing immediately before the 1956 Act should continue."

The expression "ship" or "vessel" can, therefore, encompass all property **182** on board owned by the shipowners, although it will normally be convenient to deal separately with cargo owned by the shipowner.

It will depend on the circumstances whether other items of the ship's apparel should be dealt with separately.

Property on board the ship not owned by the shipowner

Certainly, property which is not owned by the shipowner should be con- **183** sidered as distinct from the ship. This will obviously be the case with a bill of lading holder's *cargo*.[77] Likewise it is so with *bunkers* owned by charterers, as they commonly are under time charterparties.[78]

It is similarly the case with other property on board which is capable of being part of the ship or her apparel but is owned by a third party and is being *hired* by the shipowner.[79]

---

[75] [1981] 2 Lloyd's Rep. 534, 537.
[76] See *The Alexander* (1811) 1 Dods. 278, 282.
[77] See *post*, §§ 190–193.
[78] See *The Silia* [1981] 2 Lloyd's Rep. 534 (*supra*).
[79] *ibid.*, 535.

184 As shewn by the judgment in *The Silia*, however, property owned by third parties may be dealt with along with property of the shipowner in Admiralty proceedings. Sheen J. observed[80]:

> "When the Court orders that a ship is to be sold it is the duty of the Admiralty Marshal . . . to sell the ship and her contents, other than those articles which are the personal property of someone other than the owner of the ship. He permits the removal of the personal effects of the crew and equipment which is on hire: he destroys perishable food or other food which might attract vermin.
>
> In order to realise the highest price it was the practice in the past for the Marshal to sell separately from the ship such things as tinned food, stores, barometers and chronometers. The manner in which such items are sold is left to the discretion of the Marshal. Barometers and chronometers are now sold with the ship. Unbroached drums of oil are usually sold separately. But the oil in the ship's tanks must, for practical reasons, be sold with the ship. Those reasons are as follows. In some parts of this country the removal of fuel oil from a ship's tanks is prohibited because of the hazards involved. But even where that operation is permitted the oil would have to be pumped out of the tanks. In the case of a ship under arrest the need to remove the oil would be likely to occur at a time when pumps are not in operation and when no engine-room personnel are available. The oil would have to be pumped into a barge or land tanker, and the cost of the operation would have to be paid for. The quantity of oil might be too small to justify the cost of removing it. Furthermore, if the oil were to be removed from the ship it would be likely to attract import duty. On the other hand the oil will realise the current market price if it is sold in the ship. If anyone other than the owner of the ship asserts a right of property in the oil the Marshal refers that question to this court, as was done, for example, in *The Saint Anna*.[81] In that case it was not contended by the charterers that the court had no power to sell their fuel oil. The charterers only sought to recover the proceeds of its sale. It is the practice of the Admiralty Marshal to account separately for the proceeds of sale of fuel and lubricating oil sold with the ship because the brokers are entitled to commission on the price of the ship, but not on the price of the oil."

185 The common law contemplated that the interests involved in an adventure for salvage purposes were the ship, her apparel, cargo and freight. For various, not always articulated or clearly known, reasons, certain objects, such as the wearing apparel of passengers and seamen, seamen's wages, lives saved, bank notes, mails on board, and provisions were excluded. The standard authority for this attitude is *Brown v. Stapyleton*,[82] where it was held that only *merces*,

---

[80] *ibid.*, 535.
[81] [1980] 1 Lloyd's Rep. 180.
[82] (1827) 4 Bing. 119.

or cargo put on board for the purpose of commerce, was subject to a contribution.

In recent times, with the development of sophisticated and expensive wireless and navigational equipment and the installation on passenger vessels of banks, shops, night clubs and so on, there are many more interests in the common adventure than those envisaged in most of the cases, and it is unlikely that the court would confine, to *merces* or cargo, liability to contribute to salvage.

186 Not uncommonly, ships carry wireless or navigational equipment which is hired from its owners under contract. The contract frequently specifies who (generally, the shipowner) is to bear the risk of loss of the equipment and/or its rental. This may, of course, affect the question of who is liable for payment of a salvage award, although it does not answer the question whether the equipment is in the first place a subject of salvage. In the first instance, its status as a subject of salvage would appear to depend on whether it fell within one of the recognised categories. It is unrealistic to describe it as cargo, or "*merces*". But it could be counted as part of the ship or, more likely, of its apparel. Yet this again is somewhat artificial and, arguably, unnecessary if the general position is not so much that salvage is only due for preservation of something which is easily categorised under the existing heads but that it is due from all objects which are exposed to risk except those which for reasons of public policy are excluded because of their small value, the number of interests involved or the difficulties of collection. On the latter view, which seems preferable, there would be no reason for exempting radio equipment from the obligation to contribute as it is exposed to the risk, it is in most cases valuable, and it is easy to identify the owner and to collect the reward, by reference to the contract of hire. By analogy with cargo and freight, it might be proper to distinguish between the equipment at risk and its rental, although the latter sum may not be sufficiently large to justify such a distinction, particularly since in general the income-generating value of the equipment will be included in its overall salved value. In conclusion, it is submitted that radio and radar equipment should be recognised as subjects of salvage but that practical considerations, particularly of recovering salvage, and the fact that the shipowner is generally responsible for the equipment, and entitled to recover from third parties responsible for its loss, dictate that claims for salvage of such equipment should be brought against and satisfied by the shipowner.

187 The question might arise whether property which is supplied to a shipowner under a contract incorporating a *retention of title clause*, whereby the supplier purports to reserve his title to the goods, is to be treated as a separate subject of salvage. Such clauses are rarely upheld,[83] may need registration if they are

---

[83] The most recent survey is by G. McMeel, "Retention of Title: The Interface of Contract, Unjust Enrichment and Insolvency", Chap. 7 of F. D. Rose (ed.), *Restitution and Insolvency* (2000, Mansfield Press).

Subjects of Salvage

to be effective against a company,[84] and may not be enforced while a shipowning company in subject to administration proceedings.[85] The further practical problems that they are likely to present in salvage cases point to the shipowner's being responsible for payment of salvage for such goods.

Ship's provisions

188 If "ship" includes everything on board belonging to the owner, it includes food for consumption (*i.e.* not being carried as cargo) and other ship's provisions. Indeed, it has been stated that when the Admiralty Marshal carries out a court order to sell a ship, he destroys perishable food and other food that might attract vermin but sells, albeit separately from the ship, tinned food on board.[86] It was held in *Brown v. Stapyleton*[87] that provisions (in that case, victuals and ammunition) do not contribute to general average, even where the cargo of the ship consists only of passengers (in that case, convicts): only merchandise of value at destination, and not provisions attaching to the passengers, who are not themselves subjects of general average, could be included. It has previously been stated in this book,[88] citing *Brown v. Stapyleton*,[89] that ship's provisions, according to the analogy of general average, would not be liable to arrest for salvage. But the precise authority of *Brown v. Stapyleton* has been doubted in the leading work on general average, where it is pointed out that provisions carried as merchandise are included but other provisions were not clearly excluded.[90] It would not be unreasonable to exclude from salvage those provisions taken on board by passengers or members of the crew personally for consumption during the voyage.[91] But it certainly makes sense to include the owner's provisions for persons on board a large passenger ship, particularly if not all of them are likely to be consumed, and unnecessary to distinguish the owner's provisions on board non-passenger ships, even if a line could easily be drawn. On the analogy of the current view of the position in general average, therefore, ship's provisions should be taken into account as part of the ship.[92]

189 One reservation needs to be made, however. The salvor must not be permitted to recover twice in respect of the same items. Thus, in the case of passenger vessels, he should be rewarded for salvage of passage money less the cost of earning it (*i.e.* the value of ship's provisions that will be consumed

---

[84] Companies Act 1985, ss 395 *et seq.*
[85] Insolvency Act 1986, ss 15–16.
[86] *The Silia, supra,* n. 78, at p. 535.
[87] See (1827) 4 Bing. 119 and 12 Moore 334.
[88] (4th ed.), p. 384.
[89] *Supra.*
[90] Lowndes & Rudolf, §17–73.
[91] Beawes included such victuals within the exemption of passengers' personal effects. See Beawes, 243.
[92] The salved fund for rewarding salvage of lives and property from a vessel carrying troops and passengers in *The Eastern Monarch* (1860) Lush. 81 was made up partly of cargo, described in the headnote as "stores", on board at the end of the voyage.

by the passenger) but not for the value of such provisions as well. Commenting on *Brown v. Stapyleton*,[93] the editors of *Lowndes & Rudolf* state that, "If the claim to contribution had been allowed, it would have been based only on the value of the stores unconsumed at the end of the voyage."[94] Similarly in salvage.

(d) Goods

Cargo

After the ship, cargo is likely to be the next single largest item to qualify as a subject of salvage. In modern times the cargo will in most cases, particularly oil tankers, be more valuable than the ship. In Box 2 of LOF 2000, "her cargo" is listed after the vessel as the next item of "Property to be salved" to which the Lloyd's Form salvage contract applies. **190**

Cargo includes all the merchandise on the salved vessel, regardless of who its owner is. It is not necessary for it to be carried under a bill of lading or for freight to be payable for its carriage, although where freight is payable this may be an important factor in fixing the cargo's salved value. Aircraft cargo is by legislation made a subject of salvage,[95] as is hovercraft cargo.[96] **191**

The significance of cargo as a subject of salvage is that, if it is preserved, it is property which benefits from salvage services, for which benefit a contribution should be made. There is, therefore, no independent, intrinsic necessity in determining whether or not property being carried by the vessel qualifies as salvage. Thus, there is no reason to exclude from treatment as cargo aircraft or small vessels being carried as such just because, if they were travelling under their own power, they would be treated for salvage purposes as vessels or aircraft, rather than as cargo.

Likewise, it is of no consequence to the salvor that cargo being carried on deck is treated differently from other cargo as between its owner and the shipowner or other cargo-owners in other areas of maritime law.[97]

Despite the common law exclusion of human lives from the subject of salvage,[98] slaves were regarded as equivalent to other merchandise and, **192**

---

[93] *Supra.*
[94] §17–73.
[95] Civil Aviation Act 1982, s.87. *cf. Watson v. RCA Victor Co. Inc.* (1934) 50 Ll.L. Rep. 77.
[96] Hovercraft Act 1968, s.1(1)(h),(j),(3); Hovercraft (Application of Enactments) Order 1972 (S.I. 1972 No. 971), Art. 8.
[97] *e.g.* under the Carriage of Goods by Sea Act 1971, s.1(7), Sched., Art. 1(c), and in the law of general average (see Lowndes & Rudolf, *passim*) even though salvage and general average are governed by similar principles.
[98] See *post*, §§ 260 *et seq.*

Subjects of Salvage

therefore, as subjects of salvage.⁹⁹ By analogy, live animals, which are treated differently from other cargo under the Carriage of Goods by Sea Act 1971,¹ can safely be treated as cargo for salvage purposes.² There is no direct authority on the point but this is assumed to be so in practice. Animal lives have never been seen to be as important as human lives and to that extent not governed by the same policy of increasing an award against property for exertions to save lives.³ But it would arguably not be totally unjustified for slight account to be taken of additional exertions, on grounds of humanity, which are taken to avoid suffering by animals in danger.

193 The speeches of Lords Herschell and Watson in *The Gas Float Whitton No. 2*⁴ refer to goods which are or have formed part of the cargo or apparel of a ship as clear subjects of salvage. This does not mean that goods can only form subjects of salvage in cases where the vessel also is salved. The vessel need not be salved, certainly not by the cargo salvors. The identity of the vessel does not even have to be known. But some common identity with a vessel would seem necessary for, if property other than a vessel has not been on the sea during the course of navigation, it would seem to fall within the category of subjects, such as the gas float *Whitton No. 2*, which are outside the subjects of salvage.⁴ᴬ If property is being carried, then it would seem to qualify as cargo and as such a subject of salvage even if its normal identity is such that it would not. Thus, buoys being carried in a Trinity House vessel to or from repairs should be treated as cargo. Moreover, a steel space-frame structure for a drilling platform which was salved while being carried on a barge remained subject to a maritime lien even after its subsequent attachment to the sea-bed as (part of) a permanent structure.⁵

The question has arisen whether goods under tow should be treated as cargo. This is discussed below.⁶

Personal effects and luggage

194 The personal effects and luggage of passengers, master and crew are by tradition excluded from the subjects of salvage and, avoiding the possibility that the position might have been altered by the Salvage Convention 1989, are excluded from the application of the Lloyd's Form contract⁷ by its terms.⁸

---

⁹⁹ *cf. Brown v. Stapyleton* (1827) 4 Bing. 119.
¹ s.1(7), Sched., Art. 1(c).
² *cf. The Coriolanus* (1890) 15 P.D. 103.
³ See *post*, §§ 260 *et seq.*
⁴ [1897] A.C. 337, 343, 347.
⁴ᴬ See also the remarks on the Salvage Convention 1989, Art. 19, *ante*, §§ 61–63.
⁵ *Sembawang Salvage Pte Ltd v. Shell Todd Oil Services Ltd* [1993] 1 N.Z.L.R. 97 (N.Z. H.C.).
⁶ *Post*, §§ 195–200.
⁷ See further *post*, §§ 321–328.
⁸ LOF 2000, Box 2; LSSAC 2000, cl. 3.2.

Personal effects and luggage

(e) Towed property

Property which at a time of danger is being towed might normally be **195**
categorised within the established subjects of salvage (most obviously as a
ship or as cargo) or as an excluded subject (such as the gas float *Whitton
No. 2*). Whatever its normal classification, whether it is a subject of salvage
depends upon its classification at the time of the danger.

Pre-Convention law

It was suggested by Lord Herschell in *The Gas Float Whitton No. 2*[9] that **196**
the term "cargo" might extend to goods in tow:

> "Where goods are being towed from place to place, although they are
> not, strictly speaking, cargo, they yet partake of its character and are
> closely analogous to it. They are being transported from place to place by
> a vessel. Their transport is a maritime adventure of precisely the same
> nature as the carriage of goods in the body of a ship. All the grounds of
> expediency in which the law of salvage is said to have had its origin
> would seem to apply to the one case as much as to the other. It may be,
> then, that in salvage law a broad and liberal construction should be
> extended to the word 'cargo' so as to embrace goods in course of being
> transported by a vessel though not inside it. I desire to reserve my
> opinion on the point, in case it should hereafter be necessary to decide
> it."

Whether or not tug and tow are considered separately, they must each
contribute to rewarding salvage services from which they have benefited. If
they were both owned by the same person, it would in one sense be immaterial
how much he had to contribute in respect of each item of property—although,
in practice, he would need to know for which sums he is to be indemnified by
different insurers. There is, therefore, no intrinsic merit in discriminating
between a tow which is considered as part of a tug's cargo and one that is dealt
with as a distinct vessel. What is imperative is to discern whether (a) tug and
tow are both experiencing a common danger and are both benefiting from a
salvage service rendered to preserve them both from that danger or (b) they
receive different services for which they should not both be bound to
contribute.

The identity of tug and tow for general average purposes has been con- **197**
sidered in two American cases. In *The J.P. Donaldson*,[10] a tug was towing
some sailing barges, each of which had its own means of propulsion and was
under the control of a master. To save herself from grounding during a storm,

---
[9] [1897] A.C. 337, 344–345.
[10] (1897) 167 U.S. 599 (U.S. S.C.).

the tug cast off the barges, which were lost. The barge owners could not recover a general average contribution from the tug because the tug and the barges were not so connected by the contract of towage as to make the tug and the tow, while navigated under and in accordance with that contract, a single maritime adventure. The master of each barge, and not of the tug, had authority and responsibility for the barge cargo and could not affect the tug's liability by his decisions. Moreover,

> "The fact that the sum to be paid to the tug for towing each barge was measured by a certain proportion of the freight to be earned by that barge is immaterial. It did not create a partnership between the owners of the tug and the owners of the barges. Nor could it have the effect of combining the tug and the barges into a single maritime adventure, within the scope of the law of general average."[11]

The case was distinguished in *S.C. Loveland Co. v. USA*,[12] where a tug was towing two barges owned by the tug-owner. After a casualty, one of the barges was run on shore to prevent its sinking. Although this action was not taken to benefit the tug, the other barge or the cargo on board, the United States District Court held all three liable to contribute to general average to be paid to the owner of the cargo on the other barge.

198   Neither case is binding on English courts or above criticism. In particular, *S.C. Loveland* would appear to be wrongly decided, for there was no obvious common danger to justify general average. Both cases suggest that tug, tow and cargo on board a tow may, but will not always, be united in a common adventure so as to require contribution for a general average act for the common benefit, such as setting adrift a tow. But, even so, it is not easy to envisage circumstances where all three could be liable for salvage services provided to the tow and its cargo. It might in a general sense benefit the tug which was liable to be pulled on to the rocks in a storm by the tow for the tow to be taken away by a salvage tug. But that would be no real benefit in law because a tug in such circumstances is not legally bound to remain attached to the tow; the danger to the tug arises from not exercising her privilege to let go the tow, not from the storm. There would only be a common danger if tug and tow were defined to be engaged in a common adventure as an incident of the towage contract—but that is definition for the sake of definition, it does not explain why as a matter of general principle the tug should pay salvage. To deem there to be a common adventure would be to provide a gratuitous benefit to the salvor, by giving him additional rights against the tug, the value of which would presumably be brought into account. It would also impose a double burden on the tug, which could be worth much less than the tow, to require it to contribute to the reward payable for saving both tug and tow. This

---

[11] *ibid.*, 606.
[12] [1963] A.M.C. 260.

might seem even more unjust if it is recalled that the tug's presence on the voyage in the first place was to provide a service for the tow.

199 For that reason, it is less unreasonable to require the tow to contribute for a salvage service provided to the tug, especially if the tug keeps a line aboard the tow during the danger, so as to obviate even greater salvage services which would be needed by the tow if she grounded.[13] But that is no doubt justifiable anyway: not because they are regarded as participating in a common adventure, but because a benefit provided to the tug would likewise in fact probably be a benefit to the vessel it was towing.

Under the Salvage Convention 1989

200 The Salvage Convention 1989 applies to any property which is not permanently and intentionally attached to the shoreline[14] at the time at which the danger occurs. Accordingly, the Convention applies as a matter of general principle to property under tow and it is unnecessary to consider whether or not that property falls within one of the traditional headings of subjects of salvage.[15]

(f) Wreck

Former definition

201 In its most ancient sense, the description "wreck" was limited to those portions of ship and cargo which were cast up on land. The location of the property was important because, as in the case of all salvage, the jurisdiction of the ancient Admiralty Court originally only extended outside the body of a county. In the case of wreck, which could only be classified as such if cast upon land, the further fact that the high seas extended only to low-water mark might have seemed to imply that wreck could never have been within the Admiralty jurisdiction. This was certainly so when the land was within the body of a county, *i.e.* with the jurisdiction of the common law courts, and the ancient Admiralty Court was prevented from exercising jurisdiction there by prohibitions issuing from the courts of common law. It would seem that the former Admiralty jurisdiction over wreck was, at least by the end of the nineteenth century, restricted to wreck cast up abroad where no prohibition issued. However, the Admiralty jurisdiction has been extended to the body of a county, as stated above, and the salvage jurisdiction in the case of wreck

---

[13] *cf. The Rilland* [1979] 1 Lloyd's Rep. 455.
[14] Art. 1(c). See *ante*, §163.
[15] Similarly, platforms and mobile offshore drilling units under tow (and so not "on location engaged in the exploration, exploitation or production of sea-bed mineral resources") are not excluded from the Convention by Art. 3. See Shaw [1996] L.M.C.L.Q. 202, 210. *cf. post*, §§ 317–320.

which was formerly exercised within the framework of the common law in the bodies of counties has been transferred to the Admiralty jurisdiction.[16]

202   In the Admiralty Court in *The King (in his office of Admiralty) v. Forty-nine Casks of Brandy*,[17] Sir John Nicholl referred with approval to explanations of the term wreck by Coke and Blackstone and by the Court of King's Bench in *Sir Henry Constable's Case*.[18] It was resolved in *Constable's Case*: "That nothing shall be *wreccum maris*, but such goods only which are cast or left on the land by the sea."[19] According to Blackstone[20]:

> "shipwrecks ... are ... declared to be the king's property by the ... prerogative statute 17 Edw. II, c.11[21] and were so, long before, at the common law....
> It is to be observed that, in order to constitute a legal *wreck*, the goods must come to land. If they continue at sea, the law distinguishes them by the barbarous and uncouth appellations of *jetsam, flotsam*,[22] and *ligan*.... These three are therefore accounted so far a distinct thing from the former, that by the king's grant to a man of wrecks, things jetsam, flotsam, and ligan will not pass."

203   It was held by Sir John Nicholl in *The King v. Forty-nine Casks of Brandy*,[23] that all casks floating beyond the high-water mark which had never touched the ground, including those floating between the high and low water marks, were droits of the Crown in its office of Admiralty but the casks found aground, including those aground between the two water marks, were wreck and therefore within a grant to the local lord of the manor. The following year, he held, in *The King v. Two Casks of Tallow*[24]:

> " '*Wreccum maris*' is not such in legal acceptation, till it comes ashore, until it is within the land jurisdiction; whilst at sea, it belongs to the King in his office of Admiralty, as derelict, flotsam, jetsam, or ligan. Above high-water mark it belongs to the lord of the manor as grantee of the Crown; but beyond low-water mark he can have no claim; it is on the high seas and belongs to the Admiralty. It is equally clear law that between high and low-water marks it is *divisum imperium*; when the tide covers this space it is sea; when it recedes, it is again land and within the

---

[16] See *ante*, Chap. 2.
[17] (1836) 3 Hagg. 257.
[18] (1601) 5 Co. Rep. 106a.
[19] *ibid.*, 106a. See also 2 Coke, Inst., Pt II, Vol. 1, 167: "wreck, or shipwreck, legally *wreccum maris*, a wreck of the sea, in legal understanding, is applied to such goods as, after shipwreck, are by the sea cast upon the land."
[20] Bl.Com. (7th ed., 1756) Vol. i, 290, 292–293.
[21] See *ante*, Chap. 2.
[22] See also the definition of flotsam in *Palmer v. Rouse* (1858) 3 H. & N. 505, 510, *per* Martin B.; *post*, § 206.
[23] *Supra*.
[24] (1837) 3 Hagg. 294.

jurisdiction of the manor (*Constable's Case*).[25] If the article be floating, it belongs to the sea; it is not '*wreccum maris*' but 'flotsam': if it become fixed to the land, though there may be some tide remaining round it, it may be considered as '*wreccum maris*' but it having merely touched the ground, and being again floating about, its character will depend upon its state at the time it was seized and secured into possession; whether, for instance, the person who seized it, as salvor, was in a boat, or wading, or swimming.

Such, in my judgment, being the law, what are the facts? There is an affidavit from the persons who brought the goods to shore; and even supposing they were mistaken as to the state of the tide, there seems no reason to doubt that they went into the sea, and so within the admiralty jurisdiction, and that the casks, therefore, were not '*wreccum maris*', but flotsam. I cannot agree to the proposition that things having once touched the ground thereby necessarily become the property of the lord of the manor. What might be the law in the case of things having become fixed on the shore and afterwards the sea leaving them and then returning, may be a question hereafter, but it is one which does not arise at present in this case."

Flotsam, jetsam and lagan

The descriptions "flotsam, jetsam and lagan" were explained in *Sir Henry Constable's Case*[26] in terms approved by Sir John Nicholl in *The King v. Forty-nine Casks of Brandy*[27] and in the Court of Appeal in *The Cargo ex Schiller*[28]:

204

"*flotsam* is when a ship is sunk, or otherwise perished, and the goods float on the sea; *jetsam* is when the ship is in danger of being sunk, and to lighten the ship the goods are cast into the sea, and afterwards notwithstanding the ship perish. *Lagan* (*vel potius ligan*) is when the goods which are so cast into the sea, and afterwards the ship perishes, and such goods cast are so heavy that they sink to the bottom, and the mariners, to the intent to have them again, tie to them a buoy, or cork, or such other thing that will not sink, so that they may find them again, & *dicitur lig. a ligando*; and none of these goods which are called *jetsam, flotsam*, or *ligan*, are called wreck so long as they remain in or upon the

---

[25] *Supra*, n. 18.
[26] (1601) 5 Co.Rep. 106a, 106a–106b.
[27] (1836) 3 Hagg. 257.
[28] (1877) 2 P.D. 145, 148, *per* Brett L.J. See also *The Cosmopolitan* (1846) 6 N.o.C. Supp. xvii, xxvii–xxviii. In *The Cargo ex Schiller, supra*, 148, Brett L.J. continued (in his dissenting judgment) that in *Constable's Case, supra*, "the reason is given why such things were given to the king. 'Note, reader, at first the common law gave as well as wreck, jetsam, flotsam, lagan, upon the sea, as estray, &c., treasure trove, and the like, to the king, because, by the rule of the common law, when no man can claim property in any goods, the king shall have them by his prerogative'. Applying this principle to the former definitions, it seems to me that nothing can be considered to be flotsam, jetsam, or lagan, within any effective legal definition of those things, if it has never been taken possession of by any one but the true owner."

sea; but if any of them by the sea be put upon the land, then they shall be said wreck."

Flotsam, jetsam and lagan were always within the jurisdiction of the ancient Admiralty Court and the common law courts do not appear ever to have attempted to interfere by prohibition or otherwise.

Admiralty Court's current jurisdiction

205 The Admiralty Court's jurisdiction over flotsam, jetsam, lagan and derelict continues to exist, as part of the inherent Admiralty jurisdiction exercised in the Admiralty Court. However, the former jurisdiction of the common law courts over wreck within the body of a county has also been transferred to the Admiralty jurisdiction.[29]

206 For salvage purposes it is an extended feature of the identity of wreck in relation to ships or vessels that the wrecked property previously was or formed part of property which was within the classification of subjects of salvage, principally a vessel, its apparel or cargo. Thus, where planks of timber had been moored in a river above a harbour and had accidentally got adrift and floated down to the sea, the Court of Exchequer held that, as a matter of construction of the statute this was not a case where Parliament had given jurisdiction to justices to make an award for salvage of wreck under the Merchant Shipping Act 1854.[30] However, Martin B. also referred to "the well known meaning of flotsam, as stated in the *Termes de la Ley*, it refers to goods having been at sea in a ship and separated from it by some peril."[31] Similarly, a gas float moored as a beacon which had got adrift was held not to be wreck within the same Act in *The Gas Float Whitton No. 2*.[32]

207 The principal statutory provision for wreck is currently the Merchant Shipping Act 1995, Pt IX, Chap. II, which provides that in that Part of the Act, unless the context otherwise requires, "wreck" includes[33] jetsam, flotsam, lagan, and derelict found in or on the shores of the sea or any tidal water.[34]

The statutory provision is drafted within the framework of the case law relating to wreck and does not contemplate the inclusion of wreck in subjects of salvage made such by statute. Thus, salvage would not be awarded for the recovery of the dead bodies of shipwrecked persons.[35] Specific provision has

---

[29] See *ante*, Chap. 2.
[30] *Palmer v. Rouse* (1858) 3 H. & N. 505.
[31] *ibid.*, 510.
[32] [1897] A.C. 337. See *ante*, §§ 154–157.
[33] "Includes" does not mean "shall be confined to": *ex p. Ferguson* (1871) L.R. 6 Q.B. 280, 290, *per* Blackburn J.
[34] s.255(1).
[35] They do not fall within the definitions of "wreck". They are of a different nature from the subjects of salvage from which they derive: the wreck of a vessel may be said to be the vessel in a different, though less valuable form whereas a corpse falls outside the definition of a "life" and outside the statutory policy of preserving lives or valuable property in peril. Moreover, corpses have traditionally fallen outside the definition of property. See Matthews (1983) 36 C.L.P. 193.

been made for other types of wreck. So far as aircraft salvage is concerned, "wreck" is generally expressed to include any aircraft or any part or cargo thereof found derelict in or upon the seas surrounding the United Kingdom or the tidal waters thereof or upon or near the shores of the said sea and waters or found or taken possession of outside those limits and brought within them.[36] So far as the legislation relating to hovercraft is concerned, "wreck" generally includes any hovercraft or any part or cargo thereof found stranded or abandoned in or on any navigable waters, or on or over the foreshore, or place where the tide normally ebbs or flows.[37] Fishing boats or fishing gear lost or abandoned at sea and either found or taken possession of within the territorial waters of the United Kingdom or found or taken possession of beyond those waters and brought within them are treated as wreck for the purposes of Part IX of the Merchant Shipping Act 1995.[38]

Derelict

Derelict was not specifically mentioned by Lord Esher M.R. in *The Gas Float Whitton No. 2*,[39] but it was unnecessary for him to do so for the gas float in question was certainly not derelict. "Derelict" is a term legally applied to a thing which is abandoned and deserted at sea by those who were in charge of it, without hope on their part of recovering it (*sine spe recuperandi*) and without intention of returning to it (*sine animo revertendi*).[40] Derelict has always been within the Admiralty jurisdiction. The term is in practice usually applied only to a vessel, but it might properly be used of cargo also apart from a vessel.[41]

The question whether a vessel is or is not to be adjudged a derelict is decided by ascertaining, not what was actually the state of things when she was quitted by her master and crew, but what were their intentions and their

---

[36] Aircraft (Wreck and Salvage) Order 1938 (S.R. & O. 1938 No. 136), Art. 2(b). See *post*, §§ 244 *et seq.*

[37] Hovercraft (Application of Enactments) Order 1972 (S.I. 1972 No. 971), Art. 8(1). See *post*, §§ 257–259.

[38] See Fisheries Act 1968, s.17, as amended by MSA 1995, s.314(2) and Sched. 13, para. 43(b).

[39] [1896] P. 42.

[40] See *The Perla* (1857) Swab. 230, 230–231; *Cossman v. West* (1887) 13 App.Cas. 160, 180, 181; *The Aquila* (1798) 1 C.Rob. 37, 40; *The Coromandel* (1857) Swab. 205, 208, 209; *The Gertrude* (1861) 30 L.J.Adm. 130, 131; *The Cosmopolitan* (Irish) (1848) 6 Not. of Cas.Suppl. xvii, xx–xxviii; *The Zeta* (1875) L.R. 4 A. & E. 460, 462; Marvin on *Wreck and Salvage*, p. 133; *The Tubantia* [1924] P. 78, 87; *Pierce v. Bemis (The Lusitania)* [1986] Q.B. 384, 388, *per* Sheen J. ("A ship is derelict in the legal sense of the term if the master and crew have abandoned her at sea without any intention of returning to her and without hope on their part of recovering her"). See also *Bradley v. H. Newsom, Sons and Company* [1919] A.C. 16; *The Belgia* (1941) 71 Ll.L.Rep. 21, 22, *per* Langton J. In *The Heemskerk* (1941) 70 Ll.L.Rep. 35, the vessel was abandoned but the hopes and intentions of her master and crew do not appear to have been investigated.

[41] *The Samuel* (1851) 15 Jur. 407, 410; *The King v. Property Derelict* (1825) 1 Hagg. 383; *The King v. Forty-nine Casks of Brandy* (1836) 3 Hagg. 270; *The King v. Two Casks of Tallow, ibid.*, 294; *Boiler ex Elephant* (1891) 64 L.T. 543.

expectation when they quitted her.[42] The vessel is not a derelict if she is left by her master and crew temporarily, for the purpose of procuring assistance, or with the distinct intention of returning to her,[43] although the master may have given up the entire management to salvors.[44] On the other hand, a deserted vessel is not the less a derelict, because those who left her for the safety of their lives, and not for the purpose of getting assistance, meant, if they could, to send a steamer to look for her[45]; and if they intended at the time to leave her finally, a change of intention on their part, and an effort by them to regain her, are immaterial.[46]

210 In judging of the intention and expectation of the master and crew at the time of abandonment, the Admiralty Court, in the absence of any direct evidence which is satisfactory, is guided by the consideration of the surrounding circumstances, such as the fact that the vessel was then near the coast and not in the open sea,[47] or that the quitting of the ship took place without counsel or deliberation in the agony of collision,[48] or under pressure of enemy action.[49] A barge found adrift in the Thames without anyone on board is not, in the absence of further evidence of abandonment by her owners, to be treated as a derelict.[50] A vessel found at sea in a position of danger and without any one of her crew on board is prima facie a derelict.[51] But she ought not to be considered a derelict if it is shown that she had been captured by the enemy and afterwards deserted by the captor; for in such a case there is no *animus derelinquendi* imputable to the owner.[52]

---

[42] See *The Sarah Bell* (1845) 4 Not. of Cas. 144, 146. In *The Albionic* [1941] P. 99, 107, Langton J. commented on *The Sarah Bell:* "At the time when that case was determined I can well believe that there would have been few to differ from the judge's decision [that the vessel, waterlogged, aground on the Haisborough Sands and having lost her rudder, had been abandoned by her crew *sine spe revertendi*; and was thus a derelict for salvage purposes]. Today, with the vastly improved machinery of salvage, I can very easily imagine that most judges would decide the other way."

[43] *The Aquila* (1798) 1 C.Rob. 37, 40; *The Lepanto* [1892] P. 122.

[44] *Cossman v. West* (1887) 13 App. Cas. 160; *The Lepanto, supra.*

[45] *The Coromandel* (1857) Swab. 205.

[46] *The Sarah Bell* (1845) 4 Not. of Cas. 144.

[47] See *The Barefoot* (1850) 14 Jur. 841, 842; *The Florence* (1852) 16 Jur. 572; *The Heemskerk* (1941) 70 Ll.L.Rep. 35.

[48] *The Cosmopolitan* (Irish) (1848) 6 Not. of Cas.Suppl. xvii; *The Fenix* (1855) Swab. 13, 15; *The Pickwick* (1852) 1 Jur. 669, 670. And see *The Portreath* [1923] P. 155.

[49] *The F. D. Lambert* [1917] P. 232n.; *Bradley v. Newsom, infra*, in the text. But the mere fact of damage by enemy action causing abandonment is not conclusive either way: *e.g. The Amelia Lauro* (1940) 68 Ll.L.Rep. 12; *The San Demetrio* (1941) 69 Ll.L.Rep. 5; *The Belgia* (1941) 71 Ll.L.Rep. 21.

[50] *The Zeta* (1875) L.R. 4 A. & E. 460. In *The Upnor* (1826) 2 Hagg. 3, Lord Stowell rejected a claim for salvage which was preferred by persons who had found a barge, without persons on board, and with no anchor out, aground on a sandbank in the Medway. The owners satisfied the court that the two hands had only left the barge to procure assistance, and that it was a common usage to leave barges on the sand.

[51] *The Cosmopolitan, supra*; *The Pergo* [1987] 1 Lloyd's Rep. 582 (Ct Sn) (vessel abandoned on automatic pilot with engines running at half speed).

[52] *The John and Jane* (1802) 4 C.Rob. 216; *The Cosmopolitan, supra*, at pp. xxix–xxxi. But see *The Lord Nelson* (1809) Edwards 79.

In *Bradley v. Newson*,[53] while on a voyage from Archangel to Hull with a cargo of timber, the steamship *Jupiter* was attacked off the coast of Scotland by a German submarine. The master and crew were compelled by force to leave the vessel. Believing the vessel to have been sunk, the master so informed the owners. The submarine did not in fact sink the vessel, which was salved and brought into Leith. The cargo owners claimed delivery of the cargo at Leith free of freight, on the ground that the contract of affreightment had been terminated by abandonment of the vessel. The House of Lords[54] held that the circumstances in which the master and crew left the vessel were not such as to make the vessel derelict, and the cargo owners were not entitled to treat the contract of carriage as at end. In his speech, Lord Finlay L.C. said[55]:

> "The crucial question is this. Was this vessel, when she was picked up by salvors, a derelict in the legal sense of the term; or, in other words, had the master and crew *abandoned* her without any intention of returning to her, and without hope of recovery? It appears to me to be quite impossible to answer this question in the affirmative. In quitting the vessel the master and crew simply yielded to force. There was no voluntary act on their part, and the case stands exactly as it would have done if they had been carried off the vessel by physical violence on the part of the crew of the German submarine. It would be extravagant to impute to them the intention of leaving the ship finally and for good. They simply bowed to the pressure of irresistible physical force. If a British destroyer had appeared on the scene, and had driven off or sunk the submarine, they would gladly have returned to their vessel. All they intended was to save their lives by obeying the orders of the German captain. . . . The physical act of leaving the vessel is only one feature in such a case. Another and essential feature, in order to make it a case of derelict, is the state of mind of the captain and crew when they left. The question *quo animo* is decisive, and the facts seem to me to show clearly that the quitting of the ship was not under such circumstances as to make it a case of derelict".[56]

The intentions and expectations of the master and crew are judged at the time of abandonment, although evidence of this may be supported by subsequent events. In *The Lusitania*,[57] Sheen J. thought the matter was put beyond doubt by the owners of the ship claiming and being paid by underwriters on the basis of an actual total loss of the ship and (despite the unavailability until more recently of facilities for recovery) a "necessary inference" from a lapse of 67 years before the owners of the contents made

---

[53] *Bradley v. H. Newsom, Sons and Company* [1919] A.C. 16.
[54] Lord Sumner dissenting.
[55] [1919] A.C. 16, 27.
[56] For cases of vessels derelict following damage by enemy action, see *supra*, n. 49; recent peacetime cases include *The Trumpeter* (1947) 80 Ll.L.Rep. 263; *The American Farmer* (1947) 80 Ll.L.Rep. 672; *The Firethorn* (1948) 81 Ll.L.Rep. 178.
[57] *Pierce v. Bemis (The Lusitania)* [1986] Q.B. 384, 389.

Subjects of Salvage

any attempt to recover them. He held further that it is immaterial to the status of an object as derelict whether it is afloat or lying on the sea bed.[58]

Wreck under the Salvage Convention 1989

213 The Salvage Convention 1989 does not mention wreck, thereby avoiding, but not resolving, controversy during negotiations leading to the Convention whether or not wreck was, or should be, covered by it.[59] It is not a major practical concern for professional salvors, who normally operate on floating or stranded casualties; wrecks are likely to attract difficulties in dealing with local authorities and to require great expense for little reward, so that it is better to render services on a contractual[60] rather than a salvage basis.

214 A further issue is that wrecks, especially historic or cultural wrecks, may be more appropriately dealt with by a specific regime rather than as part of the law of salvage. In some countries wreck recovery is not part of the general law of salvage; and historic or cultural wrecks raise wider issues than the commercial ones normally arising in salvage cases. The Convention itself, in Article 30(1)(d), authorised signatories to disapply the Convention to maritime cultural property of prehistoric, archaeological or historic interest which is situated on the sea-bed. However, the United Kingdom has not availed itself of this power.

215 English law has traditionally included wrecks within subjects of salvage. The Convention is generally inclusive,[61] and does not provide for the exclusion of wrecks. Consequently, if as a matter of construction wrecks fall within the terms of the Convention, it will apply to them. The Convention aplies generally to any property which is not permanently and intentionally attached to the shoreline. It can therefore confidently be asserted that it applies to vessels or goods which are afloat. Property which has sunk and become attached to the shoreline should also be covered since, even if it has become permanently attached, it is unlikely to have become so attached *intentionally*. Of course, the fact that wreck falls within the description of property to which the Convention applies does not answer all difficulties. For example, the property must also be in danger[62]; and questions of ownership may have to be settled.

---

[58] Relying on *HMS Thetis* (1835) 3 Hag. Adm. 228, 235; *The Tubantia* [1924] P. 78; *The Association and The Romney* [1970] 2 Lloyd's Rep. 59, 60.

[59] See Gaskell, 21–376 to 21–377.

[60] For a daily rate or lump sum, such as Wreckcon 1993.

[61] See *ante*, § 163.

[62] In some jurisdictions, property which has come to rest is not regarded as being in danger; and some property (*e.g.* bullion) may patently be in no, or minimal, danger of deterioration at rest on the sea-bed. However, English law has traditionally regarded sunken property, of whatever nature, to be in a position of danger.

3. FINANCIAL INTERESTS

Freight and hire

Freight generally

Freight is an undoubted subject of salvage and it is included within the description of "Property to be salved" in Lloyd's Form.[63] However, the term requires closer investigation to identify exactly what type of freight is included within the description for salvage purposes, in particular whether the expression incorporates or extends to charterparty hire. This involves the further though theoretically separable questions of whose freight (shipowners', charterer's or cargo-owner's) is in issue and how that freight is valued. The latter question is frequently subsumed in the valuation of the carrying vessel and the cargo being carried; this is dealt with below in the chapter on salved values.[64] This association between freight and tangible property also raises the issue of the means by which a salvor can enforce his claim by exercise of a lien or action *in rem*, an issue of admiralty procedure generally rather than salvage *stricto sensu*.[65] **216**

Freight is not a specified subject of salvage under the Merchant Shipping Acts. However, Lord Esher M.R. in *The Gas Float Whitton No. 2*[66] identified it as such, although he did not expand on the meaning of the term. The word is used in a number of senses.[67] **217**

Freight is ordinarily regarded as the remuneration payable to the shipowner by the cargo-owner for the carriage of cargo. It is most commonly taken to refer, therefore, to the remuneration earned for carriage of cargo to destination and its arrival there for delivery in merchantable condition to its owner. Such freight is normally only payable on such cargo as actually so arrives, as *freight collect*. It is, however, possible for the full amount of freight contracted for to be *lump sum freight*, payable on arrival of the cargo even if not all of the consignment in fact arrives safely. Since freight is in principle payable for carriage to destination, it is generally not payable where goods are delivered before arrival at the originally intended destination. But, where the contract of carriage is performed by a substituted method, *pro rata freight* may be payable by agreement. Clearly distinct from freight payable on arrival is *advance freight*, which, if expressed to be payable under the contract, must be pre-paid in full on shipment and is non-returnable in the event that the cargo is lost. Ordinary freight, lump sum freight, advance freight and pro rata freight are all examples of freight which may be payable for carriage of cargo under the **218**

---

[63] Box 2.
[64] Chap. 14.
[65] See *post*, Chap. 13; Jackson, §§ 18–38 to 18–40, 20–45.
[66] [1896] P. 42, 63.
[67] See Carver, §§ 1661 *et seq.*; Scrutton. Chap. 15.

terms of a bill of lading. In modern times, tanker charterparties commonly provide for freight to be paid collect but in the dry cargo trades it is generally pre-paid.

Charterparty remuneration

219 The expression "freight" may also be used to describe the remuneration payable by the charterer under a charterparty. The method by which it is calculated and payable varies in practice and depends ultimately, of course, on the terms of the particular charterparty. There are, however, two basic variants. First, it might be calculated by relation to the amount of cargo actually carried, whether payable initially by the cargo-owner to the charterer or to the shipowner, and whether payable on delivery or in advance. Alternatively, the charterer might pay one or more stipulated sums to the shipowner. In the case of a voyage charterparty—a charter of the use of the vessel for a single voyage, which is commonly regarded as a contract for the carriage of goods by sea—the charterer's payment is invariably termed freight, however payable. In the case of a demise charterparty, under which the charterer becomes *pro hac vice* and during the term of the charter equivalent to the shipowner[68] and which is akin to the lease of the vessel for period, the charterer's payment is not inappropriately termed "hire," is calculated independently of the volume of cargo expected to be, or actually, carried, and is payable periodically. A third type of charterparty—the most recently developed of the three and nowadays, with the voyage charterparty, one of the two most important—is the time charterparty. This is not a hire of the ship but a contract whereby the owner provides the services of the master and crew in sailing the ship for the charterer's purpose, under his directions in accordance with the contract.[69]

220 It would not have been entirely wise in the very early days of time charterparties, when sail was the principal method of ship propulsion, for the charterer to have relied on the uncertainties of the elements in paying for the use of the vessel. It would therefore, have been appropriate for his remuneration to have been determined by reference to the freight payable on the cargo actually carried during the operation of the charter. That consideration, taken together with the established description of the shipowner's remuneration as freight, may help to explain why payments under time charterparties were formerly spoken of as "time freight" or "time chartered freight". As Donaldson J. has said[70]:

> "It is only in comparatively modern times that the word 'hire' has been used. It was formerly known as 'time freight' or 'time chartered freight'. Indeed, in marine insurance terminology, 'freight' still includes 'hire'."

[68] *Baumwoll Manufactur von Carl Scheibler v. Furness* [1893] A.C. 8.
[69] *Mardof Peach & Co. Ltd v. Attica Sea Carriers Corporation of Monrovia (The Laconia)* [1977] A.C. 850, 870.
[70] *Seven Seas Transportation Ltd v. Atlantic Shipping Co. S.A.* [1975] 2 Lloyd's Rep. 188, 191.

However, the change in the times has been accompanied by a change in practice. The increased use of modern motor-powered vessels meant more reliable sailing times, free from the vagaries of the weather, so that charterers could more confidently contract for the charter of vessels to be paid for at regular intervals to the period of use rather than the amount of cargo carried. Lord Denning M.R. has observed[71]:

221

> "At one time it was common to describe the sums payable under a time charterparty as 'freight'. Such description is to be found used by judges and textbook writers of great distinction. But in modern times a change has come about. The payments due under a time charter are usually now described as 'hire' and those under a voyage charter as 'freight'. This change of language corresponds, I believe, to a recognition, that the two things are different. 'Freight' is payable for carrying a quantity of cargo from one place to another. 'Hire' is payable for the right to use a vessel for a specified period of time, irrespective of whether the charterer chooses to use it for carrying cargo or lays it up, out of use. Every time charter contains clauses which are quite inappropriate to a voyage charter, such as the off-hire clause and the withdrawal clause. So different are the two concepts that I do not think the law as to 'freight' can be applied indiscriminately to 'hire'."

Potential confusion arises, as MacKinnon L.J. has observed, since[72]:

222

> "A time charterparty is, in fact, a misleading document, because the real nature of what is undertaken by the shipowner is disguised by the use of language dating from a century or more ago, which was appropriate to a contract of a different character then in use [a demise charterparty]."

Thus, Cumming-Bruce L.J. has commented[73]:

> "The term 'hire,' as MacKinnon L.J. observed, is really wholly inappropriate a description of the consideration payable by the charterer for the use of a vessel, its master and crew, put at the charterer's disposal for the purposes of the use of the vessel for the carriage of goods by sea on bills of lading signed by the master on behalf of the owners, although under most time charterparties the master acts on the direction of the charterer. If you look at the mutual obligations of owner and charterer at the time of the charterparty there is no express provision for the carriage of cargo, yet the whole object of the adventure comprised in the charterparty is an adventure for carriage of goods by sea and the provisions of the charterparty expressly make that perfectly plain. When one looks at the history of the word 'freight' as used to describe the consideration in

---

[71] *Federal Commerce & Navigation Co. Ltd v. Molena Alpha Inc. (The Nanfri)* [1978] Q.B. 927, 973.
[72] *Sea and Land Securities Ltd v. William Dickinson & Co. Ltd* [1942] 2 K.B. 65, 69.
[73] *The Nanfri, supra*, n. 71, at p. 996 (a dissenting judgment).

shipping contracts paid by the charterer, as a matter of common sense 'freight' is a more apt description of the consideration payable by the charterer on a hire charter than the term 'hire.' This explains the fact, which I regard as emerging clearly from an examination of the authorities, that that was the way in which the consideration in a hire charter was described throughout the 19th century and the early years of the 20th century. 'Freight' and 'hire' seem frequently to have been used indistinguishably in innumberable judgments."

223 The purpose for which remuneration is paid under a charterparty and the terminology used to describe it will therefore vary depending on the type of charterparty. The charterer may be liable for voyage charter freight, demise charter hire or time charter "hire," and the contract may require him to pay in arrear or in advance.

224 The preceding account sets out the basic position concerning payments by cargo-owners under contracts of carriage, which will normally be contained in the terms of a bill of lading or similar document, and by charterers under the relevant form of charterparty. The picture in practice is infinitely more complicated.

At its most straightforward, the vessel may not be under charter, in which case it is simply a question of considering the arrangements for payment of freight by shippers of cargo to the shipowner.

Equally, if the vessel is demise-chartered, the charterer becomes for all practical purposes the shipowner during the period of the charter and hire is normally payable whatever events occur during that time. It is payable and paid regardless of events necessitating salvage, so its payment is not something that will be preserved for the benefit of the owner by salvage unless the vessel is saved from imminent total loss. The benefit which the charterer normally derives from its payment is a profit-earning vessel, for the preservation of which a reward must be paid anyway, normally by the true owner, under a demise charter by the *pro hac vice* owner.[74] Since the demise charterer is *pro hac vice* owner, bill of lading freight will be payable to him in the normal way.

The position may be more complicated under voyage and time charterparties because, whatever the basic obligation to pay freight or hire, the means by which these payments are produced or secured may vary considerably, as the following paragraphs demonstrate.

225 *Sub-charterparties.* A charterer of the whole vessel may sub-charter part of it. The sub-charter may be effected by the head charterer as agent for the owner and the sub-charterer's payments may be due directly to the owner, for which the head charterer receives a commission. More likely, the payments

---

[74] Separate questions are whether the owner should contribute for preservation of a vessel of value to him after the termination of the demise charter and the effect of arrangements in the charter between the parties as to payment of salvage.

are for the benefit of the head charterer, but may be payable in the first instance to the owner, who may or may not be entitled to deduct sums due from the head charterer before paying over to him, and in any case the owner may have, though not invariably, a lien on the sub-freights for payments due from the head charterer.

226 *Bills of lading for goods on a chartered ship.* A cargo-owner normally expects to contract for the carriage of his goods with the shipowner and will be held to do so unless the position is clearly otherwise. The charterer may, however, contract with him as carrier and issue bills of lading himself. But the cargo-owner will normally wish to contract with the actual carrier and the charterparty, particularly if a time charterparty, will frequently require that ship's rather than charterer's bills of lading be issued but that the charterer will indemnify the owner for loss he may suffer as a result of issuing the bills. In such a case, the bill of lading freight will normally be paid directly to the owner. But it will depend on the terms of the charterparty whether, as between charterer and shipowner, the owner receives the freight on his own account, subject to paying a commission to the charterer, through whose efforts it was derived, or on account of the charterer, though even in this case the owner may have a lien over the cargo and the bill of lading freight for payments due from the charterer.

227 *Voyage charterparties.* A voyage charterer may be obliged to pay freight collect or in advance, and the remuneration due from him may or may not vary depending on the quantity of cargo carried. If it does depend on the volume carried, it may be collected from cargo shippers by the owner, who, after deducting the sum due from him, will pay the surplus to the charterer. It may be payable to the owner as agent for the charterer or payable directly to the charterer, but in either case the owner may have a lien on the cargo for unpaid charter freight. What is more, the shipper's obligation to pay freight in advance or collect will be independent of whether the charterer's obligation is to pay in advance or collect. Thus, the charterer may be liable for advance freight and the cargo-owner for freight collect (normally for a higher amount, otherwise the charterer will make no profit).

228 *Time charterparties.* The position is not dissimilar under time charterparties, though hire will normally be payable at a specified rate, frequently in advance and independently of bill of lading freights, which will normally be payable under the bill of lading to the shipowner but thereafter under the charterparty to the charterer. The owner will normally have a lien over the cargo for bill of lading freight, but not for unpaid hire. He may or may not have a lien for unpaid hire over the bill of lading freight when it is paid. The purpose for which a payment is made must be determined according to the particular circumstances. Thus a pre-payment, under a contract of carriage with time charterers, by cargo-owners to the shipowner of advance freight, and not on account of hire, for cargo which is never

Subjects of Salvage

shipped, cannot be retained by the shipowner as hire payable in advance under the charterparty.[75]

"Freight at risk"

229 It is a fundamental principle of the law of salvage that a contribution to the salvage reward is payable by a person who derives a benefit from salvage. Obvious beneficiaries will be the owners of tangible assets preserved by salvage, namely, the owners of the ship and its cargo. The position of freight and hire is less certain. In certain cases, it will be unnecessary to consider them as independent subjects of salvage on the same level as ship and cargo. Thus, if non-returnable advance freight has been paid by a cargo-owner, this expense will be passed on to and count towards the value of the goods at destination. Indeed, goods are commonly valued on a c.i.f. basis. The shipowner will have received the freight before salvage and will have derived no benefit from the salvage; if advance freight was payable but not in fact paid, he can recover it by action.[76] The cargo-owner's investment in the voyage, as freight, will be subsumed in the enhanced (c.i.f.) value of the cargo for which, if salved, he must contribute accordingly. Similarly, unless hire ceases to be payable in the event of salvage, the owner of a ship chartered by demise stands to suffer no loss and therefore derives no benefit from salvage.[77] The charterer's investment of hire is reflected in the value of the ship to him as a profit-earning chattel.

230 The fact that freight and hire can thus be subsumed within the value of ship or cargo and that they are in practice treated as elements of valuation obscures the issue whether they can be treated as independent subjects of salvage. Lord Esher M.R. in *The Gas Float Whitton No. 2*[78] included freight within his list of subjects of salvage without adverting to the question. The former statutory provisions governing liability for salvage do not even go so far, for they were framed as being only applicable to tangible property.[79] That freight has been assumed to be included can be deduced from those cases in which the statute has been held applicable to freight and from Brett M.R.'s comment, in delivering the judgment of the Court of Appeal in *The Renpor*,[80] that:

> "for the saving of life alone without the saving of ship *freight* or cargo salvage is not recoverable in the Admiralty Court."

---

[75] *Afro Produce (Supplies) Ltd v. Metalfa Shipping Co. Ltd. (The Georgios)* [1978] 2 Lloyd's Rep. 197.

[76] If it was payable in advance but returnable in the event of non-arrival of the cargo, it is not true advance freight but must be treated in the same way as ordinary freight collect.

[77] Whether he would suffer a loss if his ship became a total loss, and the effect of provisions in the charterparty as to salvage, is considered *post*, Chap. 6.

[78] [1896] P. 42, 63.

[79] See MSA 1894, ss 544, 546 (now repealed). See now the Salvage Convention 1989, Art. 1(c) (including "freight at risk" within the definition of "property").

[80] (1883) 8 P.D. 115, 117 (emphasis added).

But it is likely that his Lordship was only contemplating freight as an inevitable element in computing the amount of the award to be given for salvage of ship and cargo. In the great majority of cases, it will be irrelevant that the Act fails to mention freight for it must normally be taken into account in valuing the benefit received by the owners of ships and cargoes salved from danger. It is important to examine, however, the extent to which "freight", whatever that term may be deemed to encompass, can, and/or should, be regarded as an independent subject of salvage.

Conclusions

231 The question whether freight can be regarded as a subject of salvage involves consideration of the meaning of the term freight and whether it extends to voyage and/or time charter hire. Since the object of a voyage charterparty is similar to that of a contract for the carriage of goods by sea, it is not too great a step to classify voyage charter hire as freight. However, time charterparties are different in nature, and incidentally of more recent history, and different considerations may apply.

The availability and consequent pre-eminence of reliable power-driven vessels has prompted the growth of both time charterparties and professional salvors. The reliance by professional salvors on, principally, the Lloyd's Form of salvage contract and the consequent withdrawal of salvage matters from the court, for resolution confidentially by arbitrators, has no doubt deflected judicial consideration of the question whether time charterparty hire can be an independent subject of salvage.

232 The role of Lloyd's Form in this area deserves particular attention, for in the majority of cases the issue will not so much be one of principle but of construction—whether the "freight" in question, be it a form of freight or of hire, falls within the treatment of freight to which Lloyd's Form applies. In *The Pantanassa*,[81] Brandon J. assumed that a claim for salvage lay against charterers as owners of freight at risk and that voyage charterers fell within the expression "owners of freight" within Lloyd's Form. But he expressed no view as to the correctness of those assumptions nor on a further, third, assumption.

His third assumption was that a master purporting to sign Lloyd's Form on behalf of charterers had authority to do so. It can reasonably be assumed that a master signing Lloyd's Form does not, and need not, consider specifically on whose behalf he signs the form but is entitled to assume that he is acting on behalf of whomsoever is correctly described as an owner of freight and that such a person, if correctly described, is bound. That, however, requires reversion to resolution of the point at issue.

233 Two practical issues confuse resolution of the matter in hand. The first is the absence of an independent procedure *in rem* against freight or hire, though the

---

[81] [1970] P. 187, 192–193.

procedural obstacle, which does not prevent the possibility of an action *in personam*, should not *per se* affect substantive rights. It does, however, provoke recollection of the court's unwillingness to award salvage in circumstances where the danger is not directly to tangible property at risk.

The second factor to bear in mind is that, in practice, the salvor's reward for preservation of freight or hire commonly derives from the inclusion, if any, of the value of freight or hire in the salved value of a ship or cargo which is the subject of salvage. The extent to which this is or should be done is not a matter beyond controversy.[82] The modern practice is to assess the value of the ship not taking into account the charter upon which she is engaged and her profit-earning capacity. Voyage charter freight is regarded as an independent subject of salvage but, despite some judicial support,[83] time charter hire is not.

Passage money

234   Where, as the consequence of a supervening peril, a shipowner is unable to complete the carriage of passengers to their destination, a person who intervenes to enable the shipowner to complete the carriage, or who himself carries them on to the destination, may be able to recover salvage.

Passage money is normally paid to the carrier in advance and so is not at risk on the voyage. Consequently, there have been very few opportunities for the courts to consider whether its preservation justifies a salvage reward. In turn, it has not been specifically dealt with in either the Brussels Salvage Convention 1910 or the International Salvage Convention 1989. Nevertheless, it seems clear that passage money is in principle a subject of salvage at common law and that it comes within the ambit of the International Salvage Convention 1989.

The "common law"

235   The leading case is *The Medina*.[84] A steamship carrying pilgrims to Jedda for passage money of £4,000 was wrecked on a rock in the Red Sea. The *S.S. Timor* came up but refused to take off the passengers for less than £4,000. The master of the *Medina* reluctantly entered into an agreement whereby the *Timor's* master agreed "to take the whole of his passengers (pilgrims) from off the Parkin Rock and take them to the Port of Jedda . . . for the lump sum of £4,000 sterling." He performed his part and, it seems,[85] £4,000 passage money was paid to the owners of the *Medina*, which was lost with its cargo. The owners of the *Timor* sued the owners of the *Medina* to recover the sum

---

[82] See further Howard (1975) 91 L.Q.R. 502.
[83] *The Castor* [1932] P. 142; *Five Steel Barges* (1890) 15 P.D. 142.
[84] (1876) 2 P.D. 5; affirming (1876) 1 P.D. 272.
[85] See *ibid.*, 274; Kennedy (4th ed.), p. 385. This is not entirely clear from the reports, though see (1876) 45 L.J. Adm. 78, 82: "The value of the *Timor* was £45,000, and her cargo was about £90,000. The freight of the *Medina* was about £4,000." In *The Mariposa* [1876] P. 273, 279, Gorell Barnes J. said of *The Medina:* "I have been unable to ascertain upon what terms the pilgrims were being carried, and whether the passage-money was at risk and saved by the services of the salvors."

of £4,000 under the agreement in an action *in personam* in the Exchequer Division of the High Court. The action was transferred to the Admiralty Division, where Sir Robert Phillimore, whose judgment was upheld by the Court of Appeal, refused to uphold the agreement as being inequitable,[86] but he awarded the plaintiffs salvage of £1,800.

It is not clear that *The Medina* is a case on salvage rather than simply on inequitable contracts, for it is entirely consistent with the High Court's general equitable jurisdiction not to enforce an agreement for a sum which is unconscionably high but to award payment of a lower sum than the one contracted for.[87] However, the fact that the proceedings were transferred from the Exchequer Division to the Admiralty Division is evidence that the case was perceived not simply to concern the enforcement of an inequitable contract but as falling within the jurisdiction of the High Court in Admiralty to give a salvage reward for preservation of passage money for the original carriers. **236**

In such a case, two potential benefits accrue to the original carrier. He ultimately receives the passage money which he was in danger of losing. And, if he were liable to carry the passengers to their destination even after the danger, he escapes liability to them for failing to do so. In practice, this second class of benefit will be illusory: it is unlikely that the contract will have required performance absolutely, particularly other than by the originally contemplated method, and/or that the original contract will not have been frustrated. **237**

If, as is most likely in such a case, the contract of the shipowner with the passengers excludes liability to forward them on to their destination and the master tranships them, he may be held to be "acting for the benefit, and on account, and as the agent, of the passengers, and not of the" shipowner, so that remuneration for the transhipment will be payable by the passengers, not by the shipowner.[88] This need not be so. That the owner is excused from having to continue performance does not mean that he cannot do so and recover the contract remuneration accordingly or that, assuming performance of the original contract to have terminated, he could not recover from the passengers for the on-carriage he subsequently procures on the basis of an implied contract or in restitution.

Furthermore, it should not be necessary for either the salvor or the original carrier to take the passengers on to their destination. If a third party actually finishes the job on behalf of the original carrier, the salvor should be entitled to claim for his success in rescuing the passengers from the danger so as to preserve the means of earning passage money, as would be the case with freight.

---

[86] See *post*, §§ 925–952.
[87] See Goff & Jones, Chap. 12.
[88] See *The Mariposa* [1896] P. 273, in which there was held to be no danger such as to make life salvage claimable.

Subjects of Salvage

238 Assuming *The Medina* can correctly be treated as a salvage case, it supports the assertion that, where the remuneration to be earned by the voyage consists of money payable for the carriage of passengers, and the ship is lost but the passengers are saved and are carried in the saving ship to their destination, so that through the service this remuneration is earned for the owner of the lost ship, there is in that remuneration a valuable interest which is saved so that the shipowner is liable to the person preserving the passengers' lives and the passage money to pay a salvage reward.[89] If this is indeed the case, it carries three implications.

239 First, and most obviously, it implies generally that, where passage money is saved to the shipowner, even without an agreement to do so, the person responsible for its preservation will be entitled to a salvage reward in respect of the passage money. This is borne out by Dr Lushington's decision in *The Eastern Monarch*.[90] The vessel, which had voyaged from the East Indies on its way to London caught fire in Portsmouth harbour. Consolidated actions were brought for salvage of the lives, hull and cargo saved. The principal consideration was to reward life salvage. The value of the hull and cargo saved was £2,131 15s. 3d. and passage money was £2,001 3s. 0d., making a total of £4,132 18s. 3d. Bearing in mind the statutory provision authorising life salvage,[91] £1180 was awarded for life salvage and £480 for property salvage. On these figures, life and property salvage could have been paid out of the fund provided by the property preserved. But his Lordship clearly conceived that the owner's liability had to be satisfied in respect of both property and passage money, albeit he made no reference to the statute's failure to mention either freight or passage money. His decision is not inconsistent with this omission.

240 Secondly, *The Medina* suggests that freight in the form of passage money can be an independent subject of salvage. In *The Medina*, nothing was saved apart from the passengers' lives and their baggage. Human lives are not an independent subject of salvage[92] and passengers' luggage is treated as being exempt from salvage claims.[93] If passengers' luggage were regarded as prima facie a subject of salvage but merely exempt in practice, passage money would not have to be regarded as an independent subject of salvage. But it would be a blatant fiction to award salvage for the preservation of that part of the passage money earned to carry the passengers against money earned to carry both passengers and their luggage. This is particularly so since the

---

[89] See Kennedy (4th ed.), p. 384.
[90] (1860) Lush. 81.
[91] MSA 1854, s.459. See now *post*, §§ 298–310.
[92] See *post*, §§ 260 *et seq.*
[93] See *post*, §§ 321–328 *et seq.* If this exemption is merely a privilege, it might be asserted that an entitlement to salvage arises in circumstances such as those in *The Medina* for the preservation of the luggage but on the enhanced basis adopted in Admiralty for the simultaneous preservation of lives. But this would be unrealistic. The maximum amount payable would be the value of the luggage saved, which is likely to be less than the passage money. It would in practice not be collectable, or only at great inconvenience. And it would be payable by the owners of the luggage, the passengers, not by the shipowner.

greater proportion of it is presumably earned for the carriage of the passengers rather than the luggage.[94] Moreover, a different result would presumably be regarded as anomalous. The problem cannot be circumvented by treating the lives of the passengers as prima facie subjects of salvage but exempt in practice because this possibility is specifically denied by the Court of Appeal: there is no admiralty jurisdiction *in rem* against human lives.[95] Finally, if passage money is not *sui generis* but is a species of freight, it falls foul of the absence of a procedure *in rem* against freight alone.[96]

241 Thirdly, if passage money is preserved and is not doubted to be an independent subject of salvage, the salvor of the passengers' lives will be entitled to recover life salvage. This could simply be an enhanced award on common law principles against the payee of the passage money. It has been stated above that the statutory jurisdiction to award salvage does not expressly authorise a reward in respect of the salvage of freight; nor, by extension does it do so of passage money. It is doubtful, however, whether life salvage could be so recoverable by statute. The relevant provision[97] makes a reward for the salvage of life payable "by the owner of the vessel, cargo, or apparel saved" but not by the owner of "freight" saved. It may be inferred that freight is nonetheless one of the subjects of salvage covered by Brett M.R.'s comment, in delivering the judgment of the Court of Appeal in *The Renpor*,[98] that:

> "for the saving of life alone without the saving of ship *freight* or cargo salvage is not recoverable in the Admiralty Court."[99]

242 But it is likely that his Lordship was only contemplating freight as an inevitable consideration in awarding salvage in respect of ships and cargoes. In most cases, it is irrelevant that the Act fails to mention freight for it is taken into account in valuing the benefit received by the owners of ships and cargoes salved. But that does not necessarily justify a judicial rectification of this parliamentary *casus omissus*. It is, therefore, submitted that the salvor of passage money has no additional claim under statute for life salvage. If he salves passage money, he must be content with his claim in respect of that.

The International Salvage Convention 1989

243 The International Salvage Convention 1989 states that "This Convention shall apply to *any* salvage operations"[1] and that, "For the purpose of this

---

[94] The contract may provide that passengers pay only for themselves and that luggage goes free. But the courts can treat carriage of both as part of the shipowner's consideration: see Atiyah (1976) M.L.R. 335; but *cf. Esso Petroleum Co. Ltd v. Customs & Excise Commissioners* [1976] 1 W.L.R. 1.
[95] See *post*, §§ 260 *et seq.*
[96] *cf. The Kaleten* (1914) 30 T.L.R. 572.
[97] MSA 1894, s.544(1).
[98] (1883) 8 P.D. 115.
[99] *ibid.*, 117 (emphasis added).
[1] Art. 6.1 (emphasis added).

Convention—(a) Salvage operation means any act or activity undertaken to assist a vessel or any other property... " and "(c) Property... *includes* freight at risk."[2] These provisions do not clearly include or exclude passage money from the ambit of the Convention. The express incorporation of freight within a range of subject-matter which is primarily tangible property makes clear that a traditionally important subject of salvage is included. However, it does not thereby bring passage money in, since passage money is not "freight". But nor does the failure to mention passage money imply its exclusion: the definition of property is inclusive. Moreover, there is no evidence in the *travaux préparatoires* of an intention to exclude it. Accordingly, passage money may be a subject of salvage within the Convention. If it were not within the Convention, it would nevertheless seem to fall within the Admiralty jurisdiction over "any claim... in the nature of salvage not falling within" the International Salvage Convention 1989 or a contract concerning salvage.[3]

4. AIRBORNE CRAFT

(a) Aircraft

History

244 When Lord Esher M.R. proffered his description of the subjects of salvage in *The Gas Float Whitton No. 2*,[4] the first powered, sustained and controlled flight by heavier-than-air aircraft had not yet taken place[5] and it is probable that salvage services to any other form of aircraft[6] were not then considered. There seems no reason why aircraft being carried by a sea-going vessel as cargo should fall outside the court's Admiralty jurisdiction over cargo but the right to claim for salvage of aircraft in other circumstances or property on board was more controversial. Whatever the answer at common law, the growth of international air traffic in the twentieth century obviously necessitated some clear guidance on the applicability of Admiralty jurisdiction to aircraft.

Parliament first dealt with the issue in the Air Navigation Act 1920, section 11 of which provided that:

"The law relating to wreck and to salvage of life or property, and to the duty of rendering assistance to vessels in distress... shall apply to

---

[2] Art. 1(a), (c) (emphasis added).
[3] SCA 1981, s.20(2)(j)(iii). See *post*, Chap. 13.
[4] [1896] P. 42; affirmed [1897] A.C. 337; *ante*, §§ 154–157.
[5] The Wright Brothers' machine did not fly until December 17, 1903.
[6] The first aerial voyages were in 1783 by balloon, the first man-carrying glider flew about 1850, the first dirigible airship flew under power in 1852, and the first dirigible airship to use an internal combustion engine flew in 1870.

aircraft on or over the sea or tidal waters as it applies to vessels, and the owner of an aircraft shall be entitled to a reasonable reward for salvage services rendered by the aircraft to any property or persons in any case where the owner of a ship would be so entitled. . . . "

Unfortunately, the section confused the extent to which the common law of salvage was sufficiently adaptable to accommodate services of a salvage nature rendered to aircraft. The problem first arose judicially in *Watson v. RCA Victor Company Inc.*[7] A seaplane *en route* from New York to Europe was forced by bad weather onto the sea near Greenland. After sending an SOS message, she made a sea passage towards a rocky islet surrounded by an ice pack but foundered on it. The pilot and passengers scrambled on to the islet, a bare rock with no bird life, vegetation, shelter or means of communication. They were taken off by a steam trawler together with cinematograph equipment which they had succeeded in saving and in respect of which salvage was claimed.[8] It was conceded that, for the claim to succeed, the seaplane had to be regarded as of the nature of a ship or vessel or boat, which, it was held, it was not. The Sheriff-Substitute, whose judgment was upheld on appeal, said[9]:

245

> "It is common knowledge that a seaplane is in reality only a species of aircraft, and that although its construction permits of its floating on the sea, or even being navigated a short distance, its primary function . . . is navigation in the air. Its construction for the purpose of floating or moving on the water is, I understand, mainly designed for purposes of safety should it be compelled through stress of weather or mechanical defect or for other reasons to descend from the air while flying above water. In short, in popular language no one would I think describe a seaplane as a ship, or vessel, or boat. But further it is, I think, plain that a seaplane does not satisfy the definitions or descriptions of a ship or a vessel given in either the Merchant Shipping Acts or the decided cases. . . . The essential element in these definitions[10] is that ships or vessels must be structures 'used in navigation.' Plainly it cannot be predicated of a seaplane—which as pointed out is a species of aircraft—that it is 'used in navigation' in the sense in which a vessel or ship is so used. . . . But the conclusive argument against the contention that at common law aircraft such as a seaplane ought to be regarded as a ship for salvage purposes is the fact that the benefit of the law relating to wreck and to salvage of life and property was only extended to aircraft by section 11 of the Air Navigation Act 1920. . . . I may observe (a) that if at common law seaplanes, which are included in aircraft, could be

---

[7] (1934) 50 Ll.L.Rep. 77.
[8] No claim was made for life salvage.
[9] *ibid.*, 78–79, after citing Lord Esher M.R.'s conclusion in *The Gas Float Whitton No. 2* [1896] P. 42, 63: *ante*, §156.
[10] Of "vessel" and "ship" in the Merchant Shipping Act 1894, s.742. See now MSA 1995, s.313(1).

Subjects of Salvage

regarded as ships or vessels or boats for the purposes of salvage, there was no necessity for the legislature enacting the provisions of section 11 of the Act of 1920, and (b) that there is no attempt in that section to include aircraft in any definition of a ship, all that the section does being to enact that the law relating to wreck and salvage of life and property shall apply to aircraft as it applies to ships."[11]

246 There are, with respect, several flaws in this reasoning. First, it proceeds—not unreasonably, it is conceded—on the assumption that the court's inherent Admiralty jurisdiction can only be applied to one means of transport—that is, ships or similar structures—an assumption that can be questioned. It does not follow, from a finding that normally static floating objects are outside the law of salvage, that, if the Admiralty law of salvage only applies to vessels which are or are capable of being used in navigation, then it is necessarily limited to structures which can be, and are, only used in navigation in or on the sea, so as to exclude structures which are capable of being so used, especially when they must partly be so used. Just as a ship or boat normally used on inland waterways could be a subject of salvage whilst on the sea, so, arguably, should a seaplane or flying boat. This must especially be the case where the aircraft is amphibious. There is no clear evidence in the report to support the view that the seaplane's construction to float or move on the water was mainly designed as an additional safety factor—not, of course, that it would necessarily be desirable to lead distinctions between aircraft which could land on the sea, depending on whether they were designed to land primarily on the sea or mainly on land.

247 Secondly, the mere fact that the 1920 Act dealt with salvage of aircraft does not necessarily mean that the law of salvage of aircraft was only extended to aircraft by the Act, for there was no decision to deny that it did not already so apply. If aircraft did notionally fall within the common law, it does not follow that it was totally unnecessary so to enact, for statutes may advantageously clarify doubtful points of law. In fact, necessity is irrelevant for the Act was passed primarily to give effect to an international convention relating to the regulation of aerial navigation,[12] the provisions of which might or might not have reflected existing English law. The convention had provided[13] that "With regard to the salvage of aircraft wrecked at sea the principles of maritime law will apply, in the absence of any agreement to the contrary", and section 11, it seems, merely sought to reflect this, however obscurely. It did not necessarily extend merely the benefit of the law of salvage to salving aircraft, nor, since its wording was not inappropriate to specify aircraft as subjects of

---

[11] It was also said that the Air Navigation Act 1920, s.11 might have made applicable to it the law relating to salvage as if it had been a ship, if the salvage services had been rendered within the territorial waters of Great Britain, but that the statute had no application to salvage services off the coast of Greenland. It was unnecessary to consider a further point, whether the nature of the rocky islet was such that the claim failed, as being one for rescue from land.
[12] The Convention of Paris 1919.
[13] Art. 23.

Airborne Craft

salvage, was it essential to do what is in one sense ludicrous—to define aircraft as ships.

As will be seen,[14] subsequent legislation has negatived the restrictions of *Watson v. RCA Victor* but it retains some residual importance in emphasing the narrow interpretation of Lord Esher M.R.'s judgment in *The Gas Float Whitton No. 2*.[15] The case was cited, with apparent approval, in *Polpen Shipping Co. Ltd v. Commercial Union Assurance Co. Ltd*,[16] in which Atkinson J. held that an (anchored) flying boat was not a "ship or vessel" within the meaning of a marine insurance policy—quite correctly, though the case might unthinkingly be referred to in order to support the view that aircraft fall outside the inherent Admiralty jurisdiction.

248

Certainly, it is true that no claim at common law has succeeded for salvage of or from aircraft, and Hewson J. has said[17]:

> "It needs but little imagination to realise that prior to 1873[18] this court had no jurisdiction over aircraft of any kind—and certain it is that gliders did not exist in those days—and I class gliders as aircraft. It may well be that there were odd balloons blowing about, but this court had no Admiralty jurisdiction over them, so far as I am aware."

Section 11 of the Air Navigation Act 1920 was amended by the Air Navigation Act 1936.[19] By authority of the two Acts, the Aircraft (Wreck and Salvage) Order 1938[20] was made, with the clear intent of making aircraft subject to the law of salvage and to Admiralty jurisdiction.[21] In the same year, an international convention was signed primarily to tackle salvage problems resulting from the use of flying boats which landed at sea and then proceeded to ports as surface vessels.[22] The convention has, however, never come into force. Of more moment was the Civil Aviation Act 1949, s.51, which superseded the Acts of 1920 and 1936 and by virtue of which[23] the 1938 Order continued in force. The relevant statutory provisions were repealed by and re-enacted in the Civil Aviation Act 1982, the 1938 Order again continuing in force and having effect as if made under the Act.[24]

249

---

[14] *Post*, § 249.
[15] *Ante*, § 156.
[16] [1943] K.B. 161.
[17] In *In re The Glider Standard Austria S.H. 1964* [1965] P. 463, 465. He held that, classing gliders as aircraft, the Admiralty jurisdiction of the court did not extend to a claim to the possession or ownership of a glider, its jurisdiction over aircraft conferred by what is now the Supreme Court Act 1981 being confined to claims in the nature of salvage, and of towage and pilotage while the aircraft is waterborne: see SCA 1981, ss 20(2) (j)–(l), 24(1). Presumably his Lordship did not intend to include aircraft being carried purely as cargo within his *dictum*.
[18] The year of the Supreme Court of Judicature Act 1873: see *ante*, Chap. 2.
[19] s.28 and Sched. 5.
[20] S.R. & O. 1938, No. 136.
[21] Its provisions are outlined *post*, App. 21.
[22] International Convention for the Unification of Certain Rules relating to Assistance and Salvage of Aircraft or by Aircraft at Sea, Brussels, September 28, 1938. See *post*, App. 29.
[23] s.70(2).
[24] See Civil Aviation Act 1982, ss 87(4), 109, Sched. 14, para. 3, Sched. 16; Interpretation Act 1978, s.17(2)(b).

Subjects of Salvage

Application of law of wreck and salvage to aircraft

250   Under section 87(4) of the Civil Aviation Act 1982,

> "Her Majesty may by Order in Council direct that any provisions of any Act for the time being in force which relate to wreck, to salvage of life or property or to the duty of rendering assistance to vessels in distress shall, with such modifications, if any, as may be specified in the Order apply in relation to aircraft as those provisions apply in relation to vessels."

By virtue of the Aircraft (Wreck and Salvage) Order 1938,[25] the provisions of Part IX of the Merchant Shipping Act 1995 dealing with wreck and salvage, apply in relation to aircraft as they do to vessels, though with certain modifications. The principal modification is that[26] the expression "wreck" includes any aircraft or part thereof or any cargo thereof found derelict in or upon the seas surrounding the United Kingdom or its tidal waters, ports or harbours, or upon or near the shores of such seas or waters, or found or taken possession of outside the said seas and tidal waters and subsequently brought within those limits.

251   Section 87(1) of the 1982 Act specifically provides that any services rendered in assisting, or in saving life from, or in saving the cargo or apparel of, an aircraft in, on or over the sea or any tidal water, or on or over the shores of the sea or any tidal water, shall be deemed to be salvage services in all cases in which they would have been salvage services if they had been rendered in relation to a vessel. Consistently with the common law, the owner of an aircraft which has been used in providing salvage services should be as entitled to participate in a salvage reward as is a shipowner, particularly as there is no finite classification of salvage services.[27] The possibility of any contrary argument, particularly in the case of salvage of an aircraft by an aircraft, is fortunately precluded by section 87(2) of the 1982 Act, which provides that "where salvage services are rendered by an aircraft to any property or person, the owner of the aircraft shall be entitled to the same reward for those services as he would have been entitled to if the aircraft had been a vessel."

The provisions of section 87(1)–(2) of the Act have effect notwithstanding that the aircraft concerned is a foreign aircraft and notwithstanding that the services in question are rendered elsewhere than within the limits of the territorial waters adjacent to any part of Her Majesty's dominions.

---

[25] Art. 2.

[26] Except so far as concerns any claim by a person entitled to wreck other than the Crown. Such persons could not, in the absence of statute, have a right to aircraft or their cargo "cast up by the sea on land." This modification seems to be included in order to prevent their acquiring such a right under the legislation concerning aircraft.

[27] See *post*, Chap. 4.

Definition of "aircraft"

Jurisdiction in respect of aircraft

An Order in Council may be made to provide as to the courts in which **252** proceedings may be taken for enforcing any claim in respect of aircraft.[28] In particular, it may provide for conferring jurisdiction in any such proceedings on any court exercising Admiralty jurisdiction and for applying to such proceedings any rules of practice or procedure applicable to proceedings in Admiralty.[29]

To the extent that this power is not exercised, salvage or related claims will automatically fall within the High Court's Admiralty jurisdiction, which includes any claim arising the virtue of the application, by or under section 87 of the Civil Aviation Act 1982, of the law relating to salvage of aircraft, their apparel, cargo or wreck, or lives thereon.[30] It also includes claims in the nature of towage or pilotage in respect of an aircraft while the aircraft is waterborne.[31] These provisions apply in relation to all aircraft, whether British or not, and whether registered or not, and wherever the residence or domicile of their owners may be.[32] They also relate to all claims wherever arising; this includes, in the case of cargo or wreck salvage, claims in respect of cargo or wreck found on land.[33] Furthermore, in any case in which there is a maritime lien or other charge on any aircraft or other property for the amount claimed, an action *in rem* may be brought in the High Court against that aircraft or property.[34]

Definition of "aircraft"

It has been established at common law that seaplanes and flying boats are **253** not ships, vessels or boats and that they fall within the description "aircraft".[35] Further precise amplification of that term for wreck and salvage purposes is unavailable, either at common law or under statute. It is perhaps unlikely, however, that the court would depart from the "Table of General Classification of Aircraft" in the current Air Navigation Order,[36] which has effect under the Civil Aviation Act 1982,[37] the Act governing the extension of the law of wreck and salvage to aircraft. The Table includes free and captive balloons, airships, gliders and kites, aeroplanes (landplanes, seaplanes,[38] amphibians

---

[28] Civil Aviation Act 1982, s.91.
[29] *ibid.*
[30] Supreme Court Act 1981, s.20(2)(j), (6). The paragraph in fact refers to the Civil Aviation Act 1949, s.51 but must now be read as referring to the 1982 Act: see the Interpretation Act 1978, s.17(2)(a).
[31] Supreme Court Act 1981, ss.20(2)(k)–(l), 24(1).
[32] *ibid.*, s.20(7)(a).
[33] *ibid.*, s.20(7)(b).
[34] *ibid.*, s.21(3).
[35] *Ante*, §§ 244–248.
[36] Air Navigation Order 1980 (S.I. 1980 No. 1965), Sched. I, Pt. A. *cf.* Art. 95.
[37] See *ante*, § 249.
[38] In the Civil Aviation Act 1982, s.97, "seaplane" includes a flying boat and any other aircraft designed to manoeuvre on the water: s.97(7).

Subjects of Salvage

and self-launching motor gliders) and rotorcraft (helicopters and gyroplanes).

254 A more general definition applies under the Chicago Convention 1944, to which the United Kingdom is a party. It defines an aircraft as "Any machine that can derive support in the atmosphere from the reactions of the air *other than the reactions of the air against the earth's surface.*"[39] The italicised words were added specifically to exclude hovercraft from the definition; the law of salvage has, however, been made applicable to hovercraft by statutory instrument.[40]

The definition would, it has been said, exclude machines such as missiles or satellites which fly without support derived from the reactions of the air.[41] It is not necessarily the case that a reward could not be recovered for such services rendered to pilotless rocket-propelled craft not flying in space. But it is reasonable to conclude that the law of wreck and salvage would not apply to "spacecraft",[42] even if they were satellites designed for maritime activities and/or return to earth by landing on the sea. The opportunity for providing services of a salvage nature to such craft are rare but, if they did occur, the question might become a live issue, given the sophistication and potential value of such objects, particularly if reusable, as in the case of a space shuttle, which might fall within the definition of an aircraft for these purposes.

Salvage services by or to aircraft

255 Section 87(1)–(2) of the Civil Aviation Act 1982 makes it clear that any services in assisting or saving aircraft or lives or cargo on board will be salvage services if they would have been salvage services if rendered in relation to a vessel, and that both the owner and the crew of a salving aircraft may claim as salvors. No particular type of service is either excluded or necessary. The most obvious form of service that an aeroplane might perform is to seek and locate a distressed vessel.[43] Helicopters are, of course, particularly useful for lifting persons or property off distressed vessels and might even provide modest towage services in appropriate cases.

Locality

256 Salvage services within section 87 of the Civil Aviation Act 1982 may be performed in, on or over the sea or any tidal water, or on or over the shores of the sea or any tidal water,[44] and notwithstanding that they are rendered

---

[39] See Shawcross & Beaumont, para. V(1). See also *op. cit.*, paras. V(2–4).
[40] See *post*, §§ 257–259.
[41] Cheng, *The Law of International Air Transport* (1977), p. 111.
[42] See Shawcross & Beaumont, para. IV(2).
[43] See, *e.g. The American Farmer* (1947) 80 Ll.L. Rep. 672.
[44] s.87(1).

elsewhere than within the limits of the territorial waters adjacent to any part of Her Majesty's dominions.[45]

(b) Hovercraft

257 A hovercraft is defined for the purposes of the Hovercraft Act 1968 as: "a vehicle which is designed to be supported when in motion wholly or partly by air expelled from the vehicle to form a cushion of which the boundaries include the ground, water or other surface beneath the vehicle."[46] It has, therefore, not only some of the characteristics of a ship and of an aircraft but also some of those of a land vehicle. The Act, which does not attempt to lay down a completely new body of law for hovercraft, makes provision for them by enabling Orders in Council to be made extending to hovercraft or to persons, things or places connected with them the provisions of legislation affecting ships, aircraft, motor vehicles and other forms of transport, or persons, things or places connected therewith and any rules of law relating to ships or to persons, things or places connected with ships (other than rules relating to maritime liens).[47] Such legislation may be given effect as if references to ships, aircraft or motor vehicles or activities connected therewith included references to hovercraft or activities connected with hovercraft.[48] But, except as otherwise provided by or under the 1968 Act or an enactment passed before the 1968 Act was passed, a hovercraft is not to be treated as being a ship, aircraft or motor vehicle for the purposes of any such enactment or any instrument having effect by virtue of any such enactment.[49]

258 By statutory instrument made under the 1968 Act, and by the Merchant Shipping Act 1995, s.310,[50] the wreck and salvage provisions of the merchant shipping legislation have effect as if references therein, in whatever terms, to ships, vessels or boats, or activities or places connected therewith, include a reference to hovercraft, or activities or places connected therewith. "Wreck" for these purposes (except so far as concerns those other than the Crown entitled to unclaimed wreck) includes any hovercraft or any part thereof or any cargo thereof found sunk, stranded or abandoned in or on any navigable water, or on or over the foreshore, or place where the tide normally ebbs or flows.[51]

---

[45] s.87(3).
[46] s.4(1).
[47] *ibid.*, s.1(1)(h). As to maritime liens, see *post*, § 259.
[48] *ibid.*, s.1(1)(h). See further Kovats, *The Law of Hovercraft* (1975).
[49] s.4(3).
[50] Hovercraft (Application of Enactments) Order 1972 (S.I. 1972 No. 971), Art. 8(1).
[51] *ibid.*, art. 8(1).

259 Under the Hovercraft Act 1968,[52] the Acts governing the Admiralty jurisdiction of the High Court and County Courts have effect as if references to ships[53] included references to hovercraft and as if references to Her Majesty's ships included references to hovercraft belonging to the Crown in right of the Government of the United Kingdom or the Government of Northern Ireland. The law relating to maritime liens applies in relation to hovercraft and property connected with hovercraft as it applies in relation to ships and property connected with ships, and even though the hovercraft is on land at any relevant time.[54] But Orders in Council may be made restricting the extent to which the provisions mentioned in this paragraph apply in relation to hovercraft.[55]

5. LIFE SALVAGE

(a) Introduction

Definition

260 Salvage law is traditionally concerned with property. Indeed, at common law it was not possible to claim remuneration simply for services rendered to lives in peril. Under the Salvage Convention 1989 it is an open question whether payment can be obtained for such services alone. It may therefore be technically inappropriate to refer to such cases as life *salvage* rather than as saving or assisting lives. However, the expression is reasonably clear and convenient, and does no harm provided it is not used without regard to the law as it actually is, and particularly to whether the claimant has rendered a service to life alone or also to property or the environment.

The modern law

The precise effect of the International Salvage Convention 1989 on the English law on life salvage is unclear. Therefore, the English law on life salvage as it existed prior to the implementation of the Convention will be stated first. Then the possible effects of the Convention in relation to the pre-existing law will be considered.

---

[52] s.2(1), (3A). S.2(3A) was added by the SCA 1981, Sched. 5.
[53] Except references to Her Majesty's ships and the reference in para. 4(1) and the second reference in para. 8(1) of Pt I of Sched. I to the Administration of Justice Act 1956.
[54] Hovercraft Act 1968, s.2(2).
[55] *ibid.*, s.2(3).

The common law rule and practice

(b) Pre-Convention English law

The common law rule and practice

The legal rule

The general rule in Admiralty law is that human[56] life is not an independent subject of salvage.[57] As Dr Lushington said in *The Fusilier*[58]:   **261**

> "First, then, as to the old law respecting salvage of life when not connected with the salvage of property—the law before any Statute was passed on the subject. There is, I apprehend, no doubt that the law was that where no ship or cargo had been saved, no property rescued from destruction, but lives had been saved from the ship, no suit for salvage reward could be maintained."

The practice

The Admiralty Court did, however, find itself able and willing, as a matter of practice, to award a higher amount of salvage where life was saved together with property. Thus, Dr Lushington continued[59]:   **262**

> "Then as to the case where life and property had both been salved by one set of salvors, it was the practice of the Court to increase the amount of salvage which would have been given if property only had been saved, and such doctrine does, I think, rest on too high authority to be doubted."

This statement was reflected by Lord Chelmsford in the Privy Council in the same case[60]:

> "where both property and life had been saved, it was the well-established practice of the Court to increase the amount of salvage, and thus indirectly remunerate the salvors for the merit due to their having saved life as well as property."

---

[56] There appears to be no case in which it was considered that animal life might not be a subject of salvage. Traditionally animals have been treated simply as property and so would be covered by the ordinary rules relating to cargo, whether or not they were alive.

[57] *cf. The Duke of Manchester* (1847) 6 Moo. P.C. 90, 99, *per* Lord Campbell: "The very notion of saving a ship, supposes that the salvor... shall... exert himself to the utmost *for the safety of life* and property" (emphasis added).

[58] (1865) 3 Moo. P.C. (N.S.) 51, 55. His judgment was upheld by the Privy Council: *ibid.* See also *The Zephyrus* (1842) 1 W. Rob. 329, 331; *The Johannes* (1860) Lush. 182, 187.

[59] (1865) 3 Moo. P.C. (N.S.) 51, 56.

[60] *ibid.*, 70–71.

Subjects of Salvage

Moreover, the Admiralty Court's tolerance of the salvor's conduct during salvage operations was particularly generous where lives were at risk.[61]

Yet, even where the court did feel inclined to exercise its discretion to award a higher amount of salvage reward than normal, it seems it would not do so unless lives and property were subject to a common danger. Thus, referring to the recovery of crew members from pirates on payment of ransom—and not by a salvage service—and after the vessel had been salved, the court denied salvage, adding[62]:

> "I have felt it my duty to make this observation, that we may never lose sight of the principle upon which alone a salvage service can be founded, namely, a rescuing of a ship and cargo from some impending danger or distress."

Several salvors

263   If more than one salvor participated in saving both life and property, all such salvors would have benefited from this practice. But, as Dr Lushington acknowledged[63]:

> "It is true that an anomalous case did sometimes arise, where one set of salvors exclusively salved life, and another wholly distinct salved the ship and cargo; but even in these circumstances the salvors of life alone could not render the property amenable to their claims."

In *The Zephyrus*,[64] he explained away the contrary decision in *The Queen Mab*[65] on the ground that, since the vessel involved was a derelict, the judge did not have to contend with any opposition on the part of its owners to the claim for life salvage.

Liability in Admiralty law

264   It was also the practice that, as the salvage was awarded in one entire sum, the owners of all property salved—the ship, the freight and the cargo—should contribute to such increased rate of salvage, each in proportion to its value.[66]

---

[61] See *The St Blane* [1974] 1 Lloyd's Rep. 555, 560–561, *per* Brandon J.:
"The principle of the lenient approach to mistakes is an important one. It derives from the basic policy of the law relating to salvage services, which is to encourage, rather than discourage, the rendering of such services. The principle is especially important in cases involving life salvage, where its application demands that salvors should not in general be criticised if, faced with conflict between saving life on the one hand, and preserving property on the other, they err on the side of the former at the expense of the latter."

[62] *The Mary* (1842) 1 W. Rob. 448, 455–457 (bounties offered by the Lords Commissioners of the Treasury).

[63] *ibid.*, 55–56.

[64] (1842) 1 W. Rob. 329.

[65] (1835) 3 Hagg. 242.

[66] *The Fusilier* (1865) 3 Moo. P.C. (N.S.) 51, 56 (*per* Dr Lushington), 71 (*per* Lord Chelmsford).

Effect of statutory changes

There was, therefore, no independent right to a reward for life salvage in Admiralty law, though there is evidence that the government might occasionally have offered bounties to encourage life salvage in particular instances.[67] As will appear, the position under Admiralty law was altered by statute.[68] But to the extent that the legislation did not apply, both the Admiralty law rule and practice remain unchanged. It has remained the case that, where there is danger to life, its existence is one of the most important elements tending to increase the amount of the award.

Explanation of the common law position

The Admiralty Court's refusal to admit any claim for a reward for life salvage alone was not, it seems, due to a conservative reluctance to acknowledge as a ground for a salvage award a putative subject of salvage which had not previously been acknowledged, nor from an old-fashioned predilection for according more importance to property than to persons—indeed, the Victorians, who would appear to be the most obvious butt for the latter accusation, introduced the original statutory alteration of the common law rule. Admittedly, the court's attitude reflected to some extent the traditionally narrow approach of the common law courts in cases of the preservation of life and health.[69] But that does not seem to be a matter that was either considered to be relevant or likely to inhibit the Admiralty Court.

The judiciary were clearly alive to the desirability of awarding life salvage, as is revealed by their practice of giving enhanced awards where life was salved with property and statements supporting the extension of such practice. Thus, it was conceded by Dr Lushington[70]:

> "Most true it is that the preservation of human life is a much higher service than the rescuing from destruction of any property however valuable, and deserves the most ample reward for the risk and labour undergone in the performance of the service."

As he put it in a later case[70A]:

> "Such being the state of the law and the practice of the Court, the question arises, what was the grievance which required the interposition of the Legislature? That grievance clearly was, that persons who had risked their own lives, perhaps, and salved life only, or with so little property as not to afford the payment of an adequate reward, could not be justly compensated. That was the grievance intended to be remedied.

---

[67] See *The Swan* (1839) 1 W. Rob. 68.
[68] *Post*, §§ 273 *et seq.*
[69] See now Goff & Jones, 473–476.
[70] *The Johannes* (1860) Lush. 182, 187.
[70A] *The Fusilier* (1865) 3 Moo P.C. (N.S.) 51, 56.

No doubt the leading motive for a legislative enactment to remedy this grievance was to encourage the salving of life, but there was a subsidiary ground, the encouragement of salvors generally; for reward of life salvage operates as a further incentive to salvage exertions."

It was, therefore, something other than the attitude of the judges which precluded rewards for salvage of life alone at common law.

The reason given for the restrictive stance of the Admiralty Court is primarily jurisdictional. Dr Lushington stated it thus in *The Fusilier*[70B]:

"One reason for this state of the law was, that no property could be arrested applicable to the purpose. There could be no proceeding *in rem*, the ancient foundation of a salvage suit."

In *The Zephyrus*,[70C] Dr Lushington said:

"The jurisdiction of the Court, in salvage causes, is founded upon a proceeding against property which has been saved, and I am at a loss to conceive upon what principle the owners can be made answerable for the mere saving of life."

Quoting Dr Lushington's opinions in *The Zephyrus* and *The Fusilier*, it was said in *The Cargo ex Schiller*,[70D] by Brett L.J. that[70E]:

"This shews that the foundation of the Admiralty jurisdiction in the awarding of salvage is, the power of enforcing the maritime lien on property saved by salvors."

Subsequently, as Brett M.R., he put the matter slightly differently in *The Renpor*[70F]:

"there is one element invariably required by Admiralty law in order to found an action for salvage, there must be something saved more than life, which will form a fund from which salvage may be paid, in other words, for the saving of life alone without the saving of ship freight or cargo salvage is not recoverable in the Admiralty court."

In addition, he echoed a justification given for this jurisdictional approach by Dr Lushington in *The Fusilier*, that something must have been benefited by the services rendered.

[70B] *ibid.*, 55. *cf. The Elton* [1891] P. 265, 270.
[70C] (1842) 1 W. Rob. 329, 331.
[70D] (1877) 2 P.D. 145, *affirming* (1876) 1 P.D. 473.
[70E] (1877) 2 P.D. 145, 149. See also *ibid.*, 150.
[70F] (1883) 8 P.D. 115, 117.

The common law rule and practice

Life salvage by agreement

There was one further situation in which the Admiralty Court was prepared **267** to acknowledge a claim for life salvage at common law—where there was a specific agreement in relation to it. Thus, Sir Robert Phillimore once qualified the general rule thus[71]:

> "I consider it to be now a fixed principle of salvage law that, *in the absence of any* special contract, some property in the ship or cargo must be saved in order to found the liability of the owners of the ship or cargo to the payment of salvage remuneration."

Six years later, however, the Court of Appeal made it clear that the mere **268** existence of a contract would not be conclusive. In *The Renpor*,[72] by a written agreement, the master of the *S.S. Mary Louisa* agreed with the master of the *S.S. Renpor*, for a fixed sum, to stay by the *Renpor* until she was in a safe position to get to port. The *Mary Louisa* remained by the *Renpor* then, when she began to sink, took her crew on board, after which she sank. The Court of Appeal refused to award salvage on two grounds: first, because of the general Admiralty law rule against rewarding the saving of life alone; secondly, on the construction of the agreement. The second ground effectively encompassed two points—first, the question of construction itself; secondly, the question of the master's authority in making the agreement. As a matter of construction, it was held that the contract was one to pay a sum for performance by staying with the ship until either the ship, or the ship master and crew jointly, were safe, and this was not done as the ship never became safe.[73] Secondly, it was said, by Brett M.R., delivering the court's judgment[74]:

> "But there are two circumstances necessary in order to make an agreement binding on an owner; first, the contract must be made under a necessity; and secondly, it must be made for his benefit. I do not desire to say anything which may seem cruel, but I must express a doubt whether if an agreement is made only for the purpose of saving a master and a crew without regard to any saving of the property of the shipowner, though it be in a case of necessity, yet as the subject-matter is without benefit to the property of the shipowner, the master has authority to bind the owner to a money payment."

---

[71] *The Cargo ex Sarpedon* (1877) 3 P.D. 28, 34 (emphasis added). See also, in a case concerning property salvage, *The Prinz Heinrich* (1888) 13 P.D. 31, 34, *per* Butt J.; "when the captain of a ship reasonably and properly enters into an arrangement for the salvage of the ship for a particular sum he binds the shipowners to pay the agreed amount."
[72] (1883) 8 P.D. 115.
[73] It might also have been said, but was not, that, if this was a contract to salve, it could not be performed without salvage as understood under Admiralty law, *i.e.* by salvage of the ship itself.
[74] (1883) 8 P.D. 115, 118.

Subjects of Salvage

It may be inferred from his Lordship's words that such an agreement, if it is in other respects unimpeachable, may be upheld. It is nonetheless debatable whether such a cautious approach is merited.

269 Given the court's decision on the matters of construction referred to above, these words are only *dicta*, and the case's authority is not affected by their correctness. Leaving aside his Lordship's possible implication that this was a contract to save the crew alone (which it clearly was not), it may be queried whether a shipowner cannot be benefited by such an agreement. If he has a duty to take all necessary steps to protect persons on board—if not the crew, then passengers at least—he would derive a benefit from steps taken to prevent his breaching that duty in circumstances when he could have discharged it. In *The Medina*,[75] the captain of the defendant's ship, which had gone to pieces, contracted, on behalf of 550 pilgrims who were left on a rock just six feet above the water, to have them taken off for £4,000[76] with the captain of a ship who had otherwise refused to take them. The agreement was held to have been entered into as a result of illegitimate pressure[77]—from the circumstances and, in Brett J.A.'s view, from the fact that, if the stranded captain refused to accept the terms, he took upon himself the responsibility of allowing 550 human beings under his care to be left to the danger of being drowned.[78] The agreement was not enforced, being inequitable, but "there was salvage to be paid" and £1,800 was awarded against the shipowners.

270 Sir Robert Phillimore, who was judge at first instance in *The Medina*, said in *The Cargo ex Sarpedon*,[79] that he considered the contract in *The Medina* to be a salvage contract, which entitled him to resort to the power under the law of salvage to reduce the amount recoverable. In *The Cargo ex Sarpedon*, a Spanish steamship took off lives and cargo from the helpless *Sarpedon* but was unable to satisfy its master's request to save the ship. It was contended that the master was bound to contract, and did contract by implication, with the master of the steamship for saving the lives. But the judge did not consider *The Medina* as making the owners of the *Sarpedon* liable to contribute to the reward for life salvage:

> "I consider it to be now a fixed principle of salvage law that, in the absence of any special contract, some property in the ship or cargo must be saved to found the liability of the owners of the ship or cargo to the payment of salvage remuneration."[80]

In the light of this, it is more accurate to say that a contract to save life alone is not strictly speaking a salvage contract, no property needing to be salved,

---

[75] (1876) 2 P.D. 5, affirming (1876) 1 P.D. 272.
[76] The amount of their passage money.
[77] See *post*, § 930.
[78] (1876) 2 P.D. 5, 8.
[79] *The Cargo ex Sarpedon* (1877) 3 P.D. 28, 34.
[80] *ibid.*, 34.

Life salvage under statute

but that, so long as the alleged agreement is specifically to save the lives in question and not simply to salve, it will be enforced as a contract in the nature of a salvage contract and subject to similar but not identical rules.

271 The Court of Appeal in *The Renpor*[81] did not consider, and so did not deny, a further point: that a contract might be entered into, not on behalf of and for the ostensible benefit of the shipowner, but on behalf of the persons whose lives are to be saved. Assuming it is not set aside as being entered into in consequence of illegitimate pressure,[82] it should be enforced.[83]

It must be said, however, that if the shipowner or other persons are to be bound by such a contract, then, consistently with Brett M.R.'s reasoning in *The Renpor*[84] that no reward will be payable under such a contract if it is a true salvage contract, the sum payable will not be on the salvage scale but, if at large, an ordinary *quantum meruit* or, if fixed, the agreed sum, subject to adjustment downwards if unconscionably high. Moreover, the sum would be payable by the actual parties to the contract and not by the shipowner simply *qua* shipowner.

272 A stated "overriding objective" of LOF 2000 is to seek to promote safety of life at sea.[85] However, this does not appear to impose a specific duty to save, or to pay a reward for the saving of, human lives. Rather, it expresses a moral exhortation, a function which ameliorates action which is otherwise inconsistent with the objectives of salving property and averting or minimising environmental damage, and a factor which can be taken into account in favour of a salvor who has taken action to promote safety of life at sea.

Life salvage under statute

Early statutes

273 Parliament initially made statutory provision for life salvage in an Act of 1846.[85A] The relevant section (with the marginal note "reasonable salvage to be allowed to persons saving ship or goods") enacted that "every person . . . who shall act or be employed . . . in the saving or preserving of any ship or vessel in distress . . . or of the life of any person on board . . . shall . . . be paid in a reasonable reward or compensation by way of salvage for such service."

---

[81] *Supra*, n. 72.
[82] See *post*, Chap. 9.
[83] And should, moreover, not fail on the ground that there is a statutory duty to assist persons in distress for performance of an existing legal obligation may be good consideration: see *post*, Chap. 6.
[84] *Ante*, §268.
[85] The Wreck and Salvage Act (1846) 9 & 10 Vict. c. 99, s.19. Earlier Acts (The Frauds by Boatmen etc. Act (1809) 49 Geo. 3, c. 122, s.9; repeated in The Frauds by Boatmen etc. Act (1821) 1 & 2 Geo. 4, c. 75, s.8) gave jurisdiction to justices to determine salvage remuneration for services which included being instrumental in saving lives but provided no basis on which such rewards might be payable; they did not, therefore, go beyond current practice.
[85A] LSSAC 2000, cl.2(a). See generally *ante*, § 117.

Subjects of Salvage

In *The Silver Bullion*,[86] in which lives and cargo were saved and rewarded accordingly, Dr Lushington said[87]:

> "Before the passing of that statute, the law stood in a very peculiar predicament, because this Court had no power to give any remuneration whatever for the salvage of life. Certainly that was a gross anomaly, and one that ought to have been corrected; but I apprehend that it was for that purpose that the Wreck and Salvage Act was worded as it is."

Whatever the exact effect of the 1846 Act,[88] it was replaced by the Merchant Shipping Act 1854, ss.458–459.[89] Those sections, as extended by the Admiralty Court Act 1861, s.9,[90] were in turn superseded, by consolidation, in the Merchant Shipping Act 1894, ss.544–546.

Merchant Shipping Act 1894, ss.544–545

274 The 1894 Act provided for liability to pay for lives salved from British and from foreign ships, for discretionary payments to be made by the Crown in certain circumstances, and for the priority of claims for life salvage against shipowners.

Principles of interpretation

275 In the view of Dr Lushington and, later in the Privy Council, Lord Chelmsford in *The Fusilier*,[91] the legislature must have been aware of, and to have legislated so as to legitimise, though no more, the practice of the Admiralty Court of rendering the owners of ship and cargo liable to pay an enhanced award where lives were also preserved. As Lord Chelmsford indicated, this reward could not be assessed on the general principle that only the property benefited is chargeable, since it is difficult to visualise life salvage benefiting property.

Intention to save lives only

276 The Merchant Shipping Act 1894 provided for salvage claims on distinct bases—for salvage of vessel, apparel, cargo and lives. If one of these was salved, a salvage claim could be brought against the property *saved*, whether or not other claims were brought.[92] It was similarly the case that: *under the statute*, so long as some property was saved, the salvor of life could claim

---

[86] (1854) 2 Spinks 70.
[87] *ibid.*, 74.
[88] See Wiswall, pp. 43–44, who suggests that the Act was regarded as only confirming the existing practice of giving an enhanced reward in the case of life salvage, though he appears to misinterpret a dictum of Dr Lushington's in support of this view.
[89] Merchant Shipping Repeal Act 1854, s.4, Sched.
[90] And the Merchant Shipping Acts Amendment Act 1854, ss 59, 61–62.
[91] (1865) 3 Moo. P.C. 51.
[92] *e.g. The Willem III* (1871) L.R. 3 A. & E. 487.

against that property even though he only salved life and even though he only intended to salve life and was only capable of doing that.[93]

General rules

Where services were rendered in saving life[94] from any British vessel, whether in British waters or elsewhere, a reasonable amount of salvage was payable to the salvor by the owner of the vessel, cargo or apparel saved,[95] to be determined in case of dispute in the manner laid down in the 1894 Act. Salvage similarly had to be paid where such services were rendered to any foreign vessel, but only where they were rendered wholly or in part within British waters.[96] **277**

Extension to aircraft

Admiralty jurisdiction over claims in the nature of salvage was extended to include jurisdiction over claims which can be brought for services rendered in saving life from a ship or an aircraft or in preserving cargo, apparel or wreck.[97] There has so far been no reported case in which an award has been made for saving life from aircraft. The principles discussed concerning vessels apply *mutatis mutandis* to aircraft.[98] **278**

Requirement that property be saved

Liability to pay salvage is, in the absence of a special contract,[99] only a qualified and limited liability. No liability arises at all unless some property or, at all events, some interest in property has been saved for the benefit of the person whom it is sought to make responsible for the payment of salvage. Thus, Brett M.R. said in *The Renpor*[1]: **279**

> "there is one element invariably required by Admiralty law in order to found an action for salvage, there must be something saved more than life, which will form a fund from which salvage may be paid, in other words, for the saving of life alone, without the saving of ship freight or cargo salvage is not recoverable in the Admiralty Court."

---

[93] *The Coromandel* (1857) Swab. 205, 207.
[94] *cf. The Fusilier* (1865) 3 Moo. P.C. (N.S.) 51, 73, interpreting "the lives of the persons *belonging to* such ship or boat" (emphasis added) under the Merchant Shipping Act 1854, s.458 to include passengers as well as crew.
[95] MSA 1894, s.544(1).
[96] *ibid.* s.544(1). *The Cairo* (1874) L.R. 4 A. & E. 184 was such a case. See also MSA 1894, s.545.
[97] Under MSA 1894, ss 544–546, the Civil Aviation Act 1982, ss.87, 91, 109, Sched. 16, and the Aircraft (Wreck and Salvage) Order 1938. See SCA 1981, s.20(6).
[98] See further *ante*, §§ 244–259.
[99] See *post*, Chaps. 8, 9.
[1] (1883) 8 P.D. 115, 117.

Similarly, Sir James Hannen P. has said[2]: "There can be no claim for salvage services against a person; something must be saved to which the claim can attach." This rule was applicable equally to claims in Admiralty law and under the Merchant Shipping Acts.[3] Moreover, it is a clear intimation from the cases that, where property is salved with lives, a claim for life salvage will still only succeed where the property salved comes within the recognised subjects of salvage.

Thus "the wearing apparel of passengers, and other effects carried by them for their daily personal use, may properly be considered to be privileged from arrest."[4]

Interest in property saved

280 Life salvage is payable by each and every owner of vessel, cargo or apparel saved but not by the owner of any such property which is not saved. If the ship is saved but the cargo is lost, it is only from the shipowner that payment for the salvage of life can be required. If, on the other hand, the ship is lost but lives and cargo are preserved, the shipowner is under no liability to contribute to the salvage reward due to the salvors of life, and the burden of it must be borne wholly by the owners of the cargo.

In *The Cargo ex Sarpedon*,[5] the owners of cargo, which was the only property salved, argued that, since salvage services had been rendered by virtue of a salvage agreement under which the shipowners were liable *in personam*, then, although the cargo-owners might be solely liable to pay for that part of the reward given for salvage of their cargo, the shipowners were nevertheless liable to contribute to that element of the reward representing life salvage. However, Sir Robert Phillimore held, following *The Cargo ex Schiller*,[6] that "in the absence of any special contract, some property in the ship or cargo must be saved in order to found the liability of the owners of the ship or cargo to the payment of salvage remuneration,"[7] and that "the owners of the lost ship are not personally liable to pay salvage"[8] and so nor are they liable to contribute to its payment.

281 In *The Annie*,[9] the defendants' vessel sunk off the Victoria Docks as a result of a collision caused by another vessel. Acting under their statutory powers, the Thames Conservators caused the vessel to be raised and sold. The proceeds of sale being insufficient to defray the expenses of raising it, they recovered the deficiency from the defendants. The defendants on their part recovered the full value of their vessel plus the expenses paid to the Conservators from the owners of the vessel which caused the collision. The

---

[2] *The Annie* (1886) 12 P.D. 50, 51.
[3] See *post*, Chap. 8.
[4] *The Willem III* (1871) L.R. 3 A. & E. 487.
[5] (1877) 3 P.D. 28.
[6] *Infra*, n. 17.
[7] (1877) 3 P.D. 28, 34.
[8] *ibid.*, 53.
[9] (1886) 12 P.D. 50.

plaintiffs, who had preserved the lives of the defendants' crew at the time of the collision, brought an action *in rem* for life salvage, though they did not arrest the wreck. Their claim failed. Sir James Hannen P. ruled that a claim for life salvage could not attach to the defendants' claim for damages against the other vessel. The defendants' vessel was not saved and there could be no claim for salvage services against a person; something had to be saved to which the claim could attach. He went on to say that the salvors could not in any way be preferred to the Conservators' claim to the expenses to which they were entitled by statute[10]:

> "But that is a totally different transaction. I am clearly, therefore of opinion that the present plaintiffs have no claim as against the Conservators of the Thames, whose rights are superior to those of all other persons. The section which I have read[11] refers only to salvage claims, and that of the Conservators is not such a claim, but a charge for the benefit of the public."

A similar point arose in *The Chieftain*.[12] *HMS Thunderer* rendered services to the barque *Chieftain* and her cargo, in distress on the coast of Africa, and seven of the *Thunderer*'s crew were lent to her on her homeward voyage. The captains of the two ships then made an agreement by which the sum of £400 was fixed as the reward for the service rendered. The master of the barque drew a bill for that amount upon his owners, who had, however, in the meanwhile, parted with the vessel to the defendants. The vessel was lost on its way home. Dr Lushington, who doubted whether salvage services had been rendered, refused a monition against the defendants calling upon them to shew cause why the salvage reward should not be paid to the captain, officers and crew of the *Thunderer*[13]:

> "the property is actually lost and gone, and a Monition to shew cause is decreed only in cases where the property has been allowed to go into the hands of the owners, instead of the parties attaching the property itself. In no case has a Monition to shew cause issued against the owners of property which has been lost. . . . It would be to convert the jurisdiction of this Court from a proceeding *in rem* to a proceeding *in personam*, which can only be where the property is in the possession of the proprietors themselves."

Interest in property saved irrelevant to liability—the property need not have been "salved"

The owners of maritime property which is eventually saved from destruction are liable to pay a reward for life salvage, regardless of the precise nature

---

[10] *ibid.*, 52.
[11] MSA 1854, s.459; subsequently MSA 1894, s.544(2); now repealed.
[12] (1846) 4 N.o.C. 459.
[13] *ibid.*, 460.

of their property or their interest in it, and even if their property is the only property saved. And, provided that either ship, cargo or apparel in fact, either wholly or in part, escapes destruction, that which so escapes is liable to the claims of the salvors of life, although its preservation has not itself been by the life salvors[14] or even due to any salvage service.

284 In *The Cargo ex Schiller*,[15] the German steamship *Schiller* was wrecked in British waters, and the lives of 10 passengers and of some of her crew were saved by certain boats. Only small portions of the hull and stores of the *Schiller* were saved; but, some time after the ship was lost, divers employed by the owners of cargo in the steamship succeeded in recovering from the wreck a large amount of *specie*. The owners, masters and crews of the boats which had saved the passengers claimed salvage from the owners of the *specie* recovered. The Court of Appeal held, by a majority, that the plaintiffs were entitled to succeed. Its decision turned on the interpretation of the Merchant Shipping Act 1854, s.458, the forerunner of the Merchant Shipping Act 1894, ss 544–546.[16] Section 458 provided:

> "In the following Cases, (that is to say,)
> Whenever any Ship or Boat is stranded or otherwise in Distress on the Shore of any Sea or Tidal Water situate within the Limits of the United Kingdom, and Services are rendered by any Person,
> (1) In assisting such Ship or Boat;
> (2) In saving the Lives of the Persons belonging to such Ship or Boat;
> (3) In saving the Cargo or Apparel of such Ship or Boat, or any Portion thereof;
> And whenever any Wreck is saved by any Person other than a Receiver within the United Kingdom;
>
> There shall be payable by the Owners of such Ship or Boat, Cargo, Apparel, or Wreck, to the person by whom such Services or any of them are rendered or by whom such Wreck is saved, a reasonable Amount of Salvage, together with all Expenses properly incurred by him in the Performance of such Services or the saving of such Wreck, the Amount of such Salvage and Expenses (which Expenses are hereinafter included under the Term Salvage) to be determined in case of Dispute in manner hereinafter mentioned."

285 Brett L.J., who dissented, objected that the cargo was not "wreck" nor was it "salved" for, having been recovered by the cargo-owners, it could not be subject to a salvor's lien such as to give the Admiralty Court jurisdiction by

---

[14] *The Cairo* (1874) L.R. 4 A. & E. 184.
[15] (1877) 2 P.D. 145, affirming (1876) 1 P.D. 473.
[16] Now repealed and replaced by the provisions of the Salvage Convention 1989: see *post*, §§ 268–310.

virtue of an action *in rem*. Since, he said, "saved" in the Act meant "salved by salvors," the remuneration payable was not a reasonable compensation but "a reasonable amount of salvage":

> "The enactment does not give a new subject-matter on which the Admiralty [Court] may enforce a lien, but gives a new cause on service in respect of which the Admiralty [Court] may enforce a lien upon the same subject-matter as before. . . . The whole remedy is evidently founded on Admiralty remedy, which, though it does not absolutely shut out a remedy by suit *in personam* either in the Admiralty Court, or, mayhap, in some other division of the High Court, yet shews that it is a remedy for a salvage claim, which imports, as is stated in *The Zephyrus*[17] and *The Fusilier*,[18] the possibility of a suit *in rem*."[19]

He accepted the views expressed in *The Fusilier*[20] that the object of the statute was to regularise the previous practice of the Admiralty Court, and a remedy was not intended to be given by the Act for a claim which was not otherwise classifiable as a salvage claim.

286 Baggallay L.J. decided, both on an interpretation of the grammatical meaning of the words used in the statute[21] and as a matter of Parliamentary intention, that, quite simply, a reward was payable for the performance of any one of the three listed services (*i.e.* assisting the ship; saving lives; or saving cargo and apparel) by each and every owner of "property saved from destruction", however it was saved, *i.e.* even if it were "saved" but not "salved":

> "under the provisions of the Act the owners of all property saved, whether ship, cargo, or apparel, and however saved, are rendered liable, to the extent of the value of the property saved, for a reasonable amount of salvage in respect of life saved, even though the life salvors have in no respect assisted in the salvage of either ship or cargo."[22]

287 James L.J. agreed with Baggallay L.J., basing his "decision on the words of the statute as they would be understood by plain men who know nothing of the technical rule of the Court of Admiralty, or of flotsam, lagan and jetsam"[23]:

---

[17] (1842) 1 W. Rob. 329.
[18] (1865) 3 Moo. P.C. (N.S.) 51.
[19] (1877) 2 P.D. 145, 150–151.
[20] (1865) 3 Moo. P.C. (N.S.) 51. See *ante*, §275.
[21] Including MSA 1854, s.468. See now MSA 1995, s.226(1)(a): "Where salvage is due to any person under this Chapter, the receiver shall—(a) if the salvage is due in respect of services rendered—(i) in assisting a vessel, or (ii) in saving life from a vessel, or (iii) in saving the cargo and equipment of a vessel, detain the vessel and cargo or equipment." Baggallay L.J. wondered: "Why should the cargo be detained in a case in which there has been life salvage only, if the owners of such cargo are under no liability to pay or contribute to the amount due in respect of such life salvage?": *The Cargo ex Schiller* (1877) 2 P.D. 145, 156. This suggests a failure to appreciate the distinct points conflated in the section.
[22] (1877) 2 P.D. 145, 158.
[23] *ibid.*, 161.

"This seems to me quite in accordance with reason and principle. If a ship is in distress and the persons who go to its rescue busy themselves, in the first instance, as they ought to do, exclusively with the salvage of lives, and while they are doing this by a change of weather a rising tide and a favourable breeze lift the ship and waft her into a safe cove, surely it is quite as reasonable and right that the ship and cargo, saved by the aid of God, and without further expense, should pay the life salvors as if they had been saved by a steam-tug coming up at the critical moment, or by some other salvage services for which they would have further to pay."[24]

He was comforted, in making his decision, by the fact that the value of the cargo saved was very large and that a liberal allowance could, indeed should, be made to its owners for the expense of raising it.

288 It is unfortunate that the views of Brett L.J., the one member of the Court of Appeal with expertise in the law of Admiralty, did not prevail. They are consistent with the principles of interpretation of the Act adopted in *The Fusilier*[25] and do not involve such a radical departure from the general principle that salvage is payable because of the benefit derived from salvage operations at the expense of the salvor.[26] The reasoning of the majority is morally persuasive and the court's decision may in any case be justified simply as one on the true interpretation of the statute, prevailing over the pre-existing law of salvage. But it has considerably more profound implications. Section 458 of the 1854 Act provided a statutory basis for claims for services to ships and boats, cargo and apparel, as well as to lives. The reasoning of the majority could, therefore, be applied to property salvage as well as to life salvage, so as, for example, to permit salvors of cargo to claim against the vessel if that were later saved, though not salved due to their efforts. This would contravene the principles that success (*i.e.* successful *salvage*) is necessary for a salvage claim[27] and that the value of the *salved* property represents the upper limit of the fund from which salvage is payable.[28] Such ramifications would not be found acceptable. Fortunately, the relevant provisions of the Merchant Shipping Acts 1894 and 1995 have dealt with life salvage and property salvage separately.[29] The decision in *The Cargo ex Schiller*,[30] which is submitted to be misconceived, can only be justified, if at all, as based on statutory interpretation, and interpretation limited to life salvage only.

---

[24] *ibid.*, 160.
[25] (1865) 3 Moo. P.C. (N.S.) 51. See *ante*, § 275.
[26] See *ante*, §§ 33–35.
[27] See *post*, Chap. 8.
[28] See *post*, Chaps. 14–15.
[29] See MSA 1894, ss 544 and 546 respectively; and *post*, §§ 298–310.
[30] *Supra*, n. 181.

289 Although life salvors can claim a reward for life salvage against property saved, they can only claim salvage for the service which they have successfully performed. Thus, life salvors cannot participate in the reward for salvage of the property if it is salved by other salvors. In *The Eintracht*,[31] a steamer took in tow a barque which was out of control and took her crew off. She later had to cease towing and the vessel was later salved by another steamship. The life salvors could claim for life salvage only, the second steamer alone recovering for salvage of the ship. In such a case, however, life salvors who are not responsible for the eventual salvage of property, but who have contributed in some way to its preservation by others, can participate in the reward for salving the property.[32]

Saving of property immaterial if lives preserved but not salved

290 In *The Tarbert*,[33] a steamship being towed by the plaintiffs' tug collided with another ship, so her crew was taken off by the plaintiffs. The ship was subsequently lost, though some of her cargo was later raised. Hill J. refused to reward the plaintiffs for life salvage:

> "I am not prepared to say that an engaged tug which takes on board the master and crew of the ship which has engaged her is so far acting outside her duty that she can claim as a salvor."[34]

The decision in *The Cargo ex Schiller*[35] was inapplicable (though not cited) as there was no salvage service.

Extent of reward limited to value of property preserved

291 Although claims for life salvage can be made against property which is saved but not salved, it has been held, consistently with the general principle that the value of salved property provides the normal upper limit of liability to pay salvage, that the extent of the liability of the owner of the property saved to pay life salvage is limited to the value of the property as saved. In *The Cargo ex Schiller*,[36] Baggallay L.J. said:

> "I am of opinion that the liability to pay a reasonable amount of salvage to life salvors is imposed upon owners of cargo as well as upon owners of the ship, and that such liability is not a general personal liability to be enforced in any circumstances whether the ship and cargo are lost or not, but a liability limited to the value of the property saved from destruction."

---

[31] (1874) 1 Asp. M.L.C. 198. See also *The India* (1842) 1 W. Rob. 406.
[32] *The E.U.* (1853) 1 Spinks 63; *The Genessee* (1848) 12 Jur. 41.
[33] [1891] P. 372.
[34] *ibid.*, 377.
[35] *Supra*, n. 18.
[36] (1877) 2 P.D. 145, 157. See also *ibid.*, 158.

Discretionary payments of life salvage

292 The Merchant Shipping Act 1894, s.544(3) provided the Secretary of State with a residual discretion to award life salvage which could not otherwise be paid. Where the vessel, cargo, and apparel were destroyed, or the value thereof was insufficient, after payment of the actual expenses incurred, to pay the amount of salvage payable in respect of the preservation of life, the Secretary of State could, in his discretion, award to the salvor, out of monies provided by Parliament, such a sum as he thought fit in whole or in part satisfaction of any amount of salvage so left unpaid.[37]

The section enabled the Secretary of State, if he so decided, to make up any deficiency which existed in Admiralty law or under subsequent legislation, arising from the inadequacy of the fund represented by the salved property. But it went further for, both in Admiralty law and under statute, there could be no obligation to pay salvage if no property was salved. In such a case, salvage could only be paid under the section at the Secretary of State's discretion and only from monies provided by Parliament. If he did exercise his discretion to make a payment, the Secretary of State was not required by the statute to do so in a particular way, *e.g.* to award such a sum as the Admiralty Court would be likely to award if it were capable of doing so. No more, it is submitted, could the exercise of his discretion normally be circumscribed by the usual administrative law principles of *ultra vires* for, as has been intimated elsewhere, it is illogical to suggest that he should pay such a sum as an Admiralty Judge would have paid if an Admiralty Judge would not, because he could not, have awarded anything in such a case. However, payments under section 544(3) were in fact exceedingly rare and the section had minimal practical importance.[38] Its provisions have, however, survived the implementation of the Salvage Convention into English law.[39]

The lives in question

293 The Merchant Shipping Act 1854, s.458 provided for salvage rewards "in saving the lives of the persons belonging to such ship or boat", an expression which was held to include passengers as well as crew.[40] It was also held that the shipowner was liable for the payment of salvage reward to the salvors of some of the crew who had left the ship in danger in one of her boats, even though they left the ship without being ordered to do so.[41] But the judge, Sir Robert Phillimore, said that he was unwilling to countenance the idea that the section:

---

[37] MSA 1894, s.544(3), as affected by the Merchant Shipping (Mercantile Marine Fund) Act 1898, s.1(1)(b).

[38] In the absence of special agreement, the salvor could obtain reward in no other way. He had no right to reward under this provision.

[39] See *post*, § 310.

[40] *The Fusilier* (1865) 3 Moo P.C. (N.S.) 51. See also *The Medina* (1876) 2 P.D. 5; *The Cargo ex Sarpedon* (1877) 3 P.D. 28. But *cf. R. v. Kelly* [1982] A.C. 665.

[41] *The Cairo* (1874) L.R. 4 A. & E. 184.

"could be so strained as to compel the court to hold a ship liable for [life] salvage because some of her crew had deserted her without reason and contrary to orders, and had afterwards found themselves in a condition of danger, from which they had been rescued. Whether a vessel is or is not liable for life salvage is a question which can only be answered by considering the circumstances of each case."[42]

This must be correct for, in the circumstances mentioned, the ship and lives in question would not be in such common danger as would bring the law of salvage into operation.[43] But, it is submitted, if there were a common danger, it would be contrary to public policy to deny salvage simply on the ground that the master had ordered the crew not to leave the ship.

"British waters"

Rewards for salvage of lives from foreign vessels under the 1894 Act needed only to be paid for services rendered wholly or in part within "British waters".[44] It was a question of fact in each case whether the service for which salvage reward is claimed was rendered in part within British waters.

British waters were held to include the open sea within three miles of the shore, but not the high seas beyond.[45] If life salvors salved life from a foreign vessel wholly outside British waters and other salvors salved the vessel outside British waters and then each set of salvors separately brought the lives and vessel respectively into British waters, the life salvors could not claim against the vessel,[46] though the salvors of the vessel presumably could. Similarly, in *The Willem III*.[47] A French schooner picked up passengers and crew from a Dutch ship on fire outside the three-mile limit. Whilst still outside the limit, the schooner fell in with a British steamship to which the survivors were transferred, at their request, and which brought them safely to Spithead. It was held that "the circumstances that other services were afterwards performed by other persons in British waters cannot avail to bring the claim of the *Flora* [the schooner] within the provisions of the Act of Parliament".[48]

Sir Francis Jeune P. expressed reservations about *The Willem III* in *The Pacific*,[49] in which he rewarded a British steam-trawler which brought from the North Sea to Hull the crew of a drifting Norwegian barque which was itself later brought to Grimsby by other salvors. He said[50]:

[42] *ibid.*, 186.
[43] See *ante*, §263.
[44] MSA 1894, s.544(1). See now MSA 1995, s.313(2)(a) ("United Kingdom waters") and s.313(2)(b) ("national waters").
[45] *The Leda* (1856) Swab. 40. See now *The Mac* (1882) 7 P.D. 126; *General Iron Screw Collier Co. v. Schurmanns* (1860) 1 J. & H. 180; *The Johannes* (1860) Lush. 182.
[46] *The Johannes* (1860) Lush. 182.
[47] (1871) L.R. 3 A. & E. 487.
[48] *ibid.*, 494.
[49] [1898] P. 170.
[50] *ibid.*, 175.

> "It must be a question of fact in every case whether the service is rendered wholly or in part in British waters. The test of that appears to me to be whether what was done by the salvors for the purpose of saving life was done wholly or in part in British waters. I can imagine cases where people might be salved from a vessel and then might be taken very considerable distances, perhaps for a long voyage, by the vessel which salved them, and then come within British waters. It could not be said that that was a case of salvage services being performed in part in British waters, because it is evident that the salvage services finished long before the vessel came within British waters at all. It is clear that one must be guided by practical considerations in each case, and what you have to look at is whether the salving vessel in the course of effecting the salvage service is within British waters."

296 In *The Pacific*, the life salvors were held to be within British waters during the course of effecting the salvage service. But that it is always a question of fact is clear from *Jörgensen v. Neptune Steam Fishing Co. Ltd*.[51] The facts were similar to those in *The Pacific*. A British trawler took the crew from a derelict Danish schooner, which was 200 miles from the United Kingdom, to Hull and another trawler took the schooner to Aberdeen. The Court of Session rewarded the second but not the first trawler. According to Lord Trayner[52]:

> "The men were salved whenever they were taken off the disabled vessel they were abandoning and placed on the deck of another vessel which was seaworthy. They were then rescued from the peril which rendered salvage service necessary. It was not necessary that in order to be salved they should be landed in an English port, or indeed in any other port."

The Court had no original jurisdiction in such a case, and no British statute could confer jurisdiction over foreigners on the high seas beyond the realm.[53]

The Supreme Court Act 1981 declares the High Court to have Admiralty jurisdiction over any claim in the nature of salvage in relation to all ships or aircraft, whether British or not, and in relation to all claims wherever arising[54] but the Act does not extend the cases in which salvage is recoverable under the Merchant Shipping Act.[55]

Priority

297 The Merchant Shipping Act 1894, s.544(2) provided that, when payable by the owners of the vessel, salvage in respect of the preservation of life was

---

[51] (1902) 4 F. (Ct of Sn Cas.) 992.
[52] *ibid.*, 995.
[53] *The Johannes* (1860) Lush. 182, 187.
[54] SCA 1981, s.20(i)(j), (6), (7).
[55] *ibid.*, s.20(7) proviso. *cf. The Johannes* (1860) Lush. 182, 189.

payable in priority to all other claims for salvage. However, the life salvor no longer has statutory priority.[56]

(c) The Salvage Convention 1989 and English law

Current statutory provisions

The Merchant Shipping Act 1995 gives the force of law to the International Salvage Convention 1989, Art. 16, which is in similar terms to the equivalent provision in the Brussels Salvage Convention 1910[57] and which provides: **298**

> "1. No remuneration is due from persons whose lives are saved, but nothing in this article shall effect the provisions of national law on this subject.
> 2. A salvor of human life, who has taken part in the services rendered on the occasion of the accident giving rise to salvage, is entitled to a fair share of the payment awarded to the salvor for salving the vessel or other property or preventing or minimising damage to the environment."

In addition, in a special provision for English law, the 1995 Act retains the Secretary of State's discretionary power to make a life salvage payment where no, or an insufficient, sum is otherwise forthcoming.[58]

Interpretation of the Convention

Article 16 of the Convention is disappointingly obscure. First, if the second part of Article 16.1 is read literally ("*nothing* in this article shall effect the provisions of national law on this subject"[59]), it gives States parties absolute freedom to provide for life salvage. If so, it would have been better to have so stated in a separate sentence. For, although it seems clear enough that the provisions of Article 16.2 are subject to this licence, it is not clear whether it can override the opening immunity of persons saved from personal liability to pay remuneration. Fortunately, given the history of life salvage both nationally and internationally, States parties are unlikely to provide for the personal liability of persons saved. English law has not done so, and to that extent **299**

---

[56] MSA 1894, s.544 was repealed by the Merchant Shipping (Salvage and Pollution) Act 1994, s.10 and Sched. 4. But *cf.* Jackson, §2.53.

[57] The Brussels Salvage Convention 1910, Art. 9 provides:
"No remuneration is due from persons whose lives are saved, but nothing in this article shall effect the provisions of national law on this subject.
Salvors of human life, who have taken part in the services rendered on the occasion of the accident giving rise to salvage or assistance, are entitled to a fair share of the remuneration awarded to the salvors of the vessel, her cargo, and accessories."

[58] Merchant Shipping Act 1995, s.224(2), Sched. 11, Pt II, para. 5. See *post*, § 310.

[59] Emphasis added.

criticism of the drafting of Article 16.1 is of no practical significance. Moreover, for an English lawyer there is a ready explanation of the effect of Article 16.1, since it has sanctioned Parliament's continuing the Secretary of State's discretionary power to make salvage payments,[60] a provision which is not inconsistent with any of the substantial provisions of Article 16.

300 Secondly, the word "provisions" in Article 16.1 is capable of different meanings. It could encompass provisions made both before and after implementation of the Convention, and both statutory and non-statutory "provisions". To the extent that the objects of the Convention should not be undermined by relics of the pre-existing national law which it is intended to replace, it can confidently be asserted that the Convention overrides inconsistent pre-existing national law. And, given that subsequent case law should primarily be concerned with interpreting the law under the Convention, the most obviously contemplated "provisions" are national legislation such as that authorising discretionary payments by the Secretary of State.[61] However, as will be seen in the next paragraph, there may be a role for pre-existing case law which is not inconsistent with the terms of the Convention and to which resort might therefore be made as an aid to its interpretation.

301 A third difficulty with Article 16, to be discussed further below,[62] is that the circumstances in which Article 16.2 provides for payment of life salvors is patently unclear. International Conventions should be construed, first, according to their terms and, secondly, so as to achieve an internationally uniform approach; but, where the international approach is not yet apparent, and if it is legitimate to take notice of the prevalent English law and practice in the light of which the Convention was agreed—particularly since an English tribunal must give effect to the Convention in English law—in accordance with what was stated in the previous paragraph, it may be justifiable to resolve ambiguities by reference to the pre-existing law.

No personal liability

302 The pre-Convention law rule[63] is reproduced in the Convention's provision that "No remuneration is due from persons whose lives are saved".[64] More accurately, no remuneration is due from such persons simply for the saving of their lives. Although this is not specifically stated in the Convention, it should not be supposed that persons who are otherwise liable to pay a reward for the salvage of property are relieved of that obligation simply because their lives are also saved.

---

[60] *Ante*, § 292; *post* § 310.
[61] *ibid.*
[62] *Post*, §§ 304–308.
[63] *Ante*, §§ 261, 275.
[64] Art.16.1.

Entitlement to payment

Payment is due for life salvage under Article 16.2 if: (i) the claimant is "A **303** salvor of human life"; (ii) he "has taken part in the services rendered on the occasion of the accident giving rise to salvage"; and (iii) there is "payment awarded to the salvor for salving the vessel or other property or preventing or minimising damage to the environment".

Enforcing payment

Article 16.2 provides that "A salvor of human life ... is entitled to a fair **304** share of the payment awarded to the salvor for salving the vessel or other property or preventing or minimising damage to the environment."

A life salvage payment is therefore, first, dependent on the earning of what is now conventional salvage remuneration, *i.e.* for property and environmental salvage.

Secondly, the Convention refers to the payment for such conventional salvage as "the payment awarded". It would have been better if the reference had been to "the payment due". Otherwise the life salvor can be confronted with the argument that he is only entitled to payment if there has been a formal award, so being disfranchised if the salvees and the property and environmental salvors settle or if the property and environmental salvors make no claim. If the argument were valid, it might be countered by the life salvor's pursuing his own claim until he obtained an award; but that response is dependent on the life salvor's being entitled to claim against the salvee which, as will be seen next, may not be the case.

There are several possible interpretations of a life salvor's means of recov- **305** ering salvage remuneration under current English law.

First, if he can also claim for property and/or environmental salvage, he simply claims for the life salvage to be taken into account in assessing the reward in the usual way.[65] The difficulties to be discussed next arise where the claim is for life salvage alone.

Secondly, the life salvor may be able to claim directly against the property salvees. Under Admiralty law, a life salvor had no right to claim against anyone[66] but was given a right to claim against property salvees by statute.[67] That being so, it was unnecessary either to implement the terms of the Brussels Salvage Convention 1910 providing for life salvage or to introduce special national provision. Unfortunately, in enacting the Salvage Convention 1989,

---

[65] See *post*, Chap. 15.
[66] See above *ante*, §261.
[67] For the law prior to the implementation of the Salvage Convention 1989, see MSA 1894, ss 544–546; *ante*, §§ 273–297.

Subjects of Salvage

the United Kingdom conflated the existing English statutory provisions for life salvage within the Secretary of State's continued power to make discretionary payments for life salvage[68] and repealed the provisions directly authorising claims by life salvors. Therefore, if such claims remain possible, they must conform with the terms of the Salvage Convention 1989.

306 One argument might be that life salvage falls within the description of "salvage operation" as "*any* act or activity undertaken to assist a vessel or any other property in danger". Unfortunately, such an interpretation not only strains the language of the Convention[69]; but, where the life salvor's efforts are only for the sake of persons at risk, seems to contradict it. However, that may not be fatal. Life salvage is traditionally dependent on property salvage, so it is not conclusive that the definition of salvage operation omits connected claims unless it is intended to be exclusive.

Liability of one salvor to another

307 Clearly, one salvor may be liable to another salvor for breach of duty if they are in a contractual relationship or for the commission of a tort. However, absent a contract, English law is reluctant to impose liability for a failure to act. If a claim for life salvage has to be enforced in combination with a claim for property salvage,[70] it follows that a claimant of life salvage alone will only recover: (i) if the award to the property salvor includes the requisite element of life salvage remuneration (whether or not it has actually been claimed by the property salvor); or (ii) if the life salvor is entitled to claim from the property salvor a fair share of the remuneration received by the property salvor, regardless of whether the tribunal intentionally included an amount in respect of life salvage; or (iii) if the property salvor is obliged to include a claim for life salvage in his own claim and to pay over the life salvage element of the reward to the life salvor, or to be liable in damages for failure to enforce the life salvor's claim. Given English law's traditional reluctance to impose duties to act and the common law rule that each salvor's claim is only on his own behalf, together with the absence of a clear intention in the Merchant Shipping Act 1995 that property salvors should be liable to enforce claims on behalf of life salvors (whether with or without being required to do so by life salvors), it must be concluded that property salvors are not be held liable for failure to enforce life salvors' claims.

A trust of salvage proceeds?

308 Article 16.2 provides that "A salvor of human life . . . is entitled to a fair share of the payment *awarded* to the salvor for salving the vessel or other property or preventing or minimising damage to the environment."[71] It is

---
[68] See *post*, § 310.
[69] International Salvage Convention 1989, Art. 1(a) (emphasis added).
[70] This is not necessarily the case.
[71] Emphasis added.

arguable that this provision constitutes a statutory trust of all or part of the amount of the award. However, such an argument is probably impossible to sustain where the amount of the award has not yet been paid by the salvee[72] and it is hard to believe that it was intended that a property salvor was intended to hold the full reward or an uncertain proportion of it on trust once he received it. However, if a life salvor has no direct claim against a salvee and a property or environmental salvor is not obliged to enforce a life salvage claim against a salvee, the imposition of a trust on monies received may be the only way, if any, of giving effect to the entitlement accorded to a life salvor by Article 16.2.

Assessment

One of the criteria to be taken into account in fixing a salvage reward under the Salvage Convention 1989 is "the skill and efforts of the salvors in salving the vessel, other property *and life*".[73] This criterion is more easily taken into account where all potential claimants and all potential defendants are parties to and bound by an arbitration than where that is not the case. It is also not difficult to apply in the situation most obviously addressed by this wording: where a salvor is claiming in respect of his own contribution to property and life salvage. However, it is unhelpful where a salvor is only entitled to a reward in respect of life salvage *and* if his claim has to be enforced against the property or environmental salvor rather than directly against the salvee.

The Convention provides that a life salvor "is entitled to a fair share of the payment awarded to the salvor for salving the vessel or other property or preventing or minimising damage to the environment".[74]

Discretionary Governmental life salvage payment

For English law,[75] the Merchant Shipping Act 1995[76] supplements the International Salvage Convention 1989 by continuing legislative provision[77] for discretionary governmental life salvage payments. The discretion arises where:

"(a) services are rendered wholly or in part in United Kingdom waters[78] in saving life from a vessel of any nationality or elsewhere in saving life from any United Kingdom ship[79];

---

[72] There is no clear subject-matter of the trust.
[73] International Salvage Convention 1989, Art. 13.1(g) (emphasis added). See *post*, §§ 1412–1414.
[74] International Salvage Convention 1989, Art. 16.2.
[75] For the application of the Merchant Shipping Act 1995, see *ibid.*, s.315.
[76] MSA 1995, s.224(2), Sched. 11, Pt II, para. 5. This effectively reproduces the provisions of the Merchant Shipping Act 1894, s.544(3), which was repealed by the Merchant Shipping (Salvage and Pollution) Act 1994, ss 1(6) and 10, Sched. 2, para. 1(2) and Sched. 4.
[77] See *ante*, §292.
[78] For the definition of "United Kingdom waters", see the Merchant Shipping Act 1995, s.313(2)(a).
[79] For the definition of "United Kingdom ship", see the Merchant Shipping Act 1995, ss 1(3) and 313(1).

      and
  (b) either—
        (i) the vessel and other property are destroyed, or
        (ii) the sum to which the salvor is entitled under [the Convention][80] is less than a reasonable amount for the services rendered in saving life."

If these conditions are satisfied and if he thinks fit, the Secretary of State may pay to the salvor such sum or, as the case may be, such additional sum as he thinks fit in respect of the services rendered in saving life.

This discretion has been exercised rarely[81] and, it might have been thought, could have been conveniently abolished when enacting the Convention. However, it was retained at the suggestion of practitioners and provides a residual means whereby payment might be recovered where lives are saved and no adequate payment is forthcoming from salvees. It remains to be seen whether its retention encourages more frequent exercise of the discretion and, if so, on what basis the sum payable is calculated.

6. LIABILITY

311   As is noted in Chapter 4,[82] the owner of property in danger may face the prospect of liability to third parties, which may be averted by a salvage service. This aspect of the service has long been a feature tending to enhance salvage rewards and, but for the fact that salvage has historically been a service to benefit property, it is arguable that minimisation or aversion of liability was deserving of recognition as an independent subject of salvage. However, this position was not achieved by the Admiralty Court and the negotiators of the International Salvage Convention 1989, especially in their discussions on environmental services, consciously avoided the introduction of a new category of liability salvage. It remains, therefore, outside the range of independent subjects of salvage.

7. THE ENVIRONMENT

312   Large modern vessels and their cargoes may pose the threat of considerable damage to the environment, for which shipowners may risk substantial liability, *e.g.* in the case of an incident involving a large oil tanker. Intervention by salvors may prevent or minimise damage to the environment and so benefit

---

[80] International Salvage Convention 1989, Art. 16.2. See *ante*, §§ 304–308.
[81] The most recent recorded instances were in 1939 and 1951 and for modest sums—£13 10s. and £250 respectively. See *Hansard* 1956, Vol. 557, No. 204; (1994) 555 H.L.Deb., col. 695.
[82] *Post*, §§ 345–351.

Contract

both salvees and the community in general. However, since the basis of salvage is a service to property in danger, the traditional law of salvage provided no manifest basis for the salvor to be paid purely for environmental services, either by salvees or third party beneficiaries of "environmental services". In order to stimulate such services and to afford some payment for them, following on innovations in LOF 1980, the International Salvage Convention 1989 incorporated provisions designed to enhance salvage rewards and to require shipowners to make special payments for environmental services. However, the "special compensation" provided for this purpose under Article 14 of the Convention[83] is calculated with reference to the salvor's expenditure, not on normal salvage principles:

> "[T]he promoters of the Convention did not choose ... to create an entirely new and distinct category of environmental salvage[84] ... [T]he reward under Article 14 is subordinate to the reward under Article 13,[85] and its functions should not be confused by giving it a character too closely akin to salvage."[86]

Nonetheless, encouragement of and payment for environmental services are linked with salvage services and are discussed in this book where appropriate.

8. CONTRACT

Subjects may be included within or excluded from the application of a salvage contract by the terms of that contract. Thus, Box 2 of LOF 2000 defines the "Property to be salved" as: **313**

> "The vessel:
> her cargo freight bunkers stores and any other property thereon but excluding the personal effects or baggage of passengers master or crew
> (referred to in this agreement as 'the property')."

9. ROYAL FISH

So-called "salvage" in connection with royal fish is not now of real importance and is also obscure. The meaning of the term "royal fish" certainly includes whales and sturgeon found on the shore or caught near the **314**

---

[83] See *post*, Chap. 5.
[84] See also *Semco Salvage and Marine Pte Ltd v. Lancer Navigation Co. Ltd (The Nagasaki Spirit)* [1997] A.C. 455, 460 (H.L.: *per* Lord Mustill): "the solution devised in the 1980s was not to create a new institution: a kind of free-standing 'environmental salvage'."
[85] See *post*, Chap. 15.
[86] [1997] A.C. 455, 468E–H.

coasts of Great Britain and probably also grampuses, porpoises, dolphins, riggs and graspes[87] and "generally whatsoever other fish having in themselves great and immense size or fat."[88] Fish or associated mammals taken on the high seas belong to the captor in accordance with the law and custom applying in the locality.[89]

The right to royal fish is a prerogative of the Crown.[90] The right is not asserted to rest on a claim by the monarch to the sovereignty of the seas from which such fish come; but a whale found on the shore or caught near the coasts of Great Britain is considered not only as being, but also as having always been, property so inherent in the Crown that, by a species of legal fiction, it is to be restored to the monarch as its rightful owner.[91] In fact, both the King and the Queen were regarded as having rights, not as joint tenants or tenants in common but as tenants in severalty, the King being entitled to the head and the Queen to the tail (it being supposed that the tail provided whalebone for the Queen's clothing—although such bone actually comes from the head).

315   The sovereign exercised his power to make royal fish the subject of grants much in the same way as wreck. Thus, the Lord Warden of the Cinque Ports has the right within the area of the Cinque Ports.[92] It appears also that such fish elsewhere, save where by grant or prescription they belonged to lords of manors and others in definite areas, were droits of Admiralty by grant at least when the Lord High Admiral was appointed in the time of Queen Anne[93] and that when this office went out of commission[94] all previous duties, rights and privileges were included in patents to the Lords Commissioners of Admiralty.

The procedure following on capture of royal fish seems to have been as follows. Unless action was taken by the Admiralty, the captors kept royal fish. Where action was taken, it was by process in the High Court of Admiralty for condemnation of the fish, or the oil, etc., produced from it, as a droit of Admiralty. In that event, the captors could intervene in the proceedings and claim an award of salvage. Where captors claimed, it was the practice to

---

[87] Origin: *crassus piscis*.

[88] See *The Lord Warden and Admiral of the Cinque Ports v. H.M. in his Office of Admiralty, etc. (In the Matter of a Whale)* (1831) 2 Hagg. 438, 442. See also *The Case of Swans* (1592) 7 Co.Rep. 15b, 16a.

[89] *Aberdeen Arctic Co. v. Sutter* (1862) 6 L.T. 229 (HL).

[90] Statute de Praerogativa Regis (17 Edw. 2, st. 2, c.11), *temp. incert.* the Wild Creatures and Forest Laws Act 1971, s.1(1) generally abolished the prerogative right of Her Majesty to wild creatures but expressly excepted from the abolition and preserved the prerogative to royal fish and swans.

[91] *The Lord Warden* case, *supra*, n. 88, at 441.

[92] *The Lord Warden and Admiral of the Cinque Ports v. H.M. in his Office of Admiralty, etc. (In the Matter of a Whale)*, *supra*. It appears from Admiralty Court records in the Public Record Office that at various times the Court of Admiralty and the Mayor's Court were in conflict over the right to Royal Fish caught in the River Thames.

[93] *ibid.*, 442.

[94] In 1708 the function was entrusted to the Board of Admiralty. It is now discharged by the Secretary of State for Defence, the Defence Council and the Admiralty Board.

Static structures, platforms and drilling units

award salvage, at least where their claim was not contested.[95] Salvage is usually regarded as "payable",[96] although there appears to be no authority to the effect that the claim could not be contested on the ground that there is no right.

316 Royal fish are not wreck, so the provisions of the Merchant Shipping Act 1995 are inapplicable. By the provisions of the Supreme Court Act 1981, however, the Admiralty jurisdiction of the High Court includes jurisdiction to hear and determine any claim for droits of Admiralty,[97] together with any other jurisdiction which was vested in the court before the Act was passed,[98] and the jurisdiction includes any claim in the nature of salvage.

In practice, captors are at the present time allowed to keep sturgeon, which may be of considerable value, and may dispose of them as they wish. It has not infrequently happened, however, that a captor has offered a sturgeon to Her Majesty the Queen and that Her Majesty has been graciously pleased to accept such a gift.

10. EXCLUDED SUBJECTS

317 Services in the nature of salvage will not give rise to a salvage award if the subject of the service is not within the range of subjects of salvage, as recognised under Admiralty law or extended by statute, or, though prima facie within that range, is specifically excluded from it, whether by law or contract.

Static structures, platforms and drilling units

General principle

318 It was established in *The Gas Float Whitton No. 2*[99] that normally static[1] structures, even if capable of being used in navigation, are not subjects of salvage, at least if they are not classifiable as ships. The general Admiralty law principle is part of the framework of the International Salvage Convention 1989, Art. 1(c) of which states that:

---

[95] *The Lord Warden* case, *supra* n. 88, at 442.
[96] See Halsbury, Vol. 1, para. 350.
[97] s.20(1)(s). No necessity for the exercise of the jurisdiction ordinarily arises, since droits of Admiralty (usually, unclaimed wreck, flotsam, jetsam, lagan and derelict found in or on the shores of the sea or any tidal waters and derelict on the high seas beyond the limits of the U.K.) in times of peace are dealt with by the Receiver of Wreck of the district or by the Secretary of State as Receiver-General of Admiralty droits.
[98] s.20(1)(c).
[99] *Wells v. The Owners of the Gas Float Whitton No. 2 (The Gas Float Whitton No. 2)* [1897] A.C. 337; affirming [1896] P. 42; reversing [1895] P. 301. See *ante*, §§ 155–157.
[1] *i.e.* fixed or floating.

"For the purposes of this Convention ... Property means any property not permanently and intentionally attached to the shoreline ... "

The general principle finds particular application in the Convention's specific treatment of platforms and drilling units.

Platforms and drilling units under Article 3

319 Article 3 of the International Salvage Convention 1989 provides:

"This Convention shall not apply to fixed or floating platforms or to mobile offshore drilling units when such platforms or units are on location engaged in the exploration, exploitation or production of sea-bed mineral resources."

There are three criteria for the operation of the exclusion. First, the object must be a fixed or floating platform or a mobile offshore drilling unit. The exclusion applies to platforms which rest on or are attached to the sea-bed, including semi-submersibles which can raise or lower legs to or from the sea-bed, and any mobile offshore drilling unit.[2] Secondly, the subject must be on location. Thirdly, Article 3 is concerned with the designated subjects while they are employed with a specific purpose, namely on location engaged in exploration, exploitation or production of sea-bed mineral resources. The rationale behind the exclusion was apparently partly that such structures often have detailed safety and response plans which could be interfered with by a salvor having experience of ships rather than oil rigs; though, if so, the exclusion seems largely unnecessary, given the right of potential salvees to reject salvage services[3] and the salvor's inability to claim a salvage award for officious intervention.[4]

320 If platforms and drilling units are not engaged in exploration, exploitation or production of sea-bed mineral resources, the application of the Convention to them is not excluded and a salvage reward is recoverable, but only if the subject of the service qualifies under the normal rules. Thus, Article 3's exclusion of fixed or floating platforms applies the Admiralty law exclusion of static structures in *The Gas Float Whitton No. 2*[5]; so salvage is not generally recoverable in respect of such structures whether under the Convention or otherwise. However, mobile offshore drilling units seem prima facie to fall within the definition of vessel,[6] in which case they are subjects of salvage except where Article 3 applies.

---

[2] In particular, mobile oil drilling units ("MODUs"). These are defined in the IMO MODU Code, adopted by RES. A.414(XI), 15.
[3] See *post*, Chap. 10 and §§ 1228–1244.
[4] See *ante*, §§ 50–64.
[5] *Ante*, § 155.
[6] *Ante*, §§ 168–177. See Shaw [1996] L.M.C.L.Q. 202, 210.

Personal effects and luggage

The application of the Admiralty jurisdiction provisions of the Supreme Court Act 1981,[7] to goods extends to "baggage".[8] However, so far as liability to arrest and contribution to salvage are concerned, it has long been conceded that the personal effects of the master and the crew are exempt.[9] Similarly, the wearing apparel of passengers and other effects *ejusdem generis* belonging to them and carried by them for their daily use or consumption during the voyage were privileged from arrest.[10] In both cases, the property preserved would seem to benefit from the service provided and should arguably have contributed to the salvage reward. However, their exemption from liability to contribute to payment of salvage reward and to general average[11] has long been established. 321

There is a distinction, however, between possessions and valuables taken by passengers for use during the voyage, and luggage and valuables which are in the custody of the ship. There is scarcely any authority in this area but English law's position in cases of both salvage and general average has been assumed to be represented by Brown D.J.'s opinion on the law relating to general average in the United States of America in *Heye v. North German Lloyd*.[12] He noted that, if the trunks and other luggage of passengers and the effects of the master and crew were jettisoned for the common benefit, then the interests benefited should contribute in general average but, although the reciprocity principle dictated that interests which could claim general average were normally obliged to contribute when themselves preserved, this was not decisive. After an exhaustive review of the authorities, he concluded[13]: 322

> "Considering, then, the undoubted universal rule to pay for baggage sacrificed, and the quite general exception of such articles from assessment, it is necessarily to be inferred that this exemption is based upon grounds that do not affect the justice and equity of compensation for such articles when sacrificed for the rest, though they may not be called on to contribute when saved. The reasons for this exemption in the case of passengers' baggage, I have not found stated any further than its insignificance, as Loundes[14] suggests, and the reason above indicated, *viz.*, that what is upon the person is not subject to the same risk that attends the cargo, and may be saved with the person though the cargo be lost[15] but that suggestion would apply only to what is strictly attached to the

---

[7] ss 20–24. See *post*, Chap. 13.
[8] s.24(1): " 'goods' includes baggage."
[9] See Beawes, Vol. I, p. 242.
[10] *The Willem III* (1871) L.R. 3 A. & E. 487.
[11] See Lowndes & Rudolf, §§ A.82–A.83, 17.05, 17.09, 17.59, 17.60, 17.64.
[12] *Heye v. North German Lloyd* (1887) 33 Fed. Rep. 60 (District Court, S.D., of New York); affirmed (1888) 36 Fed. Rep. 705 (Circuit Court of Appeals).
[13] (1887) 33 Fed. Rep. 60, 68–69.
[14] His reference is to a previous edition of what has become Lowndes & Rudolf.
[15] Conceivably, the clothes being worn by a passenger might also be considered a part of his life, which is exempt from liability to pay salvage. See *ante*, §§ 259–310.

person, not to trunks in the baggage compartment. But, aside from that, when we consider how great annoyance and inconvenience to passengers would attend the long detention of their trunks and clothing until a general average adjustment could be had, or an average bond be given; the practical impossibility of either, where passengers with their baggage are taken on and off at intermediate ports in the course of the voyage; the difficulties attending the valuations to be put upon such articles in average adjustments, and in the collections thereon; the inquisitorial and offensive nature of such examinations; the small value of many such packages, such as those of the steerage passengers; the insignificant sums to be derived from most of the trunks and boxes, often, perhaps, less than the cost of adjustment; and the difficulty of making any distinction in the mode of dealing with the baggage of the different classes of passengers, and the natural desire to accommodate travellers in the rivalries of competing lines,—in all these considerations there seem to be practical reasons enough, without reference to the legal right, to have led, first, to the omission in practice of any assessment on passengers' baggage, and, next, to the adoption of that practice in many of the recent Codes. Whether this be the true account of the matter or not, in the light of the above authorities, and the general usage of maritime nations, it is clear that the absence of reciprocity in the right to compensation and the obligation to contribute, is not sufficient to exclude passengers' baggage from compensation. The same authorities shew, as it seems to me, that by the general maritime law, aside from the provisions of recent Codes, the only baggage exempt is apparel, and such other articles as the passengers wear, with the usual changes for the voyage, and such as they actually take with them for use, which in that sense are attached to their person[16]; not trunks delivered in the exclusive charge of the ship, and which are neither in use, nor in the passengers' possession, during the voyage.

323 The modern codes above cited differ as to the extent to which this exemption is allowed. Where, as in this country, there is no statutory provision on the subject, and no adjudication, the omission of the baggage from assessment, beyond that actually in the possession of the passenger, and in use on the voyage, must be regarded as a favour or courtesy to passengers, or as being a waiver for practical reasons, rather than a strict legal right to exemption under the general maritime law; unless, indeed, the practice not to detain and hold baggage for a general average adjustment were proved to have been so long settled and acted upon as to form one of the implied terms and conditions upon which passengers embark."

324 A further justification for exempting passengers' luggage is that it tends to diminish the amount recoverable. It is in practice preferable that a larger claim can be brought against the ship and cargo rather than that some of the liability

---

[16] See *supra*, n. 54.

to which they would be subject should be transferred to the luggage of several passengers. Each of them would individually be responsible for a small proportion and, if there is no lien on their baggage, they would not be worth suing personally even if subsequently traceable.[17]

325 It may, therefore, be posited, as a general guideline, that luggage carried not for use during the voyage will in principle be liable to contribute to general average. Such luggage will normally, but need not necessarily, be in the custody of the ship. It is not necessary that it be separately liable for freight, though that will be a relevant factor. And it should certainly be relevant that it is unaccompanied, *e.g.* where its owner travels by air, for it will not then be *passengers'* luggage or effects. The distinction is almost one between luggage carried for personal use and that carried as cargo.[18]

326 It has been said that[19]:

> "The principle upon which contribution [to general average] becomes due does not appear to [their Lordships] to differ from that upon which claims of recompense for salvage services are founded."

Assuming the correctness of Brown D.J.'s reasoning, it may, therefore, be stated that the principle of Admiralty law is that passengers' luggage which is carried for use on the voyage will be subject to contribute to salvage, but luggage carried otherwise will not.

In practice, therefore, passengers' luggage, even if not carried for use during the voyage, was not liable for salvage. However, in classifying passengers' effects as privileged, Sir Robert Phillimore said in *The Willem III*[20]:

> "Lest any difficulty arise in determining the character of any of the goods in question, the parties, if they think fit, may agree to appoint some person to act as arbitrator, who can inspect the articles and determine their character, or if necessary, the matter may be again brought before the court."

Contractual provision

327 Brown D.J.'s last possible reason for excluding passengers' luggage from salvage liability (on the basis of an implied term) is, however, inadequate. For such an implied term would not at common law bind a third party salvor. Previous editions of Lloyd's Form were unhelpful. The position of passengers

---

[17] See Lowndes & Rudolf, § 17.59.
[18] *cf. R. v. Judge of City of London Court* (1883) 12 Q.B.D. 115. Though, with respect to motor vehicles, see now *post*, § 328.
[19] *Strang, Steel & Co. v. A. Scott & Co.* (1889) 14 App.Cas. 601, 608, *per* Lord Watson, delivering the opinion of the Judicial Committee of the Privy Council.
[20] (1871) L.R. 3 A. & E. 487, 490.

depended on whether they fell within the description of persons on behalf of whom it was purported that the Form was signed, *e.g.* the owners of the vessel, her cargo, freight, bunkers, stores and any other property thereon. It remained arguable that luggage was not covered, either because luggage did not fall within one of these descriptions or because the passengers did not authorise the signature of Lloyd's Form on their behalf. But, if luggage did fall within these descriptions or if passengers were held to have authorised signature of the Form, the express terms would presumably have overridden any argument that luggage was excluded by implied terms.

The conundrum was exacerbated by the introduction of the International Salvage Convention 1989, the application of which to "Property means any property not permanently attached to the shoreline . . . ".[21]

328 The potential subjection of personal effects to the same liability as other subjects of salvage has now been specifically excluded by contract.[22] Thus, personal effects and baggage are by contract excluded from the scope of LOF 2000. Box 2 describes as the "Property to be salved" "The vessel [the name of which is to be inserted] her cargo freight bunkers stores and other property thereon but excluding the personal effects or baggage of passengers master or crew". LSSAC 2000, cl. 3.2 enlarges upon this exclusion by stating:

> " 'personal effects or baggage' as referred to in Box 2 of the Agreement means those which the passenger, Master and crew member have in their cabin or are otherwise in their possession, custody or control and shall include any private motor vehicle accompanying a passenger and any personal effects or baggage in or on such vehicle."

Humanitarian cargoes

329 As will be seen in Chapter 12,[23] under the Salvage Convention 1989, Art. 26, if a state donates a humanitarian cargo, and agrees to pay for salvage services rendered in respect of it, no provision of the Convention shall be used as a basis for its seizure, arrest or detention. Article 26 does not take humanitarian cargoes outside the range of subjects of salvage, though its effect may be to impede or even thwart a claim for a salvage reward. However, since the donors of such cargoes are usually richer states, a governmental commitment from such a state is likely to be honoured and this provision may enable the cargo in question to reach its intended recipients more quickly.[24]

---

[21] Art. 1(c).
[22] See also the York-Antwerp Rules 1994, cl. XVII: "Mails, passengers' luggage, personal effects and accompanied private motor vehicles shall not contribute in general average."
[23] *Post*, §§ 1178–1181.
[24] See Shaw [1996] L.M.C.L.Q. 202, 229.

CHAPTER 4

DANGER AND SALVAGE SERVICES

Overview

330 In English law prior to the implementation of the International Salvage Convention 1989, a salvage service was one which contributed to the preservation of a subject of salvage in danger in tidal waters and it endured until that subject was brought to a place of safety. For the purposes of the International Salvage Convention 1989[1]:

> "salvage operation means any act or activity undertaken to assist a vessel or any other property in danger in navigable waters or in any other waters whatsoever".

Danger

331 Dr Lushington has on different occasions described the foundation of a salvage claim as danger and as a service actually rendered.[2] The second observation more obviously relates to the requirement of success.[3] However, the fact that both factors can be regarded as foundations of salvage claims indicates the link between the danger which must exist before a salvage service can be rendered and the part which a salvor must play in the preservation of the casualty from danger before he can claim salvage. It is, therefore, convenient to deal with danger and salvage services together in this chapter, before concluding with consideration of the duration of salvage services.

Danger as the foundation of salvage

332 By virtue of the venture in which they are involved, the ship, cargo and freight and the persons on board are exposed to risk of loss or damage arising from perils associated with the venture. Measures must normally be taken by the owners, master and crew to reduce or to extinguish such risks; and services, such as those of pilots, may be required to assist in these objects. They will not usually give rise to a salvage claim. An operative peril, whether or not it is one that can normally be expected to be encountered during the

---
[1] MSA 1995, s.224(1)(2); Sched. 11, Pt I, Art. 1(a).
[2] See respectively *The Wilhelmine* (1842) 1 N.o.C. 376, 378; *The Ranger* (1845) 3 N.o.C. 589, 590.
[3] See *post*, Chap. 8.

venture, will generate a salvage claim only where there exists a "danger". Danger of loss or damage to the subject-matter of the service is the very foundation of a claim to salvage[4] and the degree of danger has been said to be the most important element to be considered in awarding salvage.[5] The Salvage Convention 1989, Art. 13.1(d) specifies that "the nature and degree of the danger" shall be a criterion for fixing the reward.[6] If a danger exists but the property in question, *e.g.* the cargo, is not exposed to it, its owner need not pay salvage.[7]

333 The danger necessary to found a salvage service, however it arises, has been described as a real and sensible danger.[8] On the one hand, it must not be either fanciful or only vaguely possible[9] or have passed by the time the service is rendered.[10] On the other hand, it is not necessary that distress should be actual or immediate or that the danger should be imminent[11]; it will be sufficient if, at the time at which assistance is rendered, the subject-matter has encountered any misfortune or likelihood of misfortune which might possibly expose it to loss or damage if the service were not rendered.[12] As Bucknill J. put it with regard to life salvage in *The Suevic*,[13] there must be danger or apprehension of danger. Thus, it is not necessary to shew that a stranded vessel would not or might not have got away before a reasonably apprehended peril became an actual danger; it is sufficient that she would not have come free without the services provided.[14] The possibility of a danger's becoming imminent, *e.g.* through mistake, misunderstanding or misapprehension, may be some evidence of danger.[15] Indirect danger will not be sufficient. Thus, to salvage one ship from colliding with a second ship will not be a salvage service to the second ship if it could have avoided the collision.[16] The fact that disaster would have become inevitable may be a ground for increasing the

---

[4] *The Wilhelmine, supra*, 378.
[5] *The Perfective* (1949) 82 Ll.L.Rep. 873, 875. See also Brussels Salvage Convention 1910, Art. 8 (*post*, App. 28).
[6] See *post*, Chap. 15.
[7] See, *e.g. The Geertje K* [1971] 1 Lloyd's Rep. 285, 287.
[8] Kennedy's description. See 4th ed. (1958), p. 14. *cf. Watson v. Firemen's Fund Insurance Co.* [1922] 2 K.B. 355.
[9] *The Mount Cynthos* (1937) 58 Ll.L.Rep. 18, 25.
[10] *The Ranger* (1845) 3 N.o.C. 589; *The Batavier* (1853) 1 Spinks E. & A. 169, 171.
[11] *The Aztecs* (1870) 3 Asp. M.L.C. 326, 326. In several, particularly older, cases, a service appears to have been held to be salvage because the danger was immediate or imminent. But the relevant comments, which were not infrequently made because of the court's desire not readily to impose liability to salvage, must invariably be read in context of the facts of the cases.
[12] *The Charlotte* (1848) 3 Wm. Rob. 68, 71; approved in *The Strathnaver* (1875) 1 App. Cas. 58, 65 (P.C.), and *The Mount Cynthos* (1937) 58 Ll.L.Rep. 18, 25. See also *The Albion* (1861) Lush. 282; *The White Star* (1866) L.R. 1 A. & E. 68. *cf. The Ella Constance* (1864) 33 L.J. Adm. 189, 193, and *The Bengloe* (1940) 67 Ll.L.Rep. 307, 308: "The danger was real enough, but, fortunately, it was quite remote." See also *The Fountain* (1866) L.R. 1 A. & E. 58, 60.
[13] [1908] P. 154, 158.
[14] *The Mount Cynthos* (1937) 58 Ll.L.Rep. 18.
[15] *cf. The Bengloe* (1940) 67 Ll.L.Rep. 307, 309.
[16] *The Port Caledonia and The Anna* [1903] P. 184; *The Ovre and the Conde de Zubiria* (1920) 2 Ll.L. Rep. 21. See also *The Helmsman* (1950) 84 Ll.L. Rep. 207 (motor-tanker fuelling steamship which was saved from collision could have cast off to avoid damage).

Danger

amount of a salvage award.[17] Therefore,[18] in order to warrant a salvage service, there must be such reasonable, present apprehension of danger that, in order to escape or avoid the danger, no reasonably prudent and skilful person in charge of the venture would refuse a salvor's help if it were offered to him upon the condition of his paying a salvage reward.[19] The views of the master as to the existence of danger, if bona fide and reasonable, will be strong evidence that the danger was a real one.[20] The court will be slow, with the benefit of hindsight, to find that the apprehension of danger was reasonably held but that the danger was in fact illusory.[21]

Degree of danger

It is not necessary that the subject-matter be in danger of total loss. A salvage service may be performed though the danger is easily remedied.[22] Danger of damage is sufficient, although obviously not all steps taken to avoid or reduce reasonably apprehended damage will justify a salvage reward.[23] The degree of danger will affect the salvor's ability to claim where he falls outside the traditional classification of volunteer,[24] particularly where he is habitually engaged in the performance of services in order to avoid danger to shipping. Thus, in *Akerblom v. Price, Potter, Walker & Co.*,[25] the Court of Appeal stated that in order to entitle a pilot to salvage reward he must not only show that the ship was in some sense in distress, but that she was in such distress as to be in danger of being lost and such as to call upon him to provide such a service as to make it unfair and unjust that he should be paid otherwise than upon the terms of salvage reward.[26] Where a danger is found to exist, the existence of alternative and cheaper ways of saving the property may affect the degree of danger and so may reduce the amount of the reward.[27]

334

Vessels already damaged

Where a danger does exist, the Court has tended to take a more permissive attitude to the conversion of towage services to salvage services than it does

335

---

[17] *The Mount Cynthos* (1937) 58 Ll.L. Rep. 18, 25.

[18] The remainder of this sentence was cited with approval in *The Hamtun* [1999] 1 Lloyd's Rep. 883, 889, *per* Peter Gross Q.C., sitting as a Deputy Judge of the High Court.

[19] *The Phantom* (1866) L.R. 1 A. & E. 58, 60; *The Aztecs* (1870) 3 Asp. M.L.C. 326; *The Mount Cynthos* (1937) 58 Ll.L.Rep. 18, 24–25. See also *The Suevic* [1908] P. 154, 159–160, where Bucknill J. said he had to look upon danger as an ordinary person of ordinary intelligence, acting upon certain facts, and not in the same way as lifeboatmen, who look upon danger differently from other people. *cf. The Amelia Lauro* (1940) 68 Ll.L.Rep. 12, 19.

[20] This sentence was cited with approval in *The Hamtun* [1999] 1 Lloyd's Rep. 883, 889, *per* Peter Gross, Q.C., sitting as a Deputy Judge of the High Court.

[21] See *Corry v. Coulthard* (1876) 3 Asp. M.L.C. 546; *The Wordsworth* (1898) 88 Fed. Rep. 313. The sentence in the text was cited with approval in *The Hamtun* [1999] 1 Lloyd's Rep. 883, 889, *per* Peter Gross, Q.C., sitting as a Deputy Judge of the High Court.

[22] *The Lord Dufferin* (1849) 7 N.o.C. Supp. xxxiii, xxxiv.

[23] See, *e.g. The Geertje K* [1971] 1 Lloyd's Rep. 285, 287.

[24] Chap. 7.

[25] (1881) 7 Q.B.D. 129.

[26] *ibid.*, 135.

[27] *The Werra* (1886) 12 P.D. 52, 54; *The Queen Elizabeth* (1949) 82 Ll.L.Rep. 803, 820; *The Troilus* [1950] P. 92, 108, *per* Bucknill L.J. (affirmed [1951] A.C. 820).

to the conversion of the services of other non-volunteers.[28] In *The Reward*,[29] Dr Lushington said:

> "I apprehend that mere towage service is confined to vessels that have received no injury or damage and that mere towage is payable in those cases only where the vessel receiving the service is in the same condition she would ordinarily be in without having encountered any danger or accident."

This statement and a subsequent statement of Dr Lushington in *The Princess Alice*,[30] that towage may be described as the employment of one vessel to expedite the voyage of another when nothing more is required than the accelerating of her progress, have both been judicially approved.[31] But the remarks must be read in the context of the cases in which they were uttered and of the other authorities. Just as salvage services may be rendered in order to avoid the danger of injury or damage to an undamaged vessel, a service rendered to a vessel which is already damaged will only be a salvage service as a consequence of that damage if the damage or the cause of damage places the vessel in danger from which it needs to be saved. The mere fact that a vessel has suffered damage does not mean that any services rendered to that vessel must be salvage services.

Condition of vessel

336 On the one hand, the fact that a vessel is in poor physical condition and so not as capable of withstanding potential dangers as stronger vessels may lead to the conclusion that it is in danger, particularly where there is a possibility of touching the bottom or stranding, where a more sound vessel might not be in danger, because it would be capable of getting off with minimal or no damage.[32] But there is no general rule that, where a ship is for some reason without means of propulsion, she and her cargo are necessarily in danger until she is repaired.[33] On the other hand, a salvage claim must not be disallowed merely because a vessel is tight, staunch and strong and in no obvious, present danger of damage to its physical structure. Thus, a stranded vessel in no immediate or reasonably apprehended danger of destruction but without reasonable expectation of being able to get off with ease very soon is nevertheless in a position of danger for salvage purposes because she cannot pursue her intended voyage or deal effectively with any emergency which may arise.[34] Similarly, salvage was awarded where a ship was drifting in a dangerous part of the Pacific Ocean without a crew, though there was not necessarily more than an even chance that she would be lost; it was considered

---

[28] See Chap. 7.
[29] (1841) 1 W. Rob. 174, 177.
[30] (1848) 3 W. Rob. 138, 139–140.
[31] See, *e.g. The Glaucus* (1948) 81 Ll.L.Rep. 262, 266.
[32] See *The Victoria Peak* (1947) 80 Ll.L.Rep. 527.
[33] *The Troilus* [1951] A.C. 820, 830, 833.
[34] *The National Defender* [1970] 1 Lloyd's Rep. 40 (New York District Court).

relevant that it would not have been at all easy to have found an insurer for her in that state.[35]

It may not necessarily be the case, however, that property is in danger merely because it is not currently subject to any immediate physical control[36] or means of control. In *Simon v. Taylor*,[37] the Singapore High Court refused to award salvage in respect of mercury recovered from a German U-boat which had been sunk 28 years previously, *inter alia*, it seems, because the mercury was said not to have been exposed to a present apprehension of danger.

Type of danger

The danger which threatens need not be from the normal perils of sailing on the sea. Danger from war risks is sufficient.[38] Danger to proprietary rights will also justify a reward. The salvage service may be, therefore, retention of a ship in the hands of its owner as against the threatened onslaught of pirates; or it may be recovery of a ship from the control of an enemy, pirates or mutineers and restoration to the owner.[39] Such danger may not be limited to cases where the object of the pirates is "feloniously and permanently to deprive the owner of his proprietary rights."[40] The extent to which a financial danger may be regarded as an independent head of danger rather than as one tending to enhancement of reward is a controversial issue, and will be considered more fully below.[41]

337

Provided that danger threatens, it is immaterial that the consequences which it threatens alter: *e.g.* that a ship which was in danger of being driven ashore by a storm becomes in danger of sinking while still at sea.

Danger to salvors

Dicta appearing in early authorities suggests not only that it is relevant to deciding whether or not danger exists that the service is undertaken with risk to the salvor[42] but even that danger to the salvor might *per se* be sufficient to constitute a service as one of salvage.[43] It has been established, however, that danger to the salvor alone will not found a claim for salvage. Moreover, it is

338

---

[35] *Norddeutscher Lloyd v. "Cairnhill," Cargo and Freight* (1920) 5 Ll.L.Rep. 386. The fact that a vessel is not insured, so that the owner is likely to be more prejudiced by loss than the owner of an insured vessel, would not, at least by itself, put it in a position of danger for salvage purposes. *cf. The Rosa Luxemburg* (1934) 49 Ll.L.Rep. 292, 303.

[36] See *The Homewood* (1928) 31 Ll.L.Rep. 336.

[37] [1975] 2 Lloyd's Rep. 338, especially at 345.

[38] See, *e.g. The Amelia Lauro* (1940) 68 Ll.L.Rep. 12; *The Tafelberg* (1942) 71 Ll.L.Rep. 189.

[39] *Société Maritime Calédonienne v. The Cythera and her Cargo, The Cythera* [1965] 2 Lloyd's Rep. 454 (N.S.W. S.C.); *The Beaver* (1801) 3 C.Rob. 292; *The Trelawney* (1802) 4 C.Rob. 223; *The Calypso* (1828) 2 Hagg. 209.

[40] *The Cythera*, *supra*, n. 39, at 461, where Macfarlan J. decided that the danger "included" such cases.

[41] *Post*, §§ 345–350.

[42] *The Phantom* (1866) L.R. 1 A. & E. 58, 61.

[43] See, *e.g. The Princess Alice* (1848) 3 W.Rob. 138, 140.

not necessary, for a salvor to qualify for salvage reward, that he be in any position of danger during provision of the salvage services[44] or even that the services be difficult to perform.[45] The court will, however, take account of the risks run and the difficulties incurred by salvors in assessing the amount of salvage reward.[46]

Knowledge of danger

339   A master's ignorance of the locality or other circumstances affecting the venture is not by itself a proper ground for salvage.[47] The court will not readily allow a salvage claim to be engrafted upon the local ignorance of foreigners who, as foreigners, are not very likely to be well acquainted with a locality.[48] Likewise, ignorance of an English master which necessitates the simple assistance of a pilot will not tend to found a claim for salvage or augment the rate of a salvage award, for it is the business of a pilot to supply any deficiency of a master's knowledge.[49] And where a pilot's services are engaged it may reasonably be assumed that they are for providing assistance in respect of local matters of which a ship's master can be expected to be ignorant.[50] However, a ship which might be held to be in safety if handled by a skilful master who knows the locality may be in peril if her master is not possessed of such skill and knowledge. Thus, the ignorance of persons on board may add to all the ordinary and natural perils to which a ship is prone so as to constitute the danger to the ship and the property in their charge which is essential to give rise to a salvage service.[51] On the other hand, evidence that the master and crew had no knowledge that a vessel was in danger may incline the tribunal to conclude that there was no danger.[52]

Proof of danger

340   The onus of proving the danger which is alleged to have generated the need for salvage "lies strongly and justly on the salvors."[53] The existence of danger, however, is frequently not disputed, as, for example, where it is clear on the facts that no useful purpose would be served by denial or where

---

[44] *The Henry* (1810) 1 Edw. 192, 196; *The Pericles* (1863) Br. & Lush. 80. *cf. The Tsiropinas* (1935) 51 Ll.L.Rep. 87, 89.
[45] See, *e.g. The Ellora* (1862) Lush. 550; *The Jubilee* (1879) 4 Asp. M.L.C. 275.
[46] The Salvage Convention 1989, Art. 13.1(g) includes as a criterion for fixing a salvage reward "the risk of liability and other risks run by the salvors or their equipment". See *post*, Chap. 15.
[47] *The Vrouw Margaretha* (1801) 4 C.Rob. 104; *The Eugenie* (1844) 3 Not. of Cas. 430.
[48] *The Vrouw Margaretha, supra*, at 104; *The Joseph Harvey* (1799) 1 C.Rob. 306, 309.
[49] *The Eugenie, supra*, n. 47, at 431.
[50] See, *e.g. The Mary* (1842) 1 W.Rob. 448, 454.
[51] *ibid.*, 451; and see *The Tres* (1936) 55 Ll.L.Rep. 16, 18–20. In most cases, however, it will not be unreasonable to infer that owners would not entrust their vessel other than to a reasonably competent master and crew: see *The Mary* (1842) 1 W.Rob. 448, 454.
[52] See *The Liverpool* [1893] P. 154, 162.
[53] *The Wilhelmine* (1842) 1 Not. of Cas. 376, 378. See also *The Princess Alice* (1849) 3 W.Rob. 138, 142: "if the matter be left in doubt, it is impossible for the Court to say that a salvage service has been performed, and that a salvage remuneration is due."

Danger

Lloyd's Form is signed, for signing the form will normally put the matter beyond doubt.[54] Very often, contention centres not on the existence of the danger alleged by the salvors, which would affect the very foundation of the salvage claim, but around the degree of danger, which would affect the quantum of a salvage award.[55] Either contention, however, would have to be judged in the light of all the evidence available. In a case where a ship came into a state of danger when she lost her propeller and, after being towed to a port of call by one tug, was towed therefrom by another to safety at her original destination, Bucknill L.J. said that, to defeat a salvage claim, the burden was on the owners to shew that the danger had come to an end before the second tug started to tow her.[56]

Evidence of danger

The existence and degree of danger must be judged by looking at each set of circumstances as a whole. The fact that similar circumstances in a previous case were held to constitute a danger produces no clear guide, even with respect to the same geographical locality.[57] Moreover, the older cases must be read with some circumspection in modern times. For example, the presence of fast modern means of communication may radically alter the degree of danger that would have been present in former times to a vessel which has broken down at sea.[58]

341

The following circumstances are likely, but are not bound, to indicate a greater or lesser degree of danger: the abandonment of the voyage[59]; the fact that the crew or passengers are leaving, preparing to leave or have left the vessel[60]; the reputation of an area as one of danger to shipping[61]; the fact that several other ships were in distress in the vicinity[62]; illness, exhaustion, ignorance and incompetence of the master or crew[63]; a divided command or an easily excitable master[64]; loss of anchors and chains[65]; the fact that services are demanded urgently[66]; the use of distress signals[67]; the acceptance of

---

[54] See *The Beaverford v. The Kafiristan* [1938] A.C. 136; *post*, §§ 866–875.
[55] *The Aglaia* (1888) 13 P.D. 160, 161.
[56] *The Troilus* [1950] P. 92, 103 (affirmed [1951] A.C. 820).
[57] See *The Trevorian* (1940) 66 Ll.L.Rep. 45, 48. *cf. The Anna Mazarki* (1931) 39 Ll.L.Rep. 194 with *The Glaisdale* (1945) 78 Ll.L.Rep. 403, 477; and *The Glaucus* (1948) 81 Ll.L.Rep. 262 with *The Troilus* [1951] A.C. 820.
[58] See *The Perfective* (1949) 82 Ll.L.Rep. 873, 875.
[59] *The Elizabeth* (1844) 8 Jur. 365, 366.
[60] *The Suevic* [1908] P. 154, 160–161; *The Glenmorven* [1913] P. 141; *The Roumelian* (1933) 45 Ll.L.Rep. 267; *The Tsiropinas* (1935) 51 Ll.L.Rep. 87. *cf. The Homewood* (1928) 31 Ll.L.Rep. 336.
[61] *The Prins Knud (No. 1)* (1940) 67 Ll.L.Rep. 458. *cf. The Bengloe, ibid.*, 307.
[62] *The Medora* (1853) 1 Spinks E. & A. 17.
[63] *The Swan* (1839) 1 W. Rob. 68; *The Charlotte Wylie* (1846) 2 W. Rob. 495; *The Ottercaps* (1876) Pritchard, Vol. 2, 2094. See also *The Aglaia* (1888) 13 P.D. 160. *cf. The Canova* (1866) L.R. 1 A. & E. 54; *The British Inventor* (1933) 45 Ll.L.Rep. 263.
[64] *The Dimitrios N. Bogiazides* (1930) 37 Ll.L.Rep. 27.
[65] *The Prince of Wales* (1848) 6 Not. of Cas. 39.
[66] *The Ovre and The Conde de Zubiria* (1920) 2 Ll.L.Rep. 21.
[67] *The Wilhelmine* (1842) 1 Not. of Cas. 376; *The Aglaia* (1888) 13 P.D. 160.

Danger and Salvage Services

services when offered[68]; stranding or the risk of stranding[69]; total or substantial loss of means of propulsion, with its attendant diminution in ability to negotiate difficulties[70]; and the master's representation of his vessel's being in danger.[71]

342 Evidence of the conduct and circumstances of the alleged salvor may be just as usefully adduced for the purpose of demonstrating the existence and degree of danger. Thus, it may well be unlikely that a passenger vessel with many passengers on board would voluntarily delay its voyage unnecessarily except to go to the assistance of another vessel genuinely believed to be in danger.[72] The fact that a tug demands a sum appropriate for towage, rather than salvage,[73] or that it leaves the tow, particularly if without protest from the master, crew and passengers,[74] will also be relevant.

343 It cannot be assumed that evidence which by itself may tend to suggest the presence of danger will necessarily be more than equivocal. Thus, it will be relevant that a ship has slipped her cables but not conclusive, for that is a measure of precaution which may be resorted to frequently for convenience and expedition and at small expense, since, with a buoy attached to them, they may be easily recoverable.[75] A request for pilotage assistance may be made entirely in the ordinary course of prosecuting a voyage but employment for the purpose of a person who is not a pilot[76] or outside pilotage waters[77] may raise the service to the rank of a salvage service. The original or alleged motive for the conduct, such as hoisting a signal for a pilot only, does not prevent the services rendered from being in the nature of salvage if the vessel can be proved actually to have been in danger; recipients of salvage services cannot deny that the services were in the nature of salvage.[78]

Signals

344 Where a person is induced to go out to assist a vessel by an ambiguous signal, the signal will be construed with respect to the condition of the

---

[68] *The Wilhelmine, supra,* n. 67, at 377. See also *The Mount Cynthos* (1937) 58 Ll.L.Rep. 18, 22.

[69] The cases are particularly numerous. See, *e.g. The St Patrick* (1930) 35 Ll.L.Rep. 231; *The Anna Mazarki* (1931) 39 Ll.L.Rep. 194; *The Luigi Accame* (1938) 60 Ll.L.Rep. 106; *The Driade* [1959] 2 Lloyd's Rep. 311. *cf. The Liverpool* [1893] P. 154; *The Domby* (1941) 69 Ll.L.Rep. 161. The evidence of danger may operate retrospectively: *The British Inventor* (1933) 45 Ll.L.Rep. 263 (the fact that the ship is later shown to be damaged may be evidence that she was aground and therefore in danger).

[70] *The Batavier* (1853) 1 Spinks E. & A. 169; *The Ellora* (1862) Lush. 550; *The Thomas Allen* (1886) 12 App. Cas. 118; *The Werra* (1886) 12 P.D. 52; *The Glaucus* (1948) 81 Ll.L.Rep. 262; *The Troilus* [1951] A.C. 820.

[71] *The Swan* (1839) 1 W. Rob. 68, 71.

[72] *The Wilhelmine* (1842) 1 Not. of Cas. 376, 377.

[73] *The Canova* (1866) L.R. 1 A. & E. 54, 56.

[74] *The Batavier* (1853) 1 Spinks E. & A. 169.

[75] *The Wilhelmine* (1842) 1 Not. of Cas. 376, 379.

[76] *The Aglaia* (1888) 13 P.D. 160.

[77] *The Hedwig* (1853) 1 Spinks E. & A. 19.

[78] *The Bomarsund* (1860) Lush. 77; *The Anders Knape* (1879) 4 P.D. 213.

vessel.[79] If the vessel is in need of assistance, particularly where it is damaged, the signal will be treated as a request for assistance and those answering it as salvors. Otherwise, it will be treated as a signal for ordinary services of pilotage or such like.

Non-physical danger ("liability salvage")

345 It has long been the practice to take account of non-physical dangers in assessing the extent of liability to pay salvage rewards. Thus, account has been taken of potential loss of proprietary rights,[80] the risk of destruction by a port or governmental authority,[81] the inability or reduced ability of a valuable, profit-earning asset to earn profits whilst disabled,[82] the avoidance of liability to third parties for failure to perform contracts,[83] the avoidance by an inexpensive salvage service of more expensive liability to other salvors,[84] the avoidance of tortious liability to third parties,[85] and even the risk to a shipowner's reputation from the disability of a prestigious liner.[86] The authorities illustrate these factors, even the risk to proprietary rights, as consequences of physical dangers and as tending to enhanced rewards rather than as distinct heads of danger preservation from which *per se* justifies an award. On the other hand, the cases do not deny this possibility, which must therefore be investigated. The size of modern vessels and the increasing potential harmfulness of certain cargoes, especially in the case of large oil tankers, exposes salvees to possible substantial liability to national and local governmental and harbour authorities, and to those engaged in tourist industries—liability which may significantly exceed the values of the casualty or the limitation fund.

346 Salvage services may also be beneficial to the environment in general but in pre-Convention law it was difficult to conceive of this being a relevant factor in assessment except in relation to the legal liability of a person with an interest in a recognised subject of salvage, which it is the object of the public policy underlying salvage to protect. The absence of an interest in a subject of salvage may also be the reason why a vessel which has negligently collided with an oil tanker, pollution from which has been reduced or avoided by a salvor, may be held not liable to the salvor for his having reduced the liability

---

[79] *The Mary* (1842) 1 W.Rob. 448, 452–453; *The Dosseitei* (1846) 10 Jur. 865, 866; *The Hedwig* (1853) 1 Spinks E. & A. 19; *The Felix, ibid.*, at p. 23n.; *The Little Joe* (1860) Lush. 88; *The Racer* (1874) 2 Asp. M.L.C. 317. See also *The Jubilee* (1879) 4 Asp. M.L.C. 275, 276; *The Aglaia* (1888) 13 P.D. 160.
[80] *e.g. The Cythera* [1965] 2 Lloyd's Rep. 454.
[81] *The Merannio* (1927) 28 Ll.L.Rep. 352, 353.
[82] *The Glaucus* (1948) 81 Ll.L.Rep. 262, 266; *The Troilus* [1951] A.C. 820 (*post*, §383); *The Orelia* [1958] 1 Lloyd's Rep. 441, 450.
[83] See *ante*, §§ 234–243.
[84] *e.g. The Tsiropinas* (1935) 51 Ll.L.Rep. 87, 89; *cf. The Sandefjord* [1953] 2 Lloyd's Rep. 557; *cf.* also *The Tervaete* [1922] P. 259, 271, where Scrutton L.J. seems to have regarded the existence of a maritime lien as reducing a vessel's salved value.
[85] See *post*, §§ 347–351.
[86] *The Queen Elizabeth* (1949) 82 Ll.L.Rep. 803, 820.

of the colliding vessel; however, there is no authority definitely denying the possibility of a claim directly against the colliding vessel for salvage.[87]

347 In the great majority of situations dealt with in the law reports, the defendants will be exposed to the risk of damage or destruction, the physical danger which most frequently necessitates salvage services, and this obvious danger has tended to be the predominant or only concern of the court, even though the circumstances also suggest that the defendants may be exposed to liability to third parties. Thus, in *The Vandyck*,[88] a tug was rewarded for disentangling two ships which, having been anchored, had fouled each other in a hurricane. Similarly, in *The Port Caledonia and The Anna*,[89] and in *The Ovre and The Conde de Zubiria*,[90] rewards were also given to tugs which prevented vessels which had dragged their anchors during storms from colliding with other vessels at anchor.[91] However, in *The Vandyck*, the possibility that one of the endangered vessels might have been liable for the collision was not considered. And in the other two cases, salvage claims against the stationary vessels were expressly disallowed, Hill J. pointing out in the third case that the vessel dragging her anchor had a duty to terminate the risk of damage to the stationary vessel.[92] In both cases, the stationary vessels could have preserved themselves from danger.

348 The possibility of further loss, over and above that arising from imminent physical danger, was averted to in *The Merannio*,[93] where a vessel being towed in fog was struck by another vessel, which had dragged her anchor. In awarding salvage to tugs which pulled the first vessel free of the other, Lord Merrivale P. pointed out that she had been prevented from sinking and that[94]:

> "the owners would have had the expense of removing her, or might have found themselves without either vessel or cargo, because the Port of London authorities might have thought that the proper mode of clearing the channel was to destroy her."

---

[87] Of course, subject to questions of limitation of liability, the colliding vessel will be liable to reimburse the tanker for liability for salvage and otherwise which it has caused. It is suggested that the colliding vessel could not plead the rule of remoteness of benefit in *The Annapolis* (1861) Lush. 355: see *ante*, §64.

[88] (1882) 5 Asp. M.L.C. 17 (CA), affirming Sir Robert Phillimore's judgment (1881) *ibid.*; (1881) 7 P.D. 42. The CA's judgment concentrates on another matter. See also *The Empress of Australia and The Debrett* (1947) 81 Ll.L. Rep. 24; *The Merannio* (1927) 28 Ll.L. Rep. 352; and *cf. The Saratoga* (1861) Lush. 318.

[89] [1903] P. 184.

[90] (1920) 2 Ll.L. Rep. 21.

[91] See also *The Beatsa* (1937) 58 Ll.L. Rep. 85; *The Bertil* [1952] 2 Lloyd's Rep. 176, 182; *The New Australia* [1958] 2 Lloyd's Rep. 35.

[92] See also *The Helmsman* (1950) 84 Ll.L. Rep. 207; and *cf. The Emilie Galline* [1903] P. 106.

[93] (1927) 28 Ll.L. Rep. 352, and also in *The Salawati* (1929) 34 Ll.L. Rep. 37.

[94] *ibid.*, 353.

This does not obviously contemplate risk above and beyond that of official destruction or of an expense voluntarily incurred. But in similar circumstances, in *The Gregerso*,[95] where a vessel had blocked Boston harbour, Brandon J. made his award expressly[96] "bearing in mind the potential liability of the defendants to third parties if the port had remained blocked."

349 It is perhaps not surprising that in the majority of cases cited so far in this section, there was no express consideration of liability to third parties as a distinct element of danger, because nearly all of them involved salvage services in the nature of towage, which service, it goes without saying, requires prevention of liability to third parties as well as avoidance of the potential damage or destruction which comes uppermost into the mind when salvage is required. In *The Whippingham*,[97] however, where in a gale a ship which took action to avoid a collision went out of control, fouled some yachts and risked fouling more, Bateson J., in rewarding the salving tug, said[98]:

> "I think she would have inflicted some damage on other yachts, which would have become claims, at any rate, against her. Whether she could successfully have resisted the claims—she has already got five against her—or whether she could not, is a matter, possibly, of some doubt. She might have been able to throw the blame on somebody else, but from what I have heard of the case I should think it would be very difficult for her to escape being partly to blame, at any rate, for what happened. The mere saving of a vessel from damage to other ships which might result in claims is a service, to my mind, because although the claim may not be a good one there is considerable damage attached to successfully defending a claim, because there is all the expense which you do not recover even when you are a successful defendant. I must think that in itself would be a ground of claim for salvage."

350 It is submitted, therefore, that the avoidance or diminution of the extent of potential liability to third parties is in principle capable of providing a distinct service whereby property is salved from danger, albeit it does not necessarily follow that this will normally or necessarily require a higher reward than will normally be given for preservation from the physical dangers that will almost invariably be present whenever such potential liability arises. There is support for the view that avoidance of contractual liability may ground a salvage claim.[99] But it would be a distinct departure from tradition to award salvage solely for preservation from tortious liability to a third party in the absence of risk of physical damage, particularly bearing in mind the consideration that the risk of third party liability is likely only to be borne by one party to the

---

[95] [1973] Q.B. 274.
[96] *ibid.*, 284.
[97] (1934) 48 Ll.L. Rep. 49.
[98] *ibid.*, 51–52.
[99] See *ante*, §§ 234–242.

adventure, the shipowner.[1] It is submitted, therefore, that, as a matter of law, preservation from such liability is not an independent ground for reward but a feature tending to enhance it.

351 This is confirmed by the negotiations leading to, and the consequent content of, the International Salvage Convention 1989. Negotiations to make provision for environmental services were conducted against a reluctance to recognise a new category of "liability salvage". Specific provision has been made for environmental services, both within the Convention and contractually, without establishing liability salvage as a recognised category.[2] And the Convention is silent on the point.

Property of no value

352 Salvage services are generally necessary because the danger threatens the economic value of the subject of salvage. To safeguard its value, it will be necessary to preserve the property itself, so no distinction normally needs to be made between the property and its value. If the property no longer has any value, even scrap value, salvage services will not normally be rendered or a claim for a salvage reward will not be pursued, since there will be no fund in respect of which an award can be made. However, the Salvage Convention 1989, Art. 14 authorises the payment of special compensation for environmental services[3] in cases where no reward is recoverable for property salvage. Such compensation may therefore be claimed where the property in question is no longer worth salving. In most cases, of course, especially since special compensation claims are likely to arise in respect of large oil tankers with at least some scrap value, the property in question will have some value. It is nonetheless the case that special compensation claims are essentially dependent on there being a "salvage operation"; and it must therefore be determined whether there is such an operation when the value of the property as preserved exceeds the cost of preservation, or at least where that property has no value at all.

353 The English law of salvage is founded upon property[4] and it is arguable that it is in principle sufficient that property be preserved, whatever its value. Although there is an underlying policy of encouraging salvors by generous rewards, and that policy cannot be effectively implemented when the valuelessness of the property removes the incentive, that is not conclusive, since the policy is arguably relevant to inflating the amount of the reward rather than to the general principle of recovery.[5]

---

[1] *cf. The Velox* [1906] P. 263; *post*, Chap. 13.
[2] See *post*, Chap. 5.
[3] See *post*, Chap. 5.
[4] See *ante*, Chap. 2.
[5] See further, *post*, Chap. 15.

Also relevant is the requirement of success.[6] At common law, a salvor was not entitled to a reward unless property was preserved and he made a meritorious contribution to its preservation. Under Admiralty law, therefore, it seemed prima facie sufficient that the salvor meritoriously contributed to the preservation of property. Under the Salvage Convention 1989, Art. 12, "1. Salvage operations which have had a useful result give right to a reward" and "2. Except as otherwise provided, no payment" [which means "any reward, remuneration or *compensation* due under this Convention"[7]] "is due under this Convention if the salvage operations have had no useful result." The extent, if any, to which the Convention's requirement of a useful result differs from the common law requirement of success remains to be determined: it is possible to make a contribution to the preservation of property even if the preservation of that property is otherwise not worthwhile. However, the effect of Article 12 appears to be that a salvage award is dependent on both the carrying out of a salvage operation and the achievement of a "useful result", rather than that there is only a salvage operation in cases where there is a useful result.

Consequently, it seems that, both under Admiralty law and under the Convention, there may be a danger for salvage purposes regardless of the value of the subject of salvage.

Classification of salvage services

The services listed below have been identified as capable of being salvage services. And, since the nature of such a service is that it is one which preserves from a danger of a type that founds a claim to a salvage reward, the examples given also illustrate the types of danger which have justified such awards. Many of the services listed are very common and others have appeared less frequently. It is not suggested, however, that the list is exhaustive or that there is, or could be, a closed list of classes of salvage service. The Salvage Convention 1989[8] states widely that "salvage operation" means any act or activity undertaken to assist a vessel or any property in danger in navigable waters or in any other waters whatsoever. The services listed below are merely representative of a multitude of instances referred to in other respects throughout this book.[9] Some suggested categories do not seem to have appeared in the law reports at all and are listed tentatively. Some, namely liability salvage[10] and environmental services,[11] have not traditionally been treated as independent justifications for salvage awards but as factors to be taken into account in assessing the amount of an otherwise justifiable salvage

354

---
[6] See generally *post*, Chap. 8.
[7] Art. 1(e) (emphasis added).
[8] Art. 1(a).
[9] For further salvage cases not otherwise referred to in this book, see Pritchard, pp. 1920–2123; Marsden's *Shipping and Marine Insurance Digest* (2nd ed., 1927). The Digests of Lloyd's List Law Reports, later Lloyd's Law Reports, contain summaries of the facts and awards in cases reported in those Reports.
[10] See *ante*, §§ 345–351.
[11] See *post*, Chap. 5.

award. A service will not merit a salvage reward merely because it has done so in the past. Indeed, some services, such as towage, are regularly provided without there being any question of salvage. By the same token, salvage remuneration should not be denied merely because it has not been awarded previously in a similar case. Not infrequently, entitlement to salvage will derive from the performance of a combination of services. And the owner of salved property may incur liability to different individuals for their performance of different types of salvage service.

355 In all cases, whether a service counts as salvage depends not upon any formal classification but on whether it satisfies the normal criteria in the case at hand. Thus Sir Boyd Merriman P. said in one case[12]:

> "I think that there was a perfectly definite service, and that in considering whether there was or was not a service, the whole of the circumstances must be taken into consideration. I do not think that each separate stage can be isolated and regarded by itself, although of course one must be able to say that it was one particular thing, or that thing coupled with others which constituted the service in question."

356 Similarly, of an argument that what had occurred was lightening, and not salvage, it was said in the High Court of Australia[13]:

> "It is, I think, a misconception to regard services rendered to a vessel as capable of division into neat categories, such as towage, lightening or salvage services, as is revealed by the judgment of Dr Lushington in *The Westminster*.[14] It is not the physical character of the particular services that is important but rather the circumstances in which they were being carried out; if they involve the necessary elements of salvage, they will be salvage services whether or not they take the form of lightening, towing or any other maritime operation. As was said by Lord Blackburn, at first instance, in *Nicholson v. Leith Salvage and Towage Co. Ltd*[15]
>
>> '... in many cases of pure salvage nothing more is required than towage services...'
>
> and see also *per* Isaacs J. in *The Cartela v. The Inverness-shire*[16] and *Bergher v. General Petroleum Co.*,[17] in which it was held that merely because the respective owners described the service rendered as towage,

---

[12] *The Tower Bridge* [1936] P. 30, 35–36, 38.
[13] In *The Oceanic Grandeur* [1972] 2 Lloyd's Rep. 396, 406, *per* Stephen J.
[14] (1841) 1 W. Rob. 229, 232.
[15] 1923 S.L.T. 229, 231.
[16] (1916) 21 C.L.R. 367, 404.
[17] (1917) 242 F. 967.

Classification of salvage services

this was not of moment in determining whether or not the crew of the vessel in fact rendered salvage services."

Individually and taken together, the services listed demonstrate the variety of services which can be taken into account in assessing salvage rewards. In most cases, performance will be of an overtly active kind, providing physical assistance to the vessel in distress. But it may be more passive, as with a standing by. It also seems to be established that prevention or diminution of a legal liability to third parties may be included.[18]

357

The following services may be noted.

(1) Towage.[19]

(2) Pilotage.[20]

(3) Navigating a ship into safety.[21]

(4) Standing by.[22]

(5) Getting a stranded ship afloat[23] (*e.g.* by advising on local conditions,[24] towing,[25] lightening,[26] or use of ground tackle).[27]

(6) Holding a stranded vessel in position when she is in danger (*e.g.* of being set further up as the tide makes,[28] or of slipping off and thereafter sinking in deep water, or doing damage to shipping or to property on shore and thereby exposing her owners to actions for damages)[29]; or to enable her cargo to be taken off.[30]

---

[18] See *ante*, §§ 345–351.
[19] *The Ellora* (1862) Lush. 550; *The Germania* [1904] P. 131; *Troilus (Cargo Owners) v. Glenogle (Owners, Masters and Crew) (The Troilus)* [1951] A.C. 820, affirming [1950] P. 92, affirming in part (1949) 82 Ll.L. Rep. 681 (see *ibid.*, 690: "a glorified towage"); *The Pa Mar* [1999] 1 Lloyd's Rep. 338.
[20] *The Lockwoods* (1845) 9 Jur. 1017, 1017; *The Anders Knape* (1879) 4 P.D. 213; *The Tafelberg* (1942) 71 Ll.L. Rep. 189.
[21] *Newman v. Walters* (1804) 3 B. & P. 612; *The Le Jonet* (1872) L.R. 3 A. & E. 556; *The San Demetrio* (1941) 69 Ll.L. Rep. 5.
[22] *The Maude* (1876) 3 Asp. 338; *The Comitas* (1934) 43 Ll.L. Rep. 43; *The Guernsey Coast* (1950) 83 Ll.L. Rep. 484; *The Dalewood* (1943) 75 Ll.L. Rep. 88. Standing by has been described as "the lowest footing of salvage" (*The Amelia Lauro* (1940) 68 Ll.L. Rep. 12) but as not altogether to be minimised (*The Maasdam* (1893) 7 Asp. 400, 401). *cf. The Cambrian* (1897) 8 Asp. M.L.C. 263; *The Stiklestad* [1926] P. 205, 209 (affirmed (1926) 43 T.L.R. 118); *The American Farmer* (1947) 80 Ll.L. Rep. 672, 689.
[23] A stranded ship is "from the mere fact of stranding, necessarily in some degree of danger": *The Orelia* [1958] 1 Lloyd's Rep. 441, 449.
[24] *The Africa Occidental* [1951] 2 Lloyd's Rep. 107.
[25] See *The Santipore* (1854) 1 Spinks E. & A. 231.
[26] See *The Kate B. Jones* [1892] P. 366.
[27] *The India* (1842) 1 Spinks E. & A. 63; *The Erato* (1888) 13 P.D. 163; *The Inchmaree* [1899] P. 111; *The Cayo Bonito* [1904] P. 310; *The Meandros* [1925] P. 61; *The Victoria Peak* (1947) 80 Ll.L. Rep. 527; *The Queen Elizabeth* (1949) 82 Ll.L. Rep. 803. *cf. The British Inventor* (1933) 45 Ll.L. Rep. 263.
[28] *The Driade* [1959] 2 Lloyd's Rep. 511.
[29] See *ante*, §§ 345–351.
[30] *The Madras* [1898] P. 90.

Danger and Salvage Services

(7) Beaching a vessel in danger of sinking or of being damaged.[31]

(8) Rescue by landing[32] or transhipment[33] of cargo[34] or persons[35] belonging to a ship in danger.

(9) Lightening a stranded vessel, so enabling repairs to be effected.[36]

(10) Raising a sunken ship[37] or cargo.[38]

(11) Bringing derelict[39] or wreck[40] into safety.

(12) Raising the alarm[41] and setting in motion,[42] fetching,[43] or bringing[44] assistance to a ship in danger.

(13) Searching for and locating a vessel in danger, such as by ascertaining by aircraft-search whether or not a derelict vessel had sunk, and giving information by radio that she had remained afloat and communicating her position[45]; there is no obvious reason why this should not encompass location by satellite.

---

[31] *The Tafelberg* (1942) 71 Ll.L. Rep. 189; *The Luigi Accame* (1938) 60 Ll.L. Rep. 106.

[32] *The Favorite* (1844) 2 Wm. Rob. 255.

[33] *The Columbia* (1838) 3 Hagg. 428; *The Westminster* (1841) 1 W.Rob. 229; *The Alma* (1861) Lush. 378; *The Erato* (1888) 13 P.D. 163.

[34] Salvage will not be awarded merely because cargo is taken off a vessel before, rather than after, it sinks: see *The Tarbert* [1921] P. 372.

[35] *The Suevic* [1908] P. 154 (expediting the passage of passengers from ship to shore by towing the lifeboats); *The Medina* (1876) 1 P.D. 272, affirmed (1876) 2 P.D. 5. *cf. The Cargo ex Woosung* (1876) 3 Asp. M.L.C. 50, 56, 58 (overruled on another point (1876) 1 P.D. 260, 266); *The Mariposa* [1896] P. 273. See also *The Duke of Manchester* (1847) 6 Moo.P.C. 90, 99. Saving of life alone, without property, will not found a claim for life salvage: see *ante*, §§ 260–310.

[36] *The Oceanic Grandeur* [1972] 2 Lloyd's Rep. 396 (HCA).

[37] *The Catherine* (1848) 6 Not. of Cas. Suppl. xliii. *cf. Simon v. Taylor* [1975] 2 Lloyd's Rep. 338 (Sing. HC).

[38] *The Jubilee* (1826) 3 Hagg. 43n.; *The Cadiz and The Boyne* (1876) 3 Asp. M.L.C. 332.

[39] *The Hebe* (1878) 4 P.D. 217; *The Andrina* (1870) L.R. 3 A. & E. 286; *The Janet Court* [1897] P. 59.

[40] *The Samuel* (1851) 17 L.T. (O.S.) 204.

[41] *A.B. Donaldson v. Dow & Carnie* (1922) 10 Ll.L. Rep. 572 (Ct of Sn) (pursuer gave alarm after trawler had gone ashore, the man at the wheel having fallen asleep, so enabling engines to be stopped and another vessel to be engaged to help refloat her).

[42] *The Marguerite Molinos* [1903] P. 160. See *ibid.*, 164, *per* Bucknill J. "The law is clear, that where a person does something, outside his duty, of such a nature as to be the cause of an act done by another which is a salvage act, he may himself hold the position of a salvor although he has done no more than give information." The claim in the case failed on the facts, however. Compare the kind of information in class (14), *infra*. In *The Cayo Bonito* [1904] P. 310, launchers of a lifeboat were given salvage reward. See also *The Enchantress* (1860) Lush. 93, 97; *The Cadiz and The Boyne* (1876) 3 Asp. M.L.C. 332, 334: "not only those who are actually employed, but also those who stay behind are entitled to participate."

[43] *The Ocean* (1843) 2 W.Rob. 91 (carrying of an order from a vessel in distress to a steamer to go out of harbour to assist); *The Sarah* (1878) 3 P.D. 39 (steam-tug seeing a ship ashore went out of her way to inform another steam-tug, which salved her).

[44] *The Charlotte* (1848) 3 W.Rob. 68; *The Undaunted* (1860) Lush. 90.

[45] *The Albion* (1861) Lush. 282, 284; *The American Farmer* (1947) 80 Ll.L. Rep. 672. See also the Civil Aviation Act 1982, s.87(2).

Classification of salvage services

(14) Giving advice or information in order to save a vessel from danger[46] or to facilitate its extricating itself from danger[47]; or to enable it to avoid danger.

(15) Saving persons belonging to a ship who, having taken to the boats in order to escape from danger on board ship, are afterwards picked up whilst in danger at sea.[48]

(16) Protection or rescue of a ship or her cargo or the lives of persons on board her from pirates or plunderers.[49]

(17) Saving a captured ship, and bringing her to a British port for the purpose of restoring her to her owners.[50]

(18) Quelling a mutiny or panic, making the crew do their duty and restoring or maintaining discipline.[51]

(19) Supplying officers or seamen to a ship which, through illness, exhaustion or other calamity, is dangerously short of hands to navigate or to work her competently.[52]

(20) Supplying tackle or gear to a ship, which would be imperilled by the want of it.[53]

(21) Supplying provisions to a ship with an insufficient supply. There is no reported case of salvage reward for the supply of necessary provisions alone, but there can be no doubt that it might constitute a salvage service.[54]

---

[46] *The Eliza* (1862) Lush. 536; *The Strathnaver* (1875) 1 App.Cas. 58 (PC), 62–63; see also *The Tower Bridge* [1936] P. 30; *The American Farmer* (1947) 80 Ll.L. Rep. 672; *The Africa Occidental* [1951] 2 Lloyd's Rep. 207. Mere ignorance of the master cannot of itself be a ground for salvage; it must cause the vessel to be in danger: see *The Vrouw Margaretha* (1801) 4 C.Rob. 103, 104. *cf. The Little Joe* (1860) Lush. 88, 89, where Dr Lushington doubted whether the mere giving of information or advice as to the locality, even to a foreign vessel, would amount to a salvage service.

[47] *The Tower Bridge* [1936] P. 30 (returning to an icefield and giving information as to a course to enable a vessel to clear the icefield). *cf. The Benlarig* (1888) 14 P.D. 3.

[48] *The Cairo* (1874) L.R. 4 A. & E. 184; *Five Steel Barges* (1890) 15 P.D. 142, 145.

[49] *The Erato* (1888) 13 P.D. 163; *The Cargo ex Ulysses, ibid.*, 205; *The Cythera* [1965] 2 Lloyd's Rep. 454 (N.S.W. S.C.). See also *The Calypso* (1828) 2 Hagg. 209; *The Lady Worsley* (1855) 2 Spinks 253; *The Ningpo* (1923) 16 Ll.L. Rep. 392; *The Tubantia* [1924] P. 78.

[50] *The Beaver* (1801) 3 C.Rob. 292; *The Dorothy Foster* (1805) 6 C.Rob. 89; *The Henry* (1810) Edwards 192 (purchase of a captured ship, about to be burnt, for restoration to her owners).

[51] *The Trelawney* (1802) 4 C.Rob. 223. *cf. The Governor Raffles* (1815) 2 Dods. 14, where the claimants failed because they formed part of the crew and therefore in quelling the mutiny they could not be considered volunteers, and *The Francis and Eliza* (1816) 2 Dods. 115.

[52] *The Charlotte Wylie* (1846) 2 W.Rob. 495; *The Ottercaps* (1876) Pritchard 2094. *cf. The Canova* (1866) L.R. 1 A. & E. 54; *The Golondrina* (1867) L.R. 1 A. & E. 334; *The Skibladner* (1878) 3 P.D. 24. But a ship is not necessarily in need of salvage services merely because there is currently no one on board: see *The Homewood* (1928) 31 Ll.L. Rep. 336.

[53] *The Prince of Wales* (1848) 6 Not. of Cas. 39; *The E.U.* (1853) 1 Spinks E. & A. 63, 64.

[54] See *The Aglaia* (1888) 13 P.D. 160; *The August Korff* [1903] P. 166. See also *The Cato* (1930) 37 Ll.L.Rep. 33, 37: "the *Cato* had troubles . . . through being short of provisions, because the mate of the *Cato* had to broach the cargo to the extent of using a bag of potatoes, but they disagreed with the crew and he had to get some brandy from the *Loch Nevis*."

Danger and Salvage Services

(22) Extinction of fire on board of a ship[55] or assistance in such service.[56]

(23) Rescue of life or property from a ship on fire or in the sea as a result of the fire.[57]

(24) Removal of a ship or cargo from a place where it is in imminent danger of catching fire.[58]

(25) Towing out a ship on fire and holding it till the fire burns out.[59]

(26) Extrication of a ship from an ice-floe.[60]

(27) Removal of a ship from a danger (*e.g.* separating her from an anchor, buoy, wreck or other ship which she has fouled[61] or which has fouled her[62]).

359 (28) Saving a ship from an impending collision (*e.g.* from colliding with another ship[63] or a dock,[64] or from being hit by another ship[65]).

(29) Avoiding potential liability to third parties,[66] such as for oil pollution[67] or contamination from nuclear materials.

(30) Assistance by one vessel in convoy to another, by towage services, enabling her to rejoin the convoy and securing for her the protection of the escort from hostile attack.[68]

(31) Preventing a ship from falling into the hands of revolutionaries[69] or terrorists.

(32) Watching or guarding shipwrecked property that may be the prey of wreckers or looters.[70]

---

[55] *The Rosalie* (1853) 1 Spinks E. & A. 188; *The City of Newcastle* (1894) 7 Asp. M.L.C. 546 (at quay); *The Elise* [1899] W.N. 54; *The Flore* (1929) 34 Ll.L. Rep. 172 (in dock); *The Belgia* (1941) 71 Ll.L. Rep. 21.

[56] *The Ferriby* (1948) 81 Ll.L. Rep. 246.

[57] *The Eastern Monarch* (1860) Lush. 81 (in Portsmouth harbour).

[58] *The Tees, The Pentucket* (1862) Lush. 505 (ship in dock where surrounding warehouses on fire). See also *The Demosthenes* (1926) 26 Ll.L. Rep. 99.

[59] *The Elkhound* (1931) 39 Ll.L. Rep. 15 (oil tanker in danger of exploding).

[60] *The Swan* (1839) 1 W.Rob. 68.

[61] *The Vandyck* (1881) 7 P.D. 42, affirmed (1882) 5 Asp. M.L.C. 17; *The Emilie Galline* [1903] P. 106; *The Melmore Head* (1945) 78 Ll.L. Rep. 102; *The Empress of Australia and The Debrett* (1947) 81 Ll.L. Rep. 24. *cf. The Annapolis* (1861) Lush. 355 (mere recovery of a tow which has become entangled with another ship does not *per se* entitle her tug to salvage).

[62] *The Merannio* (1927) 28 Ll.L. Rep. 352; *Five Steel Barges* (1890) 15 P.D. 142, 145.

[63] *The Port Caledonia and The Anna* [1903] P. 106; *The Ovre and The Conde de Zubiria* (1920) 2 Ll.L. Rep. 21; *The Beatsa* (1937) 58 Ll.L. Rep. 85; *The Bertil* [1952] 2 Lloyd's Rep. 176; *The New Australia* [1958] 2 Lloyd's Rep. 35. *cf. The Annapolis* (1861) Lush. 355.

[64] *The Saratoga* (1861) Lush. 318.

[65] *cf. The Port Caledonia and The Anna* [1903] P. 184; *The Ovre and The Conde de Zubiria* (1920) 2 Ll.L. Rep. 21; *The Helmsman* (1950) 84 Ll.L. Rep. 207.

[66] *The Whippingham* (1934) 48 Ll.L. Rep. 49.

[67] See *post*, Chap. 5; Salvage Convention 1989, Art. 13.1(c). *cf. The Pacific Colocotronis* [1981] 2 Lloyd's Rep. 40.

[68] *The Kangaroo* [1918] P. 327.

[69] *The Lomonosoff* [1921] P. 97.

[70] *The Favorite* (1844) 2 W.Rob. 255; *The Ningpo* (1923) 16 Ll.L. Rep. 392.

(33) Minimising a loss which does occur.

(34) Remooring a ship which has drifted from her moorings.[71]

(35) Acting promptly to prevent a perishable cargo from deteriorating.[72]

(36) Provision of moral support and encouragement.[73]

(37) Receiving an aircraft which has run out of fuel at sea and transporting it to safety.[74]

Passive salvage

360 To qualify for salvage, a service should normally evidence some form of positive action on the part of the salvor, even if it is only forebearing from possible alternative conduct, such as by standing by. This is consistent with the public policy influence on salvage remuneration, encouraging action by the salvor in response to the opportunity of a generous reward. But what if a benefit is obtained from the salvor without any action or even acquiescence on his part?

361 This question is posed by the facts of *The Alraigo*.[75] In June 1983, a Royal Navy Sea Harrier, a vertical static take-off and landing aircraft, became detached from its mother ship in the Atlantic Ocean. With only seven minutes' fuel left, the only break in the ocean to appear on the pilot's radar screen was the small Spanish cargo vessel the *Alraigo*. He flew there and landed on it with less than a minute's fuel to spare, causing some slight damage to the cargo. The crew, with his assistance, lashed down the aircraft and carried it to port. Lloyd's Form was subsequently signed, so there was no dispute as to whether a salvage service had been performed.[76] It seems that the vessel stopped engines to enable the pilot to land, which would have been a sufficient service to justify an award. Even if it had not, however, it is submitted that a salvage reward was due, because a benefit was obtained from the preservation of the aircraft from a danger at sea, and it would be unjust for the Crown, as owner of the aircraft, to be enriched by that benefit without payment.[77] This is particularly so since, under English law at least, a bailee, even an involuntary one, is not free to deal with bailed property to the detriment of the owner, such as by throwing it overboard[78]; and to encourage such conduct by denying a reward would be contrary to the public policy of encouraging salvage.

---

[71] *The MacGregor Laird* [1953] 2 Lloyd's Rep. 59.
[72] *The Velox* [1906] P. 263.
[73] *The London Merchant* (1837) 3 Hagg. 394, 399; *The Tower Bridge* [1936] P. 30, 38.
[74] This is considered in the next paragraph.
[75] [1984] 116 L.M.L.N.; [1984] 123 L.M.L.N.; [1984] 4 L.M.C.L.Q. 690. Although the *Alraigo* was the salving, rather than the salved, property, it is convenient to refer to the case by its name. The arbitration award is, of course, unpublished.
[76] See *post*, §§ 866–875.
[77] See *ante*, Chap. 1.
[78] See *Sachs v. Miklos* [1948] K.B. 23; *Munro v. Willmott* [1949] 1 K.B. 295.

Danger and Salvage Services

Moreover, even if the actual reception of the aircraft were not a salvage service, its conveyance from a place of danger to one of safety should be sufficient. A similar result should follow if a pilot parachuted from his aircraft onto a vessel and the aircraft or its wreck were subsequently saved.

Location of danger—relevant waters

Categories of location

362 There are a number of different locations in which services may be rendered to property in danger: (i) on the high seas; (ii) in tidal territorial waters; (iii) in non-tidal harbours; (iv) in docks enclosed from tidal waters by lock gates; (v) in the non-tidal waters of a river; (vi) in canals; (vii) in inland lakes; and (viii) in inland artificial lakes, whether permanent or (as in the case of a boat show) temporary. In respect of each of these locations it may be necessary to determine: (a) if remuneration can be claimed, whether as salvage or under some other cause of action; and (b) if it makes any difference to an English tribunal that, in the locality in question, there is a difference between English and foreign law on whether a claim can be maintained. The historical division between the scope of Admiralty and non-Admiralty law has made it necessary to consider the limits of claims in these different situations, which of course raises the perennial problems of how and why lines should be drawn between them. To limit the scope of Admiralty claims has the possible advantage of avoiding the application of its peculiar liability and enforcement regime and the obligation to pay remuneration on a salvage scale, though of course this is to some extent counterbalanced by removing the financial incentive to render assistance in an emergency.

Pre-Convention law

363 The general rule of Admiralty law was that salvage was concerned with services rendered in respect of danger arising in tidal waters, though it was not also necessary that the service should only be rendered on such waters. In *The Cargo ex Woosung*,[79] a ship took off, from an island on a barbarous but inhabited coast, persons who had been wrecked there but had got ashore in safety and who, although suffering privations from scarcity of water and from exposure, were not in any immediate danger. In a claim for life salvage,[80] it was argued by counsel for the defendants that, before such a claim can be enforced, there must be a removing of the lives from a position of danger which arises from the sea or from a perilous position of the ship on which the lives are.[81] The judge disallowed the claim without comment or reasons.[82]

---

[79] (1876) 3 Asp. M.L.C. 50 (the point under consideration does not appear in the report at (1876) 1 P.D. 260 nor was it considered during the appeal, which was successful: *ibid.*, 266). See also *The Mariposa* [1896] P. 273.
[80] *cf. The Renpor* (1883) 8 P.D. 115.
[81] (1876) 3 Asp. M.L.C. 50, 56.
[82] *ibid.*, 58.

Location of danger—relevant waters

Certainly, it is not the case that life salvage will not be awarded if passengers are saved from a piece of land, however small. In *The Medina*,[83] it was recovered where a ship took on board shipwrecked pilgrims from a rock in the Red Sea upon which there was barely room for them to stand. Moreover, the fact that a vessel comes to a place of temporary safety at a port, albeit still afloat, does not mean that it cannot still be at risk of danger so as to warrant salvage services.[84] Although the statutory incentive to salvage, in the enacted obligation to assist persons or vessels in distress,[85] does not extend beyond distress at sea, the general principles of public policy which motivate the encouragement of salvage will apply so that salvage reward will be forthcoming where services are rendered during the continuation of danger which is incurred by a vessel at sea and even though the subjects of the salvage are no longer strictly speaking at sea, so long as there is still risk from perils of a maritime nature.[86] Of course, it should be immaterial that the precise nature of the danger has altered: *e.g.* that shipwrecked passengers are in danger of starving rather than of drrowning. The view expressed is supported by *The Mary*,[87] in which, although the court refused salvage for the rescue of seamen from pirates on land, there was no adversion to the fact that the men were not even taken from the sea, but whilst chopping wood ashore.

The leading case on the law prior to the implementation of the International Salvage Convention 1989 was *The Goring*.[88] The *Goring* is a large passenger vessel which was lying on the River Thames in Berkshire. One night, she broke loose from her moorings and floated unmanned downstream, raising the possibility of her damaging moored pleasure craft and their occupants and then of colliding with Reading bridge and going over a weir, when she might have become a total loss. Fortunately, she was observed by a member of the Island Bohemian Club, on his way to De Montfort Island, in the middle of the river, in the club's ferry boat. Four other members were summoned and the five—three men in the boat and two ashore—got a line on board the *Goring* and hauled her to a vacant mooring. As was to be observed by Sir John Donaldson M.R. (as he then was) the service, although valuable, hardly ranked as an epic of the sea.[89] Nonetheless, the five rescuers, suing on behalf of themselves personally and of the club (the boat owner), issued a writ *in rem* claiming "remuneration for salvage services". The owners of the *Goring* responded by seeking a procedural remedy, applying to have the writ struck out, as disclosing no jurisdiction or cause of action, and it was partly the inappropriateness of the remedy which caused their defeat before Sheen J. in

364

---

[83] (1876) 1 P.D. 272; affirmed (1876) 2 P.D. 5.
[84] See *post*, §§ 382–389.
[85] See *post*, §§ 534–543.
[86] *The Rosalie* (1853) 1 Spinks E. & A. 188, 192. *cf. China-Pacific S.A. v. Food Corp. of India (The Winson)* [1982] A.C. 939.
[87] (1842) 1 W.Rob. 448.
[88] [1988] A.C. 831; discussed by D.C. Jackson [1988] L.M.C.L.Q. 449; F.D. Rose (1989) 9 O.J.L.S. 167; D.E.C. Yale [1988] C.L.J. 153.
[89] [1987] Q.B. 687, 699.

the Admiralty Court.[90] For a service which, in Donaldson M.R.'s view, could have been settled, if not for the price of a round of drinks at the Bohemian Club, at least for a relatively modest sum,[91] it may, therefore, seem surprising that there should have been an appeal to the Court of Appeal,[92] where (by Ralph Gibson and Bingham L.JJ., Donaldson M.R. dissenting) the judgment of Sheen J. was reversed, and ultimately to the House of Lords,[93] which upheld the decision of the Court of Appeal.

365 However, three fundamental questions needed to be considered: (1) whether the Admiralty Court had jurisdiction to entertain a claim for salvage services rendered in navigable, non-tidal inland waters; (2) whether, if there were such jurisdiction, the cause of action for salvage extended to such services; and (3) whether there was any basis, other than under the maritime law of salvage, for upholding a claim such as that brought by the plaintiffs. The issues, therefore, had general significance for the providers of emergency services and, in particular, the owners and insurers of property exposed to sudden dangers, not only on inland non-tidal waters, but also on dry land. They even raised doubts as to the validity of salvage awards for services rendered in docks and harbours which would be subject to the tide were they not closed off from it and within which it had hitherto been accepted that the law of maritime salvage applied.

366 The wider implications of the case were discussed in the judgments of the Court of Appeal and were canvassed at the hearing before the House of Lords, and indeed appear to have caused their Lordships some uncertainty, for it was some time after the hearing that judgment was handed down. When this did occur, however, it was essentially in the form of a single speech by Sheen J.'s predecessor as the Admiralty Judge, Lord Brandon of Oakbrook. Lord Brandon concentrated his deliberations on, first, an historical review and construction of the statutory basis of the relevant Admiralty jurisdiction and, secondly, the scope of the cause of action for salvage. He held essentially on the second ground, that the plaintiff's claim should fail. In passing, he offered an explanation of the basis upon which salvage might be awarded for services rendered in docks enclosed from tidal waters by lock gates,[94] though not in such terms as to indicate that the validity of the cause of action in such a situation was in dispute. Fortunately, a Merchant Shipping Bill was contemporaneously before Parliament and the hearing had been brought forward and the judgment given in time for an amendment to be introduced to the Bill so as to override any doubts which might exist on that score.[95]

---

[90] [1987] Q.B. 687. See Rose (1986) 102 L.Q.R. 185; [1986] L.M.C.L.Q. 276; Yale (1987) 46 C.L.J. 14.
[91] [1987] Q.B. 687, 698–699.
[92] [1987] Q.B. 687; noted R. Shaw [1987] L.M.C.L.Q. 262.
[93] [1988] A.C. 831.
[94] That the relevant waters were adjacent to and closely connected with waters which were and formed part of the complex of a basically tidal port or harbour: [1988] A.C. 831, 856.
[95] See the MSA 1988, s.48, Sched. 5, adding a new subs. (2) to the MSA 1894, s.546. See also *The Powstaniec Wielkopolski* [1989] Q.B. 279. See now *post*, §§ 369–376.

Location of danger—relevant waters

It is respectively suggested that the two points of Admiralty law upon which the Law Lords were content finally to focus their attention were dealt with correctly. What is perhaps regrettable is that the highest court in the land, composed as it is of judges with experience of different areas of the law and of different jurisdictions, should follow the practice of preferring a single speech on the narrower points of statutory construction raised by the case in hand to availing themselves of the opportunity, presented not only by the facts of the case but by the arguments before it, of considering and providing guidance on the wider issues presented, particularly as they were considered in the Court of Appeal. That this point did not entirely escape the attention of their Lordships is evident from their decision, in the closing passages of Lord Brandon's speech, that an extension of the law of salvage by way of analogy and for reasons of public policy had to be determined by reference to the statutory provisions and, therefore, by the legislature rather than judicial decision.[96] However, this is only one aspect of the third question posed above, the wider aspects of which are in fact not without immediate practical relevance to plaintiffs such as those in *The Goring*: whether the claim could be upheld other than under the Admiralty law of salvage, *i.e.* under the common law of restitution.

367 It has hitherto usually been assumed that the common law, as opposed to Admiralty law, is generally hostile to a person who confers a benefit on another to avert prejudice to that other in circumstances of necessity. However, there are undoubtedly a number of specific situations where the law has awarded payment to such interveners. Whatever the recognisable peculiarities of those situations, if the cases are examined not so much from the perspective of their particular contexts but with a view to identifying criteria of potentially general application, then, although the various sources cannot (and need not) support a rigid set of criteria for universal compliance, they nevertheless reveal a reasonably consistent body of rules which is capable of supporting a general scheme of restitution for necessitous intervention at common law.

368 The rule of English law at the time of enactment of the International Salvage Convention 1989 was, therefore, that salvage could be claimed in respect of a service rendered in tidal waters or, since they were adjacent to and closely connected with waters forming part of the complex of a basically tidal port or harbour, in docks enclosed from tidal waters by lock gates.[97]

Post-Convention law

369 With respect to the location of salvage services, the United Kingdom has exercised its liberty to make reservations to the International Salvage Convention 1989.[98] The general position under the Convention is that "salvage operation means any act or activity undertaken to assist a vessel or any other

---
[96] [1988] A.C. 831, 856–857.
[97] *The Goring* [1988] A.C. 831, 856.
[98] Permitted under the Convention, Art. 30.

property in danger in navigable waters or in any other waters whatsoever".[99] However, the Merchant Shipping Act 1995 provides that[1]:

> "(1) The provisions of the Convention do not apply—
> (a) to a salvage operation which takes place in inland waters of the United Kingdom and in which all the vessels involved are of inland navigation; and
> (b) to a salvage operation which takes place in inland waters of the United Kingdom and in which no vessel is involved.
> (2) In this paragraph 'inland waters' does not include any waters within the ebb and flow of the tide at ordinary spring tides or the waters of any dock which is directly or (by means of one or more other docks) indirectly, connected with such waters."

370 The combined effect of the general provision in the Convention and the United Kingdom's reservation thereto is to establish a general rule that an act or activity undertaken to assist property in danger in any waters will constitute a salvage operation; but the general rule does not apply if both of two conditions are satisfied, *i.e.* that (i) the waters in question are non-tidal or they are the waters of a dock not directly or indirectly connected to such waters,[2] and (ii) the operation does not involve at least one vessel[3] which is not a vessel of inland navigation.

371 The definition of "inland waters" is not entirely clear,[4] since it states two areas which are definitely excluded without stipulating what other areas might or might not be included (*e.g.* the Manchester Ship Canal—which is not a "dock"). However, in most cases in practice it is probably safe to assume that an area of water not covered by the specific exclusions will fall within the description "inland waters". Therefore, the real difficulty to be settled will be whether a vessel which is not "of inland navigation" is involved.

372 It is a remarkable, though not unusual, feature of the law that, whatever the advantages of flexibility, major issues of definition should continue to elude precise resolution. Thus, as seen above, the definition of "vessel" or "ship" for the purposes of the merchant shipping legislation remains imprecise.[5] For

---

[99] MSA 1995, s.224(1)(2); Sched. 11, Pt I, Art. 1(a).
[1] MSA 1995, s.224(2), Sched. 11, Pt II, para. 2.
[2] Obviously, a service within a dock will be in inland waters if the dock is not connected with tidal waters directly or by means of one or more other docks (*e.g.* if its connection is by a canal).
[3] For the definition of "vessel", see *ante*, §§ 168–177.
[4] *cf.* the Administration of Justice Act 1956, s.45(4), stating that "inland waters" for the purpose of collision jurisdiction in Scotland "includes any part of the sea adjacent to the coast of the U.K. certified by the Secretary of State to be waters falling by international law to be treated as within the territorial sovereignty of Her Majesty apart from the operation of that law in relation to territorial waters."
[5] *Ante*, §§ 168–177. Since navigability is a test for a vessel, services to preserve from fire a sea-going vessel moored in an artificial arena such as a boat show, and so in fact incapable of navigation, should not qualify for salvage.

present purposes it needs to be settled alongside the probably more difficult issue whether the vessel is one "of inland navigation".

A number of factors arise for consideration, *e.g.*: whether it was originally designed for inland or sea-going navigation; whether it is physically capable of inland and/or of sea-going navigation; whether it is legally capable of navigation inland and/or at sea; and whether in practice it operates inland and/ or at sea. Most vessels are in some way capable of navigation inland and at sea, so mere capacity is unlikely to be decisive; and, given the possibility of different uses, the purpose of the original design is likely to be even less important. Similarly, a vessel's potential, or even actual, versatility may not be conclusive. It is unlikely that a normally sea-going vessel which enters the Manchester Ship Canal is thereby to be categorised as a vessel of inland navigation; but it may be more difficult to decide when—and, if so, to what extent—the frequency with which a dinghy which is habitually sailed on a lake rather than occasionally at sea determines whether or not it is a vessel of inland navigation. Probably the decisive factor will be that at the time of the operation the vessel is normally used as a vessel of inland navigation. **373**

It is important to remember, however, that the general rule of the International Salvage Convention 1989 is that salvage operations may occur in any waters[6]; consequently, any doubt should be resolved in favour of the application of the Convention. The burden of proving otherwise will be on the party disputing its application.[7] **374**

Movement between inland and tidal waters

It is a conceivable, though highly remote, possibility that a service of a salvage nature might begin in circumstances where the Convention was excluded but end where it applied, *e.g.* if a sinking inland pleasure cruiser were towed from inland waters to a place of safety in a tidal harbour.[8] Similarly, a vessel of inland navigation which was temporarily at sea might salve property in danger and bring it to a place of safety in inland waters. The Merchant Shipping Act 1995 distinguishes between a salvage operation to assist property "in danger in navigable waters or in any other waters whatsoever"[9] and "a salvage operation which takes place in inland waters"[10] but does not obviously contemplate a service spread over two localities. This may be a proper way of proceeding and so should not exclude the possibility of a salvage reward altogether. **375**

---

[6] *Ante*, §369.
[7] If he fails to discharge the burden and the tribunal is led to conclude that the Convention embraces a claim falling outside the traditional understanding of what constitutes salvage, the fault, if any, for such an unfortunate result may rest in the failure of the Convention to include a mechanism for excluding trivial claims.
[8] See Gaskell, 21–431.
[9] MSA 1995, s.224(1), Sched. 11, Pt I, Art. 1(a).
[10] MSA 1995, s.224(2), Sched. 11, Pt II, para. 2(1).

376   If movement from one locality to another is a correct way of proceeding (*e.g.* because the proper place of safety is in the final locality), the salvor should not be prejudiced by his action. If it is wrongful (*e.g.* because the property was or could have been brought to a place of safety in the first locality), the salvor at least should not recover a salvage reward for that part of the service which was not necessary and is in any case liable to suffer the consequences of misconduct.[11] Otherwise, since the International Salvage Convention 1989 applies except in so far as its application is excluded, salvage should be recoverable for such part of the operation as does not fall within the exclusion.

Duration

Importance

377   It is important to identify the period during which a danger endures, for a salvage reward can only be claimed for a service rendered whilst the danger persists.[12] For services performed in the absence of danger, the claimant will only be entitled to an ordinary *quantum meruit*. Where a danger supervenes during the performance of non-salvage services, salvage reward will be payable for the period of the danger even though the original service, *e.g.* towage, is not interrupted.[13] The duration of the salvage service will be a material element to be taken into account in assessing the salvor's reward,[14] albeit the duration of the services in very many cases is not the true criterion of their value.[15] The value of the service may alter as the circumstances change: salvage may continue even though the greatest danger has ceased.[16]

It is not necessary to determine the precise moment at which a service begins.[17] It is, however, possible and may be convenient specifically to do so.[18] However, since signature of the Lloyd's Form is evidence of salvage,[19] proof of when that is signed will be evidence of at least the latest moment at which the service began. LOF 2000, cl. E provides that any salvage services rendered by the contractors before and up to the date of the agreement shall be deemed to be covered by the agreement.[20]

378   It is normally more important to determine when salvage services have terminated. The general principle is that, once the casualty has reached a place of safety, the necessary element of success,[21] and therefore the claimant's

---

[11] *Post*, Chap. 11.
[12] *The Ranger* (1845) 3 N.o.C. 589; *The Batavier* (1853) 1 Spinks E. & A. 169, 171.
[13] *The I.C. Potter* (1870) L.R. 3 A. & E. 292.
[14] See Salvage Convention 1989, Art. 13.1(f) and (h); *post*, Chap. 15.
[15] *The Strathgarry* [1895] P. 264, 270.
[16] *The Matatua* (1924) 20 Ll.L.Rep. 5.
[17] *The Tower Bridge* [1936] P. 30, 38.
[18] In *The Premuda* (1940) 67 Ll.L.Rep. 9, 13, a clause stating when the services began was added to the Lloyd's Form entered by the Admiralty.
[19] See *post*, §§ 866–875
[20] *cf.* the SCOPIC clause, which is only operative once invoked: *post*, §§ 964–965.
[21] See *post*, Chap. 8.

entitlement to salvage, has been achieved and the place at which salved values are to be determined. It is to the salvor's advantage to reach safety reasonably expeditiously, for his reward will not be diminished by a subsequent reduction in salved values.[22] On the other hand, it may be to his disadvantage to prolong his services. In *The Pinnas*,[23] salvors, a firm of shipbuilders and repairers, raised a sunken vessel and beached her in a position of safety but then improperly refused to deliver up possession to the owners until they, the salvors, had completed certain repairs prior to docking the vessel, for which they expected payment on a salvage basis. Sir James Hannen P. described the conduct of the plaintiff's managing partner as a most outrageous proceeding but said that the case must be dealt with on the footing that up to that time salvage services had been rendered. He concluded his judgment by assessing salvage at £700 and pointing out that over £650 had already been paid into court. That may have encouraged him to conclude that, having regard to the misconduct of the managing partner, he would not allow the plaintiff any costs. His attitude nevertheless reflects the fact that misconduct may well lead to a diminution in, or total deprivation of, reward.[24] Even though the burden may be on the salvee to show that salvage, once begun, has come to an end, the salvor can at least expect no encouragement to attempt to enhance his reward.

Paradoxically, it may be the salvee who seeks to deny that success has been achieved and salvage has terminated. Several reasons have been identified. Where insured values exceed salved values (which they generally will), it may be more advantageous for owners to claim for total loss. If the administrative costs, such as arranging for guarantees to enter port, are high for a badly damaged ship, shipowners may be tempted to leave that class of expenditure and work to the salvor. This is particularly so where cargo salved values exceed that of the vessel, for the shipowner will not then simply be postponing his liability to pay for such expenses but transferring a substantial proportion of liability to his fellow salvees. The problem is exacerbated where the nature of the cargo creates the burden of locating a port at which the authorities will be prepared to admit the cargo. If the salvor were simply to leave the cargo at a particular place, he might fail to prove that he has achieved success, he would certainly suffer a reduction in his security, especially if the property is deteriorating, and he would be exposed to liability for breach of duty.[25] **379**

The general rule is that salvage services terminate in respect of a particular subject of salvage once that subject has been brought finally to a place of safety, even if the other subjects have not.[26] The argument in *The Winson*[27] reflected an assumption that the salvage services rendered to the cargo owner **380**

---

[22] See *post*, Chap. 14.
[23] (1886) 6 Asp. M.L.C. 313.
[24] See *post*, Chap. 11.
[25] The salvor's duties at the termination of salvage were considered by the House of Lords in *The Winson* [1982] A.C. 939 and are discussed *post*, Chap. 10.
[26] See *post*, Chap. 1.
[27] [1982] A.C. 939. See *supra*, n. 25.

under a Lloyd's Form agreement come to an end separately in respect of each individual parcel as soon as it arrives in safety. However, Lord Diplock said that[28]:

> "I should not, however, wish to be taken as necessarily accepting that, in the absence of subsequent variation either express or to be implied from the conduct of the parties, where a Lloyd's open form of agreement is signed by the master on behalf of a single owner of the whole of a bulk cargo and the salvage services involve unloading it in whole or in part and taking it to a place or places of safety separately from the carrying ship, there is a 'termination' of the salvage services within the meaning of Lloyd's open form until either the whole of the cargo has been brought to places of safety or further attempts to salve cargo that has not yet been brought to any place of safety have been justifiably abandoned by the salvor."

381 Difficulties over the termination of salvage operations have been reduced by contractual and statutory provision.[29] LOF 2000[30] provides for the parties to agree where services under a Lloyd's Form contract terminate; the Salvage Convention 1989[31] requires salvees, when the property has been brought to a place of safety, to accept redelivery when reasonably requested by the salvor to do so; and LOF 2000, cl. F(iii) requires contracting salvees to co-operate fully with the salvage contractors in obtaining entry to the agreed or (if none is agreed) actual place of safety, thus facilitating termination of services.

If SCOPIC 2000 has been invoked, it will continue to apply until its operation is terminated. If the shipowner terminates its operation before salvage has been completed, the salvage relationship will continue. But, if the property has been brought to a place of safety, so that the salvage operation would normally terminate, the provisions of SCOPIC 2000 will nonetheless continue to apply, so that it may well be necessary for the shipowner to bring it to an end.[32]

Salvage in stages

382 A salvor does not have to effect salvage in one continuous act. Salvage is awarded to salvors who merely bring the salved property to a place of comparative safety provided that the property is subsequently brought to a place of complete safety.[33] All who meritoriously contribute to success are entitled to participate in the salvage reward. However, where services to a casualty are provided in identifiably distinct stages, this inevitably raises the

---

[28] *ibid.*, 956–957.
[29] See fully *post*, §§ 1044–1085A.
[30] Box 3 and cl. A.
[31] Art. 8.2(c).
[32] See more fully *post*, § 973.
[33] *The Troilus* [1950] P. 92, 104, *per* Bucknill L.J.

question whether salvage has terminated before the conclusion of the final stage.

This issue confronted the House of Lords in *The Troilus*.[34] In that case, a steamship was bound for Liverpool from Australia with a cargo of foodstuffs, though not strictly a perishable cargo and in no immediate danger of perishing. She lost her propeller in the Indian Ocean but was otherwise unimpaired. A motor-vessel towed her about 1,050 miles to a safe anchorage at Aden—an admitted salvage service. There were, however, no facilities at Aden for repairing the ship or discharging and storing the cargo. She was, therefore, towed to the United Kingdom by a second vessel, except that towage through the Suez Canal was carried out by the Canal Company's tugs. Repairs in the Mediterranean would have been difficult and would have involved considerable delay. It was held by the House of Lords, on appeal by the cargo-owners, that the towage by the second vessel was a salvage service.

Lord Porter, who delivered the judgment of the House, was not concerned to answer the question[35]:

> "What in this collocation is meant by a safe place? Are there only the three alternatives, either (1) a place where the ship can lie in physical safety even though she cannot be repaired there and may have to remain there for an indefinite time until some problematical tug or tugs can be procured to tow her away at a fixed contract price for the towage service; or, (2) some place where she can ultimately be repaired with or without some risk but after a very considerable delay, the cargo meanwhile being partially or wholly discharged and stored until the ship is repaired or until space in some other ship can be obtained to carry it to its destination; or, (3) the port of destination at which the cargo is to be delivered."

He did, however, state that a ship might lie at an intermediate port "safe enough for all practical purposes" but could still be in danger if a prudent master would be reasonably apprehensive of physical danger having regard to the weather to be anticipated in the locality whilst his ship lay in the anchorage which she had reached or if she continued to be so damaged that it would be unsafe for her to put to or remain at sea until she is repaired.[36] However, there is no established principle that a vessel which has no means of propulsion remains in a state of danger until she has recovered some power of propulsion, even though she has come to anchor in a safe place.[37] Essentially, the House agreed with the courts below that whether a place of safety

---
[34] [1951] A.C. 820, affirming [1950] P. 92 (CA), dismissing an appeal by cargo-owners only from the judgment of Lord Merriman P. (1949) 82 Ll.L.Rep. 681. Similar facts arose in other decisions considered in *The Troilus, viz. The Idomeneus* (1925) 22 Ll.L.Rep. 299; *The Laomedon* (1925) 23 Ll.L.Rep. 230; and in particular *The Glaucus* (1948) 81 Ll.L.Rep. 262.
[35] [1951] A.C. 820, 833–834.
[36] See *ibid.*, 829 and 831, citing *The Syria* (1874) Shipp. Gaz., July 7, 1874 (discussed more fully by Bucknill L.J. at [1950] P. 92, 104–106).
[37] [1951] A.C. 820, 833.

has been reached is a question of fact, and a place which may be a place of safety for a vessel alone need not necessarily be one if the ship is carrying cargo. Lord Porter said[38]:

> "The solution of the question whether a ship and cargo have reached a place of safety must . . . depend upon the facts of each case, one of which is the facility for repairs at the place in question, and another the possibility of safety discharging and storing the cargo and sending it on to its destination and the danger of its deterioration."

386 The pivot of the decision was the fact that the whole service, although its first stage had been completed, began as a salvage rather than as a towage service, and Lord Porter was scrupulous to avoid determining whether, if *The Troilus* had lost her propeller lying at Aden, a ship which towed her to a port of safety would be entitled to salvage.[39]

In Lord Porter's view, the case did not depend on answering only two possible questions, namely, "(1) May the master of a damaged ship which is taken in tow in a damaged condition from a position of potential danger treat the towage to his destined port as salvage services? or (2) Is the cargo only bound to pay its proportion of salvage up to the nearest position at which the ship can lie in physical safety?"[40] His Lordship decided that, bearing in mind certain considerations, "the salvage lasts so long as the master acts reasonably for the combined benefit of ship and cargo."[41] Relevant considerations are: the lesser ability of a disabled vessel to deal with emergencies such as fire or being set adrift[42]; the danger of deterioration of the ship and cargo (especially if perishable) if not removed; the facility for repairs at the place in question; the possibility of safely discharging and storing the cargo and sending it on to its destination; the possibility of expenses and the effect of delay upon both ship and cargo; and the possibility of repair at convenient ports and the time involved and safety of the operation to ship and cargo.[43] Moreover, as Willmer J. said with respect to similar facts in *The Glaucus*[44]:

> "quite apart from the physical danger, there is this to be added, that until somebody got her to a place where the necessary repairs could be executed she was completely immobilised. It is no use saying that this valuable property, worth something approaching a million pounds, is safe, if it is safe in circumstances where nobody can use it. For practical purposes, it might just as well be at the bottom of the sea."

Also relevant is the possible prejudice to a salvor if he takes a disabled vessel into a port *en route* in order to give her crew much-needed rest, or to pick up

---

[38] *ibid.*, 830.
[39] *ibid.*, 831.
[40] *ibid.*, 835.
[41] *ibid.*, 835.
[42] *The Glaucus* (1948) 81 Ll.L. Rep. 262, 266.
[43] [1951] A.C. 820, 829, 830, 834.
[44] *The Glaucus* (1948) 81 Ll.L. Rep. 262, 266.

stores, or because of bad weather, or because the salving vessel has to discharge or pick up cargo there.[45]

387 All of the appellate judges in *The Troilus* were careful not to depart from Lord Merriman P.'s decision at first instance on a matter which he stressed as being essentially a question of fact, though with some reluctance by Denning L.J. in the Court of Appeal. He alluded to the difficulty of focusing on the authority of a master where a salvage service has begun before a port of call rather than to a more objective determination of that port as a place of safety. Lord Porter subsequently said that considerable latitude ought to be allowed to a master of a casualty in deciding whether or not to accept services on a salvage basis, especially where the ship is carrying a general cargo and it is therefore a difficult task involving much delay to communicate with the various owners.[46] But, as Denning L.J. warned[47]:

> "Remuneration on such a scale cannot, however, be justified when the shipowner has, as a practical matter, a freedom of choice either to accept the proffered services or to adopt some other alternative: for then he would normally in his own interest—and should in the interest of the cargo owners—throw the other alternatives into the scale so as to reduce the remuneration to a figure which represents the time, labour and risk involved to those who render the services. If the shipowner, having a choice before him, contracts to pay for services on a salvage basis, that is his affair—it may be so important for him to fulfil his future engagements that he contracts on that basis—but he cannot by so doing make the cargo owner liable for salvage unless the services are really salvage services: *Anderson v. Ocean Steamship Co.*"[48]

388 It is particularly important where a subsequent part of an interrupted service is performed by a second salvor for all parties involved to be before the arbitrator or court. For, if the tribunal had to award salvage for the first part of a service without its being clear that the second salvor was entitled to salvage, its inclination would be to award, on salved values at the port of call, a reward which would exceed what the salvees would have to pay to the first salvor if their liability for salvage to a second tug were also being assessed.

389 On one view, certain property which has come to rest and is unlikely to deteriorate (most obviously bullion) may no longer be in danger, so that services rendered in recovering such property should not justify a salvage award. A further, though different, point is that such property (particularly, of course, where it has lain on the sea-bed for some period of time) is more appropriately dealt with under a distinct regime for wreck or maritime cultural property rather than under the law of salvage. This is not the position in

---
[45] *The Troilus* [1950] P. 92, 109.
[46] [1951] A.C. 820, 834.
[47] [1950] P. 92, 111.
[48] (1884) 10 App. Cas. 117. As to authority to bind cargo owners, see *post*, Chap. 9.

English law. All property outside the control of its owner or lawful possessor is subject to some danger, whether it be minimal deterioration, the possibility of theft or the possibility of becoming lost through the ordinary activity of and in the sea. Provided the property in question came into its current position as a result of a danger justifying a salvage service, subsequent services rendered to it to bring it to safety will support a salvage award. Thus, even though bullion at the bottom of the sea is unlikely to suffer much, if any, damage, its recovery can still be a question of salvage.[49] However, the fact that the law of salvage applies does not mean that other rules of law, particularly the law of wreck, may not also apply.

Duties on termination

390 The duties of salvor and salvee on termination of salvage services will be considered below.[50]

Services in stages

391 Just as a service may be begun and remunerated on a non-salvage basis (*e.g.* towage) and then converted into a salvage service so, obviously, once a salvage service has terminated, may the parties' relationship continue but on a non-salvage basis.[51]

---

[49] See *HMS Thetis* (1833) 3 Hagg. 228; *The Tubantia* [1924] P. 78; *The Egypt* (1932) 44 Ll.L.R. 21. The argument that property which has become valueless can no longer be in danger is considered *ante*, §§ 352–353.
[50] *Post*, Chap. 10.
[51] See, *e.g. The Pa Mar* [1999] 1 Lloyd's Rep. 338.

CHAPTER 5

ENVIRONMENTAL SERVICES

1. GENERAL

Background

Increasingly in modern times, with larger vessels and greater cargoes, ships **392** and their cargoes have enhanced potential to cause harm to the environment and thereby to expose those responsible for such harm to liability. A situation necessitating salvage operations may therefore also require services designed to prevent or minimise environmental damage. For convenience, these will be referred to as environmental services. Unfortunately, the traditional law of salvage was inadequate to provide a resolution of environmental issues which would satisfy the interests of all the parties involved when a casualty arises.[1]

First, entitlement to a salvage reward is essentially dependent upon rescuing **393** from danger property belonging to salvees, whereas the effect of environmental services is to restrict the legal liability of salvees (a doubtful subject of salvage)[1A] and/or to provide a benefit to possibly unidentifiable third parties who are not liable to remunerate the salvor with a salvage reward or possibly on any other basis. Furthermore, in modern times, services required by casualties are increasingly onerous and expensive but salvage rewards remain subject to the general requirement of "no cure—no pay",[2] so, even if a salvor were willing to consider rendering services to a casualty requiring environmental services, he might be deterred by the expense of doing so coupled with the possibility of failing to earn a reward or even recoup his outlay, leaving salvees and third parties with the prospect of no assistance to avert the dangers which have arisen. Moreover, not only might a salvor be faced with the possibility of no reward; he faced the risk that his actions after intervention might expose him to the risk of liability for contributing to or causing environmental damage. However, any attempt to overcome these problems,

---

[1] See Shaw [1996] L.M.C.L.Q. 202, 205.
[1A] See *ante*, §§ 345–351.
[2] See *post*, Chap. 8.

and to induce salvors in such situations to render salvage and environmental services, encountered the further difficulty that the basic liability for environmental damage to be overcome was that borne by shipowners and their protection and indemnity associations (P. & I. clubs), and cargo-owners and their insurers were naturally resistant to proposals to increase the liabilities of all salvees.

394 The reaction to these tensions has inevitably been compromise. First, following the grounding of the VLCC *Amoco Cadiz* on the French Atlantic coast in 1978, Lloyd's Form was extended, so that LOF 1980 incorporated a "safety net" whereby a salvage contractor rendering services to a tanker laden, wholly or partly, with a cargo of oil became eligible for a maximum payment of 115 per cent of the amount of expenses which he incurred.[3] However, salvors were understandably keen that their interests were elevated from a contractual to a legislative basis. Secondly, the Montreal CMI Draft Salvage Convention 1981, and in due course the International Salvage Convention 1989, Art. 13, amplified the criteria for fixing salvage rewards so that the skill and efforts of salvors in preventing or minimising damage to the environment became factors to be taken into account in assessing salvage rewards.[4] Thirdly, the CMI Draft and resulting 1989 Conventions incorporated "the Montreal Compromise", whereby salvors' representatives relinquished radical proposals for extending salvors' rights (such as the formal establishment of liability salvage) in return for the acceptance by representatives of shipowners, cargo-owners and their insurers of a limited level of liability for environmental services.[4A]

395 The resulting Article 14 of the Salvage Convention 1989 extended and replaced the safety net provisions of LOF 1980, establishing a system of "special compensation" which applied not only to oil tanker casualties but more widely. This was supplemented by a "Common Understanding" that the tribunal should be under no duty to fix a reward under Article 13 up to the

---

[3] LOF 1980, cl. 1(a) provided, *inter alia*, that:
"The services shall be rendered and accepted as salvage services upon the principle of 'no cure—no pay' except that where the property being salved is a tanker laden or partly laden with a cargo of oil and without negligence on the part of the Contractor and/or his Servants and/or Agents (1) the services are not successful or (2) are only partially successful or (3) the Contractor is prevented from completing the services the Contractor shall nevertheless be awarded solely against the Owners of such tanker his reasonably incurred expenses and an increment not exceeding 15 per cent of such expenses but only if and to the extent that such expenses together with the increment are greater than any amount otherwise recoverable under this Agreement. Within the meaning of the said exception to the principle of 'no cure—no pay' expenses shall in addition to actual out of pocket expenses include a fair rate for all tugs craft personnel and other equipment used by the Contractor in the services and oil shall mean crude oil fuel heavy diesel oil and lubricating fuel."

[4] MSA 1995, s.224(1), Sched. 11, Pt I, Art. 13.1(b). See *post*, § 1417. Although the Convention states that the listed criteria are to be taken into account without regard to the order in which they are presented, it is noticeable that the relevant criterion appears before most of the traditional criteria for assessing salvage rewards.

[4A] The property insurers agreed to pay normal salvage remuneration under Article 13 (see *post*, Chap. 15) *including* efforts to protect the environment (which they did not insure) in return for the P&I Clubs' accepting liability for special compensation in full: see Shaw [1996] L.M.C.L.Q. 202, 206.

maximum salved value of the salved property before assessing Article 14 special compensation. Most of the 1989 Convention's provisions on environmental damage were almost immediately given contractual effect by incorporation into LOF 1990.[5] After the enactment of the Convention into English law, the subsequent revision of Lloyd's Form included the relevant Articles of the Convention for information only.[6]

SCOPIC

Nonetheless, in the light of the House of Lords' decision in *The Nagasaki Spirit*[7] and more generally, there continued to be dissatisfaction with the degree of financial incentive to salvors, the calculation of remuneration for salvage and environmental services and the promptness with which payments were made. Accordingly, interested parties devised a separate clause, SCOPIC,[8] which could be added to, so as to override parts of, Lloyd's Form. Introduced in August 1999, it was initially envisaged that SCOPIC would be used for a trial period of two years but, following perceived difficulties of substance and drafting, it was more quickly revised, at the same time that Lloyd's Form was being revised. Thus, LOF 2000 and SCOPIC 2000 came into effect simultaneously on September 1, 2000. **396**

In all cases, salvage remuneration remains initially to be determined in accordance with the Salvage Convention 1989, Art. 13.[9] In the absence of contrary agreement, in appropriate cases, special compensation is also payable under Article 14 of the Convention. However, if two conditions are satisfied (*viz.*, first, SCOPIC is incorporated into LOF 2001 and, secondly, its terms are invoked by written notice), the SCOPIC provisions will apply. When SCOPIC is successfully invoked, Article 14 of the Convention is excluded and remuneration is payable according to a detailed scheme set out in Appendix A to the clause. SCOPIC remuneration is supplementary to that due under Article 13, unless it falls below what would be awarded under Article 13, in which case the Article 13 remuneration is discounted by 25 per cent. Though its full title is not revealed in the clause, SCOPIC is an acronym for "Special Compensation P. and I. Clause". However, it is not merely a substitute for the special compensation provisions of Article 14 of the Salvage Convention 1989 but applies more widely and in a carefully structured way. Nonetheless, it has in practice become a standard method of determining remuneration for environmental services. **397**

---

[5] See LOF 1990, cll. 1(b) ("Subject to clause 2 incorporating Convention Article 14 the services shall be rendered and accepted as salvage services upon the principle of 'no cure—no pay'") and 2 ("Article 1(a) to (e), 8, 13.1, 13.2 first sentence, 13.3 and 14 of the International Convention on Salvage 1989 ('the Convention Articles') set out hereafter are hereby incorporated into this Agreement. The terms 'Contractor' and 'services'/'salvage services' in this Agreement shall have the same meanings as the terms 'salvor(s)' and 'salvage operation(s)' in the Convention Articles").

[6] Arts. 1, 6, 8 and 13–14 were printed at the end of LOF 1995. *cf. ibid.*, cll. 1(a)(ii)–(b) and 2.

[7] [1997] A.C. 455. The case is discussed *post*, §§ 428–437.

[8] See further *post*, §§ 960–980.

[9] See *post*, Chap. 15.

Damage to the environment

398 The Preamble to the International Salvage Convention 1989 twice refers in general terms to "protection of the environment".[10] However, the terms of the Convention, and the specific concern of this chapter and the provisions to be discussed, is "damage to the environment". According to the International Salvage Convention 1989, Art. 1(d):

> "Damage to the environment means substantial physical damage to human health or to marine life or resources in coastal or inland waters or areas adjacent thereto, caused by pollution, contamination, fire, explosion or similar major incidents."

A number of elements of this definition should be noted.

The relevant damage

399 First, the definition is concerned with "damage to human health or to marine life or resources". This fairly obviously embraces damage to the health of human beings and to marine fauna and flora, whether wild or farmed; and it should also apply to water to be used in a desalination plant.[11] It should also cover natural resources which support tourist industries. The definition of "marine ... resources" may also cause difficulties. It is designed to exclude shore-based structures such as warehouses or other buildings ashore,[12] but it may extend to man-made structures inserted into the marine environment, such as a desalination plant, a fish farm or a jetty. Yet some resources appearing in a marine environment may not be regarded as true "marine resources", *e.g.* a platform for drilling oil from beneath the sea bed.

400 The requisite size of the "class" of "victim" is also unclear from the definition. The CMI Report preceding the International Salvage Convention 1989 expressed the aspiration that the definition would apply only to risk of damage of a general nature and not to damage to a particular person or installation[13] or, presumably, to a particular animal or plant. It was hoped that the employment of the words "substantial" and "major" in the definition would achieve this. But, as a matter of construction, "major" seems to describe the nature of the relevant incident[14]; and "substantial" qualifies "damage", not the size of the class of victims—it is quite possible for an

---

[10] "The States Parties to the present Convention ... Noting that substantial developments, in particular the increased concern for the protection of the environment, have demonstrated the need to review [the Brussels Salvage Convention 1910], Conscious of the major contribution which efficient and timely salvage operations can make ... to the protection of the environment ..., Have agreed ... "
[11] See Brice, §6–95.
[12] See CMI Report, 1–1.4 (*post*, App. 32).
[13] See CMI Report, 1–1.4 (*post*, App. 32).
[14] See *post*, §403.

individual person or penguin[15] to suffer substantial or non-substantial damage. Nonetheless, the use of generic phraseology to describe the classes of victims makes it sufficiently clear that it was damage to classes of, rather than individual, victims that was intended.

Secondly, the damage must be physical. Economic loss or intangible loss of amenity is excluded from the definition.   **401**

Thirdly, the damage must be "substantial", and not of a minor nature. Whether or not claims for non-substantial damage should be excluded from the Convention is no doubt a matter for debate.[16] At least it has the practical advantage of reducing or excluding from consideration during salvage operations or arbitrations losses which are not substantial.

Location[17]

The definition is concerned not with where the incident giving rise to damage occurs, but with the place where the damage occurs, which must be "in coastal or inland waters or areas adjacent thereto". Therefore, no matter how serious the incident, unless the relevant place of harm is "adjacent to" a designated locality, the definition does not extend to the high seas or even to exclusive economic zones. However, it will include incidents arising beyond the designated localities if, *e.g.* as a consequence of weather and currents, such incidents result in damage within the designated localities. The damage may occur on dry land "adjacent to" coastal or inland waters.   **402**

Cause of the damage

The Convention applies to damage "caused by pollution, contamination, fire, explosion or similar major incidents". This should embrace most serious effects imaginable following a casualty to a ship carrying hazardous or noxious substances.   **403**

It seems appropriate that the list of designated risks should be extended to something such as "similar major incidents", though it is not inconceivable that the term may pose difficulties of interpretation. One view is that the definition applies to listed causes of damage to the environment provided that the incident is, when it arises, major.[18] However, this is not what the definition provides. The location of the word "major" (within the sweeping up provision "similar major incidents") assumes that all of the previously listed acts of "pollution, contamination, fire, explosion" are inherently "major incidents", so that the sweeping up provision incorporates other "major incidents" so long as they are similar to those specified. Therefore, for the definition to apply, it is sufficient that there occurs an incident which is one of those listed. It is not also necessary that the extent of the occurrence is major. The limiting factor is that, no matter how large or small an act of, say, pollution or fire may

---

[15] See Gaskell, 21–378.
[16] *cf.* Gaskell, 21–378.
[17] *cf. ante*, §§ 362–376. See also Shaw [1996] L.M.C.L.Q. 202, 209.
[18] See Gaskell, 21–378.

be, the damage must be substantial.[19] However, in practice, the difference in degree between the extent of the occurrence and the extent of the damage is likely to be reduced by the fact that in most cases the cause will have to be substantial in order to give rise to damage which is substantial.

404 Independently of the issues where the relevant incident or damage occurs, it is an interesting feature of the Convention that, except in the case of Article 14, its provisions on damage to the environment are not expressed to be limited to damage caused by the casualty or its cargo.[20] On the other hand, Article 14 is specifically limited to claims for special compensation "in respect of a vessel which by itself or its cargo threatened damage to the environment".[21]

Responsibility for the damage

405 It should be noted that, for the purposes of the definition, it is irrelevant whether or not salvees are exposed to actual or potential liability for the relevant damage. Accordingly, a salvee may have to pay for environmental services even if he obtains no benefit in the avoidance of liability which he would otherwise incur. Conversely, a salvor who averts or minimises liability to which a salvee is subject (*e.g.* where a local authority claims clean-up costs for damage to buildings outside the definition)[22] may have no claim under the Convention.

Encouraging environmental services

406 There are a number of ways in which the International Salvage Convention 1989 encourages environmental services.

First, Article 11 imposes a general requirement on States parties to the Convention, whenever regulating or deciding upon matters relating to salvage operations such as admittance to ports of vessels in distress or the provision of facilities to salvors, to take into account the need for co-operation between salvors, other interested parties and public authorities in order to ensure the efficient and successful performance of salvage operations for the purpose of saving life or property in danger as well as preventing damage to the environment in general.[23]

407 Secondly, Article 8 imposes a duty to exercise due care to prevent or minimise damage to the environment on the salvor[24] (in carrying out his duty

---

[19] See *ante*, §400.
[20] See International Salvage Convention 1989, Arts. 1(b), 6.3, 8.1(b), 8.2(b), 11, 13.1(b), 14 and 16.2 for those Articles which deal with damage to the environment. *cf. ibid.*, Art. 9.
[21] *cf.* Art. 14.5, one (though not favoured) interpretation of which is that the disentitlement to special compensation of a salvor who has negligently failed to prevent or minimise damage to the environment is not dependent only on avoiding environmental damage arising from the casualty.
[22] See Brice, § 6–95.
[23] See further *post*, §§ 1044–1085.
[24] Art. 8.1(b).

to carry out the salvage operations with due care)[25] and on the salvee[26] (in carrying out his duty to co-operate fully with the salvor during the course of the salvage operations).[27] Thirdly, the skill and efforts of salvors in preventing or minimising damage to the environment has been made a criterion to be taken into account in fixing salvage rewards under Article 13.[28] Fourthly, where the salvage reward falls below the level laid down in Article 14, that Article gives the salvor an entitlement to special compensation in accordance with its terms[29]; and, under the "Common Understanding" attached to the Convention,[30] in fixing a reward under Article 13 or special compensation under Article 14, the tribunal is under no duty to fix an Article 13 reward up to the maximum salved value of the property before assessing Article 14 special compensation.

408 Additionally, under Article 16.2, a salvor of human life, who has taken part in the services rendered on the occasion of the accident giving rise to salvage, is entitled to a fair share of the payment awarded to the salvor for preventing or minimising damage to the environment.[31] These provisions are reinforced by Article 6, which provides generally that the application of the Convention may be expressly or impliedly excluded by contract,[32] but not where that would affect duties to prevent or minimise damage to the environment.[33]

The policy behind Article 14

409 It has long been a prominent feature of the law of salvage that it is intended not only to reimburse the successful salvor for expenses incurred and to remunerate him for his services, but to provide an additional financial incentive in order to attract the provision of salvage services.[34] However, the traditional law of salvage provide little or no incentive to provide environmental services or even salvage services where there was a risk of environmental damage, *inter alia* because the law of salvage afforded no prospect of payment for services which turned out to be unsuccessful or, even if successful in salving property, for services to the environment.

410 The International Salvage Convention 1989 attempted to remedy these deficiencies by providing "adequate incentives",[35] *inter alia* in Article 14.[36]

---

[25] See Art. 8.1(a). See *post*, § 1037.
[26] Art. 8.2(b).
[27] See Art. 8.2(a). See *post*, §§ 1055 *et seq*.
[28] Art. 13.1(b). See *post*, §§ 1417, 1421.
[29] See *post*, §§ 414 and 416.
[30] See *ante*, § 395.
[31] See further *ante*, §§ 298–310.
[32] Art. 6.1. See *ante*, §§ 77 and 80.
[33] Art. 6.3.
[34] See *ante*, Chap. 1.
[35] See the Preamble to the Convention.
[36] *cf.* Art. 13.1(b): *post*, §§ 1417 and 1421.

The House of Lords in *The Nagasaki Spirit*[37] decided that it did so[38] but to a limited extent. It provided that a salvor who had carried out salvage operations in respect of a vessel threatening damage to the environment should recover a minimum level of special compensation for expenses incurred, with the possibility of a profit element in the possible uplift of a maximum of 100 per cent of such expenses.[39] But it did not provide any additional financial incentive beyond one measured by expenses: this was indicated by including in calculation of the uplift only those criteria for fixing salvage rewards under Article 13.1 (promptness, availability, state of readiness and efficiency)[40] which can be regarded as a type of expense, and not those tending to enhance salvage rewards[41]:

> "[T]he promoters of the Convention did not choose ... to create an entirely new and distinct category of environmental salvage ... [T]he reward under Article 14 is subordinate to the reward under Article 13, and its functions should not be confused by giving it a character too closely akin to salvage."[42]

This conclusion was supported by the provisions of LOF 1980 and the *travaux préparatoires* from which the Convention provisions originated.[43] In short, salvors can not under Article 14 expect any payment measured in terms of profit or reward.

Duties to exercise due care to prevent or minimise damage to the environment

411 Both the Salvage Convention 1989 and the Lloyd's Form contract impose duties to encourage environmental services. These are considered below.[44]

2. SPECIAL COMPENSATION

(a) Conditions for payment

412 Where Article 14 of the International Salvage Convention 1989 applies, it provides for the possibility of payments[45] to a salvor of special compensation

---

[37] *Semco Salvage and Marine Pte Ltd v. Lancer Navigation Co. Ltd (The Nagasaki Spirit)* [1997] A.C. 455.
[38] *ibid.*, 467H.
[39] *ibid.*, 468A–B.
[40] Art. 13.1(h)–(j).
[41] [1997] A.C. 455, 468C.
[42] *ibid.*, 468E–H.
[43] *ibid.*, 469.
[44] *Post*, Chap. 10.
[45] Special compensation falls within the Convention's definition of "payment" in Art. 1(e) ("Payment means any reward, remuneration or compensation due under this Convention"); see *post*, § 1211.

Basic entitlement (Article 14.1)

by way of basic entitlement and also by way of a discretionary uplift, but subject to overriding upper limits.

Basic entitlement (Article 14.1)

Under Article 14.1, a salvor is entitled to special compensation in accordance with the provisions of Article 14 if the following conditions are satisfied.

(i) A threat of damage to the environment

It is necessary, first, that a vessel by itself or its cargo threatened damage to the environment.[46] However, it is not necessary for a salvor's basic entitlement to special compensation that the salvor has actually prevented or minimised damage to the environment.[47]

(ii) Performance of salvage operations

The claimant salvor must have carried out salvage operations in respect of the relevant vessel.[48] The salvor's motives for intervening (*i.e.* whether to earn a salvage reward or special compensation or both) are irrelevant.[49] But he must in fact have carried out *salvage operations*[50] before he can be awarded special compensation. However, it is not necessary that those operations in result satisfied the condition of success[51] necessary for a salvage reward under Article 13.

(iii) The incurring of expenses

Since the special compensation under Article 14 is calculated by reference to the salvor's out of-pocket and overhead expenses as defined in the Article,[52] it follows that no special compensation can be paid if there are no such expenses. In practice, it would be difficult for this requirement not to be satisfied, although in an unusual case a low level of expense may considerably inhibit an award of special compensation.

---

[46] Art. 14.1.
[47] However, actual prevention or minimisation of environmental damage is a requirement for the uplift under Art. 14.2: *post*, §§ 415–416.
[48] Art. 14.1.
[49] *cf.* Brice, §§ 6–145 to 6–147, whose view is that the salvor must initially have been bona fide concerned with undertaking a salvage operation rather than an operation to remove a wreck or the threat of environmental damage.
[50] Defined *ante*, § 18.
[51] See *post*, Chap. 8.
[52] Art. 14.3.

(iv) Article 13 reward less than basic entitlement to special compensation

The salvor must have failed to earn a reward under Article 13[53] at least equivalent to the special compensation assessable in accordance with Article 14.[54]

The Article 13 reward should be assessed in the normal way.[55] In particular, it is confirmed by a "Common Understanding" attached to the Convention and enacted in the Merchant Shipping Act 1995[56] that, in fixing a reward under Article 13 and assessing special compensation under Article 14, the tribunal is under no duty to fix a reward under Article 13 up to the maximum salved value of the vessel and other property before assessing the special compensation to be paid under Article 14.[57]

Discretionary uplift (Article 14.2)

415 Under Article 14.2 of the International Salvage Convention 1989, a salvor may obtain an increase in the special compensation payable under Article 14 if the following conditions are satisfied.

(i) Basic entitlement to Article 14.1 compensation

First, the conditions for basic entitlement to special compensation under Article 14.1 must be satisfied.[58]

In particular, the basic compensation payable should exceed the amount of any Article 13 salvage reward. If it does, as will be seen below,[59] an uplift may be granted of up to a further 100 per cent of the basic special compensation. But Article 14.2 provides that, "If, *in the circumstances set out in paragraph 1*, the salvor has ... prevented or minimised damage to the environment, the special compensation ... may be *increased* ... ".[60] Since the circumstances set out in Article 14.1 include failure to earn an Article 13 reward at least equivalent to basic special compensation as a pre-condition of such compensation, there should result such compensation before it can be "increased". It follows that, even if the total (basic and uplifted) special compensation exceeds the Article 13 reward, no special compensation at all would be payable unless the salvor's expenses exceeded the Article 13 threshold, however meritorious the salvor was in actually preventing environmental

---

[53] See *post*, Chap. 15.
[54] Art. 14.1.
[55] See *post*, Chap. 15. *cf. post*, § 1492.
[56] MSA 1995, s.224(2), Sched. 11, Pt II, 4 (redrafted to make specific reference to "arbiters" in Scotland).
[57] The Common Understanding may appear potentially confusing in that its purpose is not manifest. For there is no indication in the Convention that the position would have been any different if it had not been added. However, it was felt necessary, in order to secure agreement to the Convention, to provide assurance that this was the case. Otherwise, there might have been doubt if the salved fund were low and the salvor's expenses were high.
[58] See *ante*, §§ 413–414.
[59] *Post*, §§ 423–425.
[60] Emphasis added.

Discretionary uplift (Article 14.2)

damage. In practice, however, both the basic compensation and the uplift have been calculated before applying the Article 13 sum and awarding the difference.[61]

(ii) Prevention or minimisation of environmental damage

Secondly, the salvor by his salvage operations must actually have been successful in preventing or minimising damage to the environment.

416

(iii) Exercise of the tribunal's discretion

Whether or not a salvor receives an uplift in special compensation under Article 14.2, and the amount of that uplift, are not matters of entitlement (as under Art. 14.1) but of the exercise of the tribunal's discretion(s).[62]

(iv) Total special compensation not exceeding reward recoverable under Article 13[63]

In addition to the limit on basic entitlement to special compensation under Article 14.1,[64] Article 14.4 stipulates that the *total* special compensation under Article 14 (*i.e.* the basic entitlement under Art. 14.1 and any uplift under Art. 14.2)[65] shall be paid only if and to the extent that such compensation is greater than any reward recoverable by the salvor under Article 13.[66]

(b) The relationship between Articles 13 and 14

The object of Article 14 was to provide a means whereby a salvor could receive payment for environmental services in cases where there was no, or an inadequate, salvage reward under Article 13. Consistently with that object, any reward recoverable under Article 13 can limit or even eliminate payment(s) of special compensation under Article 14.

417

In practice, a salvage reward is assessed before consideration of what, if any, special compensation is payable under Article 14. In principle, however, for the purposes of calculating permissible special compensation, the tribunal's first task should be to identify the salvor's allowable expenses under Article 14 and then the amount of uplift, if any, it is prepared to make under Article 14.2. The resulting sum should then be reduced by the amount of reward recoverable under Article 13.[67]

---

[61] See Brice, § 6–142; Shaw [1996] L.M.C.L.Q. 202, 222–223.
[62] See further *post*, §§ 423–425.
[63] See *post*, Chap. 15.
[64] *Ante*, § 414.
[65] See *post*, §§ 423–437.
[66] Art. 14.4.
[67] This point is made twice, and therefore somewhat confusingly, in Art. 14.1 and Art. 14.4.

418   The size of the reward recoverable under Article 13 will therefore progressively reduce or eliminate the amounts of, first, basic special compensation under Article 14.1 and, then, the discretionary uplift under Article 14.2.

There are a number of common factors which may affect the initial calculation of Article 13 rewards and Article 14 special compensation. Thus, the salvor's expenses are a criterion for fixing an Article 13 salvage reward and the basic measure of calculating special compensation in accordance with Article 14.3, which also specifically requires consideration of the criteria for fixing salvage rewards listed in Article 13.1(h)–(j).[68] Moreover, Article 13.1(b) requires consideration of the skill and efforts of salvors in preventing or minimising damage to the environment, success in achieving which is the prerequisite of an Article 14.2 uplift. The uplift itself ultimately depends upon the tribunal's discretion, which, like the discretion for assessing salvage rewards, should be exercised "bearing in mind" the criteria in Article 13.1.[69]

419   The drafting of Article 14 presents the possibility that the same factor(s) may, or even should, be taken into account in assessing both salvage rewards and special compensation. This possibility is not specifically addressed by the Convention. On one view, it should be avoided, so as to avoid some form of double payment to the salvor.[70] However, the drafting of Article 14 is such that, within its terms, this should occur. Indeed, Article 14.2's directions for its second tier discretion is that it should be exercised "bearing in mind" the relevant criteria in Article 13.1, *not* bearing in mind the extent to which those criteria have already been considered in fixing a salvage reward.

420   Of course, consideration of the same factor may well not have the same numerical consequence in assessing salvage rewards and special compensation: the impact of the criteria for fixing a salvage reward will vary depending *inter alia* on the size of the salved fund and the exercise of the tribunal's discretion, whereas basic special compensation is intended to be calculated on a simple arithmetical basis. However, even if the same factor inflates both calculations, its tendency to double the salvee's liability is reduced by the requirement that sums payable by way of special compensation (and the elements by which they are constituted) are reduced by the amount of the recoverable salvage reward (and the criteria by which that is constituted). Naturally, since basic special compensation is calculated objectively, the effect of the notional setting off of a sum taken into account in assessing the two types of payment will vary depending on whether the salvage reward is calculated on a modest or a generous basis. But the effect of such variability

---

[68] *i.e.* (h) the promptness of the services, and (i)–(j) the availability, state of readiness, efficiency and value of the salvage equipment.

[69] This is, it is submitted, implicit in formulating any uplift, though only made explicit in relation to the discretion to increase the uplift beyond 30 per cent: Art. 14.2.

[70] See Brice, §§ 6–143 to 6–144.

is consistent with the policy behind special compensation, which is to endeavour to provide a minimum level of payment, decreasing from a full amount where there is no salvage reward, to nothing where the salvage reward exceeds the total special compensation which could be made.[71]

421 The necessity for independent assessment of salvage rewards and special compensation is underlined by the Common Understanding that the tribunal is not obliged to fix an Article 13 reward up to maximum salved values before assessing Article 14 special compensation.[72]

(c) Liability

422 Liability to pay Article 14 special compensation rests on the owner of the relevant vessel.[73]

(d) Amount of special compensation

423 The calculation of salvage rewards under Article 13 and of special compensation under Article 14 is subject to upper limits. In addition, the calculation of salvage rewards and the Article 14.2 uplift involve the exercise of the tribunal's discretion; but the assessment of basic special compensation under Article 14.1—and (since it is a percentage of the amount of basic compensation) the fixing of the upper limit to the uplift—is designed to be on a simple arithmetical basis, involving no discretion.

Thus, salvage rewards are assessed in the tribunal's discretion, subject to an upper limit determined by the value of the salved fund. Where a salvor has a basic entitlement to special compensation under Article 14.1, the sum is initially calculated as an amount equivalent to the salvor's expenses as defined in the Article.[74] Then, where the salvor qualifies for an uplift under Article 14.2, the tribunal has a discretion to increase the amount of special compensation up to a sum equivalent to 200 per cent of such expenses.[75] Once the total amount of special compensation has been calculated, it must then be reduced by deducting the amount of salvage reward recoverable under Article 13.[76]

---

[71] Art. 14.4.
[72] See *ante*, § 395
[73] Art. 14.1.
[74] Art. 14.1.
[75] Art. 14.2. Under Art. 14.1, basic compensation is initially calculated by reference to the salvor's allowable expenses. Under Art. 14.4, the amount payable in fact is reduced by the amount of any Art. 13 salvage reward. If this latter sum were the yardstick for calculating the uplift, it would reduce the amount of possible uplift. However, under Art. 14.2, the increment is calculated by the amount of special compensation "payable ... under paragraph 1", not by the amount of basic special compensation payable in fact after the application of Art. 14.4.
[76] Art. 14.1 and 14.4.

The discretionary uplift: a two-tier discretion

424   LOF 1980, cl. 1(a) sanctioned an uplift of up to 15 per cent of expenses incurred by salvors in rendering environmental services. Inevitably there was debate in the deliberations leading to the International Salvage Convention 1989 as to what percentage uplift (basically between 15 and 100 per cent) should be permitted by the Convention. These deliberations produced a somewhat unhappy compromise.

Where a salvor has by his salvage operations successfully prevented or minimised damage to the environment so that the tribunal has a discretion to increase the amount of Article 14 special compensation, Article 14.2 states that:

> "the special compensation ... may be increased up to a maximum of 30 per cent of the expenses incurred by the salvor. However, the tribunal, if it deems it fair and just to do so and bearing in mind the relevant criteria set out in Article 13, paragraph 1,[77] may increase such special compensation further, but in no event shall the total increase be more than 100 per cent of the expenses incurred by the salvor."

425   Article 14.2 appears to be intended to impose a two-tier discretion; but it is oddly drafted, since all that distinguishes the initial discretion (to increase the special compensation by up to 30 per cent) from the further discretion (up to 100 per cent) is that the tribunal deems it fair and just to do so and bearing in mind the relevant criteria in Article 13.1, both of which should be (and, it is submitted, are) implicit requirements of the reasonable exercise of the initial discretion. However, at the least Article 14.2 imposes a psychological restraint on the uplifting of special compensation and in practice it has been accepted as setting a maximum which should only be exceeded in special circumstances. Where there are special circumstances, an uplift may be well deserved.[78]

Salvor's expenses

426   Article 14.3 provides that, for the purposes of Article 14, salvor's expenses means:

> "the out-of-pocket expenses reasonably incurred by the salvor in the salvage operation and a fair rate for equipment and personnel actually and reasonably used in the salvage operation, taking into consideration the criteria set out in Article 13, paragraph 1(h), (i) and (j)."

---

[77] See *post*, § 1395.
[78] Brice, §§ 6–135 to 6–136, gives the example of a vessel carrying toxic chemicals on fire in a port area which, in a short operation and at minimal expense to the salvor, is towed out to sea and sinks, leaving no salved fund and no possibility of a salvage reward. Basic special compensation under Art. 14.1 and the initial uplift under Art. 14.2 would be low but the service would have been highly beneficial environmentally, justifying a further increment under the secondary discretion in Art. 14.2. For an outline of the events of the 1989 Diplomatic Conference leading to the adoption of this wording, see Shaw [1996] L.M.C.L.Q. 202, 221.

Article 14 expenses therefore comprise two elements: reasonably incurred out-of-pocket expenses; and a fair rate for equipment[79] and personnel reasonably used.

The closing words of Article 14.3 amplify the Article 14.3 definition of expenses by directing the tribunal to take into consideration certain of the criteria for fixing Article 13 salvage rewards, namely:

427

> "(h) the promptness of the service rendered;
> (i) the availability and use of vessels or other equipment intended for salvage operations;
> (j) the state of readiness and efficiency of the salvor's equipment and the value thereof."

It is not clear from the drafting of Article 14.3 whether this amplification is confined to the interpretation of "fair rate" or extends to "out-of-pocket expenses", but the sense of Article 14.3 is that it has the narrower meaning.

Although Article 14 provides for special compensation for environmental services, it does so by reference to expenses incurred "in the salvage operation" and is not limited to expenses incurred in or for the purpose of preventing or minimising damage to the environment. Thus, they may include the expense of a sub-contracted tug which does not actually participate in the removal of bunkers from a casualty.[80]

The "fair rate"

In *The Nagasaki Spirit*[81] the salvors argued that the word "compensation" had been applied to salvage remuneration in the traditional sense[82] and that "fair rate" in Article 14.3 meant:

428

> "a fair rate of remuneration having regard to the circumstances of the case, including the type of craft actually used and the type of work required (but in general terms) and a rate which acts as an incentive to the salvor (*i.e.* normally including a profit element but without amounting to a salvage reward or anything like it)."[83]

Moreover, in his dissenting judgment in the Court of Appeal, Evans L.J. formed the view that Article 14.3 meant a fair rate to both parties in the sense

---

[79] "Equipment" includes vessels. See *post*, §§ 1408–1410.
[80] Lloyd's Appeal Arbitration, 4/11/1994.
[81] *Semco Salvage and Marine Pte Ltd v. Lancer Navigation Co. Ltd (The Nagasaki Spirit)* [1997] A.C. 455, noted S. Girvin [1997] L.M.C.L.Q. 321; affirming [1996] 1 Lloyd's Rep. 449 (CA); affirming [1995] 2 Lloyd's Rep. 44 (Clarke J.).
[82] *ibid.*, 457C.
[83] *ibid.*, 467A.

of a commercial rate for the particular service, taking account of market rates when those may apply.[84]

429 However, these arguments were rejected by the House of Lords. The concept of "expenses" permeates Article 14.1–3; in its ordinary meaning "expenses" denotes either amounts disbursed or borne, not earned as profits; the addition of "fair rate" to "out-of-pocket expenses" in Article 14.3 signifies "overhead expenses"[85] and instances a quantification containing no element of profit; Article 14.2's reference (twice) to "expenses *incurred*" does not refer to something which yields a profit; and the word "compensation" normally has a flavour of reimbursement or recompense, not of profit or reward, a distinction drawn in Articles 1(e), 14.1 and 14.4.[86] This conclusion was supported by the policy behind Article 14.[87]

430 "[I]n the context of article 14 ['rate'] simply denotes an amount attributable to the equipment and personnel used, just as the expenses include an amount attributable to out-of-pockets."[88] "[T]he ascertainment of the fair rate must necessarily be performed with a fairly broad brush, albeit not so broad as the fixing of the reward under Article 13, and the uplift under Article 14.2. Quite sufficient information for such purposes could be derived from the salvor's books."[89] Accountants may be used to assist in the calculation of the fair rate,[90] though their assistance does not ensure an easy resolution of the issue.[91] Certainly, since Article 14.3 is not concerned with remuneration, authorities on the assessment of non-contractual rates of remuneration do not assist.[92]

Period

431 A threat of environmental damage may not exist at the moment at which a salvor begins to render services to a casualty but may do so at a later point in time, *e.g.* where an oil tanker taken in tow in the middle of the Atlantic Ocean runs into a dangerous storm off the English coast. It is, however, clear from the wording of Article 14.1 of the Convention that the possibility of special compensation under Article 14 arises not when the danger to the casualty arises or when salvage operations begin, but only from the time at which the threat to the environment materialises.[93] Before such time, would-be salvors have no guarantee that they will be able to earn any special compensation.

---

[84] [1996] 1 Lloyd's Rep. 449, 459.
[85] [1997] A.C. 455, 472, *per* Lord Lloyd of Berwick.
[86] [1997] A.C. 455, 467. See also *ibid.*, 458, *per* Lord Mackay of Clashfern L.C., and 471–472, *per* Lord Lloyd of Berwick.
[87] See *ante*, §§ 409–410.
[88] [1997] A.C. 455, 470–471 [*sic*.].
[89] *ibid.*, 469–470.
[90] *The Nagasaki Spirit* [1995] 2 Lloyd's Rep. 44, 59 (Clarke J.); [1996] 1 Lloyd's Rep. 449, 455, *per* Staughton L.J., 461, *per* Swinton Thomas L.J.; [1997] A.C. 455, 472, *per* Lord Lloyd of Berwick.
[91] See Brice, §6–122.
[92] [1997] A.C. 455, 470B. *cf. ibid.*, 457F.
[93] *The Nagasaki Spirit* [1995] 2 Lloyd's Rep. 44, 57, *per* Clarke J.

The deductible salvage reward

432 However, once a threat of environmental damage has arisen, Article 14 applies to expenses throughout the whole of the ensuing period of salvage operations, not only during those times when a threat to the environment exists.[94] The length of the period or periods during which the threat of environmental damage exists will be a relevant factor in exercise of the discretion(s) to award an uplift under Article 14.3. It may, however, encourage both restraint in awarding an uplift (because the duration of the threat has been brief) or generosity (because it was the effectiveness of the salvor's services which limited the duration).

The deductible salvage reward

(i) Whose reward?

433 In authorising basic special compensation, Article 14.1 provides *inter alia* that:

> "If the salvor has carried out salvage operations in respect of a vessel . . . and has failed to earn a reward under Article 13 at least equivalent to the special compensation assessable in accordance with this Article, he shall be entitled to special compensation from the owner of that vessel . . . "

An uplift under Article 14.2 is also expressed to be "payable by the owner". Neither Article 14.1 nor Article 14.2 makes clear whether the reward referred to in Article 14.1 is one payable only by the shipowner or extends to rewards payable by other salvees. On one view, the reference to the carrying out of salvage operations in respect of a vessel in Article 14.1 indicates that the Article 13 reward against which permissable special compensation is to be measured is one payable by the defendant shipowner alone. Unfortunately, the use of the word "reward" in the singular is inconclusive since, although separate awards may be made against individual salvees, it is common for a variety of salvees to be severally liable for a single award relating to a number of salved interests. An alternative view, therefore, is that the basic entitlement to special compensation is only to such amount as exceeds all the reward recoverable by the salvor as a result of the operation in issue.

434 A similar difficulty occurs with Article 14.4. That states that "The total special compensation under this Article shall be paid only if and to the extent that such compensation is greater than *any reward* recoverable by the salvor under Article 13."[95] The italicised words raise two possible uncertainties in construction. The first, as in the case of Article 14.1, is whether they refer to a reward payable by the shipowner or to rewards payable by all salvees. The second is that there may be a distinction between Article 14.1 and Article

---

[94] *The Nagasaki Spirit* [1997] A.C. 455, 471, *per curiam*; affirming [1995] 2 Lloyd's Rep. 44 (Clarke J.) and [1996] 1 Lloyd's Rep. 449 (CA).
[95] Emphasis added.

14.4, so that Article 14.1 refers to a reward payable by the shipowner alone, whereas Article 14.4 refers to any and all liabilities to pay a reward following the relevant operations. If that were right, a salvor could obtain a basic entitlement to special compensation by overcoming the limit under Article 14.1 but lose it by virtue of the higher limit under Article 14.4.

435 The placing of liability for special compensation on the shipowner and the policy of encouraging environmental services underlying Article 14 (which is better served by a lower deductible) favour a construction referring to a reward payable by the shipowner alone. However, Article 13 seems to favour "the reward" as covering the salvor's entire entitlement[96]; this was assumed to be the case in *The Nagasaki Spirit*,[97] and in practice it is accepted that it refers to the entirety of salvage reward recoverable by the salvor.

(ii) The reward "under Article 13"

436 Article 14.1 applies if the salvor has "failed to earn a reward under Article 13 at least equivalent to the special compensation payable under [Article 14]" and Article 14.4 permits payment of special compensation under Article 14 only if and to the extent that the total such compensation is greater than any reward "recoverable by the salvor under Article 13". Article 14 therefore assumes a salvage reward assessed in the normal way (albeit with the uncertainty involved in exercise of the tribunal's discretion).[98] However, the effect of Article 14.4 is contentious where this does not occur.

If the parties had come to an agreement excluding the application of Article 13 (*e.g.* where the service was to be paid for on a different basis, such as for a fixed sum or agreed rate), on one view, it would not be possible for special compensation to be payable under Article 14, for it can be argued that a salvor could not "fail to earn a reward under Article 13" in terms of Article 14.1 if he never attempted to earn such a reward.

437 The amount of a "reward under Article 13" can only be identified if it is assessed in the normal way. If this has not already been done, the tribunal assessing special compensation must incur the inconvenience and expense of such assessment. Fortunately, in practice the salvage reward will have been determined before calculation of special compensation is attempted. However, it may not have been assessed in the conventional way but settled by the parties. In such a case, if it can be objectively ascertained that the settlement was lower or higher than a reward assessable in the conventional way, it will be in the interest of the shipowner or salvor respectively to argue that the conventional rather than the agreed amount should be deducted from the special compensation. If the settlement is simply agreed by the salvor and

---

[96] See especially Art. 13.2. But *cf.* Art. 13.3.
[97] [1997] A.C. 455. However, the point was not argued.
[98] See also the "Common Understanding", which confirms that the tribunal is not obliged to fix a salvage reward up to the amount of the salved values before assessing special compensation: *ante*, § 395.

the shipowner, they will be estopped from denying that the settlement determines the reward under Article 13 for the purposes of Article 14. However, if the relevant reward is one which is only payable and agreed by parties other than the shipowner,[99] the shipowner will not be bound by the settlement and can maintain that the deductible amount is one to be determined in accordance with Article 13.[1]

(e) Salvor's misconduct

Article 18 of the International Salvage Convention 1989 provides that, **438**

"A salvor may be deprived of the whole or part of the payment due under this Convention to the extent that the salvage operations have become necessary or more difficult because of fault or neglect on his part or if the salvor has been guilty of fraud or other dishonest conduct."[2]

In addition, Article 14.5 provides that,

"If the salvor has been negligent and has thereby failed to prevent or minimise damage to the environment, he may be deprived of the whole or part of any special compensation due under this Article [14]."

However, since the word "payment" in Article 18 includes special compensation under Article 14,[3] Article 14.5 is in fact superfluous and its only function in practice, if any, is to emphasise that one of the types of misconduct mentioned in the more widely drafted Article 18 may have the effect of reducing or eliminating a potential award of special compensation.

(f) Shipowner's right of recourse

Subject to qualifications on the other party's liability,[4] a person may have **439** a right of recourse against another: by way of damages, if the other party has caused him a loss by a tort or breach of contract; or (whether or not the other party would otherwise be subject to a legal liability), if that party has by contract agreed to indemnify him.[5] Thus, if a ship negligently collides with a tanker carrying oil, the owners of the tanker and of its cargo are entitled to

---

[99] See also *post*, §§ 1488–1491.
[1] If so, a shipowner may not be able to rely on the objectively determined reward, unless the settlement was obviously wrong. See Brice, §6–148.
[2] See further *post*, Chap. 11.
[3] See also *post*, § 1211.
[4] See *post*, Chap. 12.
[5] *e.g.* under an indemnity clause under a demise charterparty, an employment and indemnity clause in a time charterparty or an indemnity clause under a towage contract.

claim against the colliding ship for losses resulting to them, including sums which they become liable to pay to third parties, *e.g.* for salvage services. Similarly, a cargo-owner may be entitled to recoup salvage expenditure from a shipowner whose breach of contract in providing an unseaworthy ship resulted in a fire necessitating salvage services.[6] And a shipowner may, depending on its proper interpretation, have a right to claim against a cargo-owner under a bill of lading contract or against a charterer under a charter-party for losses incurred as a consequence of shipping dangerous goods. Furthermore, a person who has made an extraordinary sacrifice or incurred an extraordinary expenditure for the benefit of the common adventure may claim a contribution from the beneficiaries of his act in general average.

440   Where a shipowner has a right of recourse, the International Salvage Convention 1989 makes it clear that it is unaffected by the imposition on him of liability to a salvor for special compensation under the Convention. Article 14.6 provides that "Nothing in this Article [14] shall affect any right of recourse on the part of the owner of the vessel."

By the same token, Article 14.6 does not create any right of recourse not otherwise existing. In particular, a salvor cannot claim in general average a contribution to special compensation which he is called upon to pay. This situation has been achieved, following a recommendation by the Diplomatic Conference adopting the International Salvage Convention 1989,[7] by the revision of the York-Antwerp Rules, which in practice apply to the settlement of general average. It is now provided by the York-Antwerp Rules 1994, r. VI(b), that special compensation payable under Article 14 or under any other provision similar in substance shall not be allowed in general average.[8] In fact, however, rule VI(b) does more than make clear that a shipowner has no automatic right to a general average contribution to his liability for special compensation. Its effect is that, if, under the normal principles of general average, an entitlement to such a contribution were to arise, it would be excluded by rule VI(b).[9]

---

[6] See, *e.g. The Breydon Merchant* [1992] 1 Lloyd's Rep. 373.
[7] See the International Salvage Convention 1989, Attachment 2: *post*, App. 33.
[8] See F. D. Rose, *General Average: Law and Practice* (1997), pp. 51–54.
[9] If such a right were to be created by a contract which was also subject to the York-Antwerp Rules 1994, the terms of the contract would conflict.

CHAPTER 6

ENTITLEMENT TO CLAIM

1. GENERAL CONDITIONS FOR CLAIMS

441 The public policy which encourages the provision of salvage services supports the view that all those who in any way contribute to the success of salvage operations should be entitled to claim and participate in a salvage reward.

In previous editions of this book, certain qualifications on this position have been given; namely, that the claimant: should come within the traditional classification of salvors; must not be under a pre-existing obligation to provide the service (*i.e.* he should be a "volunteer"); and does not have an interest in the salved property. Moreover, the claim may be defeated in whole or in part as a result of the salvor's misconduct or by a set-off or counterclaim.[1] However, this image needs to be revised, particularly in the light of the impact of the Salvage Convention 1989.

442 The general principle remains true and has in fact been strengthened under the Convention.[2] However, it is not and, in fact, never was, true that a salvage award will only be made if the claimant comes within a certain classification: the former "classification" of salvors merely serves to indicate the nature of the service which claimants have provided.[3] Also, a salvage reward is not subject to the claimant's proving himself to be a "volunteer". The reverse is true: *i.e.* the salvor's status is not a precondition of an award but a matter which, in a limited number of circumstances, may deprive him of the whole or part of a reward to which he is otherwise entitled.[4] Furthermore, a claimant's interest in the salved property does not *per se* disentitle him from claiming salvage.[5] It is true that misconduct or cross-claims may diminish or

---

[1] See *post*, Chap. 11.
[2] See Art. 12: "salvage operations which have had a useful result give right to a reward." See *post*, Chap. 8.
[3] *Post*, §§ 445–484.
[4] See *post*, Chap. 7.
[5] See *post*, §§ 485–510.

Entitlement to Claim

eliminate a salvage award, but these are matters more appropriately considered separately from the issue of the salvor's prima facie entitlement.[6]

Definition of salvor

443   The best known Admiralty law descriptions of salvors concentrate on their status as "volunteers" rather than define the term independently of that role.[7] The Salvage Convention 1989 defines "salvage operation" as any act or activity undertaken to assist property in danger in navigable or other waters.[8] However, it does not define the word "salvor". It does use the word in several places[9] but not as a term of art. Thus, Article 16's statement that "A salvor of human life . . . is entitled to a fair share of the payment awarded to *the salvor* for salving the vessel or other property or preventing or minimising damage to the environment"[10] describes the saver of human life as a salvor but seems to treat as the real salvor the person rendering services to property and the environment, albeit services to both life[11] and the environment[12] are not salvage within the traditional definition but a modern elaboration of matters deserving treatment within the law of salvage.[13] In short, the word "salvor" in the Salvage Convention 1989 conveniently describes a person who has rendered a useful service to either property, human life or the environment where one or more of them has been exposed to danger on water, but does not *per se* indicate the legal consequences of the service.

444   The effect of the Salvage Convention 1989 is that a salvor is any person who engages in any act or activity undertaken to assist a vessel or any other property in danger in navigable waters or in any other waters whatsoever.[14] Although its application is subject to exclusions,[15] the Convention prima facie applies[16] whatever the normal status of the person involved and whatever the nature of the act or activity undertaken. All salvors therefore become subject to the duties imposed by the Convention[17] and, if their salvage operations have had a useful result, are prima facie entitled to a salvage payment, albeit

---

[6] See *post*, Chap. 11.
[7] See *post*, §445.
[8] Salvage Convention 1989, Art. 1(a).
[9] See Salvage Convention 1989, Arts. 5.2, 8 (heading and Art. 8.1), 11, 13.1, 14 (paras 1, 3 and 4), 15 (heading and Art. 15.1), 16.2, 18, 20.1, 21 (paras 1 and 3), 22.1. and 24.
[10] Emphasis added.
[11] See *ante*, §§ 260–310.
[12] See *ante*, Chap. 5.
[13] *cf.* Art. 18 (the effect of a salvor's misconduct), stating that misconduct may deprive a "salvor" of all payment under the Convention. On one view, the term may appear to be ambiguous, since a salvor who is entitled to no payment is arguably not a salvor. However, the better view is to regard someone contributing to the preservation of the subject at risk as prima facie a salvor, but one whose entitlement to payment is subject to reduction, in part or in whole, because of his misconduct.
[14] Art. 1(a).
[15] See *post*, Chap. 12.
[16] See Art. 6.1.
[17] Art. 8. See *post*, Chap. 10.

2. Personal Service and Provision of Property ("Classification of Salvors")

(a) General

It was formerly stated in this book[19] that: **445**

"The Court of Admiralty requires of those who claim to rank as salvors that they shall be in at least one of the following four classes–
(1) Owners of a salving vessel; or
(2) demise-charterers who are, or, it seems, charterers who by the express terms of the charterparty in relation to salvage become *pro hac vice* owners of a salving vessel; or
(3) master or crew of a salving vessel; or
(4) persons who have been personally engaged in the service in respect of which they claim reward, whether or not they are also within any of the above three classes."

This categorisation of salvors may be a convenient way of dividing into groups some of the main types of persons who have proved to be successful in pursuing claims. But it is not a classification which has been formally required or approved by judicial authority, its inclusion of particular and general categories of salvor gives it a somewhat clumsy and perhaps misleading appearance, and its failure to concentrate on the general qualities to be found in potential claimants reduces its practical utility.

The absence of a previous claim, especially a successful one, by a particular **446**
class of salvor will put the tribunal on its guard against readily admitting such a claim.[20] But "There are no rigid categories of salvor. They include any volunteer who renders services of a salvage nature."[21]

It is suggested, therefore, that the cases and the principle of success—which confines claims to services which have made a real contribution to salvage which in fact proves to be successful[22]—justify the following threefold *description*, rather than definition, of persons entitled to claim salvage. A person providing a service is entitled to claim a salvage reward if he was at the time when the salvage service was provided:

---

[18] See *post*, Chap. 12.
[19] See 4th ed., p. 124.
[20] See *The Vrede* (1861) Lush. 322; *The Sava Star* [1995] 2 Lloyd's Rep. 134, 138, *per* Clarke J.
[21] *The Sava Star* [1995] 2 Lloyd's Rep. 134, 141, *per* Clarke J.
[22] See *post*, Chap. 8.

(i) personally engaged in a salvage service; or
(ii) entitled to possession of a vessel used to provide salvage service; or
(iii) the owner or the person entitled to possession of other property which was used to provide a salvage service.

447 In modern times persons providing salvage services normally do so as a result of an agreement but it is not necessary to consider an additional category: (iv) by contract. The salvage contracts currently in use assume that entitlement to salvage is basically dependent on complying with established legal requirements and if, exceptionally, the parties agreed that a contractor should be remunerated regardless of such compliance, the contract, if enforceable, would not be given effect as a salvage contract.

Two aspects of the suggested categorisation of salvors will be considered next. The first relates to personal services provided by salvors. The second concerns the necessary possessory or proprietary interest which a salvor must have in property utilised in salvage services.

(b) The rule of personal service

448 In the days of sailing ships, salvage services were generally of a personal character, and salvage was commonly performed by the despatch of men in boats to the aid of the vessel to be salved. These men were regarded as the real salvors. Thus, Dr Lushington could state in *The Charlotte*[23] that:

> "In order to entitle a person to share as salvor, he must, I conceive, have been personally engaged in the service. This principle has long prevailed as the acknowledged doctrine of this Court, and was recognised by Lord Stowell ... in *The Vine*."[24]

Refusing the claim of a coastguard officer who permitted men in boats under his command to go out and render salvage services, Lord Stowell said in *The Vine*[25] that:

> "It is, I apprehend, a general rule that a party, not actually occupied in effecting a salvage service, is not entitled to share in a salvage remuneration. The exception to this rule that not infrequently occurs is in favour of owners of vessels, which, in rendering assistance, have either been diverted from their proper employment, or have experienced a special mischief, occasioning to the owners some inconvenience and loss, for which an equitable compensation may reasonably be claimed."

---

[23] (1848) 3 W. Rob. 68, 72.
[24] (1825) 2 Hagg. 1.
[25] *ibid.*, 2; cited in *The Makedonia* [1958] 1 Q.B. 365, 373.

The rule of personal service

Lord Stowell's *dictum* suggests that the uniting principle is that a person is entitled to claim a salvage reward if he has made a real contribution to successful salvage. Thus, boat owners in *The Charlotte*[26] received "equitable compensation" *qua* boat owners but not personally, since the only other contribution to salvage they made was to permit others to effect salvage in their boats. The position was similar with the coastguard officer in *The Vine*,[27] although it may be noted that his *locus standi* to claim salvage was affected by the fact that he had a public duty to facilitate salvage. Thus, just as a boat owner could not claim salvage for doing nothing more than permitting use of his property, so the coast-guard officer could not claim without shewing that he had done more than merely discharging his public duty.[28]

449

But, even in the early nineteenth century, it was clear that such a salvor who did contribute an additional personal service, and one that he was not already obliged to provide, could claim salvage. Thus, in *HMS Thetis*,[29] Sir Christopher Robinson acceded to the proposition:

450

> "that there is no principle of constructive assistance in civil salvage, and that no admiral or commanding officer of a station, not being an actual salvor, but merely by virtue of such command, has any right to claim to share in the salvage earned by, and awarded to, a ship belonging to such station ... but that will not exclude a claim from being propounded on behalf of an admiral on special grounds of extensive contribution of assistance."

He, therefore, awarded an admiral salvage for services "much beyond ... the mere performance of official duties," in furnishing men and stores at his own responsibility and procuring some things at his own cost and credit. His Lordship stressed that it was important not to confuse the necessity of a personal *service* with mere physical *presence*:

> "If, then, admirals can be entitled at all, for anything but mere personal presence and exertion, it must be for such services as these, which were infinitely more conducive to the success, than the Admiral's own personal presence could in this instance have been."[30]

A reason for limiting salvage rewards to those providing personal service was given by Lord Stowell in *The Vine*,[31] that:

451

> "to acknowledge him as a salvor would be to introduce a sort of prize principle very inapplicable to cases of this description. In cases of

---
[26] *Supra*, n. 23.
[27] *Supra*.
[28] See *post*, Chap. 7.
[29] (1833) 3 Hagg. 14, 58; affirmed subject to variation (1834) 2 Knapp 390.
[30] (1833) 3 Hagg. 14, 60.
[31] (1825) 2 Hagg. 1, 2–3.

Entitlement to Claim

prize, a commander on shore, if the capture takes place within the limit of his station, is considered as the manager of the whole transaction, and, the property being condemned, is entitled to his proportion; but, in questions of salvage, the Court must not act on the same liberality of principle that belongs to prize cases. Here all is to be paid out of the pockets of the British owner;—he alone has to discharge all demands."

The policy which precludes a person's claiming as salvor should not, however, be confused with the method by which the salvage reward of a true salvor is assessed. Thus, Sir Christopher Robinson stated in *HMS Thetis*[32] that:

"deeming it expedient, in a case of novelty, to act as far as I am able on rules and principles in established cases, and thinking that the proportion allowed in other civil cases will not be unfit to be applied to this, I shall adopt the rule of the prize proclamation."

452 Since the advent of steam and motor-driven vessels, power has become the principal instrument in salvage, and the type of service ordinarily performed in effecting salvage has greatly altered since the days of sail, when services by towing were exceptional and services inevitably contained a more personal element.[33] Moreover, the greater size of and difficulty in manoeuvring vessels in distress renders it less likely that purely personal services will be as effective as in days gone by. It therefore seems less unusual nowadays that a shipowner who is not present in person at salvage operations should nevertheless recover the lion's share of the salvage reward. But that is not because personal service is no longer necessary. It is because there is a much greater likelihood nowadays that actual salvage will be effected more by a salving vessel than individual salvors.

453 In *The Makedonia*,[34] Pilcher J. had to consider the extent to which the incidence of taxation figured in assessing a salvage reward. In considering whether a company of professional salvors, owners of the salving vessel, should be treated in like fashion to the master and crew of a salving vessel, his Lordship said[35]:

"it is unusual, where a professional salvor is a plaintiff in an action or a claimant in an arbitration, for the master and crew of the salvage vessel involved to figure personally as plaintiffs or claimants. *The award made, however, in every salvage case is in a sense a reward for personal services.* The element of risk to the salving crew is the same whether they are on board a merchant ship or a salvage vessel. The responsibilities undertaken by the master of the salving craft is the same whatever its

---

[32] (1833) 3 Hagg. 14, 61.
[33] See further *ante*, §§ 43–47.
[34] [1958] 1 Q.B. 365.
[35] *ibid.*, 376 (italics added).

(c) Possession or ownership of salving property

Owners of salving vessels

In the nineteenth century, it was laid down in several cases where the use of smacks, rowing boats or sailing vessels made it possible for personal services to be performed by their crews, that the owners of such vessels were usually entitled to some reward if the owners' interests were affected or, at least, at risk of being affected, either by the possibility of danger to the vessel or by her detention during the services. Thus, as has been seen,[36] Lord Stowell in *The Vine*[37] acknowledged that delay or loss could justify the award of "equitable compensation", and this is what Dr Lushington purported to award in *The Charlotte*.[38] In *The Jane*,[39] Sir Christopher Robinson stated that:

454

> "the general principle of law is, that the claim of owners generally is very slight, unless, from the circumstances of the case, their property becomes exposed to danger, or they incur some real loss or inconvenience."

It was evident from his judgment, however, that awarding shipowners salvage was not merely a concession to them but was supported by the public policy of encouraging potential salvors, not only in the sense that a shipowner might be prepared for his ship to be used to assist in salvage operations, but in the sense that the master could better justify deviation from his authorised course if he had acted so that both he and the shipowner could claim salvage.[40] Thus, Dr Lushington held in *The Martin Luther*[41]:

> "I shall allot £600 to the owners, and for this reason—because their property was engaged; and also for another and obvious reason, that unless I encourage the owners of steamers that are able to perform the most efficient services, it may follow, and this has often been suggested

---

[36] *Ante*, §448.
[37] (1825) 2 Hagg. 1, 2.
[38] (1848) 3 W. Rob. 68, 72. See also *The Norden* (1853) 1 Spinks 185. *cf. The Two Friends* (1844) 2 W. Rob. 349, where Dr Lushington disallowed the claim of a shipowner whose own vessel had sunk. Members of his crew in his boats came upon the *Two Friends* but he was entitled to do nothing for services provided by his apprentices or for the fact that salvage might not have occurred but for his boats, which were "in all probability... themselves saved by the circumstances of meeting with the ship."
[39] (1831) 2 Hagg. 338, 343.
[40] *ibid.*, 343–344. *cf. The Mulgrave* (1827) 2 Hagg. 77: the owner of a smack obtained nothing for any injury he might have suffered by the detention of his vessel, for, said Lord Stowell, the master having entered into an agreement with the vessel in distress, it was a case of contract, not of salvage.
[41] (1857) Swab. 287, 290.

to the Court, that orders will be given to the masters of their ships that, except in cases of saving life, they shall never engage in any salvage service at all."

455   In *The Valverda*,[42] Lord Wright observed that in the middle of the nineteenth century it was:

> "clear from the cases that the original idea that salvage was personal still retained its force, but was in process of being weakened by the growing sense that private shipowners should in certain cases be given for the services of their steam vessels remuneration which went beyond the awards in respect of demurrage or repairs, actual expenses and perhaps risk, which constituted the limit of what was generally given in those days."

Thus, he cited *The Raikes*[43]—the first case in which salvage was awarded for a steamship's services, which Lord Stowell was eager to do to encourage the great skill and power of such vessels—as having established a special exception to the rule of personal service, a year before the general exception in the case of shipowners was recognised in *The Vine*.[44] In common with what has been suggested above, however, it is submitted that this so-called special exception was in reality not so much an exception to a general need for personal service, but more of a further example of how to satisfy the overriding requirement that a claimant's services actually contribute to success. Nowadays, of course, it has become the leading example. As Lord Wright observed in *The Valverda*[45]:

> "The world has become accustomed to heavy claims and awards for salvage being made to shipowners in respect of their vessels, which are regarded as agents or instruments of the salvage. If it were not for the powerful steam or motor vessels of modern days, with their elaborate and valuable machinery and equipment, salvage such as the tonnage of the *Valverda* could not be achieved. The personal courage and exertions of the salving officers and crew would be of little avail without the aid of the mechanical means and the power supplied by the salving vessel."

---

[42] *Admiralty Commissioners v. Valverda (Owners)* [1938] A.C. 173, 190.
[43] (1824) 1 Hagg. 246.
[44] *Ante*, §448. *cf. The Beulah* (1842) 7 Jur. 207, *per* Dr Lushington:
"Now, in former times, before steam vessels were introduced, the principle laid down was this, that the salvage remuneration was to be allotted to those by whom the salvage service had been rendered, *viz.* the master and crew of the salving vessel; it was only *incidentally*, to use Lord Stowell's words, that the owners of the vessels were allowed to take anything. Such services were generally or for the most part effected by personal labour, exertion, and risk, and therefore must necessarily be rendered by the master and crew; but in some cases, where the ship herself to which the salvors belonged had materially contributed to the success of the service, those cases formed exceptions to the rule, because it was but fair, that, as the property of the owners had been risked, they should participate in the benefit derived partly from the use and employment of their property."
See also *The Enchantress* (1860) Lush. 93, 96.
[45] [1938] A.C. 173, 190.

Possession or ownership of salving property

Where the modern power-driven vessel is the effective foundation of **456** services, as it now ordinarily is, the cost of fuel consumed in performing the service may present a substantial expense for the owner, and it is the owner who, even if not present at the time, gets the principal share of the reward.[46] Even where salvage has been performed entirely by the personal exertions of the crew of his vessel, he is usually held to be entitled to some, albeit a smaller, share. Moreover, it appears that any requirement relating to the interests of the owner being affected or at risk of being affected in order that he may claim is self-evident or taken for granted, and that any such element goes to the quantum of the award, not to the right of owners to claim reward.

It is now quite clear, therefore, that a shipowner can claim salvage in **457** respect of a salvage service provided by his ship. The reward is earned by the ship and payable to its owner. But a shipowner is not entitled to claim a reward in respect of services provided by members of his crew. The reward they earn goes to them personally, and their employer is not entitled either to take any or part of their reward or to put forward an independent claim for having in some way provided the personnel who render assistance.[47] This is so even if the services could not have been rendered without the use of a shipowner's vessel.

Chartered vessels

It has long been understood to be the general rule that, where a salvage **458** reward becomes due in respect of the services rendered by a salving vessel, the reward for those services is payable to the owner of the vessel. It was his property that was risked and which actually effected the service, and he was the one empowered to give instructions as to the vessel's employment, whether for salvage or otherwise.

Charterer not by demise and cargo-owner

In consequence, it has long been the view that, where a ship is under a **459** charterparty not amounting to a demise and silent as to salvage, it is still the owner—and not the charterer—who is entitled to salvage. Thus, in *The Waterloo*,[48] the East India Company were not entitled to avoid paying salvage for services rendered by a ship under charter to them, on the ground that they would be paying themselves. Dr Lushington said this in *The Alfen*[49]:

---

[46] *The Makedonia* [1958] 1 Q.B. 365, 373–374.
[47] *The Two Friends* (1844) 2 W. Rob. 349, 353; *The Meandros* [1925] P. 61.
[48] (1820) 2 Dods. 433. See also *The Sarpen* [1916] P. 306.
[49] (1857) Swab. 189, 190. *cf.* the *dictum* of Lord Birkenhead L.C. in *Admiralty Commissioners v. Page* [1921] 1 A.C. 137, 142; discussed *post*, §472.

"I apprehend that where a vessel is under charter, unless there be express terms in the charter-party giving the charterer the right to control salvage, and the benefit of any salvage, if performed, the charterer has no claim to reward for salvage services rendered by the ship. I conceive there are various reasons why this must be the case. In the first place, with regard to the personal exertions of the master and crew, they are wholly independent of the charterer: it would, therefore, be quite contrary to justice that the charterer should found any claim upon them—and not only so, but it would not conduce to the safety of ships at sea if it could be said that the master and crew were to be deprived of the effect of their personal exertions. I apprehend, therefore, that salvage would not belong, except in special cases, to the charterer; but, at the same time, I do not mean to say there might not arise out of the circumstances of the salvage a reason for the charterers refusing to pay the whole amount for which they chartered the ship, or a right of action against the owners of the ship for delay and loss incurred."

460 This statement does not clearly justify the proposition that charterers are unable to claim salvage. Uttered at the end of the time when salvage services were almost invariably personal services in the strict sense of the term,[50] it, with respect, mistakenly assumes that the proposed claims of owner or charterer are founded on the services of the master and crew, which they are not.[51] Individual claims are founded on the means by which salvage is effected and the claimant's actual contribution to salvage. It is, therefore, natural, particularly in the case of a general ship, that the true salvor be seen to be the person normally entitled to ownership and possession of the salving vessel, that is, the owner.

461 Does it necessarily follow that a time charterer should not be entitled to claim salvage or cannot make a contribution to salvage? These questions merit more serious consideration today, when whole ships are regularly under time charter, than in the early nineteenth century, when this was uncommon.[52] The general public policy of encouraging potential salvors to act has not led to all deviations' being treated as justifiable, so as to relieve a deviating shipowner from liability to a charterer not by way of demise or to a cargo-owner.[53] As Dr Lushington recognised in *The Alfen*,[54] owner and charterer may come to an agreement as to the provision of salvage and/or the distribution of salvage earned. But does this agreement always have to be contained in writing, in a previously concluded charterparty? It may at first blush appear unrealistic to contemplate a charterer's subsequently consenting to a deviation to effect salvage, at the very time at which the ship to be salved is in distress. But the speed of modern communications does make this easily imaginable. The

---

[50] See *ante*, §§ 448–453.
[51] See *ante*, §452. *cf.* Gaskell, 21–374.
[52] See the cases in Rose [1981] L.M.C.L.Q. 33.
[53] See generally Scrutton, pp. 256–266.
[54] *Ante*, §459.

Possession or ownership of salving property

master or shipowner who envisages the opportunity to earn a large salvage reward but does not wish simultaneously to incur great liability to a time-charterer and the risk of failing to earn any salvage at all would be well advised to obtain the charterer's prior consent before deviating. He might even seek subsequent ratification of his actions. Indeed, without his doing so, the charterer himself might of his own accord seek to adopt the acts of salvage.

The time charterer's opportunities of earning salvage may be small. A ship in distress will normally be salved by professional salvors, and a time-chartered ship which is not specifically equipped to effect salvage may be unlikely to be able to render a very effective service. Even where it is, it may be asked what contribution the time-charterer himself actually makes. He may be said to contribute the availability of the salving ship's services, risking financial losses and liabilities (to buyers and cargo-owners) and foregoing opportunities of profit. If they are too indirect to found an independent claim, as they probably would be, he may be held to have provided, jointly with the shipowner, the services of the ship itself and share accordingly in the reward earned by it. In such a case, he should recover more than he would if claiming damages for loss against a deviating shipowner. The authorities do not specifically deny his claim. *The Waterloo*[55] decided that the owner of a salved ship was liable to pay salvage for the services of a ship chartered by him, not that he should not be allowed to participate in the reward for those services.[56] In *The Alfen*,[57] the owner of the salved ship neither sought to deny his liability nor that he had contributed to services provided by the ship chartered to him.   **462**

If the authorities do not specifically deny *locus standi* to non-demise charterers or cargo-owners and if public policy generally favours their claim, then, subject to the point that a perceived extension of the law may be unnecessary—since provision for salvage may be made in the charterparty[58]—there is a case for admitting such claims in appropriate circumstances.   **463**

As indicated by Dr Lushington,[59] there are two situations in which it has been accepted that a charterer may claim salvage: where the charter is by way of demise, and where the contract so provides.

Demise charterparties

It has been stated previously in this book[60] that, if the salving ship is at the time under charter, the charterer, not the owner, is entitled to claim salvage if   **464**

---

[55] (1820) 2 Dods. 433.
[56] See *ante*, § 459.
[57] *Supra*, n. 49. *cf.* also *The Queen Elizabeth* (1949) 82 Ll.L.Rep. 803, 814.
[58] See, *e.g.* Baltime, cl. 19; N.Y.P.E. 1993, cl. 24.
[59] *Ante*, § 459.
[60] See 4th ed., p. 124 and, especially, p. 149.

Entitlement to Claim

the charterparty amounts to a demise of the ship—*locatio navis*—so that he is *pro hac vice* owner. Most of the authorities previously cited for the proposition in this book dealt with the familiar situation of the demise charterer's taking the usual place of the owner for various purposes, but they were not directly concerned with salvage.[61] It does not appear to have been necessary to determine the point except in two related cases, *Admiralty Commissioners v. Page*[62] and *Elliott Steam Tug Co. v. Admiralty Commissioners*,[63] the appeals from which—to the Court of Appeal and the House of Lords—were consolidated.

465   In *Page*, a tug named the *Conquerer* was requisitioned by the Admiralty under a time charterparty under which all salvage was to be for owners' benefit. The ship was to be deemed off-hire during the time occupied in salvage operations. The gross charterparty was superseded by a demise (net) charter under which the master and crew became servants of His Majesty, but nothing was said concerning salvage. It was held at first instance and in the Court of Appeal that the ship was a "ship belonging to His Majesty", thus entitling the Admiralty to claim salvage under the Merchant Shipping (Salvage) Act 1916, s.1.[64] Swinfen Eady M.R. in the Court of Appeal followed the Court of Appeal's approval in *The Sarpen*[65] of the intimation by Sir Robert Phillimore in *The Nile*[66] that a demise charterparty effects a temporary transfer of ownership, so that a ship demised to the Crown would become a "ship belonging to Her Majesty". The point was not considered in the House of Lords, which decided the case on the broader ground that a charterparty by demise operates to transfer the right to salvage. The result was that the Admiralty was granted a declaration, against the defendant owners, that it was entitled to the remuneration earned by salvage services rendered by the tug. According to Bailhache J.[67]:

> "Under the earlier form of charterparty the owners of the *Conqueror* had the right to salve vessels in distress and to receive any salvage award that might be made for those services; time lost during the salvage operations was of course for their account. The form of charterparty by demise says nothing about salvage operations. *The legal effect, however, of a charterparty by way of demise is that if salvage services are rendered by a vessel under such a charterparty and an award is made in respect of those services, the money goes, not to the owners, but to the charterers of the*

---

[61] See *Fenton v. City of Dublin Steam Packet Co.* (1838) 8 A. & E. 835; *Colvin v. Newberry* (1830) 7 Bing. 90, affirmed (1832) 1 Cl. & F. 283; *Schuster v. M'Kellar* (1857) 7 E. & B. 704; *Omoa and Cleland Coal and Iron Co. v. Huntley* (1877) 2 C.P.D. 464. See further Carver, §§ 582–588; Scrutton, Chap. 4.

[62] [1918] 2 K.B. 447; affirmed [1919] 1 K.B. 299, CA; affirmed [1921] 1 A.C. 137, HL.

[63] Unreported at first instance; affirmed [1919] 1 K.B. 299 (CA); affirmed [1921] 1 A.C. 137.

[64] See *post*, §663.

[65] [1916] P. 306.

[66] (1875) L.R. 4 A. & E. 449.

[67] [1918] 2 K.B. 447, 451–452.

Possession or ownership of salving property

vessel.[68] The fact that it was not present to the minds of the owners that by the alteration of the basis of hire of the vessel from a gross to a net basis they would be losing the right to an award for salvage services does not seem to me to make any difference. The legal effect of the change was to transfer the right to any salvage award from the owners to the Admiralty, who were holding the tug on demise."

The italicised passage was assented to as a proper statement of the law by Hill J. at first instance in *Elliott's* case, of which the facts were similar.[69]

Several reasons may be gleaned for the decision in *Page* and *Elliott*. In one respect, it can be explained on the particular facts of the case and the statute in question. The main point at issue, from which the decision flowed, was whether the salving ship came within the definition of "a ship belonging to His Majesty" within the Merchant Shipping (Salvage) Act 1916, s.1. The phrase has clearly been interpreted to cover ships both owned by and demised to the Crown,[70] but its wording is arguably more supportive of a claim for salvage services rendered by a ship, which would otherwise go unrewarded, than in the case where a putative salvor simply claims *qua* demise charterer. Nonetheless, the case must be taken to establish that, *vis-à-vis* the true owner, the Admiralty is entitled to claim salvage in respect of a ship demised to them.

466

The principal reason for the decision in *Page* and *Elliott* was simply a statement, without reasons or authority, of the conclusion, as appears from the above, italicised sentence in Bailhache J.'s judgment. It was assumed to be the accepted rule that, where a vessel is demised, the demise charterer automatically acquires salvage rights arising from use of the vessel. Thus, Lord Birkenhead L.C. felt able to say[71]:

467

"[the owners] are informed that a change is made in the arrangement between themselves and the Admiralty of such a character as to render it highly irrational and unusual that they should thereafter attempt to establish any claim for salvage."

---

[68] Emphasis added. In the House of Lords [1921] 1 A.C. 137, 145, Lord Shaw of Dunfermline quoted this sentence as follows:
 "The legal effect of a Charter Party which is by way of demise is that if salvage services are rendered by a vessel under such a Charter Party and an award is made for such services, the money when an award is made for such services goes not to the owners but to the charterers, who have the vessel upon time charter."
It is clear from a later passage in the judgment of Bailhache J. that the type of time charterparty to which he was referring was a "time charter... by way of demise." See [1918] 2 K.B. 447, 452.
[69] See [1921] 1 A.C. 137, 145.
[70] See *post*, §§ 668–676.
[71] [1921] 1 A.C. 137, 141.

Entitlement to Claim

468 This central proposition was, however, bolstered by reference to the normal circumstance, that under a demise charter the master and crew are normally servants not of the owner but of the charterer. As Viscount Finlay said[72]:

> "The effect was that the crew were no longer in the service of the owner; it therefore became quite impossible that salvage services should be rendered on behalf of the owner so that the owner would be entitled to receive payment for such salvage services. . . .
>
> The truth is that when the change was made and the parties agreed to the change, the owners of the tugs, and I daresay the Admiralty, never thought about its effect on salvage; but the change was made, and *the only question now is*, in the absence of any extraordinary agreement such as that suggested to vary the rights of the parties, *what in law is the effect of the transference of the crews from the service of the owners of the tugs to the service of the Crown?*"

Similarly, Lord Shaw of Dunfermline said[73]:

> "a demise to the Crown takes place; the servants become the servants of the Crown; salvage is rendered by the Crown through its servants and not through the servants of the owners."

469 In the light of what has been said above,[74] it would be misconceived to interpret these dicta as signifying that it is the transfer of the services of the master and crew *per se* which effects a transfer of salvage rights, for even the owner's claim in normal circumstances is not parasitic on his servants' contribution to salvage. The crew's acting under the directions of the demise charterer is relevant because it is by this means that he is enabled to control the disposition of the vessel, and it is the vessel which is the instrument by which the salvage reward under discussion is earned. That, of course, does not necessarily mean that it must be the demise charterer who should receive salvage, for he will nonetheless be controlling the disposition of someone else's vessel—indeed, it does not inevitably follow from the fact of demise that the charterer will assume all the liabilities of the owner *vis-à-vis* third parties.[75] The owner foregoes the freedom to utilise the vessel's services for other purposes but, in the absence of an express obligation on the charterer to indemnify him for loss, does he necessarily risk the vessel itself?

470 The dicta in *Page* and *Elliott* indicate that there are two other features of the common demise charterparty which justify a transfer of salvage rights. The first, which was stressed in the Court of Appeal, was that the Admiralty

---

[72] *ibid.*, 143–144 (emphasis added).
[73] *ibid.*, 145.
[74] *Ante*, §457.
[75] See *Manchester Trust v. Furness, Withy & Co.* [1895] 2 Q.B. 539.

acquired the right to claim salvage because it acquired the liabilities of the owner. As Duke L.J. put it[76]:

> "The effect of the transactions in this case on the part of the Crown has been to vest the vessel, at any rate for the period when the vesting and divesting occurred, absolutely and indisputably in the Crown as a King's ship, with a King's officer in command, a King's crew in charge, the whole of the expenses being at the public charge through the Admiralty, and the whole of the risk at the cost of the public."

The duty to assume the burdens of ownership was deemed to be accompanied by a correlative right to take on the benefits of it.

The second feature finds expression in the speech of Lord Birkenhead L.C. in the House of Lords[77]:

> "the latter [demise charterparty] agreement by its substance destroyed those circumstances in the earlier [time charterparty] contract which, and which alone, rendered either usual or proper the payment of salvage to the appellants [the owners]. Under these circumstances, and in the absence of any stipulation to the contrary, it must be assumed that the right of salvage on behalf of the owners disappeared when the earlier agreement was modified. It was, in other words, for the appellants who acquiesced in a charter by demise to make an express reservation or stipulation if they wished to exclude from such a charter the legal effect which it normally produces."

This dictum could be construed in two ways. On the one hand, it could be said that a reason for the decision in *Page* and *Elliott* was that the parties had, by making no express provision for the owner to have salvage where he had had it under the original charter, impliedly decided that the demise charterer should receive it in the case in hand—so that the case did not necessarily lay down a general rule for subsequent cases. But this construction is expressly rejected. Viscount Finlay put it bluntly[78]:

> "the question is what in law is the result of that change; and it is utterly immaterial that it never occurred to the owners to think of that change in its effect on salvage if salvage should be earned."

It seems quite clear, therefore, that it was the alternative meaning that was intended: that the normal rule was assumed to be that a charterparty by demise automatically carries with it the right to salvage but that the parties can contract otherwise[79] (as, of course, they could do if the normal effect were not

---
[76] [1919] 1 K.B. 299, 306.
[77] [1921] 1 A.C. 137, 142.
[78] *ibid.*, 143.
[79] See also *ibid.*, 144, *per* Viscount Finlay.

Entitlement to Claim

to transfer the right to salvage). The force of this intimation is weakened by the fact that the received view is that, in general, a charterer is not entitled to recover salvage, yet Lord Birkenhead stated that it was the circumstances in the original time charterparty "which, *and which alone*, rendered either usual or proper the payment of salvage to the [owner]."[80] He may simply have meant that it was not unusual for the owner to be entitled to salvage under a time charterparty. But, assuming the perceived general rule, denying salvage to charterers for the service of the ship, to be correct,[81] then, if the House of Lords regarded the demise charterparty rule as part of a general rule entitling all types of charterer to salvage, its decision was, with respect, clearly misconceived.[82]

473 In the final result, then, subject to contrary provision, demise charterers appear to be entitled to salvage because it has been and is assumed that this is the case. Demise charterparties are commonly regarded as putting the charterer in the position of the owner for the duration of the charterparty, so that he automatically assumes both the liabilities and rights of the owner. In fact, of course, there is merely a transfer of possession and what really provides the charterer with the right to salvage is the power given to him (additionally to the rights he would normally have under the employment and indemnity clause in a time charterparty) to order the ship to provide salvage services and to bear the risk of any loss to the vessel—for which he must indemnify the owner—during salvage. He has the right to decide on the employment of the ship, so he is able to contribute its services, and it is he who bears the risk.

474 It is for those reasons, and not simply because he acquires the appearance of ownership, that the demise charterer can claim salvage. The owner foregoes the services of and risk to the vessel during the demise and can be said to contribute nothing to salvage. Mere ownership is not enough. A person who lends towing equipment to another, on terms that the other will either return the equipment as provided or indemnify him for any loss, cannot claim a salvage reward merely because the other effects salvage with the use of his equipment.

Entitlement to salvage as between owner and charterer seems, therefore, to be well settled. The general rule might have been the reverse of what it is. But, since the general rule, whatever it may be, is always open to qualification by the terms agreed for the charterparty in question, it may be thought to be largely irrelevant what the general rule is, provided that there is a clear rule with which to begin.[83]

475 The fact that the owner may not be able to maintain his right to salvage as against the demise charterer does not necessarily mean, however, that he has

---

[80] *Supra*, text to n. 77 (emphasis added).
[81] *cf. ante*, §463.
[82] See *ante*, §458.
[83] *cf. Aries Tanker Corp. v. Total Transport Ltd* (*The Aries*) [1977] 1 W.L.R. 185, 190, *per* Lord Wilberforce.

no claim against the person whose property has been salved. If the latter were ignorant of the charterparty, then, although the demise charterer could intervene as undisclosed principal, the master would have ostensible authority to act on behalf of the owner, who could, therefore, claim as principal for the defendant, albeit he might be obliged, *vis-à-vis* the demise charterer, to transfer the reward to him. This may *a fortiori* be the case where the defendant knows of the demise charterparty but the demise charterer puts up no claim to salvage.[84]

476 Furthermore, the following argument may be put. There are normally two elements of the salvage services which a shipowner provides: the vessel itself and the use of that vessel. Where the vessel is chartered by demise, the owner obtains the benefit of the vessel's usefulness by receiving hire from the charterer; the right to the vessel's use is clearly transferred to the charterer, so he must be the one who contributes that part of the salvage service. It does not necessarily follow that the owner should go unremunerated by the owner of salved property in respect of any loss to the salving vessel. In principle, the owner should be entitled to recover for this directly, albeit any benefit received must be applied in reduction of the indemnity payable to him by the charterer according to the terms of the charterparty. In practice, it will be claimed by the charterer and it will no doubt be the charterer, and not the owner, who will be entitled to the additional element of reward due. But the owner should not go uncompensated in a case where the demise charterer fails to indemnify him, unless the charterer has already received that element of the award from the owner of the salved property. The defendant should not have to pay twice. But he should not be unjustly enriched. Indeed, Swinfen Eady M.R. in the Court of Appeal in *Page* and *Elliott*[85] thought it legitimate for owners to claim salvage in respect of tugs demised to the Admiralty at the time when the latter provided salvage services but were not entitled to claim a reward for them.

477 The view put forward is supported by the decision in *The Meandros*.[86] Salvage services were rendered to the Greek defendants' ship during requisition by the Greek Government, which therefore "were in possession of and had an interest in the ship",[87] but not its owners. No maritime lien and therefore no enforceable salvage claim were available against the Greek Government.[88] But on derequisition, a salvage action *in rem* was commenced. The owners pleaded *inter alia* that they derived no benefit from the services since, by the terms of the requisition, the vessel had to be delivered up to them in the same condition as when requisitioned, and that they were thus not liable for salvage. Pointing out that the defendants were never dispossessed of property in the vessel, Sir Henry Duke P. held them liable on the basis that they benefited from the return of their vessel rather than having merely a claim

---

[84] See Swinfen Eady M.R. in the Court of Appeal in *Page* [1919] 1 K.B. 299, 305.
[85] *ibid.*, 305.
[86] [1925] P. 61.
[87] *ibid.*, 68.
[88] See *post*, Chap. 13.

against the Greek Government. His Lordship did not attempt to lay down that the salvor's lien was existent but inchoate during the Greek Government's possession, becoming choate on derequisition, a proposition which would have contradicted then recent authorities.[89] The success of the salvor's claim therefore means that the salvor had a maritime lien against the owners (albeit not enforceable during the Greek Government's possession) in respect of the owners' separate interest in the vessel.[90]

478 *Mutatis mutandis,* it should be recognised that the owners of a demised chartered vessel have during the period of the charterparty an interest in respect of which they should be entitled to claim salvage. The possible practical difficulty of apportioning the reward between the owners and the charterers should not preclude the owners' claim, particularly if none were made by the charterer and given that the parties to the charterparty are able specifically to provide in the contract for salvage claims.

Contractual provision for salvage

479 A right to receive all or part of a salvage award may be transferred by contract.

A charterparty may either provide that the risk of using the chartered vessel for salvage and the reward for a salvage operation should be for the charterer's account or stipulate that the owner of the vessel be obliged to pay over to the charterer all or part of the reward which he, the shipowner, recovers directly from the owner of salved property. Similarly, by virtue of a contract of insurance, in *The Pickwick*[91] Dr Lushington held that underwriters who had chartered a steamer to search for and bring to safety a derelict of which they were part insurers were entitled to claim salvage.

480 In *George Booker & Co. v. Pocklington Steamship Co. Ltd.*,[92] a consecutive voyage charterparty of the steamship *Pocklington* gave the shipowners liberty to effect salvage operations. Clause 20 provided that "All derelicts and salvage shall be for owners' and charterers' equal benefit." An off-hire clause provided that, if any damage prevented the working of the vessel for more than 24 hours, hire should cease. After salvaging another steamship, the *Pocklington* had to put into dock for repairs. In an action by the charterers to recover a moiety of the salvage awarded to the owners, Bigham J. held that the latter were entitled to deduct from the amount of the award all such losses and expenses incurred by them (including loss of hire) as were attributable to the salvage services, and that the balance only ought to be divided between the owners and the charterers. He based his decision on a construction of the charterparty, in particular of clause 20:

---

[89] *The Tervaete* [1922] P. 259; *The Sylvan Arrow* [1923] P. 220.
[90] See also Thomas, *Maritime Liens,* §§ 127–128.
[91] (1852) 16 Jur. 669. The case is explained and distinguished on the ground stated in the text in *Crouan v. Stanier* [1904] 1 K.B. 87. See *post,* § 510.
[92] [1899] 2 Q.B. 690.

Possession or ownership of salving property

" 'Equal benefit' cannot be accorded to shipowner and charterer without taking into account what each has contributed towards securing the benefit. Salvage in this case does not mean the amount recovered in the suit in the Admiralty Court. It means the net pecuniary result of the salvage operations. Therefore, it follows that from the sum awarded by the Admiralty Court all the losses mentioned . . . must be deducted by the shipowner, and the balance only divided . . . It is the salvage operations which have caused the damage and the loss of hire, and the Admiralty Court, though not awarding to the ship a specific sum in respect thereof, has taken both heads of loss into consideration in fixing the amount payable by the salved vessel. In other words, if there had been no loss of hire and no damage to the vessel the award would have been proportionately less, and the charterers would have got what they get now, neither more nor less."[93]

The decision in *Admiralty Commissioners v. Page*,[94] which established the demise charterer's right to recover from the owner salvage awarded to him, is consistent with the reasoning in the *Pocklington* case.

481 In previous editions of this book,[95] the general rule in respect of a charterparty's transfer of the fruits of salvage from one of the parties to the other was expressed as follows: "If the salving ship is at the time under charter, the charterer, not the owner, is entitled to claim salvage . . . if by the express terms of the charterparty he becomes, in reference to salvage, *pro hac vice* owner." This is certainly true to the extent that the terms of the charterparty may effect a transfer to the charterer of the benefits of salvage operations which would normally accrue to the owner of the salving vessel. It is also true to the extent that it restates the received view that, where a ship is chartered by demise, it is normally the demise charterer, rather than the owner, who is entitled to salvage. But it is submitted that the sentence is misleading if it is attempted to suggest that the charterer must be made owner *pro hac vice*, in the sense that a demise charterer is, in order to sustain a claim to salvage reward *vis-à-vis* the owner, for that would be to deny the effect of the *Pocklington* case.[96]

482 The position may be otherwise where the charterer is seeking to enforce the right to salvage, given to him by the charterparty, directly against the owner of salved property. If the shipowner expressly and effectively assigns to a charterer his right to salvage earned or (more significantly) to be earned, the charterer may simply enforce against the owner of salved property his rights to the debt/obligation owed, as assignee of an existing or future debt. This is in effect what the normal demise charterparty achieves by implication. In the usual absence of such an implication, it then becomes necessary as a matter of practice for the charterer to claim as owner *pro hac vice*, for it will only be in

---
[93] *ibid.*, 694.
[94] [1921] 1 A.C. 137; *ante*, §465.
[95] See 4th ed., p. 149.
[96] *Supra*, n. 92.

229

such a case that he will be likely to be able to demonstrate the transfer to him of a right to claim salvage.

483 These points arise from a number of cases in which the same party was simultaneously owner of either the salving or salved vessel, and charterer of the other vessel. It was held by Dr Lushington in *The Maria Jane*[97] that the owner of the salving vessels in that case could not claim against the owner of a salved vessel chartered to him by demise at the time of the operations (albeit partly because the main object of the operations was to salve cargo of his aboard the salved vessel). He subsequently distinguished this decision in *The Collier*[98] and held that a salvor could claim from the owner of a salved vessel time chartered to him. His reason was that the elements of possession and control were missing from the latter charterparty. The charter did in fact expressly provide "that all derelicts and salvages should be for owners' and charterers' benefit, in moieties to each, after settling with the crew" so, unless there were a rule of law overriding the terms of the charterparty, then, provided the circumstances occurring could be regarded as governed by the terms of the charterparty, the matter was really governed by the contract anyway.

The underlying points appear neatly in *The Scout*.[99] A Mr Churchward chartered two vessels, the *Prince Frederick William* as *pro hac vice* owner and the *Scout*, it was presumed, on no special terms. Churchward and the owners, master and crew of the former vessel claimed for services rendered to the *Scout*. It was held that all except the owners were entitled to succeed.

484 In modern times, express provision in the charterparty makes it unnecessary to consider as a matter of principle, at least as between charterer and owner, whether it is the demise or time charterer or the shipowner who is entitled to receive salvage. Charterparties commonly provide how the cost of salvage is to be allocated and that in the case of a demise charter the charterer is entitled to salvage,[1] while in the case of a time charter the salvage is to be shared equally.[2]

---

[97] (1850) 14 Jur. 857.
[98] (1866) L.R. 1 A. & E. 83; following *The Waterloo* (1820) 2 Dods. 433.
[99] (1872) L.R. 3 A. & E. 512.
[1] The standard demise charter, Barecon 89, cl. 17, provides that "All salvage and towage shall be for the Charterers' benefit and the cost of repairing damage occasioned thereby shall be borne by the charterers."
[2] The New York Produce Exchange (NYPE) (1946) form, cl. 19 provides "That all derelicts and salvage shall be for Owners' and Charterers' equal benefit after deducting Owners' and Charterers' expenses and Crew's proportion . . . ". NYPE 93, cl. 24 states the same (the other matters included in the remainder of the NYPE (1946) form being dealt with in separate clauses. Baltime, cl. 19 provides that:

> "All salvage and assistance to other vessels to be for the Owners' and Charterers' equal benefit after deducting the Master's and Crew's proportion and all legal and other expenses including hire paid under the charter for time lost in the salvage, also repairs of damage and coal or oil-fuel consumed. The Charters to be bound by all measures taken by the Owners in order to secure payment of salvage and to fix its amount."

3. INTEREST IN SALVED PROPERTY

Salvor's relationship to salved property

The person rendering salvage services may be debarred from claiming **485**
salvage in respect of services rendered to the property in danger, by reason of
his legal relation to that property. The court will first determine whether a
salvage service has been rendered, prima facie entitling the salvor to a reward,
and then go on to decide whether there are circumstances rendering it impossible for him to recover.[3]

At common law, the owner or demise charterer of the salving ship is
generally disentitled from claiming from a salved vessel of which he is also
owner or demise charterer. But he may be able to claim against the cargo on
board it. And his crew will generally be able to claim against both such a
salved ship and its cargo, provided that, as must usually be the case, they
render services outside those required of them by their contracts and are not
paid for the services by their ordinary wages.[4] In *The Sava Star*[5] Clarke J.
summarised and approved[6] the rules laid down by the Admiralty Court,
stating that,

> "the following propositions have been accepted by both practitioners and
> judges over a very long period. (1) A shipowner is not entitled to claim
> salvage against himself. (2) Where ship and cargo are salved by a vessel
> in the same ownership as the salved ship, the master and crew of the
> salving ship are entitled to salvage against the owners of the salved ship
> and the owners of her cargo. (3) In such a case the shipowners are
> entitled to salvage against the owners of the cargo on the salved ship
> unless the casualty which necessitated the salvage services was wholly
> caused by an actionable breach of contract on the part of the plaintiffs, in
> which case (subject to the possible effect of limitation of liability) the
> claim falls for circuity of action. (4) Subject to (1) above, the fact that the
> salving and the salved ships are in common ownership or common
> management is relevant to the quantum of the salvage award."

However, these principles have been altered by the Salvage Convention **486**
1989, Art. 12.3. As will be seen,[7] the Convention now permits claims for
sister ship salvage, at least in certain circumstances, and may permit claims
where a shipowner renders services to his own ship without employing the
services of a sister ship.

---

[3] *The Miranda* (1866) L.R. 3 A. & E. 561, 566–7.
[4] See *post*, §§ 565–587.
[5] [1995] 2 Lloyd's Rep. 134, 139.
[6] As having been accepted as correct by the leading texts (*Kennedy's Law of Salvage* (5th ed., 1985), §§ 399, 408, 411; Brice, *The Maritime Law of Salvage* (2nd ed., 1993), §§ 1–234 to 1–236) and correctly based on sound principles. See *The Sava Star* [1995] 2 Lloyd's Rep. 134, 139–141.
[7] *Post*, §§ 504–509.

The salved cargo

487   If the owner of the salving ship is also the owner, or the owner *pro hac vice*, of the salved vessel, he may be precluded from claiming a salvage reward for salvage of cargo on board the salved vessel by reason of his legal obligations, as bailee and carrier, towards the owners of that cargo.

Whether he is so precluded or not depends in each case on whether, if the salvage service had not taken place, he would have been responsible in damages to the owners of the cargo for the loss or injury to it which was averted by that salvage service. In other words, did the salvage service become necessary owing to that which, if loss or damage had resulted from it, would have constituted a breach of duty or contract on the part of the bailee and carrier of the cargo, for which the latter would have been liable to the cargo-owner?

488   The owner of the salving ship who would, but for the salvage services, have been liable for breach of his duty as bailee or carrier to the owner of the salved cargo cannot claim salvage reward in respect of salvage services he has rendered to that cargo. In *The Glenfruin*,[8] cargo was shipped on board the *Glenfruin* under bills of lading which contained exception clauses but which did not include an exception in regard to the shipowners' implied warranty of seaworthiness. The vessel broke down at sea due to a latent defect in the crank-shaft. She was towed into safety by the *Glenavon*, of which all the owners except one, William Houston, were owners of the *Glenfruin*. The defendants, owners of cargo on board the *Glenfruin*, were held liable to pay salvage to William Houston, the masters and crew of the Glenavon but not to the other owners of the *Glenavon*, for salvage had been necessitated by their breach of their implied warranty of seaworthiness to the defendants, which warranty was not excused by the exception clauses in the bill of lading. Furthermore, they were held liable, on the counterclaim of the defendants against them, to pay to the defendants the amount of salvage which had been awarded against the defendants to the successful plaintiffs.

Butt J. based his refusal of salvage on this ground, to avoid the circuity of action which would be caused by the cargo-owner's immediately recovering back the salvage reward from the carrier-salvor as damages, whether by way of counterclaim, cross-action or set-off.[9]

489   It has further been suggested that denial of salvage can be justified as an application of the principle that no man can profit by his own wrong—that no man can earn a salvage reward by services to the life or to the property which his own wrongdoing or the wrongdoing of his servants has placed in jeopardy.[10]

---

[8] (1885) 10 P.D. 103.

[9] *ibid.*, 109. *cf. The Beaverford v. The Kafiristan* [1938] A.C. 136; *The Susan v. Luckenbach* [1951] P. 197. For the differences between counterclaim, cross-action and set-off, see Rose [1981] L.M.C.L.Q. 33.

[10] *cf. The Miranda* (1872) L.R. 3 A. & E. 561, 565; *post*, §490.

The salved cargo

If the owner of the salving ship would not be held responsible as bailee or **490** carrier of the cargo in the salved vessel for the loss or damage which would have befallen that cargo but for the salvage service, then his claim to reward as a salvor against the cargo of the salved vessel is a valid claim.[11] Thus, a cargo-owner who fails to discharge his burden of proving the shipowner's liability will be bound to pay him a salvage reward. In *The Miranda*,[12] salvage was necessitated by the breakdown at sea of machinery of a steamship carrying a cargo under bills of lading excepting liability for accidents or damage from machinery. The clause was held to apply to the circumstances of the case, so the cargo-owners had to pay for salvage by another of the carrier's ships. But Sir Robert Phillimore also said that the defendants had the burden of proving breach of the alleged implied warranty of seaworthiness and, having failed to adduce sufficient evidence that the carrying vessel was unseaworthy at the time the cargo was shipped, could not avoid liability on that ground. The salvor's claim in such a case will be upheld even if it is clearly a fault of himself or his servants which has necessitated the salvage and he only escapes responsibility for it by the special terms of the bill of lading.[13]

However, where a shipowner renders assistance to the whole adventure **491** comprised in another of his vessels and the cargo on board it, he can be said to be to some extent working in his own interest in order to maintain his trade and to keep his ship going in its regular employment, earning freight. The court is reluctant to make a large award against the cargo in such a case unless the services are very substantial.[14] However, it is, it seems, confirmed by the Salvage Convention 1989, Art. 12.3 that the salvor's claim cannot be rejected simply because he owns both the salving ship and the vessel upon which the salved cargo is being carried.[15]

It was held in *The Sava Star*[16] that in appropriate circumstances a cargo-owner could claim salvage from the owners of the carrying ship. Clarke J. said[17]:

> "I can see no logical reason why, if a shipowner is entitled to claim salvage against the owner of cargo carried in his ship, a cargo-owner should not be entitled to claim salvage against the owner of the ship carrying his cargo. That can be tested by a simple example. Suppose that a ship and her cargo were salved by two tugs, one owned by the

---

[11] *The Miranda* (1872) L.R. 3 A. & E. 561; *The Cargo ex Laertes* (1887) 12 P.D. 187; *The August Korff* [1903] P. 166; *The Theseus* (1925) 23 Ll.L.Rep. 136; *The Laomedon, ibid.*, 230; *The Sava Star* [1995] 2 Lloyd's Rep. 134.

[12] (1872) L.R. 3 A. & E. 561.

[13] *The Cargo ex Laertes* (1887) 12 P.D. 187 (breakdown at sea of carrying vessel caused by latent defect for which carrier would have been liable had not bills of lading reduced his duty to provide a seaworthy ship to a limited warranty to take reasonable care to do so).

[14] *The Miranda* (1872) L.R. 3 A. & E. 561, 567; *The Cargo ex Laertes* (1887) 12 P.D. 187, 191; *The August Korff* [1903] P. 166, 173; *The Theseus* (1925) 23 Ll.L.Rep. 136, 137.

[15] See *post*, §§ 504–509.

[16] [1995] 2 Lloyd's Rep. 134. See further *post*, § 637.

[17] [1995] 2 Lloyd's Rep. 134, 141.

shipowner and the other owned by her cargo-owner. It would make no sense to hold that the cargo-owner was liable to pay salvage to the shipowner as owner of one tug but that the shipowner was not liable to pay salvage to the cargo-owner as the owner of the other tug."

Salving crew

492 As is shewn below, the claimant of a salvage award must generally be classifiable as a volunteer; therefore, a member of the crew of a salved vessel can only claim salvage if his rendering of a salvage service goes beyond performance of his normal duties.[18] Since the duties of a member of the crew of a ship are essentially owed to the owners of his own ship and, indirectly, to the owners of the cargo carried by it, it follows that he remains a volunteer in relation to all other property, and so entitled to claim salvage for assisting in rescue of such other property from danger. "Where salvage services have been rendered by one ship to another in distress, the master and crew of the salving vessel have a claim to salvage independently of the owners."[19] This is so even though the salved property is another vessel owned by or chartered by demise to his owners or is cargo carried on board such a vessel. An inability on the part of the owner of the salving ship to recover salvage for himself, arising from his relation to the salved ship or to the salved cargo, does not *per se* affect the rights of the crew of his ship: they are held to be entitled to salvage reward for their services even though the owner of the ship is not.

493 It was pointed out in *The Sappho*[20] that the services for which the seaman claims in such a case may not strictly be described as services which he is bound to perform. True, the seaman may be subject to the moral obligation to assist ships in distress.[21] And it may be that, as an ordinary incident of a voyage, if a ship meets another vessel in distress and the master orders seamen of his ship to give assistance, they are to a certain extent bound to give assistance. Indeed, the master and crew of the salving ship may well get their chance of a salvage claim because the ships are in common ownership. But that assistance is not strictly speaking within the ordinary contract which a seaman enters, which says nothing about rendering services to another vessel.[22] The seaman is, therefore, just as entitled to the ordinary consequence of rendering extraordinary services to the other vessel where that vessel turns out to belong to his owner as where it belongs to a third party.[23] However, just as

---

[18] See *post*, Chap. 7.

[19] *Nicholson v. Leith Salvage and Towage Co.* 1923 S.C. 409, 419. *cf. The Sava Star* [1995] 2 Lloyd's Rep. 134, 141.

[20] (1871) L.R. 3 P.C. 690, 694.

[21] See *post*, § 522.

[22] Of course, *pace* their Lordships, such assistance is impliedly within the seaman's contract if he is not entitled to resist an order by his master to participate in salvage.

[23] *The Sappho* (1871) L.R. 3 P.C. 690; *The Miranda* (1872) L.R. 3 A. & E. 561, 566; *The Agamemnon* (1883) 5 Asp. M.L.C. 92; *The August Korff* [1903] P. 166, 176; *The Troilus* (1949) 82 Ll.L.Rep. 681, 684 (affirmed [1950] P. 82; [1951] A.C. 820). Note also, the master of a vessel in distress being assisted by another ship acts quite properly in telling a ship of his owners which comes up not to intervene but to stand by: *The August Korff* [1903] P. 166, 176.

the master and crew of a salving ship may reap the benefit of earning salvage from another vessel in common ownership with theirs, so must they bear the burden of that circumstance, and they cannot recover in the capacity of a salvor who against his will is prevented from completing services which he has undertaken and is able and ready to perform, if the owners choose in their own interests to ask them to desist from the service in favour of another vessel.[24]

A seaman is similarly entitled to claim salvage for services rendered to a vessel chartered to the same charterer as has chartered his own ship, whether or not either or each charter is by way of demise.[25]

Even if seamen aboard the salving ship were regarded as owing a pre-existing duty to assist another vessel of the same owner, they would not necessarily be regarded as disentitled from claiming for salvage of cargo coming into jeopardy through the fault of the shipowner as bailee or carrier. In fact, since they can usually claim for salvage of their owner's other vessel, *a fortiori* can they do so against cargo carried aboard her. Admission of the title of the master and crew of the salving ship to salvage reward for assistance rendered to cargo on board another vessel in the same ownership as the former is invariably treated as being so obvious as to be a matter of course.[26]

The court, however, does not favour such claims of seamen unless the extra-contractual service which they have rendered is of a substantial nature. In *The Agamemnon*,[27] a disabled steamship was towed a short distance by another steamship belonging to the same owners. Fifteen of the crew of the towing vessel instituted a salvage action in the sum of £5,000 against the vessel towed and arrested the vessel, cargo and freight therein. Butt J. reluctantly conceded that he was bound by authority[28] to acknowledge the crew's title to claim but noted that they received pay during performance of the services, which were slight, and had not incurred hardship in rendering them. Expressing disapprobation of the institution of the action and castigating the arrest of the vessel for the amount claimed as an attempt to obtain money by compulsion, he awarded only £1 a head to each of the claimants (a total of £15 on a salved value of £105,500) and ordered them to pay all the costs of the action.[29]

---

[24] *The Theseus* (1925) 23 Ll.L.Rep. 230.
[25] *The Collier* (1866) L.R. 1 A. & E. 83; *The Scout* (1872) L.R. 3 A. & E. 512, 515.
[26] See *The Sappho* (1871) L.R. 3 P.C. 690 (distinguishing *The Maria Jane* (1850) 14 Jur. 857); *The Miranda* (1872) L.R. 3 A. & E. 561, 566; *The Glenfruin* (1885) 10 P.D. 103, 109; *The August Korff* [1903] P. 166, 176; *The Theseus* (1925) 23 Ll.L.Rep. 136, 137; *The Troilus* (1949) 82 Ll.L.Rep. 681, 684 (affirmed [1950] P. 92; [1951] A.C. 820).
[27] (1883) 5 Asp. M.L.C. 92.
[28] *The Sappho* (1871) L.R. 3 P.C. 690.
[29] *cf. The August Korff* [1903] P. 166.

The salved ship

(i) Generally

496   If the owner of the salving ship and the salved vessel be one and the same person, the general rule at common law has been understood to be that there can be no salvage claim on his account against the salved ship herself, for the claim in such a case would be a claim against himself in relation to his own property.[30] It makes no difference that another ship would have rendered the service if another of the owner's own ships had not done so.[31] The public policy of encouraging salvage may be thought to be inapposite in the case of a salvor salving his own property, for self-interest might appear to be inducement enough.[32] Indeed, even apparently deserved reimbursement of losses suffered by the salvor might be considered a pointless exercise in transferring money from one pocket to another. Moreover, it is not clear as a matter of general principle that a prima facie right of the salvor to claim would enable him to obtain the benefit of insurance monies due.[33] The Marine Insurance Act 1906, s.65(1) provides that:

> "Subject to any express provision in the policy, salvage charges incurred in preventing a loss by perils insured against may be recovered as a loss by those perils."

But section 65(2) provides that:

> "'Salvage charges' means the charges recoverable under maritime law by a salvor independently of contract. They do not include the expenses of services rendered by the assured or his agents, or any person employed for hire by them, for the purpose of averting a peril insured against. Such expenses where properly incurred, may be recovered as particular charges or as a general average loss according to the circumstances under which they were incurred."

497   Salvage services rendered by a salvor against his own property would not be regarded as recoverable from underwriters under section 65 because they are not charges "recoverable under maritime law by a salvor independently of contract", albeit that argument has an element of circularity because it states that the charges are not recoverable because they are not recoverable. Of course, in modern times, most salvage services are rendered under contract but contracted-for salvage is irrelevant here because, even if a person were entitled to wear two hats, as salvor and owner of salved property, that would

---

[30] This was accepted as being the case in *The Caroline* (1861) Lush. 334, where a person was part-owner of both ships; *The Miranda* (1872) L.R. 3 A. & E. 561; *The Telemachus* [1957] P. 47; *The Makedonia* [1958] 1 Q.B. 365; *The Sava Star* [1995] 2 Lloyd's Rep. 134.
[31] See *The Theseus* (1925) 23 Ll.L. Rep. 230, 234.
[32] But see *post*, § 557.
[33] See Arnould. *Law of Marine Insurance and Average* (16th ed, 1982), §§ 908–915.

not enable him to contract with himself. Thus, he could not claim for salvage under the sue and labour clause normally included in marine insurance contracts, even if salvage charges were not specifically excluded from the ambit of the clause.[34]

In the section of the Marine Insurance Act 1906 dealing with the suing and labouring clause, it is stated that:

> "It is the duty of the assured and his agents, in all cases, to take such measures as may be reasonable for the purpose of averting or minimising a loss."[35]

It is not clear to what extent the assured is under such a duty in the (unusual) absence of a sue and labour clause, or in situations not covered by the clause.[36] It is at least arguable that an assured should always be under such a duty and should be encouraged to fulfil it and to preserve the property in peril by the possibility of earning salvage, particularly as the insurer may be unable to prove failure to take steps to fulfil it. This is especially so if the practical value of the salved property to its owner is negligible (where it is subject to mortgages and/or liens), although it is difficult to see how the owner could be induced to salve by the possibility of protecting any claim to salvage by a lien over his own property, especially in competition with other interests.

In practice, the matter has been dealt with by contract. Marine insurance policies generally contain sister-ship clauses enabling a shipowner to claim salvage from his insurers.[37]

(ii) Demise charterparties

The owner of the salving ship is not entitled to claim salvage from the owner of a vessel of which possession and control has passed to him under a charterparty which amounts in law to a demise of that vessel.[38] Although the salvor is not the true owner of the salved vessel, he is regarded as being in the position of owner *pro hac vice*.[39] As Dr Lushington once commented[40]:

> "The argument against a claim for salvage is founded on the supposition that the salvor is claiming in substance for the salving of his own property, which, certainly, is against reason."

Similarly, a demise charterer cannot claim salvage for services rendered by the chartered ship to a vessel owned by himself.[41]

---

[34] Marine Insurance Act 1906, s.78.
[35] s.78(4).
[36] See F. D. Rose, "Failure to Sue and Labour" [1990] J.B.L. 190; "Aversion and Minimisation of Loss", Chap. 7 of D. R. Thomas (ed.), *The Modern Law of Marine Insurance* (1996).
[37] *e.g.*, Institute Time Clauses-Hulls, cl. 9. See also *post*, § 509.
[38] *The Maria Jane* (1850) 14 Jur. 857.
[39] See, *e.g.* Kennedy (4th ed.), p. 151.
[40] *The Collier* (1866) L.R. 1 A. & E. 83, 86.
[41] *The Maria Jane* (1850) 14 Jur. 857, 858.

500 On the other hand, if the owner of the salving ship be only the charterer of the salved vessel under a charterparty which is not a demise charterparty and does not divest the owner of that vessel of the possession and control of it or expressly gives the charterer the benefit of salvage, the owner of the salving ship is entitled to claim salvage from the owners of the salved vessel.[42]

Nor is it any answer to a salvage claim made by the owner of the salving ship, against the salved vessel, that the owner of the salved vessel was at the time of the service also the charterer of the salving ship under a charterparty other than a demise charterparty.[43] Lord Stowell gave the reason for this as being that:

> "the charter... leaves the property in the vessel exactly where it found it, and in all respects, where the engagements of the charter-party do not apply, as independent a property as that in any other vessel whatever. The commander, officers, and crew are all appointed by the owner; they cannot be transferred to a Company's ship at the pleasure of the Company, as the King's officers and crew are, at the pleasure of the Crown, to another of His Majesty's ships; it is merely by the voluntary act or contract of the owner that the voyage is undertaken, for the Company had no other right so to employ her."[44]

501 The circumstances of the salvage service in such a case may possibly give rise to claims on the part of the charterer against the salvor for delay and loss occasioned to the charterer by diversion of the vessel from the chartered voyage to the performance of salvage services—but this consideration does not affect the right of the salvor, as owner of the salving ship, to claim for himself salvage reward for the services rendered to the vessel owned by the charterer.[45]

502 Where there is more than one part-owner of the salving ship and one of them (or more) is an owner of the salved vessel, the other part-owners of the salving ship are entitled to claim salvage reward against the salved ship; and the court will compute the amount to be paid to them by, first, estimating the value of the service rendered, and then, deducting from the value of the whole service the share which would be due to the owner who has shares in both vessels.[46] The same principles apply *mutatis mutandis* where more than one person owns shares in both vessels, and whether such a person is in the position of owner or owner *pro hac vice* so far as either or both vessels are concerned.

---

[42] *The Collier* (1866) L.R. 1 A. & E. 83, following *The Waterloo, infra.*
[43] *The Waterloo* (1820) 2 Dods. 433; discussed in *The Alfen* (1857) Swab. 189, wherein it was indicated that the charterer of a salving ship other than by demise could not claim for services rendered to another vessel, whether or not the latter vessel was chartered by him.
[44] *The Waterloo* (1820) 2 Dods. 433, 434–435.
[45] *The Alfen* (1857) Swab. 189, 190 (quoted *ante*, § 459).
[46] *The Caroline* (1861) Lush. 334; *The Glenfruin* (1885) 10 P.D. 103, discussed *ante*, § 488.

Dr Lushington said in *The Collier*[47] that:

> "I am not prepared to say that there may not be such a connection between two ships which, though it would not bar a claim for salvage, might affect the quantum. I shall order the 12th article to be struck out, which denies that any salvage whatever was due; but not the first three articles,[48] which, though the facts therein detailed, if proved, would not bar a claim for salvage, might possibly affect the quantum. I think it right to be upon my guard, because, no doubt, the amount and quantum of a salvage service may be affected by particular circumstances, though the claim for salvage is not barred. I speak, for instance, where fishing vessels render assistance to each other, and matters of that description."

The owner of a vessel chartered to the salvor otherwise than by demise may not, therefore, have to pay as large a salvage reward as to an independent salvor. Similarly, where the salving ship is chartered other than by demise to the owner of the salved vessel.

(iii) The Salvage Convention 1989

Contrary to the English common law position, the desirability that there should be sister-ship salvage and that it should be rewarded became widely accepted in the international maritime community, was recognised by both shipowning and hull insurance interests by provision for it in the Institute Clauses[49] and found favour in both the Brussels Salvage Convention 1910 and the Salvage Convention 1989. The Brussels Convention 1910, Art. 5[50] stipulated that, "Remuneration is due notwithstanding that the salvage services have been rendered by or to vessels belonging to the same owner." The 1910 Convention was not enacted into English law[51] but the principle is now given effect, in amended form, by the Salvage Convention 1989, Art. 12.3, which provides:

> "This chapter shall apply, notwithstanding that the salved vessel and the vessel undertaking the salvage operations belong to the same owner."

The 1910 provision was expressed to apply generally, whereas the 1989 provision is expressed with reference to the chapter of the Convention in

---

[47] (1866) L.R. 1 A. & E. 83, 86.
[48] It was alleged in these articles that the salved vessel was time chartered to the owners of the salving ship and that the salving ship was signalled by those on board the vessel in distress, knowing that the salving ship belonged to the plaintiff company and believing that it would be in the best interest of the company for its ship to render the necessary assistance.
[49] See *ante*, § 498.
[50] Which was not enacted into English law.
[51] It was, however, implemented in U.S. law: see *Kimes v. United States* [1953] A.M.C. 1335 (US CA, 2nd Circuit), 1338, *per* Clark J.

which it appears (Chapter III: Rights of Salvors),[52] though nothing appears to turn on this apparent restriction. The effect of Article 12.3 is not clear.[53]

505 One possible interpretation is that it simply recognises the traditional English common law approach: that salvage rights and liabilities are first assessed as if the parties involved have independent interests—and so, for example, where the salvor owns both the salving and salved vessels, a claim against the owner of cargo on board the salved vessel is in principle assessed independently of the fact that sister-ship vessels are involved; but the tribunal may then proceed to disallow a claim by the salving vessel against the salved vessel if they are both in the same ownership,[54] the owner nevertheless having the right to contract with his insurer for an indemnity for sister-ship salvage. However, not only would such an interpretation render Article 12.3 largely ineffective; it would, without clearly doing so, reverse the general international practice of rewarding sister-ship salvage, in an international Convention intended to promote international uniformity.

506 A second interpretation therefore seems clearly correct. Its most obvious purpose is to formalise the commonly held international understanding that, where a person owns both the salving and salved vessels, he may claim salvage not only from the owner of a third interest benefiting from salvage service, but also from himself. As a matter of language, this seems clear; and there is nothing in the Article to imply that this may not be the case. A number of consequences follow.

507 First, though such an interpretation formalises the existing practice of insurers' indemnifying assured owners of sister ships, it should be noted that, if insurers wish not to be liable, they should not simply omit such an indemnity from the policy but must positively exclude it.

Secondly, whereas the common law limitation applies equally to shipowners and demise charterers, Article 12.3 only refers to owners, thereby possibly leaving the position of demise charterers unaltered. Given the long-established tradition of treating demise charterers as equivalent to owners for many purposes, Article 12.3 may therefore create an unwelcome distinction. It may, however, be overcome if Article 12.3 is construed on the principle that a reference to a shipowner may be treated as also applicable to a demise charterer unless there is clear contrary indication.

508 Thirdly, this interpretation of Article 12.3 may heighten the concern by cargo interests that a shipowner may be tempted to use another of his ships in order to be able to claim a salvage reward from them for services which he should be providing under the contract of carriage. However, the suggested interpretation of Article 12.3 merely removes the obstacle to awarding salvage to a shipowner that he has an interest in both the salving and salved vessels;

---

[52] Arts. 12–19.
[53] This was recognised in *The Sava Star* [1995] 2 Lloyd's Rep. 134, 140, *per* Clarke J.
[54] See *ante*, §495.

Insurers

it does not purport to authorise a salvage award in circumstances where one is not otherwise available, in particular, where he cannot demonstrate that the service he provides exceeds his existing contractual duties, so as to bring him within the category of voluntariness.[55]

A wider principle? It should be noted that Article 12.3 is specifically concerned with the case where the same person owns both the salving and the salved vessels. It does not purport to express a more general principle: that the rights of salvors are to be assessed notwithstanding that the person effecting salvage and/or the owner of property used for that purpose is the same person as the owner of the property salved. This is not surprising: Article 12.3 purports to deal with the most obvious case of dual identity, *i.e.* the ownership of sister-ships. There are, however, other examples which may well arise in practice. The most obvious one is where the owner of a ship in distress renders services other than by use of a sister-ship. Another example would be where a cargo-owner renders services, in part at least, for the benefit of cargo which he owns.[56] In such situations salvage will often in practice be awarded to a third party engaged to provide the relevant service. But, if the service is provided directly by the owner of the property in danger, in neither situation can he recover a salvage award, whether at common law or under Article 12.3. It is not surprising if salvees and their insurers are reluctant to expand the subject-matter of Article 12.3 into a broader principle, though such an extension is consistent with the public policy underlying the law of salvage.

(iv) Current position

Though the law provides for sister-ship salvage, the vast majority of vessels today are owned by one-ship companies, so sister-ship salvage is *extremely* rare. Where it does occur it is commonly dealt with by private arbitration under the Institute Time Clauses-Hulls, clause 9.

Insurers

An insurer who avoids liability under the policy by himself, incurring salvage expenses which, if incurred by the assured, would be indemnifiable under the policy as sue and labour charges,[57] cannot recover those expenses from the assured as salvage.[58] In *Crouan v. Stanier*[59] Kennedy J. disallowed such a claim on two grounds: that the claimants were, as insurers, salving for themselves to prevent an insured loss; and that they were doing with the knowledge of the owner of the insured property that which he was entitled to do himself in circumstances whereby they were liable to indemnify him.

---

[55] See *post*, Chap. 7.
[56] In fact the report of *The Sava Star* [1995] 2 Lloyd's Rep. 134 states that the cargo-owners there claimed remuneration for services rendered to both ship and cargo, though the judgment only deals with the claim against the ship.
[57] See Rose, *General Average: Law and Practice* (1997), p. 4.
[58] *Crouan v. Stanier* [1904] 1 K.B. 87, distinguishing *The Pickwick* (1852) 16 Jur. 669.
[59] [1904] 1 K.B. 87.

CHAPTER 7

VOLUNTARINESS

1. GENERAL CONSIDERATIONS

(a) Voluntariness in general

The two meanings of "voluntariness"

511   A claimant's entitlement to a salvage reward depends upon whether he rendered the service in respect of which he claims "voluntarily". In the law of salvage the adjective "voluntary" has acquired a specific meaning, *viz.* that the service was not rendered by virtue of a pre-existing legal obligation, in particular a contractual or public duty. However, the word also embraces another idea, which is also relevant in the present context but must be distinguished: that the person rendering the service is doing so gratuitously, *i.e.* with the intention that he will not be paid for doing so. A claimant will fail to recover salvage for such part of the service which he was under a pre-existing obligation to render and/or if it can be shewn that he intended not to claim for the service. The major part of this chapter concerns "voluntariness" in the first of these senses. The second sense will be dealt with under the description gratuitous salvage.

Voluntariness: the general rules

512   It was established as a general rule by the Admiralty Court that a person's entitlement to salvage depended on whether or not he was a "volunteer", in the sense that the service in respect of which he claimed a reward was not rendered simply by virtue of a pre-existing legal obligation, in particular a contractual or public duty.[1] The Brussels Salvage Convention 1910 did not specifically incorporate this general rule but only a particular example of it, namely that a tug can only claim a salvage reward for exceptional services which cannot be considered as rendered in fulfilment of the contract of towage.[2] The Salvage Convention 1989 does not expressly include a general rule. However, it does so by implication, by laying down general rules for the recovery of salvage and certain qualifications.

[1] "The very notion of saving a ship, supposes that the salvor, instead of merely executing orders, shall perform some extraordinary service, and exert himself to the utmost for the safety of life and property": *The Duke of Manchester* (1847) 6 Moo.P.C. 90, 99, *per* Lord Campbell.
[2] Brussels Salvage Convention 1910, Art. 4. See further, *post*, §§ 600–624.

General rule as to voluntariness

513 In respect of "Services rendered under existing contracts", Article 17 provides that:

> "No payment is due under the provisions of this Convention unless the services rendered exceed what can be reasonably considered as due performance of a contract entered into before the danger arose."

Extending beyond the scope of the subject-matter of this chapter, Article 5 of the Convention provides more extensively for "Salvage operations controlled by public authorities":

> "1. This Convention shall not affect any provisions of national law or any international convention relating to salvage operations by or under the control of public authorities.
> 2. Nevertheless, salvors carrying out such salvage operations shall be entitled to avail themselves of the rights and remedies provided for in this Convention in respect of salvage operations.
> 3. The extent to which a public authority under a duty to perform salvage operations may avail itself of the rights and remedies provided for in this Convention shall be determined by the law of the State where such authority is situated."

514 There is no definition of salvor in the Salvage Convention 1989, and prima facie every person is entitled to claim as such if carrying out salvage operations.[3] This general position is reinforced by the provision that a master's compliance with the statutory duty to render assistance to persons in danger at sea shall not affect rights to payment under the Convention.[4] Moreover, salvage operations carried out by or under the control of public authorities are expressed to carry entitlement to salvage under the Convention.[5] The only clear exception to the prima facie rule is the provision in Article 17 that performance of a pre-existing contract without more does not justify a claim to salvage. However, the Convention is ambiguous in relation to claims by public authorities under a duty to perform salvage operations. This issue is considered below.[6]

General rule as to voluntariness

515 It was established by the Admiralty Court as a general rule that voluntariness is an essential element of salvage, and that salvors must be volunteers.[7] It has been described as the foremost of those principles entitling a person to

---

[3] See Art. 1(a).
[4] MSA 1995, s.224, Sched. 11, Pt II, para. 3(1).
[5] Art. 5.2.
[6] See *ante*, §§ 688–693.
[7] The Salvage Convention 1989 does not provide generally for voluntariness. But see *ibid.*, Arts 5.2–3, 12.3 and 17.

a salvage reward.[8] As Langton J. has pointed out, the word "volunteer" is not free from ambiguity; and he suggested that it could hardly be contended, for example, that on any occasion upon which the master of a ship called for volunteers for a specially dangerous duty the contract of service of those who answered the call would be dissolved so as to render them volunteers.[9] Lord Stowell has best expressed the guiding principle in his description in *The Neptune*[10] of a salvor as:

> "A person who, without any particular relation to a ship in distress, proffers useful service, and gives it as a volunteer adventurer, without any pre-existing covenant that connected him with the duty of employing himself for the preservation of that ship."

Thus, if a service is rendered solely under a pre-existing obligation to work for the benefit of property and life at risk, or solely in the interest of self-preservation, it is prima facie not a salvage service.[11]

Beneficiary of the pre-existing duty

516 It is not a requirement of voluntariness that the pre-existing duty be owed to the salvee. It is sufficient to deprive the claimant of an award that he is simply performing duties ordinarily to be expected of him in the capacity in which he performs them.[12] If so, he neither provides a benefit to the defendant which the latter would not receive anyway, nor responds to the incentive of reward held out by the public policy of encouraging salvage services. The terms of the Salvage Convention 1989, Art. 17 do not make it clear whether the Convention was intended to incorporate or permit deviation from this principle,[13] but the survival of the common law principle is supported by both a literal reading of Article 17 and the absence of any intention to alter the established rule.

517 Most obviously, a person under a pre-existing contractual obligation to preserve the ship, the cargo or the lives on board should not be entitled to claim. Thus, the master and crew of the ship or of a tug engaged to tow her will not ordinarily be entitled to claim. This is particularly so the more it is contemplated that such a person may need to perform his duties in the face of danger, especially if, as in the case of a pilot, he is specifically engaged to

---

[8] *The Carrie* [1927] P. 224, 230.
[9] *The Albionic* [1941] P. 99, 111 (*affirmed* [1942] P. 81).
[10] (1824) 1 Hagg. 227, 236. See also *Clan Steam Trawling Co. Ltd v. Aberdeen Steam Trawling and Fishing Co. Ltd* 1908 S.C. 651, 658, *per* Lord Ardwall: "in order to entitle a person to claim salvage remuneration, the services in respect of which he claims must have been spontaneously and voluntarily rendered, and not rendered in respect of any contractual or official duty resting on the person rendering them."
[11] *cf. Gark v. Straits Towing Ltd and Sayer* (*The Belize*) [1966] 2 Lloyd's Rep. 277.
[12] *The Sava Star* [1995] 2 Lloyd's Rep. 134, 142, *per* Clarke J., citing the example of members of a public or local authority fire brigade merely providing their ordinary or statutory duties and master and crew performing services to cargo ordinarily to be expected of them.
[13] See Gaskell, 21–421.

assist in overcoming a danger. The same rule applies where the would-be salvor is acting in discharge of a public duty owed to the defendant, as in the case of persons who are obliged by statute to render assistance to the vessel without entitlement to salvage. The position is similar where the claimant is acting solely in discharge of a duty owed only to a third party—as in the case of a Lloyd's agent, the agent of underwriters—or of a public or official duty which is not directly owed to the defendant—as in the case of members of the Armed Forces.

518 A passenger on board a ship in distress is also ordinarily unable to claim as a salvor. He is not, it is true, under any legal or official obligation to work for the safety of her ship or cargo. But in saving them he is usually both in purpose and in fact labouring for his own safety. And he is not permitted to found a title to salvage reward upon exertions to which he is driven solely by self-interest—*i.e.* the interest of self-preservation—although they may be at the same time incidentally beneficial to other interests.

There is, however, no principle that, where a person is bound up in a maritime adventure which is the subject of a casualty, *e.g.* as a passenger or cargo-owner, then he has a duty to assist ship and cargo which negatives voluntariness and debars a claim to salvage, leaving the parties' relationship to be governed only by the principles of general average and the terms of any contract or bailment.[14]

519 The main reasons for the restrictions under discussion, which will be considered in more detail later in this chapter, are: the desire not to encourage or condone a failure properly to perform existing duties (which failure might in fact cause, or contribute to, the danger necessitating salvage); and the desire to avoid the opportunity of the claimant's refusal to render services except in circumstances where he is likely to receive a salvage award.[15] In the latter case, it may also be said to be immaterial why a duty (regardless of to whomever it is owed) is rendered if, when rendered, it does not provide a service which confers any more of a benefit than the claimant should have provided anyway. In this respect, the position can be compared and contrasted with the rule in the law of contract that a plaintiff may provide consideration if he performs, or promises to perform, a duty not already owed to the defendant.[16] In modern practice, the contrast is more apparent than real in that, particularly in the case of services provided by tugs, the court has been less reluctant to award salvage and more willing to acknowledge the benefit derived by the plaintiff in having his property preserved from danger. The non-voluntary aspect of the plaintiff's service has been more significant in

---

[14] *The Sava Star* [1995] 2 Lloyd's Rep. 134, 141. Clarke J. stated there: "The problem is that such a principle would apply to debar claims by shipowners in respect of services rendered by sister-ships.... Yet... such claims are not barred." With respect, Clarke J.'s conclusion is correct but not for this reason, since in most cases a sister-ship will not be "bound up in the maritime adventure".

[15] In the case of public authorities, there is also a more general question of their entitlement to remuneration for services which they render. See *post*, §§ 688–693.

[16] See Chitty, Vol. 1, Chap. 3; Treitel, Chap. 3.

moderating the amount of his reward than in preventing its being made.

520 If, while performing a pre-existing obligation, a claimant does more than his obligation otherwise requires him to do, as *a fortiori* where he does something completely outside his pre-existing obligation, he is entitled to a salvage reward. As we shall see, before considering in detail cases when individual non-volunteers may claim, the mere presence of a pre-existing obligation does not *per se* prevent a salvage award's being made.

521 As indicated by the preceding paragraphs, the classification of salvage claimants as volunteers habitually requires consideration of whether the claimant is or is not under a pre-existing obligation to provide the service in question. If not, and he has liberty to decide whether or not to act, he can be regarded as acting voluntarily. But it must be borne in mind that classification as a salvor is not simply based on voluntariness as commonly understood and that "volunteer" and "voluntariness" have technical meanings in the law of salvage which may exclude claims by persons acting voluntarily in the ordinary sense of the word, such as lifeboatmen. The detailed classification of salvors provided in the second part of this chapter must be understood in that light. It will be preceded by a general categorisation of the different elements of voluntariness.

(b) Moral obligation

522 There is a universal moral obligation, where life or property is at peril at sea, to render every possible assistance to its preservation.[17] "It is the duty of all ships to give succour in distress; none but a freebooter would withhold it; but *that* does not discharge from liability to payment where assistance is substantially given."[18] The existence of this duty, however, does not prevent services from being voluntary[19]:

> "This moral obligation applies on land as well as on sea, and its force as a moral obligation is only greater in the case of sea perils because these are in the general case more claimant in their call for aid because of their exceptionally dangerous character. But this is an obligation which applies not to seafaring matters only, but to all circumstances in which the citizen can by timely assistance save others from danger; and even that obligation can hardly be held to exist as regards saving of corporeal objects. It applies only to persons. But whatever be the extent of it, it is plainly not an obligation in law. Its non-fulfilment cannot be visited with either

---

[17] As to the effect of deviation on the shipowner's policy of insurance or his contract of carriage, see *ante*, Chap. 6.

[18] *The Waterloo* (1820) 2 Dods. 433, 437. See also *The Beaver* (1801) 3 C. Rob. 292, 294; *The Thetis* (1869) 2 A. & E. 365, 368, *per* Sir Robert Phillimore ("the rendering of salvage services is an obligation required by the dictates of humanity, by the principle of public policy, and by the general interests of society").

[19] *The Sappho* (1871) L.R. 3 P.C. 690, 694.

public official censure or give claim in civil suit in respect of failure."[20]

What causes difficulty is the coincidence in the claimant of such moral duty and a pre-existing legal duty which does militate against salvage remuneration; the line between these duties may be difficult to draw, and the use of the word "duties" as common to both classes must not be allowed to confuse them.[21]

(c) Pre-existing duty to owner of salved property

Performance of an existing contractual or official duty owed to the owner of salved property without more does not justify a salvage award. If additional services are rendered, or if any services are rendered after frustration (probably by the danger) of the original obligation, reward may be due. The claims of persons who are obliged to perform regardless of a danger, namely the master or crew of the vessel, will, however, be particularly scrutinised. Of course, no objection can be taken to a salvage claim for the provision of services under an agreement entered into after and because the danger has arisen, even though such services thereby become legally due and not merely voluntary, for that is commonly the situation in which salvage contracts are made.[22] Furthermore, where an agreement to provide any services is made after a danger has arisen, salvage remuneration may be awarded even where the agreement purports to be other than for salvage services, *e.g.* if it is expressed to be a contract for towage services.[23] Nevertheless, care will be taken to ensure that a person engaged other than as a salvor does not take advantage of the situation by attempting, through entry into a purportedly fresh relationship, to elevate his status to that of salvor.[24] **523**

Beneficiary of pre-existing contractual or official duty

In most cases in practice, where a person discharges a contractual or official duty in providing services which would normally justify a salvage reward, he will only be disentitled from claiming a reward on that ground if the duty was one owed directly to the defendant.[25] In particular, the members of the crew of the salving ship are not precluded from claiming because they are ordered to provide the salvage service, even though the service was one which their owners contracted with the owners of the salved ship to provide.[26] In *The* **524**

---

[20] *Clan Steam Trawling Co. Ltd v. Aberdeen Steam Trawling and Fishing Co. Ltd* 1908 S.C. 651, 657.
[21] *The Leon Blum* [1915] P. 90, 96 (affirmed *ibid.* 290).
[22] See *The National Defender* [1970] 1 Lloyd's Rep. 40, 45.
[23] See *post*, §§ 600–624.
[24] *The Crusader* [1907] P. 196 (ship's agent instructed to obtain and obtaining services of tug subsequently purporting to enter agreement with ship as salvor).
[25] See *The Sava Star* [1995] 2 Lloyd's Rep. 134, 141–142.
[26] *Fisher v. The Oceanic Grandeur* (1972) 127 C.L.R. 312, 331; [1972] 2 Lloyd's Rep. 396, 405; *The National Defender* [1970] 1 Lloyd's Rep. 40, 45.

Voluntariness

Sarpen,[27] the steam tug *Simla* rendered valuable services to the *Sarpen*, which was aground in the Orkneys. The owners, master and crew of the tug claimed salvage. But the defendants pleaded that the services were not voluntary because they were rendered by the orders of the naval authorities, the tug having been requisitioned by the Admiralty. However, the tug was taken by the Admiralty upon such terms that, when it was rendering (with the permission of the naval authorities) the services for which salvage reward was claimed, it was the owners of the *Simla*, and not the Admiralty, who were incurring risks of sea damage and injury to the vessel and her crew, whose wages they paid. The Admiralty was not at risk, the requisition having been on terms not amounting to a demise and not such as to make her a ship belonging to the Crown.[28] The Court of Appeal, therefore, rejected the defence. Pickford L.J. said:

> "The test of voluntariness is only applicable as between the salvor and salved, and if the services be voluntary in relation to the salved, *i.e.* not rendered by reason of any obligation towards him, it is quite immaterial that the salvor has been ordered by someone who has control of his movements to render them. . . . [29]
>
> . . . [T]he owners of a vessel are not excluded from the right to salvage because she is in the service of the Crown and cannot render such services without its consent and the services are rendered under the instructions of the naval authorities."[30]

525 Therefore, where fire-fighting services are rendered by a publicly owned fire-brigade or fire-fighting vessel, salvage is not payable. If services be voluntary in relation to part of the salved property, *i.e.* not rendered by reason of any obligation to the owner of it, it is quite immaterial that the salvor is under a duty to some one else to render service to another part of the salved property.[31] The limitation on the plaintiff's right to claim a salvage reward only prevails to the extent that the service is rendered in discharge of that duty.[32] Similarly, it is immaterial that the salvor may render services together with another person who may be acting under a duty to do so.[33] Thus, shipowners cannot escape liability to pay salvage on the ground that the claimant was under a duty to salve the cargo. Similarly, neither a shipowner nor a cargo-owner is precluded from recovering salvage against the other

---

[27] [1916] P. 306.
[28] See *post*, §§ 669 *et seq.*
[29] *ibid.* at 315, approved in *The Carrie* [1917] P. 224, 231; *The National Defender* [1970] 1 Lloyd's Rep. 40, 45; *Fisher v. The Oceanic Grandeur* (1972) 127 C.L.R. 312, 331; [1972] 2 Lloyd's Rep. 396, 405. See also *The Solway Prince* [1896] P. 120.
[30] *ibid.*, 317, referring to *The Nile* (1875) L.R. 4 A. & E. 449; *The Bertie* (1886) 6 Asp. M.L.C. 26.
[31] *The Carrie* [1917] P. 224.
[32] See also *The Nile* (1875) L.R. 4 A. & E. 449, 455.
[33] *The Cythera* [1965] 2 Lloyd's Rep. 454, 457 (NSWSC).

merely because he owed a duty to his insurer to avert or minimise loss, under a contractual or statutory duty to sue and labour.[34]

Pre-existing custom, usage or agreement

Lord Stowell in *The Waterloo*[35] expressed his view thus as to evidence adduced in order to establish a claim of exemption from salvage liability founded upon contract or usage: **526**

> "This information is peculiarly necessary in a case where the exemption is claimed from a right otherwise universally allowed, and highly favoured in law, for the protection of those who are subjected to it; for it is for *their* benefit that it exists under the favour of the law. It is what the law calls *jus liquidissimum*, the clearest general right that they who have saved lives and property at sea should be rewarded for such salutary exertions; and those who say that they are not bound to reward, ought to prove their exemption in very definite terms, and by arguments of irresistible cogency."

The Admiralty Court has been reluctant to determine the existence of a custom without the necessity of doing so, especially so as not to discourage the rendering of salvage services for fear that no reward will be earned[36]; albeit the existence of a custom will, because it necessarily incorporates a requirement of mutuality, be of potential benefit to plaintiff and defendant.[37] It was suggested in *The Waterloo*[38] that defendant shipowners might possibly sustain their claim of exemption in cases of slight services rendered by ships chartered by them; and it was suggested in *The Margaret*[39] that salvage awards should not be encouraged where an owner's ship was assisted by another of his ships. **527**

In order to maintain successfully the benefit of such a custom, the defendant must prove, first, as a matter of law, that the alleged custom is capable of being a valid and legally binding custom.[40] **528**
Dr Lushington said in *The Swan*[41] that:

> "if the custom has any legal foundation at all, it must be founded upon the principle of mutual benefit and protection of property, and upon the assumption that the parties are embarked in common enterprise, and

---

[34] *The Sava Star* [1995] 2 Lloyd's Rep. 134, 144.
[35] (1820) 3 Dods. 433, 435–436; affirmed (1821) 2 Dods. (title page).
[36] See *The Swan* (1839) 1 W. Rob. 68, 70. *cf. The Margaret* (1828) 2 Hagg. 48n.
[37] See *infra*.
[38] (1820) 2 Dods. 433, 437.
[39] (1828) 2 Hagg. 48n.
[40] *The Harriot* (1842) 1 W Rob. 439. Of relevance is the number of years during which the trade in question has been conducted and the number of vessels in the trade.
[41] (1839) 1 W.Rob. 68, 70.

Voluntariness

whatever service is mutually rendered may be mutually required, '*dantque accipiuntque vicissim.*' "[42]

529 Secondly, the plaintiff must prove, as a matter of fact, that the alleged custom exists in the case in hand and that it governs the facts of the case.[43] Against the obviously relevant evidence of the unfulfilled opportunities for successful salvage claims in circumstances covered by the alleged custom[44] and a witness's ignorance of the alleged custom,[45] must be weighed the possibilities that salvage may have been earned but not claimed or paid.[46] The Admiralty Court has always been careful to ensure that exemption from salvage liability is only granted in circumstances within the precise ambit of the alleged custom[47] and has not uncommonly used the finding that the alleged custom did not apply on the facts as an excuse for not determining the existence of the custom.[48] A custom may bind crew members as well as their owners.[49]

530 In *The Zephyr*,[50] salvage was denied to the master, crew and the owners' assignees where the salving and salved vessels were sailing "all consorts under a special agreement to give mutual protection." Lord Stowell was:

"informed by the gentleman of the Trinity House . . . that it is agreeable to well-established usage for vessels in the Honduras trade to sail together on understandings of this sort, and that such agreements are supported by general convenience and benefit."[51]

But that is not to say that special agreements to render mutual assistance, and so to oust the right to a salvage award, must rest upon a custom in order to be upheld. Where there is a pre-existing agreement between shipowners to render mutual assistance, the owners of the salving vessel cannot recover a salvage reward, not because the contract bars a claim, but because the word "salvage" does not apply to services which the person providing them had already

---

[42] See also *The Waterloo* (1820) 2 Dods. 433, 438; *The Africa* (1854) 1 Spinks E. & A. 299 (steamship could not be bound by custom between sailing ships of which it could not, therefore, take advantage). See also n. 53, *infra*.

[43] *The Harriot* (1842) 1 W.Rob. 439.

[44] *e.g.* as to the number of years during which the relevant trade has been conducted and the number of vessels in the trade; see *The Harriot* (1842) 1 W.Rob. 439.

[45] See *The Waterloo* (1820) 2 Dods. 433, 438–439.

[46] *e.g.* for the maintenance of good relations between plaintiff and defendant: see *ibid*. at 438.

[47] See, *e.g. The Waterloo* (1820) 2 Dods. 433; *The Harriot* (1842) 1 W.Rob. 439 (custom of the South Sea Whaling trade applied at least so far as "ordinary" salvage services were concerned); *The Red Rover* (1850) 3 W. Rob. 150 (custom of Plymouth fishing boats to help each other gratuitously not binding upon owners of a boat not belonging to that port); *The Africa* (1854) 1 Sprinks E. & A. 299 (doubted whether a custom applicable to the case of services rendered by one sailing ship to another could properly be extended to the case of services rendered by a steamship).

[48] See, *e.g. The Swan* (1839) 1 W. Rob. 68. *cf. The Margaret*, *supra*, n. 36.

[49] See *The Zephyr* (1827) 2 Hagg. 43; *The Maria Jane* (1850) 14 Jur. 857; *The Sappho* (1871) L.R. 3 P.C. 690, 693.

[50] (1827) 2 Hagg. 43.

[51] *ibid.*, 46–47.

contracted to render. A pre-existing agreement may preclude salvage even though the vessels are not consorts or engaged in a common enterprise.[52] In *Clan Steam Trawling Co. Ltd v. Aberdeen Steam Trawling and Fishing Co. Ltd*,[53] two vessels were insured in the same mutual insurance company under policies containing a condition that any vessel insured with the company should, if necessary, render assistance to any other vessel insured with the same company or with two other similar associations. One of the vessels rendered assistance to the others in distress. It was admitted that the master and crew of the salving vessel were entitled to a salvage award, presumably because they were not parties to the agreement and because they had rendered services outside the ambit of their normal employment.[54] But their owners could not recover, their services being contractual and obligatory.[55]

If proof of an alleged custom or special agreement fails but the court is satisfied that there was in the circumstances of the case some cause for a belief on the part of those on board the assisted vessel that, because they are associated in a common interest, they are entitled on either ground to the assistance given, the court may take this into consideration in assessing the amount of salvage.[56]   531

Pre-existing contract for work and labour

A pre-existing contract to render services may prevent the person rendering   532
them from obtaining a salvage award. Thus, a pre-existing contract to give all towage work to the plaintiff may, despite the ease with which towage may be turned into salvage,[57] afford some disinclination to a judge to award salvage.[58] In *The Solway Prince*,[59] the plaintiffs, with the knowledge and assent of the defendant owners, undertook to lift a sunken vessel under a contract with the

---

[52] *Clan Steam Trawling Co. Ltd v. Aberdeen Steam Trawling and Fishing Co. Ltd* 1908 S.C. 651.

[53] 1908 S.C. 651.

[54] *cf. The North Goodwin No. 16* [1980] 1 Lloyd's Rep. 71. See further *post*, §§ 565–587. Particular plaintiffs may conceivably also not be bound where they do not benefit equally from a custom or usage; the owners in the *Clan Steam Trawling* case derived a mutual benefit from a lowering of premiums. *cf. The Zephyr, supra*, n. 50. As to the owners' power to bind the master and the crew by agreement, see *post*, Chap. 9.

[55] Non-fulfilment would have resulted in the invalidity of the insurance and possibly an action for damages: see 1908 S.C. 651, 661.

[56] *The Trelawney* (1802) 4 C. Rob. 223, 227–228 (less awarded than would otherwise have been because the two vessels, engaged in the slave trade, were associated in a common interest; insurgent slaves gained control of one vessel and the other vessel regained control); *The Collier* (1866) L.R. 1 A. & E. 83, 86 (where Dr Lushington thought that the quantum might be affected "where fishing vessels render assistance to each other, and matters of that description"). See also *The Glenbeg* (1940) 67 Ll.L.Rep. 437, 441 ("But one has to bear in mind that these tugs were already engaged, and that is a matter which must, at least, quantitively, be taken into account in arriving at the amount of salvage reward to be awarded").

[57] See *post*, §§ 600–624.

[58] See *The Glenbeg, supra*, n. 56, at 439–440.

[59] [1896] P. 120; distinguished in *The Goulandris* [1927] P. 182, 191.

insurers, who advanced to the plaintiffs before the work commenced 40 per cent of the amount for which the vessel was insured. The vessel was successfully raised but the operation proved more costly than anticipated and some of the underwriters had become insolvent. The plaintiffs could not, however, claim as salvors from the defendants. Sir Francis Jeune P. said[60]:

> "During the argument I doubted whether the plaintiffs should not be considered as having acted in a dual capacity, that is to say, both as salvors and as contractors with the insurers. But on reflection I have come to the conclusion that the latter capacity excludes the former, and that the plaintiffs are not, and never were, salvors, because they were employed by the insurers under an ordinary, and not a salvage contract, to do all they did do, on the terms of receiving a specified reward.
> ... If the owner made such a contract with such persons himself, provided there be no change in the nature of the service, and ... provided that the transaction is not shewn to have been inequitable ..., I think that there can be no doubt that the contracting parties could not claim a remuneration on salvage principles. Again ... if the contract of the plaintiffs with the insurers does not prevent their claiming as salvors, why should not any one of the persons employed by them also claim? But can it be supposed that any one of the servants or workmen engaged—a diver, for example, employed at his usual rate of wages—has, if the wreck be raised, a meritorious claim against the owner as a salvor?
> ... [The authorities] shew that if work be done in pursuance of a contract other than a salvage contract, it does not, under ordinary circumstances, give rise to a salvage claim."

(d) Salvage under legal duty or authority

General principles

533 In principle, the general rule on voluntariness applying to a salvor in a pre-existing contractual relationship with the salvee applies to salvors carrying out salvage operations under a legal duty or under the direction of legal authority, namely whether the salvor is providing services beyond those which he is normally expected to perform. However, in the case of such services provided by public authorities, it is necessary to consider whether they must also satisfy a financial test.

---

[60] [1896] P. 120, 126–127.

Statutory duties not precluding claims for salvage

The duties and the subjects of the duties

The Merchant Shipping Act 1995[60A] places three duties on masters of **534** vessels to render assistance at sea; namely to assist persons in danger at sea,[61] to respond to information of distress,[62] and to assist vessels with which their ship collides.[63] Breaches of these duties give rise to criminal penalties.[64] "Master" is defined so that the duty extends to "every person (except a pilot) having command or charge of a ship and, in relation to a fishing vessel, means the skipper."[65] The duties therefore extend to persons having temporary charge of a vessel, such as the officer of the watch.

The duties to respond to information of distress[66] and to assist colliding vessels[67] are imposed specifically on masters of United Kingdom ships[68] and on masters of foreign[69] ships when in United Kingdom waters, whereas the duty to assist persons in danger at sea is placed on "Every master".[70] In relation to the duty to assist persons in danger at sea only, it is specifically provided that "The owner of the vessel shall incur no liability for a breach of the duty of the master".[71]

Duty to render assistance to persons in danger at sea

The Brussels Salvage Convention 1910 implemented a general duty on **535** masters to render assistance to persons at sea in danger of being lost.[72] Article 10.1 of the Salvage Convention 1989 now provides that "Every master is bound, so far as he can do so without serious danger to his vessel and persons

---

[60A] See also the United Nations Convention on the Law of the Sea 1982, Art. 98 (*post*, App. 31).

[61] See *post*, §§ 535–536.

[62] See *post*, §§ 537–539.

[63] See *post*, §§ 540–543.

[64] Breaches occur where there is a failure to comply with the statutory duty. If he has a reasonable excuse, the master has a defence to breach of the duty to assist colliding vessels but not to breach of the other two duties; the practicality and reasonableness of the situation are relevant to the content of the duties to assist colliding vessels and to respond to information of distress, whereas the only limitation on the existence of the duty to assist persons in danger at sea is serious danger to the master's own vessel. The penalties are identical for breaches of the duties to assist persons in danger at sea and to respond to information of distress, and similar in the case of the duty to assist colliding vessels. See MSA 1995, ss 92(4), 93(6) and 224, Sched. 11, Pt II, para. 3(1).

[65] MSA 1995, s.313(1), defining "master" for the purposes of the Act.

[66] See MSA 1995, s.93(3).

[67] See MSA 1995, s.92(2).

[68] For "United Kingdom ship", see MSA 1995, ss 1(3), 313(1).

[69] For "foreign", see MSA 1995, s.313(1).

[70] Salvage Convention 1989, Art. 10.1.

[71] Salvage Convention 1989, Art. 10.3.

[72] The Brussels Convention 1910, Art. 11 was enacted in the Maritime Conventions Act 1911, s.6, which was amended by the Merchant Shipping (Registration, etc.) Act 1993, s.8(3), Sched. 4, para. 6(2), then repealed by MSA 1995, s.314 and Sched. 12 and replaced by MSA 1995, s.224, Sched. 11, Pt I, Art. 10 and Pt II, para. 3.

thereon, to render assistance to any person[73] in danger of being lost at sea." It is specifically provided that "The owner of the vessel shall incur no liability for a breach of the duty of the master under [Art. 10.1]."[74]

The duty in Article 10.1 is simply to render assistance to persons in danger of being lost at sea. It does not require assistance to property or a salvage service as such, though salvage may be carried out as a consequence of performing the duty and there is no inhibition on performing a salvage service unless carrying out salvage means that the duty in Article 10.1 is not being performed. Performance of the duty is excused so far as it would involve *serious* danger to the master's vessel and persons thereon, but should be continued (*e.g.* by standing by) so far as it does not involve such serious danger.

536 The measures necessary to enforce the duty in Article 10.1 are not laid down in the Salvage Convention 1989 but have to be adopted by the States parties.[75] The United Kingdom has provided[76] that the master of a vessel who fails to comply with the duty imposed on him by Article 10.1 commits an offence and shall be liable: (a) on summary conviction, to imprisonment for a term not exceeding six months or a fine not exceeding the statutory maximum[77] or both; and (b) on conviction on indictment, to imprisonment for a term not exceeding two years or a fine, or both.

However, "Compliance by the master of a vessel with that duty shall not affect his right or the right of any person to a payment under the Convention or under any contract."[78] This provision not only preserves the master's status as a volunteer so as to be able to claim a salvage reward at common law but, by reference to "payment under the Convention", his entitlement to a payment under the Salvage Convention 1989, Arts. 13–14[79] as well.

Duty to respond to information of distress

537 Section 93 of the Merchant Shipping Act 1995 imposes a duty on masters[80] to respond to information of distress.[81] The master of a ship, on receiving at sea a signal of distress or information from any source that a ship or aircraft is in distress, shall proceed with all speed to the assistance of the persons in

---

[73] The Brussels Salvage Convention 1910, Art. 11 specifically provided that assistance should be given to "everybody, even though an enemy" but "any person" in the Salvage Convention 1989, Art. 10.1 presumably means what it says, so as to include enemies, the reference to which was presumably omitted as being superfluous rather than because the duty was no longer intended to extend to enemies.

[74] Salvage Convention 1989, Art. 10.3.

[75] Salvage Convention 1989, Art. 10.2.

[76] MSA 1995, s.224, Sched. 11, Pt II, para. 3(1).

[77] For the statutory maximum, see Criminal Justice Act 1982, s.74.

[78] MSA 1995, s.224, Sched. 11, Pt II, para. 3(2).

[79] See *ante*, Chap. 5; *post*, Chap. 15.

[80] *i.e.* masters of U.K. ships and masters of foreign ships when in U.K. waters: MSA 1995, s.93(3).

[81] The section derives from the Merchant Shipping (Safety Conventions) Act 1949, s.22, as subsequently amended by the Merchant Shipping (Registration, etc.) Act 1993, s.8(3), Sched. 4, para. 6(2), which superseded MSA 1932, s.26, which was a response to the loss of the *Titanic*.

distress (informing them if possible that he is doing so) unless he is unable, or in the special circumstances of the case considers it unreasonable or unnecessary, to do so.[82] He is released from the obligation: as soon as he is informed of the requisition of one or more ships other than his own and that the requisition is being complied with by the ship or ships requisitioned[83]; or if he is informed by the persons in distress, or by the master of any ship that has reached the persons in distress, that assistance is no longer required.[84] Where the master of any ship in distress has requisitioned any ship that has answered his call, it is the duty of the master of the requisitioned ship to comply with the requisition by continuing to proceed with all speed to the assistance of the persons in distress.[85] But, again, he is released from this obligation if he is informed by the persons in distress, or by the master of any ship that has reached the persons in distress, that assistance is no longer required.[86]

538 The precise effect of section 93 is not entirely clear. The marginal note to the section is "Duty to assist ships, etc. in distress" and the section itself requires masters subject to the duty "to proceed with all speed to the assistance of the persons in distress". Yet it is arguable that the section is mainly concerned with ensuring that a master responds to a signal by changing course and taking his vessel to the location of the casualty, and that the section does not seem to require assistance as such.[87] This would not deprive the section of most of its practical effect, since the master would become subject to the overlapping, and more stringent, duty to assist persons in danger at sea under the Salvage Convention 1989, Art. 10.1.[88]

539 If a master fails to comply with the obligations imposed by the Act, he commits an offence.[89] The Act expressly provides, however, that compliance by the master of a ship with the provisions of the section shall not affect his right or the right of any other person to salvage.[90] Thus, salvage was awarded in *The Tower Bridge*.[91] In that case, the defendants' steamship, while bound for St John, New Brunswick, got into an extensive ice-field in which she sustained so much damage that she sent out an SOS message, as it was thought that she was in danger of sinking. The message was heard and answered by the plaintiffs' steamship *Newfoundland*, 30 miles away, which was also bound to St John and had herself encountered the ice-field but had got out of it. She turned back into the ice-field and, sustaining damage in the process, pushed herself to within six miles of the *Tower Bridge*, when it was ascertained, by wireless, that the condition of the *Tower Bridge* was not so serious as had been

---

[82] MSA 1995, s.93(1).
[83] s.93(4).
[84] s.93(5).
[85] s.93(2).
[86] s.93(5).
[87] See Gaskell, 21–115.
[88] See *ante*, §§ 535–536.
[89] s.93(6).
[90] s.93(7).
[91] [1936] P. 30.

thought. The only request then made by her was that the *Newfoundland* should stand by and see her into St John. The master of the *Newfoundland* did not think that the situation required his standing by and simply sent advice as to the course which the *Tower Bridge* should steer to clear water. This she did successfully and the plaintiffs were awarded salvage, despite the defendants' objection that the plaintiffs were merely fulfilling their statutory duty under the forerunner of section 93(1) of the 1995 Act[92] and did not provide the requested service of standing by. Sir Boyd Merriman P. conceded that, if the master had simply proceeded in response to the statute and nothing had resulted from that, a salvage award would not have been due, the reason being because no salvage service was rendered, not because one was rendered as a result of obeying the statute.[93] It does not follow that every ship responding to an SOS message is automatically entitled to a salvage award.[94] However, by coming to assist and giving advice a service had been provided[95] and it was immaterial that it was not the precise service requested.

Duty to assist colliding ship

540 Section 92 of the Merchant Shipping Act 1995 imposes a statutory duty in the case of a collision to assist the other ship involved.[96] In every case of collision between two ships, it is the duty of the master of each ship, if and so far as he can do so without danger[97] to his own ship, crew and passengers (if any) to render to the other ship, its master, crew and passengers (if any) such assistance as may be practicable and may be necessary to save them from any danger caused by the collision.[98] He must also stay by the other vessel until he has ascertained that it has no need of further assistance[99] and must give the master of the other ship the name of his own ship and also the names of the ports from which it comes and to which it is bound.[1] If the master or person in charge fails without reasonable cause to comply with the section, he commits an offence.[2] If he is a certified officer, an inquiry into his conduct may be held and his certificate cancelled or suspended.[3]

541 Unlike the statutory provisions just considered, section 92 does not expressly preserve any right to claim for a salvage service which may be provided independently of performance of the statutory duty. Certainly, it has

---

[92] The Merchant Shipping (Safety and Load Line Conventions) Act 1932, s.26(1).
[93] [1936] P. 30, 34–35.
[94] *The Stiklestad* [1926] P. 205, 210, *per* Bateson J.; affirmed (1926) 43 T.L.R. 118.
[95] [1936] P. 30, 33. See also *The Bengali (ex Theophile Massart)* (1935) 52 Ll.L. Rep. 315.
[96] The MSA 1995, s.92 derives from the MSA 1894, s.422, the Brussels Collision Convention 1910, Art. 8, the Maritime Conventions Act 1911, s.4(2), the MSA 1979, s.43, Sched. 6, Pt VII, para. 6, the Merchant Shipping (Registration, etc.) Act 1993, s.8(3), Sched. 4, para. 6(2).
[97] Compare "serious danger" in the Salvage Convention 1989, Art. 10.1: *ante*, § 535.
[98] MSA 1995, s.92(1)(a).
[99] *ibid*.
[1] *ibid.*, s.92(1)(b).
[2] s.92(4). However, the master's failure to comply with s.92 shall not raise any presumption of law that the collision was caused by his wrongful act, neglect or default: s.92(3).
[3] s.92(4).

Statutory duties not precluding claims for salvage

been held that, if a ship is in fault, either wholly or partly, for a collision, neither her owners nor her crew can maintain a claim as salvors for any services rendered by that ship, and made necessary by her fault, to the other ship or to the life an property on board her.[4] In *The Beta*,[5] Butt J. considered *obiter* whether a ship which had, without fault, collided with and thereafter towed another ship to safety was entitled to salvage remuneration. He thought it had not occurred to any of the parties that salvage might be due, and added:

> "In my view of the Act of Parliament,[6] if the steamer had not chosen to tow the schooner she would have had to stay by her a very long time, because she would not have dared to have left her. Therefore I do not think that this is a case in which any salvage ought to be awarded."[7]

However, as will be seen,[8] the view that the ship responsible for a collision cannot claim, has been doubted.[9] Moreover, it has since been stated on more than one occasion in the House of Lords that salvage may be claimed by one of two colliding ships. Thus, in language that was adopted by Lord Wright in *The Beaverford (Owners) v. The Kafiristan (Owners)*,[10] Lord Phillimore said in *The Melanie (Owners) v. The San Onofre (Owners)*[11] that:

542

> "This is, I believe, the first opportunity which this House has had of pronouncing upon a question which has, I imagine, long been treated as settled in the Courts below. Ever since the judgment of Sir Robert Phillimore in *The Hannibal and The Queen*[12]—accepted, I think, in the Privy Council, though there was another ground on which the decision was confirmed—it has been taken as law that the duty cast by the Merchant Shipping Acts upon one of the two colliding vessels to stand by and render assistance, does not prevent that vessel if she renders assistance from claiming salvage."

---

[4] See, *e.g. The Cargo ex Capella* (1867) L.R. 1 A. & E. 356; *The Glengaber* (1872) L.R. 3 A. & E. 534; *The Duc d'Aumale* [1904] P. 60; *The Beaverford (Owners) v. The Kafiristan (Owners)* [1938] A.C. 136. But see now Chap. 11.

[5] (1884) 5 Asp. M.L.C. 276. Butt J.'s judgment was upheld by the Court of Appeal, the judgment of which alone is reported at (1884) 9 P.D. 134.

[6] MSA 1873, s.16; repealed by MSA 1894, s.745 and Sched. 22.

[7] (1884) 5 Asp. M.L.C. 276, 277.

[8] *Post*, Chap. 11. See also *ante*, Chap. 6.

[9] See *The Beaverford (Owners) v. The Kafiristan (Owners)* [1938] A.C. 136, 149. *The Susan V. Luckenbach* [1951] P. 197, 200.

[10] [1938] A.C. 136, 147.

[11] [1925] A.C. 246, 261–262. The plaintiff's ship held not to be negligent: see *ibid.*, 253, 259; *The Melanie (Owners) v. The San Onofre (No. 2)* (1919) 35 T.L.R. 507; [1919] W.N. 154. See also *The Melanie (Owners) v. The San Onofre (Owners) (No. 3)* (1919) [1927] A.C. 162n.

[12] (1867) L.R. 2 A. & E. 53 (salvage awarded to tug against a ship which had collided with the tug's tow). The case was decided on the Merchant Shipping Act Amendment Act 1862, s.33: see now the MSA 1995, s.92. The wording of each section was similar.

Such dicta have not expressly extended to claims by vessels responsible for causing collisions, but it may be assumed from Lord Phillimore's speech that this was his intention.

543 However, though the master of a vessel which has collided with the casualty is not debarred from claiming a salvage reward simply by virtue of the section 92 duty to assist or because of his vessel's part in the collision, he may be deprived of the whole or part of his potential award to the extent that the salvage operations became necessary or more difficult because of his fault[13]; *i.e.* in particular if it was his fault which caused or contributed to the collision.

Duties under the Salvage Convention 1989

544 The Salvage Convention 1989, Art. 8.2 provides that:

> "The owner and master of the vessel or the owner of other property in danger shall owe a duty to the salvor—
> (a) to co-operate fully with him during the course of the salvage operations;
> (b) in so doing, to exercise due care to prevent or minimise damage to the environment; and
> (c) when the vessel or other property has been brought to a place of safety, to accept redelivery when reasonably requested by the salvor to do so."

In *The Sava Star*[14] Clarke J. opined that a cargo-owner who is doing no more than discharging his duty under Article 8.2[15] should not be treated as a volunteer.

Public duties: salvage operations by or under the control of public authorities

545 Article 5 of the Salvage Convention 1989 is headed "Salvage operations controlled by public authorities" and provides:

> "1. This Convention shall not affect any provisions of national law or any international convention relating to salvage operations by or under the control of public authorities.
> 2. Nevertheless, salvors carrying out such salvage operations shall be entitled to avail themselves of the rights and remedies provided for in this Convention in respect of salvage operations.

---

[13] Salvage Convention 1989, Art. 18. See *post*, Chap. 11.
[14] [1995] 2 Lloyd's Rep. 134, 143.
[15] The report states "Art. 8.3" but this is obviously a misprint.

3. The extent to which a public authority under a duty to perform salvage operations may avail itself of the rights and remedies provided for in this Convention shall be determined by the law of the State where such authority is situated."

Article 5 of the Salvage Convention 1989 appears to be attempting to achieve three objectives and to do so in a rather clumsy way. First, Article 5.1 appears to be designed to preserve legal provisions which are external to the Convention and which concern operations by or under the control of public authorities which relate to salvage. In this respect, Article 5.1 overlaps with Article 9, which preserves the rights of states under generally recognised principles of international law to take measures generally against pollution or the threat of pollution. The precise relationship between Articles 5.1 and 9, and the extent to which Article 9 adds anything to what is contained in Article 5.1, are unclear.[16]

Secondly, without the traditional English drafting practice of subjecting the general rule to other expressed provisions, Article 5.1 is qualified by the succeeding paragraphs. In particular, Article 5.2 preserves the rights and remedies under the Salvage Convention 1989 (continuing, in new form, the pre-Convention law) of salvors carrying out salvage operations. Article 5.2 does not purport to create rights not otherwise existing under the Convention. It therefore remains necessary for claimants to be "salvors carrying out such salvage operations". This is possible whether the claimant is a private salvor or a public authority.

However, thirdly, Article 5.3 takes particular account of the fact that different States may have different rules for public authorities which carry out salvage operations.

Most likely, Article 5.3 should simply be read as a provision of an international convention specifically recognising that States parties may make their own provision for whether public authorities can claim salvage.

A much less likely, though possible, interpretation of Article 5.3, as a term of a United Kingdom statute, is that it introduces a new rule concerning public authority salvors, of particular importance to such salvors "situated" outside the United Kingdom. On this interpretation, if the claimant is a public authority *and* it has a duty to perform salvage operations, then its rights and remedies under the Convention shall be determined not by the law prima facie governing the salvage claim, but by the law of the State where the authority is situated. Of course, if the authority is situated in the United Kingdom and the claim is governed by English law, Article 5.3 adds nothing to what would otherwise be the case. Moreover, even where the authority is situated outside the United Kingdom, Article 5.3 will not necessarily apply, for it only comes into effect where the authority has a duty to perform salvage operations, and will not therefore apply in circumstances where the authority had merely a

---

[16] See further *ante*, § 69.

power which it was not bound to exercise to carry out services of a salvage nature.

If Article 5.3 does apply on this basis, the law of the State where the authority is situated will govern its position. In the case of private persons or bodies, the governing, or proper, law has normally been identified with reference to the country where the person or body is domiciled or resident. In the case of a public body the test of "situation" may well be more appropriate and is not likely to be difficult to identify. Similarly, although the possibility of a difference between the law of the State and the law of the country (for conflict of laws purposes) where the authority is situated should be noted, in most cases at least this is not likely to lead to difficulty in practice.

548 The law applying to different categories of salvors who might be precluded from recovering salvage by the rules on "voluntariness" is set out, as laid down mostly prior to the Salvage Convention 1989, in the second Part of this chapter.[17] Clearly, so far as the law there set out constitutes *"provisions of national law...* relating to salvage operations by or under the control of public authorities",[18] it is preserved by Article 5.1. This depends on whether the Convention (which does not deal specifically with this point) embraces only certain "provisions" of national law (such as legislative materials) or all components of national law (which seems the better interpretation).[19]

The relevant public authorities

549 As a general rule a public authority may be national or local, and is a person or body entrusted with functions to perform for the benefit of the public and not for private profit, although the term may also apply where such an authority is conducting a commercial enterprise which Parliament has empowered it to undertake.[20] Public authorities therefore include the Crown and its Armed Forces,[21] magistrates and other officials,[22] Receivers of Wreck,[23] and the Coastguard[24] and other emergency services.[25] It will also include public harbour authorities, even when providing on contractual terms

---

[17] *Post*, §§ 563–705.
[18] Italics added.
[19] A contrast can be made between "provisions of national law" in Art. 5.1 and the more open-ended term "law" in Art. 5.3's reference to "the law of the State where such [public] authority is situated": see Gaskell, 21–381. However, it seems more likely that Art. 5.1 and Art. 5.3 were simply concerned with different subject-matter rather than expressing a perceived distinction between the content of the national law or law of the State.
[20] See *The Ydun* [1899] P. 236, 239, *per* Jeune P., affirmed *ibid.*, 242 (CA); *Att.-Gen. v. Company of Proprietors of Margate Pier and Harbour* [1900] 1 Ch. 749; *Parker v. London County Council* [1904] 2 K.B. 501; *Lyles v. Southend on Sea Corp.* [1905] 2 K.B. 1; *DPP v. Manners* [1978] A.C. 43.
[21] See *post*, §§ 645–682.
[22] See *post*, §§ 696–697.
[23] See *post*, §§ 694–695.
[24] See *post*, §§ 683–687.
[25] See *post*, §§ 688–693.

services such as pilotage which were formerly provided mainly by independent contractors licensed by pilotage authorities.[26]

550 A more difficult question of interpretation is whether a body authorised by statute to operate as a commercial, profit-making entity but with powers of a public nature, such as Associated British Ports, is a public authority for the purposes of Article 5. It is likely to be regarded as undesirable that ports carrying out public functions should be treated differently according to whether they fall within the definition of public authority, and a tribunal faced with the issue may be inclined to interpret the term according to the function being carried out by the body, so as to safeguard powers conferred in the public interest. However, strictly speaking, private bodies are not public authorities simply because they have statutory or other public powers and will not necessarily be categorised as such simply because this may be thought to produce a beneficial result.

551 Given that a body can only be treated as a charity if it satisfies the requirement of public benefit,[27] the Royal National Lifeboat Institute (RNLI) may be regarded as a public body; but it does not follow that it is a public *authority* for current purposes. In any event, the issue seems to be unimportant: it is unlikely that the the legal provisions preserved by Article 5.1 will apply to the RNLI; those rights which lifeboatmen do have[28] are not diminished by Article 5.1–2; and the RNLI itself does not attempt to exercise any rights of salvage which it might theoretically have, so Article 5.3 is of no practical use to it.

In practice, the definition of public authority for the purposes of the Salvage Convention 1989 may prove to be of minimal importance: there is unlikely to be a conflict between the private law based provisions of Article 5.1 and the public concerns which Article 5.1 is intended to preserve; the main potential difficulty (safeguarding the interests of salvors) is specifically dealt with by Article 5.2; and, on one interpretation, pre-Convention rights of public authorities are continued (albeit not improved) by Article 5.3.[29]

552 It should be noted that Article 5.3 of the Salvage Convention 1989 does not refer the rights under the Convention of all public authorities to the law of the State where the authority is situated, but only those of "a public authority with a duty to perform salvage operations". It is not entirely clear whether it is only public authorities discharging a duty to perform salvage operations that are unable to claim a salvage reward under Admiralty law,[30] so it is not clear how far the Convention changes the law in this respect, particularly if the Admiralty rule is wider and this rule is preserved by Article 5.1's saving of "*any* provisions of national law . . . relating to salvage operations by or under the

---

[26] See *post*, §§ 588–599.
[27] *Tudor on Charities* (8th ed., 1995), pp. 5–6.
[28] See *post*, §§ 698–705.
[29] See *post*, §§ 688–693.
[30] See *post*, §§ 688–693.

control of public authorities". What is clear is that, at least in respect of a public authority with a duty to perform salvage operations, the law may differ from the Convention.

English law on salvage operations by public authorities

553 The effect of the Salvage Convention 1989 on the Admiralty rule is unclear, for the language of Article 5 appears to be inconsistent. Article 5.1 provides that the Convention "shall not affect *any* provisions of national law or any international convention relating to salvage operations by or under the control of public authorities",[31] yet Article 5.2 goes on to provide that, "*Nevertheless*, salvors carrying out such salvage operations shall be entitled to avail themselves of the rights and remedies provided for in this Convention . . . "[32] Having thus laid down a general rule for recovery, Article 5 concludes, in Article 5.3, by providing that:

> "The extent to which a public authority under a duty to perform salvage operations may avail itself of the rights and remedies provided for in this Convention shall be determined by the law of the State where such authority is situated."

There are several ways to reconcile these provisions.

554 First, although it overlaps with Article 9,[33] Article 5.1 seems clearly designed to ensure that a public authority's general rights of intervention in cases of danger are not affected by the Salvage Convention 1989. If this is the sole purpose of Article 5.1, there is no inconsistency in Article 5.2's laying down a prima facie rule that all salvage operations *by or under the control of* public authorities give a prima facie entitlement to a salvage reward. Article 5.2 would then have effectively reversed the pre-Convention rule, so that public authorities under a duty to perform salvage operations would only be disentitled from claiming salvage by virtue of Article 5.3 if a new rule to that effect were introduced by legislation; and this has not been done. On this interpretation, public authorities now have a prima facie right to claim salvage.

555 Secondly, the combined effect of the different parts of Article 5.1 may be to lay down a general rule limiting the impact of the Salvage Convention 1989 on the general law relating to salvage operations by or under the control of public authorities, subject to a prima facie right by persons conducting salvage operations to recover salvage, which right is displaced if there is an existing (*i.e.* pre-Convention) rule denying such recovery to public authorities with a duty to perform salvage operations. On this interpretation, public authorities with a duty to perform salvage operations remain disentitled from claiming a

---
[31] Emphasis added.
[32] Emphasis added.
[33] See § 68.

Self-interest

salvage reward when exercising their statutory powers. So far as it is relevant, this interpretation has the attraction of familiarity. It is perhaps the one most likely to be adopted by an English tribunal.[34]

Salvage operations under the control of public authorities

556 The Admiralty law rule appears to be that, where a salvor who would not in the normal course of events provide a service of a salvage nature does so while acting under official orders, he is entitled to a salvage reward.[35] The Salvage Convention 1989 specifically provides that salvors carrying out salvage operations under the control of public authorities shall be entitled to avail themselves of the rights and remedies in the Salvage Convention 1989.[36]

(e) Self-interest

557 The mere presence of the interest of self-preservation, if it is not the sole interest, does not take services outside the scope of voluntariness. In *The Sava Star*[37] Clarke J. went further, holding that "Motive is irrelevant".

In *The Lomonosoff*,[38] the plaintiffs were British and Belgian soldiers in Murmansk in February 1920, on their way to take service with the government of Northern Russia. The town and port of Murmansk were seized by Bolsheviks in a rising. The plaintiffs would have been imprisoned and probably shot if they had remained in Murmansk. They could have escaped to Norway by sleigh but instead, carrying two machine guns, they boarded the *Lomonosoff*, a steamship flying the mercantile flag of the government of North Russia. A number of the crew were on shore and there was insufficient steam in the boilers for her to proceed to sea. The plaintiffs cast off the vessel from the quay, helped to raise sufficient steam, and returned heavy fire from the quay

---

[34] A third possible construction of Art. 5 is consistent with each of the previous interpretations. It depends upon whether Art. 5.3 is construed more as an enabling provision of an international Convention or (as enacted) a part of an English statute. Simply as a Convention provision, Art. 5.3 authorises States parties to lay down their own rules as to whether a public authority with a duty to perform salvage operations can claim salvage. If so, either of the first two interpretations of Art. 5 given above is possible. Alternatively, read simply as a term of an English statute, it may be read to mean that, whatever the general law to be applied by the tribunal hearing a salvage claim, the entitlement of a public authority with a duty to perform salvage operations shall be determined by the law of the State where it is situated: so that the decision which an English tribunal reaches will be different if a public authority claimant is situated outside the U.K. in a State with a different rule from the English rule. It is suggested that this interpretation is erroneous. This discussion illustrates the point that, however advantageous it may be to import Convention provisions verbatim into English law, simply scheduling them to a statute may have unfortunate consequences. Parliament could have put the point beyond doubt by exercising its liberty under Art. 5.3 to make specific provision in the MSA 1995, Sched. 11, Pt II (provisions having effect in connection with the Convention).

[35] *The Kangaroo* [1918] P. 227. See the discussion and quotation from the judgment of Hill J., *ante*, § 56.

[36] Salvage Convention 1989, Art. 5.1–2.

[37] [1995] 2 Lloyd's Rep. 134, 144, citing *The Liffey* (1887) 6 Asp.M.L.C. 255; *The Lomonosoff* [1921] P. 97, 102, *per* Hill J.; *The Theseus* (1925) 23 Ll.L. Rep. 136, 137, *per* Hill J.; *The Laomedon* (1925) 23 Ll.L. Rep. 230.

[38] [1921] P. 97.

and other ships which had surrendered to the Bolsheviks. The ship, therefore, escaped and was navigated by the plaintiffs, with assistance from its officers and crew, to Tromso, where it was handed over to its owners' representatives. Noting that the plaintiffs had had other (and, counsel argued, safer) means of escape. Hill J. awarded them salvage. He referred to the second edition of this book[39]:

> "where the learned author says: 'It is to be observed that, except in the peculiar case of the passengers on board a vessel in distress,[40] the requirement of voluntariness in the salvor is satisfied by the absence of any contractual or official obligation.' It not infrequently happens that a salvor in saving property is also saving himself: see, *e.g. Le Jonet*[41]; and where in a case like the present the salvor has two means of saving himself and elects one which also saves maritime property I have no doubt that *qua* that property he is a volunteer."[42]

(f) Gratuitous salvage

558   As stated above, awards of salvage are founded on the notion that the recipient of the benefit of the relevant service should make payment for it to its provider.[43] This is substantially bolstered, but not fundamentally explained, by the public policy of inflating remuneration for the service to encourage voluntary efforts to salve. The public interest in encouraging provision, and establishing on a professional basis the means of provision, of salvage services helps to explain the court's willingness to reward on a salvage basis tugs providing a service which is contemplated as being one of towage but which turns out to be provided to a vessel which is in danger.

559   That response to the attraction of a substantial reward is not in itself the justification for awards on a salvage basis is evidenced by the fact that a person rendering services of a salvage nature to property of which he believed himself to be the owner has not precluded recovery of a salvage award when the true facts emerged.[44] Further support is provided by *The Lomonosoff*,[45] in which, although clearly acting with the intention of preserving their own lives, the plaintiffs took a vessel from a port in the control of revolutionary forces and, having returned it to its owners, subsequently recovered salvage from them. To justify the reward on the ground that they were acting partly to effect salvage would be straining the facts and the case is better explained on the basis that they had provided the necessary service to justify salvage and that

---

[39] (2nd ed., 1907), p. 28.
[40] It is, however, possible, albeit uncommon, for a passenger to claim salvage: see *post*, §§ 632–636.
[41] (1872) L.R. 3 A. & E. 556, where the mate voluntarily remained on board the ship in danger after the order to abandon.
[42] [1921] P. 97, 103.
[43] *Ante*, §§ 33–37.
[44] See *The Liffey* (1887) 6 Asp. M.L.C. 255.
[45] [1912] P. 97; *ante*, § 557. See also *The Beaver* (1801) 3 C. Rob. 292.

Gratuitous salvage

they did not lose their prima facie entitlement to reward by intending not to be paid for their actions.

The crucial factor negating a claim in such circumstances is the element of what is known in the general law of restitution—paradoxically, or perversely—as voluntariness[46] or, more accurately perhaps, gratuitousness. If, with sufficient knowledge of the circumstances, a person performs a service of a salvage nature with the intention, however formed, of not claiming a salvage reward for that service, he *may* be dis-entitled from claiming salvage. The word "may" is used rather than "will" because the court is disinclined to deprive a person of a salvage reward for a meritorious service which would in all other respects qualify for one, even where the service is provided under a contract with a term which is apparently intended to exclude salvage.[47] Salvage may therefore be denied where the salvor is considered to be acting solely for his own benefit.[48]

This principle explains the general refusal of salvage, certainly for life salvage, to lifeboatmen, an undoubtedly meritorious class, whose claim for classification as volunteers in a lay sense is unbeatable. They are assumed to act under a duty, and it is possible to construct an argument that, at least once they have begun a particular service, their duty is one in law, to whomever it may be owed. But the reality is that they are basically gratuitous volunteers so far as the law of salvage is concerned, albeit entitled to recover for property salvage in certain circumstances.[49] But they do not act in response to the attraction of liberal remuneration. Indeed, the public interest in their concentrating on saving lives is furthered by reducing the incentive of reward for property salvage.

The principle also encompasses cases of work provided by sub-contractors and employees of sub-contractors or contractors providing services in respect of the imperilled property.[50] Such persons, by virtue of the doctrine of privity of contract, generally have no contractual claim against the salvee for services rendered. No more do they have a restitutionary claim. This denial has been explained simply on the basis that such claimants cannot claim for merely performing their normal duties.[51]

2. When Non-Volunteers may Claim

In appropriate circumstances, the provider of services of a salvage nature who falls within the general classification of volunteer may be entitled to

---

[46] See Goff & Jones, Chap. 1.
[47] See *post*, Chap. 9.
[48] See *Simon v. Taylor* [1975] 2 Lloyd's Rep. 338 (Sing HC); *ante*, § 49.
[49] See *post*, §§ 698–705.
[50] See *post*, §§ 638–642.
[51] See *The Texaco Southampton* [1983] 1 Lloyd's Rep. 94.

Voluntariness

claim salvage. Those circumstances will now be considered in respect of different types of volunteer. It is important to remember that the categories of salvor are not closed[52] and to bear in mind that there is in each case examined in the succeeding paragraphs some measure of conflict between two important principles; the one that salvage is the reward only of voluntary services, the other that efforts to save life or property in peril deserve favourable consideration in the interests of humanity and commerce. "In all cases, indeed, where duty springing from office, or arising out of contract,[53] would have legally bound the claimants to do services of the same nature as those actually rendered, the court is vigilant to protect the owners from improper claims, without neglecting what is required for the ends of justice and the encouragement of enterprise on such occasions."[54]

564 The general principles on entitlement to claim salvage have been discussed above.[55] The remainder of this chapter sets out the law in respect of individual categories of claimants whose status inhibits their entitlement to a salvage reward. The law in respect of these claimants was in the main laid down prior to the Salvage Convention 1989 and therefore needs to be read with regard to the impact which the Convention may have. Since the principal test for entitlement to a salvage reward is whether or not the claimant is doing something other than what can ordinarily be expected of him, it has formerly been unnecessary to divide the following examples of claims into groups. However, such a division will now be made for reasons of convenience and to take account of the different treatment in the Salvage Convention 1989 of contractual relationships and salvage operations controlled by public authorities.

(a) Contractual relationships

The master, officers and crew

General principle

565 "The crew of a salved vessel cannot, under ordinary circumstances, have a *persona standi* as salvors against their own vessel."[56] A claim on the part of the officers and crew to be permitted to assume the character of salvors in respect of services to their own vessel, or the lives or property on board of her,

---

[52] See *ante*, 445–446.
[53] Similar considerations apply in the case of the passenger labouring for his own safety.
[54] Maclachlan, *Treatise on the Law of Merchant Shipping* (7th ed., 1932), pp. 527–528; approved by Willmer J. in *The Mars and other Barges* (1948) 81 Ll.L. Rep. 452, 456, *supra*; Kennedy (4th ed.), p. 91; see also *The Gregerso* [1973] Q.B. 274, 281.
[55] *Ante*, Chaps. 6 and 7(1).
[56] *The Le Jonet* (1872) L.R. 3 A. & E. 556, 559, adhering to *The Neptune* (1824) 1 Hagg. 227; *The Warrior* (1862) Lush. 476.

The master, officers and crew

is always very strictly scrutinised.[57] To make the distress of their ship an avenue to reward beyond their wages might be to tempt some seamen to negligence and to unfaithfulness in the discharge of their contractual duty.[58] More fundamentally, when danger arises a seaman is already bound by his contract to render assistance to overcome the danger.[59] He not only undertakes to perform his duties in favourable weather. He is to be taken as having pledged his last ounce of strength for better or for worse.[60] Thus, in cases of shipwreck, he must remain as long as possible and exert himself to save as much of the ship and cargo as he can: in shipwreck, the contract continues to lie as long as a plank can be saved[61] and it is immaterial that the crew contribute as much as, or even more than, volunteer salvors to the safety of the vessel.[62] The master's authority survives the occurrence of the misfortune and the seaman's obligations are not discharged so long as his rights of authority exist.[63] For performance of his duties, the seaman receives his remuneration in wages.[64] But in all cases of wreck or loss of the ship, proof that he has not exerted himself to the utmost to save the ship, cargo and stores is to bar his claim to wages.[65]

The denial of salvage or a *quantum meruit* to a seaman who had preserved part of the property involved in a shipwreck (but who was, from the ship's failure to earn freight, formerly disentitled to claim in full the wages he had earned) was also justified on the grounds of simplicity and convenience (a claim for wages is one for a liquidated sum and one which cannot be exceeded) and because the property preserved remained subject to his maritime lien, which had extended over the whole part of the property involved in the venture and was therefore available so far as possible to satisfy his claim for wages already earned.[66]

566

Since it is the existence of the seaman's duties under his contract of service which normally precludes his standing as a salvor, it is therefore the nature and extent of those duties, as properly interpreted, which define the parameters of the prohibition against his so acting. Thus, a member of the crew will normally be entitled to claim salvage for assistance rendered to another ship owned by the owners of his own ship, because he will usually only be

567

---

[57] *The Albionic* [1941] P. 99, 105; (1941) 70 Ll.L.R. 257, 263. See also *The Neptune, supra*, note 56, at pp. 236–237. *cf. The San Demetrio* (1941) 69 Ll.L.R. 5, 12; *post*, §569.

[58] *The Neptune, supra*, n. 56, at 237.

[59] See *The Sappho* (1871) L.R. 3 P.C. 690, 694.

[60] *The Albionic* [1941] P. 99, 105.

[61] *The Florence* (1852) 16 Jur. 572, 573; *Newman v. Walters* (1804) 3 B. & P. 612, 615; *The Neptune, supra*, n. 56, at 236, 238, followed in *The Warrior* (1862) Lush. 476.

[62] *Newman v. Walters, supra*, n. 61, at 615; *The Neptune, supra*, n. 56, at 237; followed in *The Portreath* [1923] P. 155.

[63] *The Neptune, supra*, n. 56, at 238–239.

[64] The old rule that his entitlement to wages was dependent on freight having been earned (see *The Neptune, supra*) has been abolished by statute.

[65] *The Florence, supra*, n. 61, at 573, following *The Neptune, supra*.

[66] *The Neptune, supra*, n. 56, at 237–238.

legally[67] obliged under his contract of service to render services to his own ship.[68] Similarly, it is in principle arguable that a seaman should be able to claim from his own ship if, during performance of his contract, he renders services in excess of those ordinarily required by that contract.[69] However, the draconian nature of the performance required from a seaman is such that he is virtually incapable of exceeding the requirements of the contract while it remains on foot and, despite possible support derivable from one case,[70] this argument was rejected in *The Florence*.[71]

568 It follows that the dissolution of a seaman's contract of service is a condition precedent to his right to claim as a salvor. "The true question is whether there was a *vis major* of so permanent a character as to dissolve the contract."[72] This dissolution can be effected in any of three ways—

(a) by the act of the master in discharging him; or

(b) by the abandonment of the ship bona fide and with the master's authority; or

(c) by a hostile capture of the ship.

Discharge by master

569 The following principles were enunciated in *The Warrior*.[73] A seaman's contract may be dissolved by the act of the master giving him a discharge. This may be the case although the ship is not shewn to have been finally abandoned and although the master is guilty of misconduct in discharging the crew (which is possible even though he may not think the ship can be recovered, for he must know that he is legally entitled to have the services of the crew to rescue as much of the ship and cargo as possible). The discharge and the seaman's consequent liberty to act as a salvor will be invalid if the seaman is a party to misconduct by the master. But seamen are not generally considered capable of inquiring into the master's conduct nor obliged to do so, and any allegation of fraud on the seaman's part must be strictly proved. "This is obviously a rare class of case, but where the discharge is formal and unqualified to the degree found in this instance, and the master was clearly acting within the sphere of his authority as the owner's agent, it would seem that the decision could hardly be otherwise."[74]

---

[67] He may be morally obliged to assist the sister ship: see *The Sappho* (1871) L.R. 3 P.C. 690, 694; following Lord Stowell in *The Waterloo* (1820) 2 Dods. 433, 437, and distinguishing *The Maria Jane* (1850) 14 Jur. 857, where, according to usage in the African trade, ships and crews of the same owner were obliged to render mutual assistance to each other.
[68] *The Sappho, supra.* See also *The Telemachus* [1957] P. 47.
[69] *cf. Newman v. Walters* (1804) 3 B. & P. 612.
[70] See the discussion of *The Beaver* (1801) 3 C. Rob. 292; *post*, §582.
[71] (1852) 16 Jur. 572, 575.
[72] "permanent according to all human probability, for the law can never depend upon mere possibilities:" *The Florence, supra,* n. 61, at 575.
[73] (1862) Lush. 476.
[74] *The Albionic* [1941] P. 99, 108.

Abandonment of the vessel

570 The principles which determine when a vessel has been abandoned and when members of the crew are entitled to claim as salvors for services rendered to their own vessel subsequent to the abandonment were laid down by Dr Lushington in *The Florence*,[75] the case which has always been regarded as the *locus classicus* of this branch of the law.[76] Dr Lushington was not deterred from apparently encouraging hasty and improper abandonments since only bona fide abandonments would qualify and the occurrence of salvage by mariners who had abandoned their ship was so rare as to render the danger of temptation to abandon largely imaginary, particularly since the requirement that abandonment had to take place at sea meant that, in addition to the unlikelihood of earning salvage, the mariner would at that time have lost his wages.[77] He listed four requirements to be fulfilled, which have been consistently applied.[78] First, the abandonment must take place at sea, and not upon the coast. Secondly, it must be *sine spe revertendi aut recuperandi* (without hope of return or recovery). Thirdly, it must be bona fide and for the purpose of saving life. And, finally, it must be by order of the master in consequence of danger by reason of damage to the ship and the state of the elements. The separate components of these "four" propositions will now be considered, albeit in a different order.

571 (i) *The danger justifying abandonment.* It is one of the basic prerequisites of a salvage claim that the vessel must be in danger before a salvage service can be rendered and a salvage reward earned, and once the vessel has been finally abandoned, that fact should be conclusive in establishing the necessary danger.[79] But the mere existence of such danger as would enable third parties to provide and claim for salvage services will not *per se* justify abandonment. By their calling, seamen are bound to incur a certain amount of danger, however it arises, and it is part of their duties to work to preserve the ship and cargo from such perils that do arise. Abandonment may, however, be justified, even though it can be shewn in retrospect that, if the crew had remained on board to face the danger, they could have overcome it without any additional assistance.[80] The precise degree of danger which will justify abandonment cannot be exactly defined but three points seem to be well established: first, that there must be danger by reason of the state of the elements (which seems uncontroversial); secondly, that the ship must have been damaged; and, thirdly, that human life must be imperilled.

---

[75] (1852) 16 Jur. 572.
[76] *The Albionic, supra*, n. 74, at 107.
[77] (1852) 16 Jur. 572, 574.
[78] See *The Warrior* (1862) Lush. 476, 481–482; *The Portreath* [1923] P. 155, 160; *The San Demetrio* (1941) 69 Ll.L. Rep. 5, 12; *The Albionic* [1941] P. 99, 107, affirmed [1942] P. 81.
[79] See *ante*, Chap. 4.
[80] See *The Le Jonet* (1872) L.R. 3 A. & E. 556, 560.

Voluntariness

572 In all of the cases in which abandonment has been justified, the ship was damaged. Provided the ship was, at the commencement of the voyage, properly seaworthy to negotiate the ordinary perils of the voyage, it is reasonable to expect the crew to stand by the ship during the perils which arise and, while the ship is undamaged, to carry out their duties in trying to overcome them. However, given the stress placed upon the duty not to imperil human life, it is submitted that, in an exceptional case, abandonment should not be condemned as wrongful merely because the ship is undamaged but that that should merely be a factor to be considered in determining the extent of the danger. As Dr Lushington put it,[81] there is a limit to the risk to which a seaman is bound to expose himself; human life is more valuable in the sight of God than any property; and it is clearly a duty not to sacrifice human life. He considered the potential conflict between saving life and saving property negligible in practice on the ground that, if there were a reasonable chance of saving the ship, and consequently the cargo, there should in most cases be the same reasonable chance of saving the lives of the crew.

573 (ii) *The decision to abandon.* The master is the proper person to form a judgment as to whether or not abandonment is absolutely necessary. He is the person whom the owners voluntarily entrusted with the command of their vessel and the care of the property on board. They must be supposed to have believed him competent to discharge his duties and especially that he would not leave the property to destruction without adequate cause.[82] Thus, in *The Albionic*,[83] where the master gave the order to abandon ship without intending a final abandonment, the later act of the chief officer in giving the option of leaving the ship to those crew members who were unable to take advantage of the master's original call to abandon did not effect an abandonment, even though Langton J. confessed that the master, who was injured and ill, was really unfit to be in charge of a vessel at sea.[84]

574 Moreover, where the master himself contemplates the necessity of abandonment, he should, in pursuance of his duty to safeguard human life, implement his analysis of the situation by giving an *order* to abandon ship. In *The San Demetrio*,[85] Langton J. said that the chief of the conditions to be fulfilled before seamen could claim salvage in respect of their own vessel was "that the ship was properly abandoned under the orders of her master." However, if a vessel is so badly damaged that she is likely to founder in a matter of moments and the master and crew leave her with one accord at the best possible speed, no one could be heard to say that she was not truly and completely abandoned merely because no actual order to abandon was given by the master.[86]

---

[81] *The Florence* (1852) 16 Jur. 572, 573; *The Trelawney* (1802) 4 C. Rob. 223.
[82] *The Florence, supra,* n. 81, at 573. See also *The Warrior* (1862) Lush. 476, 482–483; *ante,* § 569.
[83] *The Albionic* [1941] P. 99; affirmed [1942] P. 81.
[84] (1941) 70 Ll.L.R. 257, 262.
[85] (1941) 69 Ll.L.R. 5, 12.
[86] *The Albionic* [1941] P. 99, 112 (affirmed [1942] P. 81).

The master, officers and crew

An order may be given expressly or inferred from the master's conduct.[87] If the order is not warranted, the master is not entitled to give the crew liberty to decide themselves whether to abandon, nor will their exercise of such an option constitute a valid abandonment.[88] The mere fact that the master or other person in charge of a vessel offers an option to members of the crew to leave or to stay with the vessel cannot by itself be the test of whether a sailor's contract is ended; at the highest it is only an option to continue or discontinue the contract of service.[89] Similarly, the fact that the master calls upon crew members who have left the ship to return voluntarily, instead of ordering them to do so, cannot be decisive as to whether their contracts had been terminated.[90]

575 The master's decision to abandon is justifiable if made bona fide, in the belief that it is necessary to save human life; in cases of bona fide abandonment, the crew are justified in obeying the orders of the master to quit.[91] Thus, the fact that abandonment is later shewn to have been unnecessary should not invalidate the abandonment or the consequent liberty of a crew member to claim salvage, even if he did not himself believe in the necessity of the order which it was his duty to obey.

Where the circumstances are doubtful, the court will be slow to infer that property of great value has been abandoned, unless it is proved that there was no reasonable hope of recovery.[92] This attitude, coupled with the need for abandonment to have been ordered bona fide, should mean that an order to abandon will be invalid if it can be shewn not to have been made bona fide, even if objectively it could be shewn to have been justifiable. However, despite the onerous nature of the seaman's obligation to perform his duty in times of peril, it is submitted that the court would be inclined to condone abandonment by the crew if a master's decision not to abandon ship could not be justified on any reasonable grounds.

576 In a particular case, an order to abandon ship may be designed to effect an immediate discharge of the crew's contracts and may achieve that result.[93] But as a general rule an order to abandon ship without more will not automatically dissolve the contracts. The ship must actually be abandoned[94]; and the question in each case must be whether the facts warrant the inference in law that

---

[87] *The Albionic* [1941] P. 81, 85. Surprisingly, perhaps, none was to be inferred from the facts of that case.
[88] *ibid.*, 85.
[89] *The Albionic* [1941] P. 99, 111, *per* Langton J. (affirmed [1942] P. 81).
[90] *The Portreath* [1923] P. 158, 161; *The Albionic* [1941] P. 99, 110–111 (affirmed [1942] P. 81).
[91] *The Florence* (1852) 16 Jur. 572, 573. *The Albionic* (1941) P. 81, 85.
[92] *The Warrior* (1862) Lush. 476, 482.
[93] See *ante*, §569; *The Warrior, supra*, where the discharges were given after abandonment and in writing.
[94] *The Albionic* [1941] P. 99; affirmed [1942] P. 81.

the vessel was abandoned.[95] Moreover, it may well be necessary to demonstrate that the leaving of the ship occurred voluntarily. In *The Albionic*,[96] where the master and half of the crew entered the lifeboats, one of the factors which suggested that the ship had not been abandoned was that the lifeboats were never cast off by the order of the captain or anyone else, but were in fact broken or drifted away from the ship's side.

A ship may be held to have been abandoned although one or two men, or possibly a handful of men, owing to special circumstances cannot get away[97] or refuse to get away.[98] A seaman's claim to salvage, therefore, depends on whether the ship has been abandoned, not on whether he has abandoned it. Where the master remains on board, it is less likely that an abandonment will be found to have taken place but his presence need not necessarily be conclusive.

577 (iii) *Final abandonment.* In *The Florence*,[99] Dr Lushington said that the abandonment must be *sine spe revertendi*, for no one would contend that a temporary abandonment, such as frequently occurs in collisions, from immediate fear, before the state of the ship is known, would vacate the contract. The judgment of Hill J. in *The Portreath*,[1] where this principle was applied, suggests that an abandonment may be revoked even if, when made, it was contemplated as being final. In the view of Hill J., "when one finds a master giving orders to his crew to abandon ship and go on board another vessel because he thinks his ship is sinking, and then within a short time, on maturer judgment, he arrives at the conclusion that the ship is not sinking there is no foundation for saying that there was any final abandonment of the ship."[2] However, Dr Lushington laid down in *The Sarah Bell*[3] that if, at the time of abandonment, it was made *sine spe revertendi*, it was immaterial that, on reflection, this view was altered. For consistency, Hill J.'s dictum must therefore be taken to indicate that a total physical abandonment will not be final where the master temporarily contemplates its revocability.[4]

It was, it seems, from the principle that the intention to abandon must have been final that Dr Lushington emphasised the requirement, drawn from the absence of any contrary examples, that the abandonment must have taken

---

[95] *The Albionic* [1941] P. 99, 112–113.
[96] *Supra.*
[97] *cf. The Herbert Fearn* (1920) 4 Ll.L.Rep. 86, 87, where, without commenting on any entitlement to claim, Hill J. expressed the hope that the owners would substantially recognise the good conduct of an able-bodied seaman who, involuntarily and unknown to his companions, had been left on board and subsequently assisted in salvage.
[98] *The Le Jonet* (1872) L.R. 3 A. & E. 556, following *The Warrior* (1862) Lush. 476 regarding abandonment; *The Albionic* [1942] P. 81, 84. In *The Florence* (1852) 16 Jur. 572, 574, Dr Lushington declined to express an opinion on the effect of the crew remaining on board against the orders of the master.
[99] (1852) 16 Jur. 572, 573.
[1] [1923] P. 155.
[2] *ibid.*, 161. See also *The Albionic* [1941] P. 99; affirmed [1942] P. 81.
[3] (1845) 4 Not. of Cas. 144.
[4] *cf.* Dr Lushington's assumption (text to n. 14, *post*) of Lord Alvanley C.J.'s view that a contract will not be terminated by a hostile capture which is soon followed by a recapture.

place "at sea". There was, he stated, a wide distinction between an abandonment at a distance from land in the open ocean and quitting the ship on the coast, where there may exist a fair expectation of returning, where the *spes recuperandi* is probable.[5] In *The Portreath*,[6] abandonment after collision of a vessel anchored near the Breaksea light-vessel was held to have occurred at sea.

578 (iv) *Summary*. A member of the crew will be entitled to claim a reward for salvage services rendered to his own ship after his contract has been discharged by abandonment. This discharge will be effected where, because of danger arising from the elements and (usually) due to damage to the ship, the ship is actually and (it seems) intentionally abandoned while at sea by the major part of the ship's complement on an order given, *sine spe revertendi aut recuperandi*, bona fide and for the purpose of saving human life, by the person in charge of the ship.

Hostile capture

579 In *The Warrior*,[7] Dr Lushington said: "There are two ways in which the contract of seamen may be dissolved. It may be dissolved by final abandonment of the ship, or by the act of the master giving the seamen a discharge." This assumption has been followed in subsequent cases[8] and reflects, no doubt, the two most common situations in which dissolution is, if at all, likely to occur. There is no clear authority which lays down that a seaman may be afforded the opportunity of earning salvage from his own ship in other circumstances but the effect of the relevant authorities is such as to suggest the distinct possibility of it in cases of hostile capture, on similar principles to those governing the settled situations.

580 In *The Florence*,[9] whilst observing that mariners are bound to incur a certain amount of danger, whether it proceeds from an enemy, pirates or the elements, Dr Lushington stated that "By capture, certainly, if there be no recapture, the contract is at once put an end to, and this, I apprehend, whether by an enemy or by pirates." Later in his judgment he discussed *Beale v. Thompson*,[10] a case concerning the crew's entitlement to wages where their ship had been temporarily detained by order of the Russian Government. Commenting that an embargo, being of a temporary character, does not dissolve the seaman's contract,[11] he referred to not entirely consistent dicta of

---

[5] *The Florence* (1852) 16 Jur. 572, 573. See also *The Warrior* (1862) Lush. 476, and Langton J.'s comment thereon in *The Albionic* [1941] P. 99, 197.

[6] [1923] P. 155.

[7] (1862) Lush. 476, 482.

[8] See *The Le Jonet* (1872) L.R. 3 A. & E. 556, 559 and *The Portreath* [1923] P. 155, 160, where Dr Lushington's dictum was quoted; and *The Albionic* [1941] P. 99, 105.

[9] (1852) 16 Jur. 572, 573.

[10] (1803) 3 B. & P. 405 (Court of Common Pleas); reversed (1804) 4 East 546 (Court of King's Bench).

[11] As was decided by the Court of King's Bench in *Beale v. Thompson, supra*. See further Temperley, §§ 204–206.

Lord Alvanley C.J. (dissenting in the Court of Common Pleas) suggesting that capture might sometimes effect a termination of a seaman's contract, then, in line with those dicta, continued:

> "The true question is, whether there was a *vis major* of so permanent a character as to dissolve the contract; permanent according to all human probability, for the law never can depend on mere possibilities ... Assuming the law to be, though I give no opinion upon it, that capture with a total loss puts an end to the contract, and that capture and recapture, the mariners remaining on board, either do not put an end to the contract or revive it, I think there is a strong distinction between capture and abandonment at sea. They are, it is true, both *vis major*; but the probability of recapture is not an unlikely event; the probability of recovering a ship abandoned at sea is so small as very seldom to occur, and cannot be[12] in the contemplation of the parties ... If capture alone puts an end to the contract, which appears to have been the leaning of Lord Stowell,[13] then, *a fortiori*, abandonment *ex necessitate* would do so."[14]

More encouragingly, a majority of the House of Lords decided in *Horlock v. Beal*,[15] in which a British ship in a German port at the outbreak of the First World War was detained, the crew being imprisoned some months later, that[16] the seaman ceased to be entitled to his wages as soon as the further performance of the contract became impossible. This disentitlement was, by a smaller majority[17] said to date from the ship's detention.

581   As indicated by Dr Lushington in *The Florence*,[18] the drift of the authorities had early been anticipated by Lord Stowell, who indicated on several occasions[19] that an act of capture can terminate the obligations under the seaman's contract of service, so that he was thereafter a volunteer, and so capable of earning salvage. In this respect, in *The Governor Raffles*,[20] he distinguished capture from mutiny, which does not release a seaman from his duties, in particular from his duty to give every assistance in his power to prevent or quell a mutiny and, short of unduly risking human life and whenever there is

---

[12] In The Law Times report, this appears as "can scarcely be": (1852) 19 L.T. (O.S.) 304, 305.

[13] In *The Governor Raffles* (1815) 2 Dods. 14.

[14] (1852) 16 Jur. 572, 575. *cf. supra*, n. 4.

[15] [1916] 1 A.C. 486, in which the Court of King's Bench's decision in *Beale v. Thompson*, *supra*, was distinguished and *The Friends*, *infra*, was cited.

[16] *per* Earl Loreburn, Lord Atkinson, Lord Shaw of Dunfermline and Lord Wrenbury, Lord Parmoor dissenting.

[17] *per* Lords Atkinson, Shaw of Dunfermline and Wrenbury. Earl Loreburn dated it from the imprisonment of the crew.

[18] *Ante*, §580.

[19] See *The Two Friends* (1799) 1 C. Rob. 271, 278; *The Friends* (1801) 4 C. Rob. 143, 144; *The Beaver* (1800) 3 C. Rob. 292; *The Governor Raffles* (1815) 2 Dods. 14, 18.

[20] (1815) 2 Dods. 14, 17–18. His Lordship distinguished *The Trelawney* (1801) 3 C. Rob. 216n.; (1802) 4 C. Rob. 223, where the reward was decreed to the crew of another ship, upon whom no duty was imposed to attempt the rescue from insurgent slaves.

a reasonable prospect of success, to use his best endeavours to preserve or recover the vessel and goods of his employers.

Curiously, his Lordship made no specific reference to the rule as to recovery of salvage under discussion in deciding the nearest case to an authority in this area, *The Beaver*.[21] He nevertheless awarded salvage to the master and a boy, his apprentice, who, after their vessel had been captured by a French privateer and the rest of the crew taken out, overthrew the prize crew of five, regained possession of the ship and, with assistance later given by a British frigate, navigated her to England.

The impact of *The Beaver* as an authority is impaired to the extent that no point appears to have been raised in relation to the possible subsistence of the contracts of service. If the contracts were found to have subsisted, then: either the master and boy should not have been entitled to salvage since, as in the case of mutiny,[22] they were merely performing their duties to recover the captured property; or the case is a unique example of seamen earning salvage by rendering services in excess of those required by their subsisting contracts.[23]

582

Reverting to the more usual analysis, *i.e.* considering whether the contracts of service were terminated by the capture, *The Beaver*, if correctly decided in law and on its facts (which is not necessarily the case), otherwise provides a fairly strong basis for the view that a sailor is, after capture, free to act as a salvor of his own ship, whether by regaining possession of it or performing other services, such as navigation; for, while rejecting the argument that the ship was a derelict, Lord Stowell said: "The vessel itself was never in the state of a derelict—the eye of the master was constantly upon it; and if I may say so, kept a possession of it for the whole time under the *spes ac animus recuperandi*."[24] Unfortunately, however, this point was not considered by Dr Lushington in his rather opaque dictum[25] that "capture followed by recapture, the mariners remaining on board, does not either put an end to or revive the contract."

583

Despite Dr Lushington's view that recovery after capture is more likely than after abandonment,[26] claims in the former case have clearly not had the significance in practice of those in the latter. However, this does not rule out the possibility of such claims and it may be worthwhile to synthesise the views discernible in the cases. First, the seaman is contractually obliged to use his best endeavours to preserve the ship and its cargo. Secondly, he is discharged from his duties by an act of pirates or enemies constituting *vis major* of so permanent a character as to dissolve his contract and so to set him

584

[21] (1801) 3 C. Rob. 292.
[22] *Ante*, §581.
[23] See *Newman v. Walters* (1804) 3 B. & P. 612, 614. *cf.* the quotation in the text to n. 24 next.
[24] (1801) 3 C. Rob. 292, 293–294.
[25] *Ante*, text to n. 14.
[26] *ibid.*

free to render salvage services as a volunteer. Neither a temporary event, such as possibly an embargo, nor a mutiny will suffice, but capture by terrorists might do so. Thirdly, in line with general principles of the doctrine of frustration,[27] although the permanence of the capture may not be apparent at first and though the crew must take reasonable steps to try to regain possession, their contracts will be dissolved from the moment when the probability of recovery of the ship appears unlikely. Fourthly, their contracts may be dissolved even though they remain on board the ship and hope to recapture her.

Salvage service

585 A salvage award cannot, of course, be made unless, after proving that his contract has been validly discharged, the plaintiff crew member also shews that he subsequently rendered a service to the vessel which was a salvage service.[28]

Parties governed by these rules

586 The majority of claimants against their own ship have been officers or other members of the crew. The master is a far less likely candidate because contracts of service continue while his authority survives and he is the last person likely to be regarded as freed from his duties to the ship, particularly as he is responsible for deciding to terminate the contracts, or at least that supervening events have necessitated termination of the contracts. However, *dicta* of the Privy Council in *The Sappho*[29] and the admittedly indecisive decision in *The Beaver*[30] establish that the master may also earn salvage in appropriate circumstances.

587 Occasionally, employees of third parties are nominally signed on ship's articles at a nominal rate of payment.[31] There has been a practice for certain telecommunication companies to supply not only equipment, but also officers to operate it, to British merchant vessels, although more recently shipowners have tended directly to employ their own officers to operate such equipment. The number of such officers carried by a vessel is dictated by its classification and tonnage.[32] Where such officers have been supplied, they have commonly been paid by the supplying company. They have, however, habitually been signed on ship's articles as Radio Officer and paid a more or less nominal sum by the shipowner. In such cases it has been a usual term of the contract between the shipowner and the company that the officer shall be deemed to be the servant of the shipowner during the currency of the articles. *The Albionic*[33]

---

[27] See *post*, §§ 608–614.
[28] *The Le Jonet* (1872) L.R. 3 A. & E. 556, 560.
[29] (1871) L.R. 3 P.C. 690.
[30] *Supra*.
[31] See, *e.g. The Coriolanus* (1890) 15 P.D. 103.
[32] *cf.* Temperley, § 1118. See now MSA 1995, s.85.
[33] [1941] P. 99; affirmed [1942] P. 81. The relevant point appears at [1941] P. 99, 104 and (more fully) at (1941) 70 Ll.L.Rep. 257, 260.

was by agreement a test action, brought by the ship's wireless officer as sole plaintiff and decided against him on the issue of abandonment. To Langton J.'s query, the parties replied that it was not considered necessary to differentiate his position from the rest of the crew just because he was employed in the first instance by the Marconi Company although his name appeared on the ship's articles as a member of the crew. His Lordship merely commented that it was customary in the Admiralty Court to give a wireless officer the standing of either the second or third officer in apportioning a reward.

Pilots[34]

588 A pilot has been defined for the purposes of the Merchant Shipping legislation[35] as meaning any person not belonging to a ship who has the conduct thereof. Pilots are habitually engaged to conduct a vessel in negotiating particular risks or dangers, most commonly of local navigation, which the master otherwise in command of the vessel may consider himself not sufficiently competent to negotiate without the assistance of a pilot.

589 By virtue of their profession, therefore, pilots are involved in the provision of services which, if they were provided by other persons, might entitle such other persons to claim a salvage reward. As Dr Lushington put it, however[36]:

> "[T]here is a striking difference between a person possessed of such monopoly [of pilotage], and entitled to charge a given sum [which is fixed on the ground of its being a monopoly], and a person voluntarily performing a duty, whether a pilotage or a salvage service, because the latter has a right to exercise his own judgment as to whether he will go out on the service or not, and may then demand a fair remuneration for whatever he does. It might happen that mere pilotage pay would be no reward at all to a person who goes out under these circumstances... Suppose there was no such danger as to prevent a pilot going out for the ordinary rate of pilotage, it would not follow that individuals who voluntarily perform that duty would be entitled to no more pay, because the grounds are totally different."

590 The guidance of a vessel under extraordinary circumstances by a person who is not a pilot may, therefore, rise to the rank of a salvage service.[37] It seems that, where a vessel is in such a condition of danger that salvage services

---

[34] See generally Rose, *The Modern Law of Pilotage* (1984); and *Current Law Statutes Annotated* 1987, c. 21.
[35] See MSA 1894, s.742; the Pilotage Act 1987, s.31(1). Under the latter Act, pilotage became a matter of port and harbour law rather than merchant shipping law, and the definition does not appear in the Merchant Shipping Act 1995.
[36] *The Rosehaugh* (1854) 1 Spinks 267, 268.
[37] See *The Aglaia* (1888) 13 P.D. 160, 162, *per* Sir James Hannen P.; *Newman v. Walters* (1804) 3 Bos. & Pul. 612 (where a passenger salvor was also justified in restraining and overriding a drunken pilot's attempt to let go the anchor); *The Eugenie* (1844) 3 Not: of Cas. 430.

might be rendered to her, any doubt as to whether a person who is not a pilot has rendered services of pilotage or salvage will, in the absence of contradictory evidence and provided the alleged salvor has otherwise satisfied his burden of proving that he has supplied salvage services, be resolved in favour of a salvage award.[38] Yet a person who is not a pilot but who renders a service of pilotage will not by that fact alone be entitled to remuneration other than on a pilotage basis.[39] In particular, such a person who is used to acting as a pilot, who contracts to act as one and who does so act, using the local knowledge and skill of a pilot, will not lightly be allowed to claim as a salvor, even though the vessel may be in some distress in circumstances enabling others to claim as salvors and even though he is assisted by a person entitled to claim as a salvor.[40]

591 The pilot on board a vessel in danger who has been engaged for reward as pilot cannot claim salvage remuneration for doing so merely because the vessel is in danger.[41] This is also true of a compulsory pilot who performs pilotage for a vessel to which others are providing salvage services for which they can claim remuneration accordingly, and even though he is required to give orders to them.[42] Nor are the services of a pilot to be deemed extraordinary for the sake of converting them into salvage services merely because they involve some degree of hazard, or even such a degree of hazard as might entitle one who performed them as a volunteer to rank as a salvor in respect of them. Pilotage is by its nature a hazardous occupation; having voluntarily taken up the occupation and its risks, and with knowledge of them, pilots must generally be content with their normal remuneration.[43] It may be that a pilotage service is rendered in circumstances of such risk that the pilot is required to render more than ordinary pilotage services and becomes entitled to claim additional remuneration.[44] And even where a pilot does assist in the provision of salvage services he will not obtain salvage renumeration for merely trifling assistance.[45]

---

[38] See *The Anders Knape* (1879) 4 P.D. 213, applying the test in *The Frederick* (1838) 1 W. Rob. 16.

[39] *The Michael* (1805), referred to in *The Columbus* (1828) 2 Hagg. 178n. *cf. The Branken Moor* (1837) 3 Hagg. 373.

[40] *The Aeolus* (1873) L.R. 4 A. & E. 29 (waterman).

[41] See, *e.g. The Joseph Harvey* (1799) 1 C. Rob. 306; *The City of Edinburgh* (1831) 2 Hagg. 333; *The Funchal* (1837) 3 Hagg. 386n; *The Johannes* (1848) 6 Not. of Cas. 288.

[42] *The Bedeburn* [1914] P. 146. It is possible that the presence of a pilot will obviate the need for others to provide salvage services and erode their claims accordingly: see *The Wilhelmine* (1842) 1 Not. of Cas. 376.

[43] See *The Joseph Harvey, supra,* n. 41, at 307.

[44] See *The Hebe* (1844) 2 W. Rob. 246, where Dr Lushington's judgment to award more than ordinary pilotage remuneration seems to betray a reluctance to award pilots salvage remuneration with the generosity that might be accorded to other categories of salvors. For further discussion, see *infra.*

[45] *The Monarch* (1886) 12 P.D. 5. *cf. The Tsiropinas* (1935) 51 Ll.L.Rep. 87, where a third pilot, whose presence was deemed to be unnecessary but who boarded in good faith and rendered some slight service, was awarded a small sum. See also *The Jonge Andries* (1857) Swab. 227, 229–230; affirmed (1857) 11 Moo. P.C. 313.

Pilots

Even where a pilot's services are classifiable as salvage services, his entitlement to salvage remuneration may be restricted by the terms of local regulation.[46]

592 The courts have long been reluctant to recognise in cases before them that pilots have performed salvage services. Thus, Sir Boyd Merriman P. said in *The Luigi Accame*[47]:

> "I regard it as of the utmost importance to the seafaring community in general that there should be no temptation to pilots to convert their ordinary pilotage duties, or the normal hazards which may arise in the course of performing their ordinary pilotage duties, into salvage services ... I agree with [Sir Samuel Evans P. in *The Bedeburn*[48] that] 'It would be undesirable [I would use a stronger adjective] for the shipping community at large, and for the respectable body of men constituting the pilots of the country, that any encouragement should be given to them to become searchers after salvage.' "[49]

Thus, Sir John Nicholl stated quite firmly in *The Johannes*[50] that if licensed pilots, to whom Parliament has given special privileges and exclusive rights, lend themselves to attempt extortion on foreigners, the court must repress them.[51] Similarly, the court will not undermine its policy of encouraging salvors by looking favourably on a claim for salvage by persons who appear to have put off efforts to provide salvage services, either through excessive regard for their own safety or where the effect of the delay may have been to prolong or to confirm the danger.[52] It will also be slow to regard the conversion of pilotage into salvage, for the reason that a master may be inclined to reject the offer of assistance for fear of exposing his owners to liability to salvage.[53]

593 The court is, however, conscious of the need to strike a balance between protecting shipowners from extortionate demands and taking great care that a person providing salvage services should be properly remunerated, pilotage rates only having been calculated as giving an adequate reward for the provision of pilotage services which the law has made compulsory for pilots to perform,[54] *i.e.* the conducting of a vessel into port in the ordinary and common course of navigation. Pilotage of a vessel being salvaged by others

---

[46] See Kennedy, 4th ed., p. 44, nn. 1–5.
[47] (1938) 60 Ll.L.Rep. 106, 110.
[48] [1914] P. 146, 151.
[49] See also *The Aeolus* (1873) 4 A. & E. 29, 31; *The Santiago* (1900) 9 Asp. 147, 149.
[50] (1835) 6 Not. of Cas. 288. See also *The Elizabeth* (1844) 8 Jur. 365, 365.
[51] See also *The Joseph Harvey* (1799) 1 C. Rob. 306, where the pilot's monstrous breach of duty in taking over the vessel in face of the master's objection was reported to Trinity House.
[52] *cf. The City of Edinburgh* (1831) 2 Hagg. 333.
[53] See *The Jonge Andries* (1857) Swab. 227, 229–230; affirmed (1857) 11 Moo. P.C. 313. See also *The Galatea* (1858) Swab. 349, 350.
[54] See *The Elizabeth, supra,* n. 50, at 365.

will only generate pilotage reward though the pilot may be unable to claim additional fees for the particular pilotage services required, but the circumstances may justify additional remuneration within the range of pilotage fees.[55] A pilot will be entitled to claim salvage where the circumstances are more difficult than those with which he will normally be expected to cope in the performance of his duties. No pilot is bound to go on board a vessel in distress to render pilot service for mere pilotage reward; if a pilot, being told he would receive pilotage only, refused to take charge of a vessel in that condition, he would be subjected to no censure, and if he did take charge of her he would be entitled to a salvage remuneration.[56] The court has always held, when pilots go on board vessels which are in a state of danger, that they are entitled to say that they go on board also as salvors, in which case they are not entitled to abandon the vessels but are entitled to be compensated by more than ordinary pilotage reward.[57] Just as there may be circumstances of such danger at the commencement of services provided by a pilot that they will be treated as salvage services from the start, so may circumstances of such danger supervene after pilotage services have commenced as to alter their character and engraft a right to salvage reward on them. Thus, on the occurrence of emergencies requiring extraordinary service, a pilot on board a ship is bound to stay by the ship but becomes entitled to salvage remuneration and not a mere pilotage fee.[58] And a pilot in charge of a vessel engaged in salving another vessel may be entitled to salvage reward from the owners of the salved vessel on the ground that he has performed pilotage services which could not be considered to be within the contemplation and scope of his contract as pilot.[59]

594   It has been said that a very clear line has to be crossed before turning a pilot's services into salvage services.[60] The cases have demonstrated, however, that a pilot's task in crossing the line will not be easy rather than that there is a clear line to be passed. Not infrequently, the test for distinguishing pilotage from salvage has been expressed in an unhelpful and circular way. Thus, in *The Santiago*,[61] Gorell Barnes J. said that:

---

[55] See *The Luigi Accame* (1938) 60 Ll.L.Rep. 106, 113, where, if it had been pilotage, although there was no licensed pilot's fee for beaching a ship and no additional fee for piloting a "lame duck" (a flotilla of salvage vessels plus the salved ship being towed by them) as against a sound ship, the pilotage fees could be increased by reason of the ship's coming within the category of ships with a deeper draught.

[56] *The Frederick* (1838) 1 W. Rob. 16, 17, applied in *The Anders Knape* (1879) 4 P.D. 213; *The Dosseitei* (1846) 10 Jur. 865, 866. cf. *The Hebe* (1844) 2 W. Rob. 246, 247–248.

[57] *The Jonge Andries* (1857) Swab. 226, 229; affirmed (1857) 11 Moo. P.C. 313. See also *The Elizabeth* (1844) 8 Jur. 365. cf. *The Joseph Harvey* (1799) 1 C. Rob. 306; *The Hebe, supra*.

[58] *The Saratoga* (1861) Lush. 318, 321; referred to in *Akerblom v. Price, Potter, Walker & Co.* (1881) 7 Q.B.D. 129, 134–135. See also *Newman v. Walters* (1804) 3 Bos. & Pul. 612, 616; *The Galatea* (1858) Swab. 349, 350; *The Aeolus* (1873) L.R. 4 A. & E. 29, 32.

[59] *The Santiago* (1900) 9 Asp. 147. The pilot was not confined merely to receiving the additional fee provided by s.593 of the Merchant Shipping Act 1894, for leading in a vessel without a qualified pilot on board.

[60] *The Bengloe* (1940) 67 Ll.L. Rep. 307, 311, per Langton J.

[61] (1900) 9 Asp. 147, 149.

"the question comes to this, Does he in any particular case run so much risk that he ought to receive some salvage in addition to what is considered to be pilotage reward?"

The test is stated with a little more precision, however, in the leading decision of the Court of Appeal in *Akerblom v. Price, Potter, Walker & Co.*[62]:

"The tribunal must determine, whether under all the circumstances of the particular case the service, which the pilot has entered upon or has unexpectedly found imposed upon him, was rendered so different in responsibility or danger or kind from the ordinary service of a pilot, as to make it impossible that any fair owner should have insisted upon his being paid otherwise than by a salvage reward; or, whether, although there was some increased responsibility or danger or unusual kind of service, any fair pilot would have refused to enter upon the service or to continue to perform the service, unless paid otherwise than by a fair compensation for pilotage services."

In the abstract, this test may not appear significantly more decisive. In practice, it is applied by taking account of various factors which are themselves tested in the light of the prevailing circumstances:

"It leaves the rule of law to be that in order to entitle a pilot to salvage reward he must not only shew that the ship was in some sense in distress, but that she was in such distress as to be in danger [of being lost],[63] and such as to call upon him to run such unusual danger, or incur such unusual responsibility, or exercise such unusual skill, or perform such an unusual kind of service, as to make it unfair and unjust that he should be paid otherwise than upon the terms of salvage reward."[64]

The relevant factors merit consideration for the purposes of deciding both whether a pilot has performed a salvage service and also the amount of reward to which a pilot salvor will be held entitled.

The danger to the vessel to be salved will be evidence of whether a pilot is required to perform a salvage service, *e.g.* if she is aground in an area known as a death trap for ships.[65] But, just as a pilot may be entitled to salvage where a vessel is not disabled, so the mere fact that she is disabled will not give a right to salvage reward.[66] A pilot may be rewarded for his courage in boarding

595

596

597

---

[62] (1881) 7 Q.B.D. 129, 134. The judgment was delivered by Brett L.J.
[63] The bracketed words must be omitted.
[64] *Akerblom v. Price, Potter, Walker & Co.* (1881) 7 Q.B.D. 129, 135.
[65] See, *e.g. The Prins Knud (No. 2)* (1941) 68 Ll.L. Rep. 100. *cf. The Prins Knud (No. 1)* (1940) 67 Ll.L. Rep. 458. For other cases of stranding, see *The Etrib* (1930) 37 Ll.L. Rep. 262; *The Driade* [1959] 2 Lloyd's Rep. 311.
[66] *The Bedeburn* [1914] P. 146, 151.

a ship in boisterous weather[67] and a pilot taking personal risks in boarding a vessel about the condition of which he is uncertain, *e.g.* where a bombed vessel may still contain unexploded bombs, may receive greater remuneration than if he merely remained on board the vessel which has come into that condition.[68] As Lord Stowell has said, "the safe conduct of a ship into port under circumstances of extreme danger may exhalt a pilotage service into something of a salvage service."[69] A pilot who risks his health to a lesser extent than exposing his life to danger, by incurring unusual strain, may be remunerated accordingly.[70] Not infrequently, a pilot will be generously rewarded for taking upon himself such responsibility that he puts his reputation at stake and risks losing his licence should his efforts prove unsuccessful or even more detrimental than if he had done nothing.[71] Where there is an ample fund from which to reward salvors, a salvor's reward may reflect his good fortune in his risk's turning out to be justified and the fund's turning out to be ample, in counterbalance to his bad fortune if the result had been otherwise.[72] But an extravagant reward will not be made where a grave risk is taken, for fear of encouraging unnecessary risks, particularly where other assistance is available.[73] Circumstances may leave one no alternative but to take a risk, and the prudent man is the man who takes justifiable risks and avoids unjustifiable risks where a choice is presented.[74] A compulsory pilot who is theoretically under the control of another, such as a local harbour board official in the position of owner, but who is in substance left to his own devices and undertakes responsibility accordingly can claim substantial salvage remuneration.[75] This may be so even though or because he assumes responsibility in the face of contrary advice.[76]

598   A pilot may be rewarded for having to apply a greater degree of skill than usual. But his reward is not to be inflated merely because, by virtue of its being derived from the profession in which he is engaged, the skill and knowledge of local conditions which he is able to apply is greater than that available from anyone else.[77] A salvage service may be provided by a pilot's

---

[67] *The King Oscar* (1848) 6 Not. of Cas. 384; *The Hebe* (1844) 2 W. Rob. 246; *The Tsiropinas* (1935) 51 Ll.L. Rep. 87. *cf. The Joseph Harvey* (1799) 1 C. Rob. 306; *The Johannes* (1835) 6 Not. of Cas. 288.
[68] See *The Amelia Lauro* (1940) 68 Ll.L. Rep. 12; *A Belgian Steamship (Salvage Claim)* (1941) 71 Ll.L. Rep. 82.
[69] *The Joseph Harvey* (1799) 1 C. Rob. 306, 306; approved by Lord Alvanley C.J. in *Newman v. Walters* (1804) 3 Bos. & Pul. 612, 616.
[70] See *The Etrib* (1930) 37 Ll.L. Rep. 262.
[71] *The Kenora* [1921] P. 90; *The Sandefjord* [1953] 2 Lloyd's Rep. 557. And see *The Luigi Accame* (1938) 60 Ll.L. Rep. 106.
[72] See *The Tafelberg* (1942) 71 Ll.L. Rep. 189, 196.
[73] *The Sandefjord* [1953] 2 Lloyd's Rep. 557, 560–561.
[74] *The Rosa Luxemburg* (1934) 59 Ll.L. Rep. 292, 303, *per* Langton J.
[75] *The Driade* [1959] 2 Lloyd's Rep. 311. And see *The Matatua* (1924) 20 Ll.L. Rep. 5. *cf. The Amelia Lauro* (1940) 68 Ll.L. Rep. 12, where the fact that operations were conducted within the harbour master's jurisdiction indicated that it was he, rather than the pilot standing by, who conducted salvage operations.
[76] See *The Matatua* (1924) 20 Ll.L. Rep. 5.
[77] *The Hertha* (1940) 67 Ll.L. Rep. 370.

acting outside his geographical area,[78] paying out an anchor and cable,[79] boarding a ship in distress,[80] beaching a ship,[81] acting without the assistance of his tug,[82] mooring a ship,[83] standing by ("the lowest footing of salvage"),[84] giving advice,[85] restoring morale and maintaining discipline,[86] minimising the loss caused by a peril,[87] and taking a ship from a place of danger to one of safety, rather than merely shifting her from one place to another.[88]

Whether or not pilotage or salvage has been performed must be decided by looking not merely to the inception of the service but by looking at matters retrospectively, to see what the circumstances actually were and what actually happened.[89] The circumstances may suggest the need for salvage services, as where the vessel is in a damaged state[90] and where a signal is made for a pilot from outside pilot grounds.[91] It will be relevant that, if the pilot had not been present, an attempt would have been made to obtain someone else to provide local knowledge, which a pilot habitually provides.[92] Although the evidence of pilots, as members of a respectable profession, is not lightly to be discredited,[93] the onus is on the salvor to prove the need for and the provision of salvage services.[94] If the evidence is equivocal, the service will be treated as pilotage.[95] The evidence must, however, be viewed as a whole and individual circumstances and services not regarded in isolation.[96] If there is continuing danger, the salvage services may continue though the greater danger is over[97] and a service may be salvage although it takes no longer than pilotage would have done.[98]

599

---

[78] See *The Hedwig* (1853) 1 Spinks E. & A. 19 and *The Luigi Accame* (1938) 60 Ll.L. Rep. 106, 111, where Sir Boyd Merriman P. stated that whether or not a pilot was acting within his geographical area was merely a factor to be considered.

[79] See *The Hebe* (1844) 2 W. Rob. 246, 248.

[80] See the cases in *supra*, n. 57.

[81] *The Tsiropinas* (1935) 51 Ll.L. Rep. 87; *The Tafelberg* (1942) 71 Ll.L. Rep. 189. It is not necessary for the pilot to have advised the beaching. See *The Luigi Accame* (1938) 60 Ll.L. Rep. 106, 110.

[82] See *The Etrib* (1930) 37 Ll.L. Rep. 262.

[83] *The Beatsa* (1937) 58 Ll.L. Rep. 85.

[84] *The Amelia Lauro* (1940) 68 Ll.L. Rep. 12, 19. *cf. The Rosa Luxemburg* (1934) 49 Ll.L. Rep. 292.

[85] See *The Matatua* (1924) 20 Ll.L. Rep. 5, 6. *cf. The General Palmer* (1830) 2 Hagg. 323.

[86] *The Tsiropinas* (1935) 51 Ll.L. Rep. 87.

[87] *ibid.*, where the pilot advised beaching without the assistance of tugs, to which salvage remuneration would have had to have been paid.

[88] *The Bengloe* (1940) 67 Ll.L. Rep. 307, 309.

[89] *The Luigi Accame* (1938) 60 Ll.L. Rep. 106, 110, *per* Sir Boyd Merriman P., applying the test in *Akerblom v. Price, Potter, Walker & Co.*, (1881) 7 Q.B.D. 129, 134 (*ante* §595).

[90] See *The Felix* (1853) 1 Spinks E. & A. 23n.

[91] *The Hedwig* (1853) 1 Spinks E.&A. 19.

[92] *The Luigi Accame* (1938) 60 Ll.L. Rep. 106, 112. The master's ignorance of local knowledge can in no way be decisive because that is precisely what it is a pilot's duty to provide: *The Joseph Harvey* (1799) 1 C. Rob. 306.

[93] See *The King Oscar* (1848) 6 Not. of Cas. 284.

[94] *The Branken Moor* (1837) 3 Hagg. 373. See also *The Funchal* (1837) 3 Hagg. 368n.

[95] See *The Joseph Harvey* (1799) 1 C. Rob. 306, 308.

[96] *The Luigi Accame* (1938) 60 Ll.L. Rep. 106, 113.

[97] See, *e.g. The Matatua* (1924) 20 Ll.L. Rep. 5.

[98] See, *e.g. The Bengloe* [1953] 2 Lloyd's Rep. 557.

Tugs

Towage

600 Like pilots, tugs are commonly engaged in order to enable a vessel to negotiate difficulties which it may not be capable, or at least not entirely capable, of negotiating unassisted. A tug may offer to provide salvage services, in which case, if the offer is accepted, there will invariably be a contract for salvage entitling the tug to remuneration on a salvage basis. More often, the tug will have contracted to provide a towage service. This has been described, although not exclusively, as the employment of one vessel to expedite the voyage of another when nothing more is required than the accelerating of her progress.[99] Or a tug may be required to perform some other service considered to be within the normal range of operations it conducts, such as holding a ship up against the tide.[1] The precise obligations of the tug will depend on the terms of the contract and the circumstances, in particular, whether the service involves berthing a ship in harbour or ocean towage. It may be that a tug provides services without any clear prior agreement. But the general rule in any case is that a tug which has provided services will only be entitled to receive remuneration on the normal basis for such services, whether by virtue of contract or on a *quantum meruit*.[2]

601 Apart from the unlikely event that a towage contract provides that services will only be provided where there is no difficulty in performing them,[3] the parties to the towage contract must be taken to have assumed that problems of one sort or another can ordinarily arise during performance of the contract and that performance will continue in such events.[4] The tug under a contract of towage is not entitled to claim greater remuneration merely because some unexpected difficulties[5] or delays[6] occur in the performance of her undertaking; or because the towage is temporarily interrupted by the breaking or the slipping of the towing-hawser[7]; or because fair or moderate weather at the

---

[99] *The Princess Alice* (1848) 3 W. Rob. 138, 139–140, *per* Dr Lushington; approved in *The Strathnaver* (1875) 1 App. Cas. 58, 63; *The Jubilee* (1879) 4 Asp. 275, 276; *The Glaucus* (1948) 81 Ll.L. Rep. 262, 266.

[1] See, *e.g. The Driade* [1959] 2 Lloyd's Rep. 311.

[2] See, *e.g. The Glaisdale* (1945) 78 Ll.L. Rep. 477, 478.

[3] On the general issue of whether such an agreement *defines* the area of contractual performance or *exempts* a contracting party from performance in certain events, and on the effects of the distinction, see Treitel, pp. 217–18; Coote, *Exception Clauses* (1964), Chap. 1; Rose [1980] L.M.C.L.Q. 396.

[4] *The Refrigerant* [1925] P. 130, 140.

[5] *The Domby* (1941) 69 Ll.L. Rep. 161, 163. As to what difficulties may be expected, see, *e.g. The Aboukir* (1905) 21 T.L.R. 200 (not unreasonable to imply a term into a contract to dock that, if difficulties arose that prevented docking, the tugs should return the ship to her anchorage).

[6] *cf. Five Steel Barges* (1890) 15 P.D. 142, 144. In *The Hjemmett* (1880) 5 P.D. 227, Sir Robert Phillimore dismissed a claim for additional remuneration for delay during performance of a contract for a specified towage service at a fixed remuneration; but he expressly guarded himself from being supposed to give an opinion as to what his decision would have been if the plaintiff's case had been a case of salvage grounded on a towing service.

[7] See, *e.g. The Liverpool* [1893] P. 154.

start changes to ordinary bad weather[8]; or because the tow touches the bottom with the risk of stranding[9]; or even possibly where the tow becomes entangled with another ship.[10] *A fortiori*, where such problems were present or apparent when the contract was made.[11] It may be that during towage the tow comes into a position which would be one of danger if she were unassisted by the tug; but this is frequently the circumstance which the tug is engaged to avoid or the risk which is contemplated as being part of its task to negotiate. Thus, in *The Homewood*,[12] it was held to have been contemplated in a contract to tow a ship without means of propulsion to Glasgow to have her engines put in that there might be bad weather, that the hawser *might* part and that the tow might have to anchor on the way, although the contract did not contemplate that the crew might have to be taken off by lifeboat and the vessel left at anchor with no one on board, that a crew might have to be put on board with exposure to danger whilst boarding, and that the vessel might have to complete the voyage to Glasgow without anchors. In *The Tarbert*,[13] Hill J. was not prepared to say that an engaged tug which took on board the master and the crew of the ship, after the ship had suffered a collision and begun to sink, was so far acting outside her duty that she could claim life salvage.

Therefore, when a tug is engaged, she will be held to have undertaken: to use her best endeavours to carry out her engagement; to bring to the task competent skill and such a crew, tackle and equipment as are reasonably to be expected in a vessel of her class; and to continue performance despite difficulties and interruptions and even if the task cannot be completed in the mode in which it was originally intended.[14] A tug cannot claim additional remuneration merely because performance turns out to be more onerous than originally contemplated.[15]

602

From towage to salvage

While it is the duty of the court to take care adequately to remunerate all salvors for salvage services in order to encourage those services to be performed, it is equally the duty of the court to see, where a towing contract has been made or where services in the nature of towage services have been provided, that a little departure from the exact mode in which the contract is to be performed or in which the services are normally provided is not

603

---

[8] *The Galatea* (1858) Swab. 349 (where the undertaking having taken the chance of bad weather, was "entirely interrupted by act of God"); *The I.C. Potter* (1870) L.R. 3 A. & E. 292; *The Slaney* [1951] 2 Lloyd's Rep. 538. *cf. The White Star* (1866) L.R. 1 A. & E. 68.
[9] See, *e.g. The Liverpool* [1893] P. 154.
[10] *The Annapolis* (1861) Lush. 355.
[11] See, *e.g. The Slaney* [1951] 2 Lloyd's Rep. 538.
[12] (1928) 31 Ll.L.Rep. 336, 340. *cf. The Glenmorven* [1913] P. 141.
[13] [1921] P. 372, 377. The main claim, for salvage of the cargo, also failed: see *post*, §735.
[14] *Ward v. McCorkill (The Minnehaha)* (1861) 15 Moo. (P.C.) 133, 153, *per* Lord Kingsdown.
[15] *The True Blue* (1843) 2 W. Rob. 176, 180.

magnified so as to convert towage into salvage services.[16] The court's reticence has the effect of keeping the parties to their contract so far as it is possible, protecting the tow from extortionate demands which may be made by the tug where the tow may be in difficulties, and protecting the tow so far as is possible from the large amount of salvage which is normally awarded to tugs by virtue of the amount of valuable property which is risked by salvors which are tugs. However, if the performance of towage is subject to uncontemplated and extraordinary perils, the tug will become entitled to claim salvage reward for the service which it renders.[17] "Where a vessel is in a distressed state, a steamer, not knowing or being informed of her state, undertaking to tow that vessel at a certain rate of remuneration, would not be bound by that rate, but be entitled to be rewarded for services in the nature of salvage."[18] Hill J. put it thus in *The Homewood*[19]:

> "To constitute a salvage service by a tug under contract to tow, two elements are necessary: (1) that the tow is in danger by reason of circumstances which could not reasonably have been contemplated by the parties; and (2) that risks are incurred or duties performed by the tug which could not reasonably be held to be within the scope of the contract."

The court or arbitrator must consider three issues when deciding whether to award salvage remuneration to a tug: first, the danger which arises; secondly, the relationship between the danger and normal services of towage and such like; and, thirdly, the burden of proof to be satisfied.

604   The most exhaustive leading statement of principle is that by Lord Kingsdown in *The Minnehaha*[20]:

> "When a steam-boat engages to tow a vessel for a certain remuneration from one point to another, she does not warrant that she will be able to do so and will do so under all circumstances and at all hazards; but she does engage that she will use her best endeavours for that purpose, and will bring to the task competent skill, and such a crew, tackle and equipments, as are reasonably to be expected in a vessel of her class.
>
> She may be prevented from fulfilling her contract by a *vis major*, by accidents which were not contemplated, and which may render the fulfilment of her contract impossible, and in such case, by the general rule of law, she is relieved from her obligations.
>
> But she does not become relieved from her obligations because unforeseen difficulties occur in the completion of her task; because the

---

[16] *The Liverpool* [1893] P. 154, 164.

[17] *The Saratoga* (1861) Lush. 318, 321; quoted in *Akerblom v. Price, Potter, Walker & Co.* (1881) 8 Q.B.D. 129, 134 (CA). See also *The Galatea* (1858) Swab. 349.

[18] *The Beulah* (1842) 7 Jur. 207, *per* Dr Lushington.

[19] (1928) 31 Ll.L.Rep. 336, 339. His statement of the law was applied in *The St Patrick* (1930) 35 Ll.L.Rep. 231; *The Glenbeg* (1940) 67 Ll.L.Rep. 437; *The Slaney* [1951] 2 Lloyd's Rep. 538; and *The Texaco Southampton* [1983] 1 Lloyd's Rep. 94.

[20] (1861) 15 Moo. (P.C.) 133, 152–154.

performance of the task is interrupted, or cannot be completed in the mode in which it was originally intended, as by the breaking of the ship's hawser. But if in the discharge of this task, by sudden violence of wind or waves, or other accidents, the ship in tow is placed in danger, and the towing-vessel incurs risks and performs duties which were not within the scope of her original engagement, she is entitled to additional remuneration for additional services if the ship be saved, and may claim as a salvor, instead of being restricted to the sum stipulated to be paid for mere towage. Whether this larger remuneration is to be considered as in addition to, or in substitution for, the price of towage, is of little consequence practically. The measure of the sum to be allowed as salvage would, of course, be increased or diminished according as the price of towage was or was not included in it. In the cases on this subject, the towage contract is generally spoken of as superseded by the right to salvage.

It is not disputed that these are the rules which are acted upon in the Court of Admiralty, and they appear to their Lordships to be founded in reason and in public policy, and to be not inconsistent with legal principles.

The tug is relieved from the performance of her contract by the impossibility of performing it, but if the performance of it be possible, but in the course of it the ship in her charge is exposed, by unavoidable accident, to dangers which require from the tug services of a different class and bearing a higher rate of payment, it is held to be implied in the contract that she shall be paid at such higher rate.

To hold, on the one hand, that a tug, having contracted to tow, is bound, whatever happens after the contract, though not in the contemplation of the parties, and at all hazards to herself, to take the ship to her destination; or, on the other, that the moment the performance of the contract is interrupted, or its completion in the mode originally intended becomes impossible, the tug is relieved from all further duty, and at liberty to abandon the ship in her charge to her fate;—would be alike inconsistent with the public interests.

The rule as it is established guards against both inconveniences, and provides at the same time for the safety of the ship and the just remuneration of the tug. The rule has been long settled; parties enter into towage contracts on the faith of it; and we should be extremely sorry that any doubt should be supposed to exist upon it.

It is said that it has never been brought before us for decision. If so, considering how often the rule has been acted upon, the necessary inference is, that it has never been made the subject of appeal because it has been universally acquiesced in."

The effect of danger supervening

Every salvage claim is founded upon danger to the subject-matter of a claim, *i.e.* in the case of towage, to the tow. But danger to the tow does not by **605**

Voluntariness

itself entitle the tug to salvage remuneration.[21] Where the tow is placed in a position of danger, then, even where this arises by some cause outside the contemplation of the contract, as a general rule, it is the duty of the tug to stand by the tow and to do all that she reasonably can to take care of and to protect the ship.[22] If she fails to do so, she may be liable in damages to the tow for necessary salvage services subsequently provided by another vessel.[23] Where in such a case the tug brings, or assists in bringing, her to safety and does so by incurring risks or by performing duties which could not reasonably be held to be within the scope of the original bargain, the towage contract does not bar a right to additional remuneration but, except where otherwise agreed,[24] is superseded by a right to salvage.[25] In Dr Lushington's view[26]:

> "these rights and obligations incident to a contract of towage are implied by law, and that the law thereby secures equity to both parties and the true interests of the owners of ships. A similar law holds with respect to a pilot."[27]

606 A danger may arise during towage which is common, to a greater or lesser extent, to both the tug and the tow. It may happen that the tug alone comes into a situation of danger. In either event, the tug may be in a position to receive salvage services—and the tow, or persons on board it, might be placed so as to be able to provide such services and to claim salvage remuneration accordingly.[28] So far as possible, even where the tug is in some danger, it must fulfil its duty to continue assisting the tow, and any risks run by it and its master and crew will form an element to be taken into account in assessing the quantum of salvage remuneration.[29] However, the tug will be entitled to cast off from the tow where not casting off would unfairly and unreasonably prevent it from

---

[21] *The Liverpool* [1893] P. 154, 160.

[22] See *The Galatea* (1858) Swab. 349, 350, *per* Dr Lushington; *The Saratoga* (1861) Lush. 318, 321; *The Minnehaha* (1861) Lush. (P.C.) 335, 347, 348; *The White Star* (1866) L.R. 1 A. & E. 68, 70; *The I.C. Potter* (1870) L.R. 3 A. & E. 292, 298; *The Thalatta, Shipping Gazette*, May 26, 1905, cited in *The Leon Blum* [1915] P. 90, 101; *The Leon Blum, ibid.*, 96 (affirmed, *ibid.*, 290); *The Refrigerant* [1925] P. 130, 140.

[23] *The Refrigerant* [1925] P. 130. Where the tow is not in immediate need of the tug's services, the tug may be justified in leaving it temporarily in order to render salvage services to another vessel which is in danger: see *The Annapolis* (1861) Lush. 355.

[24] See *post*, §620.

[25] *The William Brandt Junior* (1842) 2 Not. of Cas. Suppl. lxvii, lxviii; *Ward v. McCorkill (The Minnehaha)* (1861) 15 Moo. (P.C.) 133, 153–154.

[26] *The Saratoga* (1861) Lush. 318, 321.

[27] See *ante*, §§ 588–599.

[28] The tow has a general obligation to do whatever is reasonable on its part to facilitate performance of the towage contract: *The St Patrick* (1930) 35 Ll.L.Rep. 231, 236. If it prevents the tug from completing the towage the tug will be able to claim for the loss suffered: see *e.g. The Madras* [1898] P. 90. Similarly, it is not open to a tug, during the performance of salvage services, unreasonably to refuse assistance from the tow and then to ask for remuneration in respect of labour expended and risks run from its own choice: see *The Homewood* (1928) 31 Ll.L.R. 336, 340. Abandonment by the master and crew of a vessel being towed may entitle the tug to terminate the towage contract and turn the towage services into salvage services: *The Glenmorven* [1913] P. 141.

[29] See *post*, Chap. 15.

avoiding loss of life or injury to life or property.[30] This is so at least where it can no longer effectively render salvage services to the tow and where it does not further imperil the tow by casting off. But danger to the tug itself will in no way found any part of a salvage claim against the tow (as opposed to being a factor for consideration in quantifying a salvage award). And any salvage services provided for the purpose of extricating the tug from danger will have to find their remuneration, if any, in a claim against the tug. Once the tug is out of danger, it must of course return as soon as possible to continue the provision of services, whether of towage or salvage, to the tow.[31]

607 A tug will be eligible to claim a salvage reward even though it has not run the risk of any danger to itself, although of course a salvor will not receive such high remuneration as he would have received if he had acted with risk to himself.[32]

Provided the tug succeeds in, or contributes to, saving the ship from danger, it will be entitled to claim salvage. A tug which had originally agreed to provide towage services will normally remain obliged to bring the ship to its intended destination if possible. If not, it must bring it to some other reasonable place of safety. Where the towage contract has been abandoned and the tug tows the vessel back to the place from which the towage began, the tug cannot be denied salvage on the basis that she was obliged to do that as part of the towage service.[33]

Effect on the contract

608 If difficulties which arise are within the contemplation of a towage contract, the terms of the contract will govern the amount of remuneration to be earned for the service, which will normally be no more than the amount due where no difficulties in fact arise. It might be that the tug can, without going so far as to shew entitlement to a salvage award, shew such a departure from the normal course of towing that it should be entitled to something extra for the towage undertaken.[34] As a rule, however, the tug will either receive the towage remuneration originally agreed or salvage, with nothing in between.

609 The cases demonstrate some divergence of opinion as to the precise effect of the supervening necessity for salvage on the towage contract. It has been seen that the tug has a basic obligation to do all that is reasonable to ensure performance of the contract and the negotiation of difficulties which emerge

---

[30] See *The Annapolis* (1861) Lush. 355; *The Leon Blum* [1915] P. 90, 96 (affirmed *ibid.*, 290).
[31] *The Annapolis* (1861) Lush. 355.
[32] *The Pericles* (1863) Br. & L. 80.
[33] *The Galatea* (1858) Swab. 349, 350. *cf. The Aboukir, supra*, n. 55.
[34] See, *e.g. The Glaisdale* (1945) 78 Ll.L.Rep. 477, 478. A pilot would only be able to claim additional remuneration for pilotage services over and above those which it was originally intended he should provide by shewing that the services in fact performed were in a class meriting a higher level of fee: see *ante*, §§ 588–599.

Voluntariness

but which are within the contemplation of the contract.[35] But, when a tug engages to tow a vessel for a certain remuneration from one point to another, she does not warrant that she will be able to do so and will do so under all circumstances and all hazards.[36] Where she is prevented from fulfilling her contract by *vis major*, by accidents which were not contemplated and which may render fulfilment of her contract impossible, she is relieved from her obligations.[37]

610   Where the contract of towage is an indivisible contract which cannot be fulfilled owing to circumstances for which neither party is to blame, the position at common law was that neither party remained liable to fulfil the contract, neither party had rights against the other for the other's having failed to perform after the frustrating event supervened, and neither party had a remedy against the other for loss suffered as a result of the frustration.[38] The Law Reform (Frustrated Contracts) Act 1943[39] now provides some means for adjusting the positions of the parties as at the time of frustration, where a towage contract governed by English law has become impossible of further performance.[40] Money payable under the contract before frustration ceases to be payable and, if already paid, is recoverable, but subject to the court's discretion to allow expenses incurred in or for performance of the contract to be recovered or to be deducted from money which is repayable.[41] More often than not, however, money will not be payable or paid except at the end of the towage. That being so it is relevant that, where the tow has, by reason of anything done by the tug in or for the purpose of performing the contract, obtained a valuable benefit before frustration discharges the contract, the court has a discretion to order the tow to pay what it considers to be a just sum to the tug.[42] The operation of the Act is excluded to the extent that, upon the true construction of the contract of towage, a provision in the contract is to have effect in the case of the frustrating event and is inconsistent with an award under the Act.[43] Towage contracts not infrequently contain provisions which are to have some effect in such a case.

611   Where a towage contract is not an entire contract, payment for work done under it before salvage services become necessary might have become due on

---

[35] *Ante*, §601.
[36] *Ward v. McCorkill (The Minnehaha)* (1861) 15 Moo. (P.C.) 133, 152.
[37] *ibid.*, 153; cited as the leading statement of the law in *The Liverpool* [1893] P. 154, 159–60.
[38] *The Madras* [1898] P. 90, following *Appleby v. Myers* (1867) L.R. 2 C.P. 651. See also *Cutter v. Powell* (1795) 6 T.R. 320; *Fibrosa Spolka Akcyjna v. Fairbairn, Lawson, Combe, Barbour Ltd* [1943] A.C. 32. And see generally Chitty, Chap. 24; Treitel, Chap. 20; Goff & Jones, pp. 365–369, 564–583.
[39] *Quo vide*. The Act was discussed at length in *B.P. Exploration Co. (Libya) Ltd v. Hunt (No. 2)* [1979] 1 W.L.R. 783; [1981] 1 W.L.R. 232; [1983] A.C. 352. See Rose (1981) 131 N.L.J. 955.
[40] s.1(1).
[41] s.1(2).
[42] s.1(3).
[43] s.2(3).

an instalment basis but will much more likely be due on a *quantum meruit*[44]; in practice, a similar sum will be due on either basis.

Salvage remuneration will be assessed on the basis of the salvage services **612** provided, independently of whether or not the contract was entire, and independently of whether any sum (and, if so, how much) is payable in respect of towage services provided. It may be that a combined claim for the towage and for salvage will be presented, and the final sum awarded would be increased or diminished according to whether or not the towage remuneration was included. In principle, remuneration for the different services will be assessed separately, but it has been said that whether the larger remuneration (*i.e.* including the towage remuneration) is to be considered as in addition to, or in substitution for, the price of towage is of little consequence practically.[45]

According to Sir Robert Phillimore in *The I.C. Potter*[46]: **613**

"the true criterion by which it is to be ascertained, whether the towing vessel has become a salvor, is whether the supervening circumstances were such as to justify her in abandoning her contract."

The preponderance of authority, however, is that such circumstances do not necessarily justify the abandonment of the contract.[47] Certainly, the tug may be relieved of her obligation to tow while the supervening circumstances operate and the facts of a particular case may be such that any further performance of the towage contract becomes impossible. But the towage contract need not become permanently "superseded"[48] by the salvage services and the rights arising therefrom. Just as the tug's rendering of salvage services is not completely voluntary, in that she is obliged to render whatever salvage assistance she can, so must she resume her obligations under the towage contract when the danger is over and so far as she possibly can in the altered circumstances.[49] To that extent, the effect of the supervening danger is that the contract cannot be abandoned but performance is initially only suspended, although of course the provision of services during persistence of danger and

---

[44] See *e.g. The Glenmorven* [1913] P. 141, 147.
[45] *Ward v. McCorkill (The Minnehaha)* (1861) 15 Moo. (P.C.) 133, 153, *per* Lord Kingsdown.
[46] (1870) L.R. 3 A. & E. 292, 298–299. See also his similar statement in *The Hjemmett* (1880) 5 P.D. 227, 229–230 and his adherence to what he said in *The I.C. Potter* in *The Waverley* (1871) L.R. 3 A. & E. 369, 379. *cf. The Galatea* (1858) Swab. 349, 349–350.
[47] His Lordship did not suggest that abandonment of the tow (as opposed to the contract) would be justified, which it most certainly would not: see *ante*, §606. As to the validity of his statement as a test for distinguishing towing from salvage, see *post*, §§ 615–618.
[48] See *Ward v. McCorkill (The Minnehaha)* (1861) 15 Moo. (P.C.) 133, 153.
[49] *The Leon Blum* [1915] P. 90, (affirmed, *ibid.*, 290). See also *Five Steel Barges* (1890) 15 P.D. 142, 144; *The Thalatta*, Shipping Gazette, May 26, 1905, cited in *The Leon Blum* [1915] P. 90, 101. The standard international ocean towage agreements provide that, "Should the Tow break away from the Tug during the course of the towage service, the Tug shall render all reasonable services to re-connect the towline and fulfill this Agreement without making any claim for salvage": Towcon, cl. 15(a); Towhire, cl. 15(a).

suspension of towage may mean that the tug is not resuming towage but is providing a salvage service.

614 Where further performance of the original contract is frustrated, a new contract may be implied by the acts of the parties, giving rise to new rights[50]; or the tow may be liable on a *quantum meruit* for any benefits received from the performance of subsequent towage services.[51] On principle, if the contract is not frustrated, resumed towage operations will be remunerated according to the terms of the original agreement and despite performance's being more onerous than originally contemplated. And it will not be open to the court or arbitrator to include compensation for more arduous performance after salvage services have ceased in the assessment of the salvage reward due for rescuing the tow from danger. However, it may well be possible to recognise an implied obligation that slightly higher remuneration will be due for the rendering of additional services, on the basis of either a contractual *quantum meruit*, because the parties must have assumed that additional remuneration would be payable in such circumstances, or of a restitutionary *quantum meruit*, because the tow would in the event be unjustly enriched at the expense of the tug.[52]

The tests for salvage by tugs

615 The courts have recognised the difficulty of determining the point at which a tug's service becomes one of salvage and they have admitted the difficulty of determining when this becomes so on any given set of facts.[53] Unfortunately, no clear test has been laid down for drawing the line between towage and salvage. As has just been demonstrated, although the line will have been crossed where the circumstances justify abandonment of the towage contract, the criterion of abandonment of the contract does not have to be satisfied in order to constitute services as salvage services. Nor would that criterion by itself indicate when abandonment is justified anyway.

616 It has been said that the services must be something quite different, not only in quantity but in quality, from what the tug was engaged to do, so that they come within a different class of services.[54] While it is not decisive that the quantitative aspect is satisfied, in that salvage is not awarded merely for more onerous performance, nor is it necessary. Just as a tug which has not been engaged to tow may supply salvage services other than by towing (*e.g.* by

---

[50] *The Madras* [1898] P. 90, 94.
[51] See *Société Franco-Tunisienne D'Armement Tunis v. Sidermar SpA (The Massalia)* [1961] 2 Q.B. 278, 312–334.
[52] See Goff & Jones, Chap. 1. *cf. The Glaisdale* (1945) 78 Ll.L.Rep. 477, 478.
[53] See, *e.g. Ward v. McCorkill (The Minnehaha)* (1861) 15 Moo. (P.C.) 133, 154; *The Liverpool* [1893] P. 154, 161, quoting Lord Cranworth L.C. in *Boyse v. Rossborough* (1857) 6 H.L.C. 3, 45: "There is no possibility of mistaking midnight for noon; but at what precise moment twilight becomes darkness is hard to determine."
[54] See *The Domby* (1941) 69 Ll.L.Rep. 161, 163; *The Trevorian* (1940) 66 Ll.L.Rep. 45, 49. *cf. Five Steel Barges* (1890) 15 P.D. 142, 144.

holding up a vessel[55]), so may an engaged tug earn salvage by doing something different from, rather than more than, what was originally required, such as searching for and locating a vessel in distress.[56] Whether or not the services rendered are of a different quality or class from those contracted for will depend on defining the contract services and analysing the circumstances in which they were provided. In *The White Star*,[57] Dr Lushington said:

> "The real question is, what are the contracting parties reasonably supposed to have intended by the engagement, and what degree of alteration had they a right to expect, because to suppose that the performance of the service would always be of the same character would be absurd."

It is not, therefore, necessary that the circumstances which arise should be capable of being described as unpredictable, unforeseeable or unforeseen.[58] What has to be decided is whether, as a matter of construction, the services rendered are beyond what can be reasonably supposed to have been contemplated by the parties entering into such a contract.[59] Thus, a tug may be expected to deal with greater difficulties in winter than in summer.

617

Where difficulties do arise, however, a tug's entitlement to salvage is usually judged not so much by separate consideration of the danger arising and what was contemplated by the contract,[60] but by those two elements judged cumulatively, with particular emphasis on the danger present to the tow.[61] A further factor which is sometimes used in this process is the test whether the services which were necessary or were provided were such that an owner of reasonable prudence would have refused.[62] This introduces an objective element into determining when salvage begins, somewhat reminiscent of the test for distinguishing between pilotage and salvage.[63] The cases are not entirely congruent in that the pilotage cases have often turned on the question whether the danger was such that a pilot could have refused to act whereas the tug cases have often concerned engaged tugs which have been obliged to act, by virtue of the engagement and despite the danger, but have been entitled by the danger to recover more than towage remuneration. Their similarity lies in the court's desire to award salvage where it is merited and to

618

---

[55] See, *e.g. The Driade* [1959] 2 Lloyd's Rep. 311. *cf. The Madras* [1898] P. 90.
[56] See, *e.g. The Albion* (1861) Lush. 282. *cf. The Mount Cynthos* (1937) 58 Ll.L.Rep. 18, 25.
[57] (1866) L.R. 1 A. & E. 68, 70. See also *The Refrigerant* [1925] P. 130, 140: "In all these contracts it must be implied that the parties contemplate an interruption of the service."
[58] *cf.* Kennedy (4th ed.), pp. 52–53.
[59] *Five Steel Barges* (1890) 15 P.D. 142, 144. See also *The Saratoga* (1861) Lush. 318, 322; *Ward v. McCorkill (The Minnehaha)* (1861) 15 Moo. (P.C.) 133, 152–154; *The Lady Egidia* (1862) Lush. 513, 514; *The Liverpool* [1893] P. 154, 160, applied in *The Stanmore* (1897) 13 T.L.R. 165, *The Glenbeg* (1940) 67 Ll.L.Rep. 437, 440; *The Leon Blum* [1915] P. 90, 101.
[60] *cf. ante*, §603, text to n. 19.
[61] See *The Strathnaver* (1875) 1 App. Cas. 58, 65.
[62] See, *e.g. The H.M. Hayes* (1861) Lush. 355, 375; *The Homewood* (1928) 31 Ll.L.Rep. 336, 339.
[63] *Ante*, §595. The pilotage test looks more to reasonableness on the part of the pilot rather than the owner.

Voluntariness

judge the situation in the light of events as they actually unfold. Likewise, if the circumstances call for a salvage award, it is considered immaterial whether or not the services have been accepted by the tow[64] or whether towage has been interrupted.[65]

Towage as salvage ab initio

619   When a contract to tow is concluded and after that time a danger arises, the question for consideration is whether the services are rendered and to be remunerated under the towage contract or it has been superseded owing to the altered circumstances by a right to salvage. If, however, the contract is concluded after the occurrence of circumstances giving a prima facie right to salvage, two different questions arise. First, does the agreement effectively exclude the right to salvage?[66] Where the agreement does not expressly or by its nature purport to exclude salvage, the circumstances may automatically prompt the tribunal to classify the service as salvage.[67] Secondly, should the court refuse to give effect to the agreement as being for some reason inequitable?[68]

Towage contract providing "no salvage charges"

620   If, before a danger arises, a contract for towage is made between the owners of a tug and a tow, then, while the terms of that contract apply, no claim for salvage will normally be allowed because the owners, master and crew of the tug will be assumed to be providing services under the towage contract alone and will be regarded as "volunteers". Where circumstances arise such that the terms of the towage contract are no longer applicable or where the agreement to tow is concluded after a danger has arisen, there will be a prima facie right to salvage but it may be expressly excluded.[69] Such an exclusion will only be effective in the circumstances to which it is expressed to apply.[70] Thus, a contract to tow a partially disabled vessel with her master and crew on board "no cure, no pay, no claim to be made for salvage" was held not to exclude a salvage claim for services after the master and crew left her.[71] A similar contract purportedly concluded on behalf of the tow alone will not enure to the benefit of the cargo owners.[72] Nor, prima facie, will such a contract which is purportedly concluded on behalf of cargo owners, since the tow will not normally have authority to contract as agents of the cargo, though an

---

[64] *Ante*, §§ 50–63
[65] *The I.C. Potter* (1870) L.R. 3 A. & E. 292.
[66] See *post*, §620.
[67] See *e.g. The Charles Adolphe* (1856) Swab. 153, 157, where Dr Lushington said towing a vessel disabled and in distress "cannot by possibility be compared to an ordinary towage service." *cf. The Waverley* (1871) L.R. 3 A. & E. 369, 378.
[68] The various grounds of "inequity" are discussed *post*, Chap. 8. See *e.g. The Kingalock* (1854) 1 Spinks E. & A. 263; *The Canova* (1866) L.R. 1 A. & E. 54.
[69] *Post*, §§ 784–789.
[70] See *The Queen Elizabeth* (1949) 82 Ll.L.Rep. 803, discussed *post*, §788.
[71] *The Glenmorven* [1913] P. 141.
[72] *The Leon Blum* [1915] P. 90, affirmed, *ibid.*, 290.

attempted exclusion is unlikely to be defeated on this ground in practice as the cargo owners would no doubt ratify the agreement.[73]

Tug owners have no inherent authority to bind the master and crew of the tug by an agreement depriving them of salvage remuneration[74]; indeed, the crew's rights are expressly preserved by statute.[75] The rights of the master and crew have been stated to be not only against salved cargo, but also against ship and freight.[76]

Burden of proving conversion of towage into salvage

A person who claims a salvage reward has the burden of proving his entitlement to the reward.[77] Where there is no previous contract of towing existing between the parties, the court will not be reluctant to admit that towage services rendered to a vessel in danger qualify for a salvage reward.[78] However, where the services began under a contract of towage, a superadded claim for salvage may only be admitted upon the clearest proof of circumstances which justify such a claim. Thus, delivering the opinion of the Privy Council, Lord Kingsdown stated in *The Minnehaha*[79]:

> "When it is remembered how much in all cases—how entirely in many cases—a ship in tow is at the mercy of the tug; how easily, with the knowledge which the crews of such boats usually have of the waters on which they ply, they may place a ship in their charge in great, real or apparent peril; how difficult of detection such a crime must be, and how strong the temptation to commit it, their Lordships are of opinion that such cases require to be watched with the closest attention, and not without some degree of jealousy."

On the question of exactly what has to be proved, his Lordship said this[80]:

> "The claimants must prove their own case; they must shew that, the ship being in danger from no fault of theirs, they performed services which were not covered by their towage contract, and did all they could to prevent the danger."

---

[73] See *post*, Chap. 8.
[74] *The Leon Blum* [1915] P. 90, (affirmed, *ibid.*, 290); *The Margery* [1902] P. 157. See also *The Friesland* [1904] P. 345.
[75] MSA 1995, s.39.
[76] *The Leon Blum* [1915] P. 90, 103.
[77] See *post*, Chap. 15.
[78] See *ante*, Chap. 4.
[79] (1861) 15 Moo. P.C. 133, 155.
[80] *ibid.*, 158.
[81] (1879) 5 P.D. 54, 57; followed in *The Duc D'Aumale (No. 2)* [1904] P. 60, 71; *The St Patrick* (1930) 35 Ll.L.Rep. 231, 238. *cf. The Ratata* [1898] A.C. 513, 517.

Voluntariness

Similarly, Brett L.J. said in *The Robert Dixon*[81]:

> "The plaintiffs, being under a towage contract, bring this action, in which they assert that the towage service was altered into salvage; and it seems to me that the plaintiffs are in this position, that it lies on them to show that the change occurred without any want of skill on their part, but by mere accident over which they had no control. The burden of proof on both the affirmative and the negative issues is on the plaintiffs, that is, both that there was an inevitable accident beyond their control, and that they showed no want of skill."

623 Thus, James L.J. said in the same case[82]:

> "when an accident happens, and the original danger is found to have occurred through want of skill, the loss occasioned by the accident . . . is properly attributable to the want of skill which caused the original danger."

Brett L.J.'s passage was quoted in *The Maréchal Suchet*[83] by Sir Samuel Evans P., who said[84]:

> "The burden of proof is upon the plaintiffs. It is a twofold burden. They must show that they were not wanting in the performance of the obligations resting upon them under the towage contract; and they must also account for the stranding of the vessel by showing something like *vis major*, or an inevitable accident."

624 He also added the important point that:

> "It was argued that, apart from the allegation of insufficiency of power in the tug, the defendants did not allege negligence but it is not necessary to plead negligence in such a case to defeat a salvage claim."[85]

"In applying these principles . . . the first point for consideration is whether the [defendant's property] was ever in danger, and if she were, whether the court [is] warranted in finding . . . that the danger was owing to the misconduct of the tug."[86]

Foyboatmen

625 The word foy means local. Foyboats are small boats used on the north-east coast, especially at Shields, particularly before the introduction of steam-tugs,

---

[81] (1879) 5 P.D. 54, 57; followed in *The Duc D'Aumale (No. 2)* [1904] P. 60, 71; *The St Patrick* (1930) 35 Ll.L.Rep. 231, 238. *cf. The Ratata* [1898] A.C. 513, 517.
[82] (1879) 5 P.D. 54, 56.
[83] [1911] P. 1.
[84] *ibid.*, 12–13.
[85] *ibid.*, 14, citing *The Minnehaha, infra.*
[86] *The Minnehaha* (1861) 15 Moo. P.C. 133, 155.

to tow vessels in and out of harbour. Foyboatmen who voluntarily perform work which goes right outside the ordinary course of their day-to-day duties may be entitled to a salvage award. In *The MacGregor Laird*,[87] a vessel moored to buoys in an exposed position in the River Tyne parted her forward moorings in a gale and fell athwart the river. Seven tugs brought her back into position at the pier and held her there. Ten foyboatmen then re-moored her. One of them gave evidence that, given the exposed position in which she had to be moored and the weather conditions there prevailing, it was a day on which a ship arriving in the Tyne could not have expected foyboatmen to have followed their regular calling so as to have made her fast in the ordinary way and for the ordinary tariff rates. For Willmer J., such circumstances were capable of justifying a salvage award, particularly since the plaintiffs exposed themselves to some danger. What clinched the matter for him was that their work was a part, and a necessary part, of the whole operation which the tugs started and could not have completed without them, at least without very great expense.[88]

Lloyd's agents and ship's agents

Until the first half of the nineteenth century, Admiralty Judges resisted attempts by underwriters' agents and by ship's agents to claim as salvors. In *The Lively*,[89] Dr Lushington warned that:

626

> "it would inevitably happen that in every case where a vessel met with any misfortune in the neighbourhood of any seaport where a Lloyd's agent was established, and he was applied to by the master to hire a steam vessel or sailors to render assistance, such agent would be entitled to come to this court and sue as a salvor, he himself doing nothing to effect the salvage."

In *The Lively*, however, the plaintiff acted "in his capacity of Lloyd's agent ... and as such only discharged the duty which was properly incumbent upon him."[90] The decision is thus quite consistent with the principle that, whatever the efforts or intentions of the would-be salvor, a salvage award cannot be made for performing services which cannot properly be denominated salvage services.[91] Ship's agents have similarly, and not surprisingly, been confined to the terms of their engagements where no personal risk was incurred by themselves or by anyone else,[92] and Dr Lushington also warned that:

> "It would certain open the door to abuse if ship's agents were encouraged first to send in charges in their character of ship's agents, and then,

---

[87] [1953] 2 Lloyd's Rep. 259. *cf. The Good Helmsman* (1950) 84 Ll.L.Rep. 207.
[88] It was noted that the number of foyboatmen employed could more easily be justified than the number of tugs.
[89] (1848) 3 W. Rob. 64, 67.
[90] *ibid.*
[91] See *The Watt* (1843) 2 W. Rob. 70, 72.
[92] See *The Cargo ex Honor* (1866) L.R. 1 A. & E. 87, 91.

when those charges are disputed, to turn round and assert themselves salvors."[93]

627 However, following Lord Stowell's lead in *The Cranstoun*[94] and other authority,[95] Dr Lushington opined in *The Purissima Concepcion*[96]:

"that it is for the advantage of all parties concerned, and for the benefit of the mercantile interests in general, that the [Admiralty] court should possess the jurisdiction to entertain the suit.

In the first place, ... both the shipowner and the owners of the cargo would be benefited by the intervention of the court's authority in the matter, inasmuch that this court would take cognisance of the whole of the case, and would take care that no improper expenses were allowed, and that nothing should be taken in the nature of ship agency or of salvage which was not fairly earned, and to which the party claiming as salvor was not justly entitled. In the case of foreign owners, the advantage ... would be still greater, in enabling them to procure with greater facility the assistance of persons of this description, who are most useful in effecting and superintending services of this kind, and who might naturally hesitate to undertake the duty upon the mere personal credit of the master, or the foreign owner whom he did not know. As regards the ship agent, himself, the same consideration equally applies, because, supposing him to perform the duty fairly and assiduously, he is assured of receiving a proper reward out of the property which becomes subject to the jurisdiction of the court, and he is not left to the chance of recovering it from a foreign owner or master."

628 Further reasons for the Admiralty Court's clothing itself with jurisdiction,[97] albeit not exclusive jurisdiction,[98] were being able to consider the evidence where there was a dispute as to whether the agent were to act solely as agent and not as salvor[99] and to enable the Admiralty Court to decide proceedings already begun without requiring a fresh trial at common law.[1] In addition to the expressed desirability of acquiring jurisdiction, Dr Lushington has also reasoned, in *The Cargo ex Honor*,[2] that:

[93] *ibid.*, 91. See also *The Lively, supra.*
[94] (1827) unreported; referred to in *The Happy Return* (1828) 2 Hagg. 198, 207 and *The Purissima Concepcion* (1849) 2 W. Rob. 181, 184. It appears that the name of the vessel was as set out in Haggard and adopted in the text, *supra*. The contemporary peerage was Cranstoun. The variations in W. Rob. (Cranstone) and in earlier editions of Kennedy (Cranston) are, therefore, rejected.
[95] *The Happy Return, supra*; *The Favorite* (1844) 2 W. Rob. 255; and an anonymous, unreported decision involving a magistrate: see (1849) 2 W. Rob. 181, 184.
[96] *ibid.*, 183–184.
[97] Formerly, the Admiralty Court had no jurisdiction if the action lacked a salvage element and was based solely on a contract entered into in the circumstances of the case. In that event, the plaintiff would have been obliged to institute proceedings anew in a court of common law.
[98] See *Baring v. Day* (1806) 8 East 75; *The Happy Return, supra*, n. 94, at 205, 206.
[99] *cf. ibid.*, 198–201.
[1] See *The Favorite, supra*, n. 95, at 256.
[2] *Supra*, n. 32. It is not clear from the report, however, in what respect any of the personal services of the agent in that case could fairly be described as extraordinary.

> "it would be unjust that for extraordinary services the remuneration should be restricted to the ordinary commission allowed to ship agents of 5 per cent upon disbursements"

and that:

> "The truth is, that in cases like the present, where ship agents are employed to discharge a cargo from a vessel wrecked on a beach, it becomes a matter of nicety to draw the line between salvage services and agency services. For this reason, the Court, on previous occasions, has entertained similar applications to the present."

The result of this process was expressed to be:

> "that the Court would allow a claim as agent and a claim as salvor to be united and combined under particular circumstances."[3]

It is clear from some of the authorities that the court has awarded more modest sums than for more obviously classified salvage services, for services which, in an understandably indistinguishable way, partake partly of the character of salvage services and partly of the character of agency services,[4] or may even be admitted not to be "in the strict character of salvage services, but rather of a successful and meritorious agency."[5] But, although "an agent is not precluded from being a salvor, his position affects to some extent the question of what his precise reward and rights are."[6] In such cases, it has not proved necessary that the claimant be shewn to have incurred danger to life, or personal risk of any kind, or to have made any exertion beyond that which one might fairly suppose to have lain within the scope of his business as the agent for the ship or cargo.

The decided cases give no decisive indications as to the circumstances under which a person who is a Lloyd's agent or who has accepted the position of ship's agent and then renders services in saving the ship or cargo can claim to rank as salvor in respect of them. It is reasonably clear, though, that the court will lean to the consideration rather than the rejection of a salvage claim. Naturally, it will be more inclined to generosity where the services are of an arduous and somewhat dangerous character.[7] Moreover, where the agent owns salvage plant and has a diving staff in his employ for his own purposes, he is not precluded, by reason of his agency, from recovering salvage for the use of

---

[3] ibid.
[4] See *The Happy Return, supra; The Favorite, supra; The Purissima Concepcion, supra; The Cargo ex Honor, supra.*
[5] See *The Favorite, supra,* n. 95, at 259.
[6] *The Crusader* [1907] P. 15, 16, *per* Gorell Barnes, P. (affirmed, *ibid.*, 196), following *The Kate B. Jones* [1892] P. 366.
[7] *The Kate B. Jones* [1892] P. 366.

Voluntariness

them, particularly where his functions as agent are normally confined to providing other specific services, such as fuelling.[8]

631 In conclusion, it must be noted that, where the owners of salved property have become liable to indemnify the agent against expenses incurred by him, or to pay to him some remuneration for his services, independently of the success of the salvage operations, the court, if awarding salvage, will take account of the probability that the risk of the entire loss of their expenditure was one which the plaintiffs did not incur, and it will not make so large an award to him as it would to the ordinary salvor who incurs the risk of receiving nothing at all if his services prove unsuccessful.[9] The court will be careful not to allow a ship's agent to take advantage of the danger by allowing him to procure consent to his engagement on salvage rather than agency terms, particularly where the salvage agreement is intended to replace an existing agency agreement and even though, if on "no cure—no pay" terms, the agent might obtain nothing if salvage were unsuccessful.[10] But the fact that the putative salvor owes certain duties to the salvee is no more than a circumstance to be taken into account,[11] and the court will enforce such an agreement if just and equitable.[12]

Passengers

632 Salvage will not be awarded to a master, crew member or tug performing ordinary duties which have been contracted for. To a certain extent, a passenger is bound up with the ship upon which he is travelling because of the contract he enters under which the shipowner agrees to carry him and his property to the place of destination. But there is no engagement on his part to perform any service[13] and to that extent it is arguable that any service which he does provide in time of danger should entitle him to salvage remuneration. However, it was said by Lord Stowell in *The Branston*[14] that:

> "Where there is a common danger, it is the duty of every one on board the vessel to give all the assistance he can; and more particularly this is the duty of one whose ordinary pursuits enable him to render most effectual service."

But such a person's obligation is of a moral rather than a legal nature and performance of a service by a passenger in time of danger will normally find

---

[8] *The Charcas* (1908) *Shipping Gazette*, December 15, summarised in Kennedy (4th ed.), p. 71.

[9] *The Kate B. Jones* [1892] P. 366. *cf. The Happy Return* (1828) 2 Hagg. 198, 205, where some salvage remuneration was awarded when "it was intended that the service should be entrusted to Mr Davis in the character of agent, and that the claim for salvage should in some degree or other be limited and controlled by that understanding."

[10] *The Crusader* [1907] P. 196.

[11] *ibid.*, 210, *per* Lord Alverstone C.J. See also *ibid.*, 214, *per* Kennedy L.J.

[12] *The Prins Knud (No. 2)* (1941) 68 Ll.L.Rep. 100.

[13] *The Vrede* (1861) Lush. 322, 325.

[14] (1826) 2 Hagg. 3n. See also *Newman v. Walters* (1804) 3 Bos. & Pul. 612, 615.

its reward in the motive which presumably induced it—preservation of himself and his own property—rather than satisfaction of a salvage claim.[15] Thus, Lord Stowell continued:

> "No case has been cited where such a claim by a passenger has been established; though a passenger is not bound, like a mariner, to remain on board, but may take the first opportunity of escaping from the ship and of saving his own life."[16]

In *The Salacia*,[17] passengers comprising the crew rescued from a previously shipwrecked vessel were assumed to be entitled to salvage, in so far as their services were distinguishable from those of the *Salacia's* crew, where other salvors might not have been able to manage without their assistance; but the claim was hardly contested. In *Newman v. Walters*,[18] a merchant captain travelling as a passenger took command at the crew's request and received salvage remuneration. But the case was disapproved of, as an aberration of a court of common law, by Dr Lushington in *The Vrede*,[19] where the rarity of salvage claims by passengers, and in particular of successful ones, deterred him from "furnishing an evil precedent" by encouraging claims for "services which are of ordinary occurrence."

633

It can be inferred from his judgment that a passenger will not generally be entitled to salvage remuneration but that he may be: if he provides a service other than for his own selfish purposes; if, when means of escape from danger for himself and his property are available, he elects to remain for the purposes of providing a salvage service; and if the service he performs is more than can justifiably be expected from a passenger in his position. Thus, in the American case *Towle v. The Great Eastern*,[20] a civil and mechanical engineer travelling on board the disabled *Great Eastern* who intervened, at the risk of humiliation, to devise and, after long, skilful and exhausting endeavours, successfully to execute a plan for steering her was rewarded as a salvor. According to Shipman J.:

634

> "I think it follows, from the principles laid down by the authorities, first, that a passenger on board a ship can render salvage service to that ship when in distress at sea; secondly, that in order to do this he need not be first personally disconnected from the ship[21]; but thirdly, that these services, in order to constitute him a salvor, must be of an extraordinary character, and beyond the line of his duty, and not mere ordinary services,

---

[15] See *ante*, § 557.
[16] *The Branston* (1826) 2 Hagg. 3n.
[17] (1829) 2 Hagg. 262.
[18] (1804) 3 Bos. & Pul. 612 (Exchequer Chamber), discussed *ante*, §§ 134–138.
[19] (1861) Lush. 322.
[20] (1864) 2 M.L.C. 148 (U.S. District Court of Admiralty, Southern District of New York).
[21] See also *Newman v. Walters* (1804) 3 Bos. & Pul. 612, 614.

such as pumping and aiding in working the ship by usual and well-known means."[22]

635 The requirement that the passenger provide extraordinary services will restrict the possibility that a passenger in possession of a particular skill, and so better placed to assist in time of danger, such as a sailor travelling as a passenger, will be more easily able to obtain salvage reward than an unskilled person. In fact, the size and complexities of modern vessels minimise the circumstances in which passengers can even perform their recognised duties in time of danger, let alone provide salvage services.[23] And in no reported English case has a passenger without nautical experience successfully claimed a salvage reward from the vessel upon which he was travelling.

636 A passenger who leaves a vessel in distress but then returns to render assistance will be in a better position to put forward a salvage claim than if he had rendered the service from the first. Certainly, a passenger is ordinarily a volunteer in regard to a vessel other than that in which he is travelling. However, mere inconvenience to passengers, delayed on their voyage by reason of services performed by their carrying ship and its master and crew, is not enough[24]: it is essential that they should have assisted in and contributed to the services.[25]

Cargo-owners

637 The same principle that applies to passengers applies to cargo-owners.[26] A cargo-owner might be expected, *qua* cargo-owner, to provide information to the shipowner or to another salvor about the characteristics of his cargo; and, if he did no more than what could ordinarily be so expected of him or that was required by the terms of the contract of carriage, he should not be permitted to claim salvage, even if it would be a salvage service if rendered by a third party. But he will be entitled to claim salvage for services which go beyond those which would ordinarily be expected of a cargo-owner, such as the

---

[22] *ibid.*, 152.
[23] See *The Sava Star* [1995] 2 Lloyd's Rep. 134, 143: "what may be expected of a passenger on a cross channel ferry in the 1990s may be very different from what was expected in a sailing vessel in the 1820s or on a passenger vessel in the 1860s."
[24] *cf. The Hope* (1838) 3 Hagg. 423, 425, where, in apportioning an award amongst salvors which included passengers on board the salving vessel, whose claims to share were uncontested, Sir John Nicholl opined "that the passengers are entitled to share as able-bodied seamen; they were delayed and experienced some inconvenience." In the *Notre Dame de Fourvière* (1923) 14 Ll.L.Rep. 276, 277, Sir Henry Duke P. said that in *The Hope* the passengers rendered services. But the reports do not actually state that this was the case in either *The Hope* or *The Perla* (1857) Swab. 230, where foreign seamen on board the salving vessel as passengers were remunerated as able-bodied seamen. However, it may be reasonably inferred. In *The American Farmer* (1947) 80 Ll.L.Rep. 673, a small award was given to a "gate-crasher" who went from the salving vessel upon which he was travelling to board "in a spirit of adventure" a derelict vessel on which he was given the job of peeling potatoes.
[25] *The Coriolanus* (1890) 15 P.D. 103 (passengers on the salving vessel nominally on its books).
[26] *The Sava Star* [1995] 2 Lloyd's Rep. 134.

Sub-contractors

provision of a tug or other salving vessel or the rendering of fire-fighting services.[27] If a shipowner is entitled to claim salvage against the owner of cargo carried in his ship, it is illogical if a cargo-owner is not entitled to claim salvage against the owner of the ship carrying his cargo.[28]

Sub-contractors

638 The owners of distressed property may hire contractors to render, say, towage or lightening services on the terms that they shall be paid, if at all, under a common law contract for work and labour, thus obviating the necessity of incurring potentially greater liability for salvage. As will be seen, such contracts can validly exclude the contractors' right to salvage.[29] Under the common law doctrine of privity of contract, a third party to a contract cannot normally take a benefit under, or be bound by, a contract to which he is not a party. Thus, a seaman is not bound by an agreement by owners not to claim salvage from other owners who are fellow members of a mutual insurance association.[30] Of course, a sub-contractor may contract with a head contractor specifically on the basis that he will share in any salvage reward,[31] *e.g.* on the International Salvage Union Sub-Contract (Award Sharing) 1994.[32] Otherwise, a third party may be prevented by a term in a head contract from claiming salvage, particularly where he enters the sub-contract to provide a particular service after the distress has arisen.

In such a case, he is not entitled to a possessory lien at common law.[33] Nor is he entitled to an action *in rem*. His claim must be solely against his head contractor.[34]

639 In *The Solway Prince*[35] the plaintiffs, with the knowledge and assent of the owners, undertook to lift a sunken vessel under a contract with the insurers, who advanced to the plaintiffs before the work commenced £1,980 (being about 40 per cent of the amount of £5,000 for which the vessel was insured). The vessel was successfully raised, having an unrepaired salved value of £2,500. The operation of lifting proved more costly than anticipated and some of the underwriters in the meantime became insolvent. The plaintiffs therefore

---

[27] Moreover, having remarked that it has never been suggested that the duty to sue and labour in the Marine Insurance Act 1906, s.78(4) deprives a shipowner of his right to claim salvage against a cargo-owner in a case of salvage by a sister-ship, Clarke J. in *The Sava Star* [1995] 2 Lloyd's Rep. 134, 144, accordingly treated the existence of a cargo-owner's duties to avert or minimise loss under the Institute Cargo Clauses as irrelevant to his entitlement to claim salvage from a shipowner.
[28] *The Sava Star* [1995] 2 Lloyd's Rep. 134, 141, *per* Clarke J.
[29] *Post*, §§ 784–790.
[30] *The Margery* [1902] P. 157; *The Alice Richardson* (1865) 3 M.L.C. Dig. 68.
[31] On the use of sub-contractors by salvors generally, see *post*, Chap. 10.
[32] See *post*, App. 9.
[33] *Castellain v. Thompson* (1862) 13 C.B. (N.S.) 105.
[34] *The Solway Prince* [1896] P. 120; *The Egypt* (1932) 44 Ll.L.Rep. 21 (*obiter*, Langton J. having found that the plaintiffs in fact made no contribution to success). See also *Simon v. Taylor* [1975] 2 Lloyd's Rep. 338 (Sing HC), especially at 344.
[35] [1869] P. 120.

claimed the alleged balance due of £2,646 from the owners *in rem*. Sir Francis Jeune P. decided against the claim, saying[36]:

> "the real question ... seems ... to be: Can the plaintiffs be regarded as salvors, although employed by the insurers to do the work which they performed under an ordinary contract at common law for which the remuneration was not to depend on success? ... During the argument I doubted whether the plaintiffs should not be considered as having acted in a dual capacity, that is to say, both as salvors and as contractors with the insurers. But on reflection I have come to the conclusion that the latter capacity excludes the former, and that the plaintiffs are not, and never were, salvors, because they were employed by the insurers under an ordinary, and not a salvage contract, to do all they did do, on the terms of receiving a specified reward.

640 I think this must be so on principle. There need not, of course, in some cases of salvage, such as those of the rescue of a derelict, be any actual assent of the owner of the *res* or his servants to his property being saved—that is the characteristic difference between the legal consequences of the preservation of property by land and of some property at sea. But it appears to me impossible that the property of any owner can be salved without his sanction, express or implied, in any case in which anything that is done is done with this knowledge; and that when, as here, the owner has merely allowed some one else to employ persons to endeavour to rescue his property on the terms of being paid for their work and labour, such a sanction is certainly not expressed, and cannot be implied. If the owner made such a contract with such persons himself, provided there be no change in the nature of the service, and it may perhaps be necessary to add, provided that the transaction is not shewn to have been inequitable (here there is no question of any such change or want of equity), I think that there can be no doubt that the contracting parties could not claim a remuneration on salvage principles. Nor do I think it makes any difference if the contract is, to the knowledge and with the assent of the owners, made not with themselves but with third parties. Again, which is substantially one of the arguments advanced on behalf of the defendants before me, if the contract of the plaintiffs with the insurers does not prevent their claiming as salvors, why should not any one of the persons employed by them also claim? But can it be supposed that any one of the servants or workmen engaged—a diver, for example, employed at his usual rate of wages—has, if the wreck be raised, a meritorious claim against the owners as a salvor?

Again, which is another way of putting the same considerations, the plaintiffs are really trying to make the owners liable, because the insurers, with whom they contracted, are not able to pay them in full. It was admitted that, had the insurers fulfilled their contract, there could have

---

[36] *ibid.*, 125–126.

been no claim against the defendants. But it appears to me impossible to treat the defendants as in any sense guaranteeing the insurers' solvency."

641 It seems that the third party's claim is not ousted merely by his being contractually obliged to the head contractor to render the service in question, for acting upon the orders of a third party does not necessarily deprive salvors of the necessary element of voluntariness[37]:

> "The true rule appears . . . to be, to consider, whether the services are in themselves of the nature of salvage services; and next, whether they are services which are within the contract which the Seaman originally enters into, so that he receives remuneration for them by his ordinary wages."[38]

Despite the privity rule, the third party claim can be excluded, the apparent rationale being that he caused himself to confer the benefit without the intention of claiming salvage.

642 The mere existence of a head contract does not exclude the third party's claim, for that contract may not on its true construction purport to exclude salvage, or at least the third party's claim to salvage, *e.g.* where the owner of the casualty simply contracts to indemnify salving owners for their expenses and losses.[39]

643 In *The Texaco Southampton*,[40] the agents of the owners of a disabled vessel requested their normal sole supplier of tugs to place tugs on standby. The supply was habitually on terms providing for towage rates, with no reference to salvage. The supplier arranged with another company to send a tug to assist the disabled vessel, the master, pilot and crew of which subsequently claimed, but failed to recover, salvage. It was held by the New South Wales Court of Appeal that there was no authority touching the question whether the crew of a vessel acting under their contract could be volunteers though their employer, because he acted under his contract, could not; but that, where there exists a contract to tow making no provision for salvage and the role of the tug and crew was limited to the performance of that contract, as in the case in hand, neither the crew nor the tug could claim as salvors.

---

[37] *The Sarpen* [1916] P. 306, 315; *The National Defender* [1970] 1 Lloyd's Rep. 40, 45; *Fisher v. The Oceanic Grandeur* (1972) 127 C.L.R. 312, 331; [1972] 2 Lloyd's Rep. 396, 405.
[38] *The Sappho* (1871) L.R. 3 P.C. 690, 695; applied *Fisher v. The Oceanic Grandeur* (1972) 127 C.L.R. 312, 333; [1972] 2 Lloyd's Rep. 396, 406–407.
[39] *Fisher v. The Oceanic Grandeur* (1972) 127 C.L.R. 312; [1972] 2 Lloyd's Rep. 396. See also *Aitchison v. Lohre* (1879) L.R. 4 App. Cas. 755, 765; *The Egypt* (1932) 44 L.L.Rep. 21.
[40] [1983] 1 Lloyd's Rep. 94.

Voluntariness

Employees

644   Employees may be in a direct contractual relationship with the casualty, *e.g.* members of the crew of a salved ship,[41] or they may be in a contractual relationship with another would-be salvage claimant, *e.g.* members of the crew of a tug rendering assistance. In either case the general rule applies: *i.e.* entitlement to a reward is dependent upon their doing something over and above what can ordinarily be expected of them. They cannot therefore recover salvage simply for carrying out the terms of their engagement. And the terms of their engagement may validly require them to provide what would in the absence of such an agreement be a salvage service[42] (albeit the crew of a salvage tug would normally expect to have a contractual entitlement to a percentage of any salvage reward earned by the tug). Both at common law and under statute, the law has provided that any right which a seaman may have or obtain in the nature of salvage shall not be capable of being renounced by any agreement.[43] But the applicability of this rule depends upon whether the seaman had a right to salvage: so, even if the service he rendered were otherwise in the nature of salvage, if he rendered it under a non-salvage contractual undertaking, no right to salvage will accrue to him.

(b) Public Duties

Crown ships, officers and men

General principle

645   "It is, I think notorious," said Dr Lushington in *The Charlotte Wylie*,[44] "that it forms part of the instructions of every one of Her Majesty's vessels that they shall render assistance to British vessels in distress." Similarly, Lord Wright has said that:

> "It is true that the Admiralty in the King's Regulations have strongly inculcated on the officers and crews of His Majesty's ships that it is their duty to render assistance to vessels in distress, but that it is a moral obligation and gives no rights to the shipowner."[45]

The position of officers and men of the Royal Navy, which includes the Fleet Air Arm, requires from them, as servants of the State, the performance of certain active services of protection to British ships and to the lives and cargoes on board them. It is their duty to render such assistance as is

---

[41] See *ante*, especially §§ 565–587.
[42] MSA 1995, s.39(2).
[43] MSA 1995, s.39(1). See further *post*, §§ 1536–1540.
[44] (1846) 2 W. Rob. 495, 499.
[45] *Admiralty Commissioners v. Valverda (Owners)* [1938] A.C. 173, 184.

necessary without having in view any object of claiming salvage.[46] They cannot claim salvage reward for doing anything which fairly falls within the scope of this public duty. Since it is unlikely that those serving in the Royal Navy would be rendering a service other than when the defendant's ship is in some peril,[47] the general discouragement of salvage awards in such cases not only inhibits the possibility of their obtaining a salvage award merely for performance of their public duty but also limits the likelihood of trivial claims being brought every time an officer or man in the Royal Navy assists the defendant whilst discharging his duty.[48]

646 Nevertheless, these considerations have not eroded the general public policy of encouraging persons to provide salvage services.[49] Thus, Lord Stowell said in *The Louisa*[50]:

> "[T]hough it is certainly the duty of King's ships to afford assistance to all His Majesty's subjects whom they meet with in distress, yet I do not know that it is incumbent upon them, at the hazard perhaps of their lives, and without any prospect of reward, to take charge of a ship in a sinking state. Any hesitation in affording assistance might be of dangerous consequence to the property of persons so circumstanced; and it is therefore proper, for the encouragement of prompt and signal exertions, on the part of the King's officers and men, to hold out to them the prospect of reward."

647 Similarly, Sir John Nicholl held in *The Lustre*[51] that the mere fact that the admiral superintendent at Portsmouth gave permission for a Government ship to be used for salvage, on condition that stores expended or damaged would be paid for, did not destroy the right of the ship's commander, officers and men to a salvage reward:

> "[W]hy are officers and crews to hazard their lives, or undergo labour to save the owners of merchant ships from the expense of hiring private steamers, or resorting to other means?"[52]

Dr Lushington made the point most directly in *The Rosalie*[53]:

---

[46] See *The Francis and Eliza* (1816) 2 Dods. 115, 120, *per* Lord Stowell.
[47] In *The Charlotte Wylie* (1846) 2 W. Rob. 495, 499–500, Dr Lushington thought that Her Majesty's vessels had no inducement to assist British vessels from the habitual danger of short-handedness occurring by reason of maladies prevailing on the coast of Africa at that time except in discharge of their instructions to assist British vessels in distress; for it was necessary for the efficiency of Her Majesty's ships engaged in the suppression of the slave trade there that their commanders should retain on board their own vessels their full complement of men, and not expose them to a double danger of short-handedness.
[48] See *The Clifton* (1834) 3 Hagg. 117, 122. And see *post*, §§ 652–653.
[49] See *ante*, Chap. 1.
[50] (1813) 1 Dods. 317, 318–319. See also *The Iodine* (1844) 3 Not. of Cas. 140, 144.
[51] (1834) 1 Hagg. 154.
[52] *ibid.*, 155. See also *The Mary Ann* (1823) 1 Hagg. 158, 158.
[53] (1853) 1 Spinks E. & A. 188, 189.

Voluntariness

"It is all very well to talk of the abstract question of fulfilling duty and obeying commands; and I have no doubt that, so long as men can execute the duty and perform the commands entrusted to them, they will do so; but in cases of doubt and difficulty, and where great and extraordinary exertions have to be made, reward according to human exertions is the only great stimulus to their performance."

Similarly, he said in the following year[54]:

"What is the primary duty of the coast-guard? No doubt it is to prevent smuggling; but I apprehend it to be perfectly true that it is also to assist vessels in distress. But is it a duty not to be paid for? It is the duty of Her Majesty's vessels of war, to assist vessels in distress, and they have positive orders to do it; but we know it is the every-day practice of the Court to remunerate them. With regard to the general principles of salvage, it would be ludicrous at this time of day if I were to enter minutely into them. They are not only well known here, but by the public at large."

Provided the criteria to be discussed in this section are met, therefore, a suitable salvage award will be made in appropriate cases, even though the naval salvor might regard himself as acting only within his daily routine.[55]

Extent of duty

648 It has not proved to be possible exactly to define the extent of the public obligation of members of the Royal Navy, so as to be able to distinguish clearly between services which are performed purely by way of discharge of the public duty and services which justify a salvage award to the particular claimants under consideration. What is reasonably clear, however, is that their claim is much less likely to succeed if the danger is a risk which is within the normal duties of officers and men of the Royal Navy to overcome.[56] *A fortiori*, the risk of disfavour by the Admiralty is an ingredient tending to enhance a salvage reward.[57]

649 In *The F.D. Lambert*,[58] a cargo ship anchored off Lowestoft was preparing to get under way when German warships came in sight and began shelling the coast. One of the shells struck her and set her on fire. The master and crew thereupon took to the boats and started to row away. Meanwhile, the German ships, having been engaged by a British squadron, disappeared. Shortly

---

[54] *Silver Bullion (Cargo ex the Sir Robert Peel)* (1854) 2 Spinks E. & A. 70, 73–4.
[55] See *The Amelia Lauro* (1940) 68 Ll.L. Rep. 12, 19.
[56] See *The Cargo ex Ulysses* (1888) 13 P.D. 205. *cf. The Beaver* (1801) 3 C. Rob. 292, 294, *per* Lord Stowell: "It is the duty of every King's ship, and indeed of every other ship, to give assistance, as well against the elements as against the enemy." His remark was directed to the merit of services rendered during a storm rather than to the existence and extent of any duty existing.
[57] See *post*, § 1434.
[58] [1917] P. 232n.

afterwards, H.M. torpedo-gunboat *Dryad* came up, took the crew on board and sent a party of officers and crew to extinguish the fire and to navigate the *F.D. Lambert* to Yarmouth, where her master and crew returned to her. The defendants admitted that salvage services had been rendered. Sir Samuel Evans P. awarded salvage to the commander, officers and crew of the *Dryad*, and observed[59]:

> "It is said that there was danger from submarines. Unfortunately there was this danger; but it must be remembered that the protection by one of His Majesty's ships of a merchant vessel against submarines does not necessarily partake of a salvage nature. Patrol vessels round our coasts are expected to and do render services of that kind as part of their duties. But for such services our mercantile marine would fare very much worse than it does; and although I do not say that in no case is the protection of a ship from submarine danger to be taken into account when salvage services are rendered, yet in a case where there is no sea danger at all the Court must be very careful indeed not to lay it down that whenever such protection is afforded by one of His Majesty's ships the services thus rendered are to be rewarded by salvage remuneration."

The public duty similarly extends to rescue from piracy or hostile seizure.[60] **650** And the quelling of a mutiny on board a merchant ship is so far within the public duty that salvage will not ordinarily be awarded for such a service. Thus, Lord Stowell said in *The Francis and Eliza*[61]:

> "Certainly it has been determined by this Court, as far as its authority goes, that King's ships may acquire a title to civil salvage by assistance rendered to vessels in distress, even where that distress does not arise from the dangers of the sea, and where the assistance is not of a maritime kind; but the Court has not been in the habit of considering such services, unless they have been very splendid and extraordinary, as entitling the parties to a salvage reward."

He also said later:

> "I do not mean to say that the King's officers would universally and in all cases be excluded from salvage for services rendered by them in rescuing vessels from other than maritime dangers, but still it is their duty to render such assistance without having any such object in view; and unless they incur great personal danger and use very great exertions in the performance of the service, I must hold that they are not entitled to a pecuniary award."[62]

---

[59] *ibid.*, 233n.
[60] *cf. The Cargo ex Ulysses* (1888) 13 P.D. 205, 208.
[61] (1816) 2 Dods. 115, 117–118.
[62] *ibid.*, 120.

Voluntariness

Thus, in *The Cargo ex Ulysses*[63] the posting of sentinels on an island in the Red Sea to protect rescued cargo from looting "would not ... give rise to a high standard of service."

Type of danger and degree of performance

651 Although claims by officers and men of the Royal Navy are less likely to succeed where the danger is not a peril of the seas or a "maritime danger", the impediment to their claim does not depend on a classification of risks into marine risks as opposed to war risks and other non-marine risks,[64] or on whether or not military salvage (as opposed to civil salvage) may be awarded.[65] As Lord Stowell pointed out,[66] private citizens are capable of earning salvage remuneration for recapture from mutineers.[67] Moreover, officers and men of the Royal Navy will not necessarily obtain an award even when effecting salvage from a marine peril. Even in this case, the Admiralty Court has repeatedly expressed the opinion, as illustrated in Lord Stowell's judgment in *The Francis and Eliza*,[68] that no claim for salvage ought to be put forward on behalf of officers and men of the Royal Navy unless the service has required undoubtedly extraordinary exertions or has otherwise been of an important character.[69] The test for whether or not salvage may be claimed by officers and men of the Royal Navy is, therefore, not simply whether or not they happen to be performing their public duty, nor whether they are salving from a maritime rather than a "non-maritime" peril, but whether, in providing the service in question, they are doing more than their duty ordinarily obliges them to do, in terms of incurring greater personal risk, displaying greater skill or courage and making greater exertions than normal.[70]

Admiralty's consent to claim by commander or crew of Her Majesty's ships

652 In accordance with this judicial opinion, the Board of Admiralty, by Order of January 30, 1852, directed the officers of Her Majesty's ships not to claim reward for salvage services rendered to vessels in distress unless the service was one of real importance, or was accompanied with hazard. In order to prevent claims for salvage in respect of any but important services, the legislature has since laid down,[71] under "provisions dictated by public policy ... for considerations of State",[72] that no claim for salvage services by the

---

[63] (1888) 13 P.D. 205.
[64] See *The Lomonosoff* [1921] P. 97. *cf. The Carrie* [1927] P. 224.
[65] *The Louisa* (1813) 1 Dods. 317. See *ante*, § 20
[66] *The Francis and Eliza* (1816) 2 Dods. 115, 118.
[67] *The Trelawney* (1801) 3 C. Rob. 216n.; (1802) 4 C. Rob. 223.
[68] *Supra*.
[69] *The Clifton* (1834) 3 Hagg. 117, 121–122; *The Rapid, ibid.*, 419, 421; *The Iodine* (1844) 3 Not. of Cas. 140, 141; *The Gorliz* [1917] P. 233n; *The Carrie* [1917] P. 224.
[70] See also *The Rosalie* (1853) 1 Spinks E. & A. 188 (towage of vessel on fire, and extinguishing fire).
[71] By MSA 1854, s.485. See now MSA 1995, s.230(3)–(8).
[72] *Admiralty Commissioners v. Valverda (Owners)* [1938] A.C. 173, 185.

commander or crew, or part of the crew, of any of Her Majesty's ships[73] shall be finally adjudicated upon without the consent of the Secretary of State to the prosecution of the claim.[74] Consent would not be given for service plainly within the ordinary duty of Her Majesty's ships, such as affording protection against pirates or land robbers.[75] Any document purporting to give the consent of the Secretary of State, and to be signed by an officer of the Ministry of Defence, shall be evidence of that consent.[76]

The prohibition cannot be waived by a contract with the master of the ship to which services are rendered.[77] If a claim is prosecuted without such consent, it must be dismissed with costs.[78] Furthermore, it was held in *The Rapid*[79] that, if naval officers are in ignorance of or mistake their legal rights and delay in asserting them, it is their own fault and they must bear the consequence of having their claim dismissed.

The Queen's Regulations and Admiralty Instructions include sections which apply to claims by officers and men of the Royal Navy.[80]

653

Assessment of award

From some of the language of the judgments in early cases decided by Sir John Nicholl,[81] it might, perhaps, be thought that the salvage services of the Royal Navy should be remunerated on a somewhat lower scale than those of private salvors. Later decisions of Dr Lushington shew, however, that any such notion in regard to either officers or men would be incorrect and that officers and crews of King's ships are entitled to salvage remuneration upon the same footing as other salvors[82]:

654

---

[73] MSA 1995, s.230(7) provides that "Her Majesty's ships" is defined by MSA 1995, s.192: see *post*, § 1169. This would seem to include flying personnel of aircraft-carriers and other ships: claims by pilots and crew of shore-based aircraft appear to be covered by Queen's Regulations and Admiralty Instructions.
[74] MSA 1995, s.230(3). See also *ibid.*, s.230(8) (application to Northern Ireland). The forerunner of s.230(3) stated that no such claim should be adjudicated upon, unless this consent "is proved" but the omission of these words does not appear to be significant. The consent of the Admiralty in usual form was held to cover a claim for salvage of life as well as of property in *The Alma* (1861) Lush. 378. It may also be noted that no proceeding to enforce a claim for prize salvage on recapture may now be instituted without consent: see the Prize Salvage Act 1944.
[75] See *The Cargo ex Ulysses* (1888) 13 P.D. 205, 208 (*supra*, text to n. 63), where what elevated the service to one more deserving of a salvage reward was rescuing cargo from seriously fouled water and hauling it overland in the severe heat of the Red Sea. The case is more fully reported at (1888) 60 L.T. 111.
[76] MSA 1995, s.230(4).
[77] *Admiralty Commissioners v. Valverda (Owners)* [1938] A.C. 173, 196, *per* Lord Maugham.
[78] MSA 1995, s.230(5). In Scotland, a claim prosecuted without such consent must be dismissed with the defender being found entitled to expenses: MSA 1995, s.230(6).
[79] (1838) 3 Hagg. 419.
[80] See *post*, App. 34.
[81] See *The Clifton* (1834) 3 Hagg. 117, 121–122; *The Ewell Grove* (1835) 3 Hagg. 209, 228; *The Rapid* (1838) 3 Hagg. 419, 421. *cf. The Lustre* (1834) 1 Hagg. 154, 156.
[82] *The Wilsons* (1841) 1 W. Rob. 172; *The Iodine* (1844) 3 Not. of Cas. 140, 141.

Voluntariness

"where a service is done, and there is personal risk and labour, her Majesty's officers and seamen are entitled to be rewarded precisely in a similar manner, on the same principles, and in the same degree, as where any other persons render that service."[83]

655 In his decisions, Sir John Nicholl probably only intended to refer to the point, also alluded to more than once by Dr Lushington,[84] that, since these salvors do not risk their own property or even their own time, those elements of claim are not present so as to justify the higher award that would normally be made to a plaintiff risking his property during the service and taking time from other profitable employment.[85] The Act 12 Anne, c. 18, 1713, which was the first statute which laid down a duty on the commanders and officers both of men-of-war and merchant ships to give salvage assistance to vessels in distress and which prescribed the payment of "reasonable reward" for such services, made no distinction between the two classes as regards either the duty or the reward.[86] However, the fact that salvors are engaged in the public service may be a factor which will effect some slight reduction in the reward which they would otherwise receive.[87]

Beneficiaries of the duty

656 The public duty which limits the ability of officers and men of the Royal Navy to claim salvage has traditionally been regarded as one owed to British ships. In *The Gorliz*,[88] salvage remuneration was awarded for towing a stranded Spanish steamship and in *The Carrie*[89] an award was made for towage, away from the danger of submarine attack, of an abandoned Swedish vessel laden with munitions for the Government of France, an ally of His Majesty in the First World War. The question of the vessel's nationality does not appear to have arisen in *The Gorliz* but, assuming that the cargo in *The Carrie* was the property of the French Government and that it was the duty of the officers and crews of King's ships to protect the property of allied Governments, Hill J. held in that case that salvage could still be awarded for salving the ship. "Whatever was their duty to their own country or to France, they were under no duty to the Swedish owners to save the Swedish ship."[90] He went on to hold, however, that the plaintiffs' claims were governed by the factors which always influence claims by officers and men of the Royal Navy, in particular, that the claim could only be brought with the sanction of the

---

[83] *ibid.*, 141, *per* Dr Lushington.

[84] *The Iodine, ibid.*, 141; *The Rosalie* (1853) 1 Spinks E. & A. 188, 189; *The Earl of Eglinton* (1855) Swab. 7, 8. See also *The Cargo ex Ulysses* (1888) 13 P.D. 205, 208.

[85] But *cf. post*, §660, where part of Dr Lushington's judgment in *The Iodine, supra*, is quoted.

[86] But *cf. The Carrie* [1917] P. 224, 229. The Act and others which culminated in Pt. IX (Salvage and Wreck) of MSA 1995, are considered *ante*, in Chap. 2.

[87] See *The Belgia* (1941) 71 Ll.L.Rep. 21, 22; *The Lord Dufferin* (1849) 7 N.o.C. Supp. xxxiii, xxxvii.

[88] [1917] P. 233n.

[89] [1917] P. 224.

[90] *ibid.*, 231.

Crown ships, officers and men

Admiralty, "a sanction which is intended to enforce the rule ... that to entitle His Majesty's ships[91] to claim salvage remuneration the services must be of an important character" and that "the work done in connection with the salvage service may be no harder and no more risky than work in which they would be ordinarily engaged."[92] The effect of the two cases may be, therefore, not so much that the public duty is only owed to British vessels but that, whether or not that is so, what primarily governs the ability of officers and men of the Royal Navy to claim are the importance of the service and the degree of skill and exertions employed.[93]

However, in *The Belgia*,[94] while making an award to the Admiralty and to the master, officers and crew of two tugs which salved a Swedish steamship, Langton J. reflected that the British taxpayer should not be asked to maintain costly salvage instruments to salve Swedish vessels for nothing.[95] In assessing the award, he took account of the fact that the salved vessel was not British, so that it was unnecessary to make a discount from the services of those employed by the Admiralty on the ground that they were rendered by people in the public employ.[96] *Quaere* the extent to which naval men are, if at all, governed by statutory duties which exclude claims for salvage and the extent to which those duties inhibit claims and/or overlap with their public duties. **657**

Place of performance of duty

There appears to be no territorial limitation beyond which the public duty is not owned to British ships and their personnel.[97] Moreover, the Merchant Shipping Act 1995, s.230(2) specifically permits the Crown to recover salvage "to the same extent as any other salvor" where services are rendered on behalf of Her Majesty, whether in right of Her Government in the United Kingdom or otherwise. **658**

Claims by the Crown itself: historical development

The former position of the Crown with regard to claims for salvage services rendered by H.M. ships may be summarised as an aid to the understanding of the earlier cases, in the following way. **659**

The early cases were vague as to the *locus standi* of the Crown in relation to salvage. Where services were performed by officers and men of Royal Navy ships, the judges stated the public duty of Crown ships to be to render assistance to vessels in distress and the fact that claims could in the right circumstances be brought in respect of such services.[98] But the references in

---

[91] *Sic.*
[92] [1917] P. 224, 231, 232. See also the judgment in *The Gorliz, supra.*
[93] *cf.* also *The Lomonosoff* [1916] P. 306 (*ante*, § 557): salvage of Russian steamship by British army officers.
[94] (1941) 71 Ll.L.Rep. 21.
[95] *ibid.*, 21.
[96] *ibid.*, 22.
[97] See *China Navigation Co. Ltd v. Att.-Gen.* [1932] 2 K.B. 197.
[98] See the cases cited *ante* in §§ 645–650.

the judgments to services provided by H.M. ships did not obviously distinguish between the contribution to salvage by the ships, as opposed to that of their commanders, officers and men, who were almost invariably the only claimants.[99] And the particular role played in the service by the ship itself was normally considered with respect to the inability of its officers and men to have taken into account, in assessing their reward, the value of the Crown property risked, rather than with respect to the question whether the Crown had an independent right to claim.[1] The Crown's ability to claim might have been considered potentially weaker than that of Crown servants in that, if it is the mere performance of a public duty without more that inhibits such claims,[2] there is much less likelihood of a Crown's ship's acting otherwise than in performance of a public duty.

660   In *The Lustre*,[3] however, Sir John Nicholl commented that:

> "It is a mistake to suppose that the public force of this country is to be employed gratuitously in the service of private individuals merely to save them from expense."[4]

He went on to award salvage to officers and men of the ship used, referring to *The Mary Ann*,[5] in which he said "a King's ship was held entitled",[6] although it is not in fact clear from that decision that the Crown also recovered. In *The Iodine*,[7] in which again the Crown was not a claimant, Dr Lushington seemed to assume that the Crown might claim:

> "But, with regard to the use of the vessel, . . . a less remuneration would always be made, on account of the vessel being the property of the country, and the property of the owners under these circumstances never being risked."[8]

He was not obviously referring, however, to a claim by the Crown[9] and Lord Wright later said that the court "must have referred to the award to the officers and the crew, as they were the claimants."[10]

---

[99] See, in particular, *The Mary Pleasants* (1857) Swab. 224, which the reporter refers to as "a suit promoted by Her Majesty's steamship *Leopard*", although the judgment refers only to its captain's claim.
[1] *Admiralty Commissioners v. Valverda (Owners)* [1938] A.C. 173, 191. See also *post*, §660.
[2] But *cf. ante*, §651.
[3] (1834) 3 Hagg. 154.
[4] *ibid.*, 155.
[5] (1823) 1 Hagg. 158.
[6] (1834) 3 Hagg. 154, 155.
[7] (1844) 3 Not. of Cas. 140.
[8] *ibid.*, 141.
[9] If he did only contemplate their claims, his dictum is curious, for it assumes (perhaps because the Crown had no independent claim?) that the officers and crew of a Crown ship could have the ship taken into account so as to inflate the assessment of their reward, but to a lesser extent than a shipowner claiming independently could. This would be wrong in principle. See *The Rosalie* (1853) 1 Spinks 188, 192. The point would not arise today now that it has been established that the Crown and its servants have independent rights to salvage. See *infra*.
[10] *Admiralty Commissioners v. Valverda (Owners)* [1938] A.C. 173, 192.

The clearest support for the view that the Crown could claim salvage at **661** common law was *HMS Thetis*,[11] which is an inconclusive authority, because the claim was for expenses only, and it was admitted. Sir Christopher Robinson said[12]:

> "The claim on the part of the Admiralty for the wages and victualling of the men, and for the wear and tear of the ships, has been in some degree resisted on the part of the salvors; and it is said to be unprecedented; but I do not know that it can be essentially distinguished from claims of owners for demurrage and repairs, in cases of private salvors; and such claims have constantly been allowed. The claim is more novel in form than in principle, and new classes of cases may be expected to require new rules. The Lords of the Admiralty are but trustees for the public, in regulating the employment of H.M. ships: and they must act as they think proper in regard to the terms on which they may be permitted to engage in such services as these. There is, undoubtedly, a difference between the assistance afforded in ordinary cases, by public vessels, for which nothing has hitherto been charged, and the appropriation of them with additional supplies of men and stores, to a service of this kind, for eighteen months together. I am, however, not called upon to give any opinion on this claim, as it is not opposed, but admitted, on the part of the owners and of the Admiral: and I think the salvors have no reason to complain of being so supplied with the means of effecting this service."

It was pointed out by one judge, in *The Lord Dufferin*,[13] that there appeared to be no case in which the Crown had ever claimed more than expenses[14] and he intimated that the Government's interposal in the claim in question may simply have been to enable its servant to use its name to make the best of it he could for his own purposes.[15] But he thought that, rightly or wrongly, it would probably be held that the Government (in that case, of Bombay) would be entitled to claim salvage.

However, referring to *The Lustre*[16] and *The Iodine*,[17] Lord Wright reflected **662** in *Admiralty Commissioners v. Valverda (Owners)*[18] that:

> "These and other cases seem to me to shew clearly that no one dreamt of any claim by the Admiralty for the use of public vessels in salvage,

---

[11] (1833) 3 Hagg. 14; affirmed *sub. nom. The Thetis* (1834) 2 Knapp 390 (PC).
[12] (1833) 3 Hagg. 14, 61–62.
[13] (1849) 7 Not. of Cas. Supp. xxxiii, xxxv, xxxvi, *per* Sir T. Eskine Perry C.J. of the Bombay Supreme Court.
[14] And see *China Navigation Co. Ltd v. Att.-Gen.* [1932] 2 K.B. 197, 231, where, said Lawrence L.J., the Admiralty sometimes deducted the pay of the officers and crew employed on the salvage operations from the amount recovered by them.
[15] See also *The Mary Pleasants, supra*, n. 99.
[16] *Supra*.
[17] *Supra*.
[18] [1938] A.C. 173, 192.

Voluntariness

and that claims by the Admiralty for risk, loss or damage were for all practical purposes never made. *HMS Thetis*[19] and *The Lustre*[20] seem to be the exception which prove the rule. They may have been noticed as cases tending to introduce a new and, as it seemed, objectionable practice, which called for legislative prohibition."

663 Whatever might have been the position at common law, therefore, Parliament legislated so as to inhibit claims for salvage services rendered by H.M. ships, while permitting personal claims by commanders and crews subject to proof of consent by the Admiralty to the prosecution of their claims. The Merchant Shipping Act 1894, s.557(1) (replacing s.484 of the Merchant Shipping Act 1854, which in turn replaced s.39[21] of the Merchant Shipping Act 1853) enacted, under "provisions dictated by public policy... for considerations of State",[22] that in the case of salvage services being rendered by any ship belonging to Her Majesty or by the commander and crew thereof, no claim should be allowed in respect of any loss, damage, or risk, caused to the ship or her stores, tackle, or furniture, or for the use of any stores or other articles belonging to Her Majesty supplied in order to effect those services, or for any other expense or loss sustained by Her Majesty by reason of that service. The wording of the section seemed to indicate that it was only designed to reverse the ruling in *HMS Thetis*,[23] which permitted claims for losses and expenses. But the Act has been regarded as disallowing all possible salvage claims by the Crown, so much so that it was decided by the House of Lords in *Admiralty Commissioners v. Valverda (Owners)*[24] that section 557 could not be the subject of contracting out or of waiver and that it excluded all claims by the Admiralty, including claims for the use of a King's ship as a salvage instrument. Section 557 was qualified by the Merchant Shipping (Salvage) Act 1916, s.1, which enacted that, where the ship was a ship specially equipped with salvage plant[25] or was a tug, the Admiralty, should, notwithstanding the above provisions, be entitled to claim salvage for such

---

[19] *Supra.*
[20] *Supra.*
[21] In fact, the section numbered 39 is the fortieth section to appear in the statute, the designated s.40 being the thirty-ninth.
[22] *Admiralty Commissioners v. Valverda (Owners)* [1938] A.C. 173, 185, *per* Lord Wright. *cf. ibid.*, 196, *per* Lord Maugham: "it is legitimate to consider the position as it was in 1853 when the relevant part of s.557 was first enacted (s.40 of the Merchant Shipping Act 1853). At that date there was no such device as that of wireless communication. Is it to be supposed that the framers of the section conceived that the commander of one of Her Majesty's ships was to be at liberty, for the benefit of the Crown, to negotiate an agreement ousting the section with the master of a vessel in grievous distress on the high seas? If an answer in the affirmative were possible it would seem to follow that such a commander ought always in carrying out his duty to the Crown to do his best to secure such an agreement. In my opinion it is clear that the answer must be in the negative."
[23] *Supra.*
[24] [1938] A.C. 173. The decision of the Court of Appeal [1937] K.B. 745, reversing that of Branson J. [1936] 1 K.B. 724, was affirmed.
[25] As to the meaning of this phrase, see *The Morgana* [1920] P. 442.

services and should have the same rights and remedies as if the ship rendering such services did not belong to His Majesty.

664 The relevant part[26] of the Merchant Shipping Act 1894, s.557(1) and the whole of the Merchant Shipping (Salvage) Act 1916 were repealed by the Merchant Shipping (Salvage) Act 1940, s.4(3). Section 1 of the 1940 Act provided that, where salvage services were rendered by or with the aid of any ship, aircraft or other property whatsoever belonging to His Majesty,[27] His Majesty should be entitled to claim salvage for those services and should have the same rights and remedies in respect of those services as any other salvor would have had if the ship, aircraft or property belonged to him. It was also provided that, where salvage services were rendered by or with the aid of any requisitioned ship or aircraft, as defined in the Act, the ship or aircraft should be treated, for the purpose of any claim in respect of those services, as belonging to His Majesty and not as belonging to any other person, subject to the proviso that this should not apply if under any agreement made on behalf of His Majesty in connection with the requisition, salvage earned by the ship or aircraft was for the benefit of some person other than His Majesty. The Merchant Shipping (Salvage) Act 1940 was repealed by the Crown Proceedings Act 1947, s.89. The rights of the Crown to salvage were enacted in section 8(2) of the 1947 Act, which has now been replaced by the Merchant Shipping Act 1995, s.230(2).

Claim by the Crown itself: present position

665 The Crown's right to claim salvage[28] is now fully equiparated to that of the private salvor by the Merchant Shipping Act 1995, s.230(2). It provides that:

> "Where salvage services are rendered by or on behalf of Her Majesty, whether in right of Her Government in the United Kingdom or otherwise, Her Majesty shall be entitled to claim salvage in respect of those services to the same extent as any other salvor, and shall have the same rights and remedies in respect of those services as any other salvor."

The Act makes it clear that the Crown may claim salvage in respect of salvage services rendered by any vessel owned by the Crown, regardless of whether

---

[26] The Merchant Shipping (Salvage) Act 1940 repealed the words from the beginning of s.557(1) of the Merchant Shipping Act 1894 to "service". It left untouched the rest of the subsection, dealing with the consent of the Admiralty to claims for salvage by a commander, crew or part of a crew. See *ante*, §§ 652–653.
[27] The meaning of "Her Majesty's ships" is considered in MSA 1995, ss.192, 230(7): see *post*, §§ 668–676.
[28] This extends to Northern Ireland: MSA 1995, s.230(8).

Voluntariness

it is a vessel of the Royal Navy, and indeed for "any services rendered by or on behalf of Her Majesty."

666 The admiral of the station or of the fleet to which a Queen's ship belongs has not, by virtue merely of his command, any prerogative right to salvage reward; but if the senior naval officer in command of a locality renders any effective salvage service he may claim.[29]

Officers and crew of other Crown ships

667 Section 230(2) the Merchant Shipping Act 1995 provides that the right of the Crown to claim salvage shall be determined by the general principles governing the claims of other salvors. It does nothing, however, to clarify the applicability of one of those principles in this context. That is, is there a similar public duty on the Crown and on officers and men serving on Crown vessels other than vessels of the Royal Navy to the duty considered in respect of the Royal Navy? It has been suggested in previous editions of this book[30] that the question might perhaps be affected by the nature of the particular vessel, a subject that will be considered below.[31]

668 A related, but distinct, question concerns the applicability of section 230(3) of the Merchant Shipping Act 1995, requiring the consent of the Admiralty to salvage claims "by the commander or crew, or part of the crew, of any of Her Majesty's ships".[32] However, its applicability to claims by officers and men of Crown ships which are not Royal Navy ships has been said in previous editions of this book to appear to be doubtful.[33] What cannot be doubted, given the wording of the section, is that the necessity for the consent depends upon whether the claimants can be said to be "of any of Her Majesty's ships".

Her Majesty's ships: historical interpretation

669 There were a number of decisions interpreting the expression "ships belonging to Her Majesty" in the first part of section 557(1) of the Act of 1894 and in the Merchant Shipping (Salvage) Act 1916.[34] In one of them, *The Cybele*,[35] it was argued that there was a difference in phrases used in the

---

[29] *H.M. Thetis* (1833) 3 Hagg. 14. See also *The Nile* (1875) L.R. 4 A. & E. 449, followed by Sir James Hannen P. in *The Bertie* (1886) 6 Asp. 26. As to the principle of reward in prize, see *The Banda and Kirwee Booty* (1866) L.R. 1 A. & E. 109, 135, 250, *per* Dr Lushington.
[30] See 4th ed., p. 85.
[31] §§ 663–674.
[32] *Ante*, §§ 652–653.
[33] See 4th ed., p. 85.
[34] See *ante*, §664.
[35] (1877) 2 P.D. 224; affirmed (1878) 3 P.D. 8.

forerunners of the original two parts of section 557(1).[36] But Sir Robert Phillimore said:

> "The first contention has been that there is a distinction between 'any ship belonging to Her Majesty' ... and 'any of Her Majesty's ships' ... I am unable to follow the subtlety of that distinction. I think that the two sections are *in eadem materiâ* and both relate to those of Her Majesty's ships."[36A]

Before the first part of section 557(1) was repealed,[37] therefore, the section contained references both to "ships belonging to Her Majesty" and to "Her Majesty's ships". Yet this and the succeeding sections are headed "Salvage by Her Majesty's ships" and this was pointed out by Sir Robert Phillimore, apparently in support of his view, that there was no distinction between the two expressions.

It may, therefore, be instructive, with a view to determining the meaning of **670** "Her Majesty's ships", to consider together those decisions which have interpreted both that phrase and "ships belonging to Her Majesty". Sir Robert Phillimore said in 1875, in *The Dalhousie*,[38] that a steamer belonging to the Bombay Government, "being in the Queen's service, could not be considered as a salvor" and, in *The Cargo ex Woosung*,[39] in the following year, that "there is not much distinction to be drawn between a ship belonging to the Bombay Government and a ship belonging to the Queen."[40] In *Page v. Admiralty Commissioners*,[41] where a tug was requisitioned upon terms which amounted to a charterparty by demise and the crew became Crown servants, the Admiralty, and not the owners, was held to be entitled to the reward for salvage services. And in *The Matti*,[42] where a German steamship condemned as prize was subsequently requisitioned by the Admiralty on terms which gave the Admiralty full dominion and control over the vessel, her master and crew, she was held to be a ship "belonging to Her Majesty". Sir Samuel Evans P. stated that:

---

[36] MSA 1854, ss.484–5.
[36A] (1877) 2 P.D. 224, 227.
[37] See *ante*, §664.
[38] (1875) 1 P.D. 271n., followed by the Court of Appeal in *The Cargo ex Woosung* (1876) 1 P.D. 260.
[39] *ibid*.
[40] *ibid.*, 264.
[41] *Elliott Steam Tug Co. Ltd v. Admiralty Commissioners*; *Page v. Admiralty Commissioners* [1921] 1 A.C. 137; affirming [1919] 1 K.B. 299; affirming *inter alia* [1918] 2 K.B. 447. The Court of Appeal decided that the tug was a "ship belonging to His Majesty" within the meaning of the Merchant Shipping (Salvage) Act 1916, s.1 (repealed by the Merchant Shipping (Salvage) Act 1940) but that particular point was not argued in the House of Lords.
[42] [1918] P. 314. See *ibid.*, 320, *per* Sir Samuel Evans P.: "It is a little significant, but, of course, not in any degree conclusive, that the Admiralty themselves in their statement of claim describe the vessel as '*HMS Comet.*'" It was also held that the power in MSA 1906, s.80 to register "Government ships" (*i.e.* ships not forming part of His Majesty's Navy which belong to His Majesty, or are held by any person on behalf of or for the benefit of the Crown: *ibid.*, s.80(3)) did not give any authority to the Crown by Order in Council to declare what class of ship was or was not within the category of ships dealt with in MSA 1894, s.557.

"Temporary ownership by or for the Crown, apart from complete legal ownership, may be sufficient to constitute a ship one belonging to His Majesty."[43]

671 However, it had previously been held, in *The Sarpen*,[44] that a tug requisitioned by the Admiralty on terms not amounting to a demise was not "a ship belonging to His Majesty".[45] Swinfen Eady L.J. said:

"prima facie a ship rendering services such as the *Simla* rendered to the *Sarpen* would be entitled to a salvage award; the burden of shewing that the *Simla* was not so entitled was upon the *Sarpen*."[46]

Thus, the owners, master and crew of the ship were entitled to prosecute a claim for salvage:

"the owners of a vessel are not excluded from the right to salvage because she is in the service of the Crown and cannot render such services without its consent and the services are rendered under the instructions of the naval authorities."[47]

The fact of being under requisition does not necessarily make any difference.[48]

672 The salving ship in *Symons v. Baker*[49] was owned by the Government, entered in the Navy List and exclusively engaged, under the Admiralty, by the Devonport Dockyard Authorities in carrying coal for the Royal Navy. It was held to be a ship belonging to His Majesty,[50] although neither master nor crew were in the Royal Navy. Lord Alverston C.J. said:

"I do not understand why any distinction is to be drawn between the service of an ordinary ship of the Navy and the most useful but less dignified work which this vessel was performing."[51]

In *The Cybele*,[52] however, a vessel owned by the Board of Trade as trustees of Ramsgate Harbour was said not to be "one of Her Majesty's ships". The decision is in fact doubtful on this point; it can be supported on the ground that

---

[43] [1918] P. 314, 320. See also *ibid.*, 321: "it is settled law that possession amounting to a temporary ownership in the Crown may constitute a vessel one 'belonging to His Majesty'." See also *The Nile* (1875) L.R. 4 A. & E. 449; *The Bertie* (1886) 6 Asp. M.L.C. 26; *Master of Trinity House v. Clark* (1815) 4 M. & S. 288; *cf. Weir v. Union Steamship Co.* [1900] A.C. 525.
[44] [1916] P. 306.
[45] Under the Merchant Shipping (Salvage) Act 1906, s.1, now repealed: see *supra*, n. 18.
[46] [1916] P. 306, 314.
[47] *ibid.* at 317, *per* Pickford L.J., approving *The Nile* (1875) L.R. 4 A. & E. 449 and *The Bertie* (1886) 6 Asp. M.L.C. 26.
[48] See also *The Broadmayne* [1916] P. 64.
[49] [1905] 2 K.B. 723.
[50] Under MSA 1894, s.741.
[51] [1905] 2 K.B. 723, 728.
[52] (1877) 2 P.D. 224; affirmed (1878) 3 P.D. 8.

the Board of Trade was not strictly acting as a Government Department but as trustees of a particular trust.[53]

Her Majesty's ships: present definition

It is provided, by the Merchant Shipping Act 1995, s.230(7), that "Her Majesty's ships" means: **673**

"(a) ships of which the beneficial interest is vested in Her Majesty;
(b) ships which are registered as Government ships;
(c) ships which are for the time being demised or sub-demised to or in the exclusive possession of the Crown;
except that it does not include any ship in which Her Majesty is interested otherwise than in right of Her Government in the United Kingdom unless that ship is for the time being demised or sub-demised to Her Majesty in right of Her Government in the United Kingdom or in the exclusive possession of Her Majesty in that right."[54]

The requirement of Admiralty consent to salvage claims in section 230(3) of the Merchant Shipping Act 1995 is stated to apply to "*any* of Her Majesty's ships",[55] so the section would appear to be designed to have a wide ambit and not necessarily to be restricted to salvage claims relating only to ships of the Royal Navy. In the light of the cases just considered, however, it may be submitted that the expression "Her Majesty's ships" does not extend to ships other than those over which a government department is exercising dominion at the time of the salvage services. **674**

It may be, therefore, that officers and crews in the service of or employed by the Crown in ships owned by the Crown, *e.g.* Army personnel on board tank-landing craft or civilian officers and crews of Admiralty tugs, would be held to require Admiralty consent before claiming salvage. It may be noted, however, that the Admiralty's consent is not required except for services by "the commander or crew or part of the crew" of any of Her Majesty's ships. Thus, it will be no bar to his claim that the plaintiff was a member of Her Majesty's Armed Forces who was on board one of Her Majesty's ships but was not her commander or one of the crew,[56] unless he was the commander or one of the crew of another of Her Majesty's ships. Indeed, the section as expressed extends to all salvage services provided by commanders and crew **675**

---

[53] *Young v. S.S. Scotia* [1903] A.C. 501, 505. See *The Jassy* [1906] P. 270. At first instance, in *The Cybele*, Sir Robert Phillimore doubted whether it was the intention of the statute transferring the harbour to the Board of Trade to place the harbour's vessel in the category of Her Majesty's ships.
[54] The meaning, for the purpose of s.230, is the meaning provided by s.192(2).
[55] Italics added.
[56] *cf. The American Farmer* (1947) 80 Ll.L.Rep. 672 (U.S. Army personnel).

Voluntariness

of Her Majesty's ships, whether or not they are on board one of Her Majesty's ships, any other ship, or even on no vessel at all.

676 The section may be framed widely, in relation to the personnel it covers, because Parliament has perceived that the public duty owed by members of the Royal Navy to assist at sea extends to all types of personnel serving on all government ships. Indeed, it might conceivably extend to all public servants, at least to those in the other Armed Forces, although it is probably doubtful whether it should apply to public servants whose ordinary occupation does not normally fit them to contribute to services of a salvage nature.[57] In any event, however, the existence of the public duty alone is unlikely to be decisive as to whether or not a claim should succeed and would, therefore, only form a factor to be considered in assessing the amount of reward.

The Royal Air Force, its officers and men

677 The Merchant Shipping Act 1995, s.230(2) clearly provides that, where salvage services are rendered by or on behalf of the Crown, it shall be entitled to claim salvage in respect of those services to the same extent as any other salvor, and shall have the same rights and remedies in respect of those services as any other salvor.[58] By itself, the section would seem to provide direct authority for the proposition that the Crown may claim salvage in respect of services rendered by aircraft of the Royal Air Force. This view derives support from the Civil Aviation Act 1982, s.87(2), albeit the Act is only concerned with *civil*, and not military aviation. It provides that:

> "Where salvage services are rendered by an aircraft to any property or person, the owner of the aircraft shall be entitled to the same reward for those services as he would have been entitled to if the aircraft had been a vessel."[59]

The Crown's right to claim for salvage services rendered by RAF aircraft would, therefore, appear to be similar to its right to recover for salvage services provided by Royal Navy vessels.

678 Section 87(2) of the 1982 Act refers only to the *owner* of an aircraft. It does not cover claims by the captain and crew of RAF aircraft. It has been submitted previously in this book[60] that it would appear that the crew of any aircraft who rendered salvage services would be entitled to claim salvage for two reasons. First, apart from statute, personal services, even though not involving the use of any vessel or other equipment, may, according to the

---

[57] *cf. ante*, §633.
[58] See *ante*, §665.
[59] This section replaces the provisions of the Air Navigation Act 1920, s.11, as substituted by the Air Navigation Act 1936 (now repealed by the Civil Aviation Act 1949, s.70(1) and Sched. 12).
[60] 4th ed., pp. 87–88.

general principles of the law of salvage, be rewarded. Secondly, there is a general statutory right to a reward for salvage operations which have had a useful result,[61] which therefore prima facie extends to the captain or crew of an aircraft, whether RAF or civilian. However, these reasons are incomplete if the difficulty in establishing the right to claim of RAF personnel is more than mere doubt as to whether they are notional salvors. The vital issues, of course, are whether RAF personnel are restricted from claiming salvage by a similar public duty to the one which lies on personnel of the Royal Navy and, if so, the extent to which it affects their claims.

679 Two points of similarity between those serving in the two Forces must be noted. First, by Order in Council made under previous legislation,[62] the provisions of the Merchant Shipping Acts as to wreck and salvage have been applied to aircraft. The effect of this, for present purposes, is that: (i) no claim for salvage services by the commander or crew or part of the crew of any of Her Majesty's aircraft shall be finally adjudicated upon without the consent of the Air Council to the prosecution of the claim; (ii) any document purporting to give the consent of the Air Council for this purpose and to be signed by an officer of the Ministry of Defence shall be evidence of that consent; and (iii) if a claim is prosecuted without such consent, it shall be dismissed with costs.[63]

Secondly, Queen's Regulations and Air Council Instructions include sections which apply to claims for salvage by officers and men of the RAF, and the public duty which affects claims by naval personnel is in part founded on the inculcation into naval personnel by Queen's Regulations that it is their duty to effect salvage where necessary.[64]

680 Admittedly, there is less opportunity for the rendering of salvage services, at least of a direct kind, by members of the RAF than there is by members of the Royal Navy. And in individual cases it may more easily, though not necessarily correctly, be argued that such services as are rendered by RAF personnel are more likely to be outside their normal duties, so as more easily to qualify as salvage services. But in modern times, a line between the type of services provided by the different services becomes increasingly difficult to draw. It would be invidious to distinguish between services provided by an aircraft (particularly a helicopter) of the Royal Navy's Fleet Air Arm and one of the RAF; and between those provided by a naval vessel and an RAF Air Sea Rescue vessel.

The personnel of all three Armed Forces are treated similarly by Queen's Regulations. It is submitted, therefore, that the law applicable in the event of claims being made by officers and men of the RAF should and would, in all

---

[61] MSA 1995, s.224, Sched. 11, Pt I, Art. 12.1.
[62] The Aircraft (Wreck and Salvage) Order in Council, S.R. & O. 1938, No. 136 (now partly revoked by S.I. 1964 No. 489), made under the Air Navigation Acts 1920 and 1936.
[63] This is the effect, with respect to aircraft, of MSA 1995, s.230(3)–(6).
[64] See *ante*, §675.

probability, *mutatis mutandis* be similar to that applied where the claimants are officers and men of the Royal Navy.

681 In *The American Farmer*,[65] in response to a request from the owners of an abandoned vessel, a Liberator of RAF Coastal Command was despatched to ascertain whether the vessel was still afloat and her exact position. After this was done, the aircraft flew on to the Azores, weather conditions being unfavourable for an immediate return to the United Kingdom, and returned a day or so later, *en route* confirming the present position of the vessel, which was then being attended by two steamships. According to Pilcher J.[66]:

> "these services were services rendered at request and consequently they lack one of the most valuable characteristics of the ordinary salvage service, in that they were not voluntary. I do not think that the services rendered by the Liberator in this case actually conferred any real benefit upon the salved property. Both the *Elizabete* and the *American Ranger* found the *American Farmer* on their own ... if the Royal Air Force had never been in a position to send this Liberator to find her and had never given the position which they did give, this salvage would have taken exactly the same course as it has taken. At the same time one must remember ... that the risk involved in despatching an aircraft to go over 700 miles of sea is a very different risk from that which is involved in despatching a salvage tug to a vessel requiring assistance. Salvage tugs are accustomed to navigate in the ocean under the most arduous conditions and do so in comparative safety, but if anything goes wrong with an aircraft when hundreds of miles out over the sea not only the aircraft itself but also its crew are in grave peril. The services rendered by this aircraft are of a kind which must be encouraged."

He accordingly awarded salvage to the President of the Air Council, as nominal owner of the Liberator, and to its captain, officers and crew. The fact that the service was rendered by RAF property and personnel did not on the face of it influence the assessment of the award.

Royal Army

682 As noted above, the circumstances in which members of the Army, as opposed to members of the other Armed Forces, may be capable of effecting salvage are limited so that, although they might be regarded as under some form of public duty to effect salvage, those circumstances may be a less inhibiting factor on salvage claims than in the cases of their colleagues.[67]

Coastguard officers and personnel

683 The officers and personnel of the coastguard have historically had duties in connection with the revenue.[68] They have, in addition, duties in connection

---
[65] (1947) 80 Ll.L.R. 672.
[66] *ibid.*, 689.
[67] See *ante*, §676; *The Lomonosoff* [1921] P. 97, *ante*, §533.
[68] See, *e.g. The Clifton* (1834) 3 Hagg. 117, 121.

with salvage and wreck, which they perform under the instruction of the Secretary of State, *viz.* the duty of watching and protecting shipwrecked property, and the duty of assisting Receivers of Wreck in discharging their various functions under the Merchant Shipping Acts in regard to wreck and marine casualties. Dr Lushington put it thus[69]:

> "What is the primary duty of the coastguard? No doubt it is to prevent smuggling; but I apprehend it to be perfectly true that it is also to assist vessels in distress. But is it a duty not to be paid for? It is the duty of Her Majesty's vessels of war to assist vessels in distress, and they have positive orders to do it; but we know it is the every-day practice of the Court to remunerate them. With regard to the general principles of salvage, it would be ludicrous at this time of the day if I were to enter minutely into them. They are not only well known here, but by the public at large."

684 Where services are rendered by any officers or personnel of the coastguard service in watching or protecting shipwrecked property, then, unless it can be shewn that those services have been declined by the owner of the property or his agent at the time they were tendered, or that salvage has been claimed and awarded for those services, the owner of the property must pay remuneration in respect of those services, according to a scale fixed by the Secretary of State.[70] That remuneration is recoverable by the same means, and must be paid to the same persons, and accounted for and applied in the same manner, as fees received by Receivers.[71]

In respect of their other statutory and official duties, officers and personnel of the coastguard may become entitled, with the sanction of the Secretary of State, to remuneration which is ultimately paid by the owners of shipwrecked property; but they cannot sue for salvage.

685 However, if officers and personnel of the coastguard were to incur some risk or undertake some labour beyond the scope of their official and statutory duties—if, for example, they actually put out to sea, and with risk and labour saved property—they would be legally entitled to salvage in the same manner and to the same extent as other salvors.[72] As Sir John Nicholl said in *The Clifton*[73]:

---

[69] *Silver Bullion (Cargo ex the Sir Robert Peel)* (1854) 2 Spinks E. & A. 70, 73–74. See further on the status and possible liability of H.M. Coastguard *OLL Ltd v. Secretary of State for Transport* [1997] 3 All E.R. 897; *Skinner v. Secretary of State for Transport* [1995] T.L.R. 2; noted R. Shaw [1998] I.J.S.L. 125. See generally R. Bagshaw [1999] L.M.C.L.Q. 71.

[70] MSA 1995, s.250(1)–(2). See also *ibid.*, s.250(4). S.250 does not provide that salvage can be recovered; merely that, if there is a right to salvage, it is not taken away by the section.

[71] Under the Merchant Shipping Act 1995, s.249: see *ibid.*, s.250(3). See *post*, §695. The scale fixed by the Secretary of State must, by statute, not exceed the scale by which remuneration to officers and men of the coastguard for extra duties in the service of the Commissioners of Customs and Excise is for the time being regulated: see MSA 1995, s.250(4).

[72] *The Queen Mab* (1835) 3 Hagg. 242, 243 (the actual decision was not followed in *The Zephyrus* (1842) 1 W. Rob. 329); *The Charlotta* (1831) 2 Hagg. 361; *The Clifton* (1834) 3 Hagg. 117; *The London Merchant* (1837) 3 Hagg. 394; *Re Silver Bullion (Cargo ex the Sir Robert Peel)* (1854) 2 Spinks E. & A. 70; see also Pritchard, Vol. 2, p. 1920. *cf. The Lockwoods* (1845) 9 Jur. 1017.

[73] (1834) 3 Hagg. 117, 121–122.

"It has been admitted that the coastguard is kept for Custom House purposes—to prevent smuggling; was it not the duty of Lieut. Kelly to go out and visit or watch this vessel? Persons in the public service have, I think, a peculiar duty cast upon them to render aid to the trade of the country: they sacrifice no time from any other profitable employment; their time is paid for by the public; they risk no property; for the property they use belongs to the public. It is upon this principle that in prize salvage on recapture King's ships received less than private ships: the former received only one-eighth, while the latter, one-sixth. I do not say that individuals paid by the public are excluded altogether from remuneration when they render an important service to private property; but their being so paid ought to cast upon them a peculiar readiness to give assistance, and prevent them from setting up exaggerated demands for trivial service."

686   Coastguard personnel are, therefore, doubly impeded in any attempt to claim salvage: first, because they may be directly performing their official duties; and, secondly, because going beyond their official duties *stricto sensu*, they may be discharging a wider public duty of assisting in cases of danger at sea. But this is always subject to the public policy of encouraging and rewarding beneficial services in such circumstances. Thus, in one case, Sir John Nicholl said[74]:

"The cutter was rather an intruder: the crew were told their assistance was not wanted; and going on board for the protection of the revenue will not make them salvors: they, however, at the pilot's suggestion, put on board a cable and anchor, and though they were not used, and were taken back by them on the next day, it is always desirable to encourage due assistance, and I shall therefore award some small remuneration for this trouble."

His judgment in *The London Merchant*[75] even suggested that members of the coastguard might even be rewarded merely where discharge of their duty assists salvage:

"Lieut. Dooley exerts himself; he stations his men, in order to guard the property from plunder, in case it should be necessary to land any part of it. That was his first duty: he then goes on board himself, he imparts comfort and confidence to the alarmed passengers; he superintends and countenances the proceedings. It is true, he does not afford much personal assistance, that was unnecessary; the services of the harbour-master, boatmen, and pilots had been agreed for; but still he is to be considered as a salvor, and entitled to remuneration."

---

[74] *The Queen Mab* (1835) 3 Hagg. 242, 243–244. The actual decision was not followed in *The Zephyrus* (1842) 1 W. Rob. 329.
[75] (1837) 3 Hagg. 394, 398–399.

Statutory authorities and their servants

In certain circumstances, a principal officer of the coastguard may exercise **687** the powers of a receiver of wreck in the absence of the receiver; when so acting he is not entitled to any fees payable to receivers nor is he deprived by reason of his so acting of any right to salvage to which he would otherwise be entitled.[76]

Statutory authorities and their servants

A public or statutory authority may have a duty or a power to provide a **688** service. If it has a duty to do so, it cannot claim money in the form of tax without Parliamentary authority.[77] Indeed, it may be expressly forbidden from doing so.[78] But the mere fact that a service is provided by a public authority does not mean that it must be provided gratuitously.[79] If there is no requirement to perform a service, it is possible for a charge to be made.[80] However, it is also possible that a service provided under powers given for public purposes will be treated as rendered in discharge of the authority's public duty.[81] Moreover, where there is provision for payment in respect of the service rendered (*e.g.* for expenses incurred), that may be treated as exhaustive, so precluding a claim on any other basis.[82] The general test for whether a public authority is entitled to claim for a service provided is essentially the same as the Admiralty law test for voluntariness: whether the service provided is outside the scope of the normal performance of its public duties.[83] Thus, a harbour authority taking action for the safety of shipping is likely to be unable to claim salvage while acting within its harbour area but may be able to do so if acting elsewhere. Similarly, even a statutory inhibition on claims to remuneration[84] may be held to be inapplicable to services performed outside the authority's jurisdiction, particularly on the high seas.

---

[76] MSA 1995, s.231. See *post*, §695.

[77] *Att.-Gen. v. Wilts United Dairies Ltd* (1922) 91 L.J. (K.B.) 897 (HL).

[78] See especially the Fire Services Act 1947, s.3(4), forbidding any charge not expressly authorised by the Act. *cf.* MSA 1995, s.231(4), denying an officer discharging functions of receivers of wreck fees payable to receivers, but preserving any right of salvage to which he would otherwise be entitled.

[79] *The Lustre* (1834) 1 Hagg. 154, 155, *per* Sir John Nicholl.

[80] See the pre-Crown Proceedings Act 1947 salvage cases cited in *China Navigation Co. Ltd v. Att.-Gen.* [1932] 2 K.B. 197, 217, 231, 241.

[81] At least if it exercises the power to provide services on the basis that a charge will be made. See, *e.g. The Mars and Other Barges* (1948) 81 Ll.L.Rep. 452, 455, *per* Willmer J.: see *post*, §690.

[82] *cf.* MSA 1995, s.250, which authorises remuneration for services rendered by coastguard personnel in watching or protecting shipwrecked property, except where salvage has been awarded for such services. Alternatively, it supports the assumption that salvage may be recovered. This does not *per se* mean that salvage can be awarded for such services: the exception may have been included simply to avoid double recovery. *cf.* MSA 1995, ss.252–253, authorising harbour, conservancy and lighthouse authorities to recover expenses for wreck removal, without reference to the possibility of salvage.

[83] *Glasbrook Bros Ltd v. Glamorgan County Council* [1925] A.C. 270; *China Navigation Co. Ltd v. Att.-Gen.* [1932] 2 K.B. 197 (CA); *Harris v. Sheffield United Football Club Ltd* [1988] Q.B. 77 (CA).

[84] *e.g.* the Fire Services Act 1947, s.3(4): *supra*, n. 78.

689 It has not been uncommon for services to have been rendered by public bodies in circumstances where a claim to a salvage reward might be upheld but without its being pursued or with informal payments being made by other salvors (*e.g.* where professional salvors have enlisted the assistance of members of a fire service). However, restraints on public funding and the increased cost of modern salvage operations may encourage a reversal of these practices and an increased perception that public authorities may succeed in such claims in appropriate cases.

690 Port, harbour and lighthouse authorities invariably have statutory powers to deal with property in distress in their jurisdiction.[85] Those powers may be expressed to exist for the general benefit of third parties involved in navigation but, even so, are generally accepted to impose a duty also to the owners of the distressed vessel, *i.e.* a duty to shipping generally.[86] Even where the authority owes no such duty, it may be otherwise obliged to provide services to a casualty. As regards the duties of the Port of London Authority, Willmer J. said in *The Mars and Other Barges*[87]:

> "I doubt myself whether it is right to say that the section imposes a statutory duty. It in fact grants a permissive power. But I doubt whether this is a point of any significance, because it is well established on the authorities that if an authority armed with such a power received tolls and dues from shipping using the port, then at common law there arises a duty towards vessels paying such tolls and dues to exercise reasonable care to see that the channel is safe, and so forth."

691 The effect of such duties is to exclude altogether the possibility of a claim by the relevant authority for acts done in exercise of that duty.[88] Deciding this point, Brandon J. also expressed the view that the necessity for performance of the relevant duty also excluded the authority's power to acquire a right to salvage by conclusion of a Lloyd's Form contract[89]:

> "My provisional view is that a port authority has no such power, and this for three main reasons. First, because the statutes giving power to remove obstructions provide for the recovery of expenses only, and this excludes, by necessary implication, the recovery of salvage: this seems to have been the view of Lord Blackburn in his judgment in *The Citos*[90] . . . Second, because a 'no cure, no pay' contract is a speculative contract inappropriate for a public authority to make as a means of performing its

---

[85] See *e.g.* MSA 1995, ss.252–253; *The Gregerso* [1973] Q.B. 274, 278. As to the effect of the statutory rights as against salvors, see *The Ousel* [1957] 1 Lloyd's Rep. 151.
[86] *The Citos* (1925) 22 Ll.L. Rep. 275, 276, (Ct of Sn); *The Mars and Other Barges* (1948) 81 Ll.L. Rep. 452, 455.
[87] *The Mars and Other Barges* (1948) 81 Ll.L. Rep. 452, 455.
[88] *The Gregerso* [1973] Q.B. 274.
[89] *ibid.*, 283.
[90] (1925) 22 Ll.L. Rep. 275.

Statutory authorities and their servants

public duty.[91] ... Third, because the authority, by entering into such a contract, may create a situation in which there is a conflict between its private contractual obligation to the owners of the obstructing vessel to use their best endeavours to salve her, and its public duty owed to users of the port generally to clear the port with all reasonable expedition ...

The result at which I have arrived may appear unjust in that it means, in effect, that the defendants get the benefit of having their vessel salved by the port authority, without having to pay for such benefit on salvage terms. This result is, however, justified by the need to ensure that those who have existing public duties to perform at ordinary rates of remuneration should not be permitted to say that they will only discharge such duties if they are paid salvage for doing so.[92]

It is, perhaps, significant in this connection, that in another Scottish case, *Greenock Port and Harbours Trustees v. British Oil and Cake Mills Ltd*,[93] the view seems to have been taken that this form of 'cut price' salvage, if I may so call it, was not merely an inevitable consequence, in certain cases, of the exercise by port authorities of their statutory powers of removing obstructions, but was even one of the purposes for which such powers were conferred."

Since an authority can only discharge its duties through the agency of its **692** *servants*, it is accepted that an authority's employees, including the dock or harbour master, by joining the service of the authority, come under the same statutory duty to the public as the authority itself.[94] Even if that is not necessarily true, it is certainly the case that employees providing services which they are obliged to perform other than for a salvage reward are generally precluded from claiming salvage,[95] and particularly where the nature of their employment may require them on occasions to perform in unusually onerous circumstances.[96]

However: **693**

"it cannot be right to say that, wherever there is a duty on a public authority, then any right to salvage on the part of the servants of the

---

[91] His Lordship cited *Boston v. France, Fenwick & Co. Ltd* (1923) 15 Ll.L. Rep. 85, 90, *per* Bailhache J., who opined that a harbour authority's "no cure, no pay" salvage contract was *ultra vires*.
[92] *cf. The Citos* (1925) 22 Ll.L. Rep. 275, 277, *per* Lord Blackburn:
"In his opinion it was undesirable and dangerous that men employed on a public service of this character should be entitled to draw a fine distinction between a condition of weather which they considered too bad to require the performance of their public duty, but not too bad to hinder the voluntary performance of the same service for the purpose of earning a large salvage award."
[93] 1944 S.C. 70.
[94] *The Citos* (1925) 22 Ll.L. Rep. 275, 276. See also *The Gregerso* [1973] Q.B. 274.
[95] See *ante*, §§ 638–643.
[96] See *The Mars and Other Barges* (1948) 81 Ll.L. Rep. 452, 457. *cf. The Krypton and Other Barges* [1954] 2 Lloyd's Rep. 451; *The Buffalo and Other Barges* (1937) 58 Ll.L. Rep. 302.

Voluntariness

authority in any circumstances is gone forever.... It cannot... be right to say that the mere existence of a statutory duty automatically and of itself excludes the possibility of any claim for salvage."[97]

It is, therefore, the case that a port authority and its servants have a right to recover salvage for rendering assistance in situations which do not call for the exercise by the authority of its statutory powers, whether the services are rendered outside the port or inside it.[98] It may, however, be difficult to distinguish between services required to discharge the statutory duty and those which would have been required in the ordinary process of salvage, and a very much higher degree of service is required than in the performance of the public duty.[99] This in turn will cause the tribunal to be cautious in assessing the reward payable. Thus, Willmer J. has said[1]:

"what I have to do is to hold the balance between two aspects of public policy—one which demands that the court do nothing lightly to encourage claims of this character on the part of public servants, and the other one which prompts the court, where it is satisfied that services going beyond the public duty have been rendered, to encourage the enterprise of the men who have performed those services."

Receivers of wreck

694 Where a United Kingdom or foreign vessel is wrecked, stranded or in distress at any place on or near the coasts of the United Kingdom or any tidal water within United Kingdom waters, on being informed of the circumstance, the Receiver of Wreck[2] must proceed forthwith to the place where the vessel is, take command of all persons present, and must assign such duties and give such directions to each person as he thinks fit for the preservation of the vessel and of the lives of the persons belonging to the vessel.[3] The Receiver must not, however, interfere between the master and the crew of the vessel in reference to the management thereof, unless he is requested to do so by the master.[4]

The Act stipulates that there shall be paid to the Receiver the expenses properly incurred by him in the discharge of his functions, and such fees as

---

[97] *The Mars and Other Barges* (1948) 81 Ll.L. Rep. 452, 455–456.
[98] *The Mars and Other Barges* (1948) 81 Ll.L. Rep. 452; *The Citos* (1925) 22 Ll.L. Rep. 275; *The Gregerso* [1973] Q.B. 274, 284; *The Cawarsand* [1953] 1 Lloyd's Rep. 298: See also *The Corcrest* (1946) 80 Ll.L. Rep. 78; *Dover Harbour Board v. The Ruby* (1923) 14 Ll.L. Rep. 98; *The Cybele* (1878) 3 P.D. 8, affirming (1878) 2 P.D. 224. *cf. Symons v. Baker* [1905] 2 K.B. 723.
[99] See *The Citos* (1925) 22 Ll.L. Rep. 275, 276–277.
[1] *The Mars and Other Barges* (1948) 81 Ll.L. Rep. 452, 458.
[2] On Receivers generally, see MSA 1995, Pt IX.
[3] MSA 1995, ss.231(1), (5), 232(1)–(2). Any person intentionally disobeying the directions of the Receiver is liable to a fine not exceeding level 3 on the standard scale: *ibid.*, s.232(4).
[4] *ibid.*, s.232(3).

may be prescribed by the Secretary of State.[5] But a Receiver is not entitled to any other remuneration.[6] In addition to all other rights and remedies for the recovery of those expenses or fees, the Receiver has the same rights and remedies in respect thereof as a salvor has in respect of salvage due to him.[7]

Any function conferred on the Receiver in respect of vessels in distress under the Merchant Shipping Act 1995, ss.232–235 may be discharged by any officer of customs and excise or any principal officer of the coastguard.[8] An officer discharging such functions of the Receiver shall be treated as the Receiver's agent with respect to any goods or articles belonging to a vessel deliverable to the Receiver.[9] But he will not be entitled to any fees payable to Receivers, or be deprived of any right to salvage to which he would otherwise be entitled.[10] However, any person unjustly interfering with respect to a ship in distress, at least if convicted of doing so, will not be entitled to claim salvage.[11]

695

Receivers should, however, be able to claim as salvors if they personally render salvage services to life or property in peril which are outside the duties prescribed by statute.[12]

Magistrates and other officials

In conformity with the principles discussed in the preceding paragraphs, other persons holding a public office or appointment are entitled to salvage reward only if, and so far as, that which they do is clearly outside the scope of the duties of the office or the appointment. Thus, as Lord Stowell said in *The Aquila*[13]:

696

> "if a magistrate acting in his public duty, on such an occasion, should go beyond the limits of his official duty, in giving extraordinary assistance, he would have an undeniable right to be considered as a salvor: it will be therefore necessary to enquire what has been the extent of this gentleman's services: if they amount only to the ordinary discharge of his duty, I shall be disposed to leave him to the reward of all good magistrates, the fair estimation of his countrymen, and the consciousness of his own right conduct."

---

[5] See *ibid.*, s.249(1). Any dispute as to the amount payable to the Receiver in respect of expenses or fees is subject to final determination by the Secretary of State: *ibid.*, s.249(4).
[6] MSA 1995, s.249(2).
[7] *ibid.*, s.249(3).
[8] *ibid.*, s.231(2).
[9] Under *ibid.*, ss 231–247 ("wreck"): see *ibid.*, s.231(3).
[10] *ibid.*, s.231(4).
[11] *The Wear Packet* (1855) 2 Spinks E. & A. 256, decided on the basis of the Wreck and Salvage Act 1846, s.15 (replaced by MSA 1854, s.445), a forerunner of MSA 1995, s.231.
[12] That would not, however, justify a claim where a Receiver wrongfully interfered between the master and the crew in reference to the management of the vessel, contrary to *ibid.*, s.232(2): *ante*, §694.
[13] (1798) 1 C. Rob. 37, 46.

Voluntariness

It is salutary to note that the necessary delineation of the scope of an official's duties must be made as at the time at which he was acting, and that the older authorities may provide deceptive guidelines, for the nature of the relevant duties may change. In *The Aquila*,[14] a magistrate sent 15 men to assist a shipwrecked vessel and drive off 200 persons who had gone to plunder in accordance with "the barbarous *lex loci*". He also sent notice to the Swedish consul and to Lloyd's Coffee-house. But his claim for salvage was rejected.

697 The decision in *The Aquila* depends, at least in part, on Lord Stowell's view that the magistrate might have done more than he did, by going down to supervise personally. Moreover, "It is fit that a magistrate should know, that when a ship comes into port in the condition of this vessel, there are interests of the crown which, on behalf of the public, it is his duty to protect. Notice should have been sent also to the officers of the crown."[15] Proper discharge of official and public duties may, therefore, be a prerequisite for claiming salvage for efforts outside those duties.

In one anonymous and unreported case, Lord Stowell allotted £100 to a magistrate in Ireland for sending police officers to protect the cargo of a stranded vessel.[16]

At the time of *The Aquila*, the statutory duties of magistrates with regard to vessels wrecked or in distress were extensive.[17] These duties have since passed to the Receiver of Wreck and the police; so, save in exceptional circumstances, a magistrate would not now be precluded from claiming salvage on account of his official position in the now unlikely event that he carried out a salvage operation.

(c) Lifeboat personnel

698 The Royal National Lifeboat Institution (RNLI), founded in 1824. The RNLI is entirely supported by voluntary contributions. It is a charity[18] incorporated by Royal Charter and governed by its own regulations,[19] binding lifeboatmen in its service. The Institution is the owner of a considerable number of lifeboats stationed at suitable points on the coasts of the United Kingdom and the Republic of Ireland. The paramount purpose of the Institution is the saving of life in cases of shipwreck, and its regulations

---

[14] *ibid.*, 46–49.

[15] *ibid.*, 49.

[16] See *The Purissima Concepcion* (1849) 3 W. Rob. 181, 184, where Dr Lushington thought that Lord Stowell might have gone too far.

[17] See the Acts set out *ante*, in Chap. 2.

[18] *Re Richardson, Shuldham v. Royal National Lifeboat Institution* (1887) 56 L.J. Ch. 784. See also *Thomas v. Howell* (1874) L.R. 18 Eq. 198; *Re David Buckley v. Royal National Lifeboat Institution* (1889) 41 Ch.D. 168, affirmed (1889) 43 Ch.D. 27.

[19] For the relevant regulations, see *post*, App. 35. *cf. The Cayo Bonito* [1904] P. 310, 310n–311n; *The Marlborough* (1943) 76 Ll.L. Rep. 102 (Ct of Sn).

Lifeboat personnel

provide that lifeboats[20] must not be launched solely for property salvage.[21] The RNLI regulations provide that "The Committee of Management, Officials and Honorary Officials of the Institution, as such, will take no part in any claim against the Master, owner or underwriters of any vessel in respect of property salvage."[22] Although in an earlier case, Gorell Barnes J. appeared to think that the Institution ought to consider claiming for a service provided by a large and valuable lifeboat tug,[23] Willmer J. has subsequently declared emphatically that the Institution is unable to claim[24]:

"There is not, and cannot be, any claim in respect of the services (if there were any) rendered to the ship by the lifeboat itself."

In practice, the Institution would not wish to claim, as participation in a profit-induced venture such as salvage is likely to prejudice its charitable status. Lifeboats are not insured save at certain times when they are out of the control of the Institution, *e.g.* whilst at contractors' yards for repairs. With few exceptions, it is not the employer of lifeboat crews.

Members of such crews are volunteers and the individual composition of crews may vary from one day to another, although all lifeboat crews are invariably composed of experienced members. They are not paid wages or salaries but the Institution pays them a service allowance on a regulated scale whenever they go out in the lifeboat, except that, "If a property salvage claim is made by a lifeboat crew, service allowances will not be paid by the Institution for the whole of the service during which an engagement for property salvage was undertaken, even though no payment in respect of the claim may be received from the Master, owners or underwriters of the casualty concerned".[25] In addition, "For the attendance of the lifeboat, at the request[26] of the Master of a casualty, during any more extended salvage operations, whether assistance[27] is given in such operations or not, service allowances will not be payable by the Institution."[28] However, in cases of standing by a casualty, "Provided that (1) No claim for salvage is made on behalf of the lifeboat and: (2) The period of standing by does not exceed 12 hours; service

699

---

[20] The Regulations apply to all classes of lifeboat operated by the Institution: reg. 2.4.4.8.
[21] RNLI reg. 2.4.4.1.
[22] *ibid.*
[23] *The Cayo Bonito* [1904] P. 123, 127–128. There is no general *ultra vires* doctrine inhibiting chartered bodies: *cf. Jenkin v. Pharmaceutical Society of Great Britain* [1921] 1 Ch. 392.
[24] *The Africa Occidental* [1951] 2 Lloyd's Rep. 107, 112.
[25] RNLI reg. 2.4.4.5. As to the significance of the word "engagement", see *infra*, n. 30.
[26] This request may be implied, *e.g.* from behaviour: *The Africa Occidental* [1951] 2 Lloyd's Rep. 107, 114.
[27] In addition to the moral support and comfort afforded by the presence of a lifeboat standing by, services are frequently rendered by coxswains and crews in giving advice, based upon their local knowledge of sands and channels, for bringing stranded vessels into safety in deep water. See *The Africa Occidental* [1951] 2 Lloyd's Rep. 107.
[28] RNLI reg. 2.4.4.7.

allowances will be paid to the crew for the whole period of such a service."[29]

700 Lifeboat crews nowadays play a considerable part in saving life and property in peril, since the development of modern, manoeuvrable, power-driven lifeboats with good equipment and communications. Their usefulness is recognised by the Institution in its regulations. They provide in respect of salvage engagements[30] that:

> "the Coxswain of a lifeboat which has been launched on a lifesaving service, is at liberty, on behalf of his crew, to accept an engagement with the Master of a casualty to salve his vessel and to make use of the lifeboat and her gear for this purpose. Before accepting such an engagement the Coxswain must bear in mind that the primary aim of the Institution is the saving of life at sea; and that this aim may be adversely affected by undue hazard to his lifeboat and the crew by prolonged absence of the boat from her station on salvage operations. No lifeboat may be used for property salvage when tugs or other suitable craft are available and adequate for the task.[31] . . .
>
> When an engagement, as above, has been accepted, the position of the lifeboat crew becomes that of a party of men who have borrowed a boat for the purpose of effecting property salvage and they must, therefore, look to the Master of the casualty and not the Institution for their remuneration for the service. . . . [32]
>
> If the Coxswain of a lifeboat finds, on reaching a casualty, that other vessels are endeavouring to assist the casualty to safety, or to refloat her, if aground, the Coxswain may stand by the casualty in the lifeboat, if, in his opinion, it may be desirable for the crew of the casualty to abandon her, or if requested[33] to do so by the Master of the casualty."[34]

701 The Institution has no control over the question whether a claim shall or shall not be made by its coxswain, helmsmen or crews. They will be entitled to a reward for the performance of services outside their basic task of saving life, although the tribunal is faced with the dilemma of reconciling, on the one hand, the general policy of encouraging by reward the salving of property

---

[29] RNLI reg. 2.4.4.6. *cf. The Africa Occidental, supra,* n. 27, at 114:
"I must, of course, bear in mind that, as lifeboatmen, these men would no doubt have regarded it as their duty in any case to stand by the ship for the purpose of saving life until such time as they were satisfied that no peril any longer existed, and it may be that the standing by is something which the lifeboat would have done in any case."

[30] In *The Marlborough* (1943) 76 Ll.L.Rep. 102, 106, Lord Robertson said:
"There is no express provision in the Regulations for a case where no engagement is made with the master of a casualty because (as in the present case) he has previously left the casualty: but I think it may be inferred that in such a case any reasonable actings of the crew would be regarded and dealt with by the Institution as if an engagement had been made."

[31] RNLI reg. 2.4.4.1.
[32] RNLI reg. 2.4.4.2.
[33] See *supra,* n. 26.
[34] RNLI reg. 2.4.4.6. See also the text to n. 29, *supra.*

Lifeboat personnel

with, on the other, maintaining the particular policy of encouraging what is, despite the allowances payable, the essentially voluntary service of saving lives. This has been referred to as a duty.[35] Of course, there is no conflict with the statutorily authorised policy of saving lives,[36] but the Institution's regulations have expressly provided that:

> "The fact that lives have been rescued, in addition to the salvage of property, must not be taken into account in the formulation of salvage claims."[37]

However, regardless of such a regulation, a life salvage service would no doubt go unrewarded by the court as the provision of a voluntary benefit without intention of remuneration. Pilcher J. declared himself "anxious not unduly to encourage nor yet to discourage claims of this kind".[38] The court's prime concern is to maintain the effectiveness of the lifeboat service and only subject to that to encourage property salvage. Where the casualty could have been salved by other efficient means or where, in order to render the services, the lifeboat has been exposed to the risk of destruction or serious injury, the court has not looked with much favour upon claims arising out of such services:

702

> "Lifeboats should in the first instance be used only for saving life, because a lifeboat might be destroyed or very much injured while saving property, and consequently might not be available when wanted for saving life."[39]

Similarly, Hewson J. has said[40]:

> "I want to make it quite clear that the primary duty of lifeboatmen manning lifeboats owned by the Royal National Lifeboat Institution is the saving of life. It must be clearly understood that in the course of standing by to save life this Court is giving no encouragement to lifeboatmen to get a line on board a disabled vessel at all costs; but, nevertheless, they must be encouraged to stand by and to give such assistance, without unduly risking their craft, where necessary."

More positively, Willmer J. has said[41]:

> "[Counsel for the shipowners] ... went so far as to say that services of this nature ought rather to be discouraged. All I wish to say about that

---

[35] *The Africa Occidental* [1951] 2 Lloyd's Rep. 107, 114; *The Viscount* [1966] 1 Lloyd's Rep. 328, 333.
[36] See *ante*, Chap. 3.
[37] *cf. The Marlborough* (1943) 76 Ll.L.Rep. 102.
[38] *The Guernsey Coast* (1950) 83 Ll.L.Rep. 483, 487.
[39] *The Bushmills, Shipping Gazette,* June 19, 1906, *per* Bucknill L.J.
[40] *The Viscount* [1966] 1 Lloyd's Rep. 328, 333.
[41] *The Africa Occidental* [1951] 2 Lloyd's Rep. 107, 114. See also *The Kirby* (1934) 49 Ll.L.Rep. 50, 52; *The Ocean Hound* (1950) 84 Ll.L.Rep. 5, 7.

submission is that I do not agree with it. It seems to me that if lifeboatmen, at their own risk, go beyond what is strictly required for the performance of their main duty of saving life, what they do can only be regarded as highly meritorious, and ought to be remunerated by an award which will encourage them, and others, in the future."

703 Nonetheless, a strict burden of proof rests on the claimants[42]:

"Lifeboatmen must understand that when they have gone out to save life, as members of a lifeboat crew, the onus is on them to prove that they have afterwards become entitled to salvage reward as against the property alleged to be in peril."

In *The Golden Sands*,[43] Brandon J. treated as evidence of a case of property salvage the fact that, had the lifeboatmen's only purpose been to save the lives on board the casualty, they could have taken the men concerned on board the lifeboat and brought them in without bringing in the yacht itself. In *The Cayo Bonito*,[44] Gorell Barnes J. held that, under the then current regulations:

"those who launch the boats must contemplate that one of two things may happen—that there may only be life salvage, or there may be a change later on into salvage of property, and when they assist in the launching they take their chance of which of those two things may result."

He therefore held the launchers to have a direct claim against the casualty.[45]

704 Although the Institution does not itself claim salvage, its regulations endeavour to safeguard its position in respect of the use of the lifeboat itself. They provide[46]:

---

[42] *The Marguerite Molinos* [1903] P. 160, 164. In *The Maréchal Suchet* [1911] P. 1, a volunteer lifeboat crew who boarded a stranded ship from which the crew had been taken off, jettisoned a small quantity of cargo, laid out a small anchor, and did other slight work until told to desist, were refused salvage.
[43] [1975] 2 Lloyd's Rep. 166.
[44] [1904] P. 310, 318.
[45] *cf. The Enchantress* (1860) Lush. 93, 97:
"Local and customary agreements, if equitable, such as that, where there is a lifeboat company, those who stay shall be rewarded as those who go, the Court will always favourably consider."
In *The Auguste Legembre* [1902] P. 123, since the Regulations prohibited a steam tug lifeboat from going out without an unpowered lifeboat, the latter's crew were treated as analogous to crew members of the tug, therefore, whilst remaining fast astern of a disabled vessel towed into safety by the tug, were entitled to participate in salvage.
[46] RNLI regs. 2.4.4.3., 2.4.4.4. It was stated in Kennedy (4th ed.), p. 95, that "the . . . expenses are payable to the Institution by the crew as a *first charge* against the salvage remuneration" (emphasis added). But it is not clear that this was intended to describe other than a personal claim against the successful lifeboatmen.

"The following expenses will be recoverable from the crew whenever a property salvage claim is made:—
(1) The cost of fuel, lubricants and other consumable stores used on the service;
(2) The cost of repairs to the lifeboat, if any, necessitated by accident or other cause during the service, including transport charges and all expenses involved in the temporary replacement of the damaged lifeboat by a relief boat;
(3) The cost of repairs or replacement of stores or gear, damaged, lost or expended during the service . . .
Except as [so] provided . . . the Institution will have no claim to any part of the sum by which a claim is settled."

Since the Institution does not claim salvage, and has been said to be unable to do so,[47] it stands liable not only to fail to obtain a benefit for salvage effected with one of its lifeboats, but even to suffer a detriment for expenses and losses it incurs, particularly since the assessment of rewards to lifeboatmen tends to be restrained and awards are usually on a modest scale. Nonetheless, the tribunal does not take account of the potential interest of the Institution but merely rewards the lifeboatmen for their personal services,[48] including losses and expenses which they have actually incurred personally.[49] The fact that the lifeboatmen may have decided to pay over a portion of their reward to the Institution is irrelevant.[50] As Brandon J. said in *The Golden Sands*[51]:

"As regards the assessment of the reward, the main point to bear in mind all along is that these are personal services by the crew of the lifeboat and are not services by the owners of the lifeboat, and any award to be made must take account of that fact. It was suggested by [counsel] for the plaintiffs that lifeboatmen come somewhere between the crew of an ordinary ship and the owners, in that they have the responsibilities that I

705

---

[47] See *ante*, text to n. 24.
[48] *The Guernsey Coast* (1950) 83 Ll.L.Rep. 483, 485; *The Africa Occidental* [1951] 2 Lloyd's Rep. 107, 114; *The Geertje K* [1971] 1 Lloyd's Rep. 285; *The Boston Lincoln* [1980] 1 Lloyd's Rep. 481, 483.
[49] *The Ocean Hound* (1950) 84 Ll.L.Rep. 5; *The Africa Occidental* [1951] 2 Lloyd's Rep. 107, 114. The RNLI Regulations do not make lifeboatmen personally responsible for the risk of possible loss or damage to the lifeboat; see *The Marlborough* (1943) 76 Ll.L.Rep. 102, 106.
In *The Ocean Hound* (1950) 84 Ll.L.Rep. 5, 7, Willmer J. treated £36 for petrol, oil, payment to launchers, etc., as moneys numbered, adding it on to an award of £150, making a total of £186; see also *The Corcrest* (1946) 80 Ll.L.Rep. 78. Such expenses are, however, not normally separately itemised: see, in particular, *The Guernsey Coast* (1950) 83 Ll.L.Rep. 483, 487.
[50] See *The Geertje K* [1971] 1 Lloyd's Rep. 285, 287. The plaintiffs stated their intention of paying equal portions of the award to the Institution and all 21 members of the pool of Selsey lifeboatmen whether or not actually engaged in the operation. *cf. The Cayo Bonito* [1904] P. 310, 317, where Gorell Barnes J. made clear that, if he had not recognised that the launchers of the lifeboat had a direct claim for salvage, he would have added a sum to the lifeboatmen's reward to provide the launchers sufficient proper remuneration.
[51] [1975] 2 Lloyd's Rep. 166, 167; see also *ibid.*, 170.

Voluntariness

have mentioned, namely to pay for fuel and to pay for repairs, but it seems to me that it is an overstatement of the case for the plaintiffs. The fact that they have these liabilities must be taken into account, but that does not put them into some intermediate position. They are making a claim for personal services in the same way as the master and crew of any other ship or vessel."

CHAPTER 8

SUCCESS

1. GENERAL PRINCIPLES

It was established by the Admiralty Court that success is necessary for a salvage award in the proper sense of the term.[1] This means that, except in cases of special provision, two requirements must normally be satisfied.[2] First, property in the ship or cargo,[3] or some part of it, must ultimately be preserved.[4] Secondly, the claimant must have provided a useful and effective service (commonly referred to as a meritorious contribution) to that end. However, remuneration could also be earned under the doctrine of engaged services or under a special contract.[5] Exceptionally, discretionary payments may be made by statute for life salvage without salvage of property.[6] And payments may be made for environmental services.[7]

716

The *locus classicus*[8] of the statement of general principles applicable in this area is generally taken to be the speech of Lord Phillimore in *The Melanie (Owners) v. The San Onofre (Owners)*[9]:

717

> "On the general question several authorities have been cited at your Lordships' Bar. All those which were earlier in date than the second edition of Kennedy L.J.'s work on salvage are to be found cited under the head 'Success' in the second chapter of that work. The principles may be summed up in these words: Success is necessary for a salvage reward. Contributions to that success, or as it is sometimes expressed meritorious contributions to that success, give a title to salvage reward. Services, however meritorious, which do not contribute to the ultimate success, do not give a title to salvage reward. Services which rescue a vessel from one danger but end by leaving her in a position of as great or nearly as great danger though of another kind, are held not to contribute to the ultimate success and do not entitle to salvage reward.

---

[1] *Owners of the S.S. Melanie v. Owners of the S.S. San Onofre* [1925] A.C. 246, 262.

[2] *The Lepanto* [1892] P. 122, 128–129.

[3] Although salvage may awarded for the saving of freight, as for the saving of life, such entitlement must ultimately be parasitic on the saving of the cargo—or of the ship and cargo.

[4] See *post*, §§ 717 *et seq*. The property need not necessarily be *salved*.

[5] See *post*, §§ 728, 742–778.

[6] See *ante*, § 292.

[7] See *ante*, Chap. 5.

[8] So called by Willmer J. in *The Alenquer, The René* [1955] 1 W.L.R. 263, 266; [1955] 1 Lloyd's Rep. 101, 109.

[9] [1925] A.C. 262–263.

In considering these questions wherever the service has been meritorious, the Court has leant towards supporting a claim for salvage, as is shown by the cases of *The Jonge Bastiaan*;[10] *The E.U.*[11]; and *The Santipore*[12] among other authorities.

That partial or initial service, if it can be shown to have been a factor of or contributory to ultimate success, is a subject of salvage reward, is shown by a line of cases of which the decision of the Privy Council in *The Atlas*[13] and of Sir James Hannen in *The Camellia*[14] are good examples.

That meritorious action which does not contribute to ultimate success must go without reward is shown by such instances as *The India*;[15] *The Edward Hawkins*[16] (a decision of the Privy Council); *The Killeena*;[17] and my own decision, if I may quote it, in *The Dart*[18] and a recent decision of Hill J. in *The Tarbert*.[19] This case was not, I think, cited by counsel, but has some features of marked resemblance to the case which your Lordships are now discussing.

Such cases as *The Cheerful*,[20] *The Benlarig*,[21] and *The Lepanto*[22] are cases *a fortiori*. In them the Court found that the effect of the services was to put the vessel in a worse position than she was in before.

To the propositions which I have stated, I would add a corollary. The mere fact that the claimant has brought the ship to a position or spot where the ultimate salvor has found her, does not of itself show that the bringing to that spot was a contribution to the ultimate success. This last proposition is supported by the cases of *The India*[23] and *The Killeena*.[24] If it were otherwise, in every case where there was ultimate salvage every person who rendered any service would be a salvor. In cases like *The Camellia*[25] the view taken was that the ship had been brought into or nearer to the track of vessels, and, to use the language of Kennedy L.J.,

---

[10] (1804) 5 C. Rob. 322.
[11] (1853) 1 Spinks E. & A. 63.
[12] (1854) 1 Spinks E. & A. 231.
[13] (1862) Lush. 518.
[14] (1883) 9 P.D. 27.
[15] (1842) 1 W. Rob. 406.
[16] (1862) Lush. 515.
[17] (1881) 6 P.D. 193.
[18] (1899) 8 Asp. M.L.C. 481, 483:
"If a salvor is employed to do anything and does it, and the property is ultimately saved, he may claim a salvage award, though the thing which he does, in the events which happen, produces no good effect. If a salvor is employed to complete a salvage and does not, but, without any misconduct on his part, fails after he has performed a beneficial service, he is entitled also to a salvage award. If a salvor is employed to do a thing and does not do it, and no doubt uses strenuous exertions and makes sacrifices but does no good at all, then it seems to me he is not entitled to salvage."
[19] [1921] P. 372.
[20] (1885) 11 P.D. 3.
[21] (1888) 14 P.D. 3.
[22] [1892] P. 122.
[23] *Supra*.
[24] *Supra*.
[25] *Supra*.

into a position of greater comparative safety. On this ground also Bruce J. decided the case of *The Hestia*."[26]

718 The common law requirement of success has been expressly embodied in the description of Lloyd's Form as Lloyd's Standard Form of Salvage Agreement *"No Cure—No Pay"*.[27]

719 The Brussels Salvage Convention 1910, Art. 2 stated that:

> "Every act of assistance or salvage which has had a useful result gives a right to equitable remuneration.
>
> No remuneration is due if the services rendered have no beneficial result."

Retaining the requirement of a "useful result", the Salvage Convention 1989, Art. 12 provides:

> "1. Salvage operations which have had a useful result give right to an award.
> 2. Except as otherwise provided, no payment is due under this Convention if the salvage operations have had no useful result."

The term "useful result" looks like a conflation of the common law requirements that a salvor's entitlement to a reward was dependent on (a) successful preservation of the property from danger and (b) the claimant's having made a useful contribution to that success.[28] Indeed, it was intended that the Convention should continue the common law position.[29] Moreover, in cases where the tribunal has jurisdiction to make a salvage award, Article 13.1(c) of the Convention utilises the traditional term and lists "the measure of success obtained by the salvor" as one of the criteria to be taken into account in fixing a salvage reward.[30] On one view at least, Article 13.1(c) confirms the continuation of the old law on success. However, the meaning and effect of "measure of success" are not uncontroversial[31] and, inevitably, the change of language from "success" to "useful result" in Article 12 raises the questions whether a change in the law was intended and/or has been effected.

Useful result

720 Under Admiralty law, a salvor was not entitled to a reward unless: property was preserved[32]: and he made a meritorious contribution to its preservation. It was prima facie sufficient that the salvor meritoriously contributed to the preservation of property. The useful result required by the Convention is, as under the prior law, preservation of property. However, the different phrasing of the Conventional requirement may suggest a different attitude. Thus, in the rare case where property is preserved but it is completely valueless, the

---

[26] [1895] P. 193.
[27] Emphasis added.
[28] See *ante*, §716.
[29] See 1984 CMI Report, 20.
[30] See *post*, Chap. 15.
[31] See *post*, §§ 1450–1452.
[32] *The Renpor* (1883) 8 P.D. 115.

salvage operation[33] may be perceived to be successful in principle without achieving a useful result. But the distinction is false and the salvor is no worse off under the Convention, since in either case no reward is recoverable.

Salvage operation without useful result

721   It should be borne in mind that there may be a salvage operation without there also being a useful result. The distinction is inherent in Article 12.1. In most cases it is unimportant, since no reward will be payable. It is, however, important in that *a* payment may become due in respect of a salvage operation even though the operation does not result in an award of salvage.

Payment without useful result

722   Article 12.2's provision that "no payment is due under this Convention if the salvage operations have had no useful result" applies "Except as otherwise provided". This exception has been said to require express provision.[34] In fact, the Convention does not specify that such provision must be express, though of course it will need to be clear that the general requirement of useful result is ousted. Three examples of such contrary provision appear from the Merchant Shipping Act 1995.

723   The first and clearest is the Article 14 provision for special compensation for environmental services.[35] Provided the salvage operation is directed to salving property—which by definition it must be[36]—special compensation may be claimed even if no property is salved.[37] Indeed, the provision for special compensation is specifically designed to provide payment to a salvor involved in an unprofitable salvage operation.

Secondly, the Convention stipulates that nothing in its provision for life salvage shall affect the provisions of national law on the subject[38] and the United Kingdom has exercised its liberty under this stipulation to continue the Secretary of State's discretion to make payments where the vessel and other property are destroyed.[39] However, this power is hardly ever exercised, so is of minimal practical importance.[40]

724   Thirdly, the provisions of the Convention are generally subject to contrary agreement.[41] So far as they are lawful, contracts will be given effect according to their terms, which may therefore lead to the enforcement of an agreement

---

[33] Assuming that valueless property is in danger, so that attempts to preserve it qualify as a salvage operation: see *ante*, §§ 352–353.
[34] See Gaskell, 21–398.
[35] See *ante*, Chap. 5.
[36] See *ante*, §§ 16–18.
[37] It is therefore irrelevant whether preservation of property with no value achieves no useful result.
[38] Art. 16.
[39] MSA 1995, s.224(2), Sched. 11, Pt II, Art. 5.
[40] See *ante*, Chap. 3.
[41] Art. 6.1. But note Art. 6.3.

to make a payment regardless of its achieving a useful result in the sense in which that term is used in the Convention.[42] It is therefore possible to enforce contracts for "engaged services"[43] or under which the SCOPIC clause has been invoked.[44] This is so whether or not such contracts are governed by the Salvage Convention 1989.[45] However, Article 12.2 provides that, "Except as otherwise provided, no payment is due *under this* Convention if the salvage operations have had no useful result".[46] Thus, a contract providing for payment regardless of a Conventionally useful result will not *per se* attract provisions of the Convention which would otherwise not apply under Admiralty law, in particular those on environmental services. Such provisions may be expressly incorporated into the contract but, if so, they will be given effect as contract terms and any payment made will still not be due "under this Convention".

Preservation of property

The general rule, affirmed by the Court of Appeal in *The Renpor*,[47] is that **725** in order to maintain a claim for a salvage award, whether by proceedings *in rem* or *in personam*, the property imperilled, or at least some part of it, must have been preserved from the danger to which it was subject. It is not, however, necessary that it be finally preserved as the result of salvage operations; it is sufficient if the vessel eventually manages to save itself by its own exertions or if the danger simply passes.[48] The effect of the general rule is commonly said to be that some part at least of either ship, cargo or freight must have been preserved.[49] In practice, this must generally mean that some tangible property must have been preserved. In particular, since the general rule is that freight is earned on carriage and safe delivery of cargo to its destination,[50] preservation of freight in such a case is dependent on preservation of the cargo upon which it is earned. However, "freight" may be preserved without the preservation of property which by itself could found a claim for salvage, as where shipwrecked passengers are conveyed to their destination under an agreement between the shipowners and the salvors, the shipowners' right to passage-money being preserved in consequence.[51]

---

[42] If the service required by the contract is the exercise of best endeavours rather than the achievement of a particular result as a consequence of the exercise of those endeavours, there may of course be a "useful result" within the terms of the contract without there having to be one within the terms of the Convention.

[43] See *post*, §§ 742–778.

[44] See *post*, §§ 960–980.

[45] The extent to which contracts for engaged services are governed by the Convention is discussed separately *post*, §§ 754–755.

[46] Emphasis added.

[47] (1883) 8 P.D. 115, 117. See also *The Cargo ex Sarpedon* (1877) 3 P.D. 28, 34.

[48] See *The Nellie* (1873) 2 Asp. M.L.C. 142.

[49] See *The Renpor* (1883) 8 P.D. 115, 117.

[50] See *ante*, Chap. 3. In modern times, most freight (other than on bulk oil cargoes) is prepaid. The freight is thus included in the cargo's C. & F. value.

[51] *The Medina* (1876) 2 P.D. 5 must be explained on this ground.

726 It is not the case that salvage is earned merely because human lives alone have been saved. By statute, discretionary payments may be, though scarcely ever are, made for the saving of human life.[52] But a salvor is only entitled legally to enforce a claim for life salvage if property has also been preserved.[53] If it has been saved, it does not prejudice his claim that he only succeeded in the life salvage, provided that he made some contribution to the preservation of the property.[54]

The reasons for the rule requiring preservation of property are the fact that the Admiralty Court's jurisdiction was founded on a proceeding against property and that it was the property which was preserved that provided the fund out of which salvage remuneration was payable and which dictated the extreme limits of liability.[55] Consequently, the liability of the owner of any property imperilled is limited to the portion of his property which is preserved; and, if none of his property is preserved, he cannot be made to contribute to the liability of a defendant whose property is saved.[56]

Requested services

727 It was laid down in *The Undaunted*[57] that services which have been rendered at request may provide entitlement to remuneration even though they have not contributed to success. Although the judgment of Dr Lushington in that case is consistent with the view that eventual preservation of property is not essential to sanction such remuneration, Brett M.R. declared in *The Renpor*,[58] although expressly refraining from expressing an opinion as to the correctness of *The Undaunted*, that such preservation is as much a prerequisite of remuneration for such requested services as for purely voluntary services. The other cases on requested services conform with this view, although in none of them has it ever had to have been clearly decided. The Court of Appeal in *The Renpor*[59] also disapproved an anonymous case referred to (with some unease) by Dr Lushington in *The E.U.*,[60] in which, assuming the report

---

[52] See *ante*, § 292.
[53] *The Zephyrus* (1842) 1 W. Rob. 329; *The Cargo ex Sarpedon* (1877) 3 P.D. 28; *The Renpor* (1883) 8 P.D. 115. See also *The Fusilier* (1865) 3 Moo. (P.C.) (N.S.) 51; *The Medina* (1876) 2 P.D. 5; *The Cargo ex Schiller* (1877) 2 P.D. 145; *The Tarbert* [1921] P. 372. The apparently contradictory decision in *The Queen Mab* (1835) 3 Hagg. 242 can be explained on the ground that, as the owner of the salved vessel in that case did not defend the claim, the vessel being a derelict; the case is not a binding authority: see *The Zephyrus*, at 333, *per* Dr Lushington. Apparently contrary *dicta* of Dr Lushington himself in *The E.U.* (1853) 1 Spinks E. & A. 63, 64–65 and *The Undaunted* (1860) Lush. 90 were reconciled with the general rule by the Court of Appeal in *The Renpor, supra*, 117; see *post*, § 727.
[54] *The Zephyrus* (1842) 1 W.Rob. 329, 333.
[55] *ibid.*, 331; *The Cargo ex Schiller* (1877) 2 P.D. 145; *The Renpor* (1883) 8 P.D. 115, 117.
[56] *The Cargo ex Sarpedon* (1877) 3 P.D. 28.
[57] (1860) Lush. 90.
[58] (1883) 8 P.D. 115, 117.
[59] *ibid.*, 117.
[60] (1853) 1 Spinks E. & A. 63, 64–65.

is correct, he had decided that completed services rendered by request had to be paid for whether or not the vessel was lost.[61]

Special contracts

There may be circumstances in which the master of a ship in danger or distress is justified in binding the shipowners by a special agreement to pay for certain assistance independently of the ultimate safety of the vessel. In several such cases, where it has been agreed that remuneration shall be paid other than on a salvage basis, the court has enforced the right to remuneration for performance of the agreed services. In *The Alfred*,[62] the master, who believed there was a chance of saving his disabled ship, which a tug wished to abandon, induced the tug to remain for "as long as possible" by agreeing to pay remuneration for towage done and to be done.[63] Butt J. held the agreement to pay a few hundred pounds in the hope of saving thousands (which was less than salvage would have been) to be reasonable and enforced it despite the eventual loss of the vessel.[64] The agreed sum is payable if the terms of the agreement are fulfilled, even though there is not such success as would normally justify a salvage reward. But the agreement is nonetheless to be regarded as a salvage agreement and therefore subject to the rules normally applicable to such agreements, such as that they will not be enforced if manifestly unfair or unjust.[65]

728

The master's authority

According to the Court of Appeal in *The Renpor*,[66]

729

> "there are two circumstances necessary in order to make an agreement binding on an owner; first, the contract must be made under a necessity; and secondly, it must be made for his benefit."

Brett M.R., with whose judgment Cotton and Bowen L.JJ. concurred, continued:

---

[61] The Court of Appeal held the case to be inconsistent with *The Fusilier* (1865) 3 Moo. (P.C.) (N.S.) 51; *The Zephyr* (1827) 2 Hagg. 43; and *The Cargo ex Schiller* (1877) 2 P.D. 145. The report is too brief to indicate whether Dr Lushington's case could have been justified on the basis of a special contract: see *post*, §728.

[62] (1884) 5 Asp. 214.

[63] *cf. The Kilmaho* (1900) 16 T.L.R. 155, 156, where the Court of Appeal held that the master had no authority to pledge his owner's credit for past services. But there is no inconsistency with the general rule that past consideration will not support a binding contract if the price of obtaining the required future services is partly calculated on the basis of what has been done already, particularly if payment for the previous services was not dependent on the benefits hoped to be derived from them. See further Treitel, pp. 73–76.

[64] See also *The Strathgarry* [1895] P. 264 (remuneration due for towage performed and broken off before salvage by a third party); and *The Prinz Heinrich* (1888) 13 P.D. 31 (agreement upheld for payment of £200 per day for attendance on vessel plus an additional sum of £2.000 should salvage prove successful—which it did).

[65] *The William Lushington* (1850) 7 N.o.C. 261, 362.

[66] (1883) 8 P.D. 115, 118.

"I must express a doubt whether if an agreement is made only for the purpose of saving a master and crew without regard to any safety of the property of the shipowner, though it be in a case of necessity, yet as the subject-matter is without benefit to the property of the shipowner, the master has authority to bind the owner to a money payment."[67]

730 Three comments may be made. First, if, as in *The Alfred*,[68] the master contracts to obtain the possibility of preserving the ship, Brett M.R.'s doubt is resolved. Secondly, since the shipowners, through the master, are liable to fulfil a duty to take all reasonable steps to safeguard the lives of persons on board their vessel, the master who contracts to secure performance of that duty should be recognised as acting for the benefit of his owners.[69] Finally, the nature of the agreement (whether it is to save life or property or both, or merely to make attempts to effect the purpose) will be a question of construction of the agreement. So will the event upon which remuneration is to be payable. If the agreement is in fact a salvage agreement, preservation of the property of the principals on whose behalf the agreement is made will be a vital prerequisite of remuneration.

Salvage agreements

731 A salvage agreement has been defined as an agreement which fixes[70] the amount to be paid for salvage but leaves untouched all the other conditions necessary to support a salvage award, one of which is the preservation of some part at least of the *res*: that is, ship, cargo, or freight.[71] This definition is certainly incomplete for modern purposes and must now be modified in the light of Lloyd's Form and *The Unique Mariner (No. 2)*.[72] However, if an agreement is truly a salvage agreement, by definition, salvage must be effected before salvage remuneration can be claimed. An agreement may provide for remuneration on alternative bases without losing its character as a salvage agreement. It may provide for salvage remuneration in the event of the services' proving successful or beneficial, and for payment of expenses, loss or damage incurred if the services are not successful or beneficial. Such an agreement does not prevent the agreement as a whole from being regarded as a salvage agreement.

Loss or damage after preservation

732 The existence of a successful salvor's entitlement to salvage reward and the amount of remuneration properly due to him for services which he has

---

[67] *ibid.*, 118.
[68] *Supra*.
[69] See *post*, Chaps. 8–9.
[70] In the fourth edition of Kennedy, p. 100, "fixes" appeared as "may fix".
[71] Kennedy (1st ed.), p. 42; quoted in *The Hestia* [1895] P. 193, 199, and presumably derived from *The Renpor* (1883) 8 P.D. 115, 118. See *post*, Chap. 9.
[72] [1979] 1 Lloyd's Rep. 37, discussed *post*, §§767–778.

rendered will not be affected by any loss or damage to the property occurring subsequently to its preservation.[73]

Meritorious contributions to success

When salvage is finally effected, those who have meritoriously contributed to that result are entitled to a share in the reward, although the part they took, standing by itself, would not have produced it.[74] The initial requirements of this entitlement are that some services have been rendered, that the vessel has been salved[75] and that the services have played some part in the salvage. This will commonly be so where the vessel is brought into a position of greater comparative safety than that in which it was found,[76] although any service will suffice if it minimises an increase in the danger or in some other way facilitates eventual salvage.[77] Salvage claimants may be successful whether their attempts at salvage were interrupted because of act of God,[78] with the consent of the master of the vessel in danger,[79] in order to carry out pre-existing duties (such as to the owners of livestock at risk on board the salving vessel)[80] or for any other reason not attributable to the fault of the salvor.[81] No reward will be forthcoming to a claimant who voluntarily relinquishes attempts at salvage and who, while able to continue attempts, abandons the vessel without intending to resume operations[82] or without taking whatever steps are reasonable to procure eventual salvage, such as signalling the position of the vessel in danger.[83] To award salvage in such circumstances would expose defendants to the possibility of numerous claims for services from which they have derived no benefit as well as weakening the policy of encouraging salvage attempts in circumstances where the opportunity of earning salvage might be the only inducement to attempt salvage. If an unsuccessful salvage attempt which has not contributed to the safety of the vessel is abandoned, it makes no difference to the claimant's case that the vessel is not saved because of further salvage services provided by a third party but merely through the vessel's own efforts or because the danger passes.[84] But, if a salvor has provided assistance and broken off attempts,

733

---

[73] *The Bomarsund* (1860) Lush. 77 (vessel subsequently damaged due to pilot's negligence). *cf. The Norma* (1860) Lush. 124.

[74] *The Atlas* (1862) Lush. 518, 527; followed in *The August Korff* [1903] P. 166, 175. See, in addition to the other cases cited in this section, *The Lepanto* [1892] P. 122, 129; *Owners of the S.S. Melanie v. Owners of the S.S. San Onofre* [1952] A.C. 246, 262–263.

[75] *The Genessee* (1848) 12 Jur. 401, 402.

[76] See *The Camellia* (1884) 9 P.D. 27.

[77] See *The Jonge Bastiaan* (1804) 5 C. Rob. 322 (approved in *The Atlas* (1862) Lush. 518, 527–528); *The August Korff* [1903] P. 166, 175–176.

[78] *The Aztecs* (1870) 21 L.T. 797, 798.

[79] See ibid.

[80] *The E.U.* (1853) 1 Spinks E. & A. 63; *The Camellia* (1884) 9 P.D. 27.

[81] *The Nellie* (1873) 2 Asp. 142; *The August Korff* [1903] P. 166, 174–175.

[82] *The Edward Hawkins* (1862) 15 Moo. (P.C.) 486, distinguished in *The Aztecs* (1870) 21 L.T. 797; *The Killeena* (1881) 6 P.D. 193.

[83] See *The Hestia* [1895] P. 193.

[84] *The Edward Hawkins* (1862) 15 Moo. (P.C.) 486. *cf. The Genessee* (1848) 12 Jur. 401 (claim of the *Fame*).

Success

without intending not to resume his efforts, the mere fact that he does not intervene while he perceives a third party rendering further services which the third party can perform without his assistance will not deprive him of a salvage award.[85]

Doubt as to value of service: court favours salvors

734 Several cases shew that, if it is proved that the services of the alleged salvors have been meritorious in character but there is a doubt as to whether they have in fact contributed to the ultimate safety of the vessel in danger, the court, looking to the general maritime and commercial interest in inducing men to assist life and property in danger at sea, has leant towards the view that in fact they have so contributed and so towards supporting a claim for salvage.[86] Thus, in *The E.U.*,[87] lifeboatmen boarded a vessel in distress and got her head to the north but, with her own crew, were then forced to leave her, whereafter she was subsequently salved by a steamer. Dr Lushington admitted that putting the vessel to the north might have been greatly, or not in the slightest degree, beneficial to saving the vessel. But, looking at the case as a whole, particularly to the courage of the lifeboatmen and the general maritime interest, salvage was awarded. The court will not, however, go out of its way to adopt such a benevolent attitude if there is no genuine doubt as to whether the services performed have in fact contributed to successful salvage.

Where there is an agreement to render services to a vessel in distress, the court will similarly be willing to uphold entitlement to a *quantum meruit* on the contract, though not as salvage, so as not to discourage the provision of such necessary services.[88]

Services not contributing to success

735 The general rule is that a mere attempt to save the vessel and cargo, however meritorious or well-intentioned that attempt may be or whatever degree of risk of danger may have been incurred, cannot be considered as furnishing any title to salvage reward if it does not contribute to the ultimate, successful salvage of the property imperilled.[89] The reason is that salvage is a reward for benefits actually conferred, not for a service attempted to be rendered.[90] The jurisdiction and authority of the court is founded on a service

---

[85] *The Jonge Bastiaan* (1804) 5 C.Rob. 322.

[86] See *Owners of the S.S. Melanie v. Owners of the S.S. San Onofre* [1925] A.C. 246, 262; *The E.U.* (1853) 1 Spinks E. & A. 63, 66.

[87] *Supra*. See also *The Jonge Bastiaan* (1804) 5 C.Rob. 322; *The Genessee* (1848) 12 Jur. 401; *The Santipore* (1854) 1 Spinks E. & A. 231.

[88] *The Benlarig* (1888) 14 P.D. 3, 6; followed in *The August Korff* [1903] P. 166, 174.

[89] *The Zephyrus* (1842) 1 W. Rob. 329, 330; *The India* (1842) 1 W.Rob. 406, 408; *The Lockwoods* (1845) 9 Jur. 1017, 1018; *The E.U.* (1853) 1 Spinks E. & A. 63, 65; *The Camellia* (1884) 9 P.D. 27, 29; *The City of Chester* (1884) 9 P.D. 182, 201; *The Dart* (1899) 8 Asp. 481, 482, 483; *Owners of the S.S. Melanie v. Owners of the S.S. San Onofre* [1925] A.C. 246, 262.

[90] *The Zephyrus*, supra, n. 89, at 330–331; *The Chetah* (1868) L.R. 2 P.C. 205, 212; *The City of Chester*, supra, n. 89, at 202; *The Cargo ex Port Victor* [1901] P. 243, 247; *The Tarbert* [1921] P. 372, 376.

actually provided[91] and a proceeding against property which has been saved.[92] Thus, in *The Tarbert*,[93] no salvage was awarded where it could not be demonstrated that cargo, which was taken from a vessel which had struck a bank during towing and had become a constructive total loss, was worth more than if the vessel had been allowed to sink in deep water and the cargo taken from it there. It makes no difference to the would-be salvor that he took off the crew from a vessel which is saved by another salvor.[94] Moreover, it is immaterial that the vessel was lost after the unsuccessful salvage attempts[95] or that it was ultimately saved,[96] even if only by its own exertions,[97] or that the danger simply passed.[98] Furthermore, it will not enhance the claimant's case that he justifiably abandoned attempts at salvage[99] or that, after having abandoned the vessel, he later returned to resume his attempts, unless perhaps there was only a temporary suspension of services with the master's concurrence.[1]

Incompleted service leaving vessel in greater danger

Services which rescue a vessel from one danger but end by leaving her in a position of as great or nearly as great danger, though of another kind, are held not to contribute to ultimate success and do not justify a salvage award.[2] If, when the services of the claimants of salvage terminate, the vessel which they have sought to assist is in a position as dangerous or nearly as dangerous as that from which they rescued her, they are not entitled to any salvage reward, however meritorious may have been their exertions and although the vessel is ultimately preserved, without loss or injury, from the position in which the claimants were obliged to leave her. It makes no difference to the plaintiff's claim that he was perfectly entitled to cease rendering services, whether from inability to continue them successfully or from having to save himself from danger[3]; that he made all possible efforts to salve the vessel and suffered loss or damage in the process[4]; or that it was he who arranged for the ultimate salvor to go out and salve the vessel.[5]

736

---

[91] *The Ranger* (1845) 3 Not. of Cas. 589, 590.
[92] See *The Zephyrus* (1842) 1 W.Rob. 329, 331; *The City of Chester* (1884) 9 P.D. 182, 201–202. *cf. the* dictum of Dr Lushington in *The E.U.* (1853) 1 Spinks E. & A. 63, 65, discussed *ante*, §734. See also *The Queen Mab* (1835) 3 Hagg. 242, explained in *The Zephyrus*, *supra*, at 333.
[93] [1921] P. 372.
[94] *The India* (1842) 1 W.Rob. 406.
[95] *The Zephyrus*, *supra*.
[96] *The India, supra; The Killeena* (1881) 6 P.D. 193; *The Dart* (1899) 8 Asp. 481.
[97] *The Edward Hawkins* (1862) 15 Moo. (P.C.) 486.
[98] See *The Ranger* (1845) 3 Not. of Cas. 589.
[99] See *The E.U., supra*, n. 92, at 66.
[1] *The India, supra*.
[2] *Owners of S.S. Melanie v. Owners of S.S. San Onofre* [1925] A.C. 246, 262, *per* Lord Phillimore.
[3] See *The Cheerful* (1885) 11 P.D. 3.
[4] *cf. The Benlarig* (1888) 14 P.D. 3. See *post*, §737.
[5] See *The Benlarig, supra*.

Success

737 The rule against salvage awards where a vessel is left in a position of danger was established by Butt J. in *The Cheerful*,[6] on the basis of Dr Lushington's dictum in *The India*[7] that salvors are not entitled to reward unless they confer actual benefit on the salved property. Butt J. followed his judgment three years later in *The Benlarig*.[8] The master of the steamship *Vesta* agreed to do his best to tow the *Benlarig*, which had broken down 12 miles from Cape St Vincent, to Gibraltar. After towing her about 130 miles in that direction, one of the hawsers broke and and fouled the *Vesta's* propeller and the other had to be cut. As the vessel was disabled and considerably damaged, and as a heavy gale was continuing, the master of the *Vesta* decided that his best course was to proceed to Gibraltar and to give information as to the position and state of the *Benlarig*. This he did. Another vessel then went out and brought her in, earning substantial salvage remuneration. But, as the *Vesta* had left the *Benlarig* in a more dangerous position than when she had found her, she received no salvage.[9]

738 It is submitted that in these two decisions, and especially in the latter, the general principle of "no success, no salvage" was applied somewhat strictly against the claimants. In each case, not only had the services been undertaken at the request of the vessel in distress and had been continued as long as it was practically possible to continue them, but they had been actually beneficial, in so far as they had brought the vessel into a position which, though temporarily one of greater danger than she was in at the moment of their inception, yet was actually nearer (in the case of the *Benlarig*, very much nearer) to the place of safety into which she was ultimately taken, and also to the means of obtaining the assistance which took her there. What would have happened if the *Cheerful* or the *Benlarig* had not been taken in tow must be a matter of mere speculation.

739 The view of these cases given by Lord Phillimore, in *Owners of S.S. Melanie v. Owners of S.S. San Onofre*,[10] is that they[11] are merely *a fortiori* examples of the general rule that meritorious action which does not contribute to ultimate success must go without reward[12]; and the mere fact that the claimant has brought the ship to a spot where the ultimate salvor has found her does not of itself shew that the bringing to that spot was a contribution to the ultimate success, otherwise in every case where there was ultimate salvage, every person who rendered any assistance would be a salvor. On this view, the impact of the decisions can be ameliorated by a more generous interpretation

---

[6] (1885) 11 P.D. 3.

[7] (1842) 1 W.Rob. 406, 408. The quotation in Butt J.'s judgment at (1885) 11 P.D. 3, 5, is in fact a paraphrase of Dr Lushington's dictum in *The India*.

[8] (1888) 14 P.D. 3. See also *The Kilmaho* (1900) 16 T.L.R. 155; *Owners of S.S. Melanie v. Owners of S.S. San Onofre* [1925] A.C. 246.

[9] She did receive a smaller sum under the towage engagement.

[10] [1925] A.C. 247, 263.

[11] He referred specifically to *The Cheerful, supra; The Benlarig, supra;* and *The Lepanto, supra.* See also *The Lockwoods* (1845) 9 Jur. 1017.

[12] *Ante,* §717.

Engaged services

of the circumstances, so as to establish that a benefit has in fact been conferred, particularly where the claimant bringing the vessel nearer to the ultimate place of safety is the one who communicates to the ultimate salvor the information which prompts him to go out and enables him to earn salvage.

Such a solution would not, however, be possible on an alternative interpretation of the cases, suggested by the language used in the judgments. This is that the court will decline to hold that any benefit has actually been conferred where, no matter what salvage efforts have been undertaken and no matter how much the task of the ultimate salvor has been facilitated, the vessel is left in a position of danger which is greater than that existing at the inception of the services.[13] Judicial recognition of such a strict rule would be unfortunate where the position of greater danger arises merely incidentally to salvage attempts, particularly as it is likely to have the undesirable effect of discouraging would-be salvors.[14]

740

Effect of other remedies

LOF 2000, cl. D provides:

741

"Subject to the provisions of the International Convention on Salvage 1989 as incorporated into English law ('the Convention') relating to special compensation and to the Scopic Clause if incorporated the Contractor's services shall be rendered and accepted as salvage services upon the principle of 'no cure—no pay' and any salvage remuneration to which the Contractors become entitled shall not be diminished by reason of the exception to the principle of 'no cure-no pay' in the form of special compensation or remuneration payable to the Contractors under a Scopic Clause."

2. ENGAGED SERVICES

There exists at common law a doctrine of engaged services, whereby a person who has not contributed to salvage but who has rendered requested services to property which is ultimately saved may be rewarded on a basis similar to a salvage award. The common law of engaged services will be

742

---

[13] See *The Lepanto* [1892] P. 122, 129, *per* Jeune J.: "In these circumstances, it is impossible to say that the [plaintiff] benefited her as a question of salvage service."
[14] A consideration which comforted Butt J. in *The Benlarig, supra*, in being able to award £400 by way of *quantum meruit* for performance of engaged services. (The actual salvor received £3.500.)

discussed next. Then the impact of the Salvage Convention 1989 on the doctrine and its place, if any, in modern law and practice will be considered.

743 Judicial approval has been given to Kennedy's statement of the doctrine[15] of engaged services, which is as follows.[16] There is one distinct and exceptional class of cases in which the Court of Admiralty awards salvage remuneration for services to property in danger although in fact they have not contributed to its ultimate preservation. If the master of a ship in distress requests the performance of a service of a salvage nature—requests, for example, a steamer to stand by her in a storm, or to fetch an anchor from the shore—and that service is rendered, but the ship for which the service is requested is eventually saved through some other cause, such as a fortunate change of weather; or, secondly, if after the service has begun and whilst they are willing and able to complete it, those who have undertaken it are discharged by the master of the vessel in danger, who prefers, perchance, some other help which offers itself: the court will not suffer the act of assistance, although unproductive of benefit, to go unrewarded, if it has involved an expenditure of time, labour, or risk; and further, in the second case, may include in its award some compensation for the loss which the claimants of salvage have sustained in being prevented from completing the service which they had agreed to render.[17]

744 The leading judicial statement of these principles is that of Dr Lushington in *The Undaunted*[18]:

"There is a broad distinction between salvors who volunteer to go out and salvors who are employed by a ship in distress. Salvors who volunteer, go out at their own risk for the chance of earning reward, and if they labour unsuccessfully, they are entitled to nothing: the effectual performance of salvage service is that which gives them a title to salvage remuneration. But if men are engaged by a ship in distress, whether generally or particularly, they are to be paid according to their efforts made, even though the labour and service may not prove beneficial to the vessel ... The engagement to render assistance to a vessel in distress, and the performance of that engagement, so far as necessary or so far as possible, establish a title to salvage reward."[19]

---

[15] So called by Phillimore J. in *The Dart* (1899) 8 Asp. 481, 482.

[16] The following two sentences were adopted by Lord Merriman P. as part of his judgment in *The Hassel* [1959] 2 Lloyd's Rep. 82, 85.

[17] This sentence was approved by Gorrell Barnes J. in *The Helvetia* (1894) 8 Asp. 264n, 265n and by Willmer J. in *The Loch Tulla* (1950) 84 Ll.L. Rep. 62; and quoted by Lord Merriman P., in *The Hassel* [1959] 2 Lloyd's Rep. 82, 85. The compensation of superseded salvors is considered *post*, §§ 756–778.

[18] (1860) Lush. 90, 92; referred to in *The Nellie* (1873) 2 Asp. 142, 143; *The Killeena* (1881) 6 P.D. 193, 197–198. See also *The Dart* (1899) 8 Asp. 481, 483, *per* Phillimore J. (*ante*, §724).

[19] Quoted in *The Aztecs* (1870) 3 Asp. 326, 327; *The Nellie* (1873) 2 Asp. M.L.C. 142, 143; *The Helvetia* (1894) 8 Asp. 264n, 265n; *The Cambrian* (1897) 8 Asp. 263, 265; *The Stiklestad* [1926] P. 205, 209 (affirmed (1926) 43 T.L.R. 118).

Engaged services

The vessel must ultimately have been saved.[20] But *ex hypothesi* no benefit **745** need be conferred on the vessel by the claimant.[21] Entitlement to remuneration for such engaged services depends, therefore, on the making of a request for the services, a determination of the nature of the services requested, a finding that the claimant has performed his engagement so far as he was able to do so and the ultimate saving of the vessel. The cases in this area suggest that these four features can be identified with relative ease.

In *The Undaunted*,[22] according to Dr Lushington, a "steamer was engaged **746** to go on shore and bring off an anchor and cable to [the] ship, which ... was ... in very great danger. The engagement, as usual in such cases, was not more specific than was necessary. The true effect of it was, 'You are to go and get me an anchor and cable, and do all that is necessary for this purpose'." Remuneration was awarded to luggers employed by the steamship for this purpose which did all in their power to reach the vessel but "were only disappointed of effecting their service by the act of God".[23] Similarly, in *The Melpomene*,[24] which can be explained as coming within this group of cases,[25] Sir Robert Phillimore said "that where a vessel makes a signal of distress and another goes out with the bona fide intention of assisting that distress, and, as far as she can, does so, and some accident occurs which prevents her services being as effectual as she intended them to be, and no blame attaches to her, she ought not to go wholly unrewarded."[26] Slight remuneration was therefore given to a tug which had passed a hawser to a vessel in distress, which vessel was assisted to safety by other tugs after the hawser had come away, it not having been made fast.

In a typical situation, a vessel in distress will request assistance, services **747** will be tendered in response to that request and those services will be accepted by the vessel in danger. It would not be difficult, therefore, to infer in a majority of cases that services are classifiable as engaged services meriting remuneration accordingly. This is particularly so if the nature of the engagement can usually be described in the general terms indicated in *The Undaunted*.[27] However, it has been declared that it does not follow at all that when a ship sends out an SOS message every other ship on the sea is thereby entitled to go to that ship and ask for a salvage award. The services have to

---

[20] *The Renpor* (1883) 8 P.D. 115, 117.
[21] *The Helvetia* (1894) 8 Asp. 264n; *The Cambrian* (1897) 8 Asp. 263; *The Maréchal Suchet* [1910] P. 1, 15.
[22] (1860) Lush. 90, 92.
[23] *ibid.*, 93.
[24] (1873) L.R. 4 A. & E. 129.
[25] Kennedy (4th ed.), p. 15. *cf. infra*, n. 43. The facts might appear to suggest that the tug's position was at least similar to that of a superseded salvor: see *post*, §§756–778. Phillimore J. (who decided both cases) distinguished *The Melpomene* in *The Dart* (1899) 8 Asp. M.L.C. 481, 483, on the ground that in *The Melpomene* the fault of those on board the salved vessel alone prevented the salvor from fulfilling his engagement.
[26] (1873) L.R. 4 A. & E. 129.
[27] *Supra*.

be rendered in response to a definite request[28] and it is necessary to make sure that the plaintiff has entered upon the service, for otherwise the first condition of this type of remuneration does not arise.[29]

748 Whether or not remuneration is earned consequent upon such a definite request depends primarily upon the proper construction of the content of the service requested. In *The Tarbert*,[30] no remuneration was earned by a tug engaged to tow inshore a damaged vessel which, by misfortune, struck a bank before the towage was completed. And in *The Dart*,[31] none was earned by a ship which, during an engagement to tow to a port of safety, lost sight of the tow during the night, after the hawser had broken, and sailed on her way the next day. As Bruce J. put it in *The Hestia*[32]:

> "where there is a contract to perform a specified service for a specified remuneration, nothing becomes due under the contract until the specified service has been completely performed. Although the service may have been partly performed yet, as the contract is not divisible, no obligation arises out of it to pay any part of the stipulated remuneration, and the existence of an express contract negatives the presumption which might otherwise arise of an implied contract to pay for the work done according to its value."

749 Where the actual obligation imposed by the engagement is of a lesser kind, or more open-textured, as in *The Undaunted*,[33] it can more easily be accomplished. Thus, in *The Maude*,[34] remuneration was earned by a tug which, doubting that the vessel in distress could be towed to Hull, was engaged *to try* to tow it there.[35] The hawser parted during towing and, though the claimant was ready and willing to continue performance, the vessel engaged another vessel for a fixed sum to complete the towage to Hull, a sum which was not earned because towage to Hull in fact turned out to be not possible. It will depend on the facts of a particular case[36] whether there is, for example, a contract to salvage or a contract to tow to a particular place[37] (in which situations remuneration will, by definition, not be earned until successful completion of the engagement); or a contract to attempt such a service (under which, again by definition, remuneration will be due for whatever attempts are

---

[28] *The Stiklestad* [1926] P. 205, 210; (1926) 43 T.L.R. 118.
[29] *The Hassel* [1959] 2 Lloyd's Rep. 82, 85.
[30] [1921] P. 372.
[31] (1899) 8 Asp. 481.
[32] [1895] P. 193, 199.
[33] *Supra.*
[34] (1876) 3 Asp. 338.
[35] *cf. The Loch Tulla* (1950) 84 Ll.L.Rep. 62, where the plaintiff's undertaking was said to be to have a pull rather than actually to refloat the grounded vessel. A sufficiently open-textured engagement, *e.g.* to have a pull until either party decides to terminate the engagement, would mean that the tug would earn remuneration on a *quantum meruit* for what it has done until dismissal and that, on dismissal, it would not be able to claim compensation for loss of the opportunity to complete the salvage. See also *The Nellie* (1873) 2 Asp. 142.
[36] See *The Benlarig* (1888) 14 P.D. 3.
[37] Which can fairly readily be interpreted as salvage anyway: see *ante*, §603.

reasonably made until the time when, whilst remaining ready and willing to continue performance, the salvor is excused from further performance).

If an indivisible obligation (such as to tow to a place of safety) is not completed, then no remuneration is payable for the efforts made to fulfil that obligation either (whether the efforts are voluntarily abandoned) under the rules rewarding meritorious contributions to success[38] or (as a matter of construction) under the doctrine of engaged services.[39] Where an unsuccessful, indivisible engagement is replaced by an engagement to endeavour to effect a service, remuneration for the latter service will not be calculated so as to include any sum for the unsuccessful former engagement[40]; nor will the salvor be entitled to claim such a sum if the latter agreement stipulates for it, since the master has no authority to pledge his owners' credit for past services for which they were not liable.[41]

750

In all of the cases in which a reward has been given for engaged services, the salvor has either satisfied the requirement made of him or has been justifiably excused or prevented from further performance, such as by act of God,[42] or by being wrongfully discharged by the master of the vessel in distress.[43] The claimant has failed in cases where he has either simply failed to perform an indivisible engaged service, as in *The Tarbert*,[44] or has by his own conduct deprived himself of entitlement to an award, such as by his negligence[45] or by voluntarily abandoning performance.

751

Since remuneration has been given in cases where the claimant has provided the so-called "engaged" or "employed" service required of him,[46] it would be reasonable to infer that the remuneration is to be assessed on the basis of a contractual *quantum meruit* for work and labour done. But in fact remuneration is assessed on a similar basis to the quantification of an award for a successfully completed, engaged salvage service.[47] Remuneration is given by way of salvage reward[48] and the amount is governed by the factors

752

---

[38] *The Edward Hawkins* (1862) 15 Moo. (P.C.) 515.
[39] *The Dart* (1899) 8 Asp. 481.
[40] *The Lepanto* [1892] P. 122, 130.
[41] *The Kilmaho* (1900) 16 T.L.R. 155, 156. This is consistent with general rules of the law of contract to the effect that past consideration is not normally good consideration: see Chitty, Chap. 3(5); Treitel, pp. 73–76. But LOF 2000, cl. E (and its predecessors) provides for retrospective incorporation of services prior to signature.
[42] See, *e.g. The Undaunted* (1860) Lush. 90.
[43] See, *e.g. The Maude* (1876) 3 Asp. 338. *The Melpomene, supra,* n. 25, may perhaps be better explained on similar grounds.
[44] *Supra,* n. 30.
[45] See, *e.g. The Alenquer, The René* [1955] 1 W.L.R. 263; [1955] 1 Lloyd's Rep. 101. See further, *post,* Chap. 11.
[46] If an absolute engagement, *e.g.* to tow to a particular place, is replaced by a lesser one, such as to endeavour to effect the towage, remuneration for the unfulfilled absolute engagement will not be given as part of the reward under the later agreement: *The Lepanto* [1892] P. 122, 130; *The Kilmaho* (1900) 16 T.L.R. 155.
[47] See *post,* §764.
[48] *The Undaunted* (1860) Lush. 90, 92; *The Helvetia* (1894) 8 Asp. 264n, 265n; *The Dart* (1899) 8 Asp. 481, 483; *The Stiklestad* [1926] P. 205, 209 (affirmed (1926) 43 T.L.R. 118); *The Alenquer, The René* [1955] 1 W.L.R. 263; [1955] 1 Lloyd's Rep. 101.

normally taken into account in assessing salvage awards.[49] Moreover, subject to contrary agreement,[50] no reward appears to have been given except in cases where the basic rule of salvage has been satisfied that some part at least of the property imperilled has been saved. If the justification for the reward were simply performance of a contractual obligation, this criterion would be unnecessary, albeit the necessity for ultimate success could be incorporated into the contract as an implied term.

753 Entitlement to remuneration for engaged services on a salvage basis can be explained on contractual grounds; but that explanation is generally denied.[51] It has been said to exist on equitable principles.[52] It also has some affinity with principles of the law of restitution. However, those principles generally concentrate not so much on remunerating the plaintiff for his loss or expenditure but on the defendant's liability to pay for an incontrovertible benefit obtained by him at the expense of the plaintiff.[53] *Ex hypothesi* this would seem not to be so in the cases under discussion unless the moral support of the salvor could be counted as the salvage service.[54] If standing by can rank as a salvage service[55] this would seem quite reasonable. Similarly, the luggers' fetching of the anchor and cable in *The Undaunted*[56] and the initial towage in *The Maude*[57] both come within the accepted range of salvage services. Indeed, it would seem more consistent with principle that the provision of engaged services of endeavour,[58] which might not have been provided at all if the salvor doubted whether they would be successful, should be regarded not merely as in the nature of a salvage service but actually as a salvage service[59] and the award of salvage for meritorious contributions to success under the principles discussed above[60] regarded as remuneration for the defendant's receipt of a benefit at the plaintiff's expense in circumstances where it would be unjust for him to retain it without paying for it. Ultimately, however, whatever consistency there is between the circumstances in which rewards have been given and the various theoretical justifications for such awards, it

---

[49] See, *e.g. The Undaunted* (1860) Lush. 90, 92, 93; *The Maude* (1876) 3 Asp. 338, 339.

[50] If salvors in the performance of successful services have acted under an agreement which entitled them to some remuneration independently of success, the court will take this fact into consideration as an element reducing the amount of the reward.

[51] See, *e.g. The Hestia* [1895] P. 193, 199.

[52] See *The Norma* (1860) Lush. 124, 127.

[53] See Goff & Jones, pp. 22–25, 31–32, 483–485.

[54] See *The Stiklestad* [1926] P. 205, 209; affirmed (1926) 43 T.L.R. 118. Lloyd's arbitrators frequently cite encouragement of the salved vessel's crew as justifying salvage awards in such circumstances.

[55] See *The Undaunted* (1860) Lush. 90, 92; *ante*, §744. *cf. The Cambrian* (1897) 8 Asp. M.L.C. 263, 265.

[56] *Ante*, §746.

[57] *Ante*, §749.

[58] An engagement under an absolute engagement could be regarded as the exceptional case, where the parties exclude the possibility of remuneration in the absence of success.

[59] The language used in the 3rd and 4th editions of Kennedy prompted Lord Merriman P. in *The Hassel* [1959] 2 Lloyd's Rep. 82, 84 specifically to talk in terms of "an award in the nature of a salvage award" rather than of a salvage award *simpliciter*. See also *The Unique Mariner (No. 2)* [1979] 1 Lloyd's Rep. 37, 49.

[60] *Ante*, §733.

Engaged services today

is difficult to deny that the overriding justification for such awards is the familiar principle of the general maritime law that it is for the interests of commerce and of navigation, and also for the encouragement of salvage services generally, that some remuneration should be given for the provision of engaged services even if the services do not prove to be actually beneficial to the vessel.[61]

Engaged services today

Though commissioned on an engaged services rather than a salvage basis, performance of engaged services would appear to constitute a salvage operation[62] and fall within the normal classification of salvage services.[63] If so, and if they achieve the "useful result" required under the Salvage Convention 1989, Art. 12, they may qualify for a salvage reward *stricto sensu*. If there is no such useful result but they fulfil the Convention's requirements for special compensation for environmental services, special compensation may be paid.[64] To that extent, engaged services arguably require no separate treatment.

However, they fulfil a distinctive function in that the service provider can be remunerated, and for more than a *quantum meruit*, without contributing to a successful salvage operation. Therefore, by stipulating that at least some payment will be made, the doctrine of engaged services can be regarded as having the advantage of encouraging assistance which might otherwise not be forthcoming.

754

Yet, no matter how beneficial an engaged service may be thought to be, if there is no successful preservation of property to which the provider has meritoriously contributed, there cannot be the useful result which the Convention requires as a qualification for salvage[65] and the provider cannot claim the benefit of provisions in the Convention, *e.g.* for special compensation.

Of course, engaged services falling outside the Convention may still be provided for by contract, but the terms of the Convention will not apply to the contract except in so far as it so provides.

A further difficulty is that, in whatever form they may continue to exist, engaged services do not clearly fall either within or outside the jurisdiction of the Admiralty Court. Suffice it to say here that, if engaged services may still lawfully be provided for, albeit outside the Convention, it would be bizarre if they did not fall within Admiralty jurisdiction. Such a claim would probably be treated as a claim "in the nature of salvage" within the Supreme Court Act 1981, s.20(2)(j)(iii).

755

---

[61] *The Melpomene* (1873) L.R. 4 A. & E. 129, 131–132. See also *The Helvetia* (1894) 8 Asp. 264n, 265n; *The Cambrian* (1897) 8 Asp. 263, 265; *The Benlarig* (1888) 10 P.D. 3, 6; *The August Korff* [1903] P. 166, 174; *The Unique Mariner (No. 2)* [1979] 1 Lloyd's Rep. 37, 49.
[62] See *ante*, § 18.
[63] See *ante*, Chap. 4.
[64] See *ante*, Chap. 5.
[65] The position is the same under, the Brussels Salvage Convention 1910, Art. 2. See *Wildeboer*, 115–124; Gaskell, 21–399. *cf. Vincenzini*, 63.

Compensation for supersession of engaged services

756 The remedies of a salvor who has been prevented from completing the provision of a salvage service and so earning a normal salvage reward must be considered in two separate contexts. Where, as is common nowadays, the salvor has entered into an agreement under Lloyd's Form, his rights will be governed by the obligations under the contract, as interpreted in *The Unique Mariner (No. 2)*.[66] In other cases, his remedies will be governed by the general maritime law laid down in four authorities, *The Maude*,[67] *The Maasdam*,[68] *The Loch Tulla*[69] and *The Hassel*,[70] which cases were reviewed in *The Unique Mariner (No. 2)*.[71]

Admiralty law

757 The effect of the general maritime law was stated by Kennedy as follows. If a salvor, whose services have been accepted, and who is able and willing[72] to complete the salvage which he has entered upon, finds himself dismissed or superseded by the orders of the owner or master of the vessel in distress in favour of a second salvor, he should not forcibly resist, but should rely upon the court's recognition of these facts in dealing with his claim to salvage reward. But, in estimating the award to be given to the original salvor in such circumstances, the court will be very careful to inquire whether the owner or master of the salved vessel acted rightly or wrongly in superseding the original salvor.[73]

758 The first condition of this type of remuneration is that the salvor has entered upon the service required.[74] The mere sending out of an SOS inviting assistance from all and sundry does not necessarily amount to an engagement.[75] Nor will a willing salvor whose services are rejected necessarily be entitled to enforce a claim if his offer of services is accepted on the basis that use will only be made of them if actually required when he reaches the vessel.[76] His services must have been accepted to perform a definite engagement.[77]

---

[66] [1979] 1 Lloyd's Rep. 37.
[67] (1876) 3 Asp. 338.
[68] (1893) 7 Asp. 400.
[69] (1950) 84 Ll.L.Rep. 62.
[70] [1959] 2 Lloyd's Rep. 82.
[71] *Supra.*
[72] The word "alone" appeared after "willing" here, in the original version of this paragraph as approved by Willmer J. (see n. 73, *infra*). But, in the light of *The Hassel, infra*, n. 79, it seems correct to omit it now.
[73] This paragraph was approved by Willmer J. in *The Loch Tulla* (1950) 84 Ll.L.Rep. 62, 69. See also the clear, if slightly incomplete, statement of principle by Sir Francis Jeune P. in *The Maasdam* (1893) 7 Asp. 400, 401.
[74] *The Hassel* [1959] 2 Lloyd's Rep. 82, 85.
[75] *ibid.*; *The Stiklestad* [1926] P. 205, 209; affirmed (1926) 43 T.L.R. 118.
[76] See *The Hassel, supra.* Of course, if there actually exists an engagement to stand by and the salvor does stand by, he should be able to claim for having carried out what was required of him. See *ante*, §§743–753.
[77] *The Stiklestad* [1926] P. 205, 210; affirmed (1926) 43 T.L.R. 118.

Compensation for supersession of engaged services

Secondly, none of the cases contradict the arguably incontrovertible proposition that, in order for his claim to succeed, the salvor must have been ready and willing to render or to continue performance at the time when his engaged services were superseded. It was suggested in previous editions of this book[78] that the salvor must have been able and willing to complete the salvage alone. That this is not necessary is clear from *The Hassel*,[79] the salvor's claim succeeding where an engagement was concluded by wireless on the understanding that a second tug might also be engaged, this being commonly a desirable and prudent course of action.

759

In none of the authorities was no property saved and the ultimate salvage of some of the property imperilled has been declared to be a prerequisite of compensation,[80] unless perhaps the property would have been saved had the salvor's services not been rejected.[81] Certainly, it has been declared that the right to some compensation for supersession is not dependent on any prior benefit having been conferred.[82]

760

The judges have not matched the salvor's readiness and willingness to act with a clear requirement that it should have been wrong for the salvor to have been dismissed by the master of the vessel in distress.[83] It is not surprising that the court has not appeared to condone a rule which might hinder the chances of quick and efficient salvage, by justifying resistance to supersession by a salvor possibly better able to accomplish the task.[84] This consideration may have influenced the comment that it is not necessary to inquire whether the master or other representative of the property in peril was justified in dismissing the superseded salvor,[85] albeit in none of the cases under consideration in

761

---

[78] See *ante*, n. 72.
[79] [1959] 2 Lloyd's Rep. 82.
[80] *The Unique Mariner (No. 2)* [1979] 1 Lloyd's Rep. 37, 52.
[81] Brandon J.'s explanation of the reasons for awarding and calculating compensation would deny this: see *post*, §764.
[82] *The Unique Mariner (No. 2)* [1979] 1 Lloyd's Rep. 37, 50. *Cf. The Loch Tulla* (1950) 84 Ll.L.Rep. 62. This would seem to exclude a restitutionary theory for the availability of compensation.
[83] In *The Maude* (1876) 3 Asp. M.L.C. 338, 339, Sir Robert Phillimore said that the salvor ought not to have been discarded. In *The Maasdam* (1893) 7 Asp. M.L.C. 400, Sir Francis Jeune P. refrained from questioning the wisdom of the salvor's replacement on the arrival of a steamship belonging to the owners of the vessel in distress but appeared to think, in that particular case perhaps, that the supersession was not at all improper. In *The Loch Tulla* (1950) 84 Ll.L.Rep. 62, 69–70, Willmer J. said that the master was entitled to engage a replacement tug but that, in addition to salvage earned by it, compensation had to be paid by the superseded tug. In *The Hassel* [1959] 2 Lloyd's Rep. 82, 88, Lord Merriman P. seemed to think that the salvor had a "right" from the moment when his services were accepted.
[84] *cf.* O.W. Holmes' well-known principle of the law of contract that a contractor is entitled to breach his contract (a wrongful act in law) should he decide to do so, so long as he is prepared to compensate the other party in damages. Note also the general principle of equity that an equitable remedy, such as an injunction, will not be granted to a plaintiff where damages provide him with an adequate remedy.
[85] *The Maasdam* (1893) 7 Asp. 400, 401; *The Unique Mariner (No. 2)* [1979] 1 Lloyd's Rep. 39, 49.

Success

this section has been the dismissal been found to be so justifiable as to exclude the rejected salvor's claim for compensation.

762 Superseded salvors are entitled to remuneration (whether as salvage remuneration or as remuneration in the nature of salvage) under three heads: first, as a reward for the services which they have actually rendered before they were superseded[86]; secondly, by way of compensation for loss of the opportunity to complete the services; and, thirdly, as reward for any salvage services which were rendered after the supersession (*e.g.* where towage services are superseded and the tug is asked to remain standing by).[87]

763 It has been said that the measure of compensation to which the salvor is entitled for losing the chance of earning a substantial award must itself be a substantial sum of money[88] and that this sum is to be measured partly on what the merit of the service would have been if rendered and partly on the prospects of rendering a successful service. This approach closely resembles the general rule of the law of contract for damages for loss of opportunity.[89] However, it has also been said not to be very important to determine whether the remuneration is: compensation for services which might have been rendered and which were not; remuneration for services rendered as a whole, treating as part of those services the readiness and willingness to give help which might be available[90]; or remuneration on the basis of the public policy of encouraging the readiness and willingness of salvors to come rapidly to the assistance of vessels in distress, even though they may, after entering upon salvage services, be deprived, as a result of supersession, of the opportunity to complete them successfully.[91]

764 *Inter alia*, these remarks led Brandon J. in *The Unique Mariner (No. 2)*[92] to conclude[93] that the compensation awarded to a superseded salvor is not assessed like damages for breach of contract or duty, on the basis of *restitutio in integrum*; but that the public policy consideration is the legal basis of the right to compensation, the only criterion for assessing the amount due being what is fair and reasonable in all the circumstances in order to give the encouragement which it is the policy of the law to provide. The factors to be considered will be the amount of salvage remuneration which the superseded salvors were deprived of the opportunity of earning[94]; deductions from the

---

[86] *cf. The Unique Mariner (No. 2)* [1979] 1 Lloyd's Rep. 37, 53.
[87] *The Maude* (1876) 3 Asp. 338, 339; *The Maasdam* (1893) 7 Asp. 400, 401; *The Loch Tulla* (1950) 84 Ll.L.Rep. 62, 70; *The Unique Mariner (No. 2)* [1979] 1 Lloyd's Rep. 37, 50.
[88] *The Loch Tulla, supra*, n. 87, at 70; *The Hassel* [1979] 2 Lloyd's Rep. 82, 85, 89.
[89] See *Chaplin v. Hicks* [1910] 2 K.B. 486 and the other cases referred to by Chitty, § 27–034 and Treitel, pp. 890–891.
[90] *The Maasdam* (1893) 7 Asp. 400, 401.
[91] See *The Hassel* [1959] 2 Lloyd's Rep. 82, 89; *The Unique Mariner (No. 2)* [1979] 1 Lloyd's Rep. 37, 50.
[92] *ibid.*
[93] *Obiter*. The actual decision was based on interpreting the effects of Lloyd's Form: see *post*, §§765–766. See further Chap. 10.
[94] See *The Maude* (1876) 3 Asp. M.L.C. 338, 339.

Compensation for supersession of engaged services

notional award which would have been earned for risks not run, expenses and time saved[95]; the value of the service that would have been rendered[96]; the prospects of success[97]; and the fact that other salvors may have to be paid out of the salved fund.[98]

The reasons he listed for his conclusion were[99]:   **765**

- (i) the observation that the judges in the four authorities did not appear to be thinking in terms of damages for breach of contract or duty;

- (ii) "a claim for salvage, or, perhaps, more precisely, a claim in the nature of salvage" was one in respect of which the superseded salvors had a maritime lien on the property concerned, which they would not have had in respect of a claim for breach of contract or duty;

- (iii) the claim was one in respect of which the court had jurisdiction both *in rem* and *in personam*;

- (iv) an inference from *The Maude*,[1] that the salvor's award should be less than the notional award which would have been earned, even with deductions for risks not run, expenses and time saved and the possibility of no success;

- (v) an inference from *The Maasdam*, *The Loch Tulla* and *The Hassel*[2] that it was unnecessary to consider whether the salvor's dismissal was justified, which conclusion would be false with respect to determination of whether there had been a breach of contract or duty;

- (vi) an indication from *The Loch Tulla*[3] that regard had to be had, in assessing compensation, to the reward payable to other salvors from the salved fund, which should be irrelevant to compensation for breach of contract;

- (vii) the observation that the sums awarded in the four authorities appeared to be smaller than compensation for breach of contract or duty would have been;

- (viii) the indication that "what was claimed and awarded in all the cases **766** was not damages but salvage remuneration[4]" (In fact, the

---

[95] *The Unique Mariner (No. 2)* [1979] 1 Lloyd's Rep. 37, 50; see also *ibid.*, 49.
[96] See *The Maasdam* (1893) 7 Asp. M.L.C. 400, 402; *The Loch Tulla* (1950) 84 Ll.L.Rep. 62, 69; *The Hassel* [1959] 2 Lloyd's Rep. 62.
[97] *The Loch Tulla, supra*, n. 96, at 69.
[98] *ibid.*, 72.
[99] [1979] 1 Lloyd's Rep. 37, 49–50.
[1] *Supra*.
[2] See *ante*, §756 and n. 78; *The Maude* was not mentioned in this context.
[3] See *ante*, text to n. 98.
[4] (1876) 3 Asp. 338, 339.

indication, to be expected from the nature of the circumstances, is not at all consistent: in the first case, *The Maude*, the judge referred to reward for services rendered and compensation for the loss sustained; and even Brandon J. accepted Willmer J.'s terminology in *The Hassel*[5] drawn from Kennedy, of an award "in the nature of salvage" as more appropriate: see (ii), above);

(ix) the Admiralty Court never regarded a claim for salvage, in the absence of an express salvage agreement, as being a contractual claim but rather as a claim founded on an independent right given to salvors under the general maritime law[6];

(x) Lord Diplock's general statement in *The Tojo Maru*[7] that the Court of Admiralty, before its absorption into the High Court in 1875 (and, incidentally, before the four authorities were decided), was not in the habit of applying the concept of contract to salvage services and that, although the rendering of salvage services was consensual, there was no obligation on the salvor to continue to provide his services—this carrying the implication that both parties were free to discontinue the relationship at will. (In fact, Lord Diplock did not clearly distinguish between a salvor under a specific contract, a salvor providing other engaged services and a purely voluntary salvor; moreover, the offeree's freedom to withdraw from performance of a unilaterial contract is not generally believed to be matched by the offeror's freedom to do so after performance has begun.[8] Brandon J. said[9] that the freedom of both parties to withdraw from an engagement under the general maritime law was analogous to that which exists under a unilateral contract, quoting Chitty[10] and *Luxor (Eastbourne) Ltd v. Cooper*[11] but the analogy really points him in the opposite direction);

(xi) his decision that the compensation was really given, for reasons of public policy, under the general maritime law.[12]

Lloyd's Form

767 The principles governing the claim of a party to a contract concluded on the standard Lloyd's Form and superseded in breach of contract[13] were laid down as follows in *The Unique Mariner (No. 2)*[14] by Brandon J.

[5] [1959] 2 Lloyd's Rep. 82, 84.
[6] See *The Hestia* [1895] P. 193.
[7] [1972] A.C. 242, 292.
[8] See *Daulia Ltd v. Four Millbank Nominees Ltd* [1978] Ch. 231, 239; Treitel, pp. 35–39.
[9] [1979] 1 Lloyd's Rep. 37, 51.
[10] (24th ed.), Vol. 1, §§ 81–82. See now 28th ed., § 2–071 to 2–073.
[11] [1941] A.C. 108.
[12] See *ante*, in this §.
[13] The master of the vessel to be salved dismissed the salvor when he discovered that it was not, as he had mistakenly believed, the tug sent out by his owners. See further *The Unique Mariner (No. 1)* [1978] 1 Lloyd's Rep. 438; *post*, Chap. 9.
[14] [1979] 1 Lloyd's Rep. 37.

Compensation for supersession of engaged services

First, the rights and obligations of parties to the Lloyd's Form are governed by the terms, express and implied, of that contract; and the general maritime law of salvage only applies in so far as it is expressly or impliedly incorporated into such contract.[15]

Secondly, the proper approach to determining the obligations of contractors under Lloyd's Form is to consider, first, what would be the salvage contractor's liability under the general English law of contract and then to examine what, if any, differences flow, either in principle or on the authority of previous decisions, from the special characteristics of salvage services.[16]

Thirdly, under Lloyd's Form, the salvage contractor undertakes a continuing obligation, until the ship is lost or brought to a safe port, to use his best endeavours to salve her and to provide the equipment and labour which in the circumstances it would be reasonable for him to use for this purpose.[17] The contract is, therefore, a contract for work and labour.[18]

Fourthly, under a contract of work and labour, it is an implied term, necessary to give business efficacy to it, that, so long as the person employed is both willing and able to perform the work and labour which he has undertaken, the employer will not act in such a way as to prevent him from doing so.[19]

Fifthly, there is no evidence that the judges of the Admiralty Court before 1875[20] applied the concept of contract to salvage services or that the general maritime law was other than to the effect that a salvor assumed no obligation to continue to provide his services and that the owners of the property imperilled were equally under no obligation to continue to employ the salvors.[21] Thus, as Lord Diplock said in *The Tojo Maru*[22]:

> "[E]xcept in the case of derelicts, the rendering of salvage services was consensual. It involved the acceptance by the owner of a vessel which was in peril of an offer by the salvor to try and save it for a reward upon a *quantum meruit* in the event of success. To 20th century English lawyers this has the essential characteristics of a contract. But to lawyers in the 18th and the first part of the 19th centuries the similarities between salvage services and contracts for work and labour were less apparent. There was no room for any consensual element in the case of derelicts; and even when there was a consensual element the implied promises lacked mutuality in that the salvor assumed no obligation to continue to

---

[15] *ibid.*, 50–51; *The Beaverford (Owners) v. The Kafiristan (Owners)* [1938] A.C. 136, 144–145, 153–154, *per* Lord Wright.
[16] *The Tojo Maru* [1972] A.C. 242, 292; followed in *The Unique Mariner (No. 2), supra,* n. 95, at 50–51.
[17] *The Tojo Maru, supra,* n. 16, at 292.
[18] *The Unique Mariner (No. 2), supra,* n. 95, at 51.
[19] *ibid.*, 51, referring to Chitty (24th ed.), Vol. 1, §§788, 1491. See now 25th ed., §§13–012, 22–036.
[20] The date when it became part of the High Court.
[21] *The Unique Mariner (No. 2), supra,* n. 95, at 50.
[22] *The Tojo Maru, supra,* n. 16, at 292.

provide his services. He could withdraw at any time, yet claim a reward if his services had contributed to the successful saving of the ship. One does not, therefore find the Judges of the Court of Admiralty before 1875 applying the concept of contract to salvage services."

770   Sixthly, the difference in the obligations of salvors engaged without any express contract and contractors engaged on the terms of Lloyd's Form must be matched by a corresponding difference in the obligation of the owners of the property to be salved. Where, on the one hand, the engagement is made without any express contract, the owners of the property to be salved are under no obligation to allow the salvors to complete their services, but are entitled, if they wish, to dismiss them and supersede them by other salvors. Where, on the other hand, salvors are engaged on the terms of Lloyd's Form, the owners of the salved property must be under an obligation, so long as the salvors are both willing and able to perform the services which they have undertaken, not to act in such a way as to prevent them from doing so. There is then a bilateral contract.[23]

771   Seventhly, it is wrong to argue: that the fact that services under the Lloyd's Form are rendered on the principle "no cure—no pay" has the effect of incorporating into the contract the general maritime law of salvage so far as it is not inconsistent with the terms of Lloyd's Form; that the result of such incorporation is to give the contractors, if superseded, the same right to some compensation as they would have had under that law; and that, since this right was available to them, there was no need to imply a term that they would not be superseded so long as they were willing and able to perform the services they had undertaken. Under the general maritime law the salvors are not bound to go on with the engagement, so that it is not necessary that the owners of the property to be salved should be bound to go on with it either. But the situation under Lloyd's Form is radically different: the salvors are bound to go on, so that it is necessary to imply an obligation on the part of the owners of the salved property not to prevent them from doing so.[24]

772   Eighthly, the remedy available to superseded salvors under the general maritime law is an incomplete remedy in two respects. First, it does not give the salvors full compensation. Secondly, since what is awarded is salvage, or a sum in the nature of salvage, the right to it is dependent on the property in peril being successfully salved by the superseding salvors. Such a remedy is inadequate for salvors who have entered into a bilateral contract with the owners of the property in peril and have undertaken by it to use their best endeavours to salve such property, which includes the deployment by them of all resources reasonably required for that purpose.[25]

---

[23] [1979] 1 Lloyd's Rep. 37, 51–52.
[24] ibid., 52.
[25] ibid., 52.

Compensation for supersession of engaged services

Ninthly, it is not the case that the term in question ought not to be implied on the ground that it would make Lloyd's Form less workable rather than more workable. **773**

It was objected that the master of a ship in peril who was in doubt whether a vessel which offered salvage services on Lloyd's Form would be able to perform the services successfully would be in the difficulty that, if he accepted the offer, he would be stuck with that vessel and unable to employ other assistance in her place, even though he thought that it was for the safety of his ship to do so. But the suggested implied term would allow the master to supersede the vessel originally engaged if she was in fact unable to perform the services successfully. He would have to back his judgment about this, as about other problems with which a master has to deal.[26]

A further objection was that, where a salvage vessel had been engaged on Lloyd's Form to come out a considerable distance to assist a ship in peril and, while she was still on her way, another vessel, equally or perhaps even more suitable to render the services required, arrived on the scene earlier, the master would be in the difficulty that he could not engage the second vessel, even though the need for assistance was urgent and she could render it substantially more quickly. But, again, if the need for assistance was so urgent that the vessel first engaged could not arrive in time to render successful services, the implied term would allow the master to engage the second vessel. Again he would have to back his judgment.[27] **774**

Brandon J. also rejected the contention that, if the suggested term were implied, it would create too great a difference between the responsibilities of salved interests under Lloyd's Form and their responsibilities under the general maritime law. The reality of the matter seemed to be that Lloyd's Form is a serious commercial contract, involving mutual obligations, which should not be entered into lightly or inadvisedly. If it is entered into, the fact that the obligations under it are mutual must be accepted.[28]

Tenthly, therefore, it is an implied term of salvage agreements made on Lloyd's Form that the owners of the property to be salved will not act in such a way as to prevent the contractors from performing the services which they have undertaken so long as the latter are willing and able to do so. The obligation not to act in such a way as to prevent performance obviously includes an obligation not to dismiss or supersede.[29] **775**

---

[26] *ibid.*, 52. The same reasoning could equally be applied to supersession of services engaged other than on Lloyd's Form.

[27] *ibid.*, 52. Indeed, his duty as master would, no doubt, require that he so backed his judgment. Again, Brandon J.'s reasoning could equally be applied to supersession of services engaged other than on Lloyd's Form.

[28] *ibid.*, 52. Again, the same could be said of other engaged services. The point of distinction would, therefore, seem to be the entering into a signed contract containing a number of specific terms.

[29] *ibid.*, 52–53.

Eleventhly, the conduct of the shipowners in *The Unique Mariner (No. 2)* was a breach of obligation of such a character as to constitute a repudiation of the contract which was accepted on behalf of the contractors.[30]

776 Twelfthly, on the footing that the shipowners repudiated the salvage agreement and that the contractors accepted such repudiation, the latter are entitled to the usual remedy in damages which a party to a contract has in such a case.[31]

If they choose to claim damages, however, they are not also entitled, in Brandon J.'s view, to recover payment for the services which they actually rendered.[32] The contractors are not entitled to moneys for services actually rendered; they are entitled to damages for breach of contract.[33]

The damages to which the contractors are entitled should be assessed on the usual principle of *restitutio in integrum*. For this purpose an estimate should be made of the salvage remuneration which the contractors would have earned if they had been allowed to complete the services, and deductions should be made for risks not run and for expenses and operating time (if any) which were or could reasonably have been saved. In theory, a discount for the possibility of the contractors' not being successful should also be made if such possibility really existed.[34]

777 The fact that the contractors stood by after supersession may be relevant, depending on the facts found by the appeal arbitrator. If the appeal arbitrator finds that the standing by was a reasonably foreseeable consequence of the repudiation, and that the *Salvaliant* would otherwise have resumed her other activities earlier, the contractors are entitled to have the standing by taken into account as an additional factor in the assessment of their damages for what it is worth. If the appeal arbitrator finds that the standing by was not a reasonably foreseeable consequence of the repudiation, he will have to consider whether the contractors, if acting reasonably in mitigation of their damage, should have withdrawn earlier. His findings on that matter will be relevant to the amount of the deduction (if any) to be made, in the assessment of the contractors' damages, for expenses and operating time which were or could reasonably have been saved.[35]

The fact that the defendants have to pay the superseding salvor and the amount of such payment are both irrelevant to the assessment of the superseded salvor's damages.[36]

The dangers to which the vessel in distress would have been exposed are relevant to the estimation of the award which the contractors would have earned if they had been allowed to complete their services. So also are the facts that the superseding salvors were on hand as alternative salvors if

---

[30] ibid., 53.
[31] ibid., 53.
[32] ibid., 53. The position is different under the general maritime law: see *ante*, §762.
[33] [1979] 1 Lloyd's Rep. 37, 54.
[34] ibid., 54.
[35] ibid., 54.
[36] ibid., 54. *cf.* the position under the general maritime law: *ante*, §762.

required, and, if the appeal arbitrator so finds, that they were less skilful than the contractors.[37]

Brandon J. derived some support from his views on the effect of Lloyd's Form from *The Valsesia*.[38] Agreements for specific sums were entered that the plaintiff tugs should refloat the grounded vessel and beach her in a safe place. The tugs tried to perform the services which they had undertaken, but their efforts were defeated by the negligent failure of those on board the *Valsesia* to slip their anchor cable at the proper time. Had this been done, the services would have been successfully performed. On these facts, it was held by Hill J. that the owners, masters and crews of the two tugs were not entitled to recover the sums for salvage which it had been agreed should be paid, because they had not performed successfully the services which they had undertaken. They were, however, entitled to recover *equivalent sums* as damages for the *Valsesia's* breach of contract in failing to exercise reasonable skill and care. Brandon J. recognised that *The Valsesia* was not a case on Lloyd's Form, and that the implied obligation of the shipowners for breach of which damages were awarded was a qualified obligation to use reasonable skill and care in the combined work, rather than an absolute obligation not to act in such a way as to prevent performance. However, the case does shew, in his view, first, that, when an express contract for the rendering of salvage services is made, ordinary common law principles apply to the interpretation of such contract; and, secondly, that the obligations of the parties to such a contract are, under those ordinary common law principles, of a mutual character.[39]

778

---

[37] [1979] 1 Lloyd's Rep. 37, 54.
[38] [1927] P. 115.
[39] [1979] 1 Lloyd's Rep. 37, 53. It is arguable that the principles allowing compensation for supersession of engaged services under the general maritime law and damages for the *Valsesia's* breach of duty, which would possibly have been due whether or not the duty was contractual, are dictated by the same considerations, even if different considerations produce different levels of quantification in different circumstances and/or on different facts. It is unfortunate that neither Hill J. nor Brandon J. considered *The Valsesia* in conjunction with the supersession cases nor is it clear from the reports whether the *Valsesia* was ultimately salved and what claims had to be satisfied out of whatever fund was available.

CHAPTER 9

SALVAGE AGREEMENTS

1. TYPES OF SALVAGE AGREEMENT

Introduction

779   The principal object of this chapter is to consider the nature and effect of express agreements for salvage. Before doing so, it is necessary to distinguish between the various types of agreement that may be concluded in relation to salvage, and which attract the description of salvage agreement, and to note their relationship with the common law of salvage.

Several kinds of agreement may be made with respect to the provision of services of a salvage nature. The characteristics of the most obvious type were mentioned by Brett M.R. in *The Renpor*[1]:

> "I think, therefore, that the agreement is a proper salvage agreement; it fixes the amount of salvage to be paid both for services to life and property, but leaves untouched all the other conditions necessary to support a salvage award."

This remark seems to have provided the basis of the definition of salvage agreements given by Kennedy and referred to by Bruce J. in *The Hestia*[2]:

> "The way in which an agreement affects the question of salvage is laid down by Kennedy J. thus[3]: 'A salvage agreement is an agreement which fixes, indeed, the amount to be paid for salvage, but leaves untouched all the other conditions necessary to support a salvage award, one of which is the preservation of some part at least of the *res*, that is, ship, cargo, or freight.' "

780   However, this description of a salvage agreement is not exclusive. Former editions of Lloyd's Standard Form of Salvage Agreement made provision for the insertion of an agreed figure "unless this sum shall be afterwards objected to as hereinafter mentioned in which case the remuneration for the services

---

[1] (1883) 8 P.D. 115, 118.
[2] [1895] P. 193, 199. See also *Gark v. Straits Towing Ltd (The Belize)* [1966] 2 Lloyd's Rep. 277, 282.
[3] 1st ed., p. 42.

Introduction

shall be fixed by Arbitration in London." For this reason the Form is still commonly referred to as "Lloyd's Open Form" (generally abbreviated to "LOF"). In practice, the blank space in Lloyd's Form was very seldom filled in. Most of the cases concerning agreements fixing the salvage remuneration payable were decided before the introduction of Lloyd's Form. In modern times, such agreements remain rare. An agreement may provide for remuneration on alternative bases or even, as with LOF 2000, simply provide a means for assessing the reward (by arbitration) without losing its character as a salvage agreement. Salvage agreements are commonly made to provide for salvage remuneration in the event of services proving successful or beneficial. But an agreement governed by the doctrine of engaged services falls within the court's salvage jurisdiction; indeed, any provision for payment of expenses, loss or damage incurred if the services are not successful or beneficial does not prevent the agreement as a whole from being regarded as within that jurisdiction.[4]

In *Admiralty Commissioners v. Valverda (Owners)*,[5] the House of Lords considered the effect of the Admiralty Standard Form of Towage Agreement then in use.[6] Clause 4 provided that: "The remuneration shall, if the services are successful or beneficial, consist of a reasonable amount of salvage." But clause 5 went on to stipulate that: "If the services are not successful or beneficial, then the actual out-of-pocket expenses incurred by or on behalf of the Admiralty in the endeavours to salve or assist the said ship and her cargo and freight, together with compensation not exceeding £350 for any loss or damage incurred in such endeavours, shall be the measure of the remuneration payable to the Admiralty under this agreement, but there shall not be included in the said expenses or compensation any charge for the use of any ship or tug belonging to His Majesty." The amount of any remuneration payable was referred to arbitration. At that time, the Admiralty could claim salvage only for the services of ships specially equipped with salvage plant or of tugs,[7] other claims remaining barred.[8] The House of Lords therefore rejected the claim of the Admiralty, which had incurred considerable expenses, in respect of the services of two cruisers.[9] The agreement was a salvage agreement and the statutory provisions could not be waived or contracted out of, which in fact the agreement on its true construction did not do anyway. **781**

The House also rejected the alternative argument that the agreement was not a salvage agreement but an agreement for work and labour, and therefore **782**

---

[4] See *ante*, Chap. 8.

[5] [1938] A.C. 173.

[6] Form D.46. Lloyd's Form has taken its place since 1940. Current instructions are for Lloyd's Form to be employed whenever salvage services are rendered by H.M. ships or Admiralty-owned ships.

[7] Under M.S. (Salvage) Act 1916, replaced by the M.S. (Salvage) Act 1940, which was repealed by CPA 1947.

[8] By MSA 1894, s.557(1), repealed by CPA 1947. See now CPA 1947, s.8; *ante*, §§ 664 *et seq*.

[9] There was no dispute as to the right of the Admiralty to claim in respect of services clearly permitted by statute or as to the right of officers and men.

outside the statutory prohibition. Lord Wright, with whom the other Law Lords agreed, thought that the provisions for remuneration on a salvage basis and for a maritime lien would be sufficient to establish that the agreement was a salvage agreement. But their Lordships also had to contend with the point that the agreement provided for remuneration even if the services were not successful or beneficial. The argument that this prevented the agreement's being a salvage agreement was rejected as contrary to principle and to authority.[10] Thus, Lord Maugham said[11]:

> "The master of a commercial vessel may well be willing to enter upon a salving enterprise possessing very doubtful prospects of success if he can secure an agreement that a certain expense or loss in which the job will involve his ship will in any event be repaid. It would not be in the true interests of shipping if this were held to be impossible."

Similarly, Lord Roche said[12]:

> "It is true enough that 'no cure, no pay' is of the essence of salvage. Unless the *res* is saved and a claimant to salvage brings about or contributes to its safety he is not ordinarily entitled to salvage remuneration in the proper sense; but there is no reason in principle or upon any authority why a person should not alternatively be a salvor entitled to salvage remuneration or a labourer worthy of some hire. That alternative position may arise by reason of an agreement antecedent to any salvage services, as in the familiar case of a towage agreement: see *Five Steel Barges*.[13] In such a case salvage remuneration may be earned if the circumstances warrant it, but if it is not the towage money will be payable. Similarly with an agreement made contemporaneously with or subsequent to the rendering of services I see no obstacle in the way of alternative and truly severable stipulations for remuneration on different bases according as the facts turn out. That is the situation I find here on the plain terms of the agreement. One basis stipulated for is a salvage basis, and it does not change its character because of the presence of a stipulation for some remuneration on another basis if there is no salvage."

The salvage part of a severable agreement for remuneration on either a salvage or an alternative basis therefore takes effect as a salvage agreement, although the precise effect of such an agreement will reduce the level of

---

[10] The House approved *The Kate B. Jones* [1892] P. 366 and *The Edenmore* [1893] P. 79.
[11] [1938] A.C. 173, 197.
[12] [1938] A.C. 173, 202–203. See also *ibid.*, 187–188, *per* Lord Wright.
[13] (1890) 15 P.D. 142.

remuneration payable.[14] And if no property is ultimately in some way preserved the remuneration payable will not be salvage remuneration.

The agreements considered so far all relate to the provision of services and payment therefor. The second main group of salvage agreements includes those made by salvors *inter se* as to the allocation and apportionment of salvage remuneration. These will be considered in Chapter 17.

Agreements excluding salvage

The often repeated and frequently stressed policy of rewarding genuine salvage services is so strong that, in Lord Stowell's words, the court ought to be precisely informed as to the foundation for any claim for exemption from liability to pay a salvage reward[15]:

> "This information is peculiarly necessary in a case where the exemption is claimed from a right otherwise universally allowed, and highly favoured in law, for the protection of those who are subjected to it; for it is for *their* benefit that it exists under that favour of the law. It is what the law calls *jus liquidissimum*, the clearest general right that they who have saved lives and property at sea should be rewarded for such salutary exertions; and those who say that they are not bound to reward, ought to prove their exemption in very definite terms, and by arguments of irresistible cogency."

However, subject to its unenforceability for reasons of public policy, an agreement may be made excluding a right to a salvage award which would otherwise exist. Thus, Lord Salvesen once said[16]:

> "I do not affirm that shipowners may not, by agreement, bar themselves from any claim for salvage remuneration in respect of services rendered to each other's property. Such an agreement might conceivably be objected to as being contrary to public policy. But, assuming its validity, I think it must be clear, from the agreement, that the rendering of assistance to a vessel in distress shall not found a claim for remuneration. The right to obtain salvage remuneration is one very much favoured in law, and therefore cannot be excluded unless by express words or by very clear implication from the language used."

The ouster of a right to salvage is unlikely to be achieved by implication. As Stephen J. observed, delivering the judgment of the High Court of Australia in *Fisher v. The Oceanic Grandeur*[17]:

---

[14] See *ante*, Chap. 8.
[15] *The Waterloo* (1820) 2 Dods. 433, 435–436. See also *The Leon Blum* [1915] P. 90, 120. *cf. The Salawati* (1929) 34 Ll.L.Rep. 177, 180.
[16] *Clan Steam Trawling Co. Ltd v. Aberdeen Steam Trawling and Fishing Co. Ltd (The Clan Grant)* 1908 S.C. 651, 655n.
[17] (1972) 127 C.L.R. 312, 334: [1972] 2 Lloyd's Rep. 396, 407.

"I see no ground upon which it would be proper to imply into the arrangement such a term as would exclude an otherwise justifiable claim for salvage reward."

786 To be effective then, such an agreement should expressly exclude a salvage reward. It is possible for services to be obtained and paid for on a contractual work and labour rather than on a salvage basis, *e.g.* for lightening,[18] although where there is a serious imminent danger, the court has not been unwilling to reward the rendered services on a salvage basis, particularly in the case of towage.[19]

787 A person who attempts to exclude another's right to salvage will need the clear authority of that other to do so.[20] Statute generally prohibits the exclusion of claims by seamen.[21] It was held in *The Leon Blum*[22] that a towage agreement made on behalf of a vessel's owners "no cure, no pay; no salvage charges" did not automatically enure for the benefit of owners of cargo being carried while salvage services were rendered. In fact, cargo owners will normally not be required to pay for services provided under such a contract, though not because they are parties to it but on the separate ground that the contractors will be acting without the intention to claim salvage from cargo owners, *i.e.* as "volunteers".[23] That was not so in *The Leon Blum* because the contractors habitually contracted to tow the relevant vessels in ballast; it was fortuitous that cargo was being carried at the time in question.

788 Of course, an attempted exclusion of salvage will only be effective to the extent that it so excludes on its true construction. In *The Queen Elizabeth*,[24] there was an agreement between the Cunard Steamship Co. Ltd and certain tug owners for the hire of tugs, it being understood that for "special services" no claim on a salvage basis would be made. Willmer J. thought that the agreement prima facie appeared to indicate that the tug owners were contracting out of any right to claim on a salvage basis for work done outside the ordinary routine work of assisting Cunard's vessels in harbour. However, "special services" were expressly defined, which the judge thought meant exclusively defined, and on the facts the agreement failed to bar the claim.

789 Where an agreement is prima facie effective to exclude entitlement to salvage, it may nevertheless fail to do so if there is a change in the circumstances in which the agreement is designed to operate. In *The Glenmorven*,[25]

---

[18] See, *e.g. The Ningpo* (1923) 16 Ll.L.Rep. 392. *cf. The Pacific Colocotronis* [1981] 2 Lloyd's Rep. 40.
[19] See *ante*, Chap. 4.
[20] *Fisher v. The Oceanic Grandeur* (1972) 127 C.L.R. 312, 334; [1972] 2 Lloyd's Rep. 396, 407. See also *The Leon Blum* [1915] P. 90, affirmed *ibid.*, 290 (tug owners excluded their, but not their master's, claim). *cf. The Friesland* [1904] P. 345.
[21] MSA 1995, s.39. See *post*, §§ 1538–1539.
[22] [1915] P. 90, affirmed, *ibid.*, 290.
[23] See *ante*, §§ 600–623, especially §620.
[24] (1949) 82 Ll.L.Rep. 803.
[25] [1913] P. 141.

the plaintiffs contracted for £400 to tow a steamship from Vigo to the Tyne "no cure no pay, no claim to be made for salvage". Sir Samuel Evans P. held that this was a contract to tow a partially disabled vessel with her master and crew on board and that it was brought to an end when the master and crew left the vessel without sufficient justification, from which time the plaintiffs' services were provided not under contract but as salvage, justifying an award of £1,400, plus £300 on a *quantum meruit* for the previous towage services.

Contractual salvage

In earlier times, when navigation and direction of vessels was heavily dependent on the elements and communications were not easy, salvage operations were much less certain and controlled than they have become today and frequently took the form of unco-ordinated personal services. Such circumstances were not favourable to the prior arrangement of agreements to salve, particularly since would-be salvors could not have complete confidence in their ability successfully to undertake salvage services. However, the emergence of steam-powered vessel in the nineteenth century furnished potential salvors with more reliable and controllable means of propulsion and, therefore, more effective means of salvage. This in turn led, by the beginning of the last quarter of the century, to the establishment of specialist providers of professional towage and salvage services, the advantages of which have been reflected in the court's benevolent treatment and encouragement of professional salvors.[26] An incident to this development was the use of standard forms of salvage agreement.

Lloyd's Form of salvage agreement

In 1890, at the instance of a particular salvage contractor, a form of salvage agreement was devised by which the salvor's remuneration should be assessed by arbitration. In the same year a different form was introduced experimentally for use by another salvage organisation but no agreement was then reached with the Committee of Lloyd's for the use of the form. In 1891 a third type of form was agreed by various associations for use by any salvage contractor, and this and another type for use by two salvage contractors received the approval of Lloyd's. In the following year another salvage organisation undertook to use the same form as that used by the two already mentioned. Revisions and alterations were made in 1892 and towards the end of that year the first Standard Form was issued. This in turn was amended in 1896, 1897 and 1908, when the Committee of Lloyd's decided that there should in future be only one form of agreement and there was first published the Lloyd's Standard Form of Salvage Agreement ("No Cure—No Pay") as it is known today. Revisions to the form, sometimes radical, have been

---

[26] See *ante*, §§ 42–47.

regarded as necessary from time to time to accommodate developments in case law,[27] practice, and technological and other changes. There were revisions in 1924, 1926, 1950, 1953, 1967, 1972, 1980, 1990, 1995 and most recently in 2000, following extensive consultations with interested parties in the world of salvage, shipowning and the law. This form has long been referred to familiarly as "Lloyd's Form" and the most recent version[28] by the code "LOF 2000." Both designations are used in this book.

792 Copies of Lloyd's Form and incorporated clauses are easily obtainable.[29] They are carried on board most salvage tugs and held by Lloyd's Agents throughout the world. Lord Roche noted in the House of Lords in 1937, in *Admiralty Commissioners v. Valverda (Owners)*,[30] that:

> "Counsel for the respondents was probably not far from the mark in saying that in these days of Lloyd's salvage agreements the larger number of salvages are regulated by agreement."

This is even truer today, and the agreement forms the basis of the majority of salvage claims now made throughout the world.

Claims for salvage at common law have become extremely rare. The majority of the few reported cases concerning questions of salvage derive from points of law coming before the court from arbitrators, and those cases have become less frequent since the Arbitration Act 1979.[31]

2. Parties

General

793 The mere fact that a document purporting to have contractual effect purports to bind persons identified therein, whether expressly or more generally, will not *per se* subject those persons to liabilities under the contract. As a general rule, a person is only legally liable as a party to a contract if he has legal capacity and the contract is made with his consent or by a person acting with authority.[32] This must be borne in mind when considering the effect of the provisions appearing in the Lloyd's Form salvage contract. Persons who

---

[27] The novel appearance of the form seems clear from its apparent first reported judicial consideration in *The City of Calcutta* (1898) 8 Asp. M.L.C. 442.

[28] Which is reproduced in App. 2.

[29] Free of charge on application either in person or by post to the Salvage Arbitration Branch of Lloyd's. The text of the current form is also set out in Lloyd's Calendar and many nautical almanacs. See LOF 2000, Important Notice 2.

[30] [1938] A.C. 173, 202.

[31] See now the Arbitration Act 1996; *post*, Chap. 13.

[32] Authority is discussed in the next part of this Chapter. See *post*, §§ 796–846.

are involved in salvage operations but who are not parties to salvage contracts may of course have rights and liabilities under the general law.

A contract (even on Lloyd's Form) can be made without a written record of the parties' names. However, a written record of the would-be parties is obviously useful, not only to identify them, but possibly to exclude persons alleging themselves to be parties to the contract but not recorded as such along with parties who are named. LOF 2000 makes provision for this by providing boxes with blank spaces to be completed to identify the parties and their agents, although the small size of the box demonstrates an expectation that only one person will sign on behalf of all property to be salved.[33]

The contracting salvors

Box 1 of LOF 2000 begins with the printed words "Name of the salvage Contractors", followed by a space for insertion of the name(s) of the contracting salvor(s), then the printed words "(referred to in this agreement as 'the Contractors')". Once the box is completed, the identification of the salvage contractors should be straightforward.

794

The contracting salvees

Box 2 of LOF 2000 also contains blank spaces to be completed. Given the wider range of potential salvees, the question whether the person signing Lloyd's Form on their behalf has authority to do so is potentially more important in the case of the person signing as the salvor's agent. Box 2 is as follows.

795

"Property to be salved:

The vessel:
her cargo freight bunkers[34] stores and other property thereon but excluding the personal effects or baggage of passengers master or crew (referred to in this agreement as 'the property')."

In addition, LSSAC 2000 states that " 'Owners' means the owners of the property referred to in box 2 of the Agreement"[35] and " 'owners of the vessel' includes the demise or bareboat charterers of that vessel".[36]

---

[33] Boxes 8 and 9 contain spaces for identifying the agents. See *post*, § 797.
[34] If the person signing Lloyd's Form contracts on behalf of the owners of the bunkers without more (*i.e.* on behalf of the owners of the bunkers whether those owners be shipowners, charterers or others), this should bind the bunker owners without first having to determine their identity. *cf. The Saint Anna* [1980] 1 Lloyd's Rep. 180; *The Silia* [1981] 2 Lloyd's Rep. 534; *The Span Terza* [1984] 1 Lloyd's Rep. 119; *The Pan Oak* [1992] 2 Lloyd's Rep. 36.
[35] LSSAC 2000, cl.3.6.
[36] LSSAC 2000, cl.3.7.

3. AUTHORITY

General sources and specific provision

Pre-Convention and post-Convention law

796 Where a person enters into a contract as an intermediary, purporting to act on behalf of another, his authority to do so and the effect for his would-be principal depend initially on the general law of agency.[37] It must be remembered that the general law applies unless it is displaced. For the International Salvage Convention 1989, Art. 6.2 makes important, but not entire, provision for the consequences of acts of intermediaries in entering salvage contracts. Article 6.2 provides:

> "The master shall have the authority to conclude contracts for salvage operations on behalf of the owner of the vessel. The master or the owner of the vessel shall have the authority to conclude such contracts on behalf of the owner of the property on board the vessel."

So far as it provides, therefore, and only to that extent, the Convention displaces the general law of agency. However, the Convention itself concedes that its provisions may generally be displaced by contract.[38]

LOF 2000

797 As is to be expected, LOF 2000 contains provisions turning on the role of intermediaries. First, the closing boxes on the face of LOF 2000 provide the opportunity to identify the persons concluding the contract. Box 8 is for completion by the "Person signing for and on behalf of the Contractors" and Box 9 has space for the name of the "Captain [followed by a blank space] or other person signing for and on behalf of the property" [followed by another blank space]. At the foot of both boxes a space is indicated for the signature of the relevant persons. LOF 2000, cl. K then states:

> "*Scope of authority*: The Master or other person signing this agreement on behalf of the property identified in Box 2 enters this agreement as agent for the respective owners thereof and binds each (but not one for the other or himself personally) to the due performance thereof."

798 Three points may be made about the effect of these provisions in LOF 2000.

---

[37] See generally F. M. B. Reynolds, *Bowstead and Reynolds on Agency* (16th ed., 1996).

[38] "The Convention shall apply to any salvage operations save to the extent that a contract otherwise provides expressly or by implication" (Art. 6.1), though "Nothing in this Article shall affect the application of Article 7 [Annulment and modification of contracts] nor duties to prevent or minimise damage to the environment."

The first is that they are ineffective to *impose* liability on the would-be principal of the person entering the agreement. They will do so if he had authority; but he will not have authority simply by agreeing on the basis of a document which states that he has authority. However, by entering into an agreement stating that he had authority when this was untrue, he may incur liability for breach of warranty of authority.[39] In the vast majority of cases in practice, the intermediary will have authority and there will be no difficulty with these provisions. Their main effect, therefore, will be to *declare* or *define* the status of the intermediary.

Their definitional role may, however, have a further consequence, in *excluding* liability—by making it clear that the person signing the agreement is not acting as an agent for anyone other than the specified principals.[40]

Thirdly, LOF 2000 appears to assume that the contract will be signed on or on behalf of both parties. However, it is not necessary for LOF 2000 or any other salvage contract to be signed in order to be valid. Indeed, even where a contractual document is signed, it is not uncommon for the contract to be concluded orally and signed later.

LSSAC 2000

LSSAC 2000 is designed to remove from the main LOF 2000 agreement provisions concerning matters arising after termination of salvage operations, principally security, arbitration and payment. However, it also contains certain "General Provisions". In particular, clause 13 provides that the contractors may claim salvage on behalf of their employees and any other servants or agents who participate in the services and on behalf of authorised sub-contractors[41] including their employees, servants and agents.[42] An agreement between the Contractors and the salvees: cannot confer authority upon the Contractors to claim on behalf of designated third parties; does not create a right to salvage on behalf of those third parties if they are not otherwise entitled to claim[43]; and does not prevent such third parties enforcing their own claims. This last point is acknowledged by the fact that LSSAC 2000, cl.13 requires Contractors bringing such claims, if required by the salvees, to provide an indemnity against claims being brought directly by the relevant third parties.[44]

799

---

[39] See further *post*, § 802.

[40] In fact, the drafting of LOF 2000, cl.K opens the possibility of an argument, if an owner signs the agreement, that he will not himself be liable under it ("The Master or other person signing this agreement . . . enters this agreement as agent for the respective owners thereof and binds each (*but not . . . himself personally*) . . .)" (emphasis added). It is unfortunate that a clause obviously contemplating the role of an intermediary who was not an owner should be drafted so as to be apparently applicable to owners as well.

[41] Under LSSAC 2000, cl.13.2. See *post*, § 1036.

[42] LSSAC 2000, cl. 13.1 and 13.2.

[43] Although the Contracts (Rights of Third Parties) Act 1999, in certain circumstances, enables contracting parties to confer legally enforceable rights on third parties, the object of LSSAC 2000, cl.13 is not to do this but, as between the contracting parties, to authorise the Contractors to claim against the salvees in respect of independently valid third party salvage claims.

[44] LSSAC 2000, cl. 13.1 and 13.3.

General principles

800 The paradigm position in English law is where an intermediary, acting with authority to bind his principal, enters into a transaction with a third party which creates a binding relationship between the principal and the third party. Except in certain circumstances, the agent is not a party to a contract so concluded and therefore generally without rights against or obligations towards the third party: this is undoubtedly the position under LOF 2000, cl. K of which stipulates that the agreement does not bind him personally. However, the agent and his principal normally have rights and obligations *vis-à-vis* each other because of their relationship. An agent should, personally, carry out his instructions with due skill and care, in his principal's best interests, and indemnify him against any liability which he wrongfully causes him. For his part, the principal must pay his agent any sums due for performance of his duties and indemnify him for liabilities incurred in consequence. The agent also normally has a lien for claims against the principal over property of the principal coming into his hands during the agency.

The most important aspect in practice is the extent of an agent's authority to conclude a contract between the third party salvor and the salvee as principal.

Types of authority

Agent's actual authority, express and implied

801 An agent must perform the duties given to him *expressly*; and he must not exceed their limits, otherwise he will be liable to his principal.[45] A master's express instructions may be given generally, in his contract of employment or from his owners' standing orders, or specifically, with respect to a particular act. Inevitably, express instructions will not be given on every detail of his activities, but he has *implied* authority to do such acts as are necessary in order to enable him to discharge his express duties. Such express and implied authority, which together are commonly referred to as *actual* authority,[46] empower an agent to enter into a transaction with a third party which binds his principal and the third party. It is possible for the agent additionally to become personally bound to the third party, and to acquire rights against him, but this will not usually be the case. Of course, a third party will often be unaware of the extent of the authority which a principal has conferred upon his agent. However, if the agent has actual authority, the third party's ignorance of it is no objection to holding the transaction valid. If the agent has acted without authority, his principal should generally not be bound.

---

[45] *The Hermione* [1922] P. 162.
[46] However, authority of necessity, where present, also forms a species of actual authority: see *post*, §§ 804–808. So, in another sense, does apparent authority: see *post*, §802.

Types of authority

Breach of warranty of authority

802 Moreover, an intermediary cannot acquire authority by his own representation that he has authority.[47] In such a case, neither his principal nor the third party will be bound by the intended transaction, and the intermediary will be liable to the third party for damages for breach of warranty of authority.

Apparent, or ostensible, authority

However, if the third party acts on a representation by the principal that the intermediary does have authority, which may be in cases where the intermediary has actual authority for other purposes, the intermediary will be considered to have apparent, or ostensible, authority to bind his principal.

Usual authority

803 The doctrine of apparent authority, or a separate rule of "usual authority", may apply in the controversial situation where an agent is placed in such a position that he would usually be empowered to bind his principal. In *Watteau v. Fenwick*,[48] the purchasers of a public house appointed the vendor as their manager and he remained as licensee, his name being painted over the door. He was permitted to buy bottled ales and mineral waters for the business but expressly forbidden to buy any other goods, which were to be supplied by the owners. He nevertheless bought cigars from the plaintiffs, who were held to be entitled to recover the cost from the owners. Wills J. said[49]:

"I think that the Lord Chief Justice [Lord Coleridge C.J.] during the argument laid down the correct principle, *viz.*, once it is established that the defendant was the real principal, the ordinary doctrine as to principal and agent applies—that the principal is liable for all the acts of the agent which are within the authority usually confided to an agent of that character, notwithstanding limitations, as between the principal and the agent, put upon that authority. It is said that it is only so where there has been a holding out of authority—which cannot be said of a case where the person supplying the goods knew nothing of the existence of a principal. But I do not think so. Otherwise, in every case of undisclosed principal, or at least in every case where the fact of there being a principal was undisclosed, the secret limitation of authority would prevail and defeat the action of the person dealing with the agent and then discovering that he was an agent and had a principal."

---

[47] Except to a very limited extent, where the principal has put the agent in a position where third parties are reasonably entitled to rely on the agent's representation that he has authority to perform certain acts.
[48] [1893] 1 Q.B. 346.
[49] *ibid.*, 348–349.

However, this proposition is notoriously controversial. Authority which would usually be exercisable by an agent in the position of the intermediary in question can normally be explained in the circumstances as implied actual authority or apparent authority, rather than as an independent type of authority.[50] In any event, the proposition in *Watteau v. Fenwick* is unlikely to be of importance in a salvage case because it is only expressed to bind an undisclosed principal and the circumstances would be extremely rare where a salvor believed himself to be contracting with a person as principal when that person was intending to act as an agent.

Authority of necessity

804 The doctrine of agency of necessity, developed primarily and most opportunely in circumstances involving sea transit but which may be part of a wider doctrine of necessitous intervention, recognises that a person may be bound by acts done on his behalf in an emergency in the following circumstances.[51]

805 There must be an emergency, the force of circumstances which determine the course which has to be taken as a matter of urgency[52]—not necessarily an irresistible compelling power but, on the other hand, certainly not merely circumstances where action is expedient or generally reasonable, albeit such action as is taken must be reasonable and prudent in the circumstances. Thus, in *The Pa Mar*,[53] a case in which the vessel was experiencing problems with her generators, Clarke J. held that it did not necessarily follow from the fact that it was prudent to take towage assistance that it was prudent to take salvage assistance; but, where no towage assistance was available on commercial terms, so that the vessel would be indefinitely immobilised without engaging a tug on LOF terms, then it was necessary to take salvage assistance.

It must be impracticable, though not necessarily impossible, to obtain proper instructions from the defendant.[54] The defendant's failure to give any instructions when apprised of the situation may be sufficient.[55]

806 The plaintiff must act bona fide in the interests of the defendant and not officiously, simply out of self-interest. Thus, a lienee cannot recover expenses incurred solely to preserve his lien.[56] But a plaintiff who acts from mixed motives may be able to recover if he acts primarily for the defendant's benefit, or possibly even if he can merely shew that the defendant received *a* benefit

---

[50] See *The Rhodian River* [1984] 1 Lloyd's Rep. 373; [1978] J.B.L. 410.
[51] See generally Rose (1989) 9 O.J.L.S. 167; Goff & Jones, Chap. 17.
[52] *Australasian Steam Navigation Co. v. Morse* (1872) L.R. 4 P.C. 222, 230.
[53] [1999] 1 Lloyd's Rep. 338, 360, 361.
[54] *Beldon v. Campbell* (1851) 6 Exch. 886, 890; *The Winson* [1979] 2 All E.R. 35, 44 (affirmed [1982] A.C. 939, reversing [1981] Q.B. 403).
[55] *The Winson* [1982] A.C. 939, 961–962.
[56] *Somes v. British Empire Shipping Co.* (1860) 8 H.L.C. 338.

from his acts.[57] In *The Pa Mar*,[58] the master of a vessel in the Red Sea originally agreed an LOF 1990 contract with no specified port of delivery. The vessel's managers then agreed variations of the contract, first, with Dubai/ Colombo as optional ports of destination, then, secondly, adding as a further option Singapore, to where the vessel was eventually towed. Clarke J. held that no reasonable shipowner with the interests of his underwriters and of cargo in mind would have committed the owners of cargo to a LOF contract involving a long tow on salvage terms without carrying out further investigations such as informing class (as the rules required) and asking both the Bureau Veritas and the Salvage Association surveyors to investigate the position. Accordingly, the salvors failed to discharge the burden of proving on the balance of probabilities that the vessel's managers acted bona fide and reasonably in the interests of cargo by adding the Dubai/Colombo or Singapore options.

It has been suggested that there must be a pre-existing agency or other relationship between the parties,[59] a factor which would also negative officiousness and which is not inconsistent with the English cases. If the doctrine of agency of necessity is but the most prominent manifestation of a wider doctrine of necessitous intervention, it may suffice if the plaintiff is merely a suitable person to act and who intends to be paid for his acts. That would be consistent with cases on the preservation of life or health,[60] which themselves shew some affinity with the public policy of allowing recovery by persons intervening in an emergency to effect salvage. Of course, the law of salvage entitles a salvor to claim a salvage reward whether or not there is a pre-existing relationship with the defendant.[61] Indeed, if there is, under a pre-existing relationship, a duty to act, the claimant will, as a non-volunteer, be positively disentitled from claiming salvage,[62] although, if acting as an agent, he should be indemnified for expenditure incurred on behalf of his principal. Where three parties are involved, the intermediary is unlikely to have authority to effect relations between the defendant and the third party unless he has a pre-existing relationship with the defendant.

807

The case for the presence of an existing relationship is bolstered by dicta that the plaintiff is under a duty to act in the emergency,[63] although other dicta suggest that, at least in cases involving the preservation of life,[64] including

---

[57] *The Winson* [1982] A.C. 939, 962–963, 965–966. But *cf. Burns Philp & Co. Ltd v. Gillespie Bros. Pty. Ltd* (1947) 74 C.L.R. 148.

[58] [1999] 1 Lloyd's Rep. 338, 363–364.

[59] *Jebara v. Ottoman Bank* [1972] 2 K.B. 254, 271, *per* Scrutton L.J. (actual decision reversed [1928] A.C. 269).

[60] See, *e.g. Re Rhodes* (1890) 44 Ch.D. 94; *Matheson v. Smiley* [1932] 2 D.L.R. 787; *Greenspan v. Slate* (1953) 97 Atl. 2d. 390. *cf. Shallcross v. Wright* (1850) 12 Beav. 558; *Donnelly v. Joyce* [1974] Q.B. 454; *Cunningham v. Harrison* [1973] Q.B. 942; *Griffiths v. Kerkemeyer* (1977) 139 C.L.R. 161.

[61] See *ante*, Chap. 7.

[62] *loc. cit.*

[63] See, *e.g. Australasia Steam Navigation Co. v. Morse* (1872) L.R. 4 P.C. 222, 230; *The Cargo ex Argos* (1873) L.R. 5 P.C. 134, 164.

[64] See, *e.g. Matheson v. Smiley* [1932] 2 D.L.R. 787, 789.

animal life,[65] the duty may be one recognised as arising from the emergency as a matter of public policy. If so, the extent of such public policy may be such that, at least where the plaintiff acts to preserve life, his action could be justified even though a defendant instructed him not to act. The position is, however, more debatable where property is at risk.

808 If the agency of necessity cases are manifestations of a general doctrine of the law of restitution, requiring the defendant to pay for a benefit received at the plaintiff's expense so as to prevent unjust enrichment, the defendant would arguably be under no liability unless the defendant received a real benefit from what was done. The plaintiff would succeed unless, contrary to the requirement of success in the maritime law of salvage, the attempt to guard against the emergency were considered to be a benefit. If, however, the doctrine is a true agency doctrine, or at least there was in the given case a pre-existing agency, the plaintiff should be entitled to the normal agent's indemnity even without success.

A similar problem arises with respect to third parties. An agent is entitled to be indemnified by his principal for expenditure incurred in discharge of his duties but, if he engages a third party on his principal's behalf, the third party can claim directly from the principal. Most agency of necessity cases involve the agent's claim. But, if they are ramifications of a wider doctrine of necessitous intervention, the third party will be able to claim even if the intermediary is not an agent in the strict sense.[66]

Authority by ratification

809 Where an agent has at the relevant time purportedly acted on behalf of, but without authorisation from, a putative principal, no binding relationship is created thereby between the principal and the third party. But the purported principal can validate the transaction *ex post facto* by subsequently ratifying it, in which case it becomes as valid as if the agent initially acted with authority. This appears to be the explanation of *Newman v. Walters*.[67] Where an intermediary signs a salvage contract on behalf of a party from whom he has no authority, the latter, as a recipient of salvage services, will still be liable to pay a reward under the general law but has the opportunity of having his liability determined according to the terms of the contract by ratifying it. This course of action will, however, not be open to such a recipient where the intermediary did not purport to act on his behalf, for the doctrine of privity of contract generally prohibits persons who are not parties to a contract, or at least not designated as such at its conclusion, to take benefits thereunder.[68]

---

[65] *Great Northern Railway Co. v. Swaffield* (1874) L.R. 9 Ex. 132.
[66] See *Hastings v. Seman's Village* [1946] 4 D.L.R. 695.
[67] (1804) 3 Bos. & P. 612. See *ante*, §§ 134–149, 633. See also *post*, §840.
[68] *Keighley Maxsted & Co. v. Durant* [1901] A.C. 240.

Agency and salvage

The general principles of the English law of agency are, as is appropriate in the circumstances arising in practice, as applicable to cases of salvage as to other cases. In 1848, Dr Lushington put it succinctly[69]:

> "The rule of law is, that no person can be legally bound by any contract unless he has entered into it himself personally or through a duly authorised agent, or has by his own act subsequently ratified that contract."

More recently, the same point has emerged from the tenor, though not the precise language, of the judgment of Brandon J. in *The Unique Mariner (No. 1)*.[70]

In that case, the master of the plaintiff's unladen stranded vessel cabled for assistance to refloat her to the ship's managers, who cabled back that they were sending a tug. Another tug, owned by the defendants, offered her services, which were accepted by the plaintiff's master, on Lloyd's Form, in the belief that she was the tug sent by the managers. The plaintiffs claimed, unsuccessfully, that they were not bound by the contract, *inter alia*, on the ground that their master entered it with no authority, either actual or ostensible. Deciding that the master did have authority, Brandon J. stated[71]:

> "The principles of law applicable to this issue can, I think, be stated in three propositions as follows. First, the relevant authority of a master, for the purpose of deciding whether his owners are bound, as against a third party, by an act which he has purported to do on their behalf, is his ostensible, rather than his actual, authority. Secondly, the ostensible authority of a master is the same as his implied actual authority, unless the latter has been restricted by express instructions from his owners or their representatives, and the third party concerned is, or should be taken to be, aware of such restriction. Thirdly, the implied actual authority of a master, unless restricted by such instructions lawfully given, extends to doing whatever is incidental to, or necessary for, the successful prosecution of the voyage and the safety and preservation of the ship."

A ship's master has all the actual authority expressly conferred upon him, plus the necessary implied authority. It is unlikely to occur to the shipowner that it is necessary to confer upon the master authority to conclude salvage contracts, which may therefore properly be regarded as part of the master's implied actual authority, a necessary incident to the discharge of his primary duty to navigate the ship safely to its destination. Indeed, it may be regarded as a term implied by law into the master's contract of service that he can and

---
[69] *The Charlotte* (1848) 3 W.Rob. 68, 74.
[70] [1978] 1 Lloyd's Rep. 438.
[71] *ibid.*, 449.

even must conclude such contracts when necessary,[72] as Brandon J.'s third proposition relates. A principal is at liberty to restrict his agent's actual authority, as his Lordship notes, so prima facie a shipowner will not be liable on a contract concluded by the master without authority.

813 Such a contract is, nevertheless, likely to bind the owner as one concluded by virtue of the master's ostensible authority. Such authority is created by a principal's representation that an intermediary has authority, thereby creating an agency where none previously existed or—as in the case of the ship's master—extending the authority of an existing agent. Since the shipowner's representation estops him from denying that the master had authority, a limitation on the master's actual authority of which the third party salvor was unaware will be irrelevant to the shipowner's liability on the salvage contract (albeit the master himself will be liable to his owner for his breach of duty). If the salvor is aware of the limitation, or should be taken to be so (which will rarely be the case),[73] the relevant alleged ostensible authority simply will not, because it does not appear to, exist. In practice, the appointment of a person as a ship's master will clothe him with the ostensible authority to conclude salvage contracts and this will normally coincide with actual implied authority to do so. The master usually has such authority and indeed, the situation is analogous to that in *Watteau v. Fenwick*,[74] for what that is worth.[75] But, although the doctrine of ostensible authority normally operates to extend an agent's authority, it is, with respect, perhaps restrictive to give more prominence to a master's ostensible than his actual authority, for a principal can increase his agent's actual authority, and therefore be bound by acts so authorised, without creating any ostensible authority to do those acts. Too close adherence to Brandon J.'s first proposition is, therefore, likely to be undesirably restrictive in practice and it is submitted that his Lordship's dictum should be read as a summary of the normal application of the relevant principles to salvage situations rather than a redefinition of the generally applicable law.

Salved vessel's master's power to bind shipowner

814 The owner of the distressed vessel is, of course, the most obvious person able to bind himself by a salvage agreement. In practice, the agreement will be concluded by an agent on his behalf. In most cases, this agent will be the ship's master. But it need not be so and is less likely to be so than in the past now that instantaneous communications enable the owner or his managing agents to be quickly appraised of the circumstances and likewise able to communicate with the salvor to agree a contract. An authorised agent other

---

[72] See *Liverpool City Council v. Irwin* [1977] A.C. 239 as to the implication of terms into contracts.
[73] The courts have always set their faces against the extension of constructive notice to commercial transactions. See, *e.g. Manchester Trust v. Furness* [1895] 2 Q.B. 539.
[74] [1893] 1 Q.B. 346.
[75] See *ante*, §803.

than the master is as capable of concluding a valid salvage contract as the master.[76] There being no formal requirements in law for salvage contracts, a verbal agreement is sufficient, though it is usual for the agreement to be reduced into writing. Frequently, the master on the spot will sign Lloyd's Form to record a verbal agreement previously concluded by managing agents. The difficulties that this can cause are considered below.[77] In cases where the shipowner is not bound by a salvage contract, because it was concluded without authority, he will of course be liable at common law for salvage services provided.[78]

The master is appointed to command the ship, as the owner's agent, and his rights and liabilities are governed in general by the law of agency. In particular, Lord Blackburn has said[79]:

815

> "The contract of the shipowner is to carry the goods to their destination. In *Beldon v. Campbell*[80] it is said by Parke B. with, I think, perfect accuracy, 'There is no doubt of the power of the master by law (but some as to what extent it goes) to bind the owner. The master is appointed for the purpose of conducting the navigation of the ship to a favourable termination, and he has, as incident to that employment, a right to bind his owner for all that is necessary, that is, upon the legal maxim, *quando aliquid mandator, mandatur et omne per quod pervenitur ad illud.*' "

In *The Renpor*,[81] Brett M.R. said that:

> "there are two circumstances necessary in order to make an agreement binding on an owner; first, the contract must be made under a necessity; and secondly, it must be made for his benefit."

In *The Crusader*,[82] Kennedy L.J. said:

> "It is true, however, that a salvage agreement, in order to be binding on the shipowner, must satisfy the requirements mentioned in the judgment of Lord Esher in *The Renpor*. It must be made honestly for the benefit of ship and cargo. There must also be a necessity, in the sense not of an

---

[76] See, *e.g. Anderson Tritton & Co. v. Ocean Steamship Co.* (1884) 10 App. Cas. 107, 116. Standing orders provide for the signature of Lloyd's Form by commanders of Crown Ships. See *ante*, §781.

[77] §§ 916 *et seq.*

[78] See *The Leon Blum* [1915] P. 90 and other cases in this section. See also *Hingston v. Wendt* (1876) 1 Q.B.D. 367.

[79] *Anderson Tritton & Co. v. Ocean Steamship Co.* (1884) 10 App. Cas. 107, 116. See also *The True Blue* (1843) 2 W. Rob. 176, 179–180; *The Africa* (1854) 1 Spinks E. & A. 299, 300; *The Henry* (1851) 15 Jur. 183, 183; *The Arthur* (1862) 1 M.L.C. 228, 228; *The Waverley* (1873) L.R. 3 A. & E. 369, 378; *The Prinz Heinrich* (1888) 13 P.D. 31, 33; *The Margery* [1902] P. 157, 165.

[80] (1851) 6 Ex. 886, 889.

[81] (1883) 8 P.D. 115, 118, applied in *The Mariposa* [1896] P. 273, 280.

[82] [1907] P. 196, 215.

absolute necessity, but of that absence of reasonable alternative which most men mean, I think, when they speak of necessity in cases of this kind."

816 The point has now been enacted by implimentation of the International Salvage Convention 1989, Art. 6.2 of which now provides specifically that "The master shall have the authority to conclude contracts for salvage operations on behalf of the owner of the vessel." This authority is, however, subject to Article 6.1, which stipulates that "This Convention shall apply to any salvage operation save to the extent that a contract otherwise provides expressly or by implication."

The master's authority to take reasonably necessary action on behalf of his owner entitles him to conclude, *inter alia*: a salvage contract on Lloyd's Form, leaving the amount of reward to be determined; a contract for an agreed amount of salvage[83]; or an agreement obliging his owner to pay for towage though the vessel is lost so no salvage would have been payable, for the agreement might have avoided liability for a substantial reward if salvage had been successful.[84]

Reasonable necessity[85]

817 Although the master has no actual authority to engage non-necessary services, he may, by virtue of being the owner's representative on the spot, presumably in the best position to decide on the necessity for salvage, have ostensible authority to bind the owner. Where, in the prevailing circumstances, there is no appearance of the necessary danger, a master is more likely to attempt to conclude, say, a towage rather than a salvage contract. If, exceeding his actual authority, he opts for salvage, it is unlikely to appear to the salvor that he is acting within his ostensible authority so as to bind the owner. This is consistent with the decision in *The Crusader*.[86] A tug was engaged at £60 per day to tow a vessel off a reef but, on arrival of the tug, the master of the vessel, doubting whether the vessel could be got off, declined to accept the services of the tug except on the terms of a "no cure, no pay" agreement. After some discussion, the master and the tug owner's representative concluded an agreement for the vessel to pay £4,000 if she was refloated, which she was on the following day. It was held that the tug owners could only recover in a personal action disbursements plus agency commission, because, on the facts of the case, they were agents of the ship and it was inequitable to allow them to ratify the final agreement. (There was in fact a conflict of interest with that of the shipowner, for whom they were agents.)

---

[83] *The Mulgrave* (1827) 2 Hagg. 77.
[84] *The Alfred* (1884) 5 Asp. M.L.C. 214.
[85] See further *The Pa Mar* [1999] 1 Lloyd's Rep. 338.
[86] [1907] P. 15 (affirmed, *ibid.*, 196).

Sir Gorell Barnes P., at first instance, added[87]:

"that it was an absolutely outrageous bargain for the captain to attempt to make, and that he was acting in an extremely foolish way. I cannot myself believe—because he is stated to be an intelligent man—that he thoroughly grasped or was adequately informed of the opinion of the position which that placed him in, because it is so obvious that a trifling expense would have enabled him to see whether he was going to get the ship off or not, and he could have waited and then made his big bargain if he thought it necessary. That being so, even if the agent has had his act ratified, and acted quite straightforwardly in making the contract with the master, who was insisting upon it at the time, I do not think that this Court can allow the plaintiffs to ratify and adopt that act so as to give them a right to bring a salvage claim based upon it."

However, in the Court of Appeal, Lord Alverstone C.J., with whom Fletcher Moulton and Kennedy L.JJ. expressly concurred, said[88]:

"The only ground upon which this judgment can be affirmed is that it was not reasonable for the master of the *Crusader*, in the exercise of the full authority which ... I think he has, to enter into the bargain into which he did enter, or, to put it another way, that it was not reasonable for a man who could have got under an existing agreement practically all he got under the new agreement ... to enter into the agreement in question."

Benefit

A contract with the salvors for the purpose of saving only lives without regard to saving any property of the shipowner has been held not to bind the owner,[89] although it may be otherwise where the shipowner is under a continuing obligation to passengers to forward them to their destination.[90] The authorities on the master's power to bind his owners by agreements to settle salvage claims and to submit to arbitration depend on issues of benefit principally and also of reasonableness.

Settlement of claim

It is clear that the master has no authority to pledge his owners' credit for past services for which he is not liable.[91] However, it was accepted in the Court of Appeal in *The City of Calcutta*[92] that the master had power to bind his owners as to the amount of salvage to be paid for services already

---
[87] ibid., 27.
[88] ibid., 209.
[89] *The Renpor* (1883) 8 P.D. 115; *The Mariposa* [1896] P. 273.
[90] *The Mariposa* [1896] P. 273. See *ante*, §§ 234–243.
[91] *The Kilmaho* (1900) 16 T.L.R. 155, 156. *cf. The Alfred* (1884) 5 Asp. M.L.C. 214, 216.
[92] (1898) 8 Asp. M.L.C. 442. See also *The Cumbrian* (1887) 6 Asp. M.L.C. 151. *cf. The Chieftain* (1846) 4 N.o.C. 459.

performed. Most of the authorities on settlements assume this to be so and are principally concerned with the fairness, and therefore the enforceability of the terms of such settlements.[93] However, in *The Elise*,[94] which concerned a master's contracting on behalf of the salvor, Dr Lushington said:

> "although the master of a ship is on land as at sea agent for the crew to bind them by agreement in respect of salvage compensation, I doubt whether he is agent for the owner for that purpose, when the owner is at hand and gives him no authority."

821 In modern times, even if the owner is not present, the use of instantaneous means facilitates rapid communication between the master and the owner. For either reason, the master is unlikely to have authority of necessity, or indeed of any kind, to conclude an agreement as to the *amount* of reward to be paid. It is similarly unlikely to be immediately urgent or reasonable to conclude such an agreement in such circumstances, so the question of benefit will not arise. Of course, an unauthorised agreement which is in fact for the owner's benefit can be validated by him by ratification. If, as is very unlikely, the owner cannot reasonably be contacted and there is some necessity to conclude such an agreement, it should be upheld so long as it is for the owner's benefit.

It is, however, accepted to be the case that, after the provision of salvage services for which the owner is liable, the master has implied authority to conclude an agreement on Lloyd's Form for the resolution of the amount in the usual way. This is assumed to be so in practice and is both reasonable and beneficial to the owner. As shewn in the next paragraph, it is, however, not a point beyond some controversy.

Arbitration

822 It was doubted by the Court of Appeal in *The City of Calcutta*[95] whether a master had power to bind his owners to submit to arbitration on the terms of Lloyd's Form. The case appears to be the first in which the terms of Lloyd's Form were expressly considered and the objection seems to have been on policy grounds[96] which, in the light of arbitrations' having become the

---

[93] See *post*, §941.
[94] (1859) Swab. 436, 440. *cf. Beldon v. Campbell* (1851) 20 L.J. Ex. 342.
[95] (1898) 8 Asp. M.L.C. 442.
[96] The Court of Appeal upheld the exercise of Gorell Barnes J.'s discretion not to stay judicial proceedings. Rigby L.J. said, *ibid.*, 444–445:
> "Assuming as I do that it is not at any rate clear that the master of a vessel has authority to bind his owners to arbitration, that is a very good reason why the discretion should be exercised in the way Barnes J. has exercised it—by not forcing them to go to arbitration. The nature of the tribunal is also a reason in my mind why the discretion should be thus exercised. The character of the arbitrators is by no means called in question and they may, for anything I know to the contrary, give general satisfaction. But, supposing it had been another body of arbitrators, the law would have been the same; we cannot take cognisance of the character of the Committee of Lloyd's. Then it would have been a decided objection, to my mind, that the arbitrators had power under the agreement to raise this lay law suit, as my Lord has called it, and to adjudicate upon their own costs, if any."

Owners of salved cargo, freight, bunkers, etc.

standard means of determining salvage cases and Parliamentary approval of commercial arbitration,[97] no longer seems applicable. If the point were ever taken, it could, moreover, be settled in favour of arbitration in accordance with the principles upon which compromises of disputes claims are generally upheld.[98]

Authority of person other than master to bind salved vessel

Where the master is present and able to act, he is in general the sole person on the spot capable of concluding a salvage contract on behalf of the owner. It is a general rule of the law of agency that an agent should not and cannot delegate his authority, but this is permissible in exceptional circumstances if necessary in the principal's interests, in which case the owner will be bound.[99] Dr Lushington held in *The Crus V*[1]:   **823**

> "Undoubtedly the person who has the whole authority over a vessel is the master, but when he cannot act, from not knowing enough of the requisite language, and applied to the vice-consul of the flag to which he belongs, or to his agents, I am prepared to say that any agreement made by them for the benefit of the owners, if it is a just and equitable agreement, ought to be upheld."

Where the master cannot act, any person who is at the time properly in command of the vessel is in the same position as the master himself in regard to authority to bind the owners.[2] However, in the case of the making of a salvage agreement by some person other than the master or other servant of the shipowner properly in command of the vessel in distress, the agency, in order to bind the shipowner, must be proved. The engagement of a salvor which is unauthorised may nevertheless be ratified by the shipowner.[3]

Owners of salved cargo, freight, bunkers, etc.

The power to bind by an agreement persons, other than the shipowners, who are the owners of cargo, freight or bunkers depends as much on application of the general principles of the law of agency as does the master's power to bind the shipowners.   **824**

Shipowner acting in personal capacity

It must be noted, first, that where the shipowner or his agent purports to contract solely in his personal capacity, the contract will not bind persons who   **825**

---

[97] See the Arbitration Act 1996.
[98] See Treitel, pp. 82–86.
[99] See *De Bussche v. Alt* (1878) 8 Ch.D. 286.
[1] (1862) Lush. 583, 584.
[2] *cf. ante*, §573.
[3] This seems to be the current explanation of *Newman v. Walters* (1804) 3 Bos. & Pul. 612. See *ante*, §§ 134 *et seq.*

are not parties to the contract even if they have an interest in its successful performance. In *Anderson Tritton & Co. v. Ocean Steamship Co.*,[4] a standard form agreement was concluded on behalf of the *Achilles*, stranded on a sandbank on the river Yangtsze, and the vessel *Shanghai*, under which *inter alia* the master of the *Achilles* was to pay the master of the *Shanghai* 10,000 taels whether the *Achilles* was towed off or not. The service was completed and the necessary sums paid. The owners of the *Achilles* subsequently sought to recover from the owners of cargo on board a proportion of the sum paid as a contribution to general average, but unsuccessfully. The House of Lords conceded that the cargo owners were liable to pay to the shipowners a reasonable sum in general average but the latter had no right to make them liable for a specific sum even though it was the one demanded by the salvors and had in fact been paid. If the shipowners had sought to recover as a contribution to the contractual liability to the *Shanghai*, they would inevitably have failed since only the owners of the two vessels, and no other persons, were expressed to be parties to that contract, so the cargo owners were neither subject to its burdens nor entitled to its benefits. In fact, the shipowners failed and a new trial was ordered on the ground that the owners could not make the cargo owners liable for any stipulated sum under the contract with the *Shanghai*, though they were entitled to recover a reasonable sum. Lord Blackburn said[5]:

> "But neither the owners of the ship nor their master have authority to bind the goods, by any contract. The master has, I think, authority to make for his owners all disbursements which are proper for the general purposes of the voyage, and when once those disbursements are paid for, either by the master out of funds belonging to the owners which the master has, or by funds which the owners themselves apply to discharge a contract which they either could not dispute because the master had bound them to make it or did not choose to dispute, I think that the disbursement, in so far as it is a disbursement for the salvation of the whole adventure from a common imminent peril, may properly be charged to general average. But I think that there is neither reason nor authority for saying that the whole amount which the owners of the ship choose to pay is, as a matter of law, to be charged to general average."

826 Similarly, the shipowner who has personally undertaken to pay the whole of a specific amount of salvage cannot claim a reduction of liability to the salvor for the proportion of the value of cargo to the value of the whole property saved. Deciding this point, Butt J. said in *The Prinz Heinrich*[6]:

---

[4] (1884) 10 App. Cas. 107.
[5] (1884) 10 App. Cas. 107, 117.
[6] *The Prinz Heinrich* (1888) 13 P.D. 31, 33–34.

Owners of salved cargo, freight, bunkers, etc.

"It has also been argued on behalf of the defendants that they are not liable to pay this amount, because it is one agreed on for the whole of the salvage, and that the shipowners have only to bear the same proportion as £3,500, the value of the ship, bears to £14,000, the value of the cargo. To that proposition I could under no circumstances assent. Even if my opinion were different, I consider that the owner of *The Prinz Heinrich* have so conducted themselves as to make themselves liable. I refer to the negotiations, the appointment of arbitrators and the deposit of the sum of £2,200 in a bank, all of which circumstances would tend to make the defendants now liable for the entire sum, if they were not so originally. The result has been to put the plaintiffs to rest in this matter, to lead them to believe that this claim was safe. It is wholly unreasonable to expect them, some two years after the services have been rendered, to obtain the larger part of the reward by arresting such portions of the cargo as they might chance to find after this lapse of time. But further, I am of opinion that when the captain of a ship reasonably and properly enters into an arrangement for the salvage of a ship for a particular sum he binds the shipowners to pay the agreed amount. The cargo is on board, and the shipowners need not part with it till they have obtained security for any payments which they may have to make or have made in respect of it."

827 Just as persons who are not parties to a salvage agreement are not subject to its burdens, so they cannot take its benefits. In *The Leon Blum*,[7] a vessel carrying cargo was being towed under a contract made between the owners of the tug and of the tow on the terms "no cure, no pay, no salvage charges" when, before completion of towage, a danger arose in respect of which the tug rendered salvage services. The owners and master of the tug were held entitled to recover salvage from the *cargo* owners. Indeed, if the owner or master of a carrying vessel cannot be regarded as an agent of the cargo owners, it seems that they will be unable, even if purporting to contract for such a benefit on behalf of the cargo owners, to protect the cargo owners from liability to salvors.[8]

Authority to bind persons other than shipowner

828 *Anderson Tritton & Co. v. Ocean Steamship Co.*[9] supports the proposition that the master has no general authority to contract on behalf of cargo owners or other persons apart from the shipowner unless he is expressly authorised.

---

[7] [1915] P. 290. *cf. The Queen Elizabeth* (1949) 82 Ll.L.Rep. 803.
[8] See *Scrutton Ltd v. Midland Silicones Ltd* [1962] A.C. 446; *New Zealand Shipping Co. Ltd v. A. M. Satterthwaite & Co. Ltd (The Eurymedon)* [1975] A.C. 154; Rose (1975) 4 Anglo-Am. L.R.7; *Port Jackson Stevedoring Pty. Ltd v. Salmond & Spraggon (Australia) Pty. Ltd, The New York Star* [1981] 1 W.L.R. 138; (1981) 44 M.L.R. 336; Treitel, pp. 577–587.
[9] (1884) 10 App. Cas. 107; *ante*, §825.

The difficulty might appear to be overcome by a contract such as LOF 2000, cl. K of which states that:

> "The Master or other person signing this agreement on behalf of the property identified in Box 2 enters into this agreement as agent for the respective owners thereof and binds each (but not the one for the other or himself personally) to the due performance thereof."

However, since an agent cannot confer authority upon himself, the mere fact that the person signing Lloyd's Form purports to contract on behalf of persons other than the shipowner does not settle the problem. One possible solution lies in the fact that all interests which Lloyd's Form purports to bind can authorise the master's act *ex post facto* by ratification—but that leaves the problem posed where a particular party prefers not to be bound by its provisions, quite apart from being an unsatisfactorily indirect and half-hearted method of resolving a general issue, the practical importance of which requires a more straight-forward, acceptable solution.

829 It is certainly the case that, in the absence of express authority, the master is not ordinarily the agent of the owners of cargo laden on board his ship and has in general no authority to make contracts on behalf of the owners of cargo. The view was nonetheless accepted sufficiently widely in practice to appear beyond contradiction that, arising from his duty to safeguard the interests in goods in his possession, the master had, by virtue of the emergency which occurs, such authority of necessity as entitled him, not only to request salvage assistance so as to render cargo-owners liable for salvage at common law but, to bind the owners to the precise terms of the Lloyd's Form contract. His authority of necessity arguably existed, by virtue of the emergency, subject to the conditions set out above, one of which is that he should act reasonably in the interests of his "principals".[10] Lloyd's Form, as periodically revised, is accepted internationally as a reasonable basis upon which to perform salvage services. And the practical difficulties which would be presented by any contrary argument, which would considerably impair the efficacy of Lloyd's Form, might have seemed to be sufficient to counter such an argument.

Moreover, it is doubtful whether Lord Blackburn's dictum in the *Anderson Tritton* case[11] was intended to be as wide as it appears. It was uttered in the context of a case in which, after salvage services had terminated, the master of the salved vessel agreed to pay a certain sum to the the salvors and it was held by the House of Lords simply that the shipowners were only entitled to recover from the cargo-owners such sum as was reasonable, fair and just, and not necessarily the whole of their proportion of the sum agreed. The decision

---

[10] See *ante*, §§ 804–808.
[11] See *ante*, §825.

does not, therefore, deny the master's authority to contract on behalf of cargo in cases of necessity.[12]

Support for such authority appeared in authoritative texts[13] and is implicit in the House of Lords' decision in *The Winson*,[14] discussed fully below.[15] It was also supported by dicta in *The Gaetano and Maria*,[16] a bottomry case, of Brett and Cotton L.JJ. According to the former[17]:

830

> "I doubt myself (but it is not necessary to decide in this case) whether the master is ever the agent of the owner of the cargo. The master is the agent of the owner of the ship, and it may be that the master, as agent of the owner of the ship, has certain rights with regard to the cargo. But suppose that the master can be under circumstances of necessity the agent of the owner of the cargo, out of what does the authority of the master arise? Now this authority of the master of the ship to hypothecate the ship or cargo is peculiar. It does not arise merely out of a contract of bailment, for that contract gives no such right. It does not arise even out of a contract of carriage on land. I doubt whether it arises on a contract of sea carriage, where it is all within the realm, but it is not necessary that this should be now decided. It does arise where goods are shipped on board a ship to be carried from one country to another. That is acknowledged by the maritime law of England, and, as far as I know, is equally acknowledged in every maritime country. It arises from the necessity of things; it arises from the obligation of the shipowner and the master to carry the goods from one country to another, and from it being inevitable from the nature of things that the ship and cargo may at some time or other be in a strange port where the captain may be without means, and where the shipowner may have no credit because he is not known there, that for the safety of all concerned and for the carrying out of the ultimate object of the whole adventure, there must be a power in the master not only to hypothecate the ship but the cargo. That the power of the master does not arise out of the bill of lading nor out of the charterparty, because it may exist where there is neither bill of lading nor charterparty. It arises out of the contract of maritime carriage, by the shipment of goods on board a ship for the purpose of being carried from one country to another, and it exists the moment the goods are put on board for such a purpose. It is regulated, and often limited, by terms in the bill of lading or by terms in the charterparty; but unless such terms specifically do away with this authority of the master, the authority of the master exists by virtue of the contract which arises between the shipowner and the cargo owner by the

---

[12] This paragraph was cited with approval in *The Choko Star (No. 2)* [1989] 2 Lloyd's Rep. 42, 49, *per* Sheen J., whose judgment was, however, reversed by the Court of Appeal [1990] 1 Lloyd's Rep. 516.
[13] See, *e.g.* Scrutton (19th ed.), p. 255. *cf.* Carver (13th ed.), para. 1328.
[14] [1982] A.C. 939.
[15] *Post*, Chap. 10.
[16] (1882) 7 P.D. 137.
[17] *ibid.*, 145–146.

shipment of the goods. It is not necessary to decide whether this authority is given to the master by way of contract or by means of the law."

Cotton L.J. said[18]:

"It was said that necessity gives the authority to hypothecate. In my opinion that is putting it wrongly. Necessity is the condition of the exercise of the authority; but, in my opinion, the implied authority arises out of the contract and is not properly given by necessity."

831 The matter came for resolution before the courts in *Industrie Chimiche Italia Centrale v. Alexander G. Tsavliris & Sons Maritime Co. (The Choko Star) (No. 2)*.[19] A demise chartered vessel carrying a cargo of soya beans from Argentina grounded in the river Parana and the master entered into an LOF 1980 contract with European salvors to refloat her. Security was provided and the salvors' claim against the shipowners was subsequently settled by agreement. The cargo-owners objected that the master had no authority to engage salvors on their behalf and continued with arbitration under protest.[20] They subsequently claimed restitution of all moneys paid by reason of the appeal award or alternatively all moneys in excess of a reasonable sum. The preliminary matter of the master's authority to contract on behalf of the cargo-owners came to trial. Following the views expressed in this book, Sheen J. held that the contract of carriage gave the master implied authority, when acting reasonably in cases of necessity, to contract with salvors, and that authority could not be overridden by the cargo-owners. However, his judgment was reversed by the Court of Appeal.

832 The Court of Appeal was apprised of the practical difficulties which could arise from the master's not being able to contract on behalf of cargo-owners. However, it delivered a purist decision on the agency issue by holding that the master had no implied authority to do so, though compromised by acknowledging that the master would have such authority on the basis of agency of necessity where the requirements of that doctrine were satisfied. Apparently fearful of judicial legislation, the Court took notice that there was a proposal to resolve the issue in the then forthcoming Article 6.2 of the International Salvage Convention 1989, which has now reversed their judgment and effectively restored the view previously expressed in this book and the wise and principled judgment of Sheen J.

Accordingly, the position now is that, as Article 6.2 provides, "The master or the owner of the vessel shall have the authority to conclude [contracts for salvage operations] on behalf of the owner of the property on board the

---

[18] *ibid.*, 148–149.
[19] [1989] 2 Lloyd's Rep. 42, *per* Sheen J.; reversed [1990] 1 Lloyd's Rep. 42 (CA); noted R. Munday [1990] L.M.C.L.Q. 1.
[20] See *Industrie Chimiche Italia Centrale v. Alexander G. Tsavliris & Sons Maritime Co. (The Choko Star) (No. 1)* [1987] 1 Lloyd's Rep. 508 (CA); Shaw [1996] L.M.C.L.Q. 202, 211–212; *post*, § 1270.

vessel", subject to the saving in Article 6.1 "that a contract otherwise provides expressly or by implication."

Salving vessel

Master's power to bind owners by salvage agreement

833 The same general principles as govern a master's power to bind the owner of a salved vessel apply to the power of the master to bind the owner of the salving vessel. Obviously, however, the circumstances are not identical, so the salving master is unlikely to have any authority of necessity to bind his owners. If, as is common nowadays, the owners of the salving vessel are professional salvors, the master should have express or implied actual authority. In other cases this need not at all be the case. It is generally accepted, however, that the master does have authority to conclude a contract for the performance of salvage services which is in his owners' interests.[21]

834 However, the master has no authority to bind his owners—at least where the owners are present or there are means of communication with them[22]—by an agreement as to compensation for past services where those services if they stood alone, would give rise to a right for salvage remuneration, for such services create vested rights in the owners which the master is not competent to bargain away. Thus Dr Lushington said in *The Elise*[23]:

> "although the master of a ship is on land as at sea agent for the crew to bind them by agreement in respect of salvage compensation. I doubt whether he is agent for the owner for that purpose, when the owner is at hand and gives him no authority."

835 However, where the master's contract on behalf of his owners relates to a continuous service, where the contract relates to future as well as to past services and, even though the vessel should be subsequently salved, the part of the service already performed by itself gives no vested right, the court will give effect to the contract so far as it relates to future services.[24] Moreover, it was said by Dr Lushington in 1839 of an agreement to refer assessment for services rendered to arbitration that, although the master had no authority to bind the crew by such an agreement:

> "Now, with respect to the master and the owner of the [salving vessel], it would, I conceive, be decidedly conclusive; as it was clearly competent for the master, within the scope of the authority committed to him, to bind the interest of his employers and *a fortiori* his own."[25]

---

[21] *The Africa* (1854) 1 Spinks E. & A. 299, 300; *The Margery* [1902] P. 157, 165.
[22] *The Elise* (1859) Swab. 436, 440; *The Inchmaree* [1899] P. 111, 117.
[23] *The Elise* (1859) Swab. 436, 440.
[24] *The Inchmaree* [1899] P. 111, especially at 117 (quoted *post*, §838). *N.B.* LOF 2000, in cl.E, expressly purports to apply to both past and future services.
[25] *The Britain* (1839) 1 W. Rob. 41, 43.

Salvage Agreements

Master's power to bind officers and crew by salvage agreement

836   The authority of the master of the salving vessel to bind his officers and crew by a salvage agreement appears to be as follows. A salvage agreement made in respect of past services will not ordinarily bind the crew or the owners. But where the agreement also relates to future services, the court will give effect to so much of it as relates to those services so far as it is not inequitable. This distinction reconciles two lines of first instance authorities.

837   In *The Macgregor Laird*.[26] Sir Robert Phillimore "was of opinion that, when an agreement had been made by salvors belonging to the ordinary class of seamen with the master of the salved vessel, the Court ought to be satisfied that it was entered into with reasonable deliberation, and with adequate knowledge of its meaning and effect, in which case the Court, even if of opinion that the remuneration was too small, would not, except in very extraordinary cases, interfere with it; that when the Court was satisfied that the interests of the crew had been fairly considered, it would be disinclined to disturb such agreement, though of opinion that the sum awarded was less than they would have received at the hands of the Court." In *The Nasmyth*,[27] Butt J. uttered the "opinion that it is against public policy and much to be deprecated that seamen should endeavour to upset such an agreement." In *The Elise*,[28] in which he doubted the master's authority to bind his owners by an agreement made after the service to fix the amount of compensation, Dr Lushington mentioned in general terms that "the master of a ship is on land as at sea agent for the crew to bind them by agreement in respect of salvage compensation." However, in *The Britain*,[29] Dr Lushington opined that, "according to any principles of justice", the master had no authority to bind the crew (as opposed to the owners) by an agreement as to quantum on termination of services. Indeed, in *The Sarah Jane*,[30] after agonising over, on the one hand, depriving mariners of that reward to which they were justly entitled and, on the other, the possible prejudice to the owners of the salved vessel of laying down a rule of universal application that in no case whatever could the master or owner act on behalf of the crew, Dr Lushington went so far as to suggest that "in all ordinary cases of salvage, neither the owners nor the master have a power of binding the crew, without their previous consent."[31]

838   That the authorities support the distinction made above[32] is borne out by the more recent decision in *The Inchmaree*.[33] Tugs rendered salvage services to a

---

[26] [1867] W.N. 308.
[27] (1885) 10 P.D. 40, 43.
[28] *The Elise* (1859) Swab. 436, 440.
[29] (1839) 1 W. Rob. 40, 43–44.
[30] (1843) 2 W. Rob. 110.
[31] *ibid.*, 116.
[32] *Ante*, § 836.
[33] [1899] P. 111, followed in *The Friesland* [1904] P. 345.

Salving vessel

stranded vessel on three tides. Between the second and third tides, the masters of two salving tugs signed agreements for themselves, their owners and crews, "to accept the sum of £20 per tide, and £150 when floated, in full for all claims for rendering assistance to the stranded vessel *Inchmaree*. The agreement to apply as well to past as to future services, and such sum to be paid in full for all salvage and other claims on ship cargo and freight." These tugs would not have been further employed if the masters had not signed the agreements. The vessel came off on the third tide. Phillimore J. upheld the agreement as to services subsequent to, but not previous to, its conclusion, awarding £70, instead of £20, for the first two tides, and £150 for the last. He found that the tug masters did not agree or intend to agree to sell their past rights, then continued[34]:

> "There is the further question of the tugmasters' authority. My view about that matter is that, where there is one continuous service, and some small step has been made in that service—a step which of itself would not give any right to salvage even though the vessel should be subsequently salved—and at some epoch the master of the salved vessel says, 'Now, let us go no further without a bargain, to cover what you have done as well as what you are going to do'—then I think it is within the scope of the authority of the master of the salving vessel to enter into a bargain to cover both the past as well as the future services; because the past service does not stand by itself—it has not by itself given any right, that is to say, in such a case there is no assessable value to give to the past service. But where the service is discontinuous with hours between, in which nothing is done at all, and where the past services give—as in this case—vested rights, because if the plaintiffs' tugs had not towed the *Inchmaree* off and some other salvor had done so, the plaintiffs still would be entitled to payment, then I do not think that the master of the salving vessel has a right to bargain away the rights of his owner, or that of the crew, for those past services. Still less do I think that he has the right to make it part of the condition upon which he and his co-salvors are to be employed for the future services. That is a kind of 'truck' which seems to me to be repugnant to public policy. I think that in this case the masters had no authority to bargain away the past rights of their co-salvors for the sake of being allowed to render the rest of the service.
>
> I, therefore, come to the conclusion that that part of the contract cannot stand, both because it was not agreed to, and because the plaintiffs' masters had no authority. But I do not see why the other half of the contract cannot stand by itself. I do not see how the plaintiffs can complain of getting the sum which their masters were willing to agree to beforehand to take for the chance of rendering the future salvage service;

---

[34] [1899] P. 111, 116–117.

Salvage Agreements

and I do not see why the defendants should complain of paying that sum which they agreed to pay for the future service."

839 In the Court of Appeal in *The Cargo ex Woosung*,[35] Bagallay J.A. and Lush J. expressed the view that the statutory provisions governing salvage by Crown ships,[36] which "are entirely consistent with public policy",[37] appeared to negative the power of an officer commanding a ship belonging to Her Majesty to enter into an agreement on behalf of himself and the crew to salve for half the value of the property preserved. The claim was therefore dealt with without regard to the agreement. In recent years, standing orders have provided for Lloyd's Form to be signed wherever possible.[38]

840 Although a seaman is not bound by a contract purported to be concluded on his behalf but without authority,

"acts done by a person presuming to act as an agent, without previous authority, may become valid by the subsequent recognition of the individual whom such agent professes to represent; and this recognition may be effected either by express assent, or by some act on the part of the individual represented which necessarily carries with it the inference of his approbation and consent."[39]

He may ratify such a contract by receipt from his "agent" of part of the award paid to the latter.[40] But the mere making of an application to that person is not *per se* inevitably a ratification.[41]

Power of owners to bind master and crew

841 The general competence of the owners of a salving vessel to act on behalf of the master and the crew appears to be the same as that of the master to act for the crew. Where there is no reasonable opportunity to consult the crew, an agreement may be made on their behalf for reward for future services,[42] but the owners cannot prejudice the crew's accrued rights to salvage.[43] The owners' power has been expressed to be authority of necessity or implied authority. It does not seem to comply with the requirements of authority of necessity.[44] It is not necessary to imply such a term to give business efficacy

---

[35] (1876) 1 P.D. 260.
[36] See now MSA 1995, s.230.
[37] (1876) 1 P.D. 260, 271, *per* Lush J.
[38] See *ante*, §781.
[39] *The Sarah Jane* (1843) 2 W. Rob. 110, 116 (*per* Dr Lushington).
[40] *The Sarah Jane, supra*.
[41] *ibid*.
[42] *The Margery* [1902] P. 157, 165; *The Friesland* [1904] P. 345, 351; *Huddart Parker Ltd v. The Mill Hill* (1950) 81 C.L.R. 502, 511 (HCA).
[43] *The Inchmaree* [1899] P. 111; *The Friesland* [1904] P. 345, 351.
[44] See *ante*, §§ 804–808.

to the seaman's contract of service, although the tribunal might be encouraged to regard it as a standard implied term in such a contract,[45] given the advantages of the common means of determining salvage questions and the fact that it does not detract from the statutory protection of seamen's interests in salvage.[46] The advantages of Lloyd's Form arbitration are such that in practice owners' agreements of the first kind will be authorised by acquiescence and ratification, if not for any other reason, although Dixon J. has expressed the view in the High Court of Australia[47] that an agreement as to the forum to be available for the assertion of right in respect of salvage services lies outside the scope of any authority that can fairly be implied from the relationship of the master and crew to the owners of a tug and from the exigency of the circumstances. In a later case, the High Court of Australia held that shipowners had no authority to bind their master and crew by an agreement excluding the right to salvage reward.[48]

842 Two dicta of Sir Francis Jeune P. are particularly relevant. In the Divisional Court in *The Margery*,[49] having decided that the master and crew were not parties to, and therefore not bound by, the rules of mutual insurance clubs binding the owners of the salving and the salved vessels, Sir Francis Jeune P. opined[50]:

> "I am not at all prepared to say that under certain circumstances an agreement made by the owners on behalf of the crew might not bind them, just as an agreement made under certain circumstances by the master may bind the owners. It is clear that if, before the salvage service is rendered, the masters of the two ships meet together, they may make an arrangement by which, subject to the jurisdiction of this Court to see whether it is equitable or not, the masters can undoubtedly bind the owners. I should not be prepared to deny that an agreement made under similar circumstances by the owners on behalf of the master and crew might bind the master and crew; but the reason for that is the necessity of the case. The service has to be rendered on the spur of the moment, and if the agreement cannot be made by the only persons who are there to make it, it cannot be made at all. Therefore *ex necessitate* an agreement so made binds; but that is a very different thing from saying that, where there is no stress at all, an arrangement made by the owner binds the master and crew, without any notice to the master and crew. That

---

[45] See *Liverpool City Council v. Irwin* [1977] A.C. 239.
[46] See MSA 1995, s.39; *post*, §§ 1538–1539.
[47] *Huddart Parker Ltd v. The Mill Hill* (1950) 81 C.L.R. 502, 511, referring to *The City of Calcutta* (1898) 8 Asp. M.L.C. 442.
[48] *Fisher v. The Oceanic Grandeur* (1972) 127 C.L.R. 312, 334; [1972] 2 Lloyd's Rep. 396, 407.
[49] [1902] P. 157, on appeal from the Yarmouth County Court.
[50] *ibid.*, 165.

proposition I am not prepared to adopt, nor is that seriously contended."

843 In *The Friesland*[51] he said:

"The effect of the authorities appears to me to be this, that before such a service is performed the owners have authority to bind the masters and crew. On what principle that rests I am not very careful to inquire. It may be that it is to be put down to the principle that in the particular circumstances, if a contract is to be made it must be made by the owners without communication with the master and crew, because no communication can be made with them; and therefore it is just like a bargain made by the master *ex necessitate*, which binds the owners, in the particular circumstances of the case. That may be the principle which enables the owners to bind the master and crew for future services, though they in no way acquiesce. Again, that may not be the real principle. It may be that when the master enters into service there is an implied contract by which the owners can bind him. It can only apply, however, to ordinary services. Where there is something special, out of the course of a man's ordinary employment, I should be very slow to think that there could be any authority of that kind, and I am not sure whether all salvage would not be considered to be outside an ordinary agreement. Whatever be the principle, I think the authorities are pretty clear that as regards future services the owners can bind the master and crew by an agreement to which the master and crew are not parties,[52] but I think it is otherwise as to past services. Here services had been done, or partly done, of a salvage kind, giving independent rights, and the owners cannot bargain away the vested rights of the master and crew by a bargain in which the master and crew do not acquiesce. That, I think, is the result of the various authorities upon this point."[53]

844 Just as owners have no authority to bargain away rights to salvage already vested in the master and crew, it was held at common law,[54] and in the case of seamen confirmed by statute,[55] that owners are unable to bind the master and crew that they should not in any circumstances receive salvage remuneration. The owners' authority is only exercisable in, and not against, the interest of the master and crew.

---

[51] [1904] P. 345, 351.
[52] Presumably as principals. The agreement should not bind them at all if it is not expressed to do so.
[53] The authorities cited were *The Britain* (1839) 1 W. Rob. 40; *The Sarah Jane* (1843) 2 W. Rob. 110; *The Nasmyth* (1885) 10 P.D. 41; and *The Inchmaree* [1899] P. 111. See *ante*, §§ 833–840.
[54] *The Leon Blum* [1915] P. 90, (affirmed, *ibid.*, 290).
[55] See now MSA 1995, s.39. See *post*, §§ 1538–1539.

Agreement with one of several salvors or salvees

Where there are several salvors, or several sets of salvors, if the only **845**
relation between them is the temporary association in the work of the salvage
service, a salvage agreement made by the master of the vessel in distress with
one of them will only bind others if it has been concluded on their behalf and
with their authority. The mere accident of co-operation in the salvage service
gives no one of the salvors any implied agency to contract with the representatives
of the vessel to be salved on behalf of his co-salvors. Similarly, the
signature of a salvage agreement by one salvee or his agent will only bind
other salvees where it purports to do so on its true construction and the person
entering into it had authority to do so on their behalf.

Notification to principal

Where an agent enters into a contract on behalf of his principal with the **846**
latter's authority, the principal is generally bound by the contract as soon as
it is made, whether or not he is aware of it. However, it is of course in the
interests of both contracting parties and of the agent that all parties are aware
of the full position as soon as possible, particularly if preparations need to be
made for performing contractual obligations. Accordingly, LOF 2000 contains
an Important Notice 1, headed "Salvage security", which provides *inter alia*
that, "As soon as possible the owners of the vessel should notify the owners
of other property on board that this agreement has been made."

4. TERMS OF AGREEMENT

Parties to a contract will be bound by the express terms of their contract and **847**
by terms implied as a matter of fact and by the general law. However, the
normal scope of the agreement may be qualified by law or by the agreement
itself. These issues are discussed elsewhere in this book[56] and need not be
repeated here.

It is important to bear in mind, however, that parties are generally free by
contract to override the general law of salvage. It remains convenient to refer
to persons providing salvage and related services as salvors. But, since the
contract is the primary source of the parties' rights and liabilities, it is
appropriate that salvors contracting on the basis of Lloyd's Form and the
SCOPIC clause are designated therein as "the Contractors" or "the
Contractor".[57]

---

[56] See in particular Chaps. 8–12.
[57] LOF 2000 and SCOPIC 2000 are not consistent as to the use of the plural or the singular but
it seems to make no practical difference. In all previous editions of Lloyd's Form the singular
"Contractor" was used.

Salvage Agreements

848 In practice, salvage contracts are throughout the world entered into on the basis of well-known standard form contracts.[58] It is, nevertheless, generally the case that, no matter how familiar a standard set of terms is, it will only govern a relationship so far as the parties agree. They are generally free to choose whether to use a standard form or not; and, if a standard form is used, which type and which edition. In most instances throughout this book, references are made to the latest edition of Lloyd's Form available when the book was written. Where parties orally agree to be bound by the terms of Lloyd's Form without specifying which edition, they will be assumed to have agreed to the terms current when the contract was made.[59] However, parties are free to use an earlier or later version.[60] Moreover, whichever edition they use, they are free to modify the terms governing their relationship, though the Council of Lloyd's is unlikely to appoint an arbitrator if there is significant alteration of the standard terms.

LOF 2000

849 Earlier versions of Lloyd's Form were mainly concerned with the details of referring salvage questions for decision by arbitration plus attendant security issues. Inevitably, other terms were added and the document grew in length. An innovation with LOF 2000 is that most of the first of its two pages contains a number of boxes to be completed by the parties with the main details peculiar to their particular contract, namely: the names of the salvors[61] and vessel[62] and of the persons signing on their behalves[63]; the date[64] and place[65] of the agreement; and (if they so decide) the agreed place of safety,[66] the agreed currency of any arbitral award and security[67] and whether the SCOPIC clause is incorporated.[68] The remainder of LOF 2000 comprises 12 short clauses (A–L) plus two Important Notices.

850 There are separate sets of detailed terms on security, arbitration and procedure. These are specifically designed as part of the regime governing Lloyd's Form of salvage contract and not to have independent existence. They could therefore simply have been added to LOF 2000. However, it was thought a good idea to keep LOF 2000 itself fairly short by relegating these details to separate documents. LOF 2000 therefore always incorporates by reference[69] two further sets of terms, namely Lloyd's Standard Salvage and

---

[58] *e.g.* Lloyd's Form.
[59] *The Geestland* [1980] 1 Lloyd's Rep. 628, 629.
[60] Accordingly, reference is also occasionally made in this book to the terms of earlier editions of Lloyd's Form.
[61] Box 1.
[62] Box 2.
[63] Boxes 8 and 9.
[64] Box 5. The date of the Agreement will determine which version, if any, of the SCOPIC Clause is incorporated: LSSAC 2000, cl.3.9.
[65] Box 6.
[66] Box 3.
[67] Box 4.
[68] Box 7.
[69] LOF 2000, cl.I; LSSAC 2000, cll. 1.1 and 6.1. And see LOF 2000, Important Notice 2.

Arbitration Clauses[70] and Lloyd's Procedural Rules.[71] Again, references throughout this book are to the editions of those terms current when the book was written. The editions of LOF, LSSAC[72] and LPR current when this book was written were all published on the same day, namely September 1, 2000. All three sets of terms are subject to periodical revision. In particular, it is contemplated that the different sets of terms will not necessarily be revised simultaneously. It is, however, provided that Lloyd's Form contracts will be subject to LSSAC and LPR as revised from time to time.[73] For clarity, therefore, it is made clear throughout this book that references herein are to the 2000 editions.

Similarly, it is a matter for agreement, when a contract on LOF 2000 terms **851** is made, whether it incorporates the Scopic (or SCOPIC) Clause and, if it is incorporated, whether it will actually be invoked.[74] Again, it is stated (oddly, in the LSSAC rather than in LOF or SCOPIC itself) that " 'Scopic Clause' ... includes any replacement or revision thereof. All references to the Scopic Clause in the Agreement shall be deemed to refer to the version of the Scopic Clause current at the date the Agreement is made".[75] Again, for convenience, it is made clear throughout this book that references herein are to SCOPIC 2000.

5. EFFECT OF SALVAGE AGREEMENT

Prima facie effective

General principles

It is a general rule of thumb that a person is assumed to intend the natural **852** consequences of his own acts.[76] Moreover, parties are prima facie bound by their agreements. In particular, though considerably weakened by a large number of exceptions, the parol evidence rule, such as it is, confirms the binding nature of the written expression of an agreement where the parties reduce it to writing.[77] These observations are as applicable to salvage agreements as to other agreements. Thus, where parties have signed a salvage agreement:

[70] See *post*, App. 3.
[71] See *post*, App. 4.
[72] Officially these are referred to as "the LSSA Clauses" (*ibid.*, cl.1.1) but it seems convenient to give them a shorter description.
[73] LSSAC 2000, cll. 1.1. and 6.1. The final draft of LSSAC 2000 was amended to make clear that reference to the LSSAC meant "These clauses ... or *any* revision thereof which may be published with the approval of the Council of Lloyd's" (cl.1.1.; emphasis added). The relevant LPR are those in force at the time the arbitrator is appointed: LSSAC 2000, cl.6.1.
[74] See *post*, §§ 964–965.
[75] LSSAC 2000, cl.3.9.
[76] *cf.* Phipson on Evidence, (15th ed., 2000), §15–08.
[77] See Chitty, §§ 12–094 to 12–103; Treitel, pp. 175–183.

"*prima facie* unless the contrary be proved, they must be considered to be cognisant of the contents of the instrument, and to have intended to bind themselves accordingly to its tenor. This is the natural presumption, and is also the presumption of law."[78]

More generally, Dr Lushington has said that[79]:

"The principle upon which the Court acts is, that if satisfied that an agreement has been made, it will carry it into effect unless totally contrary to justice and the equity of the case."

In a previous case, he stated[80]:

"Now I entertain no doubt whatever, that an agreement of this description can be legally made between a master of a vessel in distress, and persons affording a salvage assistance, provided there be a clear understanding of the nature of the agreement; that it is made with fairness and impartiality to all concerned; and that the parties to it are competent to form a judgment as to the obligations to which they are binding themselves. Such an agreement, I feel no hesitation to pronounce, would be a binding instrument, not to be disturbed by a judgment of this Court. On the contrary, it would be the duty of the Court to enforce the fulfilment of such an agreement, and I am borne out in this opinion by the authority of Lord Stowell, in the case of *The Mulgrave*."[81]

The decision in *The Mulgrave*[82] was that a person who provided services under a contract for an agreed sum could not subsequently claim salvage, albeit he could have done so if there had not been a contract.[83]

Independent assessment different

853 Once a salvage agreement has been made, it should normally be given effect according to its true construction.[84] The court will not decline to give effect to a salvage contract which appears otherwise unobjectionable merely because in the circumstances which have in fact happened it would, but for the contract, have awarded as salvage a somewhat greater or less sum than that which the parties have agreed between themselves or because it turns out that

---

[78] *The True Blue* (1843) 2 W. Rob. 176, 181. See also *The Repulse* (1845) 2 W. Rob. 396, 397. The editors of *Phipson, op. cit.*, doubt whether it is now still accurately considered a presumption of law.

[79] *The Helen and George* (1858) Swab. 368, 369.

[80] *The True Blue* (1843) 2 W. Rob. 176.

[81] (1827) 2 Hagg. 77.

[82] *ibid.*

[83] This meant that the agreement precluded the court from deciding on the merits of the case, not that it deprived it of jurisdiction: *The Catherine* (1848) 6 N.o.C. Suppl. xliii. li–lii. Since the merger of the old courts into one Supreme Court in 1873, the point is no longer of any practical relevance.

[84] See *The True Blue* (1843) 2 W. Rob. 176; *The Repulse* (1845) 2 W. Rob. 396.

either one or the other of the parties might have made a more prudent bargain.[85] If they were such services as were fairly within the meaning of the contract, the mere circumstance that the ease, risk or duration has proved to be greater or less than was expected, when the contract was made, affords no ground for impeaching the validity of the contract or for the court's interference with it. An agreement which was fair and reasonable when made cannot become fair or unfair as a result of circumstances which happened afterwards.[86] The very object of such agreements is to fix by estimate that which in its nature is uncertain and cannot be the subject of accurate calculation.[87] The parties take the risk of any circumstances which may alter the extent of the stipulated service.[88] Thus, Sir Robert Phillimore said[89]:

"I feel as strongly as any of my predecessors in this chair have felt the duty and expedience of encouraging by liberal remuneration all salvage services, but I feel no less strongly the duty and expedience of not allowing a contract deliberately entered into between perfectly competent parties to be set aside by either of them, because the execution of it has turned out more difficult or more easy than was anticipated at the time of making the contract."

In extreme circumstances, however, supervening circumstances may justify the non-enforcement of a salvage agreement.[90]

True salved values different

A salvage agreement will not be set aside, at the instance of either of the parties or of a third party, merely because the salved value turns out to be less than the salvage agreed between the parties. In *The Inna*,[91] a ship exploded in Poole Harbour, damaging property, then sank. A week later, salvors agreed to tow her to Southampton for £1,250. After she was raised, the owners of the damaged property issued a writ *in rem* and arrested her. Shortly afterwards, the salvors issued a writ *in rem* and, on their motion, the court ordered her sale, which realised £578. The salvors obtained judgment for £1,250 and successfully moved the court for payment to them of the proceeds of sale. The salvors' lien had priority over the earlier damage lien of the owners of the damaged property, whose intervention to set aside the agreement was unsuccessful. According to Sir Boyd Merriman P.[92]:

854

---

[85] *The Mulgrave* (1827) 2 Hagg. 77; *The True Blue* (1843) 2 W. Rob. 176; *The Resultatet* (1853) 17 Jur. 353, 354; *The Firefly* (1857) Swab. 240.
[86] *The Strathgarry* [1895] P. 264, 271.
[87] *The Resultatet* (1853) 17 Jur. 353, 354.
[88] *The True Blue* (1843) 2 W. Rob. 176, 180.
[89] *The Waverley* (1871) L.R. 3 A. & E. 369, 380–381. See also *The Jonge Andries* (1857) Swab. 303; *The Cato* (1866) 35 L.J. Adm. 116.
[90] See *post*, §§ 957–959.
[91] [1938] P. 148.
[92] *ibid.*, 156.

"There is no question whatever that the Court can review agreements and substitute some other sum; and there is no doubt that, among other things which could be taken into account in any such review, would be the value of the property salved. But the Court must act upon some principle in these matters, and I cannot find the slightest authority for the suggestion that the mere fact that the salved value of the ship turns out to be less than the amount of the agreed reward is, of itself, any ground whatever for setting aside the agreement and substituting some other sums."

855 The applicable principle was restated by Brandon J. in the later, similar, case of *The Lyrma (No. 2)*[93]:

"In such a case it may turn out that the remuneration so agreed in advance equals, or even exceeds substantially, the value of the salved property at the time and place of termination of the services. Yet, unless the agreement can be impugned on some equitable or other ground, the salvors are entitled to proceed against the salved property in respect of the services and to obtain a judgment for the full agreed amount of remuneration against it; and the result of that will inevitably be that the salvors' judgment, if given priority, will absorb the whole of the value of the salved property, leaving nothing for other claimants of whatever category whose liens attached before the salvage services were rendered."

LOF 2000

856 The difficulties dealt with in the cases in the preceding paragraphs are largely avoided in modern times, when the great majority of salvage agreements are on Lloyd's Form. LOF 2000 purports neither to pre-estimate salved values nor to predetermine the salvage reward but refers these issues to subsequent resolution by arbitration if the parties do not agree them.

Proof

Existence of agreement

857 Since the effect of a valid salvage agreement, whilst not altering the nature of the service, is to preclude the parties from recourse to the court on the merits of the case, where there is dispute as to the conclusion of a binding agreement, the court will insist upon the clearest proof of the allegation that such an agreement has been made. Dr Lushington expressed the position thus[94]:

[93] [1978] 2 Lloyd's Rep. 30, 33–34.
[94] *The Graces* (1844) 2 W. Rob. 294, 297; *The William Lushington* (1850) 7 N.o.C. 361, 363; *The Resultatet* (1853) 17 Jur. 353, 354; *The Arthur* (1862) 1 M.L.C. 228; *The Charlotte* (1848) 3 W. Rob. 68, 72–74. See also *The Salacia* (1829) 2 Hagg. 262, 265; *The True Blue* (1843) 2 W. Rob. 176; *The Africa* (1854) 1 Spinks E. & A. 299; *The Firefly* (1857) Swab. 240; *The Viscount* [1966] 1 Lloyd's Rep. 328. *cf. The Catherine* (1848) 6 N.o.C. Suppl. xliii.

"I need scarcely observe, that the proof of the alleged agreement which has been set up rests with the party who has set it up; and that this proof must be clear and satisfactory, in order to induce the court to depart from the ordinary principles of adjudication, and introduce the agreement instead."

In a more recent, Scottish case, Lord Salveson said that, subject to contrary public policy, shipowners may bind themselves not to claim salvage from each other but that[95]:

"The right to obtain salvage remuneration is one very much favoured in the law, and therefore cannot be excluded unless by express words or by very clear implication from the language used."

This echoes the view of Lord Stowell that[96]:

"This information is peculiarly necessary in a case where the exemption is claimed from a right otherwise universally allowed, and highly favoured in law, for the protection of those who are subjected to it; for it is for *their* benefit that it exists under that favour of the law. It is what the law calls *jus liquidissimum*, the clearest general right that they who have saved lives and property at sea should be rewarded for such salutary exertions; and those who say that they are not bound to reward, ought to prove their exemption in very definitive terms, and by arguments of irresistible cogency."

However, the agreement need not be in writing.[97]

Fairness of agreement

The Admiralty Court has long been concerned that any agreement reached **858** should be fair and equitable and has long claimed jurisdiction to set aside inequitable agreements.[98] Indeed, in one case, Dr Lushington said[99]:

"that it lies upon the party setting it [an agreement for a stipulated sum] up to prove two things: first, that such an agreement was made; and, secondly, that it was just. Where there has been a definite distinct agreement, with ample time for the parties to consider what they are doing, the court would be reluctant to interfere with it, but only under these circumstances."

---

[95] *Clan Steam Trawling Co. v. Aberdeen Steam Trawling* [1908] S.C. 651, 655n.
[96] *The Waterloo* (1820) 2 Dods. 433, 435–436.
[97] *The Graces* (1844) 2 W. Rob. 294, 297; *The Arthur* (1862) 1 M.L.C. 228; *The Firefly* (1857) Swab. 240; *The Cumbrian* (1887) 6 Asp. M.L.C. 551.
[98] See *post*, §§ 925–941.
[99] *The British Empire* (1842) 6 Jur. 608.

However, later judgments of Dr Lushington and others make it clear that the party setting up an agreement does not have to prove the justice of it; the burden is on the other party to impeach it.

859 Brett L.J. made it clear that this burden was not a light one in *Akerblom v. Price, Potter, Walker & Co.*[1]:

> "If the parties have made an agreement, the Court will enforce it, unless it be manifestly unfair or unjust; but if it be manifestly unfair and unjust, the Court will disregard it and decree what is fair and just. This is the great fundamental rule. In order to apply it to particular instances, the Court will consider what fair and reasonable persons in the position of the parties respectively would do or ought to have done under the circumstances."

860 It is significant to note the concern expressed by Dr Lushington that, to be upheld, the agreement must be "honest":

> "The Court is very much indisposed to set aside an honest agreement, but it must be satisfied that the agreement is honest. Where there is any doubt its rule is to adhere to the agreement; and the Court would be just as ready, in favour of salvors, to set aside an agreement, if satisfied that it was wholly inequitable."[2]

On the other hand, it is important to bear in mind his subsequent, albeit somewhat contradictory dictum that[3]:

> "If the evidence be evenly balanced, I must pronounce against the document... but it does not follow, therefore that the document is a forgery."

It is one thing to hold that an agreement is not proved but quite another to say that serious misconduct has been proved. That not only carries an adverse imputation on the supposed forger but is likely to deprive him of his right to salvage remuneration,[4] which is normally independently assessed where no agreement is proved.

Invalidity

861 Though the court is satisfied that a valid salvage agreement has been made, between parties appearing to have been competent to contract,[5] it may nevertheless hold it ineffective because of some vitiating factor.[6] Where that is alleged, the burden of proof shifts to those who seek to invalidate it:

[1] (1881) 7 Q.B.D. 128, 133.
[2] *The Theodore* (1858) Swab. 351, 352.
[3] *The Resultatet* (1853) 17 Jur. 353, 354.
[4] See *post*, Chap. 11.
[5] See generally Chitty, Chaps. 8–11; Treitel, Chap. 13.
[6] See *post*, §§ 876–953.

Admiralty jurisdiction still applies

"The principle on which the Court acts is, that if satisfied that an agreement has been made, it will carry it into effect unless totally contrary to justice and the equity of the case; but the owner of the ship, against whom the agreement is attempted to be enforced, may show that it was improperly obtained. The owner may contend that, under the circumstances, the sum of money was grossly exhorbitant; and, *a fortiori*, if he can show that the agreement was obtained by fraud or compulsion, no Court would hold it to be binding. But when the execution of such an instrument is once proved, it is *prima facie* binding and the burden of proof falls on those who dispute the validity of the instrument."[7]

The same principle applies in relation to allegations that an agreement has been cancelled by consent[8] or that because of supervening circumstances an agreed towage service has become a salvage service.[9]

Admiralty jurisdiction still applies

Even though a salvage agreement is concluded, providing the basis of the rights and obligations of the parties, if all the other elements of salvage are present, it still falls to be applied under the Admiralty jurisdiction and according to the common law of salvage administered by the court. In Dr Lushington's words[10]:

862

"It has been argued, that the agreement was to effect the nature of the service itself: that is utterly impossible. An agreement, if entered into, might be a bar to the parties recovering a salvage reward, because they would have estopped themselves from proceeding in the suit; but to suppose that an agreement can convert that which is originally a salvage service into one of a different nature, is to suppose that which is utterly inconsistent with every principle of law. It is very true that, where a vessel is on shore, in the manner that this was, and where the owners are cognisant of it, and select their own salvors, though they cannot convert a service which from its own nature and kind is inconvertible, yet they may protect themselves against a demand for performing it, by entering into an agreement, and fixing in some way the amount of reward that they shall be paid. This they are fully at liberty to do . . . .

In order to bar [a claim for salvage], there must be a distinct agreement between the parties for a fixed sum, and in explicit terms."

In the House of Lords, Lord Roche said in *Admiralty Commissioners v. Valverda (Owners)*[11]:

863

---

[7] *The Helen and George* (1858) Swab. 368, 369. See also *The Theodore* (1858) Swab. 351, 352; *The Medina* (1876) 2 P.D. 5, 7; *Akerblom v. Price, Potter, Walker & Co.* (1881) 7 Q.B.D. 129, 132–133.
[8] *The Betsey* (1843) 2 W. Rob. 167, 170–172. See *post*, § 956.
[9] *The Betsey* (1843) 2 W. Rob. 167, 170, 172–174.
[10] *The William Lushington* (1850) 7 N.o.C. 361, 362, 363.
[11] [1938] A.C. 173, 202.

"It is true enough that the right to salvage arises independently of and is not based upon contract; but it is untrue to say that where there is a contract as to salvage it ceases to be salvage. Counsel for the respondents was probably not far from the mark in saying that in these days of Lloyd's salvage agreements the larger number of salvages are regulated by agreement. Nevertheless they do not cease to be salvages, and they are dealt with and paid for in accordance with the maritime law of salvage."

864 Special treatment is, however, accorded to an agreement providing for remuneration to be assessed on either a salvage or an alternative basis according to the events which occur. In such a case, the danger to the salvor remains the same, whether he is paid for his services or receives remuneration by means of a salvage award.[12] But the provider of the service does not, as does the ordinary salvor, bear the full risk of obtaining nothing should efforts to salve prove unsuccessful or should the vessel be salved by other means before he can act. So long as there clearly is the possibility of remuneration where there is no salvage,[13] this factor will tend to diminish the award to be made where salvage is earned.[14] As Jeune J. put it in *The Lepanto*[15]:

"the remuneration cannot be considered on what I may call the strict salvage scale, because one of the reasons why salvage is so high is, that it involves this, that unless some of the property is saved, no remuneration is obtainable at all."

865 However, the position is different again where the part of the agreement as to salvage provides for remuneration not to be settled in arrears but of a stipulated amount. In *The Prinz Heinrich*,[16] there was an agreement for £200 for each day of service and a further sum of £2,000 in the event of the stranded vessel's being got off the rocks. Butt J. gave judgment for the full £2,200, stating that he was:

"of opinion that when the captain of a ship reasonably and properly enters into an arrangement for the salvage of the ship for a particular sum he binds the shipowners to pay the agreed amount."[17]

---

[12] See *The Edenmore* [1893] P. 79, 83, *per* Gorell Barnes J.
[13] *cf. The Prometheus* (1949) 82 Ll.L.Rep. 859, where an invalid requisition meant that the shipowners were not entitled to hire from the Crown.
[14] *The Alfred* (1884) 5 Asp. M.L.C. 214; *The Raisby* (1885) 10 P.D. 114; *The Lepanto* [1892] P. 122; *The Kate B. Jones* [1892] P. 366; *The Edenmore* [1893] P. 79; *The Valverda* [1938] A.C. 173, 187–188, 203; *The Prometheus* (1949) 82 Ll.L.Rep. 859 (CA).
[15] [1892] P. 122, 130.
[16] (1888) 13 P.D. 31.
[17] *ibid.*, 30. He distinguished *The Raisby* (1885) 10 P.D. 114, where "Sir James Hannen points out that 'the so-called agreement' did not purport to extend the liability of the shipowners, and that it did not carry the matter further than if the captain of the *Raisby* had accepted the services of the salving ship."

Denial of salvage estopped

Enforcement of such an agreement for a fixed sum is, however, subject to the court's jurisdiction over unconscionable agreements.[18]

Denial of salvage estopped

As a general rule, agreement to be bound by a contract on Lloyd's Form estops the contracting parties from denying that the services provided were not salvage services.[19] In *The Beaverford v. The Kafiristan*,[20] following on a collision, a sister ship of the vessel with which the casualty collided took the casualty in tow. A month after the collision the owners of the towing vessel and the casualty signed Lloyd's Form, which provided that the services were to be rendered and accepted as salvage services on the principle of "no cure—no pay". The owners of the casualty argued that the claimants, as owners of the colliding vessel, were wholly or partly to blame for the collision and so unable to claim salvage for the services rendered by the sister ship. In the view of the House of Lords, whatever the normal position was regarding the claimants' ability to claim a salvage reward,[21] the defendants' signature of Lloyd's Form estopped them from denying that the service rendered was a salvage service meriting a salvage reward.

866

After reviewing the authorities, Lord Wright said[22]:

867

"In my opinion, even if there had not been a Lloyd's salvage agreement executed between the parties, the salvage would have been claimable. But that agreement seems to me to put the matter beyond doubt. I have already observed that its validity is not and could not be contested. It specifically provides for remuneration as salvors in the event of success; there is no reservation for the possibility that the *Empress of Britain* was in whole or in part to blame; I see no ground for implying any such reservation."

Lord Atkin agreed with the opinion of Lord Wright and said[23]:

868

"When the agreement is examined, the terms appear to make it impossible for the defendants to contend that they are not liable to pay for salvage services, whatever may be the legal position if no agreement is made. The first stipulation is by the owner of the salving ship to use his best endeavours to salve the injured ship and her cargo; and for this purpose he is by clause 2 given a licence to use the vessel's gear. The services which he renders under this obligation are to be 'rendered and accepted as salvage services upon the principle of no cure no pay.' This

---

[18] *Post*, §§ 925–953.
[19] See also *The Pa Mar* [1999] 1 Lloyd's Rep. 338.
[20] [1938] A.C. 136.
[21] See *post*, §§ 1096–1103.
[22] [1938] A.C. 136, 153.
[23] *ibid.*, 140.

obviously is intended to prevent any suggestion that they are not salvage services, *e.g.*, that they are simply towage, and I think equally precludes the idea that they are not salvage services at all or, if salvage services, are not to receive any remuneration as such because the contractor's servants have been to blame for the collision."

869 Lloyd's Form currently contains two terms on whether or not services provided are salvage services. LOF 1995, cl.1 states:

"(b) Subject to the statutory provisions relating to special compensation the services shall be rendered and accepted as salvage services upon the principle of 'no cure—no pay'.

(d) In the event of the services referred to in this Agreement or any part of such services having been already rendered at the date of this Agreement by the Contractor to the said vessel and/or her cargo freight bunkers stores and any other property thereon the provisions of this Agreement shall apply to such services."

870 The equivalent terms in LOF 2000 are as follows:

"D. **Effect of other remedies**: Subject to the provisions of the International Convention on Salvage 1989 as incorporated into English law ('the Convention') relating to special compensation and to the Scopic Clause if incorporated the Contractor's services shall be rendered and accepted as salvage services upon the principle of 'no cure-no pay' and any salvage remuneration to which the Contractors become entitled shall not be diminished by reason of the exception to the principle of 'no cure—no pay' in the form of special compensation or remuneration payable to the Contractors under a Scopic Clause.

E. **Prior services**: Any salvage services rendered by the Contractors to the property before and up to the date of this agreement shall be deemed to be covered by this agreement."

871 It is generally the case that a party is only estopped or bound by contract terms to the extent that, on the true construction of the words used, they apply to the circumstances in issue.[24] In the light of that guiding principle, five points can be made about these terms in Lloyd's Form.

First, the services referred to by these clauses are the salvage contractors' basic obligation to use their best endeavours to salve the relevant property and to take it to the place agreed, otherwise to a place of safety.[25] They do not purport to extend to anything else which the contractors might do in relation to the Lloyd's Form contract so as to entitle them to a salvage reward for it.

---

[24] See *Phipson on Evidence* (15th ed., 2000), Chap. 5.
[25] See LOF 1995, cl.1(a); LOF 2000, cl.A. See *post*, Chap. 10.

Secondly, LOF 1995, cl.1(b) and LOF 2000, cl.D make clear that, subject **872**
to the question of special compensation and SCOPIC remuneration (to be
considered below), the services rendered after conclusion of the agreement in
using best endeavours to salve the specified property and take it to the
destination in the Lloyd's Form contract are, as between the parties to the
contract, to be regarded as salvage services.

Thirdly, where the contract is concluded after the services have begun or
commenced, then: (i) in the case of LOF 1995, services rendered prior to the
conclusion of the contract are subjected to the regime laid down by the
contract; but (ii) under LOF 2000, only *salvage* services performed prior to
the conclusion of the contract are deemed to be covered by the agreement.[26]
In other words, all the relevant services performed after conclusion of the
contract are to be treated as salvage services; but, where services are performed before conclusion of the agreement, only those services which are in
fact salvage services are to be governed by the regime of the contract.

Fourthly, LOF 1995, cl.1(b) and LOF 2000, cl.D create no estoppel in **873**
respect of special compensation or (under LOF 2000) SCOPIC remuneration.[27] In fact, services designed to earn, and liability for, such payments are
ex hypothesi not for salvage, so (subject to the fifth point, below)[28] an estoppel
directed to services of a salvage nature should not expose the shipowners to
liability for a salvage reward anyway. However, both editions of Lloyd's Form
are drafted so that the estoppel provisions are set out after the statement of the
salvage contractors' two prime duties (to use best endeavours to salve, and to
prevent or minimise environmental damage); and *ex hypothesi* the estoppel
provisions are designed to treat services which might not qualify for salvage
reward as salvage services. So it was deemed to be at least prudent to make
clear that the environmental services were to be remunerated under the special
provisions relating to them, and not by salvage reward, and that remuneration
for environmental services should not affect the calculation of salvage
remuneration.

Fifthly, it may be necessary to define the range of services which are **874**
subjected to a contractual estoppel such as that contained in Lloyd's Form.
Prima facie this is a matter of construction of the contract. But there may be
a further hurdle to overcome: can a service be treated by contract as a salvage
service if it is not objectively classifiable as one? The issue is narrowed by the
terms of Lloyd's Form, since the estoppel applies to the use of "best endeavours to *salve*",[29] and not to attempts to do anything other than to salve.[30] But

---

[26] LOF 1995, cl.1(d); LOF 2000, cl.E. Though their wording differs, the effect of both clauses is identical; the latter is simply clearer and more elegant.

[27] The separate methods of calculating salvage remuneration, special compensation and SCOPIC remuneration explain the otherwise inappropriate heading of LOF 2000, cl.D as "Effect of other remedies".

[28] *Post*, § 874.

[29] LOF 2000, cl.A (emphasis added). LOF 1995, cl.1(a)(i) is virtually identical.

[30] The further duty to take the property to the agreed place or a place of safety is, it is submitted, parasitic on attempts to salve, and not an independent duty. This is assumed by the SCOPIC clause: SCOPIC 1999, cl.10.

this narrowing of the issue does not eliminate it. For the estoppel is only important for services which may not otherwise qualify as salvage services; if they clearly amount to salvage, the estoppel is unnecessary and therefore irrelevant. One possible approach might be to apply the estoppel to doubtful cases (*e.g.* to towage in circumstances in which there might or might not be the necessary danger) but not to cases where an element of salvage is clearly absent (*e.g.* where contractors under a public duty to the salvee are *ex hypothesi* not "volunteers").[31] But this distinction may be more apparent than real; for, though in the examples given a different requirement of salvage may be missing (danger in the first, voluntariness in the second), both cases turn on the same point (the absence of one of the requirements of salvage) and that is the very point to which the estoppel is directed.

875   It is unlikely that the matter under discussion will give rise to dispute in practice in the case of Lloyd's Form. If it does, two approaches are suggested: (1) that, as a matter of interpretation, the estoppel should be construed as applying to cases in which it is in doubt whether the requirements of salvage are present, rather than to cases in which they are clearly absent; and (2) if the estoppel does apply on the true construction of the agreement, then it should be given effect unless there are overriding vitiating factors (such as fraud or public policy).

6. Vitiating Factors

Introduction[32]

876   Generally, parties are entitled to enter into contracts on whatever terms they wish and judges are bound to give effect to such contracts, whatever their views on whether those contracts should have been concluded or their terms. However, in certain circumstances, the court can hold that a contract is void, voidable, unenforceable or capable of being modified. Nevertheless, the fact that a contract is not given effect, whether at all or according to its original terms, does not mean that one party may not have rights against the other party other than in accordance with their original agreement. In particular, the Admiralty Court has balanced its general willingness not to enforce unfair contracts against the general public policy of encouraging salvage by making salvage awards. Similarly, the Salvage Convention 1989 generally provides that a person carrying out salvage operations which have a useful result is entitled to a salvage payment unless the Convention otherwise provides. Likewise, the common law may allow restitution in cases of failed contracts in order to reverse unjust enrichment.

---

[31] See *Brice*, §8–35. See further *ante*, §§ 533–556.
[32] It is important to stress that the statements in the following two paragraphs are of a very general nature.

Vitiating Factors

877 Thus, where parties are in a contractual relationship, the terms upon which a service is provided will be governed by the original contract or, exceptionally, by the modified or a substituted contract. But, where parties are not bound by contract, either because none was ever made or because it is ineffective, a service provider may still be able to recover payment under the common law of restitution or the Admiralty law of salvage. Yet, just as a claim under contract may be defeated by vitiating factors, so may a claim at law. So, for example, a claimant's misconduct may have double significance: it may defeat both his claim under contract and any remaining claim he might have at law.[33]

Common law vitiating factors

878 It is well known that there are a number of vitiating factors operating in the general law of contract—namely, mistake, non-disclosure, misrepresentation, illegitimate pressure (duress and undue influence), illegality and public policy—and that they are governed by different rules rather than one overarching principle. The common law rules are well developed and therefore at the least afford guidance on similar circumstances relating to salvage contracts, and there is merit in English law's applying similar principles on vitiation to salvage and non-salvage contracts. That in itself does not mean that the two sets of rules are identical, though Brandon J.'s judgment in *The Unique Mariner (No. 1)*[34] indicates that modern commercial salvage contracts should generally be governed by the principles of the ordinary law of contract unless they are displaced by a special rule of Admiralty law or, now, by the terms of the Salvage Convention 1989.

879 A consequence of applying common law vitiating factors is that a contract may be void or avoided at the victim's option, thereby freeing him from an agreement to refer matters to arbitration and increasing the likelihood of the claimant's having no effective corresponding entitlement to payment. On the other hand, the Admiralty court's traditional power to set aside inequitable salvage agreements has always been tempered by the public policy of awarding fair sums where possible, in order to encourage salvage operations. It should therefore not be assumed that the Admiralty Court would be ready to accept the supersession of this policy by the infiltration of common law vitiating factors. The issue is now largely academic: vitiation of salvage contracts is an uncommon issue and in most cases the matter will be governed by the terms of the Salvage Convention 1989. Not only does the Convention apply a general policy of rewarding useful salvage services; by authorising the tribunal to modify, and thereby to prolong, salvage contracts governed by its terms, Article 7 expressly enables the tribunal to reward salvage services under the modified contract.

---

[33] Misconduct is dealt with specifically *post*, Chap. 11.
[34] [1978] 1 Lloyd's Rep. 438.

Salvage Agreements

Admiralty law

880 Previous editions of this book have listed several specific situations where a salvage contract has been rendered ineffective, *viz.*: that it was tainted with fraud; that the salvor was induced to enter into it by the misstatement or non-disclosure, even though non-fraudulent, of a material fact; and that the terms of the agreement were inequitable.[35] However, in *The Unique Mariner (No. 1)*[36] Brandon J. doubted the accuracy of these grounds, especially non-disclosure, or even whether they were correctly presented as separate grounds rather than as ramifications of one general Admiralty jurisdiction.

881 The Admiralty Court has always conscientiously striven to administer the law equitably; that is, fairly.[37] This is an ancient principle governing the exercise of its jurisdiction.[38] It finds expression, in judicial statements as to the proof of the validity of salvage agreements, and in attendant dicta that the court requires to be satisfied that salvage agreements are just and equitable.[39] Despite one early dictum,[40] this does not mean that the court requires it to be proved that a salvage agreement which is proved to exist must also positively be proved to be fair. It signifies the court's recognition of the propriety of disregarding an agreement which is shown for some reason to be inequitable. Nonetheless, even in such a case, the general principle persists, to maintain a balance between the parties: the party standing to be advantaged by an unfair agreement is not penalised for having been a party to such an agreement but retains his basic right to reasonable remuneration in the absence of a binding

---

[35] 4th ed., p. 304. This list there also includes the fact that the agreement has been cancelled by consent of the parties, which is more appropriately dealt with under Discharge: see *post*, § 956.
  In *The Repulse* (1845) 2 W. Rob. 396, 397, Dr Lushington said:
  "There are two ways, and two ways only, by which contracts of this description can be annulled. The first is by proving that the contract was founded in fraud and misrepresentation, in which case it would be void *ab initio*; the second, by showing that it was cancelled by mutual consent."
  As the following discussion makes clear, this statement is too narrow for accuracy. See also *The Betsey* [1843] 2 W. Rob. 167, 170; *The Inna* [1938] P. 148, 156.

[36] [1978] 1 Lloyd's Rep. 438.

[37] "Equity" in the Admiralty Court refers to fairness and justice in the general sense, rather than to the system of law developed by the Court of Chancery and now applicable in all Divisions of the High Court. See *ante*, §§ 21–25.

[38] Thus, it is laid down in the Rolle of Olayron, probably compiled in the latter part of the twelfth century, that:
  "Yf it were so, that the mayster and the marchauntes have promised to folke, that should helpe them to save the shyp and the said goodes, the thyrde parte or half of the said goodes which should be saved for the peryll that they be in, the justyce of the country ought well to regarde what payne and what labour they have done in saving them, and after that payne, notwithstanding that promise which the said mayster and the marchauntes shall have made, rewarde them. This is the judgment."
  See Twiss (ed.), *Black Book of the Admiralty*, Vol. 2, p. 437.

[39] See *e.g. The British Empire* (1842) 6 Jur. 608; *The True Blue* (1843) 2 W. Rob. 176, 181; *The Firefly* (1857) Swab. 240, 241; *The Helen and George* (1858) 368, 369; *The Arthur* (1862) 1 M.L.C. 228; *Akerblom v. Price, Potter, Walker & Co.* (1881) 7 Q.B.D. 129, 132.

[40] In *The British Empire* (1842) 6 Jur. 608, quoted *ante*, § 858.

agreement. Delivering the judgment of the Court of Appeal, Brett L.J. said in *Akerblom v. Price, Potter, Walker & Co*[41]:

> "The fundamental rule of administration of maritime law in all courts of maritime jurisdiction is that, whenever the Court is called upon to decide between contending parties, upon claims arising with regard to the infinite number of marine casualties, which are generally of so urgent a character that the parties cannot be truly said to be on equal terms as to any agreement they may make with regard to them, the Court will try to discover what in the widest sense of the term is under the particular circumstances of the particular case fair and just between the parties. If the parties have made no agreement, the Court will decide primarily what is fair and just. The rule cannot be laid down in less large terms because of the endless variety of circumstances which constitute maritime casualties. They do not, as it were, arrange themselves into classes, of which *a priori* rules can be predicated."

882 There are two possible interpretations of the Admiralty jurisdiction: one, as a general jurisdiction to modify salvage contracts; the other, as a jurisdiction to set aside unfair salvage contracts and to apply the general policy of the law in rewarding salvage on equitable terms. The latter interpretation is the better. It is consistent with Brandon J.'s decision in *The Unique Mariner (No. 1)*.[42] The effect is that vitiation of salvage contracts is generally governed by common law vitiating factors, subject to the Admiralty Court's inherent power to set the contract aside and to do what is equitable. However, this jurisdiction is of course now subject to the terms of the Salvage Convention 1989.

The Salvage Convention 1989

883 Neither the Brussels Salvage Convention 1910 nor the Salvage Convention 1989 contains a detailed list directly comparable with the range of circumstances in which contracts may be vitiated at common law. The Brussels Salvage Convention 1910, Art. 7 provided:

> "Every agreement as to assistance or salvage entered into at the moment and under the influence of danger may, at the request of either party, be annulled, or modified by the court, if it considers that the conditions agreed upon are not equitable.
>
> In all cases, when it is proved that the consent of one of the parties is vitiated by fraud or concealment, or when the remuneration is, in proportion to the services rendered, in an excessive degree too large or too

---

[41] (1881) 7 Q.B.D. 129, 132–133. See also *The Phantom* (1866) L.R. 1 A. & E. 58, 61, per Dr Lushington: "There is another matter in all agreements, when salvors are going to perform a duty, whether the agreement is just and equitable; because if it is not, however much it has been agreed upon by both parties, the Court is in the habit of overruling such an agreement if it is unjust and inequitable."

[42] [1978] 1 Lloyd's Rep. 438.

small, the agreement may be annulled or modified by the court at the request of the party affected."

884 The Salvage Convention 1989, Art. 7 (which cannot be contracted out of)[43] provides:

"A contract or any of terms thereof may be annulled or modified if:
(a) the contract has been entered into under undue influence or the influence of danger and its terms are inequitable; or
(b) the payment under the contract is in an excessive degree too large or too small for the services actually rendered."

885 Article 7 of both the 1910 and the 1989 Conventions contains similar elements but with different terminology and arrangement. The 1910 provision may therefore provide some, but only limited, guidance to the interpretation of the current Article 7, which has consciously been drafted in a different way.

It was not the intention of those preparing the 1989 Convention to suppress national rules on the invalidity of contracts or their terms.[44] However, this intention is not expressed in the Convention, which generally provides that a person carrying out salvage operations which have a useful result is entitled to a salvage payment unless the Convention otherwise provides. Therefore, whether all those circumstances in which a contract is vitiated or modified under general English law apply in cases of salvage depends upon whether: the Convention is exclusive; it permits them to continue to operate, albeit without acknowledging the fact; or it in some non-specific way embraces them within the terms used in the Convention. Most likely, the general Admiralty rules on the effect of vitiating factors on salvage contracts continue to apply except in so far as they are overridden by the terms of the Convention, most obviously by Article 7 and the duties to prevent or minimise damage to the environment.[45]

886 The central issue, therefore, is the scope of Article 7. It is most obviously concerned with contracts entered into under compulsion and/or with inequitable terms; and will be discussed fully in that context below.[46] At this point it should be noted that its provisions specifically apply to contracts "entered into under undue influence" but that, although undue influence has a fairly specific meaning in English law (in equity), in the context of the Convention it is unlikely that it will not be given a broader construction, so as to embrace at least all types of illegitimate pressure but also possibly fraud, misrepresentation and non-disclosure (even absent a general requirement of disclosure),[47] provided that the terms of the contract are inequitable. Though

[43] Art. 6(3).
[44] See CMI Report 1984, pp. 16–17.
[45] See Art. 6.3.
[46] *Post*, §§ 925–952.
[47] This would be consistent with the the provisions of the Brussels Convention 1910, Art. 7, from which the Salvage Convention 1989, Art. 7 derives. See also Gaskell, 21–387.

traditional Admiralty law vitiating factors may continue to operate outside the Convention, different consequences may follow if they operate under it, for they would then attract the Convention powers of annulment and modification, which may possibly override the victim's Admiralty law rights.[48]

The effects of vitiating factors

Under the general law,[49] contracts concluded under mistake are automatically void without the necessity of action by either party, while those induced by misrepresentation, duress and undue influence are valid but voidable *ab initio* at the option of the victim of the inducement provided he avoids the contract before one of several bars to avoidance operates.[50] Under Admiralty law, the general principle is that the court has power to set aside the terms of an unfair agreement and to impose terms which it considers just in the circumstances.[51]

887

Where the Salvage Convention 1989, Art. 7 applies, either the whole contract or part of it may be annulled or modified. The Convention does not state how this annulment or modification may occur, though it is obviously fanciful to suggest that such a power is given to the victim of the undue influence or the inequitable contract term rather than simply to the tribunal. Since the Convention has the force of law,[52] the tribunal may be not only a court but also an arbitrator, except perhaps in relation to a jurisdiction clause.[53] Under the Brussels Convention 1910, Art. 7, the power of annulment or modification was exercisable "at the request of either party" and in practice this will continue to be the case. The drafting of the current Article 7, however, is such that the tribunal could exercise the power on its own initiative.

888

A more substantive issue is that the tribunal's Convention powers may override powers which the victim might exercise at common law. Thus, at common law, a victim of illegitimate pressure may generally avoid the contract. One possible interpretation of Article 7 is that this is no longer possible in salvage cases; *i.e.* that he can no longer act unilaterally but must apply to the tribunal for it to exercise its powers on his behalf. Certainly Article 7 confers its powers on the tribunal where no unilateral action is taken by the victim. A further possibility, though, is that, even where the victim prima facie can take action unilaterally to avoid the contract, the Convention authorises the tribunal to continue it in modified form,[54] thereby giving effect to the public policy of encouraging salvage.

889

[48] See *post*, §§ 887–889.
[49] *i.e.* non-Admiralty, terrestrial common law and equity: see *ante*, Chaps. 1–2.
[50] See Treitel, Chaps. 8–9.
[51] See *supra*, §881.
[52] See *ante*, Chap. 1.
[53] See Gaskell, 21–389.
[54] *cf.* the Misrepresentation Act 1967, s.2(2), which authorises the tribunal to award damages in lieu of rescission of a contract induced by non-fraudulent misrepresentation.

890 In most cases in practice, the court's powers under Admiralty law and the statutory jurisdiction to annul or modify contracts may produce little difference in result, since in most cases salvage disputes are resolved after the event and concern the payment of money. Moreover, where the contract is rendered inapplicable to a particular matter, the general provisions of the Salvage Convention 1989 will reassert themselves. In appropriate cases, however, the power to modify is potentially far-reaching. It is not restricted to limiting contract terms but might be invoked, even before a salvage operation has been completed, to impose an obligation on the salvor to take specific action.

The circumstances in which salvage agreements may be vitiated may now be considered in turn.

Fraud or collusion

891 Judges have always regarded fraud with great circumspection. Being a serious accusation, it is not easily found proved. Once found guilty of it, however, a party has been regarded with great disfavour. At common law, a fraudulently induced agreement is voidable at the election of the victim, who is also entitled to damages for deceit for loss suffered as a result of it.[55] Likewise, the Admiralty Court has always been willing to set aside an agreement entered into as a result of a fraudulent misrepresentation.[56] "for an agreement obtained by extortion, or assented to from fraud and misrepresentation, would be null and void *ab initio*, and would bind neither party."[57] Thus, in *The Crus V*,[58] the agents of the master of the salved vessel agreed a salvage award of £600 with the salvors, bargaining at the same time for a return to them of £50, out of which they were to keep £40 for themselves and to pay £10 to the master of the tug. Dr Lushington adjudged the agreement to be corrupt and pronounced for a tender of £250, with costs. Similarly, in *The Generous*,[59] where the court found that the master of the salving vessel had been bribed to sign a salvage agreement for £55 by a promise of £10 for himself, the judge was of the opinion that the agreement could not be sustained as binding upon the owners of the salved vessel; but he thought, nevertheless, that a salvage service had been rendered, and awarded £30, but without costs.

892 However, damages for deceit are unlikely to be awarded in salvage cases. If the fraud is discovered in time, the agreement will not be upheld, so the victim will not suffer loss in having to pay excessive remuneration. If it is discovered after an award has been made, the award may be remitted or set

---

[55] See Treitel, Chap. 9.
[56] See, *e.g.* the dicta in *The Henry* (1851) 15 Jur. 183; *The Repulse* (1845) 2 W. Rob. 396, 397; *The Resultatet* (1853) 17 Jur. 353, 354; *The Helen and George* (1858) Swab. 368, 369.
[57] *The Resultatet* (1853) 17 Jur. 352, 354.
[58] (1862) Lush. 583.
[59] (1868) L.R. 2 A. & E. 57.

aside and there may be restitution of sums paid. Damages would be appropriate where an agreement was fraudulently obtained with a view to causing loss (*e.g.* by deterring the vessel in distress from enlisting alternative assistance, and then failing to provide assistance) but these would be highly unusual circumstances.

893 More important is the question whether the court will be more severe on a salvor than simply refusing to enforce the agreement, though assessing a reward independently, or by refusing costs. First, the rewards in *The Crus V* and *The Generous* being less than the agreed sum minus the amount of the bribe, it can be inferred that fraudulent conduct is a factor of which the judge can take account in limiting the notional award. Secondly, with respect to an allegation that in concluding an agreement the salvors were to pay the master of the vessel to be salved 5 per cent of the salvage award, Gorell Barnes J. said in *The Kolpino*[60] that it was "extremely probable that any arrangement of this kind between the masters of vessels would forfeit any right to salvage altogether." The allegation in *The Kolpino* was not proved. The case was, however, an appropriate one for the application of his Lordship's dictum, for he was speaking with reference to the eventual apportionment of the reward. Although it has since been clearly established that a principal may be liable for the misconduct of his servant or agent,[61] an Admiralty judge, inhibited by the public policy of rewarding salvors, is unlikely to deprive of an award a salvor (such as the owner of the salving vessel) who was not directly a party to the fraud.

894 But he need not be so restrained in the case of a direct participant in the fraud. Certainly, such a person is liable to be convicted of a criminal offence, and his principal is entitled to claim payment of any bribe actually received.[62] Further support for the view that any party who is directly a party to a fraudulent dealing, including the shipowner, is liable to forfeit salvage is provided by general statements of principle by Dr Lushington[63] and in the Privy Council[64] and in particular by a dictum of Dr Lushington in *The Westminster*[65] that he would refuse to pronounce any salvage due where an agreement was entered with the master or owners of a distressed vessel with cargo on board to salve the vessel and not the cargo:

> "why it would be an encouragement to fraudulent bargains by owners and masters of vessels, to the detriment of owners of the cargo, and of course salvors would make a bargain much more advantageous to

---

[60] *The Kolpino* (1904) 73 L.J.P. 29, 30.
[61] *Lloyd v. Grace, Smith & Co.* [1912] A.C. 716.
[62] *Mahesan v. Malaysian Government Officers' Housing Society* [1979] A.C. 374.
[63] In *The Magdalen* (1861) 31 L.J. Adm. 22, 24: see *post*, §1125.
[64] In *The Atlas* (1862) Lush. 518, 528, delivered by Sir John Coleridge: see *post*, §§1108, 1125.
[65] (1841) 1 W. Rob. 229, 235.

Salvage Agreements

the owners of the ship with the master when they are sure of obtaining his assistance to get a larger salvage from the owners of the cargo."

The burden of proving fraud is on the party alleging it.[66]

Non-disclosure

895 At common law, there is no general duty on a party negotiating to enter into a contract to disclose any facts which may be material to the contract.[67] In admiralty, however, if, before conclusion of an agreement, a material fact is not disclosed, whether intentionally or unintentionally,[68] the agreement will not be enforced against the party who has been led or allowed to contract without knowing the true state of affairs, if the result would be inequitable. The duty of disclosure applies to both parties.[69] Dr Lushington stated the principles thus in *The Kingalock*[70]:

> "An agreement to bind two parties must be made with a full knowledge of all the facts necessary to be known by both parties; and if any fact which, if known, could have any operation on the agreement about to be entered into is kept back, or not disclosed to either of the contracting parties, that would vitiate the agreement itself. It is not necessary, in order to vitiate an agreement, that there should be moral fraud; it is not necessary, in order to make it not binding, that one of the parties should keep back any fact or circumstance of importance, if there should be misapprehension, accidentally or by carelessness; we all know that there may be what, in the eye of the law, is termed equitable fraud."

896 In *The Unique Mariner (No. 1)*,[71] Brandon J. stated that the treatment of non-disclosure in the fourth edition of this book,[72] under the heading "Agreements Concerning Amount of Salvage Remuneration", appeared in the third edition in the section on "Agreements fixing the amount of the Salvage Remuneration",[73] where there was no mention of the Lloyd's Form of salvage agreement. The then current edition of Lloyd's Form made provision for the

---

[66] See *The Atlas* (1862) Lush. 518, 528 (see *post*, §1125); *The Iodine* (1844) 3 N.o.C. 140, 142; *The Henry* (1851) 15 Jur. 183; *The Helen and George* (1858) Swab. 368.
[67] *cf. The Jonge Andries* (1857) Swab. 226, 227.
[68] *cf. The Cargo ex Woosung* (1876) 1 P.D. 260, 263–264, where Sir Robert Phillimore seems to suggest that non-disclosure must be intentional.
[69] *The Unique Mariner (No. 1)* [1978] 1 Lloyd's Rep. 438, 454.
[70] (1854) 1 Spinks E. & A. 263, 265. See also *The Canova* (1866) L.R. 1 A. & E. 54, 56; *The Unique Mariner (No.1)*, *supra*, at 454.
[71] [1978] 1 Lloyd's Rep. 438.
[72] 4th ed., pp. 305–8.
[73] (3rd ed., 1936), Chap. IX, Pt. A. Pt. B related to "Agreements for the apportionment of Salvage Remuneration".

Non-disclosure

provisional fixture of an amount, although in practice assessment was normally deferred, as is provided today by LOF 2000.[74]

Brandon J. then considered *The Kingalock*,[75] in which the court held invalid an agreement for the towage of a disabled ship and awarded salvage. He then went on to say[76]:

897

> "The Admiralty Court has always exercised an equitable jurisdiction to declare invalid, and to refuse to enforce, an agreement of this kind if it considers the agreement, in all the circumstances of the case, to be seriously inequitable to one side or the other. In many of the cases where this jurisdiction has been exercised, the nature of the serious inequity on which the Court has founded its judgment has been that the sum agreed was of itself either much too large or much too small, having regard to the nature and circumstances of the assistance rendered ... There may, however, be other circumstances, besides the gross inadequacy or exorbitance of the sum agreed itself, which render an agreement of the kind under discussion so inequitable to one side or the other that it should not be allowed to stand. One such circumstance is where there is oppression or virtual compulsion arising from inequality in the bargaining position of the two parties concerned; another such circumstance is the existence of collusion of one kind or another; and a third such circumstance, in my view, is where there has been non-disclosure of material facts by one side or another, as in *The Kingalock* above."

His Lordship continued as follows[77]:

898

> "If this be the right view of the matter, as Counsel for the defendants in his most helpful argument convinced me that it was, two consequences follow. The first consequence is that *The Kingalock* is not an authority which establishes that all contracts relating to salvage services are contracts *uberrimae fidei*, and therefore voidable by either party on the ground of non-disclosure of material facts by the other. It is rather just one example of the exercise by the Admiralty Court of its equitable power to treat as invalid, on the ground of serious unfairness to one side or the other, one particular kind of salvage agreement, namely an agreement by which the amount to be paid for services, in respect of which those rendering them would otherwise have a claim for salvage at large, is fixed at a definite sum in advance. The second consequence is that some modification may be required, so far as the ground of non-disclosure is concerned, in the categorisation on p. 304 of the 4th ed. of

---

[74] See [1978] 1 Lloyd's Rep. 438, 452.
[75] *Supra*, n. 70.
[76] [1978] 1 Lloyd's Rep. 438, 454.
[77] *ibid.*, 454–455.

Kennedy of the various grounds on which the particular kind of agreement just mentioned can be avoided.

899 It is in the light of the analysis which I have made . . . that I now turn to answer the question whether contracts for the rendering of salvage services in general, and Lloyd's Standard Form of Salvage Agreement in particular, are contracts *uberrimae fidei* or not. The conclusion which I have reached is that there is no good reason in principle why such contracts, which are basically commercial contracts for work and labour,[78] should be regarded as contracts *uberrimae fidei*, and that there is further no authority, either in the case of *The Kingalock* or otherwise, for the proposition that they should."

He later stated, however, that, even if he were of opinion that such contracts were *uberrimae fidei*, the circumstance in question was not such a fact as had to be disclosed.

900 The Admiralty Court has always claimed a general jurisdiction to set aside inequitable agreements. And it may be possible to regard the jurisdiction as governed by a unified general principle with particular applications. Indeed, salvage agreements in general have been categorised with cases of duress of goods, unconscionable transactions, undue influence and undue pressure as cases "where there has been inequality of bargaining power, such as to merit the intervention of the court."[79] In doing so. Lord Denning M.R. has suggested, in a case on undue influence[80]:

> "that through all these cases there runs a single thread. They rest on 'inequality of bargaining power'. By virtue of it, the English law gives relief to one who, without independent advice, enters into a contract upon terms which are very unfair or transfers property for a consideration which is grossly inadequate, when his bargaining power is grievously impaired by reason of his own needs or desires, or by his own ignorance or informity, coupled with undue influences or pressures brought to bear on him by or for the benefit of the other. When I use the word 'undue' I do not mean to suggest that the principle depends on proof of any wrongdoing. The one who stipulates for an unfair advantage may be moved solely by his own self-interest, unconscious of the distress he is bringing to the other. I have also avoided any reference to the will of the one being 'dominated' or 'overcome' by the other. One who is in extreme need may knowingly consent to a most improvident bargain, solely to relieve the straits in which he finds himself. Again, I do not mean to suggest that every transaction is saved by independent advice. But the absence of it may be fatal. With these explanations, I hope this principle will be found to reconcile the cases."

[78] See *The Tojo Maru* [1972] A.C. 242, 292, per Lord Diplock.
[79] *Lloyd's Bank Ltd v. Bundy* [1975] Q.B. 326, 336–339, per Lord Denning M.R.
[80] ibid., 339.

Lord Denning M.R.'s synthesis of the cases did not provoke a move from specific grounds to a wider, more general ground of relief in the situations with which he dealt. Indeed, the House of Lords has rejected the principle as an inappropriate reformulation of principle in cases of undue influence and as an unnecessary innovation in the general law of contract, where Parliament has undertaken the role of implementing restrictions on freedom of contract.[81] But it is suggested that general statements of principle such as those offered by Brandon J. and Lord Denning M.R. provide useful guidance in appropriate cases. **901**

If there is any duty of disclosure in salvage contracts, the court will treat as material any fact in or relating to the property for which salvage assistance is sought if that fact affects, or not improbably may affect: the danger to the property; the risk, difficulty or duration of the salvor's service; the suitability of the salvors' vessel as an instrument of salvage or the prospects of success under a contract to use best endeavours[82]; or possibly the assessment of the potential reward.[83] **902**

In *The Kingalock*,[84] an agreement was set aside because the ship's master had not disclosed that she had suffered damage from extreme bad weather and also because the omission to state the facts could, with reasonable probability, have affected the service to be performed since, in the weather conditions prevailing, "the services might have been delayed and rendered much more arduous, much more difficult in consequence of the want of ground tackle." Therefore, the agreement was declared to be "null and void, *ab initio*". Since this was the *ratio* of Dr Lushington's decision, it provides clear authority for the proposition that an agreement may be unenforceable for non-disclosure—even if it could have been, as Brandon J. states in *The Unique Mariner (No. 1)*,[85] that it was, decided on the basis of the inequitable sum agreed. If Dr Lushington's decision is correct—and it is consistent with the jurisdiction in non-Admiralty cases to set aside agreements for non-disclosure in certain circumstances—then salvage agreements induced by material non-disclosure can be set aside even where the agreement pre-determines a fair reward to be payable. In practice, a party is unlikely to contest the agreement in such a case—but he might do so if he did not wish to be bound by any of its other provisions. **903**

The fact that agreements are rarely contested on the ground of non-disclosure is presumably nowadays due to the fact that the prime matter of contention in salvage cases—the reward—is left open in the ubiquitous Lloyd's Form for subsequent determination and concealed, but subsequently **904**

---

[81] *National Westminster Bank Plc v. Morgan* [1986] A.C. 686, 707–708.
[82] *The Unique Mariner (No.1)* [1978] 1 Lloyd's Rep. 438, 455, but not whether the salving vessel had come to the assistance of the vessel in distress by chance, rather than by reason of an arrangement between the parties' representatives; see *ibid.*, 455.
[83] This last point is controversial: see *post*, §§ 908–909.
[84] (1854) 1 Spinks E. & A. 263.
[85] [1978] 1 Lloyd's Rep. 438. See *ante*, § 898.

revealed, facts can be taken into account by the arbitrator in assessing a fair reward. That being so, the court is likely to be generally motivated to uphold the conclusion of such an agreement, which reduces the necessity for negotiation when the need for salvage services is imminent, and which provides a recognised, successful means of providing an equitable outcome.

The paucity of earlier cases on non-disclosure is presumably a product of the traditional uncommonness of agreements attempting to predetermine the amount of reward. Such cases as have been reported mostly concern the non-disclosure of facts which have not resulted in non-enforcement of the agreement, *viz.* slight damage or making water in circumstances where most vessels made water,[86] illness of the majority of the crew[87] and the value of the cargo.[88]

Misrepresentation

905   Under the general law of misrepresentation, laid down at common law and in equity and as modified by statute,[89] where a party has been induced to enter into a contract as a result of a material misrepresentation of fact, he can, provided he is not defeated by any of the recognised bars to rescission, rescind the contract, the parties being put back into the position in which they were when the contract was made. In all cases of misrepresentation, he may also obtain an indemnity for necessary expenditure in effecting rescission. If it is claimed in any proceedings arising out of a contract induced by a faultless[90] misrepresentation that the contract ought to be or has been rescinded, the court or arbitrator has a discretion to declare the contract subsisting and to award damages in lieu of rescission.[91] However, in cases of fraudulent or negligent misstatement, the party induced by the misstatement does not need to rely on the tribunal's discretion to award damages in lieu of rescission, but has a right to sue for damages. Where there was fraud, damages for deceit are payable. Where there has been negligence, he can claim damages in tort under the *Hedley Byrne & Co. Ltd v. Heller & Partners Ltd*[92] line of authorities or under the Misrepresentation Act 1967, s.2(1), the application of which is limited to contracting parties but for whom it is more advantageous. The subsection is free of the limitations of the *Hedley Byrne* rule. And the plaintiff does not need to prove negligence—the defendant must disprove it. A plaintiff could therefore recover damages from a defendant whose misrepresentation was

---

[86] *The Jonge Andries* (1857) Swab. 226 (affirmed, *ibid.*, 303).
[87] *The Canova* (1866) L.R. 1 A. & E. 54 (where in fact no danger was found to exist).
[88] *The Henry* (1851) 15 Jur. 183. *Sed quaere*: see *post*, §§ 908–909.
[89] For a full discussion, see Chitty, Chap. 6; Treitel, Chap. 9.
[90] The traditional common law distinction is between "fraudulent" and "innocent" misrepresentation. However, since *Hedley Byrne & Co. Ltd v. Heller & Partners Ltd, infra*, "innocent misrepresentation" has been sub-divided into "negligent misrepresentation" and non-negligent innocent misrepresentation, for which no convenient single adjective has received common acceptance; "faultless" seems convenient and accurate and will be used here.
[91] Misrepresentation Act 1967, s.2(2).
[92] [1964] A.C. 465.

made without fraud or negligence if the faultless defendant were unable to discharge the burden.

906 In *The Unique Mariner (No. 1)*,[93] Brandon J. said, *obiter*:

> "So far as misrepresentation is concerned I can see no reason why the ordinary principles of law relating to rescission of contracts for fraudulent and innocent misrepresentation (including the relevant provisions of the Misrepresentation Act 1967) should not apply to contracts for the rendering of salvage services, including contracts on the terms of Lloyd's Form, in exactly the same way as they apply to all other contracts, and every reason why they should. If that is right, there is no need for the exercise by the Admiralty Court of any additional equitable jurisdiction to treat such contracts as invalid by reason of mis-statement."

907 It is nevertheless true, therefore requiring some consideration here, that the Admiralty Court has always maintained, though, from the evidence of the few reported cases, infrequently needed to apply, an inherent jurisdiction not to uphold a contract induced by a misrepresentation, at least one made fraudulently.[94] Thus Dr Lushington said of the facts in *The Henry*[95]:

> "If the master had been asked to state the condition of the ship, and had given a false description of the damage done and the difficulties under which she laboured—if he had concealed the leaks which might possibly have existed in the ship, or had misrepresented the number of his anchors and cables, or the means of supplying any want, that would be a clear fraud affecting the agreement itself, upon which the Court would have been inclined to hold that it was null and void from the beginning."

908 In *The Henry*,[96] the salvors sought to upset a salvage agreement for £100 on the ground that the master of the salved vessel had misled them by fraudulently keeping back from them the true value of the cargo by representing it to consist only of fuller's earth, worth £250, whereas in fact there was cargo worth £2,000. Dr Lushington decided against the salvors, finding, first, that there was no fraud and, secondly, that the value of the cargo was an immaterial fact, so that even a positive misrepresentation in regard to it could not lead to avoidance of the salvage agreement. He said[97]:

> "I cannot assent to the proposition, that by the value of the cargo the salvors are to determine the amount of the agreement. It is perfectly true,

---

[93] [1978] 1 Lloyd's Rep. 438, 455.
[94] See, *e.g. The Resultatet* (1853) 17 Jur. 353, 354; *The Helen and George* (1858) Swab. 368, 369; *The Medina* (1876) 2 P.D. 5, 7; *The Cargo ex Woosung* (1876) 1 P.D. 260, 263–264.
[95] (1851) 15 Jur. 183, 184.
[96] *ibid.*
[97] *ibid.*, 184; continuing immediately after the quotation above, text to n. 95.

that this Court does, to a certain and limited extent, take into consideration the value of the property saved in assessing salvage compensation, with the view of making the general rate of compensation sufficient to induce persons to undertake salvage services, and, as it were, to a certain extent, making up, in cases of large value, for the impossibility of giving a complete and adequate reward in cases of small value. Salvors are not entitled to make an agreement upon any other grounds than these:—The extent of danger to which the property to be salved is exposed, the degree of labour they will have to undergo, the risk to which they themselves may be exposed, and the length of time to be occupied; but they are not to speculate on the value of the cargo. See what a dangerous principle I should encourage if I allowed this to pass without observation. Here is a packet coming from South America laden with dollars; she gets, in great distress, into the chops of the Channel; assistance is offered, but the salvors say, 'We will do nothing till we know the quantity of dollars on board.' That would, in the first place, lead to extortion; and in the second, to disputed agreements over and over again, because the master may be ignorant of the precise value of the property. It is my duty utterly to discourage such proceedings as this."

909 The authority of Dr Lushington's decision is seriously undermined by his view, repeated elsewhere but incapable of standing with the prevailing authorities,[98] that the value of the salved property does not form a substantive element in the calculation of salvage reward. However, even with all due allowance for this possible difference of view, it is difficult to believe that he intended to lay down that the court would uphold, as binding on the salvors, an agreement which was in fact obtained from them by an intentional and gross representation of the value of the property in peril, and that he meant more than that honest silence or misrepresentation on this point, at least in the absence of negligence, ought not to affect the validity of a salvage agreement.[99] Even when thus limited, the justice of the rule might appear somewhat open to question, for there is no doubt that in the Admiralty Court, if the character of the services in two cases is equally meritorious, the saving of property worth £100,000 is much more highly rewarded than the saving of property worth £10,000.

910 It is submitted that knowledge which the court deems material in adjudging the reward ought not to be treated as immaterial to a salvor fixing his reward by agreement. Faultless non-disclosure may be excused, for there is no general duty of disclosure in salvage agreements and a salvor concluding such an agreement can simply request the relevant information, leaving him free not to fix the amount if no answer is forthcoming and, it is submitted, the other party liable for misrepresentation if he answers wrongly. As to the evil of extortion which Dr Lushington seemed to fear if a salvor is entitled to have

---

[98] See *post*, Chap. 15.
[99] Immediately before the quotation *ante*, in § 907. Dr Lushington said: "he may not have known the value of the rest of the cargo." See (1851) 15 Jur. 183, 184.

correct information as to the value of the property when bargaining for the price of its rescue, this is a distinct matter which should not affect the issue of misrepresentation; the court has a separately defined jurisdiction to set aside any agreement for an exorbitant amount obtained by practical compulsion.[1] As to the suggested engendering of disputes because the master of the ship in peril may be ignorant of the precise value of the property, that is not likely to create significant practical difficulties even in those unusual cases where agreements are made to fix salvage awards, for a difference between the stated value and the real value of the property at risk should only affect the validity of the agreement where the difference is sufficiently great that it would materially affect the court's reward.

911 It is respectfully submitted that Dr Lushington's views in *The Henry*[2] should be rejected as inconsistent with the subsequently acknowledged significance of the materiality of the value of salved property. This is especially desirable since, if the general law of misrepresentation were being applied, it cannot at all realistically be supposed that the Admiralty Court would distinguish the case as an inapplicable decision of the civil law. If it were held to represent the Admiralty rule, it would, in the absence of other authorities to clarify the law, also be inconsistent with the subsequent threefold common law distinction of fraudulent, negligent and "faultless" misrepresentation (to which Dr Lushington did not address himself) and the common law rule that material misrepresentations make contracts voidable at the option of the party induced rather than, as Dr Lushington stated, "null and void from the beginning," which would equally benefit the party making the misrepresentation, in a case where he in fact concluded a contract disadvantageous to himself but from which he wished to resile.[3]

912 If *The Henry*, the strongest Admiralty case on misrepresentation, and one dealing rather with non-disclosure, can be disregarded as anomalous, there remains no obvious objection to accepting Brandon J.'s suggestion[4] that the general law of misrepresentation should govern salvage contracts. It will, of course, apply equally to both parties, as much against a salvor misrepresenting his ability to effect salvage as against the owner of salved property.

Mistake

913 The law laid down by the common law courts in relation to the effect of mistake on contracts is notoriously controversial and need not be re-examined in detail here.[5] This is in large part the result of the difficulty of reconciling, on the one hand, the courts' general desire to uphold apparently valid commercial agreements, especially so as not to prejudice third parties who act in

[1] See *post*, §§ 925–941.
[2] *Supra*.
[3] He expressed the same view in *The Resultatet* (1851) 15 Jur. 353, 354.
[4] *Ante*, § 906.
[5] For references to the relevant cases, see Chitty, Chap. 5 and, particularly, Treitel, Chap. 8, on the arrangement of which the following discussion is based.

reliance on their validity, and, on the other, the unwillingness to allow this policy to produce an unjust result in individual cases. Where mistake does operate, it operates, in Lord Atkin's words, so as to negative or, in some cases, to nullify consent,[6] and to make the contract void. However, confusion is often compounded by cases where a mistake is provoked by a misrepresentation made by one of the parties; for, as shewn above,[7] whatever effect mistake has independently of misrepresentation, misrepresentation itself makes a contract voidable. Occasionally, equity may grant relief where a contract is made as the result of a mistake which does not upset the validity of the contract at common law, *e.g.* a mistake as to the value of the subject-matter; but the courts are disinclined to upset commercial bargains by parties dealing at arms' length.[8] In *The Friesland*,[9] after their tug had begun to perform salvage services to a vessel with her shaft broken, the tugowners made a bargain with the casualty's owners that the service should be on towage rather than salvage terms. Sir Francis Jeune P. intimated that, if it could be shewn that they made the agreement in ignorance of the real facts, thinking that the vessel had nothing wrong with her, the agreement might not stand, but they did know the true facts and, being *sui juris*, the agreement stood.[10]

914 Mistake *nullifies* consent where the parties reach an agreement which is based on a fundamental mistaken assumption.[11] There is such a mistake where it is as to: the existence of the subject-matter of the contract; the identity of the subject-matter; the possibility of performing the contract; an identifying quality; and, occasionally, quantity. Such mistakes might occur in salvage cases. In *The British Inventor*,[12] the plaintiffs' services were engaged in the mistaken belief that the defendants' vessel was aground. The plaintiffs towed for 20 minutes, "a miserable service for a very short time if it was a service at all", but recovered no salvage.[13] However, the types of mistake under consideration are not likely to be common, at least where the salvee had an interest in the subject-matter of the contract when it became a casualty. Even where he subsequently acquired an interest, two particular rules of general application are likely to defeat a plea of mistake. In *McRae v. Commonwealth Disposals Commission*,[14] the plaintiffs entered a contract of sale (not salvage)

---

[6] *Bell v. Lever Bros Ltd* [1932] A.C. 161, 217.
[7] §§ 905–912.
[8] The jurisdiction might apply where the parties are mistaken as to the difficulty of salvage operations. The apparent, limited, jurisdiction in equity to set aside on terms contracts which are otherwise valid at common law (see, *e.g. Solle v. Butcher* [1950] 1 K.B. 671) is difficult to reconcile with the, itself controversial, House of Lords decision in *Bell v. Lever Bros Ltd* [1932] A.C. 161; *cf.* now *Sybron Corp. v. Rochem Ltd* [1984] Ch. 112; *Great Peace v. Tsavliris (The Great Peace)* (2001) 151 N.L.J. 1696.
[9] [1904] P. 345.
[10] *ibid.*, 350.
[11] Treitel, p. 262.
[12] (1933) 45 Ll.L.Rep. 263.
[13] Bateson J. said there was a mistake but did not clearly state its effect on the engagement. If there were no danger and no salvage service, the plaintiffs would have failed even if there had been a valid agreement to salve.
[14] (1950) 84 C.L.R. 377.

to buy an oil tanker lying on a reef and said to contain oil, and its cargo. At considerable expense, the plaintiff fitted out a salvage expedition but discovered that the property had never existed. They recovered damages for breach of contract because, first, there was an undertaking by the defendants (by implication) that the subject-matter existed (this term overriding the effect of a possible mistake) and, secondly, even if there were a mistake, it could not be relied upon if, as was held, it was induced by the fault of the defendants or their servants in recklessly and without reasonable ground inducing the mistake in the plaintiff's mind.

Mistake *negatives* consent where the parties are at such cross-purposes that they do not reach agreement, *viz.* (i) where there is a relevant type of mistake (*e.g.* one party is mistaken about the identity of the other, or intends to deal with one thing and the other party with a different one, or intends to deal on one set of terms and the other on a different set); (ii) the mistake actually induces the mistaken party to contract; and (iii) the mistaken party does not conduct himself so that a reasonable man would believe that he was assenting to the terms proposed by the other party and the other party upon that belief enters into a contract with him.[15] In practice, it would not be usual for those circumstances to occur, particularly where salvage is to be on the terms of Lloyd's Form. However, as with mistakes which nullify consent, it is possible to imagine circumstances in which such mistakes may invalidate contracts, the most likely type of situation being the one considered by Brandon J. in *The Unique Mariner (No. 1)*.[16]

915

In that case, the master of the plaintiffs' stranded vessel cabled for assistance to refloat her to the ship's managers, who cabled back that they were sending a tug. The master of another tug, owned by the defendants, offered her services, which were accepted by the plaintiffs' master, on Lloyd's Form, in the belief that she was the tug sent by the managers. The plaintiffs claimed, unsuccessfully, that they were not bound by the contract, *inter alia*, on the ground that their master intended to deal with a servant or agent of a tugowner appointed by the plaintiffs' agents, and not with the defendants, and the defendants' master was aware, or by virtue of the surrounding circumstances ought to have been aware, of the said intention. Brandon J. found on the facts that the defendants' master did not know, and should not be taken to have known, of the plaintiffs' master's mistake. His judgment assumes, without expressly stating it to be the case, that the common law of mistake applies to salvage contracts in the same way as it does to other contracts. But, by virtue of his findings, he decided that it was unnecessary to determine the logically anterior precondition of invalidity, that the mistake was sufficiently fundamental, although the decision makes it clear that it will be no easier in Admiralty cases than at common law to convince the court that a mistake is sufficiently fundamental to avoid a salvage contract.

916

[15] Treitel, pp. 273, 281.
[16] [1978] 1 Lloyd's Rep. 438.

917   Where more than one would-be salvor is competing for salvage, similar circumstances may well arise again. The cases at common law proceed on the assumption that a person is presumed to intend to contract with the person with whom he is dealing (whether by correspondence, *inter praesentes* or, no doubt, by radio or other instantaneous means of communication) but that the presumption can be rebutted by proof that the other party knew that the person did not intend to contract with him. A mistake as to a contracting party must generally be one as to his identity and not as to his attributes. A shipowner may well have reasons for discriminating between contractors, in favour of professional over non-professional salvors and for preferring certain professional salvors. But a contract should only be vitiated where the salvor clearly knows that the salvee intended not to contract with him.

918   Although the mistake in *The Unique Mariner (No. 1)* was regarded as being one as to the identity of the salvor with whom the master intended to contract on behalf of his owner, it would appear more accurate to say that the master's mistake was that he believed he was signing Lloyd's Form as a formal record of a contract already concluded between his owners, through their managing agents, and the salvors engaged by the managing agents. Since the defendants would still have been able to plead their belief that the master intended to contract with them, it is unlikely to have made any difference to the decision if the mistake were treated as relating not to the identity of the salvor but to the effect of the document. It does raise the question, however, whether the court might have been able to grant relief on some other basis.

919   In the unusual circumstances where a salvage agreement predetermines the salvage award, a mistake may have a significant effect on whether a fair reward becomes payable. Of course, in most cases in practice Lloyd's Form will be signed, so any potential unfairness resulting from a mistake can be reduced by the tribunal's consideration of the true circumstances, such as the real difficulty of the service, in assessing the reward. But even in such a case, the defendant may be at a disadvantage for, as the proceedings involving the *Unique Mariner* demonstrated, where two salvors are engaged by different agents of the shipowners and only one is permitted actually to salve, the shipowners will ultimately have to pay both a reward to one and compensation to the other.[17]

920   If the master of a casualty signs a document, it would, from the common law authorities, appear to be extremely unlikely for him successfully to plead *non est factum*: that he was at the time of signing the salvage agreement, through no fault of his own, unable to have any real understanding of its effect, which was radically different from what he supposed.[18] The defence could conceivably apply where a master who did not speak English thought

---

[17] See *The Unique Mariner (No. 1)* [1978] 1 Lloyd's Rep. 438; *The Unique Mariner (No. 2)* [1979] 1 Lloyd's Rep. 37.

[18] See Chitty, §§ 5–054 to 5–059; Treitel, pp. 301–304; *Saunders v. Anglia Building Society (on appeal from Gallie v. Lee)* [1971] A.C. 1004.

Mistake

that he was signing a towage contract as opposed to a salvage agreement.[19] But ships' masters are normally familiar with Lloyd's Form; and they are unlikely to be prejudiced if they are not—a salvage reward for basically towage services will not be high and an excessive agreed sum for a salvage service in the nature of towage may be set aside anyway as an inequitable term.[20] In any event, the defence of *non est factum* has rarely availed a person of full age and capacity at common law.

It may be, however, that the jurisdiction of the Admiralty Court is more **921** flexible. In *The Inchmaree*,[21] a vessel went aground on a sandbank. Salvage services were rendered by tugs on three tides. Between the second and third tides, the masters of two salving tugs signed agreements for themselves, their owners and crews, to accept the sum of £20 per tide and £150 when floated, in full for all claims, the agreements to apply as well to past as to future services. Phillimore J. held that the agreements could stand in respect of subsequent services but salvage could be assessed independently for past rights. He said[22]:

> "though I take the view that the defendants' servants, the master and the ship's broker, honestly believed that the contract was as appears on paper, I have also come to the conclusion that the tugmasters did not understand it. The matter was one of hurry and emergency. There was a great deal of bargaining and discussion, and the question was complicated by the position of the other two tugs, whose masters seem to some extent to have waived their rights in favour of the two tugs first in the field. It may be difficult to come to the conclusion that two people of the capability and vigour of those two tugmasters should have made a mistake. But I was impressed by their honesty in other respects; I thought them trustworthy; and I have come to the conclusion that I cannot disbelieve them, and, although the burden was very strongly against them, I hold that they did not agree, or intend to agree, to sell their past rights."

The equitable remedy of *rectification* applies as much to salvage as to other **922** mistakenly recorded contracts but will rarely be useful, for its general purpose is simply to bring the document in question into line with the prior agreement made by *both* parties, the mistake of only one party being generally insufficient.[23]

Resort to the equitable jurisdiction for *rescission* on terms of contracts **923** which are otherwise valid at law[24] is unlikely to be necessary. A similar, better

---

[19] Brice, §5–126.
[20] See *post*, §§ 905–912.
[21] [1899] P. 111.
[22] *ibid.*, 116.
[23] See Goff & Jones, pp. 298–305; Treitel, 296–301.
[24] Treitel, pp. 292–296.

established, jurisdiction has long been claimed by the Admiralty Court to set aside agreements the terms of which prove to be inequitable—though the more recent trend is to uphold freely concluded agreements so far as possible.[25]

924 Where they are not bound to each other by contract, the positions of the salvor and the salvee will not be affected by mistake. In *The Liffey*,[26] a person who rendered services of a salvage nature to a vessel of which he mistakenly believed himself to be the owner subsequently recovered salvage from the true owner. In *The Premuda*,[27] the Admiralty Salvage Department signed Lloyd's Form with the casualty's master. The Admiralty arranged for tugs, which in fact had an agreement with the Admiralty that they should participate in salvage. The casualty was unaware of this and did not specifically accept the tugs' services on a salvage basis. It was nonetheless held that salvage was payable to them, and that the defendants were not prejudiced by this decision.

Compulsion and inequity of terms

925 It is convenient to set out the Admiralty law on compulsion and inequitable contract terms before mentioning the common law rules and then considering the effect of the Salvage Convention 1989, Art. 7 in these circumstances.

Admiralty law generally

926 The older cases established as a general rule that an agreement, once made, is prima facie strong evidence of what is fair between the parties to it and enforceable because, in the absence of evidence to the contrary, it may be taken to be that which the parties who were most interested, and best able to judge, thought to be fair.[28] According to Dr Lushington in *The Henry*[29]:

> "Where agreements are made at sea between salvors and the masters of vessels, the Court will always be very desirous to confirm them, if it can do so consistently with equity and justice. The Court would be very reluctant, under ordinary circumstances, to disturb an agreement made between parties on account of the sum appearing too large or too small, but I do not say that there are not cases in which I should not hesitate for a single moment to pronounce against an agreement either on the one ground or the other. There are many reasons for this. It is obvious that both parties are fully capable of entering into a contract; the master is the representative of the owners, and the salvors are acting on their own behalf, and have ample means of so doing, because, being on the spot at

---

[25] See *post*, §§ 925–941.
[26] (1887) 6 Asp. M.L.C. 255.
[27] (1940) 67 Ll.L.Rep. 9.
[28] See, *e.g. The Iodine* (1844) 3 N.o.C. 140, 142.
[29] (1851) 15 Jur. 183, 183.

the moment, they must be cognisant of the state and condition of the vessel which requires assistance, the nature and extent of the services to be performed, and the time to be occupied in rendering them. It is very desirable that agreements of this kind should exist, and that, when just and fair, they should be upheld in these courts."

The same judge said in *The Helen and the George*[30]:

"The principle on which the Court acts is, that if satisfied that an agreement has been made, it will carry it into effect unless totally contrary to justice and the equity of the case; but the owner of the ship, against whom the agreement is attempted to be enforced, may show that it was improperly obtained. The owner may contend that, under the circumstances, the sum of money was grossly exorbitant; and, *a fortiori*, if he can show that the agreement was obtained by fraud or compulsion, no Court would hold it to be binding. But when the execution of such an instrument is once proved, it is *prima facie* binding, and the burden of proof falls on those who dispute the validity of the instrument."

More recently, Brett J.A. said in *The Medina*[31]:

"I think that the old rule of the Admiralty Court ought not to be lightly encroached upon, *viz.*, that where there is an agreement made by competent persons and there is no misrepresentation of facts the agreement ought to be upheld, unless there is something very strong to shew that it is inequitable."

However, as the quoted comments conceded, if on examination of the facts it appeared that, whilst there was no fraud or deceit in the transaction, yet one of the parties was, when he made the agreement, in such straits that he was practically compelled to accept such terms as the other party might dictate, and that other party used his opportunity to dictate them, it is obvious that the value of the agreement, as evidence of what was fair, is taken away. Where, therefore, a salvor sought to enforce a salvage agreement and the Admiralty Court found, not only that the price of the salvage services which it incorporated was disproportionate to the nature and value of those services, but also that the agreement was wrung from those in charge of the property in peril by the salvors' refusal to give on any lower terms the help which alone could save the property from destruction, the duty of the court, as a court of equity, to disregard the agreement, was far more obvious than in a case where there was no evidence of any such practical compulsion and the largeness of a stipulated reward could be attributed only to some ignorance, timidity or recklessness on the part of those who agreed to pay it.

---

[30] (1858) Swab. 368, 369.
[31] (1877) 2 P.D. 5, 7.

Salvage Agreements

929 The duty of the Admiralty Court in such cases has nowhere been more powerfully stated than by Story J. in the early American case *The Emulous*[32]:

> "No system of jurisprudence, purporting to be founded on moral, or religious, or even rational principles, could tolerate for a moment the doctrine, that a salvor might avail himself of the calamities of others to force upon them a contract, unjust, oppressive, and exorbitant; that he might turn the price of safety into the price of ruin; that he might turn an act, demanded by Christian and public duty, into a traffic of profit, which would outrage human feelings, and disgrace human justice."

930 Similarly, Sir Robert Phillimore said in *The Medina*[33]:

> "it is the practice of this Court, partly for the protection of absent owners and partly on the grounds of general policy, to control agreements made by masters when an examination of those agreements show that they are clearly inequitable."

In that case, a vessel was wrecked and her 550 passengers stranded on a rock in the Red Sea. Another vessel, the *Timor*, came up but refused to take them on to their destination for less than £4,000, for which sum an agreement was concluded. Sir Robert Phillimore's decision, which was affirmed by the Court of Appeal,[34] demonstrated that an agreement concluded as a result of practical compulsion would not be enforced, though the court would not penalise the party relying on it but would normally award such sum as he would have been entitled to if there had been no agreement. The agreement was not enforced but "it was certainly a valuable salvage service according to the principles upon which such services have always been considered"[35] and £1,800 was awarded.[36]

931 The guiding test for setting aside an inequitable agreement was given by Brett L.J. in *Akerblom v. Price, Potter, Walker & Co.*[37] His Lordship observed in that case that a person in need of salvage services is inevitably under some pressure. For the court to set aside a salvage agreement, therefore, something more was required than mere inequality between the parties. Referring to Brett L.J.'s judgment in *Akerblom*, Butt J. restated the test thus in *The Strathgarry*[38]:

---

[32] (1832) 1 Sumn. 207, 210–211.
[33] (1876) 1 P.D. 272, 275. *cf. The Cargo ex Sarpedon* (1877) 3 P.D. 28.
[34] (1877) 2 P.D. 5.
[35] (1876) 1 P.D. 272, 275–276.
[36] See also *The Theodore* (1858) Swab. 351; *The Cargo ex Woosung* (1876) 1 P.D. 260; *The Silesia* (1880) 5 P.D. 177; *The Rialto* [1891] P. 175; *The Altair* [1897] P. 105; *The Kilmaho* (1900) 16 T.L.R. 155; *The Port Caledonia and The Anna* [1903] P. 184. *cf. The Helen and George* (1858) Swab. 368; *Akerblom v. Price, Potter, Walker & Co.* (1881) 7 Q.B.D. 129; *The Prinz Heinrich* (1888) 13 P.D. 31; *The Strathgarry* [1895] P. 264.
[37] (1881) 7 Q.B.D. 129, 132–133; quoted *ante*, § 881.
[38] [1895] P. 264, 270. See also *The Altair* [1897] P. 105, 108; *The Port Caledonia and The Anna* [1903] P. 184, 189.

Compulsion and inequity of terms

"A number of cases have been cited during the argument; in some of them slightly different language has been used by the judges—sometimes the word *exorbitant* has been used—sometimes the word *inequitable*; but in substance all the cases are, I think, consistent with the rule laid down in *Akerblom v. Price* as the fundamental rule. The question, therefore, to be determined is whether the agreement was manifestly unfair or unjust."

The court would not set aside a salvage agreement merely because the parties were not of perfectly equal bargaining strength in the circumstances because "marine casualties ... are generally of so urgent a character that the parties cannot be truly said to be on equal terms as to any agreement they may make with regard to them."[39] Sir Robert Phillimore expressed the position thus in *The Cargo ex Woosung*[40]: **932**

"Now, in one sense the services of every salvor are unwillingly and under duress accepted; the lesser evil of losing a portion of the profit and property being submitted to rather than the greater evil of losing all, so that in that sense all salvage services are accepted under compulsion. But there is no compulsion of duress of a criminal character, unless, indeed, all reasonable limits are transgressed by the salvors, as there has been a use of false representation or the excitement of ungrounded fears in order to procure the acceptance of their services."

Quite apart from the traditional judicial reluctance to set aside agreements, the jurisdiction to set aside salvage agreements for illegitimate pressure was inhibited by the judicially fostered public policy of encouraging potential salvors to act. In response to the allegation of pressure exerted by the master of the salving vessel by, inconsistently with his employers' wishes, making repeated offers to assist with the stipulation that remuneration should be on a salvage basis, the High Court of Australia reacted that[41]: **933**

"the main object of the law of salvage is, by the incentive of monetary gain, to encourage seafarers to render assistance to vessels in danger and the fact that their response is, to a greater or lesser extent, the product of that incentive cannot adversely reflect upon them."

The two factors that were necessary to overcome the presumption of validity of the agreement were stated by Butt J. in *The Rialto*[42]: **934**

"What is an inequitable agreement in cases of this sort? On this point two ingredients are commonly referred to. First, the parties contracting must

---

[39] *Akerblom v. Price, Potter, Walker & Co.* (1881) 7 Q.B.D. 129, 132, *per* Brett L.J.
[40] (1876) 1 P.D. 260, 265, *per* Sir Robert Phillimore.
[41] *Fisher v. The Oceanic Grandeur* (1972) 127 C.L.R. 312, 336; [1972] 2 Lloyd's Rep. 396, 408.
[42] [1891] P. 175, 178–179, *per* Butt J.

be shown not to have contracted on equal terms. I am inclined to think that, in general, in the case of salvage services contracted for and about to be performed, the parties are on unequal terms, and, therefore, the mere fact of their standing in such a position will not invalidate the agreement. If, however, contracting on unequal terms—that is to say, the master of the salved ship being at a disadvantage—it further appears that the sum insisted upon is exorbitant, then the two ingredients exist which will induce the court not to uphold the agreement."

935 The same principles applied even if the agreement was not to salve but to provide a specified service in circumstances where salvage services were necessary. In *The Strathgarry*,[43] the master engaged a tug to tow for half an hour for £500, believing that he would be enabled to get the engines restarted and avoid the need for salvage. The agreement being performed, the £500 was payable, even though the master's expectations were not actually realised so that he in fact obtained no benefit therefrom. Butt J. said that[44]:

"in forming an opinion on the fairness or unfairness of the agreement, I think the Court must regard the position of the parties at the time the agreement was entered into. The agreement cannot become fair or unfair by reason of circumstances which happened afterwards . . . I cannot say that it was manifestly unfair or unjust for him, in order to obtain a certain fixed limit to his liability, to agree to pay the specified sum on the sole condition that the specified service was rendered."

936 The same amount of compulsion or duress which would invalidate an agreement at common law was not necessary to induce the court to refuse to enforce a salvage agreement as inequitable.[45]

937 Finally, it must be stressed that a salvage agreement could be set aside as inequitable because the remuneration fixed was either exorbitant or inadequate. The court has been just as ready in favour of salvors, as in the case of the owners of salved property, to set aside an agreement which was wholly inequitable.[46] If the level of remuneration fixed were too low, it would be increased.[47]

Admiralty law: inequitable terms alone

938 Several cases have been concerned with the question whether an agreement which was not otherwise vitiated could be set aside solely because of the inequity of its terms. In *The Mark Lane*,[48] the steamship *Crete* in the Atlantic

---
[43] [1895] P. 264.
[44] *ibid.*, 271–272.
[45] *The Mark Lane* (1890) 15 P.D. 135, 137; *The Rialto* [1891] P. 175, 178.
[46] *The Theodore* (1858) Swab. 351, 352.
[47] *The Phantom* (1866) L.R. 1 A. & E. 58; *The Westbourne* (1889) 14 P.D. 132.
[48] (1890) 15 P.D. 135.

fell in with another, the *Mark Lane*, which had lost two propellor blades, was leaking owing to the increased vibration, could not use her engines, and needed towing 350 miles to Halifax. The master of the *Mark Lane* believed, on reasonable grounds, that he would not receive assistance without agreeing with the *Crete*'s master, as he therefore did, for his owners to pay £5,000 for the service, or a sum for work done if it was not successful. £5,000 was more than one-fifth of the total value of the *Mark Lane*, her cargo and freight. Butt J. rejected the agreement as entered into under compulsion and exorbitant, and awarded £3,000 with costs. He said[49]:

> "I have said that I consider the demand exorbitant. In the cases referred to by counsel, the word 'inequitable' has been used. But I think that what is at the root of the question is this—where it is found that a wholly unreasonable price has been insisted upon by the salvors and an agreement incorporating it has been signed, the Court looks rather to the position of the parties than to the reasonableness or unreasonableness of the amount. Were the parties, in fact, contracting on equal terms?"

A short passage in the judgment of Sir Robert Phillimore in *The Cargo ex Woosung*[50] also supports the view that the court would only interfere with an agreement which fixed a grossly excessive remuneration where it was a result of one of the other established heads of "unfair dealing", such as fraud, misrepresentation or practical compulsion. However, his judgment was reversed by the Court of Appeal, where Baggallay J.A. referred[51] to:

> "the case of *The Helen and George*,[52] where it was held 'that salvage would be upheld unless proved to be very exorbitant, or to have been obtained by compulsion and fraud.' Therefore, the ground of exorbitancy of the agreement would be sufficient to set it aside."

In fact, Baggallay J.A. was referring to the paraphrase in the headnote of the report of *The Helen and George* of the less decisive dictum of Dr Lushington (who upheld the agreement in question) that[53]:

> "The owner may contend that, under the circumstances, the sum of money was grossly exorbitant; and, *a fortiori*, if he can show that the agreement was obtained by fraud or compulsion, no Court would hold it to be binding."

Dr Lushington's judgment in *The Theodore*[54] supports the view that an agreement with wholly inequitable terms may not be enforced even though

---

[49] *ibid.*, 137.
[50] (1876) 1 P.D. 260, 263–264. *cf. The Rialto* [1891] P. 175, 178–179, *per* Butt J. (inequality between the parties *plus* exorbitance of terms sufficient to set aside).
[51] (1876) 1 P.D. 260, 270. *cf. The Waverley* (1871) L.R. 3 A. & E. 369.
[52] (1858) Swab. 368.
[53] *ibid.*, 369.
[54] (1858) Swab. 351. The headnote states that the agreement was dishonestly made by the master, who was in fact said by his owners to have been dismissed for making it.

Salvage Agreements

not concluded as a result of some independent vitiating factor, such as compulsion. In that case, he set aside an agreement for an "exorbitant demand" of £200, which, in the circumstances was "scarcely consistent with any just or fair dealing", and upheld a tender for £50. The headnote states that the agreement was dishonestly made by the master, who was in fact said by his owners to have been dismissed for making it. However, although Dr Lushington emphasised the court's indisposition to set aside an agreement which it was satisfied was honest, he did not make clear that the agreement's unenforceability was a result of fraud rather than simply of its wholly inequitable terms, unless, perhaps the latter factor was *per se* sufficient evidence of fraud. It is unlikely that inequitable terms will be agreed in the absence of one of the vitiating factors already considered. But if it were and the terms were wholly unreasonable, it is submitted that the court retained its discretion not to enforce it and to assess the reward independently.

An agreement is not inequitable merely because the salved value is less than the agreed remuneration.[55]

Admiralty law: inequitable settlements

941 Just as the court would disregard an inequitable agreement made *before* salvage services began, it would also do so where, *after* the services had been rendered, an inequitable settlement was concluded. If a payment were made to the salvor and he had given a receipt in the form of a discharge of all claims, the court would nevertheless make him an award if, first, it held the payment to be very inadequate and, secondly, it found either that the salvor was not competent properly to understand the value of his salvage services (though he may have understood the meaning of the receipt)[56] or that the circumstances under which the receipt was signed were not satisfactorily explained by those who sought to set up the settlement as a bar to the salvage claim (such as where the receipt referred to only part of the salvage services rendered and the log was dishonest).[57] "[W]hen an agreement is made by salvors belonging to the ordinary class of seamen with the master of the salved vessel, the Court ought to be satisfied that it was entered into with reasonable deliberation, and with adequate knowledge of its meaning and effect, in which case the Court, even if of the opinion that the remuneration was too small, would not, except in very extraordinary cases, interfere with it."[58] Similar principles should apply where the settlement was likewise unconscionable so far as the owner of salved property was concerned.[59]

---

[55] *The Inna* [1938] P. 148.
[56] *The Silver Bullion (Cargo ex The Sir Robert Peel)* (1854) 2 Spinks E. & A. 70. Dr Lushington's judgment, referring to an uncited decision of Lord Stowell, states the court's jurisdiction as one in favour of "ignorant persons" but does not appear to contemplate ignorance other than an inability to form a proper judgment of the value of the services.
[57] *The Macgregor Laird* [1897] W.N. 308.
[58] *ibid.*, per Sir Robert Phillimore.
[59] But *cf. The Theodore* (1858) Swab. 351, where an agreement was set aside for an exorbitant demand which, in the light of the circumstances of the service, was "scarcely consistent with any just or fair dealing". However, there was no reference to any inequality between the parties, though Dr Lushington did suggest that there was an element of dishonesty.

Compulsion and unfair terms at common law

942 At common law a contract will not be upset merely because it is concluded under compulsion; the compulsion must be "illegitimate" in the sense that it is a means of which the law disapproves. A party who is induced to contract by illegitimate pressure,[60] whether or not the terms of the contract are fair, may at his option either affirm the contract or he may avoid it, and so refuse to continue performance and claim restitution if necessary.[61] If a contract is valid at common law, it may nevertheless be voidable in equity for undue influence.[62] It is sufficient for avoidance that there has been actual undue influence. However, in cases where undue influence is presumed, either from the parties' relationship falling within certain established categories or from the facts of the case, the victim must also prove that he has been manifestly disadvantaged. Both at common law and in equity, a person avoiding a contract can only do so provided he makes counter-restitution of any benefits received under it.

943 Except where manifest disadvantage is required in equity, the common law rules on illegitimate pressure are primarily concerned with the procedure of how the contract is made rather than its substance. The courts may generally not interfere with a contract because its terms appear unduly advantageous or disadvantageous to one of the parties. However, they may do so to retrain the effect of terms which purport to qualify or exclude liability, under common law rules and under the provisions of the Unfair Contract Terms Act 1977 and the Unfair Terms in Consumer Contracts Regulations 1999.[63]

The Salvage Convention 1989

944 The Salvage Convention 1989, Art. 7 (which cannot be contracted out of)[64] provides:

> "A contract or any of terms thereof may be annulled or modified if:
> (a) the contract has been entered into under undue influence or the influence of danger and its terms are inequitable; or
> (b) the payment under the contract is in an excessive degree too large or too small for the services actually rendered."

---

[60] A threat to commit a tort, crime or breach of contract.
[61] See Goff & Jones, Chaps. 10–12.
[62] See especially *Barclays Bank Plc v. O'Brien* [1994] 1 A.C. 180; *CIBC Mortgages Plc v. Pitt* [1994] 1 A.C. 200; *Royal Bank of Scotland v. Etridge (No. 2)* [2001] 3 W.L.R. 1021.
[63] See *post*, Chap. 12. Under the Unfair Terms in Consumer Contracts Regulations 1999, reg. 5(1), "unfair term" means any term which has not been individually negotiated and, contrary to the requirement of good faith, causes a significant imbalance in the parties' rights and obligations under the contract, to the detriment of the consumer; the strength of the parties' bargaining positions, inducements to agree to the term and the extent to which a supplier of services has dealt fairly and equitably with a consumer are relevant to assessing good faith (reg. 5(5), Sched. 2).
[64] Art. 6.3.

The operation of Article 7 generally differs from that of the common law in four respects: the compulsion need not be "illegitimate" (an external danger suffices)[65]; compulsion must be accompanied by inequitable terms[66]; unfair terms as to the size of payment are sufficient (without compulsion)[67]; and the contract may be either annulled or modified.

945 Unlike the Brussels Convention 1910, Art. 7, which applied to agreements as to assistance or salvage entered into at the moment and under the influence of danger, the Salvage Convention 1989, Art. 7 simply applies to contracts, without more. This does not mean that Article 7 provides a general power to annul or modify any type of contract, for the Convention applies to salvage operations.[68] It does mean, however, that a contract which is not made specifically for salvage purposes, such as a towage contract, but which prima facie applies to salvage operations[69] will be subject to Article 7. Moreover, Article 7 may apply to sub-contracts made between salvors and third parties[70] and to contracts between salvors and their employees.[71]

946 Two conditions are required to trigger the operation of Article 7(a): first, entry into the contract under "undue influence" or the influence of danger; and, secondly, inequitable terms.

As noted above,[72] the term "undue influence" appears to embrace all types of unfair pressure or influence applied, and it is therefore unfortunate that it may be necessary to avoid confusion by distinguishing it from the more familiar and specific meaning of undue influence in equity.[73] In the 1989 Convention it is a more widely expressed successor to "fraud and concealment" in the Brussels Convention 1910, Art. 7. As such, it not only applies to conduct of the salvor but could also include a salvee's failure to disclose information relevant to the terms upon which the salvor is considering entry into the contract or a salvor's failure to explain the significance of bespoke contract terms which he is proposing.

947 On one view, it is irrelevant that Article 7(a) is expressed to depend on the contract's being entered under undue influence or the influence of danger, since *ex hypothesi* salvage is always dependent on danger[74] and obviously anyone who enters into a salvage contract, however close or distant he may be

---

[65] Under Art. 7(a).
[66] Under Art. 7(a).
[67] Under Art. 7(b).
[68] See Art. 6.1.
[69] Of course, where danger requiring salvage intervenes, a pre-existing contract may not apply.
[70] *cf.* Gaskell, 21–388.
[71] *cf.* Gaskell, 21–388. Salvors' employees are in any event protected by MSA 1995, s.39; see *post*, §§ 1538–1539.
[72] *Ante*, § 944.
[73] See *ante*, § 942.
[74] See *ante*, Chap. 4; Salvage Convention 1989, Art. 1(a).

from the event, does so to some extent under the influence of danger. It appears that the equivalent provision in the 1910 Convention was designed to apply to a master at the time of peril rather than to a shipowner in a distant office,[75] but Article 7(a) is clearly not so restricted. What Article 7(a) appears to contemplate, when the contract is entered into "under undue influence or the influence of danger", are circumstances such that the will of the person affected is inordinately and unfairly impaired, above and beyond the ordinary effects of the danger necessitating salvage. Where this is the effect of the danger, it is unnecessary for the party influenced to shew that the other party either exerted, took advantage of, or was even aware of such influence. However, in cases of "undue influence" it is unlikely that the contract will be affected if the person exerting the undue influence is not doing so consciously.

948 As stated above, no matter how much he has been influenced, a party cannot claim annulment or modification unless the terms of the contract are "inequitable". However, whereas it may be assumed that Article 7(a) will generally operate where the inclusion of inequitable terms is a consequence of the relevant influence, this is not required by the drafting. Furthermore, there may be different results where, say, a master influenced within Article 7(a) concludes a contract the terms of which are inequitable for a cargo-owner but not for the shipowner, *e.g.* where the salved value of the cargo is agreed to be disproportionately high to that of the ship, potentially at least imposing a disproportionate liability on the cargo-owner under Article 13.2.[76] In such a case, since the master will be acting as agent for both cargo-owner and shipowner, both principals may be influenced but only the cargo-owner would be able to claim that he was subject to inequitable terms so as to invoke the operation of Article 7(a).

949 Whether terms are inequitable will depend on the facts: the Convention offers no guidance. If, as is commonly the case in practice, the contract is on a standard form—particularly one of long and widespread usage negotiated by a committee including underwriting representatives and primarily designed to leave matters to arbitration, such as Lloyd's Form—its terms are very unlikely to be held to be inequitable. There will be more scope for such a finding where a bespoke contract or a different standard form is used, or where a generally accepted standard form has been amended or amplified, particularly if the person proposing such a contract has employed terms designed to depart from the provisions of the Salvage Convention 1989. Examples[77] might be terms: that the salved property, or part of it,[78] have a minimum salved value; that the

---

[75] See Wildeboer, p. 176.
[76] See *post*, Chap. 16.
[77] See Gaskell, 21–387.
[78] An agreement that cargo should have a disproportionately high salved value to that of the ship would not reflect the respective liabilities under Art. 13.2: see *post*, Chap. 16.

salvor's expenses under Article 14.3[79] are agreed at a certain rate; that there is agreed to be a threat of "substantial" damage to the environment within Article 1(d)[80]; or that waters outside the normal range of coastal waters are "coastal waters" within Article 1(d) (so as to invoke the application of terms providing for payment for avoiding environmental damage).[81]

950 Article 7(a) does not state the time at which the contract's terms are to be regarded as inequitable. It is therefore arguable that it applies even where terms are not apparently inequitable when the contract is concluded but turn out to be so, particularly where performance of the contract is made more onerous. The more orthodox view is that the arguably unfair operation of contract terms is a different matter from whether the terms are inherently inequitable, which is to be judged at the time at which the contract is made.

951 There is, however, one clear case where it is the unfair operation of terms rather than their inherent inequity which subjects the contract to annulment or modification, namely under Article 7(b): where the payment under the contract is excessively large or small for the services actually rendered. In practice, Article 7(b) may be more likely to apply where one party has acted unfairly in negotiating the contract, but this is not necessary: in particular, unlike Article 7(a), the application of Article 7(b) is not dependent on whether or not a party has been unfairly "influenced" in entering the contract. Moreover, the mere fact that agreed remuneration is high or low is insufficient. Article 7(b) only applies where it is excessively so, not in the light of the circumstances existing at the time at which the contract was made, but for the services actually rendered. It is possible therefore that Article 7(b) will not apply to a sum which appears excessive at the time of contracting for what turns out to be an arduous service. Although "excessive" will presumably be measured by comparing the agreed sum with what would be awarded in the absence of an agreement, the tribunal is not bound under Article 7(b) simply to award what it would normally award. A party may therefore still benefit from a contract which is financially favourable to him but to a lesser extent; *mutatis mutandis* with an unfavourable bargain.

Inducements prohibited

952 Lloyd's Form provides that "No person signing this agreement or any party on whose behalf it is signed shall at any time or in any manner whatsoever offer provide make give or promise to provide or demand or take any form of

---

[79] See *ante*, Chap. 5.
[80] See *ante*, Chap. 5.
[81] See *ante*, § 402.

inducement for entering into this agreement."[82] The effects of non-compliance with this clause are not stated and Lloyd's Form provides no assistance in its interpretation. Under the general law, where one person gives a bribe to another person so as to affect the position of a third person, then, depending on the circumstances,[83] the victim may have a personal claim to the profits of the wrongdoing from a fiduciary bribee,[84] and possibly a proprietary claim,[85] and a claim for damages in contract and/or tort against the bribee[86] and briber.[87] At one level, the Lloyd's Form inducement clause draws attention to the legal position governing inducements, which remains applicable regardless of this clause. However, as a contractual term, it may be breached, so as to provide a remedy in damages for any loss suffered in consequence (*e.g.* where the claimant has accepted an inferior service to one he might otherwise have accepted) and possibly the opportunity to terminate performance of the contract, though the effectiveness of that remedy will depend on when the victim becomes aware of the conduct in question. The clause is drafted in wide terms, and not limited to cases where an inducement is actually provided, though in those cases there is less likely to be loss suffered as a result of breach.

Illegality

There appears to be no reported case in which illegality has arisen for consideration in a salvage case. This may be a tribute to the standards of professional salvors in acting lawfully. However, just as in many other areas of commercial activity, economic considerations may prompt conduct or contract terms in salvage cases which fall foul of the rules on illegality and public policy, *e.g.* by attempting to avoid or ignore environmental requirements. The law on this topic is complex and cannot appropriately be discussed here.[88] It may be noted, however, that a contract to do an illegal act is void and a contract which is against public policy is unenforceable.[89] Furthermore, a person who performs such a contract will not only be disentitled from enforcing the contract but will generally be unable to claim in restitution for benefits which he has conferred on the other party.[90]

953

---

[82] LOF 2000, cl.L; LOF 1995, cl.19.
[83] See generally *Petrotrade Inc. v. Smith* [2000] 1 Lloyd's Rep. 486.
[84] *Lister v. Stubbs* (1890) 45 Ch.D. 1.
[85] *Att.-Gen. of Hong Kong v. Reid* [1994] 1 A.C. 324 (PC).
[86] *Att.-Gen. v. Blake* [2001] 1 A.C. 268.
[87] *Mahesan v. Malaysia Housing Society* [1979] A.C. 374.
[88] See further the references in the following two footnotes. Note also that the Law Commission will be proposing reform of this area of the law: see Law Commission, *Illegal Transactions: The Effect of Illegality on Contracts and Trusts* (LCCP No. 154, 1999) and *The Illegality Defence in Tort* (LCCP No. 160, 2001).
[89] See Chitty, Chap. 17; Treitel, Chap. 11.
[90] Goff & Jones, Chap. 24; F. D. Rose, "Restitutionary and Proprietary Consequences of Illegality", Chap. 10 of F. D. Rose (ed.), *Consensus ad Idem (Essays on the Law of Contract in Honour of Sir Guenter Treitel)* (Sweet & Maxwell, 1996).

Salvage Agreements

7. CONSTRUCTION

LOF 2000: overriding objectives

954 LSSAC 2000, cl.2 (entitled "Overriding objective"), states that:

"In construing the Agreement[91] or on the making of any arbitral order or award regard shall be had to the overriding purposes of the Agreement namely:
   (a) to seek to promote safety of life at sea and the preservation of property at sea and during the salvage operations to prevent or minimise damage to the environment;
   (b) to ensure that its provisions are operated in good faith and that it is read and understood to operate in a reasonably businesslike manner;
   (c) to encourage co-operation between the parties and with relevant authorities;
   (d) to ensure that the reasonable expectations of salvors and owners of salved property are met; and
   (e) to ensure that it leads to a fair and efficient disposal of disputes between the parties whether amicably, by mediation or by arbitration within a reasonable time and at a reasonable cost."

8. DISCHARGE

Grounds

955 In the main, salvage agreements are discharged on the same grounds which determine discharge in the general law of contract, *viz.* by agreement, by performance, by termination after a repudiatory breach, and as a consequence of supervening circumstances.[92] Discussion of the generally applicable principles of the law of contract can be found in the standard works on the law of contract and do not require re-examination here except in so far as particular points have arisen in the law of salvage.[93] Discharge by agreement is considered in the next paragraph[94] and discharge by supervening circumstances in

---

[91] *i.e.* LOF 2000: see LSSAC 2000, cl.1.1.

[92] Discharge is not effected by *tender*. Salvors are not entitled to maintain that an otherwise valid agreement for a fixed sum is no longer binding, so as to allow them to claim a reward which, independently assessed, would be higher than the agreement sum, simply because the salvees tender a larger sum than was stipulated in the agreement: *The Waverley* (1871) L.R. 3 A. & E. 369.

[93] See in particular Chitty and Treitel.

[94] *Post*, § 956.

the following paragraphs.[95] Discharge by performance and breach are considered in the next chapter.[96]

Agreement or consent

956 Subject to a number of important qualifications, which need not be investigated in detail here, it is generally the case that an attempted variation of a contract will be ineffective at common law and the original agreement will retain its full effect, unless the variation—which may be to discharge—is founded on accord and satisfaction, *i.e.* is supported by consideration.[97] In Admiralty, however, a salvage agreement has been held to be cancellable simply by the mutual consent of the parties.[98] The cancellation may be affected either by their express agreement[99] or by implication, by conduct from which such consent ought to be inferred.[1] But the burden of proof lies heavily upon those who assert the cancellation. As Dr Lushington put it[2]:

> "whoever takes upon himself to establish the fact that an admitted agreement has been invalidated by consent of parties, is bound to prove, by clear preponderance of testimony, that it was so cancelled."

Once the agreement is cancelled, the court forms an independent view of the remuneration which the salvors should receive, and a party is not free to rely on the agreement to his advantage—so as to form an upper or lower limit to the award—but to ignore it when it is to his disadvantage.[3]

Supervening circumstances

957 A party to a contract, whether for salvage, towage or some other object, is not relieved from his duties under the contract merely because performance becomes more onerous than originally contemplated.[4] But, after a proper and valid agreement for salvage has been entered into, circumstances may supervene which, without fault on the part of either salvors or salvees, make the contracted-for service insufficient or impossible, and the salvors thereupon perform salvage services of a different kind or class from those stipulated for in the salvage contract or those which can fairly be treated as being within the reasonable contemplation of the parties, when they entered the agreement, as

---

[95] *Post*, §§ 957–959.
[96] Chap. 10. See also *ante*, Chap. 8.
[97] See Chitty, Chap. 23; Treitel, pp. 93–95.
[98] See the cases cited *infra*, in nn. 99 and 1, and *The Betsey* (1843) 2 W. Rob. 167; *The Repulse* (1845) 2 W. Rob. 396, 397; *The Cato* (1866) 35 L.J. Adm. 116, 117; *The Inna* [1938] P. 148, 156.
[99] *The Africa* (1854) 1 Spinks E. & A. 229.
[1] *The Samuel* (1851) 17 L.T. (O.S.) 204. Dr Lushington's judgment is not entirely clear on this point.
[2] *The Betsey* (1843) 2 W. Rob. 167, 172.
[3] *The Africa, supra*, n. 99, at 302; *The Samuel, supra*, n. 1, at 204.
[4] *The True Blue* (1843) 2 W. Rob. 176, 180; *The Jonge Andries* (1857) Swab. 226, (affirmed *ibid.*, 303). See also *ante*, §§ 588–624.

coming within its scope. A salvor who performs a service which he is not bound by the agreement to provide is entitled to remuneration for it.[5] The contract being inapplicable to the supervening circumstances, and salvage not being in any case dependent on contract, it is immaterial, so long as it was not because of his misconduct, that the salvor has failed to perform the agreement.[6]

958 In *The Westbourne*,[7] a steamship fell in with the *Westbourne*, which had lost her propeller about 260 miles east of Gibraltar and 60 miles from Carthagena. The weather was moderately bad. The masters concluded a parol agreement for £600 for towage to Gibraltar. After the commencement of the service, the weather became most violent, hawser after hawser parted, the grain cargo shifted and it was found to be impossible to take the *Westbourne* to Gibraltar. Against the wish of the *Westbourne*'s master, the course was changed to Carthagena. After arrival, he stated that this had been necessitated by the stress of weather and the damage to hawsers, ship and crew caused thereby. Lord Esher M.R. said[8]:

> "I am of opinion that the agreement entered into by the masters of the *Howick* and the *Westbourne* was a towage agreement, but entered into whilst the *Westbourne* was in such exceptional danger that she required salvage assistance; it was thus a towage agreement to do work in the nature of a salvage service. If that agreement became more difficult to carry out by reason of succeeding circumstances, the Court could not therefore alter it. But if, by reason of circumstances over which the salvors had no control, the difficulty of the service was so far increased as to make it in fact a wholly different service from that which was originally contemplated by the parties, or a service of a wholly different class, then the Court of Admiralty has a right to deal with the case as if the original agreement had not been made, and to make such an award as under the circumstances it may think right."

959 The general Admiralty rule is analogous to the common law doctrine of frustration,[9] though not entirely congruent with it. Frustration at common law discharges contracting parties from all obligations from the moment of frustration but the maritime law requires a party who has contracted to tow to stand by and render whatever assistance is possible after towage has become impossible, even to resume the original obligation if this again becomes

---

[5] *The Westbourne* (1889) 14 P.D. 132; *The William Brandt Junior* (1842) 2 N.o.C. Supp. lxvii (distinguished in *The Betsey* (1843) 2 W. Rob. 167, where a towage agreement was upheld, the relevant circumstances being present at the commencement of the service and not occurring during performance); *The Waverley* (1871) L.R. 3 A. & E. 369, 378–379; see also *ante*, §§ 588–624. *cf. The Phantom* (1866) L.R. 1 A. & E. 58.
[6] *The Hestia* [1895] P. 193.
[7] (1899) 14 P.D. 132.
[8] *ibid.*, 134.
[9] See Chitty, Chap. 24; Treitel, Chap. 20.

Background

possible.[10] Services rendered after frustration at common law *are* remunerated on the basis of their reasonable value—which may exceed a sum specifically agreed for the original contracted services[11]—but subsequent services rendered as salvage are remunerated on a salvage basis. It is thus the court's inherent jurisdiction to substitute its own award of reasonable salvage remuneration, independent of contract, which lies at the heart of the law relating to the setting aside of salvage agreements which it considers to be inequitable.

9. SCOPIC

Background[12]

The provisions of Article 14 of the International Salvage Convention 1989, affording special compensation for environmental services,[13] have not proved to be free of difficulty or popular in practice. Accordingly, the industry[14] has produced a clause known in LOF 2000 and LSSAC 2000 as "the Scopic Clause", though referred to in the clause itself as "the SCOPIC Clause". LSSAC 2000, cl.3.9 states: **960**

> "'Scopic Clause' refers to the agreement made between (1) members of the International Salvage Union, (2) the International Group of P.&I. Clubs and (3) certain property underwriters which first became effective on 1st August 1999 and includes any replacement or revision thereof. All references to the Scopic Clause in the Agreement shall be deemed to refer to the version of the Scopic Clause current at the date the Agreement is made."

"SCOPIC" is an acronym for "Special Compensation Protection and Indemnity Clause", although this is not revealed in the clause itself. SCOPIC has two functions. It is designed to replace the operation of most of Article 14. However, it is unfortunate that it employs within its longer name the term "special compensation" used by Article 14 to describe the payment for environmental services authorised by that Article. For the main function of SCOPIC is to provide salvors with a guaranteed form of payment to be calculated according to a specified scale, whether or not there is the threat of damage to the environment upon which Article 14 depends. **961**

The scheme of the clause is to give the salvor the option whether to trigger its provisions. The rate of payment was designed to be fair, if not generous; **962**

---

[10] *The Minnehaha* (1861) Lush. 335. See *ante*, § 605.
[11] *The Massalia* [1959] 1 W.L.R. 787; reversed, but not on this point, in *The Eugenia* [1964] 2 Q.B. 226.
[12] See generally G. Brice [2000] L.M.C.L.Q. 26.
[13] See further, *ante*, Chap. 5.
[14] By a tripartite agreement between the International Salvage Union, the International Group of P. & I. Clubs and the London insurance market.

and the SCOPIC clause affords the salvor the opportunity of earning greater remuneration than under a normal salvage reward. But he can only benefit from it in full if he invokes the clause as soon as possible. And he will not benefit at all unless his SCOPIC remuneration exceeds the normal salvage reward; for, if it does not, he will be penalised by having his salvage reward discounted, so he will be worse off than if he had not invoked the clause. The salvor who invokes the clause quickly therefore stands the greatest chance of maximising his remuneration; but he also stands a greater chance of reducing it, if he mispredicts the situation. Unfortunately, caution is deterred: the longer he waits, the less SCOPIC remuneration he earns and the more likely it becomes that he will not exceed the threshold fixed by the conventional salvage reward.

963 SCOPIC was introduced, for use in conjunction with Lloyd's Form, on August 1, 1999, initially for a two-year trial period. However, within this trial period some dissatisfaction was expressed with its terms and a new edition of Lloyd's Form was being prepared. Accordingly, the second edition of SCOPIC (SCOPIC 2000) was published on the same day as LOF 2000, *i.e.* September 1, 2000.

Application, invocation and exclusion

964 SCOPIC 2000 applies in the following circumstances.

First, the clause is expressed to be "supplementary to any Lloyd's Form Salvage Agreement 'No Cure—No Pay' ('Main Agreement') which incorporates the provisions of Article 14 of the International Convention on Salvage 1989 ('Article 14')".[15] Unlike LOF 1990 and LOF 1995 (which was current when SCOPIC was introduced), LOF 2000 does not specifically incorporate Article 14. But the Article applies under the general law and LOF 2000, cl.D acknowledges that the services under the contract are subject to the provisions of the Convention as incorporated into English law.

Secondly, Box 7 on the face of LOF 2000 asks the parties to state whether or not the SCOPIC clause is incorporated. LOF 2000, cl.C then states that, "Unless the word 'No' in Box 7 has been deleted, this agreement shall be deemed to have been made on the basis that the Scopic Clause is not incorporated and forms no part of this agreement." Mere agreement to Lloyd's Form in general, or even signature, is insufficient. The clause must be consciously incorporated.

965 However, incorporation of SCOPIC into the contract is merely the first of two necessary steps for it to have effect. Incorporation gives *the contractor* the option to *invoke* the clause. He will only be entitled to payment on SCOPIC terms if, and from the time that, he gives written notice to the owner of the vessel.[16] The mere incorporation of SCOPIC into LOF 2000 shall not of itself

---

[15] SCOPIC 2000, cl.1.
[16] SCOPIC 2000, cl.2.

be construed as a notice invoking the clause.[17] The contractor may invoke SCOPIC whenever he chooses, regardless of the circumstances and, in particular, regardless of whether or not there is a "threat of damage to the environment".[18] However, the timing of his decision whether to invoke the clause will be crucial.[19]

Parties

The incorporation of the SCOPIC clause depends on the terms of Lloyd's Form, which essentially constitutes a contract between the contractors and the salvees in general.[20] However, SCOPIC remuneration is stated to be payable only by the shipowner.[21] In practice, therefore, SCOPIC functions as a contract between the salvor and the shipowner (effectively establishing a liability to be borne by the shipowner's P. & I. Club). However, neither LOF 2000 nor SCOPIC 2000 otherwise attempt to restrict its operation to salvor and shipowner. If appropriate, therefore, its provisions may be enforced by or against any of the parties to the Lloyd's Form contract. Thus, SCOPIC 2000, cl.14, which provides that the shipowner may not claim a general average contribution to his SCOPIC liability, can be relied upon by cargo-owners as a defence to such a claim.

966

General terms

SCOPIC 2000 is not a separate contract. Its opening words state that the SCOPIC clause is "supplementary" to the "Main Agreement".[22] More accurately, however, it constitutes part of LOF 2000 though its terms are only effective when invoked.

967

The definitions in the Main Agreement are incorporated into the SCOPIC clause.[23] However, if the SCOPIC clause is inconsistent with any provisions of the Main Agreement or inconsistent with the law applicable to SCOPIC, once the clause is invoked, it overrides such other provisions to the extent necessary to give business efficacy to the SCOPIC agreement.[24]

Security, liens and time limits

The SCOPIC arrangement must be supported by security.[25] Within two working days of receiving notice that SCOPIC has been invoked, the shipowner must provide the Contractor with Initial Security of US$3 millions for

968

---

[17] LOF 2000, cl.C.
[18] SCOPIC 2000, cl.2.
[19] See *post*, §§ 971–973.
[20] See more specifically *ante*, §§ 793–795.
[21] SCOPIC 2000, cll. 6(i) and 14.
[22] SCOPIC 2000, cl.1.
[23] SCOPIC 2000, cl.1.
[24] SCOPIC 2000, cl.1.
[25] SCOPIC 2000, cll. 3–4. These are considered in a little more detail *post*, Chap. 13, §§ 1255–1264.

his claim for SCOPIC remuneration.[26] If he fails to do so, the salvor may withdraw from SCOPIC and revert to his rights under the Main Agreement.[27] If Initial Security is provided and is likely to be less or more than the anticipated SCOPIC remuneration, the shipowner or salvor respectively may require the security to be decreased or increased as appropriate.[28] For his part, the salvor agrees by invoking SCOPIC 2000 "to give an indemnity in a form acceptable to the owners of the vessel in respect of any overpayment in the event that the SCOPIC remuneration due ultimately proves to be less than the sum paid on account".[29]

SCOPIC 2000, cl.1 provides that, "For the purposes of liens[30] and time limits[31] the services hereunder will be treated in the same manner as salvage."

Appointment of SCR and Special Representatives

969 Once the SCOPIC clause has been invoked, a Shipowner's Casualty Representative (SCR) and underwriters' Special Representatives may be appointed.

The shipowners may at their sole option appoint an SCR to attend the salvage operation in accordance with the terms and conditions of Appendix B to SCOPIC.[32]

"[T]he Hull and Machinery underwriter (or, if more than one, the lead underwriter) and one owner or underwriter of all or part of any cargo on board the vessel may each appoint one special representative (hereinafter called respectively the 'Special Hull Representative' and the 'Special Cargo Representative' and collectively called the 'Special Representatives') at the sole expense of the appointor to attend the casualty to observe and report upon the salvage operation on the term and conditions set out in Appendix C hereof."[33] It is stipulated that such Special Representatives shall be technical men and not practising lawyers.[34]

Duties of parties

970 The duties of the parties to SCOPIC remain the same as under the Lloyd's Form contract[35] except as varied by the terms of the SCOPIC clause. This is in part confirmed by SCOPIC 2000, cl.10, which states that "The duties and liabilities of the Contractor shall remain the same as under the Main Agreement, namely to use his best endeavours to salve the vessel and property

---

[26] SCOPIC 2000, cl.3(i).
[27] SCOPIC 2000, cl.4. See *post*, § 972.
[28] SCOPIC 2000, cl.3(ii)–(iii). Disputes shall be resolved by the arbitrator: *ibid.*, cl.3(iv).
[29] SCOPIC 2000, cl.8(ii).
[30] See generally *post*, Chap. 13.
[31] See generally *post*, Chap. 12.
[32] SCOPIC 2000, cl.11. SCOPIC, App. B is set out *post*, App. 5B.
[33] SCOPIC 2000, cl.12. For SCOPIC 2000, App. C, see *post*, App. 5C.
[34] SCOPIC 2000, cl.12.
[35] See *post*, Chap. 10.

Period of application, withdrawal and termination

thereon and in so doing to prevent or minimise damage to the environment". Additionally, of course, the shipowner must provide security[36] and pay SCOPIC remuneration[37] in accordance with the terms of the SCOPIC clause; and the salvor must give an indemnity in respect of any amount by which any sum paid on account exceeds the assessed SCOPIC remuneration.[38]

Period of application, withdrawal and termination

Commencement of SCOPIC remuneration

As noted above, whether or not SCOPIC is invoked, rewards for the salvage operations performed are to be assessed under LOF 2000 in accordance with Article 13 of the International Salvage Convention 1989.[39] Indeed, even in a case where SCOPIC is invoked, services rendered before it is invoked remain subject to remuneration solely under Article 13.[40] **971**

However, once, and from the moment that, SCOPIC is invoked, additional remuneration becomes payable according to its terms.[41]

Withdrawal

Under SCOPIC 2000, cl.4, the contractor has an option to withdraw from the SCOPIC arrangement. This is subject to two conditions. The first is that the shipowner has not provided the required Initial Security[42] or agreed alternative security by the time of withdrawal.[43] The second is that the Contractor gives written notice to the shipowner. Once the Contractor has withdrawn, he reverts to his rights under the Main Agreement including Article 14, which shall apply as if the SCOPIC clause had not existed. **972**

Termination

Either party may terminate the operation of the SCOPIC clause if, first, the Contractor is not restrained from demobilising his equipment by an authority[44] **973**

---

[36] See *ante*, § 968.
[37] See *post*, §§ 976–978.
[38] SCOPIC 2000, cl.8(ii).
[39] SCOPIC 2000, cll.2 and 6(i). See *post*, Chap. 15.
[40] SCOPIC 2000, cl.2.
[41] SCOPIC 2000, cl.2. And see *ibid.*, cl.6(i).
[42] Under SCOPIC 2000, cl.3. See *post*, § 1257.
[43] This is the effect of SCOPIC, cl.4, though it is infelicitously drafted. It states that:
"If the owners of the vessel do not provide the Initial Security within the said 2 working days [from invocation of the clause, as required by cl.3], the Contractor ... shall be entitled to withdraw from all the provisions of the SCOPIC clause ... PROVIDED THAT this right of withdrawal may only be exercised if, at the time of giving said notice of withdrawal the owners of the vessel have still not provided the Initial Security or any alternative security which the owners of the vessel and the Contractor may agree will be sufficient."
The proviso seems to assume that the obligation to provide the Initial Security within two working days can be satisfied after the two days have passed, which is of course impossible. What the clause means is that, once the shipowner has failed to provide the Initial Security within two working days, the Contractor acquires a right of withdrawal but this is lost if Initial or agreed security is provided before the contractor exercises his right to withdraw.
[44] "Government, Local or Port Authorities or any other officially recognised body."

Salvage Agreements

with jurisdiction over the area where the services are being rendered[45] and, secondly, he complies with the conditions laid down in SCOPIC 2000, cl.9.

To save the salvor from the obligation to proceed with services for which he might not be paid, he is given a right to terminate under cl.9(i)[46] if the total cost of the necessary services would exceed the sum of the value of the property capable of being salved and all sums to which he would be entitled as SCOPIC remuneration. However, the practical importance of this right is reduced by the fact that he is entitled to security for payment under clause 3 and has a right of withdrawal where it is not provided.[47]

Under clause 9(ii), the shipowner may at any time terminate the obligation to pay SCOPIC remuneration, provided that the contractor is given at least five clear days' notice.

Under clause 9, the salvor's right is to terminate the entire contract (LOF 2000 and SCOPIC 2000), whereas the shipowner's right is to escape liability for SCOPIC remuneration. Where the shipowner terminates, he remains liable to pay remuneration for the SCOPIC services rendered before termination at the specified rate,[48] including time for demobilisation so far as this reasonably exceeded the five days' notice of termination.[49]

Relationship with Article 13 salvage reward

974   Consistently with SCOPIC's stated aim of supplementing LOF 2000,[50] salvage rewards are to be assessed under LOF 2000 in accordance with Article 13 of the International Salvage Convention 1989, whether or not SCOPIC is invoked.[51] Moreover, "The salvage award under Article 13 shall not be diminished by reason of the exception to the principle of 'No Cure—No Pay' in the form of SCOPIC remuneration."[52]

Whereas an Article 13 salvage reward is payable by all those against whom the reward is properly made, "SCOPIC remuneration as assessed under sub-clause 5 above will be payable only by the owners of the vessel and only to the extent that it exceeds the total Article 13 Award (or, if none, any potential Article 13 Award) payable by all salved interests (including cargo, bunkers,

---

[45] SCOPIC 2000, cl.9(iii).
[46] "The Contractor shall be entitled to terminate the services under this SCOPIC clause and the Main Agreement by written notice to owners of the vessel with a copy of the SCR (if any) and any Special Representative appointed if the total cost of his services to date and the services that will be needed to fulfil his obligations hereunder to the property (calculated by means of the tariff rate but before the bonus conferred by sub-clause 5(iii) hereof) will exceed the sum of:—
   (a) The value of the property capable of being salved; and
   (b) All sums to which he will be entitled as SCOPIC remuneration."
[47] SCOPIC 2000, cl.4. See *ante*, § 972.
[48] In SCOPIC 2000, App. A. See *post*, App. 5A.
[49] SCOPIC 2000, cl.9(ii).
[50] SCOPIC 2000, cl.1.
[51] SCOPIC 2000, cll. 2 and 6(i). SCOPIC 2000, cl.6(i) provides that "The salvage *services* under the Main Agreement shall continue to be assessed in accordance with Article 13" (emphasis added); more accurately, it is the salvage *reward* which is assessed under Art. 13. See generally *post*, Chap. 15.
[52] SCOPIC 2000, cl.6(iii).

lubricating oil and stores) after currency adjustment but before interest and costs even if the Article 13 Award or any part of it is not recovered."[53] Therefore, the possibility of invoking SCOPIC gives the salvor the opportunity of earning remuneration over and above the amount of the Article 13 salvage reward; however, this is subject to the risk of a penalty discount of that reward if the assessed SCOPIC remuneration turns out to be less than the Article 13 reward.[54]

"In the event of the Article 13 Award or settlement being in a currency other than United States dollars it shall, for the purposes of the SCOPIC clause, be exchanged at the rate of exchange prevailing at the termination of the services under the Main Agreement."[55]

Relationship with Article 14 special compensation[56]

975 Although the opening words of SCOPIC 2000, cl.1 state that the SCOPIC clause is "supplementary to any Lloyd's Form Salvage Agreement 'No Cure—No Pay' ('Main Agreement') which incorporates the provisions of Article 14 of the International Convention on Salvage 1989 ('Article 14')", clause 1 immediately goes on to state that, where SCOPIC 2000 applies, the salvor's right to special compensation under Article 14[57] is excluded unless he exercises his right to withdraw from SCOPIC.[58] (Nonetheless, "[t]he assessment of SCOPIC remuneration shall include the prevention of pollution as well as the removal of pollution in the immediate vicinity of the vessel in so far as this is necessary for the proper execution of the salvage.")[59] Where the salvor withdraws from SCOPIC, Article 14 "shall apply as if the SCOPIC clause had not existed".[60]

SCOPIC remuneration

Assessment

976 SCOPIC remuneration is assessed in accordance with SCOPIC 2000, cl.5 and Appendix A on the basis of detailed tariff rates.[61] In addition, it is

---

[53] SCOPIC 2000, cl.6(i).
[54] SCOPIC, cl.7. See *post*, § 977.
[55] SCOPIC 2000, cl.6(ii). On currency conversion, see further *post*, §§ 1461–1465.
[56] On Art. 14 special compensation, see generally *ante*, Chap. 5.
[57] SCOPIC 2000, cl.1 only purports to exclude Art. 14.1–14.2. Art. 14.5 deprives the salvor of Art. 14 special compensation where he has been negligent (see *ante*, § 438). By not purporting to exclude Art. 14.5, SCOPIC 2000, cl.1 impliedly preserves it. However, by excluding the possibility of Art. 14 special compensation, SCOPIC 2000, cl.1 also renders Art. 14.5 redundant. The same is true of Art. 14.6, which provides that nothing in Art. 14 shall affect the shipowner's rights of recourse.
[58] "Subject to the provisions of Clause 4 hereof, the method of assessing Special Compensation under Convention Article 14(1) to 14(4) inclusive shall be submitted by the method of assessment set out hereinafter. If this SCOPIC clause has been incorporated into the Main Agreement the Contract may make no claim pursuant to Article 14 except in the circumstances described in subclause 4 hereof."
[59] SCOPIC 2000, cl.13.
[60] SCOPIC 2000, cl.4.
[61] See *post*, Apps 5–5A.

provided that "The assessment of SCOPIC remuneration shall include the prevention of pollution as well as the removal of pollution in the immediate vicinity of the vessel insofar as this is necessary for the proper execution of the salvage but not otherwise."[62]

Discount

977 If the salvage reward under the Main Agreement, determined in accordance with Article 13 of the International Salvage Convention 1989 or by settlement (after currency adjustment but before interest and costs) is greater than the assessed SCOPIC remuneration, the salvor will be penalised, as the Article 13 award or settlement will be discounted.[63] The discount is 25 per cent of the difference between the Article 13 award or settlement and the amount of SCOPIC remuneration that would have been assessed had the SCOPIC remuneration provisions been invoked on the first day of the services.[64] (Thus, for the purpose of determining whether a discount is payable, the actual SCOPIC remuneration is used, whereas for the purpose of determining the amount of the discount it is the total possible SCOPIC remuneration which might have been earned.)

Payment

978 The date of payment of SCOPIC remuneration will vary according to the circumstances.[65] First, if there is no potential Article 13 salvage reward, the undisputed amount of SCOPIC remuneration due hereunder should be paid by the shipowner within one month of the presentation of the claim.[66] Secondly, if there is a claim for an Article 13 salvage reward as well as a claim for SCOPIC remuneration, 75 per cent of the amount by which the assessed SCOPIC remuneration exceeds the total Article 13 security demanded from ship and cargo should be paid by the shipowner within one month and any undisputed balance paid when the Article 13 salvage award has been assessed and falls due. However, in either case, if the SCR gives a report dissenting from the Salvage Master's Daily Salvage Report,[67] any initial payment due for SCOPIC remuneration shall be at the tariff rate applicable to what is in the SCR's view the appropriate equipment or procedure until any dispute is resolved.[68] Interest on sums due will accrue from the date of termination of the services until the date of payment at United States prime rate plus 1 per cent.[69]

If the sum paid on account exceeds the SCOPIC remuneration due, the salvor should make restitution of the overpayment. As noted above, by

[62] SCOPIC 2000, cl.13.
[63] SCOPIC 2000, cl.7.
[64] SCOPIC 2000, cl.7.
[65] SCOPIC 2000, cl.8(i).
[66] SCOPIC 2000, cl.8(i)(a).
[67] See SCOPIC 2000, App. B(5) (*post*, App. 5B).
[68] SCOPIC 2000, cl.8(i) and App. B(5)(c)(iv).
[69] SCOPIC 2000, cl.8(i).

invoking SCOPIC, the salvor becomes subject to a liability to give an indemnity in a form acceptable to the shipowner in respect of any overpayment in the event that the SCOPIC remuneration due ultimately proves to be less than the sum paid on account.[70]

Rights of recourse: general average

Liability to pay SCOPIC remuneration rests on the shipowner alone.[71] In respect of SCOPIC remuneration in excess of an Article 13 Award, it is specifically provided that this shall not be a General Average expense and that the shipowner shall make no claim whether direct, indirect, by way of indemnity or recourse or otherwise relating to it in General Average or under the vessel's Hull and Machinery Policy.[72]

979

Dispute resolution

Consistently with SCOPIC's function as a supplement to Lloyd's Form, disputes thereunder must be referred for determination to the Lloyd's Form arbitrator.[73]

980

---

[70] SCOPIC 2000, cl.8(ii). See *ante*, § 968.
[71] SCOPIC 2000, cll. 6(i) and 14.
[72] SCOPIC 2000, cl.14.
[73] SCOPIC 2000, cl.15 (the only clause in SCOPIC with no title) provides briefly: "Any dispute arising out of this SCOPIC clause or the operations thereunder shall be referred to Arbitration as provided for under the Main Agreement." In addition, SCOPIC 2000, cl.3(iv) states: "In the absence of agreement, any dispute concerning the proposed Guarantor, the form of the security or the amount of any reduction or increase in the security in place shall be resolved by the Arbitrator." More comprehensively, LSSAC 2000, cl.14 ("Disputes under Scopic Clause") states that: "Any dispute arising out of the Scopic Clause (including as to its incorporation or invocation) or the operations thereunder shall be referred for determination to the Arbitrator appointed under clause 5 hereof whose award shall be final and binding subject to appeal as provided in clause 10 hereof."

CHAPTER 10

DUTIES OF PARTIES

1. INTRODUCTION

987 Parties involved in salvage and related operations are subject to a number of duties. These duties may arise from a number of sources, including Admiralty law, the common law, general statutory law, the International Salvage Convention 1989 and contract, as appropriate. The relevant duties may be listed as follows.

1. *Safety at sea*: Independently of the question of salvage, the Salvage Convention 1989, Art. 10.1 imposes on every ship master a duty to render assistance to any person in danger of being lost at sea.[1]

2. *Best endeavours*: Under LOF 2000, cl. A, the Contractors agree to use their best endeavours to salve the specified property. This duty is discussed later in this chapter.[2]

3. *Negligence*: There is a common law duty to exercise due care not to cause harm to others. In addition, Article 8.1(a) of the Convention states that the salvor owes a duty to owners of the property in danger to carry out the salvage operations with due care. These duties to refrain from negligence are discussed below[3] and in Chapter 11.

988 4. *Assistance*: Under the Convention, the salvor owes the owner of the property in danger: a duty, whenever circumstances reasonably require, to seek assistance from other salvors[4]; and a duty, when reasonably requested by the owner or master of the property in danger, to accept the intervention of other salvors.[5]

5. *Co-operation*: Under the Convention, the owner of the property in danger and the master owe the salvor a duty to co-operate fully with him during the course of the salvage operations.[6] LSSAC 2000, cl. 2(c) states it to be an overriding objective of Lloyd's Form to encourage co-operation between the parties and with relevant authorities and LOF 2000, cl. F(iii) links the salvee's duty of co-operation with his duty to accept redelivery at the

---

[1] See *ante*, Chap. 7 (especially § 534). See also LSSAC 2000, cl. 2(a).
[2] *Post*, §1013.
[3] *Post*, § 1013.
[4] Art. 8.1(c).
[5] Art. 8.1(d).
[6] Art. 8.2(a).

termination of the services. No corresponding duty is imposed on the salvor; but it is arguable that such an obligation should be implied, to make the contract workable.[7] These duties are discussed later in this chapter.[8]

6. *The environment*: Under the Convention[9] and by contract[10] the salvor has duties to attempt to prevent or minimise damage to the environment. Under the Convention, in discharging his duty to co-operate with the salvor, the salvee must exercise due care to prevent or minimise damage to the environment.[11] These duties are discussed later in this chapter.

7. *Termination of services*: Under LOF 2000, cl. A, the contractor must use his best endeavours to take the property to the place agreed or, if none is agreed, to a place of safety. Under the Convention, when the property has been brought to a place of safety, the salvee must accept redelivery when reasonably requested by the salvor to do so.[12] These duties are discussed later in this chapter.[13]

8. *Notice to other salvees*: Where shipowners have become party to Lloyd's Form of salvage contract, as soon as possible after the agreement has been made, they must notify the owners of other property on board the vessel that the agreement has been made.[14] This duty is stated in Lloyd's Form under the heading "Salvage security", which is listed next.

9. *Security*: If SCOPIC 2000 is invoked and the salvor gives written notice, the shipowner must provide Initial Security.[15] More generally, LOF 2000 requires the owners of property salved to provide successful Contractors with security in accordance with its provisions.[16] The salvor's entitlement to security is reinforced by the Salvage Convention 1989[17] and the Lloyd's Form contract,[18] which provide that salved property must not be removed from the place at which salvage services terminate until security has been provided. These duties are discussed in Chapter 13.

10. *Judicial proceedings and arbitration*: The parties to Lloyd's Form agree that matters arising from their relationship will be decided by arbitration.[19] Moreover, the Lloyd's Form contract provides that the salvors shall not arrest or detain the salved property unless their security is threatened.[20] These matters are discussed in Chapter 13.

---

[7] See Shaw [1996] L.M.C.L.Q. 202, 213, 214.
[8] *Post*, §§ 1044–1085.
[9] Art. 8.1(b).
[10] LOF 2000, cl. B; SCOPIC 2000, cl. 10. See also LSSAC 2000, cl. 2(a) and SCOPIC 2000, cl. 13.
[11] Art. 8.2(b).
[12] Art. 8.2(c). See also LOF 2000, cl. F(iii).
[13] *Post*, §§ 1044–1085.
[14] LOF 2000, Important Notice 1 (a new provision).
[15] SCOPIC 2000, cl. 3(i).
[16] LOF 2000, Important Notice 1; LSSAC 2000, cl. 4.
[17] Art. 21.3.
[18] LSSAC 2000, cl. 4.8.
[19] LOF 2000, cl. I.
[20] LSSAC 2000, cl. 4.9.

Duties of Parties

11. *Payments*: Under Admiralty law, a salvee must pay a successful salvor a salvage reward. This duty is has now been superseded by duties to pay a salvage reward in accordance with Articles 12–13 of the Salvage Convention 1989 and special compensation for environmental services under Article 14 of the Convention, where that applies. The circumstances in which these duties arise are discussed generally throughout this book.[21] The recipient of services may also have to make payment under the doctrine of engaged services (discussed in Chapter 8) and/or, of course, where there is a contractual duty to do so, as when the SCOPIC clause applies (as discussed in Chapter 9).

992 As noted above, several of the duties falling upon parties involved in salvage operations are discussed in other chapters of this book. In particular, the effect of tortious duties is considered in Chapter 11. The first part of the remainder of the current chapter includes an account of the general law of contract which may affect the parties' relationship where, as is common nowadays, that relationship is governed by contract. This is followed by: specific consideration of the salvor's duty to use best endeavours; duties to provide environmental services; the salvor's duties to accept assistance; and parties' duties of co-operation and on termination of services. Exclusions, limitations and other qualifications on liability are discussed in Chapter 12.

2. Contractual Liability

(a) General matters

Introduction

993 A contract of salvage, though by its nature obviously deserving special legal treatment in relation to its context of operation, is nonetheless in principle governed by the general law of contract. It is important, therefore, to outline the effect of the general law on this particular type of contract, particularly in the light of recent developments.[22] Where a salvage service is not provided under a contract, the general law applies; so a salvage contract will not govern claims by individual salvors, such as servants of a salvage contractor, who are not party to the salvage contract.

Origins of liability

994 Contractual liability prima facie arises in two ways: from terms expressly incorporated by the parties, and from implied terms. The effect of such terms

---

[21] See *passim* and, in particular, Chaps. 5, 8, 15 and 16.
[22] No attempt is made here at an exhaustive statement of the general law of contract or of its applicability to salvage contracts. Detailed reference must be made to specialised works, such as Chitty and Treitel.

will depend on their true construction, in the light of pertinent statutory provisions. Generally speaking, implied terms may find their way into contracts in three ways: from the facts of the particular case, to give the transaction such business efficacy as the parties must have intended; by custom; or by law. Terms implied by law may arise at common law from the nature of the parties' relationship, because such terms are commonly found in such a relationship, or they may be imposed by statute. In recent years, Parliament has become noticeably more active in giving statutory recognition to, and clarification of, terms in common forms of contract, particularly under the Supply of Goods and Services Act 1982.[23]

The 1982 Act originated in the Law Commission's proposals to extend the existing statutory statement of implied terms in contracts for the supply of goods and hire-purchase[24] to other contracts for the supply of goods. The Commission's proposals[25] were substantially enacted in Parts I and III of the Act. An important feature of the 1982 Act, however, is the extension of Parliamentary intervention into the area of the supply of services, in Part II of the Act. Part II was in fact prompted by the National Consumer Council's desire for codification of the law on the supply of services, principally for the benefit of consumers, the perceived advantages being greater clarity and certainty, ease of reference, and the publicity and increased awareness that would be derived from enactment of the relevant terms[26]; it is, however, drafted in terms of general application.

Restrictions on liability

Many contracts contain clauses seeking to confine or exclude liability which might otherwise exist. In principle, such clauses should be given effect according to their true construction. In practice, however, their efficacy is subject to the particular rules of construction developed at common law and judicial attitudes to such clauses. In addition, there is now an extensive statutory framework for the control of such exculpatory terms. These matters are discussed in Chapter 12.   995

Application to salvage

The effect of recent legislation, and even of the existing common law, on contracts of salvage is uncertain for several reasons. First is the paucity and relative imprecision of the existing authorities governing contracts for services in general and of salvage in particular. Secondly, and perhaps very wisely, persons concluding contracts of salvage, and especially the draftsmen of the widespread LOF standard form, have rarely, if ever, attempted more   996

---

[23] See Palmer (1983) 46 M.L.R. 619. The Act extends to Northern Ireland but not to Scotland: s.20(b).
[24] In the Sale of Goods Act 1979 and the Supply of Goods (Implied Terms) Act 1973, respectively.
[25] See *Implied Terms in Contracts for the Supply of Goods* (1975), Law Com. No. 95.
[26] See its report, *Service Please: Services and the Law: a Consumer View* (1981).

than a modest statement of express obligations in their contracts, thereby not provoking dispute or detailed judicial investigation of the nature of the parties' liabilities. The acts of the parties during salvage operations, albeit rarely expressed in terms of obligations and breaches thereof, have traditionally influenced the assessment of the reward earned by the salvor and payable by the owner of salved property. But the uncertainty as to how far salvage operations are likely to prove successful, plus the impossibility of exact determination of the weight to be accorded to the different factors to be considered, has inhibited rigorous examination of individual liabilities. The impact of new legislation on this state of affairs is not clarified by its being framed with a view to its applicability to a variety of contracts and the lack of detailed evidence of its intended effect on contracts of salvage. But, although it is suggested that its impact is not in practice likely to be great, it may provoke more active consideration of the nature of the contracting parties' liability to each other, and the time is certainly opportune for a closer investigation of the elements of this liability than has been attempted in the past.

Definition of salvage

997 The nature of the liability of parties to salvage operations depends, of course, on an interpretation of the nature of their general relationship and, most frequently, of the nature of a salvage *contract*. The definition of salvage canvassed in Chapter 1[27] provides minimal guidance for this task. Judicial statements of salvage as a *service* are far too numerous to require citation or to enable it to be doubted that a salvor provides a service. But that does not mean that his position must invariably be framed, though not as a contract *of service*, as a contract *for services*[28] or, to use the terminology of the common law proper, a contract of work and labour. For, in many salvage operations, the salvor supplies goods or materials, such as navigational equipment or metal plates to repair damage to the vessel, to facilitate or ensure preservation from danger. This raises the questions: whether the contract is truly a contract for services; whether it is a contract for work and materials, as defined by common law; or whether the services are to be considered as provided under a contract for services and the materials under a contract for the sale or supply of goods.

998 Whatever the true definition of such contracts in principle, their practical effects will be influenced by mandatory statutory provisions, which must now be considered. As will be seen, the statutory treatment of a contract for the sale of goods, a contract for the supply of goods and a contract for the supply of a service are such that, where a particular contract contains elements of more than one of the statutorily defined classes, the appropriate provisions govern those elements of the contract falling within its purview, and the

[27] *Ante*, §§ 16–25.
[28] For the distinction between contracts of service and contracts for services, see Chitty, Chap. 29.

(b) Implied terms

Contracts for the sale of goods

Contract of sale

Whether or not the circumstances merit the provision of services under a contract of salvage, goods or materials may be obtained under a contract of sale, possibly from someone other than the provider of salvage services, in which case the transaction should be governed by the relevant provisions of the law of sale of goods.[29] A contract of sale of goods is defined by the Sale of Goods Act 1979, s.2(1) as a contract by which the seller transfers or agrees to transfer the property in goods to the buyer for a monetary consideration, called the price. The price may be fixed by the contract, left to be fixed in a manner agreed by the contract, or determined by the course of dealing between the parties.[30] Where it is not so fixed, the buyer must pay a reasonable price,[31] which is a question of fact dependent on the circumstances of each particular case.[32]

999

It may be argued that the reasonable price of goods sold to the owners of property in distress should, in the circumstances, be calculated on a salvage basis, to include the extra element of reward invariably awarded to the providers of salvage services. However, no matter how vital are the goods obtained, it is suggested that true salvage is only earned for the provision of services and not merely for goods, and the rules against illegitimate pressure[33] will prevent a seller's extorting an unfair agreement as to the price. In most cases, the provider of goods or materials to a vessel in distress will also supply services and the salvage award will pay him for all he is owed by the other party. The law of sale will, therefore, in virtually all cases be irrelevant. But, even if the provision of goods and services were to be remunerated separately, the distinct treatment accorded in other respects to contracts of sale and supply, on the one hand, and contracts for services, on the other,[34] would help ensure that only the services were remunerated on a salvage basis.

1000

---

[29] Detailed commentary on the law of sale of goods is inappropriate here. Specialised works on the subject should be consulted. See especially *Benjamin's Sale of Goods* (5th ed., 1997).
[30] s.8(1).
[31] s.8(2).
[32] s.8(3).
[33] See *ante*, Chap. 9.
[34] See *post*, §§1001, 1005, 1008–10, 1024–1026.

Implied terms

1001 For the seller's part, the Act generally implies conditions: that he has a right to sell the goods[35]; that goods sold by description correspond with the description[36]; and that, where the seller sells them in the course of a business, the goods are of satisfactory quality,[37] and are reasonably fit for any particular purpose for which they are bought.[38] There are also implied warranties that the goods are free from undisclosed charges or encumbrances and that the buyer will enjoy quiet possession of the goods.[39]

Qualification of liability

1002 A right, duty or liability which arises under a contract of sale by implication of law may be negatived or varied by express agreement, course of dealing or usage, but subject to the provisions of the Unfair Contract Terms Act 1977[40] (UCTA) and the Unfair Terms in Consumer Contracts Regulations 1999.[41] UCTA provides that liability for breach of the implied undertakings as to title[42] cannot be excluded or restricted by reference to any contract term.[43] As against a person dealing as consumer,[44] liability for breach of the seller's implied undertakings as to conformity of goods with description, or as to their quality or fitness for a particular purpose, cannot be excluded or restricted by reference to any contract term[45]; but, as against a person dealing otherwise than as a consumer, such liability can be so excluded, though only in so far as the term satisfies the requirement of reasonableness.[46]

Contracts for the supply of goods

Contracts for the transfer of property in goods

1003 Implied terms in contracts for the transfer of property in goods are now generally governed by Part I of the Supply of Goods and Services Act 1982.[47] A contract for the transfer of goods is defined as a contract under which one person transfers or agrees to transfer to another the property in goods, other than an excepted contract.[48] Excepted contracts include contracts of sale (considered above) as well as contracts of hire-purchase and contracts

---

[35] s.12(1). *cf.* s.12(3).
[36] s.13(1).
[37] s.14(2). See also s.14(6).
[38] s.14(3). See also s.15 (sale by sample).
[39] s.12(2)(a) and (b).
[40] SGA 1979, s.55(1). See also s.55(2).
[41] See *post*, Chap. 12.
[42] In SGA 1979, s.12. See text to nn. 35 and 39, *supra*.
[43] UCTA 1977, s.6(1).
[44] See *post*, § 1148.
[45] UCTA 1977, s.6(2)(a).
[46] *ibid.*, s.6(3). The requirement of reasonableness is discussed *post*, §§ 1151–1153.
[47] Pts I and III of the Act are based on the Report of the Law Commission on *Implied Terms in Contracts for the Supply of Goods* (1979), Law Com. No. 95.
[48] s.1(1).

Contracts for the supply of goods

intended to operate by way of mortgage, pledge, charge or other security (which will not be considered).[49] For the purposes of the Act, a contract is a contract for the transfer of goods whether or not services are also provided under the contract, and whatever the nature of the consideration for the transfer or agreement to transfer.[50] The supply of goods, although not of the services, under a contract of salvage is therefore governed by the provisions of Part I of the Act, and despite the peculiar nature of the remuneration payable for salvage.

Contracts for the hire of goods

Part I of the Supply of Goods and Services Act 1982 also governs terms in contracts for the hire of goods.[51] For the purposes of the Act, a contract is a contract for the hire of goods whether or not services are also provided or to be provided under the contract, and whatever is the nature of the consideration for the bailment or agreement to bail by way of hire.[52] **1004**

Implied terms

Part I of the 1982 Act implies into contracts governed by it similar conditions and warranties as to title, description, quality and fitness for purpose[53] as are to be found in contracts of sale.[54] Terms of similar nature and status, framed in accordance with the type of contract involved, are implied into contracts for the hire of goods.[55] Other implied terms may also exist in such contracts, for Part I of the Act does not prejudice the operation of any other enactment or any rule of law whereby any condition or warranty (other than one relating to quality or fitness) is to be implied in a contract for the transfer or hire of goods.[56] Part I does not, therefore, override the terms to be implied into the services part of a contract of salvage.[57] **1005**

Qualification of liability

Where a right, duty or liability would arise under a contract for the transfer, or hire, of goods by implication of law, it may be negatived or varied by express agreement, course of dealing or usage, though subject to the Unfair Contract Terms Act 1977[58] and the Unfair Terms in Consumer Contracts Regulations 1999.[59] The 1977 Act states that, where the possession or ownership of goods passes under or in pursuance of such contracts, as against a **1006**

---

[49] s.1(2).
[50] s.1(3).
[51] Defined in s.6(1)–(2).
[52] s.6(3).
[53] See ss 2–4. See also s.5 (transfer by sample).
[54] See *ante*, §§999–1000.
[55] See ss 6–10.
[56] s.11(3).
[57] *Post*, §§1008–1010.
[58] SGSA 1982, s.11(1). See also s.11(2).
[59] See *post*, Chap. 12.

person dealing as consumer,[60] liability in respect of the goods' correspondence with description, or their quality or fitness for any particular purpose, cannot be excluded or restricted by reference to any contract term excluding or restricting liability for breach of the implied obligations under consideration.[61] As against a person dealing otherwise than as a consumer, that liability can be excluded or restricted by reference to such a term, but only in so far as the term satisfies the requirement of reasonableness.[62] However, liability for breach of obligations as to title in the type of contract for the transfer of property being considered cannot be excluded or restricted by reference to any such term.[63] In other cases, liability for such terms as to title or possession cannot be excluded or restricted by reference to any such term except in so far as it satisfies the requirement of reasonableness.[64]

Contracts for the supply of a service

The contracts concerned

1007 A contract for the supply of a service, the subject-matter of Part II of the Supply of Goods and Services Act 1982, is defined as a contract under which a person ("the supplier") agrees to carry out a service.[65] A contract is a contract for the supply of a service for the purposes of the Act whether or not goods are also (a) transferred or to be transferred, or (b) bailed or to be bailed by way of hire under the contract, and whatever is the nature of the consideration for which the service is to be carried out.[66] A salvage agreement is evidently a contract for the supply of a service and so falls within the statutory definition, whether or not the salvor sells or otherwise supplies goods or materials as part of the salvage operation. The application of the Act whatever the nature of the consideration ensures that salvage is not excluded because of the unique character of the remuneration for salvage services, comprising the additional public policy motivated element of reward.[67]

Implied terms

1008 Sections 13–15 of the 1982 Act set out three terms (of care and skill; time for performance; and consideration respectively) to be implied into contracts for the supply of a service governed by the Act. However, the sections are clearly not intended to state the parties' obligations exhaustively but to provide a minimum floor of liability, for nothing in Part II of the Act prejudices any rule of law whereby a term not inconsistent with Part II is to

---

[60] See *post*, § 1148.
[61] s.7(1), (2).
[62] s.7(3).
[63] s.7(3A); inserted by SGSA 1982, s.17(2).
[64] s.7(4), as amended by SGSA 1982, s.17(3).
[65] s.12(1). A contract for service or apprenticeship is not such a contract: s.12(2).
[66] s.12(3).
[67] See *ante*, Chap. 1.

be implied in a contract for the supply of a service[68] (such as further common law implied terms), and especially not a rule of law imposing on the supplier a duty stricter than that imposed by sections 13 or 14.[69] Thus, so far as applicable, the relevant provisions of the Sale of Goods Act 1979 and the Supply of Goods and Services Act 1982 will apply to goods sold or supplied during salvage operations. Moreover, subject to contrary statutory provision, the parties may expressly increase the liabilities under the contract.[70] Parliament's apparent lack of confidence in the regime provided by Part II and its lack of conviction in the desirability of their universal application is further illustrated by the power given to the Secretary of State to provide[71] that one or more of sections 13–15 shall not apply to services of a description specified in the order, and such an order may make different provision for different circumstances.[72] However, no order has been made excluding salvage (or towage) services.

1009 These savings reflect the hasty inclusion in the Act of proposals to reform the law for the benefit of consumers, but in terms of application to particular types of contract, such as salvage, which were not obviously considered. At present, it is necessary to consider the scope of provisions which, though intended to codify the common law, have been criticised as uncertain and unambitious in scope[73] and, not having been excluded by the Secretary of State,[74] are in principle applicable to the law of salvage.

The 1982 Act does not attempt a very detailed exposition of the implied obligations in contracts for services but may stimulate more elaboration by prompting judicial interpretation and amplification of its provisions. It remains to be seen to what extent this will prove to be significant for the law of salvage.

1010 Sections 13 and 14 only apply to contracts where the supplier is acting in the course of a business. Section 18(1) defines "business" to include a profession and the activities of any government department or local or public authority. The relevant implied terms will, therefore, apply where a salvage service is provided by a professional salvor, a Crown ship or a harbour authority. But the definition of "business" is not exhaustive; nor does it require that it be the contractor's main business, or even part of his normal business, to provide salvage services. The sections will, therefore, apply to services provided by tugowners or fishermen.

---

[68] s.16(3)(b).
[69] s.16(3)(a).
[70] See *post*, §1012.
[71] By order exercisable by statutory instrument subject to annulment in pursuance of resolution of either House of Parliament: s.12(5).
[72] s.12(4). Three orders have been made, excluding s.13 in favour of: advocates and company directors (The Supply of Services (Exclusion of Implied Terms) Order 1982: S.I. 1982 No. 1771); officers of building and friendly societies (The Supply of Services (Exclusion of Implied Terms) Order 1983: S.I. 1983 No. 902); and arbitrators (Supply of Services (Exclusion of Implied Terms) Order 1985 No. 1: S.I. 1985).
[73] See, *e.g.* Palmer (1983) 46 M.L.R. 619; Murdoch [1983] L.M.C.L.Q. 652.
[74] See *supra*, n. 72.

Duties of Parties

Before examining the individual obligations arising under Part II of the Act, it is convenient to note its provisions as to possible reduction of the liability imposed.

Variation of liability

1011 An object of the Supply of Goods and Services Act 1982 is to establish a minimum floor of liability and not to reduce liability which would otherwise exist. Thus, nothing in Part II of the Act prejudices any rule of law whereby any term not inconsistent with Part II is to be implied in a contract for the supply of a service or, specifically, any rule of law imposing on the supplier a duty stricter than that imposed by section 13 or 14.[75] In addition, Part II has effect subject to any other enactment which defines or restricts the rights, duties or liabilities arising in connection with a service of any description,[76] thus preserving the limitation provisions of the merchant shipping legislation.[77]

Subject to those mandatory requirements and to the Unfair Contract Terms Act 1977, a right, duty or liability arising under a contract for the supply of a service by virtue of Part II of the 1982 Act may be negatived or varied by course of dealing, usage or an inconsistent express term.[78]

1012 This preserves the parties' freedom of contract to include whatever express terms they wish to insert in the contract, and to increase a party's liability beyond that implied by the Act—but so long as the increase in liability of one party does not operate to lessen liability of the other party which it is the intention of the 1977 and 1982 Acts to preserve. The minimal statutory obligations in contracts of salvage do not, therefore, impliedly prohibit the more onerous obligations to use best endeavours expressly imposed by LOF 2000, cl. A.

So far as concerns contracts of marine salvage, the 1977 Act's general provisions as to negligence liability,[79] liability arising in contract,[80] unreasonable indemnity clauses[81] and miscellaneous contracts under which goods pass[82] apply in favour of a person dealing as consumer.[83] None of these provisions are specifically framed in relation to the provision of the service as such.[84]

---

[75] s.16(3).
[76] s.16(4).
[77] See *post*, Chap. 12.
[78] s.16(1), (2).
[79] s.2(2). See *post*, §§ 1149, 1155–1156.
[80] s.3. See *post*, §§ 1157–1161.
[81] s.4. See *post*, § 1150.
[82] s.7.
[83] s.1(2); Sched. 1, para. 2(a). See further *post*, § 1148.
[84] *cf.* s.7, which specifically refers to goods supplied simultaneously.

Contracts for the supply of a service

Care and skill

Section 13 of the Supply of Goods and Services Act 1982 states, as a **1013** general rule, that, in a contract for the supply of a service where the supplier is acting in the course of a business, there is an implied term that the supplier will carry out the service with reasonable care and skill. In essence, the section restates the effect of the common law as laid down in *The Tojo Maru*.[85] This has now been overridden in importance by the Salvage Convention, Art. 14.1(a), which imposes a duty on salvors to carry out salvage operations with due care. In addition, under the Convention, both parties have a duty to exercise due care to prevent or minimise damage to the environment.[86]

Time for performance

Section 14 provides that, where, under a contract for the supply of a service **1014** by a supplier acting in the course of a business, the time for the service to be carried out is not fixed by the contract, left to be fixed in a manner agreed by the contract or determined by the course of dealing between the parties, there is an implied term that the supplier will carry out the service within a reasonable time. What is a reasonable time is a question of fact.

In practice, in the case of a contract for the supply of services, this will simply mean that, where the time for the service to be carried out is not fixed by the contract, which it usually is not, the service must be carried out within a reasonable time. This effectively restates the common law and does not diminish the undertaking by the contractor under LOF 2000, cl. A to use his best endeavours to salve, which may in fact require more expedition than would otherwise be considered reasonable. In any event, the promptness of the service rendered is a criterion for fixing a reward under the Salvage Convention 1989.[87] Section 14 of the 1982 Act may nonetheless prove beneficial to the owner of property in distress. Not only does it support the comparative depression of an award which would be enhanced to reflect a more expeditious service, but proof that the salvor has failed to comply with the clearly stated obligation in section 14 will render the salvor liable for any loss proved to have flown from his delay.

Section 14 may also be resorted to where the parties were in some relation- **1015** ship before salvage was effected. Thus, if through a tugowner's unreasonable delay the tug came into danger, not only would the breach of section 14 in performing the towage contract deprive the tugowner of the right to claim salvage, it would also entitle the shipowner to claim from him for any losses suffered as a result of the delay, including the cost of salvage services.

---

[85] [1972] A.C. 242.
[86] Art. 8.1(b) and 8.2(b).
[87] Art. 13.1(h). See *post*, Chap. 15.

Consideration

1016 By section 15 of the 1982 Act, where, under a contract for the supply of a service, the consideration for the service is not determined by the contract, left to be determined in a manner agreed by the contract or determined by the course of dealing between the parties, there is an implied term that the party contracting with the supplier will pay a reasonable charge. What is a reasonable charge is a question of fact. The section is not restricted to cases where the supplier is acting in the course of a business.

1017 In the great majority of salvage cases, section 15 will not come into operation, for the consideration will invariably be determined in the manner laid down by the Salvage Convention 1989, Arts. 12–13 and in accordance with long established practice.[88] In this sense the consideration will be fixed in accordance with ordinary salvage law, albeit the existence of an established legal means of determining remuneration is not *per se* a reason admitted by section 15 for excluding the section.

1018 If section 15 were considered to govern the determination of salvage consideration, it might arguably reduce the amount which a salvor could recover if the reasonable charge to which he was entitled under the Act were held to be assessable on the basis of an ordinary contract for work and labour and not as true salvage remuneration, with its enhanced, public policy dictated element of reward. It is submitted, however, that a salvage reward assessed on traditional principles could quite properly be held to be a reasonable charge in such circumstances and that it would not be right to assume that, without obviously addressing itself to the point, Parliament had, within the terms of the section, instituted a new means of assessing salvage remuneration and brought it into line with ordinary contracts for work and labour, albeit subject to the express terms of the contract and the Secretary of State's power[89] to exclude or modify the application of section 15 to salvage contracts.

Personal performance

1019 It can be inferred, from their phraseology, that sections 13–15 suggest a requirement that the parties to a salvage contract must perform personally.[90] Certainly, there is nothing remarkable about section 15's having this effect, assuming it to apply, for the requirement that "the party contracting with the supplier will pay a reasonable charge" is perfectly consistent with the personal liability of the recipient of successful salvage services to pay a reward with respect to the benefit he has received.

1020 Sections 13–14, however, might have potentially inconvenient repercussions. On one interpretation, their statement that "the supplier will carry out

---

[88] See *post*, Chap. 15.
[89] In s.12(4).
[90] See Palmer (1983) 46 M.L.R. 619, 628–630.

the service" assumes personal performance by the salvor and forbids his use of sub-contractors. In many situations, this will not matter for a salvage contractor will normally be expected to perform personally and professional salvors should by the nature of their work be sufficiently well equipped and capable of performing without assistance from sub-contractors. Moreover, there is nothing inherently objectionable from a contractual viewpoint in a decision by the party in distress, assuming he wishes the salvor to dispense with the services of a specialist sub-contractor, to minimise so far as possible the factors tending to enhance the reward, by requiring personal performance from the contractor he originally engaged. But the public policy of preserving property and life at sea would probably recognise, in the absence of an express denial, implied permission to sub-contract where this is really necessary. Indeed, the salvor's obligation under LOF 2000, cl. A to use his best endeavours is ambivalent in this respect: on the one hand, it expressly requires use of his own best endeavours; on the other, his best endeavours may be said impliedly to permit or even require him to seek further the necessary assistance, which, under the Convention, he may have to seek and accept.[91] It is unlikely that the party in distress will be prejudiced.

Whilst a new statutorily implied obligation of personal service is unlikely to have much impact in most practical situations, it could cause difficulties in circumstances such as those in *The Winson*,[92] the actual decision in which could even, on an extreme view, be argued to have been reversed. Must the salvor who has successfully salved property and become a bailee of it retain custody of it personally until the owner accepts redelivery? This will remain an unlikely consequence. At common law, a bailee cannot normally sub-delegate but no objection was raised in *The Winson* to the salvor's sub-bailing the salved cargo to a third party at the place of safety. If the salvor were considered now to be obliged to retain possession until acceptance by the owner, he is largely protected under the Salvage Convention 1989[93] by the obligation on the latter promptly to accept redelivery of the salved property at such place. It would, however, seem to be possible for the salvor to argue that, even if he could not sub-bail salved goods during performance of salvage services *stricto sensu*, he could do so afterwards, for sections 13–14 apply to contracts for the supply of a service and, whilst the services being provided may continue, the contract does not appear to do so, the House of Lords having decided in *The Winson* that on termination of salvage services the salvor became a gratuitous bailee.

1021

Successful performance

A further possible deduction that can be made from the phrase "the supplier will carry out the service" in sections 13–14 is that he is impliedly obliged to

1022

---

[91] Salvage Convention 1989, Art. 8.1(c)–(d). See *post*, §§ 1039–1043.
[92] [1982] A.C. 939. See *post*, §§ 1070–1085.
[93] Art. 8.2(c). See also Arts 20–21.

complete performance of the contract service successfully.[94] This certainly goes beyond the position at common law, under which the putative non-contractual salvor can normally cease performance at any time. It may even go further than the position under LOF 2000, by which the salvor is expressly obliged to use his best endeavours to salve, though he is not under liability if, having used his best endeavours, he fails to achieve the desired result. In the past, the courts have never insisted that contractual salvors are obliged to complete such a frequently uncertain and dangerous operation in the absence of an (unlikely) express promise to do so. And the public policy of encouraging salvage would hardly be furthered by deterring would-be salvors from assuming contractual liability for potential failure except where the service to be rendered is relatively straightforward and their services are not so necessary.

1023 It must, nevertheless, be conceded that many modern salvage operations, conducted by professional salvors, are often likely to be successful and that, in the circumstances of such a case, it is not unjust for the salvor to be obliged to perform successfully. But, even if this is not to pay more attention to the possible interpretation of the statute rather than to Parliament's more obviously declared intentions, the suggested construction is likely to have minimal practical effect. For the service which the supplier will carry out under LOF 2000, cl. A is not a service to salve successfully but to use his best endeavours to do so. Thus, he should not automatically be liable for failure. If he unsuccessfully performs a relatively straightforward service, it should not be necessary for him to be liable under statute, for he will probably be in breach of his contractual duty to use best endeavours. It is therefore unnecessary to do more than to query whether the suggested inference from sections 13–14 should properly be drawn anyway, in the absence of any clear evidence that Parliament intended or even considered it.

Common law implied terms

1024 Albeit the Sale of Goods Act 1979 and the Supply of Goods and Services Act 1982 admit the possibility of implied terms other than those contained in the Acts,[95] the statutory terms for contracts for the sale or supply of goods are of such a range as to appear comprehensive. By analogy, it is tempting to suppose that the statement of terms in contracts for the supply of a service are similarly wide. But they are not directly comparable. The implied term on consideration[96] echoes the Sale of Goods Act 1979 provision on price,[97] which is not one of the main group of implied terms in contracts of sale and is not mentioned amongst the implied terms in the 1982 Act in contracts for the supply of goods. The implied term about time for performance[98] does not

---

[94] See Palmer (1983) 46 M.L.R. 619, 628.
[95] See SGA, s.55(1) (though *cf.* s.14(1)); SGSA, s.16(3).
[96] s.15.
[97] SGA, s.8.
[98] SGSA, s.14.

Breach of contract

appear in similar form in the Sale of Goods Act 1979[99] or at all in the 1982 Act's provisions as to the supply of goods.

The remaining specific statutory implied terms in contracts for the sale or supply of goods impose strict liability as to title, description, quality and fitness for purpose.[1] The only outstanding statutory obligation in contracts for the supply of services, however, is the less onerous one of care and skill.[2] Yet the two sets of provisions are neither directly comparable nor exhaustive. First, many contracts for the supply of services may involve a transfer of goods or materials, which will be governed by the provisions as to the supply or sale of goods.[3] Secondly, parties to both groups of contracts may be liable for negligence; it is not only a form of liability for suppliers of services. Finally, it is possible to describe the liability of a supplier of services with more particularity. This is especially so if the suggestions are correct that a salvor must perform personally[4] and (more controversially) with some degree of success.[5] It can also be asserted that he impliedly undertakes that he is, in the light of the prevailing general practice, a sufficiently experienced and proficient salvor, that his methods and techniques are fit for the purpose in point, and that his services will be of a proper and workmanlike quality generally, for all of which his liability, though necessarily judged in the light of the relevant circumstances, should be strict.[6]

1025

It is very likely that in most cases the question of the existence of contractual liability or its breach will be subsumed within the general process of assessing the salvage reward. But a shipowner may on a later occasion wish to claim for a subsequently arising loss proved to have originated in the salvor's defective performance. And further judicial articulation of liabilities in contracts of service generally, provoked by interpretations of the 1982 Act, will need to be examined for their particular impact, if any, on the law of salvage.

1026

(c) *Failure of performance*

Breach of contract

Generally speaking, a party's liability for failure to perform or comply with a contractual term, whether it be express or implied, depends upon that term's

1027

---

[99] *cf.* ss.10, 17, 20(2), 29(3), 35(1), 37(1), 49(1)–(2), 50(1), 51(1).
[1] SGA, ss.13–15; SGSA, ss.2–5 (*cf. ibid.*, ss.7–10).
[2] SGSA, s.13.
[3] See *ante*, §996.
[4] See *ante*, §§1019–1021.
[5] See *ante*, §§1022–1023.
[6] See Palmer, *Bailment* (2nd ed, 1991), 892–936.

classification as a condition, warranty or so-called intermediate, or innominate, term.[7] If it is a condition, its breach entitles the innocent party to refuse to perform his part of the contract and to claim damages for his loss. If it is a warranty, he can only claim damages. Where the term is not expressly or otherwise clearly definable as a condition or a warranty, the party in breach will again be liable for damages as a matter of course, but the plaintiff will only be entitled to terminate performance of the contract where the manner and consequences of the breach have been such as to deprive him of substantially the whole benefit which it was intended that he should obtain.[8]

1028   The classification of a contractual term as a condition, warranty or intermediate term is essentially one of construction of the contract and of the parties' intention as expressed therein. This is not always an easy task, however, and certainly any description of the term in the contract is not conclusive.[9] In specific cases, statute offers firm guidance. Thus, in contracts for the sale or supply for goods, the majority of statutorily implied terms are stated to be conditions,[10] while others are expressly made warranties.[11] In all other cases it is primarily a question of construction,[12] but construction in the light of the current tendency, where there is any uncertainty, to treat terms as innominate terms and to concentrate on the effects of breach rather than on a *priori* categorisation.[13]

1029   Since the statutory implied terms in contracts for the supply of a service are, in distinction to the similar, more specifically classified terms in contracts for the sale or supply of goods, described simply as "terms", it seems reasonable in principle to conclude that the statutory implied terms in contracts for salvage, and any further common law implied terms, are innominate terms, particularly the implied term of care and skill.[14] However, this conclusion is not manifestly appropriate for the implied term on consideration,[15] payment of the correct amount of which after termination of salvage services is the primary duty of the person whose property has been salved, and therefore appears to be a condition. Furthermore, the general approach to the treatment of implied terms is subject to the effect of judicial precedent governing particular cases, which may be important in relation to the implied term on time for performance.

---

[7] This area has attracted more than its fair share of difficulty. See Chitty, Chaps. 22 and 25; Treitel, Chaps. 18–19; Rose (1981) 34 C.L.P. 235.

[8] See *Hong Kong Fir Co. Ltd v. Kawasaki Kisen Kaisha Ltd* [1962] 2 Q.B. 26.

[9] See, *e.g. L. Schuler A.G. v. Wickman Machine Tool Sales Ltd* [1974] A.C. 235, and note that the "warranties" in marine insurance contracts are similar to conditions in the normal use of that term: see Marine Insurance Act 1906, s.33.

[10] See *ante*, §§ 1001, 1005.

[11] See *ante*, §§ 1001, 1005.

[12] See, *e.g. Cehave N.V. v. Bremer Handelsgesellschaft mbH (The Hansa Nord)* [1976] Q.B. 44.

[13] See *Bunge Corporation, New York v. Tradax Export S.A., Panama* [1981] 1 W.L.R. 711. And *cf.* Law Com. W.P. No. 58 (1983): *Sale and Supply of Goods.*

[14] SGSA, s.13. See *ante*, §1013.

[15] SGSA, s.15. See *ante*, §§ 1016–1018.

Time

The Sale of Goods Act 1979 provides that, subject to contrary intention, stipulations as to time of payment are not of the essence of a contract of sale, and whether any other stipulation as to time is or is not of the essence depends on the terms of the contract.[16] In a case involving a contract for the international sale of goods, the House of Lords has held, in relation to express stipulations as to time, that the court will require precise compliance with stipulations as to time wherever the circumstances of the case indicate that this would fulfil the intention of the parties, and that broadly speaking time will be considered of the essence in mercantile contracts.[17] In other words, the term will normally have the effect of a condition. This seems a not inappropriate approach to the statutory implied term as to time in contracts for salvage services.[18] In the case of a serious delay, the eventual result in law would be the same if that implied term were regarded as an intermediate term. For less serious delays, this alternative approach might seem in fact more favourable to the shipowner, for he would clearly be entitled to claim damages for loss resulting from all delays. In practice, however, this may not put him in any better position than if his delay were merely considered by the arbitrator or judge as a factor tending to depress the amount of reward which he could have otherwise obtained.

1030

The effects of breach of a contract of salvage

In principle, the effects of breach of a term in a contract of salvage are the same as with contracts generally. Where there is a breach of condition or a sufficiently serious breach of an innominate term, provided the shipowner acts (and decides to do so) in the relatively short period of time during which salvage services are normally rendered, he can terminate performance of the contract. Where such a breach only comes to light subsequently, he can only claim damages, which are of course always payable. Consistently with the case of damages payable for the salvor's negligence, contractual damages may be set off against the salvage reward payable.[19]

1031

In practice, however, where a salvor who is in breach of contract completes his performance of salvage services, damages for his breach will not be claimed or paid as such. The extent to which he has performed his contract will be assessed in the light of any survey carried out between salvage and arbitration and will influence the tribunal's determination of the award payable. This may incline slightly to the other party's advantage as this will tend to minimise the public policy element of the reward, whereas it is conceivable that if the value of the salvage services were (assuming they could be) assessed ignoring the breach, the salvor might benefit accordingly.

1032

---

[16] s.10.
[17] *Bunge v. Tradax, supra.*
[18] SGSA, s.15. See *ante*, §§ 1014–1015.
[19] *cf. ante*, § 488 and *post*, Chap. 11.

1033   Where a breach of contract which could not reasonably have been discovered before the salvage award was made comes to light subsequently, as where materials supplied prove defective, there is in principle no reason why damages should not be claimed, provided this is done within the limitation period.[20] However, although the assessment of salvage reward is not a process which normally involves consideration of cross-claims, the salvor may well be entitled to argue that, if the other party was at the time of the arbitration aware of facts evidencing a breach of contract by the salvor, and certainly where he adduced evidence relating to those facts, then he should be regarded as having waived his right subsequently to sue for damages.

3. Best Endeavours

1034   Under Admiralty law, a salvor recovered no reward unless he was successful and was under no obligation either to begin a salvage service or to complete one which he had begun. Under LOF 2000, cl. A, however, a "Contractors' basic obligation" is laid down with reference to the details entered into the blank boxes on the face of the form:

> "The Contractors identified in Box 1 hereby agree to use their best endeavours to salve the property specified in Box 2 and to take the property to the place stated in Box 3 ['Agreed place of safety'] or to such other place as may hereafter be agreed. If no place is inserted in Box 3 and in the absence of any subsequent agreement as to the place where the property is to be taken the Contractors shall take the property to a place of safety".[21]

Under LOF 2000, salvors do not promise to salve and will not be liable simply for failing to do so. They are, however, obliged to use their best endeavours in accordance with clause A. If they fail to do so and the salvees suffer a loss, the salvors will not automatically be liable, for the loss might have occurred anyway. But the salvors will incur contractual liability if the salvees' losses result from their failure to use best endeavours.

1035   By definition, under Admiralty law, salvage is not achieved unless property in danger is brought to a place of safety. This remains the position if no place of safety is agreed when the contract is made or thereafter. However, LOF 2000 invites the parties to agree a place of safety, either by completing Box 3 or by subsequent decision. An advantage of agreeing the place of safety is to reduce the possibility of dispute as to whether the salvor has successfully

---

[20] See *post*, Chap. 12.
[21] See also SCOPIC 2000, cl. 10:
> "The duties and liabilities of the Contractor shall remain the same as under the Main Agreement, namely to use his best endeavours to salve the vessel and property thereon and in so doing to prevent or minimise damage to the environment."

completed the service by delivering to a place of safety. It also indicates where the salvee is obliged to accept delivery of the property at the termination of services.[22]

However, the drafting of clause A raises the possibility that the salvor will not have discharged his duties or become entitled to a salvage reward unless he has used his best endeavours both to "salve ... *and* to take the property to [the agreed place of safety or] ... a place of safety".[23] Probably in most cases, even if the agreed place of safety is not entirely safe, by agreeing to it the salvee will be estopped from denying that the salvor has discharged his duties. However, in exceptional cases, particularly where a place agreed has subsequently become unsafe, it may be considered unreasonable for a salvor to be entitled simply to take the property to the agreed place.

1036 Though a Lloyd's Form salvor has a duty to use best endeavours to salve, this does not displace his Convention duties to seek or accept assistance from other salvors.[24] Indeed, it may be argued that discharge of such duties complements the use of "best" endeavours.

The necessity for a salvor to use *his* best endeavours does not exclude the possibility that doing so may require his enlisting proper assistance so to do. LSSAC 2000, cl. 13.2 provides more generally that "The Contractors may engage the services of subcontractors for the purpose of fulfilling their obligations under clauses A[25] and B[26] of the Agreement but the Contractors shall nevertheless remain liable to the Owners for the due performance of those obligations."

A salvor may desist from using his best endeavours to salve in accordance with his contractual "Rights of termination" in LOF 2000, cl. G.[27]

4. ENVIRONMENTAL SERVICES

1037 At common law, parties have a duty to refrain from causing harm to others. This may involve not causing damage to the environment, but there is no general duty to take steps to avoid environmental damage. However, Article 8 of the International Salvage Convention 1989 imposes a duty to exercise due care to prevent or minimise damage to the environment[28] on: the salvor[29] (in carrying out his duty to carry out the salvage operations with due care)[30]; and the salvee[31] (in carrying out his duty to co-operate fully with the salvor during

---

[22] See further *post*, §§ 1044–1085.
[23] Emphasis added.
[24] International Salvage Convention 1989, Art. 8.1(c)–(d). See *post*, §§ 1039–1043.
[25] LOF 2000, cl. A ("Contractors' basic obligation"—to use best endeavours).
[26] LOF 2000, cl. B ("Environmental protection").
[27] See *post*, § 1068.
[28] "Damage to the environment" is defined by Art. 1(d). See *ante*, § 398.
[29] Art. 8.1(b).
[30] See Art. 8.1(a); *post*, Chap. 11.
[31] Art. 8.2(b).

the course of the salvage operations).[32] The duty on the salvor is expressed in slightly stronger terms by LOF 2000, cl. B and SCOPIC 2000, cl. 10, which state that, while performing the salvage services, the salvor must use his "best endeavours" to prevent or minimise damage to the environment.[33]

1038 A salvor whose conduct causes environmental damage may incur liability under the general law; but he should not do so simply for failing to discharge his duties under the Convention or Lloyd's Form.[34] However, in a situation where the salvee shipowner is subject to liability for causing environmental damage, a salvor who fails to carry out his environmental duties may become liable to indemnify the shipowner for the liability which he (the salvor) has failed to avert. In most cases, however, the significance of imposing environmental duties on a salvor will be to affect the payment(s) which may be made to him. Previously the performance or non-performance of environmental duties was irrelevant to the assessment of payment to the salvor. Now that there are such duties, not only will performance of them tend to enhance salvage rewards, special compensation or SCOPIC compensation,[35] but their non-performance can be taken into account as a factor tending to depress or negate such payments.

5. Assistance

1039 The primary motive for engaging in a salvage service is to earn a salvage reward, and a lone salvor has a better prospect of earning or maximising a reward than if other salvors were involved. *A fortiori*, a salvor who has been contracted to salve has a basic right to earn that reward rather than give way to or allow the intervention of other potential salvors. Indeed, a salvor who has been partially or wholly displaced by other salvors may be able to recover compensation for his lost opportunities from the salvees[36] or from intervening salvors.[37] Salvors therefore have an incentive to resist the intervention of other salvors. However, this will not necessarily be in their best interests, if they are by themselves unable to render services successfully or efficiently. And it will certainly be unhelpful to the salvees if they do not receive services promptly, efficiently and successfully.

1040 Accordingly, the International Salvage Convention 1989, Art. 8.1(c)–(d) provides:

---

[32] See Art. 8.2(a); *post*, § 1056.
[33] LOF 2000, cl. B and SCOPIC 2000, cl. 10 use slightly different language but with no obvious reason for doing so, as the effects seem identical.
[34] It is submitted that potential third party beneficiaries of the salvor's Lloyd's Form duty will not acquire rights by virtue of the Contracts (Rights of Third Parties) Act 1999.
[35] Under the Convention, Arts. 13 and 14, LSSAC 2000, cl. 2(a) and SCOPIC 2000, cl. 13 respectively. See further *post*, Chap. 15.
[36] See *ante*, §§ 756–778.
[37] See *post*, §§ 1228–1246.

"The salvor shall owe a duty to the owner of the vessel or other property in danger— ...
  (c) whenever circumstances reasonably require, to seek assistance from other salvors; and
  (d) to accept the intervention of other salvors when reasonably requested to do so by the owner or master of the vessel or other property in danger; provided, however, that the amount of his reward shall not be prejudiced should it be found that such a request was unreasonable."

Given the overlap between paragraphs (c) and (d) and their different terminology, their relationship and effects are not entirely clear.

1041 The drafting of the two paragraphs of Article 8.1(c)–(d) is awkward. It appears to require the salvor, when reasonable, to *seek* the assistance of other salvors but it only states that they should *accept* intervention which is already on offer if requested to do so by the salvees. Nevertheless, in broad terms, their combined object seems clearly to be that, when reasonable: salvors should accept the intervention of other services which are present and available; and, if such services are not present and available, they should seek assistance.

Furthermore, "reasonably" is employed in differing contexts in the two paragraphs. Paragraph (c) applies "whenever circumstances reasonably require"; and paragraph (d) "when reasonably requested to do so by [the master or salvees]." No doubt it will be possible to argue that there may be a difference between the reasonableness of circumstances and the reasonableness of a request by the master or salvees. But in practice there is unlikely to be much, if any, difference. In either case, the issue is likely to be whether in the circumstances (which may, of course, alter during salvage operations) the salvor is sufficiently equipped to render efficient services within a reasonable time.

Prima facie, a salvor's breach of his duties under Article 8.1(c)–(d) should render him liable to an action for damages for loss caused by the breach. Though he may argue that the loss resulted from the initial danger, the salvee may retort that, once a salvor has commenced salvage operations and acquired the statutory duties, loss which could have been avoided by discharging those duties is in fact caused by their non-performance. In any event, the failure to discharge them by a salvor contractually obliged to use best endeavours may render him liable for damages for breach of contract.

1042 Neither discharge nor failure to discharge Convention duties is a listed criterion in fixing an Article 13 salvage reward[38]; but failure to discharge them is at the least likely to restrain the amount of reward that could be earned and will in practice be a factor inhibiting it.

---

[38] See *post*, Chap. 15.

In fact, accepting assistance may benefit a salvor: he will not have to shoulder the full burden of providing the requisite services; and, if the services are performed more promptly and efficiently, the reward may be greater than it would otherwise have been. Against that, of course, he will have to share the reward with the intervening salvors.

1043   Article 8.1(d) states that the salvor has a duty to accept the intervention of other salvors "when reasonably requested to do so" by the master or salvees. It then provides that "the amount of his reward shall not be prejudiced should it be found that such a request was unreasonable". On first impression, the proviso may seem superfluous, as the salvor's duty does not arise if the request was unreasonable. However, if the request was unreasonable but the salvor nonetheless accepted intervention, in principle this would have meant that there eventuated more than one salvor entitled to participate in the overall reward, thus diminishing the amount which the original salvor could have earned. The proviso therefore preserves the first salvor's prima facie entitlement where a second salvor was accepted as a consequence of the salvee's unreasonable request. The final words of the proviso suggest that it is intended to apply when at a later point of time it is "found that such a request was unreasonable". However, it purports to preserve the salvor's rights to his reward without stipulating that he himself should have acted reasonably in acceding to the salvee's request.

6. CO-OPERATION AND TERMINATION OF SERVICES

1. Introduction

1044   The salvor's duty to co-operate with other salvors was discussed in the previous section. This part of the chapter embraces three distinct topics which overlap in practice and which, therefore, it is convenient to consider together. The first is the question whether parties to salvage operations are obliged to co-operate with each other and the effect of non-co-operation. The second concerns the rights which persons have to enter ports or harbours and the controls which may be placed on such entry. The third concerns the duties of salvees to accept redelivery of their property at the termination of salvage services.

2. General problems

1045   A salvor's ability to effect salvage, whether efficiently or at all, may be affected by the extent to which salvees and/or third parties are entitled to obstruct or refuse to co-operate with him during the salvage operations. Even where property has been salved, if it has been badly damaged it may be an inconvenience or a potential danger to third parties, pose a threat to the environment and be a financially unattractive proposition for its owners. Its

Entry to ports and harbours

owners may be reluctant to accept redelivery and/or port authorities may be reluctant to allow it access to a port: in traditional parlance, a casualty in such a position has become a "leper ship". The salvor is then faced with difficulties. If he cannot bring the property to the contract destination, he does not complete the salvage service and so is not entitled to a salvage reward. In the unlikely event that he can bring the service to a conclusion, if he leaves the property unattended, he relinquishes his security. In such a situation, or if he should decide to abandon the salvage service, he exposes himself to the risk of liability if the vessel should become an obstruction to other shipping. It is therefore necessary: for the salvor to obtain the co-operation of the salvees and of the relevant authorities to bring the property to the contract destination or to a place of safety; and for the salvees to accept redelivery of the cargo.

Traditionally, the law has permitted parties to pursue their own interests, provided only that they do not positively harm others. In particular, even though it is in the interest of one contracting party that the other contracting party carry out his obligations, the first party may generally decline to co-operate with the second and insist that the onus is on the latter party to discharge its duties. *A fortiori*, a State may insist that, for whatever reason they have been laid down, and whatever the effect of enforcing them, its laws be complied with. In particular, in circumstances in which salvage operations have become necessary, States may enforce laws prohibiting the operation of foreign salvors in their waters, or for protecting the environment or other interests, *e.g.* the provisions of the Merchant Shipping Act 1995, ss.94–100 in relation to unsafe ships. Such provisions may well inhibit or prevent prompt and full action by salvors.

1046

Clearly, the successful performance and completion of salvage and environmental services may require the co-operation of salvors, salvees and third parties. In fact, the recent climate has become receptive to the infiltration of the notion of co-operation into the English law of contract. Consistently with this, Lloyd's Form and the Salvage Convention 1989 contain provisions designed to promote co-operation in the performance of salvage and environmental services.[38A]

3. Entry to ports and harbours

As a general rule, ports and harbours are open to shipping subject to the payment of local charges and to other restrictions laid down by national and local laws.[39] One such restriction is the harbour master's power to give directions prohibiting the entry of a vessel into harbour under the Dangerous Vessels Act 1985, s.1. The harbour master's power is subject to the powers

1047

[38A] See Shaw [1996] L.M.C.L.Q. 202, 213–214.
[39] See, *e.g.* the Harbours, Docks and Piers Clauses Act 1847, ss.33 (harbours open to shipping subject to payment of rates) and 52 (harbour master's powers to regulate entry and movement of vessels). Provisions of the Act or equivalent provisions are incorporated into the legislation applicable to most harbour authorities.

given, for the prevention or reduction of oil pollution, to the Secretary of State under the Merchant Shipping Act 1995, s.137. Section 137 empowers the Secretary of State to give directions as respects a ship or its cargo to take or refrain from action of any kind, including salvage measures and action for the movement of vessels.

4. The duty of contracting States

1048   Under the heading "Co-operation", the Salvage Convention 1989, Art. 11 provides as follows[39A]:

> "A State Party shall, whenever regulating or deciding upon matters relating to salvage operations such as admittance to ports of vessels in distress or the provision of facilities to salvors, take into account the need for co-operation between salvors, other interested parties and public authorities in order to ensure the efficient and successful performance of salvage operations for the purpose of saving life or property in danger as well as preventing damage to the environment in general."

1049   The inclusion of Article 11 in the Salvage Convention 1989 and its drafting exemplify the spirit of compromise which usually underlies the conclusion of an international convention; and it serves a purpose as a recognition of the merit of encouraging co-operation in salvage and environmental services. However, it may be of limited utility. It represents, primarily at least, a treaty obligation between States parties to the Salvage Convention 1989 rather than an obligation enforceable at municipal level.[40] Furthermore, it is largely exhortatory, and at the very most requires States parties merely "to take into account" the need for co-operation.[40A]

Where duties or powers are intended to be imposed or conferred by statute, this is most frequently done within the body of the statute.[41] However, the general policy for implementing the Salvage Convention 1989 has been to set out its provisions verbatim in a schedule to the Merchant Shipping Act 1995. In this process, a number of articles in the Convention directed to the treaty obligations of States parties to the Convention rather than to the rights and

---

[39A] See Shaw [1996] L.M.C.L.Q. 202 at 214. Following the *Castor* incident in December 2000, the IMO decided to develop guidelines on places of refuge for vessels in distress threatening environmental damage. At its 83rd Session (October 2001), the IMO Legal Committee requested the Secretariat and the CMI to work jointly on a study of the existing international and national laws on this subject.

[40] Unlike certain provisions of European Community law, provisions of international treaties are generally not directly enforceable in English law.

[40A] Note, however, the partial response to Art. 11 in the International Convention on Oil Pollution Preparedness, Response and Co-operation 1990 ("the OPRC Convention"), in force internationally and given effect in U.K. law by MSA 1995, s.128(1)(d), the Merchant Shipping (Oil Pollution Preparedness, Response and Co-operation Convention) Order 1997 (S.I. 1997 No. 2567) and the Merchant Shipping (Oil Pollution Preparedness, Response and Co-operation) Regulations 1998 (S.I. 1998 No. 1056).

[41] *cf.* in relation to oil pollution, MSA 1995, ss.137–138, 293.

obligations of parties to salvage operations have been omitted.[42] However, the Act does include other provisions concerning the rights[43] and obligations of States[44]; and all those provisions of the Convention scheduled to the Act have the force of law.[45] Accordingly, Article 11 has the force of law. It is therefore necessary to consider the precise content of what is being enforced, by whom the duty is to be performed, when it is to be performed, and how it is to be enforced.

The content of the duty

1050 The obligation of States parties to the Convention only arises whenever they are regulating or deciding upon matters relating to salvage operations and is simply "to take into account the need for co-operation" between interested parties and public authorities for the designated purposes. States parties are not required to go further and to ensure that such co-operation actually occurs in practice.

The relevant authority

1051 The duty is stated to rest on States parties to the Convention. This is subject to two possible interpretations. The first is that the duty is to be discharged by central government, most obviously by the Secretary of State, and relates to the functions of central government, rather than extends also to those of other public authorities. If so, it will apply to the conferment of powers on other public authorities but not to their exercise of such powers. The second possibility is that the duty is to be discharged by whichever arm of government has relevant functions.[46] However, the Convention assumes a distinction between States and public authorities, rather than that the latter may be emanations of the State.[47] Accordingly, the first interpretation may be preferred.

Time for performance

1052 The duty must be discharged not only when regulating on matters relating to salvage operations but also at the time of such operations when the relevant authority decides upon matters such as admittance to ports of vessels in distress or the provision of facilities to salvors.

---

[42] Arts. 28–33 (final clauses).
[43] See Art. 25 (preserving sovereign immunity).
[44] See Art. 4.2 (States to notify the Secretary-General of the IMO of the application of the Convention to its warships) and Art. 27 (States to encourage publication of arbitral awards).
[45] MSA 1995, s.224(1).
[46] See *R. v. Charrington* (1999) Unreported (Bris. Crown Ct); noted W. Gilmore (2000) 49 I.C.L.Q. 477.
[47] See Arts. 5.3 and 11.

Enforcement of the duty

1053 Enforcement of the duty in Article 11 may be by public law or, where private rights are concerned,[48] by private law.[49]

Under public law, if the duty is not discharged during the relevant decision-making process, then the decision is subject to judicial review.[50] If the decision is found to be unreasonable, it should be corrected, so that future activities are conducted on a proper basis. But this procedure is unlikely to be helpful to parties wanting prompt co-operation at the time of the operations in issue: a court hearing an emergency application for judicial review may feel unable to decide that the omission to act is unreasonable, and it will be too late to make a difference if the court decides the matter with hindsight.

1054 If a private law remedy is sought, the claimant would need to prove both that a tort had been committed against him and that he had suffered loss as a consequence. The relevant torts are breach of statutory duty (if the statute is intended to give rise to the remedy),[51] negligence[52] and misfeasance in a public office (for deliberately or recklessly causing the loss).[53] In most cases it will be difficult to prove the main elements of the claim, in particular, that the mere failure to take account of the need for co-operation caused the loss. However, in an appropriate case, breach may, either alone or in contribution with other factors, lead to loss of the endangered property or of salvage remuneration and damages may be substantial. Moreover, there may be an appropriate alternative remedy. Thus, where a direction is given or action is taken to prevent or reduce oil pollution under the Merchant Shipping Act 1995, s.137 and the action was not reasonably necessary or was disproportionately less beneficial than the ensuing expense or damage, a person consequently incurring expense or suffering damage may recover compensation from the Secretary of State.[54]

5. Co-operation between parties to salvage operations

1055 *Ex hypothesi* property requiring salvage services is in danger and the onus is on the salvor (traditionally of his own volition, in modern times under a contractual obligation) to attempt to salve.[55] The object of a salvage operation is that the salvor should render a service. Thus, he is not necessarily obliged to "co-operate" with the salvee or his servant in carrying out the necessary

---

[48] See *O'Reilly v. Mackman* [1983] 2 A.C. 237 and subsequent cases qualifying the decision.

[49] See generally P. P. Craig, *Administrative Law* (4th ed., 1999), especially Chap. 23.

[50] See the Supreme Court Act 1981, s.31; C.P.R., Pt. 54.

[51] *cf.* the Crown Proceedings Act 1947, s.2.

[52] See, *e.g. Mersey Docks and Harbour Board Trustees v. Gibbs* (1866) 11 H.L.C. 686.

[53] See, *e.g. Micosta S.A. v. Shetland Islands Council (The Mihalis)* [1984] 2 Lloyd's Rep. 525; and especially *Three Rivers District Council v. Governor and Company of the Bank of England (No. 3)* [2000] 2 W.L.R. 1220.

[54] MSA 1995, s.138.

[55] See *ante*, Chap. 8 and §§ 1034–1036.

service, though he must accept the intervention of other salvors when reasonably requested to do so and it is arguable that the obligation to co-operate is mutual, to make the contract workable.[56]

1056 More important is the issue to what extent the recipients of salvage services must co-operate in their performance. Reproducing a provision previously introduced into Lloyd's Form,[57] the Salvage Convention 1989, Art. 8.2 provides that:

> "The owner and master of the vessel or the owner of other property in danger shall owe a duty to the salvor—
> (a) to co-operate fully with him during the course of the salvage operations;
> . . .
> (c) when the vessel or other property has been brought to a place of safety, to accept redelivery when reasonably requested by the salvor to do so."

1057 More specific duties are expressed in Lloyd's Form. Thus, LOF 1995, cl. 3 states:

> "*Owners Co-operation:*
> The Owners their Servants and Agents shall co-operate fully with the Contractor in and about the salvage including obtaining entry to the place named or the place of safety as defined in clause 1.[58] The Contractor may make reasonable use of the vessel's machinery gear equipment anchors chains stores and other appurtenances during and for the purpose of the salvage services free of expense but shall not unnecessarily damage abandon or sacrifice the same or any property the subject of this Agreement."

1058 In its statement of the overriding objectives of LOF 2000,[59] LSSAC 2000, cl. 2(c) states that, "In construing the Agreement or on the making of any arbitral order or award regard shall be had to the overriding purposes of the Agreement namely: . . . to encourage cooperation between the parties and with relevant authorities." More specifically, LOF 2000, cl. F states:

> "**Duties of property owners:**
> Each of the owners of the property shall cooperate fully with the Contractors. In particular:
> (i) the Contractors may make reasonable use of the vessel's machinery gear and equipment free of expense provided that the Contractors shall not unnecessarily damage abandon or sacrifice any property on board;

---

[56] See *ante*, §§ 1039–1043. *Cf.* Shaw [1996] L.M.C.L.Q. 202, 213.
[57] LOF 1980, cl. 2.
[58] See now *post*, § 1064.
[59] See *ante*, § 954.

Duties of Parties

(ii) the Contractors shall be entitled to all such information as they may reasonably require relating to the vessel or the remainder of the property provided such information is relevant to the performance of the services and is capable of being provided without undue difficulty or delay;

(iii) the owners of the property shall co-operate fully with the Contractors in obtaining entry to the place of safety stated in Box 3[60] or agreed and determined in accordance with Clause A."[61]

The effect of these provisions may be summarised as follows.

(a) *The person(s) owing the duty*

1059 (i) A duty to co-operate with the salvor is placed on each of the owners of the property in danger[62] by the Salvage Convention 1989[63] and Lloyd's Form.[64]

(ii) A duty to co-operate with the salvor is placed on the master of the vessel in danger by the Salvage Convention 1989.[65]

(iii) LOF 1995,[66] but not LOF 2000, also states that the duty upon the owners of the property in danger extends to their servants and agents. However, servants and agents of the property owners will normally only be bound by their contract with their principals and will not be parties to the Lloyd's Form contract so as to become subject thereunder to duties to the salvor. Accordingly, LOF 1995 simply makes clear that the duty on the property owners extends to the actions of their servants and agents.

(iv) No duty of co-operation is specifically imposed upon the salvor; but the overriding objective stated by LSSAC 2000[67] indicates that disapproval of the (in)action of a salvor who fails to co-operate with the other parties, other salvors and relevant authorities may be reflected in the arbitrator's award. Moreover, the Salvage Convention 1989 specifically requires salvors to accept the assistance of other salvors when reasonably requested to do so by the owner or master of the vessel or other property in danger.[68] It is conceivable that a tribunal could recognise a correlative implied duty of co-operation on the salvor.

---

[60] The agreed place of safety.
[61] The Contractors' basic obligation. See *ante*, §1034.
[62] The references to "the owner of the vessel or *other property in danger*" in the Salvage Convention 1989, Art. 8.1 and 8.2 make the assumption that the duty is imposed on the owners and master of the vessel only when the vessel is in danger.
[63] Art. 8.2(a).
[64] LOF 1995, cl. 3; LOF 2000, cl. F; LSSAC 2000, cl. 2(c).
[65] Art. 8.2(a).
[66] LOF 1995, cl. 3.
[67] LSSAC 2000, cl. 2(c).
[68] Salvage Convention 1989, Art. 8.1(d). See *ante*, § 1040.

(b) *The duties owed*

(i) The Salvage Convention 1989 and Lloyd's Form lay down a general duty to co-operate with the salvor.[69] This is expressed to be a duty to co-operate "fully", which, strictly speaking, makes any further elaboration of the duty otiose. However, Lloyd's Form makes clear certain important ramifications of this general duty.

(ii) Under Lloyd's Form,[70] the salvees must permit the contractors to make reasonable use of the vessel's equipment without expense; but the limited nature of this licence is made clear by its being stressed that the contractor is not entitled to cause unnecessary loss or damage to it.

1060

(iii) Under LOF 2000[71] the salvees must provide information relating to the property in danger relevant to the performance of the services, provided that it can be provided without undue difficulty or delay and provided that it may reasonably be required by the contractors. It is not clear whether the duty to provide such information must be fulfilled on the salvees' own initiative, provided that it is "such information as [the contractors] may reasonably require", or whether it needs to be triggered by the contractors' making a reasonable request. Consistently with the overriding duty to co-operate, the better view would seem to be: that the salvees should volunteer such information if they ought to realise that it should be provided; and that, on the contractors' request, they must supply such information together with any additional information which it is reasonable for the contractors to request.

1061

(iv) Under Lloyd's Form[72] the salvees[73] must co-operate fully with the contractors in obtaining entry to the contract destination. This duty should be considered together with the following duty.

1062

(v) Under the Salvage Convention 1989,[74] when the property has been brought to a place of safety, the salvees must accept redelivery when reasonably requested by the salvees to do so.

6. Termination of services

The place of safety

Under Admiralty law, a salvor is generally entitled to terminate salvage services at any time. However, to earn a salvage reward it is necessary to bring the property from danger to a place of safety.[75] Under Lloyd's Form also, no reward is earned unless the property is brought to a place of safety; but the

1063

---

[69] Salvage Convention 1989, Art. 8.2(a); LOF 1995, cl. 3; LOF 2000, cl. F.
[70] LOF 1995, cl. 3; LOF 2000, cl. F(i).
[71] LOF 2000, cl. F(ii).
[72] LOF 1995, cl. 3; LOF 2000, cl. F(iii).
[73] And, under LOF 1995, cl. 3, their servants and agents: see *ante*, §1059.
[74] Salvage Convention 1989, Art. 8.2(c).
[75] See *ante*, Chap. 8.

salvor is not free to break off his engagement and must use his best endeavours to reach such a place.

1064 LOF 2000 has on its face a box (Box 3), entitled "Agreed place of safety", to be filled in when the contract is concluded. As noted above, clause A then goes on to provide that:

> "The Contractors ... hereby agree to use their best endeavours to salve the property specified in Box 2 and to take the property to the place stated in Box 3 or to such other place as may hereafter be agreed. If no place is inserted in Box 3 and in the absence of any subsequent agreement as to the place where the property is to be taken the Contractors shall take the property to a place of safety."

Therefore, where (as is usually the case) no place of safety is agreed, the Lloyd's Form salvor must take the property to a place of actual safety. Where such a place is agreed, either at the time of contracting or subsequently, he is obliged and entitled to to take the property to the agreed place.

1065 LOF 2000, cl. H amplifies the Lloyd's Form duty to deliver, under the heading "Deemed performance", as follows:

> "The contractors' services shall be deemed to have been performed when the property is in a safe condition in the place of safety stated in Box 3 or agreed or determined in accordance with Clause A. For the purpose of this provision the property shall be regarded as being in safe condition notwithstanding that the property (or part thereof) is damaged or in need of maintenance if (i) the Contractors are not obliged to remain in attendance to satisfy the requirements of any port or harbour authority, governmental agency or similar authority and (ii) the continuation of skilled salvage services from the Contractors or other salvors is no longer necessary to avoid the property becoming lost or significantly further damaged or delayed."

Methods of termination

1066 Salvage services may be terminated in a number of ways.

(i) *Performance.* One is by performance—by the salvor's bringing the property to a place of safety. The salvor will then be entitled to payment for having done so.

(ii) *Breach of contract.* If a contracting party commits a repudiatory breach of contract, the other party has an election to "accept" the repudiatory breach and so to terminate the contract. In such a case, a salvor will earn no reward but the party not in breach will be entitled to recover damages from the other party for the loss caused by the breach.

1067 (iii) *Frustration.* By law, a salvage contract will be automatically discharged by frustration if performance of the salvage operation becomes impossible. In accordance with general contractual principle, a contractual salvor cannot plead that his contract has been frustrated simply because it has become more onerous to perform.[76] Indeed, a salvor's function is to extricate the casualty from difficult circumstances. Thus, he may be obliged to wait in order to gain entry to an agreed place of safety. If in fact it is impossible to enter an agreed place of safety, the contract should be frustrated. In that case, no salvage reward will be earned.[77] Where a salvage contract is frustrated, Lloyd's Form imposes no express or implied duty on the salvor to bring the property to an alternative place of safety. But nor is a bailee normally entitled simply to abandon property. However, once the contract has been frustrated, the salvor may be justified in claiming a salvage reward if he completes a salvage service on non-contractual principles. And the frustrated contract will probably be survived by the salvee's duty under Article 8.2(c) of the Convention "when the vessel or other property has been brought to a place of safety, to accept redelivery when reasonably requested by the salvor to do so." Certainly, under common law principles, a person who confers a benefit on another after frustration of contract is entitled to reasonable remuneration.[78]

(iv) *Other rights of termination.* Not being under an obligation to salve, a non-contractual salvor can break off at any time and can be expected to do so where it becomes clear that there is little prospect of a profitable conclusion of the services. However, a Lloyd's Form salvor is prima facie bound to continue to carry out his duty to use best endeavours to salve, even where there is little or no prospect of either party benefiting from his doing so. However, a party can terminate his contractual obligation where the contract gives him a right to do so. Accordingly, LOF 2000, cl. G provides: **1068**

"When there is no longer any reasonable prospect of a useful result leading to a salvage reward in accordance with Convention Articles 12[79] and/or 13[80] either the Owners of the vessel or the Contractors shall be entitled to terminate the services hereunder by giving reasonable prior written notice to the other."

In addition, under SCOPIC 2000, cl. 9, the Contractor may by written notice terminate his services under both SCOPIC 2000 and the Main (LOF 2000) Agreement where continuation would prove unprofitable. SCOPIC 2000, cl. 9 also affords the shipowner the right to discontinue paying SCOPIC remuneration.[81]

---

[76] *Tsakiroglou & Co. Ltd v. Noblee Thorl GmbH* [1962] A.C. 93.
[77] The general law (in particular, the Law Reform (Frustrated Contracts) Act 1943) provides for adjustment of the parties' rights and liabilities. However, its provisions are unlikely to be helpful in a salvage case. *cf. ante,* § 610.
[78] *The Massalia* [1959] 1 W.L.R. 787; affirmed [1961] 2 Q.B. 276.
[79] "Conditions for reward". See *ante*, Chap. 8.
[80] "Criteria for fixing the reward". See *post*, Chap. 15.
[81] See further *ante,* §§ 972–973.

7. Prolongation by public authority

1069 Public authorities have powers of intervention which may be exercised during salvage operations. Their intervention may have the effect of extending a salvage operation; for a salvage operation which is otherwise deemed to have terminated under LOF 2000, cl. H will not be so deemed "if Contractors are obliged to remain in attendance on a casualty to satisfy the requirements of any port or harbour authority, governmental agency or similar authority." However, such intervention by a public authority is not recognised as precluding shipowners or Contractors from exercising their rights of termination under LOF 2000, cl. G,[82] though in practice the salvors at least may be unlikely to want to terminate in such a case. On the other hand, SCOPIC 2000, cl. 9, only permits Contractors and shipowners to exercise their rights of termination under that clause (by which the Contractor can terminate the services under both SCOPIC and the Main Agreement) "if the Contractor is not restrained from demobilising his equipment by Government, Local or Port Authorities or any other officially recognised body having jurisdiction over the area where the services are being rendered." The services which a salvor continues to render at the insistence of a designated authority may, though equally it may not, qualify for payment by way of salvage reward, special compensation or SCOPIC compensation. But certainly a person otherwise entitled to a salvage reward will not be disentitled by the fact that salvage operations are controlled by public authorities.[83]

8. Non-acceptance of salved property

1070 A salvor who has completed a salvage service is entitled to a reward (previously under Admiralty law principles, now under the International Salvage Convention 1989). And a Contractor who has performed duties under an LOF 2000 or SCOPIC 2000 contract will be entitled to be remunerated in accordance with the contract. A salvor may continue to earn such payments if the salvee has not taken redelivery of his property. But, under the Salvage Convention 1989, Art. 8.2(c), when the property has been brought to a place of safety, the master and salvees owe a duty to the salvor to accept redelivery when reasonably requested by the salvor to do so. Failure to discharge this duty will entitle the salvor to claim for resulting losses. Otherwise, the position will have to be determined in accordance with the common law rules to be discussed as follows.

1071 The general position regarding the obligations and rights of a salvor after the termination of salvage services was considered by the House of Lords in *The Winson*.[84] The defendants, cargo owners, chartered the vessel for carriage

---

[82] See *ante*, § 1068.
[83] International Salvage Convention 1989, Art. 5. See *ante*, §§ 68–69.
[84] *China Pacific S.A. v. Food Corporation of India (The Winson)* [1982] A.C. 939; reversing [1981] Q.B. 403, CA; and restoring [1979] 2 All E.R. 35, *per* Lloyd J. See Rose (1982) 45 M.L.R. 568; [1982] L.M.C.L.Q. 200.

of a full cargo (37,100 tons) of wheat. The vessel had a lien on the cargo for freight, which was to be at all times at the risk of the shipowners and which was deemed earned upon arrival. On January 21, 1975, through no fault of the carrier, the ship grounded on a reef 420 miles from Manila. On the following day, the ship's managing agents contracted with the plaintiffs, professional salvors, for salvage of the ship and her cargo on Lloyd's Form (1972 edition). It provided, as does LOF 2000, that the cargo owners were to be directly liable to the plaintiffs for performance of the contract to salve the cargo.[85] It was necessary to lighten the vessel, and six separate parcels (of 15,429 tons *in toto*) of wheat were off-loaded and carried to Manila, arriving between February 10 and April 20 inclusive. Entry into the port of Manila was assumed to be into a place of safety.[86] However, it was necessary on arrival there for the wheat to be stored to prevent its rapid deterioration from exposure to the elements during the period before a decision as to what was to be done with it was reached by whomever was legally entitled to possession. The plaintiffs had no storage facilities of their own at Manila. They therefore contracted as principals for its storage by depositaries, who held it to their order and to whom they were thus personally liable for storage expenses until the cargo owners completed taking possession of it, which they did not do until August 5. On April 15 salvage operations had been justifiably suspended in view of the danger to men and equipment caused by fighting which had broken out in the vicinity on the previous day. It never became practicable to resume them and the plaintiffs formally terminated them on May 20. Nevertheless, even if completion of the charterparty had been physically possible, it would have involved such delay as would have frustrated the adventure. The shipowners had an option either to abandon the chartered voyage or to on-carry the salved wheat in other bottoms. But, on April 24, they elected formally to abandon the voyage, which thereupon terminated.

The plaintiffs obtained a salvage award for services rendered up to entry into Manila harbour and the defendants conceded liability to them for storage charges incurred subsequent to the shipowners' abandonment of the charterparty.[87] The question remained, however, of liability for storage at Manila before such abandonment. This was held to depend on the question: to whom was the salved cargo deliverable on arrival at Manila? The Court of Appeal, the judgment of which was substantially given by Megaw L.J., agreed with the defendants—that it was the shipowners. Lloyd J., however, had decided that it was the defendants. His judgment was restored by the House of Lords, the leading speech in which was given by Lord Diplock, with whom Lords Keith of Kinkel, Roskill and Brandon of Oakbrook simply agreed, Lord Simon of Glaisdale delivering a concurring speech.

1072

The nub of the House's decision was expressed thus by Lord Diplock[88]:

---

[85] LOF 1972, cl. 16. See now LOF 2000, cl. K. There was no dispute as to the defendants' agents' authority so to bind the cargo owners.
[86] But see [1982] A.C. 939, 956–957, 964.
[87] *cf.* [1981] Q.B. 403, 420.
[88] [1982] A.C. 939, 958–959.

Duties of Parties

> "Where in the course of salvage operations cargo is off-loaded from the vessel by which the contract of carriage was being performed and conveyed separately from that vessel to a place of safety by means ... provided by the salvor, the direct relationship of bailor and bailee is created between cargo owner and salvor as soon as the cargo is loaded on [the] vessels ... ; and all the mutual rights and duties attaching to that relationship at common law apply, save in so far as any of them are inconsistent with the express terms of the Lloyd's open agreement."

Lloyd J. put it this way[89]:

> "When the master actually or notionally handed over the cargo to the salvors, the old bailment came to an end and a new bailment was substituted."

Reimbursement under the salvage contract

1073 The "bailment" approach was not the only basis upon which it was argued that the defendants were liable. Thus, Lloyd J. had commented that[90]:

> "it would be absurd if, having saved a perishable cargo from maritime perils, the salvor was bound to leave the cargo on arrival so as to perish on land."

He concluded that common sense required reimbursement, just as common humanity had justified reimbursement for the railway's stabling of an uncollected horse in *GNR v. Swaffield*.[91] Similarly, but more specifically, Lord Simon said[92]:

> "if cargo, or part of it, is salved separately from the carrying vessel, it is the duty of the salvor [by implication from the Lloyd's Form contract], owed to the cargo owner, to take reasonable steps on its arrival at the place of safety to prevent its deterioration. It is also ... a necessary implication that, if the salvor incurs expense in fulfilling that duty, he is entitled to be reimbursed by the cargo owner. What I venture to submit hereafter, under the heading of 'Bailment', about the correlation of the performance of the duty to safeguard the goods on the one hand and the entitlement to reimbursement of expenses incurred thereby on the other, is relevant here; but it would be particularly unreasonable not to imply such correlationship in the context of the commercial nexus constituted by the Lloyd's Open Form."

---

[89] [1979] 2 All E.R. 35, 42.
[90] *ibid.*, 43. See also [1982] A.C. 939, 964.
[91] (1874) L.R. 9 Ex. 132.
[92] [1982] A.C. 939, 963–964.

Non-acceptance of salved property

1074 Since it was assumed that salvage had terminated on entry into Manila harbour, it was not possible to argue that the storage expenses were incurred as part of salvage, either under the maritime law of salvage or under the Lloyd's Form contract. However, it is suggested that, in similar circumstances in the future, salvors would be well advised to argue that, if they have an implied right to recover, it is for services rendered during, albeit towards the conclusion of, salvage services, especially while the salvage contract remains in operation.[93] To found their claim on something like an extension of the salvage relationship, but separate from it, is not only to expose themselves to the present uncertainties of the general law governing restitution for benefits conferred in cases of necessity, but to deprive themselves of the better-established and apparently more generous range of remedies available to those conferring benefits necessitated by emergencies arising at sea rather than on land.[94]

Duties and rights of the carrier

1075 Under the contract of carriage, whether it be a bill of lading contract or a voyage charterparty, a duty is imposed upon the carrier to carry the goods to the contract destination and to deliver them there to the proper consignee. While he has the goods in his custody, the carrier has possession of them as a bailee—invariably as a bailee for reward—and owes the cargo owner the appropriate duties to take proper care for the safety and preservation of the cargo under the law of bailment, subject to the terms of the contract of carriage and to any relevant statute. The carrier may be justified in employing as principal third parties to perform certain of his contractual duties. Even if those third parties handle the cargo while carrying out their functions, that does not necessarily make them bailees of it. In such a case, they would clearly be obliged to redeliver to the carrier and to look to him alone for payment for the services rendered, even though the services were in fact beneficial to the cargo owner. Similarly, if the carrier's employees became sub-bailees of the cargo from him, they would have to redeliver the cargo to him, not to the cargo owners. And, it is submitted, those employees might even be sub-bailees of the carrier and authorised as direct bailees of the cargo owners for the particular purpose of the engagement.[95]

1076 Supervening events may obviously make it necessary for the carrier to engage assistance to preserve the cargo from perils over and above those normally to be expected during performance of the contract of carriage. Where salvage services are necessary, the shipowner is entitled and obliged to engage the services of a salvor on behalf of the interests imperilled. But engagement of salvage services is not *per se* accompanied by termination of his rights and liabilities under the contract of carriage. The prevalent danger may justify his leaving the vessel and her cargo. But, even in such a case, he

---
[93] See *ibid.*, 956–957, 957–958, 964.
[94] See Rose (1989) 19 O.J.L.S. 167.
[95] *cf.* [1982] A.C. 939, 959.

must, if possible, attempt to resume possession of the imperilled property as soon as is convenient and to complete performance of his duties as carrier. He must normally bear the expense of performing his own duties. If one of those expenses is for storage charges incurred after completion of salvage operations and while the contract of carriage remains on foot, the carrier should be directly liable to the salvor for them. It is up to him whether he has insured himself against such liability or stipulated for the cargo owner to indemnify him for discharge of it.[96]

1077   It was not denied in *The Winson* that, *vis-à-vis* the cargo owners, the carrier had under the contract of carriage an immediate right to possession of the salved cargo and that the cargo owners would have been liable to him for damages for not allowing him to exercise that right and to earn freight by on-carriage of the cargo to destination.[97] But the carrier's rights under the contract were weakened in two respects. First, if he had wanted to on-carry, and obtaining possession from the cargo owners again proved more inconvenient than if redelivery had been to him, he could probably have recovered no damages for any resulting loss, either from the salvors or the cargo owners. Certainly, the cargo owners committed no breach of contract. Indeed, in order to escape liability to the plaintiff, they affirmed the carrier's rights, arguing that redelivery should be to him. Secondly, the carrier's uncrystallised power to secure his rights against the cargo owners by lien was, perhaps, too lightly disregarded. For Lloyd J. the point did not arise, since freight—and the lien for it—was not earned until safe arrival at port of discharge.[98] But that does not mean that cargo owners are normally at liberty to demand redelivery of their property before completion of the voyage. Lord Simon stated[99] that:

> "The shipowner, by becoming party to and implementing the salvage contract, gives up his possessory lien; and I know of no principle entitling him to repossession merely to reassert a possessory lien. As for his option to on-carry, he can exercise it merely by communication with the cargo-owner."

But if it is to be implied that loss by the shipowner of the security of his lien is in practice unimportant, this, with respect, is clearly unrealistic. Admittedly, it is misguided merely to try to enable shipowners to acquire a lien for its own sake. But if they can insist on redelivery from salvors and complete carriage to destination, they are clearly much better off than a carrier with only an unliquidated personal claim against the cargo owners.

---

[96] After salvage, it seems unlikely that he could claim a contribution for general average: *cf.* [1981] Q.B. 403, 431.
[97] See [1979] 2 All E.R. 35, 42; [1981] Q.B. 403, 430–431; [1982] A.C. 939, 957, 963.
[98] [1979] 2 All E.R. 35, 42.
[99] [1982] A.C. 939, 963. *cf. ibid.*, 959; [1981] Q.B. 403, 430–431.

Non-acceptance of salved property

1078 If the carrier remained a bailee of the cargo during salvage, it is just conceivable that he might acquire a lien over the cargo for storage expenses.[1] If so, it is not inconceivable that he might simultaneously demand to retain possession until satisfaction of the claim founding his lien, attempt to complete the contract of carriage, and eventually obtain his lien for freight. The carrier's bailment would continue if the salvor merely acquired possession of the cargo as his sub-bailee, for the period of salvage. In that case, he would obviously be bound to redeliver afterwards to the carrier, who would be liable for post-salvage expenses.

Frustration or abandonment

1079 As Megaw L.J. remarked[2]:

> "It is the duty of the shipowners ... under their contract of carriage ... to carry the goods on to the contractual destination, unless the adventure has been frustrated or is abandoned by consent of the parties to it. The adventure is not necessarily frustrated even though the vessel in which the goods were being carried may itself be unable to continue the contract voyage."

Whether frustration occurs is, as always, a question of construction of the contract. If continued carriage by the stranded vessel becomes impossible, the contract may still require on-carriage by substituted means; or it may, as in *The Winson*, give the carrier an option for this. In the former case, the carrier would be both entitled and obliged to possession for that purpose. In the latter, he would be entitled to it, until such time as he exercised his option to abandon the voyage.

If frustration does occur, the carrier will immediately be discharged from liability to complete the contract of carriage. If he still has possession of the cargo, he should redeliver it to its owners on demand, but may recover reasonable remuneration for performance, so far as possible, of his frustrated contract duties.[3] In any event, if he still has possession of the cargo, he will owe the duties of a gratuitous bailee. If, in discharging them, he incurs necessary expenditure for preservation of the property, he should be reimbursed. This should be so if the goods were currently being handled by a third party, such as a salvor, whether as a purely ministerial agent of the carrier or as a sub-bailee also. It is not unreasonable that he and his sub-bailee should remain liable to each other under their contract of bailment, for a contract of salvage is intended to take effect in circumstances under which a contract of carriage may be frustrated.

---

[1] This is contentious. A salvor has liens for his salvage claims. And it was contemplated that the person incurring liability for post-salvage storage expenses would have a lien: see [1981] Q.B. 403, 425; [1982] A.C. 939, 966; *cf. ibid.*, 962.

[2] But, so far, English law has denied a lien to necessitous benefactors. See [1981] Q.B. 403, 421D–F.

[3] *Société Franco-Tunisienne D'Armement Tunis v. Sidermar SPA (The Massalia)* [1961] 2 Q.B. 278.

Duties and rights of salvors

1080 Under the general law, a person who attempts to save property may abandon his efforts at will. But under the Lloyd's Form contract he binds himself to use his best endeavours to effect salvage. Whether he fulfils his duties is a question of fact. But, since the essence of salvage is the successful preservation of property from danger, the salvor should in principle bring the salved property to a reasonable place of safety. LOF 2000 may be completed to specify an agreed place of safety. Lloyd's Form does not take into account the possibility that different "places of safety" may be more convenient for salvors, cargo owners, and shipowners who may wish to complete carriage, although in practice the same place will often suit all parties. It is not unreasonable to suggest that the normal place of safety, if there is dispute, is the place at which the person entitled to immediate possession of the cargo—whoever he is—can reasonably be expected to resume possession; and that that person should, in principle, be the carrier.

1081 During salvage, a salvor is under a duty to the owners of property not to cause loss or damage due to his negligence. Moreover, a salvor who acquires possession of property will inescapably become a bailee of it. If a direct bailee, he clearly owes a duty of care to the owners. Indeed, as Lord Diplock remarked[4]: "A person who holds possession of goods as sub-bailee of an original direct bailee of the owner of goods also owes some duty of care towards the owner: *Morris v. C. W. Martin & Sons Ltd.*"[5] This remark followed his Lordship's suggestion that, even if the owners of the *Winson* remained *vis-à-vis* the cargo owners entitled to repossession of the cargo, it did not follow that it was the shipowners, and not the cargo owners, who were liable to reimburse the salvors for the storage expenses. But no more is it necessary to conclude that, since the salvors owed the cargo owners a duty to refrain from being negligent, then, before abandonment of the contract of carriage, any right to reimbursement for storage should be exercised against the cargo owners alone and not the carrier. The two points are distinct.

1082 On completion of salvage, the salvor can claim salvage remuneration in respect of each parcel of property salved from the owner of the respective parcel, and from him alone[6]; and this position is affirmed under Lloyd's Form.[7] His claim is supported by a maritime lien, enforceable by action *in rem*, and a possessory lien, enforceable against anyone requesting delivery of the cargo, whoever that may be and regardless of that person's liability to pay salvage remuneration.[8] In practice, the need to exercise the liens is commonly superseded by security's being put up, as it was in *The Winson*.

---

[4] [1982] A.C. 939, 957–958; and see *ibid.*, 963. But *cf.* [1979] 2 All E.R. 35, 43; [1981] Q.B. 403, 423.
[5] [1966] 1 Q.B. 716.
[6] [1979] 2 All E.R. 35, 41.
[7] See LOF 2000, cl. K.
[8] *cf.* [1982] A.C. 939, 962.

Non-acceptance of salved property

The salvor is obliged and entitled to redeliver the salved cargo to the person entitled to possession of it. That person was not specified in *The Winson* but, it has been submitted, it should as a matter of general principle normally be the carrier. However, Article 8.2(c) of the International Salvage Convention 1989 now provides that:

> "The owner and master of the vessel or the owner of other property in danger shall owe a duty to the salvor... when the vessel or other property has been brought to a place of safety, to accept redelivery when reasonably requested by the salvor to do so."

This means that the cargo owners are directly liable to the salvor to accept redelivery of the cargo, regardless of who is otherwise entitled to demand possession, and must compensate him for failure to accept redelivery. This is consistent with the direct relationship created under Lloyd's Form between the salvor and the owner of each parcel of property salved. It is arguable that this redelivery provision completely supersedes whatever rights and duties in respect of redelivery that exist at common law. But that might produce absurd results. The clause appears to contemplate a familiar situation where the owners of salved property wish to, and do, resume possession of their own property at a single place of safety to which all the salved property is brought. But it could hardly be contemplated that a salvor who assumed possession of ship and cargo during salvage operations would be obliged or even entitled to prevent resumption of the contract of carriage by taking the cargo off the ship for redelivery directly to its owner. It is submitted, therefore, that the salvor's primary duty on completion of salvage services is to attempt redelivery to the carrier and that the carrier should, *vis-à-vis* the salvor and the cargo owner, accept redelivery. Article 8.2(c) would, therefore, seem to give the salvor a right upon which to fall back should the carrier not accept redelivery.

Redelivery to whom?

Simply to state that the salvor is bound to redeliver to the person entitled to possession is to beg two questions. First, to which a general answer has already been attempted: who is entitled to possession? Secondly, what must the salvor do if he does not know the answer to the first question, particularly where there are competing claims to possession? According to Lloyd J.[9]:

> "from the plaintiff's point of view, it would make all the difference in the world... whether the voyage had been abandoned or not before the cargo reached Manila; for, if it had, obviously the plaintiffs would not be able to look to the shipowners to accept redelivery of the cargo or to be responsible for the subsequent expenses of storage. Yet in many, and perhaps most, cases the salvors could not know whether the contract of carriage had been frustrated or not, or whether, and if so when, the

[9] [1979] 2 All E.R. 35, 42–43.

Duties of Parties

voyage had been abandoned. In those circumstances, it seems to me much better that there should be a simple rule that the salvors should, throughout, look to the cargo interests to accept delivery of the cargo ... and that the salvors should not have to look to a different paymaster depending on whether the voyage had been abandoned, and (if so) when."

With respect, the reasoning of Megaw L.J. is preferable[10]:

"as a general proposition, both principle and convenience appear to me to lead to the conclusion contended for by counsel for the cargo owners. The shipowners, unless and until the voyage is abandoned or frustrated, are the persons who are entitled to the possession of the goods which they are under a contractual obligation, and are contractually entitled, to carry to the destination, which, in some cases, they have to carry to their destination in order to earn their freight ... This general principle is no doubt subject to exceptions. One state of facts which might very probably constitute a valid exception is a case in which the shipowners cannot be found when the salvor has brought the cargo to the port of safety; or ... if the shipowners, knowing that the cargo has arrived, or is likely to arrive, at the place of safety, nevertheless indicate to the salvor that they do not wish or intend to take delivery of the salved cargo."

1084 The Lloyd's Form contract contemplates a number of direct obligations to salve and to pay for salvage between the salvor and the owner of each separate parcel of property. But it does not deny the fact that the person signing the contract is acting in discharge of the carrier's duties to care for all the property imperilled; nor does it negative the conclusion that, after satisfaction of the central obligations of the salvage contract, redelivery should be to the person who initially had possession and the most obvious right to possession—the carrier. It is suggested, therefore, that until frustration or abandonment of the contract of carriage or notice to the salvor of either event, the carrier remains a bailee, and liable for the expenses of discharging his duties, and that the salvor will normally be his agent and sub-bailee during that period.

Lord Diplock stated that[11]:

"the salvors could not resist a demand for possession of the salved wheat made by the cargo-owner upon its arrival at a place of safety by relying upon *jus tertii, viz.*, the shipowner's right to possession as against the cargo-owner, at any rate until an adverse claim to possession had been made upon them by the shipowner. If demand for possession of the salved wheat had been made upon them by the shipowner (which it never

---

[10] [1981] Q.B. 403, 421, 422.
[11] [1982] A.C. 939, 959–960.

was), the salvors would have complied with it at their peril. Their only safe course would have been to interplead; whereas in returning possession to the cargo-owner or in accordance with its directions before any demand for possession was made by the shipowner, they would have run no risk of liability to the latter."

As his Lordship states, the problem did not arise. Indeed, the very opposite, for neither shipowner nor cargo-owner claimed possession. In any event, and quite apart from the assumption that it was the cargo-owner who had the better right to possession after salvage, his Lordship omitted to mention that, so far as the danger of competing claims is concerned, this has since the events of *The Winson* been dealt with by the Torts (Interference With Goods) Act 1977. Section 8 entitles a defendant in an action for wrongful interference with goods to show that a third party has a better right to possession. The position should be no different if the cargo-owner were to sue for breach of contract.

Conclusion

The House of Lords only purported to apply its analysis of the law to the particular, perceived facts of *The Winson*: namely, where cargo of the sole cargo-owner was salved separately from the vessel in circumstances where completion of the carriage contract did not occur. Its decision need not be criticised to the extent of acknowledging a liability on the part of the cargo-owners to make restitution for a factual benefit conferred on them consequent upon performance of the salvage contract entered into on their behalf. Since the House was scrupulous in confining its judgment to the particular circumstances of the case, it is suggested that that restriction should go to negative any implication that, after salvage, the carrier is not generally obliged and entitled to resume possession of the cargo and to be primarily liable for storage expenses while the contract of carriage remains on foot. The salvor should normally redeliver to the carrier. He may be entitled to claim the expenses from either carrier or cargo owner. But, subject to the terms of the contract of carriage, the carrier should, *vis-à-vis* the cargo-owner, normally discharge the liability.[12] Since the salvor was employed on behalf of the cargo-owners, it is less easy to argue that they are not secondarily liable to him, especially given the ease with which (after frustration, abandonment or the cargo-owner's refusal to give instructions) the Court of Appeal found liability transferred to the cargo-owners. But English law would find it even more difficult to find the cargo-owners primarily liable for necessitous intervention while the carrier's liability persisted.[13]

---

[12] See [1981] Q.B. 403, 422, 423, 431.
[13] See *ibid.*, 424, 425, 431; [1982] A.C. 939, 961.

9. Summary

1085A The significance to a salvor of termination of salvage services is: (1) the success of the operation is no longer conditional on further work; (2) salvage payments are due; (3) the salvor is entitled to security from each salved interest; (4) the two year time limit[14] starts to run; and (5) subsequent services give rise to further obligations to pay (as in *The Winson*)—in particular, a subsequent casualty may result in a further salvage service.[15]

---

[14] See *post*, Chap. 12(6).
[15] See generally Shaw [1996] L.M.C.L.Q. 202, 212–213.

CHAPTER 11

MISCONDUCT

1. INTRODUCTION

Range of misconduct

Misconduct may be manifested in a number of ways at the time of danger **1086**
or salvage operations, as it may in other circumstances. Thus, misconduct in
the negotiations for a salvage contract may vitiate that contract.[1] The concern
of this chapter is primarily the effect of normally tortious conduct[2] on the
rights and liabilities of salvor and salvee. Both parties are subject to the
general duty on a person in English law to take reasonable care to avoid acts
or omissions which he can reasonably foresee would be likely to injure
persons who are so closely and directly affected by his act that he ought
reasonably to have them in contemplation. Moreover, the salvor has, under the
Salvage Convention 1989, Art. 8.1(a), a statutory duty to the owners of
property in danger to carry out the salvage operation with due care.[3]

The common law duty not to be negligent is owed by salvor and salvee not **1087**
only to each other but also to third parties. Thus, the owner of a sunken barge
in the River Thames was liable to a ship which collided with the unlit wreck
and could not escape liability by having employed an independent contractor
to salve the wreck, the salvor having negligently failed to light it.[4] Similarly,
a salvor will be liable to third parties for loss or damage he causes to them
through his actionable negligence, *e.g.* to other persons involved in salvage
operations.[5] Conversely, he will not incur liability for other losses they suffer
where he owes them no contractual or other duty, *e.g.* merely because he has
begun to provide services to a casualty and fails to prevent oil pollution to
adjoining coastlines.[6] However, the relationship between salvor and salvee, in
which the duty of care may arise from contract as much as from the general
law, is the main concern in this chapter. Additionally to the duty not to be
negligent, the parties must, of course, also refrain from deliberate wrongdoing

[1] See *ante*, Chap. 9.
[2] See generally *Clerk & Lindsell on Torts* (18th ed., 2000); *Charlesworth & Percy on Negligence*, (10th ed., 2001).
[3] See *ante*, Chap. 10.
[4] *The Snark* [1900] P. 105, affirming [1899] P. 74.
[5] *The Salvital* [1998] 1 Lloyd's Rep. 185.
[6] *The Amoco Cadiz* [1984] 2 Lloyd's Rep. 304 (U.S. Dist. Ct, Illinois), especially at 336.

to each other. Thus, a salvor may be liable for trespass or wrongful interference with the salvee's property where he intervenes in a case where the salvee has prohibited him from doing so.

Effect of misconduct

1088 The International Salvage Convention 1989, Art. 18 (headed generally "The effect of salvor's misconduct") provides more specifically that:

> "A salvor may be deprived of the whole or part of the payment due under this Convention to the extent that the salvage operations become necessary or more difficult because of fault or neglect on his part or if the salvor has been guilty of fraud or other dishonest misconduct."

This reproduces in amended form the Brussels Salvage Convention 1910, Art. 8 (final paragraph) and in part the decision of the House of Lords in *The Tojo Maru*.[7] However, it was also the case under pre-Convention law that the victim of tortious or contractual misconduct can enforce the normal remedies for losses caused by actionable misconduct: in particular, a claim for damages could be enforced not only by a direct action but also by way of set-off. These possibilities are not considered by Article 18 but nor are they excluded, and there seems no reason why such potentially important rights should be treated as impliedly excluded by the Convention.

1089 The Convention also specifically provides in Article 14.5 that:

> "If the salvor has been negligent and has thereby failed to prevent or minimise damage to the environment, he may be deprived of the whole or part of any special compensation due under this Article."[8]

Again, Article 14.5 should not be treated as an exclusive statement of the consequences of salvorial misconduct. Moreover, it overlaps with Article 18 and may well be superfluous, other than as a reminder of the importance of discharging the duty to exercise due care to prevent or minimise damage to the environment.[9]

1090 In salvage cases, it is more likely to be the salvor's breach of duty which is in issue, partly because he is the more active party, and therefore with greater opportunity for misconduct, and partly because his misconduct raises not merely the question of the extent to which, if any, he should compensate the other party for the loss or damage caused by his misconduct but also the question of the extent to which, if any, his misconduct may affect his entitlement to salvage reward or its assessment. Nevertheless, the effect of the

---

[7] [1972] A.C. 242.
[8] See further *ante*, Chap. 5, especially § 438.
[9] This duty rests on both salvor and salvee. See the International Salvage Convention 1989, Art. 8.1(b) and Art. 8.2(b); *ante*, §§ 1037–1038.

salvee's negligence should not be ignored and it is convenient to deal with this first.

2. Salvee's Duty to Salvor

There is an implied duty on the part of those in charge not only of salving **1091** vessels but also of vessels accepting assistance to use ordinary care and skill in carrying out their respective parts of the combined work. Thus, in *The Glasgow*,[10] a case in which there was no clear evidence of a contract to salve, and in which the casualty collided with and sank the salving ship, Lord Atkinson said[11]:

> "The *Glasgow* called for help. She invited the *Hatfield* to come to her assistance, and in a high wind and heavy sea endeavour to perform the difficult and dangerous operation of taking her in tow. In such an operation, I think, a duty was cast upon the vessel so asking for assistance to be on the alert, to observe the movements of the vessel coming to salve her, to accommodate her own movements as far as safety would permit to those of the latter vessel, and to render aid, according to the rules of good seamanship, in assisting in the enterprise both desired to accomplish."

Where there is clear evidence of a contract to salve, the duty of the casualty **1092** to exercise due care and skill not to cause loss or damage to the salvor coexists with a contractual duty not to prevent or inhibit the salvor's performance of salvage services. If, by reason of breach of that contractual duty, the salvor is prevented from completing the agreed service, he may recover damages not only for physical loss resulting from the defendant's negligence but also for loss of his opportunity to earn salvage.[12]

In *The Valsesia*,[13] two steam-tugs orally contracted with a vessel which had **1093** grounded on rocks in Barry Roads, for £300 and £150 respectively, to beach her. During the services, those in charge of the ship negligently failed to slip their cable with the result that the ship again grounded as the tide turned and she was no better off than when the tugs took hold of her. The claim by the owners, masters and crew of the tugs for the stipulated sums was rejected "because the contract was for a lump sum in respect of completed work, and the work was not completed." Nor, there being no success, was salvage payable. But Hill J. said[14]:

---

[10] *Owners of S.S. Hatfield v. Owners of S.S. Glasgow* (*The Glasgow*) (1914) 13 Asp. M.L.C. 33.
[11] *ibid.*, 36.
[12] See *ante*, § 763.
[13] [1927] P. 115.
[14] *ibid.*, 118, 119.

> "In my view this case falls to be decided according to the ordinary principles of common law and no question peculiar to the law of salvage is involved. I think there was implied in such an agreement as this a mutual obligation at least to act with ordinary skill and care in carrying out the respective parts in the combined work. It was the duty of the tugs to obey the orders of those who were in command of the ship and to use skill and care in the handling of the tugs, and it was equally the duty of those in charge of the ship to use ordinary skill and care in carrying out their part of the contract, which was the slipping of the cable at the right time. This, indeed, was the essential part which the ship was to play in the combined operation.
>
> ... [I]f the failure to slip was due to negligence on the part of those on board the ship, the plaintiffs must be entitled in one way or another to be put in the same position as they would have been in if that negligence had never occurred, and if those in charge of the ship had carried out their duty towards the two tugs ... and in this case the damages would be exactly commensurate with the stipulated sums, because the plaintiffs had in substance completed the whole of what they had undertaken to do. They had probably been saved no expense by reason that they were not able to complete the work."

His Lordship noted that both the pilot and the tugs contemplated that the cable would be slipped, and that the failure to do this "quite ordinary matter in ship work" was prima facie evidence of negligence putting upon the defendants the duty of shewing that the failure arose without negligence on their part.

1094 Hill J. in *The Valsesia* doubted whether such a contract as was made therein (presumably meaning one for fixed sums) could be regarded as being entered on behalf of the cargo as well as the ship. "But," he continued,

> "be that as it may, I cannot find that the negligence of those in charge of the ship was negligence in any other capacity than as servants of the shipowner, and therefore I think I cannot give judgment against anybody except the shipowner."[15]

Although salvage contracts on LOF 2000 specifically purport to be made also on behalf of parties other than the shipowner,[16] Hill J.'s dictum supports the view that parties for whom a shipowner contracts on Lloyd's Form will not be vicariously liable for the ship's negligence. It would not realistically fall within the course of his employment. However, if it were held to do so, of

---

[15] [1927] P. 115, 121. See also *ibid.*, 121: "That judgment must be *in personam*, because an action arising out of the negligent performance of such a contract as this, in my view, does not give rise to a right *in rem*." Although the action was apparently initiated *in rem*, he treated it as having been defended *in personam*.

[16] See Box 2.

course, the shipowner would be bound to indemnify his principals/masters for the loss he caused them.[17]

In most cases, negligence will be relevant where it occurs during the performance of salvage. However, it was held in *The Ranger*[18] that, where through their own negligence the defendants' vessel came into danger and the plaintiff made efforts to save her but the danger was over when he got to her, although the then absence of danger precluded any claim for salvage, the fact that the plaintiff went out because of the defendants' negligence entitled him to reimbursement for his "expenses". Although there is no general proposition that a person owes to third parties a duty not to cause danger to himself by his own negligence, it seems not unreasonable, as a matter of public policy if not a duty, in a case where both parties suffer a potential detriment as a result of the fault of one of them rather than of external circumstances, that the person responsible should at least compensate the plaintiff for his losses, at least losses other than loss of opportunity to earn salvage. However, it is not clear that *The Ranger* goes this far. In his judgment, Dr Lushington clearly says that "the expenses of the lugger should be paid by [the owners of] the *Ranger*",[19] but a sidenote to one of the reports paraphrases this as "the *costs* to be paid by the owners",[20] which costs may, but not necessarily, simply have been the costs of the action.

At the other end of the scale, it is clearly right that, where a salvor has brought the salved property to safety, and as a result of the defendant's negligence the property is damaged so as to be diminished in value, the salved value is properly taken at the place of safety.[21]

3. MISCONDUCT CAUSING DANGER

Disentitlement?

Former view

The early cases demonstrate the previously well-established view that, if it is the fault of the claimants which initially gives rise to the need for services of a salvage character, those claimants will not be entitled to claim a salvage

---

[17] *Lister v. Romford Ice and Cold Storage Co. Ltd* [1957] A.C. 555.
[18] (1845) 3 N.o.C. 589.
[19] *ibid.*, 591; (1845) 9 Jur. 119, 120. Only the former report includes the words bracketed here.
[20] (1845) 3 N.o.C. 589, 591.
[21] *The Germania* [1904] P. 131 (vessel brought within reach of tug off Aberdeen, went aground after master improperly refused tug's services).

reward.[22] Thus, in *The Cargo ex Capella*,[23] where a collision had occurred between two vessels, both being to blame, Dr Lushington held that one of them could not claim for saving the other's cargo (the owners of which were, of course, wholly innocent) from perils consequent upon the collision. Similarly, he stated, the claimants could recover no reward from the other ship, the reason "founded in justice and equity" being that no man can profit from his own wrong.[24] More elaborately, in *The Minnehaha*,[25] where the fault was a breach of contract, Lord Kingsdown, in delivering the Privy Council's opinion as to the entitlement to salvage reward of a tug previously engaged to tow the vessel coming into distress, stated[26]:

> "If the danger from which the ship has been rescued is attributable to the fault of the tug; if the tug, whether by wilful misconduct, or by negligence, or by the want of that reasonable skill or equipments which are implied in the towage-contract, has occasioned or materially contributed to the danger, we can have no hesitation in stating our opinion that she can have no claim to salvage. She can never be permitted to profit by her own wrong or default.
>
> When it is remembered how much in all cases—how entirely in many cases—a ship in tow is at the mercy of the tug; how easily, with the knowledge which the crews of such boats usually have of the waters on which they ply, they may place a ship in their charge in great, real or apparent peril; how difficult of detection such a crime must be, and how strong the temptation to commit it, their Lordships are of opinion that such cases require to be watched with the closest attention, and not without some degree of jealousy."

In *The Duc d'Aumale (No. 2)*[27] Gorell Barnes J. held that the inability to claim applied to: the master who was personally responsible for the negligence necessitating salvage; the owners, who stood or fell by the negligence of their master; and the crew, because "both on principle and as a matter of good policy ... it would not be desirable to encourage a crew to recover a salvage reward in such cases of tug and tow where the master of the tug has been one of the causes of the disaster from which the ship to which salvage services has been rendered is rescued. ... it would be bad policy to encourage sailors, as it were, to hope and expect that their master might get

---

[22] *The Cargo ex Capella* (1867) L.R. 1 A. & E. 356; *The Robert Dixon* (1879) 4 P.D. 121, affirmed (1879) 5 P.D. 54; *The Altair* [1897] P. 105; *The Adam W. Spies* (1901) 70 L.J.P. 25; *The Duc D'Aumale (No. 2)* [1904] P. 60; *The Harvest Home* [1904] P. 409, varied [1905] P. 177 (in that case, the tug was refused salvage reward but recovered towage remuneration); *The Maréchal Suchet* [1911] P. 1; *The Unique* (1939) 65 Ll.L.Rep. 75 (negligence of jetty owner). See also *The Minnehaha* (1861) 15 Moo (P.C.) 133; *The Annapolis, The Golden Light, The H.M. Hayes* (1861) Lush. 355; *The Glengaber* (1872) L.R. 3 A. & E. 534, 535.

[23] (1867) L.R. 1 A. & E. 356.

[24] Described as an "old principle (which is perhaps a little out of date now)": *The Unique* (1939) 63 Ll.L. Rep. 75, 77, *per* Bucknill J.

[25] (1861) 15 Moo. (P.C.) 133.

[26] *ibid.*, 155.

[27] [1904] P. 60.

Disentitlement?

the ship he was towing into danger, so that they would have to render services for which they could recover."[28] Similar reasoning would apply where a vessel was put in danger not by the agent of the owners of the putative salving vessel but by a servant acting within the course of his employment, for whom they were vicariously liable—who might be a (temporarily employed) compulsory pilot.[29] In *The Duc d'Aumale (No. 2)* Gorell Barnes J. commented that[30]:

> "the crew did nothing more than their ordinary duties towards their owners and master with little or no risk. It may very well be that there might be a case of joint negligence producing a disaster to a tow, where a man might be put on board the tow, or be required to perform services entirely outside the ordinary duties of tug and tow. When such a case arises it can be dealt with."

It was immaterial that the acts of the claimant giving rise to the danger were unintentional or done in good faith.[31] The results were similar whether his acts arose from deliberate fault, negligent failure to take due care, or breach of contract.

But this fault should have been of such a type that would normally have been prima facie actionable at the suit of the defendant. In *The Golden Light*,[32] the *Annapolis*, towed by the tug *Storm King*, was let go by the tug and drifted into the *Golden Light*, which subsequently drifted into the *H.M. Hayes*. The tug claimed a reward for services then rendered to the *Golden Light* in preventing or diminishing damage which she might have suffered from collision with the *H.M. Hayes*. Dr Lushington rejected the claim on the ground that the services were necessitated by the tug's failure to exercise due skill and promptness in preventing the *Annapolis* from coming into collision with the *Golden Light*. The Privy Council, however, in an opinion delivered by Lord Kingsdown, reversed his decision:

> "A most important principle of law is involved in this decision, which, as far as our knowledge extends, is new: that third persons can avail themselves of the breach of contract to which they are strangers, on the ground that if it had been duly performed they would have escaped injury to which they have been subjected. But it is not necessary to pronounce a decision upon this point, for we think it is not made out in fact that the

1097

---

[28] *ibid.*, 74, 75. But note Lord Wright's reference to and apparent disapproval of, the crew's disability in this case in *The Beaverford v. The Kafiristan* [1938] A.C. 136, 151, where he spoke of "the crew being identified with the negligent master on grounds of public policy which I need not here discuss but which seem to me as at present advised to be of dubious soundness." See also *The Kauss* (1901) 20 T.L.R. 326.
[29] See Rose, *The Modern Law of Pilotage* (1984), pp. 33–39.
[30] *Supra* n. 27, at 75.
[31] See *The Robert Dixon* (1879) 4 P.D. 121; affirmed (1879) 5 P.D. 54.
[32] *The Annapolis, The Golden Light, The H.M. Hayes* (1861) Lush. 355.

collision with the *Annapolis* was caused directly or indirectly by the fault of the *Storm King*."³³

1098 In such circumstances, subject to the Contracts (Rights of Third Parties) Act 1999, the doctrine of privity of contract would normally dictate that a third party cannot complain of the breach of a contractual duty owed by one contracting party to another.³⁴ But it is possible in such a case that the third party suffers a loss for which he can sue because the party in breach of contract has *also*, simultaneously, breached a duty of care owed directly to the third party under the tort of negligence.³⁵ On that basis, Dr Lushington's judgment, which was not overruled on this precise point, supports the view that a third party can refuse to reward salvage services necessitated initially by the claimant's act in breaching a duty owed to someone else.

If the need for salvage arose from such fault on the part of the claimant as would normally disentitle him from claiming salvage, his inability to claim would be unaffected by the fact that he was not liable to the defendant for the consequences of his fault, *e.g.* where an exemption clause in a towage contract relieved the tug from the consequences of its breach of contract.³⁶

Current view

1099 The decision of the House of Lords, and in particular the speech of Lord Wright, in *The Beaverhood v. The Kafiristan*³⁷ now support the virtually incontrovertible view that, where it is the fault of salvage claimants which causes the danger in respect of which they subsequently render salvage services, that fault does not disentitle the claimants from claiming a reward but is more properly considered in assessing the amount of the reward and the claimants' liability to the salvees for damages. The simplest case is, as in *The Beaverford v. The Kafiristan*, where Lloyd's Form is signed for, whatever his rights against the salvor for damages, the salvee becomes contractually bound to pay salvage.³⁸

Secondly, the alleged disentitlement of salvors did not occur where the wrongdoing party's sister ship was the means of salvage.³⁹ But, even where the salving ship was the wrongdoing ship, Lord Wright stated that, as a matter of principle and of policy, the salvor should be entitled to claim a reward for meritorious salvage services successfully rendered and that the authorities generally support this view; in so far as they contradict it, they cannot stand.

Admittedly, the salvee remains able to claim damages from the wrongdoer for the loss flowing from his wrong, including any liability to pay salvage. If the salvor were totally to blame for the salvee's loss, his salvage claim would

---
[33] *ibid.*, 374.
[34] See Chitty, Chap. 19; Treitel, Chap. 15.
[35] See, *e.g. Junior Books Ltd v. Veitchi Co. Ltd* [1983] 1 A.C. 520.
[36] See *The Duc d'Aumale (No. 2)* [1903] P. 61, 70.
[37] [1938] A.C. 136.
[38] See *ante*, §§ 866–875.
[39] See *post*, §1103.

fail for circuity of action. If he were only to blame in part, the amount of salvage ultimately recoverable would be reduced by the proportion of his liability, since he would have to pay back to the other party as damages that amount of any salvage reward for the service resulting from his fault.

Proof

A person who claims a salvage reward has the burden of proving his entitlement to such a reward.[40] In particular, this means that, where the circumstances in which salvage services are required are such as to lay the claimant open to suspicion of having caused the need for such services by his failure to perform a duty owed to the defendant, the claimant must negative such suspicion in order to make out his case for a reward. If he was under a positive duty to take a certain amount of care of the property concerned, as is a tug under a towage contract, he must shew: that the vessel did not come into danger through any fault of his, and that he did all he could to prevent the danger; that the danger was caused by some event beyond his control; and that he performed services not required by his original duty (which, of course, may have been superseded by the peril).[41] The claimant must discharge a similar burden where his alleged breach of duty is simply not to cause loss to the defendant by his negligence. The defendant is not obliged specifically to plead negligence to defeat a salvage claim. Where the defendant counterclaims against the claimant for damages for the loss he has caused, the claimant again has the burden of proving that it was not his fault that occasioned the loss, but that of the defendant or those for whom he is responsible.[42]

1100

Effects of claimant's fault

It has been shewn that, where salvage is necessitated by the claimant's fault, he can still claim a salvage reward. But he will prima facie be liable for any loss or damage suffered as a result of his wrongful act or default.[43] The damages which he must pay to the owner of the property placed in danger include sums payable by the owner as salvage to third party salvors; the costs payable by the owner to the third parties are also computed in the damages and are not to be itemised separately on the basis that the full amount cannot be recovered as damages, since the claimant may be able to limit his liability.[44] The claimant's liability may be excluded or limited by contract or statute[45]; whether or not this is so will be a question of construction.[46]

1101

[40] See *ante*, § 340.
[41] See *ante*, §§ 621–624.
[42] See *The Robert Dixon* (1879) 5 P.D. 54, 58–59.
[43] See *Bland v. Ross (The Julia)* (1860) 14 Moo. (P.C.) 210; *Spaight v. Tedcastle* (1881) 6 App.Cas. 217; *The Undaunted* (1860) 54 L.T. 542; *The Robert Dixon* (1879) 5 P.D. 54; *The Kauss* (1904) 20 T.L.R. 326; *The Refrigerant* [1925] P. 130.
[44] *The Kauss* (1904) 20 T.L.R. 326.
[45] See *The Kauss* (1904) 20 T.L.R. 326; *The President Van Buren* (1924) 16 Asp. 444 (the liability of the PLA tug was thus excluded under the PLA (Docks Towage Conditions then in force).
[46] See *e.g. The Refrigerant* [1925] P. 130.

The contributory negligence of the vessel in danger may reduce, or even extinguish, the liability of the party at fault.[47]

1102 Even if the party at fault fails to obtain salvage from services rendered as a consequence of his fault, he may nonetheless be awarded a reasonable sum by way of *quantum meruit* for beneficial services rendered, *e.g.* as towage remuneration.[48] The claimant may be doubly disabled from recovering salvage, because he has caused the need for the service and because he may be under a statutory duty to render assistance, so as not to be acting as a volunteer.[49] But, although to deny him any remuneration whatsoever might be to enforce firmly the policy of preventing him from profiting from his own wrong, it would give that policy precedence over the more important one of encouraging services of a salvage nature in cases of danger.

Salvor's sister ship at fault

1103 Where a ship which has been damaged by collision through the negligent navigation of another ship is salved by a third ship which was unconnected with the incident, then, even if the owners of the third ship are interested in the "wrongdoing" ship, both they and their master and crew can claim salvage from the first ship.[50] This is so even where the "wrongdoing" ship was alone to blame for the collision.[51]

4. SALVOR'S NEGLIGENCE DURING SALVAGE OPERATIONS

The Tojo Maru

1104 The effect of negligence by the salvor during salvage operations was comprehensively examined and reinterpreted in the light of the modern law generally by the House of Lords in *The Tojo Maru*.[52] In 1965, after the conclusion of a salvage agreement on Lloyd's Form, salvors rendered salvage services to the vessel and her cargo. During the course of the operations and after the cargo had been discharged, the salvors' chief diver went into the

---

[47] See Marsden (12th ed., 1997), Chap. 14; *The Altair* [1897] P. 105; MSA 1995, s.187. See also *The Adam W. Spies* (1901) 70 L.J.P. 25 (though *cf.* now the Pilotage Act 1987, s.16); *The Duc d'Aumale (No. 2)* [1904] P. 60; *The Harvest Home* [1904] P. 409 (varied [1905] P. 177).

[48] See *The Harvest Home* [1904] P. 409 (varied [1905] P. 177), in which towage remuneration was awarded for services which the tug was not obliged to perform.

[49] *e.g.* where he has collided with the salved vessel. See *ante*, Chap. 7.

[50] *The Glengaber* (1872) 1 Asp. M.L.C. 401 (less fully (1872) L.R. 3 A. & E. 534); *The Beaverford v. The Kafiristan* [1938] A.C. 136, reversing the decision of the Court of Appeal [1937] P. 63, which dismissed an appeal from a decision of Bucknill J. [1937] P. 63, 64 on a special case stated by an arbitrator.

[51] *The Susan V. Luckenbach* [1951] P. 197.

[52] *The Owners of the Motor Vessel Tojo Maru v. N.V. Bureau Wijsmuller (The Tojo Maru)* [1972] A.C. 242, reversing the CA and restoring the judgment of Willmer L.J., both reported at [1970] P. 21.

water from their tug, of which he was a temporary crew member and, contrary to orders, fired a bolt into the vessel's shell plating in order to fix a patch over a hole therein. Since the vessel was not gas free, there were a series of explosions and a fire, for the extinction of which salvage assistance had to be taken. Substantial damage was caused to the vessel. In arbitration proceedings, the shipowners denied that the salvors were entitled to a salvage reward and counterclaimed for damages for losses caused by the negligence of the salvor's diver. It was held by the House of Lords, after an exhaustive review of the authorities, that a salvor's entitlement to reward and his liability to pay damages for negligence were in principle distinct matters, though they could be the subject of cross-claims, and that a salvee had a definite right to sue for damages for the salvor's negligence, which was not simply a factor for consideration in assessing a salvage reward.

The early authorities

Negligence by salvors arose in a number of cases prior to *The Tojo Maru*.[53] **1105** The effect of the authorities and the circumstances to be borne in mind when considering them was found to be as follows.

The duty of skill and care in Admiralty law

First, it was recognised before salvage under contract became common that, independently of contract:

> "when persons undertake to perform a salvage service, they are bound to exercise ordinary skill and ordinary prudence in the execution of the duty which they take upon themselves to perform . . . they must possess and exercise such a degree of prudence and skill as persons in their condition ordinarily do possess, and may be fairly expected to display."[54]

Whether the duty is discharged must be judged in the circumstances of the case.[55] Salvage operations are inherently dangerous. They may require prompt action, quick judgment and taking of risks. These factors do not excuse the failure to exercise skill and care; but they may justify conduct which, with hindsight, does not measure up to the level of performance which could have been attained in easier circumstances.

The development of the law of negligence

At the time of the early relevant judgments at least, the concept of negli- **1106** gence as a cause of action at common law was still in the formative stage. In general, the relationships giving rise to a duty of care were still in process of

---

[53] [1972] A.C. 242.
[54] *The Cape Packet* (1848) 3 W. Rob. 122, 125, *per* Dr Lushington. See also *The Lockwoods* (1845) 9 Jur. 1017, 1018; *The Magdalen* (1861) 31 L.J.Adm. 22.
[55] *The Cato* (1930) 37 Ll.L.Rep. 33, 36–37.

piecemeal classification, apart, that is, from those resulting from contract—but claims for salvage were not regarded as contractual. Moreover, salvage was commonly undertaken by fishing or other vessels which chanced to be in the vicinity and not by professional salvage contractors. More significantly, a distinction was drawn, both at common law and in Admiralty, between situations which gave rise to a liability for ordinary negligence and those which gave rise to a liability for "gross negligence" only. A failure to exercise the care of a skilled salvor (ordinary negligence) did not amount to any breach of duty on the part of the salvor; the only duty owed by the salvor to the owner of the property saved was to exercise ordinary skill and ordinary prudence, but a breach of that duty qualified as "gross negligence".[56] The distinction was rejected by the Court of Common Pleas in 1866[57] but not before it had, in combination with a jurisdictional issue, influenced the effect accorded to salvorial negligence.

The jurisdiction of the Admiralty Court

1107 The principal jurisdictional difficulty arose from Dr Lushington's belief that the Court of Admiralty had no jurisdiction to entertain claims for tortious damage to property except where it was caused by collision between two vessels.[58] But this view was rejected by the House of Lords in 1893.[59]

Counterclaims before 1873

Dr Lushington's view coexisted until 1873 with the procedural impossibility of bringing a counterclaim in Admiralty proceedings.

Dr Lushington's views on the effect of negligence

1108 These jurisdictional and procedural hurdles coalesced to preclude proper consideration's being given to the salvor's liability for negligence in determining claims for salvage and, no doubt, to the effect to be given to such negligence as a factor in the assessment of the salvage reward. The operative principles were expounded by Dr Lushington in *The Cape Packet*[60] to the effect that: (i) if neglect or misconduct was wilful there could be a forfeiture of the whole claim to salvage remuneration; (ii) if there was "gross negligence" (apart from wilful inattention) salvage remuneration might be wholly debarred; but (iii):

---

[56] See *The Cape Packet* (1848) 3 W.Rob. 122, 125; *The Tojo Maru* [1972] A.C. 242, 297.
[57] *Grill v. General Iron Screw Collier Co.* (1866) L.R. 1 C.P. 600.
[58] See *The Ida* (1860) Lush. 6 and *The Robert Pow* (1863) Bro. & Lush. 99. The inconsistency of *The Sarah* (1862) Lush. 549, in which he accepted jurisdiction, is explicable on the ground that one of the colliding vessels was not a seagoing ship: see *The Tojo Maru* [1972] A.C. 242, 296.
[59] *The Zeta* [1893] A.C. 468.
[60] (1848) 3 W.Rob. 122.

The early authorities

"There is also *another kind of negligence*, the effect of which is to diminish the amount of salvage reward, not to take it entirely away. The extent of this diminution, I may further state, is not measured by the amount of loss or injury sustained, but is framed upon the principle of proportioning the diminution to the degree of negligence, not to the consequences."[61]

1109 In *The Perla*,[62] Dr Lushington expressed the same view. But in *The Magdalen*[63] he said that an award would be reduced not by way of punishing the salvors but by way of indemnifying the owners who had been injured by the salvor's want of skill. As a general rule, however, breach of duty was normally classified with wilful misconduct and the effect accorded in the Court of Admiralty to both was punitive rather than compensatory in character, *viz.*, forfeiture of the reward. In *The Atlas*,[64] on appeal from a decision of Dr Lushington to the Privy Council, Sir John Coleridge enunciated the proposition that:

> "no mere mistake or error of judgment in the manner of procuring it, no misconduct short of that which is wilful and may be considered criminal, ... will work an entire forfeiture of the salvage. Mistake or misconduct other than criminal, which diminishes the value of the property salved, or occasions expense to the owners, are properly considered in the amount of the compensation to be awarded."

Nowadays, counterclaims may be determined simultaneously with the assessment of salvage reward, but it remains true that lack of due care and skill is relevant to examination of the quality of the salvor's work in assessing the amount of the reward that he deserves, as some of the early cases in particular illustrate.[65]

Success and the theory of "more harm than good"

1110 "Many of [the cases] are illustrations of inquiries to see whether (there having been no contract giving entitlement to a payment in any event) a salvor's services achieved some result (even though not all that he set out to do) which, being beneficial to an owner, deserved reward. If there had been such measure of achievement there would have been 'success'. In that sense and for that purpose it will often be necessary to inquire whether there has been benefit for an owner as a result of what a salvor has done."[66]

---

[61] *ibid.*, 125 (italics added).
[62] (1857) Swab. 230.
[63] (1861) 1 M.L.C. 189.
[64] (1862) Lush. 518, 528.
[65] See *post*, Chap. 15.
[66] *The Tojo Maru* [1972] A.C. 242, 276, *per* Lord Morris of Borth-y-Gest.

It is trite law that a salvor has no entitlement to a reward unless he has achieved success; and it is manifest that a salvor's negligence is likely to affect the degree of success. It was the primary task of the House of Lords in *The Tojo Maru*[67] to correct the error into which the Court of Appeal's interpretation of the authorities on this point had led it. Lord Diplock[68] summarised thus the Court of Appeal's:

> "theory of 'more harm than good'. In effect the proposition which was accepted as correct was that you look at the salvage services as a whole to see whether the salvors have done more harm than good to the property they have salved. In order to do this you assess the 'unsalved value' of the ship before the salvors started their services, the 'actual salved value' of the ship at the end of their services, and the 'undamaged salved value' which the ship would have had but for the negligence of the salvors in the course of their services. You then subtract the 'unsalved value' from the 'actual salved value' and this is the 'measure of the good' done by the salvors. Next you subtract the 'actual salved value' from the 'undamaged salved value' and this is the 'measure of the harm' done by the salvors. Damages are recoverable from the salvors only if the 'measure of the harm' exceeds the 'measure of the good'. If it does, as I understand the judgments of the Court of Appeal, the difference, and no more is recoverable by the shipowner by way of damages and the salvor is not entitled to any salvage award. This, of course, is a quite different figure from the amount of damages for negligence which would be recoverable under general English law. That would be equal to the 'measure of harm' itself and not to the difference between that and the 'measure of good'. Against this sum the salvor would be entitled to set off the amount of the salvage award to which his success, albeit only partial, entitled him.

1111 If, on the other hand, the 'measure of the good' exceeds the 'measure of the harm' the proposition adopted by the Court of Appeal requires that the measure of the harm itself should be taken into consideration in reduction of the salvor's reward, not by simple subtraction but taking also into account the degree of negligence exhibited by the salvors in causing the harm. However much the measure of harm exceeded the amount which would have been awarded to the salvor for his services in the absence of negligence, no greater effect could be given to this than to reduce the salvage award to nothing.

The Court of Appeal were not unanimous as to the way in which the necessary sums were to be done. Lord Denning M.R., with whom Karminski L.J. agreed, considered that the 'unsalved value' of the ship was to be assessed upon the basis that nothing would be done by any salvor to salve her. Salmon L.J., however, considered that regard should

---

[67] [1972] A.C. 242.
[68] *ibid.*, 298.

be had to the actual degree of risk of her becoming a total loss but for the services rendered by the salvors. This involved taking into account the likelihood of there being other salvors able to salve her."

The Court of Appeal's approach was decisively rejected by the House of Lords. It was a novel proposition, unsupported by those cases[69] in which salvors had previously been held liable to pay damages.

The contractual duty of care[70]

The agreement concluded on Lloyd's Form is a contract for work and labour entered into by a party who carries on the business of providing salvage services for reward. Before 1875, when the ancient Admiralty Court was merged in the High Court of Justice, professional salvage contractors did not exist and express contracts of the modern type were unknown, rendering it unlikely that direct assistance as to the contractual liabilities arising under the contract under consideration could be found in the decisions of the former Court of Admiralty. Although the speeches in *The Tojo Maru*[71] involved a general discussion of negligence liability, as Lord Diplock stressed, the appeal was concerned with claims arising *ex contractu* and concerned breach of a contractual rather than a general duty of care.[72]

1112

His Lordship examined the nature of the salvor's liability under the Lloyd's Form contract in the light of the three characteristics of the salvor's remuneration, that it: is not due unless he saves the property in whole or in part; cannot exceed the value of the property saved; and was always assessed on the principle of *quantum meruit*. He said[73]:

1113

"Under the general English law of contracts for work and labour by a person who carries on the business of undertaking services of the kind which he has contracted to provide, he warrants that he will use reasonable skill and care in the provision of the services; and the measure of his liability for breach of that warranty is such a sum by way of damages as will put the other party, so far as money can do so, in the same position as if the contract had been performed without such breach. . . .

These special characteristics of the remuneration payable for salvage services whether rendered under Lloyd's Standard Form of Salvage Agreement with a professional salvage contractor, or volunteered by a passing vessel and accepted without any express contract, would not in themselves appear sufficient to oust the ordinary rule of English law that a person who undertakes for reward to do work and labour upon the

---

[69] *The C.S. Butler* (1874) L.R. 4 A. & E. 178; *The Delphinula* (1947) 80 Ll.L.Rep. 459; *The Alenquer* [1955] 1 W.L.R. 263.
[70] See *ante*, §1013.
[71] [1972] A.C. 242.
[72] See *ibid.*, 290, 292–293. See also *ibid.*, 289, *per* Lord Pearson.
[73] *ibid.*, 293–294.

property of another owes to the owner of the property a duty to exercise that care which the circumstances demand and, where he holds himself out as carrying on the business or profession of undertaking services of that kind, to use such skill in the performance of them as a person carrying on such a business may reasonably be expected to possess."

Standard of care for contractual negligence

1114 The last paragraph of the quotation from Lord Diplock's speech in the previous paragraph indicates that the standard of care to be exercised is that required by the circumstances and, as befits their status, professional salvors will, in line with their calling, be under a higher duty than non-professional salvors. However, although the standard of liability is commensurate with that lying on contractors on land, the public policy of encouraging salvors and the difficulty of establishing negligence mean that salvors will not easily be held liable for negligence.

Establishing negligence

1115 A large number of factors, including the particular circumstances in which individual services are provided, contribute to making it difficult to decide whether a salvor has been negligent. Thus, Lord Diplock said in *The Tojo Maru*[74]:

> "The circumstances in which salvage services are rendered may vary greatly. So may the expertise of those who undertake them. They may be such as to involve imminent peril to the salvor and his own property as well as to the property he is trying to save. He may have had no previous experience of salvage operations and no specialised equipment for that purpose. It may be mere chance that his was the vessel nearest to the scene when the emergency occurred which endangered the other ship and those abroad her. On the other hand, the ship requiring salvage services may be in no immediate peril. To bring her to a place of safety may be a simple operation devoid of any appreciable risk to the salvor or his property. The salvors may be professional salvage contractors who have obtained the contract to salve the ship in competition with other professional salvors. All these are circumstances to be taken into consideration in determining whether a particular act or omission of the salvor constitutes a breach of his duty of care or skill."

Moreover, as Lord Morris of Borth-y-Gest observed[75]:

> "The nature of the enterprises which are undertaken are often such that some damage may accidentally be caused. It may be caused even though consummate skill is employed."

[74] *ibid.*, 294.
[75] *ibid.*, 274.

The modern law

1116 These factors, coupled with the public policy of encouraging salvors, and especially professional salvors, means that, as Lord Reid put it[76]:

> "Just as courts are very slow to hold that errors of judgment in emergencies amount to negligence, so too are courts slow to impute negligence to salvors."

Viscount Dilhorne expressed himself more firmly[77]:

> "No doubt it is, and should be, difficult for owners of salved vessels to establish that an act or omission causing damage amounts to negligence if done or not done in the course of a rescue operation."

Lord Pearson summarised the position thus[78]:

> "if a question arises as to whether salvors have been guilty of negligence in the course of salvage operations the courts will tend to take a lenient view (although there must be a finding of negligence if it is clearly proved . . .)."

In relation to a claim (which failed) by persons who had answered a signal for a pilot, the old Admiralty Court said in *The Neptune*[79]:

> "the Court is not to expect from salvors, assuming the management of vessels in cases of this kind, the same skill as would be required from regularly licensed Trinity pilots; at the same time it is equally true that in order to entitle them to a salvage award in this Court they must shew that they possessed skill commensurate with their vocation and condition in life, and adequate to the duties which they undertook to perform."

The modern law

1117 The current law relating to negligence by a salvor during the performance of salvage services, as laid down at common law and (it is submitted) reproduced in the Salvage Convention 1989, Arts 8.1 and 18, may be summarised as follows.[79A]

Duty of care

A salvor has a duty of care at common law and (where there is a contract) under contract not to be negligent.

---

[76] *ibid.*, 267.
[77] *ibid.*, 283.
[78] *ibid.*, 289.
[79] (1842) 1 W.Rob. 297, 300.
[79A] See generally Shaw [1996] L.M.C.L.Q. 202, 225–226.

Misconduct

Liability for breach of duty

A salvor who breaches his duty of care may be sued for damages in tort or (where appropriate) for breach of contract.

Effect of salvor's negligence

A salvor's negligence may affect him adversely in three ways. First, it will render him liable to pay damages. Secondly, it will depress or diminish the size of the salved fund in respect of which he is to be remunerated, either because the salved fund is measured as the unrepaired damaged salved value or (which may be more or less) the repaired salved value less the cost of repairing the damage negligently caused. Thirdly, regard is had to the salvor's conduct and misconduct in assessing his reward,[80] which will accordingly be reduced by his negligence. However, whilst proper regard must be had to the interests of the victim of the salvor's negligence, care must be exercised to avoid injustice to the latter by prejudicing him two or three times over.[81] Moreover, the negligence of one salvor will not prejudice the claim of a non-negligent salvor.[82]

Measure of damages for breach of salvage contract and assessment of salvage award

1118 The House of Lords decided in *The Tojo Maru*[83] that, in cases of salvorial negligence, the assessment of the award and the measure of damages should be determined on the following principles.

In order to avoid penalising the salvor in the assessment of both the award and the damages: the award should be calculated on the basis that the vessel had not sustained the damage caused by the salvor's negligence; and the award as so determined, which may be hypothetical, must then be deducted from the amount of damages. Alternatively, the award may be determined taking into account the limiting factor of the salvor's negligence, and a deduction made from the damages of the difference between what has been awarded and what would have been awarded if the vessel had not been damaged. In *The Tojo Maru*, it was said that the salvors had by their negligence causing great damage forfeited the right which they would otherwise have had to salvage remuneration; nonetheless, the hypothetical salvage remuneration which would have been awarded if they had duly performed their contract was deductible from the damages.[84]

1119 The measure of the damages themselves for breach of a salvage contract is the normal contractual measure. "The broad general rule is that damages for

---

[80] *The Tojo Maru* [1972] A.C. 242, 284, *per* Viscount Dilhorne.
[81] See the Salvage Convention 1989, Art. 13.1(e); *cf.* also *ibid.*, Art. 13.1(b).
[82] *The Neptune* (1842) 1 W.Rob. 297.
[83] [1972] A.C. 242, 270, 281, 288, 289–290, 300, upholding the approach at first instance of Willmer L.J. [1970] P. 21.
[84] [1972] A.C. 242, 281, 289–290.

breach of contract are intended as compensation for the breach and, therefore, should be assessed at such sum as will place the wronged party in the position in which he would have been if the wrong-doer had duly fulfilled his contract."[85] This is in principle the difference between what would have been the value of the salved property at the place of safety upon completion of the salvage services if there had been no negligence and the actual value of the salved property at the place of safety in the state in which she was as a result of the negligence: but subject to the deduction mentioned in the previous paragraph. In *The Tojo Maru*, the measure of damages was treated as being the sum which had to be spent on repairs plus other loss and damage. However, whilst this may appear to be a reasonable calculation of the loss, it need not invariably represent the correct contractual measure on the basis outlined above, and seems more akin to the measure of damages for negligence at common law.

Damages for negligence at common law

Before salvage contracts became common, it was stated that salvors had a duty not to be negligent during salvage operations[86]; and after contractual salvage became the normal practice it was established that the general principle of liability for negligence in *Donoghue v. Stevenson*[87] was applicable to salvage—a salvor has a duty to use such skill and care as is reasonable in the circumstances, and the principles of duty and liability are the same at common law and in Admiralty.[88] Having undertaken the provision of salvage services, the salvor is "under a bounden duty to adopt the least dangerous method of salving ship and cargo which [is] practicable in [the] existing circumstances" and, where there is doubt as to the cause of loss and as to whether the salvor is in breach of his duty of care, the plaintiff has the onus of shewing on a balance of probabilities that the cause must have originated in breach of the salvor's duty of care in the conduct of the operations.[89] **1120**

The common law measure of damages of loss caused by negligence is, in cases of total loss of a ship caused by negligence, as follows: "the true measure of damages in such cases is the value of the ship to her owner as a going concern at the time and place of the loss. In assessing that value regard must naturally be had to her pending engagements, either profitable or the reverse."[90] Where property is damaged, diminution in value is the normal **1121**

---

[85] *The Tojo Maru* [1972] A.C. 242, 289 (citing *Wertheim v. Chicoutimi Pulp Co.* [1911] A.C. 301, 307 and *Victoria Laundry (Windsor) Ltd v. Newman Industries Ltd* [1949] 2 K.B. 528, 539); see also [1972] A.C. 242, 281.
[86] See *ante*, §1105.
[87] [1932] A.C. 562. See also *Dorset Yacht Co. Ltd v. Home Office* [1970] A.C. 1004.
[88] *The Delphinula* (1947) 80 Ll.L.Rep. 459 (CA).
[89] See *The Delphinula, ibid.*, 480–482 (the actual cause was never clearly established).
[90] *Owners of Dredger Liesbosch v. Owners of Steamship Edison* [1933] A.C. 449, 463–464, per Lord Wright. See also *The Winkfield* [1902] P. 42 See generally *Marsden on Collisions at Sea*, (12th ed., 1998) with Supp. (1999); Clerk & Lindsell, Chap. 29.

Misconduct

measure of damages; in the case of a vessel, this is prima facie the cost of repairs.[91] In both cases, consequential loss will be recoverable.[92]

1122   In *The Delphinula*,[93] in 1943, a tanker grounded off the entrance to Alexandria harbour. The services of the local Admiralty Salvage Department, which was engaged to salve, could be employed in three possible ways: (the ideal solution) to tow off the vessel with her cargo aboard; to take off the cargo by tankers or lighters and for the vessel to proceed, whether under her own power or in tow, to dry dock in Alexandria for temporary repair; or to jettison the cargo by pumping it into the sea and for the vessel to proceed to her destination. In the war interest, to clear the harbour approaches, Captain Damant, the head of the Salvage Department at the port (over which the Royal Navy had assumed complete control for war purposes) adopted the third method and, by means of air compressors, the cargo of petrol was pumped through the ship's holed bottom into the sea. It subsequently caught fire and the ship was lost, though some of the cargo was saved. Damages for the salvor's negligence[94] were based on the sound value of the vessel subject to a deduction of the estimated cost of repairs temporary and permanent and the value of spare parts saved (thus obtaining a sum for her damaged value), to which was added a sum for loss of profits. Deductions needed to be made for contingencies or risks which had to be overcome before the owners would have an available repaired ship, which were outlined thus[95]:

> "It is, we think, necessary and legally fair to envisage a hypothetical purchaser of the *Delphinula* as she lay on the rocks on the morning of May 18, 1943, but to attribute to him such knowledge of the facts as we now possess. The following are in our view the principal elements of risk and delay and uncertainty which would tend to diminish the value of the ship to a hypothetical purchaser: (1) The chance of getting the vessel afloat without disaster from fire or other accidental causes not due to any negligence on the part of Captain Damant; (2) The prospect of getting to El Kot and beaching her there and successfully salving the cargo without mishap to the vessel; (3) The voyage from there to Alexandria; (4) The prospect of obtaining dry dock accommodation at Alexandria within a reasonable time; (5) The voyage to the United Kingdom in a partially damaged, but none the less seaworthy, condition: (6) The very slender prospect of obtaining dry dock accommodation in the United Kingdom for the period necessary to effect repairs at a time when, according to the

---

[91] *The London Corporation* [1935] P. 70.
[92] See the cases cited in Clerk & Lindsell, §§ 29–111 to 29–114. Loss of earnings were likewise recovered by the owners of the *Tojo Maru* from the salvors.
[93] (1947) 80 Ll.L.Rep. 459, CA; affirming (1946) 79 Ll.L.Rep. 611.
[94] In fact, the main proceedings involved a tort action against Captain Damant. There was also a petition of right addressed to the Crown (the Admiralty) on the basis of an implied contract that requisite skill and care taken should be taken but there was held to be no basis for a claim based upon contract.
[95] (1947) 80 Ll.L.Rep. 459, 483.

evidence, new tankers were being obtained from America in such numbers that a damaged tanker would have had no priority for dry dock accommodation in view of the demand in connection with the preparations for the invasion of Europe."

Finally, a deduction was made of the proportion payable by the ship-owners of the estimated salvage award.

Multiple claims

1123 Claims, counterclaims and set-offs may be considered together in the same arbitral or judicial proceedings. It is therefore possible that a tribunal may be asked to determine claims for a salvage reward, damages for breach of contract and damages for negligence at common law. A negligent breach of contract will give rise to both contract and tort claims, although the plaintiff will not be permitted double recovery.[96] This can be important where one form of action provides the claimant with a better measure of damages, but this factor is unlikely to be important in salvage proceedings since the object of a salvage contract is essentially to preserve the status quo (which is the object of tort damages) rather than to produce a further element of profit, as in the majority of commercial contracts. The measure of damages for negligence is therefore likely to be identical in contract and tort, to indemnify, so neither form of action will be preferable to the other.

1124 Where salvage services have achieved some measure of success but the salvor has been negligent, there are likely to be cross-claims for salvage reward and for damages. As is clear from *The Tojo Maru*,[97] the two claims can be assessed together or independently of each other and the resulting sums then set-off against each other, so as eventually to produce the same award in favour of one party, and the availability of each claim is not affected by whichever is the greater of the damages or the salvage reward. In practice, though not of necessity, a claim for damages alone may be brought where the potential damages greatly exceed the potential salvage reward (certainly this will be so where there is no success, so no possibility of reward) and, where the effect of negligence is slight, the person from whom salvage is claimed may not sue for damages but merely plead the salvor's negligence as a factor tending to reduce the reward. In either case, however, the claims should be assessed on the principles settled in *The Tojo Maru*.[98] It is unlikely that, where one party brings a claim, the other party will fail to bring his cross-claim or at least plead those circumstances supportive of a cross-claim which will reduce the sum to which the party is prima facie entitled.

---

[96] *Batty v. Metropolitan Realisations Ltd* [1978] Q.B. 554; *Midland Bank Trust Co. Ltd v. Hett, Stubbs and Kemp* [1979] Ch. 384.
[97] [1972] A.C. 242.
[98] *ibid.*

Misconduct

On the particular facts of a case, where there is a very trifling service which confers little or no real benefit, especially where negligence results in substantial damage far exceeding any sum that could possibly be awarded for salvage, salvage though awardable, may be refused.[99]

5. EFFECT OF MISCONDUCT ON REWARD

General principle

1125 "Even where essential services have been rendered to a vessel," and even though the property in peril has been wholly or in part preserved, "the subsequent misconduct of the salvor may not only diminish the amount of his reward, but his entire claim may be forfeited."[1] Dr Lushington said in *The Magdalen*[2]:

> "The principles are these: that salvage is forfeited by wilful misconduct, bad faith, an intention not to do the whole of the duty, or an intention to protract doing that duty for the purpose of piracy. In all these cases, the court would hold, as it did in the case of *The Duke of Manchester*,[3] that the whole salvage is forfeited altogether; and I shall be very desirous, whenever such a case occurs, to do that which would be a just punishment to salvors, and for the benefit of the commercial interests of this country."

Furthermore, in delivering the opinion of the Privy Council, Sir John Coleridge said in *The Atlas*[4] that:

> "where success is finally obtained, no mere mistake or error of judgment in the manner of procuring it, no misconduct short of that which is wilful and may be considered criminal, and that proved beyond a reasonable doubt by the owners resisting the claim, will work on entire forfeiture of the salvage. Mistake or misconduct other than criminal, which diminishes the value of the property salved, or occasions expense to the owners, are properly considered in the amount of compensation to be awarded. Wilful or criminal misconduct may work an entire forfeiture of it."

Misconduct causing forfeiture

1126 The right to an award was held to be forfeited in each of the following cases, where the claimants of salvage had:

---

[99] *cf. The Alenquer and The René* [1955] 1 W.L.R. 263, 290; [1955] 1 Lloyd's Rep. 101, 115 (a fuller report). The case was effectively overruled by *The Tojo Maru, supra*.

[1] "This doctrine was laid down by Lord Stowell in the case of *The Medina*", Unreported: *The Duke of Manchester* (1846) 2 W.Rob. 470, 477, *per* Dr Lushington.

[2] (1861) 31 L.J.Adm. 22, 24.

[3] (1847) 6 Moo. P.C., affirming (1846) 2 W.Rob. 470.

[4] (1862) Lush. 518, 528.

Misconduct causing forfeiture

(i) retained possession, improperly,[5] of the salved ship and cargo and dealt with the cargo by selling it in disregard of the owner's interest[6];

(ii) refused to allow the master and crew of the salved vessel, who had temporarily abandoned her in order to get assistance, to come on board her on their return[7];

(iii) forcibly resisted the exercise by the owners of their right to save the property themselves[8];

(iv) refused, after rescuing a vessel from danger, to take her master on board her, and improperly declined the assistance of a tug[9];

(v) plundered the cargo of the vessel which they had saved[10];

(vi) stolen a large quantity of property from the salved vessel,[11] and the officers had not exercised due diligence to prevent or detect the thefts[12];

(vii) created a riot and disturbance on board the salved vessel and, against the wish of her owner, tried to prevent the employment of a steamer which would more efficiently have completed the service which they had begun[13];

(viii) dispossessed, without reasonable cause, salvors already engaged in rendering salvage services.[14]

Judicial opinions have been expressed that the right to reward would also be forfeited if a claimant of salvage: **1127**

(i) entered into an agreement for the salvage of a vessel without including in the terms of the agreement cargo carried in the vessel[15];

(ii) arranged with the master of the salved vessel that the latter should be paid any portion of the award.[16]

---

[5] As to the circumstances in which a right to retain possession exists, see *post*, Chap. 13.
[6] *The Lady Worsley* (1855) 2 Spinks E. & A. 253.
[7] *The Capella* [1892] P. 70. For a case where salvors were held to have been justified in refusing to allow the master and crew of the salved vessel to go on board her before completion of the salvage services, see *The Elise* [1899] W.N. 54; see also *The Kedah* (1948) 81 Ll.L.Rep. 217.
[8] *The Barefoot* (1850) 14 Jur. 841.
[9] *The Yan Yean* (1883) 8 P.D. 147.
[10] *The Florence* (1852) 16 Jur. 576.
[11] *The Clan Sutherland* [1918] P. 332; *The Kenora* [1921] P. 90.
[12] *The Clan Sutherland, supra.*
[13] *The Martha* (1859) Swab. 489.
[14] *The Blenden-Hall* (1814) 1 Dods. 414; *The Fleece* (1850) 3 W.Rob. 278; *The American Farmer* (1947) 80 Ll.L.Rep. 672 (dispossession justified).
[15] *The Westminster* (1841) 1 W.Rob. 229, 235, *per* Dr Lushington.
[16] *The Kolpino* (1904) 73 L.J.P. 29, 30.

Misconduct

Misconduct by some salvors: effect on claims of others

1128   If a salvor is guilty of misconduct, and any of his co-salvors recognise or are privy to his misconduct, there can be no doubt that it will affect their claim. Accordingly, persons guilty of theft will forfeit salvage,[17] as will any persons privy to the theft.[18] But neither owners nor innocent crew will forfeit their share.[19] As was said in *The Boston*[20]:

> "It will be found, I believe, in the maritime jurisprudence of the whole world, that embezzlement by salvors, directly, or by connivance, is punished by a forfeiture of all claim to salvage. In morals, in general justice, in sound policy, it should be so; for what can be more inhuman, or more thoroughly without apology, than to plunder the distressed, or to add the losses of fraud to the unavoidable calamities of a shipwreck? In the American and English law the doctrine is fully recognised; and it is applied with an unfaltering firmness, whenever the fact is clearly established.... The compensation to be awarded presupposes good faith, meritorious service, complete restoration, and incorruptible vigilance, so far as the property is within the reach, or under the control, of salvors."

1129   That the question of the effect of misconduct on the award is one to be decided on the facts of each case clearly appears from *The Kedah*.[21] Services were rendered by professional salvors to a steamship which had been abandoned by her master and crew. Some time before the salvage tug made fast, the tug's master sent out a wireless message suggesting that the crew of the *Kedah* should return to man her and assist in that operation. But it had been completed by a boarding party from the tug and the vessel was proceeding comfortably in tow at about five or six knots by the time her master and crew, having put out from land in a small boat, came up with her. The master of the tug refused to allow them to go back on board their vessel and the boarding party took action rendering it impossible for them to do so. The *Kedah* was brought to safety but pilferage of ship's equipment and crew's effects occurred.

1130   Willmer J. found that it had always been the intention of the master and crew to return on board their vessel; and he observed that prima facie they had an absolute right to do so and prima facie, unless the circumstances forbade it, the salvors had no business to exclude them from access to the vessel. He thought the controlling factor in the mind of the master in acting as he did was the chance of getting a larger award if he could say the vessel was derelict; but

---

[17] *The Clan Sutherland* (1918) P. 332; *The Boston* (1833) 1 Sumn. 328, 339, 341.
[18] *The Scindia* (1865) 2 Asp. M.L.C. (o.s.) 232, 233.
[19] *The Scindia, supra*; *The Boston, supra*; *The Blaireau* (1804) 2 Cranch 240; *The Rising Sun* (1837) Ware 378; *The Missouri's Cargo* (1832) Sprague 260; *The Kenora* [1921] P. 90.
[20] *Supra*.
[21] (1948) 81 Ll.L.Rep. 217.

in no sense could this be an excuse for the refusal. In the circumstances, however, it was reasonable for the tugmaster to take the view that a reduction of speed to allow reboarding was undesirable, involving the risk of the hawser parting when speed had to be regained. He found it difficult in the circumstances to blame the master of the tug for the action he took in that regard—an action which could not be said to be wholly unreasonable having regard to the circumstances of the case and having regard particularly to the fact that the master and crew of the *Kedah*, if they had been allowed back on board, could not in fact have done anything to assist in the operation. From a practical point of view it made no difference at all to the services whether they came back on board or not. In those circumstances, seeing that the authorities laid it down quite clearly that the question was one to be decided on the facts of each case, there was no question of the award being affected by any misconduct of the salvors in relation to the refusal to allow reboarding.

With regard to pilferage, Willmer J. held that three members of the boarding party were guilty of larceny, misconduct of the gravest kind of which a salvor could be guilty; that there was no evidence of complicity by any other person; that the chief officer, who was in command of the boarding party, although not guilty of theft, was to blame for not preventing the pilferage; that, having considered the authorities, it was impossible to punish the owners for the misconduct of some of the members of the crew; and that the tugmaster, having had a good many other things to think about on arrival in port and having delegated command of the boarding party to the chief officer, was not affected by the misconduct. **1131**

Burden of proof lies on those who assert misconduct

The burden of proving misconduct so serious as to deprive successful salvors of all reward lies upon those who impute it.[22] Furthermore, the standard of proof is not the balance of probabilities, but such as leaves no reasonable doubt.[23] **1132**

Misconduct causing diminution of award

Of the diminution of the salvage reward on account of misconduct which is not of so gross a kind as to work an entire forfeiture, there are numerous examples in the Reports. **1133**

In *The Dantzic Packet*,[24] certain Essex smacksmen who in bad weather had gone to the assistance of a brig aground on the west Knock Sand and who would otherwise, in the opinion of the court (Sir John Nicholl), have been held entitled to a liberal remuneration, were awarded only a small sum, by reason of their misconduct in interfering with the employment of additional assistance, and endeavouring to exclude a second set of salvors.

[22] *The Atlas* (1862) Lush. 518, 529.
[23] *The Charles Adolphe* (1856) Swab. 153, 156.
[24] (1837) 3 Hagg. 383. See also *The Louisa* (1843) 7 Jur. 182.

In *The Dosseitei*,[25] a ship in great distress was taken by the salvors and anchored in a place of comparative safety. She might have been placed in perfect safety if the salvors had availed themselves of further assistance which was offered them; but, in order to get a greater gain for themselves, they chose to leave her for six hours at anchor in a position of some risk, whilst they proceeded to fetch ropes and spars from their own port. She was ultimately brought by them safely into harbour. Upon a value of £10,000, instead of awarding, as he would otherwise have done, a large sum for salvage on account of the salvors' misconduct, Dr Lushington awarded only £50.

Misconduct causing diminution of award and partial or total deprivation of costs

1134 Where misconduct is proved the court may give a diminished award and allow the salvor only part of his costs or deprive him altogether of costs.[26]

In *The Trumpeter*,[27] a trawler had been driven ashore in Galway Bay and her master and crew were taken off by a lifeboat, intending to return when the weather eased. On their return the *Trumpeter* was lying safely at anchor in the bay alongside a vessel which had salved her. They were prevented, by a show of force, from reboarding their vessel. The skipper of the salving vessel at about that time sent his owner a cable stating that he had salved the *Trumpeter* and that the *Trumpeter*'s crew had been taken off by lifeboat. The owner, being unaware of the return of the master and crew of the *Trumpeter* ordered his skipper to tow the *Trumpeter* to Milford Haven and not to allow anyone on board. In the result, the skipper, who had previously acted on his own responsibility, continued to exclude the master and crew of the *Trumpeter* from their vessel. The owner of the salving vessel later, on receiving further information as to the true facts and taking professional advice, countermanded his orders and the *Trumpeter* was handed back. Pilcher J. held that the services, which were well and promptly rendered and rescued the *Trumpeter* from serious danger, would have entitled the plaintiffs to a substantial award; and that the faults of the skipper and owner of the salving vessel were venial and did not amount to very much more than a misunderstanding of their rights.

Misconduct causing only deprivation of costs

1135 The court in its discretion may mark its disapproval of misconduct without either forfeiture or diminution of the salvage reward by depriving the salvor of his costs. In *The Pinnas*,[28] salvors (a firm of shipbuilders and repairers) raised a sunken vessel and beached her in a position of safety; they then improperly refused to deliver up possession of the salved property to the owners until they, the salvors, had completed certain repairs, for which they

---

[25] (1846) 10 Jur. 865.
[26] *The Glory* (1849) 14 Jur. 676.
[27] (1947) 80 Ll.L.Rep. 263.
[28] (1888) 6 Asp. M.L.C. 313.

expected payment on a salvage basis, prior to docking the vessel. Because of the misconduct of the managing partner, the plaintiffs were allowed no costs.

To affect award, misconduct need not occasion actual damage

It is not, it is to be observed, necessary in order that the amount of the salvage awarded should be reduced on account of misconduct on the part of the salvors, that the owners of the salved property should have suffered material injury by reason of it.[29] In *The John and Thomas*,[30] Lord Stowell expressed the view that even services of the highest class might be lessened, in the judgment of the court, merely by exorbitant demands.

1136

Compound interest

Clause 8.2 of LSSAC 2000 provides:

1137

"In ordinary circumstances the Contractors' interest entitlement shall be limited to simple interest but the Arbitrator may exercise his statutory power[31] to make an award of compound interest if the Contractors have been deprived of their salvage remuneration or special compensation for an excessive period as a result of the Owners[32] gross misconduct or in other exceptional circumstances."

---

[29] *The Glory* (1849) 14 Jur. 676; *The Marie* (1882) 7 P.D. 203.
[30] (1822) 1 Hagg. 157n. "Adequate rewards encourage the tendering and acceptance of salvage services: exorbitant demands discourage their acceptance, and tend to augment the risk and loss of vessels in distress. Masters determine to encounter peril rather than expose their owners to demands so unjustifiable and so large as that made in this case": *The Nimrod* (1850) 14 Jur. 942, 944, *per* Dr Lushington. The claim in that case was £8,000, bail was taken for £6,000 and the award was £600. In *The George Gordon* (1884) 9 P.D. 46, where the salvors arrested the salved ship for a claim of £3,000, Butt J. on a value of £14,000 awarded them £450, and ordered the salvors to pay all the costs and the expenses of finding bail for £3,000, as an exorbitant claim. In *The Marguerite Molinos* [1903] P. 160, the bail demanded was £2,600, the award was £500 and the salvors were ordered to pay the bail fees above £1,000.
[31] Arbitration Act 1996, s.49.
[32] *Sic*.

CHAPTER 12

RESTRICTIONS ON CLAIMS

1. GENERAL

1138 In principle, subject to the rules governing the claim and to defences, a person with a legal claim is entitled to enforce it in full. Likewise, the defendant should satisfy it in full. Of course, especially in commercial cases, many defendants are corporations and their liability is limited by the rules governing their incorporation. In particular, the ultimate liability of the holders of shares in a limited liability company extends only to the amount by which the value of their shares is unpaid, and in practice most shares are fully paid up. More serious is the fact that the practical limitation on a defendant's liability, particularly where he is subject to more than one claim, is the extent of his insurance cover, the extent to which he can claim contribution from others, the value of his assets and the rules governing insolvency. The limitations just mentioned affect the extent to which a claim may be enforced rather than diminish the magnitude of the claim in law. However, their possible application is likely to influence a potential defendant's decision whether to engage in conduct for which he may incur liability or the extent of such liability: in short, it will influence the terms upon which he is prepared to contract and even whether he is prepared to participate in trade at all.

1139 However, the principal concern of this chapter is the extent to which the normal extent of a defendant's liability may effectively be qualified and in what circumstances proceedings against a defendant may be restricted.

2. REDUCTION OF LIABILITY

Admiralty law

1140 An agreement which is alleged to exclude a right to, or a right to participate in, a salvage reward will obviously not have that effect where as a matter of construction it does not exclude the right in question[1] or the right of the party

---

[1] *The Leon Blum* [1915] P. 290. See also *The Margaret* (1828) 2 Hagg. 48n.

against whom it is pleaded.² Where it is prima facie applicable, it will not be enforced if the court considers it to be inequitable.³

The common law

Persons have frequently attempted to restrict or exclude liability. The idea of freedom of contract prima facie entitles contracting parties to incorporate in their agreement not only terms which establish liability, but also those which restrict or exclude it. Such terms should in principle be given effect in accordance with their true construction, though this is subject to particular rules of construction at common law, which often minimise the protection prima facie available. Exemption clauses are construed strictly against the person relying on them and in the sense least likely to afford protection against negligence. It is also difficult for a party who has committed a serious breach of contract to escape liability. The relevant rules are as applicable to contracts of salvage as to other contracts, but it has never been common for parties to such contracts to indulge in the various modifications of liability that have engaged the attention of the courts in other areas. So, whilst the relevant common law is potentially applicable to contracts of salvage, in practice this is unlikely to be necessary and detailed discussion of it can be left to specialised books on contract.⁴   **1141**

In the absence of contract, there are occasions when a defendant can plead consent or *volenti non fit injuria* as a defence to an action in tort, and this is equally true in respect of torts committed during salvage operations. However, the defence is not easy to prove, its most important area of potential application (death and personal injury) is now governed by statute[5] and, since it appears to have raised no especial problems for the law of salvage, resort, where necessary, can again be had to the relevant specialised tort books.[6]   **1142**

Statute

Numerous statutory provisions deal with actual or attempted reduction of liability. Of particular importance to merchant shipping are the statutory provisions for limitation of liability, discussed below.[7] Most frequently, however, Parliament has intervened not to establish but to narrow reduction of liability. Of overriding importance is the Unfair Contract Terms Act 1977.   **1143**

---

² *The Leon Blum* [1915] P. 290; *Nicholson v. Leith Salvage and Towage Co.* 1923 S.C. 409.
³ *The Ganges* (1869) L.R. 2 A. & E. 370.
⁴ See Chitty, Chaps. 12, 14; Treitel, Chap. 7.
⁵ See *post*, §1155. Special rules govern the liability of occupiers of premises.
⁶ See Charlesworth and Percy, Chap. 3(2); Clerk & Lindsell, Chap. 3(3).
⁷ See *post*, §§ 1182–1204.

Unfair Contract Terms Act 1977

General provisions

1144 The Unfair Contract Terms Act 1977[8] gives effect, with modification, to proposals of the two Law Commissions.[9] Part I of the Act, dealing with contractual and tortious liability, extends to England and Wales and to Northern Ireland; Part II, which deals with contractual liability alone, extends to Scotland only; while Part III contains provisions applying to the whole of the United Kingdom.[10] The Act contains savings for other relevant legislation, for nothing in the Act removes or restricts the effect of, or prevents reliance upon, any contractual provision which is authorised or required by the express terms or necessary implication of an enactment or, being made with a view to compliance with an international agreement to which the United Kingdom is a party, does not operate more restrictively than is contemplated by the agreement.[11]

Sections 2–4 and 7

1145 The Act's provisions are drafted in terms of general application but specific reference is made to salvage and towage with respect to sections 2–4 and 7, which deal with negligence liability, liability arising in contract, unreasonable indemnity clauses, and miscellaneous contracts under which goods pass.[12]

Generally, in the cases of both contract and tort, sections 2–7 apply only to business liability, that is, liability for breach of obligations or duties arising from things done or to be done by a person in the course of a business (whether his own business or another's) or from the occupation of premises used for business purposes of the occupier.[13]

1146 Furthermore, the operation of sections 2–4 and 7 is subject to exceptions made by Schedule 1.[14] That Schedule states that section 2(1) extends to any contract of marine salvage or towage but, subject to this, sections 2–4 and 7 do not extend to any such contract except in favour of a person dealing as consumer.[15] The Act supplies no definition of "a contract of marine salvage or towage", though it is reasonable to suppose that it applies to such contracts as fall within the court's Admiralty jurisdiction. Such a contract does not have to be described as such in order to qualify. But it does not necessarily follow that a contract which is so described will be treated as one for these purposes:

---

[8] "U.C.T.A."
[9] *Second Report on Exemption Clauses*: Law Com. No. 69, Scot. Law Com. No. 39 (1975).
[10] s.32. See also s.27, dealing with choice of law clauses. The discussion here will be confined to contracts governed by English law, which many salvage contracts are, wherever made.
[11] s.29(1).
[12] s.5 deals with guarantees of consumer goods and s.6 with sale and hire-purchase.
[13] s.1(3).
[14] s.1(2).
[15] Sched. 1, para. 2(*a*).

Status of parties

1147 In practice, the confinement of sections 2–7 to the liability of a person acting in the course of a business will generally mean a restriction on the salvor's ability to avoid liability, particularly since the business in question does not have to be that of salvage. By the same token, it must be recognised that the same restriction applies to the, admittedly far less likely, case where the other contracting party purports to avoid liability. In either case, however, the sections will not apply where the person in question is not acting in the course of a business, which may be so in the case of either party, though in such a case it may also be less likely that a contract, purporting to restrict liability, has been concluded.

1148 Although the Act's provisions in favour of consumers will generally be of more importance for land-based contracts, their express preservation for contracts of marine salvage or towage make clear their potential applicability in such cases. Section 12 of the Act provides that a party to a contract deals as a consumer in relation to another party if: he neither makes the contract in the course of a business nor holds himself out as doing so; and the other party does make the contract in the course of a business; and, in the case of a contract governed by section 7, the goods passing under or in pursuance of the contract are of a type ordinarily supplied for private use or consumption.[16] Subject to this, it is for those claiming that a party does not deal as consumer to shew that he does not.[17] The most obvious example that can be envisaged is the salvage of a boat or yacht used for private purposes—not an insignificant situation, since the vessel and its contents are nonetheless capable of representing substantial assets.

Contractual and tortious liability

1149 The Act's concern is with the exclusion of liability for non-performance of contractual obligations and for negligence. Negligence, for the purposes in point here, is defined to include the breach of any obligations, arising from the express or implied terms of a contract or from the common law, to take reasonable care or exercise reasonable skill.[18] The defence of *volenti non fit injuria* is limited by the Act's provision that, where a contract term or notice purports to exclude or restrict liability for negligence, a person's agreement to

---

[16] s.12(1).
[17] s.12(3).
[18] s.1(1).

or awareness of it is not of itself to be taken as indicating his voluntary acceptance of any risk.[19]

Relevant contractual clauses

1150 The Act's provisions relate to: exemption clauses which attempt to exclude liability altogether; clauses, such as limitation clauses, which restrict without altogether excluding liability; and clauses which have the effect of excluding or restricting liability by narrowing the initial definition of a party's obligations.[20] Section 4 extends the statutory provisions to unreasonable indemnity clauses. Were such a clause to be found in a salvage contract, a person dealing as a consumer could not by reference to any contract term be made to indemnify another person (whether a party to the contract or not) in respect of liability that may be incurred by the other for negligence or breach of contract, except in so far as the contract term satisfied the requirement of reasonableness.[21] The section applies whether the liability in question is directly that of the person to be indemnified or is incurred by him vicariously, or whether it is to the person dealing as a consumer or to someone else.[22] It is for those claiming that a contract term or notice satisfies the requirement of reasonableness to shew that it does.[23]

The requirement of reasonableness

1151 An important feature of the Act is that, in the majority of cases, it does not seek to control exemption clauses by completely banning them but by subjecting them to a requirement of reasonableness. For most purposes, in relation to a contract term, the requirement of reasonableness is that the term shall have been a fair and reasonable one to be included having regard to the circumstances which were, or ought reasonably to have been, known to or in the contemplation of the parties when the contract was made.[24]

1152 In determining for the purposes of section 6(3)[25] or section 7(3) or (4)[26] whether a contract term satisfies the requirement of reasonableness, regard must be had in particular to matters specified in Schedule 2 to the Act.[27] These guidelines include the strength of the bargaining positions of the parties, taking account of alternative means by which the customer's requirements

---

[19] s.2(3).
[20] See in particular *post*, §§ 1157–1161.
[21] s.4(1). See also *ante*, §§ 1093–1094.
[22] s.4(2).
[23] s.11(5).
[24] s.11(1).
[25] *Ante*, §1002.
[26] *Ante*, §1006.
[27] s.11(2).

Unfair Contract Terms Act 1977

could have been met and whether the customer, in accepting the term, had an opportunity of entering into a similar contract with other persons without having to accept a similar term, both of which may be relevant factors where a private individual requires salvage.[28]

In relation to a notice (not being a notice having contractual effect), the requirement of reasonableness under the Act is that it should be fair and reasonable to allow reliance on it, having regard to all the circumstances obtaining when the liability arose or (but for the notice) would have arisen.[29] "Notice" includes an announcement, whether or not in writing, and any other communication or pretended communication.[30]

1153 Where by reference to a contract term or notice a person seeks to restrict liability to a specified sum of money, and the question arises (under any Act) whether the term or notice satisfies the requirement of reasonableness, particular regard must be had to the resources which he could expect to be available to him for the purpose of meeting the liability should it arise and how far it was open to him to cover himself by insurance.[31]

Effect of breach

1154 Under section 9(1) of the Act, where for reliance upon it a contract term has to satisfy the requirement of reasonableness, it may be found to do so and be given effect, notwithstanding that the contract has been terminated either by breach or by a party electing to treat it as repudiated. And, where on a breach the contract is nevertheless affirmed by a party entitled to treat it as repudiated, this does not of itself exclude the requirement of reasonableness in relation to any contractual term.[32]

Death or personal injury

1155 Section 2(1) of the Act[33] provides that no person can by reference to any contract term or to a notice given to persons generally or to particular persons exclude his liability for death or personal injury[34] resulting from negligence. The subsection bans equally any attempt by the salvor or the other party to avoid liability by any such contract term or notice whatever, and not simply one in a salvage contract. Moreover, the Act's protection is quite rightly not

---

[28] See generally Treitel, pp. 247–253.
[29] s.11(3).
[30] s.14.
[31] s.11(4).
[32] s.9(2).
[33] See *ante*, §§ 1145–1146.
[34] "Personal injury" includes any disease and any impairment of physical or mental condition: s.14.

confined to parties to a contract of marine salvage or towage. If it were otherwise, its provisions would fail to benefit the overwhelming majority of individuals likely to be affected.

Negligence liability generally

1156 In the case of loss or damage other than death or personal injury, in favour of a person dealing as consumer, a party cannot so exclude or restrict his liability for negligence except in so far as the term or notice satisfies the Act's requirement of reasonableness.[35]

Liability arising in contract

1157 Section 3 of the Act applies as between contracting parties where one of them deals as a consumer or on the other's written standard terms of business.[36] It provides that[37]:

> "As against that party, the other cannot by reference to any contract term—
> (a) when himself in breach of contract, exclude or restrict any liability of his in respect of the breach;
> or
> (b) claim to be entitled—
> (i) to render a contractual performance substantially different from that which was reasonably expected of him,
> or
> (ii) in respect of the whole or part of his contractual obligation, to render no performance at all,
> except in so far as (in any of the cases mentioned in this subsection) the contract term satisfies the requirement of reasonableness."

1158 Even though most recipients of salvage services will not usually deal as consumers, they will normally do so on the salvor's written standard terms of business, albeit those terms are commonly the same as those used by others salvors, namely LOF 2000. LOF 2000 has no obvious exculpatory provisions which fall foul of section 3. However, section 3 also controls terms which confine the range of liability assumed by the salvor. Such terms are essentially of two types: those which genuinely seek to define, and confine, the liability which he is prepared to assume; and those which appear to do this but are in

---

[35] s.2(2) and s.1(2); Sched. 1, para. 2(a): see *ante*, §§ 1145–1146.
[36] s.3(1).
[37] s.3(2).

reality exemption clauses rephrased in hopefully more advantageous, definitional terminology. Section 3 is therefore prima facie relevant to the salvor's undertaking to use his best endeavours in LOF 2000, cl. A.

1159 This is best seen as an undertaking which genuinely sets out the traditional object of salvage contracts, to bring about a not necessarily attainable objective, that is, successful salvage. If the salvor does use his best endeavours, he commits no breach for which to exclude liability. If he does not, then, since his liability is for failing to use his best endeavours and not for failing successfully to salve, he is doubly prevented from arguing that the term as to best endeavours relieves him from liability for not salving: first, because by definition it is not an obligation successfully to salve of which he is in breach anyway; and, secondly, even if it were, by failing to use his best endeavours, he would not have complied with the requirements of the alleged exculpatory provision.

1160 If a shipowner were to argue that the salvage contractor's true obligation was indeed to salve successfully and that the statement as to best endeavours was an attempted reduction of his liability should he not do so, contrary to section 3(2)(b), the salvor who had nonetheless used his best endeavours, though unsuccessfully, might still escape liability for breach of contract if he managed to persuade the tribunal that the term as to best endeavours satisfied the requirement of reasonableness. In reality, this would constitute a direct contradiction of the shipowner's argument. If, therefore, the view is to continue to prevail that salvors are not to be regarded as undertaking to salve but merely to use their best endeavours to do so, it is better to regard the term in question as used in the first sense, discussed in the previous paragraph.

1161 Preference for the first interpretation might be said to evidence excessive reliance on an assumption which has become increasingly unrealistic in modern times—that salvors should not generally be considered to be under greater liability than to use their best endeavours because of the difficulty of ensuring successful salvage. Except for negligence and the difficulty of guaranteeing precisely the results of salvage operations, the success of many salvage operations is, however, reasonably predictable.

Unfair Terms in Consumer Contracts Regulations

1162 In compliance with the European Communities' Council Directive on Unfair Terms in Consumer Contracts,[38] the Unfair Contract Terms in Consumer Contracts Regulations 1999[39] have been enacted into English law. *Inter alia* the Regulations are designed to apply where services are supplied under

---

[38] 93/13 [1993] O.J. L95/29. The Directive is reproduced in *Blackstone's Statutes on Contract, Tort and Restitution* (12th ed., 2001), 482.

[39] S.I. 1999 No. 2083, replacing the Unfair Contract Terms in Consumer Contracts Regulations 1994 (S.I. 1994 No. 3159). The 1999 Regulations are reproduced in *Blackstone's Statutes on Contract, Tort and Restitution* (12th ed., 2001), 474.

contract by a person acting for purposes relating to his trade, business or profession[40] to a natural person who is acting outside his trade, business or profession.[41] If in such a contract a term is not "fair", then it is not binding on the consumer; while, if in writing it is not transparent (in "plain, intelligible language"), then it is construed against the supplier. The Regulations contain a number of detailed rules for their interpretation and application.

Given the types of contract to which they apply, the Regulations are unlikely to have any role in the commercial salvage operations which are the main subject-matter of the law discussed in this book. But they are clearly potentially applicable to small-scale salvage operations falling within their scope, *e.g.* in the case of salvage of a private yacht. In such a case, reference should be made to the detailed Regulations and the more extensive discussion of them to be found in more general works on the law of contract.[42]

3. SOVEREIGN IMMUNITY

Introduction

1163   The King or Queen of the United Kingdom and foreign sovereigns have traditionally enjoyed immunity from suit. This immunity has traditionally accrued to sovereigns simply by virtue of their capacity as such. It has been formalised by international convention[43] and, in turn, by statute,[44] and it is still generally treated as appropriate where the sovereign is acting in a governmental or public role. However, it is difficult to justify where the sovereign is participating in commerce, *e.g.* where State-owned vessels are operating commercially, in which case sovereign immunity can give an unfair advantage. Accordingly, in modern times, sovereign immunity is generally disapplied in commercial situations.

Where it exists, sovereign immunity is only available as a defence where the sovereign is a defendant. There is no restriction on a sovereign's ability to bring a suit against a defendant who is not a sovereign, although in practice claims by sovereigns for salvage have been uncommon.[45]

---

[40] reg. 3(1).
[41] reg. 3(1).
[42] See Chitty, Chap. 15; Treitel, pp. 244–260. There is overlap between the Regulations and the Unfair Contract Terms Act 1977. The relationship between the two sets of statutory rules is currently under examination by the Law Commission with a view to the enactment of a revised, single statutory code.
[43] (Brussels) International Convention for the Unification of Certain Rules Concerning the Immunity of State-Owned Ships 1926 (Cmnd. 5672), with Protocol 1934 (Cmnd. 5763); European Convention on State Immunity 1972 (Cmnd. 5081).
[44] State Immunity Act 1978, s.1.
[45] See generally *ante*, §§ 645–676.

Sovereign immunity

The traditional position was given specific effect in relation to salvage by the Brussels Salvage Convention 1910, Art. 14.[46] In 1967 a Protocol[47] provided for the extension of the Brussels Convention 1910 to State-owned ships but was never brought into effect. The traditional position survives as a matter of general principle, but subject to an important qualification, in the Salvage Convention 1989, Art. 4(1):

1164

> "Without prejudice to Article 5,[48] this Convention shall not apply to warships or other commercial vessels owned or operated by a State and entitled, at the time of salvage operations, to sovereign immunity under generally recognised principles of international law unless that State decides otherwise."

In practice States, including the United Kingdom,[49] have exercised their right to exclude the defence of sovereign immunity in the case of vessels engaged in commercial activities. Where they do this, they become obliged to notify that fact under the Salvage Convention 1989, Art. 4(2) of which provides:

> "Where a State Party decides to apply the Convention to its warships or other vessels described in paragraph 1, it shall notify the Secretary-General[50] thereof specifying the terms and conditions of such application."

In English law, therefore, the position of sovereigns so far as the law of salvage is concerned is now governed in the main by legislative provisions of general application—the Crown Proceedings Act 1947[51] and the State Immunity Act 1978[52]—although particular statutes sometimes contain specific provisions relating to the position of the Crown.

1165

However, the mere fact that a State becomes subject to a claim for salvage does not render it liable to be proceeded against in the same way as other

---

[46] "This Convention does not apply to ships of war or to Government ships."

[47] Art. 1 provided that the following should be substituted for the Brussels Salvage Convention 1910, Art. 14:
"The provisions of this Convention shall also apply to assistance or salvage services rendered by or to a ship of war or any other ship owned, operated or chartered by a State or Public Authority.
A claim against a State for assistance or salvage services rendered to a ship of war or other ship which is, either at the time of the event or when the claim is brought, appropriated exclusively to public non-commercial service, shall be brought only before the Courts of such State.
Any High Contracting party shall have the right to determine whether and to what extent Article 11 shall apply to ships coming within the terms of the second paragraph of this Article."
(The Brussels Salvage Convention 1910, Art. 11 required masters to render assistance to persons found at sea in danger of being lost: see *ante*, § 535.)

[48] Art. 5 deals with salvage operations controlled by public authorities. See *ante*, §§ 68–70.

[49] In the case of the U.K., this position was secured prior to the enactment of the Salvage Convention 1989. See *post*, §§ 1171–1177.

[50] Secretary-General of the International Maritime Organisation.

[51] See *post*, §§ 1166–1170.

[52] See *post*, §§ 1171–1177.

defendants. Thus, there can be no maritime lien over, or action *in rem* against, Crown property.[53] Moreover, in relation to State-owned cargoes,[54] the Salvage Convention 1989, Art. 25 provides generally that:

> "Unless the State owner consents, no provision of this Convention shall be used as a basis for the seizure, arrest or detention by any legal process of, nor for any proceedings in rem against, non-commercial cargoes owned by a State and entitled, at the time of the salvage operations, to sovereign immunity under generally recognised principles of international law."

The Crown

Description

1166 References to the Crown may be to the Sovereign in person. More commonly they are to the position of the Crown in its capacity as the Government of the United Kingdom, or other of Her Majesty's dominions. In this case, they may include reference to acts done on the Crown's behalf by Government departments, servants or officers,[55] or agents.[56] "The Crown" has no specific definition but the Crown Proceedings Act 1947, s.17 provides for publication of a list of specific Government departments for the purposes of that Act and that civil proceedings by or against the Crown in the United Kingdom[57] may be instituted by or against the appropriate authorised department or the Attorney-General.[58]

Crown liability

1167 The Crown Proceedings Act 1947 provides generally that, although the Sovereign shall be immune from personal tortious liability,[59] the Crown shall be liable in tort, for breach of contract and in other respects as if it were a private person of full age and capacity.[60] Nothing in the Act affects the law relating to prize salvage.[61] With the exception of the Merchant Shipping Act 1995 provisions for valuation, detention and sale of property by the receiver of wrecks,[62] the law relating to civil salvage, whether of life or property, shall

---

[53] See *post*, 1170.
[54] On which see further *post*, §§ 1175–1177.
[55] "Officer", in relation to the Crown, includes any servant of Her Majesty, including a Minister of the Crown: CPA 1947, s.38(2).
[56] "Agent", when used in relation to the Crown, includes an independent contractor employed by the Crown: CPA 1947, s.38(2).
[57] See ss.41–53.
[58] The list published on July 31, 2000 is contained in *Civil Procedure Autumn 2001*, 19PD–007. It includes the Board of Trade, the Ministry of Defence and the Department of the Environment Transport and the Regions.
[59] s.40(1).
[60] ss 1–2.
[61] s.40(2)(a).
[62] MSA 1995, ss 225–227.

The Crown

apply in relation to salvage services in assisting any of Her Majesty's ships, aircraft or hovercraft,[63] or in saving life therefrom, or in saving any cargo or equipment belonging to Her Majesty in right of Her Government of the United Kingdom, in the same manner as if the ship, cargo or equipment belonged to a private person.[64] Moreover, where salvage services are rendered by or on Her behalf, whether in right of Her Government or otherwise, Her Majesty shall be entitled to claim salvage in respect of those services to the same extent, and shall have the same rights and remedies in respect of those services, as any other salvor.[65]

Limitation

The provisions in the merchant shipping legislation for limitation of liability[66] and for limitation periods for salvage claims[67] apply to the Crown as they do to other salvors.   **1168**

Crown property

For the purposes of the 1947 Act and of the Supreme Court Act 1981,[68] Her Majesty's ships (or, by extension, hovercraft[69]) are ships of which the beneficial interest is vested in Her Majesty, or which are registered as Government ships for the purposes of the Merchant Shipping Act 1995, or which are for the time being demised or sub-demised to or in the exclusive possession of the Crown—but not ships in which Her Majesty is interested otherwise than in right of Her Government in the United Kingdom unless the ship is for the time being demised or sub-demised to, or in the exclusive possession of, Her Majesty in that right.[70] Nor does the Act apply to aircraft belonging to Her Majesty otherwise than in right of Her Government in the United Kingdom.[71]   **1169**

Crown proceedings

Proceedings may be instituted against the Crown in the High Court in accordance with the governing rules of court.[72] However, so far as the method of proceeding and the remedies available in maritime cases are concerned, it was established in the Admiralty Court that there can be no maritime lien over, or action *in rem* against, Crown property.[73] Furthermore, the Crown   **1170**

---

[63] Hovercraft (Application of Enactments) Order 1972 (S.I. 1972 No. 971), Art. 8.
[64] MSA 1995, s.230(1).
[65] *ibid.*, s.230(2).
[66] See *post*, Chap. 11.
[67] See *post*, §§ 1182–1204.
[68] SCA 1981, s.24(3).
[69] See *supra*, n. 63.
[70] CPA 1947, s.38(2). See further *ante*, Chap. 6. See also MSA 1995, s.192. *cf.* MSA 1995, ss 255(1), 313(1): *ante*, Chap. 3.
[71] CPA 1947, s.38(2).
[72] CPA 1947, ss 13, 15.
[73] See, *e.g. The Broadmayne* [1916] P. 64.

Proceedings Act 1947 provides that nothing in that Act authorises proceedings *in rem* in respect of any claim against the Crown, or the arrest, detention or sale of any of Her Majesty's ships, aircraft or hovercraft,[74] or of any other property belonging to the Crown, or gives to any person any lien over such property.[75] The Supreme Court Act 1981 makes similar provision[76] and the Salvage Convention 1989, Art. 25 specifically provides that the Convention cannot found proceedings *in rem* against non-commercial cargoes owned by a State entitled to sovereign immunity unless the State consents.[77]

The Crown is, therefore, by statute, liable *in personam*, but not *in rem*, for claims against it arising out of salvage operations. It is no objection to its salvage liability that Admiralty jurisdiction is originally founded on a proceeding against property.[78] Although it is not liable *in rem*, the Crown is nevertheless capable of making itself contractually liable to provide security for salvage claims by signing Lloyd's Form.

The Crown's personal liability is not identical to that of other salvors, for no injunction can be issued against it[79] where it is allegedly acting wrongfully with regard to the possession of a casualty.[80]

Where the Crown itself is the plaintiff, it may sue *in rem* or *in personam*.

State immunity

1171   As a general rule, immunity from proceedings in United Kingdom courts is available to foreign sovereigns in their personal capacity and foreign diplomats[81]; and to foreign or Commonwealth States other than the United Kingdom except as the State Immunity Act 1978[82] otherwise provides.[83] A foreign State for this purpose is the sovereign in his public capacity or the government or any department thereof.[84] It does not include a separate entity—*i.e.* an entity distinct from the executive organs of the government of the State and capable of suing or of being sued[85]—unless the proceedings relate to anything done by it in the exercise of sovereign authority and the circumstances are such that a State (or, in the case of proceedings to which the State Immunity

---

[74] Hovercraft (Application of Enactments) Order 1972 (S.I. 1972 No. 971), Art. 4, Sched. 1.
[75] s.29. See also MSA 1995, s.230(1).
[76] SCA 1981, s.24(2)(c).
[77] See also *post*, § 1249.
[78] See *ante*, § 266.
[79] CPA 1947, s.21.
[80] See *ante*, §§ 1230 *et seq.*
[81] Diplomatic Privileges Act 1964; Consular Relations Act 1968; State Immunity Act 1978, ss.14–16, 20. See Dicey & Morris, pp. 252–258.
[82] See *post*, App. 3. The Act implemented the International Convention for the Unification of Certain Rules Concerning the Immunity of State-Owned Ships signed at Brussels on April 10, 1926 (and its Protocol of May 24, 1934) and the European Convention on State Immunity signed at Basle on May 16, 1972.
[83] SIA 1978, s.1(1).
[84] *ibid.*, s.14(1).
[85] *ibid.*, s.14(1).

State immunity

Act 1978, s.10 applies,[86] a State which is not a party to the Brussels Immunity Convention[87]) would have been so immune *qua* State.[88]

Exceptions

State immunity, where it otherwise exists, is lost in the following circumstances. First, a State is not immune as respects proceedings in respect of which it has submitted to the jurisdiction of the courts of the United Kingdom.[89] A provision in an agreement that it is to be governed by "the law of the United Kingdom"[90] is not to be regarded as submission.[91] Secondly, a State is not immune as respects proceedings relating to a commercial transaction entered into by the State or an obligation of the State which by virtue of any contract falls to be performed wholly or partly in the United Kingdom,[92] unless the parties to the dispute are States or have otherwise agreed in writing.[93] A "commercial transaction" may be a contract for the supply of goods or services, any loan or other transaction for the provision of finance and any guarantee or indemnity in respect of any such transaction or of any other financial obligation, and any other transaction or activity into which it engages otherwise than in the exercise of sovereign authority.[94]

1172

Thirdly, where a State has agreed in writing to submit a dispute which has arisen, or may arise, to arbitration, then—subject to any contrary provision in the arbitration agreement and unless the arbitration agreement is between States—the State is not immune as respects proceedings in the courts of the United Kingdom which relate to the arbitration.[95] Fourthly, a State is not immune as respects proceedings in respect of death or personal injury or damage to or loss of tangible property caused by an act or omission in the United Kingdom.[96] Fifthly,[97] there are specific exceptions from immunity in respect of ships used for commercial purposes, which will be considered below.[98]

1173

The first four exceptions from immunity just mentioned are of general import but clearly apply to salvage contracts and events arising in connection

1174

---

[86] See *post*, §§ 1175–1177.
[87] See *supra*, n. 82.
[88] SIA 1978, s.14(2).
[89] *ibid.*, s.2(1).
[90] In the Conflict of Laws, it is more correct to speak of the individual laws of England and of the other "countries" in the U.K. but the statutory phrase is not inappropriate in an Act concerned with States, as opposed to constituent "countries", and it is unlikely to have been intended to achieve any result other than to apply the Act's provisions to all U.K. legal systems.
[91] *ibid.*, s.2(2).
[92] *ibid.*, s.3(1). See also *ibid.*, s.10(6).
[93] *ibid.*, s.3(2). See also *ibid.*, s.10(6).
[94] *ibid.*, s.3(3). See also *ibid.*, s.10(6).
[95] *ibid.*, s.9.
[96] *ibid.*, s.5. See also *ibid.*, s.10(6).
[97] There are other exceptions which are not of immediate relevance to salvage. See *ibid.*, ss 6–8. 11.
[98] *Post*, §§ 1175–1176.

with salvage operations, such as the putting up of security and negligence liability. It should be noted that the exceptions for contractual obligations to be performed in the United Kingdom[99] and tortious acts in the United Kingdom[1] include references to continental waters.[2]

Clearly, signature of Lloyd's Form as this amounts to a submission to arbitration and therefore excludes immunity.[2A]

Admiralty proceedings

1175 So far as concerns ships owned by foreign States, there is no State immunity for Admiralty proceedings and proceedings on any claim which could be made the subject of Admiralty proceedings as respects an action *in rem* against a ship or other property, except cargo, belonging to the State or an action *in personam* for enforcing a claim in connection with such property if, at the time when the cause of action arose, the ship was in use or intended for use for commercial purposes.[3] However, an action *in rem* can only be brought against a sister ship if, when the cause of action arose, both the ship in respect of which the claim arose and the sister ship were in use or intended for use for commercial purposes.[4]

1176 In relation to cargo it is specifically provided by the State Immunity Act 1978, s.10(4)(a) that a State is not immune to an action *in rem* against a cargo belonging to that State if both the cargo and the carrying ship were, at the time when the cause of action arose, in use or intended for use for commercial purposes. By section 10(4)(b) of the Act, "A State is not immune as respects . . . an action *in personam* for enforcing a claim in connection with such a cargo if the ship carrying it was then in use or intended for use [for commercial purposes]." This phraseology suggests that, provided in all other respects an action *in personam* is available, immunity is removed if the carrying ship alone is "commercial".[5] But if "such a cargo" in paragraph (b) of section 10(4) refers to "cargo . . . in use or intended for use for commercial purposes" in paragraph (a), the effect of the second paragraph does not remove immunity for "non-commercial" cargoes carried on commercial vessels.[6]

Specific provision is now made in relation to salvage claims by the Salvage Convention 1989, Art. 25. Where a State is generally entitled to sovereign immunity but becomes subject to a salvage claim, nonetheless, proceedings *in*

---

[99] *Supra*, text to n. 92.
[1] *Supra*, text to n. 96.
[2] SIA 1978, s.17(4).
[2A] For this reason, many states, including the U.S., refuse to agree Lloyd's Form in salvage cases but will generally sign a private submission to arbitration, duly recording that sovereign immunity is not waived.
[3] *ibid.*, s.10(1)–(2), (5). See also *ibid.*, s.10(6). See further *The Philippine Admiral* [1977] A.C. 373; *The I Congreso del Partido* [1983] 1 A.C. 244.
[4] SIA 1978, s.10(3).
[5] See, *e.g.* Jackson, p. 314.
[6] This would be a statutory reversal of *The Cargo ex Port Victor* [1901] P. 243.

rem against *non-commercial* cargoes cannot be founded on the 1989 Convention unless the State consents.[7]

1177 The general statutory provisions for Admiralty proceedings concerning ships or cargoes belonging to States include references to a ship or cargo in a State's possession or control or in which it claims an interest.[8]

4. HUMANITARIAN CARGOES

1178 The Salvage Convention 1989, Art. 26 provides that, if a State donates a humanitarian cargo, and agrees to pay for salvage services rendered in respect of it, no provision of the Convention shall be used as a basis for its seizure, arrest or detention.[8A] Article 26 has the merit of minimising loss to a cargo which may well be perishable (if food) and, more so than most cargoes, should not being delayed in reaching its destination. It does not affect entitlement to an award but is designed to restrict the procedures for pursuing the claim. Unfortunately, its imprecision means that a salvor may be impeded, or even thwarted, in pursuing his rightful claim to a reward.

1179 The operation of Article 26 is dependent on the presence of a humanitarian cargo. However, no assistance is provided by the Convention in determining what constitutes such a cargo. It may be supposed that it is cargo which is intended to relieve unusual human suffering, most obviously food to relieve famine or starvation, medical supplies and materials to provide shelter from the elements. But it could well extend to other materials intended to stimulate a weak economy and there may well be doubt whether the description embraces cargoes destined for a location where living circumstances are normally very difficult as well as the more obvious cases of emergency relief.

1180 The difficulty is reduced by the necessity to satisfy the second requirement, that the cargo is donated by a State, for States which provide humanitarian assistance are, it may be supposed, unlikely to make a donation of goods with no strings attached except in an emergency. However, there remains scope for dispute in cases where a State allegedly donates cargo but may be thought to expect some reciprocation.

The position is exacerbated by the fact that it is not specified to whom the donation is made, or when. If the donation must have preceded the casualty, Article 26 will not apply to a cargo which is bound for a destination where it

---

[7] See *ante*, § 1170.
[8] SIA 1978, s.10(5).
[8A] In the words of the Salvage Convention 1989, Art. 26: "No provision of this Convention shall be used as a basis for the seizure, arrest or detention of humanitarian cargoes donated by a State, if such State has agreed to pay for salvage services rendered in respect of such humanitarian cargoes." See further Shaw [1996] L.M.C.L.Q. 202, 229.

is to be donated but the donation has not yet occurred.[9] It is not stated to whom the donation is to be made, *i.e.* whether to the intended beneficiaries of the cargo or to an organisation conveying it to those in need of it.

1181 The third requirement for the operation of Article 26 is that the donating State has agreed to pay for salvage services rendered in respect of such cargoes. Presumably, since the State must have "agreed" to pay salvage rather than simply consenting to do so, it must have agreed with the claimant so that he has notice of the State's decision; otherwise, there is a risk that any seizure, arrest or detention of the cargo by him may be unlawful, or at least may be set aside. There is no provision as to how the agreement may be made except that it must have preceded any potential seizure, arrest or detention. If a State makes such an agreement and it transpires that any of the conditions for the operation of Article 26 are not in fact satisfied, and if the salvage claimant has altered his position in response to the State's undertaking, the State will be contractually bound to pay salvage.

Since Article 26 provides that the agreement must precede the seizure, arrest or detention, an agreement made after such an act will neither render the act unlawful nor justify the cargo's release.

5. Limitation of Liability

Rationale and history

Rationale

1182 The exact origins and initial reasons for limitation of liability are uncertain. Various reasons and justifications can be given: that it has an affinity with the earlier idea of the value of an admiralty action *in rem*'s being limited to the value of the *res*; that it encourages (or at least avoids deterring) participation in trade; that it helps defendants to obtain effective insurance cover; that claimants are more likely to be satisfied, at least in part, if liability is subject to limitation and if defendants are insured; that the practice of constituting limitation funds facilitates the fair treatment of all claimants; that limitation of liability is a long-established part of international maritime law; that it is now regulated internationally, by convention; and that it is convenient.[10]

1183 *Per se* these explanations are not conclusive. It is not necessarily the case that would-be participants in the rewards of maritime commerce would be

---

[9] In the latter case, if the cargo is owned by the State at the time of the casualty, the State might be able to plead sovereign immunity but is equally likely to be met with the argument that the cargo is a commercial cargo to which the defence does not apply. See *ante*, §§ 1163–1177.

[10] *The Bramley Moore* [1964] P. 200, 220, *per* Lord Denning M.R. ("there is not much room for justice in this rule; but limitation of liability is not a matter of justice. It is a rule of public policy which has its origins in history and its justification in convenience").

deterred by an inability to limit their liability; indeed, most of those who have found themselves in the position of claimants have clearly not been deterred by having to bear responsibility for losses caused by others beyond the amount of the limitation fund. Nor is it necessarily the case that defendants would be unable to obtain insurance, albeit at higher premiums. At present, the cost of insuring losses in excess of limitation amounts is thrown on to claimants. Without limitation of liability, the responsibility and costs would simply be shifted (back) to persons who caused loss. And to require defendants to bear full liability for their conduct might encourage higher standards. In any event, whoever bears insurance costs initially, they all tend eventually to be passed on to and borne by ultimate consumers of maritime services, most obviously by importers and purchasers of goods which have been carried by sea. Furthermore, the regulation of claims by the establishment and administration of limitation funds is not a justification of limitation of liability but a more general problem, with which a legal system has to deal regardless of the availability of limitation. Indeed, whether or not the law should permit defendants to limit liability is a question for the whole legal system and the general response has been negative.

A simple statement of arguments for and against limitation of liability is relatively easy. An appreciation of the practical advantages and disadvantages of its preservation, modification or abolition is more complex. For the present, it should be noted that the practice has become entrenched in the transport industries by international Conventions, such that it will no doubt be difficult to overturn. **1184**

History

The jurisdiction of the Admiralty Court was founded upon proceedings against property; and until 1892[11] it was accepted that the limit of liability in an action *in rem* was the value of the *res*.[12] There was therefore early support for the idea of limitation of liability, and the *in rem* rule may have encouraged the view that there should be a limit on liability for maritime claims. However, maritime claims were not generally subject to limitation of liability, so that e.g. a claim for collision damage could be brought either in Admiralty *in rem*, or at common law or in Admiralty *in personam* without any inherent limitation on the amount of the claim.[13] **1185**

The concept of limiting liability appears to have become established on the Continent at least by the seventeenth century and a law introduced in Holland for the protection of its navigation seems[14] to have prompted the introduction of the first English statute, the Responsibility of Shipowners Act 1733.[15] **1186**

---

[11] *The Dictator* [1894] P. 64, *per* Jeune J.
[12] See, *e.g. Brown v. Wilkinson* (1846) 15 M. & W. 391, 398, *per* Parke B.
[13] See *The Volant* (1842) 1 W. Rob. 383, 387, *per* Dr Lushington; *The Dundee* (1823) 1 Hagg. 109, 120, *per* Lord Stowell.
[14] See *The Dundee* (1823) 1 Hagg. 109, 120, *per* Lord Stowell.
[15] (1733) 7 Geo. II, c. 15.

Subsequent legislation was embodied in the consolidating Merchant Shipping Act 1894, s.503, which was in turn subject to several amendments. A CMI-sponsored International Limitation Convention was agreed in 1924[16] but the United Kingdom did not accede to it. A further Convention was agreed in 1957,[17] to supersede the 1924 Convention. The 1957 Convention was implemented[18] into United Kingdom law by amendment of the Merchant Shipping Act 1894, s.503. The 1957 Convention was in turn superseded by the (London) Convention on Limitation of Liability for Maritime Claims 1976 ("LLMC 1976") sponsored by the International Maritime Organisation (IMO).

1187 The terms of the 1957 Convention were rewritten when implemented into United Kingdom law by reference to existing primary legislation. However, the substantive terms of LLMC 1976[19] were implemented verbatim into United Kingdom law, by embodiment in a schedule to the Merchant Shipping Act 1979,[20] thereby fostering uniform interpretation of the Convention internationally. The schedule also contained provisions whereby the United Kingdom exercised its right to make reservations to the Convention and otherwise gave effect to the Convention municipally. LLMC 1976 and its implementing legislation have now been consolidated in the Merchant Shipping Act 1995.[21] A Protocol to amend LLMC 1976 was agreed in 1996 but has not yet come into force.[22] LLMC 1976 is of wide import but nevertheless only applies in the circumstances which it specifies. However, further circumstances are provided for in other legislation.

Scope of LLMC 1976

1188 The Merchant Shipping Act 1995, s.185(1)–(2) provides generally that, subject to Schedule 7, Pt II to the Act (containing particular rules on the application of LLMC 1976 to United Kingdom law), the provisions of LLMC 1976 as set out in Schedule 7, Pt I *shall have the force of law*[23] in the United Kingdom and that the provisions of Schedule 7, Pt II *shall have effect* in

---

[16] International Convention for the Unification of Certain Rules Relating to the Limitation of the Liability of Owners of Sea-Going Vessels. Signed at Brussels, August 25, 1924.

[17] International Convention for the Unification of Certain Rules Relating to the Limitation of the Liability of Owners of Sea-Going Ships. Signed at Brussels on October 10, 1957.

[18] By the Merchant Shipping (Liability of Shipowners and Others) Act 1958.

[19] The Final Clauses (Arts. 16–23) are omitted.

[20] MSA 1979, s.17 and Sched 4. See also *ibid.*, s.19 and Sched 5. The Convention entered into force on December 1, 1986: Merchant Shipping Act 1979 (Commencement No. 10) Order 1986 (S.I. 1986 No. 1052).

[21] s.185, Sched. 7.

[22] MSA 1995, s.185 was amended by the Merchant Shipping and Maritime Security Act 1997, s.15 to enable implementation of the Protocol. The Merchant Shipping (Convention on Limitation of Liability for Maritime Claims) (Amendment) Order 1998 (S.I. 1998 No. 1258) provides for the implementation of the Protocol and sets out the consequently revised text of the LLMC 1976 ("LLMC 1996") and the relevant provisions of MSA 1995. The Protocol will enter into force 90 days following the date on which 10 States have expressed their consent to be bound by it.

[23] The Carriage of Goods by Sea Act 1971, s.1.(2)–(3) states that the Hague-Visby Rules "shall have the force of law" to avoid the problem which had arisen of contracting out of the Hague Rules.

connection with the Convention. Now the Act and the Convention expressly provide that, in certain cases where the parties' relationship is provided for by contract, the right to limit is not available.[24] To that extent, by entering into a specified contractual relationship, the parties are permitted to avoid the potential application of the Act. However, in other cases governed by the legislation its terminology appears to prohibit contractual ouster of the Convention.[25] Nonetheless, the view has been expressed that it is possible by contract to waive the right to limit liability.[26] Moreover, Article 1, which sets out which persons are entitled to limit liability, states that they "may limit their liability" or "shall be *entitled* to do so". So a person entitled to limit his liability may choose not to invoke the protection of the Convention and is not bound to do so. Yet it also remains possible that he can rely on the statutory force of the Convention to override a contractual exclusion to which he has agreed.

1189 The Merchant Shipping Act 1995 has enacted the first part of LLMC 1976, Art. 15, which provides that "This Convention shall apply whenever any person referred to in Article 1[27] seeks to limit his liability before the Court of a State Party or seeks to procure the release of a ship or other property or the discharge of any security given within the jurisdiction of any such State."

The remainder of Article 15 has so far not been incorporated into United Kingdom legislation, but this will be done when the 1996 Protocol to the Convention comes into force.[28]

Entitlement to limitation of liability

(a) Under LLMC 1976

1190 For the purposes of the application of LLMC 1976 to United Kingdom law, the right to limit applies in relation to any ship, whether seagoing or not,[29] and references to a ship include references to any structure (whether completed or in the course of completion) launched and intended for use in navigation as a ship or part of a ship.[30]

---

[24] See MSA 1995, s.185(4) and LLMC 1976, Arts. 2–3.
[25] See also LLMC 1976, Art. 2.
[26] G. Brice, "The Scope of the Limitation Action", Chap. II of N. Gaskell (ed.), *Limitation of Shipowners' Liability: the New Law* (1986), p. 28.
[27] See *post*, § 1190.
[28] See the Merchant Shipping (Convention on Limitation of Liability for Maritime Claims) (Amendment) Order 1998 (S.I. 1998 No. 1258).
[29] MSA 1995, s.185(2) and Sched. 7, Pt. II, §2.
[30] MSA 1995, s.185(2) and Sched. 7, Pt II, para. 12. LLMC 1976, Art. 15.1 provides that each State party to the Convention may exclude wholly or partly from the application of the Convention any ship in relation to which the right of limitation is invoked or whose release is sought and which does not, whenever any person entitled to limit his liability seeks to do so or to procure the release of a ship or other property or the discharge of security given within the jurisdiction of a State Party, fly the flag of a State Party. This part of the Convention has not been incorporated into MSA 1995 and the option has not been exercised by the U.K.

Restrictions on Claims

The following are persons entitled to limitation of liability under LLMC 1976[31]:

    (i) Shipowners.[32] For this purpose in United Kingdom law, "shipowner" means the owner, charterer, manager or operator of a ship,[33] whether seagoing or not.[34] In the Convention the liability of the shipowner includes liability in an action brought against the vessel itself.[35]

    (ii) Salvors.[36] Salvor means any person rendering services in direct connection with salvage operations.[37] For this purpose "salvage operations" include operations referred to in LLMC 1976, Art. 2.1(d)–(f) (specified wreck removal activities and acts to avert or minimise liability limited under the Convention).[38]

    (iii) Persons for whose act, neglect or default the shipowner or salvor is responsible.[39]

    (iv) Insurers of liability for claims subject to limitation under the Convention.[40] Insurers are entitled to the benefits of the Convention to the same extent as the assured himself.

Claims subject to limitation under LLMC 1976

1191   LLMC 1976, Art. 2.1 stipulates that the following claims are generally subject to limitation of liability under the Convention,[41] although claims under heads (d)–(f) are not subject to limitation of liability to the extent that they relate to remuneration under a contract with the person liable[42]:

    (a) Claims in respect of loss of life or personal injury[43] or loss of or damage to property (including damage to harbour works, basins and waterways and aids to navigation)[44] occurring on board or in direct

---

[31] LLMC 1976, Art. 1. LLMC 1976, Art. 15.1 provides that each State party to the Convention may exclude wholly or partly from the application of the Convention any person referred to in Article 1 who, at the time when the rules of the Convention are invoked before the courts of that State party does not have his habitual residence in a State party. This part of the Convention has not been incorporated into MSA 1995 and the option has not been exercised by the U.K.
[32] MSA 1995, s.185(1) and Sched. 7, Pt I, Art. 1.1.
[33] MSA 1995, s.185(1) and Sched. 7, Pt I, Art. 1.2.
[34] LLMC 1976, Art. 1.2 refers to a seagoing ship but the definition of "shipowner" has been extended for the purpose of U.K. law: MSA 1995, s.185(2) and Sched. 7, Pt II, para. 2.
[35] MSA 1995, s.185(1) and Sched. 7, Pt I, Art. 1.5.
[36] MSA 1995, s.185(1) and Sched. 7, Pt I, Art. 1.1.
[37] MSA 1995, s.185(1) and Sched. 7, Pt I, Art. 1.3.
[38] See *post*, §§ 1192–1193.
[39] MSA 1995, s.185(1) and Sched. 7, Pt I, Art. 1.4.
[40] MSA 1995, s.185(1) and Sched. 7, Pt I, Art. 1.6.
[41] MSA 1995, s.185(1) and Sched. 7, Pt I, Art. 2.1.
[42] MSA 1995, s.185(1) and Sched. 7, Pt I, Art. 2.2.
[43] Which may be of crew or passengers.
[44] *e.g.* under the Harbours, Docks and Piers Clauses Act 1847, s.4.

connection with the operation of the ship or with salvage operations, and consequential loss resulting therefrom.[45]

(b) Claims in respect of loss resulting from delay in the carriage by sea of cargo, passengers or their luggage.

(c) Claims in respect of other loss resulting from infringement of rights other than contractual rights occurring in direct connection with the operation of the ship or salvage operations.

(d) Claims in respect of the raising, removal, destruction or rendering harmless of a ship which is sunk, wrecked, stranded or abandoned, including anything that is or has been on board such a ship.

1192

In principle this would apply to claims for wreck removal under the Harbours, Docks and Piers Clauses Act 1847, s.56 and the Merchant Shipping Act 1995, s.201. However, by a permitted reservation to LLMC 1976, the Merchant Shipping Act 1995 provides that this head shall not apply unless provision has been made by an order of the Secretary of State for the setting up and management of a fund to be used for the making to harbour and conservancy authorities of payments needed to compensate them for the reduction, in consequence of head (d), of amounts recoverable by them in claims of the kind there mentioned, and to be maintained by contributions from such authorities raised and collected by them in respect of vessels in like manner as other sums raised by them.[46] This has not been done, so limitation under this head is not available under United Kingdom law, the policy of which has been to preserve unlimited liability for wreck removal expenses.

(e) Claims in respect of the removal, destruction or rendering harmless of the cargo of the ship.

1193

In a loose sense, LLMC 1976 limits liability for dealing with ships which have become casualties under head (d), and with cargo which has become a casualty under head (e). However, the disapplication of head (d) to United Kingdom law and the precise wording of the heads leaves scope for confusion, since cargo may be "anything that is or has been on board a ship" under head (d). One view is that claims in respect of cargo removal qualify for limitation before the ship is sunk, wrecked, stranded or abandoned (by virtue of head (e)) but not thereafter (by virtue of head (d)).[47] Certainly, only head (d) specifically refers to "raising" its specified subject-matter. However, it does not follow that, if liability in respect of cargo were limited under heads (d) and (e) by LLMC 1976 but not limited under head

---

[45] See, *e.g. The Breydon Merchant* [1992] 1 Lloyd's Rep. 373.
[46] MSA 1995, s.185(2) and Sched. 7, Pt II, para. 3(1). See also *ibid.*, Art. 3(2).
[47] P. Griggs and R. Williams, *Limitation of Liability for Maritime Claims* (3rd ed., 1999), p. 18.

Restrictions on Claims

(d) under United Kingdom law, that it is therefore at any time unlimited under head (e) under United Kingdom law.

(f) Claims of a person other than the person liable in respect of measures taken in order to avert or minimise loss for which the person liable may limit his liability in accordance with LLMC 1976, and further losses caused by such measures.[48]

1194 Prior to LLMC 1976, limitation in English law was only available for liability to damages and not *e.g.* for liability in debt.[49] However, limitation under LLMC 1976 is available whatever the basis of liability.[50]

The issue may arise of the extent to which a defendant's ability to limit liability carries over to his right of recourse against or to an indemnity from a third party. LLMC 1976, Art. 2.2 provides that "Claims set out in [LLMC 1976, Art. 2.1]" are generally subject to limitation of liability even if brought by way of recourse or for indemnity under a contract or otherwise.[51]

One difficulty with this provision is that, on the face of it, Article 2.2 applies to claims "set out" in Article 2.1 even though the relevant liability is not in fact limited: *e.g.* because it falls within head (d) (which does not apply under United Kingdom law) or where conduct bars limitation.[52]

1195 The question may arise whether the amount of liability which might have been, but was not, limited under a head set out in LLMC 1976 (*e.g.* shipwreck removal expenses under the disapplied head (d)) could be limited in an action for recourse or an indemnity (*e.g.* in an action by the sunken ship against a colliding vessel). The answer must be no. The object of Article 2.2 appears to be to pre-empt the liability of the defendant being extended to a greater loss than the claimant has in fact suffered, not to provide an advantage to the third party in addition to whatever limitation of liability he is himself entitled anyway.

Similarly, the fact that an action for recourse or an indemnity results from a liability falling within the heads set out in Article 2.1 does not mean that the action itself therefore falls within one of those heads. Thus, a third party who was not otherwise able to limit liability should not be able to maintain that, because the claim against him was brought to indemnify a liability limited by Article 2.1, then the claim for the indemnity also fell within the relevant head of Article 2.1 and was similarly limited. This would seem unduly to stretch the language of Article 2.1.

A fortiori it would be perverse to maintain that a third party whose liability was prima facie limited (say under head (a)) should lose that protection

---

[48] See, *e.g. The Breydon Merchant* [1992] 1 Lloyd's Rep. 373.
[49] *The Stonedale No. 1 (Owners) v. Manchester Ship Canal Co.* [1956] A.C. 1 (liability in debt to harbour authority which raised wreck under statutory powers), approving *The Millie* [1940] P. 1.
[50] *i.e.* whether tortious, contractual, statutory or otherwise.
[51] MSA 1995, s.185(1) and Sched. 7, Pt I, Art. 2.2; reversing *Alsey Steam Fishing Co. Ltd v. Hillman (Owners) (The Kirknes)* [1956] 2 Lloyd's Rep. 651 (tow's duty to damage caused to tug arising not from tort or breach of contract but from contractual duty to indemnify).
[52] Under LLMC 1976, Art. 4. See *post*, §§ 1201–1204.

because his liability was to compensate for a liability which was set out under Article 2.1(d) but was in fact unlimited because of the disapplication of head (d) in United Kingdom law. This would again diverge from the policy and language of Article 2.[53]

Counterclaims

In *The Tojo Maru*[54] different views were expressed by the arbitrators and the courts as to whether, in a case of counterclaims, each claim should be assessed subject to the relevant limitation of liability and the resulting sums then set off against each other, or if the claims should first be set off against each other with limitation then being applied to the resulting amount. The issue is dealt with, but not conclusively, by LLMC 1976. Article 5 states that:

1196

> "Where a person entitled to limitation of liability under the rules of this Convention has a claim against the claimant arising out of the same occurrence, their respective claims shall be set off against each other and the provisions of this Convention shall apply to the balance, if any."

Unlimited liability

(i) Claims not subject to limitation

It is obvious, but necessary to remember, that legal liability is unlimited unless limitation is imposed. Where limitation is prima facie imposed, it then becomes necessary to identify whether a prima facie limitation is displaced.

1197

(ii) Claims excepted from limitation under LLMC 1976

LLMC 1976, Art. 3 provides that the Convention's rules do not apply in the following cases.[55]

1198

(a) Claims for salvage or contribution in general average.

Not all claims arising in connection with salvage operations or general average acts are "for salvage or general average" in their strict sense; and it is only claims properly falling within this description that are excepted from LLMC 1976. This exception does not therefore apply to a claim by a cargo-owner for a shipowner's breach of contract which resulted in the cargo-owner's having to pay a salvage reward to a third party salvor.[56] Nor does it apply to claims provided for by the International Salvage Convention 1989 but which are not claims for salvage, *e.g.* claims arising from breach of duty

---

[53] See also Gaskell, 21–363. *cf. Barameda Enterprises Pty Ltd v. O'Connor (The Tiruna)* [1987] 2 Lloyd's Rep. 666 (Qld S.C.: F.C.)

[54] *The Owners of The Motor Vessel Tojo Maru v. N.V. Bureau Wijsmuller (The Tojo Maru)* [1972] A.C. 242; reversing [1970] P. 21 (CA); reversing [1969] 1 Lloyd's Rep. 133 (Willmer L.J.)

[55] MSA 1995, s.185(1) and Sched. 7, Pt I, Art. 3.

[56] *The Breydon Merchant* [1992] 1 Lloyd's Rep. 373.

under Article 8 of that Convention.[57] However, the United Kingdom has exercised its right to make reservations to LLMC 1976 and provided that this head of exceptions extends to claims under the International Salvage Convention 1989, Art. 14 (for "environmental services")[58] and corresponding claims under a contract.[59]

The 1996 Protocol to amend LLMC 1976 adopts the first part of this extension and, when it comes into force, this head of exceptions will be: claims for salvage, including, if applicable, any claim for special compensation under Article 14 of the International Salvage Convention 1989, as amended, or contribution in general average.[60] The extension to "corresponding claims under a contract" will no longer appear in the United Kingdom legislation and is unnecessary, since liability for such claims is not subject to limitation anyway.

1199 (b) Claims for oil pollution damage within the meaning of the International Convention for Oil Pollution Damage dated November 29, 1969 or of any amendment or Protocol thereto which is in force. In United Kingdom law, these claims are claims in respect of any liability incurred under the Merchant Shipping Act 1995, s.153.[61]

(c) Claims subject to any international convention or national legislation governing or prohibiting limitation of liability for nuclear damage. In United Kingdom law, these claims are claims made by virtue of any of the Nuclear Installations Act 1965, ss 7–11.[62]

(d) Claims against the shipowner of a nuclear ship for nuclear damage.

1200 (e) Claims by servants of the shipowner or salvor whose duties are connected with the ship or the salvage operations, including claims of their heirs, dependants or other persons entitled to make such claims, if under the law governing the contract of service between the shipowner or salvor and such servants the shipowner or salvor is not entitled to limit his liability in respect of such claims, or if he is by such law only permitted to limit his liability to an amount greater than that provided for in LLMC 1976, Art. 6.[63]

The Merchant Shipping Act 1995, s.185(4) specifically provides that the provisions having the force of law under Schedule 7 to the Act (LLMC 1976 as varied under United Kingdom law) shall not apply to any liability in respect of loss of life or personal injury caused to, or loss of or damage to any property of, a person who is on board the ship in question or employed in connection with that ship or with the salvage operations in question if he is so

---

[57] Liability for these is limited under LLMC 1976, Art. 2.1(c).
[58] *Ante*, Chap. 5.
[59] MSA 1995, s.185(2) and Sched. 7, Pt II, para. 4(1).
[60] Merchant Shipping (Convention on Limitation of Liability for Maritime Claims) (Amendment) Order 1998 (S.I. 1998 No. 1258), §3. *cf.* the York-Antwerp Rules 1994, r. VI(b), which allows salvage remuneration in general average but not special compensation under the International Salvage Convention 1989, Art. 14.
[61] MSA 1995, s.185(2) and Sched. 7, Pt II, para. 4(2).
[62] MSA 1995, s.185(2) and Sched. 7, Pt II, para. 4(3).
[63] The general limits.

Conduct barring limitation

on board or employed under a contract of service governed by the law of any part of the United Kingdom.

Conduct barring limitation

The question of limitation will not arise unless a defendant has committed a legal wrong. Where he has, views may differ as to whether his liability should be subject to limitation and, if so, whether the limit placed on his liability is suitable. But, once those policy questions have been answered and limits have been set, they should be applied. There may remain a reluctance to allow a wrongdoer to reap the benefit of limitation but that alone does not justify circumventing the limits laid down. Nonetheless, it may not be inappropriate that the law providing limitation itself sets boundaries to the right to limit (or, more colloquially, states when limitation can be broken). **1201**

Until LLMC 1976, the generally accepted test was that the defendant was disentitled from limitation where "the occurrence giving rise to the claim resulted from the actual fault or privity of the owner".[64] Three main problems arose in relation to this formula. The first was the meaning of "actual fault or privity".[65] Secondly, since most defendants are not natural persons but corporations the activities of which are conducted by natural persons, it had to be determined exactly whose actual fault or privity was relevant for this purpose. In English law, the relevant persons were held to be not servants or agents for whom the defendant was liable under normal principles of vicarious liability or agency but persons whose acts constituted acts of the company itself, *i.e.*, persons who were the alter ego of the company or who controlled the relevant activity.[66] **1202**

Thirdly, there was the issue of where the burden of proof lay. Under the Limitation Convention 1957, Art. 1(6), the placing of the burden of proof was a matter for the *lex fori*; and in English law the onus was on the defendant to disprove his actual fault or privity.[67] In practice, the burden was not easy to discharge,[68] so that the practical availability of limitation was reduced.

---

[64] MSA 1894, s.503, as enacted and as amended by the Limitation Convention 1957, Art. 1(1).

[65] See, *e.g. Temperley's Merchant Shipping Acts* (17th ed., 1976), §431.

[66] *Lennard's Carrying Co. v. Asiatic Petroleum Co.* [1915] A.C. 705; *The Lady Gwendolen* [1965] P. 294; *The Garden City* [1982] 2 Lloyd's Rep. 382 (Staughton J.); *Grand Champion Tankers Ltd v. Nordpipe A/S (The Marion)* [1984] A.C. 563; *Société Anonyme des Minerais v. Grant Trading Inc. (The Ert Stefanie)* [1989] 1 Lloyd's Rep. 349. *cf. Meridian Global Funds Management Asia Ltd v. Securities Commission* [1995] 2 A.C. 500 (NZ: PC); *R. v. Rozeik* [1996] 1 W.L.R. 159 (CA); *Red Sea Tankers Ltd v. Papachristidis (The Hellespont Ardent)* [1997] 2 Lloyd's Rep. 547; *Attorney-General's Reference (No. 2 of 1999)* [2000] Q.B. 796 (CA).

[67] *Koninklijke Rotterdamsche Lloyd (N.V.) v. Western Steamship Co. Ltd (The Empire Jamaica)* [1957] A.C. 386; *Northern Fishing Co. (Hull) Ltd v. Eddom (The Norman)* [1960] 1 Lloyd's Rep. 1.

[68] See, *e.g. The Wladyslaw Lokietek* [1978] 2 Lloyd's Rep. 520.

Restrictions on Claims

1203 Under LLMC 1976 shipowners and others agreed to a higher limit of liability than under the previous law in exchange for an almost indisputable right to limit their liability.[69]

LLMC 1976, Art. 4 adopts the approach pioneered by the Warsaw Convention[70] and provides that: "A person liable shall not be entitled to limit his liability if it is proved that the loss resulted from his personal act or omission, committed with the intent to cause such loss, or recklessly and with knowledge that such loss would probably result." This formula reduces the circumstances in which limitation may be broken.

1204 First, "mere" "actual fault or privity" is insufficient. It is only in the less frequent cases where the defendant's conduct is deliberate or reckless[71] that limitation is broken.

Secondly, the bar is restricted to "a person liable" from whose "personal act or omission" the loss results. This seems more specific than the former test, though it does not *per se* overcome the fact that a corporation's "personal" acts (or omissions) can only be committed by natural persons and that the relevant natural persons still need to be identified. Nevertheless, where there are multiple defendants, it should prevent a defendant who is not personally responsible from losing his right to limit simply because of an association with, or being privy to the conduct of, a defendant who is personally responsible. However, it does not eliminate the possibility that a shipowner may be unable to limit because of the personal act or omission of a charterer, manager or operator who is treated as the shipowner's alter ego. LLMC 1976, Art. 1.6 provides that, where the defendant is an insurer of liability subject to limitation, he can limit to the same extent as the assured himself. If he insures several persons responsible for the same loss, the insurer's right to limit will only be barred in respect of the claims of those assureds whose right to limit is barred.[72]

Thirdly, the court is not required to investigate the question whether the shipowner has been guilty of conduct barring limitation[73]; and there is now "a

---

[69] *The Bowbelle* [1990] 1 W.L.R. 1330, 1335, *per* Sheen J.

[70] Convention for the Unification of Certain Rules Relating to International Carriage by Air, Warsaw, October 12, 1929 (as amended by the Hague Protocol 1955), Art. 25; enacted in the U.K. by the Carriage by Air Act 1961, s.1 and Sched. 1, Art. 25 (see also *ibid.*, Sched. 1A, Art. 25).

[71] On the meaning of "reckless", see *R. v. Caldwell* [1982] A.C. 341; *R. v. Lawrence* [1982] A.C. 510; *Goldman v. Thai Airways International Ltd* [1983] 1 W.L.R. 1186; *S.S. Pharmaceutical Co. Ltd v. Qantas Airways Ltd* [1991] 1 Lloyd's Rep. 288 (HCA). *Gurtner v. Beaton* [1993] 2 Lloyd's Rep. 368; *The Pembroke* [1995] 2 Lloyd's Rep. 290 (NZ HC); *Monarch Airlines Ltd v. London Luton Airport Ltd* [1998] 1 Lloyd's Rep. 403; *The MSC Rosa M* [2000] 2 Lloyd's Rep. 399.

[72] In the unlikely event that a loss resulted from the intentional or reckless personal act or omission of the insurer himself (*e.g.* where he was directing operations of a shipowner or salvor), the insurer could be sued *qua* wrongdoer and could not limit under LLMC 1976 because he would not fall under any of the protected classes in Art. 1 (not even Art. 1(6), for in this capacity he would not be an insurer of liability but a person liable). But, if he were sued *qua* insurer of another person against whom a resulting claim was brought, his right to limit would not be barred, because Art. 4 only bars the right of "a person liable", *semble* a person liable for the claim in question, not someone liable as insurer of the claim.

[73] *The Bowbelle* [1990] 1 W.L.R. 1330, 1335, *per* Sheen J.

very heavy burden" on the claimant to prove the facts which cause limitation to be barred.[74]

6. LIMITATION OF ACTIONS

The general position

Under the general law in the Limitation Act 1980,[75] actions for damages for personal injuries must be brought within three years and other claims in respect of torts, simple contracts, judgments and arbitration awards within six years.[76] However, the general rules do not apply to any action or arbitration for which a period of limitation is prescribed by virtue of any other enactment.[77] Such special provision is in force implementing the International Salvage Convention 1989, Art. 23.[78] Under Art. 23(1), once the limitation period has commenced, any action relating to payment under the Convention shall be time-barred if judicial or arbitral proceedings[79] have not been instituted within a period of two years.[80] **1205**

It is also provided, by LSSAC 2000, cl. 4.2,[81] that: **1206**

> "Where a claim is made or may be made for special compensation the owners of the vessel shall on the demand of the Contractors whenever made provide security for the Contractors[82] claim for special compensation *provided always that such demand is made within 2 years of the date of termination of the services.*"

A claim for special compensation is a claim for a payment under the Salvage Convention 1989 and so subject to a two-year time bar, and the object of

---

[74] See *The Bowbelle* [1990] 1 W.L.R. 1330, 1335, *per* Sheen J.; *The Capitan San Luis* [1994] Q.B. 465. See also *Goldman v. Thai Airways International Ltd* [1983] 1 W.L.R. 1186 (Warsaw Convention); *R.G. Mayor (T/A Granville Coaches) v. P. & O. Ferries Ltd (The Lion)* [1990] 2 Lloyd's Rep. 144, 149 (Athens Convention and Hague-Visby Rules).
[75] Which apply to arbitral proceedings as they apply to legal proceedings: Arbitration Act 1996, s.13. But see further *ibid.*, s.14(1) (the parties are free to agree when arbitral proceedings are commenced for the purposes of the Limitation Acts) and s.41 (tribunal's power to dismiss claim for inordinate and inexcusable delay).
[76] Limitation Act 1980, especially ss 2, 5, 9, 24.
[77] Limitation Act 1980, s.39. General reform of the law of limitation of actions has been recommended by the Law Commission, but not so as to affect specialised statutory limitation periods, in particular those deriving from international conventions. See *Limitation of Actions*: Law Com. No. 270 (2001).
[78] Replacing similar (though in some respects different) provisions in the Brussels Convention 1910, Art. 10. Unlike most of the provisions of the 1910 Convention, Art. 10 was enacted in the U.K., within the Maritime Conventions Act 1911, s.8.
[79] For the purposes of MSA 1995, "judicial proceedings" are defined *ibid.*, Sched. 11, Pt II, para. 6: see *ante*, § 74n.
[80] Art. 23.1.
[81] Emphasis added. LOF 1995, cl. 5(b) is the same except with the words "Contractor" (for "Contractors"), "Contractor's" (for "Contractors") and "two" (for "2").
[82] *sic*.

security is generally to ensure payment of a legally enforceable claim; so it may seem superfluous to impose a two-year time limit on a claim for security if the underlying claim expires anyway after two years. However, time bars are generally procedural, merely barring proceedings without extinguishing the claim. The proviso to LOF 2000, cl. 4.2 is therefore necessary to prevent dilatory Contractors from insisting on a contractual right to security and thereby coercing payment of a time-barred claim.

Commencement of limitation period(s)

1207 Under the Convention, "[t]he limitation period commences on the day on which the salvage services are terminated".[83] Where all services terminate on one date, the position is simple. Similarly, if there is a series of different incidents, time will begun to run separately in respect of each set of salvage services. However, even a single set of circumstances may not be straightforward. Thus, different salvors may cease their services at different times or different items of property may be salved at different times. Although it is convenient in practice for all claims in respect of a single casualty to be determined together, individual salvors have independent rights and the liability of individual salvees is several, not joint,[84] so it may be important to distinguish between different claims.

1208 Where different salvors render different services or different items of property are salved, it is arguable that the limitation period begins when the service in respect of the relevant property terminates. This would mean that, consequent upon a single casualty, different limitation periods could apply between different salvors and salvees. However, in practice, it will normally be sensible and convenient if the limitation period is considered to run from the date upon which the salvage operations terminate as a whole.[85] This view is strengthened by the terminology of the Convention, which refers to a single day on which "services" are terminated. It is nonetheless possible that, say, cargo is salved but salvage of the vessel is delayed, perhaps for a substantial period of time. In such a case it may not be appropriate for there to be a longer than usual limitation period in respect of the cargo; but it would certainly be wrong to treat the limitation period for all property as commencing once the cargo was in safety, with the possibility that it might expire before the ship were salved. The sensible approach in the case of protracted services may be to treat each "set" of services separately so that, in the example given, the services in respect of cargo are treated as terminating when all the cargo is salved and the services in respect of the vessel as terminating when that is

---

[83] Art. 23.1.
[84] See *post*, Chap. 16.
[85] See Brice, §2–81. This will obviously be to the advantage of salvors who have ceased their services at an earlier date but arguably not to the disadvantage of the salvee, who will only be liable when his property is brought to safety.

Claims subject to limitation

eventually salved. Such an approach would allow the time bar to be interpreted sensibly in practice without making its commencement discretionary.

Extension of limitation period

Once time has begun to run, there is no provision for the tribunal to extend it.[86] However, the Convention provides that the person against whom a claim is made may at any time during the running of the limitation period extend that period by a declaration to the claimant; and this period may in the like manner be further extended.[87] **1209**

Claims subject to limitation

A claim will be subject to limitation under the general law unless it is subject to special provision such as Article 23 of the Salvage Convention. However, the mere fact that a claim is consequent upon a salvage operation does not *per se* bring it within the terms of Article 23. **1210**

Actions relating to payment under the Convention

Article 23 applies to "Any action relating to payment under this Convention"; and Article 1(e) states that "Payment means any reward, remuneration or compensation due under this Convention". Clearly, Article 23 applies to a claim for a salvage reward *stricto sensu*[88] and to a claim for special compensation under Article 14.[89] **1211**

It is not clear whether Article 23 applies to claims which are merely "permitted" by the Convention. Thus, rewards for life salvage are stipulated to be prima facie outside the Convention but permissible under national law.[90] It is debatable whether the Convention permits the claim "under" or outside the Convention, albeit it seems sensible that, where national law provides for life salvage,[91] the claim should be pursued within the time limits for other payments sanctioned by the Convention.

---

[86] Exercising the liberties contained in both the Brussels Salvage Convention 1910, Art. 10 and the (Brussels) International Convention for the Unification of Certain Rules of Law with respect to Collision Between Vessels 1910, Art. 7, the Maritime Conventions Act 1911, s.8 subjected actions in respect of salvage services to a time bar which was subject to discretionary judicial extension. However, when enacting the Salvage Convention 1989, the Merchant Shipping (Salvage and Pollution) Act 1994 removed salvage claims from s.8 (the remainder of which was subsequently re-enacted in the Merchant Shipping Act 1995, s.190).

There are powers to extend contractual time limits in relation to arbitration in the Arbitration Act 1996, ss.12 and 79; but the limitation regime applying to arbitrations is generally subject to contrary specific legislation, such as the Salvage Convention 1989.

[87] Art. 23.2. English practitioners customarily refer to such a declaration as an "agreed extension of time".

[88] And presumably to any separate award for an item such as a salvor's expenses and damages if these could be included in a salvage reward. See Wildeboer, 95–97.

[89] *Ante*, Chap. 5.

[90] Art. 16.1 stipulates that "No remuneration is due from persons whose lives are saved, but nothing in this article shall affect the provisions of national law on this subject."

[91] As does English law.

1212　The Convention also does not make provision for, but acknowledges the possibility of payments of, interest. Thus, Article 24 provides that "The right of the salvor to interest on any payment due under this Convention shall be determined according to the law of the State in which the tribunal seized of the case is situated." The reference to "interest on any payment due" suggests that interest is different from, rather than one of the types of, payments due under the Convention. On one view, interest will not become due until the amount of payment due under the Convention is determined, and this is the appropriate date from which time should run. However, Lloyd's salvage arbitrators customarily award interest from the date of termination of the salvage service.

1213　The limitation period for claims arising from salvage contracts is also not straightforward. The Salvage Convention 1989 applies to any salvage operations save to the extent that a contract otherwise provides expressly or by implication.[92] Prima facie, therefore, an action to recover sums provided for by the Convention as a result of performance of a salvage contract must be instituted within two years.

1214　It is not clear whether Article 23 applies to the obligation to pay damages for failure to perform a duty laid down by the Convention[93] or, by extension, a duty arising under a contract governed by the Convention. Such a claim is arguably in respect of something contrary to the Convention rather than "under" it.[94] And "compensation" in Article 1(e) does not obviously embrace compensation by way of damages as well as the special compensation provided for in Article 14.[95] In any event defendants in breach of the relevant duties should not obviously be entitled to the time bar provided by the Convention where, as is likely, it is shorter than under general national laws. It is simplistic to argue that the rights of a damages claimant may be diminished for the sake of convenience or uniformity. Indeed, the argument from uniformity points at least as much in the direction of the general law, which applies to the extent that, on their true construction only, the Salvage Convention 1989 and the Merchant Shipping Act 1995, s.190[96] do not create an exceptional two-year time bar.

1215　One view is that: first, a cause of action for damages may arise both under the Convention and outside it, whether for a breach of contract or a tort; and, secondly, the claimant could choose to pursue the claim either under the

---

[92] Art. 6.1.
[93] See Arts 8 (duties of the salvor and of the owner and master), 20 (wrongful enforcement of maritime lien), 21 (duty to provide security). *cf.* Art. 10 (duty to render assistance: *ante*, §§ 535–536) and MSA 1995, Sched. 11, Pt II, Art. 3.
[94] *cf.* Art. 18 (stating that a salvor guilty of misconduct may be deprived of "payment due under this Convention") and Art. 19 (stating that services rendered though prohibited "shall not give rise to payment under this Convention"): the Convention does not provide that damages shall be paid for breach of either article but leaves the issue to be determined outside the Convention.
[95] See *ante*, Chap. 5.
[96] For claims against ships or their owners for loss.

Claims subject to limitation

Convention or outside it, thereby avoiding the (presumably) shorter Convention time bar.[97] However, even if the first point is correct, it does not follow that the mandatory Convention time bar can be ignored for actions governed by its provisions.

Further difficulties arise where there is a claim to unravel a contract otherwise governed by the Convention. If the claim is simply to set aside the contract, it is not one for payment and therefore not subject to the two-year time bar. If restitution of money paid under such a contract were claimed, it is arguable that, if such a claim arose as a consequence of circumstances where the Convention provides for annulment or modification of the contract,[98] then it is a claim for payment under the Convention. However, a claim to undo such a contract is more properly regarded not as one relating to payment under the Convention, certainly where the vitiating factor is not one provided for in the Convention. Accordingly, the restitution claim should not be subject to the two-year time bar.

The position is more complicated where, in consequence of, or in parallel with, a claim to undo or modify a contract, a claim is made for payment not under the superseded contract but under the Convention or under the modified contract. The Convention could have taken account of any likely prejudice to the victim of the vitiating factor by granting to the tribunal a discretion to extend the limitation period under the Convention. However, although such a discretion existed prior to the 1989 Convention, it has now been abolished. Accordingly, a person who wishes to claim payment unfettered by the provisions of an existing contract should normally claim the payment at the same time as claiming rescission or modification of that contract.[99] In most cases in practice, the claimant should be aware of all the relevant facts in sufficient time to do this and it is consistent with the policy of the Convention that all claims should be settled with reasonable promptness. However, in extreme cases (*e.g.* where there has been fraud which the claimant only discovers after a substantial period of time), the defendant should not be able to shelter behind the words of the Convention.[1]

1216

Rights of recourse and actions for indemnities

A person who has become liable to make a payment under the Salvage Convention 1989 may be able to recover a sum in respect of part or all of that payment from a third party. The question then arises whether his action against the third party is subject to limitation under Article 23 of the Convention, under the general law, or under some other special provision.[2]

1217

---

[97] See Gaskell, 21–427.
[98] Under Art. 7.
[99] One possibility is that a contract is rescinded because of misrepresentation as to the existence of a danger. Such a situation would not be one of salvage, so any claim for payment would not be under the Convention or subject to the two-year time bar. *cf.* Gaskell, 21–427.
[1] See F. Bennion, *Statutory Interpretation* (3rd ed., 1997), Chap. 22.
[2] Obviously, where the action against the third party is not governed by Art. 23, the limitation period may be more or less than, or the same as, under the Convention.

There are three bases upon which a claimant may wish to pursue an action against a third party. The first arises where the claimant has discharged the third party's liability to make a payment under the Convention[3] and he seeks to recover the amount from the third party ("Case 1"). The second and third arise where the claimant has had to discharge his own liability to make such a payment: he may be able to claim damages from the third party as compensation ("Case 2")[4]; or the third party (who might or might not be liable independently of contract) may be contractually obliged to indemnify him ("Case 3"). In all three cases, the claimant is likely to run out of time if he awaits determination of his liability before instituting proceedings against the third party.

1218 The Salvage Convention 1989 contemplates two types of claims against third parties: rights of recourse, and actions for indemnities. As to rights of recourse ("Case 1"), the Convention provides that a State party may in its national law provide that the payment of a reward has to be made by one of several interests liable to pay a salvage reward, subject to a right of recourse of this interest against other interests for their respective shares,[5] and that nothing in Article 14, on special compensation,[6] shall affect any right of recourse on the part of the owner of the vessel.[7] However, there is no specific provision for limitation of actions to enforce rights of recourse. On the other hand, Article 23.3 of the Convention provides that an action for an indemnity by a person liable[8] may be instituted even after the expiration of the two-year limitation period provided by Article 23.1–2 if brought within the time allowed by the law of the State where proceedings are instituted.[9] Actions for indemnity clearly fall within Case 3 above and the word "indemnity" might be argued to extend to Case 2,[10] though it is submitted that it does not do so.

1219 Case 1 is a situation in which the third party was liable to make a payment under the Convention and the claimant is seeking to recover in respect of that payment. However, it does not follow that the right of recourse is one for a payment under the Convention; if it is not, it should not be subject to the limitation period in Article 23. *A fortiori*, an action for damages ("Case 2") or for an indemnity ("Case 3") (in which the third party, now the defendant,

---

[3] *e.g.* where the shipowner has been obliged to discharge the cargo-owner's liability for salvage.
[4] *e.g.* where salvage services were necessitated by the third party's collision with the claimant's vessel.
[5] Art. 13.2. See *post*, Chap. 16.
[6] See *ante*, Chap. 5.
[7] Art. 14.6.
[8] *i.e.* liable to make a payment under the Convention.
[9] The Hague-Visby Rules make similar provision for actions of indemnity against third parties after the expiration of the one year Hague-Visby limit: see the Carriage of Goods by Sea Act 1971, Sched., Art. III, r. 6*bis*. See *Xhina Ocean Shipping Co. (Owners of Xingcheng) v. Andros (Owners of the Andros) (The Andros)* [1987] 1 W.L.R. 1213 (Hong Kong: PC).
[10] *cf.* Gaskell, 21–428.

was not primarily liable to make a Convention payment) should not be treated as an action which is prima facie subject to Article 23. If that is correct, it was unnecessary to provide in Article 23.3 that the Article 23.1 limitation period does not apply to the action for an indemnity, except for the purpose of making the position clear.[11]

---

[11] If, however, this is regarded as incorrect, it would be the Art. 23.1 limitation period that should apply *a fortiori* to Case 1 rights of recourse.

CHAPTER 13

PROCEEDINGS

1. THE GENERAL POSITION

1220   A successful salvor has a claim to a salvage reward (originally in Admiralty law, now under the International Salvage Convention 1989 and subject to contract). Individual claimants are entitled to pursue their claims independently and to recover separate awards. However, in practice, it is at least convenient for all matters arising from the same salvage operations to be settled together and for a single award to be made with individual salvors being entitled to their appropriate shares.

1221   With this in mind, LSSAC 2000, cl. 13 provides that the Contractors may claim salvage on behalf of their employees and any other servants or agents who participate in the services and on behalf of authorised sub-contractors,[1] including their employees servants and agents.[2] However, as noted above,[3] an agreement between the Contractors and the salvees cannot by itself confer authority upon the Contractors to claim on behalf of designated third parties and does not prevent such third parties enforcing their own claims. Accordingly, clause 13 requires Contractors bringing such claims, if required by the salvees, to provide a reasonably satisfactory indemnity against claims being brought directly by the relevant third parties.[4]

1222   The normal forum for settlements of claims or disputes, actual or potential, is, of course, the courts. However, if the parties agree, the matter may be referred to arbitration. Since the introduction of Lloyd's Form of salvage agreement, arbitration has become the normal method for resolution of disputes or differences concerning salvage, which is the reason why few salvage cases now appear in the law reports. In recent years there has been a growing interest in exploring alternative means of dispute resolution. Indeed, an overriding objective or purpose of LOF 2000 is "to ensure that it leads to a fair and efficient disposal of disputes between the parties whether amicably,

---

[1] Under LSSAC 2000, cl. 13.2. See *ante*, § 1036.
[2] LSSAC 2000, cl. 13.1 and 13.2.
[3] *Ante*, Chap. 9, § 799.
[4] LSSAC 2000, cl. 13.1 and 13.3. The terminology differs slightly, not always necessarily, in the two parts of cl. 13. The contractors "shall upon request" under cl. 13.1 and "shall, if called upon so to do" under cl. 13.3 provide the necessary indemnity.

The general position

by mediation or by arbitration within a reasonable time and at a reasonable cost".[5] And the latest edition of Lloyd's Procedural Rules now provides that "The Arbitrator shall ensure that in all cases the represented parties are informed of the benefit which might be derived from the use of mediation".[6] Nonetheless, at present, arbitration remains the standard method of resolving salvage issues.

Claims for salvage rewards, as extended by statute,[7] may be brought by actions *in rem* and *in personam*.[8] In support of his claim, the salvor has a possessory lien[9] and a maritime lien.[10] Moreover, the High Court has power to order the preservation of property relevant to a cause of action.[11] This is supplemented by the power of the receiver of wreck to detain the salved property until payment is made for salvage or process is issued for the arrest or detention of the property by the court.[12] The maritime lien and procedure *in rem*, with the possibility of arrest of the defendant's property, give the salvor advantages over ordinary civil actions. They are important in practice in encouraging defendants to put up security or, more commonly, to arrange for this to be done by third parties, in order to avert the application of admiralty procedures. Where a salvee has been able to avoid the jurisdiction *in rem* and has not submitted to the jurisdiction of the court or arbitrator or put up security, the salvor will have to rely on an action *in personam*.[13] However, the effectiveness of such an action depends on his being able to effect service of proceedings on the defendant and upon the prospect of effectively levying execution if any sum awarded is not paid.

1223

---

[5] LSSAC 2000, cl. 2(d).
[6] LPR 2000, r. 6.
[7] To bring within Admiralty jurisdiction claims of an extended salvage nature not falling within the Admiralty Court's recognition of salvage claims.
[8] For the procedure in Admiralty claims, see CPR 49, *Practice Direction—Admiralty; Civil Procedure 2001*, §2A.
[9] See *post*, §§ 1228–1245.
[10] See *post*, §§ 1247–1252.
[11] SCA 1981, ss 33(1) and 35.
[12] MSA 1995, s.226. See *The Fulham* [1899] P. 251 (CA). The receiver may sell property known by its owners to be detained: see MSA 1995, s.227. For the position of wreck and the receiver generally, see *ibid.*, ss 231–55.
[13] See SCA 1981, s.21. See *The Two Friends* (1799) 1 C. Rob. 271, 277, *per* Lord Stowell (a case of prize salvage); *Five Steel Barges* (1890) 15 P.D. 142, 146, *per* Sir James Hannen P. *cf. The Hope* (1801) 3 C. Rob. 215; *The Trelawney*, *ibid.*, 216n.; *The Meg Merrilies* (1837) 3 Hagg. 346; *The Rapid* (1838) 3 Hagg. 419; *The Cargo ex Schiller* (1877) 2 P.D. 145; *The Medina* (1876) 1 P.D. 272; 2 P.D. 5 (salvage agreement); *The Prinz Heinrich* (1888) 13 P.D. 31 (salvage agreement); *The Elton* [1891] P. 265; *The Cargo ex Port Victor* [1901] P. 243; and a Scottish case, *Duncan v. Dundee, Perth and London Shipping Co.* (1878) 5 R. 742.

High Court jurisdiction[14]

1224 The jurisdiction of the High Court[15] to hear and determine salvage claims is governed by the Supreme Court Act 1981 as amended.[16] In particular, the Supreme Court Act 1981, s.20(2)(j) provides that the High Court has Admiralty jurisdiction to hear and determine any claim—

"(i) under the Salvage Convention 1989;
(ii) under any contract for or in relation to salvage services; or
(iii) in the nature of salvage not falling within (i) or (ii) above;
or any corresponding claim in connection with an aircraft."

"In subsection (2)(j)—
(a) the 'Salvage Convention 1989' means the International Salvage Convention 1989 as it has effect under section 224 of the Merchant Shipping Act 1995;
(b) the reference to salvage services includes services rendered in saving life from a ship and the reference to any claim under any contract for or in relation to salvage services includes any claim arising out of such a contract whether or not arising during the provision of the services;
(c) the reference to a corresponding claim in connection with an aircraft is a reference to any claim corresponding to a claim mentioned in sub-paragraph (i) or (ii) of paragraph (j) which is available under section 87 of the Civil Aviation Act 1982."

Not every claim arising as a result of a subject of salvage being in a position of danger is a claim within section 20(2)(j). Thus, a claim for breach of the Lloyd's Form duty not to allow removal of salved cargo[17] is not within

---

[14] Salvage claims of course form only part of the wider jurisdiction of the courts over Admiralty and other claims and cannot be dealt with comprehensively in this book. See more fully on jurisdiction and procedure: *Civil Procedure 2001*; Dicey & Morris, Chap. 13; Jackson; N. Meeson, *Admiralty Jurisdiction and Practice* (2nd ed., 2000).

The general jurisdiction of the English courts is also subject to the provisions of the Brussels Convention on Jurisdiction and Enforcement of Judgments 1968 and related provisions, the application of which in English jurisdiction is at the time of writing governed by the Civil Jurisdiction and Judgments Act 1982. The Brussels Convention 1986 will be superseded from March 1, 2002 by Council Regulation (EC) No. 44/2001 of December 22, 2000 on Jurisdiction and the Recognition and Enforcement of Judgments in Civil and Commercial Matters (2000) 44 O.J. L12. The Regulation provides specifically in Art. 5.7 that:

"A person domiciled in a Member State may, in another Member State, be sued: . . . as regards a dispute concerning the payment of remuneration claimed in respect of the salvage of a cargo or freight, in the court under the authority of which the cargo or freight in question:
(a) has been arrested to secure such payment, or
(b) could have been so arrested, but bail or other security has been given;
provided that this provision shall apply only if it is claimed that the defendant has an interest in the cargo or freight or had such an interest at the time of salvage."

[15] The jurisdiction of the County Court to hear such claims has been abolished: the Civil Courts (Amendment) (No. 2) Order 1999 (S.I. 1999 No. 1011).

[16] SCA 1981, s.20(1)(a) and (2)(j).

[17] See *post*, §§ 1253–1254.

s.20(2)(j); nor was it within s.20(2)(g) (a claim for loss of or damage to goods carried in a ship) or s.20(2)(h) (a claim arising out of an agreement relating to the carriage of goods in a ship).[18] Similarly, a claim alleging negligence by salvors is not within s.20(2)(j) but it may fall within another head of Admiralty jurisdiction, *e.g.* as damage done by a ship within s.20(2)(e) or arising out of an agreement relating to the use or hire of a ship (rendering services under Lloyd's Form) under s.20(2)(h).[19]

2. SECURITY

(a) *Introduction*

1225 Once salvage services terminate, the salvor will wish to identify those persons who are liable to pay for the services rendered and their insurers, who in most cases in practice will be responsible for handling their clients' claims and arranging or providing security for the release of their property.

Claimants are entitled to use all legal means of maximising their chances of recovery, just as defendants are entitled to utilise all such means to minimise their liability. As a general rule, a claimant will only be able to force the defendant to meet a claim against him once a tribunal has decided liability. But, even then, whether the claim can be enforced in full depends on whether the defendant is willing to pay or has sufficient assets available to meet both the claim in question and claims brought by third parties. It is therefore to the claimant's advantage if he can obtain security for his claim, ensuring that it is met in full regardless of the defendant's willingness or ability to pay, either in part or in full.

1226 A defendant may be encouraged to put up security for a claim made against him in order to obtain the release of an asset held by the claimant or in order to avert action, in particular action to obtain security. But there is no general rule of English law that a defendant must provide security, even when the claim is supported by a maritime lien. However, in a limited range of circumstances, the defendant may be obliged to put up security, in particular where his property is arrested in proceedings *in rem*[20] or where a freezing (*Mareva*) injunction has been granted against him.[21] Furthermore, where in Admiralty proceedings property has been arrested or bail or other security has been given to prevent or obtain release from arrest, and those proceedings are stayed on the ground that the dispute should be submitted to arbitration, the court granting the stay may nevertheless order that the property arrested be retained as security for the satisfaction of any arbitration award given in the

---

[18] *The Tesaba* [1982] 1 Lloyd's Rep. 397.
[19] See *The Escherheim* [1976] 1 W.L.R. 430 (HL).
[20] See *ante*, §1223.
[21] See SCA 1981, s.37; CPR 25.1(1)(f).

arbitration in respect of the dispute or order that the stay be conditional on the provision of equivalent security for that purpose.[22] The Brussels Salvage Convention 1910 made no provision for security but there are now obligations to provide security both under the Salvage Convention 1989[23] and Lloyd's Form.[24]

1227 The provision of security affords an obvious benefit to the claimant, in ensuring that his claim will be met, and to the defendant, in ensuring that his assets are otherwise freely available to him. In practice it will be important because, in the case of a general cargo ship for example: the salvor is unlikely to be able easily to ascertain the range of defendants and their insurers or to be able effectively to proceed against them all; neither party will know exactly how salvage liability is going to be assessed; and salvees and third parties are likely to be prejudiced by property's being detained, deteriorating and incurring charges, pending resolution of salvage awards. The interests of all parties will hinge on a proper balance being struck between the salvor's obtaining adequate security for his legitimate demands and the avoidance of prejudice to salvees and their insurers from unreasonable or excessive demands for security.

(b) *Possession*

Introduction

1228 As we have just seen, the rights of a salvor are protected generally by his maritime lien, his rights of action *in rem* and *in personam*, and the statutory provisions for detention by a receiver of property which is liable for salvage. Seeing that the salvor is so fully protected, and that his position does not normally require to be fortified by retention of salved property, the Admiralty Court generally views with disfavour any attempt on his part to exclude from the possession or control of it the owner or the owner's agents or servants. Moreover, Lloyd's Form requires the contractor to rely on the contract's provision for security and not detain the property salved except as provided by the contract.[25] Nonetheless, it was recognised, both at common law[26] and in Admiralty, that in certain circumstances salvors in principle have possessory rights, which therefore merit some consideration here.

---

[22] Arbitration Act 1996, s.11. See further *post*, § 1271.
[23] Art. 21. See *post*, § 1256.
[24] See *post*, §§ 1255 *et seq.*
[25] See LOF 1995, cl. 6(c) and LSSAC 2000, cl. 4.9; discussed *post*, § 1265.
[26] See *ante*, Chap. 2.

Derelict

Possessory rights of first salvors

The general principles of the law governing the possessory rights of first salvors were stated thus by the Privy Council in *Cossman v. West*[27]: **1229**

> "In the case of salvors there is a distinction between a derelict and a vessel which, though in great danger, has not been abandoned by the master and crew. In the case of a derelict, the salvors who first take possession have not only a maritime lien on the ship for salvage services, but they have the entire and absolute possession and control of the vessel, and no one can interfere with them except in the case of manifest incompetence; but in an ordinary case of disaster, when the master remains in command he retains the possession of the ship, and it is his province to determine the amount of assistance that is necessary, and the first salvors have no right to prevent other persons from rendering assistance if the master wishes such aid. So unless a vessel is derelict the salvors have not the rights as against the master to the exclusive possession of it, even though he should have left it temporarily, but they are bound on the master's returning and claiming charge of the vessel to give it up to him."

Derelict

Where, therefore, a vessel is in fact derelict,[28] the first salvors taking possession of her prima facie have a right of exclusive possession. Their rights may be protected by an injunction and/or an award of damages, and possibly by a declaration. In *The Tubantia*,[29] in 1916, a Dutch steamship, believed to be carrying treasure, was sunk in the North Sea, 50 miles from the English coast. In 1922, the plaintiffs located the wreck in about 100 feet of water, attached buoyed moorings to it, and during two seasons kept craft above the wreck from which work was carried out when weather and tide permitted. There were only two possible working periods of one and three-quarter hours per working day; and there were no more than 25 working days in 1923. Also, the working plant was liable to be carried away or destroyed by the sea. Despite expenditure of over £40,000, the plaintiffs had recovered little of value when the defendants arrived with a powerful, well-equipped vessel to find the wreck and take possession. By high-handed and deliberate interference, they endeavoured to prevent further work by the plaintiffs and to establish themselves in concurrent occupation. The plaintiffs claimed a declaration to establish their alleged possessory rights, an injunction to restrain interference by the defendants with their possession of or operations upon the *Tubantia*, and damages for trespass and wrongful interference with their **1230**

---

[27] (1887) 13 App. Cas. 160, 181 (PC, NS). See also *The Dantzic Packet* (1837) 3 Hagg. 383, 385; *The Effort* (1834) 3 Hagg. 165, 167; *The Gertrude* (1861) 31 L.J. Adm. 130, 131 ("she was legally a derelict, and, consequently, when the salvors got possession they were entitled to keep possession"); *The Champion* (1863) Br. & Lush. 69, 71; *The Tubantia* [1924] P. 78, 92.

[28] See *ante*, Chap. 3.

[29] [1924] P. 78.

lawful business. Finding the things in question to be derelict, Sir Henry Duke P. also found that the plaintiffs had possession[30]:

> "A thing taken by a person of his own motion and for himself, and subject in his hands, or under his control, to the uses of which it is capable, is in that person's possession.... There was *animus possidendi* in the plaintiffs. There was the use and occupation of which the subject matter was capable. There was power to exclude strangers from interference if the plaintiffs did not use unlawful force. The plaintiffs did with the wreck what a purchaser would prudently have done. Unwieldy as the wreck was, they were dealing with it as a whole. The fact on the other side which is outstanding is the difficulty of possessing things which lie in very deep water and can only be entered upon by workmen in fine weather and for short periods of time. Must it be said that ... the vessel, and her cargo, were incapable of possession? To my mind this would be an unfortunate conclusion, very discouraging to salvage enterprise at a time when salvage, by means of bold and costly work, is of great public importance."

1231 He found the defendants guilty of trespasses to goods in the plaintiffs' possession and wilful and wrongful molestation of them in their lawful undertaking, which he said was actionable where it causes damage. He concluded[31]:

> "A possessory right is of a limited and perhaps transitory kind, and I am not minded to make a declaration which might be misconstrued as evidence of some other than a possessory right. An injunction is properly claimed when there is the threat or danger of repetition of the wrongs complained of, especially when they affect material interests, though it is to be strictly limited so as not to enlarge the rights of the one party or to infringe the rights of the other. The defendants' interference with the plaintiffs, moreover, was high-handed and deliberate, and, unless restrained, they may repeat it. I propose, therefore to restrain the defendants, their servants and agents, until further order of the Court from doing any acts at or near the wreck of the *Tubantia* whereby the plaintiffs may be prevented from or hindered in carrying on salvage operations thereon. My judgment to this effect must be with costs against the defendants. There is a claim for damages and some evidence of damage in loss of time of divers. If the plaintiffs desire a reference they must have it."

Limitations on the right

1232 Apart from having a right to possession in certain circumstances, salvors have been said to be, whilst in possession, under a duty to the owners of the

[30] *ibid.*, 89, 90.
[31] *ibid.*, 94.

salved property.[32] The nature of their duties in this respect has not been fully examined, though at least they would have duties not to be negligent or to deliver the property to someone without a valid claim to it.[33] In any event, whatever the nature of their duties, salvors' rights of possession have been expressed to be subject to qualifications. Thus, in one case, Dr Lushington said that "it is ... expedient, where it can be done, to permit a master and crew to approach their own ship."[34] In another case, he said[35]:

> "[The salvor] retained possession of the [derelict] vessel, and, under the circumstances, I am of opinion he had no right to do so. It is perfectly true it is laid down by some authorities that there is a right to possession in salvors, but that is a defence never received by this court without great consideration. I cannot conceive that there could be any rule more mischievous to the commercial interests at large, and to the property salved, than that it should be held that, under whatever circumstances, it was the duty of the salvors to retain the property."

Consistently with the principle of success,[36] the right of possession is dependent on the salvor's ability to effect successful salvage. Thus, it has been said to exist "if he alone can salve the property"[37] or "if [the salvors] thought themselves sufficient to effect the service."[38] An honest belief, reasonably held, will presumably be sufficient to justify the repulsion of further salvors. Where there is "manifest incompetence",[39] subsequent salvors will be entitled to intervene, and the first salvor ought not to refuse further efficient aid if the success of his operations comes at any time into jeopardy.[40] **1233**

Property not derelict

General rule

Where a vessel is not derelict, the general rule is that the lawful right to possession of both the ship and its cargo remains in the shipowner, and the salvor's acts are subject to the ultimate control of the master. The owner or his **1234**

---

[32] See, *e.g.* Kennedy (4th ed.), p. 364 and *The Lady Worsley* (1855) 2 Spinks E. & A. 253, 255 (quoted in this paragraph (text to n. 35)). Presumably the movement from "right" to "duty" in the judgment was intentional. Albeit a derelict is, by definition, *sine animo revertendi*, the salvors do not acquire proprietary rights, which remain with the original owner or vest in the Crown: see *e.g.* *The Dantzic Packet* (1837) 3 Hagg. 383, 385: "he takes possession indeed for the benefit of the Crown." A salvor acts to confer a benefit; otherwise, he would simply be acting in his own interest. *cf. post*, §1234. See too *The Gertrude* (1861) 30 L.J. Adm. 130, 131 "though the master and crew of ship might have come back to her, yet the salvors were not at liberty to surrender possession."
[33] See Palmer, *Bailment* (2nd ed., 1991), 45–61, 689–697.
[34] *The Gertrude* (1861) 30 L.J. Adm. 130, 131.
[35] *The Lady Worsley* (1855) 2 Spinks E. & A. 253, 255.
[36] See *ante*, Chap. 8.
[37] *The Dantzic Packet* (1837) 3 Hagg. 383, 385.
[38] *The Effort* (1834) 3 Hagg. 165, 167.
[39] *Cossman v. West* (1887) 13 App. Cas. 160, 181.
[40] *The Cambria* (December 15, 1848) *Pritchard*, Vol. 2, p. 1822 (Irish).

representative has a right to decide whether salvage assistance shall be employed or not, whether salvors in addition to those already acting should be engaged,[41] and, subject to liability for breach of a salvage contract made with the salvor,[42] whether or not salvors whose services he *has accepted* shall be superseded by others.[43] Thus, in a case where a vessel had been temporarily abandoned not so as to make her derelict,[44] Holroyd J. said[45]:

> "the subsequent taking possession by the salvors was not adverse, but an act done for the benefit of the owners, and therefore did not dispossess them. The custody of the vessel was in the salvors till the salvage was paid; but the legal possession was still in the owners."

As Dr Lushington put it in a later case[46]:

> "unless the vessel has been utterly abandoned, and is according to the legal meaning of the word a derelict, the occupying salvor is bound to submit to the orders of the master, when the master appears and claims his authority ... [A]s between the master and salvors, unless the vessel is absolutely derelict, and the master's authority at an end, he is entitled to resume charge of the ship, to employ whom he pleases, and to take what measures he thinks proper for the preservation of the ship. The occupying salvors are entitled to reward for the services they have actually rendered, but no more."

1235 Dr Lushington gave reasons for the general principle in *The Glasgow Packet*[47]:

> "In some cases, it is true, salvors have a right to retain possession to secure for themselves the compensation which may be due. But such rule has no place here, for here was no possession acquired by a completed salvage service; and what is a still more important fact (for it is the foundation upon which salvors are at any time allowed to retain possession) there was no necessity for retaining the ship to secure the demands upon the owners, for the ship could not by possibility, under the circumstances, have escaped the process of this Court. Again, it has been suggested, in vindication of their resistance that they themselves considered the further continuance of their services necessary for the final

---

[41] *The Dantzic Packet* (1837) 3 Hagg. 383.
[42] See *ante*, Chap. 8.
[43] *The Black Boy* (1837) 3 Hagg. 386n; *The Glasgow Packet* (1844) 2 W. Rob. 306, 313; *The Barefoot* (1850) 14 Jur. 841, 842; *The Samuel* (1851) 15 Jur. 407, 410; *The Martha* (1859) Swab. 489, 491.
[44] See *Cossman v. West* (1887) 13 App. Cas. 160, 177–178; *The Pinnas* (1888) 6 Asp. M.L.C. 313; *The Kedah* (1948) 81 Ll.L.Rep. 217.
[45] *Thornley v. Hebson* (1819) 2 B. & Ald. 513, 519.
[46] *The Champion* (1863) Br. & Lush. 69, 71.
[47] (1844) 2 W. Rob. 306, 312–313.

Property not derelict

preservation of the vessel; a ground of defence which, in my judgment, is still less tenable and satisfactory."

Effect of owner's/master's right to possession

1236 Retention of possession gives the master not only rights but duties. Sir John Nicholl thus declared[48]:

> "I hope it will be understood that the master, so long as he retains the command, is fully entitled to regulate the quantum of assistance to be given to his vessel; and he may be extremely blameable if he does not avail himself of all that is at hand, and he may consider necessary."

Exceptions

1237 Exceptions to the general rule have been acknowledged in some cases of possession by salvors of vessels which have been abandoned temporarily, *i.e.* which are not derelicts in the proper sense of the term.[49]

The principal exception concerns *protection of security*, that is, the case where the salvor can prove that a surrender of the salved property would mean the loss of the security for his reward. This is the foundation upon which salvors are at any time allowed to retain possession.[50]

1238 Exceptions also occur where there are *peculiar circumstances*. In exceptional cases, salvors may be entitled to resist the orders or intervention of the master of the vessel in distress. In *The Elise*,[51] the *S.S. Northumbia* came across the *Elise* on fire, her master and crew having taken to the boats. A volunteer crew from the *Northumbia* boarded her and worked during the night to bring the fire under control, on two occasions refusing the request of the master of the *Elise* to be put on board his vessel with his crew. The brief report states that "Gorell Barnes J. held that, though the master and crew of the *Elise* had a legal right to return to their vessel, the Court will not lay down any general rule, but will be guided by the circumstances of each case, and here the master of the *Northumbia* was justified in refusing to put them on board." Similarly, in a case where, in very bad weather, all but two of the crew had gone into a ship which had collided with the vessel in danger and the colliding vessel was later encountered by the salving vessel, Dr Lushington said[52]:

> "I do not say there are no circumstances in which it is in the bounden duty of the master and crew to come on board and resume the control of

---

[48] *The Dantzic Packet* (1837) 3 Hagg. 383, 386.
[49] See, *e.g.* the cases *supra* in n. 44.
[50] *The Glasgow Packet* (1844) 2 W. Rob. 306, 312–13.
[51] [1899] W.N. 54.
[52] *The Orbona* (1853) 1 Spinks E. & A. 161, 165.

their own vessel; but not under circumstances like these. Looking at the season of the year, and the state in which the vessel was in, the salvors had an undoubted right to keep possession and carry the vessel to a port of safety."

The guiding rule is summarised in a dictum of Sir James Hannen P.[53]:

"I can conceive of the possibility of such circumstances that would morally excuse a man for saying, 'You must not interfere; it is a critical moment, and if you interfere in the way you propose we shall lose the ship'. Circumstances of that kind might arise."

1239 However, the question is one to be decided on the facts of each case. In *The Kedah*,[54] some time before a professional salvage tug made fast to a vessel abandoned by her master and crew, the tug's master sent out a wireless message suggesting that the crew should return to man her and assist in the operation. But the operation had been completed by a boarding party from the tug and the vessel was proceeding comfortably in tow at about five or six knots by the time her master and crew came up with her, in a small boat from land. The tug's master refused to allow them to go back on board their vessel and the boarding party took up the means of scrambling aboard the vessel, rendering it impossible for her master and crew to do so. Willmer J. said[55]:

"*Prima facie*, they had an absolute right to return to their vessel, and, *prima facie*, unless the circumstances forbade it, the salvors had no business to exclude them from access to their own vessel."

His Lordship thought the controlling factor in the mind of the master in acting as he did was the chance of getting a larger reward if he could say the vessel was derelict—though in no sense could that excuse the refusal. However, in the circumstances it was reasonable for him to take the view that, the tow being comfortably under way, a reduction in speed to allow reboarding was undesirable, involving the risk of the hawser's parting when speed had to be regained. It could not be said that his action was wholly unreasonable having regard to the circumstances and in particular to the fact that the master and crew, if allowed back on board, could not have done anything to assist in the operation; it made no difference to the operation. Therefore, the question having to be decided on the facts of each case, such misconduct had no effect on the award.[56]

---

[53] *The Pinnas* (1888) 6 Asp. M.L.C. 313, 314.
[54] (1948) 81 Ll.L.Rep. 217.
[55] *ibid.*, 222.
[56] *cf. The Marie* (1882) 7 P.D. 203.

First salvors' rights of possession against second salvors

First salvors are entitled to possession against subsequent salvors, provided **1240** they remain capable of effecting salvage and subject to the owners' rights of supersession.[57] In *The Glasgow Packet*,[58] Dr Lushington said:

> "In ordinary cases, when the assistance of one set of salvors has been accepted, and they are competent to fulfil the service which they have undertaken, they cannot be dispossessed by subsequent salvors.
>
> But this principle has no application to the present case. Here the vessel was actually sunk, and it was impossible for the salvors to have raised her by their own unassisted exertions. And moreover, the owners were upon the spot to give the orders which they deemed best for the preservation of their own property."

Six years later, he considered the matter again in *The Glory*[59]:

> "This brings me to consider the principle of law. Ordinarily that principle is this: where salvors are in possession of a vessel, and their services have been accepted, and they are adequate to discharge what they have undertaken with safety to the vessel, and with facility, it is not competent for any other set of persons, even one of Her Majesty's vessels, to come and interfere with the salvors so engaged in such operation. But there is no principle of law that I am aware of, and I think it would be dangerous for the idea to be entertained for a single moment, that in a doubtful case, seeing that the salvors were in possession of the vessel, and their services had been accepted, they would be justified in refusing further assistance. I cannot conceive that any notion can be broached more injurious to the security of the mercantile navy of this country, than a notion, that because a man happened first to go on board a vessel, and then a steam-tug was offered, he had a right to refuse that assistance, and claim to perform the duty himself, because, by possibility, a set of salvors might heave a vessel by an anchor, or succeed in getting her off the sand . . . . Several of the affidavits say that it is a custom, from time immemorial, that when once one body of men is in possession of a vessel, they are not to be interfered with by the other. That is a mistaken notion, and never will receive the countenance of this Court."

A first salvor's right to possession or to exclude the services of later salvors **1241** only remains whilst he justifiably retains possession or attempts to provide services continuously. Thus, a second set of salvors, able to perform the

---

[57] See *ante*, §1229.
[58] *The Glasgow Packet* (1844) 2 W. Rob. 306, 313.
[59] (1850) 14 Jur. 676, 678.

salvage, is entitled to resist the claim to repossess themselves of first salvors, who had abandoned their original employment to join in rendering assistance and left with the ship's complement.[60]

Effect of salvor's conduct

1242 Where the property is not derelict but the owner or his representative either has never ceased to be in possession or has intervened after a temporary absence, a salvor who has begun operations during a temporary absence, or whose services have been accepted, is normally entitled to remuneration for his contribution to salvage before the interruption.[61] However, if he persists in obtruding his aid after the owner or his representative has dispensed with it[62] or if he tries forcibly to exclude the aid of others whom the owner or his representative deems it necessary to employ in the work of salvage,[63] his conduct or misconduct will be a relevant factor in assessing his potential reward, certainly for further services, and possibly also for past services.[64]

1243 The effects of misconduct depend on the facts of each case.[65] Thus, a salvor may not be prejudiced by his misconduct where it had no practical effect[66] or where it arose from a mistake or misunderstanding.[67] His award may be confined to expenses incurred[68]; he may be allowed only part of his costs or even altogether deprived of costs[69]; the reward may be diminished[70]; or, in a gross case, it may be forfeited entirely.[71] As to the procedure to be adopted in taking account of misconduct, Pilcher J. said, in a case of quite venial misconduct arising from a misunderstanding, *The Trumpeter*[72]:

> "In some cases which have been before this Court—cases where misconduct either grave or venial has been made out—the Court has indicated

---

[60] *The India* (1842) 1 W. Rob. 406.
[61] *The Champion* (1863) Br. & Lush. 69, 71. *cf. The Glasgow Packet* (1844) 2 W. Rob. 306, 311.
[62] *The Glasgow Packet* (1844) 2 W. Rob. 306. See also *The Dantzic Packet* (1837) 3 Hagg. 383, 385; *The Samuel* (1851) 15 Jur. 407, 410; *The Capella* [1892] P. 70.
[63] *The Dantzic Packet* (1837) 3 Hagg. 383; *The Barefoot* (1850) 14 Jur. 841, 842; *The Martha* (1859) Swab. 489.
[64] *The Barefoot* (1850) 14 Jur. 841.
[65] *The Kedah* (1948) 81 Ll.L.Rep. 217.
[66] *The Kedah, supra.*
[67] *The Trumpeter* (1947) 80 Ll.L.Rep. 263.
[68] *The Dantzic Packet* (1837) 3 Hagg. 383; *The Glasgow Packet* (1844) 2 W. Rob. 306.
[69] *The Glory* (1850) 14 Jur. 676 (two-thirds of costs allowed); *The Barefoot* (1850) 14 Jur. 841; *The Pinnas* (1888) 6 Asp. M.L.C. 313; *The Capella* [1892] P. 70. See also *The Trumpeter* (1947) 80 Ll.L.Rep. 263. *cf. The Martha* (1859) Swab. 489 (costs allowed because original conduct laudable); *The Alenquer and the René* [1955] 1 Lloyd's Rep. 101, 116.
[70] *The Glasgow Packet* (1844) 2 W. Rob. (reward for services prior to misconduct); *The Glory* (1850) 14 Jur. 676; *The Marie* (1882) 7 P.D. 203.
[71] *The Barefoot* (1850) 14 Jur. 841; *The Capella* [1892] P. 70.
[72] (1947) 80 Ll.L.Rep. 263, 271.

the sum which it would have awarded the salvors but for the misconduct and has then indicated the sum which it proposes to deduct in respect of the misconduct.[73] In other cases the Court, after dealing with the facts and taking everything into consideration, has simply awarded the salvors a sum, stating that such misconduct as has been proved has been taken into consideration in arriving at that sum. I propose in this case to follow the latter course."

A salvor will not be prejudiced merely because he has been guilty of some misconduct if it has no effect on the salvage operations.[74] Thus, in *The Trumpeter*,[75] where, operating under a misunderstanding of their rights, plaintiffs salving a vessel in Galway Bay declined to redeliver her immediately to her master and crew but, after beginning to take her to Milford Haven, eventually redelivered her at Berehaven, on the south-west coast of Ireland, they were not liable for lost fishing when, because she had lost her boat and Carley float, Lloyd's Agent at Berehaven required her to go on to Milford Haven. The last subsequent act of Lloyd's Agent was held to be through no fault of the salvors.

1244

On the other hand, misconduct may affect an award though it does not occasion material damage. In *The Marie*,[76] the captain of a small French vessel intended to signal for a pilot, which was all that he needed. Ten men came aboard and acted throughout in a violent, overbearing and threatening way, albeit not amounting to wilful or criminal misconduct. The judge[77] entertained considerable doubt whether the master of the brig sustained any pecuniary loss by what was done and saw no reason to believe that the salvors did that which occasioned any extra expenditure. But, finding it impossible to hold that their action worked a forfeiture of the whole remuneration, it was nevertheless such as to produce a diminution. Where the position is more doubtful, as where the judge cannot say with certainty that the salvors' preventing the use of a steam necessarily entailed the loss happening, misconduct may still justify diminution of the reward.[78] Indeed, Lord Stowell has expressed the view, in denying costs to salvors, that "even services of the highest class might be lessened by subsequent misconduct, and especially by

1245

---

[73] See, *e.g. The Glory* (1850) 14 Jur. 676, 677, *per* Dr Lushington: "Now, with regard to the case itself, I propose to deal with it in the following manner:— First, I shall consider it as a mere case of salvage, and then take into consideration the nature of the service rendered, and what would be the reward which ought to be given to the parties for the performance of such a service. Secondly, I shall consider whether or not the misconduct which has been attributed to the salvors is established by the evidence in the cause, and what are those principles of law which ought to guide my judgment in determining the present case."
[74] *The Kedah* (1948) 81 Ll.L.Rep. 217, discussed *ante*, §1239; *The Trumpeter* (1947) 80 Ll.L.Rep. 263.
[75] *ibid.*
[76] (1882) 7 P.D. 203.
[77] Mr A. Cohen, Q.C., judge of the Court of Admiralty of the Cinque Ports.
[78] See *The Glory* (1849) 14 Jur. 676, 678.

exorbitant demands" (as to the reward payable).[79] Thus, Dr Lushington once said[80]:

> "Adequate rewards encourage the tendering and acceptance of salvage services; exorbitant demands discourage their acceptance, and tend to augment the risk and loss of vessels in distress."

Possession and receiver of wreck

1246 The Merchant Shipping Act 1995 makes certain provisions in respect to delivery of possession of salved property to Receivers of Wreck.[81] By sections 226, 236 and 237,[82] provision is made for the delivery to the Receiver of Wrecks of all wreck found or taken possession of in United Kingdom waters or outside United Kingdom waters but brought within those waters. The receiver shall detain property in respect of which salvage is due until process of a competent court has been issued for its detention, or payment of salvage has been made, or has been adequately secured. It has been held that, after a receiver has released property on security being given, salvors have no right to detain the property or arrest it by warrant of the Admiralty Court.[83] Failure to deliver wreck to the receiver without reasonable cause involves penalties, including forfeiture of any claim to salvage. But this provision is meant to apply to a criminal and improper detention, whereby it is sought to practise a fraud upon the Crown or the owner, and not to salvors who have restored the property to the owners[84]; it does not apply to salvors who remain in possession for the safety of the vessel[85] nor to a person who takes possession of a stranded vessel under the bona fide belief that it is his property.[86]

(c) *Maritime Liens*

1247 A maritime lien[87] is a claim or privilege over maritime property which arises by operation of law simultaneously with the cause of action, and travels

---

[79] *The John and Thomas* (1822) 1 Hagg. 157n., 158n.
[80] *The Nimrod* (1850) 7 N.o.C. 570, 579 (claim for £8,000; bail taken for £6,000; reward £600). See also *The Earl Grey* (1853) 1 Spinks 180; *The George Gordon* (1884) 9 P.D. 46 (ship arrested for exorbitant sum; salvors required to pay defendants' costs and expenses in finding bail); *The Marguerite Molinos* [1903] P. 160; *The Tribels* [1985] 1 Lloyd's Rep. 128. Of course, the mere fact that a claim is disallowed will not automatically lead to the plaintiffs' not obtaining costs: see *The Bedeburn* [1914] P. 146.
[81] On receivers of wreck, see generally MSA 1995, Pt IX.
[82] See *The Fulham* [1898] P. 206; [1899] P. 251 (CA). As to the term "wreck", see s.255(1) and *ante*, Chap. 3.
[83] *The Lady Katherine Barham* (1861) Lush. 404.
[84] *The Zeta* (1875) L.R. 4 A. & E. 460.
[85] *The Glynoeron* (1905) 21 T.L.R. 648.
[86] *The Liffey* (1887) 6 Asp.M.L.C. 255.
[87] For definitions, see the dicta cited in D. R. Thomas, *Maritime Liens* (1980), §10.

Maritime liens

with the property into whosesoever's possession it comes whether or not they have notice of the claim giving rise to it. Its advantages are: that it is enforceable by an action *in rem*, so that its threatened or actual exercise acts as an inducement to the defendant to put up security; and it confers a high priority over other claims. Maritime liens have been recognised by the Admiralty Court as arising in respect of four claims, of which a claim for a salvage reward is one[88]; a fifth claim has been added by statute.[89] A salvage maritime lien has also been provided for in three international conventions on maritime liens and mortgages agreed in the twentieth century[90]; however, none of the conventions have become part of English law. The law on maritime liens is a matter of procedure, to be determined by the *lex fori*,[91] and the Salvage Convention 1989, Art. 20(1) provides that "Nothing in this Convention shall affect the salvor's maritime lien under any international convention or national law." It is nonetheless part of English law that the operation of maritime liens is affected by security arrangements made by parties, including those contained in the Convention.

The lien attaches to ship, cargo and freight which has been salved and has by statute been extended to aircraft, their cargo and apparel[92]; but not to the proceeds of sale of such property.[93] It accrues immediately, by operation of law, upon the accrual of the cause of action: and in the case of salvage, upon the successful performance of a salvage service in the traditional sense. The circumstances in which it arises and its scope may be extended by statute; but it has not been extended to other claims giving rise to a payment under the Salvage Convention 1989.[94] Maritime liens may not be created by contract for circumstances in which they do not otherwise exist at law, though their existence, regulation and discharge may be confirmed and provided for by

1248

---

[88] The earliest case appears to be *Tranter v. Watson* (1703) 2 Ld Raym. 931 (arrest of cargo for prize salvage). See also *The Two Friends* (1799) 1 C. Rob. 271, 277; *The Eleanora Charlotta* (1823) 1 Hagg. 156; *HMS Thetis* (1833) 3 Hagg. Adm. 14, 48; *The Bold Buccleugh* (1851) 7 Moo. P.C. 267. There is a maritime lien whether the salvage claim arises under Admiralty law or from a contract such as one under Lloyd's Form: see *The Goulandris* [1927] P. 182 (in which the contract, on Lloyd's Form, expressly provided for a maritime lien; see now *post*, § 1248).

[89] The other categories recognised by the Admiralty Court are: damage done by a ship; seamen's wages; and bottomry and respondentia. By statute the master has a maritime lien for remuneration, disbursements and liabilities (see now MSA 1995, s.41). Despite the approach of Dr Lushington in *La Constancia* (1846) 2 W.Rob. 404, there is no maritime lien for a towage claim (*Westrup v. Great Yarmouth Co.* (1889) 43 Ch.D. 241) and probably none for pilotage charges (see *The Ambatielos, The Cephalonia* [1923] P. 68, 72).

[90] International Convention for the Unification of Certain Rules Relating to Maritime Liens and Mortgages 1926, Art. 2(3); International Convention for the Unification of Certain Rules Relating to Maritime Liens and Mortgages 1967, Art. 4(1)(v); International Convention on Maritime Liens and Mortgages 1993, Art. 4.1(c).

[91] *Bankers Trust International Ltd v. Todd Shipyards Corp. (The Halcyon Isle)* [1981] A.C. 221 (Sing. PC).

[92] See Thomas, *Maritime Liens* (1980), §38.

[93] *The Optima* (1905) 10 Asp. M.L.C. 147. They may, however, be subject to a freezing (*Mareva*) injunction.

[94] See *ante*, § 1211; Brice, §6–111. The Convention, Art. 14 states that special compensation is payable by "the owner" of the vessel threatening environmental damage.

contract. Reproducing[95] LOF 1995, cl. 6(a), LSSAC 2000, cl. 4.7 stipulates that, "Until security has been provided as aforesaid the Contractors shall have a maritime lien on the property salved for their remuneration". However, even if the word "remuneration" were capable of being applied to payments other than for salvage rewards in the traditional sense, the clause would not be effective to create a maritime lien for special compensation.[96] Similarly, although SCOPIC 2000, cl. 1 specifically provides that "For the purposes of liens ... the services hereunder will be treated in the same manner as salvage", it is incapable of creating a *maritime* lien for services not qualifying as salvage under Admiralty law. Similarly, a person with claims for a salvage reward and for something not giving rise to a maritime lien under Admiralty law (such as special compensation)[97] against a single defendant may enforce a maritime lien over the defendant's property in respect of the salvage reward but not in respect of the other claim.[98]

1249 A maritime lien is effective even if its existence is unknown and it endures into whosoever's ownership or possession its subject-matter comes,[99] subject to the defence of sovereign or diplomatic immunity.[1]

By virtue of the lien, a salvor in possession of the *res* may retain[2] possession.[3] But possession is unnecessary for the lien to be effective[4] and is disapproved by the Admiralty Court, since the salvor has more appropriate remedies by way of judicial process and agreement. The maritime lien is a basis for the jurisdiction of the Admiralty Court and enforceable by means of an action *in rem*[5] so that, if necessary, the subject-matter may be arrested and in due course sold. The threat of judicial process constitutes the lien a form of provisional security and a means of inducing the salvee to avert arrest by acceptance and acknowledgment of service (if proceedings are begun) and in any event (either personally or, more likely, through a third party) to put up security, so that his property is either not arrested or is released from arrest. However, the privilege must not be abused and the Admiralty Court will

---

[95] With the exception that LOF 1995, cl. 6(a) used the singular "Contractor" and "his" instead of "Contractors" and "they".

[96] In fact, the Form implicitly distinguishes between salvage remuneration and special compensation, so the clause is otiose except in so far as it makes clear that the security provisions of Lloyd's Form do not *per se* override the maritime lien, which endures until security has actually been provided in accordance with the terms of LSSAC 2000.

[97] *cf.* the International Convention on Maritime Liens and Mortgages 1993 (not in force), Art. 2 of which ensures that claims for special compensation are not the subject of maritime salvage liens.

[98] *cf.* Gaskell, 21–423.

[99] Even into the hands of a bona fide purchaser without notice.

[1] See *ante*, Chap. 12.

[2] But, if out of possession, the salvor is not entitled to self help and to seize possession. See *infra*, n. 5.

[3] See *ante*, §§ 1228–1246.

[4] *The Eleanora Charlotta* (1823) 1 Hagg. 156.

[5] SCA 1981, s.21(3). "There is no other way of enforcing his lien": *The Goulandris* [1927] P. 182, 192, *per* Bateson J.

Maritime liens

express its disapproval of a lienee who makes unreasonable or excessive demands for security.[6] In fact, the need to coerce the salvee to put up security is reduced under the Salvage Convention 1989, for Article 21 imposes a duty on persons liable to make a payment due under the Convention to provide security.[7] In addition, Article 20.2 specifically provides that "The salvor may not enforce his maritime lien when satisfactory security for his claim, including interest and costs, has been duly tendered or provided" and Lloyd's Form[8] forbids the contractor from arresting or detaining the salved property except in specified circumstances. Nevertheless, the maritime lien and the procedure *in rem* will remain important where the salvee fails to discharge his duty under Article 21.

Where sufficient security is provided, the claimant should be able to obtain full satisfaction of his claim regardless of the defendant's insolvency. Where he relies on his maritime lien, his claim is traditionally given high priority. The principles and policies influencing the order of priorities are well recognised, though the Admiralty Court retains jurisdiction to apply them flexibly.[9] The prima facie order of priorities is: the costs of and consequent upon arrest; special legislative rights[10]; possessory liens (but subject to earlier maritime liens, and *semble* later salvage liens, and possibly earlier statutory liens); salvage liens; liens for damage, seamen's and master's wages, master's claims, and bottomry and respondentia (in that order); mortgages; and statutory rights *in rem* ("statutory liens").[11] Salvage liens are accorded high priority on the ground that the salvage service has preserved the *res* and therefore the fund against which competing claims are pressed.[12] Consequently, multiple salvage maritime liens take effect in inverse order of attachment: *i.e.* later salvage liens take precedence over earlier salvage liens. The effect of these principles is that a salvage maritime lien has priority over all other liens which have attached before the salvage service was rendered[13] unless it can be shewn that, on the special facts of a particular case, the application of the principle would produce a plainly unjust result.[14] A salvor's lien also ranks before maritime liens for claims for wages earned and master's

1250

---

[6] See *ante*, §1245.
[7] See *post*, §§ 1255 *et seq.*
[8] LOF 1995, cl. 6(c); LSSAC 2000, cl. 4.9. See *post*, § 1265.
[9] *The Ruta* [2000] 1 Lloyd's Rep. 359.
[10] *The Veritas* [1901] P. 304.
[11] On priorities generally see Jackson, Chap. 23; N. Meeson, *Admiralty Jurisdiction and Practice* (2nd ed., 2000), Chap. 6; W. Tetley, *Maritime Liens and Claims* (2nd ed., 1998), Chap. 24(III), pp. 1400–1402; D. R. Thomas, *Maritime Liens* (1980), Chap. 9.
[12] See, *e.g. The Gustaf* (1862) Lush. 506, *per* Dr Lushington; *The Mons* [1932] P. 109, 111, *per* Langton J.; *The Lyrma (No. 2)* [1978] 2 Lloyd's Rep. 30.
[13] *The Lyrma (No. 2)* [1978] 2 Lloyd's Rep. 30, following *The Veritas* [1901] P. 304 (earlier salvage services); *The Mons* [1932] P. 109 (earlier wages); *The Inna* [1938] P. 148 (earlier damage). See also *The Selina* (1842) 2 Not. of Cas. 18 and *The Sabina* (1842) 7 Jur. 182 (earlier wages); *Cargo ex Galam* (1863) B. & L. 167, 181 (earlier bottomry); and *The Elin* (1883) 8 P.D. 39, 129 (CA) and *The Longford* (1889) 14 P.D. 34 (earlier damage).
[14] *The Lyrma (No. 2)* [1978] 2 Lloyd's Rep. 30, 33, *per* Brandon J.

disbursements incurred after it arises,[15] before subsequent possessory liens[16] and before the Crown's right of forfeiture.[17] However, it will be postponed in favour of a lien for subsequent damage[18] or for subsequent salvage,[19] which, it seems, would including a claim subsequently arising for bottomry or for wages arising from services which preserve the *res*.[20]

1251 It was held in *The Lyrma (No. 2)*[21] that, even though the principle is to give the salvor *priority* (rather than exclusive rights) for preserving the fund against which claims are pressed and although salvage awards are not assessed for the full amount of the salved property,[22] the salvor is entitled to enforce his lien in full even though it has the effect of exhausting the fund. In *The Lyrma (No. 2)* that occurred because of failure to realise the maximum value of the salved fund at the earliest opportunity.[23] However, Brandon J. thought the situation would be the same even where the reason for exhausting the fund was that the parties to a salvage contract had fixed in advance an amount of remuneration which equalled or even substantially exceeded eventual salved values, unless the agreement could be impugned on some equitable or other ground.[24]

1252 Maritime liens are lost *inter alia*[25] by delay,[26] by the extra-judicial sale of the *res*[27] and, most commonly in practice, by agreement or the fulfilment of

---

[15] *The Lyrma (No. 2)* [1978] 2 Lloyd's Rep. 30, distinguishing *The Mons* [1932] P. 109, in which the salvors had conceded priority to wages and disbursements incurred subsequently to the salvage services. See also *The Gustaf* (1862) Lush. 506; *The Elin* (1883) 8 P.D. 39. The reason for the rule, given by Brandon J. in *The Lyrma (No. 2)* [1978] 2 Lloyd's Rep. 30, 34, was that, "but for the preservation of the salved property by the earlier services, the wages claimants would not have had the opportunity of earning the later wages, in respect of which they have a personal remedy against the shipowners as well as a maritime lien on the ship, at all." *Quaere* how many mariners will be satisfied with the knowledge that they have had the opportunity to invest time in acquiring a right which may be effectively unenforceable.

[16] *The Gustaf* (1862) Lush. 506; *The Russland* [1924] P. 55. It is immaterial that the possessory lienee's work benefits salvors: *ibid.*, 59, *per* Hill J.

[17] *Att.-Gen. v. Norstedt (The Triton)* (1716) 3 Price 97; *The Inna* [1938] P. 138, 153–154.

[18] *The Veritas* [1901] P. 304 (the principle being that a claim which arises involuntarily should have priority over one arising voluntarily).

[19] *The Veritas* [1901] P. 304.

[20] *The Selina* (1842) 2 Not. of Cas. 18 ("without the men the vessel could not have been safely brought to this country").

[21] [1978] 2 Lloyd's Rep. 30.

[22] See *post*, Chap. 15.

[23] However, a salvor who neglects to exercise his rights to the prejudice of other claimants cannot rely on the Admiralty Court's tolerance of his conduct, especially since the implementation of the policy of more efficient progress of claims underlying the Civil Procedure Rules.

[24] [1978] 2 Lloyd's Rep. 30, 33–34, following *The Inna* [1938] P. 138, in which this occurred. The possibility of impugning the agreement "on some equitable or other ground" will not avail third parties if the salvee is unable or unwilling to impugn the agreement on the basis of one of the conventional vitiating factors. They will need to demonstrate some basis on which they can have the agreement upset: see *ante*, Chap. 9.

[25] For a full list of circumstances, see Thomas, *Maritime Liens* (1980), Chap. 11.

[26] Whether by the salvor's laches (*The Royal Arch* (1857) Swab. 269, 285; *The Optima* (1905) 10 Asp. M.L.C. 147, 149) or (more likely now) by failure to exercise within the two-year limitation period (see *ante*, Chap. 12).

[27] *The Optima* (1905) 10 Asp. M.L.C. 147.

judicial process to enforce the lien.[28] Mere entry into a salvage agreement does not extinguish the lien, which prevails for services rendered both before and after entry into the agreement.[29] Whether an agreement has this effect depends upon whether it is intended to have that effect and that intention has been fulfilled.[30] In most, if not all, cases extinction of the lien will depend, not on a partial remedy but on the actual provision of security or the successful completion of judicial process to similar effect.[31] Thus, if the claim were litigated and a judgment *in personam* were obtained but unsatisfied, the salvor could still sue to enforce his maritime lien.[32] In *The Goulandris*,[33] the ship was subjected by an Egyptian court to a "*saisie conservatoire*", the ship was subsequently sold by the owners' trustee in bankruptcy (*cum onere* and not free of incumbrances, as on an English judicial sale) and an arbitration award was made but not satisfied. Since the salvors had not bargained to release their maritime lien for such partial remedies, they remained entitled to enforce it by proceedings *in rem*.

(d) Duty not to remove salved property

The Salvage Convention 1989, Art. 21.3 provides that, without the consent of the salvor, the salved vessel and other property shall not be removed from the port or place at which they first arrive after the completion of the salvage operations until satisfactory security has been put up for the salvor's claim against the relevant vessel or property. **1253**

Furthermore, once the property salved has been taken by the contractors to the place specified in the Lloyd's Form contract,[34] until security has been provided, it must not be removed from there without their written consent (which must not be reasonably withheld).[35] Where they give such consent on condition that they are provided with temporary security pending completion of the voyage, Lloyd's Form stipulates[36] that their maritime lien on the property salved shall remain in force to the extent necessary to enable them to compel the provision of security in accordance with the contract.[37]

Since the salvor's main concern is to obtain payment for the services rendered, the object of restraining movement of the salved property is to **1254**

---

[28] A maritime lien over cargo is not lost simply because it ceases to be cargo and becomes (part of) a permanent structure: *Sembawang Salvage Pte Ltd v. Shell Todd Oil Services Ltd* [1993] 1 N.Z.L.R. 97 (NZ HC) (steel space-frame structure for drilling platform salved on barge then subsequently attached to sea-bed remained subject to maritime lien).
[29] *The Goulandris* [1927] P. 182.
[30] *The Goulandris* [1927] P. 182.
[31] See *The Goulandris* [1927] P. 182.
[32] See, *e.g. The Goulandris* [1927] P. 182, especially at 193–194 and 195 ("in order to get rid of it there must be a decision in an action *in rem* or something equivalent to it").
[33] [1927] P. 182.
[34] Under LOF 1995, cl. 1(a) or LOF 2000, cl. A respectively. See *ante*, § 1064.
[35] LOF 1995, cl. 6(b); LSSAC 2000, cl. 4.8.
[36] LOF 1995, cl. 6(b); LSSAC 2000, cl. 4.8.
[37] Under LOF 1995, cl. 5(c) and LSSAC 2000, cl. 4.5 respectively.

support such payment, the normal remedy for breach of the obligations under consideration is compensation for loss by way of damages, and the loss is likely to be no more than failure to pay the sums already due, a salvor will prima facie be better off claiming damages from the salvee for breach of these obligations than he would by simply claiming the payments due.[38] However, he will acquire a right to damages against contracting parties other than the relevant debtor (most obviously against shipowners in possession of cargo) and will have a right to apply for an injunction to restrain breach, whether against a contracting salvee who has not paid or a shipowner in possession of such a person's cargo. These provisions therefore reduce any need the salvor might contemplate to take or retain possession of salved property.

(e) *Provision of security*

1255 In practice salvors will wish to secure their claims at the earliest opportunity. By statute they are generally entitled to a two-year time period in which to bring claims[39] and there is no obligation, either under the general law or the Convention, to expedite requests for security. However, contracts on LOF 2000 include an Important Notice 1, headed "Salvage security", which states:

> "As soon as possible the owners of the vessel should notify the owners of other property on board that this agreement has been made. If the Contractors are successful the owners of such property should note that it will become necessary to provide the Contractors with salvage security promptly in accordance with Clause 4 of the LSSA Clauses referred to in Clause I. The provision of General Average security does not relieve the salved interests of their separate obligation to provide salvage security to the Contractors."

LSSAC 2000, cl. 4.1 then provides that:

> "The Contractors shall immediately after the termination of the services or sooner notify the Council and where practicable the Owners of the amount for which they demand salvage security (inclusive of costs expenses and interest) from each of the respective Owners."[40]

1256 Similarly, the salvee is prima facie not obliged to provide security. But the Salvage Convention 1989, Art. 21.1 provides that, "Upon the request of the

---

[38] However, his claim will not be subject to the shorter time limits on claims for salvage reward and special compensation. See *ante*, Chap. 12. But it does not fall within Admiralty jurisdiction: see *The Tesaba* [1982] 1 Lloyd's Rep. 397; *ante*, §1224.
[39] See *ante*, Chap. 12, §1205.
[40] LSSAC 2000, cl. 4.1. LOF 1995, cl. 5(a) is the same except for the use of the singular for "Contractors" ("Contractor") and "they" ("his").

Provision of security

salvor a person liable for a payment due under this Convention shall provide satisfactory security for the claim, including interest and the costs of the salvor".[41] Article 21.1 is triggered by any "request" of the salvor, and such a request need not be made under the procedure provided by Lloyd's Form. However, the liability to provide security under Article 21.1 is imposed only on "a person liable for payment due under this Convention" and such liability only arises once the relevant service has been performed, *i.e.* either on termination of a salvage service or on prevention or minimisation of environmental damage (which may predate salvage).

Where Lloyd's Form is used, further provision of security is made for claims for special compensation as follows by LSSAC 2000, cl. 4.2[42]: **1257**

> "Where a claim *is made or may be made* for special compensation the owners of the vessel shall on the demand of the Contractors *whenever made* provide security for the Contractors[43] claim for special compensation provided always that such demand is made within 2 years of the date of termination of the services."

The clause applies only to claims for special compensation, which are also claims for payments under the Salvage Convention 1989 and therefore already within Article 21.1. However, Article 21.1 only applies once liability has arisen, whereas LSSAC 2000, cl. 4.2 authorises demands for security in anticipation of liability for special compensation accruing.[44] SCOPIC 2000 is clearer as, once it is invoked, there is automatically liability for SCOPIC remuneration and an almost simultaneous, automatic obligation to provide "Initial Security" for SCOPIC Remuneration, as follows[45]:

---

[41] In the event of an interim payment under the Salvage Convention 1989, Art. 22 (see *post*, § 1291), the security provided under Art. 21 must be reduced accordingly: Salvage Convention 1989, Art. 22.2.

[42] Emphasis added. LOF 1995, cl. 5(b) is the same except with the words "Contractor" (for "Contractors"), "Contractor's" (for "Contractors") and "two" (for "2").

[43] *Sic*.

[44] The wording is somewhat ambiguous and, it is submitted, would benefit from redrafting. Whereas the Convention, Art. 21.1 only authorises demands for security against persons who are actually *liable*, LOF 2000, cl. 4.2 could be argued to authorise them simply where *claims* are or *may be* made. This is wider than stating, as Lloyd's Form might have done, that security may be claimed against shipowners who are or may become liable for special compensation. However, it is unreasonable to suppose that the Lloyd's Form clause was designed to authorise security other than in support of a genuine belief in the actual or anticipated liability of the defendant, in which case it is presumably directed to facilitating security in anticipation of liability arising, as well as after it has done so. However, the proviso to LOF 2000, cl. 4.2 ("provided always that such demand is made within 2 years of the date of the termination of the services") is somewhat at odds with this conclusion. For, although it can apply to demands made both two years before and two years after termination of the services, and although in practice a salvor is unlikely to have to avoid demanding security more than two years in advance of termination, the wording of the proviso more naturally applies from and after the date of termination. Yet there is a pre-existing two-year time limit on Convention claims (under Art. 23: see *ante*, §1205), so that it is arguable that, to be given substance, LOF 2000, cl. 4.2 must apply to claims other than those contemplated by the Convention. However, such an argument is unlikely to succeed.

[45] SCOPIC 2000, cl. 3(i).

"The owners of the vessel shall provide to the Contractor within 2 working days (excluding Saturdays and Sundays and holidays usually observed at Lloyd's) after receiving written notice from the contractor invoking the SCOPIC clause, a bank guarantee or P.&I. Club letter (hereinafter called 'the Initial Security') in a form reasonably satisfactory to the Contractor providing security for his claim for SCOPIC remuneration in the sum of U.S.$3 million, inclusive of interest and costs."

Currency of security

1258 LOF 1995 contains a space to be completed for the currency in which security is provided to the Council of Lloyd's,[46] failing which it has to be provided in pounds sterling.[47] LOF 2000 provides for security to be provided in an agreed currency or, if none is agreed, in United States dollars. Thus, Box 4 on the face of LOF 2000 provides space for the insertion of the "Agreed currency of any arbitral award and security (if other than United States dollars)". LSSAC 2000, cl. 4 then provides that the security demanded thereunder[48] "must be demanded and provided in the currency specified in Box 4 or in United States dollars if no such alternative currency has been agreed".[49]

Amount and variation of security

1259 The amount of security demanded under Lloyd's Form must be reasonable in the light of the knowledge available to the contractors at the time when the demand is made (and, under LSSAC 2000, any further facts which come to the Contractors' attention before security is provided).[50] It has been held: that there is an implied term in Lloyd's Form that the salvor will not demand excessive security; that an injunction can be issued to restrain such a demand; and that the arbitrator could require the salvor to pay all or part of the expense of providing excessive security.[51] Under LOF 1995, the arbitrator has an absolute discretion to order the contractor to pay the whole or part of the expense of providing excessive security or security which has been unreasonably demanded for special compensation under LOF 1995, cl. 5(b) and to deduct such sum from the remuneration and/or special compensation.[52] LSSAC 2000, cl. 4.4 provides that the arbitrator may, at any stage of the proceedings, order that the amount of security be reduced or increased, as the case may be. SCOPIC 2000, when that applies, contains provision for the Initial Security to be varied in relation to the anticipated amount of SCOPIC remuneration as follows[53]:

---

[46] LOF 1995, cl. 1(e).
[47] LOF 1995, cl. 1(f).
[48] Under LSSAC 2000, cl. 4.1–4.2.
[49] LSSAC 2000, cl. 4.3.
[50] LSSAC 2000, cl. 4.4; LOF 1995, cl. 5(c).
[51] *The Tribels* [1985] 1 Lloyd's Rep. 129.
[52] LOF 1995, cl. 10(a)(iii). A similar power is implicit in LPR 2000, cl.1(c).
[53] SCOPIC 2000, cl. 3. Disputes shall be resolved by the Arbitrator: *ibid.*, cl. 3(iv).

Provision of security

"(ii) If, at any time after the provision of the Initial Security the owners of the vessel reasonably assess the SCOPIC remuneration plus interest and costs due hereunder to be less than the security in place, the owners of the vessel shall be entitled to require the Contractor to reduce the security to a reasonable sum and the Contractor shall be obliged to do so once a reasonable sum has been agreed.

(iii) If at any time after the provision of the Initial Security the Contractor reasonably assesses the SCOPIC remuneration plus interest and costs due hereunder to be greater than the security in place, the Contractor shall be entitled to require the owners of the vessel to increase the security to a reasonable sum and the owners of the vessel shall be obliged to do so once a reasonable has been agreed."

Form of security and the liability of the Council of Lloyd's

1260 Unless otherwise agreed, security provided under Lloyd's Form must be provided (i) to the Council of Lloyd's (ii) in a form approved by the Council and (iii) by persons, firms or corporations either acceptable to the Contractors or resident in the United Kingdom and acceptable to the Council.[54] No particular form of security is prescribed[55] either by Lloyd's Form or the Council of Lloyd's, but normally, except where SCOPIC is invoked, the Council will not simply accept a letter of undertaking from a P. & I. Club. Under Lloyd's Form, the Council of Lloyd's shall not be responsible for the sufficiency (whether in amount or otherwise) of any security which shall be provided nor the default or insolvency of any person, firm or corporation providing the same.[56]

Liability for security

1261 As a general rule, a person is only bound to satisfy his own liability and any obligation he has to provide security only extends to the amount of his own liability; he is not generally bound to provide security for someone else's liability or to ensure that that other person provide security. LOF 2000 attempts to notify the owners of property on board a salved vessel of their liability in "Important Notice 1" towards the end of the Form, which *inter alia* states that:

"If the Contractors are successful the owners of such property should note that it will become necessary to provide the Contractors with

---

[54] LOF 1995, cl. 5(c); LSSAC 2000, cl. 4.5.
[55] The usual form is set out *post*, See Apps 10–15.
[56] LOF 1995, cl. 5(c): LSSAC 2000, cl. 4.5.

salvage security promptly in accordance with [LSSAC 2000, cl. 4].[57] The provision of General Average security does not relieve the salved interests of their separate obligation to provide salvage security to the Contractors."

1262 However, not all cargo-owners may appreciate their liability, be easily identifiable to the Contractors or be willing to satisfy their obligations to provide security. Accordingly, without prejudice to the salvee's general duty to provide security in respect of his own liability,[58] the Salvage Convention 1989, Art. 21.2 stipulates that the owner of the salved vessel shall use his best endeavours to ensure that, before the cargo is released, the owners of the cargo provide satisfactory security for the claims against them, including interest and costs. This duty is reproduced, in similar terms, by LOF 1995, cl. 5(d), which provides that the owners of the vessel, their servants and agents[59] shall use their best endeavours to ensure that the cargo shall not be released before its owners provide their proportion of salvage security. LOF 2000, Important Notice 1 begins by stating that "As soon as possible the owners of the vessel should notify the owners of other property on board that this agreement has been made", then LSSAC 2000, cl. 4.6 expresses the shipowners' duty more widely, extending it to property other than cargo, and stipulating that none of the property shall be released until security has been provided in respect of that property as required.[60] The shipowners (whose normal entitlement to retain possession of other parties' property is as security for their own claims, if any) will be acting as the Contractors' agents for this purpose and their action will in any event be authorised against other parties to the contract.

1263 The duty to use best endeavours is higher than merely exercising due care but it is less than a strict duty. Thus, the shipowner will not be liable where he is required by a port authority to release cargo. If he does breach the duty, he will be liable for losses flowing therefrom, thereby effectively underwriting the liability of the owner of the relevant property; but he will of course be only nominally liable if no loss flows from his breach (*e.g.* if the owner of the relevant property discharges his liability to the salvor).

The arbitrator has an absolute discretion to include in the amount awarded to the Contractors the whole or part of any expenses reasonably incurred by them in: (i) ascertaining, demanding and obtaining the amount of security reasonably required[61]; and (ii) enforcing and/or protecting by insurance or otherwise or taking reasonable steps to enforce and/or protect their lien.[62]

---

[57] See *ante*, §§ 1255–1257.
[58] In the Salvage Convention 1989, Art. 21.1.
[59] This means of course that the shipowners are liable to ensure that their servants and agents fulfil the relevant duty. Unless they are parties to the contract, servants and agents cannot be personally liable to the salvage contractors for not doing so.
[60] In accordance with LSSAC 2000, cl. 4.5.
[61] In accordance with LOF 1995, cl. 5 and LSSAC 2000, cl. 4.5 respectively.
[62] LOF 1995, cl. 6(d); LSSAC 2000, cl. 6.3.

Disputes as to security

Disputes as to the security to be provided under LOF 2000 and SCOPIC **1264**
2000 are to be resolved by the arbitrator appointed under Lloyd's Form.[63]

(f) *Restriction on arrest or detention*

Lloyd's Form[64] provides that the Contractors shall not arrest or detain the **1265**
property salved unless one of the following conditions is fulfilled:

(i) security is not provided within a specified period after the date of termination of the services: under LOF 1995, the period is 14 days (exclusive of Saturdays and Sundays or other days observed as general holidays at Lloyd's); under LSSAC 2000, it is 21 days;

(ii) they have reason to believe that the removal of the property salved is contemplated contrary to the contract[65];

(iii) any attempt is made to remove the property salved contrary to the contract.[66]

3. ARBITRATION

Introduction

A reference to arbitration may be effected by an agreement which is **1266**
exclusively concerned with arbitration or by one dealing with other matters concerning the parties' relationship, such as Lloyd's Form. The Arbitration Act 1996 provides a framework of principles and rules governing arbitration.[67] In certain cases these are mandatory; but the general principle is that parties should be free to agree how their disputes are resolved, subject only to such safeguards as are necessary in the public interest.[68] This position is unaffected by the Salvage Convention 1989, which simply requires States parties to encourage the publication of salvage arbitral awards.[69] In the vast majority of cases, determination of matters arising from salvage operations is referred to arbitration and specific provision is made for aspects of the arbitral process. In particular, LOF 1995 and previous editions of Lloyd's Standard Form of Salvage Agreement, though overtly a contract dealing with salvage,

---

[63] LSSAC 2000, cl. 4.4; SCOPIC 2000, cl. 3(iv).
[64] LOF 1995, cl. 6(c); LSSAC 2000, cl. 4.9.
[65] Under LOF 1995, cl. 6(b) or LSSAC 2000, cl. 4.8 respectively. See *ante*, §§ 1253–1254.
[66] Under LOF 1995, cl. 6(b) or LSSAC 2000, cl. 4.8 respectively. See *ante*, §§ 1253–1254.
[67] *q.v.* It is not appropriate to consider them in detail in this book.
[68] Arbitration Act 1996, s.1(b).
[69] Art. 27. See *post*, § 1300.

have included substantial provisions dealing with arbitration. These have been removed from LOF 2000 and reconstituted in a separate document as Lloyd's Standard Salvage and Arbitration Clauses (referred to in this book as "LSSAC 2000"). They are supplemented by Lloyd's Procedural Rules (referred to here as "LPR 2000"). However, the three sets of rules contained in these documents do not exist independently of each other and the documents must be read together.

1267 This separation of the terms of the Lloyd's salvage agreement therefore produces some unnecessary repetition. Thus, LOF 1995, cl. 1(c) simply stated:

> "The Contractor's remuneration shall be fixed by Arbitration in London in the manner hereinafter described and any other difference arising out of this Agreement or the operations hereunder shall be referred to Arbitration in the same way."

However, LOF 2000, cl. I states:

> "The Contractors[70] remuneration and/or special compensation shall be determined by arbitration in London in the manner prescribed by Lloyd's Standard Salvage and Arbitration Clauses ('the LSSA Clauses') and Lloyd's Procedural Rules. The provisions of the LSSA Clauses and Lloyd's Procedural Rules are deemed to be incorporated in this agreement and form an integral part hereof. Any other difference arising out of this agreement hereunder shall be referred to arbitration in the same way."

Likewise, LSSAC 2000, cl. 1.1 provides:

> "These clauses ('the LSSA Clauses') are incorporated into and form an integral part of every contract for the performance of salvage services undertaken on the terms of Lloyd's Standard Form of Salvage Agreement as published by the Council of Lloyd's and known as 'LOF 2000' ('the Agreement' which expression includes the LSSA Clauses and Lloyd's Procedural Rules referred to in clause 6)."

1268 Furthermore, although the SCOPIC clause only operates in conjunction with a Lloyd's Form salvage agreement[71] (and therefore, prima facie at least, subject to its provisions for arbitration), LSSAC 2000, cl. 14 specifically states that:

> "Any disputes arising out of the Scopic Clause (including as to its incorporation or invocation) or the operations thereunder shall be

---

[70] *Sic.*
[71] SCOPIC 2000, cl. 1.

referred for determination to the Arbitrator appointed under clause 5[72] hereof whose award shall be final and binding subject to appeal as provided in clause 10[73] hereof."

Arbitration and the courts

Stay of proceedings and security

The normal intention in entering an agreement to refer matters to arbitration is that they should be dealt with exclusively by the arbitral tribunal. Accordingly, where a party commences proceedings in court in respect of a matter which under the agreement is to be referred to arbitration, the other party may apply to the court in which the proceedings have been brought to stay the proceedings so far as they concern that matter.[74] On such an application the court must grant a stay unless satisfied that the arbitration agreement is null and void, inoperative, or incapable of being performed.[75]   **1269**

However, even where there is a dispute as to the effect of an agreement to refer to arbitration, where the agreement, as in the case of Lloyd's Form, provides an established and respected procedure for referring to arbitration, that procedure should be halted only in exceptional circumstances. Accordingly, in a case where security had been provided, and cargo-owners argued that Lloyd's Form had been signed without their authority, but the balance of convenience was in favour of continuing the arbitration, an interlocutory injunction to restrain the arbitral proceedings was refused.[76]   **1270**

Where in Admiralty proceedings property has been arrested or bail or other security has been given to prevent or obtain release from arrest, and those proceedings are stayed on the ground that the dispute should be submitted to arbitration, the court granting the stay may order that the property arrested be retained as security for the satisfaction of any arbitration award given in the arbitration in respect of the dispute or order that the stay be conditional on the provision of equivalent security for that purpose.[77]   **1271**

Continuing role of the court

Even where it is acknowledged that matters between the parties should be resolved by arbitration, there remain a number of situations in which resort may be had to the courts. Thus, as has been seen, a court granting a stay of Admiralty proceedings in respect of matters agreed to be submitted to   **1272**

---

[72] LSSAC 2000, cl. 5. See *post*, § 1280.
[73] LSSAC 2000, cl. 10. See *post*, §§ 1302–1307.
[74] Arbitration Act 1996, s.9(1).
[75] Arbitration Act 1996, s.9(4).
[76] *Industrie Chimiche Italia Centrale v. Alexander G. Tsavliris & Sons Maritime Co. (The Choko Star) (No. 1)* [1987] 1 Lloyd's Rep. 508 (CA).
[77] Arbitration Act 1996, s.11. See further *ibid.*, s.11(2).

Proceedings

arbitration may nonetheless order that property arrested be retained or equivalent security provided for the satisfaction of any award given in the arbitration.[78]

Reference to arbitration under Lloyd's Form

1273 The foregoing provisions indicate that LOF 1995 and LOF 2000 have almost identical provisions for arbitration; but they are expressed in different ways. They deal with four matters: (1) a requirement that certain matters shall be settled by arbitration; (2) the matters which are to be settled; (3) the place of arbitration (London); and (4) the procedure and conduct of the arbitration.

As to (1) and (2), LOF 1995, cl. 1(c) provides that "The Contractor's *remuneration* shall be *fixed*", whereas LOF 2000, cl. I provides that "The Contractors[79] *remuneration and/or special compensation* shall be *determined*"; and both conclude by stating that "*any other difference* arising out of this agreement or the operations hereunder shall be *referred* to arbitration".[80] Nothing significant appears to turn on the different wording between the two editions of the Form, as italicised here. Both editions require that all matters should be settled by arbitration which arise from salvage operations governed by the contract, whether they be resolution of uncertainties (the amounts due as salvage remuneration or special compensation) or settlement of other differences or disputes.

Similarly, both editions require that all these matters be resolved in the manner provided by the contract, whether as terms set out in LOF itself (in LOF 1995) or as set out separately in LSSAC 2000 (in LOF 2000). The only difference is that, although they are referred to in LOF 1995, cl. 10(a)(ii), LOF 1995 is silent on the practice of complying with Lloyd's Procedural Rules, whereas LOF 2000 gives them express contractual effect.[81]

The parties involved

Participation, representation and service

1274 The mere fact that a person has been concerned in salvage operations does not bind him to the terms of, including arbitration under, a salvage contract unless such a contract has been concluded and he is a party to it. However, once parties have entered into to a contract, they are of course bound by its terms. So prima facie, if one party to a Lloyd's Form contract (*e.g.* a salvor) requests arbitration in accordance with its terms and the parties to be bound have been given a reasonable opportunity to participate in the arbitration,[82]

---

[78] Arbitration Act 1996, s.11; *ante*, text to n. 77.
[79] *Sic*.
[80] In LOF 2000, cl. I this is a separate sentence, so begins with a capital letter. This head would include a claim by a shipowner for damages for a negligent and unsuccessful endeavour to salve: *cf. The Escherheim* [1976] 1 W.L.R. 430 (HL).
[81] See also LSSAC 2000, cl. 10.6.
[82] See the Arbitration Act 1996, ss 13–14.

even those parties (in practice, most likely to be owners of cargo laden on board a general ship) who shew no interest in the arbitration will be bound by it. This is recorded by Lloyd's Form, which states that the arbitrator's award is (subject to the appeal procedure provided)[83] final and binding on all the parties concerned, whether they were represented at the arbitration or not.[84]

1275 The Arbitration Act 1996, s.36 entitles a party to arbitral proceedings to be represented by a person chosen by him unless otherwise agreed, and Lloyd's Form specifically acknowledges the right of parties to Lloyd's Form contracts to participate in and be represented during arbitrations and states the consequences of their non-participation. LOF 1995, cl. 9 and LSSAC 2000, cl. 7.1 state that any party to the agreement who wishes to be heard or to adduce evidence shall nominate or appoint a person. That person is defined broadly in LOF 1995, cl. 9 as "a person in the United Kingdom to represent him"; in LSSAC 2000, cl. 7.1 he is described more narrowly as "an agent or representative ordinarily resident in the United Kingdom to receive correspondence and notices for and on behalf of that party". In addition, LSSAC, cl. 7.1 specifies that the party making the appointment "shall give written notice of such appointment to the Council" of Lloyd's. LSSAC 2000, cl. 7.2 additionally provides that "Service on such agent or representative by post or facsimile shall be deemed to be good service on the party which has appointed that agent or representative". If a party fails to exercise such right of appointment, he is deemed to have renounced his right to be heard or to adduce evidence and the arbitrator or appeal arbitrator may proceed accordingly.[85] Nevertheless, under LPR 2000, r. 2(c)(i) the arbitrator is bound to have regard to the interests of unrepresented parties in determining the manner in which the arbitration is to be conducted.

1276 The provisions for representation in the 1995 and 2000 editions of Lloyd's Form appear on an initial reading to differ on points of detail but on closer scrutiny to differ also in substance. Both editions appear to be concerned with requiring foreign parties to appoint representatives resident in the United Kingdom. Neither edition appears to contemplate that one or more of the parties may already be present within the United Kingdom and therefore prima facie capable of acting without appointing a third party representative;

---

[83] See post, §§ 1302–1309.
[84] LOF 1995, cl. 10(c); LSSAC 2000, cl. 6.7.
[85] LOF 1995, cl. 9 states: "failing which the Arbitrator or Appeal Arbitrator(s) may proceed as if such party had renounced his right to be heard or adduce evidence." LSSAC 2000, cl. 7.3 states: "Any party who fails to appoint an agent or representative as aforesaid shall be deemed to have renounced his right to be heard or adduce evidence." Neither edition of Lloyd's Form stipulates the date on which the party loses such right of appointment.
Brice, §8–161 opines that LOF 1995, cl. 9 might be unenforceable if an arbitrator attempted to exclude the evidence or submission of a party resident abroad without a U.K. representative, since he could be said not to be acting fairly, as required by the Arbitration Act 1996, s.33. *Sed quaere* whether a party is treated unfairly simply by being held to the terms of the contract upon which the arbitration is based.

in fact, neither edition forbids a party from appointing himself as his required representative, though both assume that it will be a different person. The 1995 edition appears to contemplate that participation in the arbitration is dependent on appointing someone to act as an advocate during the hearing. On the other hand, the 2000 edition appears more concerned with the appointment of a solicitor prior to the arbitration, leaving the party to make whatever arrangements he wishes about the hearing itself, subject to the fact that he will not be able to participate at all without having first appointed someone to receive correspondence and notices. In practice these issues are unlikely to cause difficulties since the main decision for a party to Lloyd's Form will be whether or not he wishes to participate in the arbitration proceedings or simply to accept the tribunal's decision. If the decision is made to participate, the usual and sensible course is to secure the services of a solicitor and advocate within the United Kingdom.

The relationships between the parties and the Council of Lloyd's

1277 The relationship between parties who agree to submit their differences to arbitration is essentially contractual, *a fortiori* where the agreement to arbitrate is part of a manifestly contractual agreement such as that made on Lloyd's Form. The Lloyd's Form contract purports to impose obligations and confer rights on other parties, namely the Council of Lloyd's and the arbitrator and appeal arbitrator appointed to act by the Council.[86] However, it is a general rule (though subject to substantial qualifications)[87] that a contract cannot impose obligations or confer rights on third parties.[88] Prima facie, therefore, those provisions of Lloyd's Form which refer to third parties function as an agreement between salvor and salvee *inter se* authorising acts which may be done by or in relation to the designated third parties. Thus, the clause in Lloyd's Form that, on a written request from one of the parties, "the Council shall appoint an arbitrator"[89] cannot legally oblige the Council so to act but does commit the parties to the Lloyd's Form contract to resolving their differences in this way. In practice, of course, the Council's strict legal position is unlikely to be important. As the promoter and co-ordinator of Lloyd's Form salvage and arbitration, it is in its interests to act. Moreover, once it does act upon such a request, there is a contract between the Council and the parties. Similarly, once an arbitrator or appeal arbitrator has been appointed by the Council, there will be a contract between the Council and the arbitrator or appeal arbitrator, and also one between the arbitrator or appeal arbitrator and each of the parties to Lloyd's Form.[90]

---

[86] "Council" means the Council of Lloyd's: LSSAC, cl. 3.4.
[87] In particular, under the Contracts (Rights of Third Parties) Act 1999.
[88] See Chitty, Chap. 19; Treitel, Chap. 15.
[89] LOF 1995, cl. 7(a); LSSAC 2000, cl. 5.1.
[90] *cf.* Sir M. J. Mustill and S. C. Boyd, *Commercial Arbitration* (2nd ed., 1989 with Supp., 2001), pp. 219–223.

1278 LSSAC 2000 contains a number of references to the role of the Council of Lloyd's ("the Council").[91] It provides that any award, notice, authority, order or other document signed by the Chairman of Lloyd's or any other person authorised by the Council for the purpose shall be deemed to have been duly made or given by the Council and shall have the same force and effect in all respects as if it had been signed by every member of the Council.[92] However, any guidance published by or on behalf of the Council relating to matters such as the Convention and the workings and implementation of LOF 2000 is for information only and forms no part of the agreement on LOF 2000.

Place of arbitration[93]

1279 Parties are free to agree where arbitration is to take place. Where Lloyd's Form is used, it is specified that it shall be in London.[94] This is reiterated by LSSAC, cl. 6.2, which also further provides that the venue may be changed provided certain criteria are satisfied:

> "The arbitration shall take place in London unless (i) all represented parties agree to some other place for the whole or part of the arbitration and (ii) any such agreement is approved by the Council on such terms as to the payment of the Arbitrator's travel and accommodation expenses as it may see fit to impose."

It is trite contract law that, if all parties agree, even these conditions may be dispensed with.

Appointment and tenure of arbitrator

Appointment

1280 Parties are generally free to agree on the procedure for appointing arbitrators.[95] If they have contracted on Lloyd's Form, this is laid down in similar terms by LOF 1995, cl. 7(a) and LSSAC 2000, cl. 5.1.[96] LSSAC 2000, cl. 5.1 provides[97]:

---

[91] LSSAC 2000, cl. 3.4. LSSAC 2000, cl. 1.2 stipulates that "All notices communications and other documents required to be sent to the Council of Lloyd's should be sent to: Lloyd's Salvage Arbitration Branch, Lloyd's, One Lime Street, London EC3M 7HA. Tel: +44 (0) 207 327 5408/5407/5849. Fax: +44 (0) 207 327 6827/5252. Email: lloyds-salvage@lloyds.com" (punctuation added).

[92] LSSAC 2000, cl. 12.

[93] See also the Arbitration Act 1996, s.3 (the seat of the arbitration).

[94] LOF 1995, cl. 1(c); LOF 2000, cl. I.

[95] Arbitration Act 1996, s.16.

[96] The main difference, if any, is that LSSAC no longer specifies that the written request must be "by letter telex facsimile or in any other permanent form".

[97] LOF 1995, cl. 7(a) provides: "Whether security has been provided or not the Council shall appoint an Arbitrator upon receipt of a written request made by letter telex facsimile or in any other permanent form provided that any party requesting such appointment shall if required by the Council undertake to pay the reasonable fees and expenses of the Council and/or any Arbitrator or Appeal Arbitrator(s)."

"Whether or not security has been provided the Council shall appoint an arbitrator ('the Arbitrator') upon receipt of a written request provided that any party requesting such appointment shall if required by the Council undertake to pay the reasonable fees and expenses of the Council including those of the Arbitrator and the Appeal Arbitrator."

The object of the clause is that an arbitrator will be appointed if two conditions are satisfied[98]: (1) that the Council of Lloyd's has received a written request[99]; and (2) that, if required by the Council of Lloyd's to pay its reasonable fees and expenses, the person requesting the appointment has undertaken to do so.[1] It is not necessary that the request be made within a specified period of time[2] apart from the usual limitation period. The Council of Lloyd's maintains a panel of arbitrators from which it makes appointments.

Termination of arbitrator's authority and appointment

1281 The Arbitration Act 1996 contains provisions for the termination of an arbitrator's authority and appointment and consequences thereof.[3] In addition, Lloyd's Procedural Rules provide that, unless the parties otherwise agree, if a Lloyd's salvage arbitrator cannot agree, fix or maintain a hearing date in accordance with the Rules, he must relinquish his appointment and the Council of Lloyd's must appoint an arbitrator who can do so.[4]

Arbitrator's duties and powers

1282 In addition to duties imposed or the powers conferred upon him by law or by his contract with the Council of Lloyd's and/or the parties, several duties and powers are specified for a Lloyd's salvage arbitrator.

Arbitrator's duties

(i) He must conduct the arbitration in accordance with the Lloyd's Procedural Rules which are in force at the time he is appointed.[5] In

---

[98] Lloyd's Form no longer provides that, where security is given, then the Council shall automatically appoint an arbitrator in respect of the interests secured.

[99] It is not specified that the request must emanate from a party to the contract. This can be implied, though, given the sometimes laborious precision which is attempted elsewhere in the Lloyd's Form contract, the omission is perhaps surprising.

[1] In practice, the Council of Lloyd's will not require such an undertaking if security has been provided at Lloyd's in accordance with LSSAC 2000, cl. 4.5. If an undertaking is required, it should be that of a person or firm resident in the U.K. and acceptable to the Council. This is usually the Contractors' solicitors.

[2] *cf. The American Sioux* [1980] 2 Lloyd's Rep. 224 (CA) (reversing [1980] 1 Lloyd's Rep. 620, 623). Under an earlier version of Lloyd's Form, claims for arbitration had to be received by the Committee of Lloyd's within 42 days; once the 42 days were up, the security was automatically realised, although the Court of Appeal held that it could extend the time for arbitration by exercising its discretion under the Arbitration Act 1950, s.27. See now the Arbitration Act 1996, s.12.

[3] Arbitration Act 1996, ss 23–27.

[4] LPR 2000, r. 7(c). See *post*, § 1289.

[5] LSSAC 2000, cl. 6.1.

particular, in construing a Lloyd's Form contract or on the making of any arbitral order or award, he should have regard to the overriding purposes and objectives of the agreement as stated therein.[6]

(ii) He must normally conduct the arbitration in London.[7]

(iii) He must within six weeks of his appointment or so soon thereafter as is reasonable hold a preliminary meeting[8] and make such initial order for directions or consent orders as are appropriate.[9]

(iv) Under LPR 2000, r. 6, he must ensure that in all cases the represented parties are informed of the benefit which might be derived from the use of mediation.

Arbitrator's powers

In addition to other powers conferred on him by the parties or by law,[10] the arbitrator has the following powers in Lloyd's Form arbitrations.

1283

(i) He may admit such oral or documentary evidence or information as he may think fit.[11]

(ii) He may conduct the arbitration in such manner in all respects as he may think fit subject to applicable procedural rules.[12]

(iii) Under LPR 2000, it is stated that he may make any orders required to ensure that the arbitration is conducted in a fair and efficient manner consistent with the aim to minimise delay and expense and may arrange such meetings and determine all applications made by the parties as may be necessary for that purpose.[13]

(iv) Under LPR 2000, he may conduct all such meetings by means of a conference telephone call if the parties agree.[14]

(v) He may make separate awards on provisional and other matters.[15]

---

[6] LSSAC 2000, cl. 2.
[7] See LOF 1995, cl. 1(c); LOF 2000, cl. I.; LSSAC 2000, cl. 6.2; *ante*, § 1279.
[8] LPR 2000, r. 2(a). See further *post*, § 1285.
[9] See *post*, § 1285.
[10] See LPR 2000, r. 1 and the Arbitration Act 1996, s.38, empowering the provision of security, the inspection and preservation of property which is the subject of the proceedings or of evidence, and the examination of witnesses.
[11] LOF 1995, cl. 10(a)(i); LPR 2000, r. 1(a).
[12] LOF 1995, cl. 10(a)(ii); LPR 2000, r. 1(b). The applicable procedural rules are stated to be: in LOF 1995, "such procedural rules as the Council [of Lloyd's] may approve"; in LPR 2000, r. 1(b), "these Procedural Rules and any amendments thereto as may from time to time be approved by the Council of Lloyd's ('the Council')".
[13] LPR 2000, r. 1(e).
[14] LPR 2000, r. 1(f).
[15] See *post*, §§ 1291–1294.

Proceedings

(vi) Under LSSAC 2000, he may make a consent award between such parties as so consent, with or without full arbitral reasons.[16]

(vii) He may charge, and make orders as to, fees, costs and expenses.[17]

(viii) He may correct an award or make an additional award.[18]

Procedure and evidence

1284   The Arbitration Act 1996, s.34[19] provides that it shall be for the tribunal to decide all procedural and evidential matters (of which it includes an inclusive list), subject to the right of the parties to agree any matter. A number of such matters are expressly covered as a result of contracting on the basis of Lloyd's Form, under which arbitrations (and appeal arbitrations)[20] are conducted in accordance with Lloyd's Procedural Rules. These are expressly made part of the contract under LOF 2000.[21] However, whichever edition of Lloyd's Form is used by the parties, the edition of Lloyd's Procedural Rules applying to the arbitration is the one in force at the time the arbitrator is appointed.[22] The Rules enable the arbitrator to take an active role in managing the arbitral process.

Preliminary meetings and consent orders

1285   Within six weeks of his appointment or so soon thereafter as is reasonable, the arbitrator must hold a preliminary meeting.[23] LPR 2000, r. 2(a) states that this shall be a meeting with the parties for the purpose of giving directions as to the manner in which the arbitration is to be conducted. However, the arbitrator may dispense with the preliminary meeting if the represented parties agree a consent order for directions which the arbitrator is willing to approve.[24] So that he can decide whether to approve such a consent order, the arbitrator must be provided by the contractors or their representatives with a brief summary of the case in the form of a checklist, any other party providing such comments as they deem appropriate.[25]

Initial order for directions

1286   Unless there are special reasons, the initial order for directions shall include the following[26]:

---

[16] LSSAC 2000, cl. 6.4. See further *post*, § 1290.
[17] See *post*, §§ 1296–1298.
[18] LPR 2000, r. 1(g). See *post*, § 1301.
[19] *q.v.*
[20] LSSAC 2000, cl. 10.6; LPR 2000, r. 8(a).
[21] LOF 2000, cl. I; LSSAC 2000, cll. 1.1, 6.1, 10.6.
[22] This is made clear by LSSAC 2000, cl. 6.1.
[23] LPR 2000, r. 2(a).
[24] LPR 2000, r. 2(b).
[25] LPR 2000, r. 2(b).
[26] LPR 2000, r. 3.

Procedure and evidence

(a) a date for disclosure of documents, including witness statements;

(b) a date for proof of values;

(c) a date by which any party must identify any issue(s) in the case which are likely to necessitate the service of pleadings;

(d) a date for a progress meeting or additional progress meetings unless all represented parties with reasonable notice agree that the same is unnecessary;

(e) unless agreed by all represented parties to be premature, a date for the hearing and estimates for the likely time required by the arbitrator to read in advance and for the length of the hearing;

(f) any other matters deemed by the arbitrator or any party to be appropriate to be included in the initial order.

Disclosure of documents

1287 Unless otherwise agreed or ordered, disclosure shall be limited to the following classes of document[27]:

"(a) logs and any other contemporaneous records maintained by the shipowners[27A] personnel and personnel employed by the Contractors (including any subcontractors) and their respective surveyors or consultants in attendance during all or part of the salvage services;

(b) working charts, photographs, video or film records;

(c) contemporaneous reports including telexes, facsimile messages or prints of e-mail messages;

(d) survey reports;

(e) documents relevant to the proof of:

(i) out of pocket expenses;
(ii) salved values;
(iii) the particulars and values of all relevant salving tugs or other craft and equipment;

(f) statements of witnesses of fact or other privileged documents on which the party wishes to rely."

Experts, legal advisers and assessors

1288 Arbitrators are generally empowered to appoint experts, legal advisers and assessors,[28] though the power is not normally exercised in Lloyd's Form arbitrations. LPR 2000, r. 5 provides:

---

[27] LPR 2000, r. 4.
[27A] *Sic.*
[28] Arbitration Act 1996, s.37.

"(a) No expert evidence shall be adduced in the arbitration without the Arbitrators[28A] permission.

(b) The Arbitrator shall not give such permission unless satisfied that expert evidence is reasonably necessary for the proper determination of an issue arising in the arbitration.

(c) No party shall be given permission to adduce evidence from more than one expert in each field requiring expert evidence save in exceptional circumstances.

(d) Any application for permission to adduce expert evidence must be made at the latest within 14 days after disclosure of relevant documents has been effected."

The hearing

1289 In fixing or agreeing a date for the hearing of a Lloyd's Form arbitration (or appeal arbitration), unless agreed by all represented parties, the arbitrator shall not fix or accept a date unless he can allow time to read the principal evidence in advance, hear the arbitration and produce the award to the Council of Lloyd's for publication in not more than one month from the conclusion of the hearing.[29] Once a date for the hearing has been fixed, it must be maintained unless application to alter the date is made to the arbitrator within 14 days of the completion of discovery or unless the arbitrator in the exercise of his discretion determines at a later time that an adjournment is necessary or desirable in the interests of justice or fairness.[30] Unless all parties represented in the arbitration agree otherwise, if a hearing date cannot be agreed, fixed or maintained in accordance with these rules due to the arbitrator's commitments, the arbitrator must relinquish his appointment, in which event the Council of Lloyd's must appoint in his stead another arbitrator who is able to meet the requirements of these rules.[31]

The award

1290 Under LSSAC 2000, an arbitrator may make a consent award between such parties as so consent, with or without full arbitral reasons.[32]

Separate awards

Under the Arbitration Act 1996, unless otherwise agreed by the parties, the tribunal may make more than one award at different times on different aspects of the matters to be determined, in particular relating to an issue affecting the

---

[28A] *Sic.*
[29] LPR 2000, r. 7(a).
[30] LPR 2000, r. 7(b).
[31] LPR 2000, r. 7(c).
[32] LSSAC 2000, cl. 6.4.

whole claim or to a part only of the claims or cross-claims submitted to it for decision.[33]

Moreover, the Arbitration Act 1996, s.39 provides generally that, if the parties agree, but not otherwise, the tribunal has power to order on a provisional basis any relief which it would have power to grant in a final award: *e.g.* a provisional order for the payment of money, or an order to make an interim payment on account of the costs of the arbitration.[34] Particular provision is made for interim payments by the Salvage Convention 1989, which provides that: "The tribunal having jurisdiction over the claim of the salvor may, by interim decision, order that the salvor shall be paid on account such amount as seems fair and just, and on such terms including terms as to security where appropriate, as may be fair and just according to the circumstances of the case."[35] Unlike the provision in the Arbitration Act 1996, s.39, which is only triggered by the parties' agreement, the power in Article 22 exists unless the parties make contrary agreement.[36] However, Lloyd's Form puts the matter beyond doubt. LOF 1995, cl. 10(a)(iv) states that "The Arbitrator shall have power to . . . make interim Award(s) including payment(s) on account on such terms as may be fair and just". Likewise, LSSAC 2000, cl. 6.5 states that "The Arbitrator shall have power to make a provisional or interim award or awards including payments on account on such terms as may be fair and just." **1291**

The power is significant for salvors, as modern salvage often involves high initial outlay (not only of a continuing nature but also, more importantly, in relation to the salvage operations in issue) and then a delay before arbitration and payment. Arbitrators have tended to exercise their powers to make interim awards for out-of-pocket expenses incurred. Where the prospects of further payments are high (*e.g.* where liability is admitted, or admitted up to a certain amount, or salved values are high), it may well seem appropriate to advance the settlement process.[37] **1292**

However, three factors restrain the exercise of this power. The first is the general rule that the matter should be capable of separate determination, that the arbitrator should only determine the matter specifically referred to him, and that he should specify this in his interim award.[38] Secondly, in principle there should be a single hearing to resolve the matters to be determined by **1293**

---

[33] Arbitration Act 1996, s.47(1)–(2). If the tribunal exercises this power, it must specify in its award the issue, or the claim or part of a claim, which is the subject-matter of the award: *ibid.*, s.47(3).
[34] Arbitration Act 1996, s.39(1)–(2), (4). Provisional awards are subject to the tribunal's final award, which must take account of such order: *ibid.*, s.39(3).
[35] Salvage Convention 1989, Art. 22.1. In the event of an interim payment under Art. 22, the security provided under Art. 21 (see *ante*, § 1256) must be reduced accordingly: *ibid.*, Art. 22.2.
[36] Salvage Convention 1989, Art. 6.1. See *ante*, Chap. 9.
[37] To some extent this may counterbalance an arbitrator's reluctance to order the payment of compound interest. See *post*, § 1475.
[38] See, *e.g. The Kostas Melas* [1981] 1 Lloyd's Rep. 18, 26, *per* Robert Goff J.

arbitration. Given that this hearing should in any event be arranged with reasonable expedition, it needs to be demonstrated that there is good reason to depart from this practice by interim action.[39] Thirdly, the arbitration process as a whole must be properly conducted. A salvage arbitrator must act in accordance with natural justice, giving both parties proper opportunity to present their cases and not prejudging the issue; and he needs to consider all factors, including liquidated sums for out-of-pocket expenses, not as items to be reimbursed by the payment of identical amounts but as elements to be taken into account in the overall assessment of the award. This process must not be undermined by interim action. There is a delicate balance to be struck between, on the one hand, demonstrating the merits of the case for an interim award and, on the other, not predetermining the final award. Even a claim which focuses on past events (*e.g.* that excessive security has been demanded) may require anticipation of future events (the amount of the award against which the appropriateness of the security can be measured). This means that interim awards will remain unusual.

1294 *Ex hypothesi* an interim award should be taken into account in the arbitrator's final award.[40] In particular, LOF 1995, cl. 15(a) provides that "The Contractor shall reimburse the parties concerned to such extent as the Award is less than any sums paid on account or in respect of Interim Award(s)."

Open offers

1295 Since the salved property is of necessity the paying party, the costs of the arbitration before the original arbitrator will ordinarily be borne by them. To enable the salved property to protect its position and avoid the cost of arbitration where the contractor's demands for settlement are excessive, a practice of recognising a sealed offer has developed. If the respondents make a firm offer in settlement of the contractor's claim which is not subject to conditions, it is customary to treat such an offer as equivalent to a payment into court. The letter making such an offer is enclosed in an envelope, together with any other material correspondence emanating from either party, which is sealed. This sealed envelope is handed to the arbitrator's clerk by the respondents' solicitors at the conclusion of the arbitration, and the arbitrator's attention is drawn to this fact during the closing speech of the respondent's counsel. When the arbitrator has decided the amount of his award but before he makes any order as to costs, he opens the envelope and reads its contents. The costs are in the discretion of the arbitrator. But, if the parties interested in the salved property have offered to pay a sum equal to or exceeding that which he has decided to be the salvor's remuneration, the arbitrator will most likely

---

[39] Brice, §8–173 states that the power (in LOF 1995, cl. 10(a)(iv)) should only be used when it is fair and just to depart from the practice of having a single hearing. No doubt this is generally true, though it may be noted that the stated requirement to be "fair and just" in the Salvage Convention 1989, Art. 22 and Lloyd's Form relates to the terms of the award resulting from, rather than whether there should be, exercise of the power.

[40] Arbitration Act 1996, s.39(3).

direct the salvor to pay the costs of the arbitration and the costs incurred by the salvees after the date by which the offer ought to have been accepted. It is customary to allow 21 days after the offer was made for the contractors to consider its merits, but this period may be varied. The Appeal Arbitrator has directed that, to be effective, a sealed offer must deal expressly with (a) salvage remuneration, (b) interest and (c) costs. A sealed offer of even a single lump sum greater than the total amounts actually rewarded will not necessarily affect the incidence of costs.[41]

Fees, expenses and costs[42]

In general, parties are free to agree what costs of an arbitration are recoverable.[43] Under Lloyd's Form, if required by the Council of Lloyd's, a person requesting the appointment of an arbitrator must undertake to pay the reasonable fees and expenses of the Council, the Arbitrator and the Appeal Arbitrator.[44] Moreover, whether or not matters proceed to a hearing, the arbitrator, the appeal arbitrator (if any) and the Council of Lloyd's are entitled to charge reasonable fees, expenses and/or costs and all such sums shall be treated as costs of the (appeal) arbitration.[45] The (appeal) arbitrator is empowered to make fair and just orders as to costs, fees and expenses.[46] In particular, the arbitrator has an absolute discretion to include in the amount awarded to the Contractors the whole or part of any expenses reasonably incurred by them in: (i) ascertaining, demanding and obtaining the amount of security reasonably required[47]; and (ii) enforcing and/or protecting by insurance or otherwise or taking reasonable steps to enforce and/or protect their lien.[48] (Additionally, under LOF 1995 the arbitrator had an absolute discretion to order the contractor to pay the whole or part of the expense of providing excessive security or security which has been unreasonably demanded for special compensation under LOF 1995, cl. 5(b)[49] and to deduct such sum from the remuneration and/or special compensation.[50] A comparable power is contained, in general terms, in LPR 2000, cl. 1(c).) **1296**

The arbitrator may direct that the recoverable costs of the arbitration or any part of the proceedings shall be limited to a specified amount.[51] The tribunal is empowered to withhold an award except upon full payment of its fees and **1297**

---

[41] See *The Ios I* [1987] 1 Lloyd's Rep. 321; Brice [1987] L.M.C.L.Q. 172; *The Maria* [1992] 2 Lloyd's Rep. 167.
[42] See generally the Arbitration Act 1996, ss 59–65.
[43] Arbitration Act 1996, s.63.
[44] LOF 1995, cl. 7(a); LSSAC 2000, cl. 5.1.
[45] LOF 1995, cls 7(b), 10(b), 14(b); LSSAC, cls 5.2, 10.8.
[46] Arbitration Act 1996, s.64; LOF 1995, cl. 10(a)(v); LPR 2000, cl. 1(c).
[47] In accordance with LOF 1995, cl. 5 or LSSAC, cl. 4.5 respectively.
[48] LOF 1995, cl. 6(d); LSSAC 2000, cl. 6.3.
[49] See *ante*, § 1259.
[50] LOF 1995, cl. 10(a)(iii).
[51] Arbitration Act 1996, s.65; LPR 2000, cl. 1(d).

expenses.[52] The parties are jointly and severally liable to pay the arbitrator's reasonable fees and expenses.[53]

1298 LSSAC 2000, cl. 11.5 provides that, where (i) no security has been provided to the Council as required[54] or (ii) no award is made by the (appeal) arbitrator because the parties have been able to settle all matters in issue between them by agreement, the Contractors shall be responsible for the payment of the fees and expenses of the arbitrator(s) and of the Council of Lloyd's.[55] Payment of such fees and expenses must be made to the Council within 28 days of the Contractors or their representatives receiving the Council's invoice, failing which the Council shall be entitled to interest on any sum outstanding at the United Kingdom Base Rate prevailing on the date of the invoice plus 2 per cent per annum until payment is received by the Council.

Effect of awards

1299 An arbitration award (whether on Lloyd's Form or not) is (subject to the appeal procedure provided)[56] final and binding on the parties.[57] Lloyd's Form adds that this is the case whether the parties concerned were represented at the arbitration or not.[58]

An award by a tribunal pursuant to an arbitration agreement may, by leave of the court, be enforced in the same manner as a judgment or order of the court to the same effect.[59]

Publication of awards

1300 Publication of an arbitration award can occur in at least two ways: it may be published to the parties to the arbitration agreement only; or it may be published generally. One of the traditional merits of arbitration is that parties can settle their differences confidentially. Accordingly, it has traditionally been the case with Lloyd's Form awards that the arbitrator *sends* his award to the Council of Lloyd's, and the Council publishes it to the parties but not more widely.[60] Given that most English decisions on salvage are now settled by Lloyd's Form arbitrations, this limits the dissemination of knowledge of the jurisprudence and practice of salvage. The disadvantages of this are ameliorated by the fact that legal salvage issues are handled by a close community of practitioners who are familiar with the relevant law and practice. However,

---

[52] Arbitration Act 1996, s.56.
[53] Arbitration Act 1996, s.28.
[54] By LSSAC 2000, cl. 4.5. See *ante*, § 1260.
[55] Under LSSAC 2000, cll. 5.2 and 10.8.
[56] See *post*, §§ 1302–1309.
[57] Arbitration Act 1996, s.58.
[58] LOF 1995, cl. 10(c); LSSAC 2000, cl. 6.7. These provisions in Lloyd's Form seem merely to operate *ex abundanti cautela*.
[59] Arbitration Act 1996, s.66.
[60] However, an anonymous summary of Lloyd's Form awards has been published. See *Lloyd's Digest*, 3rd ed.

Appeals and cross-appeals

it is potentially detrimental to the public interest, especially where the law derives from an international convention concerned with matters of wider interest than salvage alone, namely the environmental factors to be taken into account. Accordingly, the Salvage Convention 1989, Art. 27 stipulates that "States parties shall encourage, as far as possible and with the consent of the parties, the publication of arbitral awards made in salvage cases." Article 27 is reproduced in the Merchant Shipping Act 1995.[61] Accordingly, the Government is obliged to encourage such publication but that is as much as the statute requires. Lloyd's Form (in LSSAC 2000) now states that the arbitrator's and the appeal arbitrator's awards "shall be published by the Council in London".[62]

Correction of awards and additional awards

Under LPR 2000, r. 1(g), on his own initiative or on the application of any party, the arbitrator may correct any award (whether interim, provisional or final) or make an additional award in order to rectify any mistake, error or omission, provided that (i) any such correction is made within 28 days of the date of publication of the relevant award by the Council of Lloyd's and (ii) any additional award required is made within 56 days of the said date of publication or, in either case, such longer period as the arbitrator may in his discretion allow. **1301**

Appeals and cross-appeals

Any party to an arbitration award under Lloyd's Form may appeal against it, whether or not he actively participated in the original hearing. Under LOF 1995, cl. 13(a), "Notice of Appeal if any shall be given to the Council within 14 days (exclusive of Saturdays and Sundays or other days observed as general holidays at Lloyd's) after the date of the publication by the Council of the Award and/or Interim Award(s)." Under LSSAC 2000, cl. 10.1: "Any party may appeal from an award by giving written Notice of Appeal to the Council provided such notice is received by the Council no later than 21 days after the date on which the award was published by the Council." **1302**

"Upon receipt of Notice of Appeal the Council shall refer the Appeal to the hearing and determination of the Appeal Arbitrator(s) selected by it."[63] The Council of Lloyd's is free to appoint anyone as an appeal arbitrator but has traditionally nominated a standing Appeal Arbitrator.

Lloyd's Form does not *expressly* require the Council to inform the other parties to the arbitration of the Notice of Appeal. However, in practice it does **1303**

---

[61] Sched. 11, Pt I.
[62] LSSAC 2000, cll. 6.7, 10.9. See also the opening words to LSSAC 2000, cl. 11.1: "When publishing the award ... ".
[63] LOF 1995, cl. 13(d). LSSAC, cl. 10.2 provides: "On receipt of a Notice of Appeal the Council shall refer the appeal to the hearing and determination of an appeal arbitrator of its choice ('the Appeal Arbitrator')." The effect of these two, differently worded, clauses is identical.

so, so far as it can; and the rules of natural justice require that other parties must have the opportunity to participate in the appeal if they are to be bound by the appeal arbitrator's award. Once a Notice of Appeal is given, any other party may give a Notice of Cross-Appeal. LOF 1995, cl. 13(b) provides that: "Notice of Cross-Appeal if any shall be given to the Council within 14 days (exclusive of Saturdays and Sundays or other days observed as general holidays at Lloyd's) after notification by the Council to the parties of any Notice of Appeal." Under LSSAC, cl. 10.10.3: "Any party who has not already given Notice of Appeal under clause 10.1 may give a Notice of Cross Appeal to the Council within 21 days of that party having been notified that the Council has received Notice of Appeal from another party."

1304 "Notice of Appeal or Cross Appeal shall be given to the Council by letter telex facsimile or in any other permanent form."[64] LOF 1995, cl. 13(b) and LSSAC 2000, cl. 10.4 provide in relation to Notices of Cross Appeal that: "Such notification if sent by post shall be deemed received on the working day following the day of posting." Under LSSAC 2000, cl. 10.4, this also applies to Notices of Appeal.

The court has a discretion to extend the time for giving a notice of appeal or of cross appeal; but this discretion is limited to where the circumstances were outside the contemplation of the parties when they entered the agreement and it would be just to extend the time, or to where the conduct of one party would make it unjust for the other party to be held to the strict terms of the agreement.[65] Otherwise, if a party does not give notice of appeal or cross-appeal in time, the original award becomes operative so far as he is concerned, even if the other party is not prejudiced by delay.[66]

"If any Notice of Appeal or Notice of Cross Appeal is withdrawn prior to the hearing of the appeal arbitration, that appeal arbitration shall nevertheless proceed for the purpose of determining any matters which remain outstanding."[67]

1305 It is neither necessary nor usual when giving Notice of Appeal or Notice of Cross-Appeal to give the grounds of the appeal. However, Lloyd's Procedural Rules provide as follows[68]:

(i) In any case in which a party giving notice of appeal intends to contend that the arbitrator's findings on the salved value of all or any of the salved value of the property were erroneous, or that the

---

[64] LSSAC 2000, cl. 10.4. LOF 1995, cl. 13(c) is identical except that "Cross-Appeal" is hyphenated. Additionally, and superfluously, LSSAC, cl. 10.1 states that any party may appeal from an award by giving "written" Notice of Appeal. E-mail might be considered not to be a "permanent form".

[65] Arbitration Act 1996, s.12.

[66] See *The Geestland* [1980] 1 Lloyd's Rep. 628, 629.

[67] LSSAC, cl. 10.5. LOF 1995, cl. 13(e) similarly provides: "If any Notice of Appeal or Cross-Appeal is withdrawn the Appeal hearing shall nevertheless proceed in respect of such Notice of Appeal or Cross-Appeal as may remain."

[68] LPR 2000, r. 8.

Appeals and cross-appeals

arbitrator has erred in any finding as to the person whose property was at risk, a statement of such grounds of appeal shall be given in or accompanying the notice of appeal.

(ii) In all cases grounds of appeal or cross-appeal will be given[69] within 21 days of the notice of appeal or cross-appeal unless an extension of time is agreed.[70]

(iii) Any respondent to an appeal who intends to contend that the award of the original arbitrator should be affirmed on grounds other than those relied on by the original arbitrator shall give notice to that effect specifying the grounds of his contention within 14 days of receipt of the grounds of appeal mentioned in (ii) above unless an extension of time is agreed.

It is specifically provided in LSSAC 2000, cl. 10.7 that "The Appeal Arbitrator shall conduct the appeal arbitration in accordance with Lloyd's Procedural Rules so far as applicable to an appeal."

Parties to the appeal

1306 The general rule is that only the parties to an arbitration or an appeal arbitration are bound by the award made. Thus, the appeal arbitrator in an appeal by shipowner salvees has no jurisdiction to vary the award made in respect of cargo-owner salvees.[71] Of course, the effect of the appeal arbitrator's decision may have implications for the soundness of the original arbitrator's award in respect of all of the parties concerned in salvage operations; and ideally it might seem appropriate for the appeal arbitrator to consider the entire situation. But, if a party to the original arbitration wishes to contest the original arbitrator's award in respect of more than one party to the original arbitration, he should issue a notice of appeal or cross-appeal against that party; for it is the appeal arbitrator's function only to hear the appeal before him.

1307 Repeating the general rule in relation to original awards,[72] LOF 1995, cl. 13(f) provides that: "Any Award on appeal shall be final and binding on all the parties to that Appeal Arbitration whether they were represented either at the Arbitration or at the Appeal Arbitration or not." However, this clause merely confirms that the effect of the appeal arbitrator's award on a party to the appeal is not dependent on whether or not that party was represented at the original or appeal arbitration. It does not provide that a person who is not a party to the appeal arbitration will be bound by the appeal award. The provision is omitted from LSSAC 2000.

---

[69] LPR 2000, r. 8(c) states "given to the Arbitrator on Appeal".
[70] LPR 2000, r. 8(c).
[71] *The Geestland* [1980] 1 Lloyd's Rep. 628.
[72] See *ante*, § 1299.

Appeal arbitrator's powers

1308 In addition to his other powers,[73] Lloyd's Form provides that the Appeal Arbitrator shall have the following powers.

(i) He may admit the evidence which was before the arbitrator together with the arbitrator's notes and reasons for his award and/or interim award(s), any transcript of evidence and such additional evidence or information as he may think fit.[74]

(ii) He may confirm, increase or reduce the sum(s) awarded by the arbitrator and make such order as to the payment of interest on such sum(s) as he may think fit.[75]

(iii) He may confirm, revoke or vary any order and/or declaratory award made by the arbitrator.[76]

(iv) Both the appeal arbitrator and the Council of Lloyd's have power to charge reasonable fees and expenses for their services in connection with the appeal arbitration, whether it proceeds to a hearing or not, and all such fees and expenses shall be treated as part of the costs of the appeal arbitration.[77]

(v) The appeal arbitrator may award interest on any fees and expenses charged under (iv).[78] The date from which interest may be awarded is: under LOF 1995, from the expiration of 21 days (exclusive of Saturdays and Sundays or other days observed as general holidays at Lloyd's) after the date of publication by the Council of Lloyd's of the award on appeal and/or interim award(s) on appeal; under LSSAC 2000, from the expiration of 28 days after the date of publication by the Council of the appeal arbitrator's award. Under both editions of Lloyd's Form, interest may be awarded until the date payment is received by the Council. Both dates are inclusive.

Appeal to the court

1309 The Arbitration Act 1996 contains provisions whereby a party to arbitral proceedings may apply to the court: to challenge the substantive jurisdiction of an arbitral tribunal; to challenge an arbitral award; or to appeal on a

---

[73] LOF 1995, cl. 14(a) begins: "The Appeal Arbitrator(s) in addition to the powers of the Arbitrator under clauses 10(a) and 11 shall have power ... ". LSSAC 2000, cl. 10.7 begins: "In addition to the powers conferred on the Arbitrator by English law and the Agreement, the Appeal Arbitrator shall have power ... ".
[74] LOF 1995, cl. 14(a)(i) and LSSAC 2000, cl. 10.7(i) state this in similar terms. However, LOF 1995, cl. 14(a)(i) does not include "additional information" and LSSAC 2000, cl. 10.7(i) does not refer to interim awards.
[75] LSSAC 2000, cl. 10.7(ii). LOF 1995, cl. 14(a)(ii) is in similar terms.
[76] LSSAC 2000, cl. 10.7(iii); LOF 1995, cl. 14(a)(iii).
[77] LOF 1995, cl. 14(b); LSSAC 2000, cl. 10.8.
[78] LOF 1995, cl. 14(a)(iv); LSSAC 2000, cl. 10.7(iv).

question of law.[79] However, a would-be applicant or appellant must first exhaust any available arbitral process of appeal or review.[80] Thus, a party to Lloyd's Form must first appeal to the Lloyd's Appeal Arbitrator before resort to the court.

Payment and enforcement of security under Lloyd's Form

The parties to Lloyd's Form are bound by its provisions as to payment. **1310** These provisions require payment through the medium of the Council of Lloyd's, which assumes rights and liabilities in accordance with its contracts with the parties.[81]

Both LOF 1995 and LSSAC 2000 require the Council to call upon the parties concerned to pay the sums due from them under the award.[82] Under LOF 1995,[83] the Council's duty arises if no Notice of Appeal be received by the Council within 14 days, exclusive of Saturdays and Sundays or other days observed as general holidays at Lloyd's, after the date of publication of the award by the Council.[84] Under LSSAC 2000, immediately the Council publishes the award it must call for payment within 28 days of the publication date ("the payment date").[85] Similarly, in the event of an appeal and upon publication by the Council of the appeal award, the Council must call upon the party or parties concerned to pay the sum(s) awarded.[86]

In the event of non-payment, and subject to the Contractors' providing the **1311** Council with an indemnity for the costs of doing so,[87] the Council must take steps to realise or enforce the security provided by the defaulting party.[88] Three cases are provided for:

(1) under LOF 1995, once the period for giving notice of appeal has expired[89]; under LSSAC 2000, if the sums due are not paid within

---

[79] Arbitration Act 1996, ss 67–71.
[80] Arbitration Act 1996, s.70(2)(a).
[81] See *ante*, §§ 1277–1278.
[82] LSSAC 2000, cl. 11.1 states that these sums include the fees and expenses referred to in cl. 5.2: see *ante*, § 1296.
[83] LOF 1995, cl. 15(a).
[84] *i.e.* in accordance with LOF 1995, cl. 13(a).
[85] LSSAC 2000, cl. 11.1.
[86] LOF 1995, cl. 15(b); LSSAC, cl. 11.3.
[87] LOF 1995, cl. 10(a)–(c) states that realisation of security is "subject to the Contractor first providing to the Council a satisfactory Undertaking to pay all the costs thereof". LSSAC 2000, cl. 11.2–11.4 states that it is "subject to the Contractors providing the Council with any indemnity the Council may require in respect of the costs the Council may incur in that regard". The later version is more specific but not substantially different.
[88] LOF 1995 simply refers to "the security". LSSAC 2000 specifies "the security given to the Council under clause 4.5 [see *ante*, § 1260] by or on behalf of [the defaulting] party [or parties]" (see cll. 11.2, 11.3 and 11.4, which are worded slightly differently). However, there is no change of substance in LSSAC 2000, which simply spells out the obvious point that security can only be realised or enforced for the purpose for which it is given.
[89] LOF 1995, cl. 15(a).

56 days of the publication date (or such longer period as the Contractors may allow) and the Council has not received Notice of Appeal or Cross-Appeal[90];

(2) in the event of an appeal and publication of an appeal award, in the event of non-payment after the Council has called upon the parties in question to pay the sum(s) awarded[91];

(3) if any sums(s) shall become payable to the contractors (under LOF 1995) "as remuneration for his services and/or interest and/or costs" or (under LSSAC 2000) "in respect of salvage remuneration or special compensation (including interest and/or costs)" as the result of an agreement made between the contractors and the owners or any of them.[92]

1312 If an award directs the Contractors to pay all or part of the costs of the arbitration—and/or, under LSSAC 2000, "any sum to any other party or parties"—the Council may deduct such amounts unless the Contractors provide the Council with satisfactory security to meet their liability.[93] Under LOF 1995, the deduction may be made "from the amount awarded or agreed"; under LSSAC 2000, "from sums received by the Council on behalf of the Contractors".

1313 Under LOF 1995 the Council is required to pay from the realised security to the Contractor: in the case of an (appeal) award, "the amount awarded to him to him together with interest if any"; and, in the case of an agreement to pay, "the said sum".[94] Under LSSAC 2000, "Save as aforesaid all sums received by the Council pursuant to this clause shall be paid by the Council to the Contractors or their representatives".[95]

In normal circumstances the security in question will be an undertaking to pay a sum of money and that sum of money will be the amount payable by the salvee to satisfy his liability. Accordingly, the surety should have to pay no more than is necessary to satisfy such liability. If, however, the effect of realisation of the security were to produce a surplus, the normal situation is that the amount of the surplus should be returned to the payor. Thus, under LOF 1995, the Council should return this amount to the surety. However, under LSSAC 2000, unless "all sums received ... pursuant to this clause" were interpreted to refer only to such sums as should have been received pursuant to the payment clause, the Council would be bound to pay any

---

[90] LSSAC 2000, cl. 11.2.
[91] LOF 1995, cl. 15(b); LSSAC 2000, cl. 11.3.
[92] LOF 1995, cl. 15(c); LSSAC 2000, cl. 11.4.
[93] LOF 1995, cl. 15(d); LSSAC 2000, cl. 11.6.
[94] LOF 1995, cl. 19(a)–(c).
[95] LSSAC 2000, cl. 11.7.

surplus over to the contractors. This would, however, be without prejudice to any claim to restitution to which the surety might be entitled.

LOF 1995 provides that the Contractor shall reimburse the parties concerned to such extent as the (appeal) award is less than any sums paid on account or in respect of any awards.[96] This states the position under the general law.[97] The statement is omitted from LSSAC 2000.

The receipt of the Contractors (or, as specified by LSSAC 2000, their representatives) shall be a good discharge for sums received by virtue of the payment clause.[98]

The Council is not liable for the sufficiency or reliability of security provided[99] and its liability is in any event limited to the amount of security provided to it.[1]

4. Appeals as to Amount of Salvage Awarded

Appeals from court of first instance

The principles which have been maintained[2] in dealing with appeals from the court of first instance were clearly and concisely stated by Lord Esher M.R. in delivering his judgment in the Court of Appeal in *The Star of Persia*[3]: "If this court cannot say that the learned judge has misapprehended the facts or cannot say that he has acted contrary to any principle, then, if the amount does not seem to this court to be unreasonable, it cannot interfere." "Unreasonable" means "greatly[4] in excess of, or greatly below, the sum which should have been awarded."[5]

Where the court of first instance has not misapprehended the facts of the case, and has not erred in point of principle, and therefore the success of the appeal against its award depends entirely upon proving that its wide discretion in all questions of amount of reward has been so wrongly exercised in the

---

[96] LOF 1995, cl. 15(a)–(b).
[97] *cf.* Goff & Jones, Chap. 16; Arbitration Act 1996, s.81.
[98] LOF 1995, cl. 15(a)–(c); LSSAC 2000, cl. 11.7.
[99] LOF 1995, cll. 5(c), 15(e); LSSAC 2000, cll. 4.5, 11.8. See *ante*, § 1260.
[1] LOF 1995, cl. 15(e); LSSAC 2000, cl. 11.8.
[2] Both by the Privy Council, to which appeals from the High Court of Admiralty used to lie, and by the Court of Appeal in appeals from the present Admiralty Court.
[3] (1887) 6 Asp. M.L.C. 220, 221 (Lindley and Lopes L.JJ. concurring); applied in *The Trekieve* (1942) 72 Ll.L.Rep. 1 (CA).
[4] In *The City of Lancaster* (1929) 34 Ll.L.Rep. 381 (CA), Scrutton L.J. used the terms "a very large margin" and "a serious difference".
[5] In *The Trekieve* (1942) 72 Ll.L.Rep. 1, 4, du Parcq L.J., as he then was, after citing the above passage from *The Star of Persia*, said "In Lord Justice Kennedy's book on Salvage (p. 186 of 3rd ed.) there is a gloss added (quite correctly, I think) by way of a footnote, explaining the word 'unreasonable' ". In view of this, since the 4th edition, the former footnote has been elevated to the text.

assessment of the sum awarded that the Court of Appeal ought to interfere, the appellant has a peculiarly hard task before him.[6]

1316 It is certain, from decisions in the latter part of the nineteenth century, that the difference between the amount awarded by the court below and that which the appellate tribunal thinks ought to have been awarded must be, at least, a "very considerable" difference in order to induce the latter to interfere.[7] In comparatively recent years, the words "a very large margin" and "a serious difference" have been employed.[8] In the judgment of the Privy Council in *The Glenduror*,[9] it was suggested that the minimum difference justifying interference with the award of the court below should be one-third, and this suggestion was accepted in the judgment in *The Thomas Allen*.[10] But there is no rule to this effect.

1317 Instances[11] of an increase of the award on appeal, on the ground of its being unreasonably small, are afforded by the cases of *The Thetis*,[12] *The Caledonian Steamship Co. v. Hutton (The Medora)*,[13] *The Scindia*,[14] *The True Blue*[15] and *The City of Berlin*.[16] Instances of a diminution on the ground of the award being unreasonably large are the cases of *The Chetah*,[17] *The Thomas Allen*,[18] *The Lindfield*,[19] *The Gipsy Queen*[20] and *The Prince Llewellyn*.[21]

---

[6] See *The City of Lancaster* (1929) 34 Ll.L.Rep. 381, 381–382, *per* Scrutton L.J.

[7] *The Clarisse* (1856) 12 Moo. P.C. 340, cited with approval in *The Neptune* (1856) Swab. 129, 134 (PC); (1858) 12 Moo. (P.C.) 346, 351; *The England* (1868) L.R. 2 P.C. 253, 256; *The Chetah* (1868) L.R. 2 P.C. 205; *The Glenduror* (1871) L.R. 3 P.C. 589, 592, 594; *The Amérique* (1874) L.R. 6 P.C. 468, 472; and *The Thomas Allen* (1886) 6 Asp. M.L.C. 99, 100 (PC). The judgments in *The Lancaster* (1883) 9 P.D. 14 (CA), *The Star of Persia* (1887) 6 Asp. M.L.C. 220, 221 (CA) and *The Accomac* [1891] P. 349, 354 (CA) are substantially to the same effect. This rule was also adopted in *The Port Hunter* [1910] P. 343, 351 (CA). See also to substantially the same effect *The Glengyle* [1898] P. 97; *The City of Lancaster* (1929) 34 Ll.L.Rep. 381.

[8] Statements in the Privy Council that (i) the question of quantum would not be considered "where there has been nothing to shock the conscience, nothing gross or extravagant" (*The Carrier Dove* (1863) 2 Moo.P.C. (n.s.) 243, 254) and (ii) "It is only where the amount awarded is grossly in excess of what appears to be right that their Lordships would feel justified in overruling the decision of a court below on the question or salvage" are, as appears from later judgments of the PC and Court of Appeal, *infra*, rather too strong.

[9] (1871) L.R. 3 P.C. 589, 594.

[10] (1886) 6 Asp. M.L.C. 99, 100 (PC).

[11] For some unreported cases, see Roscoe, p. 180, note (u). When the award is varied, the general rule of the Court of Appeal is to allow the successful appellant the costs of the appeal. The former general rule that an appellant succeeding in reducing an award was not allowed costs, laid down in *The Gipsy Queen* [1895] P. 176 (CA) and based on the earlier practice of the Privy Council when exercising jurisdiction in Admiralty cases, is no longer in force (see *The Port Hunter* [1910] P. 343).

[12] (1834) 2 Knapp. 390.

[13] (1847) 5 Not. of Cas. 156.

[14] (1886) L.R. 1 P.C. 241, 257.

[15] *ibid.*, 250.

[16] (1877) 3 Asp. M.L.C. 491.

[17] (1868) L.R. 2 P.C. 205.

[18] (1886) 6 Asp. M.L.C. 99.

[19] (1894) 10 T.L.R. 606.

[20] [1895] P. 176.

[21] [1904] P. 83.

When the Admiralty Court has wrongly dismissed a salvage action, the Court of Appeal, reversing that decision, should, if the facts are in evidence before it, itself award the amount of salvage due.[22]

Appeal to the House of Lords

Where an award made by the judge of the Admiralty Court has been affirmed by the Court of Appeal, the case must be "exceptional and extraordinary"[23] to induce the House of Lords to alter the award. It will only interfere where the established principles have not been satisfactorily applied.[24]

1318

---

[22] *The Melanie (Owners) v. The San Onofre (Owners)* [1925] A.C. 246. This course was taken by the Privy Council in *The Minnehaha* (1861) Lush. 335. There are some valuable remarks in the opinion in the latter case (at pp. 350–353) as to the reversal of judgments of the court of first instance on matters of fact. See also on this point *The Julia* (1861) Lush. 224, 235 (PC); *The Carrier Dove* (1863) 2 Moo. P.C. (n.s.) 243, 256; *The Alice* (1868) L.R. 2 P.C. 245, 247, 248; *The Glannibanta* (1876) 1 P.D. 283, 287 (CA); *The Melanie (Owners) v. The San Onofre (Owners)*, *supra* at 252, 268, where the decision of Bailhache J., dismissing the claim, was reversed by the (CA) and restored by the HL. See also *per* Lord Birkenhead L.C. in *The San Onofre (No. 1)* [1927] A.C. 162n. and, *per curiam*, *The Douglas*, *ibid.*, p. 164n. as to the functions of assessors on appeals.
[23] *The Glengyle* [1898] A.C. 519, 520.
[24] *ibid.*

CHAPTER 14

SALVED VALUES

1. INTRODUCTION

Issues

1319   One of the most important factors in the assessment of a salvage reward of which the amount has not been predetermined[1] is the value of the salved property. The salved value is the worth, in financial terms, of the property which has been saved for the benefit of its owners. Since the salvors' remuneration is assessed by reference to the benefit conferred by virtue of the services which have been rendered, it is axiomatic that the salvage award will not exceed the total value of the property saved.[2] To that extent ascertainment of the total value of the salved fund is the most fundamental calculation to be made in assessing the salvage reward.

It is proposed now to consider the various means by which the values of the several contributory interests which have benefited from salvage have to be calculated for the purposes of assessing the amount of the salved fund and the different liabilities to contribute. There are essentially three methods of valuation: by agreement or, where there is dispute, by determination by the arbitrator or court, or by appraisement. These three methods will be considered in turn. First, however, a few words must be said about the burden of proof.

Burden of proof

1320   In nearly all salvage proceedings the salvor is *ex hypothesi* the claimant.[3] The burden, therefore, of proving all matters in issue, including values, lies upon him.[4] As a matter of practice, however, it is customary for the owners of salved property to put forward particulars of their case on salved values with a view to agreement.[5] This is particularly convenient in those many cases where, within broad limits, the salved value will have no material effect upon

---

[1] See *ante.*, §826.
[2] See Brussels Salvage Convention, Art. 2; Salvage Convention 1989, Art. 13.3.
[3] The owner of the casualty would be the plaintiff in a claim for damages for negligence or breach of contract—though those would not be "salvage proceedings" in the usual sense.
[4] *cf. The Stella* (1867) L.R. 1 A. & E. 340.
[5] See *post*, §1321.

612

the level of remuneration, for example, where the salvage service is little more than "a glorified towage".[6] However, if agreement cannot be achieved, the parties must produce all relevant documents in their possession, custody or power which relate to the issue of values. Thereafter, the salvors, on the basis of these documents and any other evidence they are able to adduce, must prove the salved value or values to the satisfaction of the tribunal.

2. AGREED VALUATION

1321 In most cases in practice, agreement is reached as to the values of salved property. In all cases, however, it must be borne in mind that the salved values are relevant not only to the overall reward but also to the apportionment amongst the salved interests of liability to contribute to the award. Thus, difficulties can arise, for instance, where salvors reach agreement with the shipowners as to the value of the ship for the purposes of the claim but the cargo-owners do not agree that value for the purpose of apportionment. If the cargo-owners are not parties to the agreement, they are in no way bound by it.

It is, therefore, desirable that all interests should become parties to any agreement on values. Where they fail to do so, it is thought that the proper course is for the court to make an award and an apportionment on the basis of such values as may be proved regardless of the partial agreement.[7] The court may take into account the agreement as evidence of salved values, just as it may hear evidence of agreed values in marine insurance policies. But such agreements will not necessarily be reliable and the court is of course not bound by them.

In the result, the parties to the agreement may be left with no practical option but to resile from it, particularly in the face of judicial pronouncement as to different sound values. But there is in principle nothing to prevent the parties from continuing to be bound by the agreement *inter se*, if it is freely entered into and is not inequitable.[8]

3. DISPUTED VALUATION

Valuation of property by receiver

1322 The Merchant Shipping Act 1995, s.225 continues to provide that, where any dispute as to salvage arises, the receiver of wreck may, on the application

---

[6] *The Troilus* (1949) 82 Ll.L.Rep. 681, 690 (affirmed in part [1950] P. 92, affirmed [1951] A.C. 820).
[7] *cf. The Due Checchi* (1872) L.R. 4 A. & E. 35n.
[8] *cf. ante*, Chap. 9.

of either party, appoint a valuer to value the property.[9] If a valuation has been so made, the receiver must give copies of it to both parties.[10] A copy of the valuation purporting to be signed by the valuer, and to be certified as a true copy by the receiver, is admissible as evidence in any subsequent proceedings.[11]

Place and time of valuation

1323   If the salved values are the subject of dispute, the correct principle, albeit practice may not correspond universally, is to assess the value of the property, as salved, at the place where, and the time at which, the salvage service terminates, whether or not that is the port of destination.[12] The rule prescribes that salvors suing elsewhere, such as at the place of destination, shall be entitled there to the same amount of salvage as if they had sued in the place where their services terminated.[13] "[T]he law is that when a vessel is brought into port and her cargo arrested, the price to be taken is the price at the time of the arrest, which is as if the Marshal had to sell the ship and the cargo at that time."[14]

1324   In most cases, there is no dispute about where and when salvage services ended. Indeed, the termination of the service is often marked by the signature of a certificate of delivery by the master of the casualty, confirming that his vessel is in safety and that no further services are required. On the other hand, the salvors' assistance may be terminated unilaterally at the behest of the salved property, *e.g.* because the casualty is able to proceed on her voyage under her own means or because more potent assistance is available.[15]

If there is a dispute, the question to be determined is: When and where was the salved property brought into a position of safety? This must always be a question of fact, depending upon the particular circumstances of the case.[16] As shewn elsewhere,[17] the guiding principle is whether or not the vessel, at a particular place and time, requires further assistance which would fall within the recognised categories of salvage service. If the answer is affirmative, the casualty is not in safety.

---

[9] MSA 1995, s.225(1). The person applying for a valuation must pay such fee as the Secretary of State may direct: *ibid.*, s.225(4).

[10] *ibid.*, s.225(2).

[11] *ibid.*, s.225(3).

[12] *The George Dean* (1857) Swab. 290 (derelict; cargo; freight); *The Norma* (1860) Lush. 124, 126–127; *The Cargo ex Loodianah*, Pritchard, Vol. 2, p. 1854; *The Stella* (1867) L.R. 1 A. & E. 340; *The James Armstrong* (1875) 3 Asp. M.L.C. 46, 49; *The Clara, Shipping Gazette*, November 22, 1905; *The Sunheath* (1925) 22 Ll.L.Rep. 361; *The Gaupen* (1925) 22 Ll.L.Rep. 371; *The Lyrma (No. 2)* [1978] 2 Lloyd's Rep. 30, 33; *The Yolaine* [1995] 2 Lloyd's Rep. 7, 11. See also *The Germania* [1904] P. 131; *The Teh Hu* [1970] P. 106, 114–115; but see now *post*, §§ 1461–1465 *cf. The Georg* [1894] P. 330.

[13] *The Norma* (1860) Lush. 124, 127.

[14] *The Gaupen* (1925) 22 Ll.L.Rep. 271, 375.

[15] See *The Sunheath* (1925) 22 Ll.L.Rep. 361, where it was intended that salvage towage should determine off Karachi harbour, where the vessel could get tug assistance to get in.

[16] See, *e.g. The Ningpo* (1923) 16 Ll.L.Rep. 392, considered *post*, §1326.

[17] See *ante*, Chap. 4.

The principle will not be allowed to operate, however, to deprive the plaintiff of a salvage claim or to diminish the fund represented by the property which he has sought to preserve where the owner of the casualty has been guilty of misconduct. In *The Germania*,[18] a steam trawler found the steamship *Germania* lying disabled in the North Sea and towed her to a position off Aberdeen. There, as the master of the trawler was unwilling in the bad weather then prevailing to incur the risk of taking her into harbour, signals were made for a pilot and tug. In response to the signals, a tug came up and her master offered to pilot and tow the *Germania* into the harbour. His services were refused by the *Germania*—improperly, as the court found—and subsequently the trawler was told to go ahead. As she was doing so, the hawser parted. The *Germania* then dropped anchor and steps were taken to make the trawler fast again but, before this could be done, she drifted ashore. The cost of floating her amounted to £1,150 and expenditure of £5,600 was rendered necessary for repairs. She ultimately proved to be worth £1,750, which her owners contended to be her value for the purposes of a salvage award to the trawler. It seemed to Gorell Barnes J. that the trawler had done what she could to bring the casualty into a place of safety and that if the tug had been taken there would have been no difficulty. The vessel had been brought from a position where, if unassisted, she would have been in danger of going ashore at a spot more northerly than Aberdeen to a place where she could get a tug and the value at that time, namely £8,500, was the basis on which the award should be calculated.

Several salvage services

In *The Ningpo*,[19] Hill J. adverted to the importance of fixing a single time and place for valuation. On April 11, 1921, the vessel stranded on a reef in the China Sea. An armed guard from HMS *Tamar* went on board for four days to prevent looting and the owners engaged a number of persons on a contractual, as distinguished from a "no cure—no pay", basis to work on the vessel, which they did until May 23. From April 23–26, a working and diving party from HMS *Colombo* rendered services. On May 23, by which time the owners had occurred £8,000 in expenses, she was floated off and towed by H.M. tug *Hesper* to Wei-hai-Wei, where she was beached. A further £6,000 was expended then, on June 20, she was towed to Shanghai, where she was later sold for £11,600. The result was that the owners were over £3,000 worse off than if they had abandoned her in the first place. The Admiralty, as owners, and the officers and crew of the *Hesper*, the members of the armed guard from the *Tamar*, and the captain and working parties from the *Colombo* claimed salvage. The owners argued that the salved value should be what the vessel realised in Shanghai less, in respect of each claim, the expenses incurred after the termination of the services of the respective claimants. But this contention was rejected. Hill J. said that in a case where there was a claim of salvors one

---

[18] [1904] P. 131.
[19] (1923) 16 Ll.L.Rep. 392.

could only take one value, and that value had to be determined on the beach at Wei-hai-Wei, which is presumably when and where he regarded the vessel as being in safety.

1327 It clearly makes sense where several salvors have participated in a continuous series of endeavours to preserve property from loss that the amount of the reward and their shares in it should so far as possible be assessed together. This suggests a single time and place for valuation. That is convenient and saves expense. In addition, it helps to ensure that cumulative salvage awards to individual salvors, which of course are designed to contain an element of reward over and above ordinary remuneration for the services, do not outweigh the amount of the fund remaining in the defendant's hands after the award; otherwise he derives no benefit from salvage.[20]

1328 However, where separate and distinct salvage services are rendered to a vessel on different occasions, so as to give rise to independent salvage claims, each salvage service should be assessed and rewarded separately. Thus, if each salvage service merits an award of more than 50 per cent of the salved value, the total of the two awards may exceed the value of the ship.[21] This is so even if the services are rendered by the same salvor within a short compass of time. But it may not be inappropriate in a given case for a later salvage service to be taken into account in assessing the earlier, or vice versa.

Events after termination

1329 Since the salvage award is to be assessed on the benefit conferred as at the termination of the service, it follows that, as a general principle, nothing which occurs after the reward falls due should operate so as to increase or decrease the salved values to be assessed as at that time or, indeed, be taken into account in the assessment of the award. Thus, Brandon J. said in *The Teh Hu*[22]:

> "It may happen that, after services have terminated, events unconnected with them occur which can in one sense be said to increase or reduce (or even nullify altogether) the benefit conferred by the services on the owners of the salved property. For instance, a war may break out, which results in greatly enhanced freight rates being earned by a salved ship; or a salved ship may be damaged or lost in consequence of a fresh casualty.[23] These events may supervene within a few days of the termination of the services. If the financial realities as at the date of fixing the salvage award are regarded, events like these have a highly important bearing on

---

[20] But see *post*, §1328.
[21] Likewise, in a different context, successive losses may eventually enable an assured to recover from his insurer more than the total value of the subject of a marine insurance policy.
[22] [1970] P. 106, 115. His judgment was affirmed by the CA, *ibid.* at 117. But the actual decision must now be read subject to the cases in §§ 1461–1465.
[23] See also *The Sunheath* (1925) 22 Ll.L.Rep. 361, 363.

Place and time of valuation

the benefit 'really' enjoyed by the owners of the salved property. Yet such matters are invariably disregarded in assessing such benefit for the purpose of fixing the salvage award. The reason for this is that the benefit is looked at as at the date of termination of the services, and not as at a later date when fresh events, unconnected with the original casualty, or the services rendered in consequence of it, have supervened."

In particular, the value of salved cargo is unaffected by subsequent changes in its market value.[24]

Moreover the salvor should not be prejudiced by the defendant's failure to take proper and expeditious steps to preserve the value of the salved property.[25] And it is immaterial that subsequent expenditure on a vessel means that the total expenditure on it from the time of the danger to its eventual sale exceeds its value on sale.[26]

1330

It is not harsh on the defendant to ignore subsequent diminution in value of the salved property because he is always able to insure himself against losses arising as a result of the salvage danger and subsequently. In *The Josefina Thorden*,[27] Admiralty vessels in 1941 salved a derelict Finnish tanker, which had been set on fire by German aircraft and abandoned. After the owners had put up security and the salvors' lien was released, and while the ship was undergoing repairs, the Government declared Finland to be territory in enemy occupation, the ship was seized as prize, and later released by the Prize Court to the Ministry of War Transport. Atkinson J. held[28]:

1331

> "If she is lost, whether by marine or war risks, the salvors' rights are unaffected. The owner cannot be heard to say either that the claim *in rem* or the claim *in personam* has been defeated. If the salvors were other than the Admiralty I can see no difference between seizure in prize and loss by any other war risk. ... The repairs were not yet sufficiently advanced to enable the vessel to be moved, but they were being effected for the benefit of the owners in pursuance of the promise to tow the vessel to the Tyne. The owners were then free to negotiate for future charters, or requisition, and in fact they did so negotiate. They had a ship which they could insure against marine and war risks. ... The only point that has worried me is the identity of the ... salvors and the authority seizing, both acting on behalf of the Crown. The benefit which had accrued to the ship was taken by the salvors. Can they both take back the benefit and claim payment for that benefit? ... I think the answer is this. If a shipowner gets his ship released by paying security to meet a claim for

---

[24] *The Gaupen* (1925) 22 Ll.L.Rep. 371.
[25] *The Stella* (1867) L.R. 1 A. & E. 340; *The James Armstrong* (1875) L.R. 4 A. & E. 380, 385 (deterioration of cargo from delay); *The Germania* [1904] P. 131.
[26] *The Ningpo* (1923) 15 Ll.L.Rep. 392.
[27] cf. *Admiralty Commissioners v. Owners of M.V. Josefina Thorden and her cargo (The Josefina Thorden)* [1945] 1 All E.R. 344.
[28] *ibid.* at 348.

salvage services, all risks attaching to the ship are his. The salvors' rights against the ship are exchanged for their rights against the security. This was a known risk. The owners' agent had asked for an undertaking that the ship would not be seized, and that undertaking had been refused. Knowing of the possibility of seizure the owners nevertheless preferred to prevent the arrest of their ship and to obtain the chance of making profitable arrangements for the future of their ship by securing for the salvors a banker's guarantee to pay whatever might be awarded for the salvage services rendered."

Qualifications on the general principle

1332   The general principle as to the time of valuation must not be applied categorically and is subject to a number of qualifications.[29]

The court must take account of events which, being the necessary and inevitable consequence of the casualty or the services rendered, go to demonstrate the extent to which the vessel has not been preserved from the consequences of the casualty. Thus, if the salved cargo consists of perishable food in a vessel which has become unseaworthy, it may prove impossible to arrange for transhipment of the cargo or to dispose of it locally after the termination of the service, due to the remoteness of the place of safety. In such a case, the cargo might be regarded as having no salved value despite the fact that the difficulties only arise after the termination of the service. The salvor's efforts will in one sense have been successful but he will not of course, albeit through no fault of his own, have succeeded in preserving the cargo from the risk of loss at being landed at a remote place of safety. The result will be consistent with assessing the reward according to the benefit obtained by the defendant.

1333   The position is similar with other events which are merely the natural and foreseeable consequence of the casualty or the services rendered. Thus, the owners of the cargo, acting prudently and without fault,[30] may realise less for the cargo than they might otherwise have done because of the time involved in assessing the prospects of on-shipment or transhipment. The sum realised, however, might still be regarded as the salved value of the cargo.

A most important factor in modern times, which had necessitated a change in the law, is the change in the value of money brought about by the continuous fluctuation in currencies. This will be discussed more fully below.[31]

Evidence of salved values

1334   In assessing salved values, the tribunal should take account of all the evidence put before it and may place whatever weight on that evidence it

---

[29] See further, *post*, §1338.
[30] *cf. ante*, §1325.
[31] *Post*, §§ 1461–1465.

considers appropriate. Although not bound by decisions on the available evidence reached by other tribunals or parties to the salvage operation, it may, however, take them into consideration.[32]

Thus, the court will take into consideration the fact that a sum of money has been ordered by another court of competent jurisdiction to be paid to other salvors, who had rendered services on the same occasion, out of the proceeds of the salved property.[33]

Similarly, where the salvors' claims in respect of one or more salved interests have been settled out of court and the action continued only against the remainder, the judgment of the court as to the value of the services rendered to the remainder cannot be governed by any transaction which has taken place out of court.[34] The court will take due note of the true salved value of the interests who have settled. As Dr Lushington has observed[35]: **1335**

> "It is obvious that this is the correct course to be adopted, from the consideration that in a case of this description many reasons may exist why, though the act is done by the common consent of the parties, it may not form a fair estimate of the real value of the service to be rewarded. For instance, as in this case, the small value of the ship, and the desire to get the matter expeditiously settled without awaiting the decision of this Court, in order to avoid the expense of litigation, both these considerations may be sufficient to have influenced the motives of the parties between themselves in making the arrangement in question out of Court; at the same time it is clear that they can furnish no safe rule for the guidance of my judgment upon the present occasion."

In one case, the defendants were ordered to amend their pleading by leaving out the amount paid to the plaintiffs but no further, since it was not objectionable to plead the settlement in order to inform the court that the claim was against cargo only.[36]

Where salved values have been appraised by the Admiralty Marshal, the general rule is that the appraisement is conclusive.[37]

Sales

The broad principle may be stated in this way. The salved value is the price which a willing buyer would be prepared to pay for the property in the position and condition that it finds itself at the termination of the services. The **1336**

---

[32] The court may accept another tribunal's finding of the amount of salvage to be awarded where it is considering another question, such as the distribution of the reward. See *The Calypso* (1828) 2 Hagg. 209, 211–212 (salvage awarded by American court).
[33] *The Antilope* (1873) L.R. 4 A. & E. 33.
[34] *The Emma* (1844) 2 W. Rob. 315; *The Due Checchi* (1872) L.R. 4 A. & E. 45n.
[35] *The Emma* (1844) 2 W. Rob. 315, 318–319.
[36] *The Due Checchi* (1872) L.R. 4 A. & E. 35n.
[37] See *post*, §1386.

property saved is rarely in fact sold at this moment so accordingly the exercise is a hypothetical one in the vast majority of cases.

There are occasions, however, when the property is sold shortly after the termination of the services and the proceeds of such a sale will constitute evidence of the salved value. The cogency of the evidence will depend on a variety of factors, *viz.*;

(a) the nature of the sale (auction, private treaty, etc.,)

(b) the extent to which the sale was advertised;

(c) the fluctuations in the market since the services terminated.

1337   It is not uncommon for such sales to be effected through the courts, thereby giving unencumbered title to the purchaser. Such sales are generally to be regarded as "forced" sales, which do not necessarily give a true reflection of the market value of the property, and/or the price being affected by the facts that:

(a) subject to reserve, the sale is between a "willing" buyer but an "unwilling" seller;

(b) the purchaser will usually have to pay in cash, without any credit terms;

(c) the condition of the property will be suspect in view of the forced nature of the sale; and

(d) there will be limited scope for inspection and survey.

Objective or subjective valuation

1338   It is convenient to discuss the basic principles of valuation for salvage purposes in the context of ship's value, but the principles are equally applicable to all classes of salved property.

Where no sale has actually taken place, the salved value must be assessed indirectly. The right approach is for the salvor to have his reward assessed on the basis of a salved value calculated by reference to the value of the vessel in sound condition less the costs of placing her in sound condition or, alternatively, the scrap value of the vessel less the reasonable costs of realising her as scrap, whichever is the greater.

Sound value

1339   Taking the first alternative it is easy enough to assess the cost of repairs, but it is less easy to assess the sound value of the vessel. Most of the vessels which are the subject of salvage services are trading ships. Their value is a reflection of their earning power. Indeed, the value is essentially a capitalisation of the

Sound value

potential earnings of the vessel over its trading life.[38] Since marked fluctuations occur in the profitability of vessels, it is important to know whether a vessel which has been salved should be valued by reference to the open market at that time or by reference to her actual commitments, if any. The problem can be expressed in this way. A disadvantageous long-term time charter may cause a ship with an open market value of £2,000,000 to have a value of only £500,000. The choice between the two values, particularly where repair costs are high, would be very material in the assessment of the salvor's reward.

The distinction is neatly mirrored by a conflict in the authorities. In *The San Onofre*,[39] the salved vessel had been chartered for 16 years at a low rate of hire. Her owners valued her, with her charter commitment, at £160,000. On the other hand, the Admiralty Marshal valued the vessel on the open market at over £360,000. Sir Samuel Evans P. fixed the award on the basis that the action was an action *in rem* and, if security had not been provided to the court, the vessel would have been sold charter free and the funds available to satisfy the salvors' award:

1340

> "The ground of this application is that the *San Onofre* cannot be regarded as an ordinary vessel at all, but must be looked at as a wholly exceptional vessel, having regard to the contractual obligations which had been entered into between the shipowners and the charterers. In no case, so far as I am aware, have the charters of a vessel been taken into account in assessing the value of a salved ship in salvage proceedings; and I think it would be very undesirable from all points of view if there should be introduced into valuations in salvage cases any element of that kind, which would make a reference to the Registrar and merchants necessary in order to ascertain the value of the salved ship.
>
> The ship is salved, and may be arrested as she is, as the salvors are entitled to arrest the *res*. If bail is not given the ship may be sold. She would not be sold subject to charterparties, but as she existed to any one who wanted to buy a ship of her description.
>
> In this case an undertaking was given to put in bail in ordinary form; and the writ as issued was directed to the owners of the *San Onofre*, her cargo and freight, and all persons interested in the vessel. The Court has nothing to do with the relationship between the shipowners and the charterers; nor in my opinion have the salvors anything to do with any such question."

On the other hand, in *The Castor*,[40] Lord Merrivale P. considered that a charterparty which had a further seven years to run was an element of value proper for consideration in determining the value of the *Castor* to her owners as a going concern. The court therefore found the value to be £85,000, as

1341

---

[38] *cf. The Argentina* (1888) 13 P.D. 191, 201, *per* Bowen L.J.
[39] [1917] P. 96.
[40] [1932] P. 142.

compared with the figure of £72,000 put forward by her owners as her open market value:

> "So far as I am able to see, there is nothing in *The San Onofre* which in any way infringes, or was intended to infringe, the principle laid down in *The Hohenzollern*.[41] All parties interested in the *res* were before the Court, and were interested in the salvage claim and the amount of the award. Two sets of rights, proprietory and possessory, had been benefited, and an award was made on the footing of the full value of the whole. The actual judgment does nothing exceptional. Upon an appraisement salvage was awarded. In what proportions the sum payable was divided as between the owners and charterers is not reported. Apparently they did not differ about it. As the vessel was not sold by auction it did not become necessary to determine whether by virtue of such sale the owners would become entitled to the whole balance of the purchase money on the footing that the charter-party had become discharged by operation of law. Had such a claim been made I cannot doubt that the equitable nature of the Admiralty jurisdiction in cases of salvage would have been vindicated.
>
> As in the case of *The Hohenzollern*, what has to be determined here is what is the value of the *Castor* to her owners as a going concern? What was she worth in her damaged state to her owners? The view I have expressed seems to me consistent with the judgments of the Court of Appeal in the recent case of *The Edison*,[42] to which both parties referred. There, in the case of a vessel lost by collision damage, Scrutton L.J. cited the judgment of Lord Gorell in *The Harmonides*,[43] and added words which directly affect the present inquiry. 'The value of the ship', he said, 'is an estimate, or rough capitalization, of the earning power of the ship for its life', and he added this: 'You cannot give both the value of the ship and the profits it would probably earn.'
>
> Bearing the authorities in mind, what seems to me fallacious in the contention for the plaintiffs here is that, after an appraisement which was manifestly based on some earning power, they assert a right to enhance the appraised value by adding thereto the capitalized value of the ship's whole earning power under a charterparty. On the other hand, it seems to me inconsistent with authority and wrong in principle to exclude from consideration the earning power of the *Castor* under the charterparty, under which so long as it subsists she could alone earn money for her owners. The appraisement, as I have said, proceeds on the footing that the ship is an employed ship likely to be employed. To determine whether the agreed employment enhances the value so arrived at I have made the necessary further inquiries of the valuer. He advises me that the rate of hire is not exceptional so as to call for any adjustment on that ground, but that the agreed duration of the charterparty is an element of

[41] [1906] P. 339.
[42] [1932] P. 52 especially at 149–151.
[43] [1903] P. 1.

value proper for consideration in determining the *Castor's* value to her owners as a going concern. Acting to the best of my judgment upon the valuer's advice, I determine the salved value of the *Castor* at 85.000*l*."

Despite the valiant attempt of Lord Merrivale P. in *The Castor*, it is difficult to reconcile these two decisions.[44] It is of course, possible that the salvors are entitled to claim against either the value subject to charter commitments or the open market value, whichever is the higher. But there seems to be no logical reason why the salvors should be favoured in this way. On the contrary, such an approach would appear to impose an unnecessary and unfair burden on the salved interest.

There is a body of opinion favouring *The Castor* over *The San Onofre*. The attitude is reinforced by the reference in several authorities to the need to assess the value of the vessel concerned "to her owners".[45] It is thought right that the court should accordingly take account of the financial effect of the charterparties to which the owners have committed their vessel.

Valuation for damages assessment

A close analogy is drawn[46] between the valuation of a vessel for salvage purposes and the valuation of the same vessel for the purposes of recovering damages for total loss following a collision. Reference can be made to the speech of Lord Wright in *Owners of Dredger Liesbosch v. Owners of Steamship Edison*[47]:

"The true rule seems to be that the measure of damages in such cases is the value of the ship to her owner as a going concern at the time and place of the loss. In assessing that value regard must naturally be had to her pending engagements, either profitable or the reverse. The rule, however, obviously requires some care in its application; the figure of damage is to represent the capitalized value of the vessel as a profit-earning machine, not in the abstract but in view of the actual circumstances.... The assessment of the value of such a vessel at the time of loss, with her engagements, may seem to present an extremely complicated and speculative problem. But different considerations apply to the simple case of a ship sunk by collision when free of all engagements, either being laid up in port or being a seeking ship in ballast, though

---

[44] *cf.* Howard, "Valuation in Salvage Cases—Damage, Damages and Remoteness" (1975) 91 L.Q.R. 502.
[45] *The Harmonides* [1903] P. 1.
[46] See *The Hohenzollern* [1906] P. 339.
[47] [1933] A.C. 449, 463–465. See also *The Harmonides* [1903] P. 1, 6, *per* Gorell Barnes J.: "The real test ... is what is the value" of the vessel "to the owners, as a going concern, at the time the vessel was sunk"; and the Lord Justice continues: "I should add, 'at that place', for if the vessel had to be replaced at Petras, expense and time might have been added to the cost of the vessel replaced."

intended for employment, if it can be obtained, under charter or otherwise. In such a case the fair measure of damage will be simply the market value, on which will be calculated interest at and from the date of loss, to compensate for delay in paying for the loss. But the contrasted cases of a tramp under charter or a seeking tramp do not exhaust all the possible problems in which must be sought an answer to the question what is involved in the principle of *restitutio in integrum*. I have only here mentioned such cases as a step to considering the problem in the present case. Many, varied and complex are the types of vessels and the modes of employment in which their owners may use them. Hence the difficulties constantly felt in defining rules as to the measure of damages. I think it impossible to lay down any universal formula. A ship of war, a supply ship, a lightship, a dredger employed by a public authority, a passenger liner, a trawler, a cable ship, a tug boat (to take a few instances), all may raise quite different questions before their true value can be ascertained. . . .

. . . Just as in the other cases considered, so in this, what the Court has to ascertain is the real value to the owner as part of his working plant, ignoring remote considerations at the time of loss. If it had been possible without delay to replace a comparable dredger exactly as and where the *Liesbosch* was, at the market price, the appellants would have suffered no damage save the cost of doing so, that is in such an assumed case the market price, the position being analogous to that of the loss of goods for which there is a presently available market."

This analogy, however, is not as close as might first appear. In the first place, the underlying principle of salvage is to reward a salvor for conferring a benefit upon an owner, whilst the underlying principle in a claim for damages for negligence is *restitutio in integrum*. Secondly, the value of a vessel will presumably, have no effect on whether or not a collision would occur, but the value may have a decisive influence on whether a potential salvor will undertake salvage operations. It is one thing to form a view as to the open market value of the vessel, quite another to take into account effects of the owners' contractual commitment with third parties. Thirdly, the salved value is a reflection of both the sound value of a vessel and the costs of repairing her, whilst the damage claim will only reflect the one or the other. Indeed, the greater the damage, the higher the claim in tort but the lower the salved value. Furthermore, there can be serious practical difficulties about taking account of the charterparty commitments of a vessel.

Charterparty commitments

1344   A typical problem in taking account of charterparty commitments in assessing a vessel's salved value is that, in the case of a serious casualty, the salved value of a vessel may be affected dramatically by the question whether the, say, unfavourable charterparty under which the vessel was operating has been frustrated and, further, whether the moment of frustration occurred before or after the termination of the services.

Again, although at first glance it is attractive to support the proposition that the owner is only liable for the value of his vessel to him, this does not take full account of the overall situation and in particular the position of the charterer, who, in the case of a charterparty unfavourable from the owners' point of view, may gain enormous financial advantage from the successful conclusion of a salvage service.

1345 This position has already been discussed.[48] As has been seen, the question whether and, if so, to what extent the interest of the charterer in the maritime adventure can be a subject of salvage is intimately entwined in the present issue as to whether, for example, values should be assessed in the light of the financial commitments of the owner of the property concerned.

If, for instance, time charter hire can be the subject of a salvage claim, then, by the same token, it is thought that the courts would more readily assess the ship value in the light of that charter rather than on the open market. To do otherwise would be to impose a substantial salvage liability on a shipowner assessed on the basis of market value when the ship could be worth very much less to him.

1346 Equally, if some charter hire cannot be the subject of a salvage claim, it is thought that the courts would more readily assess the ship value on the open market. To do otherwise would be to deprive the salvors of any return for the overall benefit conferred when the vessel was operating under a very onerous charterparty from the owner's point of view. As is so often the case, the final consideration is when to draw the line. Which factors bearing upon the value of a vessel to her owners are relevant to the assessment of the salved value? These are some examples:

   (i) There are factors which *directly* affect the earning capabilities of a vessel, *e.g.* where there is a time charter.

   (ii) There are factors which *indirectly* affect the earning capability of a ship, *e.g.* restrictive trading limits by reason of nationality.

   (iii) There are factors which *directly* affect the capital cost of the hull, *e.g.* onerous interest charges under a mortgage.

   (iv) There are factors which *indirectly* affect the capital cost of the hull, *e.g.* a restriction on the owners against the importation of a replacement vessel.

1347 A good example of the difficulties that arise is presented by *The Eisenach*.[49] After salvage services, the vessel had been sold for 550,000 German marks by her German owners. The plaintiffs contended that this figure should be

---
[48] *Ante*, Chap. 3.
[49] (1936) 54 Ll.L.Rep. 354, especially at 362–363. *N.B. post*, §§ 1461–1465.

converted at the rate of 12.2 marks to the pound. The owners challenged both the figure of 550,000 marks as representing the salved value and the rate of exchange. Bucknill J. dealt with the matter in the following way:

"The Court has to assess the pecuniary benefit conferred by the salvors upon the owners of the salved property, and in order to make this assessment, fixes, as one of the essential factors in that pecuniary benefit, the value of the property to the owners at the time of the service. It may be said with accuracy that the sound value of the *Eisenach* to her owners at the time of the service was the figure of 550,000 marks, credited to them as the proceeds of the sale of the ship. But the nature of the transaction with the Bulgarian buyers was such that the owners of the *Eisenach* were obliged by law to spend the proceeds of sale on building new tonnage in Germany. They were not allowed by their law to convert the proceeds of sale into sterling—even if they had been able to do so. In any case, I do not think, having regard to the evidence which was placed before me, that they could have converted this sum into sterling at the rate of 12.2 to the £, or anything like it.

Now, the judgment of this Court is in sterling, and in order to assess in sterling the pecuniary benefit received by the owners of the salved property, the value of the salved property to the owners must also be fixed in sterling. The difficulty of arriving at the salved value in sterling of the *Eisenach* is that the ship is a German ship, and the relative values of the mark and the £ sterling appear to be, on the evidence, in a very fluid and uncertain state, so far as transactions like the sale and purchase of a ship are concerned. I do not think there is any reliable standard by which I can convert this sum of 550,000 marks into sterling. I therefore have to look at the other evidence before me as to the value of the *Eisenach*, to see what assistance it provides.

One fact which emerged in the evidence is that it would cost the owners of the ship roughly $1\frac{1}{2}$ million marks to build a ship like the *Eisenach* today. Comparing marks with marks, if the owners received roughly half a million marks for the ship from the buyers, it appears that the ship was worth to them about one-third of the cost price of a new ship. The cost in sterling to build a new ship like the *Eisenach* was given in evidence by the plaintiffs before me as £93,500 and by the defendants as £82,000.

Fixing the value of the *Eisenach* on the basis of the cost of building a new ship like her, I think the sum of £30,000 would be a proper sum to take as her sound value when the services ended. This figure of £30,000 is rather less than the figure of £33,500 which the plaintiffs suggested would be the market value of the ship, based on the cost price of £93,500 less 5 per cent depreciation per annum for each of the 13 years of the *Eisenach's* age.

The market value of the ship, based on the sales of other vessels, is the usual method of assessing the value of the ship. But in this case the evidence is that if the ship had been lost to her owners, it would have

Charterparty commitments

been difficult for the German owners to replace her by purchase from any foreign owners in the open market, because of the shortage in Germany of foreign exchanges wherewith to pay the purchase price. Also, there is really no comparable sale of a like ship about the time of the salvage as a guide to the market value of the *Eisenach*, if sold, for instance, by the Admiralty Marshal. Such evidence as was put forward indicated to me that the ship if so sold would probably fetch something in the neighbourhood of about £29,000. Ships belonging to the Norddeutscher Lloyd are known to be thoroughly well built and well maintained. My view also is that to the German owners of the *Eisenach* the vessel was worth rather more than her market value, because of the difficulty which they would have of replacing her by purchase abroad."

The matter is clearly in need of judicial guidance. But it is suggested that, whilst government restrictions should always be regarded as material, purely contractual obligations or the general economic circumstances of an owner should not.

In the first place, salvage is essentially a cause of action which has its roots in an action *in rem*. In simple terms, these services are rendered to, and the claim made against, the salved property and not its owners. Since the court can sell the vessel free of any encumbrances, it is illogical that the salved value may depend upon whether the owner chooses to enter an appearance in the action or not. In the second place, it can be said that the salvor should not be concerned with the owner's contractual arrangements, which are in the category *res inter alios acta*. It would seem unreasonable that a shipowner could claim that his own interest in a vessel was reduced by reason of the terms of the contract by which he has chosen to hire out the vessel. Suppose, for instance, that for fiscal purposes one company within a huge group chose to charter out its vessel to another company within the same group at a wholly unrealistic and suppressed rate of hire. Should the salvor be faced with an assertion that the ship has no or next to no value to her owners? Thirdly, it has already been suggested that only those with a proprietary or possessory interest in the adventure can be the defendants to a salvage claim. As has been pointed out, that conclusion alone would probably incline a court to the view that the charter free market value of the vessel is the proper basis of the salved value. Indeed, it is striking to note that the decision in *The Castor*[50] may have been based on the wrongful assumption that a time charterer has a possessory interest in the vessel.

1348

Fourthly, the assessment of salved values by reference to the market value has the attraction of simplicity. It avoids the need to consider whether a particular commitment has survived the casualty. It avoids the need to assess which commitments are to be considered and which not. Furthermore, it will avoid the necessity of considering events following the termination of the

1349

---

[50] [1932] P. 142; *ante*, §1340.

services, for often it is only then that the effects of the owners' obligations and economic circumstances can be assessed. It also avoids the need for the salvor to enquire whether the vessel is on charter and to obtain security from the time charterer. The "market value" approach is therefore considered preferable.[51] In this connection, it is to be noted that Rule XVII of the York-Antwerp Rules, which deals with contributory values in general average, clearly provides:

> "The value of the ship shall be assessed without taking into account the beneficial or detrimental effect of any demise or time charterparty to which the ship may be committed."

No sale

1350 In the absence of sale, the market value of a vessel has to be established by expert evidence. The opinion of an expert should preferably be based upon the sale prices of similar vessels sold at about the time of the termination of the services. It is, of course, helpful to the court if details of these comparable sales are produced, together with an explanation of what allowances have been made in respect of differing ages, sizes, speeds and so on. Furthermore, that valuer should if possible have had an opportunity of surveying the vessel in order to gauge the general standard of maintenance and so on.

In the absence of any information about sales of similar vessels, evidence of the market value can be gleaned from an estimate of the cost of replacement. Such an estimate must perforce reflect an allowance for depreciation over the period in which the salved vessel has been in use.[52]

1351 Although it is not thought that evidence of the insured value is inadmissible as being irrelevant, such evidence cannot be regarded as having much significance. In particular it is common to over-insure vessels with the approval, if not the insistence, of underwriters.

If it was considered relevant, the valuers must be given details of the vessel's trading commitments in so far as they may differ from the state of the freight market as a whole. While many considerations weigh in the purchase price of a vessel, her capacity to pay her way, and amortise the sale price, is probably dominant.

Deductions

1352 One of the vexing problems in the assessment of salved values is the scope of the deductions which are properly allowable from the market value. It is often helpful in considering a potential deduction to consider the vessel from the point of view of a potential purchaser. Is the deduction an expense for which the purchaser would make allowance or is it an expense which will fall upon the seller in any event?

---

[51] The point is touched on again in the consideration of cargo and freight values, *infra*.
[52] See *The Eisenach* (1936) 54 Ll.L.Rep. 354 (cited *ante*, §1347).

The following are thought to be proper deductions: 1353

  (i) the costs of survey;
 (ii) the costs of delivery to a repair port;
(iii) the costs of discharge of the cargo if such activity is the responsibility of, and paid for, by the shipowners;
(iv) the costs of repairing the damage to the vessel, whether occasioned by the casualty or already caused prior to it[53];
 (v) ancillary costs, such as drydocking, gas freeing, and so on;
(vi) port charges, pilotage and towage;
(vii) costs of superintendence during repairs;
(viii) agent's charges at repair port;
(ix) running expenses during repairs, *e.g.* skeleton crews' wages, bunkers and so on;
 (x) additional insurance premiums during the repair period.

The following have been considered not to be proper deductions: 1354

  (i) outstanding claims against the vessel which gave rise to a maritime or statutory lien[54];
 (ii) liability for crew's wages earned prior to salvage[55];
(iii) costs incurred in prosecuting wreckers who had forcibly dispossessed the salvage claimants.[56]

The position as regards other matters, such as repatriation costs and loss of use during repairs, has yet to be resolved.

Scrap value

When the cost of repairing a damaged vessel and putting her back in sound 1355 condition exceeds her sound market value or the balance is less than the scrap value of the ship, then the salvor is entitled to have his award assessed on the net scrap value. The net scrap value is a question of fact. It is usually proved

---

[53] Where a yacht owner could reasonably be expected not to sell the vessel in her damaged condition but to arrange for repairs, the salved value is likely to be more than the amount for which she can be sold in her damaged condition. Accordingly, in *The Yolaine* [1995] 2 Lloyd's Rep. 7, Clarke J. assessed the salved value as the sound value less the reasonable cost of repairs.
[54] *The Hebe* (1847) 7 N.o.C. Supp. i, iii (Ir.).
[55] *The Selina* (1842) 2 N.o.C. 16, 18. See also *The Sabrina* (1842) 7 Jur. 182.
[56] *The Fleece* (1850) 3 W.Rob. 278, 281.

by obtaining evidence of the price obtainable from a scrap yard and deducting the cost of taking the vessel to that yard.[56A]

Doubts exist as to whether the costs of a comprehensive survey in order to assess the repairs required to place the vessel in sound condition are a proper deduction from the scrap value.

Freight

1356   It is convenient before considering the position of cargo value to deal with the position of "freight". It has already been suggested that freight cannot be an independent subject of salvage. There must be a tangible *res* in existence whose owner is at risk for the freight.[57] It follows that for the purposes of salvage, the "freight" must be at the risk of the shipowner or cargo-owner in order for the salvor to claim a reward in respect of it. If the situation is such that the costs of the voyage are at the risk of another person concerned with the venture, then the salvors have no claim against them.

At risk of ship

1357   The freight is at the risk of the ship if it is only payable if the ship reaches her destination. The whole of the freight will be added to the ship value if the salvage services terminate at the port of destination and the freight is then payable. This is typical in the oil tanker trades.

Where salvage services terminate at port of destination

1358   If the salvor's services continue until arrival at the port of destination of salved cargo upon which freight is chargeable collect, he is entitled to have valued as a contributory interest the whole net freight which was unpaid and at risk at the time of the service, and was preserved by the service for the shipowner. It is true that, if salvage services are rendered near the end of the voyage, the greater part of the effort in earning the freight may be attributable to the shipowner rather than the salvor. But if freight is payable collect, none of it is earned until arrival at destination, so a salvor who preserves from danger freight which was at risk of being lost entirely will be able to claim against the full amount. In practice, freight may be valued separately or included in the valuation of the cargo.

Where salvage services terminate short of the port of destination

1359   If salvage services terminate at a port or any other place short of the cargo's original port of destination, the shipowner will not then have earned his right to recover freight which is payable collect, at destination. It will depend upon the circumstances, therefore, whether or not there is any freight against which

---

[56A] Scrap value prices are usually fixed by reference to the vessel's light displacement tonnage.
[57] *The Kaletan* (1914) 13 T.L.R. 572.

Freight

the salvor can claim. Two situations must be considered: first, where the salved cargo is not carried on; and, secondly, where it is carried on.

If cargo salved is not carried on

If the cargo salved is not carried on to its destination, by transhipment or other means, no freight at all is earned except in two cases. First, if the reason why the cargo is not carried on is that its owner has himself prevented the shipowner from carrying it on and completely performing the contract of carriage, the whole freight is payable.[58] Secondly, if the reason is that the cargo-owner, having the choice, has preferred to take delivery of the cargo where it is rather than at its original destination, he is liable to pay freight *pro rata itineris* according to the terms of a new agreement which, if not expressed, will be implied from the circumstances.[59]

1360

If there is no such agreement and the cargo-owner wrongfully prevents the shipowner from completing the original contract when by virtue of a salvage service he has been enabled to do so, the shipowner will be entitled to claim damages for loss of his opportunity to earn full freight, which will be equivalent to the freight he would have earned less any amount by which his loss has, or could have been, mitigated.[60] The cargo-owner's liability will be for damages, not for freight, although of course his ability to recover such damages will be due in part to the salvage service.

If cargo salved is carried on

If cargo is carried on to its destination from the port where the salvor's services end, the shipowner, upon completion of the voyage and delivery of the cargo, is entitled to the whole of the stipulated freight which was at risk when the salvage service was rendered. Since freight is not apportionable at common law, no part of the freight can be said to have been earned at the port of refuge where the salvage services terminated and where salved values must be assessed. However, in order to prevent injustice to the salvor whose services have, in some measure at least, benefited those concerned in the freight by preserving, as far at least as the port of refuge, the property upon the safety of which the possibility of earning freight depends, Admiralty departs from the common law doctrine and, "on purely equitable principles",[61] accords to the salvor a right to salvage upon part of the freight, estimated, so far as it can be, for the portion of the voyage so far completed.

1361

In *The Dorothy Foster*,[62] Lord Stowell held:

---

[58] *The Cargo ex Galam* (1863) 2 Moo. (N.S.) 216 (PC).
[59] *Christy v. Row* (1808) 1 Taunt. 300; *Hunter v. Prinsep* (1808) 10 East 378; *Vlierboom v. Chapman* (1844) 3 M. & W. 230; *Hopper v. Burness* (1876) 1 C.P.D. 137; *Metcalfe v. Britannia Ironworks Co.* (1877) 2 Q.B.D. 423 (CA); *Mitchell v. Darthez* (1836) 2 Bing N.C. 555; *The Soblomsten* (1866) L.R. 1 A. & E. 293.
[60] See the cases *supra*, in n. 40.
[61] *The Norma* (1860) Lush. 124, 127, *per* Dr Lushington.
[62] (1805) 6 C.Rob. 89, 91.

> "The Court, in giving salvage on freight, makes no separation as to minute portions of the voyage. If a commencement has taken place, and the voyage is afterwards accomplished, the whole freight is included in the valuation of the property on which salvage is given."

Subsequent decisions have not gone so far, however.

1362 The leading case on the subject is *The Norma*.[63] A vessel on a voyage from Honduras to England, becoming disabled, was towed by salvors to Bermuda. She was refitted there for £1,822 and afterwards carried her cargo to England. The gross freight, of £2,210, upon which salvage was claimed hardly, if at all, exceeded the expenses at Bermuda, the wages home and the port charges in England. Dr Lushington's judgment affords the classic exposition of the general rule[64] that salved values should be ascertained at the place where salvage terminates. But, he continued, it was not conclusive that freight is not earned at the port of refuge:

> "But in salvage we have to decide on purely equitable principles, and the question here is not so much what freight was earned at Bermuda, but what services in respect of the contract for freight the salvors had then rendered. Judging by this test, the salvors are entitled to salvage upon a considerable part of the total freight, for it is clear that a large portion of the voyage had been performed before the salvage services, and that the entire benefit of so much was preserved to the shipowners by the salvors, not indeed absolutely, for expenses had been incurred, and the perils of the voyage from Bermuda home had yet to be undergone, but preserved from immediate and total loss."[65]

1363 It is important to understand the precise import of this judgment and to make clear that the salvor, whose services terminate at a port of refuge, cannot claim to have a value put upon the freight for the carriage of goods up to that point simply *pro rata itineris peracti*, and without regard to the expenses which the completion of the shipowner's contract of affreightment involves, and which he is obliged to incur in order that he may become entitled to any freight at all. It will, however, depend upon the facts as to what extent such considerations ought to affect the value to be put upon the salvor's services to freight.

1364 In *The Norma*,[66] Dr Lushington rejected the shipowner's contention that the whole freight had been swallowed up by the expenses of earning it, concluding[67]:

---

[63] (1860) Lush. 124.
[64] Which he laid down and applied in *The George Dean* (1857) Swab. 290, 291.
[65] (1860) Lush. 124, 127.
[66] *Supra.*
[67] *ibid.* at 127–128.

"I do not think it necessary to enter into detailed calculation upon this question of the value of the salvors' services to freight, how far the Bermuda expenses are to be taken into account, what items are proper items of deduction, and so on: my judgment must after all be a *rusticum judicium*. It is enough to say that the services of the salvors in respect to freight were considerable. I shall reckon the value of the freight saved at £1,000, that, with the agreed values of ship and freight makes a total value of property saved £5,000, and I award to the salvors one-third part of the whole."

It is doubtful whether *The Norma* can now be regarded as good law, particularly in light of the subsequent decision of the Admiralty Court in *The James Armstrong*,[68] where the court adopted a more mathematical approach. In that case, the destination of the cargo was London, and the salvor's services terminated in Scilly, whence the cargo was afterwards transhipped to London. For the purpose of estimating the figure at which the freight should be put in the salvage action, the registrar and merchants took the freight payable in London and subtracted from it the expenses attending the transhipment in Scilly and the conveyance of it thence to London. Then, to the sum of £813 0s. 5d., which was the result of this subtraction, they added an estimated sum which brought up the total to £1,000, because they held that, since the termination of the salvage services, there had been great delay (which would of course involve expense) in the transhipment and conveyance to London. In his judgment Sir Robert Phillimore approved and adopted this method of calculation.

1365

The judgment pays little regard to the distinction between deductions from the ship's salved value and deductions from the freight. Repairs to the salved vessel at the port of refuge ought to have formed deductions from the ship's salved value since they represent the capital sum by which a willing buyer would discount the value of the vessel were he to purchase her at the port of termination of the services.

On the other hand, it is clear that a deduction must be made from the salved value of the gross freight, representing the cost of earning that freight subsequent to the completion of the salvage services. Since, however, the shipowner always bears the risks of performing the voyage, it is not wholly realistic simply to deduct the bare expense to the shipowner of earning the freight for the whole voyage. An appropriate allowance should also be deducted to reflect the overhead expenses of running the vessel and the risks undertaken by it, which are possibly best reflected by the proportion of insurance costs represented by the period of the remainder of the voyage.

1366

When freight has to be paid by the owners of cargo whether or not the ship reaches her destination ("ship lost or not lost"), that freight cannot accurately

1367

---

[68] (1875) 3 Asp. M.L.C. 46.

Salved Values

be described as being "at risk". Account is taken of such freight when the value of the cargo is assessed.

Cargo salved value

1368   As with the salved vessel, the general principle is that the salved cargo must be valued as at the time and place of the termination of the services. It is relatively easy to assess the value of the cargo in the vast majority of cases because, by the nature of things, the cargo has been, is being, or will be, sold in the course of trade in any event.

1369   Where the services terminate in the port of destination, if the goods are carried to their destination the value of the cargo can be assessed in one of two ways:

   (a) (i) the f.o.b. price of the goods at the port of shipment, plus a sum in respect of the cost of insurance during, and freight for, the voyage;

   (ii) the c.i.f. price of the goods at the port of shipment, together with a margin of, say, 10 per cent to reflect the anticipated profit of the merchant importing the cargo;

   (b) the value of sales of comparable goods at the port of destination (including if available the actual shipment).

No account should be taken of freight if the freight was at risk of the ship.

Where salvage services terminate short of the port of destination

1370   If the cargo salved is not carried on to destination but sold locally, the proceeds of sale will form prima facie the salved cargo value less the costs of discharge and arranging sale. Again, evidence may be adduced to establish that this does not represent the true market value of the cargo in question, or that a higher price could have been obtained for the cargo by carrying it forward to destination or to another place where a market for such goods exists. In the latter circumstances, the test must be whether it was reasonable to sell the cargo as it then lay rather than incur the risks involved in transhipment and on forwarding. Again, pro rata freight may have to be deducted from these proceeds of sale if this is not at the risk of cargo interests.

1371   If cargo is carried on to destination in the salved vessel, the value of the cargo at its port of destination is customarily taken as the basis for valuation of cargo, subject to a deduction of the cost, if any, of getting that cargo to its destination. Repairs and port of refuge expenses incurred by the shipowners in making good the damage which rendered the salvage services necessary will generally form a deduction from the ship salved value, and the cost of proceeding from port of refuge to port of destination is deductible from the freight.

If cargo is carried on to destination in another vessel, cargo is valued as follows. The shipowner is obliged, under his contract of carriage, to carry the cargo to the port of destination named in the bill of lading. Where, however, the circumstances of the casualty frustrate the contract of carriage the shipowner is entitled to arrange transhipment and on-forwarding of cargo to destination, but he is not obliged to do so. If the cargo arrived safely at the port of destination, the cost of transhipment and on-forwarding forms a deduction from the salved value of the freight. Where, however, the freight has been prepaid, and is therefore at the risk of cargo interests, the value of cargo at the port of destination is customarily adopted as the salved cargo value, and the costs of on-carriage are deducted from that value. These costs will include transhipment expenses, costs of surveying and superintending the transhipment operation, and the freight on the on-carrying vessel. Expenses incurred at the port of refuge which are not exclusively referable to the transhipment operation may form a deduction from the ship value but not from the value of cargo. **1372**

Deductions from cargo salved value

Expenses reasonably incurred in realising the value of salved cargo may properly be deducted from this value in arriving at the cargo's proportion of the salved fund. These expenses may include all or any of the following. **1373**

(i) *Damage or shortage:* If damage is found on discharge of salved cargo, the cost of making good this damage forms a deduction from the sound value of this cargo provided that the damage in question existed at the termination of the salvage services. Where, however, cargo is damaged either on board the salved vessel or in the course of a transhipment operation subsequent to the salvage services, the amount of this damage is not a proper deduction since it is not referable to the value of the cargo in question at the time of termination of the services. An exception to this principle, however, concerns damage necessarily incident to necessary transhipment and on-carrying operations.

(ii) *Survey fees:* Where, following a casualty, there is a reasonable apprehension of damage to cargo, the expense of arranging a survey of that cargo in order to assess damage, if any, forms a deduction from the salved value of that cargo. Such surveys may take place either at the port of destination, or at a port of refuge, or both. **1374**

(iii) *Cost of on-carriage:* Where it is necessary following salvage services to carry the salved cargo either to the port of destination or to another place where there is a market for such cargo, the reasonable cost of getting the cargo to that place will form a deduction from the cargo salved value. Where, however, the freight is at the risk of the ship owner, the freight element will form a deduction from the salved freight and not from the salved cargo value.

1375 (iv) *Sale expenses:* If salved cargo should be sold not by the merchant to whom it was consigned but by other parties (*e.g.* by the shipowner or by order of the court), then the reasonable expenses incurred in disposing of the cargo and realising its value form a deduction from the proceeds of sale in arriving at the salved value.

(v) *Freight:* As has been mentioned earlier, the value of cargo at the port of destination always reflects the cost of getting it to that place; and, if the freight is at the risk of the shipowners, then the amount of such freight, less any appropriate deductions, must be deducted from the salved cargo value in order to assess the financial interest at risk of those concerned in the cargo at the time of the salvage services.

Other financial interests

1376 As has been noted, there are other financially interested parties who may well benefit from a successful salvage operation but whose financial interest is not included in the value of the salved properties, notably time charterers and the underwriters. Furthermore, we have also seen that the saving of a shipowner from third party claims is relevant to the assessment of a salvage award. Logically, this aspect of the services and liability for damages should be matched by a fund representing the amount at risk. However, no account is taken of such factors in the assessment of salved values.

1377 The salvor may agree in *advance* with the respondent interests a minimum salved fund out of which the salvor's remuneration is to be assessed. Such arrangements do occur in practice, although they are exceptional. They do, however, cause practical problems since all respondent interests must agree and this generally means that the ship- and cargo-owners must also obtain the approval of the underwriters. This may be possible where there is no great degree of urgency. But when, as in the majority of salvage operations, prompt action is essential to ensure a successful outcome, the salvor may not be able to state his terms and the respondents carry out the necessary consultations in the limited time available.

Derelicts

1378 Where a vessel has been abandoned by her crew *sine animo revertendi* this generally marks the abandonment likewise of the voyage by the shipowner, and the obligation of ship and cargo interests under the contract of carriage thereupon terminate.[69] If the derelict is subsequently brought by salvors to a

---

[69] See *Bradley v. H. Newsom, Sons & Co.* [1917] 2 K.B. 112; [1918] 1 K.B. 271 (CA); [1919] A.C. 16 (HL). See also Carver, §§1247–1248 and cases there cited.

place of safety, it must be decided upon careful analysis of all the material facts whether the voyage has been frustrated or whether the shipowner is under an obligation to repair his ship and resume the voyage.

1379 If the salvage services terminate at a port at or close to the destination of the vessel, then the salved value of the cargo will be the market value of the cargo at the port of termination less any deductions in respect of damage and cost of discharge. The value of the cargo will contain a freight component and, even if under the contract of carriage the freight is at the risk of shipowner, it is difficult to see how the cargo interests could successfully deduct the amount of such freight if they are not obliged themselves to pay it to the shipowner due to frustration of the contract of carriage.

1380 Similar considerations will apply where the salvage services terminate at a port of refuge other than the port of destination. If on the facts the contract of carriage has been frustrated or the shipowner is deemed to have repudiated his contract of carriage, then those concerned in cargo are entitled to claim that cargo at the port of refuge without payment of any freight which would have been payable at the port of destination. It is submitted, however, that the value of the cargo at the port of refuge must form the basis of cargo's contributions to the salvor's remuneration, and again this value will contain a freight component reflecting the difference between the market value for such cargo at the port of loading and the market value at the port of refuge.[70]

Freight in salvage of derelict

1381 There may be no freight against which the salvor may claim where the property salved is derelict.

Abandonment

Performance of the contract of affreightment may be brought to an end by frustration. But the shipowner cannot put an end to it by his own act. If he attempts to abandon the contract, he gives an election to the cargo-owner, who can either affirm or disaffirm the contract. If the abandonment is justified, such as by distress, he will incur no liability for it, as he will for wrongful abandonment. But he will not earn freight which is payable at destination. Nor will pro rata freight be payable without an express or implied contract to pay it, which is unlikely.[71]

Abandonment of the ship by the shipowner will not necessarily put an end to the contract of affreightment; certainly, where the abandonment is wrongful, the shipowner will remain liable to the cargo-owner for performance of

---

[70] See *The Cito* (1881) 7 P.D. 5; *The Argonaut*, Shipp. Gaz. W.S., 3rd Dec. 1884; *The Leptir* (1885) 5 Asp. M.L.C. 411; *The Arno* (1895) 8 Asp. M.L.C. 5. See also *The Kathleen* (1874) L.R. 4 A. & E. 269 and *Guthrie v. North China Insurance Co. Ltd* (1900) 6 Com. Cas. 25, *affirmed* (1902) 8 Com. Cas. 130.

[71] See, *e.g. The Arno* (1895) 8 Asp. M.L.C. 5.

the contract.[72] However, "by an abandonment of a ship without any intention to retake possession of it, the shipowner has so far as he can abandoned the contract, so as to allow the other party to it, the cargo owner, to treat it as abandoned."[73]

Therefore if, after abandonment of the contract of carriage and before the shipowner attempts to resume performance of it, a derelict vessel is brought by salvors to a port other than its port of destination and arrested by them, the persons interested in the cargo are, on putting up security, entitled to apply for an order of the court for delivery of the cargo without payment of any freight to the shipowner, either in full or pro rata.[74]

1382 If the owners of cargo on board a derelict have applied for delivery of it at the port to which the salvor brought the derelict and offered bail for its value, but the court has ordered the ship to proceed with the cargo to its original destination, the cargo-owners are not liable to pay either freight pro rata to the port at which salvage services terminated, or even the expenses of carriage onward to the port of destination or the expenses of delivery there.[75]

In *The Arno*,[76] where the salved property was brought to safety at its port of destination by the salvor and not by the shipowner, it was held that, once the cargo-owner has elected to exercise his right to treat an abandonment as determining performance of the contract of affreightment, the subsequent recovery of the vessel at the port of discharge by the shipowner does not revive the contract so as to disentitle the cargo-owner from having the cargo delivered to him without payment of freight.

1383 The fact that a shipowner shews an inclination to do everything in his power to carry out the contract is not enough to annul the abandonment or to prevent the owners of the cargo from exercising their election. However, it is possible, although the point has not been decided,[77] that if, after the vessel has been brought by the salvor to a place of safety and before the cargo-owner has intervened and claimed his right to the cargo where it lies and not at the port of delivery, the shipowner puts up security for the ship and the cargo and proceeds to carry the cargo to the port of destination without any fresh agreement, he may be able to claim freight.[78] Certainly, the shipowner is not obliged to tranship the cargo and carry it on.[79] And it has been said that an agreement entered into between the shipowner and the salvor, without the knowledge and consent of the cargo-owners, for the salvor to hold the ship for

---

[72] See, *e.g. The Cito* (1881) 7 P.D. 5, 8; *The Leptir* (1885) 5 Asp. M.L.C. 411, 412.
[73] *The Cito* (1881) 7 P.D. 5, 8–9.
[74] *The Cito* (1881) 7 P.D. 5; *The Kathleen* (1874) L.R. 4 A. & E. 269.
[75] *The Argonaut, Shipping Gazette W. S.*, December 3, 1884.
[76] (1895) 8 Asp. M.L.C. 5. See also *Guthrie v. North China Insurance Co. Ltd* (1902) 7 Com. Cas. 130.
[77] See *The Cito* (1881) 7 P.D. 5, 9; *The Arno* (1895) 8 Asp. M.L.C. 5, 7.
[78] *Bradley v. H. Newsom, Sons & Co.* [1919] A.C. 16, 42.
[79] See *Guthrie v. Northern China Insurance Co. Ltd* (1902) 7 Com. Cas. 130.

the shipowner, cannot take away the cargo-owners' right of election.[80] Vaughan Williams L.J. has said that[81]:

> "the cargo owner has a right to retake possession of his cargo without paying freight in a case where the ship and cargo have ceased to be in the possession or control of the shipowner and the shipowner has not actual or constructive possession of the ship and cargo."

If, however, the shipowner has been compelled by circumstances lawfully to abandon performance of the contract but makes every effort, successfully, to enable himself to complete performance of the contract, there would seem to be no reason why he should not be able to earn the freight which the cargo-owner originally agreed to pay. The parties will receive no more than was originally contemplated. Moreover, the salvor will be rewarded for his efforts in preserving the freight; otherwise he will not be rewarded for freight, nor will be receive the freight itself, for there will have been no contract under which he could earn it.[82] This does not mean that the cargo-owner need lose his right of election so easily where abandonment is wrongful, and a breach of contract.

No valid abandonment

1384 The rule in cases of abandonment[83] does not apply where there is no valid abandonment of the vessel.

In *The Leptir*,[84] the master and crew of a brig in distress left her and went across to a barque which had come up. The following day, they were refused permission to return and members of the barque's crew went over, the two vessels proceeding in company to a port of safety. Butt J. held that on the facts an abandonment was not intended and did not occur. Therefore, the owners of cargo, who claimed its delivery at the port of refuge, were bound to pay a pro rata freight.

In *Bradley v. H. Newsom, Sons & Co.*,[85] the master and crew were compelled to leave the ship by an enemy submarine which then, unsuccessfully, attempted to sink her. On receipt of a telegram from the master that the ship had been sunk by a submarine (which he believed to be true), the owners wrote to the ship's agents a letter for communication to the cargo-owners, advising them of the loss of the ship. She was, however, salved and delivered to the receiver of wreck. On hearing that the ship was afloat, bill of lading endorsees intervened and intimated to the receiver of wreck that they elected to take possession of the cargo where the ship lay, although, by arrangement, the shipowners delivered the cargo at the port of destination without prejudice

---

[80] *The Arno* (1895) 8 Asp. M.L.C. 5, 8.
[81] *Guthrie v. Northern China Insurance Co. Ltd* (1902) 7 Com. Cas. 130.
[82] See *The Arno* (1895) 8 Asp. M.L.C. 5, 7.
[83] *Ante*, §§ 1381–1383.
[84] (1885) 5 Asp. M.L.C. 411.
[85] [1919] A.C. 16.

Life salvage

1385 In assessing life salvage, no account is taken of any supposed pecuniary value of lives saved.[86] No more is it necessary—nor even may it be practicable—to ascertain the number of lives saved with precise accuracy.[87] Furthermore, a liberal award is given in cases of life salvage.[88] Therefore, salved values are not determined in respect of salvage of life, though of course the number of lives in danger and saved will be a factor to be taken into account in assessing life salvage.

4. APPRAISEMENT

1386 If the salved property is arrested, the salvors are entitled to have the values appraised by the Marshal of the Admiralty Court—but at the risk of their having to bear the cost, if the appraised values do not substantially exceed the values stated by the owners.[89] The general rule is that the appraisement is conclusive.[90]

---

[86] See, *e.g. The Suevic* [1908] P. 154, 161.
[87] *The Eastern Monarch* (1860) Lush. 81, 83.
[88] See, *e.g. ibid.* at 84.
[89] See Admiralty Practice Direction (CPR 49 F PD), §8.
[90] *The San Onofre* [1917] P. 96.

CHAPTER 15

ASSESSMENT

1. CLAIMS GENERALLY

Types of claims

The range of circumstances discussed in this book may give rise not only **1387**
to claims for salvage rewards but also to other claims, *e.g.* for payment for
engaged services, for special compensation for environmental services, for
SCOPIC payment and for damages for loss caused by negligence. Such claims
may be pursued independently of each other or in the same set of proceedings.
Either way, it is important to recognise the difference between such claims and
the principles determining the amount payable in satisfaction of them, in
particular that different types of claim may well be governed by different
principles. At the same time, it must recognised that conduct relevant to one
type of claim (*e.g.* negligence giving rise to a claim for damages) may be
relevant in the assessment of another type of claim (*e.g.* as evidence of the
skill and efforts of salvors which is taken into account in assessing a salvage
reward). Tribunals must therefore be careful not to allow such overlapping
factors to operate cumulatively or to be overlooked, to the prejudice or
advantage one of the parties.

It should be noted that it is not the object of this chapter to discuss the **1388**
assessment of all claims which might arise in situations of a salvage nature.
Thus, special compensation under Article 14 of the Salvage Convention 1989
is discussed in Chapter 4 and SCOPIC remuneration is discussed in Chapter
9.[1] The focus will be on the assessment of salvage rewards.

It does, however, need to be borne in mind that tribunals are generally
conscious of related claims, in order to ensure that parties are neither doubly
advantaged nor doubly disadvantaged by related or overlapping factors. However, the drafters of Lloyd's Form have been careful to maintain the basic
entitlement of salvors to salvage rewards. Thus, in considering the "Effect of
other remedies", LOF 2000, cl. D provides:

"Subject to the provisions of the International Convention on Salvage
1989 as incorporated into English law ('the Convention') relating to

---

[1] *Ante*, §§ 976–978.

Assessment

special compensation and to the Scopic Clause if incorporated the Contractors [*sic*.] services shall be rendered and accepted as salvage services upon the principle of 'no cure—no pay' and any salvage remuneration to which the Contractors become entitled shall not be diminished by reason of the exception to the principle of 'no cure—no pay' in the form of special compensation or remuneration payable to the Contractors under a Scopic Clause."

2. SALVAGE REWARDS IN GENERAL

Salvage agreements and assessment

1389   It is possible for parties to conclude a binding agreement for the assessment of payment due for performance of services of a salvage nature. Such an agreement is liable to be set aside if inequitable,[2] in which case assessment will be made as described in this chapter. Otherwise, the agreement will be enforced, even if the amount should exceed the salved fund.[3] However, such agreements are rare. Accordingly, the remainder of this chapter is devoted to the situation where there is no agreement fixing the amount of a salvage reward.

Of course, far more common than agreements which purport to fix the amount of a salvage reward are agreements such as those made on Lloyd's Form. In *The Tojo Maru*,[4] Lord Diplock described these as contracts for work and labour for which the salvor is entitled to a *quantum meruit* or reasonable remuneration. However, this reasonable remuneration is not assessed on the ordinary common law contractual basis for contracts of work and labour. "This is not a claim for ordinary work and labour, but for salvage."[5] In principle, the agreement in Lloyd's Form is for assessment according to principles of the law of maritime salvage. The criteria for fixing the reward are now laid down by statute, implementing Article 13 of the International Salvage Convention 1989, to which LOF 2000 is expressly subject.[6]

The framework for assessment

1390   Traditionally, salvage rewards have been assessed by the Admiralty Court or, in the vast majority of cases nowadays, by arbitrators. Inevitably, the reported decisions of the Admiralty Court indicate the processes by which assessments were made in earlier times. Such processes have been far less transparent since it became usual for salvage to be settled in accordance with

---

[2] See *ante*, Chap. 9.
[3] *The Inna* [1938] P. 148, especially at 157; *The Lyrma (No. 2)* [1978] 2 Lloyd's Rep. 30, especially at 33–34.
[4] [1972] A.C. 242, 293–294, 299–300.
[5] *The Duke of Manchester* (1847) 6 Moo.P.C. 90, 99, *per* Lord Campbell.
[6] LSSAC 2000, cl. J.

contracts such as Lloyd's Form, providing for determination by arbitrators, whose awards are generally confidential. However, "the implied term of confidentiality in LOF arbitration agreements is qualified by the custom and practice of awards being made available to LOF arbitrators and Counsel in other LOF cases, with a view to promoting uniformity and consistency within the LOF system of arbitration. That qualification to the implied term of confidentiality in LOF arbitration agreements is capable of being extended and ... should be extended for the same reasons, to cover LOF awards being made available to the Judge sitting in the Admiralty Court."[7]

1391 The International Salvage Convention 1989, Art. 27 requires States parties to encourage, as far as possible and with the consent of the parties, the publication of arbitral awards made in salvage cases; and LOF 2000 now provides that awards by arbitrators and appeal arbitrators shall be published by the Council of Lloyd's.[8] Accordingly, it could become easier to discover the processes by which assessments are made in individual cases in modern times, although at present this seems unlikely, as publication by Lloyd's is currently only to the parties. Nevertheless, the general methods by which salvage has been, and will no doubt continue to be, assessed have remained fairly common since they were first developed by the Admiralty Court. Indeed, proceedings before and by Lloyd's arbitrators have been conducted by a small group of practitioners whose familiarity with them has ensured a common approach in principle, underlined by the practice of having a single appeal arbitrator for all such arbitrations, thus ensuring consistency on matters of principle and the level of awards.

1392 "[T]he assessment of salvage has never been an exact science"[9]: "each case depends on its own circumstances"[10] and the assessment of salvage rewards is not made in accordance with an absolute rule or fixed scale.[11] Indeed, given the factors which have been recognised as necessary to weigh in determining the amount of an award, the application of a fixed scale would be more likely to obstruct rather than to facilitate a just solution in many cases; and the Admiralty court long ago rejected the notion of employing such an approach.[12]

---

[7] *The Hamtun* [1999] 1 Lloyd's Rep. 883, 900, *per* Peter Gross, Q.C., sitting as a Deputy Judge of the High Court.
[8] LSSAC 2000, cll. 6.7, 10.9.
[9] *Semco Salvage and Marine Pte Ltd v. Lancer Navigation Co. Ltd (The Nagasaki Spirit)* [1997] A.C. 455, 467, *per* Lord Mustill.
[10] *The Ewell Grove* (1835) 3 Hagg. 209, 221–222, *per* Sir John Nicholls.
[11] *The Ewell Grove* (1835) 3 Hagg. 209, 222, *per* Sir John Nicholls ("in civil salvage, for mere assistance to ships in distress, there is no fixed proportion applying to all cases—there is a discretion"). *cf. The Oscar* (1829) 2 Hagg. 257, 259–260. Different rules or practices have existed in much earlier times but the current position has been judicially confirmed since the beginning of the nineteenth century at least.
[12] See *The Salacia* (1829) 2 Hagg. 262, 264, *per* Sir Christopher Robinson ("The rule of proportion ... is a rule which the Court has not recognised, and will not adopt on any recommendation"); *The Ewell Grove* (1835) 3 Hagg 209, 231, *per* Sir John Nicholl.

Assessment

It has been said that the amount of a salvage reward is dependent upon the discretion of the court (or arbitrator) or "what Lord Stowell used to call it, a *rusticum judicium*".[13] But this is misleading. Obviously the tribunal must make a decision in the particular circumstances before it. But it does not have a freewheeling discretion. It should take account of those factors which have been recognised as relevant to the assessment of salvage rewards, evaluating them in the light of the particular facts[14] and also of its professional experience of the prevailing practice of assessing salvage rewards. In this way it should produce "a conventional award", *i.e.* one which is just on the individual facts and consistent with established principles, judicial decisions and current practice.[15]

Material circumstances

1393 Previous editions of *Kennedy* have recorded a classification of "material circumstances"[16] to be taken into account in assessing salvage rewards, as follows:

"A. As regards the salved property:

(1) The degree of danger, if any, to human life.
(2) The degree of danger to the property.
(3) The value of the property as salved.

B. As regards the salvors:

(1) The degree of danger, if any, to human life.
(2) The salvors' (a) classification, (b) skill and (c) conduct.
(3) The degree of danger, if any, to property employed in the salvage service and its value.
(4) The (a) time occupied and (b) work done in the performance of the salvage service.
(5) Responsibilities incurred in the performance of the salvage service, such, *e.g.* as risk to the insurance, and liability to passengers or freighters through deviation or delay.
(6) Loss or expense incurred in the performance of the salvage service, such, *e.g.* as detention, loss of profitable trade, repair of damage caused to ship, boats, or gear, fuel consumed, etc."

---

[13] *The Thomas Fielden* (1862) 32 L.J.Adm. 61, 62, *per* Dr Lushington.

[14] "the estimate of services, labour, and enterprise, requires to be made as minutely as possible under an infinite variety of particulars": *The Oscar* (1829) 2 Hagg. 257, 260, *per* Sir Christopher Robinson.

[15] In *The City of Chester* (1884) 9 P.D. 182, 202, Lindley L.J. stated that "the court has for its guidance a long course of judicial decision to assist in coming to a proper conclusion in each particular case." Of course, this observation was more pertinent towards the end of the judicially-led nineteenth century development of salvage law than in modern times.

[16] See *The Charlotte* (1848) 3 W.Rob. 68, 71, *per* Dr Lushington; *The City of Chester* (1884) 9 P.D. 182, 202, *per* Lindley L.J.

The framework for assessment

Likewise, the Brussels Salvage Convention 1910, Art. 8 provided[17]: **1394**

"The remuneration is fixed by the court according to the circumstances of each case, on the basis of the following considerations:

(a) first, the measure of success obtained, the efforts and deserts of the salvors, the danger run by the salved vessel, by her passengers, crew and cargo, by the salvors, and by the salving vessel;
the time expended, the expenses incurred and losses suffered, and the risks of liability and other risks run by the salvors, and also the value of the property exposed to such risks, due regard being had to the special appropriation (if any) of the salvors' vessel for salvage purposes;
(b) secondly, the value of the property salved."

The Brussels Salvage Convention largely restated English law and was not **1395** enacted in the United Kingdom. However, the English law of salvage is now subject to the International Salvage Convention 1989, Article 13.1 of which sets out specific "criteria for fixing the reward"[18]:

"The reward shall be fixed with a view to encouraging salvage operations, taking into account the following criteria without regard to the order in which they are presented below—

(a) the salved value of the vessel and other property;
(b) the skill and efforts of the salvors in preventing or minimising damage to the environment;
(c) the measure of success obtained by the salvor;
(d) the nature and degree of the danger;
(e) the skill and efforts of the salvors in salving the vessel, other property and life;
(f) the time used and expenses and losses incurred by the salvors;
(g) the risk of liability and other risks run by the salvors or their equipment;
(h) the promptness of the services rendered;
(i) the availability and use of vessels or other equipment intended for salvage operations;
(j) the state of readiness and efficiency of the salvor's equipment and the value thereof."

The content of these lists and the relative importance of the different factors are discussed below.[19]

---

[17] Art. 8 is set out in the style which follows for convenience.
[18] Art. 13.2 is concerned with who is liable to pay and is discussed *infra*, Chap. 16, §1488.
[19] See *post*, §§1407–1460.

Assessment

General approach

The "salved fund"

1396   The values of salved property are traditionally referred to as "the salved fund". This is a figurative expression. The salvor acquires no interest in the property preserved; nor is it necessary that payment be made out of the salved property or its proceeds.[20] It is also not necessary to constitute a distinct fund for payment.

The value of the salved fund

1397   It is an overriding limitation on the assessment of a salvage reward—historically derived from the foundation of Admiralty jurisdiction as one over property,[21] stated in the Brussels Salvage Convention 1910[22] and now embodied in the International Salvage Convention 1989, Art. 13.3[23]—that no salvage reward may exceed the value of the property salved.

In earlier times it was the practice to award "a moiety" (one half) of the salved value, at least in the case of derelicts, and there are nineteenth century decisions ruling that the upper limit of a salvage reward should be no more than a moiety.[24] However, it is clear that neither approach applies nowadays. Whatever function it may have had, the moiety is now irrelevant. In an appropriate case, a very large proportion of the salved fund may be awarded.[25] Indeed, in *The Louisa*,[26] the salvors recovered the whole of the fund remaining in court after the appraisement and sale of a salved derelict and the deduction of the costs of appraisement and sale.

The limit imposed by the salved fund is upon *salvage rewards*, "exclusive of any interest and recoverable legal costs that may be payable thereon",[27] which are assessed independently.[28]

Guiding policies and principles

1398   Before making a salvage award the tribunal must, first, establish that the claimant is entitled to a reward (*i.e.* that he has satisfied the conditions for an award) and, secondly, assess the amount of the reward. Logically the two steps

---

[20] This may be a consequence of the exercise of Admiralty jurisdiction and remedies; but that is a different matter. See *ante*, Chap. 13.

[21] See *ante*, Chaps. 1–2. *cf. The Tojo Maru* [1972] A.C. 242, 273, *per* Lord Diplock.

[22] Art. 2: "In no case shall the sum to be paid exceed the value of the property salved."

[23] "The rewards, exclusive of any interest and recoverable legal costs that may be payable thereon, shall not exceed the salved value of the vessel and other property."

[24] *L'Esperance* (1811) 1 Dods. 48, 49, *per* Sir W. Scott; *The Frances Mary* (1827) 2 Hagg. 90; *The Inca* (1858) 12 Moo.P.C. 189. See also *The Elliotta* (1815) 2 Dods. 75.

[25] See, *e.g. The Boiler ex Elephant* (1891) 64 L.T. 543 (£50 awarded to five salvors of a derelict boiler with a low salved value of £58); *The Bluebird* [1971] 1 Lloyd's Rep. 229 (£400 awarded on a salved value of £550).

[26] [1906] P. 145. See also *The Boiler ex Elephant* (1891) 64 L.T. 543; *The Arthur, Shipping Gazette*, May 2, 1901; *The Georg* [1894] P. 330.

[27] International Salvage Convention 1989, Art. 13.3.

[28] *Post*, §§ 1466–1476.

General approach

should be related, for the process of assessment is to ascertain the amount of reward to which the claimant is entitled. The process of assessment may be closely defined or flexible; but, either way, it should be conducted in accordance with the aims of the underlying claim or with exceptions which are both identifiable and intelligible.

Subject to the limit of the salved fund, the process of assessing a salvage reward in English law is flexible and is a matter for the tribunal's discretion, which should be exercised to determine a conventional award. The exercise of the tribunal's discretion has traditionally involved the interrelated application of three principles: that the salvee should pay for the benefit received; that the salvor should be rewarded for the service provided; and that the reward should reflect public policy. Attention is traditionally focused on the second and third of these principles but they operate subject to the first.

The implementation of public policy in the law of salvage is familiar from the practice of making awards on a generous scale, in order generally to encourage the provision of salvage services.[29] However, other specific policies have been brought into the assessment process. In earlier times the most noticeable was the exceptional practice of enhancing rewards to reflect the efforts of salvors in the interests of human lives,[30] a practice which retains residual effect as a factor to be taken into account in fixing rewards in the International Salvage Convention 1989, Art. 13.1(e).[31] The most striking example is the requirement of the International Salvage Convention 1989, Art. 13.1(b) that the reward should take account of the skill and efforts of the salvors in preventing or minimising damage to the environment. The policies of encouraging salvage generally and also environmental services are consistent with the principle of requiring the salvee to pay for benefits received; for, without such encouragements, salvees might receive no service at all. However, encouraging life salvage is not *per se* advantageous to the salvee; if anything, it imposes a burden on him.

1399

The policies implemented by Admiralty law and statute are contractually repeated and slightly adumbrated in LOF 2000 arbitrations, for they are subject to the "overriding objective(s)" of Lloyd's Standard Salvage and Arbitration Clauses, cl. 2.[32] This states that "In construing the Agreement or on the making of any arbitral order or award regard shall be had to the overriding purposes of the Agreement namely: (a) to seek to promote safety of life at sea and the preservation of property at sea and during the salvage operations to prevent or minimise damage to the environment; ... (c) to encourage cooperation between the parties and with relevant authorities; ...

1400

---

[29] See *ante*, Chap. 1.
[30] On life salvage generally, see *ante*, Chap. 3.
[31] "the skill and efforts of the salvors in salving the vessel, other property *and life*" (emphasis added).
[32] LOF 2000, cl. I; LSSAC 2000, cl. I. The heading of LSSAC, cl. 2 is in the singular ("overriding objective") but the clause records several "purposes".

Assessment

(d) to ensure that the reasonable expectations of salvors and owners of salved property at sea are met. . . . "

1401 The relative prominence of the above policies and principles depends on the circumstances, for "every case must be decided upon its own facts"[33] to determine "the real value of the the services rendered".[34] Thus, where the salved fund is large and the circumstances appropriate, the salvor can be amply rewarded on a generous scale.[35] But, if the salved fund is very small and below the level necessary for an otherwise appropriate reward, the salvor may be denied a generous assessment or even an award at the level of a common law *quantum meruit*; otherwise the salvee would receive little or no benefit from the service, and in practice might even be worse off than if no service had been rendered.[36]

Taking account of individual circumstances

1402 Judicial opinions have been expressed as to the relative importance of certain of the factors to be considered in assessing a salvage reward; but these have not been consistent.[37] Indeed, as noted above, the Admiralty Court has eschewed the formal weighting of factors.[38] Moreover, the International Salvage Convention 1989, Article 13.1 specifically states that account is to be taken of the Convention's criteria for fixing the salvage reward "*without regard to the order in which they are presented*".[39]

In a general sense, the weight attributable to different factors depends upon the extent to which they give effect to the guiding principles identified above.[40] Translated into specific examples, in practice, those principles provide that the primary features in any assessment are the dangers to the property salved, the nature and burden of the services provided by the salvors, and the salved values, the consequent notional award also taking account of the policies of encouraging salvage services and "environmental services" and promoting the safety of human lives. The other recognised factors are effectively emanations of these primary factors.

In practice, weighting those factors which are present is less important than the number of factors in a given case and the degree to which they are present. Where many or all of the relevant factors are found to exist, or some of them are found to exist to a high degree, a large reward is given; where few of them are found, or they are present only in a low degree, the award is comparatively small.

---

[33] *The Bluebird* [1971] 1 Lloyd's Rep. 229, 231, *per* Brandon J.
[34] *The General Palmer* (1844) 5 Not. of Cas. 159n., *per* Dr Lushington.
[35] *The Bluebird* [1971] 1 Lloyd's Rep. 229, 231, *per* Brandon J.
[36] *cf. The Tojo Maru* [1972] A.C. 242, 299, *per* Lord Diplock.
[37] See, *e.g. The Duke of Manchester* (1846) 2 W.Rob. 470, 475, *per* Dr Lushington ("the two main ingredients in all salvage services are, 1st, the danger to which the property is exposed; 2ndly, the danger encountered by the salvors in the rescue of that property").
[38] See *ante*, §§ 1390–1392.
[39] Emphasis added.
[40] *Ante*, §1400.

General approach

1403 A difference between the law before and after the implementation of the International Salvage Convention 1989 is that prior to the Convention the normal procedure would be for the tribunal to take account of those factors which were shewn to be present in the case in hand, whereas the Convention prescribes, in Article 13.1, that the tribunal "*shall* be fixed with a view to encouraging salvage operations, taking into account the following criteria . . .".[41] On one view, the prescriptive wording of the Convention has little practical significance, since the required consideration of factors which are listed but found not to be present in the case in question will simply have no effect on the reward. Nonetheless, the absence of a listed factor may have some influence on the tribunal's assessment: *e.g.* a salvor who could have exerted skill and efforts in the interests of human life and the environment may appear less deserving than he could have been. However, a more serious interpretation is that, where relevant factors are considered and found not to be present, their absence may not simply fail to enhance the notional award but may be a reason for depressing it. However, there is no evidence that the Convention was intended to reverse the previous position and to penalise salvors for omitting to do what they might do but are not obliged to do. Indeed, it would be counterproductive to discourage an otherwise meritorious service from which one or more of the listed factors was absent.

Eligible and "additional" circumstances

1404 A further issue which arises in compiling a list of factors to be taken into account in assessing a salvage reward is whether the Convention's catalogue of factors is exhaustive. The position is complicated because in fact there are two categories of circumstances to be found in the Convention which may be relevant to the assessment of a salvage reward. The first is manifest. Article 13.1 directs that "The reward *shall* be fixed with a view to encouraging salvage operations, taking into account the following criteria",[42] which are then specifically listed. However, the Convention also contains an unformalised range of other factors which might be eligible for consideration as relevant to assessment of a salvage reward. For example, Article 8.1(d) provides that "The salvor shall owe a duty to the owner of the vessel or other property in danger . . . to accept the intervention of other salvors when reasonably requested to do so by the owner or master of the vessel or other property in danger; provided however that the amount of his reward shall not be prejudiced should it be found that such a request was unreasonable." The Convention does not prescribe the sanction for non-performance of such a duty[43] but one possibility is that it may constitute a factor to be taken into account in assessing a salvage reward. Indeed, the proviso to Article 8.1(d) specifically assumes that unreasonable refusal of assistance by other salvors

---

[41] Emphasis added.
[42] Emphasis added.
[43] A party who fails to perform a Convention duty may be subject to sanction by way of damages. If so, it will be necessary to consider the relationship between claims for salvage rewards and claims for damages: see *ante*, Chap. 11.

counts in the assessment and so generally implies that a circumstance not listed in Article 13.1, at least if it features somewhere in the Convention, is a valid factor for consideration in assessment.

1405 One view is that the directive terminology of Article 13.1 is exhaustive: that it prescribes those factors which shall, and shall exclusively, be taken into account in fixing a salvage reward. Arguably, confining the list of factors to those stated in the Convention will promote the international uniformity which the Convention was designed to promote.[44] If that view were correct, and the Convention's list of factors were nominally finite, it would still be possible for non-listed factors to be taken into account if they could properly be interpreted as falling under the heads laid down in the Convention; if they did not, they would obviously have to be ignored. Thus, avoidance of danger to navigation was recognised as a material circumstance in *The Johanne Dybwad*[45] but is not a criterion listed in the International Salvage Convention 1989, Art. 13.1. It might be regarded as a feature of encouraging salvage services,[46] preventing or minimising damage to the environment,[47] the nature and degree of the danger[48] and/or salving other property.[49] But that would stretch the content of such criteria so as to render them unreliable. That may be permissible. But it is preferable if either unlisted criteria are ejected from the assessment of salvage rewards or, if that approach would exclude legitimate candidates such as safeguarding the safety of navigation, accept that the Convention's list of criteria is not exclusive.

1406 Certainly, the CMI Report preceding the Convention contemplates that the Convention is not exhaustive; and the Convention certainly does not purport to abrogate the flexibility with which salvage assessments have historically been made. Indeed, the opening words of Article 13 specifically contemplate a flexible application of the listed factors. Moreover, the drafting of Article 8.1(d)[50] indicates that the factors listed in Article 13.1 are not contemplated as being exclusive. It is possible to argue that the combined total of factors mentioned in the Convention is exhaustive; but *semble* the basis for such an argument would be to extend the application of the initial words of Article 13.1 beyond their proper domain. The better view therefore is that the circumstances listed in Article 13 or appearing elsewhere in the Convention is not finite. Nonetheless, the consideration of non-specified factors should be limited to those which are consistent with the underlying principles and policies governing entitlement to and assessment of salvage awards.

---

[44] *cf. Westar Marine Services v. Heerema Marine Contractors* (1985) 621 F.Supp. 1135 (Cal. DC: Lynch Dist. J.); Brice, §2–124.
[45] (1926) 25 Ll.L.Rep. 119, 123. See further *post*, §1416.
[46] Art. 13.1. See *post*, §1453.
[47] Art. 13.1(b). See *post*, §1417.
[48] Art. 13.1(d). See *post*, §§ 1411–1417.
[49] Art. 13.1(e).
[50] *Supra*, §1040.

3. Material Circumstances in Detail

1407 The circumstances which may be taken into account in assessing a salvage reward may now be examined individually. No formal classification of such circumstances has been recognised. Indeed, circumstances often do not fit neatly into different classes.[51] Nevertheless, it will be convenient to consider them in groups in accordance with general principle and with a view to considering how far controversial circumstances are eligible for consideration in assessing a reward.

1408 First, however, it will be convenient to ascertain the meaning of the terms "vessel"[52] and "equipment" in Articles 13 and 14.[53] Amongst the considerations for fixing salvage remuneration under the Brussels Salvage Convention 1910, Article 8 listed "the danger run ... by the salving *vessel*; ... the value of *the property* exposed to [risks of liability and other risks run by the salvors], due regard being had to the special appropriation (if any) of the salvor's *vessel* for salvage purposes".[54] The equivalent criteria for fixing a reward under the International Salvage Convention 1989, Art. 13.1 are: "(g) the risk of liability and other risks run by the salvors or their *equipment*; ... (i) the availability and use of *vessels or other equipment* intended for salvage operations; (j) the state of readiness and efficiency of the salvor's *equipment* and the value thereof."[55] In addition, Article 14.3 of the 1989 Convention includes "a fair rate for equipment" in the expenses to be considered in awarding special compensation.[56] Both Conventions therefore use more than one term to refer to the property used by the salvor, raising, in particular, the question whether in the 1989 Convention there is a significant distinction between "vessel" and "equipment".

1409 If there were, it would mean that the 1989 Convention had eliminated the Brussels Convention's inclusion of danger or risks to salving vessels from consideration under Article 13.1(g). Moreover, it would, under Article 13.1(j), take account of the state of readiness and efficiency of the salvor's equipment except in the case of vessels. Furthermore, there would be a shift from considering the value of the property exposed to risk (in the Brussels Convention) to the value of equipment alone. Since there are differences of terminology and construction between the two Conventions, it is arguable that they

---

[51] Thus the presence of passengers on board a casualty or salving vessel may be material because of the risks to the passengers themselves and because the risk or inconvenience to passengers may increase the anxiety of the master of the casualty (so enhancing the danger to the casualty) and the anxiety of the master of the salving vessel. See *The Southsea* (1933) 44 Ll.L.Rep. 373, 377.
[52] For the meaning of "vessel" generally, see *ante*, Chap. 3.
[53] See also Gaskell, 21–404 and 21–405.
[54] Emphasis added.
[55] Emphasis added.
[56] See *ante*, Chap. 5.

signify substantive changes. However, there are good reasons for concluding that "equipment" in the 1989 Convention embraces vessels.

1410 First, it would be ridiculous to take account of risks to salvors and to their equipment but to exclude risks to their vessels; and the Convention should not be interpreted as bringing about such a change in the absence of clear evidence of such intention. Secondly, to take account of the state of readiness and efficiency of the salvor's equipment except in the case of vessels would be to ignore the item of property most needing to demonstrate these features. Similarly, there is no good reason to take account of the value of equipment only other than vessels. As a matter of interpretation, equipment would seem to embrace vessels. Since the Brussels Convention takes account of the value of salving vessels, the appearance of "the salvor's equipment and the value thereof" in Article 13.1(j) of the 1989 Convention suggests an intention to enlarge the scope of the valued property. *A fortiori* the use of "or other" in Article 1.1(i) indicates that paragraph's assumption that the potentially more embracing term ("equipment") includes the narrower ("vessel"). The advantage of the drafting of paragraph (i) is to make clear that that paragraph is not limited to an alternative, narrower, construction of "equipment", *i.e.* equipment of, or other than, vessels. At the expense of relative brevity, paragraphs (g) and (j) would therefore have been clearer if they had referred to both vessels and equipment. A better solution might have been to have extended the Brussels Convention's use of the wider term "property" to encompass both vessels and other equipment; but that would have carried the risk, particularly on the drafting of Article 13.1(g) and (j), of being construed as limited to chattels owned by the salvor and so to exclude account being taken of important equipment employed by the salvor but not owned by him. In short, therefore, "equipment" in Articles 13 and 14 of the 1989 Convention should be construed to include vessels.

Dangers

Danger to maritime property[57]

1411 "[T]he nature and degree of the danger" are specifically identified as material circumstances by the International Salvage Convention 1989, Art. 13.1(d).

---

[57] Danger to the subject of salvage is a long-established prerequisite of a salvage reward (see *ante*, Chap. 4). Indeed, in *The Duke of Manchester* (1846) 2 W.Rob. 470, 475, Dr Lushington described the danger to which the property is exposed as one of the two main ingredients in all salvage services. See also *The Pergo* [1987] 1 Lloyd's Rep. 582 (Ct Sn), 585, *per* Lord Davidson. However, other dangers—to human lives, to salvors and to the property of salvors—have also traditionally been relevant factors in the assessment of salvage rewards. The Convention does not specify which dangers are contemplated by Art. 13.1(d). But Art. 13.1 lists, as separate criteria for fixing the reward, the skill and efforts of the salvors in preventing or minimising environmental damage (Art. 13.1(b)) and salving life (Art. 13.1(e)), as well as other risks run by the salvors' equipment (Art. 13.1(g)), so Art. 13.1(d) seems to be concerned specifically with dangers to maritime property.

Dangers

On one view, the Convention distinguishes between the "nature" and the "degree" of the danger.[58] But there seems to be no point in emphasising such a distinction, for in reality the Convention recognises differing aspects of the threat(s).

The types of danger to which casualties may be subject are infinitely varied. The majority of casualties fall into three categories: engine breakdown, stranding or fire. Thus, the principal general threats are physical loss (whether of destruction or damage) and immobilisation (causing loss of time).[59] The former involves an *ex post facto* assessment of the risk of loss or damage in the absence of assistance. The latter is essentially a pecuniary risk reflecting the fact that, whilst *e.g.* a ship is immobilised, both the vessel and any cargo are infructuous. The potential duration of the danger and its likely impact and consequences are therefore highly relevant.[60] Of course, all relevant circumstances must be considered, *e.g.*: the particulars of the vessel; her seaworthiness and motive power[61]; the number, availability, efficiency, capacity and morale of the crew; the nature of the locality[62]; the season of the year; the condition of the wind, weather and the tides and the likelihood of their worsening[63]; and the character of the cargo, in particular if it is perishable or has any dangerous propensities.

The prospect, suitability and cost of alternative means of assistance may be considered as a factor tempering or enhancing the initial view of the danger.[64]

The safety of human lives

The nature of modern vessels (as opposed to sailing vessels) and modern communications and life-saving appliances have greatly reduced the occasions where the saving of life is a significant factor in salvage services. However, where there is danger to human life, whether on board the casualty

1412

---

[58] Brice, §2–135.
[59] *The Glaucus* (1948) 81 Ll.L.Rep. 262; *The Troilus* [1950] P. 92. See *The National Defender* [1970] 1 Lloyd's Rep. 40, 44; *The Oceanic Grandeur* [1972] 2 Lloyd's Rep. 396.
[60] See, *e.g. The Andalusia* (1865) 12 L.T. 584, 584.
[61] Including the availability of alternative means of propulsion, *e.g.* in the case of steam trawlers with sails: see *The Perfective* (1949) 82 Ll.L.Rep. 873; *The Ebor Jewel* (1950) 83 Ll.L.Rep. 64.
[62] *e.g.* in *The Eastern Moon* (1927) 28 Ll.L.Rep. 22, the most important factor was holding the vessel off from a reef. See also *The Eisenach* (1936) 54 Ll.L.Rep. 354.
[63] See, *e.g. The Graces* (1844) 2 W.Rob. 294, 296; *The Edenmore* [1893] P. 79; *The Modavia* (1931) 39 Ll.L.Rep. 58.
[64] *The General Palmer* (1844) 5 Not. of Cas. 159n.; *The Werra* (1886) 12 P.D. 52, 54; *The Merannio* (1927) 28 Ll.L.Rep. 352, 354; *The Queen Elizabeth* (1943) 82 Ll.L.Rep. 803, 820; *The Troilus* [1950] P. 92, 108, *per* Bucknill L.J. (affirmed [1951] A.C. 820); *The Geertje K* [1971] 1 Lloyd's Rep. 285. See also *The Cheerful* (1885) 11 P.D. 3, 5; *The Cato* (1930) 37 Ll.L.Rep. 33, 37; *The St Melante* (1947) 80 Ll.L.Rep. 588, 590. *cf. The Perla* (1857) Swab. 230, 231 (*per* Dr Lushington: "As to any chance of her [a derelict] being picked up by another vessel and brought into a port of safety, that is a matter which the Court never takes into consideration"); *The Rilland* [1979] 1 Lloyd's Rep 455, 458 (where Sheen J. held that, where there is no or little prospect of such assistance, it is disregarded rather than treated as something tending to enhancing the reward).

Assessment

or on board the salving vessel, a high value is attached to it,[65] and services to passenger vessels are treated with particular generosity.

Human lives were not, under Admiralty law, subjects of salvage; but acts done to preserve them were factors prompting enhancement of awards by the Admiralty Court. Remuneration for life salvage has now been provided for by statute,[66] but life salvage also remains a factor to be considered in assessing a reward for property salvage.[67] Under the International Salvage Convention 1989, Art. 13.1(e), "the skill and efforts of the salvors in salving ... life" are a criterion for fixing the salvage reward payable by the owners of maritime property salved.[68] Article 13.1(e) has a twofold effect, for it takes account of the existence of danger to human life and of the skill and efforts employed to avert the danger.

1413 A traditional factor in assessing salvage rewards is the danger run by salvors to their own lives.[69] This is not covered by Article 13.1(e) (exposure to danger is not salving life) and is not specifically mentioned by the Convention. However, Article 13.1(g) states that "other risks run by the salvors" is a criterion for fixing the reward, and this should be interpreted to include risks to salvors' personal safety.

Article 13.1(g) ("other risks") can be interpreted more widely than Article 13.1(e) ("salving ... life"), for it can encompass risk of personal injury short of risk of death alone. The Convention does not overtly provide that risk of personal injury is a factor in the assessment of salvage rewards. However, in many cases in practice it will be impossible or unrealistic to attempt to distinguish between danger of death and other danger of personal injury. Even if the distinction could be made, it would be ridiculously formalistic to provide that the only relevant danger to the personal safety of persons on board a casualty was of death, especially if other personal dangers were a material circumstance in the case of salvors.

1414 Danger to human life is not only relevant *per se* but is often an indication, especially in modern times, of a high degree of danger to property.

The presence of passengers on board casualties and/or salving vessels is a material consideration because it tends to increase the anxiety of the masters (of the dangers faced by the casualty and the risks run by the salvors)[70] and because of the profit-earning capacity of a passenger vessel.[71]

---

[65] *The Thomas Fielden* (1862) 32 L.J.Adm. 61.
[66] See *ante*, Chap. 3.
[67] *The Bartley* (1857) Swab. 198.
[68] *cf. The Duke of Manchester* (1847) 6 Moo.P.C. 90, 99.
[69] See, *e.g. The Pergo* [1987] 1 Lloyd's Rep. 582 (Ct Sn), 587, *per* Lord Davidson.
[70] *The Southsea* (1933) 44 Ll.L.Rep. 373. See also *The Westminster* (1841) 1 W.Rob. 229, 234 ("the disappointment of the passengers might work subsequent inconvenience to the owners": *per* Dr Lushington); *The Werra* (1886) 12 P.D. 52, 55.
[71] *The Ardincaple* (1834) 3 Hagg. 151, 153. *cf. The London Merchant* (1837) 3 Hagg. 394, 400.

Risk of legal liability

Averting or minimising the risk of a casualty's liability to third parties has not *per se* been recognised as a subject of salvage.[72] However, prior to the International Salvage Convention 1989, it has been treated as a valid factor in assessing a reward for salvage of property.[73]

1415

Danger to navigation

In *The Johanne Dybwad*,[74] a case of a derelict which had drifted across Atlantic shipping lanes, Hill J. held that "The second matter which I am entitled to take into account, and *bound to take into account* apart altogether from the benefit to the owners of the property, is the benefit to navigation in general." Promoting safe navigation is not stated by the International Salvage Convention 1989 as a criterion recognised for fixing a salvage reward. But it is difficult to imagine—particularly in a case of manifest, imminent danger, as in *The Johanne Dybwad*—that it would not be treated as a permissible, even desirable, material circumstance.

1416

Damage to the environment

The threat of environmental damage is an important factor in modern salvage law; and is the basis of awards of special compensation under Article 14 of the Salvage Convention 1989.[75] However, it is not *per se* a criterion for fixing a salvage reward under Article 13, though "the skill and efforts of the salvors in preventing or minimising damage to the environment" is.[76]

1417

Salvors' classification

Previous editions of *Kennedy*[77] have listed the salvors' classification as an ingredient to be considered in assessing a salvage reward. The International Salvage Convention 1989 does not as such identify the salvor's classification as a criterion for fixing a reward. However, the cases previously discussed in *Kennedy* under this head all involve the special favour with which the Admiralty Court looked upon salvors who maintained equipment suitable for salvage operations, in particular professional salvors, features which continue to receive overt treatment in the Convention[78] and which it is appropriate to

1418

---

[72] See *ante*, §311.
[73] *The Whippingham* (1934) 48 Ll.L.Rep. 49 (risk of collision damage to vessel in the anchorage); *The Merannio* (1927) 28 Ll.L.Rep. 352, 353 (possibility of liability for wreck raising expenses). See also, in relation to passenger vessels, *The Westminster* (1841) 1 W.Rob. 229, 234 ("the disappointment of the passengers might work subsequent inconvenience to the owners": *per* Dr Lushington); *The Werra* (1886) 12 P.D. 52, 55. *cf. The Beatsa* (1937) 58 Ll.L.Rep. 85.
[74] (1926) 25 Ll.L.Rep. 119, 123 (emphasis added).
[75] See *ante*, Chap. 5.
[76] Under Art. 13.1(b). See *post*, §1421.
[77] See *Kennedy*, 5th ed., §§ 1129–1130.
[78] See Art. 13.1(i)–(j).

consider as elements of the public policy of encouraging salvage demonstrated both under the pre-Convention law and under the Convention.[79] The Convention does not otherwise take account of salvors' status as such, though it does take account of further evidence of status in listing salvors' skills as criteria for fixing the reward. Nonetheless, there may remain other elements of status which can be taken into account. Thus, in *The Sava Star*[80] Clarke J. said that, "Subject to [the fact that a shipowner is not entitled to claim salvage against himself], the fact that the salving and the salved ships are in common ownership or common management is relevant to the quantum of the salvage award."

The services provided

The skill and efforts of the salvors

1419   Although under the International Salvage Convention 1989[81] the salvors' classification is no longer specifically acknowledged as an ingredient in the assessment of a salvage reward, it still finds expression in *inter alia* the criterion of skill which salvors manifest in performing salvage services.

1420   Labour expended is an element in salvage service which is to be recognised in the award. Where, however, it is not enhanced by the exhibition of scientific or nautical skill,[82] or by the accompaniment of responsibility or danger, and derives its title to rank in the category of salvage services only from the perilous condition or position of the property to which it is applied, it forms at once the lowest and the most easily assessable of the elements to be considered in the calculation of salvage remuneration. The ship's agent, for example, who superintends salvage operations which consist in the mere discharge, landing and safe custody of the cargo of a stranded ship, if he is entitled to salvage at all, is entitled only to a very moderate reward,[83] and those who may volunteer to assist him by purely manual labour would receive a still smaller one. Similarly, as will be seen, when the question of apportionment is hereafter considered,[84] the sailor ordinarily receives less than the officer of the salving ship.

1421   In the case of all salvors, the salvage reward always reflects the knowledge, skill and work displayed in the performance of the salvage service.[85] Thus, the good conduct, promptitude, courage, energy and diligence of salvors will, according to the degree in which these qualities are displayed, enhance their

---

[79] See *The Hamtun* [1999] 1 Lloyd's Rep. 883, 889. See *post*, §1455.

[80] [1995] 2 Lloyd's Rep. 134, 139. The claim was based on LOF 1990, which incorporated the International Salvage Convention 1989, Art. 13.

[81] See *ante*, §1418.

[82] As to the contrast between ordinary labour and labour involving nautical skill, see *The Duke of Clarence* (1842) 1 W.Rob. 346.

[83] See *The Watt* (1843) 2 W.Rob. 70; *The Purissima Concepcion* (1849) 3 W.Rob. 181.

[84] See *post*, Chap. 17.

[85] See, *e.g. The Pergo* [1987] 1 Lloyd's Rep. 582, Ct Sn at 587, *per* Lord Davidson.

claim to a liberal award. This is declared in the International Salvage Convention 1989, Art. 13.1(e), which lists "the skill and efforts of the salvor in salving the vessel, other property and life" as a criterion for fixing the reward. In addition, Article 13.1(b) includes "the skill and efforts of the salvors in preventing or minimising damage to the environment".

The two criteria as designated by the Convention focus on the application of skill and efforts by salvors rather than on their consequences, which are more properly considered as elements of "success".[86]

1422 Traditionally, persons undertaking salvage services have been expected to demonstrate the knowledge and skill appropriate to their stations in life[87] in the circumstances occurring[88] and to be rewarded accordingly. Since skill is more likely to be demonstrated by professional, rather than non-professional, salvors, these criteria emphasise the traditional favour shewn as a matter of public policy towards professional salvors.[89] Indeed, though the Admiralty Court has looked with favour on the intervention of unqualified salvors where qualified salvors are unavailable, it has similarly looked with disapproval on them where better qualified persons are able to act.[90]

1423 Salvors' failure to display the skill and competence reasonably to be expected of them, negligence and *a fortiori* more serious misconduct will tend to depress[91] and may preclude altogether[92] a reward.[93] Failure of skill and care amounting to negligence causing loss to the salvee will expose the salvee to

---

[86] See *ante*, Chap. 8, and *post*, §§ 1450–1452.
[87] *The Lockwoods* (1845) 9 Jur. 1017, 1018, *per* Dr Lushington. See also *The Cape Packet* (1848) 3 W.Rob. 122, 125. See also *The Magdalen* (1861) 31 L.J.Adm. 22.
[88] *The Cheerful* (1885) 11 P.D. 3. See also *The St Blane* [1974] 1 Lloyd's Rep. 555, 561–562.
[89] See further *post*, §§ 1453–1456.
[90] *The Dygden* (1841) 1 Not. of Cas. 115.
[91] *The Cape Packet* (1848) 3 W.Rob. 122; *The Rosalie* (1853) 1 Spinks E. & A. 188; *The Perla* (1857) Swab. 230.
[92] *The Neptune* (1842) 1 W.Rob. 297 (claim of first salvors); *The Lockwoods* (1845) 9 Jur. 1017; *The Duke of Manchester* (1846) 2 W.Rob. 470, especially at 477 ("it is, I apprehend, an undoubted proposition, that salvors may be curtailed or even deprived altogether of their salvage remuneration through error misconduct, or want of skill and capacity in the performance of a salvage service": *per* Dr Lushington), affirmed (1847) 6 Moo.P.C. 90; *The Cheerful* (1885) 11 P.D. 3; *The Alenquer* [1955] 1 W.L.R. 263; [1955] 1 Lloyd's Rep. 101. In *The Atlas* (1862) Lush. 518, 528, the Privy Council (*per* Sir John Coleridge) held quite firmly that, "where success is obtained, no mere mistake or error of judgment in the manner of procuring it, no misconduct short of that which is wilful and may be considered criminal, and that proved beyond a reasonable doubt by the owners resisting the claim, will work an entire forfeiture of the salvage"; but, despite the high and clear authority of the case, it is not treated as the rule.
[93] In *The Cape Packet* (1848) 3 W.Rob. 123, 125, Dr Lushington stated that the extent of the diminution of the salvage reward "is not measured by the amount of loss or injury sustained, but is framed upon the principle of proportioning the diminution to the degree of negligence, not to the consequences"; but in *The Magdalen* (1861) 31 L.J.Adm. 22, he thought that the relevant measure was the loss caused to the salvee. Without citing either case, the Privy Council followed the latter approach in *The Atlas* (1862) Lush. 518, 528, holding that: "Mistake or misconduct other than criminal, *which diminishes the value of the property salved*, or occasions expenses to the owners, are properly considered in the amount of compensation [*i.e.* reward] to be awarded" (emphasis added). However, these dicta predate the development of the modern law on salvorial negligence and the modern practice is not to apply a fixed approach. See further *ante*, Chap. 11.

the possibility of a reduced reward or none at all, and to liability to pay damages; and the tribunal may need to consider the relationship between these two potential consequences, so that the salvor is not doubly prejudiced.[94] Similarly, where there has been serious misconduct, the reward is liable to be forfeited[95] and the salvee may be liable for damages for loss caused. However, the tribunal will weigh the skill and conduct of the claimant in the light of the public policy of encouraging salvage and the circumstances occurring. In considering whether a salvor has shewn such a want of reasonable skill and knowledge as ought materially to affect the court's award, or is guilty of only an error of judgment, the court will incline to the lenient view, and will take into favourable consideration any special circumstances which tend to exonerate the salvor from blame, such as *e.g.* a request for help, the suddenness of the emergency or the absence of more efficient means of succour.[96] As Brandon J. has said[97]:

"Before examining these particular charges in relation to the facts of this case, it is, I think, desirable to say something about the general approach of the Court to charges of negligence against persons who render or try to render assistance at sea. As to this, it is well established that the Court takes a lenient view of the conduct of salvors and would-be salvors, and is slow to find that those who try their best, in good faith, to save life or property in peril at sea, and make mistakes or errors of judgment in doing so, have been guilty of negligence. Nevertheless it is not in doubt that the Court may, in a proper case, after making all allowances, find negligence against salvors and, having done so, award damages against them in respect of it. *The Alenquer*, [1955] 1 Lloyd's Rep. 101; [1955] 1 W.L.R. 263; *The Tojo Maru*, [1972] A.C. 242; [1971] 1 Lloyd's Rep. 341. In deciding such matters the Court looks at all the circumstances of the case, including the status of the salvors—whether amateur or professional—and the question whether they have acted at request or on their own initiative. This principle of the lenient approach to mistakes is an important one. It derives from the basic policy of the law relating to salvage services, which is always to encourage, rather than discourage, the rendering of such services. The principle is especially important in cases involving life salvage, where its application demands that salvors should not in general be criticised if, faced with an actual or potential conflict between saving life on the one hand, and preserving property on the

---

[94] See *ante*, §§ 1108, 1117.
[95] See *ante*, §§ 1125–1137.
[96] This sentence (from *Kennedy's Law of Civil Salvage* (3rd ed., 1936), p. 162) was cited with approval in *The Alenquer* [1955] 1 W.L.R. 263, 269; [1955] 1 Lloyd's Rep. 101, 112, *per* Willmer J. See also *The Cheerful* (1885) 11 P.D. 3; *The C.S. Butler* (1874) 2 Asp. M.L.C. 237; *The St Blane* [1974] 1 Lloyd's Rep. 555, 560–561; *The Pergo* [1987] 1 Lloyd's Rep. 582 (Ct Sn), 587 (failure to display navigation lights revealing a degree of astuteness calling for no more than a modest discount). *cf. The Dygden* (1841) 1 Not. of Cas. 115.
[97] *The St Blane* [1974] 1 Lloyd's Rep. 555, 560–561.

other, they err on the side of the former at the expense of the latter. I approach the charges of negligence in this case in the light of the principle of leniency stated above."

Risks run by salvors

In *The Duke of Manchester*[98] Dr Lushington described as one of "the two main ingredients in all salvage services"[99] "the danger encountered by the salvors in the rescue of [the] property."

Reproducing the same expression in the Brussels Salvage Convention,[1] the International Salvage Convention 1989, Art. 13.1(g) lists "the risk of liability and other risks run by the salvors or their equipment" as a criterion for fixing the reward. The paragraph comprehends a multitude of circumstances and could have been expressed more accurately if expressed more concisely as "the risks run by the salvors", with the possible addition (to make it clear that it is not limited to personal risks) of "or their equipment".[2]

1424

Inevitably, claimants of a salvage reward (for convenience, "the primary claimants") may expose not only themselves or their own property to risk, but also other persons (most obviously employees) or the property of other persons (*e.g.* property hired by the salvors). Where other persons face the risk of personal injury or property damage or loss, those persons may themselves be entitled to claim salvage, in which case the risks to which they have been exposed can appropriately be considered in assessing any reward due to them. However, without more, those risks should not count in the assessment of rewards due to the primary claimants, for *ex hypothesi* they are risks run by other persons, not by the primary claimants. Nevertheless, they will be legitimate elements in rewarding the primary claimants to the extent that, by the very act of exposing other persons to risk, the primary claimants may themselves run risks, most obviously of liability to those other persons under, say, a contract of employment or of hire.

1425

The risks run by salvors may be taken into account whether they are undertaken unintentionally or intentionally.

Where the salvor has run risks which have materialised into losses, the tribunal should normally take into consideration the loss suffered rather than the risk run and should in any event ensure that the claimant is not doubly advantaged.

---

[98] (1846) 2 W.Rob. 470, 475.
[99] The first being "the danger to which property is exposed".
[1] With one amendment. The Brussels Salvage Convention 1910, Art. 8 lists "the *risks* of liability and other risks run by the salvors or their equipment" (emphasis added); *i.e.* it refers to plural "risks of liability" rather to a single such risk. However, this does not seem to have been intended to effect any other than a stylistic change.
[2] On the scope of the term "equipment", see *ante*, §§ 1408–1410.

Assessment

Risk of death and personal injury

1426 Salvage operations are inherently liable to be dangerous, so the risk to salvors of death, personal injury or ill health[3] are factors to be taken into account.

Risk of physical loss or damage

1427 Article 13.1(g) of the 1989 Convention specifically recognises "risks run by the salvors or their equipment" as a criterion for fixing a reward. This is, of course, particularly important where the salvor is a professional risking dedicated expensive equipment in the operation.

1428 The degree of danger, where danger exists, to property used in the performance of the salvage service, and the value of that property, are elements in the character of the salvage claim which are best considered in connection with each other. Both are obviously matters which deserve recognition in the assessment of salvage reward,[4] not only in justice to the owner of the salving vessel in the particular case,[5] but also in the public interest, and in order that the owners of vessels, particularly large and valuable ones, may be encouraged to permit them to render salvage services.[6]

It is, however, only where it is very great that the value of the salving ship has an important bearing upon the amount of the reward. It is never the measure or, like the value of the salved property,[7] the limit of the reward. If the salvor's property is of trifling value, however, this does not necessarily detract from the value which the court sets upon the service. It can never be an argument against the amount to be awarded to the salvors, that it exceeds the value of the property put in peril in performing the services.[8]

The value of the cargo on board the salving ship is material only as it affects the degree of risk and responsibility which the salvor incurs in rendering the salvage service—elements of merit which will be considered later in this chapter.

1429 *Different risks to ship, cargo and freight.* It may happen that the various interests of which the salved property is made up—ship, cargo, and freight—have been exposed to different kinds of danger.[9] In such a case the court may depart from its usual course of awarding a gross sum as salvage remuneration

---

[3] *The Rosalie* (1861) 1 Spinks E. & A. 188, 192.

[4] See, *e.g. The Pergo* [1987] 1 Lloyd's Rep. 582 (Ct Sn), 587.

[5] The value would not be relevant in the event the salvors borrowed the vessel concerned: *The Boston Lincoln* [1980] 1 Lloyd's Rep. 481.

[6] *The City of Chester* (1884) 9 P.D. 182. *cf. The De Bay* (1883) 8 App.Cas. 559, an instance of depreciation owing to engine damage by straining. *cf.* also *The Benlarig* (1888) 14 P.D. 3, 6, *per* Butt J.

[7] See *The City of Chester* (1884) 9 P.D. 182, 202, *per* Lindley L.J.

[8] *The Fusilier* (1865) Br. & L. 341, 350, PC.

[9] Such cases are rare. *cf. The Lista* (1946) 79 Ll.L.Rep. 401, decided before the Crown Proceedings Act 1947. See further *ante*, Chap. 12.

to the values of each interest; it may instead make a separate award against each portion of the salved property so as to impose a greater proportion of the gross award upon that interest which faced the more pressing danger. In *The Velox*,[10] for example, a steamship, while on a voyage from Gravingsund to Hull with a cargo of herrings, ran short of coal, and had to take assistance in order to reach port. If the cargo of herrings on board her had remained at sea 48 hours longer than they in fact did, they would have become valueless. To reflect the fact that, while both ship and cargo were immobilised, the cargo was in imminent danger of total loss, the court required the cargo to pay a sum over twice as great as that payable by ship, although the cargo was worth only slightly more than half the value of the ship. On the other hand, the general principle is that salvage remuneration is borne rateably according to the values salved; and differences in the degree of risk from which one portion of the salved property has been salved as compared with another portion affords no ground for distinction in liability to salvage.[11]

The most recent discussion of the issue does not clearly resolve it. In *The M. Vatan*[12] an ultra-large crude carrier with a cargo of about 400,000 tonnes of oil was struck by an Exocet missile and caught fire. The master signed an LOF 1980 contract, adding that "cargo owners are not authorising us to give instructions regarding cargo salvage." It was necessary to salve cargo in order to salve the vessel, but the cargo-owners disclaimed liability and took no part in the arbitration. The total salved fund was U.S.$77,290,499, of which the ship's value was only 4.6 per cent. The arbitrator decided that, if all the salved property and salved values had been before him, he would have awarded the salvors U.S.$4,750,000, of which 4.6 per cent is U.S.$221,350. Noting the possibility that no, but possibly some, salvage remuneration was recoverable from the cargo-owners, he made an award against the shipowners of U.S.$850,000. However, the appeal arbitrator reduced this to U.S.$350,000 and the appeal award was upheld by Sheen J.

1430

Two factors influenced his decision: one was doubt whether differential awards should be payable according to whether different property was exposed to different risks; the other was the desirability of avoiding intricate litigation and problems of great nicety as to whether different parcels of cargo were exposed to different risks. In conclusion, Sheen J. expressed a preference for the general rule that the liability of each salvee should be assessed pro rata and one salvee should not be liable to pay more because the salvors may have difficulty in recovering a salvage reward from the owners of other salved property. He disapproved of the decision in *The Velox*,[13] though left open the

---

[10] [1906] P. 263; *The Beatsa* (1946) 79 Ll.L.Rep. 401.
[11] *The Longford* (1881) 6 P.D. 60. Equally no distinction would be accepted to those cases where the services to one person were effectively complete a long time before services to another: *e.g.* lightening a stranded tanker. *cf.* also *The Emma* (1881) 6 P.D. 60.
[12] [1990] 1 Lloyd's Rep. 336.
[13] [1906] P. 263.

possibility that it might survive as an exception to the general rule, doing "broad justice".

1431 However, two issues are present here. Once the liability of individual salvees has been determined, it is surely right that, as a general rule, one salvee should not be made to bear a share of another salvee's liability. But it is a different question how the individual liabilities are assessed in the first place. As a matter of principle it should be the case that the danger and the value of the service to individual salvees should be separately assessed. It is a further question whether the policy of investigating the merits of individual claims and liabilities, convenient though it undoubtedly is, should override the matter of principle in every case.

1432 *The case of derelict.*[14] It was undoubtedly the ancient practice of the Admiralty Court to award to salvors of derelict one-half of the value of the salved property.[15] Even in judgments of the nineteenth century, language is to be found which seems to recognise the title of salvors of derelict to this scale of reward and so to exempt this case from the exercise by the court of that discretion which it uses in all other salvage cases.[16] It is now clearly settled, however, that there is no rule entitling the salvors of derelict, as of right, to any such proportion of the value of the salved property; the service, as in any other case of salvage, is to be rewarded adequately, according to the degree in which the various allowable ingredients of a salvage claim are found to be present.[17] As the fact of a vessel's being derelict generally implies a high degree of danger to it, the salvors of such a vessel will usually, on that score, be entitled to a high rate of reward.[18] But the reward is to be assessed upon the same[19] principles as the reward in any other case of salvage service; and danger to the property salved is only one ground, although, of course, a very important ground, for a large reward. It is quite possible that in other respects, as, for example, in respect of their danger, skill, and loss of time, the merit of the salvors of derelict may be less than in many cases of non-derelict.

---

[14] As to what is "derelict" see *ante*, Chap. 3.
[15] This former practice under "the old law" was referred to and distinguished from current (1814, 1834) practice in *The Blenden-Hall* (1814) 1 Dods. 414, 421; *The Effort* (1834) 3 Hagg. 165, 167; *The Thetis* (1834) 2 Knapp 390, 410 (PC). The practice was one of great antiquity in maritime courts. See *The Good Customs of the Sea* (Les Bones Costumes de la Mar) (probably about A.D. 1350). Twiss (ed.), *Black Book of the Admiralty*, Vol. iii, pp. 439, 441, 619; *The Wisby Town-Law on Shipping* (Wisby Stadslag van Sciprechte) (A.D. 1320–1361), c.xiii; *ibid.*, Vol. iv. p. 405.
[16] See, *e.g. The Watt* (1843) 2 W.Rob. 70, 71, *per* Dr Lushington.
[17] *The Janet Court* [1897] P. 59. *cf.* also *The Aquila* (1798) 1 C.Rob. 37; *The Florence* (1852) 16 Jur.572; *The Martin Luther* (1857) 2 M.L.C. 216; *The Anna Helena* (1883) 5 Asp. M.L.C. 142; *The True Blue* (1866) L.R. 1 P.C. 250.
[18] See, *e.g. The Pergo* [1987] 1 Lloyd's Rep. 582 (Ct Sn), 587.
[19] See *The Mars* (1921) Ll.L.Rep. 567; *The Julia Maria* (1921) 7 Ll.l.Rep. 23; *The Hoffman* (1922) 10 Ll.L.Rep. 13; *The Cambria* (1923) 14 Ll.l.Rep. 170; *The Uranus* (1924) 18 Ll.l.Rep. 439; *The Atlantic* (1925) 27 Ll.l.Rep. 196; *The Pampa* (1925) 22 Ll.l.Rep. 496; *The Johanne Dybwad* (1926) 25 Ll.l.Rep. 119.

Risk of financial loss

A person who engages in salvage operations may forego or delay commercial opportunities. Where such opportunities are inchoate, the tribunal must estimate the potential value of the chance missed, taking account of any evidence that they might not materialise or be as fruitful as they are alleged to be.[20] Where the sum lost is quantifiable, as where the salvor has desisted from performing a fixed engagement, the tribunal may accept the evidence given as to the value of the loss.[21] In both cases, however, the tribunal needs to estimate the value of the opportunity and the probability of its not materialising.

A particularly important financial risk run by the salvor, in theory at least, is that, whether or not it is a breach of a pre-existing contract, engaging in salvage services may trigger the automatic termination of contractual rights. Thus, as a matter of general principle, an unjustifiable deviation by a shipowner discharges a cargo-owner from liability under a contract of carriage[22] and an insurer from liability under a contract of insurance—though deviations to save imperilled lives or property are nowadays usually permitted.

Risks of responsibility or liability

The "responsibility" which a salvor incurs in performing a salvage service may be taken into account in assessing a reward. Thus, in *The Ewell Grove*,[23] where the service had been rendered by HMS *Rhadamanthus*, Sir John Nicholl laid great stress upon the responsibility which her commander undertook in delaying his ship in order to perform salvage. Particular credit has been given for the responsibility of the master of a vessel carrying mails and/or passengers in delaying or deviating from the voyage upon which his vessel was engaged.[24]

---

[20] See *The Perfective* (1949) 82 Ll.L.Rep. 873, 876. *cf. The Louisa* (1848) 3 W.Rob. 99, 100. See also *The Pubnico Virgo* [1975] 1 Lloyd's Rep. 448 (Can FC), 451.

[21] See *The Salacia* (1829) 2 Hagg. 262, 269–270.

[22] See, *e.g. Scaramanga v. Stamp* (1880) 5 C.P.D. 295.

[23] (1835) 3 Hagg. 209, 225–226:
"There was considerable risk of ... responsibility. The steam-vessel was on a service requiring despatch; she was under positive orders to return by a certain time, and it was not till after much consideration and doubt that Captain Evans takes upon himself the responsibility, and sends an excuse to the commodore. But if any untoward accident had happened, this conduct might have deeply involved the captain, and perhaps also his officers; and I think, therefore, that the incurring such a responsibility was equal to a personal risk of life; but, however that may be, it forms a strong feature of this case."
See also *The Salacia* (1829) 2 Hagg. 262, 270; *The Thetis* (1834) 2 Knapp 390, 409; *The Domira* (1914) 30 T.L.R. 521 (the risk run by the commander of HMS *Melpomene* of incurring possible disfavour with the Admiralty with possible "disagreeable consequences").

[24] *The Martin Luther* (1857) Swab. 287. The anxiety of the masters where passengers are present on salving and salved vessels is a material circumstance: *The Southsea* (1932) 44 Ll.L.Rep. 373 (services rendered by one passenger steamship to another). Where mails are being carried, the material circumstance may translate from "mere" responsibility to legal liability: see *The Silesia* (1880) 5 P.D. 177; *The Ionic, Shipping Gazette W.S.*, July 28, 1893.

Assessment

The majority of risks previously discussed in this book under the description of responsibilities are more precisely described as ones of legal liability. Salvors may run the risk of a variety of such liabilities.

It has been long established that, given the existence of danger to the property salved, potential third party liability is also a material and enhancing consideration to the assessment of an award.[25] This principle has been confirmed in *The Gregerso*,[26] where the potential liability to third parties was that which would have arisen in the event that the port, the entrance to which the stranded casualty had blocked, remained closed. Similarly, the avoidance or reduction of third party liability for oil pollution would also be an enhancing feature.[27]

Time used and losses and expenses incurred by salvors

1435 Article 13.1(f) of the Salvage Convention 1989 includes "the time used and expenses and losses incurred by the salvors" as a criterion for fixing a salvage reward.

Time: promptness and duration

1436 It was established by the Admiralty court that the tribunal may take account of not only the time taken in rendering a salvage service but the promptness of responding to the situation, the time and expense of going out to the casualty[28] and, in the case of a professional salvor's tug, the time taken in returning to her salvage station. Likewise, dilatoriness may depress a notional award. Time factors are listed by the International Salvage Convention 1989, Art. 13.1 under heads (h) (the promptness of the services rendered) and (f) (the time used and expenses and losses incurred by the salvors).

1437 However, "The duration of salvage services in very many cases is not the true criterion of their value."[29] The length of time taken in rendering the service is not *per se* a reason for enhancing a reward. A service, though

---

[25] *cf. The Whippingham* (1934) 48 Ll.l.Rep. 49 (risk of causing collision damage to vessel in the anchorage); *The Merranio* (1927) 28 Ll.l.Rep. 352 (risk of wreck raising expenses); see also *The Beatsa* (1937) 58 Ll.l.Rep. 85; *The Bertil* [1952] 2 Lloyd's Rep. 176; *The Johanne Dybwad* (1926) 25 Ll.l.Rep. 119, 123; *The Empress of Australia and The Debrett* (1947) 81 Ll.l.Rep. 24; *The New Australia* [1958] 2 Lloyd's Rep. 35.

[26] [1973] 1 Q.B. 274.

[27] It is because third party risks are treated as collateral to the dangers to the salved property itself and not sufficient on their own to form the basis of a salvage claim that the principles outlined in *The Velox* (*post*, §§1500–1504) do not apply so as to impose the burden of paying the salvage remuneration attributable to the work done to limit third party liability upon, say, the shipowner. *cf. The Bosworth (No. 3)* [1962] 1 Lloyd's Rep. 483.

[28] *The Graces* (1844) 2 W.Rob. 294, 301.

[29] *The Strathgarry* [1895] P. 264, 270, *per* Butt J. See also *The Thomas Fielden* (1862) 32 L.J.Adm. 61, 62, *per* Dr Lushington.

protracted, may not contain any important element of risk or skill on the part of the salvors, *e.g.* in the case of a long but easy towage of a disabled ship by a powerful salving vessel in favourable weather. Indeed, a promptly rendered service may well be more deserving of a valuable reward. In *The General Palmer*[30] the short period of time occupied by the service was unsuccessfully urged in support of a small tender, Dr Lushington observing: "I am at a loss to conceive why a patient should complain of the shortness of an operation . . . It is not the mere time occupied; it is not the mere labour, but the real value of the services rendered."

1438 Time is therefore an element of the value of services. However, in listing together "the time used and expenses and losses incurred by the salvors", the International Salvage Convention 1989, Art. 13.1(f) accurately recognises that, in many cases in practice, the significance of time taken is more an item of the salvor's expenses and losses[31] rather than evidence of the value of the service.

The ability to reward promptness and efficiency and the real value of the service provided means that a salvor should not be encouraged to protract the service by the hope of increasing the award. On the other hand, a salvee who delays accepting redelivery will expose himself to liability to pay for losses resulting to the salvor, including those resulting from loss of time.[32]

Losses and expenses incurred by the salvors

1439 With regard to the salvor's right to compensation for damage, expenses and loss of earnings or profits by the performance of the salvage service, the effect of the judgments in the leading cases of *The Sunniside*,[33] *The De Bay*[34] and *The City of Chester*[35] fairly read together appears to be as follows.

(i) The fact that damage, expense or loss of profits has been caused by the performance of the salvage service is a fact which the court ought never to disregard in assessing the amount of the reward.

---

[30] (1844) 5 Not. of Cas. 159n. See also *The Andalusia* (1865) 12 L.T. 584, 585, *per* Dr Lushington ("Respecting the duration of the service, it was short, and did not exceed eight hours; but that is a question, where steam-vessels are employed, which the court does not consider operates against the claim for remuneration, because the court has held that it is better the service should occupy a short space of time than the length of time it used to occupy from the delay which arose to make the manoeuvres requisite to perform the services"); *The Strathgarry* [1895] P. 264; *The Modavia* (1932) 39 Ll.L.Rep. 58 (where £5,000 reward was given to a tug which, by a very short service, "snatched" a vessel from a position of danger).
[31] See, *e.g.* *The Norden* (1853) 1 Spinks E. & A. 185; *The Andalusia* (1865) 12 L.T. 584, 585.
[32] See the International Salvage Convention 1989, Art. 8.2(c); *ante*, §1070.
[33] (1883) 8 P.D. 137.
[34] (1883) 8 App.Cas. 559, PC; followed in *The Baku Standard* [1901] A.C. 549 (PC).
[35] (1884) 9 P.D. 182 (CA).

Assessment

(ii) All the circumstances, of which this is only one, must be considered together.

(iii) It does not follow, necessarily, that because the salvor proves such damages, expenses, or losses, the court should fix the sum awarded high enough to cover them.

(iv) On the contrary, the salvage service may itself be so trivial as to make it unjust, or the property salved may be of so small a value as to make it impossible,[36] to cast the burden of such an indemnity upon the owner of the salved property.

(v) If the court sees that this is the case, it may properly refuse to receive evidence, either before itself, or by means of a reference to the registrar and merchants, as to the particulars of damage, expenditure, or loss of earnings or profits incurred by the salvor.

1440

(vi) Where, however, meritorious salvage services have occasioned to the salvors serious pecuniary loss, and where the value of the property saved is ample not only to defray loss sustained by a salvor, in addition to an adequate sum for salvage proper, but also to leave a substantial surplus for the owner of the property saved, the salvor should be remunerated with a sum sufficient both to reward him for his risk, labour, skill, and conduct, and also to cover damages, expenses, and losses incurred through rendering the service.[37] Evidence of such damages, expenses, and losses, where not agreed, ought to be received by the court, so that they may be ascertained with some precision, although not necessarily to examine them with the precision which would be legitimate in a common law action for work and labour done.[38]

(vii) The amounts of damage, expense or loss ought not under ordinary circumstances to be taken as "moneys numbered" to be added to the amount of the reward for actual salvage services. If the court gives the amount of the damage, loss or expense specifically, it will take care not to give the amount twice over by again considering

---

[36] See, for an example of the latter case, *The Erato* (1888) 13 P.D. 163, in which the repairs of the damage incurred in the salvage service by one alone out of several sets of salvors cost £4,700, and the total value of salved property in court was £3,750. In *The Tower Bridge* [1936] P. 30, the salved value was £10,000, the salving vessel was alleged to have been damaged to the extent of £4,000, and the award to her owners was £1,500.

[37] See, *e.g. The Jupiter*, Shipping Gazette W.S., August 9, 1901, where the salvor's losses and expenses amounted to £2,157, and on a value of £54,900 an award of £9,550 was given, of which £7,500 was apportioned to the owners; *The Baku Standard* [1901] A.C. 549 (PC), where an award of £1,000 salvage and £1,316 for damage was upheld by the PC; in *The Melanie* (1924) 40 T.L.R. 236, where the salving ship sustained damage to the amount of £19,696, Sir Henry Duke P. awarded to the owners £21,500.

[38] *The Pinnas* (1888) 6 Asp. M.L.C. 313, 315. See also *The Hektor* (1930) 36 Ll.L.Rep. 264.

Time used and losses and expenses incurred by salvors

them when it comes to fix the amount due for salvage remuneration proper; that is, the remuneration for risk and so on in the service.[39]

It may be taken that, at the present time, the court will be careful to award, wherever possible, a sufficient sum to salvors to cover the expenses they have incurred and to give them a reasonable additional amount as compensation for their services. If, however, the salved values are too low to allow such an amount and to leave an adequate amount for the owners of the salved property, the salvors may, in extreme cases, find themselves out of pocket.[39A] This risk is an element which is taken into consideration to enhance awards to salvors in cases where, by meritorious service, they have salved property of high value.

1441

If the court is requested, on making an award, to apportion it between owners, master and crew, which it has not infrequently been asked to do, any losses and expenses which have fallen upon the owners can be taken into account in the proportion of the award which is apportioned to them. Owners of salving vessels generally receive a high proportion of an award[40] and this may be higher when expenses and any losses are on a greater scale than usual. In such a case, according to the circumstances, it may be desirable and proper to make a separate assessment[41] or it may be unnecessary. Another such case is where the owner of the salving ship has suffered loss of profit, or has had to pay for repairs to the salving ship, and after making the award the court does not apportion. Apportionment between the owners of the salving ship and the master and crew may then have to be made later. In such a case, unless the court's allowance to the owner for the damage and loss of profits has been separately awarded, there will be a danger of part of that which was intended to recoup the owner for the damage and the loss of profits going to the master and crew, who have no title to any share in it. Again, there may be, as there was in the case of *The Sunniside*,[42] antecedent agreement between the different salvors to share the salvage reward in certain proportions; and it would be obviously unjust that, at the expense of one salvor whose ship has been injured in the performance of the salvage service, his co-salvors should, by reason of

1442

---

[39] See on this *The De Bay* (1883) 8 App.Cas. 557, 566; *The Sunniside* (1884) 9 P.D. 182 (CA); *The Lycaon* (1949) 82 Ll.L.Rep. 691.

[39A] However, if the salved vessel threatened environmental damage (as most do), the hardship will be mitigated if special compensation is awarded under the Salvage Convention 1989, Art. 14: see *ante*, Chap. 5.

[40] Ordinarily about three-quarters; see *post*.

[41] *The City of Chester* (1884) 9 P.D. 182, 204; *The Saltburn* (1894) 7 Asp. 474; *The James Brand, Shipping Gazette W.S.*, July 17, 1903.

[42] (1883) 8 P.D. 143. In this case one of the salvors had agreed beforehand to pay over to another one-third of the salvage reward decreed to him. He had claims, which the court assessed at £100, for loss of profits and for repairs. To prevent the obvious injustice of one-third of this compensation being paid over to the other salvor under the bargain, Sir James Hannen P. awarded separately the £100 for loss of profits and for repairs, and the £200 found due to the same salvor for salvage reward pure and simple. See also *The Wilhelm Tell* [1892] P. 337.

Assessment

an award in gross, derive a benefit from the award being enhanced by an allowance for the loss which he had sustained.

1443 The tribunal may compensate the salvor for: (i) losses occurring in and as a result of, and expenses properly[43] incurred in the furtherance, and before termination,[44] of the salvage service; and (ii) losses and expenses directly occasioned by performance of the salvage service.

Indemnifiable losses occurring during the performance of salvage services include[45]: the diminution in value of property involved in the salvage service, most obviously as a result of damage to the salving vessel[46] or the salvor's equipment[47] (in practice this will be the cost of repairs)[48]; loss of equipment[49]; loss of salvors' clothes[50]; and demurrage while a damaged salving vessel is being repaired.[51]

1444 "The Court will always recognise where, in rendering salvage services, damage is occasioned to one of the salving vessels, that that has to be taken into account as actual damage."[52] Where the salvor's vessel is lost or damaged whilst engaged in the salvage service, it is presumed that the loss, and also subsequent losses from delay, were caused by the necessities of the service, and not by the default of the salvors; and the burden of proof lies on the salvees to shew that the loss was caused by the salvor's fault.[53]

1445 No allowance will be made for losses which are not the proximate result of the service.[54] Thus, once the salvage service has terminated, a distinction must be made between losses proximately caused by the service and remote losses. Salvors may recover in respect of expenses incurring at the termination of services, *e.g.* for harbour or dock dues.[55] However, such expenses may be recoverable "independently of salvage".[56] Certainly, losses or expenses

---

[43] *The Pinnas* (1888) 6 Asp.M.L.C. 313, 315.
[44] *The Pinnas* (1888) 6 Asp.M.L.C. 313, 314.
[45] See generally *The Fairport* [1912] P. 168, 171–172.
[46] *The Saratoga* (1861) Lush. 318, 322; *The De Bay* (1883) 8 App. Cas. 559, 565–556 (general depreciation); *The Baku Standard* [1901] A.C. 549.
[47] See, *e.g. The James Armstrong* (1875) 3 Asp.M.L.C. 46, 48.
[48] *The Mud Hopper No. 4* (1879) 4 Asp.M.L.C. 103; *The Sunniside* (1883) 8 P.D. 137; *The Baku Standard* [1901] A.C. 549.
[49] *The Madras* [1898] P. 90, 96.
[50] *The Rosalie* (1861) 1 Spinks E. & A. 188, 192.
[51] *The Mud Hopper No. 4* (1879) 4 Asp.M.L.C. 103; *The Fairport* [1912] P. 168.
[52] *The Fairport* [1912] P. 168, 171, *per* Bargrave Dean J.
[53] *The Thomas Blyth* (1860) Lush. 16; *The Baku Standard* [1901] A.C. 549, PC.
[54] *The Cornelius Grinnell* (1864) 2 M.L.C. 140 (NY SD) (damage from grounding on arrival at low, rather than high, water).
[55] *e.g. The Baku Standard* [1901] A.C. 549 (PC); *The Louisa* [1906] P. 145; *The Mari Chandris* [1941] P. 94. See also *The Andrina* (1870) L.R. 3 A. & E. 286.
[56] See *The Le Jonet* (1872) L.R. 3 A. & E. 556, 559. In that case Sir Robert Phillimore awarded out of the proceeds of sale of the salved vessel expenses incurred by the salvors after the arrest of the vessel in hiring men to pump the salved ship, "although, strictly speaking, [the sum] ought to have been defrayed by the master".

incurred after the termination of salvage services should be claimed not as salvage reward but, if at all, on common law principles.[57]

Engagement in a salvage service may result in the termination of a salvor's **1446** existing contractual rights and expose him to liability for breach of contract. Thus, in principle, an unjustifiable deviation will result in termination of cover under insurance policies[58] and the discharge of contracts of carriage, together with liability in damages to cargo-owners.[59] The common law rule, which treated deviations as unjustifiable unless they were to save life,[60] directly opposed the policy of encouraging property salvage promoted by the Admiralty Court,[61] which included the shipowner's loss, or risk of such loss,[62] within the circumstances to be considered in assessing a salvage reward.[63] In modern times salvors are less likely to suffer as a result of unjustifiable deviations: contracts of carriage contain provisions giving liberty specifically to salve or more generally to take a course which would otherwise be unjustifiable[64]; contracts governed by the Hague-Visby Rules permit "[a]ny deviation in saving or attempting to save life or property at sea or any reasonable deviation"[65]; statutory provisions require intervention in cases of danger[66]; and marine insurance policies normally permit what would otherwise be, or hold the assured covered in the event of, deviation and other breaches of warranty.[67] Indeed, it might be argued, in the unusual case where a shipowner has failed to obtain the contractual protection available in the

---

[57] See especially *The Winson* [1982] A.C. 939; discussed *ante*, Chap. 9.
[58] Marine Insurance Act 1906, s.46.
[59] *Scaramanga v. Stamp* (1880) 5 C.P.D. 295.
[60] *Scaramanga v. Stamp* (1880) 5 C.P.D. 295. A deviation may be justifiably made with the object of saving life even though it is initially to investigate whether life is in danger and even if it additionally involves saving property.
[61] See *Scaramanga v. Stamp* (1880) 5 C.P.D. 295, 305–306, *per* Cockburn C.J.
[62] *The Farnley Hall* (1881) 4 Asp. 499.
[63] See, *e.g. The De Bay* (1883) 8 App. Cas. 559 (PC); *The Waterloo* (1820) 2 Dods. 433, 443; *The Jane* (1831) 2 Hagg. 338, 344–345; *Papayanni v. Hocquard (The True Blue)* (1866) L.R. 1 P.C. 250, 254–255; *Carmichael v. Brodie (The Sir Ralph Abercrombie)* (1866) L.R. 1 P.C. 454, 461; *Scaramanga v. Stamp* (1880) 5 C.P.D. 295, 305. *cf. The Orbona* (1853) 1 Spinks E. & A. 161, 166; *The Thetis* (1869) 2 A. & E. 365, 368.
[64] See, *e.g. The Thetis* (1869) 2 A. & E. 365, 368–369; *The Silesia* (1880) 5 P.D. 177, 184.
[65] Carriage of Goods by Sea Act 1971, s.1(2), Sched., Art. IV, r. 4.
[66] See the duties to render assistance at sea considered *post*, §§ 534–544.
[67] The Institute Time Clauses Hulls (1/11/95), cl. 1.1 states that: "The vessel is covered subject to the provisions of this insurance at all times and has leave . . . to assist and tow vessels or craft in distress, but it is warranted that the vessel shall not be towed, except as is customary or to the first safe port or place when in need of assistance, or undertake towage or salvage services under a contract previously arranged by the Assured and/or Owners and/or Managers and/or Charterers . . . ". The Institute Voyage Clauses Hulls (1/11/95), cl. 2 (Change of Voyage) provide: "Held covered in case of deviation or change of voyage or any breach of warranty as to towage or salvage services, provided notice be given to the Underwriters immediately after receipt of advices and any amended terms of cover and any additional premium required by them be agreed." The Institute Time Clauses Hulls (1/11/95), cl. 3 (Breach of Warranty) provide: "Held covered in case of any breach of warranty as to cargo, trade, locality, towage, salvage services or date of sailing provided notice be given to the Underwriters immediately after receipt of advices and any amended terms of cover and any additional premium required by them be agreed." Additional premiums so payable may be taken into account as an element in fixing a reward or in the portion of it to be awarded to the person who has paid the premium: *The Edenmore* [1893] P. 79.

market, that the tribunal should not take account of a loss unreasonably incurred. However, since a salvor owes no duty to the salvee to have negotiated such protection, and since a salvor intervening without such protection clearly takes a greater risk than one who has it, it should remain a legitimate consideration in assessing a salvage reward.

1447 Similarly, a salvor can have account taken of lost opportunities of profit-earning, whether fixed[68] or inchoate. However, the salvor will not be allowed double recovery.[69] Thus, the tribunal may take account of the fact that a claimant has carried out a salvage service at a time when he could have been pursuing his normal employment; but he cannot have the unearned earnings from his normal employment counted as a loss arising from the salvage service. "When seamen render salvage services they abandon their ordinary occupation for the purpose of another occupation, which is salvage, and they cannot be paid for both, although the Court will recognise the fact in making its award."[70] However, the tribunal may consider as specific items of loss: financial loss to the salvor's existing property[71]; profits lost after and as a consequence of performing salvage services, such as cancelled charter-parties.[72]

1448 Where the salvor has contractually agreed to pay a sum to a third party in the event of his engagement in salvage services, that sum may be taken into

---

[68] *The Silesia* (1880) 5 P.D. 177, 184 (cancelled charterparty); *The Edenmore* [1893] P. 79, 84.

[69] *The Sunniside* (1883) 8 P.D. 137, 142, *per* Sir James Hannen P.

[70] *The Fairport* [1912] P. 168, 170–171, *per* Bargrave Dean J. In relation to loss of fishing, Willmer J. in *The Perfective* (1949) 82 Ll.L.Rep. 873, 876, approved the following statement (derived from *The Louisa* (1848) 3 W.Rob. 99, 100, and *The Fairport* [1912] P. 168, 170–171) from Kennedy, 3rd ed., pp. 184–185: " if the salvor has been merely deprived of the employment of his vessel in the ordinary occupation of fishing, since he has been earning salvage remuneration during that time, loss of profits will not be allowed, though the Court will recognise the fact in making its award." See also *The Oscar* (1829) 2 Hagg. 257, 258; *The Nicolai Heinrich* (1853) 17 Jur. 329 (where Dr Lushington opined that, "if persons engaged in fishing are employed in a service of this [salvage] description, which is not really important, and afterwards think they can induce the Court to give them any possible amount of profit which they think they might have acquired, they had better get on with the latter, and not afford their services"); *The James Armstrong* (1875) 3 Asp.M.L.C. 46, 47 (§13); *The Sunniside* (1883) 8 P.D. 137, 142; *The Cato* (1930) 37 Ll.L.Rep. 33, 38; *The Comitas* (1934) 49 Ll.L.Rep. 43, 50; *The Tresco* (1944) 77 Ll.L.Rep. 514; *The St Melante* (1947) 80 Ll.L.Rep. 588, 591 ("It is well established now that, while the pecuniary sum which represents, or which is alleged to represent, the loss of catch due to the performance of the salvage service is an element which has to be taken into consideration in making the salvage award, it is also well recognised that any sum which the tribunal thinks would be an appropriate sum in respect of that is not given, in any sense of the word, as moneys numbered, but merely forms an element of the reward."); *The Ebor Jewel* (1950) 83 Ll.L.Rep. 64; *The Pubnico Virgo* [1975] 1 Lloyd's Rep. 448 (Can FC); *The Ben Gairn* [1979] 1 Lloyd's Rep. 410 (Ct Sn). In *The Salacia* (1829) 2 Hagg. 262, 270–271, specific "compensation" was awarded for quantified loss of profits from fishing; but that is clearly not the practice nowadays. See also *The Hektor* (1930) 36 Ll.L.Rep. 264 (discussed *infra*, n. 71).

[71] See *ante*, §§ 1444–1445. In *The Hektor* (1930) 36 Ll.L.Rep. 264, Hill J. awarded a liquidated sum for diminution in value and loss of market caused by the salvor's delay in getting fish to market as a result of engaging in the salvage service; but that was a loss to the salvor's existing property (fish which had already been caught) rather than a missed opportunity to catch and sell fish. *cf. The St Melante* (1947) 80 Ll.L.Rep. 588.

[72] *The De Bay* (1883) 8 App. Cas. 559, 564–565.

account in assessing the reward recoverable from the salvee; but the tribunal is not bound to reimburse the salvor for such sum exactly or independently of the global salvage award.[73]

Lloyd's Form provides that the arbitrator has an absolute discretion to include in the amount awarded to the Contractors the whole or part of any expenses reasonably incurred by them in: (i) ascertaining, demanding and obtaining the amount of security reasonably required[74]; and (ii) enforcing and/or protecting by insurance or otherwise or taking reasonable steps to enforce and/or protect their lien.[75]

1449

The measure of success

Reproducing, with slight modification of language, a consideration listed in the Brussels Salvage Convention,[76] the International Salvage Convention 1989, Art. 13.1(c) lists, as a criterion for fixing the reward, the measure of success obtained by the salvor.

1450

The Admiralty Court has from the beginning required "success" as a condition for claiming a salvage reward.[77] However, the Salvage Convention 1989 expresses the requirement differently. Article 12 provides that a reward may be claimed if and only if salvage operations have had a "useful result".[78] There are at least two possible interpretations of Article 12. One is that it reproduces the Admiralty law rule that if, and only if, there has been successful salvage of the subject-matter, a claimant is entitled to a reward if he has made a meritorious contribution to the operations, even though he was not himself ultimately responsible for their success. A second (less convincing) interpretation is that a useful result justifies a salvage reward even without success in the traditional sense.[79]

---

[73] In *The Silesia* (1880) 5 P.D. 177, a mail steamer had agreed to carry mail for the Belgian Government under a contract imposing penalties for deviation and delay. Sir Robert Phillimore made an award of salvage in addition to the amount of the penalties. But this does not mean that the tribunal will order precise reimbursement of such sum. First, a contract to pay a penalty (as opposed to liquidated damages) will not be enforced (*Dunlop Pneumatic Tyre Co. Ltd v. New Garage & Motor Co. Ltd* [1915] A.C. 79); and a third party to such an arrangement should remain no more subject to its consequences in a salvage action than a party to the original agreement. Secondly, Sir Robert Phillimore did not hold that the penalties should be reimbursed in full independently of the general salvage reward (*cf. Kennedy's Law of Salvage* (5th ed.), §1144; Brice (3rd ed.), §2–195); for the parties had come to an arrangement about the penalties ((1880) 5 P.D. 177, 184), so the judge only had to consider the amount remaining due for salvage. Thirdly, as a matter of principle, it is in the tribunal's discretion to decide whether to make a global award or to award certain sums specifically: see *post*, Chap. 17. As to mail contracts, see also *The Ionic Shipping Gazette W.S.*, July 28, 1893. See also *The Louisa* (1848) 3 W.Rob. 99.

[74] In accordance with LOF 1995, cl. 5 and LSSAC, cl. 4.5 respectively. See *ante*, §§ 1255–1259.

[75] LOF 1995, cl. 6(d); LSSAC 2000, cl. 6.3.

[76] Brussels Salvage Convention 1910. Art. 8: "the measure of success obtained ... by the salvors, and by the salving vessel."

[77] See *ante*, Chap. 8.

[78] International Salvage Convention 1989, Art. 12.1–12.2.

[79] See the discussion *ante*, Chap. 8.

1451 The use of the word "success" in Article 13.1(c) does not resolve this issue for, unlike Article 12, Article 13 does not purport to prescribe "conditions for reward" but merely "criteria for fixing the reward" to be taken into account; and it is possible to take into account the measure of success whether or not there has been any success.[80] However, the better view is that Article 13.1(c) confirms that the traditional requirement of success has survived and must have been satisfied.[81]

1452 Even so, there remain at least two interpretations of the meaning of "*measure of* success". The obvious one is that it is concerned with the extent to which the salvor's input into the operation has resulted in successful preservation of the casualty from the consequences threatened by the danger, *i.e.* the extent to which there has been success. Indeed, the result may well be considered more important than the salvor's input: *e.g.* where, after a long and difficult effort to fight a fire, the vessel is eventually worth only her scrap value.[82] However, in such a case the tribunal would need to be careful not to allow the outcome doubly to prejudice the salvor, for the notional reward would already be reduced by taking account of the low salved value.

Another interpretation of "measure of success" is that it is concerned with the proportion in which the salvor's input has contributed to success. This interpretation may be applied in varying circumstances. For example, success may be achieved in different degrees by the efforts of a variety of salvors, some of whom may have made only a small contribution to the operation without remaining until its completion, by the efforts of the salvees and their employees, and by favourable changes in the weather and tides. The tribunal will be concerned, in fixing the reward, to assess the extent to which the salvors have achieved success or made a useful contribution.

The interpretation is likely to be more important in practice than the first, given the limiting effect of salved values. But both interpretations may usefully be employed in their proper role—simply as factors to be taken into account by the tribunal in its flexible consideration of all criteria in fixing the reward.

Public policy considerations

1453 The International Salvage Convention 1989 confirms the judicially promoted policy of encouraging salvage operations by the prospect of assessment of the reward in a generous way.[83] In advance of listing the criteria to be taken into account in fixing the reward (which are expressly stated not to be in any order of importance), Article 13.1 states a requirement not set out in the Brussels Salvage Convention 1910, namely that "The reward *shall be* fixed

---

[80] *cf.* Brice, §2–133.
[81] See also Gaskell, 21–403; Brice, §2–133.
[82] See Brice, §§ 2–133 to 2–134.
[83] See, *e.g. The Magdalen* (1861) 31 L.J.Adm. 22, 24. See especially *ante*, Chap 1.

Public policy considerations

with a view to encouraging salvage operations".[84] In addition, Article 13.1 lists three criteria founded on public policy considerations, *viz.*: (b) the skill and efforts of the salvor in preventing or minimising damage to the environment; (i) the availability and use of vessels or other equipment intended for salvage operations; and (j) the state of readiness and efficiency of the salvor's equipment and the value thereof.

Salvage services

The Admiralty Court not only developed the general policy of encouraging salvage operations but overtly took on board the additional value of encouraging persons who were particularly able to render effective services, especially where they held themselves in readiness to provide services of a dedicated salvage nature.[85] Four classes of salvor are recognisable: those who would normally not expect to render salvage services; those, like harbour authorities, whose normal work is not salvage but who might on occasions render salvage services as an incident of their normal work; those for whom salvage is a part of their normal activities, albeit not their exclusive concern (and who may hire in salvage equipment or sub-contractors to work with their salvage superintendent); and the full professional salvor who maintains specially equipped salvage vessels, pumps and other equipment in a state of readiness allowing for quick reaction to disasters. The tribunal will react progressively more favourably the further along this scale the claimant is; and in salvage arbitrations it is the practice for claimants to adduce evidence of their status, listing their tugs and other equipment, their cost, the work they do and their market or replacement value.

1454

Article 13.1 does not specifically refer to the status of the salvors themselves but focuses on the nature of their vessels and equipment.

1455

Article 13.1(j) is applicable whatever the status of the claimant and exhorts the tribunal to take account of the extent to which the salvor keeps equipment[86] in a state of readiness, its efficiency (whether or not it is designed or maintained specifically for salvage purposes) and its value. This can be done whether the equipment is owned or hired by the salvor; it will no doubt be a factor to be considered by a claimant in agreeing to the charge to be paid to

---

[84] Emphasis added. See also the preamble to the International Salvage Convention 1989: *post*, Appx 33.

[85] An advance in the Admiralty Court's attitude came with the arrival of steam tugs towards the end of the nineteenth century. See, *e.g. The Envoy, Shipping Gazette W.S.*, February 28, 1888; *The Glengyle* [1898] P. 97; [1898] A.C. 519.

Professional salvors have become the dominating influence on the salvage scene. During the twentieth century, particular generosity came to be given to those who were in business to save vessels in danger. See *The Modavia* (1931) 39 Ll.L.Rep. 58; *The Umberleigh* (1931) 39 Ll.L.Rep. 155; *The Pacific* (1931) 41 Ll.L.Rep. 83; *The Scheldestad* (1933) 46 Ll.L.Rep. 269; *The Rosa Luxemburg* (1934) 49 Ll.L.Rep. 292; *The Topa* (1935) 50 Ll.L.Rep. 211; *The Dalewood* (1943) 75 Ll.L.Rep. 88; *The Eastwood* (1943) 75 Ll.L.Rep. 91; *The American Farmer* (1947) 80 Ll.L.Rep. 672; *The Queen Elizabeth* (1949) 82 Ll.L.Rep. 803; *The Granhill* [1951] 2 Lloyd's Rep. 13.

[86] "Equipment" includes vessels: see *ante*, §§ 1408–1410.

Assessment

a person from whom he hires equipment, though naturally the tribunal will look more generously on a claimant who is contributing and risking his own equipment. Criterion (j) does not require that the equipment in question be dedicated salvage equipment but refers generally to the equipment used by the salvor and holds out encouragement to a potential salvor to be prepared to divert equipment from commercial to salvorial use. By considering the efficiency of that equipment, the tribunal can take account not only of how well the equipment operates but, more importantly, how up-to-date and suitable for the operation it is, thereby encouraging professional salvors to maintain a programme of investment, replacement and improvement.

Though Article 13.1(j) applies whatever the salvor's status, it contemplates salvors whose work, whether or not exclusively, involves or is likely to involve salvage operations. On the other hand, Article 13.1(i) directly encourages the availability and employment of dedicated salvage equipment by such persons.

Environmental services

1456 The International Salvage Convention 1989 endeavours to encourage environmental services. However, the only element of environmental services constituting a criterion for fixing a salvage reward under the Convention is "the skill and efforts of the salvors in preventing or minimising damage to the environment".[87] Except in so far as it constitutes evidence of the exercise of such skill and efforts (which of course it may well do), no other element of environmental services (*e.g.* the extent to which they have been successful)[88] is mentioned by the Convention as material to the assessment of a salvage reward. They will, however, be material for the assessment of special compensation under Article 14 or under contract.[89]

Value of salved property

1457 Though placed last here (for it is only after the operation of the factors listed above that the property can be salved and its value ascertained), "the salved value of the vessel and other property" is the first criterion for fixing a salvage reward listed in the Salvage Convention 1989.[90]

"The value of the property saved is a most material and important consideration",[91] "for in proportion to that value is the benefit to the owners, and

---

[87] International Salvage Convention 1989, Art. 13.1(b).
[88] Interestingly, the measure of success obtained by the salvor is the next criterion listed (in Art. 13.1(c)) by the Convention after the skill and efforts of the salvors in preventing or minimising damage to the environment. But, apart from the fact that the criteria for fixing the reward are to be taken into account without regard to the order in which they are presented (Art. 13.1), the proximity of Art. 13.1(c) is irrelevant, for the criteria in Art. 13 are criteria for fixing a reward for salvage, not for environmental or other services.
[89] See *ante*, Chap. 5.
[90] Salvage Convention 1989, Art. 13.1(a).
[91] *The Lindfield* (1894) 10 T.L.R. 606, *per* Lord Esher M.R. See also *The Geestland* [1980] 1 Lloyd's Rep. 628, 630.

Value of salved property

that is one of the primary principles in settling the amount of remuneration"[92]; but "the court must not be induced by it to award a sum which is out of proportion to the services of the salvors."[93]

Where the property salved is large, the amount of the reward usually bears a much smaller proportion to the value of the property than in cases where the property saved is small. The reason for this is that in the case of property of small value a small proportion would not hold out a sufficient consideration; whereas in cases of considerable value a small proportion would afford no inadequate remuneration.[94]

> "It is obvious that whilst a small percentage on a very large value might be an ample remuneration in one case, a very large percentage on a small value might be a very inadequate remuneration in another case. The risk of getting little by reason of the comparatively small value of the property saved is one of those risks which salvors always run."[95]

It would not, however, be correct to say, as has been sometimes argued, that this greatness of value will be regarded by the Admiralty Court only for the single purpose of remembering that the court is enabled thereby out of an ample fund to remunerate meritorious services well performed. In the important case of *The Amérique*,[96] upon the question of the remuneration awarded in the case of derelicts, the Privy Council distinctly rejected any such view, and enunciated the law in the following terms[97]:

> "The rule seems to be that though the value of the property salved is to be considered in the estimate of the remuneration, it must not be allowed to raise the quantum to an amount altogether out of proportion to the services actually rendered."

Of crucial importance is whether there is any risk of damage or loss encroaching on the fund in the absence of assistance.

In *The Queen Elizabeth*,[98] claims for salvage were made in respect of services rendered to the *Queen Elizabeth*, which ran aground just outside Southampton Water in April 1947. Her salved value was £5,983,000. Willmer

1458

---

[92] *The Ewell Grove* (1835) 3 Hagg. 209, 221, *per* Sir John Nicholl.
[93] *The Glengyle* [1898] P. 97, 103, *per* Gorell Barnes J.; affirmed, *ibid.*, 103 (CA); [1898] A.C. 519 (HL). In *The Port Hunter* [1910] P. 343 (CA), where the salved value was £269,700, the CA reduced the award by Bargrave Deane J. of £10,000 to £6,000, on the ground that undue weight had been given to the value of the salved property.
[94] See *The Blenden-Hall* (1814) 1 Dods.414, 421, where Lord Stowell uses similar words. The passage from his judgment (with one word altered) is quoted with approval in the opinion of the Privy Council in *The Amérique* (1874) L.R. 6 P.C. 468, 475.
[95] *The City of Chester* (1884) 9 P.D. 182, 202, *per* Lindley L.J. See also to the same effect *The Glengyle* [1898] P. 97, 103, *per* Gorell Barnes J.
[96] (1874) L.R. 6 P.C. 468; referred to *supra*.
[97] *ibid.*, 475.
[98] (1949) 82 Ll.L.Rep. 803.

Assessment

J. said, having referred to passages above as set out in the third edition of this work[99]:

> "In those circumstances, where one has, as we do have in this case, a practical certainty of continuing expense, coupled with a possibility, even if it is not much more than a bare possibility, of a much more serious loss, one has to give some real effect to the very high value of the salved property. By that I mean that one must give some effect to it, beyond saying to oneself merely that this is a case in which the value of the salved property at least provides a sufficient and abundant fund out of which to reward the salvors."

1459 Where the property salved is of great value the court, in assessing the reward, looks not merely at the merits of the service or the benefit to the owner of the salved property but at the larger considerations of public interest, as has already been noticed. As meritorious services are not infrequently rendered when the fund at the disposal of the court is insufficient, without depriving the owners of the salved property of all benefit from its preservation, to enable it to decree an adequate reward,[1] the court may, when the property salved is of great value, in consideration of this, and for the general encouragement of salvage services, and not merely because the benefit to the owner of the property has been great, consider the value of the property as entitling the salvor to an enhanced reward.[2]

Agreement for reward independently of success

1460 It was held under pre-Convention law that, if salvors in the performance of successful services had acted under an agreement which entitled them to some remuneration independently of success, the court would take this fact into consideration as an element reducing the amount of the award.[3] In *The Lepanto*,[4] Sir Francis Jeune P. said that one of the consequences of such an agreement was that "the remuneration cannot be considered on what I may call the strict salvage scale, because one of the main reasons why salvage remuneration is so high is, that it involves this, that unless some of the property is saved, no remuneration is obtainable at all." The justice of the rule

---

[99] *ibid.*, 821.
[1] See, *e.g. The Erato* (1888) 13 P.D. 163.
[2] See *The Earl of Eglinton* (1855) Swab. 7, 8.
[3] *The Lepanto* [1892] P. 122; *The Kate B. Jones* [1892] P. 366; *The Edenmore* [1893] P. 79. The two latter cases were expressly approved in *The Valverda* [1938] A.C. 173. See also *The Prometheus* (1949) 82 LL.L.Rep. 859 (CA), affirming the decision of Willmer J., *ibid.*, 172. It is to be noted that the Admiralty as salvor no longer uses the Admiralty Standard Form of Salvage Agreement, Form D.46, of which clause 5 provided for certain remuneration in the event of non-success, referred to in *The Prometheus, supra,* at 861. It was discontinued in 1940 in favour of Lloyd's Standard Form "no cure—no pay." Current instructions are for the latter to be employed whenever salvage services are rendered by H.M. ships or Admiralty-owned ships. See also with particular reference to *The Valverda, supra,* the Crown Proceedings Act 1947, which repealed MSA 1894, s.557(1) and the M.S. (Salvage) Act 1940.
[4] [1892] P. 122, 130.

Value of salved property

is clear. But it is very difficult to say what precise effect the existence of such an agreement ought to have in reducing the award: the danger to the salvors remains the same, whether they are paid for their services or receive remuneration by means of a salvage award.[5] There has, however, been some reduction of the risk of receiving nothing in the event of failure to preserve any property, or of the vessel being saved by other means before the arrival of the prospective salvors.

Article 13.1(g) of the Convention invites the tribunal to take account of "the risk of liability and other risks run by the salvors" but not the absence of a risk. However, the absence or reduction of risk is obviously a factor which diminishes the risk which is actually being run.[5A]

4. Currency

Currency correction

However carefully salvage payments may be calculated in sterling, in an international environment parties are particularly susceptible to incidental profits or losses according to whether sums are expressed in different currencies or are effected by inflation. It is possible for adjustments to be made to take account of such factors. Thus, LOF 1995 provides space in which the parties may stipulate a currency in which salved values are to be,[6] failing which it is to be in pounds sterling.[7] No such specific provision for salved values is contained in LSSAC 2000. However, both editions of Lloyd's Form contain a currency correction clause. Thus, LSSAC 2000, cl. 9 states[8]:

1461

> "In considering what sums of money have been expended by the Contractors in rendering the services and/or in fixing the amount of the award and/or appeal award the Arbitrator or Appeal Arbitrator shall to such an extent and insofar as it may be fair and just in all the circumstances give effect to the consequences of any change or changes in the relevant rates of exchange which may have occurred between the date of termination of the services and the date on which the award or appeal award is made."

Naturally, care must be taken to ensure that an adjustment in respect of one factor does not duplicate one in respect of another. The cases have tended to be concerned with the prejudice to the salvor of currency movements. But, of course, currency movements may potentially prejudice or benefit either party.

---

[5] *The Edenmore* (1893) P. 79, 83, *per* Gorell Barnes J.
[5A] *cf.* LOF 2000, cl. D.
[6] LOF 1995, cl. 1(e).
[7] LOF 1995, cl. 1(f).
[8] *cf.* LOF 1995, cl. 12:
"In considering what sums of money have been expended by the Contractor in rendering the services and/or in fixing the amount of the Award and/or Interim Award(s) and/or Award on Appeal the Arbitrator or Appeal Arbitrator(s) shall to such an extent and in so far as it may be fair and just in all the circumstances give effect to the consequences of any change or changes in the relevant rates of exchange which may have occurred between the date of termination of the services and the date on which the Award and/or Interim Award is made."

Similarly, the exercise of the discretion contained in LOF 1995, cl. 12 to take account of movements in exchange rates produce either an increase or a reduction in the base figure of the award.[9]

Currency of award

1462   In *The Teh Hu*[10] the Court of Appeal reluctantly applied the then prevailing rule that judgment in a salvage claim, as with all claims, could only be given in pounds sterling as at the time at which the cause of action arose, *i.e.* when the salvage service terminated. Thus, amounts calculated in foreign currencies had to be converted at the rate of exchange then prevailing. The former rule was subsequently overturned, so that an English court or arbitrator may now give judgment or make an award for an amount expressed in foreign currency.[11] Accordingly *The Teh Hu* would be decided differently today.[12] The general rules of English law now are that: a claim for an unliquidated debt or damages must prima facie be calculated in the currency in which the loss was felt or borne by the person suffering it, having regard to the currency in which he operates or with which he has the closest connection[13]; but in the case of restitution for unjust enrichment, the award will be made in the currency in which the defendant's benefit can be most fairly and appropriately valued.[14] If salvage rewards are restitutionary,[15] the latter rule should prima facie apply to them and this should even prima facie be the case where salvage is carried out under contract if the intention in such a contract is that the salvage reward should be calculated on Admiralty law principles.[16]

1463   Where a contract on its true construction makes express provision for the issue, then that will prevail.[17] LOF 1995 contains a space which can be filled in if the parties wish to specify the currency in which an award should be

---

[9] See, *e.g. The Pa Mar* [1999] 1 Lloyd's Rep. 338, 341.

[10] [1970] P. 106. See also *The Eastern Moon* (1927) 28 Ll.L.R. 22; *The Eisenach* (1936) 54 Ll.L.R. 354 (salved property valued in sterling at date of termination of service; *Noreuro Traders Ltd v. E. Hardy & Co.* (1923) 16 Ll.L.R. 319 (date of general average adjustment at termination of voyage).

[11] *Miliangos v. George Frank (Textiles) Ltd* [1976] A.C. 443; *Services Europe Atlantique Sud (SEAS) v. Stockholms Rederiaktiebolag SVEA (The Folias)* [1979] A.C. 685. See Dicey & Morris, p. 1604 (rule 211(1)).

[12] *Services Europe Atlantique Sud (SEAS) v. Stockholms Rederiaktiebolag SVEA (The Folias)* [1979] Q.B. 491, 516, per Lord Denning M.R., citing *Miliangos v. George Frank (Textiles) Ltd* [1976] A.C. 443, 468, per Lord Wilberforce.

[13] See Dicey & Morris, p. 1590 (rule 209(4)), pp. 1596–1598 and the cases there cited, especially *The Despina R* [1979] A.C. 685 and *Services Europe Atlantique Sud (SEAS) v. Stockholms Rederiaktiebolag SVEA (The Folias)* [1979] A.C. 685.

[14] *B.P. Exploration Co. (Libya) Ltd v. Hunt (No. 2)* [1979] 1 W.L.R. 783, 840–841; affirmed [1981] 1 W.L.R. 232; affirmed [1983] 2 A.C. 352; Dicey & Morris, pp. 1568, 1608.

[15] See *ante*, §§ 33–35.

[16] See *ante*, §§ 31–32.

[17] The Lloyd's Form currency correction clause (*ante*, §1461) does not provide for the currency in which an award is to be made, except in so far as it relates to expenses incurred by the salvor. Its effect is that, once that currency has been determined, there is a discretion to give effect to movements in exchange rates occurring between the dates of the salvor's expenditure and/or the termination of the service and the date of the award.

made[18]; if no express choice is made, then the award shall be in pounds sterling. LOF 2000 contains a box[19] in which the "Agreed currency of any arbitral award and security (if other than United States dollars)" can be inserted, simultaneously providing for United States dollars by default. This is repeated slightly more elaborately by LSSAC 2000, cl. 6.6, which states that "awards in respect of salvage remuneration or special compensation (including payments on account) shall be made in the currency specified in Box 4 or in United States dollars if no such alternative currency has been agreed."

Inflation

The value of liquidated sums is fixed at the date on which the cause of action arises.[20] This principle was applied to sums payable as salvage rewards in *The Teh Hu*.[21] In that case, sterling was devalued by 14 per cent between the date of the salvage service and the date of the salvage award. Yet it was held that there was a general rule of English law that the amount for which a judgment was entered was not to be affected by any change in the value of sterling since the cause of action accrued and that this rule applied to salvage cases. Lord Denning M.R. dissented and in *The Folias*[22] pointed out that the decision in *The Teh Hu* on another ground (that salvage awards could not be given in a foreign currency) was no longer correct.[23] Moreover, it has subsequently been held that damages for non-economic loss (*e.g.* personal injuries) are calculated at the date of trial, taking into account the effect of inflation, though with an accompanying reduction of the interest on those damages to avoid the plaintiff's being over-compensated.[24] This appears to be the general principle for unliquidated sums and therefore supports the view of Lord Denning M.R. in *The Teh Hu*[25] that, if expenses and salved values are to be assessed at the time the services are concluded, then salvage remuneration should also be calculated as at that time but that, when the award is actually made, the figure should be uplifted so that the salvors receive the same remuneration as they would have received if there had been no devaluation; therefore, neither party would be better or worse off as a result of inflation. Such an "equitable uplift" has been applied in the United States.[26]

1464

---

[18] LOF 1995, cl. 1(e) and Note 3.
[19] Box 4.
[20] The principle of nominalism. See F.A. Mann, *The Legal Aspect of Money* (5th ed., 1992), Chap. IV.
[21] [1970] P. 106.
[22] *Services Europe Atlantique Sud (SEAS) v. Stockholms Rederiaktiebolag SVEA (The Folias)* [1979] Q.B. 491, 516.
[23] Citing *Miliangos v. George Frank (Textiles) Ltd* [1976] A.C. 443, 468, *per* Lord Wilberforce. See *ante*, §1462. See also F.A. Mann, *The Legal Aspect of Money* (5th ed., 1992), p. 117.
[24] *Birkett v. Hayes* [1982] 1 W.L.R. 816 (CA); *Wright v. British Railways Board* [1983] 2 A.C. 773.
[25] [1970] P. 106, 125.
[26] *B.V. Bureau Wijsmuller v. United States of America (The Pioneer Commander)* (1983) 702 F.2d 333 (USCA, 2nd Cir.), 341. See also *Waterman S.S. Corp. v. Dean (The Fairisle)* (1948) 171 F.2d 408 (USCA, 4th Cir.).

Assessment

1465 In practice, it has been unnecessary for further litigation on the point in England. In *The Teh Hu*,[27] Brandon J. and the majority of the Court of Appeal recommended the amendment of Lloyd's Form. Consequently a currency correction clause was introduced into the Form. This clause, currently LSSAC 2000, cl. 9,[28] does not address inflation directly but enables arbitrators to take account of it by conferring upon them a discretion to give effect to movements in exchange rates occurring between the dates of the salvor's expenditure[29] and/or the termination of the service and the date of the award.

5. INTEREST[30]

1466 Interest is money payable for the use of a principal sum. It is intended to represent "the time value"[31] of money and is awarded to compensate the claimant for the loss of use of the money and/or to reverse the defendant's unjust enrichment from use of the money; it is not awarded to punish the defendant for non-payment.[32] As a general principle, where the parties are in a contractual relationship, whether or not interest is payable is generally determined by the law applicable to the contract.[33] The Salvage Convention 1989, Art. 24 provides that "The right of the salvor to interest on any payment under this Convention shall be determined according to the law of the State in which the tribunal seized of the case is situated."

1467 As a general rule, interest on money not paid or paid late is not recoverable at common law. It is, however, recoverable in exceptional cases at common law (by contract and by custom or usage), in equity, in Admiralty,[34] under statute,[35] and under the courts' inherent powers on payments made under judgments later reversed or set aside. Except where stipulated by contract or statute, its award and the terms of the award are in the court's discretion.

As a general rule, where interest is payable, simple interest (*i.e.* at a fixed, conventional rate) will normally be awarded, though compound interest (*i.e.*

---

[27] [1970] P. 106, 116F–G, *per* Brandon J., at 132E–F, *per* Salmon L.J., at 135H, *per* Karminski L.J.

[28] Set out *ante*, §1461.

[29] *Quaere* whether "expenditure" extends to costs of a continuing nature arising independently of the salvage operation in issue, such as maintenance of professional salvage tugs. *cf.* Kennedy, (5th ed.), §1151, n. 24. *Semble* the point is unlikely to be important in practice as the (real) cost of maintaining salvage equipment is in any event a factor to be taken into account in assessing a salvage reward: see *ante*, Chap. 15.

[30] See generally F.D. Rose, "Interest", Chap. 11 of P.B.H. Birks and F.D. Rose, *Lessons of the Swaps Litigation* (Mansfield Press, 2000).

[31] The term is used in *B.P. Exploration Co. (Libya) Ltd v. Hunt (No. 2)* [1979] 1 W.L.R. 783, 799, 804, *per* Robert Goff J., and in the Explanatory Memorandum to the Late Payment of Commercial Debts (Interest) Bill 1997 (see now the 1998 Act, *infra*, n. 35).

[32] See Rose, *supra*, n. 30, at 306–307.

[33] See generally Dicey & Morris, pp. 1454–1464 (rule 196).

[34] See, *e.g. The Dundee* (1827) 2 Hagg. Adm. 137, *The Hector* (1833) 3 Hagg. 90, 95, and the cases cited in *The Aldora* [1975] Q.B. 748.

[35] See the Judgments Act 1838; SCA 1981, s.35A; the County Courts Act 1984, ss.69, 74; the Arbitration Act 1996, s.49; and the Late Payment of Commercial Debts (Interest) Act 1998.

interest on the principal sum with interest payable on the interest) may be payable by contract, by usage, in equity or by statute. It seems that the equitable jurisdiction to award compound interest is finite, and therefore it cannot be awarded under the "common law" of the Admiralty Court.[36] However, by statute[37] compound interest may be awarded by an arbitral tribunal.

1468 The Admiralty Court has an inherent power to award interest in salvage actions.[38] In addition, under the Supreme Court Act 1981, s.35A, the courts have a general statutory discretion to award interest in proceedings for the recovery of a "debt or damages".[39] This includes "any sum of money which is recoverable by one party from another, either at common law or in equity or under a statute ...".[40] Within the meaning of the Act at least, the expression "any debt" has been held to include a claim for a salvage reward[41] and should also include any claim for a payment under the Salvage Convention 1989.[42] However, a party who wants "post-award" interest must apply for it to be awarded by the arbitrator or for a correction or further award.[43]

1469 The rate at which interest can be awarded is as the court thinks fit or as rules of court provide and it may be calculated at different rates in respect of different periods. It may be awarded on all or any part of the debt or damages in respect of which judgment is given or payment is made after the institution of proceedings but before judgment. And it may be awarded for all or any part of the period between the date when the cause of action arose and the date of payment or judgment, whichever is sooner.

Where the Arbitration Act 1996 applies, a tribunal may award simple or compound interest from such dates, at such rates and with such rests as it considers meet the justice of the case, on the whole or part of any amount claimed and unpaid at the date at which the arbitration proceedings commence until the payment or award of the relevant amount, whichever is sooner.[44] However, the Act is subject to the parties' freedom to agree on the powers of the tribunal as regards the award of interest.[45]

---

[36] See *Westdeutsche Landesbank Girozentrale v. Islington LBC* [1996] A.C. 669. According to Lord Lloyd of Berwick, *ibid.*, 739–740, this was the effect of the House of Lords' decision in *President of India v. La Pintada CNSA (La Pintada)* [1985] A.C. 104, 116, *per* Lord Brandon of Oakbrook: "the Admiralty Court never, and Courts of Chancery *only in two special classes of case*, awarded compound, as distinct from simple, interest" (Lord Lloyd's emphasis).
[37] Arbitration Act 1996, s.49.
[38] *The Aldora* [1975] Q.B. 748, not following *The De Bay* (1883) 8 App. Cas. 559 (PC). *The Aldora* was applied in *Bruce's Stores (Aberdeen) Ltd v. Richard Irvin & Sons Ltd (The Ben Gairn)* [1979] 1 Lloyd's Rep. 410 (Ct Sn), *per* Lord Allanbridge.
[39] See also the County Courts Act 1984, s.69.
[40] *B.P. Exploration Co. (Libya) Ltd v. Hunt (No. 2)* [1983] 2 A.C. 352, 373; affirming [1981] 1 W.L.R. 232; affirming [1979] 1 W.L.R. 783.
[41] *The Aldora* [1975] Q.B. 748. *cf. The Ben Gairn* [1979] 1 Lloyd's Rep. 410, 423.
[42] As to the meaning of "payment under [the] Convention", see *ante*, §1211.
[43] *Walker v. Rowe* [2000] 1 Lloyd's Rep. 116.
[44] Arbitration Act 1996, s.49.
[45] *ibid.*, s.49(1)–(2).

Assessment

1470 Under Lloyd's Form interest is not dependent on an arbitrator's exercising a discretion to award it: there is a right to interest on sums awarded in the arbitration unless the arbitrator in his discretion decides otherwise.[46] Such interest is payable from the date of termination of the services (though LOF 1995 provides the arbitrator with an absolute discretion to decide otherwise) until the date of publication by the Council of Lloyd's of the award[47] at a rate[48] to be determined by the arbitrator. The Lloyd's Appeal Arbitrator has power to make such order as he thinks fit as to the payment of interest on the sum(s) which he decides to be payable.[49]

1471 By virtue of the Arbitration Act 1996, s.49 and LOF 1995, cl.11(i), Lloyd's salvage arbitrators are empowered to award compound interest; but they have been reluctant to exercise this power except in special circumstances. Such reluctance generally derives from a misconceived feeling that an unliquidated liability does not have to be discharged until its extent is ascertained and that defendants should not be penalised simply for late payment; but it overlooks that fact that the duty to discharge a liability arises from the creation of the liability, not from the time that its extent is determined, and that parties involved in commerce, whether claimants or defendants, generally earn or have to pay interest at compound rates. The extent to which an unpaid salvor is prejudiced by not recovering compound interest is in practice reduced by the exercise of the arbitrator's power to make provisional awards. Otherwise, where LOF 2000 is used, LSSAC 2000, cl.8.2 makes express provision as to certain circumstances in which compound interest is payable:

> "In ordinary circumstances the Contractors' interest entitlement shall be limited to simple interest but the Arbitrator may exercise his statutory power to make an award of compound interest if the Contractors have been deprived of their salvage remuneration or special compensation for an excessive period as a result of the Owners gross misconduct or in other exceptional circumstances."

---

[46] LOF 1995, cl.11(i); LSSAC 2000, cl.8.1. Under the 1995 edition of the Form, whichever party is awarded a sum in the arbitration has a prima facie right to interest; the 2000 edition limits this right to the contractor/salvor (who is, of course, in the majority of cases in practice, the only party likely to receive an award) but does not exclude the salvee's opportunity of an award of interest under the general law. Likewise, the 1995 edition makes interest payable on "any sum awarded", whereas the 2000 edition limits the right to "any sums awarded in respect of salvage remuneration or special compensation". Both editions require the arbitrator to take into consideration any sums already paid (the 2000 edition adding "to the Contractors on account").

[47] "and/or Interim Award(s)" is added in LOF 1995, cl.11(i).

[48] LOF 1995, cl.11 states "at rates per annum to be fixed by the Arbitrator". LSSAC 2000, cl.8.1 states "at a rate to be determined by the Arbitrator". The 1995 edition therefore contemplates the possibility of different rates being payable on different sums awarded, whereas the 2000 edition contemplates (though not unequivocably) a single rate.

[49] This is stated in the appeal clause: LOF 1995, cl.14(a)(ii); LSSAC 2000, cl.10.7(ii); see further *ante*, § 1308. The 1995 edition of Lloyd's Form also specifically provides in the interest clause that the arbitrator's determination of interest is subject to appeal as provided in the Agreement (LOF 1995, cl.11(i)) but this is superfluous and the statement is omitted from the LSSAC 2000 interest clause (cl.8).

Date from which interest may be awarded

Lloyd's salvage arbitrators follow the practice of the Admiralty Court in **1472** determining the rate at which interest is payable. The practice of the Admiralty Court is to award simple interest at commercial rates, normally 1 to 2 per cent above the current base borrowing rate. It seems that the rate at which interest is awarded is a matter for the *lex fori*.[50] However, this has been doubted and it has been held that, where interest is payable by one contracting party to another and the claimant would normally borrow at a foreign commercial borrowing rate, then that may be the appropriate rate of interest.[51] The two approaches may be reconciled if the true principle is that it is for the *lex fori* to determine the issue and the principle of the English *lex fori* is that interest should reflect the actual loss to the claimant in being kept out of his money, which may be measured by English or foreign rates depending on the circumstances. However, where salvage is *non*-contractual there then arises a further difficulty. If non-contractual salvage is awarded not to compensate the claimant for his loss but to reverse the defendant's unjust enrichment,[52] and if the defendant has been enriched at a foreign rate of interest, then that is the rate at which interest should be awarded against him. Nonetheless, in practice, such difficulties are likely to be avoided by reluctance to depart from the normal commercial rate of interest applying in the forum.

Date from which interest may be awarded

The general principle upon which interest is available is that it is payable **1473** from the date upon which the cause of action arises. Thus, interest was awarded from the date of termination of the salvage service in *The Aldora*[53] in 1974 and in *The Ben Gairn*[54] in 1978. As just stated, LOF 1995, cl.11(i) specifies that the prima facie starting point is "the date of termination of the services"[55] but that the arbitrator has an absolute discretion to decide otherwise. However, in 1978, in *The Rilland*[56] Sheen J. stated that: one of the principal factors to be taken into account in assessing a salvage reward is the value of the property salved, and that this might take weeks or months to determine; it was therefore unreal and absurd to think that the salvor could in any circumstances be paid at that moment, and that "In a commercial setting, it would be proper to take account of the manner in which and the time at which persons acting honestly and reasonably would pay"[57]; and interest is

---

[50] *Miliangos v. George Frank (Textiles) Ltd (No. 2)* [1976] 2 Lloyd's Rep. 434; Dicey & Morris, p. 1454 (Rule 196(2)).
[51] *Helmsing Schiffahrts GmbH & Co. A.G. v. Malta Drydocks Corp.* [1977] 2 Lloyd's Rep. 444.
[52] See *ante*, §§33–35; Rose, *supra*, n. 30.
[53] [1975] Q.B. 748.
[54] [1979] 1 Lloyd's Rep. 410 (Ct Sn, *per* Lord Allanbridge).
[55] The "date of termination of the services" could be the date when all services in respect of the casualty terminate. But LOF is a contract applying only to its parties and should therefore refer to the services provided by the claimant salvor. This may mean that different claimants could be paid interest from different dates. This will obviously be a factor to be considered in the exercise of the tribunal's discretion.
[56] [1979] 1 Lloyd's Rep. 455, 459.
[57] [1979] 1 Lloyd's Rep. 455, 459, citing the words of Lord Wilberforce in *General Tyre and Rubber Co. v. Firestone Tyre Co. Ltd* [1975] 1 W.L.R. 819, 836.

not awarded as a punishment for withholding payment. Accordingly, the principle was adopted that interest was payable from the time at which it was possible to ascertain the facts on which an informed view of an appropriate reward could be based, and it became the practice for Lloyd's arbitrators and the courts to award interest from about six months after termination of the services.[58] The practice was noticed by Clarke J. in 1995 in *The Yolaine*[59] but he held that, as a consequence of changes to Lloyd's Form, the practice of Lloyd's salvage arbitrators had changed, and that it was therefore appropriate for the Admiralty Court to exercise its discretion in the same way as Lloyd's salvage arbitrators. Accordingly, in general both Lloyd's arbitrators and the Admiralty Court should exercise their discretion by awarding interest from the termination of the services, save in special circumstances. As a result, general principle, the terms of Lloyd's Form and practice now coincide.

1474 In fact the principle applied by Sheen J. in *The Rilland* was misconceived in so far as it is based on a desire to avoid punishing the defendant for non-payment: for the fact that the salvee's liability and the salvor's right cannot be ascertained precisely until some time after they arise does not mean either that the salvee is being punished for having to discharge that liability over the whole of its existence or that the salvor should lose the value of use of his right to be paid while the quantum remains unascertained. However, in exercising his discretion under the current approach, Clarke J. in *The Yolaine*[60] awarded interest from a little after the termination of the services because it appeared to him that "it would have taken some time for the defendant—or, more accurately, his insurers—to assess the position."

Interest upon judgments and arbitral awards

1475 The above discussion concerns interest which may be awarded over the period from which the cause of action arises until judgment or the making of an arbitral award. Once the quantum of the defendant's liability for the principal sum and any interest thereon has been determined, the general rule is that interest is then payable on that sum from the time of judgment or award.[61] Interest on judgment debts is fixed by statutory instrument.[62] Under

---

[58] Sheen J. awarded interest after six months in *The Rilland* [1979] 1 Lloyd's Rep. 455; *The Ilo* [1982] 1 Lloyd's Rep. 39; and *The Helenus and Motagua* [1982] 2 Lloyd's Rep. 261. The practice of Lloyd's arbitrators was noted in *The Yolaine* [1995] 1 Lloyd's Rep. 7, 14, *per* Clarke J. The principle was applied by Lord Davidson in *Fairbairn v. Vennootschap G. Ver Vries ZN (The Pergo)* [1987] 1 Lloyd's Rep. 582 (Ct Sn: OH), 588, after a period of 15 weeks and one day, on the ground that it would not have taken *the defenders* very long to ascertain all the facts upon which an informed view as to an appropriate award could be based.

[59] [1995] 1 Lloyd's Rep. 7, 14.

[60] [1995] 2 Lloyd's Rep. 7, 15.

[61] The Judgments Act 1838 enacted that judgment debts should bear interest from date of entry. From the absorption of the Admiralty Court into the High Court by the Judicature Act 1873, the 1838 Act has applied to judgments for salvage: *The Jones Brothers* (1877) 3 Asp. M.L.C. 478.

[62] See *Civil Procedure 2001*, §40.8. Judgments entered on or after April 1, 1993 carry interest at 8 per cent.

the Arbitration Act 1996, s.49(4), an arbitral tribunal has a general power to award simple or compound interest from the date of the award (or any later date) until payment, at such rates and with such rests as it considers meets the justice of the case, on the outstanding amount of any award.[63] However, the Act is subject to contrary contractual provision[64] and specific provision is made by Lloyd's Form. Lloyd's Form stipulates that salvees shall have a certain number of interest-free days in which to satisfy an award in favour of the contractor; but, if they fail to pay the sums awarded (including fees and expenses) within the given time, interest is payable thereafter until payment is made, at rates determinable in the arbitrator's discretion.[65] Thus LOF 1995, cl.11(ii) provides that:

> "Interest at rates per annum to be fixed by the Arbitrator shall (subject to Appeal as provided in this Agreement) be payable on any sum awarded taking account any sums already paid ... from the expiration of 21 days (exclusive of Saturdays and Sundays or other days observed as general holidays at Lloyd's) after the date of publication by the Council of the Award and/or Interim Award(s) until the date payment is received by the Contractor or the Council both dates inclusive."[66]

LSSAC 2000, cl.8.3 states:

> "If the sum(s) awarded to the Contractors (including the fees and expenses referred to in clause 5.2)[67] are not paid to the Contractors or to the Council by the payment date specified in clause 11.1[68] the Contractors shall be entitled to additional interest on such outstanding sums from the payment date until the date payment is received by the Contractors or the Council both dates inclusive and at a rate which the Arbitrator shall in his absolute discretion determine in his award."

It has been the practice of Lloyd's salvage arbitrators normally to award **1476** such interest at 1 to 2 per cent per annum above current base borrowing rates, which is the same rate normally applied prior to publication of the award.

---

[63] The relevant outstanding amount includes any award of interest under s.49(3) and any award as to costs.

[64] s.49(1).

[65] The arbitrator should determine whether to award such interest and the rate at which it is payable, when he makes his award. This is made clearer by LSSAC 2000, cl.8.3 than by LOF 1995, cl.11(ii). If the arbitrator has not done so, he may only do so at a later date (under the Arbitration Act 1996, s.49(4)) if the clause for post-award interest is not exclusive and he retains jurisdiction to do so.

[66] For this purpose, "sum awarded" includes the fees and expenses of the arbitrator and Council of Lloyd's provided for in LOF 1995, cl.10(b).

[67] See *ante*, §1296.

[68] See *ante*, §1310.

Assessment

6. TAXATION

1477 On the grounds that it was a consequence of the public policy of encouraging salvage and consistent with taking account of expenses necessarily incurred in the performance of a salvage service, Willmer J. in *The Telemachus*[69] applied the rule recently stated in *British Transport Commission v. Gourley*[70] for awarding damages to an injured plaintiff, by holding that the possible impact of taxation was a proper element to take into account in assessing the reward for a plaintiff who had performed personal salvage services. One year later, in *The Makedonia*,[71] Pilcher J. opined that the position should be the same in the case of services rendered by a merchant or salvage vessel owned by a corporation. However, he went on to hold that the rule in personal injuries cases applied to judgments for amounts which were not subject to tax[72] and should not be extended so that "salvors, personal, mercantile or professional, should ... be entitled to off-load all or some of their liability to tax onto the shoulders of the owners of salved property."[73] "If it is right that awards made to salvors, which are already assessed on generous lines, should be exempted in whole or in part from liability to tax, this seems to me to be a matter for consideration by the legislature."[74] *Obiter* in *The Frisia*,[75] Willmer L.J. reasserted his view that, in the light of increased living costs and high incidence of taxation, in the case of personal services at least, taxation should be a factor. But Hodson L.J. (whose view Devlin L.J. favoured) thought that Willmer L.J.'s approach was not a necessary incident of *BTC v. Gourley* and that it would tend to cause injustice to salvees and between individual salvors.[76] Though the point is technically still open, the arguments against taking account of taxation are convincing and in practice it is not done.

Salvage, towage and pilotage services are zero rated for the purposes of value added tax.[77]

---

[69] *Tantalus (Master and Crew) v. Telemachus, Her Cargo and Freight (The Telemachus)* [1957] P. 47.
[70] [1956] A.C. 185.
[71] *Island Tug and Barge Ltd v. S.S. Makedonia (Owners) (The Makedonia)* [1958] 1 Q.B. 365.
[72] A "sufficient and necessary condition": see H. McGregor, *McGregor on Damages* (16th ed., 1997), §575.
[73] [1958] 1 Q.B. 365, 377.
[74] [1958] 1 Q.B. 365, 379; followed in *Parsons v. BNM Laboratories Ltd* [1964] 1 Q.B. 95, 138–139, *per* Pearson L.J.
[75] [1960] 1 Lloyd's Rep. 90, 95–96.
[76] [1960] 1 Lloyd's Rep. 90, 94, *per* Hodson L.J., 96, *per* Devlin L.J. As Hodson L.J. pointed out, individual salvors might be subject to different tax regimes but also entitled to consequent benefits.
[77] Value Added Tax Act 1994, s.30, Sched. 8, Group 8, Items 7–8.

CHAPTER 16

LIABILITY FOR PAYMENT

Introduction

For salvage to be awarded, it must first be shewn that a benefit has been conferred, by provision of a service which preserves from danger. Then, the salvor will need to identify the recipients of the benefit and the persons liable to pay the reward: these will usually, but perhaps not necessarily, be the same persons. Where several salvees are involved, they must contribute to payment of the salvage reward. Two questions then arise: (i) what, if any, is their individual liability to the salvor? and (ii) what is the liability between the contributories *inter se*? **1478**

1. LIABILITY TO SALVOR

General rule

All interests in property benefited contribute

The general rule is "that salvage reward is for benefits actually conferred, not for a service attempted to be rendered",[1] *i.e.* that there must be success,[2] governs not only the circumstances in which a salvor may claim but also the liability of those who must contribute to his reward. As Lord Chelmsford said, delivering the opinion of the Privy Council in *The Fusilier*[3]: **1479**

> "The general rule as to the parties liable to pay salvage is, that the property actually benefited is alone chargeable with the salvage recovered."

This means, in more general terms, that every interest in that property which is benefited by the salvage service must contribute to the salvage reward. In particular, it is not only the property salved which is chargeable with salvage, by an action *in rem*, but every person with an interest in that property whose

---

[1] *The Zephyrus* (1842) 1 W.Rob. 329, 330–331.
[2] See *ante*, Chap. 8.
[3] (1865) Br. & L. 341, 352 (PC). See also *The Fleece* (1850) 3 W. Rob. 278, 282.

Liability for Payment

interest is preserved by the salvage service is liable *in personam* to contribute.[4]

Life salvage

1480 Since the general rule is expressed in terms referring to property salvage, life salvage is by definition not covered by it. The rule might have evolved as one of wider scope, in the sense that there is a discernible, albeit imperfectly applied, principle in English law that a person receiving an incontrovertible benefit at the expense of another must make restitution to that other if not to do so would mean that the recipient of the benefit was unjustly enriched.[5] There are examples in the common law of persons recovering for benefits conferred to preserve life and health in cases of necessity[6] and the Admiralty Court has always maintained a policy of liberality towards salvors of life.[7] The Admiralty Court might, therefore, have in some way brought life salvage within a general principle of rewarding all benefits conferred by salvors.

1481 However, the Admiralty Court was restrained from developing any jurisdiction to reward salvage of life *per se* by its perception of its jurisdiction's being founded on a proceeding against property.[8] This attitude has survived the statutory institution of jurisdiction to reward life salvage.[9] Thus, after uttering the words quoted above,[10] Lord Chelmsford continued[11]:

> "But this rule is inapplicable in the case of life salvage, because it is difficult to imagine a case where the saving of the lives, either of the crew or of the passengers of a vessel in distress would be of any benefit, either to the vessel or to the cargo. The Legislature therefore could not have intended that the benefit to property should be the criterion of the liability to the payment of life salvage."

His meaning is, of course, clear and consistent with the law on life salvage both previously and subsequently applied. But it is obviously true that lives can and do benefit from salvage. The point is that the lives themselves are not bound to contribute for benefiting from salvage of their lives and that owners of property may now be bound to contribute for that benefit to others, but not because the contributories have also benefited; nor is the reward for life salvage calculated according to any precisely quantifiable benefit to lives preserved.

---

[4] See *Admiralty Commissioners v. Owners of M.V. Josefina Thorden and her Cargo (The Josefina Thorden)* [1945] 1 All E.R. 344, 347.
[5] See *ante*, §§ 28–30.
[6] See *ante*, § 807.
[7] See *ante*, Chap. 3.
[8] See *ante*, § 273.
[9] See now *ante*, Chap. 3.
[10] *Ante*, § 1479.
[11] *The Fusilier* (1865) Br. & L. 341, 352.

Exceptions to the general rule

Life salvage

As just stated, lives at risk may in a real sense benefit from salvage but in a legal sense they are outside the general rule, which is framed solely with reference to interests in property. To that extent, life salvage does not form a true exception to the general rule. It does, however, form an exception to the extent that interests in property may be liable to contribute to reward for life salvage despite not benefiting from it themselves.

1482

Personal effects of passengers, master and crew

The personal effects of the master and crew, and at least such wearing apparel and personal effects of passengers as are being worn or are taken on board for use or consumption during the voyage, are privileged in being exempt from having to contribute to salvage. This was considered in detail above.[12]

Bottomry or respondentia

In extreme circumstances of necessity, the master may borrow money for repairs and other necessary expenditure to enable completion of the voyage, giving in return a bottomry bond, whereby he pledges the keel or bottom of the vessel, as a symbol for the whole vessel, for repayment. He may similarly pledge the cargo as security by giving a respondentia bond. The lender upon bottomry or respondentia is entitled to recover from the interests to whom he has advanced a loan in full if the ship completes the voyage safely, and without liability to contribute to general average or salvage.[13] This is, however, of no practical significance, for both bottomry and respondentia are obsolete.

Crown proceedings

Proceedings for salvage of Crown property are governed by special rules, discussed above.[14]

1483

Sovereign immunity

Foreign sovereigns and foreign sovereign States are often immune from salvage proceedings. The rules governing their immunity and the practical

---

[12] *Ante*, Chap. 3.
[13] Park, pp. 896–899, quoting Lord Mansfield's judgment in *Joyce v. Williamson* (1782) 3 Doug. 164 and Lord Kenyon's judgment in *Walpole v. Ewer*, Sitt. after Trin. Term, 1789.
[14] *Ante*, Chap. 12.

problems this imposes in assessing salvage rewards was considered above.[15]

Defendants outside the jurisdiction

1484 A person with an interest in salved property may be outside the jurisdiction of the court, so that neither an action *in rem* nor possibly an action *in personam* may successfully be brought to recover a salvage reward or salvage contribution from him. Moreover, the absence of the property from the jurisdiction will tend to make the court's task in assessing salved values and salvage reward more difficult.[16] The court must nevertheless, so far as it is able, take account of the absent interest in determining the proportion of liability to be borne by the party or parties before it. And the absent interest will still remain in principle liable for his share of the reward.[17] Moreover, in many cases, there can and should be service on the defendant out of the jurisdiction.[18] The practical difficulty of enforcing a claim does not therefore provide an exception to the general principle that the absent interest should contribute to salvage for the benefit received.

Misconduct by salvor

As shewn above, a salvor who has been guilty of misconduct towards a particular plaintiff may not only be liable in damages but may also forfeit part or the whole of the reward to which he would otherwise be entitled.[19]

Salvor's remedies[20]

1485 The salvor, whose reward is calculated according to the value of ship, cargo, freight and other tangible property salved, may arrest tangible property to enforce his claim against it. He may also arrest tangible property to secure his claim against an intangible interest which benefits from salvage of it. In the majority of cases, this means that he can secure his claim for salvage of freight by arresting the ship, the property of the person usually benefiting from salvage of freight at risk,[21] or the cargo, the property upon the safety of which the possibility of earning freight depends.[22]

1486 So far as claims against cargo and freight are concerned, freight may either be included in the valuation of cargo, or it may be deducted from the value of the cargo and treated as a separate and distinct item.[23] No obvious advantage

---

[15] *Ante*, Chap. 12.
[16] See, *e.g. The Erato* (1888) 13 P.D. 163.
[17] See *The Raisby* (1885) 10 P.D. 114.
[18] See *The Elton* [1891] P. 265, especially at 271.
[19] See *ante*, Chap. 11.
[20] See also *ante*, Chap. 13.
[21] See, *e.g. The Raisby* (1885) 10 P.D. 114.
[22] See *The Leo* (1862) Lush. 444; *The Lady Durham* (1835) 3 Hagg. 196, 200.
[23] *The Charlotte Wylie* (1846) 2 W.Rob. 495, 497; *The Fleece* (1850) 3 W. Rob. 278, 282. See also *Cox v. May* (1815) 4 M. & S. 152, discussed *post*, §§ 1516–1518. *cf. The Westminster* (1841) 1 W. Rob. 229, 233.

to the parties attends the latter mode of proceeding. In fact, it makes no practical difference, so far as regards the owner of the cargo, whether the one course or the other is adopted. If, after paying to the shipowner the freight which was at risk when the salvage service was rendered, the cargo-owner is compelled to pay to the salvors the whole of the amount assessed upon the cargo, including the freight, he will be entitled to recover from the shipowner so much of that amount as he has paid for salvage which the owner of the freight ought to bear. If he has not paid the freight, but has paid the salvage falling on the cargo and freight assessed together, he will be entitled, when the shipowner afterwards claims payment of freight, to deduct and keep back, out of the freight, the amount which he has paid for the salvage properly chargeable to freight.

1487 Similarly, if salvage on freight is paid by the shipowner, as the beneficiary of the salvage of freight at risk, he can normally ensure that he really does benefit from preservation of freight by exercising his lien for freight on the cargo before delivering it to the cargo-owner.

In neither case, therefore, does liability fall fortuitously on the party who actually has to pay for salvage of freight. Nor can the salvor recover twice over for salvage of freight by claiming against more than one party. Although more than one party may in principle be liable to him in one set of proceedings, only one assessment will be made of reward for salvage of freight. Whoever pays the salvor, whether after single proceedings or after being held liable in a separate action, another party will then be able to plead as against the salvor that liability for salvage of freight has been discharged.[24]

Payment of salvage by shipowner

If the shipowner were to pay the whole of the salvage in the first instance, he could recover from other interests any part of the amount which he has paid on their behalf.[25]

Liability to pay salvage

1488 Under the traditional Admiralty law of salvage,[26] the International Salvage Convention 1989, Art. 13.2[27] and LOF 2000,[28] the liability of interests in ship

---

[24] *cf.* Goff & Jones, p. 17.
[25] *Post*, §§ 1493–1496.
[26] *China-Pacific S.A. v. Food Corporation of India (The Winson)* [1979] 2 All E.R. 35, 41 (the case is discussed *ante*, Chap. 9); *The Gestland* [1980] 1 Lloyd's Rep. 628, 630–631. See also *The Raisby* (1885) 10 P.D. 114, 116.
[27] This is assumed by Art. 13.2: "Payment of a reward fixed according to paragraph 1 [see *ante*, § 1395] shall be made by all of the vessel and other property interests in proportion to their respective salved values."
[28] LOF 2000, cl. K: "The Master or other person signing this agreement on behalf of the property identified in Box 2 enters into this agreement as agent for the respective owners thereof and binds each (but not the one for the other or himself personally) to the due performance thereof."

and cargo to pay salvage are several, in the sense that each interest is liable to pay its own proportionate share of the salvage remuneration. The shipowner is neither primarily liable to pay salvage, nor liable in respect of interests who are in principle liable but from whom the salvor has failed to recover salvage.[29] Thus, if a salvor of both ship and cargo brings an action *in rem* against the ship alone, he will only get judgment for such an amount of reward as the court finds to be due in respect of the value of that property which is before the court.[30]

1489 In *The Raisby*,[31] the masters of the salving and distressed vessels entered into an agreement for the vessel to be towed into St Nazaire, which done, the master of the salved vessel delivered the cargo without requiring security from the cargo-owners for salvage of the cargo. The salvors recovered salvage from the shipowners in an action *in rem* for salvage of ship and freight but their action in France against the cargo-owners failed. They, therefore, brought proceedings against the shipowners *in personam* for salvage of the cargo or, alternatively, for damages for not taking a proper bond to secure salvage from the cargo-owners. It was held that the shipowners were not primarily—or, indeed, even secondarily—liable to pay salvage in respect of the cargo, that it was not their duty to obtain security from the cargo-owners for their proportion of the reward, and that the mere entry into a salvage agreement without more did not make the shipowners liable to pay reward in respect of salvage of other interests, nor disentitle them from claiming a contribution from other interests for payment of it.

1490 The salvor should, therefore, take the appropriate steps to secure his claim against all salved interests while he has the opportunity of doing so. Moreover, he should always attempt to bring all parties before the court or he may suffer in costs.[32] If he does take the necessary steps but still, through no fault of his own, is unable to recover remuneration despite his conferment of an unequivocal benefit, still the shipowner is not liable for the unrecovered salvage. Thus, where cargo is not in fact liable to salvage because its owner can plead sovereign immunity, the court will, with great inconvenience, consider as a whole the services rendered to ship and cargo, and will estimate the amount of salvage reward according to the value of the ship and cargo taken together. But:

---

[29] *The Raisby* (1885) 10 P.D. 114. Note, however, that: under the Salvage Convention 1989, Art. 21.2, the owner of the salved vessel must use his best endeavours to ensure that the owners of cargo provide satisfactory security for the claims against them, including interest and costs, before the cargo is released; and, under LSSAC 2000, cl. 4.6, shipowners must use their best endeavours to ensure that none of the salved property is released until security has been provided. *cf. The Tesaba* [1982] 1 Lloyd's Rep. 397. See *post*, § 1262.

[30] *The Pyrennée* (1863) Br. & L. 189.

[31] (1885) 10 P.D. 114. *cf. Anderson, Tritton & Co. v. Ocean Steamship Co.* (1884) 10 App.Cas. 107.

[32] See *The Elton* [1891] P. 265, 270–271.

Agreements for fixed sum

"It is contrary to all principles of justice, if a cargo has received and been benefited by the services so rendered, that the whole burden of the salvage remuneration should fall on the ship itself."[33]

The court must, therefore, do the best it can in assessing the sum due from the defendants in respect of their own interests.

In Scotland, the Court of Session has held a salvor entitled to sue *in personam* the owners of the salved ship for reward in respect of the cargo as well as the ship, in a case where the shipowner, by the terms of the contract of carriage, would have been liable to the owner of the cargo for any loss arising from the peril from which it has been preserved by the salvage service.[34] In the circumstances of the case, the shipowners themselves received benefits (in being able to earn freight on the cargo and in avoiding liability for non-delivery) the value of which was at least equivalent to the value of the cargo.[35]

1491

The court stressed the convenience of the salvor's not having to sue the cargo-owners but did not purport to make the shipowners liable for salvage of the interests of the cargo-owners themselves, nor did it deny that the salvor could sue the cargo-owners directly if he wished.[36] He could even have recovered against the cargo-owners as well as against the shipowners for preservation of their respective interests in the cargo. This would not have provided the salvor with double recovery for salvage of the cargo, for he would be recovering from salvage of different interests in the cargo.

Defences

The International Salvage Convention 1989, Art. 13.2 (apportioning liability for awards according to salved values) provides that "Nothing in this Article shall prevent any right of defence."

Agreements for fixed sum; agreements by shipowner to pay all salvage in first instance

It has been seen that the mere fact that a shipowner enters a salvage agreement with the salvor does not impose on him liability to pay the proportion of the reward due from other salved interests.[37] In practice, in effect where LOF 2000 applies, the shipowner expressly enters salvage agreements on behalf of all of the principal interests in danger.[38]

1492

If, however, the shipowner agrees with the salvor to discharge personally the liability of other salved interests, he cannot subsequently plead against the

---

[33] *The Mary Pleasants* (1857) Swab. 224–225.
[34] *Duncan v. Dundee, Perth and London Shipping Co.* (1878) 5 R. 742.
[35] See *post*, §§ 1505–1513.
[36] That they would also be liable is shewn by *The Meandros* [1925] P. 61, discussed *post*, §§ 1512–1513.
[37] See *ante*, §§ 1489–1490.
[38] See LOF 2000, Boxes 2 and 9 and cl. K; *ante*, Chap. 9.

salvor that he is only liable for salvage of his own property. In particular, where the salvors and the master of the salved vessel enter into a valid salvage agreement which fixes the amount of the reward, the master in making it is the shipowners' agent and must be taken to pledge their liability and credit. The owners may therefore be sued, either *in personam* or in an action *in rem* against the ship, for the whole sum due under the agreement and not merely for that portion of it which, as between ship, freight and cargo, would be contributed by the ship and freight.[39] He must rely on his remedies against the other interests for reimbursement.[40] Of course, if the other interests are not privy to such an agreement, the salvor will retain his right to sue them directly for their proportion of the reward.

Estoppel

A shipowner may by his conduct make himself liable to the salvor to pay all the salvage due, *e.g.* during negotiations, by the appointment of arbitrators and the deposit of sums in a bank.[41]

Shipowner's remedies for reimbursement

1493 It is a general principle of law that a person can claim restitution for discharging another's liability under legal compulsion.[42] The following remedies ensure that, whether or not the shipowner is legally compellable in the first instance to pay the proportion of salvage due from cargo-owners, he will not personally be prejudiced.

He can do so safely if the cargo remains in his possession, for payment of reward on behalf of the owner of each parcel of cargo liable to contribute entitles him to a possessory lien over the relevant parcel for the proportion of the total reward paid for the benefit of its owner.[43] In the decision recognising this rule, *Hingston v. Wendt*,[44] it was suggested that this would not be so where the acts of the claimant, in that case the ship's agent, were done for the benefit of the shipowner rather than of the cargo-owner. But that limitation should be confined to acts done as part of the shipowner's normal duty to take care of cargo and not extended to true acts of salvage which are not simply voluntary benefits and which do confer a real benefit on the cargo-owner.

1494 Similarly, where the shipowner provides security for the proportion of salvage payable by the owner of cargo, he acquires a right to reimbursement plus a lien over and an insurable interest in the cargo.[45]

---

[39] *The Cumbrian* (1887) 6 Asp. M.L.C. 151; *The Prinz Heinrich* (1888) 13 P.D. 31.
[40] See *post*, §§ 1493–1494.
[41] *The Prinz Heinrich* (1888) 13 P.D. 31, 34.
[42] See generally Goff & Jones, Chap. 15.
[43] See *Hingston v. Wendt* (1876) 1 Q.B.D. 367, especially at 373; *The Prinz Heinrich* (1888) 13 P.D. 31, 34.
[44] *Supra*.
[45] *Briggs v. Merchant Traders' Ship Loan and Insurance Association* (1849) 13 Q.B. 167.

General rule

In practice, the shipowner will generally release his lien on cargo in return for the cargo-owner's providing him with security for payment of his proportion of the reward.

Although as a general rule a person is under no liability to reimburse someone who has voluntarily conferred a benefit upon him,[46] even though a shipowner voluntarily agrees with the salvor to undertake personal liability to discharge the liability of interests for which he is not liable,[47] he will not be assumed to forego his normal rights and remedies against those interests in the absence of clear and binding reasons for such intention. He will, therefore, normally be entitled to exercise his lien over cargo until he is reimbursed or receives security for his claim.[48]

2. CONTRIBUTION RATEABLY ACCORDING TO SALVED VALUES

General rule

It is the general rule, in ascertaining the extent to which different salved interests must contribute to payment of the salvage reward, that each part of the salved property contributes rateably according to its value as salved. Thus, Dr Lushington said that[49]:

1495

> "the ordinary usage of the [Admiralty] Court, which is well known to every person who has practised in it, is to take the whole value of the ship and cargo, and assess the amount of the remuneration upon the whole, each paying its due proportion."

Similarly, Sir Robert Phillimore has stated that[50]:

> "It appears to me that the Court would be involved in great difficulty if it admitted any other principle in salvage cases than that every description of property salved must, whatever be its nature, contribute equally in proportion to its value towards payment of the amount of salvage remuneration awarded."

More importantly now, Article 13.2 of the International Salvage Convention 1989 states that:

1496

> "Payment of a reward fixed according to paragraph 1[51] shall be made by all of the vessel and other property interests in proportion to their respective salved values."

---

[46] See *ante*, § 560.
[47] As in *The Prinz Heinrich* (1888) 13 P.D. 31.
[48] *ibid.*, 34. *cf. ante*, § 440 on the exclusion of claims for contribution in general average for liability for Article 14 special compensation.
[49] *The Emma* (1844) 2 W.Rob. 315, 319.
[50] *The Longford* (1881) 6 P.D. 60, 67.
[51] See *ante*, § 1395.

In addition, the Merchant Shipping Act 1995[52] also reproduces the following sentence in Article 13.2:

> "However, a State party may in its national law provide that the payment of a reward has to be made by one of these interests, subject to a right of recourse of this interest against the other interests for their respective shares."

The inclusion of this sentence is a consequence of the nearly wholesale reproduction of the Convention into United Kingdom legislation. It has no direct relevance to English law, other than to make clear that, in the rare case where an English court may be called upon to enforce a foreign court's ruling in accordance with the sentence, there is no inherent objection in English law to doing so.

Different degrees of risk or difficulty

1497 Therefore, difference in the degree of risk from which, or in the degree of difficulty or the type of service with which, a particular piece of salved property has been preserved, as compared with the rest of it, affords no ground for distinction in the rate of contribution.[53]

Silver or bullion

1498 In *The Emma*,[54] Dr Lushington applied the general rule in a case where, after the sunken ship and cargo had been refloated, the cargo and freight interests attempted to contend that the benefit conferred on them was less than that conferred on the shipowners, the reason given being that the cargo was not so susceptible to damage by immersion. However, he stated that an exception was admitted in the case of gold and bullion on the basis that they were more easily rescued and preserved than more bulky articles of merchandise.[55]

However, Lord Stowell's earlier decision in *The Jonge Bastiaan*[56] was not cited to him. In this case the distinction was not admitted and the fact that bullion had been taken off the distressed vessel before it had sunk was treated as irrelevant. In *The Longford*,[57] Sir Robert Phillimore considered that, if there were substance in Dr Lushington's suggestion, something similar would have appeared in the report of *The Jonge Bastiaan*. He refused to admit it in *The Longford*, in which the owners of bullion were not permitted any lower rate of contribution than that which had to be borne by the owners of other cargo which, from its nature, might have been lost or destroyed if the salvage service

---

[52] s.224(1), Sched. 11, Pt I, Art. 13.2.
[53] *The Vesta* (1828) 2 Hagg. 189; *The Emma* (1844) 2 W. Rob. 315; *The Longford* (1881) 6 P.D. 60. See also *The Jonge Bastiaan* (1804) 5 C. Rob. 322.
[54] (1844) 2 W. Rob. 315.
[55] ibid., 319–320.
[56] (1804) 5 C. Rob. 322.
[57] (1881) 6 P.D. 60.

had not been rendered. This latest decision on the point, which is consistent with the general rule, can now be considered as authoritatively rejecting the supposed exception.

Justifications of the general rule

As Sir Christopher Robinson commented in relation to the salvage of the ship and a cargo of timber in *The Vesta*[58]:

"It is said that it [a distinction] might be made with reference to the difference of danger to which the property was exposed; but that would be a difficult criterion to be applied in most cases. The buoyancy of articles may vary in different places—in the sea or in the river; and on the high seas, the consequence may not be very different to the owner, whether the articles sink or float away. It might be adopted on a computation of the difference of labour employed in the constant attempts to float the ship, which were ineffectual for so long a time, and the comparative facility of floating the deals: but I do not think that would be a safe criterion in general cases. Suppose, for instance, a casket of jewels on board, and which might be saved with great facility; it could not in such a case be contended that the salvors would only be entitled to a small gratuity for carrying it on shore. To uphold such a notion would lead to preferences in saving one part of a cargo before another. The more usual rule has been to make a valuation of the ship and cargo, and I think that would be the more convenient practice."

More generally, Dr Lushington has said[59]:

"Such a distinction, if acknowledged, would in many cases lead to intricate litigation and to questions of great nicety, which it would be exceedingly difficult for the Court to adjust."

It would also multiply points of contention and would tend to make the whole process of assessment longer, more difficult and more expensive.

A further difficulty, which was touched on in argument in *The Longford*,[60] where there were passengers on board, is that, where lives are salved, "a reasonable amount of salvage" is payable by the owners of property saved,[61] whether the property saved be salved or not.[62] It would tend further to complicate assessment of life salvage if distinctions existed in the rate of contribution for property salvage and also it needed to be considered to what extent they applied to contribution to life salvage.

---

[58] (1828) 2 Hagg. 189, 193–194.
[59] *The Emma* (1844) 2 W.Rob. 315, 319.
[60] (1881) 6 P.D. 60.
[61] MSA 1894, s.544(1).
[62] *The Cargo ex Schiller* (1877) 2 P.D. 160. See further *ante*, Chap. 3.

Different risks

1500 According to the decision of Sir Gorell Barnes P. in *The Velox*,[63] the ordinary rule requiring contribution rateably according to salved values does not apply where the different interests have been subject to different dangers or risks, so as to justify separate awards being assessed against each portion of the salved property.

The Velox ran short of coal in consequence of bad weather and had to be towed to her destination. If the cargo of herrings on board her had remained at sea 48 hours longer than they in fact did, they would have become valueless. His Lordship said[64]:

> "I propose to take a course in this case, which is not perhaps common, but which seems to me to be in accordance with sound principles. I propose mainly to have in view in making my award the real danger from which the different properties were rescued. The ship was not rescued from anything like the same danger as the cargo, because she was rescued from the possibility of floating about and getting ashore, or of being picked up by somebody else. The cargo was rescued not merely from that particular risk, but also from the risk of floating about until it became rotten and perfectly valueless."

On salved values of £1,875, £1,060 and £136 on ship, cargo and freight respectively, he thought that[65]:

> "the proper award to make is to award separately against the ship £180, and against the cargo and freight—because the freight would have perished with the cargo—£420."

Cargo and freight therefore contributed more than their salved values bore to the whole fund.

1501 There was no precedent for the course adopted in *The Velox*, aside from the authorities requiring conformity with the general rule. The weight of the decision is further open to doubt in that, all the salved property being in common ownership and therefore represented by the same solicitors and counsel, there was no competition between salved interests, the bone of contention being whether the whole reward tendered was sufficient, which the salvors sought to dispute by reference to the imminent danger of total loss to the perishable cargo and the impending loss of freight.[66] It has stood unchallenged, though *The Beatsa*,[67] in which it was considered though not applied on the facts, perhaps indicates that it will rarely be followed. *The Beatsa*'s anchor

---

[63] [1906] P. 263.
[64] *ibid.*, 266–267.
[65] *ibid.*, 267.
[66] See Brice, §§ 6–30 to 6–31.
[67] (1937) 58 Ll.L.Rep. 85.

dragged, causing a risk of collision. It was not unlikely that the ship might have been damaged but not the cargo, yet Sir Boyd Merriman P. held that, if there were reasonable risk of damage to the cargo as well as to the ship, there was no ground for differentiating against the ship and in favour of the cargo. Indeed, counsel had only requested separate awards if the risk to the cargo had been quite negligible. He took account in making his award of the fact that the risk in relation to the cargo was small, but made his award against all salved interests.

In *The Lista*,[68] salvage services were rendered to the stranded S.S. *Lista* and Government-owned cargo, not at that time subject to the jurisdiction of the court.[69] Their salved values were £65,000 and £2,000,000 respectively. In proceedings against the ship, Pitcher J. was requested to indicate the sum which would have been awarded had both ship and cargo been before the court. He awarded £1,600 against the ship, then stated that, if the whole fund had been before him, he would have awarded £3,000:

1502

> "The reasons which would have led me to make that award would have been that while I think the ship was in considerable danger, I do not think the cargo was exposed to quite the same danger."[70]

His approach is reminiscent of *The Velox*,[71] although no authorities are cited in the report, but he did not go so far as to indicate that he would have made separate awards against ship and cargo.

It has been argued that *The Velox* is out of step with American case law, alien to the idea of common adventure underlying the law of salvage and would produce further complications.[72] Thus, where cargo in one hold or container were subject to wetting, whereas other similar cargo were not, because for example it was behind watertight bulkheads, it would be necessary to distinguish not only between ship and cargo, but between different parcels of cargo, particularly if they were in different ownerships.

1503

The problem with *The Velox* is, in reality, not that the approach is unreasonable but that the circumstances dealt with are not materially different from those governed by the general rule of rateable contribution and that there is little or no substance in the supposition that the different risks considered in the case were not simply manifestations of the different degrees of risk normally coming within the rule.

The approach in *The Velox*[73] and *The Lista*[74] is not altogether unprincipled. If the underlying principle of the law of salvage is that interests should

1504

---

[68] (1946) 79 Ll.L.Rep. 401.
[69] See now CPA 1947, discussed *ante*, Chap. 12.
[70] (1946) 79 Ll.L.Rep. 404.
[71] *Supra*, n. 63.
[72] Brice, §§ 6–37 to 6–38.
[73] *Supra*, n. 63.
[74] *Supra*, n. 68.

contribute to a reward for the benefits they receive, it would seem to follow that their contributions should be assessed with reference to the actual benefit received by each interest. This would require taking account not only of the salved value of each interest but also the actual danger to which it was exposed, the degree of risk to which it became subject and the extent of services necessary to preserve it. In fact, these are all factors taken into account in assessing the total award. What the court has not done is to take the logical next step of assessing more precisely the benefit derived by each interest. Considerations of practical convenience have prevented this. What the court tends to do is to consider whether a benefit has been provided—but not the precise extent of that benefit—and to assess a reasonable reward according to the exertions of the salvors and the salved fund available.

1505 Sheen J. in *The M. Vatan*[75] has disapproved the decision in *The Velox*[76] and applied the general rule that the court should not order the owners of one part of the salved property to pay more than its liability calculated pro rata, merely because the salvors appear to be having difficulty in recovering a salvage reward from the owners of the other salved property. However, as stated above,[77] that is a separate question from how the individual liabilities should be assessed in the first place.

Interests in salved property

1506 The paradigm and most obvious case of a person liable to contribute to a salvage reward is the legal owner of the ship or other property preserved. But references to "owners" in maritime law are not necessarily framed deliberately to be restricted to those with full legal title. Thus, for the purpose of deciding that the Admiralty Court had, under the legislation then prevailing, no jurisdiction over a salvage dispute "between the owners of any such ship, boat, cargo, apparel or wreck ... and the salvors", Dr Lushington held that[78]:

> " the effect of the statute is to forbid the exercise of jurisdiction by this Court in all cases of salvage where the value of the property saved does not exceed £1,000. I do not think this position at all altered by the fact that the party defending this cause is not the owner of the ship, but the mortgagee. If it is necessary to put an interpretation upon the word 'owners' in the 460th section of the Merchant Shipping Act,[79] I think it extends to all interested in the property."

Dr Lushington's definition of "owners" does not, of course, necessarily provide a definition for all salvage purposes, but his methodology is of general

---

[75] [1990] 1 Lloyd's Rep. 336.
[76] [1906] P. 263.
[77] *Ante*, §1431.
[78] *The Louisa* (1863) Br. & L. 59, 60.
[79] MSA 1854, s.460, as amended by MSA (Am.) A. 1862, s.49. See now *ante*, Chap. 13.

Interests in salved property

import. He perceived the identity of the litigants as secondary to his primary task of giving effect to the object of the statute, which was to deal with jurisdiction in all cases where the salved value was below a certain sum. Similarly, since the underlying criterion for a salvage reward is the conferment of a benefit, it follows that those who are liable to contribute are all those recipients of a legally recognisable benefit, so that liability to the salvor's claim is not confined to the legal ownership of salved property. It is a corollary of this that a person may be liable for salvage even though he cannot be sued in an action *in rem* but only in an action *in personam*.

The leading authority is *Five Steel Barges*.[80] The defendants had contracted with the Government to make and deliver five barges. The plaintiffs contracted to tow the barges, each of which had two bargemen on board. During the towage, it became necessary for the plaintiffs to render salvage services to the barges and in respect of certain of the bargemen. The plaintiffs claimed salvage in an action *in rem* against three of the barges, against which they had asserted their maritime lien and which were still in the defendants' possession, and in an action *in personam* against the remaining two, which had been delivered to the Government before the plaintiffs had asserted their lien. The plaintiffs' claims for property and life salvage succeeded. Sir James Hannen P. said[81]:

> "As to the two which have been given up to the Government, I think it is perfectly clear on the authorities that an action *in personam* lies against the owners of a vessel which has been saved, even though the property has been transferred to others, and the lien lost. In this case, however, the property does not appear to have been in the defendants, because it would, I think, under the contract, to which reference has been made, be in the Government. But on this point I am of opinion that the right to sue *in personam* is not confined to the case of the defendant, being the actual legal owner of the property saved. *I think it exists in cases where the defendant has an interest in the property saved, which interest has been saved by the fact that the property is brought into a position of security. The jurisdiction which the Court exercises in salvage cases is of a peculiarly equitable character. The right to salvage may arise out of an actual contract; but it does not necessarily do so. It is a legal liability arising out of the fact that property has been saved, that the owner of the property who has had the benefit of it shall make remuneration to those who have conferred the benefit upon him, notwithstanding that he has not entered into any contract on the subject. I think that proposition equally applies to the man who has had a benefit arising out of the saving of the property.* In this case the defendants were under contract with the Government to supply them with barges at a certain price. Payment was to be made by certain instalments, of which only one remained unpaid at the

---

[80] (1890) 15 P.D. 142.
[81] *ibid.*, 146–147 (emphasis added).

time of the services. I think, if Mr Barnes' argument is well founded—*viz.*, that those instalments were all paid on condition that the barges should be delivered all within twelve months of the date of the contract—it would follow that, if defendants had not been in a position to deliver the barges within the twelve months, then either they would have been liable in damages for not performing the contract, or liable to make restitution of the instalments which had been paid them on conditions not fulfilled by them. It appears to me, therefore, that they had substantially an interest to the full amount of the barges at the time of the services, and that the same moral obligation to which the law has given force in the case of an owner applies to those who have an interest in the property. That is certainly the business-like view of the matter; and I do not forget that the defendants insured themselves to the full value of these barges, and described themselves as being the owners. In conclusion, I award £200, as salvage, independently of the towage contract."

1508 A decision similar to that in *Five Steel Barges*[82] had previously been reached by the Court of Session in *Duncan v. Dundee, Perth and London Shipping Co.*[83] The pursuers salved the defenders' ship plus cargo on board, shipped by 200 to 300 shippers. The Court's decision was to the effect that, where a general cargo is carried coastally by a shipowner who is liable as a common carrier, and not by special contract under bills of lading, the shipowner could be sued *in personam* not only for salvage of the ship but also of the cargo. The shipowner derived a double benefit from the salvage of cargo in such a case. He was enabled to fulfil his contract so as, first, to earn the freight which he charged for the goods and, secondly, to avoid liability for failing to discharge his absolute responsibility to deliver the goods. With regard to the second point, the majority view was that it was unnecessary for the salvor to prove any fault which would deprive the shipowner of reliance on the common carrier's exceptions from liability to the cargo-owners, one judge pointing out the difficulty of doing so without the cargo-owners being before the court.

The decision was justified as obviating unnecessary inconvenience and expenditure. There was a multitude of cargo-owners and a large number of pieces of cargo, many of which might be worthless and in respect of each of which it would be necessary to decide whether to sue as the true owners the persons who sent them or the persons to whom they were addressed. The result also avoided the need to arrest cargo and to decide which and how many cargo-owners needed to come forward for the goods to be released, how they were to find security and how the remedy *in rem* would have to be worked out in practice.

1509 It was thought that these difficulties would more easily be overcome in the case of foreign-going vessels carrying goods shipped under charterparties or

[82] *Supra.*
[83] (1878) 5 R. 742.

Interests in salved property

bills of lading, on which their Lordships refrained from expressing a view. That was the type of situation which came before the English courts in *The Cargo ex Port Victor*,[84] where Sir James Hannen P.'s judgment in *Five Steel Barges*[85] was approved by the Court of Appeal.

In *The Cargo ex Port Victor*,[86] under a time charterparty, by which the negligence of the master and servants of the owners or charterers was mutually excepted, the master was to sign bills of lading at the charterers' direction and the charterers were to indemnify the owners from any consequences of his doing so. The charterers entered into a contract of carriage with a Government department to carry Government stores. The contract was subject to Admiralty regulations which provided that:

> "The term 'owners' ... is to be understood as signifying the party or parties who engage to carry the stores under the agreement for freight or charter-party"

and that:

> "The owners will be held responsible for the safe delivery of the ... stores...."

The stores were shipped under bills of lading which were subject to the terms of the charterparty and the charterers' contract with the Government, and which did not exempt the shipowner from liability for negligence. The master was negligent and the ship collided with another vessel, thus requiring salvage assistance to put back to the port of shipment, where the stores were returned to the Government department. As Crown property, the salvors could not enforce a maritime lien or action *in rem* against their owner, but successfully brought an action *in rem* against the charterers.[87]

At first instance, Sir Francis Jeune P. said[88]: **1510**

> "I do not think it is necessary in this case to define exhaustively the classes of persons against whom, under various circumstances, claims for salvage might be made. There is no doubt the authority of eminent judges in the courts of common law for saying that contribution cannot be

---

[84] [1901] P. 243.
[85] *Ante*, §1507, particularly the test contained in the italicised words.
[86] [1901] P. 243.
[87] The charterers were also liable to indemnify the shipowners against the loss sustained by them through not being able to obtain a general average contribution from the owner of the goods by reason of the bills of lading not containing a negligence clause. See *Milburn & Co. v. Jamaica Fruit Importing Co. of London* [1900] 2 Q.B. 540.
[88] [1901] P. 243, 249–250.

Liability for Payment

required by an owner from the lender on bottomry, or at respondentia[89].... On the other hand, Dr Lushington in *The Louisa*[90] held that mortgagees come within the term 'owners' in the sections of the Merchant Shipping Act of 1854 relating to salvage. It is, however, easy to see that the contingent interest of persons who make advances by way of mortgage, or otherwise, on property, or of insurers, is of a different character from that of persons who have a direct interest in its safe delivery, and may negative, or, at least impose different conditions on, the right of a salvor against some of these persons.

It may be, therefore, that it will become necessary hereafter to consider what is the exact definition of the interest in the property saved which gives rise to a claim for salvage; but, in the present case, I have no doubt that the defendant has such an interest, and my judgment must, therefore, be for the plaintiff."

1511 His decision was affirmed by the Court of Appeal,[91] the judgment of which was substantially that of Lord Alverstone C.J., who said[92]:

"I think the defendants were bailee of these goods. It is perfectly true that they were put, not upon their own ship, but upon a hired ship; but they were put there in pursuance of a contract made with the defendants and for the purpose of earning freight which was to go into the pocket of the defendants, and under a contract whereby the defendants undertook ... in the event which happened to deliver these goods. Now, when the accident happened, which led to the salvage, what were the real interests which were at risk and at stake? There were the interests of the owners of the ship, the interests of the owner or charterer in the freight—because the charterers' freight may be an entirely different thing from the owner's freight—in fact, it is quite possible that the chartered freight would not be at risk at all, because it might be something paid for the hire of the ship in advance—and then there is the interest of the owner of the goods. In my opinion, that includes, for the purpose of the case which we have to consider, all the persons who were collectively or singly the owners of goods for the purpose of that adventure. I do not think it all necessary to go through the cases which counsel ... put of persons whose contracts may be affected more or less indirectly by the destruction of the goods.[93] I think that in a common maritime adventure of this kind at least the persons who have the interest of owners in the goods by virtue of the

---

[89] He cited Park, *A System of the Law on Marine Insurances* (8th ed., 1842) (ed. Hildyard). Vol. II, p. 898 and the decisions reported there of Lord Mansfield in *Joyce v. Williamson* (1783), *ibid.*, pp. 896–897, and of Lord Kenyon in *Walpole v. Ewer* (1789) *ibid.*, p. 899. Lord Mansfield said that "it is clear by the law of *England* there is neither average nor salvage upon bottomry bond"; similarly, Lord Kenyon said, "By the law of *England*, a lender upon *respondentia* is not liable for average losses" (italics added).

[90] *Supra*, n. 78.

[91] [1901] P. 243, 250.

[92] *ibid.*, 255–256.

[93] Those persons being: mortgagees of a ship not in possession, pledgees of bills lading, and vendors of cargo having a lien, but not underwriters.

Interests in salved property

contract they have made for the purpose of delivery have an interest for the purpose of salvage.

I agree that in all salvage cases there must be some *res* saved[94] . . . I agree with the argument that you must have property saved so as to represent a fund out of which the salvors can be remunerated; but when once you get that, I consider that at any rate at the present day proceedings against the persons who properly can be made liable to pay that salvage may be either *in rem* or *in personam*."

The cases so far discussed demonstrate, at the least, that a salvage action *in personam* is maintainable against a defendant with a possessory though not a legal interest in salved property. There is a stronger case for liability where the defendant does not have possession at the time of the casualty but is, nevertheless, the legal owner. That this is so, but that complications might arise to cast doubt on the general proposition, was shewn in *The Meandros*.[95]

The *Meandros* was requisitioned by the Greek Government under terms that the ownership remained with the defendant owners but that possession and control passed to the Greek Government. Furthermore, the crew became conscripts in the Greek forces. Salvage services were rendered to the ship during requisition but, since the Government had state immunity,[96] neither a maritime lien nor an action *in rem* could be maintained against it. On derequisition, however, an action *in rem* was successfully brought against the owners. The owners pleaded that they derived no benefit from the services since, by the terms of the requisition, the vessel had to be delivered up to them in the same condition as when requisitioned. But the judge, Sir Henry Duke P., held otherwise: they did derive a benefit because they were able to recover the ship itself and were not left simply with a claim against the Greek Government for the value of the ship which, but for the services, would probably have been a total loss. He added[97]:

"It has been said, more widely than it is necessary to express an opinion upon in this case, that any person whose interest in the property is real—though it fall short of ownership—may be liable in respect of salvage, and it has been said, further, in comprehensive terms, that 'owner' includes all persons who are collectively or singly owners. The defendants in this case were the owners in the true sense, and at all material times. . . . "

The effect of the cases can be summarised as follows. First of all, property must be salved as a precondition to a maritime lien, an action *in rem* or an action *in personam* in respect of it.[98] Secondly, an action *in rem* can be brought against the person who was the legal owner of salved property at the

---

[94] He referred to *The Renpor* (1883) 8 P.D. 115 and Kennedy (1st ed., 1891), p. 13.
[95] [1925] P. 61.
[96] See *ante*, Chap. 12.
[97] [1925] P. 61, 68.
[98] *The Renpor* (1883) 8 P.D. 115.

time of the casualty, whether or not he has the possession, control or use of the property at the time of the casualty.[99] Thirdly, an action *in personam* can be brought against a person with a possessory interest in the salved property at the time of the casualty.[1]

Fourthly, if an action *in rem* is available at the time of the casualty in principle but not in fact, because the person in possession of the property has a good defence, such as sovereign immunity, that action can still be brought after the defence has ceased to be effective.[2] If, however, the action *in rem* did not become available at the time of the casualty—for example, because the property was at the time owned by a person entitled to plead sovereign immunity—it cannot be considered to exist even in principle, and therefore cannot "revive" so as to be available against a subsequent purchaser of sovereign-owned property.

Contribution to life salvage

1514 Where services are rendered in saving life, persons interested in property saved must contribute rateably to the payment of those who are entitled to reward for the salvage of life in accordance with the provisions of the Merchant Shipping Act 1995. The exact scope and application of those provisions are considered above.[3] It may be mentioned here that it is immaterial whether the interests liable to contribute have been preserved by the exertions of the same persons who preserved life, or by other salvors, or without other salvage assistance. However, it is important to note that, since it is not necessary and may even not be practicable to ascertain accurately the number of lives saved, and since a liberal award is given for the salvage of life,[4] life salvage is assessed independently of any notional pecuniary value of lives saved,[5] and the contributions payable by property interests are proportioned according to the value of those property interests saved.

3. Division of Liability

Introduction

1515 It has been shewn that the proportion of the total salvage reward payable to the salvor by individual interests is determined by the proportion that the value of the individual interests bears to the total salved fund. Similarly, where the whole reward has been paid by one interest, in practice the shipowner, he

---

[99] *The Meandros* [1925] P. 61.
[1] *The Five Steel Barges* (1890) 15 P.D. 142; *Duncan v. Dundee, Perth and London Shipping Co.* (1878) 5 R. 742; *The Cargo ex Port Victor* [1901] P. 243.
[2] *The Meandros* [1925] P. 61.
[3] *Ante*, Chap. 3.
[4] See *The Eastern Monarch* (1860) Lush. 81, 83, 84.
[5] See *The Suevic* [1908] P. 154, 161.

may, as a general rule, claim reimbursement in general average from other interests of the proportion for which they are primarily liable.[6]

It is possible, however, that for one or more of the reasons now to be discussed, one interest may be entitled to require that his burden of the salvage reward be borne by another interest. The most obvious example is where the cargo-owner can insist that his liability to the salvor must be borne by the shipowner.

Interest not in fact benefited

As liability to bear part of the cost of salvage depends, in principle, upon the receipt of some benefit from the salvage service, a person with an interest in salved property, as between himself and other salved interests, ought to be called upon to contribute to the salvage reward only if the salvage service has actually been beneficial to him.

1516

In *Cox v. May*,[7] a ship was chartered for a voyage out and home at a monthly freight payable in three instalments, two of which were paid, the last of which was to fall due three months after the arrival of the ship at London on the homeward voyage. On her way home, she was captured, then recaptured, and the ship and cargo subsequently sold with the consent of all the parties. The Admiralty Court decreed restitution of the ship and cargo to the shipowner and charterer respectively on payment of salvage. The plaintiffs, the shipowner's assignees in bankruptcy, paid the proportion of salvage and of the charges of establishing the claim to the salved property and procuring the decree of restitution due in respect of the ship. The residue of these expenses and charges was paid out of the proceeds of the cargo owned by the defendant charterers. An action being brought for an unpaid balance of the chartered freight, the defendants claimed a set-off in respect of the moneys paid out of the proceeds of the cargo.

It was held, first, that the plaintiffs alone were liable for salvage, as the owners of the ship and the persons entitled to freight, so to that extent the defendants succeeded. Delivering the judgment of the Court of King's Bench, Lord Ellenborough C.J. said[8]:

1517

> "the persons to contribute to salvage are the persons who would have borne the loss had there been no such rescue, and who of course reap the benefit of that rescue."

To form a judgment who would have borne the loss had there been no rescue and to whom the rescue was beneficial, it was necessary to look at each party's interest. The plaintiffs had interests in the ship, to the extent of its value, and in its arrival in London, to the extent of the freight which would become due

---

[6] See generally Lowndes & Rudolf.
[7] (1815) 4 M. & S. 152.
[8] *ibid.*, 159.

(namely £16,145 13s. 7d.). The defendants were interested in the goods to the amount of £14,351 18s. 2d. His Lordship continued[9]:

> "but as the ship's arrival would subject them to the payment of the £16,145 13s. 7d., the loss by the capture would have been on the whole beneficial to them, and they of course derived no advantage, but on the contrary receive a prejudice by the event of the rescue. The salvage therefore, though computed upon ship and cargo, ought to be borne wholly by ship and freight, which is to be received by the ship owners, and the cargo ought to contribute nothing. It is very true that by this means the freight is made to bear that salvage, which was paid to the recaptors in respect of the cargo saved, and the ship owner has a much higher salvage to pay than would have been the case had the ship returned in ballast; but as it was in the contemplation of all parties that the ship was to come home loaded, the ship owners have no right to complain of any consequence which results from what was so contemplated."

1518   However, it was held, secondly, that the defendants could not set off their contribution to the charges of establishing the claim to the cargo and procuring the decree for its restitution. The plaintiffs derived no benefit from that for they earned their freight on the ship's arrival, which the defendants then had to pay. The restitution of the cargo was considered to be for their benefit alone, as affording them with a fund wherewith to pay the freight.

---

[9] *ibid.*, 160.

CHAPTER 17

APPORTIONMENT OF SALVAGE PAYMENTS[1]

1. GENERAL MATTERS

How the question of apportionment may arise

The apportionment of salvage reward may arise in three ways: 1519

(i) on the performance or enforcement of an agreement to apportion the salvage reward[2];

(ii) following a request in the course of or immediately after the close of determination of a salvage claim[3]; or

(iii) as the subject of proceedings[4] of which the substantive object is to obtain an apportionment of an amount already ascertained.[5]

The court will recognise a valid agreement or a binding arbitration award apportioning salvage or an equitable tender, in which cases it will not intervene to substitute its own decision on apportionment.[6] Otherwise, it may exercise its own jurisdiction to apportion.

Jurisdiction and general principle on apportionment

Power to apportion salvage remuneration amongst salvors has always been 1520
incidental to the jurisdiction of the Admiralty Court.[7] "The ancient law of the

---

[1] A long list of cases of apportionment, classified according to the nature of the salvage, will be found in Pritchard, Vol. 2, pp. 2119–2123. See also Lloyd's Reports Digests.

[2] The effect of these agreements will of course depend on their enforceability (on which see *ante*, Chap. 9) and on which parties are bound by them.

[3] See, *e.g. The Firethorn* (1948) 81 Ll.L.Rep. 178.

[4] The proceeding was formerly an action for distribution of salvage. The proceedings may be against the salvees or against other salvors who have successfully obtained a reward, or a judicial or arbitral decision for a reward, in which the claimant is entitled to participate. Clearly, the claimant would have no entitlement where the award was not designed to reward his contribution to salvage.

[5] See, *e.g. The Rosario* (1876) 2 P.D. 41; *The Petter* (1942) 72 Ll.L.Rep. 134 (sum agreed).

[6] The general principle governing the court's statutory function in apportionment was stated thus in *The Enchantress* (1860) Lush. 93, 95, *per* Dr Lushington: "I conceive a duty is hereby imposed upon me to decree, upon application made, what in my judgment is an equitable apportionment of salvage, unless I am barred by one of two circumstances—either an equitable agreement between the parties, or an equitable tender." This statement was approved in *The Afrika* (1880) 5 P.D. 192, 194, *per* Sir Robert Phillimore.

[7] It was not maintainable at common law: *Atkinson v. Woodall* (1862) 31 L.J.M.C. 174.

court in questions of this kind was undoubted—*viz.*, that whenever any sum had been allotted by way of salvage, it was competent to any party dissatisfied with the distribution by the owners or master to apply to this court for the apportionment of that sum of money."[8] The jurisdiction is now governed in English law by the Merchant Shipping Act 1995.

The general principle governing apportionment follows from the general principle guiding the tribunal's discretion in assessment of salvage rewards, *i.e.* that the reward or share of the reward payable to individual salvors should not be determined on any fixed scale but should be assessed in accordance with the value of their contribution to salvage.[9]

Salvage under £5,000

1521 The Merchant Shipping Act 1995, s.228 provides that, where the aggregated amount of salvage payable in respect of salvage services rendered in United Kingdom waters[10] has been finally determined and does not exceed £5,000 but a dispute arises as to the apportionment of the amount among several claimants, the person liable to pay the amount may apply to the receiver of wreck[11] for leave to pay it to him.[12] If he thinks fit, the receiver shall receive the amount; and, if he does, he must give the person paying it a certificate stating the amount paid and the services in respect of which it is paid.[13] Such a certificate is a final discharge and indemnity to the person by whom it was paid and to his vessel, cargo, equipment and effects and against the claims of all persons in respect of the services mentioned in the certificate.[14] The receiver must with all convenient speed distribute any amount received by him under section 228 among the persons entitled to it, on such evidence and in such shares and proportions as he thinks fit[15] on the basis of the criteria for fixing salvage reward contained in the International Salvage Convention 1989, Art. 13.[16] However, he may retain any money which appears to him to be payable to any person who is absent.[17] A distribution

---

[8] *The Pride of Canada* (1863) 1 M.L.C. 406, 406, *per* Dr Lushington; followed in *The Rosario* (1876) 2 P.D. 41, 44, *per* Sir Robert Phillimore.

[9] In Admiralty law, see, *e.g. The General Palmer* (1830) 2 Hagg. 323; *The Louisa* (1843) 2 W.Rob. 22, 25, *per* Dr Lushington ("I extremely doubt ... whether it would be practicable, looking at the varying circumstances of this class of cases, to establish any rule of Court on the subject which could be binding in all cases. It is necessary to look to the particular services rendered in each case, and then to apportion the salvage reward according to the facts and circumstances emerging from that investigation."). Under the International Salvage Convention 1989, Arts. 13 and 15, see MSA 1995, ss.228(5), 229(2).

[10] For the definition of United Kingdom waters, see MSA 1995, s.313(2)(a).

[11] Appointed under MSA 1995, s.248: see *ibid.*, s.255(1).

[12] MSA 1995, s.228(1).

[13] MSA 1995, s.228(2).

[14] MSA 1995, s.228(3).

[15] MSA 1995, s.228(4) provides that the receiver shall make the distribution "as he thinks fit". However, as the International Salvage Convention 1989 has the force of law (MSA 1995, s.224(1): see *ante*, Chap. 1), the receiver is bound to apply the law governing apportionment provided by Art. 15.2 of the Convention, where applicable (see *post*, § 1523).

[16] MSA 1995, s.228(4)–(5). On the criteria for fixing rewards in the International Salvage Convention 1989, Art. 13, see *ante*, Chap. 15.

[17] MSA 1995, s.228(6).

made by the receiver under section 228 is final and conclusive as against all persons claiming to be entitled to any part of the amount distributed.[18]

Apportionment by the court

The Merchant Shipping Act 1995, s.229 gives the court[19] power to apportion a salvage reward where the aggregate amount has been finally determined[20] and there has been delay or a dispute over apportionment.[21] Section 229(1) provides that:

1522

"Where—
(a) the aggregate amount of salvage payable in respect of salvage services rendered in United Kingdom waters[22] has been finally determined and exceeds £5,000; or
(b) the aggregate amount of salvage payable in respect of salvage services rendered outside United Kingdom waters (of whatever amount) has been finally determined; but
(c) in either case, any delay[23] or dispute arises as to the apportionment of the amount,
the court may cause the amount of salvage to be apportioned among the persons entitled to it in such manner as it thinks just."

The statute confirms the principle established by the Admiralty Court that "The apportionment must in each case depend upon the particular circumstances".[24] However, although the court has a discretion, it is now bound to exercise it in accordance with the criteria for fixing salvage reward contained in the International Salvage Convention 1989, Art. 13.[25] Nonetheless, for the purpose of making an apportionment under section 229, it may: appoint any person to carry that apportionment into effect; compel any person in whose hands or under whose control the amount may be to distribute it or to pay it

---

[18] MSA 1995, s.228(7).

[19] In MSA 1995, s.229, "the court" is the High Court or, in Scotland, the Court of Session or a sheriff: *ibid.*, s.229(4). A claim for apportionment of salvage must be commenced in the Admiralty Court: CPR 49; PD49F, §§ 1.4(e), 1.5(e).

[20] The final determination may be by a court (see, *e.g. the Firethorn* (1948) 81 Ll.L.Rep. 178) or by arbitration (see, *e.g. The Nicolaou Georgis* [1951] 2 Lloyd's Rep. 215).

[21] Where there has not been a final determination, the claimant should bring a salvage claim in the normal way. If there has been a final determination but no delay or dispute, the salvor must await that eventuality before applying to the court under s.229.

[22] For the definition of U.K. waters, see MSA 1995, s.313(2)(a).

[23] In *The Spirit of the Age* (1857) Swab. 286, 287, Dr Lushington observed that "it is more convenient that such applications should be made while the circumstances of the case are fresh in the mind of the court" but held that "A party dissatisfied with the tender made in apportionment of salvage is not precluded from coming here at any reasonable time after salvage decreed; and the question of time cannot be pressed against a person in the present applicant's class of life [a seaman]."

[24] *The Gipsy Queen* [1895] P. 176, 177, *per* Lord Esher M.R.

[25] MSA 1995, s.229(2). On the criteria for fixing rewards in the International Salvage Convention 1989, Art. 13, see *ante*, Chap. 15.

into court to be dealt with as the court directs; and issue such process as it thinks fit.[26]

Governing law

1523 Furthermore, it is now provided by the International Salvage Convention 1989, Art. 15 that:

> "1. The apportionment of a reward under Article 13[27] between salvors shall be made on the basis of the criteria contained in that Article.
> 2. The apportionment between the owner, master and other persons in the service of each salving vessel shall be determined by the law of the flag of that vessel. If the salvage has not been carried out from a vessel, the apportionment shall be determined by the law governing the contract between the salvor and his servants."

The remainder of this chapter discusses apportionment under English law.

2. Detailed Instances of Apportionment

1524 In the following paragraphs, the case of apportionment between the various parties who comprise a single set of salvors is considered, primarily the owner, master and crew of a salving vessel, whether it is the only salving vessel rendering the service or is one of two or more vessels performing it. Apportionment as between several salving vessels or independent sets of salvors, to each of which the court may make a separate allotment out of the total sum awarded for salvage, will be considered later.[28]

Apportionment amongst owners, master and crew of a salving vessel

Share of owner of a salving vessel

1525 In modern times, the principal salvage service is most frequently provided by salving vessels and the Admiralty Court has considered it equitable that the owners, on whom the chief risk and expense falls, should accordingly receive a high proportion of the reward.[29]

Since 1883, owners have received three-quarters so frequently that this may fairly be called the ordinary apportionment.[30] The three-quarters share, however, is by no means the invariable apportionment to the owners of the salving

---
[26] MSA 1995, s.229(3).
[27] See *ante*, Chap. 15.
[28] See *post*, §§ 1532–1534.
[29] See *The Enchantress* (1860) Lush. 93, 96, *per* Dr Lushington.
[30] See *The Livietta* (1883) 8 P.D. 24. In *The Cleopatra* (1877) 3 P.D. 145, the owner's proportion was three-fifths.

vessel at the present time. With reference to apportionment made on that basis, Lord Esher M.R. remarked in *The Gipsy Queen*[31]: "That may be a very good working principle; but there is no such rule. The apportionment must in each case depend upon the particular circumstances."

Master's share

The master of the salving ship not only takes his share in the actual work, but also has a peculiar burden of responsibility[32] in undertaking and conducting the salvage enterprise and, therefore, under ordinary circumstances he is held to be entitled to receive out of the salvage reward a special separate recompense.[33] The share allotted to him is usually about one-third[34] of what remains after deducting the amount apportioned to the owners. There is, however, no rule,[35] and the amount of the recompense will vary according to the particular facts of each case.

Crew's share; officers and seamen

As to the officers and seamen, the apportionment usually takes the form of a lump sum to be shared by them according to their rates of remuneration. An exception may be made in favour of navigating officers, whose rating is lower than that of engineers, by a direction that for the purpose of apportionment they should be treated as rated equally with the corresponding rank of engineers.[36]

Special directions may be given in the rare case nowadays of radio officers where they are not paid by the ship, and it has been said that they are to rank

---

[31] [1895] P. 176, 177. An award reduced by the CA to £800 was apportioned: £620 to owners, £50 to the master and £130 to the crew.

[32] In *The Tees, The Pentucket* (1862) Lush. 505, the manager of the company owning the salvage vessel was given a larger award than the master; he, the manager, was in charge of the operation of rescuing vessels from a dock fire and thereby incurred responsibility. An apportionment to two marine superintendents was made in *The Petter* (1942) 72 Ll.L.Rep. 134 and the master received no special apportionment, being ranked with the crew according to his and their wages.

[33] See *The Martin Luther* (1857) Swab. 289, 290, *per* Dr Lushington; *The Himalaya* (1857) Swab. 515, 518; *The Charles* (1872) L.R. 3 A. & E. 536, 538, *per* Sir Robert Phillimore.

[34] Roscoe, p. 163.

[35] *The Gipsy Queen* [1895] P. 176, 177, *per* Lord Esher M.R.; *The Goldean Falcon* [1990] 2 Lloyd's Rep. 366 (NSW SC).

[36] See *The Italia* (1906) 10 Asp. M.L.C. 284; *The Birnam* (1907) 10 Asp. M.L.C. 462, not following *The Bremen* (1906) 10 Asp. M.L.C. 229; *The Larpool* (1941) 70 Ll.L.Rep. 72, 78. In *The M. Arnus*, November 11, 1918, cited in Roscoe, p. 164, n. (g), where the crew of the salving vessel, the *Maplemore*, were of three classes in regard to rates of pay (*viz.*, those engaged in the U.K., those engaged at a higher rate in the U.S., and those on naval ratings, partly paid by the owners and partly by the Admiralty), the share of the crew was divided on the basis of the U.K. rate. In *The Empire Gulf* [1948] P. 168, Willmer J. held that war bonus payments, which every member of the crew was receiving during and for some time after the Second World War irrespective of rank or status, should not be taken into consideration in apportioning the crew's share of the salvage award; the correct method of apportionment was on the footing of their respective basic wages. See also *The Southern Venturer* [1953] 1 Lloyd's Rep. 428 (Ct Sn.), where Lord Sorn held that bonus payments calculated in proportion to the success of a whaling expedition were to be disregarded in apportioning among the crew; awards should be based on basic wages.

as second or third officers.[37] The position of radio officers on the ship's articles but neither employed by the shipowner, save as regards the contractual relationship between him and the wireless company, nor paid by him,[38] would seem to be a matter of doubt. It is the general practice of salvage law that the rule of participation in salvage awards does not extend beyond those who are really in the employ of the owner of the salvage ship, even if, as in *The Coriolanus*,[39] they are on the ship's articles, unless they perform personal services. Whether they are an exception to this rule and, as officers, are entitled to share in awards to officers and crews, who do not have to perform personal services, or whether, not being an exception, they can only share if they actually render personal services, *e.g.* in cases where the radio installation has been of use in the salvage or where they perform duties not connected with radio and outside their ordinary work, does not appear to have been the subject of judicial decision.[40] In the latter event, it would seem that they might have been able to sue as separate plaintiffs, and might also be unaffected by the disabilities which ordinarily preclude a master and crew from claiming salvage.[41]

1527 The rule of participation can best be illustrated by reference to the cases. It has extended to other non-navigating members of the crew. In *The Spree*,[42] the doctor, four stewards, stewardesses, two cooks, a baker and two cabin boys on board the salving steamship who took no part in the navigation of the ship were awarded half shares according to their rating. In contrast, in the absence of a special direction by the court the rule of participation does not appear to extend beyond those who are really in the employ of the shipowner. In *The Coriolanus*,[43] a steamship, laden with cattle and having on board a number of men who were paid by the owners of the cattle but were nominally on the ship's books, salved a derelict ship. The salvage service prolonged the voyage by nearly two days, but the keepers of the cattle did not assist in it in any way. It was held by Sir James Hannen P. that they were not entitled to participate in the salvage award.

Passengers

1528 Passengers cannot ordinarily claim salvage either against the vessel in which they are travelling or against another vessel assisted by her; but in

---

[37] *The Albionic* (1941) 70 Ll.L.Rep. 257, *per* Langton J., who in *The Larpool* (1941) 70 Ll.L.Rep. 72, 78, ranked a wireless operator with the third officer.
[38] See *ante*, § 587.
[39] (1890) 15 P.D. 103.
[40] See *The Elpenor* (1933) 47 Ll.L.Rep. 183. *cf. The Southern Venturer* [1953] 1 Lloyd's Rep. 428, a Scottish case, where the wireless officer participated in the award to officers and ratings but was refused a special award. "To justify a special award there must be special merit, special risk or special exertion": *per* Lord Sorn.
[41] See *ante*, §§ 565–587.
[42] [1893] P. 147. In *The Punta Lara* (1910) 26 T.L.R. 268 the master's wife, who was on the articles as stewardess, rated at one shilling a month, was refused any share. See also *The Noordland* [1893] P. 153n.; *The Minneapolis* [1902] P. 30; *The Dunbar Castle* [1902] W.N. 70; *The Toscana* [1905] P. 148.
[43] (1890) 15 P.D. 103; followed in *The Malin Head, Shipping Gazette*, November 20, 1903. But see *The Minneapolis* [1902] P. 30.

special circumstances they may do so.[44] In this latter event, their reward will depend upon the part which they take in the enterprise. They are not entitled to a share unless they have assisted in the service.[45] Claims of this nature appear to be rare.[46]

Extra shares

The court may order that boats' crews,[47] engineers,[48] or individuals[49] are to receive extra shares for additional work or hardship.[50]

Special rewards

Cases sometimes occur in which justice to the special gallantry or special labour of an officer or seaman requires that, instead of receiving a mere extra share,[51] he should be specially rewarded.[52] The Admiralty Court has always been prompt to recognise a claim of this nature and it has, in some cases of

---

[44] See *ante*, §§ 632–636.

[45] *The Coriolanus* (1890) 15 P.D. 103, 104, *per* Sir James Hannen P.

[46] See, *e.g. The Hope* (1838) 3 Hagg. 423, 425; it does not appear from the report that the passengers assisted in the service but this is explained in *The Coriolanus* (1890) 15 P.D. 103. In *The Notre Dame de Fourvière* (1923) 14 Ll.L.Rep. 276, 277, Sir Henry Duke P. said that in *The Hope* passengers rendered services. As stated, however, this does not appear from the report in *The Hope*. See also *The Perla* (1857) Swab. 230, 232; *The Salacia* (1829) 2 Hagg. 262.

[47] See, *e.g. The Saint Nicholas* (1860) Lush. 29 (double shares to those of crew who performed boat service at great peril); *The Santiago* (1900) 9 Asp. M.L.C. 147 (treble shares to crew who performed boat service and were nearly drowned); *The Mari Chandris* (1941) 69 Ll.L.Rep. 166, 169 (high proportion to whole crew; wartime; insurance referred to; $1\frac{1}{2}$ shares to boat's crew, hard work, handling of wires arduous and very difficult). It may be necessary to board the salved vessel, *e.g.* where she is a derelict, in order to establish towage connection, or where she is short of hands owing to illness or other causes and they require augmenting to establish connection and/or to navigate the salved vessel.

[48] *The Dunottar Castle* [1902] W.N. 70 (engineer staff reckoned as if rated at $1\frac{1}{2}$ their actual rating on account of having double watches during the towing).

[49] See, *e.g. The Cambria (sub nom. Asama v. Cambria)* (1923) 15 Ll.L.Rep. 170 (award to be shared equally between (a) owners, and (b) master and crew; quadruple shares to three volunteers who boarded derelict by boat, and despite considerable hardship, exposure and danger remained there during towage); *The Firethorn* (1948) 81 Ll.L.Rep. 178 (apportionment weighted in favour of crew as a whole; no extra shares to boat's crew but double share to mate, one of boat's crew). Compare *The Mount Cynthos* (1937) 58 Ll.L.Rep. 26 (scratch crew manned tug; ordinary rules of apportionment held inapplicable either as between owners and scratch crew or amongst that crew).

[50] In the days of sail, when those who "went out" to do the "active work" of "the salvage service", *e.g.* boats' crews, were regarded as the "actual salvors", the position was stated in the form that their "associates", the rest of the crew, except in the case of vessels employed in the public service, were also entitled to some share of the reward unless they had refused to concur in undertaking the salvage service: *The Baltimore* (1817) 2 Dods. 132; *The Sarah Jane* (1843) 2 W.Rob. 110, 115; *cf. The August Legembre* [1902] P. 123.

[51] See previous sentence.

[52] For instances of the apportionment of special sums for special services, see *The Jane* (1831) 2 Hagg. 338; *The Nicolina* (1843) 2 W. Rob. 178; *Carmichael v. Brodie (The Sir Ralph Abercrombie)* (1867) L.R. 1 P.C. 454; *The Andrina* (1870) L.R. 3 A. & E. 286; *The Sarah* (1878) 3 P.D. 39; *The Craigs* (1880) 5 P.D. 186; *The Killeena* (1881) 6 P.D. 193; *The Elise* [1899] W.N. 54; *The Santiago* (1900) 9 Asp. M.L.C. 147; *The Minneapolis* [1902] P. 30; *The Elkhound* (1931) 39 Ll.L.Rep. 15; *The Castor* [1932] P. 142 (£300 to an injured seaman); *The Elpenor* (1934) 47 Ll.L.Rep. 183 (special award to wireless operator, £50).

this type, apportioned to a mate or to a common seaman an amount exceeding the reward of the master of the salving vessel.[53]

Crown ships

1529 Section 8(2) of the Crown Proceedings Act of 1947 provides:

> "Where after the commencement of this Act salvage services are rendered by or on behalf of His Majesty, whether in right of His Government in the United Kingdom or otherwise, His Majesty shall be entitled to claim salvage in respect of those services to the same extent as any other salvor, and shall have the same rights and remedies in respect of those services as any other salvor."

There appears to be no reported case in which the Admiralty or those on board Crown ships have claimed salvage for services to which the Crown Proceedings Act 1947 has applied.[54] However, claims by the Crown under the auspices of Lloyd's Form are commonplace.

Since 1854,[55] the Admiralty has had the duty of deciding whether individuals shall be allowed to claim salvage. This position has not been altered by any subsequent Act. The nature of the consent appears to have followed the circumstances of each case. In cases where the commanding officer and crew have claimed, the crew's award has not been apportioned amongst them by the court, although the court has power to do so. The apportionment would seem to have been effected by the Admiralty itself. Provisions as to this are to be found in Queen's Regulations.[56]

Pilot

1530 The share of a pilot, when he is entitled to salvage reward,[57] depends upon the extent and character of the services rendered by him outside the scope of his duties.[58]

---

[53] *The Golondrina* (1867) L.R. 1 A. & E. 334; *The Rasche* (1873) L.R. 4 A. & E. 127; *The Skibladner* (1877) 3 P.D. 24; *The Watt* (1843) 2 W. Rob. 70; *The Minneapolis* [1902] P. 30; *The San Demetrio* (1941) 69 Ll.L.Rep. 5; *The Planet, Shipping Gazette W.S.*, January 31, 1902.

[54] Current instructions are that Lloyd's Form shall be used. But there may be cases in which the salved vessel would refuse to concur.

[55] See *ante*, § 663.

[56] See *ante*, § 654.

[57] See *ante*, §§ 588, 599.

[58] See, e.g. *The Santiago* (1900) 9 Asp. M.L.C. 147 (pilot of salvor £40 out of £1,000); *The Sardonyx, Shipping Gazette W.S.*, April 4, 1901 (£500 out of £8,850); *The Kenora* [1921] P. 90 (pilot boarding salved vessel, £400); *The Matatua* (1924) 20 Ll.L.Rep. 5 (tender of £700 upheld to pilot standing by after collision); *The Etrib* (1930) 37 Ll.L.Rep. 262 (pilot on vessel aground in River Avon, £90); *The Roumelian* (1933) 45 Ll.L.Rep. 267 (boarding and beaching damaged vessel £150 out of £650); *The Rosa Luxemburg* (1934) 49 Ll.L.Rep. 292 (boarding damaged vessel, £600 out of £10,450); *The Tsiropinas* (1935) 51 Ll.L.Rep. 87 (three pilots boarding damaged vessel in response to wireless call, £650). *The Hudson Light* [1970] 1 Lloyd's 166 (£325 for supervision of tugs in refloating operation); *The Ilo* [1982] 1 Lloyd's Rep. (£2,000 for co-ordination of tugs); *The Helenus and The Montagua* [1982] 2 Lloyd's Rep. 261.

Apportionment amongst various salving vessels or sets of salvors

Lifeboatmen

As has already been stated, the Royal National Lifeboat Institution treats lifeboat crews who have become salvors of property as ordinary salvors who have borrowed the lifeboat for the purpose of the service. Consequently, its regulations make no provision for division of a salvage award among the crew. They are left to settle their shares by agreement; or the court may make an apportionment.

Coastguard

The court has, no doubt, the same power as to apportionment in regard to the officers and men serving in the coastguard, as to whose share in salvage rewards rules have, it is believed, been laid down by the Secretary of State.

Apportionment amongst individual salvors not associated, *e.g.* as a crew

1531 When apportionment has to be made among several salvors, and they are not persons between whom there is an association outside the salvage service such as exists between the members of the crew of a salving[59] vessel, the court will fix the share of each salvor in the salvage fund by ascertaining, as well as it can, what have been the value of his services, including, for example, any responsibility incurred in superintending others[60] and any skill displayed or risk or hardship incurred, as compared with those of his co-salvors. Each case has to be considered according to its particular circumstances.[61]

Apportionment amongst various salving vessels or sets of salvors

1532 So far, only the case of apportionment between the various parties who compose a single set of salvors, principally the owners, master and crew of a salving vessel, has been considered. But it frequently happens that there are engaged in the salvage service several salving vessels or independent sets of salvors,[62] to each of which the court has to make a separate allotment.

Where services contemporaneous

Where the services of the salving vessels or sets of personal salvors have been practically contemporaneous in their inception, and not successive, the proportion of the total salvage which is allotted to each is generally determined by the same considerations as affect the assessment of the total salvage.[63]

---

[59] See *The San Demetrio* (1941) 69 Ll.L.Rep. 5, where the salvors were or had been the crew of the vessel, salved after abandonment on the orders of the master; rating was taken into account.
[60] See, *e.g. The Nicholas Witzen* (1837) 3 Hagg. 369.
[61] See, *e.g. The Mount Cynthos* (1937) 58 Ll.L.Rep. 18.
[62] The principles stated, *mutatis mutandis*, apply to both.
[63] As to these, see *ante*, Chap. 15.

Priority in time; general principle

1533 Where the services of the different salving vessels or sets of persons have not begun together, but the second or further vessels or sets of persons have either joined at a later stage in the prosecution of the salvage adventure or have taken up a salvage service which the first salvors, after rendering some assistance, have been obliged by the force of circumstances, and without fault on their part, to discontinue, the relative share of each in the total award will be affected by the consideration that first salvors, if they have acted meritoriously, are on grounds of public policy always to be treated with especial liberality in the apportionment. The favour with which the court regards the efforts of first salvors has been demonstrated by cases where, although it has been difficult to say that those efforts have contributed much, if anything, to the salvage which is ultimately effected by other salvors, they have been rewarded by the court by a substantial portion of the total award.[64]

Such liberality is in two different ways of general benefit. It serves, in the first place, to encourage that adventurous promptitude in rendering assistance to life or property in distress which is always praiseworthy, the more so if life is also in danger, and is often necessary for the accomplishment of the rescue. It serves, in the second place, to prevent a jealousy of second or later salvors which might otherwise exist, and tempt first salvors, injuriously to the interests to be saved, to shun co-operation when co-operation would ensure, or, at least, materially expedite, the success of the salvage undertaking.

The observance of this principle of favourable inclination towards first salvors by no means ranks as the principal factor in the determination of the apportionment of the total salvage between rival salvors. The priority in point of time is merely one of the points which the court has to consider in the distribution; and it will not count for much where the balance of efficacy or merit is decisively in favour of the second salvors.[65] It may here be noted that, where several tugs render salvage services to a vessel, factors which may affect their shares of the award include their respective horse-power, their values, and the number of crew on board each of them.[66]

Wrongful dispossession; effect

1534 However, if the claim of a salving vessel or set of salvors to a share in the salvage reward is based upon the dispossession, against their will, of others at the same time continuously engaged in salving the vessel in distress, and willing to persevere in the service already begun, the court allows the claim only if it clearly proved that there was reasonable cause for the dispossession.

---

[64] See, *e.g. The E.U.* (1853) 1 Spinks E. & A. 63; *The Genessee* (1848) 12 Jur. 401; *The American Farmer* (1947) 80 Ll.L.Rep. 672.

[65] See on the subject of first salvors, *e.g. The Jonge Bastiaan* (1804) 5 C. Rob. 222; *The Santipore* (1854) 1 Spinks E. & A. 231; *The Livietta* (1883) 8 P.D. 24; *The Anna, Shipping Gazette*, May 30, 1905; *The E.U.* (1853) 1 Spinks E. & A. 63; *The Genessee* (1848) 12 Jur. 401; *The American Farmer* (1947) 80 Ll.L.Rep. 672.

[66] See, *e.g. The Madoera* (1946) 79 Ll.L.Rep. 486, 491; *The Queen Elizabeth* (1949) 82 Ll.L.Rep. 803.

Share due to deceased salvor

In the absence of such proof, the burden of which lies upon the second or later alleged salvors,[67] the court holds the dispossession to be wrongful and treats the subsequent services rendered by the wrongdoers as enuring wholly to the benefit of those who have been dispossessed, not as entitling the wrongdoers to any share in the salvage reward.

Where the dispossession of the first by a second salvor is deemed by the court to have been necessary and proper, because there was no fair probability of the first salvor being able to bring the vessel into port in safety in due time, but the services of the first until such dispossession have been of a praiseworthy character, and he was willing to continue them, the court, whilst treating the second salvor as the principal and efficient cause of the success, and therefore entitled to the larger share of salvage, will give a liberal share also to the first.[68]

Share due to deceased salvor is awarded to his personal representatives

If a salvor dies before the court adjudicates upon the salvage claim, the share to which he would have been entitled is secured to his personal representatives.[69]

1535

3. AGREEMENTS FOR APPORTIONMENT

Parties involved in maritime operations—whether shipowners, masters, seamen or others—may enter into agreements as to the apportionment of remuneration earned. Thus, it has not been uncommon for those who are interested in salvage, either before[70] or after[71] the performance of the salvage service, to agree amongst themselves as to apportionment. The court is reluctant to disturb arrangements which have been acquiesced in by the parties to it and will enforce them if equitable.[72] However, as a matter of construction, and consistently with the principles governing "voluntariness",[73] a pre-existing arrangement as to apportionment of remuneration may not be applied in exceptional cases, *e.g.* in cases of great personal risk and extraordinary labour.[74] Moreover, the court is prepared to exercise its inherent jurisdiction

1536

---

[67] See *The Eugene* (1834) 3 Hagg. 156, 160, *per* Sir John Nicholl. *cf. The Blenden-Hall* (1814) 1 Dods. 414, 416, *per* Lord Stowell.

[68] *The Pickwick* (1852) 16 Jur. 669; *The Magdalen* (1861) 31 L.J.Adm 22; *The American Farmer* (1947) 80 Ll.L.Rep. 672.

[69] See, *e.g. The Marquis of Huntly* (1835) 3 Hagg. 246; *The Anna Helena* (1883) 5 Asp. M.L.C. 142; *The San Demetrio* (1941) 69 Ll.L.Rep. 5.

[70] See, *e.g. The Louisa* (1843) 2 W.Rob. 22; *The James Armstrong* (1875) 3 Asp. M.L.C. 46; *The Sunniside* (1883) 8 P.D. 137; *The Wilhem Tell* [1892] P. 337.

[71] See, *e.g. The Afrika* (1880) 5 P.D. 192.

[72] *The Beulah* (1842) 7 Jur. 207, 208, *per* Dr Lushington; *The James Armstrong* (1875) 3 Asp. M.L.C. 46.

[73] *Ante*, Chap. 7.

[74] *The Beulah* (1842) 7 Jur. 207, 207, *per* Dr Lushington.

to set aside an agreement which it considers to be in any way inequitable,[75] *a fortiori* one procured by any fraudulent or other improper action.[76] However, the court will not set aside agreements merely on the ground that it might have awarded a different amount.[77]

Customary agreements for apportionment

1537 There have been instances of alleged customary agreements for apportionment—*i.e.* agreements which the court has been asked to recognise as implied from the usage of a particular occupation or a particular locality and as determining the rights of persons involved in the relevant occupation or locality to apportionment.[78] However, the effectiveness of such customary agreements, if proved, was held to be subject to the Admiralty Court's inherent jurisdiction over salvage matters,[79] in particular to set aside inequitable agreements, albeit such customary agreements were regarded more favourably than special agreements for apportionment.[80] Moreover, the Court of Session[81] has doubted the legitimacy of an alleged customary dispensation with the statutory preservation of seamen's rights to apportionment.[82] Certainly the court would not sanction a custom by which one who actually rendered salvage service would be shut out from all share in the reward.

Seamen's salvage rights

1538 An agreement purporting to exclude or restrict a seaman's right to, or right to participate in, a salvage reward may fail to do so as a matter of construction or if the person alleged to be bound by the agreement has not authorised it.[83] Even if on its true interpretation it applies, the Admiralty Court has always recognised the fact that mariners are liable to be placed at a disadvantage in dealing with the owner or master of their ship as to the division of salvage and has accordingly scrutinised alleged contracts of apportionment with special

---

[75] *The Beulah* (1842) 7 Jur. 207, 208, *per* Dr Lushington; *The Enchantress* (1860) Lush. 93, 95 *per* Dr Lushington (quoted *supra*, § 703 n. 45; *The Afrika* (1880) 5 P.D. 192, 194, *per* Sir Robert Phillimore. On inequitable agreements generally, see *ante*, Chap. 9.

[76] *The Afrika* (1880) 5 P.D. 192, 196, *per* Sir Robert Phillimore.

[77] *The Afrika* (1880) 5 P.D. 192, 196, *per* Sir Robert Phillimore.

[78] For instance, the Hull Trawler Owners used to have an agreement whereby the crew took 34 per cent of any salvage remuneration after deduction of any special expenses that might be allowed; this 34 per cent was divided as to 10 per cent to the skipper, 7 per cent to the mate, and the remaining 17 per cent to the other members of the crew in agreed proportions.

[79] Thus, in *The Ganges* (1869) L.R. 2 A. & E. 370, 372, Sir Robert Phillimore had to balance the policy of encouraging seamen to render salvage services by the prospect of a generous reward against the policy of encouraging shipowners to have in readiness vessels and crews peculiarly fitted for rendering salvage services.

[80] *The Enchantress* (1860) Lush. 93, 97, *per* Dr Lushington. *cf. The Sarah* (1878) 3 P.D. 39; *The Sandsend, Shipping Gazette W.S.*, May 22, 1903.

[81] *Nicholson v. Leith Salvage and Towage Co.* 1923 S.C. 409, 421.

[82] In MSA 1995, s.39(1): see *post*, §§ 1538–1539.

[83] *The Leon Blum* [1915] P. 290 (CA); *The Oceanic Grandeur* (1972) 127 C.L.R. 312 (HCA), 334; [1972] 2 Lloyd's Rep. 396, 407. *cf. The Queen Elizabeth* (1949) 82 Ll.L.Rep. 802, where certain tug-owners were under contract with the shipowners to reimburse the latter for any awards given through the courts to tugmasters and crew.

care in respect of their interests.[84] "The policy of the law is to protect seamen from improvident arrangements, and to encourage their exertions to save life and property."[85]

Thus, the Merchant Shipping Act 1995, s.39(1) provides that any right a seaman[86] may have or obtain in the nature of salvage shall not be capable of being renounced by any agreement.[87] This is so whether the agreement is made before or after[88] the salvage operation, and whether it is simply an agreement to apportion or a purported assignment by way of valuable consideration of a right to share in the reward.[89] Section 39(1) also invalidates an agreement purporting to authorise owners to make deductions for repairs and loss of profits before apportioning the remainder of a global reward.[90] Furthermore, a seaman's previous failure to assert his rights against his employer under section 39(1) will not preclude his doing so on a later occasion.[91] However, the section does not apply where a settlement has been affected by a solicitor employed by the seaman to negotiate with the owners as to the seaman's share of salvage money.[92]

Section 39(2) alters the position where a seaman is specifically employed on "salvage articles": section 39(1) does not affect such of the terms of any agreement made with the seamen belonging to a ship which, in accordance with the agreement, is to be employed on salvage service, as provide for the remuneration to be paid to them for salvage services rendered by that ship.[93] However, this exception only applies where the terms of the agreement provide for remuneration on a ship employed to render a salvage service, not

1539

---

[84] See especially *The Pride of Canada* (1863) 1 M.L.C. 406.

[85] *The Wilhelm Tell* [1892] P. 337, 348, *per* Gorell Barnes J. See also *The Louisa* (1843) 2 W.Rob. 22, 23, *per* Dr Lushington.

[86] "Seaman" includes every person (except masters and pilots) employed or engaged in any capacity on board any ship: MSA 1995, s.313(1). A steward is a seaman: *Thompson v. H. & W. Nelson Ltd* [1913] 2 K.B. 523.

[87] In full, MSA 1995, s.39(1) states that: "A seaman's lien, his remedies for the recovery of his wages, his right to wages in case of the wreck or loss of his ship, and any right he may have or obtain in the nature of salvage shall not be capable of being renounced by any agreement."

[88] See, *e.g. The Rosario* (1876) 2 P.D. 41.

[89] *The Rosario* (1876) 2 P.D. 41.

[90] *The Saltburn* (1894) 7 Asp. M.L.C. 474 (at 476, Bruce J. said: "If the owners are themselves to be at liberty to assess the amount of the damage ... , there can be no security that the assessment would be fair and partial. If, on the other hand, the damage is to be assessed by the registrar of this court, or by a referee to be agreed on by the parties, much expense and delay would be incurred in many cases of apportionment."); *The Wilhelm Tell* [1892] P. 337, 351. *cf. The Spirit of the Age* (1857) Swab. 286; *The Sarah* (1878) 3 P.D. 39, 42.

[91] *Nicholson v. Leith Salvage and Towage Co.* 1923 S.C. 409, 420. Indeed, the Admiralty Court would generally retain the right to reopen previous dealings to this effect, although a seaman who unduly delayed to enforce his rights with knowledge of their existence could lose them.

[92] *The Afrika* (1880) 5 P.D. 192.

[93] MSA 1995, s.39(2). The agreement in question need not be in writing, but the onus lies strictly on the party alleging that there has been such an agreement to prove that the seamen were fully aware of what they were entering: *The Pride of Canada* (1863) 1 M.L.C. 406; see also *The Saltburn* (1894) 7 Asp. M.L.C. 474, 475; *The Oceanic Grandeur* (1972) 127 C.L.R. 312, HCA, 340; [1972] 2 Lloyd's Rep. 396, 410. In practice, most crews employed on salvage terms would expect contractually to receive a percentage of any salvage reward earned by their tug.

where the term as to salvage is incidental to the normal employment of the vessel.[94]

Section 39 of the Merchant Shipping Act 1995 supplements, and does not extinguish, the Admiralty Court's inherent jurisdiction to refuse to enforce inequitable agreements. Thus, an agreement which is not illegal and void under section 39 may be validly concluded if equitable but will still be denied enforcement under the court's inherent jurisdiction if it is inequitable.[95]

Salvors other than seaman

1540 The Merchant Shipping Act 1995, s.39 only applies to seamen. Therefore, it does not apply to salvors other than seamen, whether or not they be employees of another salvor.

In particular, masters and pilots are not within the statutory definition of seamen[96] and therefore the statutory preservation of seamen's salvage rights in section 39[97] does not extend to them.[98] However, claims of masters are subject to the Admiralty Court's inherent jurisdiction to set aside agreements on the ground that they are inequitable.[99] Otherwise, an honestly made and equitable agreement made by a master or a pilot to forego his right to salvage reward, or an assignment or sale by him of his share of salvage reward before its accrual, will be binding on him.

Prior act of apportionment

The court's power to set aside either an agreement for or act of apportionment cannot be restricted by a payment already made under a prior decision to apportion.[1] A person who advances money in accordance with such a decision takes the risk as to whether he can obtain restitution of all or part of such an advance, in particular that it may be treated as a voluntary payment.[2]

---

[94] *The Wilhelm Tell* [1892] P. 337, 347 ("She was, in fact, to be employed, according to the terms of the agreement, in trawling in the North Sea, and the clause as to salvage was only inserted in orde to deal with the case of an apportionment of any salvage which she might have the good fortune to earn."). *cf. The Saltburn* (1894) 7 Asp. M.L.C. 474.
[95] *The Pride of Canada* (1863) 1 M.L.C. 406; *The Ganges* (1869) L.R. 2 A. & E. 370; *The Wilhelm Tell* [1892] P. 337.
[96] MSA 1995, s.313(1).
[97] *Ante,* §§ 1538–1539. The Act does, however, confer on both seamen and masters similar protection of rights and remedies for wages, etc.: MSA 1995, ss 39, 41.
[98] *The Wilhelm Tell* [1892] P. 337, 347.
[99] *The Ganges* (1869) L.R. 2 A. & E. 370; *The Wilhelm Tell* [1892] P. 337, 347, 349; *Nicholson v. Leith Salvage and Towage Co.* 1923 S.C. 409. See also *The Leon Blum* [1915] P. 290.
[1] *The Louisa* (1843) 2 W.Rob. 22.
[2] See *The Louisa* (1843) 2 W.Rob. 22, 26, *per* Dr Lushington.

APPENDICES

A. SALVAGE DOCUMENTS

1. Lloyd's Standard Form of Salvage Agreement (LOF 1995)
2. Lloyd's Standard Form of Salvage Agreement (LOF 2000)
3. Lloyd's Standard Salvage and Arbitration Clauses
4. Lloyd's Procedural Rules
5. SCOPIC 2000 Clause
5A. SCOPIC 2000 Appendix A
5B. SCOPIC 2000 Appendix B
5C. SCOPIC 2000 Appendix C
6. ISU Lumpsum Sub-Contract Agreement
7. Code of Practice between ISU and International Group of P&I Clubs
8. Code of Practice between International Group of P&I Clubs and London Property Underwriters Regarding the Payment of the Fees and Expenses of the SCR under SCOPIC
9. International Salvage Union Sub-Contract (Award Sharing) 1994
10. Guarantee [for a Single Guarantor] to the Corporation of Lloyd's and to the Contractor in Connection with a Salvage Agreement on Lloyd's Form
11. Guarantee [for Two or More Guarantors] to the Corporation of Lloyd's and to the Contractor in Connection with a Salvage Agreement on Lloyd's Form
12. Guarantee [for a Single Guarantor (Insured)] to the Corporation of Lloyd's and to the Contractor in Connection with a Salvage Agreement on Lloyd's Form [With Indemnity]
13. Indemnity in Connection with a Salvage Agreement on Lloyd's Form [For Use with Guarantee by a Single Guarantor (Insured)]
14. Guarantee [for Two or More Guarantors (Insured)] to the Corporation of Lloyd's and to the Contractor in Connection with a Salvage Agreement on Lloyd's Form [With Indemnity]
15. Indemnity in Connection with a Salvage Agreement on Lloyd's Form [For Use with Guarantee by Two or More Guarantors (Insured)]
16. Salvage Guarantee Form I.S.U. 1
17. Salvage Guarantee Form I.S.U. 2
18. Salvage Guarantee Form I.S.U. 3
19. Salvage Guarantee Form I.S.U. 4
20. Salvage Guarantee Form I.S.U. 5

B. UNITED KINGDOM LEGISLATION

21. Aircraft (Wreck and Salvage) Order 1938
22. Hovercraft (Application of Enactments) Order 1972
23. Protection of Wrecks Act 1973
24. Civil Aviation Act 1982
25. Protection of Military Remains Act 1986

Appendices

26. Merchant Shipping Act 1995
27. Merchant Shipping and Maritime Security Act 1997

C. INTERNATIONAL CONVENTIONS

28. (Brussels) Convention for the Unification of Certain Rules of Law respecting Assistance and Salvage at Sea 1910
29. (Brussels) International Convention for the Unification of Certain Rules relating to Assistance and Salvage of Aircraft or by Aircraft at Sea 1938
30. (Brussels) Protocol to Amend the Convention for Unification of Certain Rules of Law relating to Assistance and Salvage at Sea 1967
31. United Nations Convention on the Law of the Sea 1982
32. CMI Report to the International Maritime Organization
33. International Convention on Salvage 1989

D. RULES AND REGULATIONS

34. The Queen's Regulations for the Royal Navy
35. Royal National Lifeboat Institution Regulations

APPENDICES

A. Salvage Documents

No. 1

LOF 1995

LLOYD'S

NOTES
1. Insert name of person signing on behalf of Owners of property to be salved. The Master should sign wherever possible.
2. The Contractor's name should always be inserted in line 4 and whenever the Agreement is signed by the Master of the Salving vessel or other person on behalf of the Contractor the name of the Master or other person must also be inserted in line 4 before the words "for and on behalf of". The words "for and on behalf of" should be deleted where a Contractor signs personally.
3. Insert place if agreed in clause 1(a)(i) and currency if agreed in clause 1(e).

STANDARD FORM OF

SALVAGE AGREEMENT

(APPROVED AND PUBLISHED BY THE COUNCIL OF LLOYD'S)

NO CURE - NO PAY

On board the...
Dated.................................

+ See Note 1 above

IT IS HEREBY AGREED between Captain +..." her cargo freight bunkers stores and any other property thereon (hereinafter collectively called "the Owners") and .... for and on behalf of ....

* See Note 2 above

.... (hereinafter called "the Contractor"*) that:-

1. (a) The Contractor shall use his best endeavours:-

See Note 3 above

(i) to salve the "..."and/or her cargo freight bunkers stores and any other property thereon and take them to #.. or to such other place as may hereafter be agreed either place to be deemed a place of safety or if no such place is named or agreed to a place of safety and

(ii) while performing the salvage services to prevent or minimize damage to the environment.

(b) Subject to the statutory provisions relating to special compensation the services shall be rendered and accepted as salvage services upon the principle of "no cure - no pay."

(c) The Contractor's remuneration shall be fixed by Arbitration in London in the manner hereinafter prescribed and any other difference arising out of this Agreement or the operations thereunder shall be referred to Arbitration in the same way.

(d) In the event of the services referred to in this Agreement or any part of such services having been already rendered at the date of this Agreement by the Contractor to the said vessel and/or her cargo freight bunkers stores and any other property thereon the provisions of this Agreement shall apply to such services.

(e) The security to be provided to the Council of Lloyd's (hereinafter called "the Council") the Salved Value(s) the Award and/or any Interim Award(s) and/or any Award on Appeal shall be in

See Note 3 above

#... currency.

(f) If clause 1(e) is not completed then the security to be provided and the Salved Value(s) the Award and/or Interim Award(s) and/or Award on Appeal shall be in Pounds Sterling.

(g) This Agreement and Arbitration thereunder shall except as otherwise expressly provided be governed by the law of England, including the English law of salvage.

15.1.08
3.12.24
13.10.26
12.4.50
18.6.53
20.12.67
25.2.72
21.5.80
5.9.90
1.1.95

Appendix A—Salvage Documents

PROVISIONS AS TO THE SERVICES

2. *Definitions*: In this Agreement any reference to "Convention" is a reference to the International Convention on Salvage 1989 as incorporated in the Merchant Shipping (Salvage and Pollution) Act 1994 (and any amendment thereto). The terms "Contractor" and "services"/"salvage services" in this Agreement shall have the same meanings as the terms "salvor(s)" and "salvage operation(s)" in the Convention.

3. *Owners Cooperation*: The Owners their Servants and Agents shall co-operate fully with the Contractor in and about the salvage including obtaining entry to the place named or the place of safety as defined in clause 1. The Contractor may make reasonable use of the vessel's machinery gear equipment anchors chains stores and other appurtenances during and for the purpose of the salvage services free of expense but shall not unnecessarily damage abandon or sacrifice the same or any property the subject of this Agreement.

4. *Vessel Owners Right to Terminate*: When there is no longer any reasonable prospect of a useful result leading to a salvage reward in accordance with Convention Article 13 the owners of the vessel shall be entitled to terminate the services of the Contractor by giving reasonable notice to the Contractor in writing.

PROVISIONS AS TO SECURITY

5. (a) The Contractor shall immediately after the termination of the services or sooner notify the Council and where practicable the Owners of the amount for which he demands salvage security (inclusive of costs expenses and interest) from each of the respective Owners.

(b) Where a claim is made or may be made for special compensation, the owners of the vessel shall on the demand of the Contractor whenever made provide security for the Contractor's claim for special compensation provided always that such demand is made within two years of the date of termination of the services.

(c) The amount of any such security shall be reasonable in the light of the knowledge available to the Contractor at the time when the demand is made. Unless otherwise agreed such security shall be provided (i) to the Council (ii) in a form approved by the Council and (iii) by persons firms or corporations either acceptable to the Contractor or resident in the United Kingdom and acceptable to the Council. The Council shall not be responsible for the sufficiency (whether in amount or otherwise) of any security which shall be provided nor the default or insolvency of any person firm or corporation providing the same.

(d) The owners of the vessel their Servants and Agents shall use their best endeavours to ensure that the cargo owners provide their proportion of salvage security before the cargo is released.

6. (a) Until security has been provided as aforesaid the Contractor shall have a maritime lien on the property salved for his remuneration.

(b) The property salved shall not without the consent in writing of the Contractor (which shall not be unreasonably withheld) be removed from the place to which it has been taken by the Contractor under clause 1(a). Where such consent is given by the Contractor on condition that the Contractor is provided with temporary security pending completion of the voyage the Contractor's maritime lien on the property salved shall remain in force to the extent necessary to enable the Contractor to compel the provision of security in accordance with clause 5(c).

(c) The Contractor shall not arrest or detain the property salved unless:-

   (i) security is not provided within 14 days (exclusive of Saturdays and Sundays or other days observed as general holidays at Lloyd's) after the date of the termination of the services or
   (ii) he has reason to believe that the removal of the property salved is contemplated contrary to clause 6(b) or
   (iii) any attempt is made to remove the property salved contrary to clause 6(b).

(d) The Arbitrator appointed under clause 7 or the Appeal Arbitrator(s) appointed under clause 13(d) shall have power in their absolute discretion to include in the amount awarded to the Contractor the whole or part of any expenses reasonably incurred by the Contractor in:-

   (i) ascertaining demanding and obtaining the amount of security reasonably required in accordance with clause 5.
   (ii) enforcing and/or protecting by insurance or otherwise or taking reasonable steps to enforce and/or protect his lien.

LOF 1995

PROVISIONS AS TO ARBITRATION

7. (a) Whether security has been provided or not the Council shall appoint an Arbitrator upon receipt of a written request made by letter telex facsimile or in any other permanent form provided that any party requesting such appointment shall if required by the Council undertake to pay the reasonable fees and expenses of the Council and/or any Arbitrator or Appeal Arbitrator(s).

(b) Where an Arbitrator has been appointed and the parties do not proceed to arbitration the Council may recover any fees costs and/or expenses which are outstanding.

8. The Contractor's remuneration and/or special compensation shall be fixed by the Arbitrator appointed under clause 7. Such remuneration shall not be diminished by reason of the exception to the principle of "no cure - no pay" in the form of special compensation.

REPRESENTATION

9. Any party to this Agreement who wishes to be heard or to adduce evidence shall nominate a person in the United Kingdom to represent him failing which the Arbitrator or Appeal Arbitrator(s) may proceed as if such party had renounced his right to be heard or adduce evidence.

CONDUCT OF THE ARBITRATION

10. (a) The Arbitrator shall have power to:-
  (i) admit such oral or documentary evidence or information as he may think fit
  (ii) conduct the Arbitration in such manner in all respects as he may think fit subject to such procedural rules as the Council may approve
  (iii) order the Contractor in his absolute discretion to pay the whole or part of the expense of providing excessive security or security which has been unreasonably demanded under Clause 5(b) and to deduct such sum from the remuneration and/or special compensation
  (iv) make Interim Award(s) including payment(s) on account on such terms as may be fair and just
  (v) make such orders as to costs fees and expenses including those of the Council charged under clauses 10(b) and 14(b) as may be fair and just.

(b) The Arbitrator and the Council may charge reasonable fees and expenses for their services whether the Arbitration proceeds to a hearing or not and all such fees and expenses shall be treated as part of the costs of the Arbitration.

(c) Any Award shall (subject to Appeal as provided in this Agreement) be final and binding on all the parties concerned whether they were represented at the Arbitration or not.

INTEREST & RATES OF EXCHANGE

11. *Interest*: Interest at rates per annum to be fixed by the Arbitrator shall (subject to Appeal as provided in this Agreement) be payable on any sum awarded taking into account any sums already paid:-
  (i) from the date of termination of the services unless the Arbitrator shall in his absolute discretion otherwise decide until the date of publication by the Council of the Award and/or Interim Award(s) and
  (ii) from the expiration of 21 days (exclusive of Saturdays and Sundays or other days observed as general holidays at Lloyd's) after the date of publication by the Council of the Award and/or Interim Award(s) until the date payment is received by the Contractor or the Council both dates inclusive.

For the purpose of sub-clause (ii) the expression "sum awarded" shall include the fees and expenses referred to in clause 10(b).

12. *Currency Correction*: In considering what sums of money have been expended by the Contractor in rendering the services and/or in fixing the amount of the Award and/or Interim Award(s) and/or Award on Appeal the Arbitrator or Appeal Arbitrator(s) shall to such an extent and in so far as it may be fair and just in all the circumstances give effect to the consequences of any change or changes in the relevant rates of exchange which may have occurred between the date of termination of the services and the date on which the Award and/or Interim Award(s) and/or Award on Appeal is made.

PROVISIONS AS TO APPEAL

13. (a) Notice of Appeal if any shall be given to the Council within 14 days (exclusive of Saturdays and Sundays or other days observed as general holidays at Lloyd's) after the date of the publication by the Council of the Award and/or Interim Award(s).

Appendix A—Salvage Documents

(b) Notice of Cross-Appeal if any shall be given to the Council within 14 days (exclusive of Saturdays and Sundays or other days observed as general holidays at Lloyd's) after notification by the Council to the parties of any Notice of Appeal. Such notification if sent by post shall be deemed received on the working day following the day of posting.

(c) Notice of Appeal or Cross-Appeal shall be given to the Council by letter telex facsimile or in any other permanent form.

(d) Upon receipt of Notice of Appeal the Council shall refer the Appeal to the hearing and determination of the Appeal Arbitrator(s) selected by it.

(e) If any Notice of Appeal or Cross-Appeal is withdrawn the Appeal hearing shall nevertheless proceed in respect of such Notice of Appeal or Cross-Appeal as may remain.

(f) Any Award on Appeal shall be final and binding on all the parties to that Appeal Arbitration whether they were represented either at the Arbitration or at the Appeal Arbitration or not.

CONDUCT OF THE APPEAL

14. (a) The Appeal Arbitrator(s) in addition to the powers of the Arbitrator under clauses 10(a) and 11 shall have power to:-

   (i) admit the evidence which was before the Arbitrator together with the Arbitrator's notes and reasons for his Award and/or Interim Award(s) and any transcript of evidence and such additional evidence as he or they may think fit.
   (ii) confirm increase or reduce the sum awarded by the Arbitrator and to make such order as to the payment of interest on such sum as he or they may think fit.
   (iii) confirm revoke or vary any order and/or Declaratory Award made by the Arbitrator.
   (iv) award interest on any fees and expenses charged under paragraph (b) of this clause from the expiration of 21 days (exclusive of Saturdays and Sundays or other days observed as general holidays at Lloyd's) after the date of publication by the Council of the Award on Appeal and/or Interim Award(s) on Appeal until the date payment is received by the Council both dates inclusive.

(b) The Appeal Arbitrator(s) and the Council may charge reasonable fees and expenses for their services in connection with the Appeal Arbitration whether it proceeds to a hearing or not and all such fees and expenses shall be treated as part of the costs of the Appeal Arbitration.

PROVISIONS AS TO PAYMENT

15. (a) In case of Arbitration if no Notice of Appeal be received by the Council in accordance with clause 13(a) the Council shall call upon the party or parties concerned to pay the amount awarded and in the event of non-payment shall subject to the Contractor first providing to the Council a satisfactory Undertaking to pay all the costs thereof realize or enforce the security and pay therefrom to the Contractor (whose receipt shall be a good discharge to it) the amount awarded to him together with interest if any. The Contractor shall reimburse the parties concerned to such extent as the Award is less than any sums paid on account or in respect of Interim Award(s).

(b) If Notice of Appeal be received by the Council in accordance with clause 13 it shall as soon as the Award on Appeal has been published by it call upon the party or parties concerned to pay the amount awarded and in the event of non-payment shall subject to the Contractor first providing to the Council a satisfactory Undertaking to pay all the costs thereof realize or enforce the security and pay therefrom to the Contractor (whose receipt shall be a good discharge to it) the amount awarded to him together with interest if any. The Contractor shall reimburse the parties concerned to such extent as the Award on Appeal is less than any sums paid on account or in respect of the Award or Interim Award(s).

(c) If any sum shall become payable to the Contractor as remuneration for his services and/or interest and/or costs as the result of an agreement made between the Contractor and the Owners or any of them the Council in the event of non-payment shall subject to the Contractor first providing to the Council a satisfactory Undertaking to pay all the costs thereof realize or enforce the security and pay therefrom to the Contractor (whose receipt shall be a good discharge to it) the said sum.

(d) If the Award and/or Interim Award(s) and/or Award on Appeal provides or provide that the costs of the Arbitration and/or of the Appeal Arbitration or any part of such costs shall be borne by the Contractor such costs may be deducted from the amount awarded or agreed before payment is made to the Contractor unless satisfactory security is provided by the Contractor for the payment of such costs.

LOF 1995

(e) Without prejudice to the provisions of clause 5(c) the liability of the Council shall be limited in any event to the amount of security provided to it.

GENERAL PROVISIONS

16. *Scope of Authority*: The Master or other person signing this Agreement on behalf of the property to be salved enters into this Agreement as agent for the vessel her cargo freight bunkers stores and any other property thereon and the respective Owners thereof and binds each (but not the one for the other or himself personally) to the due performance thereof.

17. *Notices*: Any Award notice authority order or other document signed by the Chairman of Lloyd's or any person authorised by the Council for the purpose shall be deemed to have been duly made or given by the Council and shall have the same force and effect in all respects as if it had been signed by every member of the Council.

18. *Sub-Contractor(s)*: The Contractor may claim salvage and enforce any Award or agreement made between the Contractor and the Owners against security provided under clause 5 or otherwise if any on behalf of any Sub-Contractors his or their Servants or Agents including Masters and members of the crews of vessels employed by him or by any Sub-Contractors in the services provided that he first provides a reasonably satisfactory indemnity to the Owners against all claims by or liabilities to the said persons.

19. *Inducements prohibited*: No person signing this Agreement or any party on whose behalf it is signed shall at any time or in any manner whatsoever offer provide make give or promise to provide demand or take any form of inducement for entering into this Agreement.

For and on behalf of the Contractor	For and on behalf of the Owners of property to be salved.
.... (To be signed by the Contractor personally or by the Master of the salving vessel or other person whose name is inserted in line 4 of this Agreement)	.... (To be signed by the Master or other person whose name is inserted in line 1 of this Agreement)

INTERNATIONAL CONVENTION ON SALVAGE 1989

[Articles 1, 6, 8 and 13–14 of the Convention are set out for information only.]

Appendix A—Salvage Documents

No. 2

LOF 2000

LLOYD'S

LLOYD'S STANDARD FORM OF
SALVAGE AGREEMENT
(APPROVED AND PUBLISHED BY THE COUNCIL OF LLOYD'S)

NO CURE - NO PAY

1. Name of the salvage Contractors:	2. Property to be salved.
	The vessel:
	her cargo freight bunkers stores and any other property thereon but excluding the personal effects or baggage of passengers master or crew
(referred to in this agreement as "the Contractors")	(referred to in this agreement as "the property")
3. Agreed place of safety:	4. Agreed currency of any arbitral award and security (if other than United States dollars)
5. Date of this agreement:	6. Place of agreement:
7. Is the Scopic Clause incorporated into this agreement? State alternative : Yes/No	
8. Person signing for and on behalf of the Contractors	9. Captain or other person signing for and on behalf of the property
Signature:	Signature:

A. **Contractors' basic obligation:** The Contractors identified in Box 1 hereby agree to use their best endeavours to salve the property specified in Box 2 and to take the property to the place stated in Box 3 or to such other place as may hereafter be agreed. If no place is inserted in Box 3 and in the absence of any subsequent agreement as to the place where the property is to be taken the Contractors shall take the property to a place of safety.

B. **Environmental protection:** While performing the salvage services the Contractors shall also use their best endeavours to prevent or minimise damage to the environment.

(continued on the reverse side)

LOF 2000

C. **Scopic Clause:** Unless the word "No" in Box 7 has been deleted this agreement shall be deemed to have been made on the basis that the Scopic Clause is not incorporated and forms no part of this agreement. If the word "No" is deleted in Box 7 this shall not of itself be construed as a notice invoking the Scopic Clause within the meaning of sub-clause 2 thereof.

D. **Effect of other remedies:** Subject to the provisions of the International Convention on Salvage 1989 as incorporated into English law ("the Convention") relating to special compensation and to the Scopic Clause if incorporated the Contractors' services shall be rendered and accepted as salvage services upon the principle of "no cure - no pay" and any salvage remuneration to which the Contractors become entitled shall not be diminished by reason of the exception to the principle of "no cure - no pay" in the form of special compensation or remuneration payable to the Contractors under a Scopic Clause.

E. **Prior services:** Any salvage services rendered by the Contractors to the property before and up to the date of this agreement shall be deemed to be covered by this agreement.

F. **Duties of property owners:** Each of the owners of the property shall cooperate fully with the Contractors. In particular:
   (i) the Contractors may make reasonable use of the vessel's machinery gear and equipment free of expense provided that the Contractors shall not unnecessarily damage abandon or sacrifice any property on board;
   (ii) the Contractors shall be entitled to all such information as they may reasonably require relating to the vessel or the remainder of the property provided such information is relevant to the performance of the services and is capable of being provided without undue difficulty or delay;
   (iii) the owners of the property shall co-operate fully with the Contractors in obtaining entry to the place of safety stated in Box 3 or agreed or determined in accordance with Clause A.

G. **Rights of termination:** When there is no longer any reasonable prospect of a useful result leading to a salvage reward in accordance with Convention Articles 12 and/or 13 either the owners of the vessel or the Contractors shall be entitled to terminate the services hereunder by giving reasonable prior written notice to the other.

H. **Deemed performance:** The Contractors' services shall be deemed to have been performed when the property is in a safe condition in the place of safety stated in Box 3 or agreed or determined in accordance with Clause A. For the purpose of this provision the property shall be regarded as being in safe condition notwithstanding that the property (or part thereof) is damaged or in need of maintenance if (i) the Contractors are not obliged to remain in attendance to satisfy the requirements of any port or harbour authority, governmental agency or similar authority and (ii) the continuation of skilled salvage services from the Contractors or other salvors is no longer necessary to avoid the property becoming lost or significantly further damaged or delayed.

I. **Arbitration and the LSSA Clauses:** The Contractors' remuneration and/or special compensation shall be determined by arbitration in London in the manner prescribed by Lloyd's Standard Salvage and Arbitration Clauses ("the LSSA Clauses") and Lloyd's Procedural Rules. The provisions of the LSSA Clauses and Lloyd's Procedural Rules are deemed to be incorporated in this agreement and form an integral part hereof. Any other difference arising out of this agreement or the operations hereunder shall be referred to arbitration in the same way.

J. **Governing law:** This agreement and any arbitration hereunder shall be governed by English law.

K. **Scope of authority:** The Master or other person signing this agreement on behalf of the property identified in Box 2 enters into this agreement as agent for the respective owners thereof and binds each (but not the one for the other or himself personally) to the due performance thereof.

L. **Inducements prohibited:** No person signing this agreement or any party on whose behalf it is signed shall at any time or in any manner whatsoever offer provide make give or promise to provide or demand or take any form of inducement for entering into this agreement.

IMPORTANT NOTICES:

1. **Salvage security.** As soon as possible the owners of the vessel should notify the owners of other property on board that this agreement has been made. If the Contractors are successful the owners of such property should note that it will become necessary to provide the Contractors with salvage security promptly in accordance with Clause 4 of the LSSA Clauses referred to in Clause I. The provision of General Average security does not relieve the salved interests of their separate obligation to provide salvage security to the Contractors.

2. **Incorporated provisons.** Copies of the Scopic Clause; the LSSA Clauses and Lloyd's Procedural Rules may be obtained from (i) the Contractors or (ii) the Salvage Arbitration Branch at Lloyd's, One Lime Street, London EC3M 7HA.

Tel.No. + 44(0)20 7327 5408

Fax No. +44(0)20 7327 6827

E-mail: lloyds-salvage@lloyds.com.

www.lloyds.com

15.1.08
3.12.24
13.10.26
12.4.50
10.6.53
20.12.67
23.2.72
21.5.80
5.9.90
1.1.95
1.9.2000

LLOYD'S

Appendix A—Salvage Documents

No. 3

LLOYD'S

LLOYD'S STANDARD FORM OF SALVAGE AGREEMENT

(APPROVED AND PUBLISHED BY THE COUNCIL OF LLOYD'S)

LLOYD'S STANDARD SALVAGE AND ARBITRATION CLAUSES

1. **INTRODUCTION**
   1.1. These clauses ("the LSSA Clauses") or any revision thereof which may be published with the approval of the Council of Lloyd's are incorporated into and form an integral part of every contract for the performance of salvage services undertaken on the terms of Lloyd's Standard Form of Salvage Agreement as published by the Council of Lloyd's and known as LOF 2000 ("the Agreement" which expression includes the LSSA clauses and Lloyd's Procedural Rules referred to in Clause 6).

   1.2. All notices communications and other documents required to be sent to the Council of Lloyd's should be sent to:

   Salvage Arbitration Branch
   Lloyd's
   One Lime Street
   London EC3M 7HA

   Tel: +44 (0) 20 7327 5408/5407/5849
   Fax: +44 (0) 20 7327 6827/5252
   E-mail: lloyds-salvage@lloyds.com

2. **OVERRIDING OBJECTIVE**
   In construing the Agreement or on the making of any arbitral order or award regard shall be had to the overriding purposes of the Agreement namely:

   (a) to seek to promote safety of life at sea and the preservation of property at sea and during the salvage operations to prevent or minimise damage to the environment;

   (b) to ensure that its provisions are operated in good faith and that it is read and understood to operate in a reasonably businesslike manner;

   (c) to encourage cooperation between the parties and with relevant authorities;

   (d) to ensure that the reasonable expectations of salvors and owners of salved property are met and

   (e) to ensure that it leads to a fair and efficient disposal of disputes between the parties whether amicably, by mediation or by arbitration within a reasonable time and at a reasonable cost.

3. **DEFINITIONS**
   In the Agreement and unless there is an express provision to the contrary:
   3.1. "award" includes an interim or provisional award and "appeal award" means any award including any interim or provisional award made by the Appeal Arbitrator appointed under clause 10.2.

   3.2. "personal effects or baggage" as referred to in Box 2 of the Agreement means those which the passenger, Master and crew member have in their cabin or are otherwise in their possession, custody or control and shall include any private motor vehicle accompanying a passenger and any personal effects or baggage in or on such vehicle.

   3.3. "Convention" means the International Convention on Salvage 1989 as enacted by section 224, Schedule II of the Merchant Shipping Act 1995 (and any amendment of either) and any term or expression in the Convention has the same meaning when used in the Agreement.

3.4. "Council" means the Council of Lloyd's

3.5. "days" means calendar days

3.6. "Owners" means the owners of the property referred to in box 2 of the Agreement

3.7. "owners of the vessel" includes the demise or bareboat charterers of that vessel.

3.8. "special compensation" refers to the compensation payable to salvors under Article 14 of the Convention.

3.9. "Scopic Clause" refers to the agreement made between (1) members of the International Salvage Union (2) the International Group of P&I Clubs and (3) certain property underwriters which first became effective on 1st August 1999 and includes any replacement or revision thereof. All references to the Scopic Clause in the Agreement shall be deemed to refer to the version of the Scopic Clause current at the date the Agreement is made.

4. **PROVISIONS AS TO SECURITY, MARITIME LIEN AND RIGHT TO ARREST**

4.1. The Contractors shall immediately after the termination of the services or sooner notify the Council and where practicable the Owners of the amount for which they demand salvage security (inclusive of costs expenses and interest) from each of the respective Owners.

4.2. Where a claim is made or may be made for special compensation the owners of the vessel shall on the demand of the Contractors whenever made provide security for the Contractors claim for special compensation provided always that such demand is made within 2 years of the date of termination of the services.

4.3. The security referred to in clauses 4.1. and 4.2. above shall be demanded and provided in the currency specified in Box 4 or in United States Dollars if no such alternative currency has been agreed.

4.4. The amount of any such security shall be reasonable in the light of the knowledge available to the Contractors at the time when the demand is made and any further facts which come to the Contractors' attention before security is provided. The arbitrator appointed under clause 5 hereof may, at any stage of the proceedings, order that the amount of security be reduced or increased as the case may be.

4.5. Unless otherwise agreed such security shall be provided (i) to the Council (ii) in a form approved by the Council and (iii) by persons firms or corporations either acceptable to the Contractors or resident in the United Kingdom and acceptable to the Council. The Council shall not be responsible for the sufficiency (whether in amount or otherwise) of any security which shall be provided nor the default or insolvency of any person firm or corporation providing the same.

4.6. The owners of the vessel including their servants and agents shall use their best endeavours to ensure that none of the property salved is released until security has been provided in respect of that property in accordance with clause 4.5.

4.7. Until security has been provided as aforesaid the Contractors shall have a maritime lien on the property salved for their remuneration.

4.8. Until security has been provided the property salved shall not without the consent in writing of the Contractors (which shall not be unreasonably withheld) be removed from the place to which it has been taken by the Contractors under clause A. Where such consent is given by the Contractors on condition that they are provided with temporary security pending completion of the voyage the Contractors maritime lien on the property salved shall remain in force to the extent necessary to enable the Contractors to compel the provision of security in accordance with clause 4.5.

4.9. The Contractors shall not arrest or detain the property salved unless:
 (i) security is not provided within 21 days after the date of the termination of the services or
 (ii) they have reason to believe that the removal of the property salved is contemplated contrary to clause 4.8. or
 (iii) any attempt is made to remove the property salved contrary to clause 4.8.

5. **APPOINTMENT OF ARBITRATOR**

5.1. Whether or not security has been provided the Council shall appoint an arbitrator ("the Arbitrator") upon receipt of a written request provided that any party requesting such appointment shall if required by the Council undertake to pay the reasonable fees and expenses of the Council including those of the Arbitrator and the Appeal Arbitrator.

5.2. The Arbitrator and the Council may charge reasonable fees and expenses for their services whether the arbitration proceeds to a hearing or not and all such fees and expenses shall be treated as part of the costs of the arbitration.

6. **ARBITRATION PROCEDURE AND ARBITRATORS POWERS**

6.1. The arbitration shall be conducted in accordance with the Procedural Rules approved by the Council ("Lloyd's Procedural Rules") in force at the time the Arbitrator is appointed.

6.2. The arbitration shall take place in London unless (i) all represented parties agree to some other place for the whole or part of the arbitration and (ii) any such agreement is approved by the Council on such terms as to the payment of the Arbitrator's travel and accommodation expenses as it may see fit to impose.

Appendix A—Salvage Documents

6.3. The Arbitrator shall have power in his absolute discretion to include in the amount awarded to the Contractors the whole or part of any expenses reasonably incurred by the Contractors in:
    (i) ascertaining demanding and obtaining the amount of security reasonably required in accordance with clause 4.5
    (ii) enforcing and/or protecting by insurance or otherwise or taking reasonable steps to enforce and/or protect their lien

6.4. The Arbitrator shall have power to make but shall not be bound to make a consent award between such parties as so consent with or without full arbitral reasons

6.5. The Arbitrator shall have power to make a provisional or interim award or awards including payments on account on such terms as may be fair and just

6.6. Awards in respect of salvage remuneration or special compensation (including payments on account) shall be made in the currency specified in Box 4 or in United States dollars if no such alternative currency has been agreed.

6.7. The Arbitrator's award shall (subject to appeal as provided in clause 10) be final and binding on all the parties concerned whether they were represented at the arbitration or not and shall be published by the Council in London.

7. REPRESENTATION OF PARTIES

7.1. Any party to the Agreement who wishes to be heard or to adduce evidence shall appoint an agent or representative ordinarily resident in the United Kingdom to receive correspondence and notices for and on behalf of that party and shall give written notice of such appointment to the Council.

7.2. Service on such agent or representative by post or facsimile shall be deemed to be good service on the party which has appointed that agent or representative.

7.3. Any party who fails to appoint an agent or representative as aforesaid shall be deemed to have renounced his right to be heard or adduce evidence.

8. INTEREST

8.1. Unless the Arbitrator in his discretion otherwise decides the Contractors shall be entitled to interest on any sums awarded in respect of salvage remuneration or special compensation (after taking into consideration any sums already paid to the Contractors on account) from the date of termination of the services until the date on which the award is published by the Council and at a rate to be determined by the Arbitrator.

8.2. In ordinary circumstances the Contractors' interest entitlement shall be limited to simple interest but the Arbitrator may exercise his statutory power to make an award of compound interest if the Contractors have been deprived of their salvage remuneration or special compensation for an excessive period as a result of the Owners gross misconduct or in other exceptional circumstances.

8.3. If the sum(s) awarded to the Contractors (including the fees and expenses referred to in clause 5.2) are not paid to the Contractors or to the Council by the payment date specified in clause 11.1 the Contractors shall be entitled to additional interest on such outstanding sums from the payment date until the date payment is received by the Contractors or the Council both dates inclusive and at a rate which the Arbitrator shall in his absolute discretion determine in his award.

9. CURRENCY CORRECTION

In considering what sums of money have been expended by the Contractors in rendering the services and/or in fixing the amount of the award and/or appeal award the Arbitrator or Appeal Arbitrator shall to such an extent and insofar as it may be fair and just in all the circumstances give effect to the consequences of any change or changes in the relevant rates of exchange which may have occurred between the date of termination of the services and the date on which the award or appeal award is made.

10. APPEALS AND CROSS APPEALS

10.1. Any party may appeal from an award by giving written Notice of Appeal to the Council provided such notice is received by the Council no later than 21 days after the date on which the award was published by the Council.

10.2. On receipt of a Notice of Appeal the Council shall refer the appeal to the hearing and determination of an appeal arbitrator of its choice ("the Appeal Arbitrator").

10.3. Any party who has not already given Notice of Appeal under clause 10.1 may give a Notice of Cross Appeal to the Council within 21 days of that party having been notified that the Council has received Notice of Appeal from another party.

10.4. Notice of Appeal or Cross Appeal shall be given to the Council by letter telex facsimile or in any other permanent form. Such notification if sent by post shall be deemed received on the working day following the day of posting.

10.5. If any Notice of Appeal or Notice of Cross Appeal is withdrawn prior to the hearing of the appeal arbitration, that appeal arbitration shall nevertheless proceed for the purpose of determining any matters which remain outstanding.

10.6. The Appeal Arbitrator shall conduct the appeal arbitration in accordance with Lloyd's Procedural Rules so far as applicable to an appeal.

10.7. In addition to the powers conferred on the Arbitrator by English law and the Agreement, the Appeal Arbitrator shall have power to:
    (i) admit the evidence or information which was before the Arbitrator together with the Arbitrator's Notes and Reasons for his award, any transcript of evidence and such additional evidence or information as he may think fit;
    (ii) confirm increase or reduce the sum(s) awarded by the Arbitrator and to make such order as to the payment of interest on such sum(s) as he may think fit;
    (iii) confirm revoke or vary any order and/or declaratory award made by the Arbitrator;
    (iv) award interest on any fees and expenses charged under clause 10.8 from the expiration of 28 days after the date of publication by the Council of the Appeal Arbitrator's award until the date payment is received by the Council both dates inclusive.

LSSAC 2000

10.8. The Appeal Arbitrator and the Council may charge reasonable fees and expenses for their services in connection with the appeal arbitration whether it proceeds to a hearing or not and all such fees and expenses shall be treated as part of the costs of the appeal arbitration.

10.9. The Appeal Arbitrator's award shall be published by the Council in London.

11. PROVISIONS AS TO PAYMENT

11.1. When publishing the award the Council shall call upon the party or parties concerned to pay all sums due from them which are quantified in the award (including the fees and expenses referred to in clause 5.2) not later than 28 days after the date of publication of the award ("the payment date")

11.2. If the sums referred to in clause 11.1 (or any part thereof) are not paid within 56 days after the date of publication of the award (or such longer period as the Contractors may allow) and provided the Council has not received Notice of Appeal or Notice of Cross Appeal the Council shall realise or enforce the security given to the Council under clause 4.5 by or on behalf of the defaulting party or parties subject to the Contractors providing the Council with any indemnity the Council may require in respect of the costs the Council may incur in that regard.

11.3. In the event of an appeal and upon publication by the Council of the appeal award the Council shall call upon the party or parties concerned to pay the sum(s) awarded. In the event of non-payment and subject to the Contractors providing the Council with any costs indemnity required as referred to in clause 11.2 the Council shall realise or enforce the security given to the Council under clause 4.5 by or on behalf of the defaulting party.

11.4. If any sum(s) shall become payable to the Contractors in respect of salvage remuneration or special compensation (including interest and/or costs) as the result of an agreement made between the Contractors and the Owners or any of them, the Council shall, if called upon to do so and subject to the Contractors providing to the Council any costs indemnity required as referred to in clause 11.2 realise or enforce the security given to the Council under clause 4.5 by or on behalf of that party.

11.5. Where (i) no security has been provided to the Council in accordance with clause 4.5 or (ii) no award is made by the Arbitrator or the Appeal Arbitrator (as the case may be) because the parties have been able to settle all matters in issue between them by agreement the Contractors shall be responsible for payment of the fees and expenses referred to in clause 5.2 and (if applicable) clause 10.8. Payment of such fees and expenses shall be made to the Council within 28 days of the Contractors or their representatives receiving the Council's invoice failing which the Council shall be entitled to interest on any sum outstanding at UK Base Rate prevailing on the date of the invoice plus 2% per annum until payment is received by the Council.

11.6. If an award or appeal award directs the Contractors to pay any sum to any other party or parties including the whole or any part of the costs of the arbitration and/or appeal arbitration the Council may deduct from sums received by the Council on behalf of the Contractors the amount(s) so payable by the Contractors unless the Contractors provide the Council with satisfactory security to meet their liability.

11.7. Save as aforesaid all sums received by the Council pursuant to this clause shall be paid by the Council to the Contractors or their representatives whose receipt shall be a good discharge to it.

11.8. Without prejudice to the provisions of clause 4.5 the liability of the Council shall be limited to the amount of security provided to it.

GENERAL PROVISIONS

12. **Lloyd's documents:** Any award notice authority order or other document signed by the Chairman of Lloyd's or any person authorised by the Council for the purpose shall be deemed to have been duly made or given by the Council and shall have the same force and effect in all respects as if it had been signed by every member of the Council.

13. **Contractors personnel and subcontractors.**

    13.1. The Contractors may claim salvage on behalf of their employees and any other servants or agents who participate in the services and shall upon request provide the owners with a reasonably satisfactory indemnity against all claims by or liabilities to such employees servants or agents.

    13.2. The Contractors may engage the services of subcontractors for the purpose of fulfilling their obligations under clauses A and B of the Agreement but the Contractors shall nevertheless remain liable to the Owners for the due performance of those obligations.

    13.3. In the event that subcontractors are engaged as aforesaid the Contractors may claim salvage on behalf of the subcontractors including their employees servants or agents and shall, if called upon so to do provide the Owners with a reasonably satisfactory indemnity against all claims by or liabilities to such subcontractors their employees servants or agents.

14. **Disputes under Scopic Clause.**
    Any dispute arising out of the Scopic Clause (including as to its incorporation or invocation) or the operations thereunder shall be referred for determination to the Arbitrator appointed under clause 5 hereof whose award shall be final and binding subject to appeal as provided in clause 10 hereof.

15. **Lloyd's Publications.**
    Any guidance published by or on behalf of the Council relating to matters such as the Convention the workings and implementation of the Agreement is for information only and forms no part of the Agreement.

1.9.2000

LLOYD'S

Appendix A—Salvage Documents

No. 4

LLOYD'S

LLOYD'S STANDARD FORM OF SALVAGE AGREEMENT

(APPROVED AND PUBLISHED BY THE COUNCIL OF LLOYD'S)

PROCEDURAL RULES

(pursuant to Clause I of LOF 2000)

1. **Arbitrators Powers**

    In addition to all powers conferred by the Arbitration Act 1996 (or any amendment thereof) the Arbitrator shall have power:

    (a) to admit such oral or documentary evidence or information as he may think fit;

    (b) to conduct the arbitration in such manner in all respects as he may think fit subject to these Procedural Rules and any amendments thereto as may from time to time be approved by the Council of Lloyd's ("the Council");

    (c) to make such orders as to costs, fees and expenses including those of the Council charged under clauses 5.2 and 10.8 of the Lloyd's Standard Salvage and Arbitration Clauses ("the LSSA clauses") as may be fair and just;

    (d) to direct that the recoverable costs of the arbitration or of any part of the proceedings shall be limited to a specified amount;

    (e) to make any orders required to ensure that the arbitration is conducted in a fair and efficient manner consistent with the aim to minimise delay and expense and to arrange such meetings and determine all applications made by the parties as may be necessary for that purpose;

    (f) to conduct all such meetings by means of a conference telephone call if the parties agree;

    (g) on his own initiative or on the application of a party to correct any award (whether interim provisional or final) or to make an additional award in order to rectify any mistake error or omission provided that (i) any such correction is made within 28 days of the date of publication of the relevant award by the Council (ii) any additional award required is made within 56 days of the said date of publication or, in either case, such longer period as the Arbitrator may in his discretion allow.

2. **Preliminary Meeting**

    (a) Within 6 weeks of being appointed or so soon thereafter as may be reasonable in the circumstances, the Arbitrator shall convene a preliminary meeting with the represented parties for the purpose of giving directions as to the manner in which the arbitration is to be conducted.

    (b) The Arbitrator may dispense with the requirement for a preliminary meeting if the represented parties agree a consent order for directions which the Arbitrator is willing to approve. For the purpose of obtaining such approval, the Arbitrator must be provided by the contractors or their representatives with a brief summary of the case in the form of a check list, any other party providing such comments as they deem appropriate so that the Arbitrator is placed in a position to decide whether to approve the consent order.

    (c) In determining the manner in which the arbitration is to be conducted, the Arbitrator shall have regard to:

     (i) the interests of unrepresented parties;

     (ii) whether some form of shortened and/or simplified procedure is appropriate including whether the arbitration may be conducted on documents only with concise written submissions;

     (iii) the overriding objectives set out in clause 2 of the LSSA clauses.

3. **Order for Directions**

    Unless there are special reasons, the initial order for directions shall include:-

    (a) a date for disclosure of documents including witness statements (see Rule 4);

    (b) a date for proof of values;

LPR 2000

    (c) a date by which any party must identify any issue(s) in the case which are likely to necessitate the service of pleadings;

    (d) a date for a progress meeting or additional progress meetings unless all represented parties with reasonable notice agree that the same is unnecessary;

    (e) unless agreed by all represented parties to be premature, a date for the hearing and estimates for the time likely to be required by the Arbitrator to read evidence in advance and for the length of the hearing;

    (f) any other matters deemed by the Arbitrator or any party to be appropriate to be included in the initial order.

4. Disclosure of documents

Unless otherwise agreed or ordered, disclosure shall be limited to the following classes of document:

    (a) logs and any other contemporaneous records maintained by the shipowners personnel and personnel employed by the Contractors (including any subcontractors) and their respective surveyors or consultants in attendance during all or part of the salvage services;

    (b) working charts, photographs, video or film records;

    (c) contemporaneous reports including telexes, facsimile messages or prints of e- mail messages;

    (d) survey reports;

    (e) documents relevant to the proof of:
        (i) out of pocket expenses
        (ii) salved values
        (iii) the particulars and values of all relevant salving tugs or other craft and equipment

    (f) statements of witnesses of fact or other privileged documents on which the party wishes to rely.

5. Expert Evidence

    (a) No expert evidence shall be adduced in the arbitration without the Arbitrators permission.

    (b) The Arbitrator shall not give such permission unless satisfied that expert evidence is reasonably necessary for the proper determination of an issue arising in the arbitration.

    (c) No party shall be given permission to adduce evidence from more than one expert in each field requiring expert evidence save in exceptional circumstances.

    (d) Any application for permission to adduce expert evidence must be made at the latest within 14 days after disclosure of relevant documents has been effected.

6. Mediation

The Arbitrator shall ensure that in all cases the represented parties are informed of the benefit which might be derived from the use of mediation.

7. Hearing of Arbitration

    (a) In fixing or agreeing to a date for the hearing of an arbitration, the Arbitrator shall not unless agreed by all represented parties fix or accept a date unless the Arbitrator can allow time to read the principal evidence in advance, hear the arbitration and produce the award to the Council for publication in not more than 1 month from conclusion of the hearing.

    (b) The date fixed for the hearing shall be maintained unless application to alter the date is made to the Arbitrator within 14 days of the completion of discovery or unless the Arbitrator in the exercise of his discretion determines at a later time that an adjournment is necessary or desirable in the interests of justice or fairness.

    (c) Unless all parties represented in the arbitration agree otherwise the Arbitrator shall relinquish his appointment if a hearing date cannot be agreed, fixed or maintained in accordance with rule 7(a) and/or (b) above due to the Arbitrator's commitments. In that event the Council shall appoint in his stead another arbitrator who is able to meet the requirements of those rules.

8. Appeals

    (a) All references in these Rules to the Arbitrator shall include the Arbitrator on Appeal where the circumstances so permit.

    (b) In any case in which a party giving notice of appeal intends to contend that the Arbitrator's findings on the salved value of all or any of the salved property were erroneous, or that the Arbitrator has erred in any finding as to the person whose property was at risk, a statement of such grounds of appeal shall be given in or accompanying the notice of appeal.

    (c) In all cases grounds of appeal or cross-appeal will be given to the Arbitrator on Appeal within 21 days of the notice of appeal or cross- appeal unless an extension of time is agreed.

    (d) Any respondent to an appeal who intends to contend that the award of the Original Arbitrator should be affirmed on grounds other than those relied upon by the Original Arbitrator shall give notice to that effect specifying the grounds of his contention within 14 days of receipt of the grounds of appeal mentioned in (c) above unless an extension of time is agreed.

LLOYD'S

Appendix A—Salvage Documents

No. 5

SCOPIC 2000

SCOPIC CLAUSE

1. **General**
   This SCOPIC clause is supplementary to any Lloyd's Form Salvage Agreement "No Cure - No Pay" ("Main Agreement") which incorporates the provisions of Article 14 of the International Convention on Salvage 1989 ("Article 14"). The definitions in the Main Agreement are incorporated into this SCOPIC clause. If the SCOPIC clause is inconsistent with any provisions of the Main Agreement or inconsistent with the law applicable hereto, the SCOPIC clause, once invoked under sub-clause 2 hereof, shall override such other provisions to the extent necessary to give business efficacy to the agreement. Subject to the provisions of Clause 4 hereof, the method of assessing Special Compensation under Convention Article 14(1) to 14(4) inclusive shall be submitted by the method of assessment set out hereinafter. If this SCOPIC clause has been incorporated into the Main Agreement the Contractor may make no claim pursuant to Article 14 except in the circumstances described in sub-clause 4 hereof. For the purposes of liens and time limits the services hereunder will be treated in the same manner as salvage.

2. **Invoking the SCOPIC Clause**
   The Contractor shall have the option to invoke by written notice to the owners of the vessel the SCOPIC clause set out hereafter at any time of his choosing regardless of the circumstances and, in particular, regardless of whether or not there is a "threat of damage to the environment". The assessment of SCOPIC remuneration shall commence from the time the written notice is given to the owners of the vessel and services rendered before the said written notice shall not be remunerated under this SCOPIC clause at all but in accordance with Convention Article 13 as incorporated into the Main Agreement ("Article 13").

3. **Security for SCOPIC Remuneration**
   (i) The owners of the vessel shall provide to the Contractor within 2 working days (excluding Saturdays and Sundays and holidays usually observed at Lloyd's) after receiving written notice from the contractor invoking the SCOPIC clause, a bank guarantee or P&I Club letter (hereinafter called "the Initial Security") in a form reasonably satisfactory to the Contractor providing security for his claim for SCOPIC remuneration in the sum of US$3 million, inclusive of interest and costs.
   (ii) If, at any time after the provision of the Initial Security the owners of the vessel reasonably assess the SCOPIC remuneration plus interest and costs due hereunder to be less than the security in place, the owners of the vessel shall be entitled to require the Contractor to reduce the security to a reasonable sum and the Contractor shall be obliged to do so once a reasonable sum has been agreed.
   (iii) If at any time after the provision of the Initial Security the Contractor reasonably assesses the SCOPIC remuneration plus interest and costs due hereunder to be greater than the security in place, the Contractor shall be entitled to require the owners of the vessel to increase the security to a reasonable sum and the owners of the vessel shall be obliged to do so once a reasonable sum has been agreed.
   (iv) In the absence of agreement, any dispute concerning the proposed Guarantor, the form of the security or the amount of any reduction or increase in the security in place shall be resolved by the Arbitrator.

4. **Withdrawal**
   If the owners of the vessel do not provide the Initial Security within the said 2 working days, the Contractor, at his option, and on giving notice to the owners of the vessel, shall be entitled to withdraw from all the provisions of the SCOPIC clause and revert to his rights under the Main Agreement including Article 14 which shall apply as if the SCOPIC clause had not existed. PROVIDED THAT this right of withdrawal may only be exercised if, at the time of giving the said notice of withdrawal the owners of the vessel have still not provided the Initial Security or any alternative security which the owners of the vessel and the Contractor may agree will be sufficient.

5. **Tariff Rates**
   (i) SCOPIC remuneration shall mean the total of the tariff rates of personnel; tugs and other craft; portable salvage equipment; out of pocket expenses; and bonus due.
   (ii) SCOPIC remuneration in respect of all personnel; tugs and other craft; and portable salvage equipment shall be assessed on a time and materials basis in accordance with the Tariff set out in Appendix "A". This tariff will apply until reviewed and amended by the SCR Committee in accordance with Appendix B(1)(b). The tariff rates which will be used to calculate SCOPIC remuneration are those in force at the time the salvage services take place.
   (iii) "Out of pocket" expenses shall mean all those monies reasonably paid by or for and on behalf of the Contractor to any third party and in particular includes the hire of men, tugs, other craft and equipment used and other expenses reasonably necessary for the operation. They will be agreed at cost, PROVIDED THAT:
   (a) If the expenses relate to the hire of men, tugs, other craft and equipment from another ISU member or their affiliate(s), the amount due will be calculated on the tariff rates set out in Appendix "A" regardless of the actual cost.
   (b) If men, tugs, other craft and equipment are hired from any party who is not an ISU member and the hire rate is greater than the tariff rates referred to in Appendix "A" the actual cost will be allowed in full, subject to the Shipowner's Casualty Representative ("SCR") being satisfied that in the particular circumstances of the case, it was reasonable for the Contractor to hire such items at that cost. If an SCR is not appointed or if there is a dispute, then the Arbitrator shall decide whether the expense was reasonable in all in the circumstances.
   (iv) In addition to the rates set out above and any out of pocket expenses, the Contractor shall be entitled to a standard bonus of 25% of those rates except that if the out of pocket expenses described in sub-paragraph 5(iii)(b) exceed the applicable tariff rates in Appendix "A" the Contractor shall be entitled to a bonus such that he shall receive in total
   (a) The actual cost of such men, tugs, other craft and equipment plus 10% of that rate, or
   (b) The tariff rate for such men, tugs, other craft and equipment plus 25% of the tariff rate
   whichever is the greater.

6. **Article 13 Award**
   (i) The salvage services under the Main Agreement shall continue to be assessed in accordance with Article 13, even if the Contractor has invoked the SCOPIC clause. SCOPIC remuneration as assessed under sub-clause 5 above will be payable only by the owners of the vessel and only to the extent that it exceeds the total Article 13 Award (or, if none, any potential Article 13 Award) payable by all salved interests (including cargo, bunkers, lubricating oil and stores) after currency adjustment but before interest and costs even if the Article 13 Award or any part of it is not recovered.

1.8.1999
1.9.2000

SCOPIC 2000

(ii) In the event of the Article 13 Award or settlement being in a currency other than United States dollars it shall, for the purposes of the SCOPIC clause, be exchanged at the rate of exchange prevailing at the termination of the services under the Main Agreement.
(iii) The salvage award under Article 13 shall not be diminished by reason of the exception to the principle of "No Cure - No Pay" in the form of SCOPIC remuneration.

7. Discount
If the SCOPIC clause is invoked under sub-clause 2 hereof and the Article 13 Award or settlement (after currency adjustment but before interest and costs) under the Main Agreement is greater than the assessed SCOPIC remuneration then, notwithstanding the actual date on which the SCOPIC remuneration provisions were invoked, the said Article 13 Award or settlement shall be discounted by 25% of the difference between the said Article 13 Award or settlement and the amount of SCOPIC remuneration that would have been assessed had the SCOPIC remuneration provisions been invoked on the first day of the services.

8. Payment of SCOPIC Remuneration
(i) The date for payment of any SCOPIC remuneration which may be due hereunder will vary according to the circumstances.
  (a) If there is no potential salvage award within the meaning of Article 13 as incorporated into the Main Agreement then, subject to Appendix B(5)(c)(iv), the undisputed amount of SCOPIC remuneration due hereunder will be paid by the owners of the vessel within 1 month of the presentation of the claim. Interest on sums due will accrue from the date of termination of the services until the date of payment at US prime rate plus 1%.
  (b) If there is a claim for an Article 13 salvage award as well as a claim for SCOPIC remuneration, subject to Appendix B(5)(c)(iv), 75% of the amount by which the assessed SCOPIC remuneration exceeds the total Article 13 security demanded from ship and cargo will be paid by the owners of the vessel within 1 month and any undisputed balance paid when the Article 13 salvage award has been assessed and falls due. Interest will accrue from the date of termination of the services until the date of payment at the US prime rate plus 1%.
(ii) The Contractor hereby agrees to give an indemnity in a form acceptable to the owners of the vessel in respect of any overpayment in the event that the SCOPIC remuneration due ultimately proves to be less than the sum paid on account.

9. Termination
(i) The Contractor shall be entitled to terminate the services under this SCOPIC clause and the Main Agreement by written notice to owners of the vessel with a copy to the SCR (if any) and any Special Representative appointed if the total cost of his services to date and the services that will be needed to fulfil his obligations hereunder to the property (calculated by means of the tariff rate but before the bonus conferred by sub-clause 5(iii) hereof) will exceed the sum of:-
  (a) The value of the property capable of being salved; and
  (b) All sums to which he will be entitled as SCOPIC remuneration
(ii) The owners of the vessel may at any time terminate the obligation to pay SCOPIC remuneration after the SCOPIC clause has been invoked under sub-clause 2 hereof provided that the Contractor shall be entitled to at least 5 clear days' notice of such termination. In the event of such termination the assessment of SCOPIC remuneration shall take into account all monies due under the tariff rates set out in Appendix A hereof including time for demobilisation to the extent that such time did reasonably exceed the 5 days' notice of termination.
(iii) The termination provisions contained in sub-clause 9(i) and 9(ii) above shall only apply if the Contractor is not restrained from demobilising his equipment by Government, Local or Port Authorities or any other officially recognised body having jurisdiction over the area where the services are being rendered.

10. Duties of Contractor
The duties and liabilities of the Contractor shall remain the same as under the Main Agreement, namely to use his best endeavours to salve the vessel and property thereon and in so doing to prevent or minimise damage to the environment.

11. Shipowner's Casualty Representative ("SCR")
Once this SCOPIC clause has been invoked in accordance with sub-clause 2 hereof the owners of the vessel may at their sole option appoint an SCR to attend the salvage operation in accordance with the terms and conditions set out in Appendix B.

12. Special Representatives
At any time after the SCOPIC clause has been invoked the Hull and Machinery underwriter (or, if more than one, the lead underwriter) and one owner or underwriter of all or part of any cargo on board the vessel may each appoint one special representative (hereinafter called respectively the "Special Hull Representative" and the "Special Cargo Representative" and collectively called the "Special Representatives") at the sole expense of the appointor to attend the casualty to observe and report upon the salvage operation on the terms and conditions set out in Appendix C hereof. Such Special Representatives shall be technical men and not practising lawyers.

13. Pollution Prevention
The assessment of SCOPIC remuneration shall include the prevention of pollution as well as the removal of pollution in the immediate vicinity of the vessel insofar as this is necessary for the proper execution of the salvage but not otherwise.

14. General Average
SCOPIC remuneration shall not be a General Average expense to the extent that it exceeds the Article 13 Award; any liability to pay such SCOPIC remuneration shall be that of the Shipowner alone and no claim whether direct, indirect, by way of indemnity or recourse or otherwise relating to SCOPIC remuneration in excess of the Article 13 Award shall be made in General Average or under the vessel's Hull and Machinery Policy by the owners of the vessel.

15. Any dispute arising out of this SCOPIC clause or the operations thereunder shall be referred to Arbitration as provided for under the Main Agreement.

Appendix A—Salvage Documents

No. 5A

SCOPIC 2000

APPENDIX A (SCOPIC)

1. **PERSONNEL**

    (a) The daily tariff rate, or pro rata for part thereof, for personnel reasonably engaged on the contract, including any necessary time in proceeding to and returning from the casualty, shall be as follows:

Office administration, including communications	US$ 1,000
Salvage Master	US$ 1,500
Naval Architect or Salvage Officer/Engineer	US$ 1,250
Assistant Salvage Officer/Engineer	US$ 1,000
Diving Supervisor	US$ 1,000
Diver	US$ 750
Salvage Foreman	US$ 750
Riggers, Fitters, Equipment Operators	US$ 600
Specialist Advisors – Fire Fighters, Chemicals, Pollution Control	US$ 1,000

    (b) The crews of tugs, and other craft, normally aboard that tug or craft for the purpose of its customary work are included in the tariff rate for that tug or craft but when because of the nature and/or location of the services to be rendered, it is a legal requirement for an additional crew member or members to be aboard the tug or craft, the cost of such additional crew will be paid.

    (c) The rates for any personnel not set out above shall be agreed with the SCR or, failing agreement, be determined by the Arbitrator.

    (d) For the avoidance of doubt, personnel are "reasonably engaged on the contract" within the meaning of Appendix A sub-clause 1(a) hereof if, in addition to working, they are eating, sleeping or otherwise resting on site or travelling to or from the site; personnel who fall ill or are injured while reasonably engaged on the contract shall be charged for at the appropriate daily tariff rate until they are demobilised but only if it was reasonable to mobilise them in the first place.

    (e) SCOPIC remuneration shall cease to accrue in respect of personnel who die on site from the date of death.

2. **TUGS AND OTHER CRAFT**

    (a) (i) Tugs, which shall include salvage tugs, harbour tugs, anchor handling tugs, coastal/ocean towing tugs, off-shore support craft, and any other work boat in excess of 500 b.h.p., shall be charged at the following rates, exclusive of fuel or lubricating oil, for each day, or pro rata for part thereof, that they are reasonably engaged in the services, including proceeding towards the casualty from the tugs' location when SCOPIC is invoked or when the tugs are mobilised (whichever is the later) and from the tugs' position when their involvement in the services terminates to a reasonable location having due regard to their employment immediately prior to their involvement in the services and standing by on the basis of their certificated b.h.p.:

For each b.h.p. up to 5,000 b.h.p.	US$ 2.00
For each b.h.p. between 5,001 & 10,000 b.h.p.	US$ 1.50
For each b.h.p. between 10,001 & 20,000 b.h.p.	US$ 1.00
For each b.h.p. over 20,000 b.h.p.	US$ 0.50

    (ii) Any tug which has aboard certified fire fighting equipment shall, in addition to the above rates, be paid:

    US$500 per day, or pro rata for part thereof, if equipped with Fi Fi 0.5
    US$1,000 per day, or pro rata for part thereof, if equipped with Fi Fi 1.0

    for that period in which the tug is engaged in fire fighting necessitating the use of the certified fire fighting equipment.

    (iii) Any tug which is certified as "Ice Class" shall, in addition to the above, be paid US$1,000 per day, or pro rata for part thereof, when forcing or breaking ice during the course of services including proceeding to and returning from the casualty.

    (iv) For the purposes of paragraph 2(a)(i) hereof tugs shall be remunerated for any reasonable delay or deviation for the purposes of taking on board essential salvage equipment, provisions or personnel which the Contractor reasonably anticipates he shall require in rendering the services which would not normally be found on vessels of the tugs size and type.

    (b) Any launch or work boat of less than 500 b.h.p. shall, exclusive of fuel and lubricating oil, be charged at a rate of US$3.00 for each b.h.p.

    (c) Any other craft, not falling within the above definitions, shall be charged out at a market rate for that craft, exclusive of fuel and lubricating oil, such rate to be agreed with the SCR or, failing agreement, determined by the Arbitrator.

    (d) All fuel and lubricating oil consumed during the services shall be paid at cost of replacement and shall be treated as an out of pocket expense.

    (e) For the avoidance of doubt, the above rates shall not include any portable salvage equipment normally aboard the tug or craft and such equipment shall be treated in the same manner as portable salvage equipment and the Contactors shall be remunerated in respect thereof in accordance with Appendix A paragraphs 3 and 4 (i) and (ii) hereof.

1.8.1999
1.9.2000

P.T.O.

SCOPIC 2000 Appendix A

(f) SCOPIC remuneration shall cease to accrue in respect of tugs and other craft which become a commercial total loss from the date they stop being engaged in the services plus a reasonable period for demobilisation (if appropriate) PROVIDED that such SCOPIC remuneration in respect of demobilisation shall only be payable if the commercial total loss arises whilst engaged in the services and through no fault of the Contractors, their servants, agents or sub-contractors.

3. **PORTABLE SALVAGE EQUIPMENT**

(a) The daily tariff, or pro rata for part thereof, for all portable salvage equipment reasonably engaged during the services, including any time necessary for mobilisation and demobilisation, shall be as follows:

Generators		Rate – US$
Up to 50 kW		60
51 to 100 kW		125
101 to 300 kW		200
Over 301 kW		350

Portable Inert Gas Systems		
1,000m³/hour		1,200
1,500m³/hour		1,400

Compressors		
High Pressure		100
185 Cfm		150
600 Cfm		250
1200 Cfm		400
Air Manifold		10
Blower; 1,500m³/min.		850

Pumping Equipment		
Air		
2"		75
Diesel		
2"		50
4"		90
6"		120
Electrical Submersible		
2"		50
4"		150
6"		500
Hydraulic		
6"		600
8"		1,000

Hoses		
Air Hose		
¾"per	30 metres or 100 feet	20
2"per	30 metres or 100 feet	40
Layflat		
2"	per 6 metres or 20 feet	10
4"	per 6 metres or 20 feet	15
6"	per 6 metres or 20 feet	20
Rigid		
2"	per 6 metres or 20 feet	15
4"	per 6 metres or 20 feet	20
6"	per 6 metres or 20 feet	25
8"	per 6 metres or 20 feet	30

Fenders		
Yokohama		
1.00m. x 2.00m.		75
2.50m. x 5.50m.		150
3.50m. x 6.50m.		250
Low Pressure Inflatable		
3 metres		70
6 metres		70
9 metres		150
12 metres		250
16 metres		250

Welding & Cutting Equipment		Rate – US$
Bolt Gun		300
Gas Detector		100
Hot Tap Machine, including supporting equipment		1,000
Oxy-acetylene Surface Cutting Gear		25
Underwater Cutting Gear		50
Underwater Welding Kit		50
250 Amp Welder		150
400 Amp Welder		200

Pollution Control Equipment		
Oil Boom, 24", per 10 metres		30
Oil Boom, 36", per 10 metres		100
Oil Boom, 48", per 10 metres		195

Lighting Systems		
Lighting String, per 50 feet		25
Light Tower		50
Underwater Lighting System, 1,000 watts		75

Winches		
Up to 20 tons, including 50 metres of wire		200

Storage Equipment		
10' Container		25
20' Container		40

Miscellaneous Equipment		
Air Bags, less than 5 tons lift		40
5 to 15 tons lift		200
Air Lift 4"		100
6"		200
8"		300
Air Tugger, up to 3 tons		75
Ballast/Fuel Oil Storage Bins, 50,000 litres		100
Chain Saw		20
Damage Stability Computer and Software		250
Echo Sounder, portable		25
Extension Ladder		20
Hydraulic Jack, up to 100 tons		75
Hydraulic Powerpack		75
Pressure washer,	water	250
	steam	450
Rigging Package,	heavy	400
	Light	200
Rock,	Drill	50
	Splitter	400
Steel Saw		20
Tirfors, up to 5 tonnes		10
Thermal Imaging Camera		250
Tool Package, per set		175
Ventilation Package		20
VHF Radio		10
Z Boat, including outboard up to 14 feet		200
	over 14 feet	350

Appendix A—Salvage Documents

Shackles	Rate – US$.	Protective Clothing	Rate – US$.
Up to 50 tonnes	10	Breathing Gear.	50
51 to 100 tonnes	20	Hazardous Environment Suit	100
101 to 200 tonnes	30		
Over 200 tonnes	50	**Diving Equipment**	
		Decompression Chamber,	
Distribution Boards		2 man, including compressor	500
Up to 50 kW	60	4 man, including compressor	700
51 to 100 kW	125	Hot Water Diving Assembly	250
101 to 300 kW	200	Underwater Magnets	20
Over 301 kW	350	Underwater Drill	20
		Shallow Water Dive Spread	225

(b) Any portable salvage equipment engaged but not set out above shall be charged at a rate to be agreed with the SCR or, failing agreement, determined by the Arbitrator.

(c) The total charge (before bonus) for each item of portable salvage equipment, owned by the contractor, shall not exceed the manufacturer's recommended retail price on the last day of the services multiplied by 1.5.

(d) Compensation for any portable salvage equipment lost or destroyed during the services shall be paid provided that the total of such compensation and the daily tariff rate (before bonus) in respect of that item do not exceed the actual cost of replacing the item at the Contractors' base with the most similar equivalent new item multiplied by 1.5.

(e) All consumables such as welding rods, boiler suits, small ropes etc. shall be charged at cost and shall be treated as an out of pocket expense.

(f) The Contractor shall be entitled to remuneration at a stand-by rate of 50% of the full tariff rate plus bonus for any portable salvage equipment reasonably mobilised but not used during the salvage operation provided

    (i) It has been mobilised with the prior agreement of the owner of the vessel or its mobilisation was reasonable in the circumstances of the casualty, or

    (ii) It comprises portable salvage equipment normally aboard the tug or craft that would have been reasonably mobilised had it not already been aboard the tug or craft.

(g) SCOPIC remuneration shall cease to accrue in respect of portable salvage equipment which becomes a commercial total loss from the date it ceases to be useable plus a reasonable period for demobilisation (if appropriate) PROVIDED that such SCOPIC remuneration in respect of demobilisation shall only be payable if the commercial total loss arises while it is engaged in the services and through no fault of the Contractors, their servants, agents or sub-contractors.

4. **DOWNTIME**

If a tug or piece of portable salvage equipment breaks down or is damaged without fault on the part of the Contractor, his servants, agents or sub-contractors and as a direct result of performing the services it should be paid for during the repair while on site at the stand-by rate of 50% of the tariff rate plus uplift pursuant to sub-clause 5(iv) of the SCOPIC clause.
If a tug or piece of portable salvage equipment breaks down or otherwise becomes inoperable without fault on the part of the Contractor, his servants, agents or sub-contractors and as a direct result of performing the services and cannot be repaired on site then:

(a) If it is not used thereafter but remains on site then no SCOPIC remuneration is payable in respect of that tug or piece of portable salvage equipment from the time of the breakdown.

(b) If it is removed from site, repaired and reasonably returned to the site for use SCOPIC remuneration at the standby rate of 50% of the tariff rate plus bonus pursuant to sub-clause 5(iv) of the SCOPIC clause shall be payable from the breakdown to the date it is returned to the site.

(c) If it is removed from the site and not returned SCOPIC remuneration ceases from the breakdown but is, in addition, payable for the period that it takes to return it directly to base at the stand-by rate of 50% of the tariff rate plus bonus pursuant to sub-clause 5(iv) of the SCOPIC clause.

SCOPIC 2000 Appendix B

No. 5B

SCOPIC 2000

APPENDIX B (SCOPIC)

1. (a) The SCR shall be selected from a panel (the "SCR Panel") appointed by a Committee (the "SCR Committee") comprising of representatives appointed by the following:

    - 3 representatives from the International Group of P and I Clubs
    - 3 representatives from the ISU
    - 3 representatives from the IUMI
    - 3 representatives from the International Chamber of Shipping

    (b) The SCR Committee shall be responsible for an annual review of the tariff rates as set out in Appendix A.

    (c) The SCR Committee shall meet once a year in London to review, confirm, reconfirm or remove SCR Panel members.

    (d) Any individual may be proposed for membership of the SCR Panel by any member of the SCR Committee and shall be accepted for inclusion on the SCR Panel unless at least four votes are cast against his inclusion.

    (e) The SCR Committee shall also set and approve the rates of remuneration for the SCRs for the next year.

    (f) Members of the SCR Committee shall serve without compensation.

    (g) The SCR Committee's meetings and business shall be organised and administered by the Salvage Arbitration Branch of the Corporation of Lloyd's (hereinafter called "Lloyds") who will keep the current list of SCR Panel members and make it available to any person with a bona fide interest.

    (h) The SCR Committee shall be entitled to decide its own administrative rules as to procedural matters (such as quorums, the identity and power of the Chairman etc.)

2. The primary duty of the SCR shall be the same as the Contractor, namely to use his best endeavours to assist in the salvage of the vessel and the property thereon and in so doing to prevent and minimise damage to the environment.

3. The Salvage Master shall at all times remain in overall charge of the operation, make all final decisions as to what he thinks is best and remain responsible for the operation.

4. The SCR shall be entitled to be kept informed by or on behalf of the Salvage Master or (if none) the principal contractors' representative on site (hereinafter called "the Salvage Master"). The Salvage Master shall consult with the SCR during the operation if circumstances allow and the SCR, once on site, shall be entitled to offer the Salvage Master advice.

5. (a) Once the SCOPIC clause is invoked the Salvage Master shall send daily reports (hereinafter called the "Daily Salvage Reports") setting out:-

    - the salvage plan (followed by any changes thereto as they arise)
    - the condition of the casualty and the surrounding area (followed by any changes thereto as they arise)
    - the progress of the operation
    - the personnel, equipment, tugs and other craft used in the operation that day.

    (b) Pending the arrival of the SCR on site the Daily Salvage Reports shall be sent to Lloyd's and the owners of the vessel. Once the SCR has been appointed and is on site the Daily Salvage Reports shall be delivered to him.

01.8.1999
01.9.2000

P.T.O.

Appendix A—Salvage Documents

- (c) The SCR shall upon receipt of each Daily Salvage Report:-

    - (i) Transmit a copy of the Daily Salvage Report by the quickest method reasonably available to Lloyd's, the owners of the vessel, their liability insurers and (if any) to the Special Hull Representative and Special Cargo Representative (appointed under clause 12 of the SCOPIC clause and Appendix C) if they are on site; and if a Special Hull Representative is not on site the SCR shall likewise send copies of the Daily Salvage Reports direct to the leading Hull Underwriter or his agent (if known to the SCR) and if a Special Cargo Representative is not on site the SCR shall likewise send copies of the Daily Salvage Reports to such cargo underwriters or their agent or agents as are known to the SCR (hereinafter in this Appendix B such Hull and Cargo property underwriters shall be called "Known Property Underwriters").

    - (ii) If circumstances reasonably permit consult with the Salvage Master and endorse his Daily Salvage Report stating whether or not he is satisfied and

    - (iii) If not satisfied with the Daily Salvage Report, prepare a dissenting report setting out any objection or contrary view and deliver it to the Salvage Master and transmit it to Lloyd's, the owners of the vessel, their liability insurers and to any Special Representatives (appointed under clause 12 of the SCOPIC clause and Appendix C) or, if one or both Special Representatives has not been appointed, to the appropriate Known Property Underwriter.

    - (iv) If the SCR gives a dissenting report to the Salvage Master in accordance with Appendix B(5)(c)(iii) to the SCOPIC clause, any initial payment due for SCOPIC remuneration shall be at the tariff rate applicable to what is in the SCR's view the appropriate equipment or procedure until any dispute is resolved by agreement or arbitration.

- (d) Upon receipt of the Daily Salvage Reports and any dissenting reports of the SCR, Lloyd's shall distribute upon request the said reports to any parties to this contract and any of their property insurers of whom they are notified (hereinafter called "the Interested Persons") and to the vessel's liability insurers.

- (e) As soon as reasonably possible after the Salvage services terminate the SCR shall issue a report (hereinafter call the "SCR's Final Salvage Report") setting out:

    - the facts and circumstances of the casualty and the salvage operation insofar as they are known to him.
    - the tugs, personnel and equipment employed by the Contractor in performing the operation.
    - A calculation of the SCOPIC remuneration to which the contractor may be entitled by virtue of this SCOPIC clause.

    The SCR's Final Salvage Report shall be sent to the owners of the vessel and their liability insurers and to Lloyd's who shall forthwith distribute it to the Interested Persons.

6.
   - (a) The SCR may be replaced by the owner of the vessel if either:
       - (i) the SCR makes a written request for a replacement to the owner of the vessel (however the SCR should expect to remain on site throughout the services and should only expect to be substituted in exceptional circumstances); or
       - (ii) the SCR is physically or mentally unable or unfit to perform his duties; or
       - (iii) all salved interests or their representatives agree to the SCR being replaced.
   - (b) Any person who is appointed to replace the SCR may only be chosen from the SCR Panel.
   - (c) The SCR shall remain on site throughout the services while he remains in that appointment and until the arrival of any substitute so far as practicable and shall hand over his file and all other correspondence, computer data and papers concerning the salvage services to any substitute SCR and fully brief him before leaving the site.
   - (d) The SCR acting in that role when the services terminate shall be responsible for preparing the Final Salvage Report and shall be entitled to full co-operation from any previous SCRs or substitute SCRs in performing his functions hereunder.

7. The owners of the vessel shall be primarily responsible for paying the fees and expenses of the SCR. The Arbitrator shall have jurisdiction to apportion the fees and expenses of the SCR and include them in his award under the Main Agreement and, in doing so, shall have regard to the principles set out in any market agreement in force from time to time.

SCOPIC 2000 Appendix C

No. 5C

SCOPIC 2000

APPENDIX C (SCOPIC)
The Special Representatives

1. The Salvage Master, the owners of the vessel and the SCR shall co-operate with the Special Representatives and shall permit them to have full access to the vessel to observe the salvage operation and to inspect such of the ship's documents as are relevant to the salvage operation.

2. The Special Representative shall have the right to be informed of all material facts concerning the salvage operation as the circumstances reasonably allow.

3. If an SCR has been appointed the SCR shall keep the Special Representatives (if any and if circumstances permit) fully informed and shall consult with the said Special Representatives. The Special Representatives shall also be entitled to receive a copy of the Daily Salvage Reports direct from the Salvage Master or, if appointed, from the SCR.

4. The appointment of any Special Representatives shall not affect any right that the respondent ship and cargo interests may have (whether or not they have appointed a Special Representative) to send other experts or surveyors to the vessel to survey ship or cargo and inspect the ship's documentation or for any other lawful purpose.

5. If an SCR or Special Representative is appointed the Contractor shall be entitled to limit access to any surveyor or representative (other than the said SCR and Special Representative or Representatives) if he reasonably feels their presence will substantially impede or endanger the salvage operation.

01.8.1999
01.9.2000

Appendix A—Salvage Documents

No. 6

INTERNATIONAL SALVAGE UNION: LUMPSUM SUB-CONTRACT AGREEMENT "SALVCON"

1. Date and Place of Agreement:	INTERNATIONAL SALVAGE UNION: LUMPSUM SUB-CONTRACT AGREEMENT "SALVCON" PART I	
2. Hirer; Place of Business:	3. Owner; Place of Business: (Part II—Clause 1.3)	
4. Detail and Specification of Vessel hired under this Agreement; (Part II—Preamble and Clauses 1.2, 1.3 and 27).		
5. Name of Owner's P&I Association:		
6. Details of Casualty; (Part II—Preamble, Clauses 1.1, 8.1 and 8.3). a) Name: b) Flag: c) Place of Registry: d) Owners: e) Length: f) Beam: g) Maximum draft: h) Displacement: i) Details and Nature of Cargo: j) Any other Casualty's details relevant to this Agreement:		
7. Condition of Casualty; (Part II—Clause 3.1)		
8. Location of Casualty; (Part II—Clause 3.1)		
9. Nature of Services to be provided by the Owner; (Part II—Clauses 2, 3.1, 3.6, 8.1 and 12)		
INTERNATIONAL SALVAGE UNION: LUMPSUM SUB-CONTRACT AGREEMENT	"SALVON"	PART I

10. Payment Details; (Part II—Clauses 3.1, 3.2, 3.3 and 14.1)
 a) Lumpsum Price:
 b) Stage Payments; (i)
               (ii)
               (iii)		

11. Free Time; (Part II—Clause 4)		
12. Delay Payment Rates; (Part II—Clauses 3.5, 5 and 14.1 a) At Sea: b) In Port: c) At Anchor:		

13. Payment Details; (Part II—Clause 3.4) Currency: Bank: Address: Sort Code: Account Number: Account Name: Reference:	

14. Time for Payment and Interest; (Part II—Clause 15)   Monies not paid within   calendar days of presentation of the Owner's invoice shall attract interest of   percent per month.

15. Extra Costs; (Part II—Clause 16.2) Handling Charge of percent to be applied.	16. Security Requirements; (Part II—Clauses 3.7, 17.1 and 17.2)

17. Law and Arbitration; (Part II—Clauses 25 and 26)   Arbitration to take place at: If this Box left blank then Part II, Clause 25.1 shall apply.

18. Number of Additional Clauses:

The undersigned warrant that they have full power and authority to sign this Agreement on behalf of the parties represented by them. In the event of a conflict of terms and conditions, the provisions of Part I and any additional clauses, if agreed, shall prevail over those of Part II to the extent of such conflict but no further.

....

FOR AND ON BEHALF OF   FOR AND ON BEHALF
THE HIRER   OF THE OWNER

PART II

"Salvcon" International Salvage Union Agreement (Lump Sum)

WHEREAS the Hirer is engaged, or is about to become engaged, in rendering salvage services to the casualty described in Box 6, Part I of this Agreement,

AND WHEREAS the Hirer wishes to hire from the Owner, the vessel described in Box 4, Part I of this Agreement.

NOW IT IS HEREBY AGREED that the terms and conditions of Parts I and II of this Agreement, and any additional clauses and/or annexes hereto shall apply, as follows:

1. Definitions

(a) The term "Casualty" shall include any vessel, craft, property, or part thereof, of whatsoever nature, including anything contained therein or thereon, such as but not limited to cargo and bunkers, as described in Box 6, Part I of this Agreement, in respect of which the Hirer is contracted to render salvage services.

Appendix A—Salvage Documents

(b) The Term "Vessel", in Box 4 of Part I, and in Part II of this Agreement, shall include, but not be limited to, harbour tugs, offshore/diving support vessels, anchor handling/supply tugs, salvage/ocean going tugs, floating cranes/sheerlegs, barges and any other vessel, and/or any substitute vessel provided under Clause 13 of this Agreement.

(c) The term "Owner", in Box 3, Part I and in Part II of this Agreement, shall include any Owner, Manager, Operator or Charterer of the vessel described in Box 4, Part I of this Agreement.

2. Nature of Services to be Provided by the Owner

The services to be provided by the Owner are set out in Box 9, Part I of this Agreement, and/or in any accompanying Annexe.

3. Price and Conditions of Payment

(a) The Hirer shall pay the Owner the sum set out in Box 10, Part I of this Agreement, (hereinafter referred to as the "Lumpsum"). The lumpsum price is based upon the condition of the casualty, the location of the casualty and the nature of the services to be provided as set out in Boxes 7, 8 and 9, Part I of this Agreement, and any Annexe(s) to this Agreement.

(b) The Lumpsum shall be payable as set out in Box 10(b), Part I of this Agreement.

(c) The Lumpsum and all other sums payable to the Owner under this Agreement shall be payable without any discount, deduction, set-off, lien, claim or counter claim, each instalment of the Lumpsum shall be fully and irrevocably earned at the moment it is due as set out in Box 10, Part I of this Agreement, vessel and or casualty lost or not lost, and all other sums shall be fully and irrevocably earned on a daily basis.

(d) All payments by the Hirer shall be made in the currency and to the bank account specified in Box 13, Part I of this Agreement.

(e) Any delay payment due under this Agreement, as set out in Box 12 of Part I of this Agreement, shall be paid to the Owner as and when earned on presentation of the invoice.

(f) Within 14 days of termination or completion of the Services set out in Box 9, Part I of this Agreement, and/or any Annexe(s) hereto, the Owner shall return any overpayments to the Hirer.

(g) If any amount payable under this Agreement has not been paid within seven, (7), calendar days of the due date, or if the security required in accordance with Box 16, Part I of this Agreement and Clause 17 below, is not provided within five, (5), banking days of the request by the Owner, then at any time thereafter the Owner shall be entitled to terminate this Agreement without prejudice to the sums already due from the Hirer and to any further rights or remedies which the Owner may have against the Hirer. Provided always that the Owner shall give the Hirer at least three, (3), working days notice of its intention to exercise this right.

4. Free Time

The Owner will set out in Box 11, Part I of this Agreement the amount of free time allowed to the Hirer within his lumpsum price, and the specific purposes for which this free time may be utilised.

ISU Lumpsum Sub-Contract (Salvcon)

5. Delay Payments

The Owner will also set out in Box 12 of Part I of this Agreement, the delay payment rates to be applied and the circumstances when such delay payments will be applicable.

6. Employment and Area of Operations

The Vessel shall be employed in activities which are lawful in accordance with the law of the place of the vessel's flag and of the place of operations. Such place of operations shall always be within Institute Warranty Limits which shall not be exceeded without the prior written approval of the Owners, and any necessary adjustment to the rate of hire. The hirer does not warrant the safety of the place of operations, or any other port or place to which they direct the vessel, but they will exercise care in issuing orders to the vessel, as if the vessel were their own property. (See also Clause 8.1 hereof).

7. Master and Crew

(a) The Master shall carry out his duties promptly and the vessel shall perform these services by day and by night in accordance with the Hirer's requirements.

(b) The navigation and management of the vessel shall be in the exclusive control and command of its Owners, Master and Crew.

8. The Owner's Obligations

(a) The Owner agrees to render the services set out in Box 9, Part I of this Agreement, or as otherwise reasonably requested by the Hirer during the services to the casualty identified in Box 6, Part I of this Agreement, and shall, subject to the provisions of Clause 6 hereof, carry out the reasonable instructions of the Hirer in relation to such services.

(b) Insofar as it is not inconsistent with the nature of the services to be rendered under this Agreement, the Owner and his Master and crew will exercise due care to prevent or minimise damage to the environment.

(c) The Owner accepts that the services to be rendered pursuant to this Agreement are in the nature of salvage services to the casualty identified in Box 6, Part I of this Agreement.

(d) In consideration of the payment of the sums due under this Agreement, the Owner confirms that neither, he, nor any of his servants or agents, nor any of his sub-contractors or their servants or agents, will make any claim for salvage and/or special compensation against the casualty, the subject of salvage services by the Hirer, or against any other property in the same ownership as the said casualty.

(e) The Owner further agrees to indemnify the Hirer against the consequences of any such salvage claim by any of his servants or agents or his sub-contractors or their servants or agents, including interest and costs reasonably incurred in respect of such claim, provided that the Hirer gives notice in writing of such claim to the Owner as soon as they become aware of same. See Clause 17.3 hereof.

9. Hirer's Representative

A representative of the Hirer, who will be in operational control of the services with full authority to act on behalf of the Hirer, will be available during the salvage operations on the casualty.

Appendix A—Salvage Documents

10. Permits

The Hirer shall obtain and maintain at its own cost all necessary licenses, approvals, authorizations or permits required to enable the Owner's vessel to undertake and complete the services without let or hindrance. The Owner shall provide the Hirer with all reasonable assistance in connection with the obtaining of such licenses, approvals, authorizations or permits.

11. Towering Gear and Equipment

Subject to the provisions of Clause 16.1(v) hereof the Owner agrees to provide, free of cost to the Hirer, all tow wires, pennants, chains, springs, hawsers, shackles, bridles, any other towing gear and all salvage equipment carried on board the vessel.

12. Seaworthiness of the Vessel

The Owner will exercise due diligence to tender the vessel to the Hirer at the commencement of this Agreement in a seaworthy condition and in all respects ready to perform the services set out in Box 9, Part I of this Agreement, but the Owner gives no other warranties, express or implied.

13. Substitution of the Vessel

The Owner shall at all times have the right to substitute any vessel for any other vessel of adequate power, type and capability for the intended services, and shall be at liberty to supply a vessel belonging to others for the whole or part of the services under this Agreement. Provided however that the main particulars and capabilities of the substituted vessel shall be subject to the Hirer's prior approval, which approval shall not be unreasonably withheld.

14. Termination

(a) The Hirer has the right to terminate the services to be carried out by the Owner under this Agreement at any time, provided always that notice of such termination is given to the Owner in writing. In such event the Owner is entitled to be paid all stage payments due at that time, and a proportion of the balance of the Lumpsum price, calculated on a pro rata basis up to the time of termination, and any other amounts due in accordance with the provisions of Boxes 10 and 12, Part I of this Agreement, and Clause 16 hereof.

(b) Such termination of the services will be carried out with all reasonable despatch by the Owner, subject always to permission from the relevant local authority and to the safety of personnel and equipment involved in the services. Any additional expenses arising directly as a consequence of the instructions to discontinue or terminate the services shall be for the account of the Hirer.

15. Time for Payment and Interest

The Owner shall promptly invoice the Hirer for all sums payable under this Agreement. If any sums which become due and payable are not actually received by the Owner within the period specified in Box 14, Part I of this Agreement, they shall attract interest in accordance with the rate set out in Box 14, Part I.

16. Extra Costs

(a) The following expenses/costs, other than those normally payable by the Owner at the ports or places of mobilisation and demobilisation, shall be paid by the Hirer as and when they fall due:

ISU Lumpsum Sub-Contract (Salvcon)

- (i) all port expenses, pilotage charges, harbour and canal dues and all other expenses of a similar nature levied upon or payable in respect of the Owner's vessel arising out of these services.
- (ii) all costs in connection with clearance, agency fees, visas, guarantees and all other expenses of such kind relating to these services.
- (iii) all taxes and social security charges (other than those normally payable by the Owner in the country where it has its principal place of business and/or where the vessel is registered), stamp duties, or other levies payable in respect of or in connection with this Agreement, any import—export dues and any customs or excise duties.
- (iv) all costs incurred due to the requirements of governmental or other authorities over and above those costs which would otherwise be reasonably incurred by the Owner in the execution of this Agreement.
- (v) all costs incurred by the Owner in respect of towing gear, salvage equipment, other portable equipment, materials, or stores which are lost, damaged or sacrificed during the services, provided that such loss, damage or sacrifice is immediately notified in writing to the Hirer's representative, and provided any loss or damage does not arise as a result of negligence on the part of the Owner, his servants or agents.
- (b) If any such expenses/costs are in fact paid by or on behalf of the Owner, (notwithstanding that the Owner shall under no circumstances be under any obligation to make such payments on behalf of the Hirer), the Hirer shall reimburse the Owner on the basis of the actual cost to the Owner plus a handling charge of the percentage amount indicated in Box 15, Part I of this Agreement, upon presentation of invoice.

17. Security

- (a) The Hirer shall provide on signing of this Agreement, an irrevocable and unconditional bank guarantee in the sum and at the place indicated in Box 16, Part I of this Agreement, or other security to the satisfaction of the Owner. (See also Clause 3.7 hereof).
- (b) Whether Box 16 of Part I be completed or not, the Owner may at any time require reasonable security, or reasonable further security, to be provided by the Hirer to the satisfaction of the Owner for all or part of any amount which may be or become due under this Agreement. Such security shall be given on one or more occasions as and when required by the Owner.
- (c) In the event of a claim arising under the provisions of Clause 8.5 hereof, the Owner will provide the Hirer with security in respect of such claim. Such security shall be reasonable as to both amount and form.

18. Insurance

- (a) In entering into this Agreement, the Owner warrants to the Hirer, that he is carrying adequate and sufficient insurances on his vessel for the nature of the services to be carried out under this Agreement.
- (b) Such insurances will include, but not necessarily be limited to the following:
    - (i) Hull insurance up to a level appropriate to the value of the vessel.
    - (ii) Protection & Indemnity Insurance.
    - (iii) Pollution Liability Cover up to at least US$ 500 million.
    - (iv) Employer's Liability Cover in accordance with the law of the flag of the vessel and/or the principal place of business of the Owner.
    - (v) Public Liability Cover in accordance with the law of the flag of the vessel and/or the principal place of business of the Owner.

Appendix A—Salvage Documents

(vi) Third Party Liability Cover in accordance with the law of the flag of the vessel and/or the principal place of business of the Owner.

19. Liabilities

(a) The Owner will indemnify and hold the Hirer harmless in respect of any liability adjudged due or claim reasonably compromised arising out of injury or death occurring during the services hereunder to any of the following persons:

— any servant or agent of the Owner
— any other person at or near the site of the operations for whatever purpose on behalf or at the request of the Owner.

(b) The Hirer will indemnify and hold the Owner harmless in respect of any liability adjudged due or claim reasonably compromised arising from injury or death occurring during the services hereunder to any of the following persons:

— any servant or agent of the Hirer, or of the casualty.
— any other person at or near the site of the operations for whatever purpose on behalf or at the request of the Hirer.

(c) The following shall be for the sole account of the Owner without any recourse to the Hirer, its servants, or agents, whether or not the same is due to breach of contract, negligence or any other fault on the part of the Hirer, its servants or agents:

(i) Subject to the provisions of Clause 16.1(v) hereof, loss or damage of whatsoever nature, howsoever caused to or sustained by the Owner's own or hired-in vessel.
(ii) Loss or damage of whatsoever nature caused to or suffered by third parties, or their property by reason of contract with the Owner's own or hired in vessel or obstruction created by the presence of such vessel.
(iii) Loss or damage of whatsoever nature suffered by the Owner or by third parties or their property in consequence of the loss or damage referred to in (i) and (ii) above.
(iv) Any liability in respect of wreck removal or in respect of the expense of moving or lighting or buoying the Owner's own or hired-in vessel or equipment, or in respect of preventing or abating pollution originating from the Owner's own or hired in vessel or equipment.

The Owner will indemnify and hold the Hirer harmless in respect of any liability adjudged due to a third party or any claim by a third party reasonably compromised arising out of any such loss or damage. The Owner shall not in any circumstances be liable for any loss or damage suffered by the Hirer or caused to or sustained by the casualty in consequence of loss or damage howsoever caused to or sustained by the vessel.

(d) The following shall be for the sole account of the Hirer without any recourse to the Owner, its servants or agents, whether or not the same is due to breach of contract, negligence or any other fault on the part of the Owner, its servants or agents:

(i) Loss or damage of whatsoever nature, howsoever caused to or sustained by the Hirer's own or other hired in vessel or equipment, or the Casualty, the subject of these services.
(ii) Loss or damage of whatsoever nature caused to or suffered by third parties or their property by reason of contact with the Hirer's own or other hired in vessel or equipment, or the casualty or obstruction created

ISU Lumpsum Sub-Contract (Salvcon)

      by the presence of the Owner's own or other hired in vessel or equipment, or the casualty.
- (iii) Loss or damage of whatsoever nature suffered by the Hirer or by third parties or their property in consequence of the loss or damage referred to in (i) and (ii) above.
- (iv) Any liability in respect of wreck removal or in respect of the expense of moving or lighting or buoying the Hirer's own or other hired in vessel or equipment, or the casualty, the subject of these services, or in respect of preventing or abating pollution from the Hirer's own or other hired in vessel or equipment, or from the casualty, the subject of these services.

      The Hirer will indemnify and hold the Owner harmless in respect of any liability adjudged due to a third party or any claim by a third party reasonably compromised arising out of any such loss or damage. The Hirer shall not in any circumstances be liable for any loss or damage suffered by the Owner or caused to or sustained by the vessel in consequence of loss or damage howsoever caused to or sustained by the casualty.

- (e) Save as otherwise expressly stipulated in this Agreement neither the Owner nor the Hirer shall be liable to the other party for loss of profit, loss of use, loss of production or any other indirect or consequential damage for any reason whatsoever.
- (f) Notwithstanding any provisions of this Agreement to the contrary the Owner and the Hirer shall both have the benefit of all limitations of, and exemptions from liability, accorded to the owners, charterers, managers or operators of vessels by any applicable statute or rule of law for the time being in force and the same benefits are to apply regardless of the form of signatures given to this Agreement.

20. Himalaya Clause

      All exceptions, exemptions, defences, immunities, limitations of liability, indemnities, privileges and conditions granted or provided by this Agreement for the benefit of the Owner or the Hirer shall also apply to and be for the benefit of their respective subcontractors, operators, masters, officers and crews and to and be for the benefit of all bodies corporate parent of, subsidiary to, affiliated with or under the same management as either of them, as well as all directors, officers, servants and agents of the same and to and be for the benefit of all parties performing services within the scope of this Agreement for or on behalf of the Owner or the Hirer as servants, agents and subcontractors of such parties. The Owner or the Hirer shall be deemed to be acting as agent or trustee of and for the benefit of all such persons, entities and vessels set forth above but only for the limited purpose of contracting for the extension of such benefits to such persons, bodies and vessels.

21. Evidence

      The Owner confirms that he will provide all necessary assistance to the Hirer in respect of the presentation of the Hirer's salvage claim by the provision and retention of all evidence in his possession or control relating to the salvage services and to their contribution to same, including the provision of witness statements/reports, photographs, and any other relevant documentary evidence. The Hirer agrees that he will pay the Owner's reasonable costs relating to the provision of the above evidence.

22. Confidentiality

      The terms and conditions of this Agreement are confidential between the parties hereto. Neither party shall disclose such matters to any third party without the prior

Appendix A—Salvage Documents

approval of the other party to this Agreement. Provided always that the Hirer may provide details of this Agreement in any Arbitration or other Legal proceedings relating to his salvage claim against the Casualty, the subject of these services.

23. General

(a) If any one or more terms, conditions or provisions in this Agreement or any part thereof shall be held to be invalid, void or of no effect for any reason whatsoever, the same shall not affect the validity of the remaining terms, conditions or provisions which shall remain and subsist in full force and affect.

(b) For the purpose of this Agreement unless the context otherwise requires the singular shall include the plural and vice versa.

(c) Any extension of time granted by the Owner to the Hirer or any indulgence shown relating to the time limits set out in this Agreement shall not be a waiver of the Owner's right under this Agreement to act upon the Hirer's failure to comply with the time limits.

24. Time for Suit

Save for the indemnity provisions under Clauses 8.5, 19 and 20 hereof, any claim which may arise out of or in connection with this Agreement or any of the services performed hereunder shall be notified by telex, facsimile, cable or otherwise in writing to the party against whom such claim is made, within 6 months of completion or termination of the services hereunder, and any suit shall be brought within one year of the time when the cause of action first arose. If either of these conditions is not complied with the claim and all rights whatsoever and howsoever shall be absolutely barred and extinguished.

25. Law and Arbitration Procedure

(a) In the event that Box 17 of Part I is not completed then clauses 25.2 to 25.6 hereof shall apply.

(b) This Agreement shall be governed by and construed in accordance with English law and any dispute arising out of this Agreement shall be referred to Arbitration in London in accordance with the Arbitration Acts 1950 and 1979 or any statutory modification or re-enactment thereof for the time being in force.

(c) Any dispute arising hereunder shall be referred to the arbitrament of a sole Arbitrator, to be selected by the first party claiming arbitration from the persons currently on the panel of Lloyd's Salvage Arbitrators with a right of appeal from an award made by the Arbitrator to either party by notice in writing to the other within 28 days of the date of publication of the original Arbitrator's Award.

(d) The Arbitrator on appeal shall be the person currently acting as Lloyd's Appeal Arbitrator, or by agreement of the parties, another member of the Lloyd's Panel of Salvage Arbitrators.

(e) Both the Arbitrator and Appeal Arbitrator shall have the same powers as an Arbitrator and an Appeal Arbitrator under LOF 1995 or any standard revision thereof, including a power to order a payment on account of any monies due to the Owner pending final determination of any dispute between the parties hereto.

(f) No suit shall be brought before another Tribunal, or in another jurisdiction, except that either party shall have the option to bring proceedings to obtain

ISU Lumpsum Sub-Contract (Salvcon)

conservative seizure or other similar remedy against any assets owned by the other party in any state or jurisdiction where such assets may be found.

26. Alternative Law and Arbitration Procedure

(a) If Box 17 of Part I is completed and the parties nominate a place outside of England, then the provisions of clause 26.2 hereof shall apply.

(b) Any dispute arising out of this Agreement shall be referred to Arbitration at the place indicated in Box 17, Part I, of this Agreement, subject to the procedures applicable there. The laws of the place indicated in Box 17, Part I shall govern this Agreement.

27. Warranty of Authority

If at the time of making this Agreement or providing any services under this Agreement at the request, express or implied, of the Hirer, the Owner is not the actual owner of the vessel identified in Box 4, Part I, the Owner warrants that it is authorised to make this Agreement.

INTERNATIONAL SALVAGE UNION
SUB-CONTRACT LUMPSUM AGREEMENT "SALVCON"
GUIDANCE NOTES

This Agreement is intended to be used by a Salvor working under Lloyd's Form, or similar contract, who wishes to engage additional assistance, but on a Lumpsum, non-award sharing basis, as distinct from the widely used ISU Award Sharing Sub-Contractors Agreement, or under the terms of the SALVHIRE Daily Hire Agreement.

Equally a Tugowner who wishes to hire out his tug to a Salvor, may offer its services on the basis of SALVCON.

The format of the document is very similar to the BIMCO/ISU Towage Agreements, TOWCON/TOWHIRE and the BIMCO/ISU Wreck Removal Agreements, WRECKCON/WRECKHIRE. There being two Parts to the Agreement.

Part I consists of the Boxes, in which will be entered Operational and Financial Matters. Part II contains the 27 Clauses which make up the Standard Terms and Conditions.

It will be seen that the content of the Agreement closely follows TOWCON, which until now has often been utilised by salvors when engaging additional assistance on a Lumpsum basis.

Set out below are some notes intended to assist those using SALVCON.

Part I

(a) Boxes 1, 2 and 3 require no comment.

(b) Box 4 requires details and specifications of the hired vessel(s). These could be annexed to the Agreement if, for example, a brochure exists in respect of the vessel, or, such details could be set out in a separate annex.

(c) Box 5 is for the name of the Owner's P&I Association.

(d) Boxes 6, 7 and 8 are concerned with the Details, Condition and Location of the Casualty. **The Hirer should ensure that he properly completes these details, as the owner of the vessel to be provided is entitled to rely upon this information as representing the actual state of affairs in respect of the casualty to which services are to be provided.**

Appendix A—Salvage Documents

(e) Box 9 will set out the services to be provided by the Owner.

(f) **As this is a Lumpsum Agreement it is most important that the Nature of the Services is set out as precisely as possible, as in the alternative there will be scope for the disputes between the parties as to whether what had to be done was within, or outside, the lumpsum price.**

(g) Box 10 deals with the Lumpsum Price, and any stage payments.

(h) Box 11 is for the Free Time, pursuant to Clause 4 of Part II. Again it is important that the parties agree on the use of Free Time, and whether it is fully reversible, i.e. can be used either at the commencement or completion of the services.

(i) Box 12 deals with Delay Payment rates, and it will be seen that there is provision for a Sea Rate, an in Port Rate and an At Anchor Rate.

(j) Box 13 sets out the Payment Details.

(k) Box 14 deals with the Time for Payment, and any interest to be paid in the event of late payment.

(l) Box 15 is in respect of Extra Costs, and the handling charge the Owner may levy if he pays these costs on behalf of the Hirer.

(m) Box 16 is concerned with the Security Requirements of the Owner, details.

(n) Box 17 is in respect of Law and Arbitration. **It should be noted that if this Box is left blank, English law with Arbitration in London will apply.** Whilst, in the majority of cases it is likely that the Hirer will be rendering services to the casualty under Lloyd's Form, there is every possibility that the Hirer may be engaged under some other contract, so there is provision for the parties to Arbitrate any dispute in another place, subject to the laws of that place.

(o) Box 18 is for the numbers of any additional Clauses to Part II of the Agreement.

Part II

This section begins with a standard preamble, setting out the reason for the Agreement between Hirer and Owner.

(a) **Clause 1: Definitions**; sets out a definition of "Casualty" which includes anything on the casualty, including the cargo, bunkers, etc. "Vessel!" being the Owner's tug or other equipment is also defined, as is the "Owner".

(b) **Clause 2: Nature of the Services to be Provided by the Owner**; this Clause confirms that the services are as set out in Box 9 of Part I, and any Annexe to the Agreement.

(c) **Clause 3: Price and Conditions of Payment**; deals with the financial aspects of the Agreement. Under Clause 3.3 the Hirer may not make any deductions from the lumpsum price, and under Clause 3.7 the Owner may terminate the Agreement under certain identified situations.

(d) **Clause 4: Free Time**; this clause requires the Owner to set out the amount of Free Time included within the Lumpsum Price, and the specific purposes for which the Free Time may be utilised.

(e) **Clause 5: Delay Payments**; refers back to Box 12 of Part I.

(f) **Clause 6: Employment and Area of Operations**; requires that the salvage activities must be lawful and restricts the "area of operations" to within Institute Warranty Limits. If the services are to take place outside these limits

ISU Lumpsum Sub-Contract (Salvcon)

then permission must be obtained, in writing, and there may be additional insurance costs. The clause also confirms that no warranties are given by the Hirer regarding the safety of the place of operations.

(g) **Clause 7: Master and Crew**; confirms that the Master and Crew of the Vessel are to carry out their duties promptly and that the navigation and management of the Vessel remains under the control of Owners, Master and Crew.

(h) **Clause 8: Owner's Obligations**; this clause records that the reasonable instructions of the Hirer must be complied with; that the Owner, Master and Crew will exercise due care to protect the environment; that the services to be rendered are in the nature of salvage services; that no claims for salvage are to be made against the salved property; and that the Owner agrees to indemnify the Hirer against the consequences of any such salvage claims.

(i) **Clause 9: Hirer's Representative**; requires the Hirer to have a representative in operational control of the salvage services.

(j) **Clause 10: Permits**; provides that the Hirer is responsible for obtaining any Licences, Approvals, Authorizations or Permits, but is entitled to reasonable assistance from the Owner.

(k) **Clause 11: Towing Gear and Equipment**; provides that the Owner will allow the Hirer to use all the towing and salvage equipment on the tug at no extra charge, unless there is loss or damage which is not due to the negligence of the Owner, his servants or agents.

(l) **Clause 12: Seaworthiness of Vessel**; is a warranty by the Owner that his vessel will be tendered in a seaworthy condition, fit for the services to be rendered, but no other warranties, express or implied, are given by the Owner.

(m) **Clause 13: Substitution of the Vessel**; allows the Owner to provide a substitute vessel of his own, or belonging to others, provided it is of adequate power and capability. The Hirer's approval of such substitution must be obtained but that approval shall not be unreasonably withheld.

(n) **Clause 14: Termination**; provides for the termination of the services by the Hirer, and the obligation of the Hirer with regard to payment to the Owner, as well as the obligations on the Owner in such a situation.

(o) **Clause 15: Time for Payment and Interest**; relates to time for payment by the Hirer, and the rate of interest to be charged in the event of late payment.

(p) **Clause 16: Extra Costs**; deals with extra costs which are payable by the Hirer, and as such is similar to the similar clause in the Towing and Wreck Removal Agreements.

(i) It should however be noted that 16.1 (vi) deals with the Owner's towing gear, salvage equipment, portable equipment, materials or stores, lost damaged or sacrificed during the services, which costs are recoverable from the Hirer, provided such loss or damage was not as a consequence of negligence on the part of the Owner, his servants or agents.

This wording has been introduced following suggestions that the position in WRECKCON is ambiguous as between Clauses 12.6 and 14.2.1 (i) of Part II of that agreement.

(q) **Clause 17: Security**; is concerned with the provision of security for the monies due to the Owner under the Agreement. It is similar to such clause in TOWCON, etc.

Appendix A—Salvage Documents

(i) It should be noted that in the event of any salvage claims against the salved property being made by owners, master, crew, etc. of the Vessel, then the Owners are obliged to provide the Hirer with security in respect of such claims.

(r) **Clause 18: Insurance**; is a new clause under which the Owner warrants that he is carrying adequate and sufficient insurances on his vessel(s) appropriate to the services he is being engaged to perform. The clause identifies the types of insurance cover to be in place on the Vessel.

(i) It should be noted that the Pollution Liability Cover referred to under 17.2 (iii), is not available to all tug owners/operators. Owners should be careful to advise the Hirer if this cover does not exist. Equally the Hirer should be careful to ascertain if this cover is in place for the tug/vessel in question.

(s) **Clause 19: Liabilities**; deals with Liabilities and the clause is taken from TOWCON/TOWHIRE with necessary amendments. It follows the standard "knock for knock" liability principles which are widely accepted today.

(t) **Clause 20: Himalaya Clause**; this is a standard Clause as is to be found in TOWCON, etc. It gives an extension of the defences, etc. within the agreement granted to the Hirer and Owner, to their respective servants, agents, sub-contractors, etc.

(u) **Clause 21: Evidence**; this Clause is specific to SALVCON and SALVHIRE. It requires the Owner to assist the Hirer with regard to the retention and provision of evidence to support the Hirer's salvage claim.

(v) **Clause 22: Confidentiality**; this clause requires the parties to honour the confidentiality of the Agreement, but does allow for the details to be disclosed in Court or Arbitration proceedings relating to the casualty.

(w) **Clause 23: General**; this is a standard clause to be found in many similar agreements.

(x) **Clause 24: Time for Suit**; it should be noted that any claim by one party to the contract, against the other, must be notified within 6 months and any suit must be brought within one year. Failing this the claim is barred absolutely. This time limit is the same as in TOWCON and TOWHIRE, but is shorter than the time limit prescribed in WRECKCON and WRECKHIRE.

This is considered reasonable as within 6 months of completion of the services the Hirer/Contractor will usually be close to finalising his claim against the salved property.

The indemnity provisions within Clauses 8.5, 19 and 20 are excluded from this time limit.

(y) **Clause 25: Law and Arbitration Procedure**; this clause makes the Agreement subject to English law.

(i) It is anticipated that the majority of users of this Agreement will be involved in rendering services to a casualty under Lloyd's Standard Form of Salvage Agreement. For this reason, any dispute between the parties is to be referred to a member of the panel of Lloyd's Salvage Arbitrators.
(ii) There is provision for an appeal to the Lloyd's Appeal Arbitrator.
(iii) There is provision for the parties to commence proceedings in another jurisdiction for the purpose of obtaining security.
(iv) In addition, the Owner may apply to the Arbitrator or Appeal Arbitrator for a payment on account pending determination of any disputes.

(z) **Clause 26: Alternative Law and Arbitration Procedure**; this clause recognises the fact that a number of salvage services are performed under contracts

ISU Lumpsum Sub-Contract (Salvcon)

other than Lloyd's Form. Under this clause the parties have the right to nominate another place for the hearing of any Arbitration. In such an event the Arbitration will be subject to the procedures and laws of that place.

(aa) **Clause 27: Warranty of Authority**; is the standard warranty of authority clause in relation to the person signing the Agreement in respect of the Vessel being hired.

It should be noted that these Notes are intended to be used as a general guide. In the event of any conflict between the Notes and the contents of SALVHIRE, the latter will prevail over the Notes.

Appendix A—Salvage Documents

No. 7

CODE OF PRACTICE BETWEEN INTERNATIONAL SALVAGE UNION AND INTERNATIONAL GROUP OF P&I CLUBS

In the spirit of co-operation, the following Code of Practice is agreed between the International Salvage Union and the International Group of P&I Clubs in relation to all future salvage services to which Article 14 of the 1989 Salvage Convention is applicable or under Lloyd's Form where the Special Compensation P&I Club's (SCOPIC) Clause has been invoked by the Contractor.

1. The salvor will advise the relevant P&I Club at the commencement of the salvage services, or as soon thereafter as is practicable, if they consider that there is a possibility of a Special Compensation claim arising.

2. In the event of the SCR not being appointed under the SCOPIC clause, the P&I Club may appoint an observer to attend the salvage and the salvors agree to keep him and/or the P&I Club fully informed of the salvage activities and their plans. However, any decision on the conduct of the salvage services remains with the salvor.

3. The P&I Club, when reasonably requested by the salvor, will immediately advise the salvor whether the particular Member is covered, subject to the Rules of the P&I Club, for any liability which he may have for Special Compensation or SCOPIC Remuneration.

4. The P&I Clubs confirm that, whilst they expect to provide security in the form of a Club Letter either in respect of claims for special compensation (under Article 14 of the 1989 Salvage Convention) or SCOPIC remuneration (under the SCOPIC Clause), as appropriate, it is not automatic. Specific reasons for refusal to give security to the Contractor will be non-payment of calls, breach of warranty rules relating to classification and flag state requirements or any other breach of the rules allowing the Club to deny cover. The Clubs will not refuse to give security solely because the Contractors cannot obtain security in any other way.

5. In the event that security is required by a port authority or other competent authority for potential P&I liabilities in order to permit the ship to enter a port of refuge or other place of safety, the P&I Clubs confirm that they would be willing to consider the provision of such security subject to the aforementioned provisos referred to in para. 4 above and subject to the reasonableness of the demand.

6. The Contractors will accept security for either special compensation or SCOPIC remuneration by way of a P&I Club letter of undertaking in the attached form - "Salvage Guarantee form – ISU 5" - and they will not insist on the provision of security at Lloyd's.

7. The P&I Club concerned will reply to any request by the salvors regarding security as quickly as reasonably possible. In the event that salvage services are being performed under Lloyd's Form incorporating the SCOPIC clause, the P&I Club concerned will advise the Contractor within two (2) working days of his invoking the SCOPIC Clause whether or not they will provide security to the Contractor by way of a Club Letter referred to in para. 6 above.

8. In the event that salvage services are being performed under Lloyd's Form incorporating the SCOPIC clause, the P&I Clubs will advise the owners of the vessel not to exercise the right to terminate the contract under SCOPIC Clause 9(ii) without reasonable cause.

9. It is recognised that any liability to pay SCOPIC remuneration is a potential liability of the shipowner and covered by his liability insurers subject to the Club Rules and terms of entry. Accordingly, in the event of such payment of SCOPIC remuneration in excess of the Article 13 award, neither the shipowner not his liability insurers will seek to make a claim in General Average against the other interests to the common maritime adventure whether in their own name or otherwise and whether directly or by way of recourse or indemnity or in any other manner whatsoever.

10. The P&I Clubs, if consulted, and the ISU will recommend to their respective Members the incorporation of the SCOPIC clause in any LOF.

11. This is a Code of Practice which the ISU and the International Group of P&I Clubs will recommend to their Members and it is not intended that it should have any legal effect.

1.8.1999

Code of Practice regarding SCOPIC

No. 8

CODE OF PRACTICE BETWEEN INTERNATIONAL GROUP OF P&I CLUBS AND LONDON PROPERTY UNDERWRITERS REGARDING THE PAYMENT OF THE FEES AND EXPENSES OF THE SCR UNDER SCOPIC.

The following understanding has been reached between the International Group of P&I Clubs (hereinafter called "Liability Underwriters") and members of the Lloyd's Underwriters' Association and the International Underwriters Association of London (hereinafter called "Property Underwriters") in relation to all future salvage services under Lloyd's Form where the Special Compensation P&I Clubs (SCOPIC) Clause has been invoked by the Contractor.

1. Whereas the primary liability for paying the fees and disbursements of the Shipowner's Casualty Representative ("SCR") rests upon the owner of the vessel, it is agreed that the owner of the vessel shall be reimbursed such fees and disbursements, subject always to the Club Rules and the terms and conditions of Club cover and the terms of any insurance policy or policies covering the salved property, in the following proportions:-

    - 50% by Liability Underwriters;

    - 50% by Property Underwriters (subject to Clause 2 hereof).

2. (a) Property Underwriters shall pay for 50% of the SCR's fees and disbursements in proportion to the salved value of the subject matter insured.

   (b) Should 50% of the SCR's fees and disbursements exceed the salved value of the ship and cargo less the Article 13 award, Liability Underwriters agree to reimburse such excess proportion of the said SCR's fees and disbursements to the owners of the vessel.

3. This is a Code of Practice which Liability Underwriters and Property Underwriters shall recommend to their Members and it is not intended that it should have any legal effect.

1.8.1999

Appendix A—Salvage Documents

No. 9

INTERNATIONAL SALVAGE UNION
SUB-CONTRACT (AWARD SHARING) 1994

BETWEEN

The Contractor

—and—

The Sub-Contractor

THIS AGREEMENT is made the   day of   19

Between:

for and on behalf of ("the Contractor") and

for and on behalf of ("the Sub-Contractor")

WHEREAS:
(1) The Contractor is presently or is about to become engaged in rendering salvage services to the "   ", her cargo, freight, bunkers, stores and any other property thereon under a Lloyd's Standard Form of Salvage Agreement "No Cure—No Pay" dated   ("the LOF") and the Contractor wishes to engage the services of the Sub-Contractor on "No Cure—No Pay" terms to assist him in the performance of his obligations under the LOF.
(2) The Sub-Contractor is willing to assist the Contractor and will provide the personnel, equipment and services set out in the schedule, together with any further personnel equipment or services which may reasonably be requested by the Contractor from time to time during the performance of the services.

NOW in consideration of the mutual promises and undertakings contained herein it is agreed as follows:

Definitions

1. In this Agreement the following expressions shall have the following meanings:—

(a) "ISU Terms" means award sharing terms which are the same (mutatis mutandis) or substantially the same as the terms of this Agreement;

(b) "Non Award Sharing Terms" means terms which provide for the remuneration of a Sub-Contractor otherwise than by way of a share of the Salvage Remuneration payable under the LOF;

(c) "Relevant Sub-Contract" means a Sub-Contract whereby the Contractor engages the service of a Sub-Contractor on ISU Terms to assist him in the performance of his obligations under the LOF;

(d) "Salvage Remuneration" means any and all remuneration plus interest thereon paid or payable whether awarded, agreed or received in respect of services rendered under the LOF, including out of pocket expenses, interim payments, special compensation and costs.

ISU Sub-Contract (Award Sharing) 1994

Obligations of Contractor

2. The Contractor agrees:

   (a) To engage the Sub-Contractor on "No Cure—No Pay" terms to assist him in the performance of his obligations under the LOF and to include in his claim for Salvage Remuneration the agreed services rendered by the Sub-Contractor;

   (b) To share with the Sub-Contractor the Salvage Remuneration as finally awarded under the LOF or as agreed by the parties thereto and received by the Contractor;

   (c) To use his best endeavours to recover, as part of those legal costs as finally awarded to him under the LOF, or as agreed between the parties thereto, such legal costs (calculated on the standard basis) incurred by the Sub-Contractor in and about the provision and presentation of evidence by him for use in the LOF proceedings, and thereafter to account to the Sub-Contractor for his legal costs recovered as aforesaid;

   (d) As soon as is reasonably practical to instruct solicitors in London to open an identified interest bearing client deposit account established in accordance with the Solicitors Act 1974 (as amended) (the "Trust Account") and to hold in the Trust Account any and all such remuneration as may be received pursuant to the LOF as stakeholder on trust for the Contractor and the Sub-Contractor with authority, upon final agreement or determination of the share due to each party, to release such share on being requested in writing by such party so do to; and

   (e) As soon as reasonably practicable to inform the Council of Lloyd's and the owners of the salved property and the Guarantors of the existence of this Agreement, the identity of the Sub-Contractor and to give them irrevocable instructions to pay any and all monies due under the LOF to the Trust Account.

Obligations of Sub-Contractor

3. The Sub-Contractor agrees:—

   (a) To use his best endeavours to assist the Contractor in the Performance of his obligations under the LOF, including the provision of such personnel, equipment and services as are set out in the attached schedule or as are reasonably requested by the Contractor during the performance of the service;

   (b) To assist the Contractor in the presentation of the claim for Salvage Remuneration by the provision and retention of evidence relating to the salvage services and to the Sub-Contractor's contribution to the same;

   (c) Not to claim Salvage Remuneration and/or special compensation against the Owner(s) of the property salved or any part thereof, nor to make any claim for Salvage Remuneration in respect of the services rendered pursuant to this Agreement, save insofar as this Agreement provides; and

   (d) To provide a satisfactory indemnity to the Contractor against any successful claim for Salvage Remuneration made by the Sub-Contractor's servants and/or agents and/or Sub-Contractors (and/or the servants and/or agents of the same) against the Owner(s) of such property.

Trust

4.(a) From the time when this Agreement is concluded, all sums paid or payable by way of Salvage Remuneration due under the LOF or this Agreement shall be owned in law by the Contractor and the Sub-Contractor jointly and shall be

Appendix A—Salvage Documents

subject to a trust in favour of the Contractor and Sub-Contractor as beneficiaries. Save as is expressly provided in this Agreement, neither party shall have the right to assign or otherwise dispose of or deal with such sums or any part thereof or any interest therein.

(b) In the event of either party receiving any sum howsoever on account of or in payment of Salvage Remuneration in respect of any of the services rendered under the LOF or this Agreement, such sum shall be held on trust as aforesaid for the Contractor and the Sub-Contractor and shall forthwith be paid into the Trust Account.

Conduct of LOF Arbitration

5.(a) The arbitration under the LOF and/or any negotiation for an amicable settlement shall be conducted solely by the Contractor but the Sub-Contractor agrees to provide all necessary evidence and assistance in connection therewith.

(b) The Contractor shall keep the Sub-Contractor fully advised as to the amount of the security demanded from the Owner(s) of the salved property and as to the nature and form of the guarantees received and the identity of all guarantors.

(c) The Contractor, so far as the circumstances reasonably permit, shall consult with the Sub-Contractor and keep the Sub-Contractor informed at all significant stages of the Arbitration or of any settlement negotiations, but failing agreement by the Sub-Contractor the Contractor shall be entitled at his discretion to proceed with the Arbitration or to conclude a bona fide settlement.

(d) The Sub-Contractor shall be entitled to attend the Arbitration as an observer but at his own cost.

Assignment

6.(a) The Contractor shall not without the consent in writing of the Sub-Contractor (such consent not to be unreasonably withheld) make or purport to make any assignment of the benefit of the LOF or of the whole or any part of the Salvage Remuneration.

(b) Neither the Contractor nor the Sub-Contractor shall without the consent in writing of the other (such consent not to be unreasonably withheld) make or purport to make any assignment of the benefit of this Agreement or of the share of the Salvage Remuneration to which it is entitled under the joint operation of the LOF and this Agreement or of its interest under the trust hereinbefore contained.

Indemnities

7.(a) The Contractor agrees to indemnify fully and hold harmless the Sub-Contractor, his servants and/or agents against any claim by the Owner(s) of the property salved or by any other person (other than the Sub-Contractor's own servants and/or agents) for loss or damage caused by the negligence in the salvage operations of the Contractor, his servants or agents and/or by any defects (other than latent defects) in any equipment of the Contractor used in the salvage operation.

(b) The Sub-Contractor agrees to indemnify fully and hold harmless the Contractor, his servants and/or agents against any claim by the Owner(s) of the property salved or by any other person (other than the Contractor's own servants and/or agents) for loss or damage caused by the negligence in the salvage operation of the Sub-Contractor, his servants or agents and/or by any defects (other than latent defects) in any equipment of the Sub-Contractor used in the salvage operation.

(c) The Contractor will make no claim against the Sub-Contractor, his servants and/or agents for loss or damage sustained by the Contractor's equipment or by

ISU Sub-Contract (Award Sharing) 1994

any servant or agent of the Contractor caused by the negligence of the Sub-Contractor, his servants or agents and/or by defects in the Sub-Contractor's equipment and hereby agrees to indemnify fully and hold harmless the Sub-Contractor in respect of any such claim made by the Contractor's servants and/or agents.

(d) The Sub-Contractor will make no claim against the Contractor, his servants and/or agents for loss or damage sustained by the Sub-Contractor's equipment or by any servant or agent of the Sub-Contractor caused by the negligence of the Contractor, his servants and/or agents and/or by defects in the Contractor's equipment and hereby agrees to indemnify fully and hold harmless the Contractor in respect of any such claim made by the Sub-Contractor's servants and/or agents.

Limitation of Liability

8. Notwithstanding anything contained herein, and in particular Clause 7, either party to this Agreement shall be entitled to limit any liability to the other party which he and/or his servants and/or agents may incur in and about the services under this Agreement in the manner and to the extent provided by English Law, save that this Clause shall not apply to any liability under Clause 3(d) above.

Trustee Exoneration

9. Neither the Contractor nor any other trustee of the trust hereinbefore contained shall be liable for or for the consequences of any error or mistake (whether by way of commission or omission and whether on the part of the Contractor or other trustee himself, or on the part of any agent or adviser employed or instructed by the Contractor or other trustee) made or committed in or about the agreement or ascertainment or recovery of the Salvage Remuneration receivable under the LOF, or the obtaining enforcement or release of any security therefor or otherwise in or about the execution of the trust hereinbefore contained unless such error or mistake shall be proved to have occurred or been committed in personal conscious bad faith of the party sought to be made liable.

Relationship to Other Sub-Contracts

10.(a) Save as may be specifically advised, the Contractor hereby warrants that he has not hitherto engaged the services of any other party to assist him in the performance of his obligations under the LOF except upon ISU Terms or Non-Award Sharing Terms.

(b) The Contractor may at any time hereafter engage the services of such other parties as he may think fit to assist him in the performance of his obligations under the LOF, but the terms upon which every such party is engaged shall either be ISU Terms or Non-Award Sharing Terms.

(c) Where in relation to the performance of his obligations under the LOF, the Contractor has entered or hereafter enters into any engagement with another party on ISU Terms or Non-Award Sharing Terms he will, at the request of the Sub-Contractor, furnish to the Sub-Contractor all information in his possession concerning the identity and address of every such other party.

(d) In case this Agreement is not the only Relevant Sub-Contract, the following provisions shall apply—
  (i) Clause 2(d) (release of money from the Trust Account pursuant to written direction), Clause 4 (declaration of trust by this Agreement) and Clause 11 (quantification of the shares of the Contractor and the Sub-Contractor in the Salvage Remuneration) shall have effect as if references to every Sub-

Appendix A—Salvage Documents

        Contractor under all Relevant Sub-Contracts were substituted for references to the Sub-Contractor;
- (ii) The Contractor will so instruct Solicitors in London that a single account becomes the Trust Account in relation to every Relevant Sub-Contract;
- (iii) Whenever a matter or dispute has to be determined or resolved by arbitration pursuant to this Agreement and an Arbitrator has already been appointed to determine or resolve the same, or an equivalent matter or dispute under another Relevant Sub-Contract, then notwithstanding anything to the contrary in Clause 11(a) of this Agreement, that matter or dispute shall be referred to the same Arbitrator (if he so consents) and so far as possible he will determine or resolve that matter in relation to every Relevant Sub-Contract in a single arbitration.

Arbitration

11.(a) Any dispute arising hereunder, including any dispute as to the shares of the Salvage Remuneration due to the Contractor and Sub-Contractor, shall be referred to the arbitrament of an Arbitrator, to be selected by the first party claiming arbitration from the persons currently on the panel of Lloyd's Salvage Arbitrators with a right of Appeal from an award made by the Arbitrator to either party by notice in writing to the other within 28 days of the date of publication of the original Arbitrator's Award.

(b) The Arbitrator on appeal shall be the person currently acting as Lloyd's Appeal Arbitrator.

(c) Both the Arbitrator and the Appeal Arbitrator shall have the same powers as an Arbitrator and Appeal Arbitrator respectively would have under the LOF 1980 or any standard revision thereof, including a power to order a payment on account of a share due to a party pending final determination of any dispute between the parties hereto.

(d) For the purposes of any apportionment between the parties the term "Salvage Remuneration" as defined in Clause 1(d) shall include all expenses, unrecovered costs and brokers' commissions. The Arbitrator or Arbitrator on Appeal, unless he/she considers it unfair or unjust so to do, in determining the shares of the aforesaid Salvage Remuneration, shall first apportion to the Contractor and/or Sub-Contractor(s) all sums specifically awarded other than the sums for Salvage Remuneration and interest under LOF and all reasonably incurred out of pocket expenses, unrecovered but customary costs and brokers' commissions. Where interest has been awarded or earned in respect of any of the foregoing by reason of the LOF Award or Award on Appeal, and/or by reason of being held in the Trust Account, the said interest shall be included in the initial apportionment.

Relevant Law

12. This Agreement shall be governed and construed in accordance with English Law.
AS WITNESS the hands of the duly authorised representatives of the parties hereto.

For and on behalf of the	For and on behalf of the
Contractor	Sub-Contractor
....	....

SCHEDULE OF PERSONNEL, EQUIPMENT AND SERVICES

Guarantee to the Corporation of Lloyd's

No. 10

For a <u>Single</u> Guarantor.

GUARANTEE

TO THE CORPORATION OF LLOYD'S AND TO THE

CONTRACTOR

IN CONNECTION WITH A

SALVAGE AGREEMENT ON LLOYD'S FORM.

NAME OF VESSEL	
DATE OF SALVAGE AGREEMENT	(the "Agreement")
TOTAL LIABILITY NOT TO EXCEED	
REMUNERATION TO WHICH THIS GUARANTEE RELATES	SALVAGE*/SPECIAL COMPENSATION UNDER CONVENTION ARTICLE 14* *delete as applicable

PROPERTY TO WHICH THIS GUARANTEE RELATES (THE "PROPERTY SALVED"):

continue overleaf if necessary

In consideration of the Contractor refraining from arresting or otherwise detaining the property to secure his remuneration the undersigned

NAME AND ADDRESS OF GUARANTOR.	

guarantees to the Corporation of Lloyd's and also to the Contractor that in the event of non-payment by the party or parties concerned called upon to pay by the Council of Lloyd's in accordance with clause 15 of the Agreement, the undersigned will upon the demand of the Council pay to the Corporation of Lloyd's the amount so payable.

Any monies so paid shall be deemed to have been paid by the undersigned as surety for the party or parties by whom the Contractor's remuneration shall be payable, provided that the liability of the undersigned on the one hand and the Corporation of Lloyd's and the Contractor on the other shall be that of a principal debtor and the undersigned shall not be released by time being given or other indulgence shown to the party or parties hereby guaranteed or by any other act matter or thing whereby the undersigned if liable as a surety only would or might have been released.

This Guarantee may be enforced by and in the name of the Corporation of Lloyd's alone or the Contractor alone or by and in the joint names of the Corporation of Lloyd's and the Contractor. In the event of this Guarantee being enforced the fees and/or expenses of the Council of Lloyd's and any Arbitrator or Appeal Arbitrator(s) shall be paid in full before payment of any other sums hereby guaranteed.

The total liability of the undersigned inclusive of any liability for costs, expenses and interest shall in no case exceed the amount indicated above.

The .... day of .... 19 ....

1.2.24
3.10.26
12.4.50
23.2.72
5.9.90
1.1.95

Appendix A—Salvage Documents

No. 11

For <u>Two or More</u> Guarantors.

GUARANTEE

TO THE CORPORATION OF LLOYD'S AND TO THE

CONTRACTOR

IN CONNECTION WITH A

SALVAGE AGREEMENT ON LLOYD'S FORM.

NAME OF VESSEL	
DATE OF SALVAGE AGREEMENT	*(the "Agreement")*
TOTAL LIABILITY NOT TO EXCEED	
REMUNERATION TO WHICH THIS GUARANTEE RELATES	SALVAGE*/SPECIAL COMPENSATION UNDER CONVENTION ARTICLE 14* *delete as applicable*

PROPERTY TO WHICH THIS GUARANTEE RELATES (THE "PROPERTY SALVED"):

continue overleaf if necessary

In consideration of the Contractor refraining from arresting or otherwise detaining the property to secure his remuneration the undersigned

NAME AND ADDRESSES OF GUARANTORS.	

jointly and severally guarantee to the Corporation of Lloyd's and also to the Contractor that in the event of non payment by the party or parties concerned called upon to pay by the Council of Lloyd's in accordance with clause 15 of the Agreement, the undersigned will upon the demand of the Council pay to the Corporation of Lloyd"s the amount so payable. Any monies so paid shall be deemed to have been paid by the undersigned as surety for the party or parties by whom the Contractor's remuneration shall be payable, provided that the liability of the undersigned on the one hand and the Corporation of Lloyd's and the Contractor on the other shall be that of a principal debtor and the undersigned shall not be released by time being given or other indulgence shown to the party or parties hereby guaranteed or by any other act matter or thing whereby the undersigned if liable as a surety only would or might have been released.

This Guarantee may be enforced by and in the name of the Corporation of Lloyd's alone or the Contractor alone or by and in the joint names of the Corporation of Lloyd's and the Contractor. In the event of this Guarantee being enforced the fees and/or expenses of the Council of Lloyd's and any Arbitrator or Appeal Arbitrator(s) shall be paid in full before payment of any other sums hereby guaranteed.

The total liability of the undersigned inclusive of any liability for costs, expenses and interest shall in no case exceed the amount indicated above.

The .... day of .... 19 ....

1.2.24
3.10.26
12.4.50
23.2.72
5.9.90
1.1.95

....

Guarantee to the Corporation of Lloyd's

No. 12

For a <u>Single</u> Guarantor.

GUARANTEE
TO THE CORPORATION OF LLOYD'S AND TO THE
CONTRACTOR

IN CONNECTION WITH A

SALVAGE AGREEMENT ON LLOYD'S FORM.

NAME OF VESSEL	
DATE OF SALVAGE AGREEMENT	(the "Agreement")
TOTAL LIABILITY NOT TO EXCEED	
REMUNERATION TO WHICH THIS GUARANTEE RELATES	SALVAGE*/SPECIAL COMPENSATION UNDER CONVENTION ARTICLE 14* *delete as applicable

PROPERTY TO WHICH THIS GUARANTEE RELATES (THE "PROPERTY SALVED"):

continue overleaf if necessary

In consideration of the Contractor refraining from arresting or otherwise detaining the property to secure his remuneration the undersigned

NAME AND ADDRESS OF GUARANTOR.	

guarantees to the Corporation of Lloyd's and also to the Contractor that in the event of non payment by the party or parties concerned called upon to pay by the Council of Lloyd's in accordance with clause 15 of the Agreement, the undersigned will upon the demand of the Council pay to the Corporation of Lloyd's the amount so payable.

The undersigned also agrees with the Coporation of Lloyd's and with the Contractor within 3 days from the date hereof to deliver to the Council a duly stamped policy or other instrument indemnifying the Corporation of Lloyd's and the Contractor against any default or omission of the undersigned to observe and perform his obligations hereunder which policy or instrument shall be in such form as the said Council may require and shall be given and subscribed by such Underwriters or other persons only as the said Council may approve.

Any monies so paid shall be deemed to have been paid by the undersigned as surety for the party or parties by whom the Contractor's remuneration shall be payable, provided that the liability of the undersigned on the one hand and the Corporation of Lloyd's and the Contractor on the other shall be that of a principal debtor and the undersigned shall not be released by time being given or other indulgence shown to the party or parties hereby guaranteed or by any other act matter or thing whereby the undersigned if liable as a surety only would or might have been released.

This Guarantee may be enforced by and in the name of the Corporation of Lloyd's alone or the Contractor alone or by and in the joint names of the Corporation of Lloyd's and the Contractor. In the event of this Guarantee being enforced the fees and/or expenses of the Council of Lloyd's and any Arbitrator or Appeal Arbitrator(s) shall be paid in full before payment of any other sums hereby guaranteed.

The total liability of the undersigned inclusive of any liability for costs, expenses and interest shall in no case exceed the amount indicated above.

The .... day of .... 20......

1.2.24
3.10.26
12.4.50
23.2.72
5.9.90
1.1.95

....

769

Appendix A—Salvage Documents

No. 13

For use when the Guarantee is given by a <u>Single</u> Guarantor.

To be completed by the insurance broker and insured within the Lloyd's market.

INDEMNITY

IN CONNECTION WITH A

SALVAGE AGREEMENT ON LLOYD'S FORM.

NAME OF VESSEL	
DATE OF SALVAGE AGREEMENT	
	(the "Agreement")

In consideration of a premium at the rate of .... per cent on the amounts of our respective subscriptions hereto we the undersigned, each in the proportion which his separate subscription hereto bears to the sum of .... and each being responsible in respect of his own subscription only and not for any other or others, do hereby indemnify the Corporation of Lloyd's and the Contractor named in the above-mentioned Agreement against any default or omission from any cause whatsoever of the Guarantor named in the Guarantee dated the .... day of .... 20........ fully and punctually to observe and perform his obligations and engagements under the said Guarantee.

Any monies payable by the undersigned shall be paid to the Council of Lloyd's or as they may direct, and the receipt of the Council of Lloyd's for any such monies shall be a good discharge to the undersigned : and any monies so paid by the undersigned shall be deemed to have been paid by them as sureties for the said Guarantor.

This Indemnity may be enforced by and in the name of the Corporation of Lloyd's alone or the Contractor alone or by and in the joint names of the Corporation of Lloyd's and the Contractor. In the event of this Indemnity being enforced the fees and/or expenses of the Council of Lloyd's and any Arbitrator or Appeal Arbitrator(s) shall be paid in full before payment of any other sums hereby insured.

The total liability of the undersigned inclusive of any liability for costs, expenses and interest shall in no case exceed .... and the total liability of each of the undersigned hereunder inclusive of any liability for costs, expenses and interest shall be expressly limited to the amount of his subscription hereto.

10.9.90
1.1.95

Indemnity in connection with Lloyd's Form

No. 14

For <u>Two or More</u> Guarantors.

GUARANTEE

TO THE CORPORATION OF LLOYD'S AND TO THE CONTRACTOR

IN CONNECTION WITH A

SALVAGE AGREEMENT ON LLOYD'S FORM.

NAME OF VESSEL	
DATE OF SALVAGE AGREEMENT	(the "Agreement")
TOTAL LIABILITY NOT TO EXCEED	
REMUNERATION TO WHICH THIS GUARANTEE RELATES	SALVAGE*/SPECIAL COMPENSATION UNDER CONVENTION ARTICLE 14* *delete as applicable

PROPERTY TO WHICH THIS GUARANTEE RELATES (THE "PROPERTY SALVED"):

continue overleaf if necessary

In consideration of the Contractor refraining from arresting or otherwise detaining the property to secure his remuneration the undersigned

NAMES AND ADDRESSES OF GUARANTORS.	

jointly and severally guarantee to the Corporation of Lloyd's and also to the Contractor that in the event of non payment by the party or parties concerned called upon to pay by the Council of Lloyd's in accordance with clause 15 of the Agreement, the undersigned will upon the demand of the Council pay to the Corporation of Lloyd's the amount so payable.

The undersigned also agrees with the Corporation of Lloyd's and with the Contractor within 3 days from the date hereof to deliver to the Council a duly stamped policy or other instrument indemnifying the Corporation of Lloyd's and the Contractor against any default or omission of the undersigned to observe and perform their obligations hereunder which policy or instrument shall be in such form as the said Council may require and shall be given and subscribed by such Underwriters or other persons only as the said Council may approve.

Any monies so paid shall be deemed to have been paid by the undersigned as surety for the party or parties by whom the Contractor's remuneration shall be payable, provided that the liability of the undersigned on the one hand and the Corporation of Lloyd's and the Contractor on the other shall be that of a principal debtor and the undersigned shall not be released by time being given or other indulgence shown to the party or parties hereby guaranteed or by any other act matter or thing whereby the undersigned if liable as a surety only would or might have been released.

This Guarantee may be enforced by and in the name of the Corporation of Lloyd's alone or the Contractor alone or by and in the joint names of the Corporation of Lloyd's and the Contractor. In the event of this Guarantee being enforced the fees and/or expenses of the Council of Lloyd's and any Arbitrator or Appeal Arbitrator(s) shall be paid in full before payment of any other sums hereby guaranteed.

The total liability of the undersigned inclusive of any liability for costs, expenses and interest shall in no case exceed the amount indicated above.

The .... day of 19

....

1.2.24
3.10.26
12.4.50
23.2.72
5.9.90
1.1.95

....

Appendix A—Salvage Documents

No. 15

For use when the Guarantee is given by *Two or more* Guarantors.

To be completed by the insurance broker and insured within the Lloyd's market.

INDEMNITY

IN CONNECTION WITH A

SALVAGE AGREEMENT ON LLOYD'S FORM.

NAME OF VESSEL	
DATE OF SALVAGE AGREEMENT	*(the "Agreement")*

In consideration of a premium at the rate of .... per cent on the amounts of our respective subscriptions hereto we the undersigned, each in the proportion which his separate subscription hereto bears to the sum of .... and each being responsible in respect of his own subscription only and not for any other or others, do hereby indemnify the Corporation of Lloyd's and the Contractor named in the above-mentioned Agreement against any default or omission from any cause whatsoever of the Guarantors named in the Guarantee dated the .... day of .... 19 .... fully and punctually to observe and perform his obligations and engagements under the said Guarantee.

Any monies payable by the undersigned shall be paid to the Council of Lloyd's or as they may direct, and the receipt of the Council of Lloyd's for any such monies shall be a good discharge to the undersigned : and any monies so paid by the undersigned shall be deemed to have been paid by them as sureties for the said Guarantors.

This Indemnity may be enforced by and in the name of the Corporation of Lloyd's alone or the Contractor alone or by and in the joint names of the Corporation of Lloyd's and the Contractor. In the event of this Indemnity being enforced the fees and/or expenses of the Council of Lloyd's and any Arbitrator or Appeal Arbitrator(s) shall be paid in full before payment of any other sums hereby insured.

The total liability of the undersigned inclusive of any liability for costs, expenses and interest shall in no case exceed .... and the total liability of each of the undersigned hereunder inclusive of any liability for costs, expenses and interest shall be expressly limited to the amount of his subscription hereto.

10.9.90
1.1.95

Salvage Guarantee Form I.S.U. 1

No. 16

SALVAGE GUARANTEE FORM I.S.U.1

To :

Dear Sirs,

" .... " Salvage
Lloyd's Standard Form of Salvage Agreement dated .... ("the LOF")

1. In consideration of your refraining from calling for the completion of security by means of a guarantee in the form prescribed by the Council of Lloyd's in connection with your claim for salvage remuneration (but not any claim for Art. 14 Special Compensation or SCOPIC Remuneration) in respect of salvage services rendered to the "..." the LOF we hereby undertake to pay to you on demand any sum or sums, together with interest and costs which may be agreed between you and the owners of the salved property or which may be awarded to you in respect of the said salved property by an arbitrator or appeal arbitrator appointed by the Council of Lloyd's under the terms of the said LOF.

2. In the event of an amicable settlement of your claim under the LOF being reached, and in the absence of any agreement as to date of payment and interest accruing thereafter, it is hereby agreed that payment of the settlement monies will be effected within 28 calendar days after the date of such settlement and, in the event of non-payment within that period, we undertake to pay, in addition to the principal sum, interest thereon at the rate of .... % per annum from and including the day after the due date for payment specified above until and including the date upon which payment is received and credited for value to your account with .... Bank, at ....

3. Any monies paid by the undersigned hereunder shall be deemed to have been paid by the undersigned as surety for the party or parties hereby guaranteed, provided that, notwithstanding anything hereinbefore contained, the liability of the undersigned as between the undersigned on the one hand and you on the other hand shall be that of a principal debtor, and the undersigned shall not be released by time being given or other indulgence shown to the party or parties hereby guaranteed or by any other act, matter or thing whereby the undersigned, if liable as a surety only, would or might have been released.

4. This undertaking shall be governed by and construed in accordance with English law and we undertake, when called upon to do so, to give irrevocable instructions to English solicitors to accept service of proceedings issued by you against us in relation to this undertaking

5. Provided always that our liability under this guarantee shall not exceed the sum of $................. inclusive of interest and costs.

6. This undertaking is given in respect of ....

Signed this   day of   20
By ....
Authorised signatory of ....

SEE OVER FOR NOTES ON COMPLETION OF THIS GUARANTEE FORM

1.10.91
1.11.94
1.5.01

Appendix A—Salvage Documents

**GUIDANCE NOTES ON THE COMPLETION
OF SALVAGE GUARANTEE I.S.U.1**

1. The guarantee should be addressed to the contractors named in the LOF.

2. **Paragraph 1**
   Insert the general identity of the party on whose behalf the guarantee is given, e.g. m.v. ".." her cargo, freight, bunkers and stores and any other property thereon;
   or
   the bunkers aboard m.v. ".."
   or
   the cargo aboard m.v. ".."

   Insert the date of the LOF Agreement.

   The guarantee is designed for a single guarantor. If there are two or more guarantors amend the 4th line to read "we hereby **jointly and severally** undertake to pay you.."

3. **Paragraph 2**
   Insert the appropriate rate of interest.

   At the end of this paragraph insert the name of the company or firm, or the bank and account number to whom the contractors wish payment to be made. If unknown amend to read "for value to an account to be specified by you".

4. **Paragraph 5**
   Insert the amount in the currency for which the guarantee is given, inclusive of interest and costs.

5. **Paragraph 6**
   Insert details of the salved property on whose behalf the guarantee is given
   e.g. m.v.".." her cargo, freight, bunkers, stores and any other property thereon;
   or
   the bunkers aboard m.v. " .... ";
   or
   the cargo aboard m.v. " .... ";
   or
   the cargo aboard m.v. " .... ", carried under Bills of Lading New York to London Nos. 1, 4, 8, 9.

1.10.91
1.11.94
1.5.01

Salvage Guarantee Form I.S.U. 2

No. 17

SALVAGE GUARANTEE FORM I.S.U.2

To:

Dear Sirs,

"..." **Salvage**

Lloyd's Standard Form of Salvage Agreement dated ....("the LOF")

1. In consideration of your not causing delay to the "......................................" at the port or ports of .... by the detention or arrest of the cargo and/or other salved property described in paragraph 5 ("the Unsecured Property") for the purpose of obtaining security from the Unsecured Property in connection with your claim for salvage remuneration in respect of salvage services rendered pursuant to the LOF in accordance with the requirements of Clause 4.5 of the Lloyd's Standard Salvage and Arbitration Clauses (the "LSSA Clauses") we hereby undertake to pay to you on demand any sum or sums together with interest and costs which may either be agreed between you and the owners of the Unsecured Property or which may be awarded to you in respect thereof by an arbitrator or appeal arbitrator appointed by the Council of Lloyd's under the LOF provided always that:-

    (a) you will continue your efforts to obtain from the owners of the Unsecured Property security in accordance with your requirements such efforts to comprise:-

        (i) notifying your security requirements to the Council of Lloyd's in accordance with Clause 4.1 of the LSSA Clauses

        (ii) liaising with the owners and/or charterers of the vessel to ensure that none of the Unsecured Property is released to its owners until security has been provided to you in respect of it in accordance with Clause 4.5 of the LSSA Clauses;

        (iii) if so requested by the owners and/or charterers of the vessel taking such action as may be possible to enforce your maritime lien (the right to which is not to be affected by this agreement) against the Unsecured Property at the port or ports where it is discharged

    (b) our liability hereunder inclusive of any liability for interest and/or costs shall not exceed the sum of ....………......and we shall cease to have any liability in respect of Unsecured Property when security has been provided in respect of it in accordance with your requirement.

2. In the event of an amicable settlement of your claim under the LOF being reached, and in the absence

1.10.91
1.11.94
20.3.95
1.5.01

Appendix A—Salvage Documents

of any agreement as to date of payment and interest accruing thereafter, it is agreed that payment of the settlement monies will be effected within 28 calendar days after the date of such settlement and, in the event of non-payment within that period, we undertake to pay, in addition to the principal sum, interest thereon at the rate of........................percent per annum from and including the day after the due date for payment specified above until and including the date upon which payment is received and credited for value to your account with .... Bank, at ....

3. Any monies paid by the undersigned hereunder shall be deemed to have been paid by the undersigned as surety for the party or parties hereby guaranteed, provided that, notwithstanding anything hereinbefore contained, the liability of the undersigned as between the undersigned on the one hand and you on the other hand shall be that of a principal debtor; and the undersigned shall not be released by time being given or other indulgence shown to the party or parties hereby guaranteed or by any other act, matter or thing whereby the undersigned, if liable as a surety only, would or might have been released.

4. This undertaking shall be governed by and construed in accordance with English law and we undertake, when called upon to do so, to give irrevocable instructions to English solicitors to accept service of proceedings issued by you against us in relation to this undertaking.

5. This undertaking is given in respect of ....

Signed this   day of   20

By ....

Authorised signatory of ....

SEE OVER FOR NOTES ON COMPLETION OF THIS GUARANTEE FORM

1.10.91
1.11.94
20.3.95
1.5.01

Salvage Guarantee Form I.S.U. 2

**GUIDANCE NOTES ON THE COMPLETION
OF SALVAGE GUARANTEE I.S.U. 2**

1. The guarantee should be addressed to the contractors named in the LOF.

2. **Paragraph 1**

    Insert the name of the salved vessel, e.g. m.v "...".

    Insert the date of the LOF.

    The guarantee is designed for a single guarantor. If there are two or more guarantors amends the 6th line to read "we hereby **jointly and severally** undertake to pay you on demand ...."

3. **Paragraph 1 (b)**

    Insert the amount of the guarantee in words and figures.

4. **Paragraph 2**

    Insert the appropriate rate of interest.

    At the end of this paragraph insert the name of the company or firm, or the bank and account no to whom the contractors wish payment to be made. If unknown amend to read "for value to an account to be specified by you".

5. **Paragraph 5**

    (a) Insert details of the salved cargo and/or other salved property on whose behalf the Guarantee is given, e.g.

    the bunkers aboard m.v. "..";

    or

    the cargo aboard m.v. "...";

    or

    the cargo aboard m.v. "................................", carried under Bills of Lading, New York to London Nos. 1, 4, 8, 9.

3

1.10.91
1.11.94
20.3.95
1.5.01

777

Appendix A—Salvage Documents

No. 18

SALVAGE GUARANTEE FORM I.S.U.3.

[Now withdrawn Replaced with I.S.U. 4]

To:
Dear Sirs,

"..." Salvage
Lloyd's Standard Form of Salvage Agreement dated ....

1. In consideration of your refraining from calling for the completion of security by means of a Guarantee in the form prescribed by the Council of Lloyds in connection with your claim for special compensation for services rendered to the "......................................" under the terms of Lloyds Standard Form of Salvage Agreement "No Cure - No Pay" dated........................., we hereby undertaking to pay to you on demand any special compensation together with interest and costs which may be agreed between you and the Owners of the vessel in respect of which this undertaking is given or which may be awarded to you by an Arbitrator or Appeal Arbitrator appointed by the Council of Lloyds under the terms of the said Lloyds Standard Form of Salvage Agreement "No Cure - No Pay".

2. In the event of an amicable settlement being reached, and in the absence of any agreement as to date of payment and interest accruing thereafter, it is hereby agreed that payment of the settlement monies will be effected within 28 calendar days after the date of such settlement and, in the event of non-payment within that period, we undertake to pay, in addition to the principal sum, interest thereon at the rate of .... per annum from and including the day after the due date for payment specified above until and including the date upon which payment is received and credited for value to your account with...

3. Any monies paid by the undersigned hereunder shall be deemed to have been paid by the undersigned as surety for the party or parties by whom your remuneration shall be payable provided that, not withstanding hereinbefore contained, the liability of the undersigned as between the undersigned on the one hand and you on the other hand shall be that of a principal debtor and the undersigned shall not be released by time being given or other indulgence shown to the party or parties hereby guaranteed or by any other act, matter or thing whereby the undersigned, if liable as a surety only, would or might have been released.

4. This undertaking shall be governed by and construed in accordance with English law and we undertake, when called upon to do so, to give irrevocable instructions to English Solicitors to accept service of proceedings issued on your behalf against us in relation to this undertaking.

5. Provided always that our liability hereunder shall not exceed the sum of .... inclusive of interest and costs.

Signed this   day of   2001

By ....

Authorised signatory of ....

SEE OVER FOR NOTES ON COMPLETION OF THIS GUARANTEE FORM

Salvage Guarantee Form I.S.U. 3

**GUIDANCE NOTES ON THE COMPLETION
OF SPECIAL COMPENSATION GUARANTEE I.S.U. 3**

**N.B. See ISU4 for alternative wording to the above which was agreed
with the International P&I Club in 1996**

1. The Guarantee should be addressed to the Contractors named on the Lloyd's Form.

2. **Paragraph 1:**

    (a) Insert name of vessel

    (b) Insert the date of the LOF Agreement

    (c) Insert total liability under the Guarantee

    (d) The guarantee is designed for a single Guarantor. If there are two Guarantors amend the 5th line to read "................. we hereby **jointly and severally** undertake to pay you ...."

3. **Paragraph 2:**

    (a) Insert the appropriate rate of interest.

    (b) At the end of this paragraph insert the name of the company or firm, or the Bank and Account No. to whom the Contractor wishes payment to be made.

    If unknown amend to read "........... for value to an account to be specified by you".

Appendix A—Salvage Documents

No. 19

SALVAGE GUARANTEE FORM ISU 4

Article 14 Special Compensation

To:

Dear Sirs,

"..." Salvage

Lloyd's Standard Form of Salvage Agreement dated.. ("the LOF")

1. In consideration of, and upon condition that, you refrain from arresting or otherwise detaining the ".." or any other ship or property in the same beneficial or associated ownership or management, and that you refrain from calling for the completion of security by means of a guarantee in the form prescribed by the Council of Lloyds in connection with your claim for Art. 14 Special Compensation for services rendered to the "................................" under the terms of the LOF we hereby undertake to pay to you on demand any Special Compensation together with interest and costs in relation thereto, which may be due to you whether by final unappealable award or judgement or by written agreement between you, the undersigned and the owners of the m.v. "................................"

2. In the event of an amicable settlement of your Article 14 being reached, and in the absence of any agreement as to date of payment and interest accruing thereafter, it is hereby agreed that payment of the settlement monies will be effected within 28 calendar days after the date of such settlement and, in the event of non-payment within that period, we undertake to pay, in addition to the principal sum, interest thereon at the rate of .... per annum from and including the day after the due date for payment specified above until and including the date upon which payment is received and credited for value to your account with ....

3. Any monies paid by the undersigned hereunder shall be deemed to have been paid by the undersigned as surety for the party or parties hereby guaranteed provided that, notwithstanding anything hereinbefore contained, the liability of the undersigned as between the undersigned on the one hand and you on the other hand shall be that of a principal debtor, and the undersigned shall not be released by time being given or other indulgence shown to the party or parties hereby guaranteed or by any other act, matter or thing whereby the undersigned, if liable as a surety only, would or might have been released.

4. This undertaking shall be governed by and construed in accordance with English law and we undertake, when called upon to do so, to give irrevocable instructions to English solicitors to accept service of proceedings issued by you against us in relation to this undertaking.

5. Provided always that our liability hereunder shall not in any circumstances exceed the sum of .... inclusive of interest and costs.

Signed this   day of   20
By ....
Authorised signatory of ....

SEE OVER FOR NOTES ON COMPLETION OF THIS GUARANTEE FORM

19.03.96
12.06.01

Salvage Guarantee Form I.S.U. 4

GUIDANCE NOTES ON THE COMPLETION
OF Article 14 SPECIAL COMPENSATION GUARANTEE ISU 4

N.B. The wording of this undertaking was agreed with the International Group of P&I Clubs for use in Article 14 special compensation cases in accordance with the term of "Understanding between the International Group of P&I Clubs and the ISU"

1. The guarantee should be addressed to the contractors named in the LOF

2. **Paragraph 1:**

    (a) Insert name of vessel

    (b) Insert the date of the LOF

    (c) The guarantee is designed for a single guarantor. If there are two guarantors amend the 5th line to read "...........we hereby **jointly and severally** undertake to pay you ...."

3. **Paragraph 2:**

    (a) Insert the appropriate rate of interest.

    (b) At end of this paragraph insert the name of the company or firm, or the bank and account no. to whom the contractor wish payment to be made. If unknown amend to read "..................................... for value to an account to be specified by you".

4. **Paragraph 5:**

    Insert the currency and amount in words and numbers of the limit of liability of the guarantee.

HFW2\418882-1

19.03.96
12.06.01

Appendix A—*Salvage Documents*

No. 20

**SALVAGE GUARANTEE FORM ISU 5
(SCOPIC REMUNERATION)**

To:

Dear Sirs,

".." Salvage
Lloyd's Form of Salvage Agreement incorporating the
SCOPIC Clause dated........................ (the "LOF")

1. In consideration of, and upon condition that, you refrain from arresting or otherwise detaining the "..........................." or any other ship or property in the same beneficial or associated ownership or management in connection with your claim for SCOPIC remuneration for services rendered to the "............................" under the terms of the LOF, we hereby undertake to pay to you on demand any liability on the part of the owners for SCOPIC remuneration, to the extent that it exceeds any actual or potential Article 13 award, together with interest and costs in relation thereto, which may be due to you whether by final unappealable award or judgement or by written agreement between you, the undersigned and the owners of the m.v. "..............................".

2. Any monies paid by the undersigned hereunder shall be deemed to have been paid by the undersigned as surety for the party or parties hereby guaranteed, provided that, not withstanding anything hereinbefore contained, the liability of the undersigned as between the undersigned on the one hand and you on the other hand shall be that of principal debtor, and the undersigned shall not be released by time being given or other indulgence shown to the party or parties hereby guaranteed or by any other act, matter or thing whereby the undersigned, if liable as a surety only, would or might have been released.

3. This undertaking shall be governed by and construed in accordance with English law and we undertake, when called upon to do so, to give irrevocable instructions to English solicitors to accept service of proceedings issued by you against us in relation to this undertaking.

4. Provided always that our liability hereunder shall not in any circumstances exceed (including interest and costs) the sum of US$..........................

Signed this...............day of 20
By..
Authorised signatory of.............................

SEE OVER FOR NOTES ON COMPLETION OF THIS GUARANTEE FORM

01.08.99
12.06.01

Salvage Guarantee Form I.S.U. 5

GUIDANCE NOTES ON THIS
COMPLETION OF SALVAGE GUARANTEE ISU 5

N.B.   The wording of this Undertaking has been agreed with the International group of P&I Clubs in accordance with clause 6 of the Code of Practice between the International Salvage Union and the International Group of P&I Clubs dated 1.8.99

1. The guarantee should be addressed to the contractors named in the Lloyds Form.

2. **Paragraph 1**

   Insert the identity of the ship or property which is/has been arrested or is threatened with arrest and thereafter the name of the ship to whom the services were rendered.

3. **Paragraph 4**

   Insert amount to which the undertaking is limited.

01.08.99
12.06.01

B. United Kingdom Legislation

No. 21

Aircraft (Wreck and Salvage) Order 1938

Whereas under the provisions of section 28 of the Air Navigation Act, 1936, and of the Fifth Schedule to that Act, in lieu of section 11 of the Air Navigation Act, 1920, the following section shall have effect as from such date as His Majesty may by Order in Council appoint—

"11.—(1) Any services rendered in assisting, or in saving life from, or in saving the cargo or apparel of, an aircraft in, on or over the sea or any tidal water, or on or over the shores of the sea or any tidal water, shall be deemed to be salvage services in all cases in which they would have been salvage services if they had been rendered in relation to a vessel; and where salvage services are rendered by an aircraft to any property or person, the owner of the aircraft shall be entitled to the same reward for those services as he would have been entitled to if the aircraft had been a vessel.

The preceding provisions of this subsection shall have effect notwithstanding that the aircraft concerned is a foreign aircraft, and notwithstanding that the services in question are rendered elsewhere than within the limits of the territorial waters adjacent to any part of His Majesty's dominions.

"(2) His Majesty may by Order in Council direct that any provisions of any Act for the time being in force which relate to wreck, to salvage of life or property or to the duty of rendering assistance to vessels in distress shall, with such exceptions, adaptations and modifications, if any, as may be specified in the Order, apply in relation to aircraft as those provisions apply in relation to vessels.

"(3) For the purposes of this section any of the provisions of an Act which relate to vessels laid by or neglected as unfit for sea service shall be deemed to be provisions relating to wreck, and the expression 'Act' shall be deemed to include any local or special Act and any provisions of the Harbours, Docks, and Piers Clauses Act, 1847, as incorporated with any local or special Act, whenever passed."

And whereas by section 14, subsection (2), of the Air Navigation Act, 1920, it is provided that His Majesty may, by Order in Council, make provision as to the courts in which proceedings may be taken for enforcing any claim under that Act, or any other claim in respect of aircraft, and in particular may provide for conferring jurisdiction in any such proceedings on any court exercising Admiralty jurisdiction and applying to such proceedings any rules of practice or procedure applicable to proceedings in Admiralty:

And whereas by section 35, subsection (1), of the Air Navigation Act, 1936, it is provided that that Act shall be construed as one with the Air Navigation Act, 1920, and that the two Acts may be cited together as the Air Navigation Acts, 1920 and 1936:

And whereas by section 30, subsection (2), of the Air Navigation Act, 1936, it is provided that an Order in Council made under any of the provisions of the Air Navigation Acts, 1920 and 1936, may contain such incidental and supplementary provisions as appear to His Majesty in Council to be necessary or expedient for the purposes of the Order:

Aircraft (Wreck and Salvage) Order 1938

And whereas it appears to His Majesty expedient to provide for the taking effect of the section substituted by the Air Navigation Act, 1936 for section 11 of the Air Navigation Act, 1920, and to apply in relation to aircraft the provisions of the several Acts relating to wreck to salvage of life or property or to the duty of rendering assistance to vessels in distress, more particularly referred to in this Order, with the exceptions, adaptations and modifications hereinafter specified, and to confer jurisdiction in such matters as hereinafter appears:

And whereas the provisions of section 1 of the Rules Publication Act, 1893, have been complied with:

Now, therefore, His Majesty, by virtue of the powers in this behalf by the Air Navigation Acts, 1920 and 1936, or otherwise in Him vested, by and with the advice of His Privy Council is pleased to order, and it is hereby ordered, as follows:—

1. [...]

2. The provisions of Part IX of the Merchant Shipping Act, 1894, as amended by subsequent legislation, shall apply in relation to aircraft as those provisions apply to vessels, with the following exceptions, adaptations and modifications that is to say:—

(a) The words "vessel" and "ship" shall respectively include aircraft.

(b) The expression "wreck" (save and except in so far as relates to the claims of any Admiral, Vice-Admiral, Lord of the Manor, heritable proprietor duly infeft, or any other person to unclaimed wreck for his own use) shall include any aircraft or any part thereof or cargo thereof found derelict in or upon the seas surrounding the United Kingdom or the tidal waters thereof or any ports or harbours thereof or upon or near the shores of the said seas and waters or found or taken possession of outside the United Kingdom and the said seas and tidal waters and subsequently brought within those limits.

(c) The word "master" shall include the commander or other person in charge of an aircraft.

(d) The word "shipwrecked" shall include aircraft wrecked.

(e) Section 516, subsection (1), shall have effect as though the words "commissioned officer on full pay in the air service of His Majesty" were inserted after the words "justice of the peace."

(f) The provisions of section 517 shall not apply in the case of aircraft.

(g) The provisions of sections 538 to 543, both inclusive, shall not apply in the case of aircraft.

(h) In their application to aircraft, sections 548(2) and 550(3) shall have effect as though for the word "maritime" there were substituted the word "aeronautical."

(i) [...]

3.—(1) Sections 56 and 57 of the Harbours, Docks and Piers Clauses Act, 1847, as incorporated with any local or special Act, whenever passed, and the provisions relating to the same subject matters as those sections of any local or special Act for the time being in force, and sections 13, 14 and 15 of the Dockyard Ports Regulation Act, 1865, shall apply in relation to aircraft as those provisions apply to vessels, and the expressions "wreck" and "vessel" in those sections shall be deemed to include wreckage of or from aircraft and aircraft respectively.

(2) In the application in relation to aircraft of the provisions of the said sections, the expression "owner" shall mean the owner of the aircraft at the time when it was wrecked or laid by or neglected.

Appendix B—United Kingdom Legislation

4. Every court having Admiralty jurisdiction shall have jurisdiction over claims under section 11 of the Air Navigation Act, 1920, and this Order.

5. The jurisdiction conferred by the last preceding article may be exercised either by proceedings in rem or by proceedings in personam, provided that where the jurisdiction of any court is limited as to the amount of the claim or as to the value of the property saved, the jurisdiction so conferred shall be limited in the like manner.

6. The powers of all such courts and the rules of practice and procedure for the time being in force in regard to the Admiralty jurisdiction of those courts shall apply and extend to claims under section 11 of the Air Navigation Act, 1920, and under this Order.

7.—(1) The Interpretation Act, 1889, shall apply to the interpretation of this Order as it applies to the Interpretation of an Act of Parliament.

(2) This Order shall come into operation on the First day of April 1938, and as from that date the Aircraft (Wreck and Salvage) Orders in Council, 1921 and 1935 shall be revoked.

(3) This Order may be cited as the Aircraft (Wreck and Salvage) Order, 1938.

Amendments

Art. 1, which provided for the substitution of the Air Navigation Act 1920, s.11 by the Air Navigation Act 1936, Sched. 5 (both repealed) is now spent. Art. 2(i) was revoked by S.I. 1964 No. 489. Arts 4 and 5 have been superseded by the Admiralty jurisdiction provisions in the Supreme Court Act 1981 and the County Courts Act 1984.

The Merchant Shipping Act 1894, Pt IX was repealed and replaced by the Merchant Shipping Act 1995, Pt IX; the Interpretation Act 1889 was repealed and replaced by the Interpretation Act 1978; the Air Navigation Act 1920, s.11 was repealed; see now the Civil Aviation Act 1982, s.87.

Hovercraft (Application of Enactments) Order 1972

No. 22

Hovercraft (Application of Enactments) Order 1972

8. Wreck, salvage and distress

(1) The following enactments and instruments shall have effect as if any reference therein, in whatever terms, to ships, vessels or boats, or activities or places connected therewith, included a reference to hovercraft, or activities or places connected with hovercraft namely—

(a) Sections 510 to 516, 518 to 537 and [551 to 571] of the Merchant Shipping Act 1894.

(b) Section 72 of the Merchant Shipping Act 1906.

(c) [...]

(d) Section 24 of the Merchant Shipping (Safety and Load Line Conventions) Act 1932.

(e) Section 8 of the Crown Proceedings Act 1947.

[(f) The Merchant Shipping (Navigational Warnings) Regulations 1980.]

[(g) The Merchant Shipping (Signals of Distress) Rules 1992.]

In relation to the above enactments, as so applied, the expression "wreck" (save and except in so far as relates to the claims of any Admiral, Vice-Admiral, Lord of the Manor, heritable proprietor duly infeft, or any person other than her Majesty and Her Royal Successors to unclaimed wreck for his own use) shall include any hovercraft or any part thereof or cargo thereof found sunk, stranded or abandoned in or on any navigable water, or on or over the foreshore, or place where the tide normally ebbs or flows.

(2)(a) Sections 56 and 57 of the Harbours, Docks and Piers Clauses Act 1847 (1847, c.27) as incorporated with any local or special Act, whenever passed, and the provisions relating to the same subject matters as those sections of any local or special Act for the time being in force, shall apply in relation to hovercraft as those provisions apply to vessels, and the expressions "wreck" and "vessel" in those sections shall be deemed to include wreckage of or from hovercraft, and hovercraft, respectively;

(b) In the application in relation to hovercraft of the provisions of the said sections, the expressions "owner" shall mean the owner of the hovercraft at the time it was wrecked or laid by or neglected.

(3) [...]

Amendments

Paras. (1)(c), (3) were revoked and para. (1)(f), (g) and the words in square brackets in para. (1)(a) were substituted by S.I. 1995 No. 1299.
The Merchant Shipping Act 1894, ss 510–516, 518–537, 551–571, the Merchant Shipping Act 1906, s.72, the Merchant Shipping (Safety and Load Line Conventions) Act 1932, s.24 and the Crown Proceedings Act 1947, s.8 were all repealed and replaced by the Merchant Shipping Act 1995. S.I. 1980 No. 534 and S.I. 1992 No. 1582 were revoked; see now S.I. 1996 No. 1815 and S.I. 1996 No. 75 respectively.

Appendix B—United Kingdom Legislation

No. 23

Protection of Wrecks Act 1973

1. Protection of sites of historic wrecks

(1) If the Secretary of State is satisfied with respect to any site in the United kingdom waters that—

  (a) it is or may prove to be, the site of a vessel lying wrecked on or in the sea bed; and

  (b) on account of the historical, archaeological or artistic importance of the vessel, or of any objects contained or formerly contained in it which may be lying on the sea bed in or near the wreck, the site ought to be protected from unauthorised interference.

he may by order designate an area round the site as a restricted area.

(2) An order under this section shall identify the site where the vessel lies or formerly lay, or is supposed to lie or have lain, and—

  (a) the restricted area shall be all within such distance of the site (so identified) as is specified in the order, but excluding any area above high water mark of ordinary spring tides; and

  (b) the distance specified for the purposes of paragraph (a) above shall be whatever the Secretary of State thinks appropriate to ensure protection for the wreck.

(3) Subject to section 3(3) below a person commits an offence if, in a restricted area, he does any of the following things otherwise than under the authority of a licence granted by the Secretary of State—

  (a) he tampers with, damages or removes any part of a vessel lying wrecked on or in the sea bed, or any object formerly contained in such a vessel; or

  (b) he carries out diving or salvage operations directed to the exploration of any wreck or to removing objects from it or from the sea bed, or uses equipment constructed or adapted for any purpose of diving or salvage operations; or

  (c) he deposits, so as to fall and lie abandoned on the sea bed, anything which, if it were to fall on the site of a wreck (whether it so falls or not), would wholly or partly obliterate the site or obstruct access to it, or damage any part of the wreck;

and also commits an offence if he causes or permits any of those things to be done by others in a restricted area, otherwise than under the authority of such a licence.

(4) Before making an order under this section, the Secretary of State shall consult with such persons as he considers appropriate having regard to the purposes of the order; but this consultation may be dispensed with if he is satisfied that the case is one in which an order should be made as a matter of immediate urgency.

(5) A licence granted by the Secretary of State for the purposes of subsection (3) above shall be in writing and—

(a) the Secretary of State shall in respect of a restricted area grant licences only to persons who appear to him either—

    (i) to be competent, and properly equipped, to carry out salvage operations in a manner appropriate to the historical, archaeological or artistic importance of any wreck which may be lying in the area of any objects contained or formerly contained in the wreck, or

    (ii) to have any other legitimate reason for doing in the area that which can only be done under the authority of a licence;

(b) a licence may be granted subject to conditions and restrictions, and may be varied or revoked by the Secretary of State at any time after giving not less than one week's notice to the licensee; and

(c) anything done contrary to any condition or restriction of a licence shall be treated for purposes of subsection (3) above as done otherwise than under the authority of the licence.

(6) Where a person is authorised, by a licence of the Secretary of State granted under this section, to carry out diving and salvage operations, it is an offence for any other person to obstruct him, or cause or permit him to be obstructed, in doing anything which is authorised by the licence, subject however to section 3(3) below.

Amendments

As to the transfer of functions in relation to Wales from Ministers of the Crown to the National Assembly for Wales, see the National Assembly for Wales (Transfer of Functions) Order 1999 (S.I. 1999 No. 672).

2. Prohibition on approaching dangerous wrecks

(1) If the Secretary of State is satisfied with respect to a vessel lying wrecked in United Kingdom waters that—

(a) because of anything contained in it, the vessel is in a condition which makes it a potential danger to life or property; and

(b) on that account it ought to be protected from unauthorised interference,

he may by order designate an area round the vessel as a prohibited area.

(2) An order under this section shall identify the vessel and the place where it is lying and—

(a) the prohibited area shall be all within such distance of the vessel as is specified by the order, excluding any area above high water mark of ordinary spring tides; and

(b) the distance specified for the purpose of paragraph (a) above shall be whatever the Secretary of State thinks appropriate to ensure that unauthorised persons are kept away from the vessel.

(3) Subject to section 3(3) below, a person commits an offence if, without authority in writing granted by the Secretary of State, he enters a prohibited area, whether on the surface or under water.

3. Supplementary provisions

(1) In this Act—
    "United kingdom waters" means any part of the sea within the seaward limits of United kingdom territorial waters and includes any part of a river within the ebb and flow of ordinary spring tides;

Appendix B—United Kingdom Legislation

"the sea" includes any estuary or arm of the sea; and references to the sea bed include any area submerged at high water of ordinary spring tides.

(2) An order under section 1 or section 2 above shall be made by statutory instrument subject to annulment in pursuance of a resolution of either House of Parliament and may be varied or revoked by a subsequent order under the section; and the Secretary of State shall revoke any such order if—

(a) in the case of an order under section 1 designating a restricted area, he is of opinion that there is not, or is no longer, any wreck in the area which requires protection under this Act;

(b) in the case of an order under section 2 designating a prohibited area, he is satisfied that the vessel is no longer in a condition which makes it a potential danger to life or property.

(3) Nothing is to be regarded as constituting an offence under this Act where it is done by a person—

(a) in the course of any action taken by him for the sole purpose of dealing with an emergency of any description; or

(b) in exercising, or seeing to the exercise of, functions conferred by or under an enactment (local or other) on him or a body for which he acts; or

(c) out of necessity due to stress of weather or navigational hazards.

(4) A person guilty of an offence under section 1 or section 2 above shall be liable on summary conviction to a fine of not more than [the prescribed sum], and on conviction on indictment to a fine, and proceedings for such an offence may be taken, and the offence may for all incidental purposes be treated as having been committed, at any place in the United Kingdom where he is for the time being.

4. Citation

This Act may be cited as the Protection of Wrecks Act 1973.

Amendments

The words in square brackets in subsection (4) were substituted by the Magistrates' Courts Act 1980, s.32(2).

No. 24

Civil Aviation Act 1982

87. Application of law of wreck and salvage to aircraft

(1) Any services rendered in assisting, or in saving life form, or of saving the cargo, or apparel of, an aircraft in, on or over the sea or of tidal water, or on or over the shores of the sea or any tidal water, shall be deemed to be salvage services in all cases in which they would have been salvage services if they had been rendered in relation to a vessel.

(2) Where salvage services are rendered by an aircraft to any property or person, the owner of the aircraft shall be entitled to the same reward for those services as he would have been entitled to if the aircraft had been a vessel.

(3) Subsections (1) and (2) above, shall have effect notwithstanding that the aircraft concerned is a foreign aircraft and notwithstanding that the services in question are rendered elsewhere than within the limits of the territorial waters adjacent to any part of Her Majesty's dominions.

(4) Her Majesty may by Order in Council direct that any provisions of any Act for the time being in force which relate to wreck, to salvage of life or property or to the duty of rendering assistance to vessels in distress shall, with such modifications, if any, as may be specified in the Order apply in relation to aircraft as those provisions apply in relation to vessels.

(5) For the purposes of this section—

(a) any provisions of an Act which relate to vessels laid by or neglected as unfit for sea service shall be deemed to be provisions relating to wreck; and

(b) "Act" shall include any local or special Act and any provisions of the Harbour Docks and Piers Clauses Act 1847, as incorporated with any local or special Act, whenever passed.

91. Jurisdiction in civil matters

Her Majesty may by Order in Council make provision as to the courts in which proceedings may be taken for enforcing any claim in respect of aircraft, and in particular may provide—

(a) for conferring jurisdiction in any such proceedings on any court exercising Admiralty jurisdiction; and

(b) for applying to such proceedings any rules of practice or procedure applicable to proceedings in Admiralty.

Appendix B—United Kingdom Legislation

No. 25

Protection of Military Remains Act 1986

1. Application of Act

(1) This Act applies to any aircraft which has crashed (whether before or after the passing of this Act) while in military service.

(2) Subject to the following provisions of this section, the Secretary of State may by order made by statutory instrument—

  (a) designate as a vessel to which this Act applies any vessel which appears to him to have sunk or been stranded (whether before or after the passing of this Act) while in military service;

  (b) designate as a controlled site any area (which in the United Kingdom, in United Kingdom waters or in international waters) which appears to him to contain a place comprising the remains of, or of a substantial part of, an aircraft to which this Act applies or a vessel which has so sunk or been stranded;

and the power of the Secretary of State to designate a vessel as a vessel to which this Act applies shall be exercisable irrespective of whether the situation of the remains of the vessel is known.

(3) The Secretary of State shall not designate a vessel as a vessel to which this Act applies unless it appears to him—

  (a) that the vessel sunk or was stranded on or after 4th August 1914; and

  (b) in the case of a vessel which sank or was stranded while in service with, or while being used for the purposes of, any of the armed forces of a country or territory outside the United Kingdom, that remains of the vessel are in United Kingdom waters.

(4) The Secretary of State shall not designate any area as a controlled site in respect of any remains of an aircraft or vessel which has crashed sunk or been stranded unless it appears to him—

  (a) that less than two hundred years have elapsed since the crash, sinking or stranding;

  (b) that the owners and occupiers of such land in the United Kingdom as is to be designated as, or as part of, that site do not object to the terms of the designating order which affect them; and

  (c) where the aircraft or vessel crashed, sank or was stranded while in service with, or while being used for the purposes of, any of the armed forces of a country or territory outside the United Kingdom, that the remains are in the United Kingdom or in United Kingdom waters.

(5) An area designated as a controlled site shall not extend further around any place appearing to the Secretary of State to comprise remains of an aircraft or vessel which has crashed, sunk or been stranded while in military service than appears to him

Protection of Military Remains Act 1986

appropriate for the purpose of protecting or preserving those remains or on account of the difficulty of identifying that place; and no controlled site shall have a boundary in international waters any two points on which are more than two nautical miles apart.

(6) For the purposes of the Act a place (whether in the United Kingdom, in United Kingdom waters or in international waters) is a protected place if—

(a) it comprises the remains of, or of a substantial part of, an aircraft, or vessel to which this Act applies; and

(b) it is on or in the sea bed or is the place, or in the immediate vicinity of the place, where the remains were left by the crash, sinking or stranding of that aircraft or vessel;

but no place in international waters shall be a protected place by virtue of its comprising remains of an aircraft or vessel which has crashed, sunk or been stranded while in service with, or while being used for the purposes of, any of the armed forces of a country or territory outside the United Kingdom.

(7) The power to designate any land as, or as part of, a controlled site shall be exercisable in relation to Crown land as it is exercisable in relation to other land.

(8) The Secretary of State may by order made by statutory instrument substitute references to a later date for the reference in subsection (3)(a) above to 4th August 1914 or for any reference to a date which is inserted by an order under this subsection; and a statutory instrument containing an order under this subsection shall be subject to annulment in pursuance of a resolution of either House of Parliament.

2. Offences in relation to remains and prohibited operations

(1) Subject to the following provisions of this section and to section 3 below, a person shall be guilty of an offence—

(a) if he contravenes subsection (2) below in relation to any remains of an aircraft or vessel which are comprised in a place which is part of a controlled site;

(b) if, believing or having reasonable grounds for suspecting that any place comprises any remains of an aircraft or vessel which has crashed, sunk or been stranded while in military service, he contravenes that subsection in relation to any remains by virtue of which that place is a protected place;

(c) if he knowingly takes part in, or causes or permits any other person to take part in, the carrying out of any excavation or diving or salvage operation which is prohibited by subsection (3) below; or

(d) if he knowingly uses, or causes or permits any other person to use, any equipment in connection with the carrying out of any such excavation or operation.

(2) A person contravenes this subsection in relation to any remains—

(a) if he tampers with, damages, moves, removes or unearths the remains;

(b) if he enters any hatch or other opening in any of the remains which enclose any part of the interior of an aircraft or vessel; or

(c) if he causes or permits any other person to do anything falling within paragraph (a) or (b) above.

(3) An excavation or diving or salvage operation is prohibited by this subsection—

(a) if it is carried out at a controlled site for the purpose of investigating or recording details of any remains of an aircraft or vessel which are comprised in a place which is part of that site; or

(b) if it is carried out for the purpose of doing something that constitutes, or is likely to involve, a contravention of subsection (2) above in relation to any remains of an aircraft or vessel which are comprised in a protected place or in a place which is part of such a site; or

(c) in the case of an excavation, if it is carried out for the purpose of discovering whether any place in the United Kingdom or United Kingdom waters comprises any remains of an aircraft or vessel which has crashed, sunk or been stranded while in military service.

(4) In proceedings against any person for an offence under this section, it shall be a defence for that person to show that what he did or, as the case may be, what he caused or permitted to be done was done under and in accordance with a licence under section 4 below.

(5) In proceedings against any person for an offence under this section in respect of anything done at or in relation to a place which is not part of a controlled site it shall be a defence for that person to show that he believed on reasonable grounds that the circumstances were such that (if those had been the circumstances) the place would not have been a protected place.

(6) In proceedings against any person for an offence under this section it shall be a defence for that person to show that what he did or, as the case may be, what he caused or permitted to be done was urgently necessary in the interests of safety or health or to prevent or avoid serious damage to property.

(7) A person who is guilty of an offence under this section shall be liable—

(a) on summary conviction, to a fine not exceeding the statutory maximum;

(b) on conviction on indictment, to a fine.

(8) Nothing in this section shall be construed as restricting any power to carry out works which is conferred by or under any enactment.

(9) References in this section to any remains which are comprised in a protected place or to any remains which are comprised in a place which is part of a controlled site include references to remains other than those by virtue of which that place is a protected place or, as the case may be, to remains other than those in respect of which that site was or could have been designated.

3. Extraterritorial jurisdiction

(1) Where a contravention of subsection (2) of section 2 above occurs in international waters or an excavation or operation prohibited by subsection (3) of that section is carried out in international waters, a person shall be guilty of an offence under that section in respect of that contravention, excavation or operation only—

(a) if the acts or omissions which constitute the offence are committed in the United Kingdom, in United Kingdom waters or on board a British-controlled ship; or

(b) in a case where those acts or omissions are committed in international waters but not on board a British-controlled ship, if that person is—

(i) a British citizen, a British Dependent Territories citizen or a British Overseas citizen; or

(ii) a person who under the British Nationality Act 1981 is a British subject; or

(iii) a British protected person (within the meaning of that Act); or
(iv) a company within the meaning of the Companies Act 1985 or the Companies Act (Northern Ireland) 1960.

(2) Subject to subsection (1) above, an offence under section 2 above shall, for the purpose only of conferring jurisdiction on any court, be deemed to have been committed in any place where the offender may for the time being be.

(3) Where subsection (1) above applies in relation to any contravention, excavation or operation, no proceedings for an offence under section 2 above in respect of that contravention, excavation or operation shall be instituted—

(a) in England and Wales, except by or with the consent of the Director of Public Prosecutions;

(b) in Northern Ireland, except by or with the consent of the Director of Public Prosecutions for Northern Ireland.

4. Licences to carry out prohibited works, operations, etc.

(1) The Secretary of State shall have power to grant licences authorising the doing of such things as are described (whether generally or specifically) in the licences for the purpose of enabling those things to be done without the commission of any offence under section 2 above.

(2) A licence under this section shall be capable of being granted to a particular person, to persons of a particular description or to persons generally; and such a licence may be contained in an order designating a controlled site.

(3) The Secretary of State in granting a licence under this section may impose such conditions with respect to the doing of anything authorised by the licence as he may specify in the licence for any purpose connected with protecting or preserving any remains to which the licence relates.

(4) A licence under this section shall continue in force, subject to any amendments made from time to time by the Secretary of State, until the expiration of such period as is specified in the licence or until revoked, whichever is the earlier.

(5) Where a licence (other than a licence contained in an order designating a controlled site) is granted, amended or revoked under this section, the Secretary of State shall, as he thinks fit, either—

(a) send a copy of the licence, amendment or revocation to the licensee; or

(b) publish such a copy in such manner as he considers appropriate for the purpose of bringing it to the attention of persons likely to be affected by the licence, amendment or revocation.

(6) The grant of a licence under this section is without prejudice to the rights of any person (including the Crown)—

(a) as the owner of an interest in any land where any remains of an aircraft or vessel are, or are thought to be, situated; or

(b) as the owner of, or the person entitled (whether under any enactment or rule of law or otherwise) to claim, an interest in any such remains.

5. Supplemental provision with respect to licence applications

(1) A person shall be guilty of an offence if, for the purpose of obtaining a licence under section 4 above (whether for himself or another or for persons of any description), he—

(a) makes a statement, or furnishes a dominant or information, which he knows to be false in a material particular; or

(b) recklessly makes a statement or representation, or furnishes a document or information, which is false in a material particular.

(2) A person who is guilty of an offence under subsection (1) above shall be liable—

(a) on summary conviction, to a fine not exceeding the statutory maximum;

(b) on conviction on indictment, to a fine.

(3) The Secretary of State may by order made by statutory instrument require an application made to him for a licence under section 4 above to be accompanied in such circumstances as may be specified in the order, by a fee of an amount so specified.

(4) A statutory instrument containing an order under subsection (3) above shall be subject to annulment in pursuance of a resolution of either House of Parliament.

(5) Any fees received by the Secretary of State by virtue of an order under subsection (3) above shall be paid into the Consolidation Fund.

6. Powers of boarding by authorised persons

(1) Subject to the following provisions of this section, an authorised person shall be entitled for the purpose of determining whether an offence under this Act is being, has been or is to be committed to board and search—

(a) any vessel which is in United Kingdom waters; or

(b) any vessel which is in international waters and is a British-controlled ship.

(2) An authorised person shall not board a vessel under this section unless at the time he made his first request to board the vessel he had reasonable grounds for believing—

(a) in the case of a vessel other than a British-controlled ship, that an offence under this Act was being committed on board the vessel; or

(b) in the case of a British-controlled ship, that such an offence was being, had been or was to be so committed.

(3) An authorised person who has boarded a vessel under this section may seize anything which is on board the vessel if he has reasonable grounds for believing—

(a) that it is evidence of an offence under this Act or has been obtained in consequence of the commission of such an offence; and

(b) that it is necessary to seize it to prevent its being concealed, lost, altered or destroyed.

(4) An authorised person may use such force as is reasonably necessary for the purpose of exercising any power conferred on him by this section and may do anything else reasonably necessary for that purpose, including ordering a vessel to stop.

(5) A person on whom a power is conferred by this section shall, if required to do so by the master of the vessel, produce his authority before exercising the power.

(6) Any person who intentionally obstructs a person who is exercising any power conferred by this section shall be liable on summary conviction to a fine not exceeding level 3 on the standard scale.

(7) For the purpose only of conferring jurisdiction on any court, an offence under subsection (6) above shall be deemed to have been committed in any place where the offender may for the time being be.

(8) In this section "authorised person" means a person authorised in writing by the Secretary of State to exercise the powers conferred by this section (whether in all cases or only in cases specified or described in the authority) or a person of a description of persons so authorised.

7. Supplemental provisions with respect to offences

(1) [Section 143 of the Powers of Criminal Courts (Sentencing) Act 2000] and [Article 11 of the Criminal Justice (Northern Ireland) Order 1994] (power to deprive offenders of property used, or intended for use, for purposes of crime) shall have effect in England and Wales and in Northern Ireland respectively as if an offence under section 2 above were an offence punishable on indictment with imprisonment for a term of two years or more.

(2) Where a body corporate is guilty of an offence under this Act and that offence is proved to have been committed with the consent or connivance of, or to be attributable to any neglect on the part of, any director, manager, secretary or other similar office of the body corporate or any person who was purporting to act in any such capacity he, as well as the body corporate, shall be guilty of that offence and shall be liable to be proceeded against and punished accordingly.

(3) Where the affairs of a body corporate are managed by its members, subsection (2) above shall apply in relation to the acts and defaults of a member in connection with his functions of management as if he were a director of the body corporate.

Amendments

The words in square brackets in subsection (1) were substituted by the Criminal Justice (Northern Ireland) Order 1994 (S.I. 1994 No. 2795) (N.I. 15), art. 26(1). The words in double square brackets in subsection (1) were substituted by the Powers of Criminal Courts (Sentencing) Act 2000, s.165(1), Sched. 9, para. 100.

8. Administrative expenses

There shall be paid out of money provided by Parliament any administrative expenses incurred by the Secretary of State in consequence of the provisions of this Act.

9. Interpretation

(1) In this Act, except in so far as the context otherwise requires—

"aircraft" includes a hovercraft, glider or balloon;
"British-controlled ship" means a ship registered in the United Kingdom or a ship exempted from such registration under the [Merchant Shipping Act 1995];
"controlled site" means any area which is designated as such a site under section 1 above;
"Crown land" has the same meaning as in section 50 of the Ancient Monuments and Archaeological Areas Act 1979;
"international waters" means any part of the sea outside the seaward limits of the territorial waters adjacent to any country or territory;
"military service" shall be construed in accordance with subsection (2) below;
"nautical miles" means international nautical miles of 1,852 metres;
"protected place" shall be construed in accordance with section 1(6) above;
"remains", in relation to, or to part of, an aircraft or vessel which has crashed, sunk or been stranded, includes any cargo, munitions, apparel or personal

Appendix B—United Kingdom Legislation

effects which were on board the aircraft or vessel during its final flight or voyage (including, in the case of a vessel, any aircraft which were on board) and any human remains associated with the aircraft or vessel;

"sea" includes the sea bed and, so far as the tide flows at mean high water springs, any estuary or arm of the sea and the waters of any channel, creek, bay or river;

"sea bed" includes any area submerged at mean high water springs;

"United Kingdom waters" means any part of the sea within the seaward limits of the territorial waters adjacent to the United Kingdom.

(2) For the purposes of this Act an aircraft or vessel shall be regarded as having been in military service at a particular time if at that time it was—

(a) in service with, or being used for the purposes of, any of the armed forces of the United Kingdom or any other country or territory; or

(b) in the case of an aircraft, being taken from one place to another for delivery into service with any of the armed forces of the United Kingdom.

(3) Where a place comprising the remains of, or of a substantial part of, an aircraft or vessel which has crashed, sunk or been stranded while in military service is situated only partly in United Kingdom waters, this place shall be treated for the purposes of this Act as if the part which is situated in United Kingdom waters and the part which is situated in the United Kingdom or in international waters were separate places each of which comprised the remains of a substantial part of the aircraft or vessel.

Amendments

The words in square brackets in subsection (1) were substituted by the Merchant Shipping Act 1995 s.314(2), Sched. 13, §76.

10. Short title, commencement and extent

(1) This Act may be cited as the Protection of Military Remains Act 1986.

(2) This Act shall come into force at the end of the period of two months beginning with the day on which it was passed.

(3) This Act extends to Northern Ireland.

(4) Her Majesty may by Order in Council make provision for extending the provisions of this Act, with such exceptions, adaptations and modifications as may be specified in the Order, to any of the Channel Islands or any colony.

Merchant Shipping Act 1995

No. 26

Merchant Shipping Act 1995

PART III

WAGES AND SEAMEN

Wages etc.

39. Protection of certain rights and remedies

(1) A seaman's lien, his remedy for the recovery of his wages, his rights to wages in case of the wreck or loss of his ship, and any right he may have or obtain in the nature of salvage shall not be capable of being renounced by any agreement.

(2) Subsection (1) above does not affect such of the terms of any agreement made with the seamen belonging to a ship which, in accordance with the agreement, is to be employed on salvage service, as provide for the remuneration to be paid to them for salvage services rendered by that ship.

PART IV

SAFETY

Assistance at sea

92. Duty to ship to assist the other in case of collision

In every case of collision between two ships, it shall be the duty of the master of each ship, if and so far as he can do so without danger to his own ship, crew and passengers (if any)—

(a) to render to the other ship, its master, crew and passengers (if any) such assistance as may be practicable, and may be necessary to save them from any danger caused by the collision, and to stay by the other ship until he has ascertained that it has no need of further assistance; and

(b) to give the master of the other ship the name of his own ship and also the names of the ports from which it comes and to which it is bound.

(2) The duties imposed on the master of a ship subsection (1) above apply to the masters of United Kingdom ships and to the masters of foreign ships when in United Kingdom waters.

(3) The failure of the master of a ship to comply with the provisions of this section shall not raise any presumption of law that the collision was caused by his wrongful act, neglect, or default.

(4) If the master fails without reasonable excuse to comply with this section, he shall—

Appendix B—United Kingdom Legislation

(a) in the case of a failure to comply with subsection (1)(a) above, be liable—

   (i) on summary conviction, to a fine not exceeding £50,000 or imprisonment for a term not exceeding six months or both;
   (ii) on conviction on indictment, to a fine or imprisonment for a term not exceeding two years or both; and

(b) in the case of a failure to comply with subsection (1)(b) above, be liable—

   (i) on summary conviction, to a fine not exceeding the statutory maximum;
   (ii) on conviction on indictment, to a fine;

and in either case if he is a certified officer, an inquiry into his conduct may be held, and his certificate cancelled or suspended.

93. Duty to assist ships, etc. in distress

(1) The master of a ship, on receiving at sea a signal of distress or information from any source that a ship or aircraft is in distress, shall proceed with all speed to the assistance of the persons in distress (informing them if possible that he is doing so) unless he is unable, or in the special circumstances of the case considers it unreasonable or unnecessary, to do so, or unless he is released from this duty under subsection (4) or (5) below.

(2) Where the master of any ship in distress has requisitioned any ship that has answered his call, it shall be the duty of the master of the requisitioned ship to comply with the requisition by continuing to proceed with all speed to the assistance of the persons in distress.

(3) The duties imposed on the master of a ship by subsection (1) and (2) above apply to the masters of United Kingdom ships and to the masters of foreign ships when in United Kingdom waters.

(4) A master shall be released from the duty imposed by subsection (1) above as soon as he is informed of the requisition of one or more ships other than his own and that the requisition is being complied with by the ship or ships requisitioned.

(5) A master shall be released from the duty imposed by subsection (1) above, and, if his ship has been requisitioned, from the duty imposed by subsection (2) above, if he is informed by the persons in distress, or by the master of any ship that has reached the persons in distress, that assistance is no longer required.

(6) If a master fails to comply with the preceding provisions of this section he shall be liable—

(a) on summary conviction, to imprisonment for a term not exceeding six months or to a fine not exceeding the statutory maximum, or both;

(b) on conviction on indictment, to imprisonment for a term not exceeding two years or to a fine, or both.

(7) Compliance by the master of a ship with the provisions of this section shall not affect his right, or the right of any other person, to salvage.

94. Meaning of "dangerously unsafe ship"

(1) For the purposes of sections 95, 96, 97 and 98 a ship [in port] is "dangerously unsafe" if, having regard to the nature of the service for which it is intended, the ship is, by reason of the matters mentioned in subsection (2) below, unfit to go to sea without serious danger to human life.

[(1A) For the purposes of those sections a ship at sea is "dangerously unsafe" if, having regard to the nature of the service for which it is being used or is intended, the ship is, by reason of the matters mentioned in subsection (2) below, either—

Merchant Shipping Act 1995

(a) unfit to remain at sea without serious danger to human life, or

(b) unfit to go on a voyage without serious danger to human life.]

(2) Those matters are—

(a) the condition, or the unsuitability for its purpose of—

(i) the ship or its machinery or equipment, or
(ii) any part of the ship or its machinery or equipment;

(b) undermanning;

(c) overloading or unsafe or improper loading;

(d) any other matter relevant to the safety of the ship;

and are referred to in those sections, in relation to any ship, as "the matters relevant to its safety".

(3) Any references in those sections to "going to sea" shall, in a case where the service for which the ship is intended consists of going on voyages or excursions that do not involve going to sea, be construed as a reference to going on such a voyage or excursion.

Amendments

The words in square brackets in subsection (1) were inserted and subsection (1A) was added by the Merchant Shipping and Maritime Security Act 1997, s.9, Sched. 1, para. 1.

95. Power to detain dangerously unsafe ships

[(1) Where a ship which is—

(a) in a port in the United Kingdom, or

(b) at sea in United Kingdom waters,

appears to a relevant inspector to be a dangerously unsafe ship, the ship may be detained.]

(2) [Subject to subsection (2A) below] The power of detention conferred by subsection (1) above is exercisable in relation to foreign ships as well as United Kingdom ships.

[(2A) The power of detention conferred by subsection (1)(b) is not exercisable in relation to a qualifying foreign ship while the ship is exercising—

(a) the right of innocent passage, or

(b) the right of transit passage through straits used for international navigation.]

(3) The officer detaining the ship shall serve on the master of the ship a detention notice which shall—

(a) state that the relevant inspector is of the opinion that the ship is a dangerously unsafe ship;

(b) specify the matters which, in the relevant inspector's opinion, make the ship a dangerously unsafe ship; and

Appendix B—United Kingdom Legislation

(c) [require the ship to comply with the terms of the notice] until it is released by a competent authority.

(4) In the case of a ship which is not a British ship the officer detaining the ship shall cause a copy of the detention notice to be sent as soon as practicable to the nearest consular officer for the country to which the ship belongs.

(5) In this section—

"competent authority" means any officer mentioned in section 284(1); and
"relevant inspector" means any person mentioned in paragraph (a), (b) or (c) of section 258(1).

Amendments

Subsection (1) and the words in square brackets in subsection (3)(c) were substituted, the words in square brackets in subsection (2) were inserted, and subsection (2A) was added by the Merchant Shipping and Maritime Security Act 1997, s.9, Sched. 1, para. 2.

PART IX—SALVAGE AND WRECK

CHAPTER I—SALVAGE

224. Salvage Convention 1989 to have force of law

(1) The provisions of the International Convention on Salvage, 1989 as set out in Part I of Schedule 11 (in this Chapter referred to as "the Salvage Convention") shall have the force of law in the United Kingdom.

(2) The provisions of Part II of that Schedule shall have effect in connection with the Salvage Convention, and subsection (1) above shall have effect subject to the provisions of that Part.

(3) If it appears to Her Majesty in Council that the Government of the United Kingdom has agreed to any revision of the Salvage Convention She may by Order in Council make such modifications of Parts I and II of Schedule 11 as She considers appropriate in consequence of the revision.

(4) Nothing in subsection (1) or (2) above shall affect any rights or liabilities arising out of any salvage operations started or other acts done before 1st January 1995.

(5) Nothing in any modification made by virtue of subsection (3) above shall affect any rights or liabilities arising out of any salvage operations started or other acts done before the day on which the modification comes into force.

(6) As respects any period before the entry into force of the Salvage Convention nay reference in the Salvage Convention to a State Party to the Convention shall be read as a reference to the United Kingdom.

(7) A draft of an Order in Council proposed to be made by virtue of subsection (3) above shall not be submitted to Her Majesty in Council unless the draft has been approved by a resolution of each House of Parliament.

225. Valuation of property by receiver

(1) Where any dispute as to salvage arises, the receiver may, on the application of either party, appoint a valuer to value the property.

(2) When the valuation has been made the receiver shall give copies of it to both parties.

(3) A copy of the valuation purporting to be signed by the valuer, and to be certified as a true copy by the receiver, shall be admissible as evidence in any subsequent proceedings.

(4) There shall be paid in respect of the valuation by the person applying for it such fee as the Secretary of State may direct.

226. Detention of property liable for salvage by receiver

(1) Where salvage is due to any person under this Chapter, the receiver shall—

    (a) if the salvage is due in respect of services rendered—

        (i) in assisting a vessel, or
        (ii) in saving life from a vessel, or
        (iii) in saving the cargo and equipment of a vessel,

    detain the vessel and cargo or equipment; and

    (b) if the salvage is due in respect of the saving of any wreck, and the wreck is not sold as unclaimed under this Chapter, detain the wreck.

(2) Subject to subsection (3) below, the receiver shall detain the vessel and the cargo and equipment, or the wreck, as the case may be, until payment is made for salvage, or process is issued for the arrest or detention of the property by the court.

(3) The receiver may release any property detained under subsection (2) above if security is given—

    (a) to his satisfaction, or

    (b) where—

        (i) the claim for salvage exceeds £5,000, and
        (ii) any question is raised as to the sufficiency of the security, to the satisfaction of the court.

(4) Any security given for salvage under this section to an amount exceeding £5,000 may be enforced by the court in the same manner as if bail had been given in that court.

(5) In this section "the court" means the High Court or, in Scotland, the Court of Session.

(6) As respects Scotland the reference in subsection (2) to process being issued for arrest shall be construed as a reference to warrant for arrestment being granted.

227. Sale of detained property by receiver

(1) The receiver may sell any detained property if the persons liable to pay the salvage in respect of which the property is detained are aware of the detention, in the following cases.

(2) Those cases are—

    (a) where the amount is not disputed, and payment of the amount due is not made within twenty days after the amount is due;

    (b) where the amount is disputed, but no appeal lies from the first court to which the dispute is referred, and payment is not made within twenty days after the decision of the first court;

    (c) where the amount is disputed and an appeal lies from the decision of the first court to some other court, and within twenty days of the decision of the first court neither payment of the sum due is made nor proceedings are commenced for an appeal.

(3) The proceeds of sale of detained property shall, after payment of the expenses of the sale, be applied by the receiver in payment of the expenses fees and salvage and any excess shall be paid to the owners of the property or any other persons entitled to it.

(4) In this section "detained property" means property detained by the receiver under section 226(2).

228. Apportionment of salvage under £5,000 by the receiver

(1) Where—

  (a) the aggregate amount of salvage payable in respect of salvage services rendered in United Kingdom waters has been finally determined and does not exceed £5,000; but

  (b) a dispute arises as to the apportionment of the amount among several claimants,

the person liable to pay the amount may apply to the receive for leave to pay it to him.

(2) The receiver shall, if he thinks fit, receive the amount and, if he does, he shall give the person paying it a certificate stating the amount paid and the services in respect of which it is paid.

(3) A certificate under subsection (2) above shall be a full discharge and indemnity to the person by whom it was paid, and to his vessel, cargo, equipment and effects against the claims of all persons in respect of the services mentioned in the certificate.

(4) The receiver shall with all convenient speed distribute any amount received by him under this section among the persons entitled to it, on such evidence, and in such shares and proportions, as he thinks fit.

(5) Any decision by the receiver under subsection (4) above shall be made on the basis of the criteria contained in Article 13 of the Salvage Convention.

(6) The receiver may retain any money which appears to him to be payable to any person who is absent.

(7) A distribution made by a receiver under this section shall be final and conclusive as against all persons claiming to be entitled to any part of the amount distributed.

229. Apportionment of salvage by the court

(1) Where—

  (a) the aggregate amount of salvage payable in respect of salvage services rendered in United Kingdom waters has been finally determined and exceeds £5,000; or

  (b) the aggregate amount of salvage payable in respect of salvage services rendered outside United Kingdom waters (of whatever amount) has been finally determined; but

  (c) in either case, any delay or dispute arises as to the apportionment of the amount;

the court may cause the amount of salvage to be apportioned among the persons entitled to it in such manner as it thinks just.

Merchant Shipping Act 1995

(2) Any decision of the court under this section shall be made on the basis of the criteria contained in Article 13 of the Salvage Convention.

(3) For the purpose of making that apportionment, the court may—

    (a) appoint any person to carry that apportionment into effect;

    (b) compel any person in whose hands or under whose control the amount may be to distribute it or to pay it into court to be dealt with as the court directs; and

    (c) issue such process as it thinks fit.

(4) In this section "the court" means the High Court or, in Scotland, the Court of Session or a sheriff.

230. Salvage claims against the Crown and Crown rights of salvage and regulation thereof

(1) Subject to section 29 of the Crown Proceedings Act 1947 (exclusion of proceedings *in rem* against the Crown) (so far as consistent with the Salvage Convention) the law relating to civil salvage, whether of life or property, except sections 225, 226 and 227, shall apply in relation to salvage services in assisting any of Her Majesty's ships, or in saving life therefrom, or in saving any cargo or equipment belonging to Her Majesty in right of Her Government in the United Kingdom, in the same manner as if the ship, cargo or equipment belonged to a private person.

(2) Where salvage services are rendered by or on behalf of Her Majesty, whether in right of Her Government in the United Kingdom or otherwise, Her Majesty shall be entitled to claim salvage in respect of those services to the same extent as any other salvor, and shall have the same rights and remedies in respect of those services as any other salvor.

(3) No claim for salvage services by the commander or crew, or part of the crew, of any of Her Majesty's ships shall be finally adjudicated upon without the consent of the Secretary of State to the prosecution of the claim.

(4) Any document purporting to give the consent of the Secretary of State for the purposes of subsection (3) above and to be signed by an officer of the Ministry of Defence shall be evidence of that consent.

(5) If a claim is prosecuted without the consent required by subsection (3) above the claim shall be dismissed with costs.

(6) The reference in subsection (5) above to dismissal with costs shall in Scotland be construed as a reference to dismissal with the defender being found entitled to expenses.

(7) "Her Majesty's ships" has the same meaning in this section as in section 192.

(8) In the application of this section to Northern Ireland, any reference to Her Majesty's Government in the United Kingdom includes a reference to Her Government in Northern Ireland.

Chapter II—Wreck

Vessels in distress

231. Application of, and discharge of functions under, sections 232, 233, 234 and 235

(1) Sections 232, 233, 234 and 235 apply in circumstances where a United Kingdom or foreign vessel is wrecked, stranded, or in distress at any place on or near the coasts of the United Kingdom or any tidal water within United Kingdom waters.

(2) Where any function is conferred on the receiver by any of those sections that function may be discharged by any officer of customs and excise or any principal officer of the coastguard.

(3) An officer discharging any such functions of the receiver shall, with respect to any goods or articles belonging to a vessel the delivery of which to the receiver is required by any provision of this Chapter, be treated as the agent of the receiver.

(4) However, an officer discharging such functions shall not—

  (a) be entitled to any fees payable to receivers, or
  (b) be deprived of any right to salvage to which he would otherwise be entitled.

(5) In any of those sections "shipwrecked persons", in relation to a vessel, means persons belonging to the vessel.

232. Duty of receiver where vessel in distress

(1) In circumstances in which this section applies by virtue of section 231 in relation to any vessel the receiver shall, on being informed of the circumstances, discharge the following functions.

(2) Subject to subsection [(3)] below, the receiver shall—

  (a) forthwith proceed to the place where the vessel is;
  (b) take command of all persons present; and
  (c) assign such duties and given such directions to each person as he thinks fit for the preservation of the vessel and of the lives of the shipwrecked persons.

(3) The receiver shall not interfere between the master and crew of the vessel in reference to the management of the vessel unless he is requested to do so by the master.

(4) Subject to subsection (3) above, if any person intentionally disobeys the direction of the receiver he shall be liable, on summary conviction, to a fine not exceeding level 3 on the standard scale.

Amendments

The words in square brackets in subsection (2) were substituted by the Merchant Shipping and Maritime Security Act 1997, s.29, Sched. 6, para. 14.

233. Powers of receiver in case of vessel in distress

(1) [Subject to subsection (1A) below,] in circumstances where this section applies by virtue of section 231 in relation to any vessel the receiver may, for the purpose of the preservation of shipwrecked persons or of the vessel, cargo and equipment—

  (a) require such persons as he thinks necessary to assist him;
  (b) require the master, or other person having the charge, of any vessel near at hand to give such assistance, with his men, or vessel, as may be in his power; and
  (c) require the use of any vehicle that may be near at hand.

[(1A) The receiver may not under subsection (1) above impose any requirements on the master or other person having the charge of a vessel owned or operated by the Royal National Lifeboat Institution.]

Merchant Shipping Act 1995

(2) If any person refuses, without reasonable excuse, to comply with any requirement made under subsection (1) above he shall be liable, on summary conviction, to a fine not exceeding level 3 on the standard scale.

Amendments

The words in square brackets in subsection (1) were inserted and subsection (1A) added by the Merchant Shipping and Maritime Security Act 1997, s.21.

234. Power to pass over adjoining land

(1) In circumstances where this section applies by virtue of section 231 in relation to any vessel, all persons may, subject to subsections (3) and (4) below, for the purpose of—

(a) rendering assistance to the vessel,

(b) saving the lives of shipwrecked persons, or

(c) saving the cargo or equipment of the vessel,

pass and repass over any adjoining land without being subject to interruption by the owner or occupier and deposit on the land any cargo or other article recovered from the vessel.

(2) The right of passage conferred by subsection (1) above is a right of passage with or without vehicles.

(3) No right of passage is conferred by subsection (1) above where there is some public road equally convenient.

(4) The rights conferred by subsection (1) above shall be so exercised as to do as little damage as possible.

(5) Any damage sustained by an owner or occupier of land in consequence of the exercise of the rights conferred by this section shall be a charge on the vessel, cargo or articles in respect of or by which the damage is caused.

(6) Any amount payable in respect of such damage shall, in case of dispute, be determined and shall, in default of payment, be recoverable in the same manner as the amount of salvage is determined and recoverable under this Part.

(7) If the owner or occupier of any land—

(a) impedes or hinders any person in the exercise of the rights conferred by this section;

(b) impedes or hinders the deposit on the land of any cargo or other article recovered from the vessel; or

(c) prevents or attempts to prevent any cargo or other article recovered from the vessel from remaining deposited on the land for a reasonable time until it can be removed to a safe place of public deposit;

he shall be liable, on summary conviction, to a fine not exceeding level 3 on the standard scale.

235. Liability for damage in case of plundered vessel

(1) Where, in circumstances in which this section applies by virtue of section 231 in relation to any vessel, the vessel or any part of its cargo and equipment is plundered, damaged or destroyed by persons in circumstances in which those persons commit the offence of riot or, in Scotland, of mobbing and rioting, compensation shall be made to

Appendix B—United Kingdom Legislation

the owner of the vessel, cargo or equipment in accordance with the following provisions of this section.

(2) Compensation under subsection (1) above in England and Wales shall be made by the compensation authority in the manner provided by the Riot (Damages) Act 1886 with respect to claims for compensation under that Act.

(3) Where the vessel, cargo or equipment is not within a police area, the plundering, damage or destruction shall be treated for the purposes of subsection (2) above as taking place within the nearest police area.

(4) Compensation under subsection (1) above in Scotland shall, as if entitlement to it arose under section 10 of the Riotous Assemblies (Scotland) Act 1822, be made by the council constituted under section 2 of the Local Government etc. (Scotland) Act 1994 within whose area, or nearest to whose area, the plundering, damage or destruction took place.

(5) Compensation under subsection (1) above in Northern Ireland shall be made in pursuance of an application under the Criminal Injuries to Property (Compensation) Act (Northern Ireland) 1971 as modified for the purposes of this section by the Transfer of Functions (Criminal Injuries to Vessels) (Northern Ireland) Order 1973.

Dealing with wreck

236. Duties of finder etc. of wreck

(1) If any person finds or takes possession of any wreck in United Kingdom waters or finds or takes possession of any wreck outside United Kingdom waters and brings it within those waters he shall—

(a) if he is the owner of it, give notice to the receiver stating that he has found or taken possession of it and describing the marks by which it may be recognised;

(b) if he is not the owner of it, give notice to the receiver that he has found or taken possession of it and, as directed by the receiver, either hold it to the receiver's order or deliver it to the receiver.

(2) If any person fails, without reasonable excuse, to comply with subsection (1) above he shall be liable, on summary conviction, to a fine not exceeding level 4 on the standard scale and if he is not the owner of the wreck he shall also—

(a) forfeit any claim to salvage; and

(b) be liable to pay twice the value of the wreck—

(i) if it is claimed, to the owner of it; or
(ii) if it is unclaimed, to the person entitled to the wreck.

(3) Any sum payable under subsection (2)(b) above to the owner of the wreck or to the persons entitled to the wreck may, in England and Wales and Northern Ireland, be recovered summarily as a civil debt.

(4) In Scotland any sum payable under subsection (2)(b) above to the owner of the wreck or to the persons entitled to the wreck shall, for the purposes of the sum's recovery, be regarded as a debt due to the owner or, as the case may be, to those persons.

237. Provisions as respects cargo, etc.

(1) Where a vessel is wrecked, stranded, or in distress at any place on or near the coast of the United Kingdom or any tidal water within United Kingdom waters, any

cargo or other articles belonging to or separated from the vessel which are washed on shore or otherwise lost or taken from the vessel shall be delivered to the receiver.

(2) If any person (whether the owner or not)—

    (a) conceals or keeps possession of any such cargo or article, or

    (b) refuses to deliver any such cargo or article to the receiver or to any person authorised by the receiver to require delivery,

he shall be liable, on summary conviction, to a fine not exceeding level 4 on the standard scale.

(3) The receiver or any person authorised by him may take any such cargo or article (if necessary by force) from any person who refuses to deliver it.

238. Receiver to give notice of wreck

(1) Where the receiver takes possession of any wreck he shall within 48 hours—

    (a) make a record describing the wreck and any marks by which it is distinguished; and

    (b) if in his opinion the value of the wreck exceeds £5,000, also transmit a similar description to the chief executive officer of Lloyd's in London.

(2) The record made by the receiver under subsection (1)(a) above shall be kept by him available for inspection by any person during reasonable hours without charge.

(3) The notice sent under subsection (1)(b) above the chief executive officer of Lloyd's shall be posted by him in some conspicuous position for inspection.

239. Claims of owners to wreck

(1) The owner of any wreck in the possession of the receiver who establishes his claim to the wreck to the satisfaction of the receiver within one year from the time when the wreck came into the receiver's possession shall, on paying the salvage, fees and expenses due, be entitled to have the wreck delivered or the proceeds of sale paid to him.

(2) Where—

    (a) a foreign ship has been wrecked on or near the coasts of the United Kingdom, or

    (b) any articles belonging to or forming part of or of the cargo of a foreign ship which has been wrecked on or near the coasts of the United Kingdom are found on or near the coast or are brought into any port,

the appropriate consular officer shall, in the absence of the owner and of the master or other agent of the owner, be treated as the agent of the owner for the purposes of the custody and disposal of the wreck and such articles.

(3) In subsection (2) above "the appropriate consular officer", in relation to a foreign ship, means the consul general of the country to which the ship or, as the case may be, the owners of the cargo may have belonged or any consular officer of that country authorised for the purpose by any treaty or arrangement with that country.

240. Immediate sale of wreck in certain cases

(1) The receiver may at any time sell any wreck in his possession if, in his opinion—

Appendix B—United Kingdom Legislation

(a) it is under the value of £5,000;

(b) it is so much damaged or of so perishable a nature that it cannot with advantage be kept; or

(c) it is not of sufficient value to pay for storage.

[(1A) The receiver may also sell any wreck in his possession before the end of the year referred to in section 239(1) if—

(a) in his opinion it is unlikely that any owner will establish a claim to the wreck within that year; and

(b) no statement has been given to the receiver under section 242(1) in relation to the place where the wreck was found.]

(2) [Subject to section 3 below] the proceeds of sale shall, after defraying the expenses of the sale, be held by the receiver for the same purposes and subject to the same claims, rights and liabilities as if the wreck had remained unsold.

[(3) Where the receiver sells any wreck in a case falling within subsection (1A) above, he may make to the salvors an advance payment, of such amount as he thinks fit and subject to such conditions as he thinks fit, on account of any salvage that may become payable to them in accordance with section 243(5).]

Amendments

The words in square brackets in subsection (2) were inserted and subsections (1A) and (3) added by the Merchant Shipping and Maritime Security Act 1997, s.22.

Unclaimed wreck

241. Right of Crown to unclaimed wreck

Her Majesty and Her Royal successors are entitled to all unclaimed wreck found in the United Kingdom or in United Kingdom waters except in places where Her Majesty or any of Her Royal predecessors has granted the right to any other person.

242. Notice of unclaimed wreck to be given to persons entitled

(1) Any person who is entitled to unclaimed wreck found at any place in the United Kingdom or in United Kingdom waters shall give the receiver a statement containing the particulars of his entitlement and specifying an address to which notices may be sent.

(2) Where a statement has been given to the receiver under subsection (1) above and the entitlement is proved to the satisfaction of the receiver, the receiver shall, on taking possession of any wreck found at a place to which the statement refers, within 48 hours, send to the specified address a description of the wreck and of any marks distinguishing it.

243. Disposal of unclaimed wrecks

(1) Where, as respects any wreck found in the United Kingdom or in United Kingdom waters and in the possession of the receiver, no owner establishes a claim to it within one year after it came into the receiver's possession, the wreck shall be dealt with as follows.

(2) If the wreck is claimed by any person who has delivered the statement required by section 242 and has proved to the satisfaction of the receiver his entitlement to

receive unclaimed wreck found at the place where the wreck was found, the wreck shall, on payment of all expenses, costs, fees and salvage due in respect of it, be delivered to that person.

(3) If the wreck is not claimed by any person in accordance with section 242, the receiver shall sell the wreck and pay the proceeds as directed by subsection (6) below, after making the deductions required by subsection (4) below and paying to the salvor's the amount of salvage determined under subsection (5) below.

(4) The amounts to be deducted by the receiver are—

(a) the expenses of the sale;

(b) any other expenses incurred by him; and

(c) his fees.

(5) The amount of salvage to be paid by the receiver to the salvors shall be such amount as the Secretary of State directs generally or in the particular case.

(6) The proceeds of sale (after making those deductions and salvage payments) shall be paid by the receiver for the benefit of Her Majesty—

(a) if the wreck is claimed in right of the Duchy of Lancaster, to the receiver-general of the duchy or his deputies as part of its revenues;

(b) if the wreck is claimed in right of the Duchy of Cornwall, to the receiver-general of the duchy or his deputies as part of its revenues; and

(c) in any other case, into the Consolidated Fund.

244. Effect of delivery of wreck etc. under this Part

(1) Delivery of wreck or payment of the proceeds of sale or wreck by the receiver under this Chapter shall discharge the receiver from all liability in respect of the delivery or payment.

(2) Delivery of wreck by the receiver under this Chapter shall not, however, prejudice or affect any question which may be raised by third parties concerning the right or title to the wreck or concerning the title to the soil of the place at which the wreck was found.

Offences in respect of wreck

245. Taking wreck to foreign port

(1) A person commits an offence if he takes into any foreign port and sells—

(a) any vessel stranded, derelict or otherwise in distress found on or near the coasts of the United Kingdom or any tidal water within United Kingdom waters;

(b) any part of the cargo or equipment of, or anything belonging to, such a vessel; or

(c) any wreck found within those waters.

(2) A person who is guilty of an offence under this section shall be liable, on conviction on indictment, to imprisonment for a term not exceeding five years.

246. Interfering with wrecked vessel or wreck

(1) Subject to subsection (2) below, a person commits an offence if, without the permission of the master, he boards or attempts to board any vessel which is wrecked, stranded or in distress.

(2) No offence is committed under subsection (1) above if the person is the receiver or a person lawfully acting as the receiver or if he acts by command of the receiver or a person so acting.

(3) A person commits an offence if—

    (a) he impedes or hinders or attempts to impede or hinder the saving of—

        (i) any vessel stranded or in danger of being stranded, or otherwise in distress, on or near any coast or tidal water; or

        (ii) any part of the cargo or equipment of any such vessel; or

        (iii) any wreck;

    (b) he conceals any wreck;

    (c) be defaces or obliterates any mark on a vessel; or

    (d) he wrongfully carries away or removes—

        (i) any part of any vessel stranded or in danger of being stranded, or otherwise in distress, on or near any coast or tidal water;

        (ii) any part of the cargo or equipment of any such vessel; or

        (iii) any wreck.

(4) The master of a vessel may forcibly repel any person committing or attempting to commit an offence under subsection (1) above.

(5) A person who is guilty of an offence under this section shall be liable on summary conviction—

    (a) in the case of an offence under subsection (1) above, to a fine not exceeding level 3 on the standard scale;

    (b) in the case of an offence under subsection (3) above, to a fine not exceeding level 4 on the standard scale.

247. Powers of entry etc.

(1) Where the receiver has reason to believe that—

    (a) any wreck is being concealed by or is in the possession of some person who is not the owner of it; or

    (b) any wreck is being otherwise improperly dealt with,

he may apply to a justice of the peace for a search warrant.

(2) Where a search warrant is granted under subsection (1) above to the receiver, the receiver may, by virtue of the warrant—

    (a) enter any house, or other place (wherever situated) or any vessel; and

    (b) search for, seize and detain any wreck found there.

(3) If any seizure of wreck is made under this section in consequence of information given by any person to the receiver, the person giving the information shall be entitled, by way of salvage, to such sum, not exceeding £100, as the receiver may allow.

Chapter III—Supplemental

Administration

248. Functions of Secretary of State as to wreck

(1) The Secretary of State shall have the general superintendence throughout the United Kingdom of all matters relating to wreck.

(2) The Secretary of State may, with the consent of the Treasury, appoint one or more persons to be receiver of wreck for the purposes of this Part and a receiver so appointed shall discharge such functions as are assigned to him by the Secretary of State.

(3) Such public notice of appointments to the office of receiver shall be given as appears to the Secretary of State to be appropriate.

249. Expenses and fees of receivers

(1) There shall be paid to the receiver the expenses properly incurred by him in the discharge of his functions and also, in respect of such matters as may be prescribed by regulations made by the Secretary of State, such fees as may be so prescribed.

(2) The receiver shall not be entitled to any other remuneration.

(3) The receiver shall, in addition to all other rights and remedies for the recovery of those expenses and fees, have the same rights and remedies in respect of those expenses and fees as a salvor has in respect of salvage due to him.

(4) Whenever any dispute arises as to the amount payable to the receiver in respect of expenses or fees, that dispute shall be determined by the Secretary of State whose decision shall be final.

Coastguard services

250. Remuneration for services of coastguard

(1) Subject to subsection (2) below, where services are rendered by any officers or men of the coastguard service in watching or protecting shipwrecked property the owner of the property shall pay in respect of those services remuneration according to a scale fixed by the Secretary of State.

(2) No liability in respect of those services arises under subsection (1) above where—

   (a) the services have been declined by the owner of the property or his agent at the time they were tendered; or

   (b) salvage has been claimed and awarded for the services.

(3) Remuneration under this section shall—

   (a) be recoverable by the same means,

   (b) be paid to the same persons, and

   (c) be accounted for and applied in the same manner,

as fees received by the receiver under section 249.

(4) The scale fixed by the Secretary of State shall not exceed the scale by which remuneration to officers and men of the coastguard for extra duties in the ordinary

service of the Commissioners of Customs and Excise is for the time being regulated.

Release from customs and excise control

251. Release of goods from customs and excise control

(1) The Commissioners of Customs and Excise shall, subject to taking security for the protection of the revenue in respect of the goods, permit all goods saved from any ship stranded or wrecked on its homeward voyage to be forwarded to the port of its original destination.

(2) The Commissioners of Customs and Excise shall, subject to taking such security, permit all goods saved from any ship stranded or wrecked on her outward voyage to be returned to the port at which they were shipped.

(3) In this section "goods" includes wares and merchandise.

Removal of wrecks

252. Powers of harbour and conservancy authorities in relation to wrecks

(1) Where any vessel is sunk, stranded or abandoned in, or in or near any approach to, any harbour or tidal water under the control of a harbour authority or conservancy authority in such a manner as, in the opinion of the authority, to be, or be likely to become, an obstruction or danger to navigation or to lifeboats engaged in lifeboat service in that harbour or water or approach thereto, that authority may exercise any of the following powers.

(2) Those powers are—

(a) to take possession of, and raise, remove or destroy the whole or any part of the vessel and any other property to which the power extends;

(b) to light or buoy the vessel or part of the vessel and any such other property until it is raised, removed or destroyed; and

(c) subject to subsections (5) and (6) below, to sell, in such manner as the authority think fit, the vessel or part of the vessel so raised or removed and any other property received in the exercise of the powers conferred by paragraph (a) or (b) above;

(d) to reimburse themselves, out of the proceeds of the sale, for the expenses incurred by them in relation to the sale.

(3) The other property to which the powers conferred by subsection (2) above extend is every article or thing or collection of things being or forming part of the equipment, cargo, stores or ballast of the vessel.

(4) Any surplus of the proceeds of a sale under subsection (2)(c) above shall be held by the authority on trust for the persons entitled thereto.

(5) Except in the case of property which is of a perishable nature or which would deteriorate in value by delay, no sale shall be made under subsection (2)(c) above until at least seven days notice of the intended sale has been given by advertisement in a local newspaper circulating in or near the area over which the authority have control.

(6) At any time before any property is sold under subsection (2)(c) above, the owner of the property shall be entitled to have it delivered to him on payment of its fair market value.

(7) The market value of property for the purposes of subsection (6) above shall be that agreed on between the authority and the owner or, failing agreement, that determined by a person appointed for the purpose by the Secretary of State.

(8) The sum paid to the authority in respect of any property under subsection (6) above shall, for the purposes of this section, be treated as the proceeds of sale of the property.

(9) Any proceeds of sale arising under subsection (2)(c) above from the sale of a vessel and any other property recovered from the vessel shall be treated as a common fund.

(10) This section is without prejudice to any other persons of a harbour authority or conservancy authority.

253. Powers of lighthouse authorities in relation to wrecks

(1) Where—

   (a) any vessel is sunk, stranded or abandoned in any fairway or on the seashore or on or near any rock, shoal or bank in the United Kingdom or any of the adjacent seas or island; and

   (b) there is no harbour authority or conservancy authority having power to raise, remove or destroy the vessel;

the general lighthouse authority for the place in or near which the vessel is situated shall, if in the authority's opinion the vessel is, or is likely to become, an obstruction or danger to navigation or to lifeboats engaged in lifeboat service, have the same powers in relation thereto as are conferred by section 252.

(2) Where a general lighthouse authority have incurred expenses in the exercise of their powers under this section in relation to any vessel, then—

   (a) if the proceeds of any sale made under section 252 in connection with the exercise of those powers in relation to the vessel are insufficient to reimburse the authority for the full amount of those expenses, the authority may recover the amount of the deficiency from the relevant person, or

   (b) if there is no such sale, the authority may recover the full amount of those expenses from the relevant person.

(3) Any expenses so incurred which are not recovered by the authority either out of the proceeds of any such sale or in accordance with subsection (2) above shall be paid out of the General Lighthouse Fund, but section 213 shall apply to those expenses as if they were expenses of the authority falling within subsection (1) of that section other than establishment expenses.

(4) In this section "the relevant person", in relation to any vessel, means the owner of the vessel at the time of the sinking, stranding or abandonment of the vessel.

254. Referral of questions as to powers between authorities

(1) If any question arises between a harbour authority or conservancy authority and a general lighthouse authority as to their respective powers under sections 252 and 253 in relation to any place in or near an approach to a harbour or tidal water, that question shall, on the application of either authority, be referred to the Secretary of State for his decision.

(2) Any decision of the Secretary of State under this section shall be final.

Interpretation

255. Interpretation

(1) In this Part—

   "receiver" means a receiver of wreck appointed under section 248;

Appendix B—United Kingdom Legislation

"salvage" includes, subject to the Salvage Convention, all expenses properly incurred by the salvor in the performance of the salvage services;
"the Salvage Convention" has the meaning given by section 224(1);
"salvor" means, in the case of salvage services rendered by the officers or crew or part of the crew of any ship belonging to Her Majesty, the person in command of the ship;
"tidal water" means any part of the sea and any part of a river within the ebb and flow of the tide at ordinary spring tides, and not being a harbour;
"vessel" includes any ship or boat, or any other description of vessel used in navigation; and
"wreck" includes jetsam, flotsam, lagan and derelict found in or on the shores of the sea or any tidal water.

(2) Fishing boats or fishing gear lost or abandoned at sea and either—

(a) found or taken possession of within United Kingdom waters; or

(b) found or taken possession of beyond those waters and brought within those waters;

shall be treated as wreck for the purposes of this Part.
(3) In the application of this Part in relation to Scotland, any reference to a justice of the peace includes a reference to a sheriff.

PART XIII

SUPPLEMENTAL

Application of Act to certain descriptions of ships, etc.

310. Application of Act to hovercraft

The enactments and instruments with respect to which provision may be made by Order in Council under section 1(1)(h) of the Hovercraft Act 1968 shall include this Act (except Parts I and II) and any instrument made thereunder.

Final provisions

313. Definitions

(1) In this Act, unless the context otherwise requires—
"British connection" has the meaning given in section 9(9);
"British citizen", "British Dependent Territories citizen", "British Overseas citizen" and "Commonwealth citizen" have the same meaning as in the British Nationality Act 1981;
"British ship" has the meaning given in section 1(1);
"commissioned military officer" means a commissioned officer in Her Majesty's land forces on full pay;
"commissioned naval officer" means a commissioned officer of Her Majesty's Navy on full pay;
"conservancy authority" includes all persons entrusted with the function of conserving, maintaining or improving the navigation of a tidal water (as defined in section 255);

"consular officer", in relation to a foreign country, means the officer recognised by Her Majesty as a consular officer of that foreign country;
"contravention" includes failure to comply (and "failure" includes refusal);
"Departmental inspector" and "Departmental officer" have the meanings given in section 256(9);
"fishing vessel" means a vessel for the time being used (or, in the context of an application for registration, intended to be used) for, or in connection with fishing for sea fish other than a vessel used (or intended to be used) for fishing otherwise than for profit; and for the purposes of this definition "sea fish" includes shellfish, salmon and migratory trout (as defined by section 44 of the Fisheries Act 1981);
"foreign", in relation to a ship, means that it is neither a United Kingdom ship nor a small ship (as defined in section 1(2)) which is a British ship;
"Government ship" has the meaning given in section 308;
"harbour" includes estuaries, navigable rivers, piers, jetties and other works in or at which ships can obtain shelter or ship and unship goods or passengers;
"harbour authority" means, in relation to a harbour—

    (a) the person who is the statutory harbour authority for the harbour, or
    (b) if there is no statutory harbour authority for the harbour, the person (if any) who is the proprietor of the harbour or who is entrusted with the function of managing, maintaining or improving the harbour;]

"master" includes every person (except a pilot) having command or charge of a ship and, in relation to a fishing vessel, means the skipper;
["Minister of the Crown" has the same meaning as in the Ministers of the Crown Act 1975;]
"port" includes place;
"proper officer" means a consular officer appointed by Her Majesty's Government in the United Kingdom and, in relation to a port in a country outside the United Kingdom which is not a foreign country, also any officer exercising in that port functions similar to those of a superintendent;
["qualifying foreign ship" has the meaning given in section 313A;]
"the register" and "registered" have the meaning given in section 23(1);
"the registrar", in relation to the registration of ships, has the meaning given in section 8;
"registration regulations" means regulations under section 10;
"relevant British possession" means—

    (a) the Isle of Man;
    (b) any of the Channel Islands; and
    (c) any colony;

"safety regulations" means regulations under section 85;
"seaman" includes every person (except masters and pilots) employed or engaged in any capacity on board any ship;
"ship" includes every description of vessel used in navigation;
["statutory harbour authority" means—

    (a) in relation to Great Britain, a harbour authority within the meaning of the Harbours Act 1964; and
    (b) in relation to Northern IReland, a harbour authority within the meaning of the Harbours Act (Northern Ireland) 1970.]

"superintendent" means a mercantile marine superintendent appointed under section 296;
"surveyor of ships" has the meaning given in section 256(9);
"the tonnage regulations" means regulations under section 19;
"United Kingdom ship" (and in Part V "United Kingdom fishing vessel") has the meaning given in section 1(3) except in the contexts there mentioned; and

"wages" includes emoluments.

(2) In this Act—

(a) "United Kingdom waters" means the sea or other waters within the seaward limits of the territorial sea of the United Kingdom; and

(b) "national waters", in relation to the United Kingdom, means United Kingdom waters landward of the baselines for measuring the breadth of its territorial sea.

[(2A) In this Act "right of innocent passage", "right of transit passage" and "straits used for international navigation" shall be construed in accordance with the United Nations Convention on the Law of the Sea 1982.]

(3) A vessel for the time being used (or intended to be used) wholly for the purpose of conveying persons wishing to fish for pleasure is not a fishing vessel.

Amendments

The definition of "harbour authority" was substituted, those of "Minister of the Crown", "qualifying foreign ship" and "statutory harbour authority" were inserted in subsection (1), and subsection (2A) was added, by the Merchant Shipping and Maritime Security Act 1997, s.29(1), Sched. 6, para. 19.

[313A. Meaning of "qualifying foreign ship"

(1) In this Act "qualifying foreign ship" means any ship other than—

(a) a British ship, or

(b) a ship which is not registered under Part II and which although not by virtue of section 1(1)(d) a British ship)—

(i) is wholly owned by persons falling within subsection (2) below, and
(ii) is not registered under the law of a country outside the United Kingdom.

(2) The following persons fall within this subsection, namely—

(a) British citizens,

(b) British Dependent Territories citizens,

(c) British Overseas citizens,

(d) persons who under the British Nationality Act 1981 are British subjects,

(e) British Nationals (Overseas) (within the meaning of that Act),

(f) British protected persons (within the meaning of that Act), or

(g) bodies corporate incorporated in the United Kingdom or in any relevant British possession and having their principal place of business in the United Kingdom or in any relevant British possession.]

Amendments

This section was added by the Merchant Shipping and Maritime Security Act 1997, s.29(1), Sched. 6, para. 20.

Merchant Shipping Act 1995

Section 224(1)(2) SCHEDULE 11

INTERNATIONAL CONVENTION ON SALVAGE 1989

PART 1

CHAPTER 1—GENERAL PROVISIONS

Article 1. Definitions

For the purpose of this Convention—

(a) Salvage operation means any act or activity undertaken to assist a vessel or any other property in danger in navigable waters or in any other waters whatsoever.

(b) Vessel means any ship or craft, or any structure capable of navigation.

(c) Property means any property not permanently and intentionally attached to the shoreline and includes freight at risk.

(d) Damage to the environment means substantial physical damage to human health or to marine life or resources in coastal or inland waters or areas adjacent thereto, caused by pollution, contamination, fire, explosion or similar major incidents.

(e) Payment means any reward, remuneration or compensation due under this Convention.

(f) Organisation means the International Maritime Organisation.

(g) Secretary-General means the Secretary-General of the Organisation.

Article 2. Application of the Convention

This Convention shall apply whenever judicial or arbitral proceedings relating to matters dealt with in this Convention are brought in a State Party.

Article 3. Platforms and drilling units

This Convention shall not apply to fixed or floating platforms or to mobile, offshore drilling units when such platforms or units are on location engaged in the exploration, exploitation or production of sea-bed mineral resources.

Article 4. State-owned vessels

1. Without prejudice to article 5, this Convention shall not apply to warships or other non-commercial vessels owned or operated by a State and entitled, at the time of salvage operations, to sovereign immunity under generally recognised principles of international law unless that State decides otherwise.

2. Where a State Party decides to apply the Convention to its warships or other vessels described in paragraph 1, it shall notify the Secretary-General thereof specifying the terms and conditions of such application.

Article 5. Salvage operations controlled by public authorities

1. This Convention shall not affect any provisions of national law or any international convention relating to salvage operations by or under the control of public authorities.

2. Nevertheless, salvors carrying out such salvage operations shall be entitled to avail themselves of the rights and remedies provided for in this Convention in respect of salvage operations.

3. The extent to which a public authority under a duty to perform salvage operations may avail itself of the rights and remedies provided for in this Convention shall be determined by the law of the State where such authority is situated.

Article 6. Salvage contracts

1. This Convention shall apply to any salvage operations save to the extent that a contract otherwise provides expressly or by implication.

2. The master shall have the authority to conclude contracts for salvage operations on behalf of the owner of the vessel. The master or the owner of the vessel shall have the authority to conclude such contracts on behalf of the owner of the property on board the vessel.

3. Nothing in this article shall affect the application of article 7 nor duties to prevent or minimise damage to the environment.

Article 7. Annulment and modification of contracts

A contract or any terms thereof may be annulled or modified—

(a) the contract has been entered into under undue influence or the influence of danger and its terms are inequitable; or

(b) the payment under the contract is in an excessive degree too large or too small for the services actually rendered.

CHAPTER II—PERFORMANCE OF SALVAGE OPERATIONS

Article 8. Duties of the salvor and of the owner and master

1. The salvor shall owe a duty to the owner of the vessel or other property in danger—

(a) to carry out the salvage operations with due care;

(b) in performing the duty specified in subparagraph (a), to exercise due care to prevent or minimise damage to the environment;

(c) whenever circumstances reasonably require, to seek assistance from other salvor; and

(d) to accept the intervention of other salvors which reasonably requested to do so by the owner or master of the vessel or other property in danger; provided however that the amount of his reward shall not be prejudiced should it be found that such a request was unreasonable.

2. The owner and master of the vessel or the owner of other property in danger shall owe a duty to the salvor—

(a) to co-operate fully with him during the course of the salvage operations;

(b) in so doing, to exercise due care to prevent or minimise damage to the environment; and

(c) when the vessel or other property has been brought to a place of safety, to accept redelivery when reasonably requested by the salvor to do so.

Article 9. Rights of coastal States

Nothing in this Convention shall affect the right of the coastal State concerned to take measures in accordance with generally recognised principles of international law to protect its coastline or related interests from pollution or the threat of pollution following upon a maritime casualty or acts relating to such a casualty which may reasonably be expected to result in major harmful consequences, including the right of a coastal State to give directions in relation to salvage operations.

Article 10. Duty to render assistance

1. Every master is bound, so far as he can do so without serious danger to his vessel and persons thereon, to render assistance to any person in danger of being lost at sea.
2. The States Parties shall adopt the measures necessary to enforce the duty set out in paragraph 1.
3. The owner of the vessel shall incur no liability for a breach of the duty of the master under paragraph 1.

Article 11. Co-operation

A State Party shall, whenever regulating or deciding upon matters relating to salvage operations such as admittance to ports of vessels in distress or the provision of facilities to salvors, take into account the need for co-operation between salvors, other interested parties and public authorities in order to ensure the efficient and successful performance of salvage operations for the purpose of saving life or property in danger as well as preventing damage to the environment in general.

CHAPTER III—RIGHTS OF SALVORS

Article 12. Conditions for reward

1. Salvage operations which have had a useful result give right to a reward.
2. Except as otherwise provided, no payment is due under this Convention if the salvage operations have had no useful result.
3. This chapter shall apply, notwithstanding that the salved vessel and the vessel undertaking the salvage operations belong to the same owner.

Article 13. Criteria for fixing the reward

1. The reward shall be fixed with a view to encouraging salvage operations, taking into account the following criteria without regard to the order in which they are presented below—

   (a) the salved value of the vessel and other property;
   (b) the skill and efforts of the salvors in preventing or minimising damage to the environment;
   (c) the measure of success obtained by the salvor;
   (d) the nature and degree of the danger;

Appendix B—United Kingdom Legislation

    (e) the skill and efforts of the salvors in salving the vessel, other property and life;

    (f) the time used and expenses and losses incurred by the salvors;

    (g) the risk of liability and other risks run by the salvors or their equipment;

    (h) the promptness of the services rendered;

    (i) the availability and use of vessels or other equipment intended for salvage operations;

    (j) the sate of readiness and efficiency of the salvor's equipment and the value thereof.

2. Payment of a reward fixed according to paragraph 1 shall be made by all of the vessel and other property interests in proportion to their respective salved values. However, a State Party may in its national law provide that the payment of a reward has to be made by one of these interests, subject to a right of recourse of this interest against the other interests for their respective shares. Nothing in this article shall prevent any right of defence.

3. The rewards, exclusive of any interest and recoverable legal costs that may be payable thereon, shall not exceed the salved value of the vessel and other property.

Article 14. Special compensation

1. If the salvor has carried out salvage operations in respect of a vessel which by itself or its cargo threatened damage to the environment and has failed to earn a reward under article 13 at least equivalent to the special compensation accessable in accordance with this article, he shall be entitled to special compensation from the owner of that vessel equivalent to his expenses as herein defined.

2. If, in the circumstances set out in paragraph 1, the salvor by his salvage operations has prevented or minimised damage to the environment, the special compensation payable by the owner to the salvor under paragraph 1 may be increased up to a maximum of 30 per cent of the expenses incurred by the salvor. However, the tribunal, if it deems it fair and just to do so and bearing in mind the relevant criteria set out in article 13, paragraph 1, may increase such special compensation further, but in no event shall the total increase be more than 100 per cent of the expenses incurred by the salvor.

3. Salvor's expenses for the purpose of paragraphs 1 and 2 means the out-of-pocket expenses reasonably incurred by the salvor in the salvage operation and a fair rate for equipment and personnel actually and reasonably used in the salvage operation, taking into consideration the criteria set out in article 13, paragraph 1(h), (i) and (j).

4. The total special compensation under this article shall be paid only if and to the extent that such compensation is greater than any reward recoverable by the salvor under article 13.

5. If the salvor has been negligent and has thereby failed to prevent or minimise damage to the environment, he may be deprived of the whole or part of any special compensation due under this article.

6. Nothing in this article shall affect any right of recourse on the part of the owner of the vessel.

Article 15. Apportionment between salvors

1. The apportionment of a reward under article 13 between salvors shall be made on the basis of the criteria contained in that article.

2. The apportionment between the owner, master and other persons in the service of each salving vessel shall be determined by the law of the flag of that vessel. If the

salvage has not been carried out from a vessel, the apportionment shall be determined by the law governing the contract between the salvor and his servants.

Article 16. Salvage of persons

1. No remuneration is due from persons whose lives are saved, but nothing in this article shall effect the provisions of national law on this subject.
2. A salvor of human life, who has taken part in the services rendered on the occasion of the accident giving rise to salvage, is entitled to a fair share of the payment awarded to the salvor for salving the vessel or other property or preventing or minimising damage to the environment.

Article 17. Services rendered under existing contracts

No payment is due under the provisions of this Convention unless the services rendered exceed what can be reasonably considered as due performance of a contract entered into before the danger arose.

Article 18. The effect of salvor's misconduct

A salvor may be deprived of the whole or part of the payment due under this Convention to the extent that the salvage operations have become necessary or more difficult because of fault or neglect on his part or if the salvor has been guilty of fraud or other dishonest misconduct.

Article 19. Prohibition of salvage operations

Services rendered notwithstanding the express and reasonable prohibition of the owner or master of the vessel or the owner of any other property in danger which is not and has not been on board the vessel shall not give rise to payment under this Convention.

CHAPTER IV—CLAIMS AND ACTIONS

Article 20. Maritime lien

1. Nothing in this Convention shall affect the salvor's maritime lien under any international convention or national law.
2. The salvor may not enforce his maritime lien when satisfactory security for his claim, including interest and costs, has been duly tendered or provided.

Article 21. Duty to provide security

1. Upon the request of the salvor a person liable for a payment due under this Convention shall provide satisfactory security for the claim, including interest and costs of the salvor.
2. Without prejudice to paragraph 1, the owner of the salved vessel shall use his best endeavours to ensure that the owners of the cargo provide satisfactory security for the claims against them including interest and costs before the cargo is released.
3. The salved vessel and other property shall not, without the consent of the salvor, be removed from the port or place at which they first arrive after the completion of the salvage operations until satisfactory security has been put up for the salvor's claim against the relevant vessel or property.

Article 22. Interim payment

1. The tribunal having jurisdiction over the claim of the salvor may, by interim decision, order that the salvor shall be paid on account such amount as seems fair and just, and on such terms including terms as to security where appropriate, as may be fair and just according to the circumstances of the case.

2. In the event of an interim payment under this article the security provided under article 21 shall be reduced accordingly.

Article 23. Limitation of actions

1. Any action relating to payment under this Convention shall be time barred if judicial or arbitral proceedings have not been instituted within a period of two years. The limitation period commences on the day on which the salvage operations are terminated.

2. The person against whom a claim is made may at any time during the running of the limitation period extend that period by a declaration to the claimant. This period may in the like manner be further extended.

3. An action for indemnity by a person liable may be instituted even after the expiration of the limitation period provided for in the preceding paragraphs, if brought within the time allowed by the law of the State where proceedings are instituted.

Article 24. Interest

The right of the salvor to interest on any payment due under this Convention shall be determined according to the law of the State in which the tribunal seized of the case is situated.

Article 25. State-owned cargoes

Unless the State owner consents, no provision of this Convention shall be used as a basis for the seizure, arrest or detention by any legal process of, nor for any proceedings in rem against, non-commercial cargoes owned by a State and entitled, at the time of the salvage operations, to sovereign immunity under generally recognised principles of international law.

Article 26. Humanitarian cargoes

No provisions of this Convention shall be used as a basis for the seizure, arrest or detention of humanitarian cargoes donated by a State, if such State has agreed to pay for salvage services rendered in respect of such humanitarian cargoes.

Article 27. Publication of arbitral awards

States Parties shall encourage, as far as possible and with the consent of the parties, the publication of arbitral awards made in salvage cases.

PART II

PROVISIONS HAVING EFFECT IN CONNECTION WITH CONVENTION

1. Interpretation

In this Part of this Schedule "the Convention" means the Convention as set out in Part I of this Schedule and any reference to a numbered article is a reference to the article of the Convention which is so numbered.

2. Claims excluded from Convention

(1) The provisions of the Convention do not apply—

(a) to a salvage operation which takes place in inland waters of the United Kingdom and in which all the vessels involved are of inland navigation; and

(b) to a salvage operation which takes place in inland waters of the United Kingdom and in which no vessel is involved.

(2) In this paragraph "inland waters" does not include any waters within the ebb and flow of the tide at ordinary spring tides or the waters of any dock which is directly or (by means of one or more other docks) indirectly, connected with such waters.

3. Assistance to persons in danger at sea

(1) The master of a vessel who fails to comply with the duty imposed on him by article 10, paragraph 1 commits an offence and shall be liable—

(a) on summary conviction, to imprisonment for a term not exceeding six months, or a fine not exceeding the statutory maximum or both;

(b) on conviction on indictment, to imprisonment for a term not exceeding two years or a fine, or both.

(2) Compliance by the master of a vessel with that duty shall not affect his right or the right of any other person to a payment under the Convention or under any contract.

4. The reward and special compensation: the common understanding

In fixing a reward under article 13 and assessing special compensation under article 14 the court or arbitrator (or, in Scotland, arbiter) is under no duty to fix a reward under article 13 up to the maximum salved value of the vessel and other property before assessing the special compensation to be paid under article 14.

5. Recourse for life salvage payment

(1) This paragraph applies where—

(a) services are rendered wholly or in part in United Kingdom waters in saving life from a vessel of any nationality or elsewhere in saving life from any United Kingdom ship; and

(b) either—
  (i) the vessel and other property are destroyed, or
  (ii) the sum to which the salvor is entitled under article 16, paragraph 2 is less than a reasonable amount for the services rendered in saving life.

(2) Where this paragraph applies, the Secretary of State may, if he thinks fit, pay to the salvor such sum or, as the case may be, such additional sum as he thinks fit in respect of the services rendered in saving life.

6. Meaning of "judicial proceedings"

References in the Convention to judicial proceedings are references to proceedings—

(a) in England and Wales, in the High court or the county court;

(b) in Scotland, in the Court of Session or in the sheriff court;

(c) in Northern Ireland, in the High Court;

and any reference to the tribunal having jurisdiction (so far as it refers to judicial proceedings) shall be construed accordingly.

7. Meaning of "State Party"

(1) An Order in Council made for the purposes of this paragraph and declaring that any State specified in the Order is a party to the Convention in respect of a specified country shall, subject to the provision of any subsequent Order made for those purposes, be conclusive evidence that the State is a party to the Convention in respect of that country.

(2) In this paragraph "country" includes "territory".

Section 314   SCHEDULE 14

Transitory, Saving and Transitional Provisions

11. Wreck and salvage: Cinque ports

Nothing in Part IX shall prejudice or affect any jurisdiction or powers of the Lord Warden of any officers of the Cinque ports or of any court of those ports or of any court having concurrent jurisdiction within the boundaries of those ports; and disputes as to salvage arising without those boundaries shall, subject to the Salvage Convention as set out in Schedule 11, be determined in the manner in which they have been hitherto determined.

Merchant Shipping and Maritime Security Act 1997

No. 27

Merchant Shipping and Maritime Security Act 1997

Protection of wrecks

24. Implementation of international agreements relating to protection of wrecks

(1) The Secretary of State may by order made by statutory instrument make such provision as he considers appropriate for the purpose of giving effect to any international agreement—

    (a) to which the United Kingdom is, or at the time when the order takes effect will be, a party, and

    (b) which relates to the protection of wrecks outside United Kingdom waters.

(2) Without prejudice to the generality of subsection (1), an order under this section may include—

    (a) provision designating a wreck, or an area in which a wreck is situated, for the purposes of the order,

    (b) provision prohibiting or restricting access to that wreck or are or interference with that wreck,

    (c) provision for the granting of licences by the Secretary of State,

    (d) provision authorising a person authorised by the Secretary of State in accordance with the order to board and search—

        (i) any ship which is in United Kingdom waters, and

        (ii) any United Kingdom ship which is in international waters,

    (e) provision authorising such a person to seize anything found in the course of a search authorised under the order,

    (f) provision that, subject to subsection (3), a contravention of a requirement imposed by the order shall be an offence punishable on summary conviction by a fine not exceeding the statutory maximum or on conviction on indictment by a fine, and

    (g) such incidental, supplementary and transitional provision as appears to the Secretary of State to be appropriate for the purposes of the order.

(3) No person shall be guilty of an offence under an order under subsection (1) unless—

    (a) the acts or omissions which constitute the offence are committed in the United Kingdom, in United Kingdom waters or on board a United Kingdom ship, or

    (b) in a case where those acts or omissions are committed in international waters but not on board a United Kingdom ship, that person is—

Appendix B—United Kingdom Legislation

    (i) a British citizen, a British Dependent Territories citizen or a British Overseas citizen,
    (ii) a person who under the British Nationality Act 1981 is a British subject,
    (iii) a British National (Overseas) (within the meaning of that Act),
    (iv) a British protected person (within the meaning of that Act), or
    (v) a company within the meaning of the Companies Act 1985 or the Companies (Northern Ireland) Order 1986.

(4) In subsection (3), "United Kingdom ship" means a ship which—

    (a) is registered in the United Kingdom; or

    (b) is not registered under the law of any country but is wholly owned by persons each of whom is a person mentioned in paragraph (b)(i) to (v) of that subsection.

(5) Subject to subsection (3), any offence under an order under subsection (1) shall, for the purpose only of conferring jurisdiction on any court, be deemed to have been committed in any place where the offender may for the time being be.

(6) No proceedings for an offence under any order under subsection (1) shall be instituted—

    (a) in England and Wales, except by or with the consent of the Director of Public Prosecutions;

    (b) in Northern Ireland, except by or with the consent of the Director of Public Prosecutions for Northern Ireland.

(7) A statutory instrument containing an order under subsection (1) shall be subject to annulment in pursuance of a resolution of either House of Parliament.

(8) In this section—

"international waters" means any part of the sea outside the seaward limits of the territorial sea of any country or territory;
"ship" includes any description of vessel used in navigation;
"United Kingdom waters" means the sea or other waters within the seaward limits of the territorial sea of the United Kingdom;
"wreck" means the wreck of any ship other than a ship which, at the time it sank or was stranded, was in service with, or used for the purpose of, any of the armed forces of the United Kingdom or any other country or territory.

C. INTERNATIONAL CONVENTIONS

No. 28

CONVENTION FOR THE UNIFICATION OF CERTAIN RULES OF LAW RESPECTING ASSISTANCE AND SALVAGE AT SEA, SIGNED AT BRUSSELS, SEPTEMBER 23, 1910

His Majesty the King of the United Kingdom of Great Britain and Ireland and of the British Dominions beyond the Seas, Emperor of India; His Majesty the German Emperor, King of Prussia, in the name of the German Empire; the President of the Argentine Republic; His Majesty the Emperor of Austria, King of Bohemia, etc., and Apostolic King of Hungary, for Austria and Hungary; His Majesty the King of the Belgians; the President of the United States of Brazil; the President of the Republic of Chile; the President of the Republic of Cuba; His Majesty the King of Denmark; His Majesty the King of Spain; the President of the United States of America; the President of the French Republic; His Majesty the King of the Hellenes; His Majesty the King of Italy; His Majesty the Emperor of Japan; the President of the United States of Mexico; the President of the Republic of Nicaragua; His Majesty the King of Norway; Her Majesty the Queen of the Netherlands; His Majesty the King of Portugal and the Algarves; His Majesty the King of Roumania; His Majesty the Emperor of All the Russias; His Majesty the King of Sweden; the President of the Republic of Uruguay;

Having recognised the desirability of determining by agreement certain uniform rules of law respecting assistance and salvage at sea, have decided to conclude a Convention to that end, and have appointed Plenipotentiaries who, having been duly authorised to that effect, have agreed as follows:

Article 1

Assistance and salvage of seagoing vessels in danger, of any things on board, of freight and passage money, and also services of the same nature rendered by seagoing vessels to vessels of inland navigation or vice-versa, are subject to the following provisions, without any distinction being drawn between these two kinds of service (*viz.*, assistance and salvage), and in whatever waters the services have been rendered.

Article 2

Every act of assistance or salvage which has had a useful result gives a right to equitable remuneration.
No remuneration is due if the services rendered have no beneficial result.
In no case shall the sum to be paid exceed the value of the property salved.

Article 3

Persons who have taken part in salvage operations notwithstanding the express and reasonable prohibition on the part of the vessel to which the services were rendered, have no right to any remuneration.

Article 4

A tug has no right to remuneration for assistance to or salvage of the vessel she is towing or of the vessel's cargo, except where she has rendered exceptional services which cannot be considered as rendered in fulfilment of the contract of towage.

Article 5

Remuneration is due notwithstanding that the salvage services have been rendered by or to vessels belonging to the same owner.

Article 6

The amount of remuneration is fixed by agreement between the parties, and, failing agreement, by the court.

The proportion in which the remuneration is to be distributed amongst the salvors is fixed in the same manner.

The apportionment of the remuneration amongst the owner, master and other persons in the service of each salving vessel shall be determined by the law of the vessel's flag.

Article 7

Every agreement as to assistance or salvage entered into at the moment and under the influence of danger may, at the request of either party, be annulled, or modified by the court, if it considers that the conditions agreed upon are not equitable.

In all cases, when it is proved that the consent of one of the parties is vitiated by fraud or concealment, or when the remuneration is, in proportion to the services rendered, in an excessive degree too large or too small, the agreement may be annulled or modified by the court at the request of the party affected.

Article 8

The remuneration is fixed by the court according to the circumstances of each case, on the basis of the following considerations: (a) firstly, the measure of success obtained, the efforts and deserts of the salvors, the danger run by the salved vessel, by her passengers, crew and cargo, by the salvors, and by the salving vessel; the time expended, the expenses incurred and losses suffered, and the risks of liability and other risks run by the salvors, and also the value of the property exposed to such risks, due regard being had to the special appropriation (if any) of the salvors' vessel for salvage purposes; (b) secondly, the value of the property salved.

The same provisions apply for the purpose of fixing the apportionment provided for by the second paragraph of Article 6.

The court may deprive the salvors of all remuneration, or may award a reduced remuneration, if it appears that the salvors have by their fault rendered the salvage or assistance necessary or have been guilty of theft, fraudulent concealment, or other acts of fraud.

Article 9

No remuneration is due from persons whose lives are saved, but nothing in this article shall affect the provisions of the national laws on this subject.

Salvors of human life, who have taken part in the services rendered on the occasion of the accident giving rise to salvage or assistance, are entitled to a fair share of the remuneration awarded to the salvors of the vessel, her cargo, and accessories.

Article 10

A salvage action is barred after an interval of two years from the day on which the operations of assistance or salvage terminate.

The grounds upon which the said period of limitation may be suspended or interrupted are determined by the law of the court where the case is tried.

The High Contracting Parties reserve to themselves the right to provide, by legislation in their respective countries, that the said period shall be extended in cases where it has not been possible to arrest the vessel assisted or salved in the territorial waters of the State in which the plaintiff has his domicile or principle place of business.

Article 11

Every master is bound, so far as he can do so without serious danger to his vessel, her crew and her passengers, to render assistance to everybody, even though an enemy, found at sea in danger of being lost.

The owner of a vessel incurs no liability by reason of contravention of the above provision.

Article 12

The High Contracting Parties, whose legislation does not forbid infringements of the preceding Article, bind themselves to take or to propose to their respective Legislatures the measures necessary for the prevention of such infringements.

The High Contracting Parties will communicate to one another as soon as possible the laws or regulations which have already been or may be hereafter promulgated in their States for giving effect to the above provision.

Article 13

This Convention does not affect the provisions of national laws or international treaties as regards the organisation of services of assistance and salvage by or under the control of public authorities, nor, in particular, does it affect such laws or treaties on the subject of the salvage of fishing gear.

Article 14

This Convention does not apply to ships of war or to Government ships appropriated exclusively to a public service.

Article 15

The provisions of this Convention shall be applied as regards all persons interested when either the assisting or salving vessel or the vessel assisted or salved belongs to a State of the High Contracting Parties, as well as in any other cases for which the national laws provide.

Provided always that—

1. As regards persons interested who belong to a non-contracting State the application of the above provisions may be made by each of the contracting States conditional upon reciprocity.

2. Where all the persons interested belong to the same State as the court trying the case, the provisions of the national law and not of the Convention are applicable.

3. Without prejudice to any wider provisions of any national laws, Article 11 only applies as between vessels belonging to the States of the High Contracting Parties.

Article 16

Any one of the High Contracting Parties shall have the right, three years after this Convention comes into force, to call for a fresh Conference with a view to possible amendments, and particularly with a view to extend, if possible, the sphere of its application.

Any Power exercising this right must notify its intention to the other Powers, through the Belgian Government, which will make arrangements for convening the Conference within six months.

Article 17

States which have not signed the present Convention are allowed to accede to it at their request. Such accession shall be notified through the diplomatic channel to the Belgian Government, and by the latter to each of the Governments of the other Contracting Parties; it shall become effective one month after the despatch of such notification by the Belgian Government.

Article 18

The present Convention shall be ratified.

After an interval of at most one year from the date on which the Convention is signed, the Belgian Government shall place itself in communication with the Governments of the High Contracting Parties which have declared themselves prepared to ratify the Convention, with a view to decide whether it should be put into force.

The ratifications shall, if so decided, be deposited forthwith at Brussels, and the Convention shall come into force a month after such deposit.

The Protocol shall remain open another year in favour of the States represented at the Brussels Conference. After this interval they can only accede to it in conformity with the provisions of Article 17.

Article 19

In the case of one or other of the High Contracting Parties denouncing this Convention, such denunciation shall not take effect until a year after the day on which it has been notified to the Belgian Government, and the Convention shall remain in force as between the other Contracting Parties.

In witness whereof, the Plenipotentiaries of the respective High Contracting Parties have signed this Convention and have affixed thereto their seals.

Done at Brussels, in a single copy, September 23, 1910.

Signatories: Great Britain, Germany, Argentine, Austria/Hungary, Austria, Hungary, Belgium, Brazil, Chile, Cuba, Denmark, Spain, United States of America, France, Greece, Italy, Japan, Mexico, Nicaragua, Norway, Netherlands, Portugal, Roumania, Russia, Sweden, Uruguay.

Convention for Assistance and Salvage of Aircraft

No. 29

INTERNATIONAL CONVENTION FOR THE UNIFICATION OF CERTAIN RULES RELATING TO ASSISTANCE AND SALVAGE OF AIRCRAFT OR BY AIRCRAFT AT SEA, SIGNED AT BRUSSELS, SEPTEMBER 28, 1938

Having recognised the utility of adopting certain uniform rules relating to assistance and salvage of and by aircraft at sea, the Parties have named for that purpose their respective Plenipotentiaries who, being thereto duly authorised, have concluded and signed the following Convention:

Article 1

The High Contracting Parties agree to take the necessary measures to give effect to the rules established by this Convention.

Article 2

1. Every person exercising the functions of commander on board an aircraft is bound to render assistance to everybody who is at sea in danger of being lost, in so far as he can do so without serious danger to the aircraft, its crew, its passengers, or other persons.
2. Every master of a vessel is bound, subject to the conditions stated in paragraph 1, and without prejudice to any more extended obligations imposed upon him by laws and conventions in force, to render assistance to everybody who is at sea in danger of being lost in an aircraft or as the consequence of accident to an aircraft.
3. For the purposes of this Convention, assistance means any help which may be given to a person at sea in danger of being lost, even by the mere giving of information, regard being had to the different conditions governing maritime navigation and air navigation.
4. The obligation of assistance shall exist only when the aircraft or the vessel is in the course of a voyage or ready to depart, and only if it is reasonably possible for it to render useful aid.
5. The obligation of assistance ceases only when the person bound thereby has knowledge that assistance is being rendered by others under similar or better conditions than it could be by himself.
6. The national legislations shall determine the measures necessary to give effect to this undertaking and the High Contracting Parties will communicate to one another, through diplomatic channels, the texts of such laws.
7. No liability shall rest with the owner or the manager of the vessel or with the owner or operator of the aircraft, as such, by reason of contravention of the foregoing provision except in the case where he has expressly forbidden its observance.

Article 3

1. Assistance rendered pursuant to the obligation defined in the preceding Article gives a right to an indemnity in respect of expenses justified by the circumstances and of losses suffered in the course of the operations.
2. If the assistance was rendered in the absence of any obligation to do so, the person rendering it shall have no right to indemnity unless he has obtained a useful result by saving persons or by contributing thereto.
3. The indemnity shall be payable by the operator of the aircraft assisted, or by the owner or manager of the vessel assisted and in the latter case in accordance with the national law or any contracts relating to such vessel.

4. The indemnity shall not exceed the sum of 50,000 francs for each person saved, or a total sum of 50,000 francs if no rescue has been effected.

In any case, the obligation of the aircraft operator shall be limited to the sum of 500,000 francs.

The sums fixed in this paragraph shall be deemed to refer to the gold franc containing $65\frac{1}{2}$ milligrams of gold of a standard of fineness of 900/1,000. These sums may be converted into any national currency in round figures.

Furthermore, the owner or manager of the vessel shall not be liable beyond the limits fixed by the laws and conventions in force with respect to his liability for maritime salvage.

5.(a) Where assistance has been rendered by several vessels or aircraft, and the total sum of the indemnities due exceeds the limit fixed in the foregoing paragraph 4, a proportional reduction of the indemnities shall be made.

(b) The persons who have rendered assistance must in such case take action to enforce their rights or give notice of their claims to the party who is bound to pay the indemnity within a maximum period of six months from the day of the assistance.

(c) When this period has expired, the payment of the indemnities may be proceeded with; parties who have allowed this period to expire without taking action to enforce their rights or giving notice of their claims may not exercise their rights except in respect of any balance which may not have been distributed.

Article 4

1. In case of salvage of an aircraft at sea in danger of being lost or of the property on board the same, a salvor by vessel or aircraft shall be entitled to remuneration assessed on the basis of the following considerations—

(a) First, the measure of success obtained, the efforts and the deserts of the salvors, the danger run by the salved aircraft, its passengers, crew and cargo, by the salvors and the salving aircraft or vessel, the time expended, the expenses incurred and losses suffered, and the risks of liability and other risks run by the salvors, and also the value of the property exposed to such risks, due regard being had, the case arising to the special adaptation, if any, of the salvor's equipment;

(b) Second, the value of the property salved.

2. No remuneration is due if the services rendered have no beneficial result.

3. In no case shall the sum to be paid exceed the value of the property salved at the conclusion of the operations of salvage.

4. Remuneration is due notwithstanding that the aircraft or the vessels belong to the same operator or to the same owner or manager.

5. In case of salvage by several vessels or aircraft, the remuneration shall be divided among the salvors on the bases established in paragraph 1 of this Article.

6. The same rules shall apply in case of salvage at sea by an aircraft of a vessel in danger or its cargo, in which case the owner or manager of the vessel shall retain the right to avail himself of the limitation of his liability as determined by laws and conventions in force governing maritime salvage.

Article 5

In case indemnities and remuneration are payable by reason of Articles 3 and 4 of this Convention, there shall be an equitable apportionment, upon the bases and within the limits of the said Articles, of the expenses incurred and the losses suffered.

Article 6

The apportionment of the remuneration among the operator and other persons in the service of each salving aircraft is determined by the law of the flag.

Convention for Assistance and Salvage of Aircraft

Article 7

In case of assistance to persons together with salvage of property, the salvors of human life are entitled to a fair share of the remuneration awarded for the salvage of property, without prejudice to the right to indemnity which he acquires under Article 3.

Article 8

1. No indemnity or remuneration is payable if the assistance was rendered or salvage effected in spite of the express and reasonable prohibition on the part of the vessel or aircraft to which services were rendered.
2. The court may reduce or deny the indemnity or the remuneration if it appears that the salvors have, by their fault, rendered the salvage or assistance necessary, or increased the loss, or have been guilty of theft, receiving stolen goods or other acts of fraud.

Article 9

1. The remuneration due for the operations of salvage shall be payable by the operator of the salved aircraft, or by the owner or manager of the salved vessel and in the latter case in accordance with the national laws or with contracts relating to such vessel.
2. The operator of the aircraft has a right of recourse against the owners of goods for such part of the remuneration as pertains to the salvage of such goods; provided that such recourse shall be denied or reduced if it appears that the salvage of the goods has been rendered necessary by an act of the operator of such a nature as to render him responsible to the owners of such goods.
3. The owner of the goods may, in every case, on payment of that part of the remuneration which relates to the salvage of his goods, or on giving good security or its payment, obtain delivery of the goods by the operator and the vacation of any arrest which may have been effected.
4. The recourse of the owner or of the manager of the vessel against owners of goods remains subject to maritime rules.

Article 10

Neither the personal effects of baggage of the crew or passengers, nor articles transported under the regime of postal conventions or of agreements relating to the postal service, are included in the property, either for the purpose of calculating the remuneration or in respect of the recourse to be exercised.

Article 11

1. Indemnity and remuneration actions must be brought within two years from the day on which operations of assistance or salvage are terminated.
2. The recourse of the operator against the owners of goods is limited to one year from the date of the payment of the remuneration for salvage.
3. The method of calculating the period of limitation, as well as the grounds upon which the said period of limitation may be suspended or interrupted are determined by the law of the court where the case is tried.

Article 12

Every agreement as to assistance or salvage entered into at the moment and under the influence of danger can, at the request of either party, be annulled or modified by the court if it considers that the conditions agreed upon are not equitable, and in an excessive degree too large or too small in proportion to the services rendered.

Article 13

1. Action for indemnity or remuneration may be brought at the option of the plaintiff and in conformity with the rules of procedure and jurisdiction of each state, either before the judicial authorities of the defendant's domicile, or before those of the place where the operations of salvage were effected, or if there has been an attachment of the aircraft or of the cargo, before the judicial authorities of the place of such attachment.

2. If different salvors being actions before courts situated in different countries, the defendant may, before each of them, put in a statement of the total amount of the claims made upon him, with a view to preventing the limits of his liability being exceeded.

Article 14

Any person who has the right of disposal of, and who uses the aircraft for his own account shall be termed "operator of the aircraft".

If the name of the operator is not inscribed in the aeronautical register or on some other official document, the owner is deemed to be the operator until proved to the contrary.

Article 15

Any person who, without having the right to dispose of the aircraft, makes use of it without the consent of the operator, shall be liable for the indemnities and remuneration, and the operator who has not taken the proper measures to avoid the unlawful use of his aircraft shall be liable jointly and severally with him, each of them being bound on the conditions and within the limits provided for in the foregoing Articles.

Article 16

With exception of the provisions of Article 13 relative to jurisdiction, this Convention shall apply to Government vessels and aircraft, other than military, customs and police vessels or aircraft, to which the rights and obligations resulting from the foregoing provisions do not apply.

Article 17

1. The provisions of the present Conventions shall be applied as regards all the persons interested when either the assisting or salving vessel or aircraft, or the vessel or aircraft assisted or salved, is registered in the territory of one of the High Contracting Parties.

2. The expression "territory of a High Contracting Party" includes every subject to sovereignty, suzerainty, protectorate, mandate or authority of that High Contracting Party in respect of which the latter is a party to the Convention.

3. Provided, however:

(a) That as regards interested persons who are nationals of a non-Contracting State, the application of the above provisions may be made subject by each of the Contracting States to the condition of reciprocity;

(b) That where all the interested persons are nationals of the same state as that of the court trying the case, the Convention shall not be applicable.

(c) That in a case where both vessels and aircraft are engaged in the same operation of assistance, this Convention shall not apply to relations between the vessels.

No. 30

PROTOCOL TO AMEND THE CONVENTION FOR THE UNIFICATION OF CERTAIN RULES OF LAW RELATING TO ASSISTANCE AND SALVAGE AT SEA, SIGNED AT BRUSSELS ON SEPTEMBER 23, 1910, DONE AT BRUSSELS ON MAY 27, 1967

The contracting parties,
Considering that it is desirable to amend the Convention for the unification of certain rules of law relating to assistance and salvage at sea, signed at Brussels on September 23, 1910.
Have agreed as follows:

Article 1

Article 14 of the Convention for the unification of certain rules of law relating to assistance and salvage at sea, signed at Brussels on September 23, 1910, shall be replaced by the following:
"The provisions of this Convention shall also apply to assistance or salvage services rendered by or to a ship of war or any other ship owned, operated or chartered by a State or Public Authority.
A claim against a State for assistance or salvage services rendered to a ship of war or other ship which is, either at the time of the event or when the claim is brought, appropriated exclusively to public non commercial service, shall be brought only before the Courts of such State.
Any High Contracting Party shall have the right to determine whether and to what extent Article 11 shall apply to ships coming within the terms of the second paragraph of this Article".

Article 2

This Protocol shall be open for signature by the States which have ratified the Convention or which have adhered thereto before May 17, 1967, and by any State represented at the twelfth session of the Diplomatic Conference on Maritime Law.

Article 3

1. This Protocol shall be ratified.
2. Ratification of this Protocol by any State which is not a Party to the Convention shall have the effect of accession to the Convention.
3. The instruments of ratification shall be deposited with the Belgian Government.

Article 4

1. This Protocol shall come into force one month after the deposit of five instruments of ratification.
2. This Protocol shall come into force, in respect of each signatory State which ratifies it after the deposit of the fifth instrument of ratification, one month after the date of deposit of the instrument of ratification of that State.

Article 5

1. States, Members of the United Nations or Members of the specialized agencies, not registered at the twelfth session of the Diplomatic Conference on Maritime Law, may accede to this Protocol.
2. Accession to this Protocol shall have the effect of accession to the Convention.
3. The instruments of accession shall be deposited with the Belgian Government.
4. The Protocol shall come into force in respect of the acceding State one month after the date of deposit of the instrument of accession of that State, but not before the date of entry into force of the Protocol as established by Article 4.

Article 6

1. Any contracting state may denounce this Protocol by notification to the Belgian Government.
2. This denunciation shall have the effect of denunciation of the Convention.
3. The denunciation shall take effect one year after the date on which the notification has been received by the Belgian Government.

Article 7

1. Any contracting state may at the time of signature, ratification or accession to this Convention or at any time thereafter declare by written notification to the Belgian Government which among the territories under its sovereignty or for whose international relations it is responsible, are those to which the present Protocol applies. The Protocol shall one month after the date of the receipt of such notification by the Belgian Government extend to the territories named therein, but not before the date of the coming into force of the Protocol in respect of such State.
2. This extension also shall apply to the Convention if the latter is not yet applicable to those territories.
3. Any contracting state which has made a declaration under § 1 of this Article may at any time thereafter declare by notification given to the Belgian Government that the Protocol shall cease to extend to such territory. This denunciation shall take effect one year after the date on which notification thereof has been received by the Belgian Government: it also shall apply to the Convention.

Article 8

The Belgian Government shall notify the States represented at the twelfth session of the Diplomatic Conference on Maritime Law, the acceding States to this Protocol, and the States parties to the Convention, of the following:

1. The signatures, ratifications and accessions received in accordance with Articles 2, 3 and 5.
2. The date on which the present Protocol will come into force in accordance with Article 4.
3. The notifications with regard to the territorial application in accordance with Article 7.
4. The denunciations received in accordance with Article 6.

In witness whereof the undersigned plenipotentiaries, duly authorized, have signed this Protocol.

Done at Brussels, this 27th day of May 1967, in the French and English languages, both texts being equally authentic, in a single copy, which shall remain deposited in the archives of the Belgian Government, which shall issue certified copies.

UNITED NATIONS

CONVENTION ON THE LAW OF THE SEA

(1982)

Article 98. Duty to render assistance

1. Every State shall require the master of a ship flying its flat, in so far as he can do so without serious danger to the ship, the crew or the passengers:

   (a) to render assistance to any person found at sea in danger of being lost;

   (b) to proceed with all reasonable speed to the rescue of persons in distress, if informed of their need of assistance, in so far as such action may reasonably be expected of him;

   (c) after a collision, to render assistance to the other ship, its crew and its passengers and, where possible, to inform the other ship of the name of his own ship, its port of registry and the nearest port at which it will call.

2. Every coastal State shall promote the establishment, operation and maintenance of an adequate search and rescue service regarding safety on and over the sea and, where circumstances so require, by way of mutual regional arrangements co-operate with neighbouring States for this purpose.

Article 221. Measures to avoid pollution arising from maritime casualties

1. Nothing in this Part shall prejudice the right of States, pursuant to international law, both customary and conventional, to take and enforce measures beyond the territorial sea proportionate to the actual or threatened damage to protect their coastline or related interests, including fishing, from pollution or threat of pollution following upon a maritime casualty or acts relating to such a casualty, which may reasonably be expected to result in major harmful consequences.

2. For the purposes of this article, "maritime casualty" means a collision of vessels, stranding or other incident of navigation, or other occurrence on board a vessel or external to it resulting in material damage or imminent threat of material damage to a vessel or cargo.

Appendix C—International Conventions

No. 32

CMI REPORT

**Comité Maritime International
Report
to
the International Maritime Organization—IMO**

on

the draft international convention on salvage
approved by the XXXII International Conference of the CMI held in
Montreal, May 1981

and designed to replace

the International Convention for the Unification of Certain Rules of
Law Relating to Assistance and Salvage at Sea made in Brussels on 23
September 1910

This report has been prepared by Mr. Bent Nielsen upon instructions of
the Executive Council of the CMI and has been approved by the
General Assembly of the CMI on 6 April 1984

Introduction

In March 1978 the "Amoco Cadiz" carrying approx. 220,000 tons of crude oil was wrecked on the coast of France and caused the hitherto largest oil pollution accident.

At its 35th session the Legal Committee of IMO requested its secretariat to prepare a report on the legal questions arising out of the "Amoco Cadiz" incident. In this report of September 1978 various aspects of salvage are extensively dealt with. The report raises the questions whether the existing international law of salvage contained in the 1910 Brussels Convention should be revised, and whether a new salvage convention to supersede the 1910 Convention should be prepared.

Following consideration of the subject of salvage at the CMI Assembly in March 1979, where it was concluded that the matter required immediate attention, CMI offered IMO its cooperation for the study of the subject of salvage and in particular to explore whether new rules should be prepared in order to cover those casualties which may cause a threat of pollution, thereby creating a direct and primary interest of the coastal State in the salvage operations.

Having again considered the subject of salvage and the offer for cooperation made by the CMI, the Legal Committee of IMO at its 40th session in June 1979 decided that the CMI should be requested to review the private law principles of salvage.

Informed of this decision, the CMI in September 1979 decided to set up an international Sub-Committee under the chairmanship of Professor Erling Chr. Selvig (Norway) to study the subject of salvage and to prepare a report for the consideration of the XXXII International Conference of the CMI to be held in Montreal on May 24th–29th 1981.

During 1980–81 the Sub-Committee had 3 meetings with considerable attendance including representatives of IMO and organisations for shipowners, salvors, insurers and P&I clubs, as well as Sub-committee members from the maritime law associations of more than 20 countries. At the meetings reports and drafts prepared by the Chairman and a working group set up by the Sub-Committee were considered, and in February 1981 a draft convention was approved for submission to the Montreal Conference. This draft, together with the Chairman's final report to the Conference, has been printed in CMI Documentation 1981, Montreal I.

At the Conference the subject was first dealt with by a commission under the chairmanship of the Chairman of the international Sub-Committee. The recommendations of the commission were then put before the plenary session of the Conference, and the final draft, which is now submitted for the consideration of IMO, was adopted by the votes of 31 out of 32 national Maritime Law Associations; there were no votes against and only one delegation abstained.

Explanatory notes

General Comments

The current international law of salvage is based on the Brussels Convention for the Unification of Certain rules of Law Relating to Assistance and Salvage at Sea, 1910. This Convention (together with the Collision Convention) was the first international convention in the field of maritime law. It has been almost universally accepted, and unlike most other maritime law conventions it has not so far been subject to any substantial revisions.

The basic rules of the 1910 Convention provide that a service undertaken to save property in danger at sea gives a right to equitable remuneration if, and only if, it has had a beneficial result. Such remuneration is not fixed as a compensation for the labour expended, but is usually more generous; however, it must not exceed the value of the property saved.

Since the 1910 Convention was formulated the technical and economic development in international shipping has, of course, been very significant. The dangers to ship and cargo have been reduced while the dangers which ship and cargo represent vis-à-vis third party interests, in particular relating to the environment, have substantially increased.

The values of ship and cargo have increased drastically resulting in a heavy concentration of risks on fewer keels. To the professional salvors this means fewer, but more valuable opportunities.

Salvage techniques have improved substantially, but have become far more capital intensive. This has had a certain adverse effect on the ready availability of adequate salvage equipment along the sea routes of the world.

The "Amoco Cadiz" incident demonstrates the need for rules prescribing the duties on the owners and the master of the vessel in danger as well as on the salvor, in similar situations.

It also became clear that the existing rules of salvage did not offer sufficient incentives to induce the salvor to render salvage services in cases where there is very little prospect of succeeding in saving the property while, on the other hand, major salvage operations might be urgently needed to prevent or minimize damage to the environment.

A general revision of the traditional rules of salvage as contained in the 1910 Convention was also needed in the light of the age of these rules and the substantial developments since they were formulated.

The most important new rules proposed in the draft convention are the following:

1. Art. 3-2.1. provides that the reward shall be fixed with a view to encouraging salvage operations. Although this principle has often been followed under the regime of the 1910 Convention, it was felt important to stress in the Convention itself that the encouragement of salvors is the basic consideration, which

Appendix C—International Conventions

must always be in the minds of the tribunals when salvage rewards are fixed.

Further, in Art. 3-2.1. (b) it is provided that the successful salvor of property is entitled to an enhancement for his skill and efforts in preventing or minimizing damage to the environment. This is a new consideration, which is expected to be a very important incentive to salvors when they are deciding whether to undertake salvage operations concerning casualties which threaten to damage the environment and deciding how the salvage operations should be carried out in such cases.

2. Art. 3-3 provides special compensation to salvors, who without success attempt to salve a vessel and her cargo, when these threaten environmental damage.

   Such compensation covers the salvors' expenses and may, when damage to the environment is actually prevented or minimized, also include an additional special remuneration fixed according to the circumstances of each case, but never to exceed the expenses.

   This special compensation is linked to the traditional reward in the sense that the special compensation is due only if the traditional reward is not earned or is below the special compensation.

3. Chapter II provides rules concerning the duties in salvage situations of the owner and the master, the salvor and public authorities. The owners and the master of the vessel in danger shall take timely action to arrange for salvage operations, and the salvor shall use his best endeavours to salve the vessel. It is also specifically prescribed that these parties have a duty to use their best endeavours to prevent or minimize damage to the environment. Certain rules are proposed concerning cooperation of public authorities in such cases.

4. A number of new rules have been introduced to improve the position of the salvors, in particular professional salvors, and thereby increase the incentives to undertake salvage operations. Thus, in Art. 2-1.3. it is made a duty for the owners to accept re-delivery when the salved property is brought to a place of safety. In Art. 4-1.3. the salvor is given the right to prevent the removal of the salved property from the port or place of safety until security has been provided. In Art. 4-2. certain rules are introduced facilitating the provision of security for the salvage reward. In Art. 4-3. the salvor is given the right to claim an interim decision under which he is paid an amount on account of the salvage reward. This will improve the salvor's cash flow situation while he is awaiting the final decision of the tribunal concerning his remuneration. In Art. 4-5. certain rules on jurisdiction are given to facilitate recovery of salvage rewards, and in Art. 5-1. contracting States recommended to give the salvors the right of limitation of liability provided for in the 1976 Convention on the limitation for maritime claims.

The draft convention deals with many matters which have not been provided for in the 1910 Convention. Nevertheless, the draft convention is not intended to set out the law of salvage in any exhaustive manner. The CMI considers that as regards certain questions the solution adopted in the various national laws on salvage differ to such an extent that the acceptability of the draft convention might be reduced if an attempt were made now to bring about international uniformity by provisions which also deal with such matters. One such matter is the question: who is liable for salvage rewards?

The question whether any of the rules of the Convention should be mandatory has been thoroughly debated and considered. Rules on the limits of contractual freedom have been proposed in Art. 1-5., but in Art. 1-4. it has been provided in general that the application of the rules of the Convention may be excluded by agreement between the parties.

It has been pointed out from some quarters that at least the rules relating to the prevention or minimization of damage to the environment should be compulsorily applicable, particularly to avoid haggling and the resulting delay when urgent action is required of the kind illustrated by the "Amoco Cadiz" incident.

However, it was strongly felt within the CMI that such limits should not be put on contractual freedom. In support of this it was in particular pointed out that other rights or methods of compensation provided for by contracts in given cases might be better incentives or instruments to avoid damage to the environment. For example, a salvor may in some cases for instance prefer an agreement under which he is secured the immediate payment of an agreed daily rate to the much later payment of the more uncertain sum fixed under the rules in Art. 3-3. Further, it was feared that the introduction of mandatory rules would severely jeopardize the prospects for the fast and wide international implementation of the Convention.

It is estimated that more than 80% of all salvage operations at sea are carried out under a salvage contract. Lloyd's standard form of Salvage Agreement (LOF) is by far the most frequently used standard contract.

In 1979–80 the LOF was thoroughly revised with special regard to the problems caused by oil pollution. The CMI has taken due note of the innovations of the new LOF 1980 and important parts of the draft convention are harmonized with LOF 1980.

One of the most important problems, viz. how to compensate salvors for avoidance of environmental damage if no property is salved, was solved in the LOF 1980 by the introduction of the so-called "safety net" provision, on the basis of which the draft convention, Art. 3-3. is modelled.

Other solutions were considered during the work of the CMI, but it became obvious that the "safety net" model should be preferred mainly on the grounds that it expresses a compromise among all the interested parties. Thus the compromise is a balanced solution which is not dominated by any of the interests involved, and works in the general interest of the public.

Appendix C—International Conventions

Special Comments

CHAPTER I

GENERAL PROVISIONS

Art. 1-1. Definitions

1–1.1. *Salvage operations* means any act or activity undertaken to assist a vessel or any property in danger in whatever waters the act or activity takes place.

This definition means that the scope of international salvage has been extended so as to include not only ships, but also any other structure capable of navigation as well as any other property in danger in variable and other waters, such as oil rigs, floating docks, buoys, and fishing gear. In this contract note was taken of the proposal in respect of salvage relating to off-shore mobile craft adopted at the CMI Rio Conference of 1977.

The substitution of the words "assistance and salvage" in Art. 1 of the 1910 Convention with "any act or activity undertaken to assist" is to be considered only as a redrafting of the principle, also applicable under the 1910 Convention, that any act or activity can give rise to a salvage reward if it contributes to the saving of property in danger at sea.

The definition includes salvage operations relating to vessels engaging in inland navigation, but according to Art. 1-2.2. (a) the Convention is not applicable if all the vessels involved are engaged in inland navigation.

The words "in whatever waters" are in particular incorporated to bring in the Great Lakes. However, the words make it clear that salvage operations in all inland waters are covered by the Convention. This should be kept in mind when choosing the title of the Convention, which should not, as the title of the 1910 Convention did include any reference to "assistance et sauvetage maritimes" (the words "en mer" were inserted also, it is assumed unintentionally, in the title of the French text of the Montreal draft).

It is worth noting that the words "in whatever waters" are not referring to the assistance, but to the vessel or property in danger. Therefore, salvage operations conducted from land are also covered by the definition.

It is generally felt to be an important element of salvage that it must be voluntary, but this term may be ambiguous and, therefore, it has not been included in the definition itself. The cases where salvage operations are carried out on the basis of a pre-existing duty are dealt with in Art. 1-3. which contains provisions for salvage operations controlled by public authorities and in Art. 3-6., in which it is made clear that services which are rendered in due performance of a contract entered into before the danger arose shall not be compensated under the rules of the Convention.

1-1.2. *Vessel* means any ship, craft or structure capable of navigation, including any vessel which is stranded, left by its crew or sunk.

The last part of this paragraph makes it clear that assistance to abandoned vessels will be governed by the Convention. It should be noted, however, that Art. 1-2.2. (d) provides that removal of wrecks is not governed by the Convention and is thus left for regulation at national level. The distinction between removal of wreck which is not governed by the Convention and salvage services to "stranded" and "sunk" ships, to which the Convention applies, may depend upon the particular facts of each case.

However, the criterion may often be that there is some initiative from a public authority.

1-1.3. *Property* includes freight for the carriage of the cargo, whether such freight be at the risk of the owner of the goods, the shipowner or the charterer.

The corresponding provision of the draft convention submitted by the Sub-Committee to the Montreal Conference contained the following general definition of property: "any property in danger in whatever waters the salvage operations take place". In Montreal, however, this was felt to be superfluous as it was only a repetition of the provision in Art. 1-1.1. The general definition of property, therefore, must be found in Art. 1-1.1., and Art. 1-1.3. is only retained to make it clear how freight should be dealt with. Freight does not include charter hire unless in the particular case the provision on the freight for the actual carriage of the goods is contained in the charter party.

1-1.4. *Damage to the environment* means substantial physical damage to human health or to marine life or resources in coastal or inland waters or areas adjacent thereto, caused by pollution, explosion, contamination, fire or similar major incidents.

This is a key concept in the draft convention. It is used in Art. 3-2.1. (b) and Art. 3-3. where the relevant considerations are the endeavours of the salvors to prevent or minimize such damage or the extent to which this has been done. In these provisions it is not the damage itself which is relevant, but the fact that a *risk* of such damage exists emanating from a ship in danger.

Art. 1-1.4. refers to physical damage to persons or property, not to the economic consequences thereof.

By using the words "substantial" and "major" as well as the reference to "pollution, explosion, contamination, fire" it is intended to make it clear that the definition does not include damage to any particular person or installation. There must be a risk of damage of a more general nature in the area concerned, and it must be a risk of substantial damage.

During the Montreal Conference the words "to human health or to marine life or resources" were added to exclude further from the concept cases where there may only be a risk of substantial physical damage to other property, *e.g.* warehouses or other buildings ashore.

The use of the words "coastal or inland waters" serves to make it clear that cases where there is only a risk of damage to the environment on the high seas are excluded. This is felt to be important since there would often be a possibility of speculative and inflated claims based on loose assertions that general environment damage to fishing or other ecology was involved. It must be stressed, however, that damage in coastal waters emanating from a ship in danger on the high seas is not excluded.

As can easily be seen, the definition includes much more than pollution. It is not limited to risk of damage caused by oil or other specific cargoes. The use of the words "explosion" and "fire" in particular shows that it is the intention to cover all major incidents comprehensively.

1-1.5. *Payment* means any reward, remuneration, compensation or reimbursement due under the provisions of this Convention.

The purpose of this definition is to introduce a general word covering payment in respect of expenses as well as payment in respect of a property award.

The Sub-Committee has also proposed the following definition: "owner of the goods means the person entitled to the goods". This definition was deleted in Montreal as being superfluous. On the same grounds proposals from some national MLAS for definitions of "owner" and "salvor" were not adopted.

Appendix C—International Conventions

Art. 1-2. Scope of application

1-2.1. This Convention shall apply whenever judicial or arbitral proceedings relating to matters dealt with in this Convention are brought in a contracting State, as well as when the salvor belongs to, or the salving vessel or the vessel salved is registered in a contracting State.

The CMI is of the view that the Convention should be given as wide a scope of application as possible. While the 1910 Convention is only applicable when either the salved vessel or the salving vessel is registered in a contracting State, the draft convention provides in addition for its application also if proceedings are brought in a contracting State and if the salvor belongs to a contracting State.

The rule that the Convention is applicable if proceedings are brought in a contracting State is based on the principles expressed in the 1976 Limitation Convention, Art. 15.1. In most jurisdictions this rule will make it superfluous also to have rules concerning the application of the Convention in the other cases mentioned. However, in a few countries the addition of these connecting factors could give the Convention a broader application, and for this reason they have been included.

1-2.2. However, the Convention does not apply:

(a) when all vessels involved are vessels of inland navigation,
(b) when all interested parties are nationals of the State where the proceedings are brought,
(c) to warships or to other vessels owned or operated by a State and being used at the time of the salvage operations exclusively on governmental non-commercial services,
(d) to removal of wrecks.

Warships and similar ships were excluded from the 1910 Convention. In the Protocol to this Convention dated Brussels, May 27th, 1967, the Convention was made applicable for such vessels. In particular, in view of the rather limited acceptance of this Protocol, it has been felt that these problems should not be regulated in the new Convention, but left for separate regulation.

During the work of the CMI it has been suggested that there should be a protocol modelled on the 1967 Protocol enabling contracting States to apply the Convention to vessels of inland navigation and/or warships and similar vessels if they should so wish.

Art. 1-2.2 (a) is mentioned above in the comments concerning Art. 1-1.1., and Art. 1-2.2. (d) in the comments concerning Art. 1-1.2.

Art. 1-3. Salvage operations controlled by Public Authorities

1-3.1 This Convention shall not affect any provisions of national law or international convention relating to salvage operations by or under the control of public authorities.

The draft convention does not deal directly with questions related to salvage operations by or under the control of public authorities, nor does it deal with the rights of salvors to payment in such cases from the authority concerned. This is in accordance with the system of the 1910 Convention, and Art. 1-3.1. has in fact the same wording as part of Art. 13 of the 1910 Convention.

1-3.2. Nevertheless, salvors carrying out such salvage operations shall be entitled to avail themselves of the rights and remedies provided for in this Convention in respect of salvage operations.

In this provision it is now made clear that the fact that a salvor has performed salvage operations under the control of a public authority shall not prevent him from exercising any right or remedy provided for by the Convention against the private interests to which salvage services are being rendered by him. Whether the salvor is entitled to recovery from such private interests depends upon whether, according to the facts, the conditions for recovery set out in the provision of the Convention have been met.

It should be remembered that according to Art. 1-2.2. (d) the Convention does not apply to removal of wrecks. Therefore if on the national level it is felt that a salvor engaged in wreck removal under supervision of a "public authority" should be entitled to the rights provided for in the Convention, a provision to this effect should be included in national law.

1-3.3. The extent to which a public authority under a duty to perform salvage operations may avail itself of the rights and remedies provided for in this Convention shall be determined by the law of the State where such authority is situated.

The present law varies from State to State as to whether for instance the coast guard or the fire service may recover in salvage. It is intended that this position should be preserved.

Art. 1-4. Salvage contracts

1-4.1. This Convention shall apply to any salvage operations save to the extent that the contract otherwise provides expressly or by implication.

It is here provided that the rules of the Convention shall not be mandatory save for the rather limited scope of the rules concerning invalid contracts in Art. 1-5. As mentioned, some national associations did put forward proposals relating to the mandatory character of one or more of the articles in the Convention, but these proposals did not receive the necessary support. The discussion within the CMI concerning this subject is summarized above in the general comments.

1-4.2. The master shall have authority to conclude contracts for salvage operations on behalf of the owner of the vessel and of property thereon.

This rule is new. So far it has been left to national law to provide if the master has such an authority, and in fact such authority is not always implied. This may in many cases have caused delay due to communication between owners and salvors or the master, and the proposed rule is considered important to prevent any such delay. Further, the rule improves the salvors' position and is in certain cases expected to increase the element of encouragement.

1-4.3. Nothing in this article shall affect the application of the provisions of Art. 1-5.

Art. 1-5. Invalid contracts or contractual terms

A contract or any terms thereof may be annulled or modified if:

(a) the contract has been entered into under undue influence or the influence of danger and its terms are inequitable or,

(b) the payment under the contract is in an excessive degree too large or too small for the services actually rendered.

This article mainly reflects in a modernized language the principles of the 1910 Convention, Art. 7. This article does not prevent the application of national rules relating to the invalidity of contracts or contractual terms.

Appendix C—International Conventions

CHAPTER II

PERFORMANCE OF SALVAGE OPERATIONS

Art. 2-1. Duty of the owner and master

2-1.1. The owner and master of a vessel in danger shall take timely and reasonable action to arrange for salvage operations during which they shall co-operate fully with the salvor and shall use their best endeavours to prevent or minimize danger to the environment.

This provision is new, as are the other provisions of chapter II, except Art. 2-3.

As mentioned above, the "Amoco Cadiz" incident made it clear that it was important to impose duties on the various private and public parties concerned, for the purposes of ensuring the efficient carrying out of salvage operations and also with a view to avoiding damage to the environment.

The duties as proposed by the CMI in the draft convention will, of course, have certain, and in some cases considerable, effects on the legal relationships between the parties, *e.g.* owners, salvors and public authorities, but it should be noted that the CMI has not felt that it is within its mandate to consider or to propose what measures could be adopted within the scope of public law, either in national law or by convention, to enforce these duties.

As an exception, however, the draft convention in Art. 2-3.2. deals with such public law rules concerning the master's duty to save human lives in danger at sea. The reason for this is that such rules are already contained in the 1910 Convention, Art.12.

During the work of the CMI it was asserted that problems frequently arose when attempts were made to take vessels into ports or coastal areas during salvage operations because public authorities required guarantees of some kind, and it was prolonged that owners should be obliged to provide any such guarantees. The CMI did not, however, feel that it would be reasonable or practical to impose such a duty, the consequences of which seem to be unclear and maybe very far-reaching. Therefore the proposal was not adopted.

2-1.2. The owner and master of a vessel in danger shall require or accept other salvor's salvage services whenever it reasonably appears that the salvor already effecting salvage operations cannot complete them alone within a reasonable time or his capabilities are inadequate.

The cases where several salvors may be available are dealt with here and in the corresponding article concerning the salvor's duty, Art. 2-2.2. in such cases it is provided that the owner and master as well the salvor may have a duty to obtain assistance from such other salvor; these provisions are based on the idea that the law should encourage cooperation between the several salvors available rather than consider them as competitors. It is envisaged that when assessing the payment due to each of them (*cf.* Arts. 3-2. and 3-3.) the tribunal may take due account of the fact that one of the salvors may have commenced the operation before others arrived to take part.

2-1.3. The owner of vessel or property salved and brought to a place of safety shall accept redelivery when reasonably requested by the salvors.

This is one of several new provisions introduced to facilitate the salvors' working conditions to increase the elements of encouragement.

Convention on the Law of the Sea

Art. 2-2. Duties of the salvor

2-2.1. The salvor shall use his best endeavours to salve the vessel and property and shall carry out the salvage operations with due care. In so doing the salvor shall also use his best endeavours to prevent or minimize damage to the environment.

While according to Art. 2-1.1. the owner and master of a vessel in danger each has the duty, separately and independently, to use best endeavours to prevent or minimize damage to the environment, the salvor's duty, according to his provision, to avoid damage to the environment is in addition to the duty to salve and not independent from it.

There is, of course, a close relationship between this new duty and the rules in Art. 3-2.1(b) concerning enhancement of the salvage reward in such cases as well as the rules in Art. 3-3. providing for special compensation for salvage operations in cases where the environment was in danger.

2-2.2. The salvor shall, whenever the circumstances reasonably require, obtain assistance from other available salvors and shall accept the intervention of other salvors when requested so to do by the owner or master pursuant to paragraph 2 of Article 2-1; provided, however, that the amount of his reward shall not be prejudiced should it be found that such intervention was not necessary.

The provision contains the duty of a salvor to obtain assistance from other salvors, and reference is made to the comments to the corresponding duty of the owners provided for in Art. 2-1.2.

Art. 2-3. Duty to render assistance

2-3.1. Every master is bound, so far as he can do so without serious danger to his vessel and persons thereon, to render assistance to any person in danger of being lost at sea.
2-3.2. The contracting States shall adopt the measures necessary to enforce the duty set out in the preceding paragraph.
2-3.3. The owner of the vessel shall incur no liability for a breach of the duty of the master under paragraph 1.

The whole of this provision corresponds in a modernized language and form to the rules provided in the 1910 Convention, Arts. 11 and 12.

The draft convention contains in Art. 3-5. rules regarding salvage of persons corresponding to Art. 9 of the 1910 Convention.

Art. 2-4. Co-operation of contracting States

A contracting State shall, whenever regulating or deciding upon matters relating to salvage operations such as admittance to ports of vessels in distress or the provision of facilities to salvors, take into account the need for co-operation between salvors, other interested parties and public authorities in order to ensure the efficient and successful performance of salvage operations for the purpose of saving life of property in danger as well as preventing damage to the environment in general.

The discussions within the CMI revealed that co-operation from public authorities of costal States would often be indispensable to the success of the salvage operations. On the other hand, it was recognized that the drafting of provisions on this subject was a most delicate matter. Art. 2-4 should be read in the light of this.

Appendix C—International Conventions

Chapter III

Rights of Salvors

Art. 3-1. Conditions for reward

3-1.1. Salvage operations which have a useful result give right to a reward.
3-1.2. Except as otherwise provided, no payment is due under this Convention, if the salvage operations have no useful result.

These provisions are in accordance with the 1910 Convention, Art. 2, paragraph 1. The rules establish the important principle of "no cure no pay".

The salvors have a clear preference for a system in which rewards are based on the "no cure no pay" principle rather than daily rate systems in the normal cases of salvage, and there is a strong conviction within the CMI that this principle should be retained as the main scheme of compensation in the law of salvage.

It should be noted that the "no cure no pay" principle is not fully retained if there is a risk of damage to the environment where, as mentioned, the salvors may be entitled to a special compensation according to the rules of Art. 3-3.1., even if there is no useful result, while the additional compensation according to Art. 3-3.2. is governed by the rules of Art. 3-1.2.

The fact that salvors under the "no cure no pay" system run the risk that they may not recover normal compensation for their services or may only recover part of that compensation, is an important factor to take into account when the payment for successful services comes to be fixed according to Art. 3-2. or Art. 3-3.2.

3-1.3. This chapter shall apply, notwithstanding that the salved vessel and the vessel undertaking the salvage operations belong to the same owners.

This rule corresponds to Art. 5 of the 1910 Convention. It has importance, in particular in cases where under national law according to Art. 3-4.2. apportionment of a reward shall be made between the owner, the master and other persons of the salving vessel. Further the rule makes it clear that the owner of the salving vessel is also in such cases also entitled to receive payment of the cargo's share of the salvage reward and normally entitled to claim payment of the vessel's share from his own underwriters.

Art. 3-2 The amount of the reward

3-2.1. The reward shall be fixed with a view to encouraging salvage operations, taking into account the following considerations without regard to the order in which presented below:

(a) the value of the property salved,

(b) the skill and efforts of the salvors in preventing or minimizing damage to the environment,

(c) the measure of success obtained by the salvor,

(d) the nature and degree of the danger,

(e) the efforts of the salvors, including the time used and expenses and losses incurred by the salvors,

(f) the risk of liability and other risks run by the salvors or their equipment,

(g) the promptness of the service rendered;

(h) the availability and use of vessels or other equipment intended for salvage operations,

(i) the State of readiness and efficiency of the salvor's equipment and the value thereof.

This provision is to a considerable extent in accordance with Art. 8.1. of the 1910 Convention and the practices followed in the application thereof. Certain amendments or additional provisions have, however, been introduced.

As mentioned above in the general comments some redrafting has taken place compared with the 1910 Convention, in particular in order to take into account subsequent developments in practice, but new factors have also been introduced in sub-paragraphs (b), (g), (h) and (i).

The CMI felt that it would be preferable to enumerate the relevant considerations without attempting to lay down rules as to when a particular consideration should be relevant or as to the weight to be given to it, particularly in relation to other relevant considerations. It is expressly stated that the order in which the particulars are enumerated is not intended to provide a guidance on such matters.

As mentioned above in the general comments, it has been felt important to say expressly that the reward shall be fixed with a view to encouraging salvage operations.

As explained above in the general comments and below under sub-paragraph (b) no rules have been given as to who is liable to pay the reward, this means that this is left to be decided by national law.

Re: (a)

Consideration was given to whether it would be more appropriate to provide that the relevant value was the amount for which the property is insured and not the value of the property salved, but it was felt that this was too uncertain a measure. Similarly, it was not felt appropriate to introduce rules under which the value of the loss of time saved for the salved vessel should have any direct relevance apart from the new sub-paragraph (g), where it has been provided that due regard shall be given to the promptness of the service renders.

Re: (b)

Here reference is made to the skill and efforts of the salvors in preventing or minimizing damage to the environment. In the practice of many countries this consideration is already a factor, which normally produces a certain enhancement of the salvage reward. It is, however, felt very important in the new convention to draw attention specifically to this consideration and to leave it to future practice to decide the particular weight to be given to it.

Like the 1910 Convention the draft convention refrains from dealing with the question of the person(s) liable to pay rewards due under Art. 3-2., and in particular also any enhancement awarded according to sub-paragraph (b).

The CMI proposes that this question should still be solved at national level and by agreement.

One reason for this is that the solutions adopted in the various national laws differ to such an extent that the acceptability of the draft convention might be reduced if an attempt was not made to bring about international uniformity.

Another important reason is that there is presently a general understanding between most of the world marine insurers that on the one hand the ship's liability insurers should fund the special compensation payable under the safety net rule of the LOF 1980 while, on the other hand, the property underwriters, *i.e.* hull and cargo insurers, shall fund the total reward for property salvage including any enhancement for preventing or minimizing oil pollution. It is envisaged that a similar compromise may be reached in relation to the distribution of payments according to the draft convention. This, in particular, was an important reason for following the safety net model of the LOF 1980.

The Association of European Average Adjusters have in report approved by their XIIth General Assembly in Copenhagen in September 1983 entitled "Salvage—LOF 1980 and the CMI Draft Convention" dealt in detail with this so-called "funding agreement" and laid down suggestions for a common approach to the problem of the treatment in General Average of any elements of such enhancement in the rewards payable for successful salvage. See "AIDE Copenhagen Report 1983".

Re: (f)

By virtue of the "no cure no pay" system the salvors run the risk that they may never recover their expenditure, and this is usually an important factor to be taken into account when the reward is fixed, in particular if the expenses have been substantial.

The salvor does not run the risk of losing his expenses under the "no cure no pay" rule if the vessel or its cargo threatens damage to the environment, as according to Art. 3-3.1. the salvor will always receive payment for his expenses. Therefore in such a case it could be argued that the reward should be fixed at a lower level.

It is, however, not the intention that the introduction of the rules of Art. 3-3.1. shall have such an effect. This must be kept in mind when fixing the general level of salvage rewards and in particular when considering the effect of sub-paragraph (b) relating to prevention of damage to the environment.

Re: (h)

This rule is of particular importance for professional salvors. The use of the word "availability" in this context, suggests that consideration is to be given to the salvage positioning of the salvage company, which involves keeping their tugs and other equipment available for salvage work and consequently suffering the burden of all the expenses incurred throughout the time during which the tugs and other equipment are not usefully employed.

3-2.2. The reward under paragraph 1 of this Article shall not exceed the value of the property salved at the time of the completion of the salvage operations.

This rule restated the important principle contained in the 1910 Convention, Art. 2, paragraph 3.

Art. 3-3. Special compensation

3-3.1. If the salvor has carried out salvage operations in respect of a vessel which by itself or its cargo threatened damage to the environment and failed to earn a reward under Art. 3-2. at least equivalent to the compensation assessable in accordance with Art. 3-3., he shall be entitled to compensation from the owner of that vessel equivalent to his expenses as herein defined.

3-3.2. If, in the circumstances set out in paragraph 1 of Art. 3-3. hereof, the salvor by his salvage operations has prevented or minimized damage to the environment, the compensation payable by the owner to the salvor thereunder may be increased, if and to the extent that the tribunal considers it fair and just to do so, bearing in mind the relevant criteria set out in paragraph 1 of Art. 3-2. above, but in no event shall it be more than doubled.

Art. 3-3. gives the salvors new remedies in cases where salvage operations in respect of ship and cargo are carried out also in order to prevent damage to the environment occurring. In such cases the salvor is entitled to recover from the shipowner firstly expenses involved as defined in Art. 3-3. and secondly an additional special reward contingent upon actual avoidance of such damage. The reward is to be fixed taking into account as applicable the criteria enumerated in Art. 3-2.1., but shall not exceed the salvor's expenses. This means that the total compensation under Arts. 3-3.1. and 3-3.2. will not be more than twice the salvor's expenses.

In cases, where these provisions apply and no or insufficient property has been salved so as to allow adequate recovery under Art. 3-2., it is important for the salvor that the person liable is one against whom the claim is easily enforceable. Therefore, it has been provided that the special compensation payable under Arts. 3-3.1. and 3-3.2. must be paid by the shipowner.

Art. 3-3. together with Art 3-2.2 (b) must be considered as part of a compromise. The shipowners' willingness to accept the funding of the compensation and to accept the broad definition of salvor's expenses in Art. 3-3.3. is clearly connected with the salvors' acceptance of the limit in Art 3-3.2. and his acceptance that he will not insist on any rules in the new convention as to who should be liable for the rewards payable under Art. 3-2. Equally, the fact that these provisions should not be made mandatory was an important part of the compromise.

Art. 3-3.1. provides that the shipowner shall pay the costs of salvage operations carried out in respect of a casualty if it threatens to cause damage to the environment. If this condition is met all costs of all salvage operations are included, whether or not the costs had any relation to the environment, the only condition being that the costs are reasonably incurred as provided in Art. 3-3.3.

The special reward according to Art. 3-3.2. is only payable if a useful result has been obtained. The reward cannot exceed a sum equivalent to the expenses. It is important to keep in mind that this is only an upper limit and that, even if damage to the environment has been prevented or minimized, the tribunal may decide that the salvor shall have no special compensation on top of the reimbursement of his costs, or that he shall only have as such special compensation of his costs. The tribunal is free to decide what it considers fair and just taking into account the same considerations as if the tribunal were fixing a traditional salvage reward under Art. 3-2.

3-3.3. "Salvor's expenses" for the purpose of paragraphs 1 and 2 of this Article means the out of pocket expenses reasonably incurred by the salvor in the salvage operation and a fair rate for equipment and personnel actually and reasonably used in the salvage operations, taking into consideration the criteria set out in paragraph 1(g), (h) and (i) of Article 3-2.

This definition of the salvor's expenses is rather broad and in fact it comes very close to the definition proposed by salvors' representatives. It covers out of pocket expenses as well as compensation for the salvor's own equipment and personnel. The reference to the criteria set out in Art. 3-2.1.(g), (h) and (i) is important, in particular because it is thereby made clear that due account shall be taken of the salvor's standing costs, overheads, etc. when determining what is a fair rate in the particular case.

3-3.4. Provided always that the total compensation under this Article shall be paid only if and to the extent that such compensation is greater than any reward recoverable by the salvor under Article 3-2.

This rule provides that the payment under Arts. 3-3.1. and 3-3.2. shall be made only if the award under Art. 3-2. is insufficient to meet the expenses of the salvor under Art. 3-3.1. and any increased compensation under Art. 3-3.2. An example may serve to illustrate more clearly the relationship between Arts. 3-2. and 3-3.: If the property salved is valued at $100,000 and a property award of $10,000 is made under Art. 3-2. and expenses of $5,000 have been incurred, there would be no separate compensation under Art. 3-3. However, if the expenses incurred amount to, say $12,000, then $2,000 will be recoverable under Art. 3-3.1. Further, if an increased compensation is awarded under Art. 3-3.2. the same pattern will be followed. For example, if expenses of $6,000

Appendix C—International Conventions

were incurred under Art. 3-3.1. and increased compensation of $5,000 awarded under Art. 3-3.2., making $11,000 in all, then, assuming an award under Art. 3-2. of $10,000 against the property salved of $100,000, $1,000 would be payable under Art. 3-3.

3-3.5. If the salvor has been negligent and has thereby failed to prevent or minimize damage to the environment, he may be deprived of the whole or part of any payment due under this Article.

Negligence by the salvor in relation to damage to the environment has by this rule been given a rather strict effect. This is in contrast to the broad rule concerning salvor's misconduct in Art. 3-7. It is expected that Art. 3-3.5. will increase the level of caution of the salvors in relation to damage to the environment.

3-3.6. Nothing in this Article shall affect any rights of recourse on the part of the owner of the vessel.

While the shipowner has a duty towards the salvor to pay the compensation according to Arts. 3-3.1. and 3-3.2. under Art. 3-3.6. he is allowed to seek any recovery from other parties as appropriate, in particular cargo owners or charterers.

Art. 3-4. Apportionment between salvors

3-4.1. The apportionment of a reward between salvors shall be made on the basis of the criteria contained in Article 3-2.

This provision is in accordance with the rules of the 1910 Convention, Art. 6, paragraph 2, and Art. 8, paragraph 2. It should be kept in mind that the new convention in Arts. 2-1.2. and 2-2.2. provides that the owners and the master of the ship involved in casualty as well as the salvors, when this is reasonable, have a duty to obtain assistance from other available salvors. Therefore, this rule becomes more important under the regime of the new convention.

3-4.2. The apportionment between the owner, master and other persons in the service of each salving vessel shall be determined by the law of the flag of that vessel. If the salvage has not been carried out from a vessel the apportionment shall be determined by the law governing the contract between the salvor and his employees.

This is a restatement of the provision in Art. 6, paragraph 3, of the 1910 Convention. The last part of the provision is new and takes into account the increasing number of cases where salvage is not carried out from a vessel.

The law concerning apportionment between the owners and the crew of a salvage reward varies from State to State. The CMI did not consider that much could be gained by a unification of the rules concerning this subject, which is rather controversial.

Art. 3-5. Salvage of persons

3-5.1. No remuneration is due from the person whose lives are saved, but nothing in this Article shall affect the provisions of national law on this subject.

This is a restatement of Art. 9, paragraph 1, of the 1910 Convention.
The provision must be read together with the draft convention, Art. 2-3. which provides that every master has a duty to render assistance to persons in danger at sea.

3-5.2. A salvor of human life, who has taken part in the services rendered on the occasion of the accident giving rise to salvage, is entitled to a fair share of the remuneration awarded to the salvor for salving the vessel or other property or preventing or minimizing damage to the environment. This rule restates Art. 9, paragraph 2, of the 1910 Convention.

An addition has been made, however, to make it clear that the life salvor shall have a share of any compensation for preventing or minimizing damage to the environment under the proposed new rules of Art. 3-2.1.(b) as well as Art. 3-3.2.

If there was a danger of damage to the environment, it follows from Art. 3–3.1. that the life salvor, who has taken part in the salvage operations, shall have his reasonable expenses paid.

The draft convention submitted by the Sub-committee to the Montreal Conference contained rules under which the salvor of human life should have remedies similar to those given to the salvor in Art. 3-3. for avoidance of damage to the environment. Thus it was proposed that the life salvor should in all cases receive compensation for his expenses and in cases of success should be paid a special compensation. The liability for such payments should be imposed on the shipowner or the State of register of the vessel as determined by the law of that State, in which connection it was noted that the law of some countries already had rules on this subject.

The Montreal Conference, however, did not adopt this proposal. It was felt that the commercial aspects in the proposal were too strongly emphasized. It was feared that the proposed rules could lead to new problems, and, on the other hand, it was felt that the present system, under which salvage at sea of human lives is often not compensated, was generally functioning satisfactorily.

Art. 3-6. Services rendered under existing contracts

No payment is due under the provisions of this Convention unless the services rendered exceed what can be reasonably considered as due performance of a contract entered into before the danger arose.

This is a general restatement of the principle in the 1910 Convention, Art. 4. As mentioned above, the rule forms part of the important principle under which a salvage service must be voluntary to give right to the remedies of the Convention.

Art. 3-7. The effect of salvor's misconduct

A salvor may be deprived of the whole or part of the payment due under the provisions of this Convention to the extent that the salvage operations have become necessary or more difficult because of fault or neglect on his part or if the salvor has been guilty of fraud or other dishonest conduct.

This rule is based on the principle expressed in the 1910 Convention, Art. 8, paragraph 3. A special and more far-reaching rule concerning salvor's negligence with relation to damage to the environment is contained in the draft convention, Art. 3-3.5.

Art. 3-8. Prohibition by the owners or master

Services rendered notwithstanding the express and reasonable prohibition of the owner or the master shall not give rise to payment under the provisions of this Convention.

This is a restatement of the principle expressed in the 1910 Convention, Art. 3. The rule, however, must in the regime of the draft convention be read in conjunction with Art. 2-1.1., under which the owner and master of the casualty shall take timely and reasonable action to arrange for salvage operations.

Appendix C—International Conventions

Chapter IV

Claims and Actions

Art. 4-1. Maritime lien

4-1.1. Nothing in this Convention shall effect the salvor's maritime lien under any international convention or national law.

In most states the salvors will have a maritime lien or a similar right over the salved ship and its cargo. With respect to the salved vessel this is provided in the International Conventions for the Unification of Certain Rules Relating to Maritime Liens and Mortgages, 1926, Art. 2.3., and 1967, Art. 4.1-(V). Consideration was given to whether a rule providing for a maritime lien should be included in the new convention, but it was decided not to do so because these rules were felt to have their proper place in other conventions and because the advantage would be rather limited in view of the already widespread acceptance of such a right.

4-1.2. The salvor may not enforce his maritime lien when satisfactory security for his claim, including interest and costs, has been duly tendered or provided.

In most jurisdictions maritime liens cannot be enforced if satisfactory security has been provided. However, the CMI considers it practical to have an express rule to this effect in the new convention.

4-1.3. The salved property shall not without the consent of the salvor be removed from the port or place at which the property first arrives after the completion of the salvage operations until satisfactory security has been put up for the salvor's claim.

This rule entitled the salvor to retain the possession of the salved property or to prevent it from being removed until he has obtained security. The rule is considered important in cases where there is no maritime lien or no practical way of obtaining the authorities' assistance to enforce a maritime lien in time, *e.g.* during a holiday. There is already a similar rule in the legislation of some states.

Art. 4-2. Duty to provide security

4-2.1. Upon the request of the salvor a person liable for a payment due under the provisions of this Convention shall provide satisfactory security for the claim, including interest and costs of the salvor.

From a practical point of view security provided by the person liable or his insurer is of great importance; hence this article imposes a duty on the person liable to provide security upon request.

As mentioned above, the draft convention does not provide who shall be liable to pay salvage rewards according to Art. 3-2. Once, however, a person is liable according to national law or Art. 3-3. he has a duty under the draft convention to provide security.

4-2.2. Without prejudice to paragraph 1 of this Article, the owner of the salved vessel shall use his best endeavours to ensure that the owners of the cargo provide satisfactory security for the claims against them, including interest and costs before the cargo is released.

This rule has special application in the jurisdictions where the owner of the ship involved in casualty is not liable for salvage remuneration due from the cargo.

The Sub-Committee's draft to the Montreal Conference contained a third paragraph of Art. 4-2. in which it was proposed that in cases of failure to meet the request to produce security the salvors may bring an action directly against the insurer of the person liable. For practical reasons this provision was not adopted by the Montreal Conference.

Art. 4-3. Interim payment

The court or arbitral tribunal having jurisdiction over the claim of the salvor may by interim decision order that the salvor shall be paid such amount on account as seems fair and just and on such terms including terms as to security where appropriate as may be fair and just according to the circumstances of the case. In the event of an interim payment the security provided under Article 4-2. shall be reduced accordingly.

This provision is new. It improves the salvors' cash flow and is considered to be of some importance. It is inspired by present arbitral practice.

Art. 4-4. Limitation of actions

4-4.1. Any action relating to payment under the provisions of this Convention shall be time-barred if judicial or arbitral proceedings have not been instituted within a period of two years. The limitation period commences on the day on which the salvage operations are terminated.

This provision retains the two year time-bar of the 1910 Convention, Art. 10.

4-4.2. The person against whom a claim is made may at any time during the running of the limitation period extend that period by a declaration to the claimant. This period may in the like manner be further extended.
4-4.3. An action for indemnity by a person liable may be instituted even after the expiration of the limitation period provided for in the preceding paragraphs, if brought within the time allowed by the law of the state where proceedings are instituted. However, the time allowed shall not be less than 90 days commencing from the day when the person instituting such action for indemnity has settled the claim or has been first adjudged liable in the action against himself.
4-4.4. Without prejudice to the preceding paragraphs all matters relating to limitation of action under this Article are governed by the law of the State where the action is brought.

These paragraphs are modelled on corresponding provisions in modern maritime law conventions, *e.g.* the 1968 Protocol to the 1924 Bills of Lading Convention.

It is made clear that the limitation period may be extended by declaration to the claimant, which is a widespread practice. Further, a practical rule is given concerning the time-bar with relation to actions for indemnity and, finally, it is stated that limitation under this article is governed by the law of the State where the action is brought, a rule which corresponds very well with Art. 1-2.1. concerning the application of the draft convention.

Art. 4-5. Jurisdiction

4-5.1. Unless the parties have agreed to the jurisdiction of another court or to arbitration, an action for payment under the provisions of this Convention may, at the option of the plaintiff, be brought in a court which, according to the law of the State where the court is situated, is competent and within the jurisdiction of which is situated one of the following places:

Appendix C—International Conventions

(a) the principal place of business of the defendant,

(b) the port to which the property salved has been brought,

(c) the place where the property salved has been arrested,

(d) the place where security for the payment has been given,

(e) the place where the salvage operations took place.

Within the CMI it was much debated whether provisions concerning jurisdiction should in fact be included in the draft convention.

It was, however, realized that such rules are contained in most modern conventions and also that there is a need to protect salvors' rights by providing for jurisdiction where this is most suitable and practical for the salvor.

In the first line of the provision it is said that the rules of jurisdiction shall only have application if the parties have not agreed to the jurisdiction of another court or to arbitration. The CMI finds it important to stress that the widespread use of salvage contracts, in which arbitration or jurisdiction clauses are essential elements, is, in the opinion of all commercial parties as well as the CMI, vital for the industry, and should not be abolished or limited.

4-5.2. With respect to vessels owned by a contracting State and used for commercial purposes, each State shall be subject to suit in the jurisdiction set forth in paragraph 1 of this article and shall waive all defences based on its status as a sovereign State. In the case of a vessel owned by a State and operated by a company which in that State is registered as the ship's operator, owner shall for the purpose of this paragraph mean such company.

This paragraph uses that language of the 1969 Convention on Civil Liability for Oil Pollution Damage, Arts. 1.3. and 11.2.

4-5.3. Nothing in this Article constitutes an obstacle to the jurisdiction of a contracting State for provisional or protective measures. The exercise by the salvor of his maritime lien whether by arrest or otherwise against the property salved shall not be treated as a wavier by the salvor of his rights, including the right to have his claim for salvage remuneration adjudicated by court or arbitral proceedings in another jurisdiction.

This provision was proposed by representatives of the salvors to the Montreal Conference and accepted without much debate.

Art. 4-6. Interest

4-6.1. The right of the salvor to interest on any payment due under this Convention shall be determined according to the law of the State in which the court or arbitral tribunal seized of the case is situated.

This provision on interest leaves the matter to the *lex fori*. The Sub-Committee had proposed to the Montreal Conference a further provision that interest should commence to run upon the request for security according to Art. 4-2. This proposal was not adopted.

Art. 4-7. Publication of arbitral awards

Contracting States shall encourage, as far as possible and if need be with the consent of the parties, the publication of arbitral awards made in salvage cases.

This rule recognizes the fact that most decisions on matters of salvage are arbitral awards. This means that in practice it is often difficult for the parties to ascertain the actual legal position, and the extent to which international uniformity is in fact achieved cannot be appreciated. Therefore the need for adequate information on arbitral practice was recognized by the CMI. There were, however, different views as to the appropriate remedy. The Montreal Conference preferred the rather vague rule of the draft convention to a duty to make arbitral awards public, mainly on the grounds that privacy is often an important part of the advantages of arbitration and that all commercial parties involved felt it appropriate and reasonable to retain the right to keep arbitral decisions private if they so wish.

CHAPTER V

LIABILITY OF SALVORS

Art. 5-1. Limitations of liability

5-1.1. A contracting State may give salvors a right of limitation equivalent in manner and extent to the right provided for by the 1976 Convention on the Limitation of Liability for Maritime Claims.

It was generally recognized that salvors ought to be able to engage fully in difficult salvage operations without fears of subsequently being held liable without limitation. The system of the 1976 London Limitation Convention was considered to provide an adequate solution to this problem which is in particular relevant in cases where the salvage services are not performed from a salvage vessel. The Sub-Committee had proposed to the Montreal Conference that it should be a duty to the parties to the new convention to establish a right equivalent to the 1976 Convention concerning limitation for salvors. This was much debated, and on the strength of the arguments of many national MLA delegations that such a rule might make the draft convention unacceptable, it was decided only to propose a recommendation to this effect.

It should, of course, be noted that the provision is only intended to cover the situation where a contracting State is only a party to the 1976 Convention.

The draft of the Sub-Committee also contained an Article 5-2 concerning damage caused during salvage operations, which was not adopted. For further information in this respect reference is made to the report of the Chairman of the Sub-Committee.

Appendix C—International Conventions

No. 33

INTERNATIONAL CONVENTION ON SALVAGE, 1989

CHAPTER V

[*Article 1–27 are enacted into United Kingdom law by the Merchant Shipping Act 1995 and are reproduced* ante, *pp. 818–823. The remaining provisions of the Convention are set out here.*]

FINAL CLAUSES

Article 28. Signature, ratification, acceptance, approval and accession

1. This Convention shall be open for signature at the Headquarters of the Organization from 1 July 1989 to 30 June 1990 and shall thereafter remain open for accession.
2. States may express their consent to be bound by this Convention by:

(a) signature without reservation as to ratification, acceptance of approval; or

(b) signature subject to ratification, acceptance or approval, followed by ratification, acceptance or approval; or

(c) accession.

3. Ratification, acceptance, approval or accession shall be effected by the deposit of an instrument to that effect with the Secretary-General.

Article 29. Entry into force

1. This Convention shall enter into force one year after the date on which 15 States have expressed their consent to be bound by it.
2. For a State which expresses its consent to be bound by this Convention after the conditions for entry into force thereof have been met, such consent shall take effect one year after the date of expression of such consent.

Article 30. Reservations

1. Any State may, at the time of signature, ratification, acceptance, approval or accession, reserve the right not to apply the provisions of this Convention:

(a) when the salvage operation takes place in inland waters and all vessels involved are of inland navigation;

(b) when the salvage operations take place in inland waters and no vessel is involved;

(c) when all interested parties are nationals of that State;

(d) when the property involved is maritime cultural property of prehistoric, archaeological or historic interest and is situated on the sea-bed.

2. Reservations made at the time of signature are subject to confirmation upon ratification, acceptance or approval.

3. Any State which has made a reservation to this Convention may withdraw it at any time by means of a notification addressed to the Secretary-General. Such withdrawal shall take effect on the date the notification is received. If the notification states that the withdrawal of a reservation is to take effect on a date specified therein, and such date is later than the date the notification is received by the Secretary-General, the withdrawal shall take effect on such later date.

Article 31. Denunciation

1. This Convention may be denounced by any State Party at any time after the expiry of one year from the date on which this Convention enters into force for that State.
2. Denunciation shall be effected by the deposit of an instrument of denunciation with the Secretary-General.
3. A denunciation shall take effect one year, or such longer period as may be specified in the instrument of denunciation by the Secretary-General.

Article 32. Revision and amendment

1. A conference for the purpose of revising or amending this Convention may be convened by the Organization.
2. The Secretary-General shall convene a conference of the States Parties to this Convention for revising or amending the Convention, at the request of eight States Parties, or one fourth of the States Parties, whichever is the higher figure.
3. Any consent to be bound by this Convention expressed after the date of entry into force of an amendment to this Convention shall be deemed to apply to the Convention as amended.

Article 33. Depositary

1. This Convention shall be deposited with the Secretary-General.
2. The Secretary-General shall:
   (a) inform all States which have signed this Convention or acceded thereto, and all Members of the Organization, of:
      (i) each new signature or deposit of an instrument or ratification, acceptance, approval or accession together with the date thereof;
      (ii) the date of the entry into force of this Convention;
      (iii) the deposit of any instrument of denunciation of this Convention together with the date on which it is received and the date on which the denunciation takes effect;
      (iv) any amendment adopted in conformity with article 32;
      (v) the receipt of any reservation, declaration or notification made under this Convention;
   (b) transmit certified true copies of this Convention to all States which have signed this Convention or acceded thereto.

3. As soon as this Convention enters into force, a certified true copy thereof shall be transmitted by the Depositary to the Secretary-General of the United Nations for registration and publication in accordance with Article 102 of the Charter of the United Nations.

Article 34. Languages

This Convention is established in a single original in the Arabic, Chinese, English, French, Russian and Spanish languages, each text being equally authentic.

Appendix C—International Conventions

IN WITNESS WHEREOF the undersigned* [*Signatures omitted.] being duly authorized by their respective Governments for that purpose have signed this Convention.

DONE AT LONDON this twenty-eighth day of April one thousand nine hundred and eighty-nine.

ATTACHMENT 1

Common Understanding concerning Articles 13 and 14 of the International Convention on Salvage, 1989

It is the common understanding of the Conference that, in fixing a reward under article 13 and assessing special compensation under article 14 of the International Convention on Salvage, 1989 the tribunal is under no duty to fix a reward under article 13 up to the maximum salved value of the vessel and other property before assessing the special compensation to be paid under article 14.

ATTACHMENT 2

Resolution requesting the amendment of the York-Antwerp Rules, 1974

[THE INTERNATIONAL CONFERENCE ON SALVAGE, 1989]

HAVING ADOPTED the International Convention on Salvage, 1989,

CONSIDERING that payments made pursuant to article 14 are not intended to be allowed in general average,

REQUESTS the Secretary-General of the International Maritime Organization to take the appropriate steps in order to ensure speedy amendment of the York-Antwerp Rules, 1974, to ensure that special compensation paid under article 14 is not subject to general average.

ATTACHMENT 3

Resolution on international co-operation for the implementation of the International Convention on Salvage, 1989

[THE INTERNATIONAL CONFERENCE ON SALVAGE, 1989]

IN ADOPTING the International Convention on Salvage, 1989 (hereinafter referred to as "The Convention"),

CONSIDERING IT DESIRABLE that as many States as possible should become Parties to the Convention,

RECOGNIZING that the entry into force of the Convention will represent an important additional factor for the protection of the marine environment,

CONSIDERING that the international publicizing and wide implementation of the Convention is of the utmost importance for the attainment of its objectives,

International Convention on Salvage 1989

I RECOMMENDS:

(a) that the Organization promote public awareness of the Convention through the holding of seminars, courses or symposia;

(b) that training institutions created under the auspices of the Organization include the study of the Convention in their corresponding courses of study.

II REQUESTS:

(a) Member States to transmit to the Organisation the text of the laws, orders, decrees, regulations and other instruments that they promulgate concerning the various matters falling within the scope of application of the Convention;

(b) Member States, in consultation with the Organization, to promote the giving of help to those States requesting technical assistance for the drafting of laws, orders, decrees, regulations and other instruments necessary for the implementation of the Convention; and

(c) the Organization to notify Member States of any communication it may receive under paragraph II(a).

D. RULES AND REGULATIONS

No. 34

The Queen's Regulations for the Royal Navy, Chapter 51*

SALVAGE AND SPECIAL SERVICES

SECTION IV

SALVAGE OF PRIVATE SHIPS

5141. Aid to ships in danger

J.1. Assistance should be rendered to a ship or an aircraft endangered at sea, in tidal waters, or on the shores thereof, on occasions where it is within the reasonable power of any ship or aircraft belonging to the Armed Forces of the Crown, or any shore-based personnel. (*Navy only*—The best efforts of personnel are to be used to save and protect property on board any vessel in danger or distress and, if necessary, to remove the property to a place of safety, but though there may be other and overriding considerations in war, in peace public economy and policy require that H.M. ships and vessels should not take such action if to do so would be to the detriment of any vessel registered in the British Commonwealth present and capable of affording effective help).

2. When assistance from Ministry of Defence (Navy) sources is accepted and there is reasonable hope of saving the vessel or her cargo, salvage is to proceed without delay in order to prevent any deterioration in the vessel's position. (*See also* **5124**).

3. In general, a vessel's owner or his representative has a right to decide whether salvage assistance shall be employed and whether salvors whose services he has accepted initially shall subsequently be superseded or supplemented by others. If, after salvage has begun, the master insists that other salvors should be employed, whether in complete substitution for, or in conjunction with, naval assistance, his wishes are to be complied with and no action is to be taken to prevent the other salvors from taking over either wholly or partly. If the first salvor objects to the action taken, a protest is to be lodged with the master. Its terms are to be based on the first salvor's assessment of the effects of the intervention on the ultimate success of the venture as a whole.

4. Efficient aid from outside sources should not be refused if the operations would otherwise be jeopardized. The Ministry of Defence should be consulted, if time permits, about the terms on which aid is engaged. But if, in emergency, the other party will only assist as a co-salvor under Lloyd's Open Form (*see* **5142.**1), this must be accepted. The most important consideration is that whether or not the services are being rendered under Lloyd's Open Form, no award can be earned unless some of the salved property is ultimately brought to a place of safety (*see* Clause 7).

---

* © Crown Copyright. Reproduced with the permission of the Controller of Her Majesty's Stationery Office.

Queen's Regulations for the Royal Navy

5. For derelicts, i.e., vessels abandoned and deserted at sea by those in charge of them, Clause 4 applies, but Clause 3 does not. It is the recognized general rule that the salvor who first takes possession of a derelict has the entire and absolute possession of the vessel with which no other party, not even the owner, can interfere. A derelict taken in tow by one of Her Majesty's ships or vessels may, therefore, properly remain in naval custody pending agreement with the owners or agents about the terms of salvage and the lodging of satisfactory security (*see* **5142**.3 and **5146**). When there is doubt whether a vessel may be treated as a derelict, full particulars of the circumstances in which it was found abandoned and anything known about the movements of the master and the crew should be reported to the Ministry of Defence immediately in addition to the general information required by **5144**.1.

J6. In any case where the owner of the salvaged vessel or aircraft does not want to take possession of it, reference should be made to the Ministry of Defence before action is taken to dispose of it, even if such disposal action has been suggested by the owner.

7. The "place of safety" (*see* Clause 4) is normally determined by agreement between the salvors and the owners or their representatives. If agreement cannot be reached the following considerations should be taken into account:

   (a) The condition of the distressed vessel and the time required to make her seaworthy.

   (b) The degree of exposure to weather and tidal conditions, and season of the year.

   (c) The distance from a port where permanent repairs may be undertaken.

When in doubt or difficulty Ministry of Defence instructions are to be sought.

8. Aid which qualifies as a salvage service and for which an award can be claimed can, and wherever practicable should, also be rendered from the shore by units from naval shore establishments, e.g., dockyard fire parties.

5142. Terms of salvage services

1. Whenever possible, salvage services by Her Majesty's ships or vessels, including those hired by the Ministry of Defence (Navy) on demise charter, and by shore-based units from naval establishments, are to be governed by Lloyd's Open Form unless other terms may subsequently be agreed with the owners by the Ministry of Defence or on Ministry of Defence instructions. Whenever, therefore, H.M. ships or vessels salve a private vessel, the latter's master, owner or agent is to be asked to sign Lloyd's Open Form, a supply of which should be kept on board all vessels likely to require them. The Commanding Officer, or other officer of Her Majesty's ship or vessel concerned who signs Lloyd's Open Form should do so on behalf of "The Ministry of Defence and personnel of [*the ship(s) and/or parties concerned*]" the appropriate words being inserted in third line of the form. For salvage by shore-based units the form is to be signed on behalf of "The Ministry of Defence and personnel of [*the units taking part*]". Irrespective of the number of vessels and/or units taking part, only one Lloyd's Form is required for any one salvage operation, and it should normally be signed by the officer in overall charge at the commencement of the operation. If the parties are too numerous to be inserted in line three of the form, they are to be listed under the word "Annex" on the reverse of the form and the words "parties named in the Annex overleaf" written in line three.

2. It is important for the form to be signed before the operations start, if reasonably possible. If insistence on this condition would endanger life, however, or is otherwise impracticable, every endeavour is to be made to make it clear at the time to the owner or master that the services are subject to the terms of the form, which is to be signed

Appendix D—Rules and Regulations

later and, if practicable, before the salvage operations end. At the time the form is signed a sixpenny British stamp is to be affixed in the space provided and is to be endorsed with the date. The signed Lloyd's Open Form is to be sent to the Ministry of Defence by the quickest means.

3. For derelicts, the signature of Lloyd's Open Form will be obtained by the Ministry of Defence.

4. A salvor is entitled to claim for the services which he performs notwithstanding that other salvors eventually take over, provided that the property is ultimately saved.

5143. Right to claim salvage

J.1. Under section 8(2) of the Crown Proceedings Act 1947, the Crown is entitled to claim salvage in respect of services rendered by any ship or aircraft belonging to the Crown. Service personnel engaged in salvage operations may make a claim for salvage, but only with the written sanction of the Ministry of Defence. (*Navy only*—In the context of this paragraph service personnel includes civilians employed by the Navy Department.) No court of law or arbitrator can finally adjudicate on salvage claims without the production of written evidence of the Ministry of Defence consent. The need for Ministry of Defence consent, however, does not debar the salvors from taking the preliminary steps which are given below.

2. There is no absolute rule or fixed scale of salvage remuneration. Each claim is dealt with on its merits, taking into account such factors as the degree of danger from which the property saved, its salved value, the risks and responsibilities incurred by the salvors, the time occupied, and the skill displayed by them and losses or expenses incurred by them from the time the salvage starts until the distressed vessel or cargo is placed in a position of safety.

5144. Reports to the Ministry of Defence

1. A short report of all services or assistance to a private vessel (other than purely life-saving services) is to be made immediately to the Ministry of Defence and the local Operational and Administrative Authorities by signal, irrespective of whether the personnel wish to claim salvage. The signal is to include

  (a) the name of the private vessel, the name of her owners, her port of registry and the nature of her cargo;

  (b) a brief description of the services which have been, or are being performed (*see* Clause 2);

  (c) the vessel's position;

  (d) whether Lloyd's Open Form has been signed (*see also* **5142.**2) or it is desired that this should be done in London;

  (e) whether bail or security has been offered and for what amount; (*see* Note)

  (f) if Lloyd's Open Form has not been signed, whether the vessel or property has been arrested (*see also* **5146**);

  (g) whether any personnel wish to claim;

  (h) whether they wish the Treasury Solicitor to represent them (*see* **J.5145**.2);

  (j) whether a ship's agent is being instructed and, if so, his name.

Note: Advice should always be sought from Ministry of Defence (Navy) before bail or security is agreed. The Commanding Officer, or other officer of Her Majesty's ship or vessel concerned must not in any circumstances on his own account offer a tow or other salvage assistance free of charge.

2. The report is to be made without delay after the services have started. It is to be supplemented by signalled reports of progress and the prospects of success, giving as good an idea as possible of the remaining value of the vessel, cargo and freight. The terms of the salvage agreement will be kept under review at the Ministry of Defence in the light of progress reports bearing in mind that

   (a) success is necessary to obtain a salvage award and on this "no cure no pay" basis of salvage there is no right to recover expenses incurred in a salvage enterprise which ultimately fails to preserve a vessel, cargo or freight;

   (b) the awards are based on the fund provided by the salved value of the vessel, cargo and freight and rarely exceed half this value;

   (c) the Lloyd's Open Form binds the salvor to use his best endeavours to achieve successful salvage, but nevertheless care must be taken not to persist with salvage services which may result in financial loss to the Crown.

J.3. So that the presentation of salvage claims may be considered, a full report of the circumstances is to be submitted whenever Service personnel, or ships or aircraft belonging to the Crown, perform a service entitling them to salvage money.

(*Navy only*)—When the services are complete the report is to be made without delay. It is to be addressed to the Treasury Solicitor at 3 Central Buildings, Matthew Parker Street, London, S.W.1 and sent by the quickest means. A copy is to be sent to the appropriate Administrative Authority or appropriate Senior Officer. He is to send it to the Deputy Under-Secretary of State (Naval), Naval Law Division, with his comments. Each vessel concerned is to report separately.

4. The report is to be accompanied by a copy of the Ship's Log for the relevant period. It is to be a factual narrative account arranged in chronological order, quoting times as well as dates. It is to cover in detail all the operations and services. It is to be complete in itself without reference to other communications or documents. It is to show the following:

   (a) On whose instructions the services were undertaken (copies of any relevant messages or requests are to be attached).

   (b) The name and description of the distressed vessel; name and address of her owners and/or local agents; the cause of the distress; the position (1) in which it occurred, and (2) in which assistance was first given.

   (c) The degree of disablement or damage, including all factors relevant to assessing the dangers which the vessel would have encountered if the services had not been given, and the fullest possible description of the condition of the vessel, including details of flooded compartments, draught, stability and trim.

   (d) For the periods immediately before and after the salvage service as well as for the period of the service itself, the conditions of weather, including changes in barometric pressure, wind force and direction, and state of sea, and how these conditions made operations more difficult or dangerous.

   (e) Details of any condition other than those already mentioned which made the work or any part of it more arduous or dangerous (but *see* Clause 5).

   (f) Whether any personnel wish to claim salvage and, if so, a complete and verified list in duplicate of every person on board at the time of the operation and of those of the ship's company who on the material date were absent, with the full names and Service Numbers of naval ratings and R.M. other

Appendix D—Rules and Regulations

ranks who performed special services, e.g., boat, boarding and steaming parties.

(g) Details of all expenses incurred, including the cost of fuel and lubricants, stores consumed, damaged, or lost, and claims for damage to clothing and other items of expenditure arising directly from the services: (the compensation granted for damage to clothing will be deemed part of the salvage award, if any, and deducted from the amount received before distribution).

(h) Whether any salvage agreement has been signed and the date it was sent to the Ministry of Defence.

(j) Full details of assistance given by other vessels, naval, dockyard or other working parties.

5. Opinions on the conduct of the operation or of individuals are to be given in separate reports and are not to be included in the factual report to the Treasury Solicitor. The supplementary reports are to be sent to the appropriate Administrative Authority or Senior Officer to send to the Ministry of Defence with a copy of the main report.

J.5145. Prosecution of personal salvage claims

1. The Treasury Solicitor acts for the Ministry of Defence in the presentation of Salvage claims on the Ministry's behalf and is also prepared to accept instructions from ships' agents. (*Navy only*) If a claim for salvage is to be made by personnel of ships which have a ship's agent (*see* **5102**) the Commanding Officer is recommended to communicate with the ship's agent by telegram as soon as possible after the commencement of the salvage operation. The agent is to be told the salved ship's name, her owners, details of her cargo, short particulars of where she is and the nature of the services. When more than one of Her Majesty's ships is concerned, it is suggested that the ship's agent of the senior officer's ship should be asked to act for all the salvors, the other ships' agents being informed accordingly, as it is desirable that all claims for a particular salvage should be dealt with through one agency. The Treasury Solicitor, who normally prosecutes the Ministry of Defence's claim will be prepared to accept instructions and a Retainer from the ship's agent to negotiate a claim on behalf of all personnel concerned on the terms that

(a) no personal liability will rest on the personnel for the costs concerned, but any costs not recovered from the salved interests will be deducted from the award before distribution;

(b) the Treasury Solicitor will not enforce, compromise or withdraw their claims or any of them without the ship's agents' instructions, but in the event of a difference of opinion arising between the Ministry of Defence and the personnel as to whether any claim should be enforced, compromised or withdrawn, the Treasury Solicitor's advice shall be accepted.

2. The Treasury Solicitor is also prepared to act for personnel of ships which do not have a ship's agent, such as ships hired by the Ministry of Defence on demise charter, and for personnel attached to shore establishments. Before he can act for such personnel he requires a letter of retainer on Form S.1522 signed by the Commanding Officer or other officer. It is to be sent to the Treasury Solicitor with the full written report. His services will be given only on the terms that he may enforce, compromise or withdraw the claim as he in his absolute discretion may think advisable and without prior communication with the personnel.

3. When a lump sum is recovered for the joint claims of the Ministry of Defence and of personnel represented by the Treasury Solicitor, the apportionment of that sum

between the respective claimants or groups of claimants by the Ministry of Defence and the Treasury Solicitor will be accepted without question. A nominal roll giving particulars of those on whose behalf the claim is to be made is to be provided in duplicate and reference is to be made to those who perform special services. This list is required in addition to the one forwarded with the full written report. *See* **5144.J3**.

4. The Ministry of Defence has the right to put forward a claim in respect of salvage performed by ships or aircraft belonging to the Crown in its name alone.

(*Navy only*)—and to withhold permission for personnel to claim separately. When this right is exercised the Ministry of Defence will consider granting personnel a share of any award received.

5146. Enforcement of claims—general

1. When salvage is completed, the first step is to obtain bail or security for the amount of the likely award to the Ministry of Defence and personal salvors. Subject to Clause 4, the salvors are not to consent to the release of the salved vessel or property until they have been informed that proper security has been given. This is especially important when the salvage relates to a foreign ship. The Treasury Solicitor normally obtains bail to cover the claims of the Ministry of Defence and personnel he is to represent. The ship's agent is responsible for obtaining bail for the services of the personnel he represents. If he intends to instruct the Treasury Solicitor the latter will obtain sufficient bail to cover the claims of all parties.

2. If a Lloyd's Open Form has not been signed and it is likely that the salved ship or cargo will be removed before a satisfactory guarantee can be obtained and before the Treasury Solicitor can offer advice, the salvors are, subject to Clause 4, to get the salved ship and cargo arrested or detained by the local court or nearest detaining officer until bail or security is given.

3. If a Lloyd's Open Form has been signed, the provisions of its Clause 5 must be carefully observed. Only if an attempt is made, or is known on good evidence to be contemplated, to remove the salved property without Ministry of Defence consent before security has been given, is it justifiable to arrest or detain the vessel and/or cargo. If such an attempt is made, or is believed to be contemplated, the first step to be taken to enforce the lien conferred on the Ministry of Defence by Clause 5 of the Form is to place an officer on board the salved ship, if this can be done without exercising force. Only when it is clear that the removal of the vessel or cargo is still intended may the vessel/or cargo be detained by legal process until bail or security is given.

4. Salved vessels must never be arrested or detained without Ministry of Defence authority when they belong to

(a) British owners of good standing and reputation;

(b) owners other than those at (a), of good standing and reputation, when a Lloyd's Open Form has been signed.

5147. Detention of ships abroad

1. The salvor may, subject to **5146**.4, detain the property salved if he cannot obtain an agreement from the master or a satisfactory guarantee from the owners or agents for the payment of any salvage which may be awarded. He must take the vessel to a port where there is a consular officer, or a Court of Admiralty or a Vice-Admiralty Court. In so doing, he is, so far as his primary duty to the Queen's service permits, to be guided by the convenience of the vessel salved. Within 24 hours of arrival at the port, the salvor, and the master, or other persons in charge of the alleged salved property, are each to deliver to the consular officer or to the judge of the Court of Admiralty, or Vice-Admiralty Court, a statement containing so far as possible the particulars required by

Appendix 14, Part 4. The statement must be on oath. Within four days of receiving these statements, the consular officer or judge must proceed to fix a bond sufficient to cover the probable demand for salvage and costs.

2. If either party fails to make the statement referred to in Clause 1 within 24 hours of arrival, the consular officer or judge may proceed *ex parte*. He should not, however, except in pressing circumstances, do so without giving notice, and, if the property or vessel salved is to be sold, he must allow a reasonable time for particulars of the sale to be given. He can never require the cargo to be unladen.

3. If the consular officer or judge requires additional information, he may examine the parties or witnesses upon oath. A written version of the additional evidence will accompany the original statements.

4. When the consular officer or judge has determined the amount, he instructs the parties to prepare a bond as in Appendix 14, Part 3. If the parties wish adjudication in any court of Admiralty, or Vice-Admiralty Court in the British Dominions, the name of the court, and the place for which it acts, is to be inserted in the bond. If not, the High Court in England will adjudicate. The bond must be executed by the master in the presence of the consular officer or judge, and must be attested by him. The consular officer or judge then delivers it to the salvor. Thereupon the salvor's lien on the property ceases.

5. For salved property owned by residents of foreign countries such additional security must be given as the consular officer or judge may approve. When executed and attested this additional security must be given to the consular officer or judge, or if the salvor wishes, placed in the joint possession of the consular officer, the judge, and any other person appointed by the salvor.

6. If those in charge of the salved property do not execute the bond, the salvor can take proceedings in the appropriate court having jurisdiction over the place where the salved vessel or property is at the time proceedings are instituted. He may detain the salved vessel or property through the proper officer of the court until the claim is satisfied or security given.

7. For the detention of ships in collision cases, *see* **3496**. *See also* **2815**—*Foreign Enlistment Act.*

5148. Salvage awards and distribution

1. Salvage awards for the service of Ministry of Defence (Navy) personnel, irrespective of whether they result from a decision of a court, an arbitrator, a settlement out of court, or from voluntary gift of the owners, are not to be accepted without Ministry of Defence consent.

2. Awards are distributable solely by the Director General of Defence Accounts. He distributes them according to the Order in Council relating to them and in force at the time of the services, unless the award is made by a court or arbitrator and its terms include a special apportionment, or unless there are other special circumstances. The current Order in Council is in Appendix 14, Part 2. (*See also* **5162**.3 and **5173** to **5178**).

3. When various ships or personnel engaged in the same service perform different work, recommendations for specially apportioning an ultimate award between them are to be sent to the Ministry of Defence.

4. The £5 per cent due to the naval prize cash balance under Section 17 of the Naval Agency and Distribution Act, 1894 and approved expenses incurred by the salvors in obtaining an award, including the ship's agent's commission (*see* **5102**) and any legal costs (over and above the party costs usually ordered to be paid by the salved vessel) are deducted from the award before distribution.

5. Income Tax is payable on salvage awards.

6. *See also* **5103**.3, **5107** and **5108**.

5149–5160. Unallocated

Section V

SALVAGE OF PRIVATE PROPERTY

5161. Articles found

1. All articles, other than those belonging to the Crown, found in or on the shores of the sea or any tidal waters of the United Kingdom are to be delivered to the Receiver of Wreck for the district. Abroad, application is to be made to consular or other appropriate authorities for disposal instructions.

2. A report is to be sent to the Ministry of Defence stating whether the personnel wish to claim salvage, unless an award offered by a Receiver of Wreck is accepted under **5162**.

5162. Awards from Receivers of Wreck

1. Flag Officers and Naval Officers-in-Charge may, without reference to the Ministry of Defence, sanction the acceptance of awards offered by Receivers of Wreck for salved property not owned by or entirely at risk of, the Crown. Permission to accept is not normally to be withheld even though the circumstances may have been fortuitous and the service performed during the normal course of duty. When acceptance is permitted, the reward offered by the Receiver of Wreck is to be accepted without questioning the amount. The Ministry of Defence is to be informed whenever permission is withheld.

2. When the reward exceeds £20 the Ministry of Defence is to be informed of the circumstances of the salvage, and the names and rank or rating of the salvors. The Ministry of Defence will allocate the award in part or in full to the salvors. The allocation will be distributed by the Director General of Defence Accounts according to the Order in Council in force at the time of the service or as otherwise directed. The current Order in Council is in Appendix 14, Part 2.

3. The authority sanctioning acceptance of awards within a limit of £20 is to distribute them in full according to the Order in Council in force at the time of the service, unless there is justification for a special apportionment. The current Order in Council is in Appendix 14, Part 2. When the award is so small that distribution is hardly practicable, the distributing authority may empower the Commanding Officer to pay the award at his discretion either to the Ship's Fund or a suitable charity. When local distribution occurs the charge of £5 per cent referred to in **5108**.3 will be waived.

4. Particulars of participants in local distributions and the amounts paid to them are to be sent to the Director General of Defence Accounts.

5163–5170. Unallocated

Appendix D—Rules and Regulations

No. 35

Royal National Lifeboat Institution Regulations
(Revised January 1992)

[Section 2]

Station Branches and Operations

2.4.4. Property Salvage

2.4.4.1. General Conditions. The Committee of Management, Officials and Honorary Officials of the Institution, as such, will take no part in any claims against the Master, owner or underwriters of any vessel in respect of property salvage. Lifeboats must not be launched solely for property salvage but subject to the regulation in this chapter, the Coxswain of a lifeboat which has been launched on a lifesaving service, is at liberty, on behalf of his crew, to accept an engagement from the Master of a casualty to salve his vessel and to make use of the lifeboat and her gear for this purpose. Before accepting such an engagement the Coxswain must bear in mind that the primary aim of the Institution is the saving of life at sea; and that this aim may be adversely affected by undue hazard to his lifeboat and the crew by prolonged absence of the boat from her station on salvage operations. No Lifeboat may be used for property salvage when tugs or other suitable craft are available and adequate for the task. The Committee of Management wishes to discourage claims for property salvage being made when a lifeboat is used so far as it lies in their power to do so.

2.4.4.2 Status of Crew. When an engagement as above, has been accepted, the position of the lifeboat crew becomes that of a party of men who have borrowed a boat for the purpose of effecting property salvage and they must, therefore, look to the Master of the casualty and not to the Institution for their remuneration for the service.

2.4.4.3 Expenses Payable by the Crew. The following expenses will be recoverable from the crew whenever a property salvage claim is made:

(1) The cost of fuel, lubricants and other consumable stores used on the service.

(2) The cost of repairs to the lifeboat, if any, necessitated by accident or other cause during the service, including transport charges and all expenses involved in the temporary replacement of the damaged lifeboat by a relief boat.

(3) The cost of repairs or replacement of stores or gear, damaged, lost or expended during the service.

2.4.4.4 Salvage Claims. Official writing paper of the Institution, of any of its Branches or Offices, shall not be used for correspondence for or on behalf of the crews in connection with any property salvage claim. Except as provided in Regulation 2.4.4.3 the Institution will have no claim on any part of the sum by which a claim is settled.

2.4.4.5 Service Allowances. If a property salvage claim is made by a lifeboat crew, service allowances will not be paid by the Institution for the whole of the service during which the engagement for property salvage was undertaken, even though no

R.N.L.I. Regulations

payment in respect of the claim may be received from the Master, owners or underwriters of the casualty concerned.

2.4.4.6 Standing by Casualty. If the Coxswain of a lifeboat finds, on reaching a casualty, that other vessels are endeavouring to assist the casualty to safety, or to refloat her, if aground, the Coxswain may stand by the casualty in the lifeboat, if, in his opinion, it may be desirable for the crew of the casualty to abandon her, or if requested to do so by the Master of the casualty. Any such request should be obtained in writing, if possible, and should be attached to the normal Return of Service forwarded to Headquarters by the Honorary Secretary. Provided that:

(1) No claim for salvage is made on behalf of the lifeboat, and

(2) The period of standing by does not exceed 12 hours.

Service allowances will be paid to the crew for the whole period of such a service.

2.4.4.7 For the attendance of the lifeboat, at the request of the Master of the casualty, during any more extended salvage operations, whether assistance is given in such operations or not, service allowances will not be payable by the Institution.

INDEX

[References in this index are to paragraph numbers.]

AB INITIO, TOWAGE AS SALVAGE, 619
ABANDONMENT,
  bona fide, 575
  collisions, 577
  contracts,
    discharge of, 574, 576
    tug and tow, 613
  danger justifying, 571, 578
  decision to abandon, 573–576
  derelict, 208–212
  final, 577
  freight, 1381–1384
  intention, 1382
  life, imperiling, 571–572
  masters, 573–577
  non-acceptance of salved property, 1072, 1079–1081
  perils, 572
  possession, 1234, 1237
  requirements for, 570
  reward, 578
  salved value, 1378, 1381–1384
  seamen, 570–579, 584
  success, 733
  tug and tow, 613
  unnecessary, 575
ABERDEEN, 1325
ACCEPTANCE. *See also* NON-ACCEPTANCE OF SALVED PROPERTY
  accepted services, 758
  assistance, 1039–1043
  benefits, 50, 134
  best endeavours, 1035
  common law salvage, 134
  compensation, 1082
  delivery, 1035
  officiousness, 50–63
  redelivery, 989, 1045, 1082
  remoteness of benefit, 64
  reward, 50–63
  urgency, 53
ACCIDENTS, meaning of, 70n
ACCORD AND SATISFACTION, 956
ACTS OF GOD, 733
ACTUAL FAULT OR PRIVITY, 1202–1203
ADEN, 383
ADMIRALTY COURT, 1, 14. *See also* ADMIRALTY JURISDICTION
  appeals, 98, 117
  apportionment, 1522, 1528, 1536, 1538–1540
  arbitration, 118
  assessment of rewards, 1390–1391

ADMIRALTY COURT—*cont.*
  Chancery Court, influences of, 6, 22–25
  civil law, 95
  common law, 109
    influences of, 6
    relationship with, 90–93, 95, 97
    salvage, 146, 149
  contracts, 97
  custom, 527
  equity, 21–25
  fraud by boatmen, 114–115
  High Court of Admiralty, 96
  high and low water mark, 91
  history of, 90–102
  interest, 1468, 1472–1473
  judges of, 14, 94, 99
  Judicature Acts, 96, 98
  life salvage, 1480
  locality, 91
  Lord High Admiral, 90
  maritime liens, 1247
  material circumstances, 1432
  practice and procedure, 95
  prize, 94
  Probate, Divorce and Admiralty Court, 14, 95, 96, 99
    abolition of, 125
  public policy, 36, 41
  Queen's Bench Division, part of, 101
  reallocation of business, 101
  record, court of, 111
  reward, 91
  salved value, 1457
  sovereign immunity, 1175–1177
  statute law, 93
  success, assessment of, 1450
  time, 1436
  types of salvage, 20
  vitiating factors, 879, 881
  voluntariness, 512, 515, 527, 529
  wrecks, 91, 107
ADMIRALTY INSTRUCTIONS, 654
ADMIRALTY JURISDICTION, 2–3, 21, 28–29, 103–128
  accepted services, 755
  Act of 1713, 110–111
  Act of 1753, 112
  Act of 1809, 113
  Admiralty Court Act 1840, 116
  Admiralty Court Act 1861, 119
  aircraft, 126, 246, 247, 251
  alteration of, 103
  anchors, saving, 113

875

Index

ADMIRALTY JURISDICTION—cont.
appeals, 115
arbitration, 124
arbitrators, decisions over, 104
assessment of reward, 117
bunkers, 126
Cinque Ports, 115
civil, 104
Civil Jurisdiction and Judgments Act 1982, 124
common law,
  influences of, 6
  relationship with, 90–93, 95, 97, 109
  salvage, 144–145, 147
compulsion, 925–941
containers, 126
county, body of a, 103, 115, 117–118
County Courts Admiralty Jurisdiction Act 1868, 121, 122
county courts, transfer to, 122
criminal, 104
definition, 104
EC law, 124
encouragement of salvage, 41
endangering ships, 112–113
exclusive, 143
extension of, 103, 115, 126
flotsam, jetsam, lagan and derelict, 109, 111, 204–207
frauds by boatmen, 114–115
function of, 104
High Court, 124
high seas, serviced rendered on, 103, 116
hire, 126
hovercraft, 126
in personam claims, 104
inequity of terms, 925–941
inherent, 103, 117
interests in salved property, 1506
justices of the peace, 118, 122
land, 109
life salvage, 1481
Lloyd's Open Form, 127–128
locality, 103
Lord High Admiral, 90
maritime liens, 1249–1250
Merchant Shipping Act 1854, 118
Merchant Shipping Act 1894, 122–127
mistake, 921–922
Naval Agency and Distribution Act 1864, 120
negligence, 1107
non-disclosure, 902
power-driven vessels, 126
prize, 104
Probate, Divorce and Admiralty Court, abolition of, 124
Proceedings, 1224
property, preservation of, 726
reallocation of admiralty business, 101
Records, Courts of, 115, 119
restrictions on, 91

ADMIRALTY JURISDICTION—cont.
reward, 109–111, 126
  assessment of, 117
Royal Navy, 120
salvage agreements, 858, 862–866
salvage subjects, 126
sources of, 103
special, 118
standard forms of contract, 126
statute law, 93, 103, 104, 123–124, 152
Statute of Westminister, 111
stranding, 112
subjects of salvage, 126, 152–154
time charterparties, 126
transfer of salvage jurisdiction to, 113
treaties and conventions, 127
usurping, 91–92
vitiating factors, 880–882, 889–890
wreck, 201–202
  early jurisdiction over, 105–108
  extension of jurisdiction over preservation from, 109–112
Wreck and Salvage Act 1846, 117
ADMIRALTY LAW,
English law, 15
judges' development of, 99
life salvage, 264
locality, 362–363, 367
reduction in liability, 1140
sources of modern salvage law, 15
systemisation of, 95
ADMIRALTY MARSHAL, 1386
ADMIRALTY REGISTRY, 95
ADVANCE FREIGHT, 218, 227, 228–229
AGENTS,
authority, 796, 800–815, 823–825, 828–829
  masters, as, 814–815, 829, 832
  seamen, 842
common law salvage, 137, 144
co-operation, 1059
expenses, 631
liens, 800
Lloyd's, 626–631
masters, 814–815, 829, 832
owners, 631
pre-existing, 807–808
principal, 801–803, 809, 829
  notification, 846
  undisclosed, 803
redelivery, 1084
remuneration, 137
salvage services, 629
salvors, 626–631
seamen, 840
shipowners, 815
ships, 626–631
skill and care, 800
statutory authorities, 692
voluntariness, 626–631

876

Index

AGREEMENTS. *See* CONTRACTS, SALVAGE AGREEMENTS
AIR FORCE PERSONNEL, ROYAL, 677–681
AIRBORNE CRAFT. *See also* AIRCRAFT
   subjects of salvage, 244–259
AIRCRAFT,
   Admiralty jurisdiction, 126, 246, 247, 252
   airmen, 677–681
   Chicago Convention, 254
   common law salvage, 248, 251
   definition, 253–254
   flying boats, 253
   history, 244–250
   hovercrafts, 254
   life salvage, 278
   locality, 256
   navigation, used in, 246
   owners, 678
   proceedings, 1224
   reward, 254
   Royal Air Force, 677–681
   salvage law, application to, 250–253
   salvage services, 254–255
   seaplanes, 245–246, 249, 253
   spacecraft, 254
   statute law, 244–245, 249
   subjects of salvage, 152, 244–257
   voluntariness, 677–681
   Warsaw Convention, 1203
   wreck, 250–254
AIRMEN, 677–681
ALEXANDRIA, 1122
ALTERNATIVE DISPUTE RESOLUTION, 1222
AMMUNITION, 188
ANCHORS, 113, 341
ANIMALS, 190, 261n
ANNULMENT, 892
APPAREL, 150, 179
APPEALS,
   Admiralty Court, 98, 117
   Admiralty jurisdiction, 115
   arbitration, 1302–1309
      courts, to, 1309, 1315–1317
      House of lords, to, 1318
      notice of, 1302–1305
      parties, 1306
      time limits, 1304
   assessment of rewards, 1390–1391
   Chancery Court, 98
   common law, 98, 115
   Court of Appeal, 96
   courts, to, 1309, 1315–1317
   equity, 98
   House of Lords, 98, 1318
   Lloyd's open form, 1306
   notice, 1302–1305
   parties, 1306
   Privy Council, 98
   time limits, 1304
APPLICABLE LAW,
   governing law, 72
   jurisdiction, 74

APPLICABLE LAW—*cont.*
   Salvage Convention 1989, 74
APPORTIONMENT, 2, 1519–1540
   £5, 000, under, 1521
   Admiralty court, by, 1522, 1528, 1536, 1538–1540
   agreements, 1519, 1536–1538
      customary, 1537
      setting aside, 1540
   arbitration, 1519
   assistance, 1533
   coastguards, 1530
   Crown ships, 1529
   danger, 1533
   delay, 1522
   demise charterparties, 478
   detailed instances of, 1524–1535
   engineers, 1526
   English law, 1520, 1524–1540
   expenses, 1442
   extra shares, 1528
   fraud, 893
   governing law, 76, 1523
   individual salvors, amongst unassociated, 1531
   inequity of terms, 1539–1540
   jurisdiction, 1519–1522
   lifeboatmen, 1530
   masters, 1525, 1540
   officers, 1526, 1529
   participation rule, 1527
   parties, 1524
   passengers, 1528
   personal representatives, 1535
   personal services, 1526
   pilots, 1530, 1540
   prior act, 1540
   priorities, 1533
   radio officers, 1526
   remuneration, 783, 1520, 1539
   rescue, 1533
   restitution, 1540
   reward, 2, 76, 1528
   salvage agreements, 783
   salvage articles, 1539
   Salvage Convention 1989, 76, 1521–1523
   salvage services, 1525
      contemporaneous, 1532
   salved value, 1386
   salvors,
      deceased, 1535
      first, 1533
      several, 1524, 1532–1534
      seamen, other than, 1540
      wrongful dispossession, 1534
   seamen, 1526, 1529, 1531, 1538–1539
   shipowners, share of, 1524
   special rewards, 1528
   time, 1533
   usage, 1537
   vessels, amongst salving, 1532–1534
   voluntariness, 1536

Index

APPORTIONMENT—*cont.*
  wrongful dispossession, 1534
APPRAISEMENT, 1386
ARBITRATION, 2. *See also* ARBITRATORS, LSSAC 200
  Admiralty Court, 118
  Admiralty jurisdiction, 125
  agreements, 1266, 1269–1270,1277, 1299–1300
  appeals, 1302–1309
    assessment of rewards, 1390–1391
    courts, to, 1309, 1315–1317
    House of lords, to, 1318
    notice of, 1302–1305
    parties, 1306
    time limits, 1304
  apportionment, 1519
  arrest, 1271–1272
  assessment of rewards, 1390–1391
  assessors, 1288
  authority, 819, 822, 835, 841
  awards, 1290–1294
    additional, 1301
    correction of, 1301
    currency, 1461–1463
    effect of, 1299
    final and binding, 1274, 1306
    interim, 1291–1292
    provisional, 1293–1294
    publication of, 67, 1266, 1300
    separate, 1290–1294
    variation of, 1306
  bail, 1271
  cargo-owners, 1270
  consent orders, 1285
  costs, 1291, 1295, 1296–1298, 1311–1312
  Council of lloyd's,
    awards and, 1299–1300, 1310
    parties relationship with, 1277–1278
  courts and, 1269–1272
    appeals, to, 1309, 1315–1317
  cross-appeals, 1302–1304
  currency, 1461–1463
  directions, initial order for, 1286
  disclosure of documents, 1287
  English law, 75
  environment, 1300
  evidence, 1284–1294
  expenses, 1293, 1296–1298, 1449
  experts, 1288
  fees, 1296–1298
  governing law, 73, 75
  hearings, 1289
  House of lords, to, 1318
  indemnities, 1311
  injunctions, 1270
  interest, 1469–1473, 1475–1475
  interim payments, 1291–1292
  legal advisers, 1288
  Lloyd's Open Form, 6, 8, 78, 791–792, 822, 989, 1266–1267,1299, 1300–1303

ARBITRATION—*cont.*
  Lloyd's Open Form—*cont.*
    appeals, 1306
    hearings, 1289
    interim awards, 1291
    parties involved, 1274–1278
    place of arbitration, 1279
    procedure, 1284
    provisional awards, 1294
    references under, 1273
    security, payment and enforcement of, 1310–1314
  Lloyd's procedural rules, 1267, 1284–1285, 1301, 1305
  LOF 2000, 1267, 1273, 1276, 1278
  London, 73
  Lssac 2000, 1266–1268, 1273, 1275, 1278–1279,1291, 1298, 1304, 1310–1314
  open offers, 1295
  participation, 1274–1276
  parties, 1274–1278
    appeals, 1306
    duties of, 991
  place of, 1279
  preliminary meetings, 1285
  proceedings, 1222, 1266–1318
  procedure, 1284–1294
  reference to, 1273
  remuneration, 1267, 1273
  representation, 1274–1276,1288
  reward, 8
  salvage agreements, 1274
  Salvage Convention 1989, 67, 1266, 1300
  salvors, 1292
  Scopic, 1268
  sealed offers, 1295
  security, 1264, 1266–1318
  service, 1274–1276
  sources of modern salvage law, 6, 8
  sovereign immunity, 1173–1174
  special compensation, 1273, 1311
  stay of proceedings, 1269–1271
  time limits, 1205, 1289, 1304
ARBITRATORS,
  Admiralty jurisdiction, 104
  appointment, 1280
    termination of, 1281
  authority, 1281
  Council of Lloyd's, 1280–1281
  duties, 1282
  functions of, 14
  Lloyd's Open Form, 1280, 1283
  Lloyd's Procedural Rules, 1222, 1281–1282
  LSSAC 2000, 1280, 1283
  powers, 1283
ARMED FORCES. *See also* ROYAL NAVY, ROYAL AIR FORCE
  public authorities, 549
  Royal Army, 682

Index

ARREST,
  arbitration, 1271–1272
  cargo, 1508
  in rem actions, 1223
  maritime liens, 1249
  salvors, 1485
  security, 1226, 1265
ASSESSMENT OF REWARD, 2, 1389–1406. *See also* MATERIAL CIRCUMSTANCES
  adjustments, 111
  Admiralty court, 1390–1391
  Admiralty jurisdiction, 117, 1397
  arbitrators, 1390–1391
  arbitration awards,
    availability of, 1390–1391
    appeals, 1390–1391
    publication of, 1390–1391
  confidentiality, 1390–1391
  Crown ships, 654–655
  currency fluctuations, 25
  danger, 377
  discretion, 1392, 1398
  division of liability, 1515–1518
  eligible and additional circumstances, 1404–1406
  engaged services, 752, 757
  English law, 1398
  environment, 396–397, 410, 1399
  equity, 25
  framework for, 1390–1395
  guiding policies and principles, 1398–1401
  individual circumstances, taking account of, 1402–1403
  justices of the peace, 117
  life salvage, 309
  Lloyd's open form, 1389–1390
  LSSAC 2000, 1400
  moiety, 1397
  quantum meruit, 1389
  personal services, 451
  professional salvors, 45
  public policy, 27, 37–38, 1399, 1453–1456
  quantum meruit, 37–38
  salvage agreements, 31, 780, 864
    setting aside, 1389
  Salvage convention 1910, 1397
  Salvage convention 1989, 1389, 1399, 1402–1406
  salved fund, 1396
    value of, 1397
  salved value, 1457–1459, 1499, 1504
  SCOPIC clause, 974–976
  special compensation, 420–421, 436–437
  success, measure of, 1450–1452
  supply of services, 1018
  third parties, 1448
  work and labour, 1389
ASSESSORS, 1288
ASSISTANCE,
  acceptance, 1039–1043
  apportionment, 1533, 1533
  best endeavours, 1036, 1041

ASSISTANCE—*cont.*
  co-operation, 1069
  damages, 1041
  danger, 988, 1411
  definition of salvage, 17
  failure to discharge duties, 1041–1042
  loss of opportunity, 1039
  misconduct, 1091, 1133
  parties, duties of, 988, 1039–10–43
  possession, 1234, 1241
  property, 18
    non-acceptance of salved, 1072, 1076
  reasonableness, 1041, 1043
  reward, 1039, 1042–1043
  safety at sea, 987
  Salvage Convention 1989, 988, 1040–1043
  salvors, intervention of other, 1039–1043
  supervening events, 1076
ASSUMPSIT, 135
ATTACHMENT, 1250
ATTORNEYS, 95
AUTHORITY,
  actual, 801, 812–813, 817
  agency, 796, 800–815, 823–825, 828–829
    masters, as, 814–815, 829, 832
    seamen, 840
  apparent, 802, 803
  arbitration, 819, 822, 835, 841
  benefit, 819
  breach of warranty of, 802
  bunkers, 824–832
  cargo-owners, 824–832
  continuing services, 835
  contractors, 879
  Crown ships, 839
  delegation, 823
  disbursements, 817
  emergencies, 804–808
  exclusions, 787, 798
  express, 801
  freight, 824–832
  future services, 838
  general average, 825
  general principles, 800
  implied, 801, 812, 841, 845
  indemnities, 808
  instructions, 801, 805
  intermediaries, 796–798, 800–809
  legal duty or, salvage under, 533–543
  liability, 798
  Lloyd's Open Form, 806, 822, 828–829, 841
  LOF 2000, 797–799, 846
  LSSAC 2000, 799
  masters, 565, 729–730, 796–797, 812–813
    agents, as, 814–815, 829, 832
    cargo-owners, 831–832
    officers, binding, 836–840
    persons other than, 823
    power of shipowners to bind, 841–844
    ratification, 828
    seamen, binding, 833–835

Index

AUTHORITY—cont.
  masters—cont.
    shipowners, binding, 814–823, 833–835, 841–844
    mutual insurance, 842
    necessity, 804–808, 817–818, 821, 829, 832, 841
    no cure no pay, 827
    officers, masters binding, 836–840
    ostensible, 802, 813
    passengers, 819
    past services, 838
    pre-Convention and post-Convention law, 796
    principal, 801–803, 809, 829
      notification, 846
      undisclosed, 803
    privity of contract, 809
    public policy, 807, 837, 839
    ratification, by, 808, 821, 823, 828, 840
    reasonable necessity, 817
    remuneration, 834, 837, 839
    restitution, 808, 831
    rewards, 807, 809, 815, 821
    salvage agreements, 796–846
    Salvage Convention 1989, 796, 816, 832
    salvage services, 838
    salving vessels, 833–845
    salvors, agreement with one or several, 845
    scope of, 797
    seamen,
      agents, 840
      masters binding, 833–840
      ratification, 840
      shipowners' binding, 841–844
    self-interest, 806
    settlement of claims, 820–821
    shipowners,
      binding persons other than, 828–832
      masters' binding, 814–823, 833–835, 841–844
      personal capacity, acting in, 835–827
      power of owners to bind masters and crew, 841–844
      ratification, by, 823
      seamen, power to bind, 841–844
    skill and care, 800
    success, 729–730, 808
    third parties, 879–802
    tug and tow, 805, 827, 838
    types of, 801–809
    usual, 803
AVERAGE. *See* GENERAL AVERAGE
AVOIDANCE, 889
AWARDS,
  arbitration, publication of, 1290–1294
  additional, 1301
  correction of, 1301
  effect of, 1299
  final and binding, 1274, 1306
  interim, 1291–1292

AUTHORITY—cont.
  arbitration, publication of—cont.
    provisional, 1293–1294
    publication of, 67, 1266, 1300, 1390–1391
    separate, 1290–1294
    variation of, 1306
  assessment of rewards, 1390–1391
  availability of, 1390–1391
  breach of contract, 1033
  confidentiality, 1390–1391
  diminution in, 1133–1135
  fraud, 893
  incomplete services, 736–737
  law reports, 6
  life salvage, 117
  misconduct, 1133–1136
  performance, 133
  publication, 67, 1266, 1300, 1390–1391
  Salvage Convention 1989, 67
AZORES, 681

BAIL, 1271
BAILMENT,
  cargo, 487–488
  gratuitous, 1021, 1079
  liens, 1078
  non-acceptance of salved property, 1072–1075, 1078–1079, 1081
  redelivery, 1084
  security, 1226
  sub, 1021, 1078, 1081, 1084
  supply of services, 1007, 1021
BAREBOAT CHARTERS. *See* DEMISE CHARTERPARTIES
BARGAINING POWER, INEQUALITY OF, 902, 932
BARGE, 197, 210, 1507
BAROMETERS, 184
BARRY ROADS, 1093
BASES OF SALVAGE, 26
BEACHING, 357
BEACONS, 155–158
BENEFICIARIES OF SERVICES. *See* RECIPIENTS OF SERVICES
BENEFIT,
  acceptance, 50, 64, 134
  authority, 821
  common law salvage, 130, 134
  intention, 48–49
  interest not receiving, 1516–1518
  life salvage, 1480–1482
  property, 26
  remoteness of, 64
  remuneration, 54
  salved value, 1504
  salvees, 28–30
BEREHAVEN, 1244
BERMUDA, 1362
BEST ENDEAVOURS,
  acceptance, 1035
  assistance, 1036, 1041

Index

BEST ENDEAVOURS—*cont.*
  contractors, 987, 1034
  contracts, 1034–1036
  engaged services, 772
  environment, 1037
  estoppel, 871–872, 874, 1035
  Lloyd's Open Form, 1036, 1080
  LOF 2000, 987, 1034–1036
  LSSAC 2000, 1036
  non-acceptance of salved property, 1080
  oil pollution, 70
  parties, duties of, 987, 1034–1036
  place of safety, 1035
  reward, 1034–1035
  safety, place of, 1063
  Salvage Convention 1989, 1036
  salvors, 1034–1036
  seamen, 584
  security, 1262–1263
  sub-contractors, 1036
  success, 1034
  supply of services, 1014, 1020, 1022–1023
  termination, 1063
  tug and tow, 602
  unfair contract terms, 1159–1161
BILLS OF LADING, 226, 228
BILLS OF SALE, 112
BOARD OF TRADE, 673
BOARDING, 598
BOATMEN, FRAUDS BY, 114–115
BOATS,
  flying, 253
  owners of, 449
  personal services, 449
  subjects of salvage, 168–173
BOMBS, 597
BOMBAY, 661, 670
BOTTOMRY, 1250, 1482
BREACH OF CONTRACT, 1027–1029, 1031–1033, 1066, 1446
BREACH OF STATUTORY DUTY, 1054
BREAD AND BUTTER SERVICES, 46
BREAKSEA, 577
BRITISH WATERS,
  Crown ships, 656, 658
  definition, 294–296
  life salvage, 294–296
BRUSSELS IMMUNITY CONVENTION, 1171
BRUSSELS CONVENTION 1968, 1224n
BRUSSELS SALVAGE CONVENTION 1910. *See* SALVAGE CONVENTION 1910
BULLION, 1498
BUNKERS, 126, 180–181, 797n, 826–834
BUOYS, 157, 174, 193, 204, 343

CABLE CUTTING, 113
CANCELLATION,
  remuneration, 956
  salvage agreements, 861, 956

CANON LAW, 15, 89
CAPTURE, 579–584, 650
CARE AND SKILL. *See* SKILL AND CARE
CARGO, 6. *See also* CARGO-OWNERS
  Admiralty jurisdiction, 126
  animals, 192
  arrest, 1418
  bailment, 487–488
  common law salvage, 133
  damages, 487
  dangerous goods, 439
  deck, 191
  deductions, 1486
  freight, 190, 219, 221
  goods, 193
  humanitarian, 329, 1178–1181
  in personam actions, 1489
  interests in salved property, 487–491
  liens, 133, 1494
  life salvage, 192
  limitation of liability, 1193
  maritime liens, 1252n
  material circumstances, 1428–1430
  reward, 490
  salved,
    interests in, 487–491
    value, 1332–1333, 1360–1375, 1378–1379, 1382–1384, 1500, 1503
  seaworthiness, 490
  security, 1489
  shipowners, 487–491
  sister ships, 508, 509
  slaves, 192
  subject salvage, 190–193, 329
  time limits, 1208
  tug and tow, 193
  wrongdoing, profiting by, 489
CARGO-OWNERS,
  arbitration, 1270
  authority, 824–832
  claims of, 462
  exclusions, 787
  freight, 1356
  inequity of terms, 948
  interests in salved property, 1509
  masters, 831–832
  non-acceptance of salved property, 1075–1077, 1085
  salvage services causing liability to, 1446
  salved values, 1321, 1381–1382, 1384
  SCOPIC clause, 962
  security, 1262
  shipowners, 1493–1494
  special compensation, 439
  voluntariness, 544, 637
CARRIERS, 1075–1078
CARTHAGENA, 958
CASTOR, 1048
CASUALTIES,
  danger, 1411
  limitation of liability, 1193
  oil pollution, 70

881

Index

CASUALTIES—*cont*.
 Shipowners' Casualty Representative, 969, 978
CENTRAL GOVERNMENT, 1051
CHAINS, LOSS OF, 341
CHANNEL, 688, 908
CHANCERY COURT, 96
 Admiralty Court, influences of, 6, 22–25
 appeals, 98
 Chancery Division, change into, 96, 101
 common law, 89
 equity, 22–25, 89
CHANGE OF CIRCUMSTANCES, 789
CHARGES,
 public authorities, 688
 set-off, 1518
 ships, salved, 496–497
 supply of services, contracts for, 1018–1019
 tug and tow, 620
CHARITIES, 551
CHARTERPARTIES. *See also* DEMISE CHARTERPARTIES, TIME CHARTERPARTIES, VOYAGE CHARTERPARTIES
 Admiralty jurisdiction, 126
 claims of charterers, 458–484
 freight,
  demise, 219, 224
  remuneration, 219–224
  sub, 225
  time, 219–222, 224, 228, 232
  voyage, 219, 223, 224, 227, 231
 hire, 126, 229
 interests in salved property, 1509
 personal services, 458–484
 remuneration, 126, 219–224
 salved value, 1340–1342, 1344–1351
 seamen, 493
 special compensation, 439
 sub, 225
 time, 126, 219–222, 224, 228, 232
CHARTS, 106n
CHICAGO CONVENTION, 254
CHIEF OFFICER, 573
CHINA SEA, 1326
CHRISTIAN DUTY, 927
CHRONOMETERS, 184
CIF VALUE, 229
CIGARS, 803
CINQUE PORTS, 115, 315
CIRCUITY OF ACTION, 488
CIVIL DROITS OF ADMIRALTY, 107–108, 117, 315–316
CIVIL LAW, 15, 89, 95, 97, 104
CIVIL PROCEEDINGS. *See* PROCEEDINGS
CIVIL SALVAGE, 20
CIVILIANS, 95
CLAIMS. *See also* IN PERSONAM ACTIONS, IN REM ACTIONS, RESTRICTIONS ON CLAIMS
 cargoes, 462
 charterparties, 458–484
 Crown ships,

CLAIMS—*cont*.
 demise charterparties, 464–467, 481–484
 general conditions for, 441–442
 harbour authorities, 886
 lifeboats, 700–703
 limitation of liability, 1191–1200
 multiple, 1122–1124
 overlapping factors, 1387–1388
 personal services, 458–484
 related claims, 1388
 reward, 1220, 1223
 settlement, 820–821, 941, 1222
 shipowners, 458–484
 time, 461–462
 time limits, 1210–1218
 types of, 1387–1388
 voluntariness, 563–715
CLOTHES. *See* PERSONAL EFFECTS
COAL, 1500
COASTAL WATERS, 402
COASTGUARD,
 apportionment, 1530
 official duties, 684, 686
 personal services, 448
 public authorities, 549
 public policy, 686
 remuneration, 684
 salvage services, 684
 statutory duties, 684
 voluntariness, 683–689
 wreck, 683, 684, 687, 688n
CODIFICATION, 82
COCKET, 106n
COLLISIONS,
 abandonment, 577
 danger, 347
 criminal offences, 540
 duty to assist, 540–543
 masters, 543
 misconduct, 1103
 voluntariness, 540–543
COMMANDING OFFICERS, 450
COMMERCE, 1122, 1175–1176
COMMERCIAL COURT, 100
COMMISSION, 628
COMMISSIONERS OF ADMIRALTY, 117
COMMON LAW. *See also* COMMON LAW SALVAGE
 Admiralty Court,
  influences of, 6
  relationship with, 90–93, 95, 97
 Admiralty jurisdiction, 109
 appeals, 98, 115
 attorneys, 95
 Chancery Court, 89
 compulsion, 942–943
 courts, 89
 definition, 15
 engaged services, 742, 757
 English law, 89
 equity, 15, 89
 export of, 89

Index

COMMON LAW—cont.
general average, 6
governing law, 72
implied terms, 994, 1024–1026
inequity of terms, 942–943
interest, 1467
Lloyd's Open Form, 79
mistake, 913, 916–917
non-disclosure, 895
passage money, 235
possession, 1228
prohibition, writs of, 92
reduction in liability, 1141–1142
Roman civil law, 89
sister ships, 507
solicitors, 95
sources of English law, 89
sources of modern salvage law, 6, 15
stricto sensu, 15, 89
success, 719
supply of services, contracts for, 1024–1026
vitiating factors, 878–879, 889
wrecks, 108
COMMON LAW SALVAGE,
Admiralty Court, 131, 149
recognition of, 146
Admiralty jurisdiction, 147
Admiralty law, 144–145
agents, 138, 144
aircraft, 248, 251
benefit, 130, 134
cargo, 133
contracts, 144–145
recovery in absence of, 134, 136
danger, 140
defence, 130–132
detention, 129
detinue, 130
emergencies, 142
English law, 89
flotsam, 139
general average, 145
history, 129–149
in personam actions, 131
in rem actions, 142
indebitatus assumpsit, 135
justices of the peace, 129
liens, 132
maritime, 142
possessory, 130, 132, 139
life salvage, 261–272
Lloyd's Open Form, 143–144
maritime liens, 142
possessory liens, 130, 132, 139
property, 132
quantum meruit, 136, 142
rafts, 139
ransom, 131
ratification, 144
remedies, 134, 139
remuneration, 137–138, 142

COMMON LAW SALVAGE—cont.
restitution, 130
rewards, 130, 141, 145
right to, 129–149
sale, 129
salvage services, 144
seamen, 142, 144, 147–148
sources of modern salvage law, 6, 15
subjects of, 153, 155
sue, right to, 131, 141
trover, 130
COMMON OWNERSHIP, 150
COMMON PLEAS, 96
COMMUNICATIONS, 1
COMPENSATION. *See also* DAMAGES, SPECIAL COMPENSATION
accepted services, 756–772, 1082
assessment, 763–766
damages, referred to as, 2n
equitable, 454
expenses, 1439, 1441, 1443
losses, 1443
earnings, of, 1439
opportunity, of, 1039
profits, of, 1439
misconduct, 1095
personal services, 454
property, duty not to remove, 1254
redelivery, 1082
time limits, 1214, 1217
COMPOUND INTEREST, 1137, 1467, 1476
COMPULSION,
Admiralty jurisdiction, 925–941
common law, 942–943
enforcement, 929–930, 936
illegitimate pressure, 942–943
inducement, 942
manifest disadvantage, 942–943
Salvage Convention 1989, 944
undue influence, 942
vitiating factors, 923–953
CONDITIONS, 1001, 1005, 1027–1028, 1031
CONFLICT OF LAWS. *See also* GOVERNING LAW
uniformity, 73
unjust enrichment, 74
CONSENT,
arbitration, 1284
danger, 54
orders, 1284
reward, 51
CONSIDERATION,
price, 999
sale of goods, contracts for, 999
supply of services, contracts for, 1007, 1016–1018
CONSULAR OFFICER, 696
CONSUMERS,
dealing as, 1002, 1148, 1150, 1156, 1158
sale of goods, 1002
supply of goods, 1009

Index

CONTAINERS, 126
CONTRACTORS, 13
  best endeavours, 987, 1034
  co-operation, 1054
  Lloyd's Open Form, 847
  SCOPIC, 847
  security, 990, 1255
  terms of salvage agreement, 847
CONTRACTS. *See also* CONTRACTORS, IMPLIED TERMS, LLOYD'S OPEN FORM, SALVAGE AGREEMENTS, STANDARD FORMS OF CONTRACT, SUB-CONTRACTORS, UNFAIR CONTRACT TERMS
  Admiralty Court, 97
  annulment, 890
  application to salvage, 996
  apportionment, 1519, 1536–1538
    customary, 1537
    setting aside, 1540
  avoidance, 889
  breach of, 1027–1029, 1066, 1446
    salvage, effect on, 1031–1033
  charterparties,
    demise, 481–484
    voyage, 480–481
  common law salvage, 134, 136, 144–145
  conditions, 1001, 1005, 1027–1028, 1031
  construction, 995, 1028
  Crown ships, 653
  currency, 1461–1463
  definition of salvage, 997–998
  demise charterparties, 481–484
  deviation, 1446
  employees, 644
  engaged services, 752, 755, 763–764, 767–778
    work and labour, 768
  frustration, 610, 614, 959, 1067, 1344, 1372, 1378, 1381
  governing law, 72
  hire, 480
  hostilities, 131n
  implied, 108n
  innominate terms, 1027–1029, 1031
  interest, 1466, 1467
  liability, 993–1033
    origins of, 994
    restrictions on, 995
  masters, 653, 728
  material circumstances, 1433
  misconduct, 1092–1094, 1098
  negligence, 1112–1114, 1119–1120
  parties, duties of, 993–1033
  passengers, 632
  performance, failure of, 1027–1033
  personal effects, 327
  privity of, 811, 1098
  proceedings, 1224
  quasi-contracts, 35
  remuneration, 728
  repudiation, 1066
  rescission, 905–906, 923

CONTRACTS—*cont.*
  reward, 35
    transfer by, 479–481
  sale of goods, 999–1002, 1030
  Salvage Convention 1989, 80
  salvage services, 997
  salved value, 1348
  salvors, 31, 447, 479–485
  seamen, 567–568, 574, 576, 579–584, 586
  service, of, 567–568, 574, 576, 579–584, 586
  services, for, 997, 1007–1026
  setting aside, 882, 903, 931–933, 937–938, 940, 1540
  sovereign immunity, 1174
  special, 728
  statutory provisions, 998
  subject of salvage, 159, 178, 313
  success, 728
  supply of goods, for, 998, 1003–1006
  supply of services, for, 1007–1026
  termination of, 1433
  time, 1030
  tug and tow, 601, 603, 605, 619–620
    abandonment, 613
    effects on, 608–611
    supervening events, 608–611
  void, 887, 891
  voidable, 887, 911
  voluntariness, 532, 565–637
  voyage charterparties, 480–481
  warranties, 1001, 1005, 1027–1028
  work and labour, 108n, 532, 768, 997
CONTRIBUTION. *See* PAYMENT, LIABILITY FOR
CONVENTIONS. *See* PARTICULAR CONVENTIONS (eg SALVAGE CONVENTION 1989), TREATIES AND CONVENTIONS
CONVICTS, 188
CONVOY, 56, 359
CO-OPERATION,
  agents, 1059
  assistance, 1069
  breach of statutory duty, 1054
  central government, 1051
  contracting states, duty of, 1048–1055
    content of, 1050
    enforcement of, 1053
  contractors, 1060
  damages, 1054
  decision-making, 1053
  environment, 989, 1037, 1049
  equipment, 1060
  harbours, entry to, 1047
  information, 1061
  'leper ships', 1045
  Lloyd's Open Form, 1056–1057, 1059–1060, 1062
  LOF 2000, 1058–1059, 1061
  LSSAC 2000, 1058–1059
  masters, 1059
  negligence, 1054
  obstruction, liability for, 1045

Index

CO-OPERATION—*cont.*
parties, duties of, 988, 1044–1062
performance, time for, 1052
ports, entry to, 1047
property owners, duties of, 1058–1059
public authorities, 1049–1051
public/private law, 1053–1054
redelivery, acceptance of, 1045
relevant authority, 1051
remuneration, 1054
Salvage Convention 1989, 67, 988, 1048–1056, 1059–1062
salvage operations, objects of, 1055
salvees, 1046, 1055–1056, 1060–1062
salvors, 1044–1062
Secretary of State, 1051
security, 1045
shipowners, 1057
states, 67
  duties of contracting parties, 1048–1055
  statute, duties conferred by, 1049
third parties, 1046
CORONER'S COURT, 105n, 108
CORPSE, 108, 207
CORRECTION CLAUSES, 1465
COSTS,
arbitration, 1291, 1295, 1296–1298, 1311–1312
deprivation of, 1134–1135
misconduct, 1134–11–35
salved value, 1354, 1374
COUNCIL OF LLOYD'S, 1260, 1277–1278, 1280–1281, 1299–1300, 1310
COUNTERCLAIMS, 1107, 1109, 1196
COUNTY, BODY OF A, 103, 115, 117–118, 201
COUNTY COURTS, 121
COURT OF APPEAL, 96
COXSWAIN, 700
CRASSUS PISCIS, 314n
CRANES, 161
CREW. *See* SEAMEN
CRIMINAL OFFENCES,
Admiralty jurisdiction, 104
collisions, 540
distress, 539
fraud, 894
voluntariness, 534, 539–540
CROWN. *See also* CROWN SHIPS, ROYAL FISH
beneficial interests, 1169
delegation, 89
demise charterparties, 465–466, 1169
description, 1166
Government, 1166, 1169
high seas, 107
liability, 1167, 1170
limitation of liability, 1168
Lord High Admiral, 90
payments, liability for, 1483
prize, 1167
proceedings, 1170, 1483, 1529
property, 1169

CROWN—*cont.*
public authorities, 549
reward, 2
Royal Air Force, 677
Salvage convention 1989, 1170
salvors, 1167
ships, 1169
sovereign immunity, 1166–1170
time limits, 1168
tortious liability, 1167
wrecks, 105, 107–108, 1167
CROWN PROCEEDINGS, 1170, 1483, 1529
CROWN SHIPS,
Admiralty's consent to claim, 652–653, 668, 674–675
apportionment, 1529
assessment of reward, 654–655
authority, 839
beneficiaries of the duty, 656–657
British ships, to, 656, 658
claims by Crown itself, 659–676
contracts with master, 653
danger, 651
definition, 670
demise charterparties, 670–671
expenses, 661
extent of duty, 648–650
extraordinary exertions, 651
foreign ships, 656–657, 670
hostile capture, 650
officers, 645–676, 1529
  other Crown ships, of, 667–676
performance, degree of, 651
piracy, 650
place of performance of duty, 658
public policy, 646, 663
remuneration, 651, 654, 656
requisition, 670–671
reward, 645, 647, 652, 655, 666
Royal Navy, 645, 648, 651, 654, 656, 659, 665, 667, 674, 676
salvage services, 646, 648–650, 652, 659, 663–664
seamen, 645–676, 1529
  other Crown ships, of, 667–676
sovereign immunity, 1164
voluntariness, 645–676
CRUISERS, 781
CULTURAL PROPERTY, 214, 389
CURRENCY, 1461–1465
arbitration awards, 1461–1463
cause of action, accrual, 1464
contracts, 1463
correction, 1461–1465
dollars, 1463
English law, 1462, 1464
exchange rates, 1461–1462, 1465
fluctuations, 25
foreign, 1462
inflation, 1461, 1464–1465
Lloyd's open form, 1461, 1463, 1465
LOF 2000, 1463

Index

CURRENCY—cont.
  movements, 1461
  remuneration, 1463, 1464
  restitution, 1462
  reward, 25, 1464
  special compensation, 1463
  sterling, 1461
  termination, 1462
  unjust enrichment, 1462
CUSTOM,
  Admiralty Court, 527
  apportionment, 1537
  pre-existing, 525–531
  voluntariness, 525–531
CUSTOMS, 111, 695

DAMAGE,
  danger, 334–335
  economic loss, 400
  engaged services, 777
  environment, 398–405
    cause of, 403–404
    minimising, 407, 1456
    preventing, 407, 1456
    relevant, 399–401
    responsibility, 405
    substantial, 400–401
  expenses, 1439–1440
  loss of amenity, 400
  material circumstances, 1427–1428
  misconduct, 1136
  physical, 400
  possession, 1245
  salved value, 1373
  special compensation,
    prevention or minimising of, 416, 418, 424, 427
    threats of, 413, 431–432
  success, 732
  vessels, 1444
DAMAGES,
  assistance, 1041
  breach of contract, 1027, 1031–1033
  cargo, 487
  common law, 1120–1123
  compensation referred to as, 2n
  deceit, 891–892
  engaged services, 763–764, 776–778
  fraud, 891–892
  life salvage, 281
  material circumstances, 1411–1417, 1424, 1428
  measure of, 1118–1122
  misconduct, 1088, 1093, 1099–1101
  misrepresentation, 905
  negligence, 1104, 1111, 1117
    common law, 1120–1123
    measure of, 1118–1122
    set-off, 1124
  non-acceptance of salved property, 1077
  performance, 1027, 1031–1033
  possession, 1230

DAMAGES—cont.
  salvage services and liability to, 1446
  salved value, 1343
  set-off, 1031, 1124
  special compensation, 439
  taxation, 1477
  time limits, 1033, 1205, 1214–1215
  tug and tow, 605
DANGER,
  abandonment, 571–572, 578
  aircraft, 361
  apportionment, 1533
  apprehension of, 333
  assessment of rewards, 377
  assistance, 988, 1411
  casualties, 1411
  common law salvage, 130
  collision, 347
  consent, 54
  Crown ships, 651
  cultural property, 389
  damage, of, 334
    vessels already suffering, 335
  degree of, 334
  duration, 377–389
    importance of, 377–381
  environment, 346, 351–352, 1417
  evidence of, 341–343
  exclusions, 788
  foundation of salvage, 332–333
  immoblisation, 1411
  incompleted services leaving vessel in greater, 736–741
  knowledge of, 339
  liability, risk of legal, 1415
  life salvage, 1412–1414
  lightening, 356
  location, categories of, 362–376
  maritime property, 1411
  masters, 387
  misconduct, 1095–1103
  navigation, 1416
  necessity for existence of, 1
  negligence, 987
  non-physical, 345–353
  officiousness, 62
  passengers, 634–635
  passive salvage, 360–361
  physical loss, 1411
  pilots, 343, 590–591, 597
  proceedings, 1224
  proof of, 340
  property, 1414
    no value, of, 352–359
  public authorities, 554
  quantum meruit, 377
  reward, 360
  reasonable apprehension of, 333
  safety of human lives, 1412–1414
  Salvage Convention 1989, 62, 351–352, 381, 1411, 1415–1416

886

Index

DANGER—*cont.*
  salvage services, 311
    classification of, 354–359
    termination of, 378–381, 390
  salvors, to, 338
  SCOPIC, 381
  seamen, 571
  signals, 344
  special compensation, 352
  stages, salvage in, 382–389, 391
  subjects of salvage, 330–390, 1411n
  success, 733, 735
    incomplete services leaving vessel in greater, 736–741
  third parties, 347–350, 357, 1415
  tug and tow, 335, 601, 613, 618, 623–624
    normal services and, 603
    supervening, 605–607
    tugs, in, 605–607, 618
  type of, 337
  undue influence, 947
  vessels,
    conditions of, 336
    damage, already suffering, 335
  voluntariness, 517
    persons in, duty to, 535–536
  war risks, 337
  wreck, 389
DANGEROUS GOODS, 439
DANGEROUS VESSELS, 1047
DARKNESS, 615n
DEATH, 1155, 1426, 1413, 1535
DECEIT, 891–892
DECK CARGO, 191
DECLARATIONS, 1250
DEDUCTIONS,
  cargo, 1486
  freight, 1365–1366, 1486
  salved value, 1352–1354, 1372–1375, 1379
DEFINITION OF SALVAGE, 16–18, 997–998
DELAY,
  apportionment, 1522
  damages, 1030
  performance, 1030
DELEGATION,
  authority, 823
  Crown, 89
  Secretary of State, 70n
DELIVERY. *See also* REDELIVERY
  acceptance, 1035
  best endeavours, 1035
  freight, 1360
  non-acceptance of salved property, 1075
DEMISE CHARTERPARTIES,
  apportionment, 478
  claims of, 464–477, 481–484
  contracts, 481–484
  Crown, 465–466, 1169
    ships, 670–671
  freight, 219, 224
  hire, 476

DEMISE CHARTERPARTIES—*cont.*
  indemnities, 476
  interests in salved property, 485
  masters, 468–469
  requisitioned vessels, 477
  reward, 469, 476, 478
  seamen, 468–469
  shipowners, transfer of rights from, 464–477
  ships,
    salved, 499–500, 503
    sister, 507
DEODANDS, 108
DEPREDATIONS, 113
DERELICT,
  abandonment, 108–212
  Admiralty jurisdiction, 208
  definition, 208
  material circumstances, 1432
  possession, 1230, 1234–1245
  property not, 1234–1245
  salved value, 1378–1384
  subjects of salvage, 208–215
  temporary, 208
  wrecks, 108, 109, 111
DESCRIPTION, 1001, 1002
DETENTION OF PROPERTY,
  common law salvage, 129
  security, 1265
DETINUE, 130
DEVIATION,
  contracts, 1446
  losses, 1446
  marine insurance, 1446
  material circumstances, 1432
  property salvage, encouragement of, 1446
  salvage services, 1446
  time charterparties, 461
DEVONPORT, 672
DIMINUTION IN VALUE, 1133–1136, 1331
DINGHIES, 176–177
DIPLOMATIC IMMUNITY, 1171
DIRECTIONS,
  arbitration, 1286
  oil pollution, 70
  Secretary of State, 70
DISBURSEMENTS, 817
DISCHARGE OF SALVAGE AGREEMENTS,
  accord and satisfaction, 956
  agreement, by, 956
  cancellation, 956
  consent, by, 956
  grounds for, 955
  remuneration, 956
  salvage agreements, 950–959
  supervening circumstances, 950, 957–959
  variation, 956
DISCLOSURE. *See* NON-DISCLOSURE
DISCOUNTS, 977
DISTRESS,
  criminal offences, 539
  engaged services, 747, 777

887

DISTRESS—*cont.*
  information on, duty to respond to, 537–539
  pilots, 593, 596
  price, reasonable, 1000
  quantum meruit, 734
  sale of goods, contracts for, 999
  tug and tow, 616
  voluntariness, 534, 537–539
  wrecks, 694
DIVERS, 532, 1104
DIVISION OF PAYMENT, 1515–1518
DOCKS, 672, 692
DOCTOR'S COMMONS, 90, 95
DOCTORS OF CIVIL LAW, 95
DOLLARS, 1463
DOLPHINS, 314
DREDGERS, 174
DRILLING UNITS, 318–320
DROITS, 107–108, 117, 315
'DUCK, LAME', 593
DURATION OF SALVAGE SERVICES, 1436–1438
DURESS, 887

EARNINGS, LOSS OF, 1439, 1447
EAST INDIA COMPANY, 459
EC LAW,
  Admiralty jurisdiction, 124
  Brussels Convention 1968, 1224n
  Civil Jurisdiction and Judgments Act 1982, 124
  unfair contract terms, 1162
ECCLESIASTICAL COURTS, 95
ECONOMIC LOSS, 401
ELEMENTS OF THE LAW OF SALVAGE, 2
EMBARGOES, 580, 584
EMERGENCIES,
  authority, 804–808
  common law salvage, 141
EMPLOYEES,
  contracts, 644
  reward, 644
  salvage services, 644
  seamen, 587
  statutory authorities, 690–693
  voluntariness, 562, 644, 690–693
ENDANGERING SHIPS, 113
ENEMIES, 210
ENGAGED SERVICES,
  acceptance, 758
  Admiralty jurisdiction, 755
  assessment of rewards, 752, 757
  best endeavours, 772
  common law, 742, 757
  compensation for supersession of, 756–772
    assessment, 763–766
  continuing obligations, 768
  contracts, 752, 755, 763–764, 767–778
    work and labour, 768
  damage, mitigation of, 777
  damages, 763–764, 776–778
  distress, 747, 777

ENGAGED SERVICES—*cont.*
  environment, 754
  expenses, 777
  Lloyd's Open Form, 756, 767–778
  masters, 761, 773–774
  no cure no pay, 771
  property, 743, 755, 760
  quantum meruit, 752, 754
  remedies, 772
  remuneration, 743, 746–758, 762–764
  repudiation, 776–777
  requests, 742–743, 747–748
  restitution, 753
  reward, 751, 756–757
    assessment of, 752, 757
  salvage agreements, 780
  Salvage Convention 1989, 754
  salvage operations, 754
  skill and care, 778
  special compensation, 754
  success, 724, 742–778
  tug and tow, 748–749, 778
  useful result, 754
ENGINEERS, 1526
ENGLISH LAW,
  Admiralty law, 15
  application of, 6
  apportionment, 1520, 1524–1540
  arbitration, 75
  canon law, 15, 189
  currency, 1462, 1464
  governing law, 75
  history of, 89
  interpretation, 83–84
  jurisdictions, law in other, 4
  laws of Oleron, 3
  life salvage, 260–299, 307h, 310
  limitation of liability, 1194
  Lloyd's Open Form, 75
  locality, 368
  maritime liens, 1247
  precedent, 83
  restitution, 33–35
  Roman law, 89
  Salvage Convention 1910, 11, 66, 85, 127
  salved value, 1496
  security, 1226
  sources of, 89
  sovereign immunity, 1165
  subjects of salvage, 161
  wrecks, 215
ENVIRONMENT, 440
  arbitration, 1300
  assessment of reward, 396–397, 410
  best endeavours, 1037
  class, size of, 400
  coastal waters, 402
  co-operation, 989, 1037, 1049
  damage to the environment, 398–405
    cause of, 403–404
    minimising, 407, 1456
    preventing, 407, 1456

Index

ENVIRONMENT—*cont.*
  damage to the environment—*cont.*
    relevant, 399–401
    responsibility, 405
    substantial, 400–401
  danger, 346, 351–352, 1417
  economic loss, 401
  engaged services, 754
  environmental services, encouraging, 406–408, 411
  estoppel, 873
  expenses, 394n
  indemnities, 1038
  inland waters, 402
  liability, risk of, 393
  life salvage, 408
  Lloyd's Open Form, 128, 394–396, 410, 1038
  location, 402
  loss of amenity, 400
  major incidents, 403
  misconduct, 1089
  Montreal CMI Draft Convention 1981, 394
  Montreal Compromise, 394
  no cure no pay, 393
  parties, duties of, 989, 1037–1038
  policy behind article 14, 409–410
  public policy, 1456
  remuneration, 396, 409
  rewards, 407–408, 410, 1038
    assessment of, 396–397, 410
  Salvage Convention 1989, 12, 312, 395–440, 989, 1037–1038, 1417, 1456
  salvors, 443
  SCOPIC, 396, 967, 976
  special compensation, 18, 312, 352, 395, 397, 404, 410, 412–440, 1038
  subjects of salvage, 159, 162, 312
  success, 723
  supply of services, contracts for, 1013
  victims, size of, 400
EQUIPMENT,
  co-operation, 1060
  definition, 1408, 1410
  material circumstances, 1432 1408, 1410, 1427
  navigational, 186–187
  professional salvors, 42, 45
  public policy, 1454–1455
  readiness, in state of, 1455
  salvors, 1424, 1455
  subjects of salvage, 179, 186–187
  wireless, 186–187
EQUITY, 21–25
  Admiralty Court, 21–25
  appeals, 98
  Chancery Court, 22–25, 89
  common law, 15, 89
  compensation, 454
  forfeiture, 21
  High Court, in, 97

EQUITY—*cont.*
  illegitimate pressure, 23
  interest, 1467
  jurisdiction, 28
  moral support, as, 21
  prize salvage, 21
  rewards, assessment of, 25
  sources of modern salvage law, 3
ESSEX, 1133
ESTOPPEL,
  best endeavours, 871–872, 874, 1035
  construction, 880
  environment, 873
  Lloyd's Open Form, 869, 873–875
  LOF 2000, 866–875
  payment, liability for, 1492
  remedies, effect of other, 870
  salvage agreements, 866–875
  salvage services, 866–867, 872–874
    prior, 870, 872
  shipowners, 1492
  special compensation, 883
ESTUARIES, 109
EUROPEAN UNION. *See* EC LAW
EXCHANGE RATES, 1347, 1461–1462, 1465
EXCHEQUER, 96, 98
EXCLUSIONS. *See also* REDUCTION OF LIABILITY
  agreements excluding salvage, 784–789
  authority, 787, 798
  cargo-owners, 787
  change in circumstances, 791
  construction, 790
  contractual provisions, 327–328
  danger, 788
  drilling units, 318–320
  exemption clauses, 1141, 1150, 1158
  humanitarian cargoes, 329
  luggage, 321–328
  no cure no pay, 787, 789
  personal effects, 321–328
  platforms, 318–320
  public policy, 785
  reduction in liability, 1141
  reward, 784, 786
  salvage agreements, 784–789
  SCOPIC clause, 964, 973
  seamen, 787
  special services, 788
  static structures, 318–320
  subjects of salvage, 150, 162, 317–329
  supply of goods, contracts for, 1006
  work and labour, 786
EXECUTION, 1223
EXEMPTION CLAUSES, 1141, 1150, 1158
EXPENSES,
  agents, 631
  apportionment, 1442
  arbitration, 1293, 1296–1298, 1449
  compensation, 1439, 1441, 1443
  Crown ships, 661
  damage, 1438–1439, 1442

889

Index

EXPENSES—cont.
  definition, 427, 429
  definition of salvage, 16
  engaged services, 777
  environmental services, 394n
  fair rate, 426–430
  freight, 1364, 1366
  indemnities, 631
  lifeboats, 704–705
  loss of earnings, 1439
  loss of profits, 1439, 1442
  marine insurance, 510
  material circumstances, 1439–1452
  misconduct, 1095
  non-acceptance of salved property, 1076, 1081, 1085
  out-of-pocket, 414, 426–427, 429–430
  owners, 631
  possession, 1243
  professional salvors, 45
  sale, 1381
  salvage agreements, 781
  salved value, 1327, 1371, 1373, 1375
  security, 1263
  special compensation, 414, 417–418, 423–432
  storage, 1074, 1076
  sue and labour, 510
  termination, 1445
  tug and tow, 610
  wrecks, 694
EXPORTERS, 106n
EXPLOSIONS, 856
EXTORTION, 603

FAILURE OF PERFORMANCE, 1027–1033
FAMILY DIVISION, 101
FEES,
  arbitration, 1296–1298
  survey, 1374
FINANCIAL INTERESTS, 1376–1377
FINLAND, 1331
FIRE, 358, 386, 1331
FIRE-BRIGADE, 525
FISH. See ROYAL FISH
FISHERMEN, 1010
FISHING VESSELS, 207, 1106
FIXED OBJECTS, 160
FIXED SUMS, 1492
FLAG, 823
FLEET AIR ARM, 680
FLOTSAM, JETSAM AND LAGAN,
  Admiralty jurisdiction, 204–207
  definition, 204
  subjects of salvage, 204–207
  wrecks, 108, 109, 111, 139, 204–207

FLYING BOATS, 253
FOG, 348
FOOD, 184, 188
FOREIGN CURRENCY, 1462
FOREIGN LAW, 72
FOREIGN SHIPS,
  Crown ships, 656–657, 670
  interests in salved property, 1509
  life salvage, 277
FOREIGNERS, 339, 627, 656–657, 920
FORFEITURE,
  equity, 22
  misconduct, 1126–1128, 1133, 1135
FORGERY, 860
FOYBOATMEN, 625
FRANCE, 582, 657
FRANCHISE COURT, 108
FRAUD,
  apportionment, 893
  awards, limiting, 893
  boatmen, by, 115
  criminal offences, 894
  damages, 891–892
  inducement, 891
  masters, 893
  misconduct, 893, 1101–1102
  misrepresentation, 905, 908, 911
  remuneration, 892
  vitiating factors, 891–894
  void contracts, 891
FREEBOOTERS, 522
FREEZING INJUNCTIONS, 1226
FREIGHT,
  abandonment, 1381–1384
  advance, 218, 227, 228–229
  authority, 824–832
  bills of lading, 226, 228
  cargo, 190
    amount of, 219, 221
    carried on, 1361–1367
    not carried on, 1360
    owners, 1356
  charterparties,
    demise, 219, 224
    remuneration, 219–224
    sub, 225
    time, 219–222, 224, 228, 232
    voyage, 219, 223, 224, 227, 231
  collect, 227
  damages, 1360
  deductions, 1365–1366, 1486
  definition, 218, 231
  delivery, 1360
  expenses, 1364, 1366
  hire, 219, 222, 230
  in personam actions, 233
  in rem actions, 233
  Lloyd's Open Form, 232
  lump sum, 218
  maritime property, 166
  masters, 232
  material circumstances, 1429

890

Index

FREIGHT—cont.
  non-acceptance of salved property, 1077
  passage money, 240–241
  port of destination, reaching, 1357–1359
  port of refuge, 1361, 1363
  pro rata, 219
  professional salvors, 232
  property,
    non-acceptance of salved, 1077
    preservation of, 725
  remedies, 1485–1487
  risk, at, 229–230, 232
  salvage services, 1358–1361, 1366
  salved value, 1356–1367, 1370, 1375, 1379–1384, 1500
  set-off, 1517–1518
  ship, at risk of, 1357
  shipowners, 1356, 1487
  subjects of salvage, 216–233, 242
  tangible property, 216
  termination, 1357–1359, 1363
FRIGATES, 582
FRUSTRATION,
  non-acceptance of salved property, 1079
  supervening circumstances, 959
  termination, 1067
  tug and tow, 610, 614
FUEL, 704
FULLER'S EARTH, 908
FURNITURE, 663

GALWAY BAY, 1244
GAS FLOATS, 155–158
GENERAL AVERAGE
  authority, 825
  common law, 6
    salvage, 133, 145
  contributions, 1198
  limitation of liability, 1198
  maritime adventure, involvement in, 160
  personal effects, 321–325
  SCOPIC clause, 966, 979
  security, 1261
  special compensation, 439–440, 1494
  York-Antwerp Rules, 440
GERMANY, 580, 649, 670
GIBRALTAR, 737, 958
GLASGOW, 601
GLIDERS, 248
GOD, ACTS OF, 733
GOLD, 1498
GOODS,
  cargo, 193
  dangerous, 439
  land, cast up on, 107
  robbery, 106n,
  sale of, contracts for, 999–1002, 1030
  subjects of salvage, 190–194
  supply of, contracts for, 1003–1006
  trespass to, 1231
  wreck, 106n, 109

GOVERNING LAW, 72–80
  applicable law, 72, 74
  apportionment, 76, 1523
  arbitration, 73, 75
  common law, 72
  contracts, 72, 78–80
  English law, 75
  foreign law, 72
  jurisdiction, contesting, 74
  Lloyd's Open Form, 75, 77
  London arbitration, 73
  public authorities, 76, 547
  Salvage Convention 1910, 73
  Salvage Convention 1989, 72–73, 76–77
  sovereign immunity, 1171
  statutory provisions, 72
GOVERNMENT, 1051, 1166, 1169
GRAMPUS, 314
GRASPES, 314
GRATUITOUS SERVICES,
  bailment, 1021, 1079
  intention, 49
  life salvage, 49
  lifeboats, 49
  public authorities, 688
  public policy, 49
  rescuers, 49
  voluntariness, 511
GREECE, 1512
GREENLAND, 245n

HANSARD, 86
HARBOUR AUTHORITIES,
  claims by, 688
  co-operation, 1047
  dangerous vessels, 1047
  entry to, 1047
  public policy, 1454
HALIFAX, 942
HAWSERS, 601, 746, 748, 749, 958
HEALTH, RISKS to, 597
HER MAJESTY'S SHIPS. *See* CROWN SHIPS
HIGH COURT OF ADMIRALTY, 96
HIGH COURT OF JUSTICE, 96, 97, 111, 124, 1170, 1224
HIGH SEAS,
  Admiralty jurisdiction, 103, 115
  Crown, 107
  definition, 91n
  salvage services, 117–118
  wrecks, 107
HIGH-WATER MARK, 91, 114, 201–203
HIRE,
  charterparties, 229
    demise, 476
  contracts, 480, 1004, 1005, 1006
  freight, 219, 222, 230
  reward, 126
  subjects of salvage, 216–233
  supply of goods, contracts for, 1004, 1005, 1006
  time charterparties, 126

891

Index

HIRE-PURCHASE, 994, 1003
HISTORY, 89–149
   Admiralty Court, 90–102
   common law salvage, 129–149
   English law, 89
   Scotland, 1089n
   wreck, 105–109
HM SHIPS. *See* CROWN SHIP
HOLDING UP, 616
HONDURAS, 1362
HORSES, 1073
HOSTILE CAPTURE, 579–584, 650
HOSTILITIES, 131n, 359
HOUSE OF LORDS, 98, 1318
HOVERCRAFT,
   Admiralty jurisdiction, 126
   aircraft, 254
   definition, 257
   maritime liens, 259
   statute law, 257–259
   subjects of salvage, 152, 257–259
   wreck, 258
HULL, 749
HUMILIATION, RISK OF, 634
HUMANITARIAN CARGO, 329, 1178–1181
HUMANITARIAN CONSIDERATIONS, 27

ICE-FIELDS, 540
ICE-FLOES, 358
ILLEGALITY, 953
ILLEGITIMATE PRESSURE, 23, 889, 933, 942–943
ILLNESS, 904
IMMOBILISATION, 1411
IMMUNITY. *See* STATE IMMUNITY
IMPORTATION RESTRICTIONS, 1346
IMPOSSIBILITY, 1067
IMPLIED TERMS,
   breach of contract, 1029
   business efficacy, 994
   common law, 994, 1024–1026
   conditions, 1001
   Law Commission, 994
   liability, origins of, 994
   sale of goods, contracts for, 1001–1002
   statute imposing, 994
   supply of goods, contracts for, 1003, 1005
   supply of services, contracts for, 1008–1010, 1014, 1021, 1024–1026
   time of the essence, 1030
IN PERSONAM RIGHTS, 2, 1223
   admiralty jurisdiction, 104
   cargo, 1489
   common law salvage, 131
   Crown proceedings, 1170
   freight, 233
   interests in salved property, 1506–1508, 1512–1513
   jurisdiction, defendants outside the, 1484
   limitation of liability, 1187
   maritime liens, 1252
   payment, liability for, 1479

IN PERSONAM RIGHTS—*cont.*
   property, preservation of, 725
   Scotland, 1491
   sovereign immunity, 1175
IN REM RIGHTS, 2, 1223
   arrest, 1223
   common law salvage, 142
   Crown proceedings, 1170
   freight, 233
   interests in salved property, 1506–1508, 1512–1513
   jurisdiction, defendants outside the, 1484
   life salvage, 285
   limitation of liability, 1182, 1185
   maritime liens, 1247, 1252
   payment, liability for, 1479
   property, preservation of, 725
   sovereign immunity, 1165, 1175–1176
INCOMPLETE SERVICES,
   awards, entitlement to, 736–737
   danger, leaving vessel in greater, 736–741
   meritorious action, 739
   reward, 737
   tug and tow, 737–738
INDEBITATUS ASSUMPSIT, 135
INDEMNITIES,
   arbitration, 1311
   authority, 810
   demise charterparties, 476
   environment, 1038
   expenses, 63
   limitation of liability, 1194
   losses, 1443
   misrepresentation, 905
   proceedings, 1221
   SCOPIC clause, 968, 970, 978
   sister ships, 505, 507
   time limits, 1217–1218
   unfair contract terms, 1150
INDUCEMENT,
   compulsion, 942
   fraud, 891
   illegitimate pressure, 942
   Lloyd's Open Form, 952
   misrepresentation, 905
   mistake, 914–915
   vitiating factors, 952
INEQUALITY OF BARGAINING POWER,
   inequity of terms, 932
   non-disclosure, 900
INEQUITY OF TERMS,
   Admiralty jurisdiction, 925–941
   annulment, 951
   apportionment, 1539–1540
   cargo-owners, 948
   common law, 942–943
   compulsion, 940
   illegitimate pressure, 933
   inequality of bargaining power, 932
   modification, 951
   public policy, 933

Index

INEQUITY OF TERMS—cont.
  remuneration, 933
    exorbitant or inadequate, 937–939, 941, 951
    salved value, less than, 940
    Salvage Convention 1989, 948–952
    salved value, 940
    setting aside contracts, 931–933, 937–938, 940
    settlements, 941
    standard form contracts, 949
    undue influence, 948
    unfair contract terms, 943
    unfair operation of, 951
    vitiating factors, 925–953
INFLATION, 1461, 1464–1465
INJUNCTIONS, 1226, 1230, 1272
INLAND WATERS,
  definition, 371
  environment, 402
  locality, 364–365, 371, 373
    tidal waters, movement between, 375–376
  Salvage Convention 1989, 81
  subjects of salvage, 161
  tidal waters, movement between, 375–376
INNOMINATE TERMS., 1027–1029, 1031
INSPECTIONS, 1337
INSURANCE. *See* MARINE INSURANCE, MUTUAL INSURANCE
INTENTION,
  benefit, 48–49
  gratuitous services, 49
  mistake, 48
  reward, 48–49
  tug and tow, 48
  voluntariness, 48–49
INTEREST, 1466–1476
  Admiralty court, 1468, 1472–1473
  arbitration, 1469–1473, 1475–1476
  common law, 1467
  compound, 1137, 1467, 1471
  contract, 1466, 1467
  date from which awarded, 1473
  discretion, 1458, 1470, 1474
  equity, 1467
  foreign rate, 1472
  judgments, 1469, 1475–1476
  Lloyd's open form, 1470, 1474, 1475
  LOF 2000, 1471
  Lssac 2000, 1471, 1475
  misconduct, 1137
  purpose of, 1466
  remuneration, 1137
  Salvage convention 1989, 1466, 1468
  special compensation, 1137
  statute law, 1467
  termination, 1470, 1473
  time limits, 1212
  unjust enrichment, 1466, 1472
INTERESTS IN SALVED PROPERTY,
  Admiralty jurisdiction, 1506

INTERESTS IN SALVED PROPERTY—cont.
  benefit, not receiving, 1516–1518
  cargo, salved, 487–491
  cargo-owners, 1508
  charterparties, 1509
  demise, 485
  disentitlement to claim, 485–510
  foreign vessels, 1509
  in personam actions, 1506–1508, 1512–1513
  in rem actions, 1506–1508, 1512–1513
  insurers, 510
  maritime liens, 1507, 1509, 1512–1513
  ownership, 485–510
  payment, liability for, 1506–1513
  possession, 1512–1513
  requisition, 1512
  rescue, 1517
  Salvage Convention 1989, 486
  salved value, 1506–1513
  salvors, relationship with salved property of, 485–510
  seamen, 485, 492–495
  shipowners, 1506, 1508
  ships,
    salved, 485, 496–509
    sister, 486
  sovereign immunity, 1513
INTERIM AWARDS, 1291–1292
INTERMEDIARIES, 787–788, 800–809. *See also* AGENTS
INTERMEDIATE TERMS, 1027–1029, 1031
INTERNATIONAL CONVENTION ON SALVAGE. *See* SALVAGE CONVENTION 1989
INTERNATIONAL CONVENTIONS. *See* PARTICULAR CONVENTIONS (eg SALVAGE CONVENTION 1989), TREATIES AND CONVENTIONS
INTERNATIONAL LAW, 65, 81. *See* CONFLICTS OF LAW,
INTERPRETATION,
  codification, 82
  common law, 82
  domestic law,
    implementation in, 83
    previous, reference to, 84
  English law, 83–84
  Hansard, 86
  implementation, rewritten for domestic, 83
  judicial, 84
  Parliamentary materials, reference to, 86
  precedent, 83
  preparatory works, reference to, 86–88
  Salvage Convention 1910, 85
  Salvage Convention 1989, 82–88
  statutory, 82–84, 87
  travaux preparatoires, 88
  treaties and conventions, 83
  uniform, 83

Index

INVALIDITY, 863
IRELAND, 697, 698

JET SKIS, 176
JETSAM. *See* FLOTSAM, JETSAM AND LAGAN
JEWELS, 1499
JUDGES,
    Admiralty Court, of, 14, 94
    admiralty law, development of, 99
    interpretation, 84
    'Judge in Admiralty', 100
    life salvage, 266
    nautical assessors, 99
    Queen, deputy of, as, 90n
JUDGMENTS, INTEREST ON, 1469, 1475–1476
JUDICATURE ACTS, 96, 98
JUDICIAL PROCEEDINGS, 74n, 76n, 1205n
JURISDICTION. *See also* ADMIRALTY JURISDICTION
    applicable law, 74
    apportionment, 1519–1522
    Commercial Court, 100
    equity, 28
    governing law, 74
    High Court, 1224
    locality, 91
    outside the, defendants, 1484
    payment, liability for, 1484
    Probate, Divorce and Admiralty Court, 98
    public policy, 41
    Queen's Bench Division, 100
    restrictions on, 91
    statute law, 93
    wrecks, 91
JUSTICES OF THE PEACE, 108, 111, 117–118, 122, 129

LACHES, 25
LAGAN. *See also* FLOTSAM, JETSAM AND LAGAN
LAKES, 161
LAND,
    Admiralty jurisdiction, 109
    goods cast up on, 107, 118
    wrecks, 107
LAUNCHERS, 703
LAW REPORTS, 6
LAWS OF OLERON, 3
LEGAL DUTY OR AUTHORITY, SALVAGE UNDER, 533–543
LEGISLATION. *See* STATUTE LAW
LEPER SHIPS, 1045
LIABILITY. *See* LIMITATION OF LIABILITY, PAYMENT, LIABILITY FOR
LIABILITY SALVAGE, 158, 311
LIENS. *See also* MARITIME LIENS, POSSESSORY LIENS
    agents, 800
    bailment, 1078
    cargo, 133, 1494
    common law salvage, 132–133

LIENS—*cont.*
    non-acceptance of salved property, 1077–1078, 1082
    SCOPIC clause, 968
LIFE SALVAGE,
    Admiralty court, 1480
    Admiralty jurisdiction, payment, liability for, 1480
    Admiralty law, liability in, 264
    agreement, by, 267–273
    aircraft, extension to, 278
    animals, 192, 261n
    assessment, 309
    awards, 117
    benefit, 1480–1482
    cargo, 190
    common law, 261–272
    damages, 281
    danger, 1214–1216
    death, 1413
    definition, 260
    discretionary payments of, 292, 310
    enforcement of payment, 304–308
    English law, 260–299, 307h, 310
    environment, 4–8
    foreign vessels, 277
    general rules, 277
    Governmental discretionary payments, 310
    gratuitous services, 49
    in rem actions, 285
    intention, 276
    interest in property and, 280–291
    interpretation, 275
    judiciary, attitude of, 266
    liability, 302, 307
    lifeboats, 49, 700, 702
    lives in question, 293
    Lloyd's Open Form 2000, 272
    locality, 363
    officiousness, 51–53
    overriding objective, 272
    passage money, 239–241
    payment,
        enforcement of, 304–308
        entitlement to, 303
        liability for, 1480–1482, 1514
    pecuniary value of, 1514
    personal effects, 279
    personal injuries, 1413
    personal liability, 302
    practice, 262
    priority, 297
    property requirement, 262–263, 279–282, 307, 1414
        interest in property and, 280–291
        preservation, 726
        saving immaterial where lives preserved but not salved, 290
    public policy, 41, 51
    remuneration, 299, 302, 305, 1412
    rescuers, 49

Index

LIFE SALVAGE—*cont.*
  rewards, 26, 266, 271, 283, 286, 289, 291, 305
  Salvage Convention 1989, 259, 298–310, 1412–1413
    interpretation of, 299–301
  salvage operations, 306
  salved value, 287, 1385, 1499
  salvors, 443
    several, 263
  slaves, 190
  statutory changes, effect of, 265
  statute law, 265, 273–291, 298
  subjects of salvage, 152, 158, 162, 260–310, 1412
  success, 716
  trust of proceeds, 308
  tug and tow, 601
  unjust enrichment, 1480
LIFEBOATS,
  apportionment, 1530
  crews,
    claims made by, 700–703
    composition of, 699
  expenses, 704–705
  gratuitous services, 49
  life salvage, 49, 700, 702
  property salvage, 698, 700–701, 703
  public authorities, 551
  public policy, 40
  remuneration, 702
  reward, 701, 705
  Royal Naval Lifeboat Institution, 698
  salvage services, 698–705
  service allowances, 699
  voluntariness, 561, 698–705
LIGHT VESSELS, 577
LIGHTENING, 356
LIGHTHOUSES, 38n, 690
LIGHTSHIPS, 155
LIMITATION OF LIABILITY, 1182–1204
  actual fault or privity, 1202–1203
  Admiralty jurisdiction, 1185
  burden of proof, 1202
  cargo, 1193
  casualties, 1193
  claims not subject to, 1197–1200
  claims subject to, 1191–1195
  conduct barring, 1201–1204
  contribution, 1198
  Convention on the Limitation of Liability for Maritime Claims, 127, 1186–1204
  Crown, 11, 68
  counterclaims, 1196
  English law, 1194, 1202
  entitlement to, 1190
  general average, 1198
  history, 1185–1187
  in personam actions, 1185
  in rem actions, 1182, 1185
  indemnities, 1194
  limitation funds, 1182–1183

LIMITATION OF LIABILITY—*cont.*
  Limitation of liability convention 1976, 127, 1186–1204
    scope of, 1188–1189
  Lloyd's Open Form, 127
  marine insurance, 1183, 1204
  natural persons, 1204
  nuclear installations, 1199
  oil pollution, 1199
  rationale, 1182–1183
  recourse, right of, 1194–1195
  Salvage convention 1989, 1198
  salvors, 127
  shipowners,
    meaning of, 1190
  servants of, 1200
  treaties and conventions, 1186–1204
  United kingdom, 1187, 1199
  unlimited liability, 1197–1200
  vicarious liability, 1202
  Warsaw convention, 1203
  wreck, 1192, 1195
LIMITATION PERIODS. *See* TIME LIMITS
LINERS, 345
LIVESTOCK, 192, 261n
LLOYD'S AGENTS, 626–631
LLOYD'S OPEN FORM. *See also* LOF 2000
  access to copies of, 792
  Admiralty jurisdiction, 127–128
  appeals, 1306
  arbitration, 6, 8, 78, 793–794, 824, 991, 1266–1267, 1299, 1300–1303
    appeals, 1306
    hearings, 1289
    interim awards, 1291
    parties involved, 1274–1278
    place of arbitration, 1279
    procedure, 1284
    provisional awards, 1294
    references under, 1273
    security, payment and enforcement of, 1310–1314
  arbitrators, 1280
  assessment of rewards, 1389–1390
  authority, 806, 822, 828–829, 841
  background to, 791
  best endeavours, 1036, 1080
  bunkers, 795n
  common law, 79
    salvage, 143–144
  contractors, 847
  co-operation, 1056–1057, 1059–1060, 1062
  currency, 1461, 1463, 1465
  engaged services, 756, 767–778
  English law, 75
  environment, 128, 394–396, 1038
  estoppel, 869, 873–875
  express terms, in, 996
  general law of salvage, incorporation of, 78
  governing law, 75, 77

895

Index

LLOYD'S OPEN FORM—*cont.*
  inducement, 958
  interest, 1470, 1474, 1475
  life salvage, 272
  limitation of liability, 127
  maritime liens, 1248–1249
  misconduct, 1094
  mistake, 920, 924
  negligence, 1112–1113
  non-acceptance of salved property, 1080, 1082
  non-disclosure, 896, 904
  proceedings, 1222, 1224
  professional salvors, 6, 32
  redelivery, 1084
  remuneration, 780, 791
  revisions, 791
  safety, place of, 1063
  Salvage Convention 1989, 65, 128, 410
  salvage services, 869, 874
  security, 990, 1226, 1258–1259, 1262, 1264–1265
  sovereign immunity, 1174
  statutory authorities, 691
  success, 718
  termination, 1063, 1068
  unfair contract terms, 1157–1158
LLOYD'S PROCEDURAL RULES,
  arbitration, 1267, 1284–1285, 1301, 1305
  arbitrators, 1222, 1281–1282
  LOF 2000, 852–853
LLOYD'S STANDARD SALVAGE AND ARBITRATION CLAUSES. *See* LSSAC 2000
LOCALITY,
  Admiralty Court, 91
  Admiralty law, 362–363, 367
  Admiralty jurisdiction, 103
  aircraft, 256
  arbitration, 1279
  categories of, 362
  Crown ships, 658
  danger, 362–376
  English law, 368
  environment, 402
  inland waters, 364–365, 371, 373
    tidal waters, movement between, 375–376
  jurisdiction, 91
  life salvage, 363
  Salvage Convention 1989, 368, 374
    reservations to, 369–370
  salvage operations, 369
  wrecks, 106, 108
LOCATION. *See* LOCALITY
LOF. *See* LLOYD'S OPEN FORM, LOF 2000
LOF 2000, 6, 858. *See also* LLOYD'S OPEN FORM; SCOPIC CLAUSE
  arbitration, 1267, 1273, 1276, 1278
  authority, 797–799, 846
  best endeavours, 987, 1034–1036
  construction, 954

LOF 2000, 6, 858—*cont.*
  co-operation, 1058–1059, 1061
  currency, 1463
  estoppel, 866–875
  freight, 232
  interest, 1471
  Lloyd's Procedural Rules, 850–851
  LSSAC 2000, 850–851
  overriding objective, 954
  payment, liability for, 1488
  performance, deemed, 1065
  personal effects, 328
  reference, incorporation by, 850
  remedies, 1388
  revision, 850
  safety, place of, 1064
  salvees, 795
  salvors, 794
  security, 1255, 1257n, 1258, 1261–1262
  shipowners, 795
  signatures, 799
  success, 741
  termination, 989, 1064–1065, 1068
  terms of salvage agreements, 849–851
  time limits, 1206
LONDON ARBITRATION, 73
LOOTING, 359
LORD HIGH ADMIRAL, 90
LORD OF THE MANOR, 108
LOSSES,
  amenity, of, 401
  compensation, 1443
  deviation, 1446
  earnings, of, 1439, 1447
  indemnities, 1443
  material circumstances, 1439–1452
  opportunity, 1039, 1095, 1363, 1447
  physical, risk of, 1427–1428
  profits, of, 1439, 1442, 1447
  proximate result, 1445
  third parties, to, 1448
  vessels, 1444
LOW-WATER MARK, 114
LOWESTOFT, 649
LSSAC 2000,
  arbitration, 1266–1268, 1273, 1275, 1278–1279,1291, 1298, 1304, 1310–1314
  arbitrators, 1280
  authority, 799
  best endeavours, 1036
  co-operation, 1058–1059
  interest, 1471, 1475
  LOF 2000, 850–851
  negligence, 1137
  overriding objectives, 954
  proceedings, 1221
  salvees, 795
  SCOPIC clause, 960
  security, 1255, 1257–1259, 1261–1262
  shipowners, 795
  time limits, 1206

Index

LUGGAGE,
  passage money, 240
  subjects of salvage, 194, 321–328
LUMP SUM FREIGHT, 218

MAGISTRATES,
  officials, of, 696–697
  rewards, 696
  voluntariness, 696–697
  wrecks, 697
MAIL, 185
MANAGING AGENTS, 916, 918
MANIFEST DISADVANTAGE, 942–943
MANILA, 1071
MANOR, LORD OF THE, 108
MAREVA INJUNCTIONS, 1226
MARINE ENVIRONMENT. See ENVIRONMENT
MARINE INSURANCE,
  deviation, 1446
  expenses, 510
  ships,
    salved, 496, 498
    sister, 507
  limitation of liability, 1183, 1204
  Special Representatives, 969
  underwriters, 969
MARINE POLLUTION. See OIL POLLUTION
MARINE POLLUTION CONTROL UNIT, 70n
MARITIME LIENS, 2
  Admiralty court, 1247
  Admiralty jurisdiction, 1249–1250
  arrest, 1249
  attachment, order of, 1250
  bottomry, 1250
  cargo, 1252n
  common law salvage, 142
  definition, 1247
  English law, 1247
  extinction of, 1252
  hovercraft, 259
  in personam actions, 1252
  in rem actions, 1247, 1252
  insolvency, 1250
  interests in salved property, 1507, 1509, 1512–1513
  laches, 25
  Lloyd's open form, 1248–1249
  non-acceptance of salved property, 1082
  possession, 1249
  priorities, 1250
  remedies, 1249
  remuneration, 1248, 1251
  reward, 1248
  saisie conservatoire, 1252
  sale, 1252
  salvage agreements, 1252
  Salvage convention 1989, 1247–1249
  salved value, 1251
  seamen, 566
  security, 1226, 1247–1253
  sovereign immunity, 1165, 1249
  treaties and conventions, 1247

MARITIME LIENS—*cont.*
  vitiating factors, 1251n
  wages, 1250
MARITIME PROPERTY,
  definition, 163, 166
  freight, 166
  navigable property, 168–177
  Salvage Convention 1989, 163
  subjects of salvage, 163–243
MARKS, 106n
MARSHAL, ADMIRALTY, 1386
MASTERS,
  abandonment, 573–577
  agents, 814–815, 829, 832
  apportionment, 1525, 1540
  authority of, 565, 729–730, 796–797, 812–813
    agents, as, 814–815, 829, 832
    cargo-owners, 831–832
    officers, binding, 836–840
    persons other than, 823
    power of shipowners to bind, 841–844
    ratification, 828
    seamen, binding, 833–835
    shipowners, binding, 814–823, 833–835, 841–844
  cargo-owners, 831–832
  collisions, 543
  common law salvage, 148
  contracts, 653
    special, 728
  co-operation, 1059
  Crown ships, 653
  danger, 387
  definition, 534
  demise charterparties, 468–469
  engaged services, 761, 773–774
  fraud, 893
  freight, 232
  misconduct, 569, 1096, 1130–1131
  mistake, 920
  negligence, 1096
  officers, binding, 836–840
  personal effects, 1482
  persons other than, 823
  possession, 1236
  pressure on, 26n
  protests, 56, 60
  ratification, 830
  reward, 494
  safety at sea, 987
  seamen, 565, 833–840
    binding, 833–835
    discharge of, 569, 579
  shipowners, binding, 814–823, 833–835, 841–844
  success, 729–730
  tug and tow, 620
  undue influence, 948
  voluntariness, 517, 523, 530, 534–540, 543, 565–587
  wrecks, 694

897

Index

MATERIAL CIRCUMSTANCES, 1407–1460
  Admiralty court, 1432
  cargo, 1428, 1430
    risks to, 1429–1430
  classification of, 1393, 1407, 1418–1419
  contracts, termination of, 1433
  damage, risk of, 1427–1428
  danger, 1411–1417, 1424, 1428
  death, 1426
  derelict, 1432
  deviation, 1433
  discretion, 1432
  equipment, 1427
    meaning of, 1407, 1410
  expenses, 1439–1452
  financial loss, risks of, 1433
  freight, risks to, 1429
  labour expended, 1420
  list of, 1393, 1395
  losses, 1439–1452
    risk of physical, 1427–1428
  misconduct, 1423
  negligence, 1423
  passengers, 1407n, 1434n
  personal injuries, 1426
  professional salvors, 1422, 1428
  public policy, 1453–1456
  responsibility or liability, risk of, 1434
  Salvage Convention 1910, 1394–1395, 1407–1408, 1410, 1424
  Salvage Convention 1989, 1407–1408, 1418, 1421, 1424
  salvage services, 1419–1423
  salved value, 1419–1423, 1457–1459
  salvees, 1431
  salvors,
    classification, 1478
    risks run by, 1424–1425
    skill of, 1419–1423
  ships, risks to, 1429
  skill and care, 1419–1423
  success, agreement for award independent of, 1460
  time used, 1436–1438
  vessels, meaning of, 1407
MAYOR'S COURT, 315n
MEDIATION, 1222
MERCES, 185
MERCHANTABLE QUALITY, 1001
MERCURY, 336
MERITORIOUS SERVICES, 717, 720, 733, 739, 1459
METAL PLATES, 997
MIDNIGHT, 615n
MILFORD HAVEN, 1244
MILITARY SALVAGE. *See* PRIZE SALVAGE
MISCONDUCT, 1, 1086–1137
  assistance, 1091, 1133
  awards, causing diminution of, 1133–1136
  collisions, 1103
  compensation, 1095
  compound interest, 1137

MISCONDUCT—*cont.*
  contracts, 1092–1094
    privity of, 1098
  costs, deprivation of, 1134–1135
  damage, occasioning actual, 1136
  damages, 1088, 1093, 1099–1101
  danger, 1095–1103
  disentitlement, 1096–1099
  effect of, 1088–1095
  environment, 1089
  expenses, 1095
  fault, 1097–1103
  forfeiture, 1126–1128, 1133, 1135
  fraud, 95, 1101–1102
  Lof 2000, 1094
  masters, 569, 1096, 1130–1131
  material circumstances, 1423
  negligence, 1087, 1089–1097, 1100, 1103
    salvors during salvage operations, 1104–1124
  payment, liability for, 1484
  performance, 1095
  possession, 1243–1245
  privity of contract, 1098
  proof, 1100, 1132
  quantum meruit, 1102
  remuneration, 1133, 1137
  reward, 50, 1096–1101
    effect on, 1125–1137
  safety, place of, 1133
  Salvage convention 1989, 1086–1088
  salvage operations, salvors' during, 1104–1124
  salvage services, 1101
    creating need for, 1100
  salved value, 1095, 1325
  salvees, 1087
    salvors, duty to, 1091–1095
  salvors, 438, 1087–1089, 1484
    effect on other, 1128–1131
    negligence during salvage operations, 1104–1124
    salvees' duty to, 1091–1095
    sister ships, of, 1103
    some salvors, by, 1128–1131
  seamen, 569
  sister ships, 1099, 1103
  skill and care, 1091–1092, 1097
  special compensation, 438, 1137
  supervening circumstances, 957
  theft, 1128–1129, 1131
  third parties, 1087, 1098, 1101
  time limits, 1215n
  trespass, 1087
  tug and tow, 625, 1100, 1130–1131
  vicarious liability, 1094, 1096
  volunteers, 1102
  wrongful interference with property, 1087
MISREPRESENTATION,
  damages, 905
  fraud, 905, 908, 911
  indemnity, 901

Index

MISREPRESENTATION—*cont.*
inducement, 905
material, 910–911
mistake, 913
negligence, 905, 911
non-disclosure, 910, 912
rescission, 905–906
salved value, 908–909
vitiating factors, 887, 905–912
voidable contracts, 911
MISTAKE,
Admiralty jurisdiction, 921–922
common law, 913, 916–917
consent,
   negativing, 915
   nullifying, 914
inducement, 914–915
intention, 48
Lloyd's Open Form, 920, 924
masters, 920
misrepresentation, 913
non est factum, 920
presumption, 917
public policy, 41
rectification, 922
rescission, 923
reward, 921
salvees, 924
salvors, 924
   competing, 917–918
   identity of, 917–918
subject-matter, 914
tug and tow, 920, 924
vitiating factors, 887, 913–924
MOBILE OFFSHORE DRILLING UNITS, 319
MOIETY, 27n
MONEY, 16
MONEY HAD AND RECEIVED, 147–148
MONEYS NUMBERED, 1440
MONITION, 282
MONTREAL CMI DRAFT SALVAGE CONVENTION 1989, 394
MONTREAL COMPROMISE, 395
MOORING, 174
MORAL OBLIGATIONS, 522
MORAL SUPPORT, 22
MOTOR VEHICLES, 161
MULTIPLE CLAIMS, 1123–1124
MUNITIONS, 656
MUTINY, 358, 584
MUTUAL ASSISTANCE, 503, 530
MUTUAL INSURANCE,
authority, 842
sub-contractors, 638
voluntariness, 530

NATIONAL CONSUMER COUNCIL, 994
NAUTICAL ASSESSORS, 99
NAVIGATION,
aircraft, 246
danger, 1416
definition, 174–176

NAVIGATION—*cont.*
dinghies, 177–178
equipment, 186–187
flying boats, 178
involvement in, 155–156, 158, 160–161, 168–177
jet skis, 176
'messing about in boats', 176
mooring, effect of, 174
ships or vessels, 175
subjects of salvage, 155–156, 158, 160–161, 168–177
NAVY LIST, 672
NECESSITY,
authority, of, 804–808, 817–818, 821, 829, 832, 841
reasonable, 817
NEGLIGENCE,
admiralty jurisdiction, 1107
breach of duty, 1117
contracts, 1112–1114, 1119–1120
co-operation, 1054
counterclaims, 1107, 1109
damages, 1104, 1111, 1117
   common law, 1120–1123
   measure of, 1118–1122
   set-off, 1124
danger, 987
development of law of, 1106
duty of care, 1117–1118
establishing, 1115
gross, 1106, 1108
harm than good, more, 1110–1111
Lloyd's open form, 1112–1113
Lssac 2000, 1137
masters, 1096
material circumstances, 1423
misconduct, 1087, 1089–1097, 1100, 1103
salvors during salvage operations, 1104–1124
misrepresentation, 905, 911
modern law, 1117–1124
multiple claims, 1123–1124
non-acceptance of salved property, 1081
parties, duties of, 987
professional salvors, 1114
public policy, 1116
quantum meruit, 1113
reduction in liability, 1141
reward, 1104, 1108–1110, 1112
salvage convention 1989, 987
salved value, 1343
salvors during salvage operations, 1104–1124
set-off, 1124
skill and care, 1105–1106, 1109, 1120
standard of care, 1114
success, 1110–1111
supply of services, contracts for, 1012
unfair contract terms, 1149, 1150, 1156

Index

NEW BRUNSWICK, 537
NIGHT, 615n
NO CURE NO PAY,
  authority, 827
  engaged services, 771
  environment, 393
  exclusions, 787, 789
  SCOPIC clause, 974–975
  special compensation, 1388
  success, 718, 741
NON-ACCEPTANCE OF SALVED PROPERTY,
  abandonment, 1072, 1079–1081
  assistance, 1076
  bailment, 1072–1075, 1078–1079, 1081
  best endeavours, 1080
  cargo-owners, 1075–1077, 1085
  carriers, duties and rights of, 1075–1078
  damages, 1077
  delivery, 1075
  expenses, 1076, 1081, 1085
  freight, 1077
  frustration, 1079
  liens, 1077–1078, 1082
  Lloyd's open form, 1080, 1082
  maritime liens, 1082
  negligence, 1081
  owners, 1081
  parties, duty of, 1070–1085
  possessory liens, 1092
  redelivery, 1070, 1077, 1079, 1082–1084
  reimbursement, 1073–1974
  remuneration, 1070, 1082
  restitution, 1085
  rewards, 1070
  safety, place of, 1070, 1080, 1082
  salvage agreements, reimbursement under, 1073–1974
  Salvage Convention 1989, 1070, 1082
  salvage services, 1076
  salvors, duties and rights of, 1080–1082
  storage, 1071–1073, 1081, 1085
  supervening events, 1076
  termination, 1071
  third parties, 1075
NON-DISCLOSURE,
  Admiralty jurisdiction, 900
  common law, 895
  inequality of bargaining power, 900
  Lloyd's Open Form, 896, 904
  materiality, 895
  misrepresentation, 910, 912
  remuneration, 896
  reward, 904
  setting aside contracts, 903
  undue influence, 900
  utmost good faith, 891
  vitiating factors, 895–904
  weather, 903

NON EST FACTUM, 920
NOON, 615n
NORTH SEA, 1325
NOTICE,
  arbitration, 1302–1305
  SCOPIC, 965, 972
  security, 990
  unfair contract terms, 1152
NUCLEAR MATERIALS, 359, 1199

OARS,
  propelled by, 168n, 172–173
  subjects of salvage, 172–173
OBSTRUCTION, 1045
OFF-HIRE CLAUSE, 221
OFFICERS,
  apportionment, 1526, 1529
  authority, 836–840
  chief, 573
  commanding, 450
  Crown ships, 645–676, 1529
  masters, binding, 836–840
  radio, 587, 1526
  voluntariness, 565–587, 645–676
OFFICIAL DUTY,
  coastguard, 686
  pre-existing, 524–525
  voluntariness, 524–525
OFFICIALS,
  magistrates, 696–697
  voluntariness, 696–697
OFFICIOUSNESS,
  acceptance, 50–63
  danger, 62
  life salvage, 51–53
  owners, 63
  protests, 56
  public policy, 51
  recipients' wishes, overriding, 50–63
  reward, 50–63
  Salvage Convention 1989, 51, 61–63
  submarines, 49n
OFFSHORE DRILLING PLATFORMS, 162
OIL POLLUTION. *See also* ENVIRONMENT
  best endeavours, 70
  casualties, 70
  directions, 70
  limitation of liability, 1199
  Marine Pollution Control Unit, 70n
  public authorities, 69, 546
  Salvage Convention 1989, 69
  Secretary of State, 70
  special compensation, 70
OIL RIGS, 319
OLERON, LAWS OF, 3
OPEN OFFERS, 1295
OPPORTUNITIES, LOSS OF, 1039, 1095, 1363, 1447
ORDERS, 574
OVERPAYMENTS, 978
OWNERS. *See also* SHIPOWNERS
  agents, 631

Index

OWNERS—*cont.*
  aircraft, 678
  common, 150
  co-operation, 1058–1059
  expenses, 631
  interests in salved property, 485–510
  non-acceptance of salved property, 1081
  officiousness, 63
  personal services, 454–485
  property, 1058–1059
  salving vessels, 454–485
  sister ships, 504–508
  subjects of salvage, 150
OXFORD, 95n

P&I. *See* SCOPIC
PANIC, 358
PARLIAMENT,
  Hansard, 86
  interpretation, 86
  preparatory material, 86
PAROL EVIDENCE RULE, 852
PARTIES. *See also* PARTICULAR PARTIES (eg SALVORS, SHIPOWNERS)
  arbitration, 991, 1274–1278, 1306
  assistance, 988, 1039–1043
  best endeavours, 987, 1034–1036
  contractual liability, 993–1033
  co-operation, 988, 1044–1062
  Council of Lloyd's, 1277–1278
  duties of, 987–1085
  environment, 989, 1037–1038
  judicial proceedings, 911
  negligence, 987
  payments, 991–992
  performance, failure of, 1027–1033
  property, nonacceptance of salved, 1070–1085
  public authorities, prolongation by, 1069
  reward, 991
  safety at sea, 987
  salvage agreements, 793–795
  salvage services, termination of, 989, 1063–1069
  SCOPIC, 966, 970
  security, 990
  unfair contract terms, 1147–1148
PASSAGE MONEY,
  common law, 235
  freight, 240–243
  life salvage, 239–241
  luggage, 240
  remuneration, 237–238
  reward, 239, 241
  Salvage Convention 1989, 234
  subjects of salvage, 234–242
  transhipment, 237
  unconscionability, 236
PASSENGERS,
  apportionment, 1528
  authority, 819
  contracts, 632

PASSENGERS—*cont.*
  danger, 634–635
  material circumstances, 1407n, 1434n
  passage money, 234–242
  personal effects, 194, 321–328, 1482
  remuneration, 632–634
  rewards, 635
  salvage services, 632, 634–636
    extraordinary, 635
  seamen, 633
  self-interest, 518
  voluntariness, 518, 632–636
PASSIVE SALVAGE, 360–361
PAYMENT, LIABILITY FOR, 1478–1518. *See also* APPORTIONMENT
  bottomry, 1482
  bullion, 1498
  Crown proceedings, 1483
  different risks, 1500–1505
  division of liability, 1515–1518
  estoppel, 1492
  fixed sum, agreements for, 1492
  general average, 1198
  in personam actions, 1479
  in rem actions, 1479
  interests in property benefited, contributions from all, 1479
  jurisdiction, defendants outside, 1484
  life salvage, 1480–1482, 1514
  limitation of liability, 1198
  LOF 2000, 1488
  misconduct, 1484
  personal effects, 1482
  property, interests in salved, 1506–1513
  remedies, 1485–1494
  respondentia, 1483
  reward, 2, 28
  reimbursement, 1493–1494
  risk or difficulty, different degrees of, 1497
  Salvage convention 1989, 1488, 1491
  salved value, contribution rateably according to, 1495–1514
  salvees, 2
  salvors, 1479–1494
  shipowners, payment by, 1488–1494
  silver, 1498
  sovereign immunity, 1483
PERFORMANCE,
  awards, 1032–1033
  conditions, 1027–1028, 1031
  construction, 1028
  contracts, 1027–1029
  co-operation, 1052
  damages, 1027, 1031–1033
  deemed, 1065
  defective, 1026
  delays, 1030
  failure of, 1027–1033
  implied term, 1029
  innominate terms, 1027–1029, 1031
  LOF 2000, 1065
  misconduct, 1095

Index

PERFORMANCE—*cont.*
  parties, duties of, 1027–1033
  personal, 1019–1021
  public policy, 1032
  rewards, 1032
  skill and care, 1029
  successful, 1022–1023
  supply of services, contracts for,
    1014–1015, 1019–1024, 1026
  termination, 1027, 1031, 1065–1066
  time for, 1014–1015, 1024, 1052
  time limits, 1033
  warranties, 1027–1028
PERIL. *See* DANGER
PERSONAL EFFECTS,
  contractual provisions, 327–328
  general average, 321–325
  life salvage, 279
  Lloyd's Open Form 2000, 328
  masters, 321, 1482
  passengers, 194, 321–328, 1482
  payment, liability for, 1482
  Salvage Convention 1989, 327
  salvage subjects, 194, 321–328
  seamen, 321, 1482
  valuables, 321
PERSONAL INJURIES, 1155, 1205, 1413
PERSONAL REPRESENTATIVES, 1535
PERSONAL SERVICES,
  additional, 450
  apportionment,, 1526
  assessment of rewards, 451
  boat owners, 449
  coastguards, 448
  charterers, claims of, 458–484
  compensation, equitable, 454
  crew, 457
  owners of salved vessels, 454–485
  performance, 1019–1021
  physical presence, 450
  power-driven vessels, 452, 456
  reasons for limiting to, 451
  remuneration, 447n
  reward, 454–485
    assessment of, 451
  rule of, 448–453
  salvage agreements, 790
  salving vessels, ownership and possession
    of, 458–484
  salvors, classification of, 445–484
  shipowners, claims of, 458–484
  supply of services, 1019–1021
  taxation, 453
PIERS, 174
PILFERAGE, 1131
PILOTS,
  apportionment, 1530, 1540
  compulsory, 591, 593, 597
  danger, 343, 590–591, 597
  defined, 588
  distress, 593, 596
  public authorities, 549

PILOTS—*cont.*
  public policy, 39
  remuneration, 590–591, 593, 597
  reward, 589, 593–594, 596–599
  salvage services, 590–595, 597–599
  skill and care, more than usual, 598
  voluntariness, 588–599
PIRACY, 650
PLACE OF SAFETY, 1035, 1063–1067
PLATFORMS, 162, 318–320
PLEDGES, 1003
PLUNDERERS, 109, 111, 358
POLLUTION. *See* OIL POLLUTION
POOLE HARBOUR, 854
PORPOISES, 314
PORT OF LONDON AUTHORITY, 688
PORTS,
  co-operation, 1047
  entry into, 1047
  freight, 1357–1359, 1361, 1363
  port of destination, reaching, 1357–1359
  port of refuge, 1361, 1363
  public authorities, 550
  statutory authorities, 690, 693
PORTSMOUTH, 647
POSSESSION,
  abandonment, 1234, 1237
  assistance, 1234, 1241
  common law, 1228
  conduct, 1242–1245
  damage, 1245
  damages, 1230
  declarations, 1230
  derelict, 1230, 1234
    property not, 1234–1245
  exceptions, 1237–1239
  exclusive, 1230
  expenses, 1243
  injunctions, 1230
  interests in salved property, 1512–1513
  limitations, 1232–1233
  maritime liens, 1249
  masters, 1236
  misconduct, 1243–1245
  redelivery, 1083–1084
  remuneration, 1242, 1245
  salvors, 1232–1233
    conduct, 1242–1245
    first, 1229, 1240–1241
    second, 1240–1241
    subsequent, 1233
  security, 1228–1246
  shipowners, 1234, 1236
  success, 1233
  trespass to goods, 1231
  wrecks, receivers of, 1246
POSSESSORY LIENS,
  common law salvage, 130, 133, 139
  non-acceptance of salved property, 1092
  sub-contractors, 638
  wrecks, 108

Index

POSSESSORY RIGHTS, 1348. *See also*
   POSSESSORY LIENS
POWER-DRIVEN VESSELS, 38, 126, 452, 456
PRECEDENT, 83
PRE-EXISTING DUTIES,
   property, 523
   voluntariness, 512–525, 532–543, 561
PREPARATORY WORKS, 86–88
PRICE,
   consideration, 999
   distress, 1000
   sale of goods, contracts for, 999–1000
   supply of services, contracts for, 1024
PRIORITIES,
   apportionment, 1533
   maritime liens, 1250
   time, 1533
PRINCIPAL, 801–803, 809, 829
   notification, 846
   undisclosed, 803
PRIVATE INTERNATIONAL LAW. *See* CONFLICT OF LAWS
PRIVY COUNCIL, 98
PRIZE SALVAGE, 15
   Admiralty Court, 94
   Admiralty jurisdiction, 104
   civil salvage and, 20
   Crown, 1167
   equity, 21
   remuneration, 20
   reward, 20
PRO RATA FREIGHT, 1218
PROBATE, DIVORCE AND ADMIRALTY COURT, 14, 95, 96, 99, 125
PROCEEDINGS, 1220–1318. *See also* IN PERSONAM ACTIONS, IN REM ACTIONS
   Admiralty jurisdiction, 1224
   aircraft, 1224
   alternative dispute resolution, 1222
   arbitration, 1222, 1266–1318
   arrest, 1223, 1265
   Brussels convention 1968, 1224
   contracts, 1224
   danger, 1224
   detention, 1265
   execution, 1223
   High court jurisdiction, 1224
   indemnities, 1221
   Lloyd's open form, 1222, 1224
   LOF 2000, 1222
   Lssac 2000, 1221
   maritime liens, 1247–1252
   mediation, 1222
   possession, 1228–1246
   property,
      preservation of, 1223
      remove, duty not to, 1253–1254
   rewards, claims for, 1220, 1223
   Salvage convention 1989, 1224
   salvage services, 1224
   security, 1225–1265
   settlements, 1222

PROCEEDINGS—cont.
   subcontractors, 1221
   third parties, 1221, 1223
   wrecks, 1223
PROCTORS, 95
PROFESSIONAL SALVORS, 42–47
   advantages of, 43
   equipment, 42, 45
   expenses, 45
   freight, 232
   Lloyd's Open Form, 6, 32
   material circumstances, 1422, 1428
   negligence, 1114
   public policy, 1422, 1454
   reasons for, 43
   remuneration, 47
   reward,
      assessment of, 45
      scale of, 42, 44–45
   salvage industry, 6
   salvage services as part of work, 46–47
   salvage stations, network of, 43
   stand by, 45
   success, 1023
   supply of services, contracts for, 1010, 1020, 1023
   time, 1436
   tug and tow, 43n, 47
PROFIT, LOSS OF, 1439, 1442, 1447
PROHIBITED SERVICES, 51n
PROHIBITION, 92, 109, 201, 204
PROPELLERS, 340, 383, 737
PROPER LAW,
   governing law, 74
   Salvage Convention 1989, 76
   unjust enrichment, 74
PROPERTY. *See also* INTERESTS IN SALVED PROPERTY, NON-ACCEPTANCE OF SALVED PROPERTY
   Admiralty jurisdiction, 726
   ancillary, 178–182
   assistance, 18
   benefits to, 26
   common law salvage, 130, 132
   compensation, 1254
   co-operation, 1058–1059
   Crown, 11 69
      proceedings, 1170
   cultural, 214, 389
   danger, 1414
   definition of salvage, 16
   deviation, 1446
   engaged services, 743, 755, 760
   freight, 216, 725
   in personam actions, 725
   in rem actions, 725
   life salvage, 262–263, 279–282, 307, 726
      interest in property and, 280–291
      saving immaterial where lives preserved but not salved, 290
   lifeboats, 698, 700–701, 703
   maritime, 163–243

903

Index

PROPERTY—cont.
pre-existing duties, 523
preservation, 725–727, 1223
   loss or damage following, 732
proceedings, 1223
remove, duty not to, 1253–1254
   consent, 1253
remuneration, 726
retention of title, 187
rewards, 26
Salvage Convention 1989, 1253
salvors, 443, 445–4894
security, 1253–1254
shipowner, not owned by, 183–187
subjects of salvage, 158, 160
   ancillary, 178–182
   maritime, 163–243
   shipowner, not owned by, 183–187
success, 716, 720, 725–727
   loss or damage after, 732
third parties, owned by, 183–187
transfer of, 1003
voluntariness, 523
wrecks, 215
wrongful interference with, 1087
PROPULSION, 341, 385, 601
PROTECTION AND INDEMNITY. See SCOPIC
PROTECTION OF WRECKS
PROTESTS,
masters, 56, 60
officiousness, 56
reward, 56
PROVISIONS, 188–189
PUBLIC AUTHORITIES,
armed forces, 549
charges, 688
charities, 550
coastguard, 549
co-operation, 1049–1051
Crown, 549
danger, 554
definition, 551–552
English law, 547, 553–555
governing law, 76, 547
gratuitous services, 688
interpretation, 547, 550, 555
intervention by, 1069
lifeboats, 551
local, 549
location, 547
national, 549
national law, 553
oil pollution and, 69, 546
parties, duties of, 1069
pilots, 549
ports, 550
prolongation by, 1069
public benefit, 551
public nature, bodies with powers of, 550
reward, 556, 689
rights and duties of, 67–69
Salvage Convention 1910, 68n

PUBLIC AUTHORITIES—cont.
Salvage Convention 1989, 67–69, 545–551
salvage operations, 69, 552–556
termination, 1069
UK, outside, 547
voluntariness, 513–514, 545–556, 564
wreck receivers, 549
PUBLIC DUTIES, 550
PUBLIC HOUSES, 805
PUBLIC INTERNATIONAL LAW, 65, 81
PUBLIC POLICY, 36–41
Admiralty Court, 36, 41
assessment of awards, 1453–1456
authority, 807, 837, 839
benefits, 36
coastguard, 686
Crown ships, 646, 663
encouragement of salvage, 37–38, 1454–1455
environment, 1456
equipment, 1454–1455
exclusions, 785
gratuitous services, 49
harbour authorities, 1454
inequity of terms, 934
jurisdiction, 41
life salvage, 41, 51
lifeboatmen, 40
material circumstances, 1453–1456
meritorious services, 37–38, 41
mistakes, 41
negligence, 1116
officiousness, 51
pilots, 39
professional salvors, 1422, 1454
quantum meruit, 37–38
remuneration, 34n
reward, 2, 1032
   assessment of, 27, 37–38
Salvage Convention 1910, 1453
Salvage Convention 1989, 1453, 1455
salvage services, 36
   encouraging, 1453–1454
salved values, 37
salvors,
   discrimination against less capable, 39
   encouraging, 1453–1454
   types of, 1454–1455
sub-contractors, 1020
success, 38
supply of services, contracts for, 1020
taxation, 1477
towage, conversion into salvage services, 40
tugs, 1454–1455
vessels, power-driven, 38
volunteers, 40

QUANTUM MERUIT,
assessment of reward, 37–38, 1389
common law salvage, 135
danger, 377

904

Index

QUANTUM MERUIT—cont.
  distress, 734
  engaged services, 752, 754
  misconduct, 1102
  negligence, 1113
  public policy, 37–38
  tug and tow, 611, 614
QUASI-CONTRACT, 35
QUEEN, DEPUTY OF THE, 90n
QUEEN'S BENCH DIVISION, 14, 96, 100
QUEEN'S REGULATIONS, 653, 679–680, 1529

RADAR, 186
RADIO, 358
RADIO OFFICERS, 587, 1526
RAFTS, 173
RANSOM, 131
RATEABLE CONTRIBUTION, 1495–1514
RATES OF EXCHANGE, 1347, 1461–1462, 1465
RATIFICATION,
  authority, 809, 821, 823, 828, 840
  masters, 828
  seamen, 840
  shipowners, 823
RECEIVERS OF WRECKS, 549, 683, 684, 687, 694–695
  functions of, 695
  possession, 1246
  salved value, 1322
  salvors, as, 695
RECIPIENTS. See SALVEES
RECORDS, COURTS OF, 115, 119
RECTIFICATION, 924
REDELIVERY,
  acceptance, 989, 1045, 1082
  agents, 1084
  bailment, 1084
  compensation, 1082
  co-operation, 1045
  Lloyd's Open Form, 1084
  non-acceptance of salved property, 1070, 1077, 1079, 1082–1084
  possession, persons entitled to, 1083–1084
  salvors, 1083
  termination, 989
REDUCTION OF LIABILITY, 1140–1162
  Admiralty law, 1140
  common law, 1141–1142
  construction, 1141
  exclusion of liability, 1141
  exemption clauses, 1141
  negligence, 1141
  statute law, 1143–1162
  unfair contract terms, 1144–1162
  volenti non fit injuria, 1142
REFUGE, PLACE OF, 69
REIMBURSEMENT, 2, 1073–1074, 1515
RELATED CLAIMS, 1388
REMEDIES. See also COMPENSATION, DAMAGES
  arrest, 1475
  cargo, 1486

REMEDIES—cont.
  common law salvage, 134, 139
  engaged services, 772
  estoppel, 870
  freight, 1485–1487
  LOF 2000, 1388
  maritime liens, 1249
  payment, liability for, 1493–1494
  reimbursement, 1493–1494
  salvors, 2, 1485–1491
  shipowners, 1493–1494
REMOTENESS, 64
REMOVAL, 1253–1254
REMUNERATION. See also REWARD
  agents, 136
  apportionment, 783, 1520, 1539
  arbitration, 1267, 1273
  arrears, in, 865
  authority, 834, 837, 844
  benefits, 54
  cancellation, following, 956
  charterparties, 126, 219–224
  coastguard, 684
  common law salvage, 141
  compound interest, 1137
  contracts, 727
  co-operation, 1054
  Crown ships, 651, 654, 656
  currency, 1463, 1464
  date of payment, 84
  discounts, 977
  engaged services, 743, 746–758, 762–764
  environment, 396, 409
  exorbitant, 937, 939, 940, 951
  fraud, 892
  freight, 219–224
  inadequate, 937, 941
  inequity of terms, 933, 937, 939, 940–941, 951
  life salvage, 299, 302, 305, 1412
  lifeboats, 702
  lighthouses, 38n
  Lloyd's Open Form, 780, 791
  maritime liens, 1248,. 1251
  maximising, 961
  misconduct, 1095, 1133, 1137
  non-disclosure, 896
  overpayments, 978
  passage money, 237–238
  passengers, 632–634
  personal services, 447
  pilots, 590–591, 593, 597
  possession, 1242, 1245
  prize salvage, 20
  professional salvors, 47
  property, preservation of, 726
  public policy, 34n
  reasonable, 2
  reducing, 967
  requests, 727

905

Index

REMUNERATION—cont.
salvage agreements, 731, 780–782, 864–865
apportionment, 783
cancellation, 956
discharge of, 957
salved value, 1320, 1327, 1377, 1457
SCOPIC Clause, 962, 966, 968, 970, 976–978
assessment of, 976
commencement of, 971
date of payment, 978
discounts, 977
maximising, 961
overpayments, 978
reducing, 961
seamen, 565–566
security, 1259
sister ships, 504
supervening circumstances, 957, 959
supply of services, contracts for, 1007, 1017–1018
termination, 1063, 1067
tug and tow, 600–603, 605–609, 612–614, 728
standard forms, 779
United States, 33n
vitiating factors, 881
voluntariness, 523, 558
wages, 565–566
wrecks, 695
REPAIRS,
bottomry, 1482
saved value, 1339, 1353n, 1354, 1371
REPUDIATION,
engaged services, 776–777
termination, 1066
REPUTATION, 597
REQUESTS,
engaged services, 742–743, 747–748
remuneration, 727
success, 727
REQUISITIONS,
Crown ships, 670–671
demise charterparties, 477
interests in salved property, 1512
voluntariness, 538
RESCISSION,
misrepresentation, 905–906
mistake, 923
RESCUERS,
apportionment, 1533
gratuitous services, 49
interests in salved property, 1517
life salvage, 49
RESPONDENTIA, 1483
RESTITUTION,
apportionment, 1540
authority, 808, 831
common law salvage, 130
currency, 1462
engaged services, 753

RESTITUTION—cont.
English law, 33–35
non-acceptance of salved property, 1085
SCOPIC clause, 978
set-off, 1518
sources of modern salvage law, 3
unjust enrichment, 3, 33–35, 74
vitiating factors, 876–877
voluntariness, 560, 562
RESTRICTIONS ON CLAIMS, 1138–1219. *See also* EXCLUSIONS, LIMITATION OF LIABILITY, TIME LIMITS
humanitarian cargo, 1178–1181
reduction of liability, 1140–1162
sovereign immunity, 1163–1177
RETENTION OF TITLE, 187
REVOLUTIONARIES, 359
REWARD, 1389–1406. *See also* APPORTIONMENT OF REWARD, ASSESSMENT OF REWARD, REMUNERATION
abandonment, 578
acceptance, 50–63
Admiralty Court, 91
Admiralty jurisdiction, 109–111, 126
aircraft, 254
anchors, saving, 113
apportionment, 2, 76, 1528
arbitration, 8
assistance, 1039, 1042–1043
authority, 807, 809, 815, 821
benefits, receipt of, 28–30
best endeavours, 1034–1036
common law salvage, 130, 141, 145
consent, 51
contracts, 35, 479–481
contributions, 2, 28
Crown, 2
ships, 645, 647, 652, 655, 666
currency, 25, 1464
date of payment, 991
demise charterparties, 469, 476, 478
disentitlement, 1096–1099
employees, 644
engaged services, 751, 756–757
enhanced, 141
environment, 407–408, 410, 1038
exclusions, 784, 786
frustration, 1067
hire, 126
incompleted services, 737
intention, 48–49
life salvage, 26, 266, 271, 283, 286, 289, 291, 30
lifeboats, 701, 705
magistrates, 696
maritime liens, 1249
masters, 494
misconduct, 50, 1096–1101, 1125–1137
mistake, 923
negligence, 1104, 1108–1110, 1112, 1123
non-acceptance of salved property, 1070

906

Index

REWARD—*cont.*
  officiousness, 50–63
  parties, duties of, 991
  passage money, 239, 241
  passengers, 635
  payment, 991
  performance, 1032
  pilots, 589, 593–594, 596–599
  prize salvage, 20
  proceedings, 1220, 1223
  professional salvors, 42, 44–45
  property,
    non-acceptance of salved, 1070
    benefits to, 26
  protests, 56
  public authorities, 556, 689
  public policy, 2, 36, 1032
  quasi-contract, 33–35
  sale of goods, contracts for, 1000
  salvage agreement, 31
  SCOPIC clause, 974–976
  seamen, 492, 494
  set-off, 1031
  shipowners, 458
  ships, salved, 502
  sovereign immunity, 12
  special, 1528
  special compensation,
    assessment of, 420–421, 436–437
    deductible, 433–437
    greater than, 434, 436
    inadequate, 417
    less than entitlement to, 414
    not exceeding recoverable, 416
    reduced by, 420
    size of, 418
  subjects of salvage, 160
  success, 719–720, 733, 735
    independent of, agreements, 1460
  time, 1436
  time limits, 1218
  tug and tow, 603, 607
  unjust enrichment, 33–35
  upper limit of, 2
  voluntariness, 559–560
  wrecks, 108, 109–110
RIGGS, 314
RIGHT TO SUE, 131, 142
RNLI (ROYAL NATIONAL LIFEBOAT INSTITUTION), 698
ROBBERY, 106n,
ROMALPA CLAUSES, 187
ROMAN LAW, 15, 89
ROYAL AIR FORCE,
  aircraft, 677–681
    owners of, 678
  Crown, 677
  officers and men, 677–681
  Royal Navy, 681
  salvage services, 677, 680–681
  salvors, 678
  voluntariness, 677–681

ROYAL ARMY, 682
ROYAL FISH,
  Cinque Ports, 315
  definition, 314
  droits of Admiralty, 316
  grants, 315
  subjects of salvage, 314–316
ROYAL NATIONAL LIFEBOAT INSTITUTION, 698
ROYAL NAVY, 120
  Crown ships, 645, 648, 651, 654, 656, 659, 665, 667, 674, 676
  Royal Air Force, 681
RUSSIA, 580

SAFETY AT SEA,
  assistance, 987
  best endeavours, 1035
  human lives, 1412–1414
  masters, 987
  misconduct, 1133
  non-acceptance of salved property, 1070, 1080, 1082
  parties, duties of, 987
  place of safety, 1035, 1063–1067, 1133
SAIL, DAYS OF, 1
SAISIE CONSERVATOIRE, 1252
SALE. *See also* SALE OF GOODS
  common law salvage, 129
  contracts of, 999–1000
  expenses, 1385
  maritime liens, 1252
  salved value, 1336–1337
    expenses, 1385
    no, 1350–1351
SALE OF GOODS,
  consideration, 999
  consumers, dealing as, 1002
  contracts, 999–1002, 1030
  description, 1001, 1002
  distress, 1000
  implied terms, 1001–1002
  merchantable quality, 1001
  price, 999–1000
  qualification of liability, 1002
  reward, 1000
  time, 1030
  unfair contract terms, 1002
  warranties, implied, 1001
SALVAGE AGREEMENTS, 1, 779–980. *See also* LLOYD'S OPEN FORM, TERMS OF SALVAGE AGREEMENTS, VITIATING FACTORS
  accord and satisfaction, 962
  Admiralty jurisdiction, 858, 862–866
  apportionment, 783
  arbitration, 1274
  assessment of rewards, 31, 780, 864, 1389
  authority, 796–846
  cancellation, 861, 956
  construction, 954
  contractual salvage, 790–792
  definition, 731, 779

907

SALVAGE AGREEMENTS—*cont.*
  denial of salvage, 866–875
  discharge, 955–959
    agreement, by, 956
    consent, by, 956
  effect of, 852
  engaged services, 780
  estoppel, 866–875
  excluding salvage agreements, 784–789
  existence of agreement, 857–860
  expenses, 781
  fairness of, 858–860
  independent assessments, 853
  invalidity, 861
  life salvage, 267–273
  maritime liens, 1252
  non-acceptance of salved property, 1070, 1082
  parol evidence rule, 852
  parties, 793–795
  personal services, 790
  prima faecie effective, 863–856
  professional salvors, 790
  proof, 857–861
  reimbursement, 1073–1074
  remuneration, 731, 780–782, 864–865
    apportionment of, 783
    cancellation, following, 956
  reward,
    assessment of, 31, 780, 1389
  salvage articles, 1539
  salved values, 757–854
  salvees, 795
  salvors, 794
  SCOPIC, 960–980
  setting aide, 1389
  standard forms, 781
  success, 731, 780
  supervening circumstances, 861, 955, 951–954
  supply of services, contracts for, 1007
  time limits, 1213–1216
  tug and tow, 600, 781
  types of, 779–792
  unconscionability, 862
  variation, 956
  work and labour, 782
SALVAGE COMMISSIONERS, 117
SALVAGE CONVENTION 1910, 11
  English law, 11, 66, 85, 127
  governing law, 73
  interpretation, 85
  manned and unmanned vessels, 17
  material circumstances, 1394–1395, 1407–1408, 1410, 1424
  prohibited services, 51n
  public authorities, 68n
  public policy, 1454
  Salvage Convention 1989, 85
  security, 1226
  sister ships, 504
  sovereign immunity, 1164

SALVAGE CONVENTION 1910—*cont.*
  success, measure of, 1450
  vitiating factors, 885, 885
  voluntariness, 512, 535
SALVAGE CONVENTION 1989, 1
  applicable law, 74
  apportionment, 76, 1521–1523
  arbitration, 1300
    awards, publication of, 67
  assessment of rewards, 1389–1390
  assistance, 988, 1040–1043
  authority, 796, 816, 832
  best endeavours, 1036
  compulsion, 944
  contents, 66
  contracting states, duty of, 1048–1055
    content of, 1050
    enforcement of, 1053
  contracts, 80
  co-operation, 67, 988, 1048–1056, 1059–1062
  Crown proceedings, 1170
  danger, 62, 351–352, 381, 1411, 1415–1416
  denunciation, 66
  departure from provisions of, 81
  draft, 128
  drilling units, 319–320
  enforcement, 74, 1053
  engaged services, 754
  English law, 66
  entry into force, 65
  environment, 12, 312, 395–440, 989, 1037–1038, 1417
  exclusion of, 77
  extent of the application of, 81
  general maritime law of salvage, incorporation of, 80
  governing law, 72–73, 76–77
  humanitarian cargo, 329, 1178
  implementation, 65, 81
  inequity of terms, 944–952
  inland waters, 81
  interest, 1466, 1468
  interpretation, 82–88
  languages of, 66n
  life salvage, 259, 298–310, 1412–1413
    interpretation of, 299–301
  limitation of liability, 1198
  Lloyd's Open Form, 128, 410
  locality, 368, 374
    reservations to, 369–370
  LOF 1990, 65
  maritime liens, 1247–1249
  material circumstances, 1395, 1407–1408, 1418, 1421, 1425
  misconduct, 1086–1088
  negligence, 987
  officiousness, 51, 61–63
  oil pollution,
  public authorities and, 69
  passage money, 234

908

Index

SALVAGE CONVENTION 1989—*cont.*
  payment, liability for, 1488, 1491
  platforms, 319–320
  proceedings, 1220, 1224
  prohibition under art 19, 61–62
  proper law, 76
  property, duty not to remove, 1253
  public authorities, 67–69, 545–551
  public international law, 65, 81
  pubic policy, 1453, 1455
  ratification, 81
  reservations, 66, 81, 369–370
  revision, 66
  Salvage Convention 1910, 85
  salvage operation, definition of, 18–19
  salvage services, prohibition of, 61–63
  salved value, 1457, 1496
    little or no, 19
  salvors, 443–444
  SCOPIC, 970, 977, 980–981, 983
  security, 990, 1226, 1256, 1262
  ships,
    meaning of, 169
    salved, 504–508
    sister, 504–508
  sister ships, 504–508
  sources of modern salvage law, 12
  sovereign immunity, 68, 1164, 1176
  special compensation, 1388
  standard form contracts, 77
  states, 67–69
    immunity of, 68
  status of, 66
  subjects of salvage, 159, 161–162
  success, 719–724, 741, 1450–1451
  supply of services, contracts for, 1013, 1014, 1017
  time, 1436, 1438
  time limits, 1205–1206, 1209–1219
  travaux preparatoires, 410
  tug and tow, 200
  undue influence, 952–954
  United Kingdom, in, 66
  vitiating factors, 878, 880–881, 885–888, 890, 892
  voluntariness, 512–514, 516, 535–536, 544–556, 564
  wrecks, 213–215
SALVAGE OPERATIONS,
  co-operation, 1055
  definition of, 18–19, 69, 306
  engaged services, 754
  life salvage, 306
  misconduct, 1104–1124
  negligence, 1104–1124
  prolongation of, 1069
  public authority control of, 69, 552–556, 1069
  salved values, 19
  salvors' misconduct, 1104–1124
  special compensation, 413
  time limits, 1210

SALVAGE OPERATIONS—*cont.*
  unfair contract terms, 1162
  useful result, 19
SALVAGE SERVICES, 1. *See also* GRATUITOUS SERVICES, TERMINATION OF SERVICES
  agents, 620
  aircraft, 253–254
  apportionment, 1525
    contemporaneous, 1532
  authority, 837, 840
  breach of contract, exposure to, 1446
  cargo-owners, liability to, 1446
  coastguard, 684
  contemporaneous, 1532
  continuing, 837
  contractual liability, 997, 1446
  Crown ships, 646, 648–650, 652, 659, 663–664
  damages, liability in, 1446
  danger, 311
    classification of, 354–359
    termination of, 378–381, 390
  definition of, 16
  deviation, 1446
  duration, 1436–1438
  employees, 644
  encouragement of, 56, 1453–1454
  estoppel, 868–869, 874–876
  exclusions, 789
  future, 840
  high seas, 117–118
  lifeboats, 698–705
  Lloyd's Open Form, 869, 874
  material circumstances, 1419–1423
  misconduct, 1100–1101
  non-acceptance of salved property, 1076
  non-necessary, 60
  objects of, 13
  passengers, 632, 634–636
    extraordinary, 635
  past, 838
  pilots, 590–595, 597–599
  prior, 870, 872
  proceedings, 1224
  prohibited, 51n
  promptness, 1436–1438
  public policy, 1453–1454
  refusal of, 50–63
  Royal Air Force, 677, 680–681
  salved value, 1321–1328, 1380
  seamen, 144
  security, 1255
  ships, salved, 496–501
  special, 788
  success, 735, 741
  termination of, 378–381, 390
  time limits, 1208
  tug and tow, 600, 606, 611, 613
    burden of proof of conversion into, 621–624
    conversion into, 40, 603–604, 615–618, 621–624

909

Index

SALVAGE SERVICES—*cont.*
  voluntary, 16
SALVAGE STATIONS, 43
SALVAGE SUBJECTS. *See* SUBJECTS OF
  SALVAGE
SALVED VALUE, 1319–1386
  abandonment, 1378, 1381–1384
  Admiralty court, 1457
  Admiralty Marshal, 1386
  advance, agreement in, 1377
  agreed valuation, 1321, 1377
  apportionment, 1321
  appraisement, 1386
  assessment of reward, 1457–1459, 1499, 1504
  benefit, 1343, 1504
  bullion, 1498
  burden of proof, 1320
  calculation of, 2
  cargo, 1332–1333, 1360–1375, 1378–1379, 1382–1384, 1500, 1503
  cargo-owners, 1321, 1381–1382, 1384
  charterparties, 1340–1342, 1344–1351
  contracts, 1348
  costs, 1354, 1374
  county courts, 121
  damage, 1373
  damages assessment, 1343
  deductions, 1352–1354, 1372–1375, 1379
  definition, 1319
  derelicts, 1378–1384
  diminution of value, 1331
  disputed valuation, 1323–1384
  documents, 1320
  doubt as to, 734
  English law, 1496
  evidence of, 1334–1335, 1351, 1370
  exchange rates, 1347
  expenses, 1327, 1371, 1373, 1375
  financial interests, 1376–1377
  freight, 1356–1367, 1370, 1375, 1379–1384, 1500
  frustration, 1344, 1372, 1378, 1381
  inequity of terms, 940
  interests in salved property, 1506–1513
  issues, 1319
  life salvage, 287, 1385, 1499
  little or no, 19
  maritime liens, 1251
  market value, 1349–1350, 1370
  material circumstances, 1419–1423, 1457–1459
  meritorious services, 1459
  misconduct, 1095, 1325
  misrepresentation, 908–909
  negligence, 1343
  objective, 1338
  on-carriage, costs of, 1374
  payment, liability for, 1495–1514
  place of valuation, 1323–1333
  proprietary or possessory interests, 1348

SALVED VALUE—*cont.*
  qualifications on the general principle, 1332–1333
  rateable contribution, 1495–1514
  remuneration, 1320, 1327, 1377, 1457
  repairs, 1339, 1353n, 1354, 1371
  risk or difficulty, different degrees of, 1497
  risks, different, 1500–1505
  sales, 1336–1337
    expenses, 1385
    no, 1350–1351
  salvage agreements, 854–855
  Salvage convention 1989, 19, 1457, 1496
  salvage operations, 19
  salvage services, 1380
    several, 1326–1328
  salvage subjects, 1345
  scrap value, 1355
  security, 1381
  shipowners, 1383
  shortage, 1373
  silver, 1498
  sound value, 1339–1342
  subjective, 1338
  success, 19, 734
  survey fees, 1374
  termination, 1336, 1349–1350, 1368–1369, 1373, 1380
    events after, 1329–1331
    port of destination, at, 1369, 1379–1380
    short of port of destination, 1370–1372, 1379
  time of, 1323–1333
  trading commitments, 1351
  wrecks, receivers of, 1322
SALVEES,
  benefits, receipt of, 28–30
  contributions, 2
  co-operation, 1046, 1055–1056, 1060, 1062
  duties of, 1
  LOF 2000, 797
  LSSAC 2000, 797
  material circumstances, 1431
  misconduct, 1087
    salvors, duty to, 1091–1095
  mistake, 924
  officiousness, 50–63
  overriding wishes of, 50–63
  salvage agreements, 797
  salvors, duty to, 1091–1095
  security, 1227, 1255, 1252
SALVORS, 441–510. *See also* REMEDIES OF
  SALVORS
  apportionment,
    deceased, 1535
    first, 1533–1534
    several, 1524, 1532–1534
    seamen, other than, 1540
    wrongful dispossession, 1534
  arbitration, 1292
  arrest, 1485

Index

SALVORS—cont.
  assistance, 1039–1043
  authority, 845
  best endeavours, 1034–1036
  classification, 441–442, 445–484
  competing, 917–918
  conduct, 1242–1245
  contracts, 447, 479–485
    independent of, 31
  co-operation, 1044–1062
  Crown, 1167
  danger, 338
  death, 1535
  definition, 443–444, 514
  discrimination against less capable, 39
  disentitlement to claim, 485–510
  duties of, 1
  encouraging, 26, 1453–1454
  entitlement to claim, 441–510
  environment, 443
  equipment, 1455
  first, 1229, 1240–1241, 1533–1534
  general conditions of claims, 441–442
  identity of, 917–919
  individual salvors, unassociated, 1531
  interests in salved property, 485–510
  intervention, 1039–1043
  life salvage, 443
  limitation of liability, 127
  Lloyd's agents, 626–631
  LOF 2000, 794
  loss of opportunity, 1039
  material circumstances, 1419–1425, 1478
  misconduct, 438, 1087–1089, 1484
    effect on other, 1128–1131
    negligence during salvage operations, 1104–1124
    salvees' duty to, 1091–1095
    sister ships, of, 1103
    some salvors, by, 1128–1131
  mistake, 917–919
  negligence during salvage operations, 1104–1124
  non-acceptance of salved property, 1080–1082
  non-contractual, 1069
  payment, liability for, 1479–1494
  personal representatives, 1535
  personal services, 445–484
  possession, 1232–1233
    conduct, 1242–1245
    first, 1229, 1240–1241
    second, 1240–1241
    subsequent, 1233
  property, 443–484
    interests in salved, 484–510
    non-acceptance of salved, 1080–1082
    relationship with salved, 485–510
  public policy, 1453–1454
  redelivery, 1083
  remedies, 1485–1491
  rights of, 31

SALVORS—cont.
  Royal Air Force, 678
  salvage agreements, 794
  Salvage Convention 1989, 443–444
  salvees' duty to, 1091–1095
  seamen, 141, 565
  several, 1524, 1532–1534
  ships,
    agents, 626–631
    interests in, 496–509
    sister, 504–508, 1103
  skill and care, 1419–1423
  special compensation, 438
  subsequent, 1233
  success, 447, 734
  termination, 1069
  undue influence, 946
  volunteers, 441–443
  wrecks, receivers of, 695
  wrongful dispossession, 1534
SANDBANK, 825
SATELLITES, 358
SCILLY, 1365
SCOPIC CLAUSE, 6
  application of, 964–966
  arbitration, 1292
  assessment of rewards, 974–976
  cargo-owners, 966
  contractors, 847
  danger, 381
  discounts, 977
  dispute resolution, 980
  environment, 396, 961, 982
  exclusion, 964–966
  functions, 961
  general average, 966, 979
  general terms, 967
  incorporation, 964–965, 967
  indemnities, 968, 970, 978
  introduction of, 963
  invocation, 964–966
  liens, 968
  LSSAC 2000, 960
  no cure no pay, 974–975
  notice, 965, 972
  overpayments, 978
  parties, 966
    duties of, 970
  payment, date of, 978
  recourse, rights of, 979
  remuneration, 962, 966, 968, 970, 976–978
    assessment of, 976
    commencement of, 971
    date of payment, 978
    discounts, 977
    maximising, 960
    overpayments, 978
    reducing, 961
    restitution, 978
  reward, 974–976
    relationship with Article 13 salvage, 974
  salvage agreements, 960–980

Index

SCOPIC CLAUSE—cont.
  Salvage Convention 1989, 964, 971, 974–975, 977
  scheme of clause, 962
  security, 968, 970, 972–973, 990,1257, 1259
  shipowners, 966, 972, 974
  Shipowners' Casualty Representative, 969, 978
  special compensation, 961, 975
  Special Representatives, 969
  success, 739
  termination, 979, 1068
  time limits, 968
  underwriters, 969
  withdrawal, 972, 975
SCOTLAND,
  history, 189n
  in personam actions, 1491
  Roman law, 189
  sources of law, 189n
SCRAP VALUE, 1355
SEALED OFFERS, 1295
SEAMEN. *See also* MASTERS, OFFICERS
  abandonment, 570–579, 584
  agents, 840
  apportionment, 1526, 1529, 1531, 1538–1539
  authority, 833–835
    agents, 840
    masters binding, 836–840
    ratification, 840
    shipowners' binding, 841–844
  best endeavours, 584
  charterparties, 493
  common law salvage, 141, 144, 147–148
  contract of services, 567–568, 574, 576, 579–584, 586
  Crown ships, 645–676, 1529
  danger, 571
  demise charterparties, 468–469
  discharge of, 569, 579–584
  duties, 565–587
  embargoes, 580
  employees of third parties, 587
  exclusions, 787
  hostile captures 579–584
  interests in salved property, 485, 492–495
  lifeboatmen,
    claims made by, 700–703
    composition of, 699
  maritime liens, 566
  masters, 565
    binding, by, 835–842
    discharge by, 569, 579
  misconduct, 569
  personal services, 457
  pre-existing duties, 492–495, 565
  radio officers, 587
  ratification, 840
  remuneration, 565
  reward, 492, 494

SEAMEN—cont.
  salvage articles, 1539
  salvage services, 585
  salvors, 141, 565, 568
  salvage services, 144
  shipowners,
    binding, 841–844
    duties to, 492–495
  substantial services, 495
  third parties, employees of, 587
  tug and tow, 620
  voluntariness, 492, 517, 523, 524, 530, 565–587, 645–676, 683–689
  wages, 565–566
  wrecks, 565, 694
SEAPLANES, 245–246, 249, 253
SEARCHES, 358
SEAWORTHINESS, 490
SECRETARY OF STATE,
  co-operation, 1051
  delegation, 70n
  directions, 70
  functions, 70n
  Marine Pollution Control Unit, 70n
  oil pollution, 70
SECURITY,
  amount of, 1259
  arbitration, 1264, 1266–1318
  arrest, 1226, 1265
  bailment, 1226
  best endeavours, 1262–1263
  cargo, 1489
  cargo-owners, 1262
  contractors, 990, 1255
  co-operation, 1045
  Council of lloyd's, 1260
  currency of, 1258
  detention, 1265
  disputes as to, 1264–1265
  English law, 1226
  excessive, 1259
  expenses, 1263
  form of, 1260
  freezing injunctions, 1226
  general average, 1261
  liability for, 1261–1262
  Lloyd's Open Form, 990, 1226, 1258–1259, 1262, 1264–1265, 1310–1314
  LOF 2000, 1255, 1257n, 1258, 1261–1262
  Lssac 2000, 1255, 1257–1259, 1261–1262
  maritime liens, 1226, 1247–1253
  marine insurance, 1227
  notice, 990
  parties, duties of, 990
  possession, 1228–1246
  prejudice, 1227
  proceedings, 1225–1265
  property, duty not to remove salved, 1253–1254
  remuneration, 1259
  Salvage convention 1910, 1226

912

Index

SECURITY—*cont.*
Salvage Convention 1989, 990, 1226, 1256, 1262
salvage services, 1255
salved value, 1381
salvees, 1227, 1255, 1262
SCOPIC Clause, 968, 970, 972–973, 990, 1257, 1259
shipowners, 1494
special compensation, 1257, 1259
termination, 1225
time limits, 1206, 1255, 1265
variation of, 1259
SELF-INTEREST,
authority, 806
passengers, 518
voluntariness, 518, 557–562
SELF-PRESERVATION, 518
SERVICE, CONTRACTS OF, 567–568, 574, 576, 579–584, 586
SERVICE OF PROCESS, 1274–1276
SERVICES. *See also* SALVAGE SERVICES
contracts, for, 997, 1007–1026
supply of, 998, 1007–1026
SET-OFF,
charges, 1518
damages, 1031, 1124
freight, 1517–1518
negligence, 1124
restitution, 1518
reward, 1031
SETTLEMENT OF CLAIMS,
authority, 820–821
inequitable, 941
proceedings, 1222
SHANGHAI, 1326
SHELL-FIRE, 649
SHIPOWNERS
agents, 815
authority, 814–823, 833–835, 841–844
binding persons other than, 828–832
masters' binding, 814–823, 833–835, 841–844
personal capacity, acting in, 835–837
power of owners to bind masters and crew, 841–844
ratification, by, 823
seamen, power to bind, 841–844
binding persons other than, 828–832
cargo, 487–491
cargo-owners, 1493–1494
claims of, 458–484
co-operation, 1057
definition, 1190
demise charterparties, transfer of rights to, 464–477
estoppel, 1492
first instance, payment of all salvage in, 1492
freight, 1356, 1487
interests in salved property, 1506, 1508
limitation of liability, 1190

SHIPOWNERS—*cont.*
LOF 2000, 795
LSSAC 2000, 795
masters, binding, 814–823, 833–835, 841–844
payment, liability for, 1488–1494
personal capacity, acting in, 835–837
personal services, 454–484
possession, 1234, 1236
power of owners to bind masters and crew, 841–844
ratification, by, 823
recourse, right of, 439–440
reimbursement, 1493–1494
remedies, 1493–1494
reward, 458
salved value, 1383
salving vessels, 454–484
SCOPIC Clause, 966, 972, 974
seamen, 492–495, 841–844
security, 1494
Shipowners' Casualty Representative, 969, 978
ships, 485, 496–509
special compensation, 433, 435
recourse, right of, 439–440
SHIPOWNERS' CASUALTY REPRESENTATIVE, 969, 978
SHIPS. *See also* BOATS, FOREIGN SHIPS, SISTER SHIPS, VESSELS
adapted or designed for use at sea, 169n
apparel, 150, 179
bunkers, 181
charges, 496–497
Crown, 169
definition, 169–173, 176, 183
demise charterparties, 499–500, 503
endangering, 113
interests in salved property, 485, 496–509
marine insurance, 496, 498
material circumstances, 1429
navigation, used in, 175
oars, propelled by, 168n, 172–173
provisions, 188–189
ransom, 131n
reward, 502
Salvage Convention 1989, 169, 504–508
salvage services, 496–501
salved, interests in, 485, 496–509
salvors, 496–509
shipowners, 485, 496–509
subjects of salvage, 168–174, 176, 181–182, 188–189
sue and labour clauses, 497–498
SHIPS' AGENTS, 626–631
SHIPWRECKS. *See* WRECKS
SHORTAGE, 1373
SIGNALS, 344, 540
SILVER, 1498
SISTER SHIPS,
cargo interests, 508, 509
common law salvage, 507

913

Index

SISTER SHIPS—*cont.*
  demise charterparties, 507
  indemnities, 505, 507
  interests in salved property, 486
  marine insurance, 507
  misconduct, 1099, 1103
  ownership, 504–508
  remuneration, 504
  reward, 505
  Salvage Convention 1910, 504
  Salvage Convention 1989, 504–508
  salvors, 504–508
  third parties, 509
SKILL AND CARE,
  agents, 800
  authority, 800
  engaged services, 778
  material circumstances, 1419–1423
  misconduct, 1091–1092, 1097
  more than usual, 598
  negligence, 1106–1107, 1109, 1120
  pilots, 598
  salvors, 1419–1423
  supply of services, contracts for, 1013, 1025
  tug and tow, 602
SLAVES, 192
SMACKS, 454
SOLDIERS, 682
SOLICITORS, 95
SOS MESSAGES, 540
SOSREP, 70
SOUTH AMERICA, 908
SOUTHAMPTON, 854
SOVEREIGN IMMUNITY, 1163–1177
  admiralty proceedings, 1175–1177
  arbitration, 1173, 1174
  coastal states, 68
  commercial activities, vessels engaged in, 1164
  commercial transactions, 1172, 1175
  contractual obligations, 1174
  Crown, 1166–1170
  damage, 1123
  death, 1123
  defence, as, 1163
  diplomats, 1171
  English law, 1165
  exceptions, 1172–1174
  foreign state, meaning of, 1171
  governing law, 1171
  humanitarian cargo, 1180n
  in personam proceedings, 1175
  in rem actions, 1165, 1175–1176
  interests in salved property, 1513
  Lloyd's open form, 1174
  maritime liens, 1165, 1249
  payment, liability for, 1483
  personal injuries, 1123
  reward, 2
  Salvage Convention 1910, 1164
  Salvage Convention 1989, 68, 1164, 1176

SOVEREIGN IMMUNITY—*cont.*
  state-owned ships, 1164
  United kingdom, 1171–1174
SOURCES OF ENGLISH LAW, 89
SOURCES OF MODERN SALVAGE LAW, 3–12
  Admiralty jurisdiction, 103
  Admiralty law, 15
  arbitration, 6, 8
  bottomry, 4
  civil law, 15
  common law, 6, 15
  equity, 3
  jurisdictions, law in other, 4
  Oleron, laws of, 3
  prize, 3
  restitution, 3
  Roman law, 3
  Salvage Convention 1989, 12
  Scotland, 189n
  statute law, 15
  treaties and conventions, 11
SPACECRAFT, 253
SPAIN, 656
SPECIAL COMPENSATION,
  amount of, 423–427
  arbitration, 1273, 1311
  assessment of rewards, 420–421, 436–437
  basic entitlement, 413, 415
  cargo-owners, 439
  charterparties, 439
  Common Understanding, 414
  compound interest, 1137
  conditions for payment, 412–416
  currency, 1563
  damage,
    prevention or minimising of, 416, 418, 424, 427
    threats of, 413, 431–432
  damages, 439
  danger, 352
  dangerous goods, 439
  discretionary uplift, 415–416, 418, 423–425, 432–433
  double payment, 419
  engaged services, 754
  environment, 18, 312, 352, 395, 397, 404, 410, 412–440, 1038
  estoppel, 883
  expenses, incurring of, 414, 417–418, 423–432
  general average, 439–440
  liability, 422
  misconduct, 438, 1137
  no cure no pay, 1388
  oil pollution, 70
  period, 431–432
  reward,
    assessment of, 420–421, 436–437
    deductible, 433–437
    greater than, 434, 436
    inadequate, 417
    less than entitlement to, 414

914

Index

SPECIAL COMPENSATION—*cont.*
  reward—*cont.*
    not exceeding recoverable, 416
    reduced by, 420
    size of, 418
  Salvage Convention 1989, 1388
  salvage operations, performance of, 413
  salvees, more than one, 433
  salvors, more than one, 438
  SCOPIC Clause, 961, 975
  shipowners, 433, 435
    recourse, right of, 439–440
  success, 723, 741
  time limits, 1206
  York-Antwerp Rules, 440
SPECIAL COMPENSATION P&I CLAUSE. *See* SCOPIC
SPECIAL REPRESENTATIVES, 969
SPECIAL SERVICES, 790
SPEED, 1130
ST JOHN, 537
ST VINCENT, CAPE, 737
STAGES, SALVAGE IN, 382–389, 391
STAND BY, 45, 357
STANDARD FORMS OF CONTRACT. *See also* LLOYD'S OPEN FORM
  Admiralty jurisdiction, 126
  inequity of terms, 949
  salvage agreements, 781
  Salvage Convention 1989, 77
  terms of, 848–851
  tug and tow, 780
  unfair contract terms, 1157
STATE IMMUNITY. *See* SOVEREIGN IMMUNITY
STATE-OWNED VESSELS, 1164
STATES. *See also* SOVEREIGN IMMUNITY
  co-operation, 67, 1048–1055
  rights and duties of, 67–69
  Salvage Convention 1989, 67–69
    contracting states, duty of, 1048–1055
STATIC STRUCTURES, 318–320
STATUTE LAW,
  Admiralty Court, 93
  Admiralty jurisdiction, 103, 104, 123–124, 153
  aircraft, 243–245, 249
  co-operation, 1049
  governing law, 73
  hovercraft, 257–259
  interest, 1467
  interpretation, 82–84, 87
  life salvage, 265, 273–291
  reasons for legislation, 82
  reduction in liability, 1143–1162
  sources of modern salvage law, 15
  unfair contract terms, 1144–1162
  wrecks, 105–106
STATUTE OF WESTMINISTER, 111
STATUTORY AUTHORITIES,
  agents, 692
  employees, 690–693
  harbour authorities, 690

STATUTORY AUTHORITIES—*cont.*
  lighthouse authorities, 690
  Lloyd's Open Form, 691
  ports, 690, 693
  voluntariness, 690–693
STATUTORY DUTY, 534–544
STEAM, SALVAGE IN DAYS OF, 38n
STERLING, 1463
STORAGE,
  expenses, 1074, 1076
  non-acceptance of salved property, 1071–1073, 1081, 1085
STRANDING, 112, 357
STURGEON, 314
SUB-CONTRACTORS, 562, 638–643
  best endeavours, 1036
  contracts, privity of, 638, 641
  mutual insurance, 638
  possessory liens, 638
  proceedings, 1221
  public policy, 1020
  supply of services, contracts for, 1020
  tug and tow, 643
SUBJECTS OF SALVAGE, 150–390
  Admiralty jurisdiction, 126, 152–154
  airborne craft, 244–259
  aircraft, 152, 244–256
  apparel of ships, 150, 179
  assessment, 151
  beacons, 155–158
  boats, 168–173
  bunkers, 180
  cargo, 190–193, 329
  common law salvage, 153, 155
  common ownership, property in, 150
  contracts, 159, 178, 313
  cranes, 161
  danger, 330–390, 1411
  definition, 154, 162
  derelict, 208–215
  drilling units, 318–320
  English law, 161
  environment, 159, 162, 312
  equipment, 179, 186–187
  exclusions, 150, 162, 317–329
  fixed objects, 160
  flotsam, 204–207
  freight, 216–233, 243
  gas floats, 155–158
  goods, 190–194
  hire, 216–233
  hovercraft, 152, 257–259
  humanitarian cargo, 329
  identification, 151
  inland waters, 161
  jetsam, 204–207
  lagan, 204–207
  lakes, 161
  law of salvage and, 1
  liability salvage, 158, 311
  life salvage, 152, 158, 162, 260–310
  luggage, 194, 321–328

915

SUBJECTS OF SALVAGE—cont.
  motor vehicles, 161
  navigation,
    equipment, 186–187
    involvement in, 155–156, 158, 160–161, 168–177
  new, 153
  oars, propelled by, 172–173
  offshore drilling platforms, 162
  passage money, 234–242
  personal effects, 194, 321–328
  platforms, 162, 318–320
  prohibition of salvage, 61–63
  property, 158, 160
    ancillary, 178–182
    maritime, 163–243
    shipowner, not owned by, 183–187
  provisions, 188–189
  retention of title, 187
  reward, 160
  royal fish, 314–316
  Salvage Convention 1989, 159, 161–162
  salved value, 1345
  ships, 168–174, 176, 181–182
    provisions, 188–189
  static structures, 318–320
  time charterparties, 232
  towed property, 195–200
  unjust enrichment, 153
  vessels, 168–171, 177, 182
  voyages, involved in, 160
  wireless equipment, 186–187
  wreck, 201–215
SUBMARINES, 49n
SUCCESS, 1, 716–778
  abandonment, 733
  Acts of God, 733
  Admiralty Court, 1450
  agreements independent of, 1460
  assessment of reward, 1450–1452
  authority, 808
  best endeavours, 1034
  common law, 719
  construction, 1452
  contracts, special, 728
  damage, 732
  danger, 733, 735
    incomplete services leaving vessel in greater, 736–741
  discretionary payments, 716
  engaged services, 724, 742–778
  environment, 723
  general principles, 716–741
  life salvage, 716
  Lloyd's Open Form, 718
  LOF 2000, 741
  masters' authority, 729–730
  material circumstances, 1460
  measure of, 1450–1452
  meritorious action, 717, 720, 733, 739
  negligence, 1110–111
  no cure no pay, 718, 741

SUCCESS—cont.
  possession, 1233
  professional salvors, 1023
  property, preservation of, 716, 720, 725–727
    loss or damage after, 732
  public policy, 38
  requested services, 727
  reward, 719–720, 733, 735
    agreement independent of success, 1460
  salvage agreements, 731, 780
  Salvage Convention 1450, 1450
  Salvage Convention 1989, 719–724, 741, 1450–1451
  SCOPIC Clause, 741
  salvage operations, 721
  salvage services, 741
    not contributing to, 735
  salved value, 19
  salvors, 447, 734
  special compensation, 723, 741
  supply of services, contracts for, 1022–1023
  third parties, 733
  United Kingdom, 723
  'useful result', 719–720
    without, 721–724
  value of service, doubts as to, 734
SUE AND LABOUR CLAUSES,
  expenses, 510
  ships, salved, 497–498
SUE, RIGHT TO. See RIGHT TO SUE
SUEZ CANAL, 383
SUMMER, 617
SUNKEN PROPERTY, 357
SUPERSESSION, 756–772
SUPERVENING CIRCUMSTANCES,
  assistance, 1076
  danger, 605–607
  frustration, 959
  misconduct, 957
  non-acceptance of salved property, 1076
  performance, more onerous, 957
  remuneration, 957, 959
  salvage agreements, 857, 955, 957–959
    discharge of, 955, 957–959
  tug and tow, 605–611
  weather, 958
SUPPLY OF GOODS,
  conditions, 1005
  contracts, 1003–1006
  exclusion clauses, 1006
  hire, 1004, 1005, 1006
  implied terms, 1003, 1005
  qualification of liability, 1006
  reasonableness, 1006
  transfer of property in, 1003
  unfair contract terms, 1006
  warranties, 1005
SUPPLY OF SERVICES,
  assessment of reward, 1018
  bailment, 1007, 1021

Index

SUPPLY OF SERVICES—cont.
  best endeavours, 1014, 1020, 1022–1023
  charges, 1018–1019
  common law, 1024–1026
  consideration, 1007, 1016–1018
  consumers, 1009
  contracts for, 998, 1007–1026
  course of a business, 1010, 1014, 1016
  definition, 1007
  environment, 1013
  implied terms, 1008–1010, 1014, 1021, 1024–1026
  negligence, 1012
  performance,
    defective, 1026
    personal, 1019–1021
    successful, 1022–1023
    time for, 1014–1015, 1024
  personal services, 1019–1021
  price, 1024
  professional salvors, 1010, 1020, 1023
  public policy, 1020
  reduction of liability, 1011–1012
  remuneration, 1007, 1017–1018
  salvage agreements, 1007
  Salvage Convention 1989, 1013, 1014, 1017
  skill and care, 1013, 1025
  sub-contractors, 1020
  success, 1022–1023
  tug and tow, 1015
  unfair contract terms, 1011
SUPREME COURT OF JUDICATURE, 96, 98
SURVEY FEES, 1374
SWEDEN, 656–657, 696

TACKLE, 357
TANK-LANDING CRAFT
TAXATION, 453, 1477
TENDER, 938
TERMINATION OF SERVICES,
  best endeavours, 1063
  breach of contract, 1027, 1031, 1066, 1446
  currency, 1462
  expenses, 1445
  freight, 1357–1359, 1363
  frustration, 1067
  impossibility, 1067
  interest, 1470, 1473
  Lloyd's Open Form, 1063, 1068
  LOF 2000, 989, 1064–1065, 1068
  non-acceptance of salved property, 1071
  parties, duties of, 989, 1063–1069
  performance, 1066
  deemed, 1065
  public authorities, 1069
  redelivery, acceptance of, 989
  remuneration, 1068
  reward, 1063, 1067
  safety, place of, 1063–1067
  salved value, 1336, 1349–1350, 1368–1369, 1373, 1380

TERMINATION OF SERVICES—cont.
  salved value—cont.
    events after, 1329–1331
    port of destination, at, 1369, 1379–1380
    short of port of destination, 1370–1372, 1379
  salvors, non-contractual, 1069
  SCOPIC, 1068
  security, 1225
TERMINOLOGY, 13–14
TERMS OF SALVAGE AGREEMENTS, 843–847.
  See also INEQUITY OF TERMS
  contractors, 847
  LOF 2000, 849–851
  salvors, 847
  standard form contracts, 848–851
TERRORISTS, 359, 584
THAMES, 315n
THEFT, 1128–1129, 1131
THIRD PARTIES,
  assessment of rewards, 1448
  authority, 799–802
  co-operation, 1046
  danger, 347–350, 357, 1415
  losses, 1448
  misconduct, 1087, 1098, 1101
  proceedings, 1221, 1223
  property,
    non-acceptance of salved, 1075
    owned by, 183–187
  seamen, 587
  sister ships, 509
  success, 733
  time limits, 1217–1219
TIDAL WATERS, 375–376
TIMBER, 206
TIME. See also DELAY, TIME LIMITS
  Admiralty court, 1436
  apportionment, 1533
  co-operation, 1052
  Crown, 1168
  duration, 1436–1438
  essence, of the, 1030
  implied terms, 1030
  losses, 1438
  material circumstances, 1436–1438
  performance, 1030, 1052
  priorities, 1533
  professional salvors, 1436
  promptness, 1436–1438
  reward, increase in, 1436
  Salvage convention 1989, 1436, 1438
  salved value, 1323–1333
TIME CHARTERPARTIES,
  Admiralty jurisdiction, 126
  arbitration, 1304
  claims of, 461–462
  contribution to salvage, 461–462
  deviation, 461
  freight, 219–222, 224, 228, 232
  hire, 126
  remuneration, 126

917